A HISTORY OF
ISLAMIC SOCIETIES

A HISTORY OF
ISLAMIC SOCIETIES

IRA M. LAPIDUS

Professor of History, University of California, Berkeley

The right of the
University of Cambridge
to print and sell
all manner of books
was granted by
Henry VIII in 1534.
The University has printed
and published continuously
since 1584.

CAMBRIDGE UNIVERSITY PRESS

Cambridge

New York   New Rochelle   Melbourne   Sydney

Published by the Press Syndicate of the University of Cambridge
The Pitt Building, Trumpington Street, Cambridge CB2 1RP
32 East 57th Street, New York, NY 10022, USA
10 Stamford Road, Oakleigh, Melbourne 3166, Australia

First published 1988

Printed in Great Britain by the University Press, Cambridge

British Library cataloguing in publication data
Lapidus, Ira M.
  A history of Islamic societies.
  1. Civilization, Islamic
  I. Title
  909'.097671   DS35.62

Library of Congress cataloguing in publication data
Lapidus, Ira M. (Ira Marvin)
  A history of Islamic societies.

  Bibliography.
  Includes index.
  1. Islamic countries – History. 2. Islam – History.
  I. Title
  DS35.63.L37 1988 909'.097671 87–11754

ISBN 0 521 22552 3

CONTENTS

v

PART III THE MODERN TRANSFORMATION:
MUSLIM PEOPLES IN THE NINETEENTH
AND TWENTIETH CENTURIES

ILLUSTRATIONS

Picture research by Sandra Assersohn

FIGURES

MAPS

TABLES

PREFACE

Islam is the religion of peoples who inhabit the middle regions of the planet from the Atlantic shores of Africa to the South Pacific, from the steppes of Siberia to the remote islands of South Asia: Berbers, West Africans, Sudanese, Swahili-speaking East Africans, Middle Eastern Arabs, Turks, Iranians, Turkish and Persian peoples of Central Asia, Afghans, Pakistanis, many millions of Indians and Chinese, most of the peoples of Malaysia and Indonesia, and minorities in the Philippines – some 900,000,000 people adhere to Islam. In ethnic background, language, customs, social and political organization, and forms of culture and technology, they represent innumerable variations of human experience. Yet Islam unites them. Though Islam is not often the totality of their lives, it permeates their self-conception, regulates their daily existence, provides the bonds of society, and fulfills the yearning for salvation. For all its variousness, Islam forges one of the great spiritual families of mankind.

This book is the history of how these multitudes have become Muslims and what Islam means to them. In this book we ask: What is Islam? What are its values? How did so many peoples, so different and dispersed, become Muslims? What does Islam contribute to their character, to their way of living, to the ordering of their communities, and to their aspirations and identity? What are the historical conditions that have given rise to Islam and to Islamic religious and cultural values; what are the manifold ways in which it is understood and practiced? To answer these questions we shall see how religious concepts about the nature of reality and the meaning of human

xix

experience, embedded at once in holy scripture and works of commentary, and as thoughts and feelings in the minds and hearts of Muslim believers, have given shape to the lifestyles and institutions of Muslim peoples, and how reciprocally the political and social experiences of Muslim peoples have been given expression in the values and symbols of Islam. Our history of Islam is the history of a dialogue between the realm of religious symbols and the world of everyday reality, a history of the interaction between Islamic values and the historical experiences of Muslim peoples that has shaped the formation of a number of different but interrelated Muslim societies.

Part I examines the formative era of Islamic civilization from the revelation of the Quran to the thirteenth century. It begins with the Prophet Muhammad, and continues with the classical Islamic era which gave rise to Arabic literature, Islamic religious teaching and cosmopolitan cultural achievements – a tripartite complex of tribal-ethnic, religious and courtly-aristocratic cultures from which all later versions of Islamic civilization derive. Part I attempts to explain the development of this civilization in terms of the relationship of Islamic cultures to the established institutional patterns of Middle Eastern empires, economies and monotheistic religions, and in terms of the cultural effects of the formation of new empires, urbanization, and social change. Part I concludes with the history of Iraq and Iran from the tenth to the thirteenth centuries, to explain the transformation of Islam from a complex of doctrines and cultural systems into the operative principles of a Middle Eastern society. This was the age in which Islam became the religion of the masses of Middle Eastern peoples. In this period, Muslim peoples formed new state and communal institutions (Shiʿi "sects," Sunni schools of law, and Sufi fraternities) and defined the relations of political regimes to religious bodies. In this era, Islamic values gave rise to the "mass societies," ordered by parallel political and religious institutions.

In its turn the Islamic version of Middle Eastern society became a paradigm for the creation of similar societies in other parts of the world. Part II traces the diffusion of the Middle Eastern Islamic paradigm. From the seventh to the nineteenth centuries, Islam became the religion of peoples in the Arab Middle East, Inner Asia and China, India, Southeast Asia, Africa, and the Balkans. Part II considers the forces behind the diffusion of Islam, and the interaction between Islamic religious values and established cultures and societies. It also examines the consolidation of Islamic regimes including the Mughal, the Ottoman and the Safavid empires, and Islamic states in Southeast Asia, Africa and elsewhere, and their varied ways of integrating political regimes, Islamic religious institutions, and non-Islamic values and forms of community.

By the eighteenth century the Middle Eastern paradigm for an Islamic society had been replicated, multiplied, and modified into a worldwide system of related but different societies. Each of them, in the view to be set forth in this volume, was one of a family of societies, for each was a recognizable variant upon a similar underlying structure of familial-communal, religious, and state institutions. Each of them was a variant upon the ways in which Islamic belief, culture, and social institutions have interacted with the still broader complex of human organization including the non-Islamic institutions of political regimes, systems of economic production and exchange, non-Islamic forms of kinship, tribal, and ethnic communities, and pre-Islamic or non-Islamic modes of culture. Here we explore the degree to which the Middle Eastern paradigm was transferred to new Islamic societies. What was the relation of Islamic to pre-Islamic institutions in these regions? What were the similarities and differences among these numerous Islamic societies?

The transformation of Islamic societies from the eighteenth century to the present tests the resiliency of the historical templates and the identity of the Islamic world system. In Part III we see how Islamic societies were profoundly disrupted by the breakup of Muslim empires, economic decline, internal religious conflict, and by the establishment of European economic, political, and cultural domination. These forces led to the creation of national states, to the modernization of agriculture and industrialization, to major changes in class structure, and to the acceptance of secular nationalist and other modern ideologies. In the course of these changes Islamic thought and Islamic communal institutions have been radically altered.

The legacy of eighteenth- and nineteenth-century historical change, however, is not a unilinear movement toward "modernization," but a heritage of continuing conflict in Muslim countries over political, economic, and cultural goals, and of different courses of change in different Muslim societies. Political decline and European intervention have led to a struggle among political elites, scholarly (*'ulama'*) and mystical (Sufi) religious leaders, and revivalist movements for political and social power. While secularized political elites tend to favor modernization in Western forms, and the redefinition of Islam to make it consistent with modern forms of state and economy, religious reformers espouse the revitalization of moral values and formation of new political communities on Islamic principles. By examining the historic forms of political and religious organization, the impact of European imperialisms, and the political and ideological struggles of competing elites in Muslim countries, this book will attempt to explain the structure of present-day regimes, and the role of historic Islamic institutions and reformist movements in the shaping of contemporary Muslim societies.

The basic problems in analyzing these developments are both evolutionary and comparative. Has the impact of the West and of modern technical civilization generated a new form of society or do the historic political and religious templates still regulate the destiny of new Muslim nations? Do present conditions basically reflect the cultural and political qualities of the imperial, sectarian, and tribal societies of the eighteenth century or have the nineteenth- and twentieth-century transformations of economy, class structure, and values generated a new evolutionary stage in the history of Islamic societies? To deal with these issues the history of Islamic societies will be presented in two dimensions: one historical and evolutionary, an effort to account for the formation of Islamic societies and their change over time; the other analytic and comparative, an effort to understand the variations among them.

This approach is based on a number of historical and methodological assumptions. The first is that the history of whole societies may be presented in terms of their institutional systems. An institution, be it an empire, a mode of economic exchange, a family, or a religious practice is a human activity carried out in a patterned relationship with other human beings as defined and legitimated in the mental world of the participants. An institution encompasses at once an activity, a pattern of social relations, and a set of mental constructs.

The second assumption is that the history of Islamic societies may be told in terms of four basic types of institutions: familial, including tribal, ethnic, and other small-scale community groups; economic, the organization of production and distribution of material goods; cultural or religious concepts of ultimate values and human goals and the collectivities built upon such commitments; and political, the organization of domination, resolution of conflict, and defense. These institutions have characteristic qualities in each society and are interrelated in a patterned way.

The third assumption is that the institutional patterns characteristic of Islamic societies had their origin in ancient Mesopotamia in the third millennium B.C. The constellation of lineage and tribal, religious, and political structures created by the Mesopotamian city states and empires set the foundations for the later evolution of Middle Eastern societies before and during the Islamic era, and was either reproduced or diffused from the Middle East to other Islamic societies. Thus the Middle Eastern Islamic society was based upon the infusion of more ancient institutions with an Islamic cultural style and identity. These Middle Eastern Islamic institutions in turn interacted with the institutions and cultures of other world regions to create a number of variant Islamic societies. In the modern era these variant societies were again transformed, this time by interaction with Europe. Modern Islamic countries are each the product of the interaction of a particular regional form of Islamic society with different forms of European imperial, economic and cultural influences. The variation among modern Islamic societies may be traced to older patterns.

In this volume primary emphasis will be placed upon the communal, religious, and political institutions of Islamic societies rather than upon technologies and economies, for this is what distinguishes them from other societies which have similar ecological characteristics and similar modes of production. I subordinate economic to non-economic institutions because the distinctive historical developments in Islamic societies in the last millennium have been cultural and political; and because changes in the realm of culture and institutions differentiate Islamic societies from each other and from other human civilizations. I further assume that cultural and sociopolitical institutions and economic and technological forces can act autonomously and that each may be a causal factor in historical change, but that in the history of Islamic societies cultural and institutional factors have been the significant locus of historical individuation.

For the purpose of this presentation I also assume that the basic forms of economic production and exchange in Muslim societies were set down in the pre-Islamic era. The forms of agricultural and pastoral production, handicrafts, manufacturing, prevailing systems of exchange, and technological capacities are all older than, and continue through, the Islamic era in their inherited forms. This is not to deny that there has been considerable variation in economic activity in and among Muslim societies, such as in the relative role of pastoral, agricultural, commercial, and manufacturing activities, or in degrees of poverty and prosperity, or in the distribution of wealth; nor that these differences have important cultural and political implications, nor that economic considerations are an essential aspect of all human values and social action. Still, in my judgment the fundamental modes of economic production and exchange were basically unaltered until the modern era, and economic and technological changes were not the primary sources of political and cultural variation or of changes in class structure and social organization. Until the modern era economic activity remained embedded in communal and political structures, and class divisions in society did not determine, but were inherent in, state and religious organizations. Even in the nineteenth and twentieth centuries, when European capitalism and profound economic and technological changes have influenced Islamic societies, economically derived classes such as merchants and proletariats are weakly developed in Muslim countries, and political and religious elites, institutions and cultural values continue to play a predominant role in the modernization of these societies. Whether twentieth-century technological and economic change now call into question the existence of an Islamic group of societies is a moot point.

These assumptions, presented here in a very schematic and simplistic form, derive from a variety of historical, social scientific, and philosophic sources. As an historian, however, my primary interest is not in theory but in the adaptation of the theoretical assumptions to the needs of a coherent and meaningful exposition. The central problem of this book is how to present a history of enormous diversity – the history of societies which to sight and sound are utterly different – and yet preserve some sense of their historical and institutional relatedness. For the reader this book is intended to provide a coherent overview of Islamic history. As a teacher I have long come to the conclusion that the endless everyday flow of events and news confuses rather than enlightens us and that a large "map" of the subject as a whole is essential to understand particular occurrences. Only from a large point of view can we acquire the poise, the distance, and the perspective that make it possible to identify basic structural factors and long-term historical trends and distinguish them from accidental and short-term considerations.

This is not, it should be clear, an effort to define an essential Islam but rather an effort to develop a comparative method of assessing the role of Islamic beliefs, institutions, and identities in particular historical contexts. The mechanism I have adopted to do this – the expository framework – is based on the assumptions that Islamic societies are built upon institutions and that these institutions are subject to internal variation, to variations in the relationships among them, and to variations over time. The limited number of institutional factors imposes a constraint that allows us to conceive this large subject in some ordered way, but also allows for the depiction of individual societies as concrete and different entities. By exploring the variation of institutions in differing contexts, we may be able to comprehend why Islamic societies are similar in general form and yet differ so much in specific qualities.

A few comments about the organization of the book may help the reader find his or her way through this large volume. First, the reader should be cautioned that the factual narrative approach of this book conceals great uncertainties in the problematics of historical judgment, incomplete knowledge, conflicts of opinion and interpretation among experts, and constantly changing research which brings new knowledge and new points of view to the fore. Little has been said about the degree of reliability or the margin of error in the presentation of information, but the book is based upon the most reliable and up-to-date research and intepretation. Indeed, some conclusions are based upon current unpublished research. The reader should thus be aware that parts of the work are provisional and exploratory in nature, and represent the author's best judgment about particular subjects.

The book is organized into three parts, each of which has an introduction and conclusion which deal with the organizing concepts upon which the book is based and summarize the important themes which come up in the narrative chapters. For an overview of the evolution of Islamic societies, these introductory and concluding chapters may be read separately or in conjunction with selected period or regional histories. This arrangement adds flexibility for the reader in choosing an approach to the book but involves a certain amount of repetition, for which I ask the indulgence of attentive readers of the whole volume.

Each of the three main divisions deals with a particular epoch in Islamic history – the origins, diffusion and modern transformation of Islamic societies. This means that Islamic culture, arts, literatures, and religious values are discussed primarily in Part I, and are only referred to in a summary way in Parts II and III. The latter tend to emphasize the institutional aspects. Also regional histories are ordinarily divided into two or three sections. The history of Middle Eastern Islamic societies is divided among all three parts; the histories of other Islamic societies are divided among Parts II and III. There are, however, a number of exceptions. While Part I deals generally with the formation of Middle Eastern Islamic societies from the seventh to the thirteenth century, for narrative convenience the early history of the Arab Middle East, of North Africa and of Spain is grouped with the corresponding regional histories in Part II; portions of these chapters may usefully be read in conjunction with Part I. Similarly, the entire history of the Arabian peninsula, Libya and the Caucasus is found in Part III rather than being scattered through the volume. The history of all these societies concludes in the present era around 1980, although there are references to developments as late as 1984. The use of the present tense in Part III refers to the period from 1970 to the present.

The definition of geographic regions also requires some arbitrary simplifications. Muslim world areas are by and large defined in regional terms such as Middle East, North Africa, Indian subcontinent, Southeast Asia, West and East Africa, and so on. For convenience of reference, and despite the obvious anachronism, these areas or parts of them are commonly identified by the names of present national states such as India, Indonesia, or Nigeria. This is to simplify identification for readers unfamiliar with the geography of these vast regions and to avoid such cumbersome locutions as "areas now part of the state of —," but it should be clear that the use of these terms does not necessarily imply any similarity of state and social organization or of cultural style between pre-modern and contemporary times. Also it should be noted that I have placed the history of Libya in the chapter on North Africa and the Sudan in East Africa though these countries also belong to the Arab Middle East. Finally, not all Muslim regions are covered in this book. Muslim minorities in mainland Southeast Asia, the Philippines, Ceylon, Europe and the Americas, for example, are not discussed.

Transliterations from the numerous native languages of Muslim peoples have been simplified for the convenience of English readers not familiar with these languages. In general I have tried to follow standard scholarly usage for each world area, modified by the elimination of diacritical marks and sometimes adapted to give a fair sense of pronunciation. Certain standard Arabic terms and names are given in their original, usually Arabic, literary form despite actual variations in spelling and pronunciation the world over. Dates are given in the Christian era.

In the preparation of the book I have been greatly aided by my students, research assistants, and colleagues. They have helped me, depending upon their skills and my background in a given world area: by the preparation of bibliographies; reading, review, and preparation of digests on relevant literatures; research into particular themes and topics in both secondary and source materials; summaries or translations of materials in languages I do not read, and discussion of historiographical or methodological problems in their particular fields or disciplines. They have made an important contribution to my understanding of the role of Islam in several world areas, and have enormously facilitated the completion of the book.

I would like to thank David Goodwin, Margaret Malamud, Ann Taboroff, Sahar von Schlegell (Islamic history and Sufism); James Reid (Iran); Corrine Blake (Arab Middle East); Elaine Combs-Schilling (North Africa); Sandria Freitag and David Gilmartin (India); Mary Judd and Allan Samson (Indonesia); William McFarren and Leslie Sharp (Africa); Rose Glickman and Mark Saroyan (Russian Inner Asia), and John Foran and Michael Hughes (modernization and political economy). I am also grateful for the bibliographical help of Melissa MacCauly and Susan Mattern.

For the selection of illustrations, I benefited from the advice and assistance of Guitty Azarpay, Jere Bacharach, Sheila Blair, Jonathan Bloom, Herbert Bodman, Gordon Holler, Thomas Lentz, Kim Lyon, Amy Newhall, and

Labelle Prussin. I warmly thank the individuals and institutions by whose kind permission they are reproduced here. I am grateful to Cherie A. Semans of the Department of Geography, University of California, Berkeley, for the preparation of the designs and sketch maps upon which the maps in this volume are based.

Many friends and colleagues have read portions or even the whole of the manuscript and have given me invaluable corrections, suggestions and reflective thoughts. Each of them has enriched this volume, though none of them is responsible for the remaining faults. It gives me great pleasure to thank Jere Bacharach, Thomas Bisson, William Brinner, Edmund Burke III, Elaine Combs-Schilling, Shmuel Eisenstadt, Sandria Freitag, David Gilmartin, Albert Hourani, Suad Joseph, Barbara Metcalf, Thomas Metcalf, Martha Olcott, James Reid, Richard Roberts, William Roff, Allan Samson, Stanford Shaw, David Skinner, Ilkay Sunar, Ilter Turan, Abraham Udovitch, Lucette Valensi and Reginald Zelnik. As much as the writing, the friendship and generosity of these people have blessed the last seven years.

Several colleagues have had a particularly strong effect on the development of my understanding and have generously shared with me their views and unpublished work on various aspects of this book. In particular I would like to thank Barbara Metcalf (India), Elaine Combs-Schilling (North Africa), Suad Joseph (women's studies), Martha Olcott (Soviet Inner Asia), James Reid (Iran and Inner Asia), Allan Samson (Indonesia), Warren Fusfeld (for his dissertation on the Naqshbandiya in India), and Sandria Freitag and David Gilmartin (India). Morris Rossabi has graciously allowed me to see a copy of an unpublished article by Joseph Fletcher on the Naqshbandiya in China.

I am equally indebted to the many people who have helped prepare the manuscript and the published book. The staff of the Center for Advanced Studies in the Behavioral Sciences, Stanford, California prepared an early draft of the manuscript. Muriel Bell edited several of the chapters. Lynn Gale helped to arrange the transmission of this material to the word processor of the Institute of International Studies at Berkeley, where Nadine Zelinski and Christine Peterson have worked with great skill on the preparation of the manuscript and have given me endless friendly support; they are among the close collaborators to whom I owe this book. The staff of Cambridge University Press, Elizabeth Wetton, editor, Susan Moore, subeditor, and Jane Williams, designer, have been especially helpful. Finally, but not least, I am grateful to my wife Brenda Webster for her amazed, and amazing, patience as this book grew larger and larger, for her suggestions and criticism, and above all, for her faith in the work.

The research for this project has been generously supported by the Institute of International Studies of the University of California, Berkeley. I would like to express my thanks to Professor Carl Rosberg, Director of the Institute, to Mrs Karin Beros, Management Services Officer of the Institute, and to the Institute staff, who have been generous and gracious in their support. The preparation of this volume has also been made possible by a year in residence at the Center for Advanced Studies in the Behavioral Sciences, Stanford, California, with the support of the National Endowment for the Humanities, and by a research grant from the Hoover Institution, Stanford University. The completion of this work has been made possible by a grant from the Division of Research of the National Endowment for the Humanities, an independent federal agency. To these institutions I express my deep appreciation for affording me the opportunity to concentrate upon research and writing.

IRA M. LAPIDUS

University of California, Berkeley
March 15, 1985

ACKNOWLEDGEMENTS

Information and ideas for the maps in this book are derived from R. Roolvink, *Historical Atlas of the Muslim Peoples*, Cambridge, Mass., 1957; J. L. Bacharach, *A Middle East Studies Handbook*, Seattle, Wash., 1984; W. C. Bryce, *An Historical Atlas of Islam*, Leiden, 1981; F. Robinson, *Atlas of the Islamic World*, Oxford, 1982; J. D. Fage, *An Atlas of African History*, New York, 1978.

With the permission of the publishers extensive passages have been quoted or adapted from my previous publications:

"Adulthood in Islam: Religious Maturity in the Islamic Tradition," *Daedalus*, Spring 1976, pp. 93–108.

"Islam and the Historical Experience of Muslim Peoples," *Islamic Studies: A Tradition and Its Problems*, ed., Malcolm H. Kerr, Malibu, California: Undena Publications, 1980, pp. 89–102.

"Arab Settlement and Economic Development of Iraq and Iran in the Age of the Umayyad and Early Abbasid Caliphs," *The Islamic Middle East, 700–1900: Studies in Economic and Social History*, ed., A. L. Udovitch, Princeton: Darwin Press, 1981, pp. 177–208.

"The Arab Conquests and the Formation of Islamic Society," *Studies on the First Century of Islamic Society*, ed., G. H. A. Juynboll, Carbondale, Ill.: Southern Illinois University Press, 1982, pp. 49–72.

"Knowledge, Virtue and Action: The Classical Muslim Conception of Abad and the Nature of Religious Fulfillment in Islam," *Moral Conduct and*

Authority in South Asian Islam, ed., Barbara Metcalf, Berkeley: University of California Press, 1984, pp. 38–61. © 1984, The Regents of the University of California.

Contemporary Islamic Movements in Historical Perspective, Policy Papers No. 18, Institute of International Studies, University of California, Berkeley, 1983.

"Mamluk Patronage and the Arts in Egypt," *Muqarnas*, II (1984), New Haven, Conn.: Yale University Press, pp. 173–81.

PUBLISHER'S PREFACE

Scholars and students throughout the world recognize multi-volume Cambridge Histories as an outstanding reference series of unique authority. *The Cambridge History of Islam* was published in two volumes in 1970.

For their *A History of Islamic Societies*, the Press Syndicate commissioned Professor Ira Lapidus to prepare a single-volume history for a broader readership as a supplement to this series. His is a unique enterprise, a monumental work with the status of a Cambridge History, but by one hand and integrated by one coherent vision.

PART I

THE ORIGINS OF ISLAMIC CIVILIZATION: THE MIDDLE EAST FROM c. 600 TO c. 1200

1 The Ka‘ba

INTRODUCTION: MIDDLE EASTERN SOCIETIES BEFORE THE ADVENT OF ISLAM

Islamic societies were built upon the framework of an already established and ancient Middle Eastern civilization. From the pre-Islamic Middle East, Islamic societies inherited a pattern of institutions which would shape their destiny until the modern age. These institutions included ordered small communities based upon family, lineage, clientage and ethnic ties, agricultural and urban societies, market economies, monotheistic religions, and bureaucratic empires. The civilization of Islam, though born in Mecca, also had its progenitors in Palestine, Babylon, and Persepolis.

Islamic societies developed in an environment that since the earliest history of mankind had exhibited two fundamental, original, and persisting structures. The first was the organization of human societies into small, often familial, groups. The earliest hunting and gathering communities lived and moved in small bands. Since the advent of agriculture and the domestication of animals, the vast majority of Middle Eastern peoples have lived in agricultural villages or in the tent camps of nomadic pastoralists. Even town peoples were bound into small groups by ties of kinship and neighborhood with all that implies of strong affections and hatreds. These groups raised the young, arranged marriages, arbitrated disputes, and formed a common front vis-à-vis the outside world.

The second was a contrary evolutionary tendency toward the creation of unities of culture, religion, and empire on an ever-larger scale. In prehistoric times this tendency was manifested in the expansion of trade and the acceptance of common decorative styles and religious ideas, but its most important early manifestation was the emergence of the city-state in ancient Mesopotamia

3

(3500 B.C. – 2400 B.C.). The formation of cities in lower Iraq was a revolution in the history of mankind: it brought about the integration of diverse clans, villages, and other small groups into a single society. Beyond that, the merger of peoples led to a new order of cultural and artistic achievement – the invention of writing, the creation of great works of myth and religion, the construction of architectural masterpieces, and the fashioning of sensuous sculpture.

In the formation of Mesopotamian civilization two forces were at work that would ever after shape Middle Eastern societies: religion and empire. The first cities developed from the integration of small village communities into temple communities built upon shared commitment to the service of the gods. The Sumerians, the people of southern Iraq, believed that the lands they inhabited were the property of the gods, and that their primary duty was the construction of a great temple to worship the forces of the universe. The priests who presided over the worship were also judges and "political" chiefs. Moreover, the temple-cities were necessarily communities of economic as well as religious interests. The construction of the great temples required contributions of labor and the organization of masses of workers; their rituals required specialists in administrative, professional, and artisanal activities. The earliest cities were then communities in which religious leaders and religious ideas governed the economic and political affairs of the temples' adherents.

Beginning about 2400 B.C., the temple-cities of Mesopotamia were superseded by new unifying institutions – kingship and empires. Kingship in ancient Mesopotamia emanated from two sources: the warrior or warlord houses of the ancient Sumerian cities and the tribal peoples of northern Mesopotamia. Between 2700 B.C. and 2500 B.C., city kings established ephemeral states among their neighbors. About 2400 B.C., Sargon of Akkad, the chief of pastoral peoples in northern Mesopotamia, founded the first of the world's empires. Sargon's empire soon failed, and the temple-cities temporarily regained their independence. From Sargon to Hammurapi, the great lawgiver (d. 1750 B.C.), Mesopotamian empires rose and fell, but each one, though relatively short-lived, reinforced the institutions of kingship and of multi-city regimes.

Kingship as it developed from Sargon to Hammurapi increasingly assumed a sacred aura. Kings usurped the authority of priests and became the chief servants of the gods. They took over the priestly functions of mediating between the gods and the people. Ever after, in Middle Eastern conceptions, kingship was justified as the expression of the divine plan for the ordering of human societies. Sacred or sacralized political power, as well as religious community, became a vehicle for the unification of disparate peoples.

The successive empires of this ancient period also established the institutions that would henceforth be the medium for imperial rule. At the center was the ruler's household, the king surrounded by his family, retainers, soldiers, servants, and palace administrators. Standing armies were founded; feudal grants of land were awarded to loyal retainers. Governors, administrators, and spies were assigned to control cities and provinces.

The superimposition of empires upon smaller communities transformed local life. Temples were reduced to cogs in the imperial machine, and priests lost their judicial and political authority. The empires also intervened in small communities by freeing individuals from their commitments to clans and temples. To defend, administer, and maintain communications across wide territories required some decentralization of authority and greater mobility and autonomy for individuals. Warriors and administrators were assigned land and became independent proprietors. Merchants became entrepreneurs working with their own capital. Craftsmen began to work for the market rather than for the temple or royal household. A market economy emerged to facilitate exchanges among independent producers and consumers and progressively supplanted the older forms of household redistributive economy. The spread of markets and the introduction, by the seventh or sixth century B.C., of money as the medium of exchange transformed the economic structures of the ancient world. For increasing numbers of people the cash nexus replaced patrimonial authority as the mechanism which regulated the way they earned a living.

Empires also fostered the emergence of social individuality by providing the linguistic, religious, and legal conditions that freed individuals from absorption into clans, temples, and royal households, enabling them to function in a more open society. The language of the dominant elites became the language of the cosmopolitan elements of the society; the remote and powerful gods of the king and the empire – the gods of the cosmos, organized into a pantheon – superseded the intimate gods of individual localities. Imperial law regulated the distribution of property, economic exchange, and relations between the strong and the weak. Ancient empires, then, were not only political agencies, but provided the cultural, religious, and legal bases of society. Alongside religion they were a powerful force for the cultural integration of Middle Eastern civilization.

For ancient peoples, the empires symbolized the realm of civilization. The

function of empires was to defend the civilized world against the barbarians
outside and to assimilate them into the sphere of higher culture. For their part,
the barbarians, mostly nomadic peoples, wanted to conquer empires, share in
their wealth and sophistication, and win for themselves the status of civilized
men. Empires commanded allegiance because they were a coalition of civilized
peoples against the darkness without. They commanded allegiance because
kingship was thought of as a divine institution and the king was a divinely
selected agent, a person who, if not himself a god, shared in the aura,
magnificence, sacredness, and mystery of the divine. The ruler was God's
agent, his priest, the channel between this world and the heavens, designated
by the divine being to bring justice and right order to men so that they might
in turn serve God. The king thus assured the prosperity and well-being of his
subjects. Magically he upheld the order of the universe against chaos.

From these earliest empires to the eve of the Islamic era, the history of the
Middle East may be summarized as the elaboration and expansion of the
institutions formed in this early period. While parochial communities and local
cultures were a continuing force in Middle Eastern society, empires grew
progressively larger, with each wave of expansion and contraction bringing
new peoples into the sphere of imperial civilization. Empires came and went,
but the legacy of interchange of populations – the movement of soldiers,
administrators, merchants, priests, scholars, and workers – left a permanent
imprint of cosmopolitan culture and a heritage of shared laws, languages,
scripts, and social identity.

From Sargon to Hammurapi, Middle Eastern empires were restricted to
Mesopotamia, but later Hittite, Kassite, and other "barbarian" empires
brought Mesopotamia, Anatolia, and Iran into a common network. The empire of Assyria (911 B.C. – 612 B.C.) brought Iraq, western Iran, and, for a
time, Egypt into a single state. The Acheminid empire (550 B.C. – 331 B.C.)
incorporated eastern Iran and formed the first universal Middle Eastern
empire – the first to include all settled peoples from the Oxus River to the Nile
and the Dardanelles.

With the destruction of the Acheminid empire by Alexander the Great, the
Middle East was divided into two empires. Iraq and Iran as far as the Oxus
River belonged to the Persian or eastern empires – the Parthian empire
(226 B.C. – 234 A.D.) and its successor, the Sasanian empire (234 A.D. – 634
A.D.). In the west the successor states to the empire of Alexander became part
of the Roman empire. The Late Roman empire, called the Byzantine empire,
governed southern Europe, the Balkans, Anatolia, northern Syria, and parts
of Mesopotamia, Egypt, and North Africa.

The development of more encompassing empires and empire-wide civilizations was paralleled by the transformation of religions. The earliest religions were religions of nature and place, associated with small communities. With the increasing scale of social interaction, different peoples accepted the same gods. The gods of Middle Eastern peoples were, in ancient times, the gods of families, tribes, villages, and towns, but with the growing connections between peoples, universal gods came to be recognized. The gods of empires, the gods of dominant peoples, the gods of conquerors, travelers, merchants, and priests whose activities were not circumscribed by a single locality, came to be worshiped over large areas. The tendency toward syncretism and unification was also expressed by the conception of a pantheon and hierarchy of gods, which allowed different peoples to share in the same universe while preserving local cults and forms of worship.

From the universal supremacy of the great gods it was but one step, an inspired leap, to the revelation that there was but one God, who was the God of the whole universe and of all mankind. The oneness of God was preached first by the prophets of ancient Israel and then, in the seventh century B.C., by the Iranian prophet Zoroaster. Christianity, and later Islam, would also teach the unity of God, the universality of his sway, and the obligation of all of mankind to acknowledge his glory.

The history of how Judaism, Zoroastrianism, and Christianity became the religions of almost all peoples in the Roman-Byzantine and Sasanian empires cannot be told here. Suffice it to say that the missionary force of the new ideas and doctrines, the widening net of contacts between Middle Eastern peoples, and the support of the great empires meant that by the eve of Islam, pagan religions had been supplanted by universalist ones. Some of Iraq and all of Iran adhered to the Zoroastrian religion, including its main heresies, Manichaeanism and Mazdaism. Parts of Iraq and all the regions of the Byzantine empire to the west adhered to one of the several forms of Christianity. On the eve of Islam, the Coptic church was the church of Egypt; the Jacobite was the church of Syria; the Nestorian church prevailed in Iraq. The population of Armenia followed the Armenian church, while the populations of Anatolia and the Balkans adhered in the main to the Greek Orthodox church. In addition, Jewish communities and a few pagan enclaves were scattered throughout the area.

The monotheistic faiths held similar beliefs. Judaism taught that there was a single God of the universe who commanded his people, Israel, to fulfill his holy law, and who would judge them in this world and the next. Zoroastrianism held to a belief in a supreme God, Ahura Mazda, the creator of the world, a God of light and truth. The destiny of the world was thought to be decided by God's struggle with the forces of evil and darkness. Man was a part of this struggle: he had the obligation to contribute to the victory of the Good and Light by his actions and beliefs, and would be judged at the day of judgment. Zoroastrianism, like Judaism, was a religion of individual ethical responsibility. While Christianity held many similar beliefs, it was a religion of a different type. The central Christian doctrine is faith in a triune God – God the Father, the Son, and the Holy Spirit, the Son being the *logos*, Christ incarnate, who was crucified so that believers may be saved. Christianity has a strong ethical strand, but its central aspiration is salvation through faith in Christ from the evil and suffering that is inherent in man's nature.

Though different in orientation, Judaism, Zoroastrianism and Christianity had certain basic features in common. All were transcendental. They held that beyond the world of this life there is a higher world, the realm of the divine, to be attained either through ethical action or through faith in God. Through sacrifice, prayer, and sacrament, they sought salvation from sin and death, and entrance for men into the eternal reality beyond the ephemeral appearances of this world. Furthermore, they were universal religions, believing that God had created and continued to govern the whole universe and all men. Before God, believers are individually responsible for their faith and their ethical character. Believers are thus brothers in a common religious way of life and common quest for salvation.

This sense of identity and the common ways of life were more than sentiments. Religious belief inspired the formation of religious associations of which the best examples were the Christian churches. A church was a spiritual and administrative hierarchy in which the highest authority in both doctrinal and organizational matters belonged to a supreme head, who communicated with the body of believers through a territorially organized hierarchy. Popes and patriarchs held supreme authority. They appointed the bishops who administered the districts called dioceses, and the bishops appointed the parish priests. The Zoroastrians had their *mobads* or fire priests, and at some time in the third century acquired a chief mobad, and thus a similar hierarchy of clergy. These hierarchies integrated different localities into a common body, which defined the doctrines and principles by which all the members lived.

The parish implemented the church's principles at the local level. At this level Christian churches wielded considerable authority in the lives of their communicants in what we would now consider secular as well as religious matters. Church courts had jurisdiction in many areas of civil law such as family, property, commerce, and even in some matters of criminal law. The church was also an important educational institution. Bishops were sometimes the governors and administrators of the cities in which their dioceses were located. The church was not only an organization of the body of believers, it was an organization for the management of communal life in the fullest sense. With bishops as its magistrates, a church was a kind of civic corporation based on religion. The churches did not separate the secular from the religious. Religion, then, provided the over-arching concepts by which man could comprehend the social and natural universe that surrounded him, and was the institution through which the needs of worship, justice, education, and local administration could be served.

Jewish communities were also organized as the equivalent of local parishes. The Jews formed communities which combined belief and worship with the civil administration of law, education, and charity. The heads of the Jewish communities also represented them before the state authorities. Jews, however, did not have a hierarchical ecclesiastical organization, but were linked together by informal ties to and respect for the great academies of learning. Both the organized Christian churches and the decentralized Jewish communities were precedents for the later organization of Muslim religious associations.

On the eve of Islam, then, the Middle East was divided into two great realms of polity and culture, Byzantine and Sasanian, and two overlapping spheres of religious belief, Christian and Zoroastrian. Despite profound differences, the two realms of Middle Eastern civilization shared certain underlying similarities in the organization of empires, in religious beliefs, and in the structures of religious and communal life. Within each civilization, a myriad of small communities retained their social and cultural distinctiveness. Their headmen, chiefs, and elders mediated their integration into the over-arching realms of common religion and empire. Religion and empire were also closely related. The empires sustained, patronized, endowed, and enforced the organized worship of the churches. The Sasanian empire, however, was by and large more tolerant of the several religions under its jurisdiction than the Byzantine empire was of the schismatic churches in its control. In turn the religious communities legitimized the emperors' reigns and helped govern the subjects in their name.

The two political and religious regions, with their common institutional forms, would soon be drawn into a single Middle Eastern civilization. The Arab conquests of the seventh century and the Islamic era which followed preserved the continuity of Middle Eastern institutions. Family lineage, clientele, and ethnic communities continued, despite historical change, to be the building blocks of society. The regional ecology continued to be based upon

Table 1. *Islam in world history*

Early village farming communities	c. 7000 B.C.
Cities	c. 3000 B.C.
Empires	c. 2400 B.C.
Axial-age and monotheistic religions	c. 800 B.C.
Muhammad	c. 570–632
Middle Eastern Islamic societies	622 – c. 1200
Worldwide diffusion of Islam	c. 650 to present
Rise of European world empires	1200–1900
Modern transformation of Islamic societies	1800 to present

agrarian and urban communities, and the economy functioned on the basis of marketing and money exchanges. The basic forms of state organization, including bureaucratic administration, and the predominant style of religious life, focusing upon universal and transcendental beliefs and a parish-like community organization were also maintained. Islam, however, redefined the religious beliefs and the cultural and social identity of Middle Eastern peoples and reorganized the empires that ruled them.

This transformation took place in three main phases: first, the creation of a new Islamic community in Arabia as a result of the transformation of a peripheral region with a predominantly lineage society into a Middle Eastern type of monotheistic and politically centralized society. The second phase began with the conquest of the Middle East by this new Arabian-Muslim community, and led to the generation, in the period of the early Caliphate (to 945), of an Islamic empire and culture. Finally, in the post-imperial or Sultanate period (945 – c. 1200) the institutional and cultural prototypes of the Caliphal era were transformed into new types of Islamic states and institutions. In this era Islam became the religion and the basis of communal organization of the mass of Middle Eastern peoples. In the first phase we see the emergence of Islam in a tribal society. In the second we consider Islam as it becomes the religion of an imperial state and urban elite. In the third phase we see how Islamic values and elite groups transformed the masses of Middle Eastern peoples.

THE PREACHING OF ISLAM

CHAPTER 1

ARABIA

On the eve of the Islamic era, Arabia stood on the periphery of the Middle Eastern imperial societies in a state of development equivalent to the ancient rather than the evolved condition of the rest of the region. Here the primary communities remained especially powerful, while urban, religious, and royal institutions, though not absent, were less developed. Whereas the imperial world was predominantly agricultural, Arabia was primarily pastoral. While the imperial world was citied, Arabia was the home of camps and oases. Whereas the imperial peoples were committed to the monotheistic religions, Arabia was largely pagan. While the imperial world was politically organized, Arabia was politically fragmented.

At the same time, Arabia was always in close contact with and strongly under the influence of the imperial regions. There were no physical boundaries between Arabia and the Middle East proper. No rigid ethnic or demographic frontier isolated Arabia from the rest of the region; nor did great walls or political boundaries. Arabian peoples migrated slowly into the Middle East and themselves made up much of the population of the north Arabian desert and of Syria. Arabs in the fertile crescent region shared political forms, religious beliefs, economic connections, and physical space with the societies around them. Arabia was further connected to the rest of the region by itinerant preachers, who introduced monotheism into the largely pagan peninsula; by merchants who brought textiles, jewelry, and foodstuffs such as grain and wine into Arabia and stimulated the taste for the good things of life; and by the agents of the imperial powers who intervened diplomatically and politically to extend their trading privileges, protect sympathetic religious

Map 1. The Middle East on the eve of the Muslim era

WESTERN
TURKISH
KHANATE

Arabian Sea

Jaxartes R. (Syr Darya)

SOGHDIANS

Aral Sea

TRANSOXANIA

Bukhara •
Samarqand •
Oxus R. (Amu Darya)

• Marw

Herat •

• Nishapur

KHAZARS

Caspian Sea

• Ardabil

• Isfahan

FARS

OMAN

Persian Gulf

BAHRAIN

Jundishapur •
• Ctesiphon   • Ubulla

ARMENIA

Lake Urmiya

Nasibin •
Tigris R.

IRAQ

• al-Hira

Euphrates R.

MESOPOTAMIA

KINDA

A R A B I A

HADHRAMAUT

• Najran

YEMEN   Aden •

Black Sea

Constantinople •

• Nicaea

ANATOLIA

Edessa •
• Aleppo

Antioch •

SYRIA

• Palmyra

Damascus •

• Jerusalem

• Petra

HIJAZ

Medina •

• Mecca   • al-Ta'if

Red Sea

CYPRUS

Gaza •
• Babylon

Alexandria •

EGYPT

Nile R.

Athens •

Salonika •

Dardanelles

Danube R.

Mediterranean Sea

NUBIA

ABYSSINIA

500 km
500 miles

Byzantine empire
Sasanian empire
Ghassanids
Lakhmids

populations, and advance their strategic interests. The Byzantines and the Sasanians disputed control of Yemen, and both were active in creating spheres of influence in North Arabia. They also exported military technique to the Arabs. From the Romans and the Persians the Arabs obtained new arms, and learned how to use mail coats of armor. They learned new tactics, and the importance of discipline. This seepage of military technique came through the enrollment of Arabs as auxiliaries in the Roman or Persian armies, and sometimes through the unhappy experience of being repulsed by superior forces on the frontiers of the empires.

Thus the civilization of the Middle Eastern empires was seeping into Arabia as happened everywhere where developed empires maintained frontiers with politically and culturally less organized societies. These influences and the need to mobilize the power and resources required to maintain political autonomy, or to carry on trade with empires, stimulated in less developed societies the same processes of stratification, specialization, and of community and identity formation by which the empires had themselves come into being. They generated in peripheral areas just those conditions which allowed for the eventual amalgamation of empire and outside areas into a single society. By the late sixth century, however, these inducements to evolutionary change had not gone so far as to absorb Arabia into the general civilization of the Middle East, or to inspire in it the birth of a new civilization.

From the beginning of camel domestication and the occupation of the central Arabian desert in the twelfth and thirteenth centuries B.C., until the rise of Islam in the seventh century, the balance between parochial, local elements and the unifying forces of religion and empire lay heavily on the side of small, relatively isolated communities. Families and clans, often pastoralists and camel herders, and the confederations built upon them, were the basic units of society. The bedouins raised camels and migrated seasonally in search of pasturage. They also provided caravans with animals, guides, and guards. They passed the winter in desert reserves, migrating to seek spring pasturage at the first signs of rain. In the summer they usually camped near villages or oases, where they exchanged animal products for grain, dates, utensils, weapons, and cloth.

The migratory peoples lived in tight-knit kinship groups, patriarchal families formed of a father, his sons, and their families. These families were further grouped into clans of several hundred tents, which migrated together, owned pasturage in common, and fought as one in battle. Each clan was fundamentally an independent unit. All loyalties were absorbed by the group, which acted as a collectivity to defend its individual members and to meet their responsibilities. If a member was harmed, the clan would avenge him. If he did harm, it would stand responsible with him. As a consequence of this group solidarity, called ʿasabiya, the bedouin clan regarded itself as a complete polity and recognized no external authority. The clans were led by a *shaykh* (chief) who was usually selected by the clan elders from one of the prominent families and who always acted in accord with their counsel. He settled internal disputes according to the group's traditions, but he could not legislate or command. The shaykh had to be wealthy and show generosity to the needy and to his supporters; he had to be a man of exquisite tact and prudence – forbearing, resolute, and practical. Above all he had to have the good judgment to avoid antagonizing his sensitive followers.

The clan defined the mental universe of the bedouin. Poetry expressed a fundamental devotion to the prestige and security of the group; without the clan, the individual had no place in the world, no life of his own. The language of the bedouins offered no way to express the concept of individuality or personality. The term *wajh* (face), although applied to the chief, was really a concept designating the persona of the group rather than the individuality of the shaykh as a person.

In certain conditions the bedouins could be integrated into more inclusive, often stratified, bodies. At the points of contact between the fertile parts of Arabia and the desert, at oases in Yemen, and in the northern margins where the Arabian desert touches the fertile crescent, confederations could arise to organize caravans and trade. Different groups might also be integrated on the basis of religion. The formation of a *haram*, a common sanctuary, allowed for worship of the same gods, economic exchange, sociability, and political bargaining.

Only in the peripheral zones did monarchies and kingdoms take shape. In south Arabia, royal authority was first established about 1000 B.C. and lasted until the Muslim era. By the fifth century B.C., Yemen was organized into kingdoms with monarchs, landed elites, a religious pantheon, and organized temple worship of the gods, which encompassed agriculture, trading, and pastoral peoples. In Yemen the political elite was drawn from aristocratic tribes and controlled extensive landed estates. Temples also had substantial holdings, while the commoners were organized into clans that were obliged to provide agricultural and military services to the elites. Tributary and vassal tribes extended the power of the Yemeni kingdoms well into the interior of Arabia. In the north, kingdoms were less fully institutionalized. For example, the ancient Nabatean kingdom (sixth century B.C. – 106 A.D.) was ruled by a king who claimed divinely granted authority and had some centralized administration, but really depended on a supporting coalition of clan and tribal chiefs. In 85 B.C., the new kingdom, with its capital at Petra, controlled much of Jordan and Syria. It traded with Yemen, Egypt, Damascus, and the coastal cities of Palestine. The kingdom lasted until 106 A.D., when it was destroyed by the Romans. Palmyra succeeded Petra, extending monarchical control over the deserts and surrounding border areas. An urban capital, elaborate temples, wide commercial networks, and a strong Hellenistic culture marked Palmyran supremacy. These kingdoms maintained economic and political order throughout the peninsula, and brought the bedouins of the desert interiors into the political and cultural frameworks of the periphery. Nomads provided trading links with settled places in the interior and at the same time belonged to larger political coalitions sponsored by the peripheral powers.

The degree to which the individual clan was the predominant historical actor and the degree to which confederated or large-scale societies were dominant was historically variable. The main factor regulating this balance was the degree to which sedentarized forms of economy and society imposed upon or were overwhelmed by pastoral forms. The history of Arabia was governed by the tension between the settled and the pastoral zones. From about 1000 B.C. until about 300 A.D. Yemen, the Hijaz, and the northern periphery successfully organized the interior of the peninsula and kept bedouin life subordinate to the agricultural and commercial economies of the settled kingdoms, but the dominance of the peripheral kingdoms did not last. The opening of sea routes for international trade in the first century B.C. brought financial and political disaster to Yemen. Political power in the south weakened with the failure of overland routes; bedouins interfered in internal conflicts, pushed in against agricultural areas, and cut off Yemeni influence in the Hijaz and in central Arabia. In 328 A.D., Imru al-Qays b. ᶜAmr, King of the Arabs, took control of Najran. In the north, Palmyra was destroyed in 271 A.D. – the victim, as were the Nabateans, of Roman efforts to incorporate northern Arabia directly into the empire. By the end of the third century, the peripheral kingdoms' grip on the center of the peninsula was broken.

From the early fourth century to the end of the sixth century, there were several efforts to reestablish the dominance of peripheral kingdoms, restore order in the desert, and protect trade and oasis cultivation. In Yemen, the Himyarite kingdom was reestablished, but without the effective powers of its predecessor. Yemeni influence extended over the bedouins of the Hijaz and central Arabia, mediated by the tribal confederation of Kinda, which came into being at some time in the fifth century, and lasted about 100 years. Similar efforts were made under Roman and Persian auspices. After the destruction of

Petra and Palmyra, the Romans attempted to defend these provinces by recruiting Arab confederates to guard them against other Arabs and the Sasanians. At the end of the fifth century the Ghassan, an Arab-Christian people, were mobilized to prevent penetration by the bedouins into Syria and Palestine, and to defend the empire against the Persians and their clients. The Sasanian empire also maintained a buffer state – the kingdom of Lakhm, a coalition of Aramean and Christian tribes along the border between Iraq and the desert organized under the leadership of the Lakhm family whose capital was at al-Hira, on the lower reaches of the Euphrates.

The new peripheral regimes, however, were less powerful than their predecessors. Kinda and Ghassan were not strongly organized archaic kingdoms but tribal confederations. Though Lakhm had its capital at al-Hira, a monarchy differentiated from its tribal base, and strong support from the Sasanians, it was severely hampered by Sasanian control and Arab competition.

In the course of the sixth century the peripheral kingdoms all disintegrated. In 525 Yemen was conquered by Abyssinia. Kinda broke up in 529. The Abyssinians attacked central Arabia in 535 and penetrated the Hijaz in 570, but in 572 the Sasanians expelled them from Yemen. Even the Sasanians, however, could not stem the decline of the south. In the intervening period, the south Arabian economy crumbled, and political unity was completely lost. In the north, the Romans and Persians removed their vassals and attempted to absorb north Arabia into their respective empires. Ghassan was deprived of Roman backing in 584, and Lakhm was replaced by a Sasanian governor in 602. In the early seventh century the Byzantine and Sasanian empires engaged in mutually exhausting wars. The middle-period confederations were thus destroyed by outside powers who could not replace even their ephemeral contributions to political and economic order.

In the sixth century, only Mecca stood against the trend to political and social fragmentation, and provided the one major focus of social and economic order. A religious sanctuary, whose shrine, the Kaʿba, attracted pilgrims from all over Arabia, Mecca became the repository of the various idols and tribal gods of the peninsula, and the destination of an annual pilgrimage. The pilgrimage also entailed a period of truce, which served not only for religious worship, but also for the arbitration of disputes, the settlement of claims and debts, and, of course, trade. The Meccan fairs gave the Arabian tribes a common identity and gave Mecca moral primacy in much of western and central Arabia.

These fairs were the origin of Mecca's commercial interests. The people called the Quraysh, who took control of Mecca in the fifth century, became a skilled retailing population. In the sixth century they found a place in the spice trade as well, as difficulties with other international trade routes diverted traffic to the overland Arabian route. Byzantine sea power in the Red Sea and the Indian Ocean was on the decline; piracy was endemic in the Red Sea. At the same time, the Persian Gulf–Tigris–Euphrates route was harassed by Sasanian exploitation, and was frequently disrupted by Lakhm, Ghassan, and Persian–Roman wars. By the mid-sixth century, as heir to Petra and Palmyra, Mecca became one of the important caravan cities of the Middle East. The Meccans carried spices, leather, drugs, cloth, and slaves which had come from Africa or the Far East to Syria, and returned money, weapons, cereals, and wine to Arabia. The trade required treaties with Byzantine officials and with the bedouins to assure safe passage of the caravans, protection of water and pasture rights, and guides and scouts. Such arrangements eventually gave Mecca a sphere of political as well as commercial influence among the nomads and created a confederation of client tribes. In association with the Tamim tribes, a loose Meccan diplomatic hegemony was established in the desert. With the decline of Abyssinia, Ghassan, and Lakhm, Meccan influence was about the only integrative political force in late sixth-century Arabia.

In most of Arabia, however, the failure of the border powers to restore effective control over the center of the peninsula resulted in progressive, but not uninterrupted, bedouinization. As bedouin communities were set free of the political and commercial controls once exerted by the border kingdoms, they made inroads upon the settled areas of south Arabia. In the fourth, fifth, and sixth centuries, large-scale migrations of bedouin peoples into the north Arabian desert and the margins of the fertile crescent were underway. Within Arabia, violent conflict between clans and tribes became more frequent. Progressively, pastoral interests overcame agricultural interests. Bedouin migrations converted marginal regions in Yemen and on the borders of Iraq and Syria back to pasturage. Bedouin marauders harassed the caravan trade, and the sedentary population drifted into pastoralism. The bedouinization of Arabia did not, of course, occur all at once. It was a gradual and cumulative process, shifting the ever-delicate balance between organized polities and clan societies in favor of the latter.

The confrontation between strengthened small communities and trading and religious confederacy was reflected in the cultural as well as the political life of Arabia in the late sixth century. Just as the political realm was beset by the tension among different types of political and economic organization, cultural life was beset by incompatible visions of human life, human society, and conflicting concepts of the cosmos and the gods.

The poetic and religious culture of the clans remained a fundamental element in bedouin life. By and large, the Arabian bedouin was an animist and polytheist who believed that all natural objects and events were living spirits who could be either helpful or harmful to man. The universe of the Arabs was peopled with *jinn* (demons), who had to be propitiated or controlled and defeated by magic. By magical practices, the bedouin might determine his fate or coerce these forces, but he had no sympathetic relation with them. They were another tribe, not his own, though they penetrated his existence. The bedouins also worshiped ancestors, moon and star gods, and gods in the form of stones or trees placed in protective sanctuaries. Otherwise, their religion did not entail a philosophic vision of the universe, though it expressed their sense of the sacred as vested mysteriously in the plethora of forces that dominated the natural world and the being of man.

The religions of the politically more complex confederations and kingdoms were also polytheistic, but they expressed a more differentiated concept of the divine, the natural, and the human worlds. The tribal harams and the temples of archaic kingdoms were devoted to regularized cultic worship. The Meccan Kaᶜba, for example, the center of a pilgrimage, was the sanctuary of numerous gods arranged in a hierarchy. These gods were no longer simply identified with nature; they were defined as distinct persons separate from the natural forces that, as willful beings, they controlled. Such gods had to be propitiated by sacrifices; one could communicate with them as persons.

In an environment of shared sanctuaries, new conceptions of collective identity emerged. The annual trade and religious fairs at Mecca and other places of pilgrimage brought the numerous families and tribes of the peninsula together, focused the worship of tribal peoples upon common cults, allowed them to observe each others' mores, and standardized the language and customs by which they dealt with each other. Awareness of common religious beliefs and lifestyles, recognition of aristocratic tribes and families, agreed institutions regulating pasturage, warfare, commerce, alliance and arbitration procedures, a poetic *koinē* used by reciters of poems throughout Arabia – marked the development of a collective identity transcending the individual clan.

In another sense, however, there was profound similarity between the cultic confederation of Mecca and the fragmented life of the bedouin clans. The bedouin mentality and Meccan polytheism presented the same view of the person, society, and the universe. This view afforded no coherent conception of the human being as an entity. In ancient Arabic there was no single word meaning the person. *Qalb* (heart), *ruh* (spirit), *nafs* (soul), *wajh* (face) were the several terms in use, none of which correspond to the concept of an integrated personality. The plurality of the gods reflected and symbolized a fragmented view of the nature of man, of society, and of the forces that governed the cosmos. In the pagan view the self was without a center, society without wholeness, and the universe without overall meaning.

The monotheistic religions stood for something other. They were introduced into Arabia by foreign influences: Jewish and Christian settlements, traveling preachers and merchants, and the political pressure of the Byzantine empire and Abyssinia. By the sixth century, monotheism already had a certain vogue. Many non-believers understood the monotheistic religions; others, called *hanif* in the Quran, were believers in one God but not adherents of any particular faith. Christians were numerous in Yemen in small oases, and in the border regions of the north, where they were in the minority but profoundly influential and, to many people, deeply appealing, both by the force of their teaching and by force of representing what was felt to be a more powerful, more sophisticated, and more profound civilization. The new religions taught that there was a single God who created the moral and spiritual order of the world; a God who made men individually responsible for their actions and faith; a God who made all men brethren, whatever their race or clan; and a God who made their salvation possible.

Thus, the monotheists differed profoundly from the polytheists in their sense of the unity of the universe and the meaningfulness of personal experience. Whereas the polytheists could see only a fragmented world, composed of numerous, disorderly, and arbitrary powers, the monotheists saw the universe as a totality grounded in, and created and governed by, a single being who was the source of both material and spiritual order. Whereas the polytheists envisaged a society in which people were divided by clan and locality, each with its own community and its own gods, the monotheists imagined a society in which common faith made men brothers in the quest for salvation. Whereas in the polytheistic view the human being was a concatenation of diverse forces without any moral or psychic center, a product of the fates, in the monotheistic view he was a moral, purposive creature whose ultimate objective was redemption. In the view of the monotheistic religions, God, the universe, man, and society were part of a single, meaningful whole.

Nowhere was this confrontation of worldviews more important than in Mecca. Mecca was one of the most complex and heterogeneous places in Arabia. Here society had grown beyond the limitations of the clan and tribe to afford some complexity of political and economic ties. Mecca had a council of clans (*mala*), though this council held only a moral authority, with no independent powers of enforcement. Mecca was also one of the few places in Arabia to have a floating, nontribal population of individual exiles, refugees, outlaws, and foreign merchants. The very presence of different peoples and clans – people belonging to no clan, foreigners, people with diverse religious convictions, differing views of life's purposes and values – moved Meccans away from the old tribal religions and moral conceptions. New conceptions of personal worth and social status and new social relationships were fostered in this more complex society. On the positive side, the imperatives of commercial activity, and Arabia-wide contacts and identifications set individuals free from the traditions of their clans and allowed for the flourishing of self-conscious, critical spirits, who were capable of experimenting with new values, and who might conceive a universal God and universal ethics. On the negative side, society suffered from economic competition, social conflict, and moral confusion. Commercial activities brought in their wake social stratification on the basis of wealth, and morally unassimilable discrepancies between individual situations and the imperatives of clan loyalty. The Quran would condemn the displacement of tribal virtues by the ambition, greed, arrogance, and hedonism of the new rich. Mecca, which had begun to give Arabia some measure of political and commercial order, was losing its moral and social identity.

Arabia was in ferment: a society in the midst of constructive political experiments was endangered by anarchy; strong clan and tribal powers threatened to overwhelm the fragile forces of agricultural stability, commercial activity, and political cohesion. It was a society touched by imperial influences but without a central government; marked by the monotheistic religions but without an established church; susceptible to Middle Eastern ideas but not permeated by them. Arabia had yet to find its place in the Middle Eastern world. Everything was in question. Nothing was decided. Here Muhammad was born, was raised, was vouchsafed the Quran, and here he became the Prophet of Islam.

CHAPTER 2

THE LIFE OF THE PROPHET

Prophecy is an extraordinary phenomenon, and all the more rare is the prophet whose influence permanently transforms the lives of his people and leaves as a legacy one of the world's great religions. Thus to achieve some understanding of Muhammad and the rise of Islam, we have to understand the religious vision and its relation to the Prophet's worldly action. Here we shall discuss the teaching of the Quran, the unfolding of Muhammad's life, the context in which he lived, and the impact of the Quran revealed and the activities of the Prophet upon his own society.

Compared with the history of other great founders of religions, the sources of our knowledge of the Prophet's life are abundant. We have the Quran itself, Muslim scripture, believed by Muslims to have been revealed by God through the angel Gabriel to Muhammad – the direct revelation of God's word and will, the ultimate source of Muslim belief, and the inspiration to live in the way in which God requires of human beings. In the Muslim view the Quran is the final revelation and supersedes the previous Jewish and Christian dispensations. Muhammad's recitations of the Quran were copied down and the Prophet himself probably began the process of compiling a written scripture by dictating to scribes and instructing them on how to order the verses of the revelation. The Quran was fully compiled after the Prophet's death and an official version promulgated by the Caliph ʿUthman (644–656). Because of various problems of script and variant non-ʿUthmanic traditions, small points of detail remained in dispute until the tenth century, when Muslim scholars agreed to consider seven variant readings equally valid.

The *hadith*, or sayings of the Prophet, form a second source of knowledge

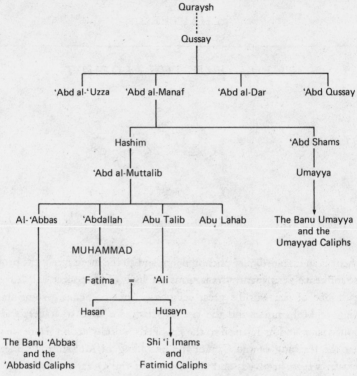

Fig. 1. The family of the Prophet.

of the Prophet's life and teaching. These are separate from the Quran and most of them constitute, in the Muslim view, Muhammad's own, albeit inspired utterances, as opposed to Quranic utterances. Hadith deal mainly with ritual, moral, and other religious matters. The third principal source of the Prophet's life is the biography compiled by Ibn Ishaq (d. 768–9) on the bases of oral tradition and partial written accounts and then edited and revised by Ibn Hisham (d. 833–4). Materials not included in the edition of Ibn Hisham are found in other later Muslim sources.

From these sources we know that the Quran was revealed over the last two decades of Muhammad's life, from about 610 until his death in 632. As it unfolded over time the Quran dealt with specific historical circumstances; later Muslim commentators provide us with information about the events associated with particular revelations. Verses of the Quran deal with Muhammad's debate with the Meccans and his handling of political and social problems in Medina, and provide concrete guidance for ritual, moral, legal and political matters. The Quran, viewed as an historical document, shows how Muhammad's vision developed in direct response to concrete circumstances. In his biography we do not see Muhammad as propounding a fixed system of belief. He was a judge rather than a legislator, a counselor rather than a theorist. We see the Prophet as a man to whom the revelation has given a new direction in life, a direction whose implications and possibilities ever unfold before him. In this chapter we shall follow, then, the progressive deepening and fulfillment of the Prophet's life over time and attempt to assess the nature of his teachings and their impact upon Arabian society.

The revelations began around the fortieth year of Muhammad's life. He was born around 570 A.D. into the once prominent clan of Banu Hashim. His ancestors had been guardians of the sacred well of Zamzam in Mecca, but by his time the clan, though engaged in commerce, was not among those that controlled the most lucrative aspects of the caravan trade. Muhammad's father died before he was born. He was raised by his grandfather and then by his uncle, Abu Talib. Muhammad worked as a caravaner, and at twenty-five married his employer, Khadija, a rich widow. They had four daughters and several sons; all the boys died in infancy.

Muhammad was a man with a religious bent. In the years before the revelations he was wont to retreat to the mountains outside of Mecca to pray in solitude. A tradition which is reported as coming from Ibn Ishaq but is not found in the recension of Ibn Hisham indicates that Muhammad received advice and support from a hanif – an Arabian monotheist, a believer in one God though not a Jew or a Christian – who taught him about the futility of worshiping idols. Thus, before the revelation of the Quran Muhammad was already a seeker after religious truth.

About the year 610, he received his first revelations. They came upon him like the breaking of dawn. The first words revealed to him were the opening five lines of *sura* (chapter) 96: "Recite: In the Name of thy Lord who created, created Man of a blood-clot. Recite: And thy Lord is the Most Generous, who taught by the Pen, taught Man that he knew not." His consciousness of the presence of the divine brought awe, fear, and foreboding.

In the early years the content of these revelations was the vision of a great, just God, Allah, who would on the day of judgment weigh every man's works and consign him to bliss or damnation. The early revelations emphasized the fear of the last judgment, piety and good works, and warnings against neglect of duties and heedlessness of the final day of reckoning. Opposed to the worship of God and fear of the last judgment were presumption, pride in human powers, and attachment to the things of this world. This was the false pride of the Meccans, that led them to the sin of avarice – neglect of the poor, neglect of almsgiving and of support for the weaker members of the community. In addition to preaching these ideas, Muhammad instituted ritual prayer. Eschatological piety, ethical nobility, and prayer formed the basis of early Islam.

The revelation in the Quran bore important similarities to Christianity and Judaism. For Muhammad the revelations came from the same source. Christian parallels are evident in the articulation of Muhammad's vision of the last judgment – the prediction that it would come with thunder, trumpets, and earthquakes, that the world would be destroyed and the dead resurrected, that it would be a terrifying moment when, one by one, all men passed before God (the angels interceding only for the good). These details are found in the preaching of itinerant Syrian monks and missionaries at the fairs of Arabia. Ideas similar to Judaism, such as rigid monotheism, belief in written revelations, the conception of a prophet sent to a chosen people, and certain specific religious practices are also prominent in the Quran. Yet Muhammad was certainly not a convert either to Christianity or to Judaism. Both his inspiration and the language in which it was couched were original. Muhammad had been vouchsafed a personal knowledge of God's being and will. He must have understood his revelation in the sense of the Arabian monotheists, who believed in a transcendent God but were neither Jews nor Christians.

For three years after the first revelations, Muhammad remained a private person, coming to terms with God's message. He related his experiences to his family and friends, and the force of inspiration and the compelling language in which it was clothed persuaded them that his visions were indeed divine revelations. A small group of people accepted his ideas and gathered around him to hear and recite the Quran. These were the first converts, and they included his wife Khadija, Abu Bakr and ʿAli, later to be Caliphs (the Prophet's successors as leaders of the Muslims), and others.

After three years the time had come for a public mission. About 613 Muhammad received the revelation that begins "Rise and warn." He began to preach publicly, a first step toward injecting religious ideas into the actualities of social and political life. Significantly, the first converts were rootless migrants, poor men, members of weak clans, and younger sons of strong clans – those people most dissatisfied with the changing moral and social climate of Mecca, for whom the Prophet's message proved a vital alternative.

Still, the early years of Muhammad's public mission were disappointing. Apart from his small following, Muhammad's preaching met with almost universal opposition. From the Quran we know that the Quraysh, the traders who dominated Meccan life, belittled Muhammad's revelations. They scoffed at the bizarre notion of a last judgment and resurrection, and asked for miracles as proof of the truth of his message. Muhammad's only response – still the Muslim response – was that the Quran itself, with its unique beauty of language, is a miracle and a sign of revelation. Nonetheless the Quraysh denounced Muhammad as a *kahin*, a soothsayer, a disreputable sort of magician or madman. Then came insults, harassment of Muhammad and his followers, and an economic boycott that extended to keeping the Muslims from purchasing food in the markets.

This opposition was apparently couched on religious grounds, but Muhammad's preaching was in fact a threat to the whole fabric of family and community associated with the beliefs of the Quraysh. The revelation was an implicit challenge to all the existing institutions of the society – worship of gods and the economic life attached to their shrines, the values of tribal tradition, the authority of the chiefs and the solidarity of the clans from which Muhammad wished to draw his followers. Religion, moral belief, social structure, and economic life formed a system of ideas and institutions inextricably bound up with one another. To attack them at any major point was to attack the whole society root and branch. The opposition of the Quraysh was thus inevitable.

Faced with this opposition, the revelations of the Quran provided Muhammad with a response. He was not just a private person to whom a vision of the divine being had been vouchsafed, but a prophet coming in a long succession of Old and New Testament and Arabian prophets; he was a prophet sent to declare God's will in Arabic. He was justified in his preaching because he was sent by God to rescue his people from ignorance and guide them on the path to righteousness. At this stage Muhammad included Christians and Jews, as well as pagans, in his mission. Only later did it become clear that his preaching would establish a new religion alongside Judaism and Christianity.

As Muhammad's mission unfolded it became clear that it involved not only the presentation of the Quranic revelation, but the leadership of the community. The opposition of the Quraysh showed that a community's life cannot be separated from its religious beliefs. Prophecy implied eschatological vision and knowledge of God's will, which in turn entailed right guidance and social leadership. As early as 615 we have a concrete sign that Muhammad had become the leader of a community, and that those who believed in his teachings constituted a group set apart from other Meccans. In that year, a group of his followers departed for Abyssinia. For the sake of religion people were willing to leave their families and clans and take up life together in a foreign land. The bonds of common belief were stronger than the bonds of blood. In this way, the new religion threatened to dissolve the old order of society and to create a new one.

The opposition to Muhammad revealed yet another dimension of the relations between religion and society. It exposed the extent to which Muhammad's very survival in Mecca, to say nothing of his preaching, depended on his uncle, Abu Talib, and his clansmen, the Banu Hashim, who protected him because he was their kinsman. With this support, Muhammad could, despite harassment, continue preaching. But from about 615 or 616, he no longer made many converts. He had by then about 100 followers, but the Meccan boycott made clear that to join Muhammad was to invite hardship. The truth of his message and his oratorical, poetical, and personal qualities were no longer as persuasive because the man himself was insulted, hounded and ostracized. For his mission to succeed, Muhammad would have to be in a more prominent, even powerful, position. People would not be moved by ideas alone, but only by ideas propounded with commanding prestige.

In 619 Muhammad resolved to seek support outside of Mecca. By then his situation had become precarious. His wife Khadija and his uncle Abu Talib were dead; the support of his clan greatly diminished. He finally decided to go to al-Taʾif, a nearby oasis, and call on the people there to accept him as Prophet. This venture proved naive. Muhammad was ridiculed and driven out. He also tried to find support among the bedouins, but again met no success. The times, after all, did not clamor for the man. By 619 Muhammad understood that to protect himself and his followers, to overcome the resistance of the Quraysh, and to gain a hearing from Arabians beyond the small circles spontaneously attracted to him, some kind of political base was necessary.

At this juncture, the situation of Medina was a godsend. Medina was an agricultural oasis. Like Mecca it was inhabited by various clans and not by a single tribe, but unlike Mecca, it was a settlement racked by bitter and even anarchic feuding between the leading tribal groups – the Aws and the Khazraj. Prolonged feuding threatened the safety of men in the fields and called into question Medina's very existence. Unlike the bedouins, Medinans had to live as neighbors and could not move from place to place.

Moreover, like Mecca, Medina was undergoing social changes that rendered the underlying bedouin form of kinship society obsolete. Agricultural rather than pastoral needs governed the economy of Medina. Its social life came increasingly to be governed by proximity in space rather than by kinship.

Also, Medina had a large Jewish population, which may have made the populace as a whole more sympathetic to monotheism.

At a crucial impasse in his own life Muhammad made his first converts in Medina, and after a protracted set of negotiations was invited to come to the troubled city. In 620 six men of Khazraj accepted him as Prophet. In 621 a dozen men representing both Khazraj and Aws pledged to obey Muhammad and to avoid sin, and in 622 a delegation of 75 Medinans paved the way for his coming to Medina by taking the pledge of al-ʿAqaba – the pledge to defend Muhammad.

Behind these agreements lie both acceptance of the Quranic revelation and Arabian precedents. In a society with no common law or government and no authority higher than the chiefs of individual clans, feuding clans often selected someone reputed to have religious vision and be just, politic, tactful, and of course disinterested, to be their arbitrator or *hakam*. Because the hakams had no means of enforcing their decisions, it was common practice for them to interview the disputants and assure themselves that the disputants would accept their decisions.

With the guarantee provided by the pledge, Muhammad and his followers made the journey to Medina – the most dramatic event in Muslim history. The community of Islam originated at that time, and the Muslim calendar dates the Christian year 622 as the year 1. The journey is called the *hijra*, which simply means "migration." For Muslims the word has come to mean not only a change of place, but the adoption of Islam and entry into the community of Muslims. The hijra is the transition from the pagan to the Muslim world – from kinship to a society based on common belief.

In Medina Muhammad and his Medinan hosts also came to a formal political agreement. Muhammad and his Meccan followers were to form one political group with the clans of Medina, called an *umma* – still the word for the community of Muslims. Meccans and Medinans would act as one in the defense of Muhammad and of Medina against outsiders. No clan would make a separate peace. No one would aid the Quraysh of Mecca, the presumptive enemy. The charter specified that all disputes would be brought before Muhammad. For Muhammad, moreover, the agreements were but the first step toward creating a sense of community among all the various clans, establishing his own authority and prestige, and ultimately converting political followers into religious believers. The political situation in Medina was highly favorable to this enterprise. Divided into small clans without unity or effective leadership, the people were frightened by the continuous feuds. Muhammad's opponents were too divided to resist the consolidation of his power, and the pagan clans yielded to his primacy and were converted to Islam.

In the consolidation of Muhammad's power, a crucial step was the elimination of the Jewish clans which proved hostile to his mission. In his early vision of himself as a Prophet, Muhammad was sent by God to all Arabians – Jews and Christians as well as pagans. He was to restore the purity of the faith already revealed, preach a renewal, and end the corruption that had crept into daily life. Thus in Medina Muhammad wanted to include the Jews in his nascent community. Specific religious practices such as an equivalent to the Jewish Day of Atonement and Jerusalem as the direction of prayer should have been appealing to the Jews. The Jewish clans, however, rejected Muhammad's claims to being a Prophet in the Hebrew tradition. They challenged his legitimacy and disputed his accounts of sacred history. In the course of this struggle with the Jews, the Quran denounced the Jews for having broken their covenant and revealed more about Abraham as the Prophet par excellence, who taught the pure religion of God, the first hanif, the builder of the Ka°ba, and the father of the Arabs. The Quran now revealed that Muhammad was sent to restore the pure monotheism of Abraham. Thus Muhammad bypassed the Jewish and Christian scriptural legacy. His community would no longer include Jews and Christians, but would be a distinct religion superseding Judaism and Christianity. To carry out his mission, Muhammad went on to exile or execute the Jewish clans in Medina and to seize their property for his followers. By winning over the Medinan pagans and destroying his opponents, including the Jewish clans, Muhammad made all of Medina a Muslim community under his rule.

In the years that followed, Muhammad worked to create a community based on shared religious beliefs, ceremonies, ethics, and laws – a community which would transcend the traditional social structure based on families, clans, and tribes and would unite disparate groups into a new Arabian society. This work proceeded on several levels.

On the ritual and religious level the existence of a Muslim community of individual worshipers was expressed by numerous ritual and social laws set down in the Quran. These include the five pillars of the faith – *salat* (ritual prayer), *zakat* (almsgiving), *hajj* (pilgrimage), the fast of Ramadan, and *shahada* (the obligation to bear witness to the unity of God and the Prophethood of Muhammad). The five pillars were derived from Arabian, Christian, and Jewish precedents and were public rituals that, when collectively performed, reinforced the collective awareness of the Muslim community and its members' consciousness of a special destiny. Brothers in religion shared alms just as clan brothers shared their livelihoods. Prayer, fasting, and the bearing of witness humbled men before God and made them open to his will. The pilgrimage was derived from an ancient Arabian rite. The almsgiving requirement was a symbol of the renunciation of selfish greed and acceptance of responsibility for all members of the community of faith.

The Quran also defined the social norms of the new community. Indeed its teachings on family law were the crux of a social and metaphysical revolution. In pre-Islamic Arabian society, the basic family unit was the patriarchal agnatic clan, the group of people descended directly through the male line from a common ancestor and under the authority of the eldest male or chief member of the family. This was an extended family of several generations, and several groups of married couples and their offspring, with collaterals and clients all considered part of one household. Women were of inferior status and were not full members of the group. A good marriage brought honor to the clan; if its female members were violated, the clan was dishonored. Even for men, status, duties, and rights stemmed entirely from the clan. Property was regulated by the customs of the group. Marriages were arranged by the heads of the families with a view to the interests of the families rather than the wishes of the couple to be married. The group was responsible for defending the other members and making restitution in case of any crime committed by a member.

However, alongside of the agnatic clan, various forms of polyandrous marriage of one woman to several men with varying degrees of permanence and responsibility for paternity, including temporary "marriages," were also known in Arabia. Polygamous arrangements varied from multiple wives in one residence to arrangements in which a man had several wives living with their own tribes whom he would visit on a rotating basis. No single norm was universally accepted. Less and less could people be held to the ideal obligations regarding the distribution of property, the protection of women, or the guardianship of children.

In conditions of institutional confusion and individual disregard for family obligations, the Quranic teachings attempted to strengthen the patriarchal agnatic clan. The Quranic rules against incest were crucial for the viability of group life, for biological heredity, and for the creation of marriage bonds between families. Divorce, though still relatively easy, was discouraged. Polyandrous marriages were condemned because they undermined patriarchal family stability. Since the family descended through its male heirs, the Quran provided rules to assure knowledge of paternity. For example, in the event of divorce, a woman could not remarry for three menstrual periods.

Further, the family ideal was protected by a clear definition of its collective duties in the all-important matter of responsibility for crimes. As in pre-Islamic times, all the male kin were held responsible for the protection of family members, but the Quranic teachings tried to reduce the devastating effects of the blood feuds that often resulted from this obligation. They urged that the aggrieved party accept compensation in money rather than blood, and ruled that if blood retaliation were insisted upon, only the culprit himself could be slain rather than any male relative. This modification did not end the law of blood revenge or the strong common responsibilities of family members to one another, but by restricting feuds it gave security to family groups, who no longer had to fear that the indiscretion of one member would in the end destroy all.

Furthermore, in the context of the patriarchal family the Quran provided for moral and spiritual reform and introduced a new freedom and dignity to individual family members. In particular, it enhanced the status of women and children, who were no longer to be considered merely chattels or potential warriors but individuals with rights and needs of their own. For the benefit of women, marriage was recognized as having important spiritual and religious values. It was a relationship sanctioned by the will of Allah. In marriage women were recognized as persons to be respected. The Quran urged respect for their modesty and privacy, that they be treated as feeling persons. The Quran also granted women certain specific rights that they did not enjoy in pre-Islamic Arabia. Women were now able to hold property in their own name and were not expected to contribute to the support of the household from their own property. They were given the right to inherit up to a quarter of their husband's estate, and, in case of divorce, retained the agreed-upon bridal gift.

In addition, the Quran tried to protect women from hasty and willful divorces, by urging delay, reconciliation, and mediation efforts by the families. The waiting period following a divorce also served to assure a woman of interim support and of support for a future child if she were pregnant. Finally, to help equalize the situation, at least some possibility was opened for a divorce on the woman's initiative.

Nonetheless, despite the emphasis on the security and status of women, the Quran did not establish equality of rights for men and women. While the prerogatives of the males were left fundamentally intact, the spirit of its teaching encouraged mutuality between husband and wife, a greater sensitivity to the personal and moral worth of individuals, and the relative autonomy of individuals in the family context. The Quranic ideal and Muhammad's example were probably much more favorable to women than later Arab and Muslim practice.

This idea of the family is at the core of the Muslim conception of the umma, the community of believers. The family ideals reinforced the concept of individuality by stressing the religious importance of individuals as God's creatures rather than as mere objects in the clan system of society, and by stressing the individual's responsibility for moral relations within the family. This sense of individuality was essential for a true appreciation of the Quranic teachings about the oneness of God and the responsibility of human beings before him at the last judgment. Only the ethical individual who acted out of inner choices could comprehend the transcendence and unity of God. Thus, the family teachings were essential to ethical individuality, which was in turn the basis of religious insight. Conversely, religious insight cultivated ethical responsibility, which in turn influenced the organization and conduct of family life. The teachings of the Quran, in contrast to the pagan view, cultivated a sense of the wholeness of the world, the unity of society, and the integrity of the person as aspects of a single transcendent vision of reality.

Apart from family laws and morals, the Quran dealt with many other kinds of communal problems. Norms for business transactions were set down – injunctions to deal justly, honor contracts, give true witness, and not take usurious interest. These were not, strictly speaking, laws but ethical norms. For example, the prohibition of usury did not specify a maximum rate of interest on loans, but taught that no one should exploit people in need or take advantage of their hardship. Such norms were also given for the conduct of war, the treatment of prisoners, and the distribution of booty. There were moral prohibitions against gambling and the consumption of intoxicating beverages, probably because these practices were associated with paganism.

Thus, one dimension of Muhammad's work was to communicate the shared beliefs, common social norms, and common rituals that were the basis of a community transcending the clan and tribe. The other aspect of his work in Medina was to build the political confederation that would extend his reforms to Mecca and to the rest of Arabia. This was part of Muhammad's religious ambition, but it was also a matter of political necessity. If Mecca were opposed to Muhammad, she could eventually crush him in Medina. However, to bring Mecca under his influence required controlling the tribes of Arabia as well. Meccan wealth and power derived from trading operations which depended on the cooperation of the Arabian tribes. In short, both religious ambition and the political logic of Muhammad's removal to Medina required an Arabian as well as a Medinan confederation.

Muhammad's policy toward Mecca began with unremitting hostility. From the very first, small parties of the *muhajirun*, the exiled Meccans, raided Meccan trade caravans for booty. At first only Meccans were involved in the raids, but by 624 Muhammad's boldness, and the temptations of booty, enabled him to assemble a large force of Meccan exiles and Medinan supporters to attack an important Meccan caravan. At the battle of Badr, Muhammad defeated a larger Meccan force, decimated Mecca's leadership, and won tremendous prestige everywhere in Arabia. The battle was widely taken to be a sign of divine favor, and led to the defection of some of the bedouin tribes that protected Mecca's caravan lines, and thus cut the major trade routes between her and the north.

In the following years the initiative passed to the Meccans, who twice attacked Muhammad and Medina, first at the battle of Uhud (625) and then at the battle of the Ditch (627). The former was a defeat for Muhammad and the latter a stalemate, but Muhammad profited from both battles. He had survived the worst Mecca could do, and even managed on each occasion either to exile or execute some of the remaining Jewish clans, confiscate their property, and expand his influence over the Arabian desert tribes.

From this point, however, Muhammad relaxed rather than intensified the pressure on Mecca, for his object was not to fight Mecca to the death but to convert her people to Islam. In 628 Muhammad and a large group of followers made the pilgrimage to the Ka'ba, where they proposed to adopt the ceremonies of pilgrimage, in modified form, as part of Islam. They did this to show that Islam was an Arabian religion and would preserve the pilgrimage rites in which Mecca had so great a stake. The Meccans, however, were wary of Muhammad's intentions and intercepted him at a place called al-Hudaybiya. There Muhammad concluded a truce in which the Meccans agreed to admit the Muslims for the pilgrimage, but Muhammad had to drop his demand that he be recognized as the Prophet of God. Further, he even agreed to an unequal arrangement whereby children who left Mecca to become Muslims would have to be returned if they did not have parental consent, while Muslim apostates would not be returned. At one level the treaty was an embarrassment to Muhammad, but at another he made tremendous gains. Meccan hostility was allayed, and the treaty confirmed what Meccan failures at the battles of Uhud and the Ditch had shown – that Muhammad was a power to contend with and that Mecca had given up her efforts to defeat him. Sniffing the wind, Arabian tribes continued to throw in their lot with Muhammad.

Two years later, in 630, Muhammad completed his triumph over Mecca. A dispute between client tribes of Mecca and Medina broke the truce, but Meccan leaders surrendered the city. Muhammad gave amnesty to almost everyone and generous gifts to the leading Quraysh. The idols of the Ka'ba were destroyed, and it was declared the holiest shrine of Islam.

The victory over Mecca was also the culmination of Muhammad's tribal policy. Throughout the eight-year struggle, Muhammad had tried to gain control of the tribes in order to subdue Mecca. Missionaries and embassies were sent throughout Arabia, factions loyal to Muhammad were supported, and tribes were raided to compel them to pay allegiance and zakat, the alms tax, to Muhammad. Muhammad regarded the tax as a sign of membership in the Muslim community and acceptance of himself as Prophet. The bedouins looked on it as a tribute plain and simple and conspired to evade it as soon as they could. Muhammad's successes resulted in the cutting off of Mecca's trade. Then with Mecca finally subdued, even the recalcitrant Arabian tribes fell under Muhammad's influence. With the only power strong enough to contest Muhammad's authority allied with him, many Arabian tribes accepted Islam. By the end of his life Muhammad had created, for the first time in centuries, a large-scale Arabian federation of oases and tribes, and had provided a solution to the destructive anarchy of Arabian life.

By the time of his death in 632, Muhammad had provided his followers with the design for a political community based on religious affiliation, and a conception of a way of life grounded in the vision of the oneness of God. Muhammad was the agent of a great historical change. In the revelations of the Quran he brought a synthesis of Arabian religious ideas, Judaism, and Christianity, along with new and distinctly Islamic ideas, into a new monotheism. The eschatological piety and fear of hellfire recall Syriac monastic preaching. The concept of the role of a prophet, the significance of written revelations, obedience to God's commands, and stress on communal life as the context of religious fulfillment all parallel Judaic ideas. The revelation expanded in parallel with Muhammad's growing engagement in public life. As the Quran revealed more and more of the history of prophecy, Muhammad assumed an ever larger social responsibility. Also, in the move from Mecca to Medina, the audience for the mission changed too. At first it involved Jews, Christians, and pagans; but in time it was redirected toward pagan Arabians, with the object of establishing a new community. The new religion was affiliated with the old, but it claimed to be the final revelation of God's full and correct will.

Though elements of the Quranic teaching resembled Jewish and Christian beliefs, Muhammad's unique religious vision and the formation of a community based upon that vision made Islam a new religion. The stress on God's utter transcendence, God's majesty, God's omnipotence and untrammeled will, and upon submission of one's own will to God's, surrender to God's commands, and acceptance of God's judgment, gave Quranic teachings a special originality within the framework of the monotheistic religions. The translation of monotheistic religious values into the principles of a reformed Arabian society and the formation of a new community with its own congregational life and ritual and legal norms, made Islam a new religious community alongside the established ones.

Islam, as a new faith and community, implied a radical transformation of the existing Arabian society. The central problem of Arabia was to create some overall order and harmony in a bedouin society racked by fratricidal conflict and fragmented by conflicting values. Muhammad created a new kind of community – the umma, the brotherhood that integrated individuals, clans, cities, and even ethnic groups into a larger community in which superordinate religious loyalties encompassed all other loyalties without abolishing them, and in which a new common law and political authority could be built to regulate the affairs of the populace as a whole.

The umma served as a basis for cooperation in political and social life, but this was not a new principle. Rather it was an adaptation of traditional Arabian concepts. The umma redefined the meaning of the tribe as a group that defended its brothers to include religious as well as blood brothers. The umma also came under the leadership of a shaykh, a person who had the prestige to arbitrate because he represented the divine will rather than custom, and was governed by a new *sunna* – the authoritative example of the Prophet – rather than tribal tradition. The law of blood revenge was accepted, but now the umma as a whole was substituted for the clan. Within the umma Muhammad counseled restraint, forgiveness, and the mediation and control of the shaykh. In family life, the patriarchal clan was reaffirmed as the ideal Muslim family, but redefined to include a new concern for women and children, the stability of marriages, individuality, and decency.

In the realm of individual morality, a similar reshaping of values took place. The traditional Arab virtues were vested with new Islamic meanings. Bedouin courage in battle, reckless bravery in defense of one's tribe, became persistent dedication to the new faith of Islam and the capacity for disciplined sacrifice in the name of the new community. Patience in the face of adversity (*sabr*), became unshakable faith in God in the face of trials and temptations. Generosity was shorn of its impulsive quality, of the penchant for showing off and display, and was transmuted into the virtue of almsgiving and care for the weak and the poor as part of a pious and restrained, but regular, commitment. The Quranic teachings and Muhammad's leadership extracted the virtues of the bedouin culture from the context of *jahl* (passion, ignorance, and

thoughtlessness), to reestablish them on the basis of *hilm* (self-control) and
caql (rational judgment), based on *Islam* (submission to Allah).

In short, the new religion reaffirmed the Arabian moral tradition. But in a
society that had already failed to realize its own ideals, this could only be
accomplished through new religious concepts of brotherhood and authority.
Islam gave to traditional virtues and social institutions a new meaning that
could command allegiance and elicit participation. By giving old concepts new
meaning, it made possible a new religious sensibility and the integration of
disparate peoples into a new community. When one looks at Arabian society
before and after Muhammad, the outward movement was small, but the inner
journey was immeasurable.

What made Muhammad so rare a figure in history, what made him a
Prophet, was his ability to convey his vision to people around him so that
concepts long known to everyone took on the power to transform other
people's lives as they had transformed his. This was accomplished by direct
preaching about God, but also by changing family life and institutions, and by
introducing new ritual practices, social mores, and political loyalties. Muhammad was a Prophet who caused a religious vision to operate in the body
of a whole society.

In the Quran and Muhammad's teachings and example, Muslims have ever
after found a revelation of the spiritual reality of God's transcendence and
man's humble place in the universe. They find a revelation of the laws by
which people should live in a community of fellow believers, dedicated to the
care of the weak and the poor, to education, and to social reform. Equally they
are dedicated to a political community organized to administer justice, to
defend itself, and to wage war in the name of the true faith. Islam proved
particularly effective in unifying tribal societies and in motivating militant
struggle in the interests of the religious community as a whole. To this day,
to be a Muslim implies a combination of personal religious belief and a sense
of membership in the community of fellow believers.

Thus the Quranic revelation and Muhammad's leadership brought to
Arabia the same type of religious beliefs and sociopolitical organization as
those characteristic of the Middle East as a whole. In a fragmented society he
integrated the otherwise anarchic small clans into a larger confederacy on the
basis of religious loyalty, built a state structure through which political and
economic order might eventually be achieved, and resolved the conflict of
bedouin familial and Meccan commercial values in a new religious point of
view. Islam fused tribal society, the monotheistic religious mentality, with

religious community, trading confederacy and political organization to create a new society built upon a "church"-like religious community and incipient imperial organization. Thus the formation of the Islamic community in Arabia established in a hitherto marginal region a type of religious polity which had already been created under Jewish, Christian, and Zoroastrian auspices throughout the Middle East. While Arabia maintained a unique identity it was becoming a society of a Middle Eastern type – committed on the basis of a familial or lineage structure to a universal confessional religion and to political unity.

CHAPTER 3

THE ARAB CONQUESTS AND THE SOCIO-ECONOMIC BASES OF EMPIRE

The Arab-Muslim community did not long remain confined to the peninsula but within decades conquered much of the Middle East. Thereby it created the arena for the construction of a new form of Islamic civilization – not only in the peripheral region of Arabia but in the core areas of already developed Middle Eastern civilization. The conquests began the long historical process that culminated in the absorption of both the Sasanian empire and the eastern regions of the Byzantine empire into an Islamic empire, and the eventual conversion of the majority of Jewish, Christian, and Zoroastrian peoples to Islam. In the first instance the conquest led to the formation of a new regime, to the migration and settlement of large numbers of Arabians in the cities and towns of the Middle East, and to extensive urbanization and economic development. Arab settlement also promoted social change and the progressive, but partial, integration of Arab and non-Arab populations into new cosmopolitan communities. Urbanization, economic change, and the formation of new communities in turn made available resources for the organization of a new and powerful empire and the new elites of city and empire gave birth to new forms of Islamic religious and imperial culture. Islamic civilization, then, was the cultural expression of the elites thrown up by the forces of economic and social change generated by the Arab conquests.

CONQUEST AND EMPIRE

The Arab conquests are popularly understood to have been motivated by a lust for booty or by a religious passion to subdue and convert the world to

Islam. Whatever the motives involved, they were in part the outcome of deliberate state policy and in part accidental. Upon Muhammad's death in 632 the whole of his life work was threatened. In the absence of an agreement in regard to a successor, the Muslim community, a conglomeration of diverse elements, threatened to break up. The Khazraj of Medina decided to elect their own chief. Other Muslims, especially exiled Meccans, weaker Medinan clans, and many individuals who had abandoned their clans to join Muhammad, saw that this would lead to the resumption of feuding. They tried to head off the Khazraj, and in the course of an all-night debate the idea of a succession was born, and Abu Bakr, one of Muhammad's closest associates and his father-in-law, was elected to be Caliph. He was successor to the Prophet, but not himself a Prophet. He was rather to be a shaykh or chief, who led the collectivity, arbitrated disputes, and followed the precedents set by Muhammad. Selected by a minority with no special competence, Abu Bakr had his nomination ratified the following day by the community as a whole. In the mosque Abu Bakr said simply that he would obey the sunna (precedent) of the Prophet and that people should obey him as long as he obeyed it.

Having preserved its existence, the Muslim community asserted its authority in the rest of Arabia. At Muhammad's death many of the Arabian tribes that had been forced into his confederation sought to regain their independence; some of them put forth prophets and religions of their own. The claim of Islam to be the Arabs' only true religion was in jeopardy. Abu Bakr thus refused any concessions to the demand for relief from taxes, waged war on recalcitrant tribes, forced them into subjection, and even expanded the sphere of Muslim power beyond what it had been in Muhammad's time. At the battle of al-Aqraba (633) the Muslims defeated a rival tribal confederation and extended their power over eastern Arabia.

The immediate outcome of the Muslim victories was turmoil in Arabia. Medina's victories led allied tribes to attack the non-aligned to compensate for their own losses. The pressure drove tribes as far as Hadhramaut and Yemen in the south, Bahrain and Oman in the east, and then across the imperial frontiers. The Bakr tribe, which had defeated a Persian detachment in 606, joined forces with the Muslims and led them on a raid in southern Iraq to Ubulla and al-Hira, the former Lakhm capital. A similar spilling over of tribal raiding occurred on the Syrian frontiers. Abu Bakr encouraged these movements, for they no doubt corresponded to Muhammad's intentions and helped recruit bedouins for campaigns in the north.

At first the small tribal groups were searching for booty but Arab raids forced the Byzantines to send a major expedition into southern Palestine. The raiding parties had to concentrate their forces east of Gaza, and there, under the leadership of Khalid ibn al-Walid, sent by Abu Bakr from Iraq to take the generalship of the Arab clans, they defeated a Byzantine army at the battle of Ajnadayn (634). This was the first battle in which the Arabs acted as an army rather than as separate raiding parties. With this victory their ambitions became boundless; they were no longer raiders on the soil of Syria seeking booty, but contenders for control of the settled empires. What began as large-scale intertribal skirmishing to consolidate a political confederation in Arabia ended as a full-scale war against the two empires.

In the wake of the battle of Ajnadayn, the Arabs moved against the Byzantine province of Syria. They took Damascus in 636. Baalbek, Homs and Hama soon surrendered. The rest of the province, however, continued to resist. Only in 638 was Jerusalem taken. Caesarea fell in 640. Finally, in 641, the Arabs took the northern Syrian and Mesopotamian towns of Harran, Edessa, and Nasibin. The conquest of Syria took so long because victories over Byzantine armies did not necessarily bring about the surrender of fortified towns, which had to be reduced one by one.

The next Byzantine province to fall to the Arabs was Egypt. Egypt's attractions were her position as the granary of Constantinople, her proximity to the Hijaz, important naval yards, and a strategic location for further conquests in Africa. The Arab general, ʿAmr b. al-ʿAs, on his own initiative, began the conquest of the province in 641. Within the year he had taken Heliopolis and Babylon, and the whole of the country, except Alexandria, which capitulated in 643, was in his hands. Because Egypt was politically centralized and scarcely urbanized, the conquest was virtually instantaneous. The next Arab objective was North Africa. Tripoli was taken in 643, but the subjugation of all of North Africa took another 75 years. Instead of sudden, dramatic victories, painfully prolonged wars were waged to establish Arab suzerainty.

Within a decade the Arabs had captured Syria and Egypt, but the Byzantine empire retained its richest and most populous provinces, Anatolia and the Balkans, and would engage in almost continuous border warfare on land and on sea, always threatening to retake territories that had for 600 years been part of the Roman and for 300 years part of the Christian world. Their victories over Byzantium left the Arabs with a contested and dangerous frontier and a permanent barrier to their expansion.

The Sasanian empire, by contrast, was utterly destroyed. The Arabs defeated the Persians at the battle of Qadisiya (637), seized the capital of the empire, Ctesiphon, and forced the last emperor, Yazdagird, to flee to the protection of

Map 2. The Arab-Muslim empire to A.D. 750.

Turkish princes in Inner Asia. All Iraq fell into Arab hands. With the collapse
of the empire, the Arabs were faced in Iran with a number of small and weak
but inaccessible principalities, protected by mountains and deserts. The problem in conquering Iran was not a strong resisting state, but the large number
of remote areas that had to be invaded, absorbed, and occupied. It took decades
to subdue all the quasi-independent principalities that had comprised the
Sasanian empire. From the garrison base of Kufa the Arabs moved north,
occupying Mosul in 641. Nihawand, Hamadhan, Rayy, Isfahan, and all the
main cities of western Iran fell by 644. Azarbayjan, to the west of the Caspian
Sea, was captured about the same time. Other forces operating from Basra
captured Ahwaz (Khuzistan) in 640, but it took until 649 to complete the
conquest of Fars. Only then did the conquest of more outlying regions, such
as Armenia and Khurasan, begin. Khurasan was conquered in 654.

This first wave of conquests was followed several decades later by new
campaigns on a world scale. To the west, North Africa was conquered between
643 and 711; Spain was invaded and absorbed by the Arabs between 711 and
759. In the north, the Arabs attacked Anatolia and launched three great but
failed expeditions in 660, 668, and 717 to capture Constantinople. They fought
against the Khazars in the Caucasus. The capitals of Transoxania, Bukhara,
and Samarqand fell in 712 and 713. The Arabs conquered for the first time in
history the whole of the Middle East, and incorporated North Africa, Spain,
and Transoxania into their empire as well. Thus they established the geographical arena for the eventual diffusion of a common culture and a common
sociopolitical identity in the name of Islam.

The reasons for the relatively rapid success of the Arab-Muslim conquests
are not hard to find. The Byzantine and Sasanian empires were both militarily
exhausted by several decades of warfare prior to their collapse in the face of
the Arab-Muslim invasions. Their Christian populations were strongly dis-
affected from imperial rule and withheld support. The Copts in Egypt, the
Monophysites in Syria, and the Nestorians in Iraq all had long histories of
troubled relations with their Byzantine and Sasanian overlords. Their dis-
affection was important in the cases where Christian-Arab border tribes and
military auxiliaries joined the conquerors and where fortified cities capitulated.
The conquests, then, were due to military triumphs over militarily weakened
powers, and were consolidated in the first decades of Arab rule because local
populations were content to accept the new regime.

The conquests were further secured by a large migration of Arabian peoples
into the empire regions. With the defeat of the Byzantine and Sasanian empires,
a frontier between populations broke down, leading to a movement of peoples

from Arabia into the lands of the Middle East. These migrations were the culmination of a centuries-long infiltration of peoples from Arabia into the settled lands. When they drifted in slowly, bedouins were either assimilated piecemeal or formed border kingdoms, such as the Nabatean, the Ghassanid, and the Lakhmid. The scale and speed of the seventh-century migrations, however, made the piecemeal assimilation of masses of migrants impossible.

Responsibility for controlling the Arabian migrants, and for governing and exploiting the conquered sedentary peoples, fell to the new Caliphs and the aristocracy of Meccan and Medinan merchants and soldiers who were the mainstay of the Muslim regime. From the outset, the chiefs of the Islamic community in Medina sought to channel the bedouin migrations for both their own and the common advantage. Medinans decided on the two basic principles of the post-conquest government: that the bedouins would be prevented from damaging the agricultural society and that the new elite would cooperate with the chiefs and notables of the conquered population. The necessary arrangements between conqueror and conquered were implemented in the reign of the second Caliph, ʿUmar (634–44).

The first principle of ʿUmar's settlement entailed the transformation of the Arab conquerors into an elite military caste who carried on further conquests and garrisoned the subdued areas. They were not to take up any of the labors or professions of the subject population, either as landowners or as peasants. To prevent the bedouins from raiding indiscriminately, forestall the destruction of the productive agricultural lands, and to segregate the Arabs from the conquered peoples, the bedouins were settled in garrison cities (sing. *misr*, pl. *amsar*). The three most important were new cities founded in Iraq and Egypt. Basra, founded at the head of the Persian Gulf, was strategically located for easy communication with Medina and for Arab expeditions into southern Iran. Kufa, founded on the Euphrates River to the north of the marshes near al-Hira, became the administrative capital of northern Iraq, Mesopotamia, and northern and eastern Iran. Fustat, the new capital of Egypt, was located just below the delta of the Nile, and served as the base for Arab expansion into North Africa until Qayrawan (Tunisia) was founded in 670. In other provinces the Arabs did not usually found new cities, but settled in towns, suburbs, and villages on the outskirts of existing towns. Important Arab bases in Iran were Hamadhan, Isfahan, and Rayy. A new eastern garrison was established at Marw in 670.

The amsar served not only to house the bedouin migrants and organize the armies, but to distribute the spoils of victory. As conquerors, the Arabs were entitled to a stipend paid out of the taxes collected from peasants and the tribute paid by townspeoples. In principle no Arab soldiers or clans were permitted to seize landed property as their own. Conquered property (*fay*) was considered the permanent possession of the community; the revenues, but not the land, could be distributed to the conquerors. These arrangements both protected the cultivated areas from pillaging and distributed the spoils of victory more equitably. In the formation of the great garrisons, Islam was a crucial factor, not because it motivated people to conquer, but because the faith made strangers willing to cooperate in a common cause. Islam facilitated acceptance of the Caliphate and justified its authority.

The second principle of ʿUmar's settlement was that the conquered populations should be as little disturbed as possible. This meant that the Arab-Muslims did not, contrary to reputation, attempt to convert people to Islam. Muhammad had set the precedent of permitting Jews and Christians in Arabia to keep their religions, if they paid tribute; the Caliphate extended the same privilege to Middle Eastern Jews, Christians, and Zoroastrians, whom they considered "Peoples of the Book," the adherents of earlier written revelations. At the time of the conquest, Islam was meant to be a religion of the Arabs, a mark of caste unity and superiority. The Arabs had little missionary zeal. When conversions did occur, they were an embarrassment because they created status problems and led to claims for financial privileges.

Just as the Arabs had no interest in changing the religious situation, they had no desire to disturb the social and administrative order. The Caliphate sent governors to oversee the collection of tributes and taxes, supervise the distribution of tax revenues as salary to the troops, and lead the Arabs in war and in prayer, but otherwise, local situations were left in local hands. The old elites and the administrative machinery of the Byzantine and Sasanian empires were incorporated into the new regime. Iranian, Aramean, Coptic, and Greek scribes and accountants worked for their new masters as they had for the old. The old landowners, chiefs, and headmen kept their authority in the villages and assisted in collecting taxes. The whole of the former social and religious order was left intact.

In practice, the relationship established between the Arabs and local elites varied from region to region, depending on the circumstances of the Arab conquests and on the available social and administrative machinery. Many provinces gained complete autonomy. Places that had stubbornly resisted Arab incursions forced the invaders to concede favorable terms in return for local compliance. Hosts of formal treaties were made by the Arabs with their subjects, the notables of towns or the chiefs and princes of small provinces, promising to leave the old elites in power, allow them autonomy in local administration, and respect their property and their religion, in return for the payment of a tribute, usually a fixed sum, which the notables could continue to collect from their subjects. In these cases, the Arabs simply collected taxes from sub-rulers who were their vassals. In most of Khurasan, in the citied areas of upper Mesopotamia and Syria, and elsewhere, the Arabs were remote suzerains.

However, the arrangements made in the wake of the conquests were not permanent. As the Arabs consolidated their power, they sought to increase their control over local affairs. Arab administration varied from province to province. In Mesopotamia and Syria, uniform administration superseded special treaties as the Arabs refused to renegotiate tributes and insisted on payment of taxes in direct proportion to the populations and resources of the areas. In this region Arab government separated town and rural administration, and gave the coup de grâce to the ancient city-states. Since classical antiquity the Mediterranean region had been divided into autonomous, self-governing city-states. The Roman empire evolved a form of administration in which the cities remained autonomous in local matters while Rome monopolized military power. Though the municipalities eventually became cogs in the machine of the Roman bureaucracy, the city-state with its surrounding rural area continued to be a basic element in Roman administration. Rome and Byzantium had begun the transformation of free city-states into units of imperial administration; now the Arabs completed the work of destroying the city-state as a political form and placed Syria and Mesopotamia under a regular territorial bureaucracy.

In Iraq and Egypt, which were administered by centralized bureaucracies, the Arabs simply set the bureaucratic machinery of the old regimes to work for the new. In Iraq the Caliph ʿUmar confiscated the land that once had belonged to the Sasanian crown, along with the estates of notables who fled with the defeated Sasanian emperor, and made them part of the Caliphal domains. In Egypt the Arabs simplified the administrative system by abolishing the fiscally independent estates (*autopragia*) and municipalities as separate units of administration. In Khurasan and other parts of Iran, however, only the loosest suzerainty and tributes were imposed, and virtually complete autonomy was conceded to local peoples.

In each province the Arabs adopted the system of taxes already in use. In Iraq they adopted the Sasanian system of collecting both a land tax (*kharaj*) and a poll tax (*jizya*). The land was measured and a tax was fixed for every *jarib* or 2,400 square meters. The actual rate of taxation per jarib varied with the quality of land, the crop, the expected productivity, and the estimated value of the produce. The rates varied also with distance from market, availability of water, type of irrigation, transportation, and so on. In addition everyone was expected to pay a poll tax in gold coins. In Syria and Mesopotamia, land taxes were levied on the basis of the *iugum*, or the amount of land that could be worked by one man and a team of animals in a day. A special poll tax was levied on urban, non-farming populations. In Egypt too there were both land and poll taxes but the poll tax was assessed on the whole village population and then divided up internally by the villagers. For provinces such as Khurasan, where there was no centralized administration, and taxation and tribute payments were left in the hands of local notables, we have no conclusive information about the nature of the tax system.

Everywhere the economic repercussions of taxation were considerable. Taxes on peasants often reached 50 percent of the value of their produce, and at such levels the incidence of taxation determined whether life for the mass of the people would be tolerable. Taxation affected the attention given to the soil and the level of investment to maintain productivity. It influenced the choice of crops. It determined whether or not the peasants would stay in the villages and work the land, or flee, leaving their homes and lands to decay. Furthermore, taxation defined social structure. Taxes were duties levied on some classes of the population for the support of others. Peasants, workers, and merchants paid taxes. Landowners, administrators, clergymen, soldiers, and emperors collected them. To pay taxes was not only an economic burden – it was a sign of social inferiority.

The Arab conquests thus followed a pattern familiar from bedouin or nomadic conquests of settled regions. The conquering peoples were the dominant military elite, and the settled societies were exploited to support them. The governing arrangements were a compromise between the elites of the conquering peoples and those of the conquered or settled peoples, in which the interests of the former in military power and adequate revenues were assured in exchange for permitting the latter to retain their local political, religious, and financial autonomy. Both groups, of course, leaned on the tax-paying peasantry.

ECONOMIC CHANGE AND THE NEW URBAN SOCIETIES

Despite conservative intentions, the Arab conquests, the settlement of large Arab populations in numerous garrisons and the consolidation of a new imperial regime set in motion vast changes in patterns of international trade, urban commerce, and agriculture. By the unification of the former Sasanian and Byzantine parts of the Middle East into one polity, political and strategic barriers to trade were removed, and the foundations for a major commercial revival were laid. The Euphrates frontier between the Persian and the Roman worlds disappeared, and Transoxania, for the first time in history, was incorporated into a Middle Eastern empire. However, a new frontier was drawn between Syria and Anatolia, which had formerly been part of a single state. Commercial considerations inspired Arab expansion in Inner Asia and India and city development in northern Syria, Iraq, Iran, and Transoxania. Basra and, later, Baghdad became two of the leading trading cities in the world. Samarqand, Bukhara and Nishapur prospered.

The conquests also had dramatic effects on agriculture and regional development. Iraq, on the eve of the Arab conquests, suffered from neglect of irrigation, exploitative taxation and the severe wars with the Roman empire. In southern Iraq the irrigation works were allowed to degenerate, and in 627–28, on the eve of the Arab conquests, a major agricultural disaster took place. In a year of high water flow, the dikes in the Tigris River system of canals burst, and there was a major shift in the river bed. The Tigris flowed westward through the canals into the Euphrates at a point to the north and west of its previous channel, creating a desert in the east, but flooding the lower course of the Euphrates, which remains a marsh to the present day. Agricultural production also declined seriously in the Diyala region, which depended upon state-maintained irrigation.

Arab rule, however, provided a stable government and encouraged recovery. Wherever the Arabs established administrative capitals and garrison towns, as at Basra, Kufa, Mosul, al-Wasit and other places, efforts were made to stimulate agricultural output and develop new sources of food for the new cities. The swamps around Kufa were drained and brought under cultivation. In the early eighth century areas in the upper Euphrates region were irrigated. Basra was planted with date palm forests. To the east of Basra salt marshes were reclaimed by Caliphs, Arab governors, and rich tribal shaykhs, encouraged by a policy of land and tax concessions. Caliphs and governors in particular sought to generate private revenues apart from taxation. To work the new lands, they imported slaves from East Africa in large numbers, thus creating the only plantation-type economy in the Middle East. These investments, however, were highly selective and favored new areas to the detriment of old areas of production whose revenues were already assigned to peasants, local landowners, and the garrison armies. The net effect of the Arab effort was to restore regions in Iraq which had Arab settlements and allow others to decay. Nonetheless, the total output of Iraq was probably below the best levels of Sasanian times.

In Iran, the Arab conquest and migrations also favored urban and agricultural development. Security, trade, a new population, and Arab policies regarding settlement, city building and irrigation stimulated economic growth. In Iran, the Arabs did not found new cities, but settled in already established places. Important places like Hamadhan, Isfahan, Qazvin, Rayy, Nishapur, and Marw received Arab garrisons. These garrisons were usually housed in newly constructed quarters, and in villages surrounding the town centers.

Moreover, in Iran, construction and settlement continued beyond the initial conquest. Throughout the seventh and eighth centuries Caliphs and governors added new quarters to the old cities. Each important governor imported his own clientele of guards, soldiers and administrators, and built new quarters, palaces, mosques, barracks, gardens, and canals. Surrounding agricultural lands were brought into cultivation. Later Caliphs also constructed walls and defined administrative jurisdictions, and thus converted groups of quarters and villages into cities. By this process, Isfahan, Rayy, and Qazvin became large cities. Qum grew from a simple complex of agricultural villages into a major town. Whole regions, such as the districts around Samarqand and Bukhara, favored with new quarters and villages, irrigation works, and walls to defend them against Turkish nomads, prospered. Khwarizm, the delta of the Oxus River, which before the Arab conquests was settled in small hamlets and farmsteads interspersed with feudal castles, became highly urbanized and densely settled.

Not all provinces flourished. In Syria, Mesopotamia, and Egypt the Arab conquest adversely affected the long-term prospects for economic development. For a time the location of the Caliphate at Damascus increased the prosperity of Syria, but the creation of a new frontier with Anatolia stifled its economy. The region north of Aleppo, formerly a center of olive growing and the manufacture of olive oil, was abandoned because Syria was cut off from its markets in Anatolia. The region east of a line from Raqqa to Damascus to ᶜAqaba, which specialized in grape growing and wine making, similarly declined owing to the loss of export markets in Anatolia and the end of Christian pilgrimages to Palestine. The migration of Arab bedouins also damaged the economies of northern Syria and Mesopotamia. In most places, Arab migrants had been forced to settle in cities, quarters or villages, but in this region bedouins were allowed to occupy unused steppe lands. Soon the nomads began to attack towns and villages. Agriculture and commerce were seriously set back by pastoralism. In Egypt exploitative taxation led to serious peasant revolts in 697, 712, and 725–26, which represented both economic protest and Coptic resistance to Muslim rulers. Thus, the net effect of the Arab conquests and empire was prosperity in Iran, a redistribution of the pattern of development in Iraq, and the economic decline of Mesopotamia, Syria and Egypt.

Under pressure of war, migration, and intensive economic change the fundamental assumption of the conquest empire, that Arab and non-Arab populations would be segregated, with the former serving as a military elite and the latter as producers and taxpayers, proved untenable, and gave way to a mutual assimilation of conquered and conquering peoples on the basis of new communities and new Islamic identities. Sedentarization itself created pressures for the assimilation of Arabs into the surrounding societies. At Isfahan, Marw, Nishapur, and Balkh, the Arab garrisons were settled in villages and rapidly became landowners or peasants. Of the 50,000 families initially settled in Marw in 670, only 15,000 were still in active military service by 730. Most of the Arab army had by then left active service for civilian occupations. In Azarbayjan, parties of Arabs from Basra and Kufa seized lands and villages and established themselves as a local landowning aristocracy. In Kirman, Arab migrants reclaimed abandoned lands, founded new villages and settled as a peasant population. In Iraq Arab chiefs from Basra and Kufa became landowners. In all these provinces an Arab landowning elite came into being, and Arabs refused to take up military duties, and to live isolated from other peoples, and found themselves, though in principle an elite caste, in fact absorbed into the occupations of the subject population. Furthermore, in Iran occupational assimilation was accompanied by social assimilation. While some Persians were converted to Islam, the Arabs by and large assimilated to the Persian milieu. Arabs spoke Persian, dressed like Persians, celebrated Persian holidays, and married Persian women.

Furthermore, the garrison towns themselves became centers of social change. Out of the matrix of Arabian kinship and lineage societies came a more socially stratified, occupationally differentiated and communally organized Arab urban society which was assimilated into non-Arab populations to form a new type of cosmopolitan community. Basra, for example, founded to be a camp city for migrant bedouin soldiers, proved to be a melting pot of peoples. At the founding of Basra each major clan or tribal group had its own quarter, mosque, cemetery, and meeting-place. Over time, however, the tent dwellings were replaced by reed huts; the huts were reinforced with earthen walls and then replaced with mud brick houses. The bedouins, used to moving whenever the climate proved unpropitious, found themselves immured in brick.

The military and administrative system also generated profound changes. They required that the natural units of Arabian society be rearranged into artificial groups. To make uniform regiments and pay units of about 1,000 men, big clans were subdivided and smaller ones combined. In 670, tens of thousands of families were removed from Basra (and Kufa) to garrison Marw in Khurasan, and all the remaining groups had to be reorganized. Also, newcomers who came in continuous streams to partake in the Arab wars had to be integrated into the basic units. Even though the military units kept their clan and tribal names, and may have kept a kinship core, they no longer represented the pre-Islamic Arabian social structure.

Furthermore, class distinctions divided the chiefs and the ordinary tribesmen. Military and administrative functions widened the gap between the chiefs and their followers. Privately owned palaces and agricultural estates suggest that the chiefs were living apart from and enjoying wealth, privileges, and a style of life far removed from that of the mass of their clansmen. The military elites began to form a new class stratum fortified by marriage ties. Class distinctions emerged in what once had been cohesive and integrated groups. Tribal society was breaking down in favor of a society stratified on the basis of wealth and power.

Settlement also entailed the transformation of bedouins and soldiers into an economically differentiated working population. As Basra developed as an important administrative capital and center of cloth manufacturing and as a trading city connected with Iran, India, China, and Arabia, Arab settlers became merchants, traders, artisans, and workers, supplementing their meager military allotments with new incomes. With the withdrawal of Arab townspeople from active military duty at the end of the seventh century, the working and commercial population must have been strengthened. Similarly, the new religion of Islam offered opportunities for social mobility through careers in teaching, scholarship, and legal administration.

At the same time, settlement also helped to break down the barriers between Arab and non-Arab populations. As a capital and commercial center Basra attracted non-Arab settlers. The soldiers and administrators of the old regime came to Basra to seek their fortune with the new. Iranian regiments were enlisted en masse. Arab governors brought back troops from the east to serve as police and bodyguards. Clerks, tax collectors, estate managers, and even village chiefs and landowners flocked to the center of government. In addition, merchants in lucrative, long-distance trade, and humble workers, including bath attendants, weavers, and spinners, migrated to the new town. Slaves, captured and purchased, itinerant construction workers, fugitive peasants and migrant laborers, seeking employment and relief from the harshness of the countryside, flooded the new city. This non-Arab population was extremely diverse. The most important elements were Iranians and Arameans, the people of Iraq. Most of them were originally Nestorian Christians. Many were Jews. Indians, Malays, Gypsies, Negroes and Turks also came in small numbers from remote areas.

The absorption of this non-Arab population had important repercussions on Arab society. The Arabs tried to absorb the newcomers into the old clan structure as clients. The concept of client (sing. *mawla*, pl. *mawali*) was inherited from pre-Islamic Arabia, where a client was an inferior associate of an Arab clan. Very often, he was a former slave who was freed and then raised to the level of client, though many people were adopted directly into the status. The client was almost a member of the clan; his heirs were also clients. Mawali could expect support and protection and would be helped in arranging marriages. The protection of the powerful was exchanged for the loyalty of the subordinates. However, as they absorbed mawali, Arab clans became less and less kin units and more and more stratified political and economic groups built around a kinship core. The gap between aristocratic and plebeian clans widened. For example, in the Tamim tribe, the noble clans acquired former Persian cavalry units as their clients, while others had slave laborers and weavers as theirs.

Clientage also generated class conflicts between the mawali and their overlords. Even the mawali who carried on skilled professions in war, administration, commerce, medicine, and religious life were held to be social inferiors. They were exploited economically, and could not intermarry with the Arabs or inherit equally. The active soldiers resented exclusion from the military payrolls (*diwans*), for enrollment in the diwans was not only a financial benefit, but was a symbol of social privilege. The mawali wanted to be recognized as part of the elite, but to the Arabs this was unthinkable. They clung to their status and privileges and resented the importance of the clients in the army and administration, their religious precocity, their commercial skill, and the shadow they cast over Arab primacy.

Thus within fifty years, the founding of new cities, the transfer of economic opportunities and political power to new peoples and new places stimulated the interpenetration of Arab and non-Arab peoples. Non-Arabs permeated the Arab-Muslim military caste as converts and associates, and Arabs became landowners, merchants, and settlers. The pressures generated by sedentarization and urbanization, by the teachings of Islam, and by contact with other Middle Eastern peoples weakened the old tribal society, fostered new group and communal structures, intensified the stratification of society and the division of labor, and led to the formation of new mixed Arab and non-Arab communities. Social change also made possible the formation of new religious associations built around family chiefs descended from the Prophet, charismatic preachers, Quran readers, scholars, and mystics. The breakdown of lineage structure made possible new forms of social organization.

Social change took cultural expression through conversions to Islam and acceptance of Arabic or Persian as shared languages. Conversion, however, was a very slow process. Though the original assumption of Muslim and Western writers was that the Middle East was quickly and massively converted to Islam, nowhere in the Arab sources is there explicit information about the conversion of large numbers of people, and certainly not of whole villages, towns, and regions. The available evidence points, rather, to a slow and uneven process of social and religious adjustment.

The earliest converts to Islam were those Christian-Bedouin tribes living on the margin of the fertile crescent who were swept up in the great migrations. Later in the first century of Arab rule other Mesopotamian Arab tribes also accepted Islam, but many such tribes remained Christian. Once the Arab conquests were secure, elites of the former Sasanian empire – soldiers, officials, and landowners – made common cause with the conquerors and accepted Islam. Insofar as it was Arab policy to reestablish the old administration, officials and landowners accepted the new religion. Conversions implied the ratification of old privileges and paved the way for entry into the dominant elite. In these cases, conversions seemed to involve mobile individuals and not classes or whole communities. Converts were made among client soldiers and scribes serving the Arab elite, and among other strata of the population attracted to the Arab garrisons.

From the very beginning of the Islamic era, the Arab-Muslim elite assumed that they would form a dual society in which the conquerors would constitute an aristocracy and the conquered peoples a subject population, the former Muslim, the latter not. The early Muslim regime was not only tolerant of the non-Muslim populations but actually helped reorganize Christian churches. The Nestorian church in Iraq resumed its important role in the educational, judicial, and even political administration of the Christian population. In Egypt, the Muslim authorities took a paternalistic attitude toward the Coptic church. Christian scribes served in the administration of both Iraq and Egypt.

For the sake of political inclusiveness and effective administration, the empire collaborated with non-Muslim elites, permitted them partial access to power, and protected them against disruptive social and economic changes.

Only after a century was this attitude reversed. By then widespread Arab assimilation into the general population had led many Arabs to accept the equality of Arabs and non-Arabs, and to value Muslim as well as Arab identifications. Thus ʿUmar II (717–20) changed the standing policy of the Caliphate and sought to put the empire on a Muslim, rather than a strictly Arab, basis. He accepted the fundamental equality of all Muslims, Arab and non-Arab, and promulgated new laws giving fiscal equality to Muslims regardless of origin. The wars in Transoxania reinforced this reversal of attitude. Protracted struggles against local princes and against Turkish rivals for control of the region prompted the Caliphate to offer fiscal benefits to converts. Though this policy was eventually abandoned as politically unfeasible, the sporadic attempts at encouraging conversion to Islam marked a turning point in the Arab conception of the relation of the Arabs to conquered peoples. In general, by the middle of the eighth century, there was a steady progress of conversions in Iraq, Egypt, Syria, Khurasan, and Transoxania. Significant numbers of converts were to be found in and around the Muslim garrison centers. However, outside the garrison towns the mass of Middle Eastern people remained non-Muslims.

Along with conversion to Islam common languages emerged in the new communities. In general, Arabic became the language of written communication in administration, literature, and religion. Arabic also became the predominant spoken dialect in the western parts of the Middle East – Egypt, Syria, Mesopotamia, and Iraq – where languages close to Arabic, such as Aramaic, were already spoken. The spread of Arabic was faster than the diffusion of Islam, but this is not to say that the process was rapid or complete. For example, Coptic was still spoken in Fustat in the eighth century. In Syria and Iraq there continued to be Aramaic-speaking populations.

In Iran the situation varied. In western Iran Arab settlers were absorbed into the local populations and became bilingual. In Khurasan, where the Arabs were assimilated to Persian manners, mores and dress, they used local Persian dialects. Not only did Arabs learn Persian, but the Arab-Muslim conquest became the vehicle for the introduction of Persian as the lingua franca of the peoples east of the Oxus. In Transoxania, Persian, the spoken language of Arabs in eastern Iran, replaced Soghdian as the common language for Arabs, Persians, and Soghdians.

Thus within a century of the Arab-Muslim conquests, the basic principles on which the empire was organized were no longer valid. The conquerors had assumed that Arabs and non-Arabs, Muslims and non-Muslims, would be segregated from each other, and that Arab Muslims would rule over conquered and "protected" peoples. In the first nomadic kingdom organized by the Caliph ʿUmar, Arabian peoples were to constitute a "nation in arms," settled in garrison centers, segregated from the subject peoples, restricted to military activities, and barred from commerce and agriculture. Membership in Islam was their prerogative. Non-Arab peoples were to keep their communal ties and religions and continue to work in the productive occupations which enabled them to support the ruling elite.

Nonetheless, in the course of the first Muslim century, the Arabs were changed from a clan or tribal people into an "urban" people, mingled with non-Arab peoples, abandoned military affairs, took on civilian occupations, and lost their monopoly on Islam. Correspondingly, non-Arab peoples entered the military and government services, converted to Islam, adopted the Arabic language, and claimed a place in the government of the empire in which they were initially subjects. Economic and social change in the garrison centers, conversions, and shared languages paved the way for the formation of new communities and for the society of the future, no longer divided between Arab conqueror and conquered peoples, but united on the basis of their integration, committed to Islam, sharing an Arabic and/or Persian linguistic identity. This mutual assimilation of peoples and the emergence of Islamic Middle Eastern communities took place, however, only in a restricted number of garrison centers. The rest of the Middle Eastern population remained outside the influence of the new societies, still bound to their more ancient heritage.

Though the mass of the population remained outside these currents of change, the cosmopolitan communities set the tone of Middle Eastern politics and culture for centuries to come. These economic and social changes were the forces which made the Arab empire possible. They generated the economic and human resources which would sustain the new imperium. However, they also generated the social conflicts between Arabs and mawali, tribal and administrative chiefs, religious and political elites, peasants and land-owners, which would bedevil the Muslim imperium and eventually destroy it altogether.

CHAPTER 4

THE CALIPHATE

The rapid transformation of the Middle East in the first century of Arab-Muslim rule generated intense conflicts fueled by the changing composition of the Arab elites, and especially by the divisions between active soldiers and settlers, the claims of the mawali, the assimilation of Arabs and non-Arabs, and the rise of sectarian religious associations. These conflicts drove the Caliphate to transform itself from a coalition of nomadic conquerors into a new form of Middle Eastern empire defined and legitimized in Islamic terms. Thus the history of the Caliphate went through several phases coinciding with the *Rashidun*, or Rightly-guided Caliphs (632–61), the Umayyad dynasty (661–750), the early ʿAbbasid empire (750–833), and the ʿAbbasid empire in decline (833–945). In this chapter we shall follow the changing concept and practice of empire until the great crisis of the mid-ninth century, in which the demands for religious legitimacy and the requirements of political efficacy proved impossible to reconcile, and left as their legacy a lasting tension between the precepts of religion and the actualities of political power.

FROM NOMADIC KINGDOM TO SYRIAN MONARCHY

The first phase in the construction of the Caliphal regime was the period of the Rashidun in which the companions of the Prophet, Abu Bakr (632–34), ʿUmar (634–44), ʿUthman (644–56), and ʿAli (656–61), ruled by virtue of their personal connection with the Prophet, and the religious and patriarchal authority derived from loyalty to Islam. The conquests made the Caliphs the

Table 2. *Outline chronology of early Islamic history*

Muhammad	c. 570–632
Rashidun Caliphs	632–61
First civil war	656–61
Umayyad Caliphs	661–750
Reign of Mu^cawiya	661–80
Second civil war	680–92
Reign of ^cAbd al-Malik	685–705
Reconstruction of regime	685–744
Third civil war	744–50
^cAbbasid Caliphs	750–1258
Consolidation of empire	750 – c. 850
Reign of al-Ma^ᵓmun	813–33
Breakup of empire	c. 833–945
Independent succession states	945 – c. 1220
Mongol invasions	c. 1220 – c. 1260

military and administrative chiefs of the newly conquered lands. In this role they claimed to be the deputies of God.

The early Caliphate was politically based on the Muslim community of Arabia and upon the Arab tribal forces who conquered its Middle Eastern empire. Almost from the outset the divisions within the Arab-Muslim elite threatened to undermine the regime. The elite was divided among those who held a Muslim and those who held an Arab concept of the Caliphate. In organizing the new empire the Caliph ^cUmar pursued an "Islamic" policy. In Mecca and Medina he favored the Meccan companions of the Prophet and the *ansar* – his Medinan helpers. In the garrison towns he favored the clans who had supported Medina in the Arabian wars and had been early participants in the conquest of Iraq. ^cUmar appointed these people to governorships, generalships, and administrative offices, gave them the highest stipends, and allowed them to administer the *sawafi* – the abandoned Sasanian crown lands – in their own interest. The opposition was equally powerful. In Medina and Mecca, the Quraysh aristocracy chafed under ^cUmar's policies. In the provinces the continuing influx of migrants from Arabia brought to the garrison towns large and prestigious Arabian clans and even the former chiefs of the earlier tribal opposition now converted to Islam. They claimed their share of power. By the end of ^cUmar's reign a fierce conflict of interests had already developed.

^cUthman, who succeeded ^cUmar, was a Meccan aristocrat of the Umayya clan. He reversed ᶜUmar's policies and favored Umayyad and other Meccan interests at the expense of the companions of the Prophet and the Medinans. He redistributed revenues in the interests of the newly migrant large clans. To accomplish this redistribution of power, ᶜUthman asserted an increased central control over provincial revenues and required a closer accounting of the sawafi lands. He also took initiatives in religious matters, including the promulgation of a standard edition of the Quran, which was resented by those Muslims who felt themselves to be the custodians of the holy book. ᶜUthman thus stood for a reassertion of the pre-Islamic coalition of Meccan and Arabian tribal aristocrats against the new elements produced by Islam, and claimed an enlarged authority for the Caliph to effect social, economic and religious changes.

In implementing these policies, ᶜUthman provoked bitter opposition, conspiracies and eventually in 656 his murder by a party of about 500 Arabs from Fustat. In the wake of this murder, ᶜAli was elected Caliph. ᶜAli opposed the centralization of Caliphal control over provincial revenues and favored an equal distribution of taxes and booty among the Arabs. As the cousin and son-in-law of Muhammad as well as one of the earliest converts to Islam, ᶜAli based his claim on personal piety and closeness to the Prophet. For decades he had claimed the Caliphate on the basis of his devotion to Muhammad and Islam, but now he compromised himself by coming to power with the support of ᶜUthman's assassins.

The civil war continued through the whole of ᶜAli's reign and was the most fateful event in Islamic history. It began as a struggle between conflicting Arab interests, and it ended in the permanent religious and political division of the Muslim community. At the outset ᶜAli was supported by the Medinan ansar and by the Kufans and Egyptians who had participated in the assassination of ᶜUthman; he even had the temporary support of the great tribal chiefs. Opposed to ᶜAli was a faction led by the Meccan aristocrats Talha and Zubayr, and the Prophet's favorite wife ᶜAᵓisha. ᶜAli defeated them at the battle of the Camel in 656. ᶜAli was also opposed by Muᶜawiya, ᶜUthman's cousin and the governor of Syria, who refused ᶜAli's demands for allegiance and called for revenge for ᶜUthman and the punishment of his killers.

The opponents and their armies met at the battle of Siffin (657), where after months of desultory confrontation and negotiations, the moderates forced an agreement to arbitrate the question of whether ᶜUthman's murder was justified. Some of ᶜAli's supporters, called the Kharijis (secessionists), saw ᶜAli's agreement to arbitrate as a defeat for their own hopes in his Caliphate and a violation of religious principles. They turned against him and were defeated in battle, but this new round of bloodshed further alienated Muslim support.

Fig. 2. The Banu Umayya and the Umayyad Caliphs.

When the negotiators met at Adhruh in January 659 they agreed that the murder of ʿUthman was not justified, and that a *shura* or council should be called to elect a new Caliph. ʿAli rejected the outcome, but to no avail. His coalition disintegrated and the great tribal chiefs of Kufa failed to support him. Moreover, the protracted struggle had begun to threaten the security of the empire and the flow of revenues. As rebellions in eastern Iran cut off the payment of taxes to the tribesmen of Basra and Kufa, Arab opinion favored the succession of Muʿawiya to the Caliphate because he was backed by disciplined forces, and because it seemed that he could maintain order within the Arab-Muslim elite and Arab control over the empire. After ʿAli's assassination by a Khariji, Muʿawiya declared himself Caliph and was accepted by the dominant interests.

The civil war settled some of the outstanding questions of the moment. It confirmed the office of the Caliphate in the hands of the Quraysh and the Umayyad family; it reduced the importance of Mecca and Medina by moving the seat of the Caliphate to Damascus; it confirmed the power of the great Arabian tribes as opposed to the early Muslim elite.

The civil war also created permanent divisions within the Muslim community. Henceforth, Muslims were divided over who had the legitimate right to occupy the Caliphate. Muslims who accepted the succession of Muᶜawiya and the historical sequence of Caliphs after him are called the Sunnis. Those who held that ᶜAli was the only rightful Caliph and that only his descendants should succeed him are called the Shiᶜa. The Shiᶜa tended to stress the religious functions of the Caliph, and to deplore its political compromises. The Sunnis tended to circumscribe the religious role of the Caliph and to be more tolerant of its political involvements. The Kharijis held that the Caliph should not descend in either family, but that he should be elected by the community of Muslims at large and hold his position only so long as he was upright and sinless in the conduct of his office. Out of the civil war came disagreements that would grow into the great sectarian divisions of Islam. As these early differences were vested with ever-widening religious importance, Sunnis, Shiᶜa, and Kharijis developed separate versions of Islam and formed distinct religious bodies within the community as a whole.

Upon coming to power, Muᶜawiya (661–80) began a new cycle of efforts to reconstruct both the authority and the power of the Caliphate, and to deal with factionalism within the ruling elite. Muᶜawiya began to change a coalition of Arab tribes into a centralized monarchy. He expanded the military and administrative powers of the state and devised new moral and political grounds for loyalty to the Caliphate. First, he tried to regulate military policy to keep the upper hand over the Arab tribal warriors. To satisfy the interests of the tribal chiefs, the conquests were resumed in North Africa and eastern Iran. On the Syrian front Muᶜawiya kept peace with the Byzantine empire so that he could hold Syrian forces in reserve for purposes of internal policing. Further, he sought to build up the revenues from private incomes, from confiscated Byzantine and Sasanian crown lands, and from investments in reclamation and irrigation. Muᶜawiya also emphasized the patriarchal aspects of the Caliphate; his growing police and financial powers were cloaked by the traditional Arab virtues of conciliation, consultation, generosity, and respect for the forms of tribal tradition. Muᶜawiya's own qualities of person were more important than any institutions. He is legendary for his *hilm*, a talent for dealing with his followers so that they cooperated without feeling that their dignity had been offended. It meant clemency and patience, and the power to do harm restrained by forbearance. If the Caliphate of ᶜUmar was fundamentally based on his closeness to Muhammad and great religious integrity,

Mu‘awiya's reign was based on his unsurpassed ability to exemplify the Arab tribal patriarch. His reign marked an effort to centralize state power and develop the non-Islamic appeal of the Caliphate, but it was still based on networks of personal and clientele ties.

The decades of Mu‘awiya's rule did not do away with the causes of the first civil wars. Medinans resented the Quraysh for usurping their place. The Shi‘a aspired to the control of the Caliphate. Arab factional conflict simmered beneath the surface. Mu‘awiya had managed to control the Arabs by his personal qualities combined with the threat of force, but when he died, civil war broke out again. This time it lasted from 680 to 692.

The second Arab civil war was a maelstrom of conflicting interests. It turned around three issues: the struggle among Arab aristocrats for the control of the Caliphate, factional rivalries, and sectarian religious rebellions. At Mu‘awiya's death, his son and successor, Yazid (680–3) had to contend with new Meccan and ‘Alid aspirants to the Caliphate. ‘Abdallah b. al-Zubayr, the son of a man killed by ‘Ali in the battle of the Camel in 656, rallied support in Arabia and in Kufa. His forces were defeated. At the same time, ‘Ali's son Husayn attempted to come from Medina to Kufa to take the lead of his followers, but his small party was intercepted at Karbala (Iraq) and destroyed before his Kufan followers could help him. At the moment the episode had few repercussions, but over time, Husayn's death took on the significance of martyrdom. Today Husayn's shrine at Karbala is one of the great pilgrimage sites of the Muslim world. As much as the defeat of his father, Husayn's death at the hands of the Umayyads divides Muslims more than any dispute over law or theology or any antipathy between tribes, races, and linguistic groups. ‘Ali is the ancestor of Shi‘ism; Husayn is its martyr.

Apart from these direct challenges to the Umayyad Caliphate, the civil war period was marked by widespread factional fighting among Arab groups. Whereas the factions of the first civil war were based on Islamic versus tribal loyalties, the new factions were based upon ad hoc alliances between clans which had come together in the insecure and changing societies of the garrison towns. Though defined in tribal terms the warring coalitions were probably composed of older- and younger-generation migrants. The Syrian tribal coalitions, which had for decades been the mainstay of Mu‘awiya's reign, fell into two warring coalitions called Yemen (or Kalb) and Qays. The fighting spread to Iraq, where the factions were called Mudar and Tamim; and to Khurasan where they were called Qays and Rabi‘a.

In the meantime, the Kharijis who had repudiated ‘Ali after the battle of Siffin also rebelled. The Kharijis formed small bands, usually of 30 to 100 men.

Each group was at once a terrorist band and a fanatical religious sect. They were held together by the conviction that they were the only true Muslims, and that their rebellions had profound religious justification. One group of Kharijis, called Azariqa, took to marauding in the province of Khuzistan. Another group of Kharijis, called Najda, controlled a good part of Arabia including Bahrain, Oman, Hadhramaut, and Yemen before they were finally crushed. These Khariji bands were most likely formed by uprooted individuals looking for communal affiliation through sectarian movements.

In the end the Umayyads prevailed, not by consensus, but by force of arms. The Caliph ʿAbd al-Malik (685–705), backed by Syrian Yemeni armies, eventually crushed his numerous opponents. The new Caliph and his successor al-Walid (705–15), now faced with endemic messianic religious opposition, both Shiʿa and Khariji, and tribal factionalism provoked by the stress of social change in the garrison-cities, had to devise an alternate strategy to rule. Their response was to accelerate the centralization of the state, but to make the regime, rather than the person of the Caliph, the focus of political and ideological loyalty. The first aspect of ʿAbd al-Malik's policy after defeating his opponents was to demilitarize the Arabs in the garrison cities of Iraq. Henceforth, Syrian forces replaced Iraqi forces in all the eastern campaigns. A Syrian army policed Iraq from a new garrison town built at al-Wasit. The Arabs of Kufa and Basra would be treated as pensioned subjects of the empire they had founded. Al-Hajjaj, the governor of Iraq (692–715), no longer sought to conciliate the tribesmen, but threatened to make heads roll. The result of this draconian policy was 40 years of internal peace.

Though the regime was essentially based upon the household of the ruler and his military and scribal clients, a small elite governing a highly decentralized empire, the Caliphate worked to further centralize administrative power. ʿAbd al-Malik and al-Walid arranged for the translation of the tax registers from Greek and Persian into Arabic. Résumés, copies, and reports now appeared in Arabic. The changeover was made in 697 in Iraq, in 700 in Syria and Egypt, and shortly after in Khurasan. The Caliphs then proceeded to reorganize the finances of various regions. Under ʿUmar II (717–20), the Caliphate proposed a major revision of the rules and principles of taxation for the sake of greater uniformity and equity. The Caliph Hisham (724–43) tried to implement ʿUmar's policies in Khurasan, Egypt, and Mesopotamia. Umayyad administration also began to develop an organizational identity. In the first decades of the Arab empire, administration had been carried on by Greek- and Persian-speaking officials inherited from the older empires. By 700, however, a new generation of Arab-speaking clients who, though trained as administrators by their predecessors, were loyal to the Caliphate, came to power. The new scribal elite and their descendants formed the secretarial backbone of the Arab-Muslim empire until the tenth century.

In line with these administrative developments, the Caliphal court was also reorganized. The days when Mu'awiya was surrounded by Arab chiefs were over. Now a court chamberlain kept visitors in order and regulated daily business. The officials of the chancery, the officer of the royal seal, guards and scribes, as well as Arab favorites, surrounded the ruler. Important governorships were still assigned to Arab leaders, but the business of government was no longer ordered by councils of Arab chiefs, but rather by professional administrators. From patriarchal rule, the Caliphate transformed itself into an imperial government.

The most important policy of the freshly consolidated Caliphal regime was the resumption of the Arab conquests on a world scale. The early conquests resulted from tribal migrations and from the annual campaigns of Arab forces based in the garrison cities. The new phase of conquests was inspired by imperial ambitions and entailed planned attacks on remote places, carried out with the aid of non-Arab forces. The new wars were not wars of tribal expansion, but imperial wars waged for world domination. These were the wars which made North Africa, Spain, Transoxania, and Sind part of the Muslim empire.

The administrative and military dimensions of later Umayyad statism were backed by a new ideological policy. In the reign of 'Abd al-Malik, the Caliphate for the first time began to mint its own coins in place of Byzantine and Sasanian coins. The new Arab coins did away with Christian and Zoroastrian symbolism, and introduced gold and silver coins with Arabic script to symbolize the sovereignty of the state, and its independence from and equality with, if not superiority to, the previous empires. Furthermore, the state also symbolized its sovereignty by undertaking monumental constructions. Under 'Abd al-Malik, Jerusalem was appropriated as a holy place for Islam, and the Dome of the Rock was built on the site of the ancient Hebrew temple. Under al-Walid, new mosques were built in Medina and Damascus. Their decoration symbolized the glory of the Arabs and testified to the splendid services of the state to the faith. They symbolized the primacy of the state and its indispensability to the Muslim community.

The later Umayyad Caliphs, from 'Abd al-Malik to Hisham (724–43), built an imperial government resting not on the Arab movement but upon the force of picked Syrian armies, an increasingly powerful and rationalized administrative apparatus, and an ideology of obedience to the state. Whereas the early

2 The Dome of the Rock

Caliphate had been a series of individual reigns deeply dependent upon the personal religious or patriarchal qualities of the Caliphs, the new Caliphate was an institution independent of individual office holders. The Umayyads had managed to turn the Caliphate into a state regime, but at the same time they had kept alive and incorporated into the symbolism of the empire its specifically Islamic heritage.

Despite the Islamic tone, however, the inspiration for this solution was not purely Umayyad. The parallels between the measures taken by ᶜAbd al-Malik and al-Walid and the practices of the Byzantine and Sasanian empires are striking. In Syria and Egypt the whole administrative apparatus, including the revenue administration, and even the form of chancery documents, was Byzantine in origin. Syrian military organization also followed Byzantine models. In Iraq the Sasanian pattern of administrative organization, the fourfold division of finance, military, correspondence, and chancellery services, was adopted by Arab administrators. The sublimity of the emperor Caliph, the official support of the state for religion and the construction of monumental churches, or, in this case, mosques, was Byzantine in inspiration. The Umayyads borrowed Greek motifs and even Greek builders and artists to decorate their mosques and took Sasanian designs and decorations for their palaces. Yet in borrowing the ideas of the previous empires, the Umayyads transformed the traditional motifs and provided old forms with a new content to create a specifically Islamic symbolism of state. The statist ideology derived from the previous empires, but its expression was characteristically Islamic.

However, the assertion of a new form of Arab-Muslim imperium did not allay unrest brewing in the garrison cities. The mawali who served as soldiers in the armies and as administrators in the government bureaucracy demanded equality of status and privilege with the Arabs. Soldiers claimed the right to be enrolled on the military diwans. Peasant converts claimed the right to exemption from discriminatory taxes levied against the non-Muslims.

Among the Arabs, bitter factional struggles continued. After the second civil war the tribal factions developed more concrete political and economic orientations. The Yemenis represented those demilitarized Arabs who were assimilated to civilian pursuits, and were becoming city dwellers engaged in trade, or village landowners and cultivators. These Arabs accepted the assimilation of Arab and non-Arab populations in the army and favored the accommodation of converts' interests. They desired peace rather than continued wars of expansion, financial equality for Arabs and converts, and decentralization of Caliphal power. They tended to stress Islamic rather than purely Arab identifications. By contrast, the Qays represented those Arabs who were actively engaged in the army and who depended for their incomes on conquests, government administration, and tax revenues. They pushed for a centralized political power, military expansion, and the preservation of Arab privileges at the expense of sedentarized Arabs, converts, and non-Muslim interests.

In the period from ʿAbd al-Malik to Hisham, the Caliphate maintained a delicate balance amidst these competing interests, but the struggle among them came to a head in the reign of ʿUmar II (717–20). ʿUmar II had the genius to appraise the situation realistically, and to propose what was in fact the ultimate and perhaps the only possible solution. ʿUmar realized that the domination of one ethnic caste over other peoples was anachronistic. The peoples who filled the armies and staffed the administration, the merchants and artisans who took a leading part in the propagation of Islam, would have to be accepted as participants in the empire. The antagonisms of Arabs and non-Arabs would have to be dissolved in a universal Muslim unity. As ʿUmar saw it, the problem was not just to placate the converts while retaining Arab supremacy. Rather, he held that the empire could no longer be an Arab empire but had to be the imperium of all Muslims. He thus stood for the conversion of all of the peoples of West Asia to Islam, and their acceptance as equals of the Arabs.

In his actual policies, ʿUmar showed a pragmatic approach enlightened by principle. His aim was not only to satisfy the claims of the converts, but to reconcile their demands with the interests of the state. ʿUmar proposed to satisfy the complaints of the mawali fighting alongside the Arab forces by fully accepting their claim that all active Muslim soldiers, Arabs or not, were entitled to be enrolled in the diwans. In Khurasan, ʿUmar ordered the enrollment of 20,000 mawali. He also established new principles for taxation based on the concept of equality among Muslims, but implemented them in ways which protected the interests of the regime. While converts claimed exemption from land and poll taxes as a form of equality with Arabs, ʿUmar ruled that taxes were not a function of the status of the individuals. Converts were expected to pay full taxes on land, and Arab landlords would also henceforth have to pay taxes at full rather than privileged rates. Thus, the tax burdens were equalized, but at higher levels – at the expense of relatively few Arab landlords. As for the poll tax, ʿUmar established the principle, not always heeded, that it was to fall on non-Muslims only. Arab settlers and converts were excused from this tax. At the same time, however, they were all expected to pay the *sadaqat* or Muslim alms tax, which partially compensated the state for the loss of poll tax revenues.

Later Caliphs attempted to implement these principles, but with very limited success. Throughout the late Umayyad period the interest in reconciliation and justice conflicted with the interest in the maintenance of the status quo, and Caliphal policy oscillated between tax concessions and cancellation of concessions.

In these circumstances the stage was set for the opposition and for yet a third Muslim civil war. In Sunni religious circles there was a deep suspicion of and hostility to the Caliphate. While supporting the regime in principle as the expression of the Muslim community, many Sunni religious leaders were alienated by the military and administrative policies of the regime, by its evident assumption of a royal authority, and by its politically motivated intervention in religious affairs. Sunni thinkers wished to dissociate themselves from the regime and its political compromises, but not from the concept of the Caliphate and its religious meaning.

The Shiʿa also nourished unsatisfied hopes for the reign of the family of ʿAli. They claimed that the Caliphate rightly belonged to the members of their family, chosen by God to teach Islam and to rule the Islamic community. They raised the hopes of many disgruntled Arabs and converts that a *mahdi*, a savior, would come of this family. If Banu Hashim had borne Muhammad and ʿAli, might they not bear the messiah to come? Since the second civil war, however, the ᶜAlid branch of the family of the Prophet was scarcely manifest in public, but various members were diligently organizing underground conspiracies against the Umayyads. Between 736 and 740, Shiᶜi agitation finally broke out in Kufa, where a number of Kufans were seized by the police and executed. In 740 Zayd ibn ᶜAli, a grandson of Husayn, rebelled and was promptly defeated.

In the meantime, another branch of the Banu Hashim, the ᶜAbbasids, bided their time. The ᶜAbbasids, like the ᶜAlids, were descended from an uncle of Muhammad, named ᶜAbbas; but their immediate claim to the Caliphate rested upon the allegation that a great-grandson of ᶜAli, Abu Hashim, had bequeathed them leadership of the family and of the opposition movement. While the ᶜAlid branch of the family concentrated on Kufa with no success, the ᶜAbbasid branch proselytized in Khurasan, sending a succession of missionary or revolutionary organizers to create a popular front of all opponents of the Umayyads. ᶜAbbasid agents agitated for revenge for ᶜAli, for the overthrow of the Umayyads, and for a new era of peace and justice. Over time, the leading ᶜAbbasid agent, Abu Muslim, built up an elaborate underground movement and organized military support in Khurasan.

With the death of Hisham in 743 the Umayyad regime again collapsed, and ᶜAlids, ᶜAbbasids, Kharijis, tribal factions, and disgruntled governors all entered the fray. The reasons for this outbreak lay in the military exhaustion of the Syrian state. The late Umayyad Caliphs had increasingly used the military power of Syria to control other Arabs and to stiffen the armies fighting on the frontiers of the empire with reliable, professional, battle-hardened and uncomplaining troops. Garrison duties exposed Syrian troops in these areas to the brunt of warfare precisely at a time when the Arabs were suffering temporary setbacks. The Turks drove the Arabs from Transoxania. The Khazars, a nomadic people living beyond the Caucasus, broke through Arab defenses, defeated the Arabs at Ardabil, invaded Armenia and penetrated as far as Mosul in 730. In 740 the Greeks won a decisive victory over Arab invaders at Acrazas in Anatolia and destroyed a major Syrian army. Arab and Berber invaders were defeated in central France in 732, and Berber rebellions under the banner of Kharijism broke out in North Africa and destroyed a Syrian army of 27,000 men. What remained of this army made its way to Spain where parts of it helped establish the Spanish Umayyad dynasty. It took yet another Syrian army to quell these rebellions in 742. These defeats brought an end to the imperial phase of Arab empire-building and left Syria militarily exhausted. Having based a century of rule on the ever increasing power of the state, the Umayyad dynasty now found itself without the military basis for effective

Fig. 3. The ʿAbbasid Caliphs to the disintegration of the empire.

central government. Now a few thousand troops might prevail. From 744 to 750 Shiᶜas, Kharijis and tribal factions struggled to seize the throne. Marwan b. Muhammad (744–50), the former governor of Armenia, gained the upper hand and claimed the title of Caliph, but despite his military victories, no one accepted Marwan's claim to rule. His authority extended only as far as his armies.

By 747, the ᶜAbbasids were ready to move. In the villages of Khurasan, especially around Marw, Abu Muslim, the ᶜAbbasid agent, found the support he needed. These were the villages settled by the initial Arab conquerors of Khurasan who had become agriculturalists, only to find themselves burdened with taxes and treated as a subject population. These were the people who had been promised tax reform by the Umayyads and had been betrayed. Now they were ready to fight. Khurasan was in a fever of political agitation and eschatological expectation. The imminent end of the world, the coming of the mahdi, and the beginning of a new era of world justice was expected. Popular apocryphal writings called *Jafr* and *al-Malahim* foretold fateful battles, harbingers of the Last Day, and the coming of the mahdi. In this atmosphere Abu Muslim showed the black banner, the sign of his advent, to rally peoples aggrieved by loss of status and by unjust taxes. About 3,000 fighting men rallied to the cause. They defeated rival factions in Khurasan, raised Yemeni support in western Iran, crushed Marwan in Iraq, and so seized the Caliphate.

The ᶜAbbasid revolt was supported largely by Arabs, mainly the aggrieved settlers of Marw, with the addition of the Yemeni faction and their mawali. Further support came from Shiᶜi factions that were confused as to the identity of the ᶜAbbasid leadership and took up the cause as their own. They were later to be bitterly disappointed by the proclamation of Abu al-ᶜAbbas, the head of the ᶜAbbasid house, as the new Caliph. At first the ᶜAbbasids represented no more than one of a number of factions which had competed for the office. On coming to power, they would again have to face the Umayyad problem of translating the title of Caliph into institutions of effective dynastic rule. How the ᶜAbbasids would do this was still an open question in 750. The answer amounted to a revolution.

THE ᶜABBASID EMPIRE: SOCIAL REVOLUTION AND POLITICAL REACTION

Almost the first venture of the new regime was the creation of a new capital. Ever since ancient times, Middle Eastern regimes had built new cities as headquarters for their armies and administrative staffs, and to symbolize the

Map 3. Iraq and Baghdad in the early ʿAbbasid era.

advent of a new order. The rulers of the Assyrian empire created the famous cities of Nineveh and Nimrod; the Sasanians founded Ctesiphon. In a strategic location on the main routes between Iraq, Iran and Syria, in one of the most fertile parts of Iraq with ready access to the Tigris–Euphrates water system, the ʿAbbasids built Baghdad to be their palace and administrative base.

Like its predecessors, Baghdad rapidly transcended the intentions of its founders and grew from a military and administrative center into a major city. The very decision to build the administrative center, called City of Peace (*Madinat al-Salam*), generated two large settlements in the near vicinity. One was the extensive camp of the ʿAbbasid army in the districts to the north of the palace complex, called al-Harbiya, and the other to the south was al-Karkh, inhabited by thousands of construction workers brought from Iraq, Syria, Egypt, and Iran. Here were markets to provision the workers and their families, workshops to produce their clothes, utensils, and tools, and factories to supply the building materials for the construction project. The original Baghdad, then, was a three-part complex – the troop settlement in al-Harbiya, the working populations in al-Karkh, and the administrative city itself, Madinat al-Salam. No sooner was Madinat al-Salam completed than the decisions of the Caliphs to build additional palace residences and administrative complexes in the immediate vicinity stimulated the growth of additional quarters. Across the Tigris the new palace district of al-Rusafa also promoted urban development.

Never had there been a Middle Eastern city so large. Baghdad was not a single city, but a metropolitan center, made up of a conglomeration of districts on both sides of the Tigris River. In the ninth century it measured about 25 square miles, and had a population of between 300,000 and 500,000. It was ten times the size of Sasanian Ctesiphon, and it was larger than all of the settled places – cities, towns, villages and hamlets combined – in the Diyala region. Baghdad was larger than Constantinople, which is estimated to have had a population of 200,000, and larger than any other Middle Eastern city until Istanbul in the sixteenth century. In its time, Baghdad was the largest city in the world outside of China.

Its vast size is an index of its incomparable importance in the formation of the ʿAbbasid empire, society, and culture. As a capital city it was the center of economic opportunity. Baghdad grew into a great city of international trade and of immensely productive textile, leather, paper, and other industries. Most important in Middle Eastern history, however, was the cosmopolitan character of its population. Jews, Christians, and Muslims, as well as secret pagans, Persians, Iraqis, Arabs, Syrians, and Central Asians made up its populace.

Soldiers and officials, the workers who built the new city, the people who lived
in the surrounding villages, merchants from Khurasan and the East who
engaged in the India traffic through the Persian Gulf, also settled in Baghdad.
Basrans seeking intellectual contacts and business fortunes, notables and landowners from Ahwaz, cloth workers from Khuzistan, prisoners of war from
Anatolia, scholars from Alexandria, Harran, and Jundishapur, and Nestorian
Christians from villages all over Iraq, made Baghdad their home. Baghdad,
then, was the product of the upheavals, population movements, economic
changes, and conversions of the preceding century; the home of a new Middle
Eastern society, heterogeneous and cosmopolitan, embracing numerous Arab
and non-Arab elements, now integrated into a single society under the auspices
of the Arab empire and the Islamic religion. Baghdad provided the wealth and
manpower to govern a vast empire; it crystallized the culture which became
Islamic civilization.

The creation of Baghdad symbolized the ʿAbbasids' effort to cope with the
various problems which had beset and eventually destroyed the Umayyad
dynasty. Upon coming to power the new dynasty faced the problems which
had troubled the old: building effective governing institutions, and mobilizing
adequate political support from Arab Muslims, converts, and from the non-
Muslim communities which paid the empire's taxes. The new dynasty had to
secure the loyalty and obedience of its subjects for a rebel regime and justify
itself in Muslim terms.

To cope with these problems the new dynasty returned to the principles of
ʿUmar II. The ʿAbbasids swept away Arab caste supremacy and accepted the
universal equality of Muslims. They did away with the anachronism of the
Arab "nation in arms," and frankly embraced all Muslims as their supporters.
The new regime committed itself to the deliberate recruitment of a wide and
representative spectrum of Middle Eastern elites, and promoted them to the
highest military and administrative offices. Arab caste supremacy had lost its
political meaning, and only a coalition regime, uniting Arab and non-Arab
elements, could govern a Middle Eastern empire. The propagation of Arabic as
a lingua franca, the spread of Islam and the conversion of at least some
proportion of the population, the tremendous expansion of commercial activities, and the economic and demographic upheavals which set people free
from their old lives and launched them on new careers in new cities such as
Baghdad, made possible an empirewide recruitment of personnel and of
political support for the new regime. Under the ʿAbbasids the empire no
longer belonged to the Arabs, though they had conquered its territories, but
to all those peoples who would share in Islam and in the emerging networks

of political, social, economic, and cultural loyalties which defined a new cosmopolitan Middle Eastern society.

The new regime expressed its orientation in the organization of new armies and new cadres of administration. The ᶜAbbasids abolished the military privileges of the Arabs and brought new forces into being, which though partly Arab in composition, were recruited and organized so that they would be loyal to the dynasty alone and not to tribal or caste interests. The Umayyads had already begun to replace provincial Arab forces with Syrian troops, non-Arab converts to Islam, mawali, and even local non-Arab–non-Muslim forces, as in Khurasan and Transoxania, and tended to concentrate military and political power in the hands of picked Syrian regiments loyal to each particular Caliph. Yet the Umayyads were never able to declare in principle or to complete in practice the transition from the Arab "nation in arms" to professional armies. Throughout the Umayyad period Arab forces were still needed for the world conquests to which they were committed.

Conversely, while the ᶜAbbasids continued to use Arab troops in Yemen, India, Armenia, and on the Byzantine frontiers, the end of the conquests meant that Arabs in Iraq, Khurasan, Syria, and Egypt could be retired from military service. The ᶜAbbasids no longer needed vast reserves of manpower. Rather they required only limited frontier forces, and a central army to make occasional expeditions against the Byzantines, and to suppress internal opposition. For this purpose the ᶜAbbasids used the army with which they had captured the state – the Khurasanian Arabs and their clients and descendants, a professional force loyal to the Caliphs who paid them.

In administration the openness of the ᶜAbbasid regime was particularly evident. Many of the scribes in the expanding ᶜAbbasid bureaucracy were Persians from Khurasan, who had begun to enter the central government under the late Umayyads. Nestorian Christians were powerfully represented, probably because they made up a large proportion of the population of Iraq. Certain smaller minorities such as Jews were active in tax and banking activities. Shiᶜi families were also prominent. Arabs did not altogether lose their important place. The ᶜAbbasid dynasty was Arab; the ᶜAbbasid armies were composed of Arabs, and the judicial and legal life of Baghdad and other important cities was in Arab hands. The prominence of Arabs, however, was no longer a prescriptive right, but was dependent upon loyalty to the dynasty.

A revolutionary social policy was accompanied by the continuation of Umayyad administrative and governmental organization. The ᶜAbbasids continued the Umayyad effort to centralize political power in the hands of the Caliph and the ruling elite. Just as the Umayyads had inherited Roman and

Sasanian bureaucratic precedents and even the remnants of the old organizations, the ʿAbbasids inherited the traditions, the practices, the skills, and even the personnel of Umayyad administration. Personal and clientele ties to the Caliphs themselves were the essence of government organization. At first the ministries were just the clerical staffs of the leading officials, and the Caliphs were consulted about everything. In time, however, the ad hoc, household character of the Caliphate was substantially, though by no means entirely, superseded by a more rationalized form of administration. The business of the government became more routinized and three types of services or bureaus (diwans) developed. The first was the chancery, the *diwan al-rasaʾil*, the records and correspondence office. The second was the bureaus for tax collection, such as the *diwan al-kharaj*. Third, there were bureaus to pay the expenses of the Caliphs' armies, court, and pensioners; the army bureau, *diwan al-jaysh*, was the most important of these. As time went on, the conduct of business grew more elaborate and more specialized. Each function – revenue, chancery, disbursement – was subdivided into a host of offices, and each office was subdivided into divisions to carry on auxiliary activities.

Alongside of the bureaucratic staffs, the Caliphs also appointed *qadis* or judges. The qadis were usually selected from among the leading scholars of Muslim law, and their duty was to apply this law to the civil affairs of the Muslim population. Other judicial officials dealt with state-related issues; customary law continued to be used in small communities.

With this elaboration of functions and offices, the Caliphs found themselves less and less able to supervise the business of the state. To keep the organization responsive to the will of the ruler special measures were adopted. The first was the elaboration of internal bureaucratic checks. Financial affairs were watched by the *diwan al-azimma*, the controller's office, which was originally attached to each diwan and which later evolved into an independent bureau of the budget. Correspondence had to go through the hands of the drafting agency, the *diwan al-tawqiʿ*, for countersignature, and the *khatam*, the keeper of the seal. In a special administrative court, the *mazalim*, the Caliph advised by leading judges, adjudicated fiscal and administrative problems. The *barid*, the official messenger and information service, spied on the rest of the government.

Finally, the office of the *wazir* was developed to coordinate, supervise, and check on the operations of the bureaucracy. Wazir was the title originally applied to the secretaries or administrators who were close assistants of the Caliph and whose powers varied according to the wishes of their patron. Under the Caliphs al-Mahdi (775–85) and Harun al-Rashid (786–809), the

Barmakid family rose to particular prominence. Originally a Buddhist priestly family from Balkh, they were made generals and provincial governors, and served as the tutors of young princes. Still, however powerful, the Barmakids were not chiefs of the whole administration, but depended on the changing impulses of the Caliphs for their positions. In 803 Harun al-Rashid executed the leading members of the family. Not until the middle of the ninth century did the wazir become the chief of administration, with the combined duties of controlling the bureaucracy, nominating provincial officials and sitting on the mazalim court.

The elaborate central government was the nerve center of the empire, and from Baghdad the Caliphs maintained communications with the provinces. But despite the propensities of the central administration, the provinces were not all governed in a bureaucratic manner. The degree of control ran from the most loosely held suzerainty to the most elaborately centralized administration. The variations maximized the influence for the central government; the empire was tolerant and inclusive rather than monolithic.

The directly controlled provinces were Iraq, Mesopotamia, Egypt, Syria, western Iran, and Khuzistan – the provinces physically closest to the capital. Khurasan was sometimes, but not always, one of this group. These provinces were organized to maximize the obedience of officials to the will of the central government and to assure the remittance of tax revenues from the province to the center. Governors' appointments were limited to a very short term so that their careers would be entirely at the mercy of the Caliph. Governors were rapidly rotated to prevent them from developing local support which they might use against the central government. In addition the powers of government were often divided among several officials. The governor himself was usually the military commander, and a different man was appointed by the central treasury to be in charge of taxation and financial affairs; yet another official headed the judiciary. These separate officials checked each other's powers, and all officials were subject to the supervision of the barid.

The ideal of frequent rotation of governors, separation of civil and military powers, and inspection by the barid was hard to implement. Governors were often appointed to pay off political debts to warlords, generals, and members of the royal family who acquiesced in the accession of a Caliph or in his succession plans, and Caliphs had to give these appointees a wide latitude in the administration of their provinces. In such cases, frequent rotation and the separation of civil and military functions might be waived.

Outside of the directly administered provinces were affiliated regions that were scarcely, if at all, controlled by the central government. Geographically these were the provinces of the Caspian highlands – Jilan, Tabaristan, Daylam, and Jurjan; the Inner Asian provinces – Transoxania, Farghana, Ushrusana, and Kabul; and most of North Africa. In some peripheral provinces the Caliphs appointed a supervising military governor and assigned a garrison to see to the collection of taxes and the payment of tribute. For example, until the middle of the ninth century, Armenia and Tabaristan had Arab governors who overawed the local rulers and collected tribute. These governors had no direct administrative contact with the subject people; the actual collection of taxes was in local hands.

In other cases, the Caliphate merely confirmed local dynasties as "governors of the Caliph." Khurasan, which until 820 was directly ruled by Caliphal appointees, came under the control of the Tahirid family (820–73). Officially the Tahirids were selected by the Caliphs, but the Caliphs always confirmed the family heirs to the office. The Tahirids paid very substantial tributes, but no one from the central government intervened to assure the payments or to inspect their administration. Transoxania under the Samanids was governed in the same way. The Samanids had been a local ruling family since Sasanian times, but in the wake of the incorporation of Transoxania into the Islamic empire, they converted to Islam. In the Caliphate of al-Maʾmun (813–33), the ruling members of the family were named hereditary governors of Samarqand, Farghana and Herat, without further supervision or control.

Local government was similarly varied. Iraq was divided into a hierarchy of districts, called *kura*, *tassuj* and *rustaq*. The rustaq was the bottom unit in the hierarchy and consisted of a market and administrative town surrounded by a number of villages. The same hierarchy and even the same names were used in parts of Khurasan and western Iran. In Egypt the structure of administration was similar.

Local government was organized for taxation. Surveys were taken in the villages to determine the amount of land under cultivation, the crops grown, and their expected yield, and the information was passed up to the central administration. The taxes for whole regions would be estimated, the sums divided up for each district, and the demand notices sent out describing the responsibilities of each subdivision. Each subunit received its bill and divided it among the smaller units. In the next stage, taxes were collected, local expenses deducted, and the balances passed upwards until the surplus eventually reached Baghdad.

This hierarchical administration did not encompass all cultivated lands. The crown lands, which included the estates of older Middle Eastern empires, church properties, reclaimed wastelands and lands purchased or confiscated by the Caliphate, were not part of the usual provincial administration. Such lands were very extensive in Iraq and western Iran.

Other lands, called *iqta*, were cut off from regular provincial administration. One type of iqta was called *iqta tamlik*, which was a concession of land with a three-year grace period and long-term reduction of taxes, usually given to individuals who were expected to reclaim the land and assure its cultivation. Iqtas of this sort were frequently, though not always, ceded out of wastelands, for the sake of stimulating agricultural investment. Ultimately such lands became private property, since whoever received such a concession could pass it on to his heirs.

A second type of iqta, called *iqta istighlal*, resembled a tax farm. In this case, lands already in cultivation and part of the general revenue administration were assigned to private individuals who agreed to pay the treasury a fixed sum of money in return for the right to tax the peasantry. The assignee's payment was assessed at the *ushr* or 10 percent rate, but he was permitted to exact from the peasants full taxes at the kharaj, land tax rates, which usually amounted to a third or a half of the value of the crop. The benefit given the assignee was the difference between what the peasants paid him and what he paid the government.

There were several reasons for making these kinds of grants. Such lands were conceded as a way of paying off political debts to the ʿAbbasid family, important courtiers, officials, and military officers who had claims on the state for rewards, pensions, or bribes for their support and cooperation. Such grants also simplified administration by obviating the need for collecting revenues in the provinces, bringing the specie to Baghdad, and redistributing the income through still other bureaus. Instead of keeping surveys and records for large areas, all that was necessary was the description of the assignment and the amount due. Still, before the middle of the ninth century, iqtas were assigned with relative restraint, for they represented an important concession of state revenues and state powers. Never in this period were they assigned in lieu of payment of military salaries.

Furthermore, whatever the organizational forms of local government, local administration and tax collection posed delicate political problems. Despite the immense power of the bureaucratic organization, it was extremely difficult to make that power effective in the villages. The bureaucracy was admirably suited to the communication of orders and to clerical and financial tasks, but in the villages, the power of the state was limited by ignorance. How could the government tax the peasantry without knowing who owned the land, how much was produced, who had money, and who did not? How was the state to work its way through the millennia-old complications of land ownership, water rights, and other legal matters? How was the state to know if crops were concealed? The state came to the villages with staffs of technical specialists such as surveyors to make land measurements, weighers and measurers to estimate the size of crops, and bankers and money changers to convert currencies or to give credits. It came with legal specialists, judges to adjudicate disputes, witnesses to transactions, registrars of deeds, and the like. Alongside the technicians, it came with specialists in violence, collectors, soldiers, police, extortionists, stool pigeons, and thugs. Fear was no small part of the business of tax collection.

Yet, with all this, the potential for passive resistance and the problem of inadequate information were insuperable without the cooperation of local people. These included family patriarchs, village headmen (such as the *raᵓis* in Iran, or the *shaykh al-balad* in Egypt), and village landowners, who controlled a large part of the village land and were much richer than the average peasant, but not so wealthy as the great estate or iqtaᶜ holders. In Iraq and Iran, the *dihqans* included native elites and Arabs who had acquired land, village-dwelling and town-dwelling absentee landlords, grain merchants, and money-changers who bought the peasants' crops, or lent them money to pay their taxes.

Money-lenders, landowners, and village chiefs played an important inter-mediary role in the taxation process. As the most powerful people connected with the villages, they handled negotiations, made a deal on behalf of the peasants, and paid the taxes. The arrangement suited everyone. The bureau-cratic agents were never absolutely sure how much money they could raise, and wished to avoid the nuisance of dealing with individuals. The peasants did not have to directly confront the exorbitant demands of the tax collectors. The elite underestimated the taxes to the state and overestimated them to the peasants and benefited from the difference. ᶜAbbasid officials understood perfectly well the importance of these people, whom they called their aᶜwan (helpers). They understood that for the ultimate tasks of assessment, division and collection of taxes, the bureaucracy had to depend on people who were not subordinates, who could not be given orders, but whose cooperation had to be enlisted nonetheless.

Thus, the ᶜAbbasid imperial organization was a complex bureaucracy highly elaborated at the center and in touch with provincial and local forces throughout the empire. Yet the arrangements between the central government and the provincial and local levels were not simply hierarchical. At each level, the business of administration was carried on by independent people. In some cases these were princes or independent governors who controlled whole provinces, and in other cases they were the local village chiefs and landowners without whom the central and provincial governments were helpless. Since the ties of government were not strictly hierarchical, a complex system of constraints and opportunities, obligations and loyalties, bound the central, provincial, and local notables to the regime.

These ties depended first of all upon the fact that the army, the police, and the inspectors of the barid could compel obedience. Also, self-interest dictated collaboration because the village chiefs and landowners found that participation in the tax-collecting apparatus consolidated their local position. It increased their political importance, conferred upon them the prestige, authority, and respect accorded the state, and gave them financial opportunities. Collaboration was in their interest because in the end all power and status derived from association with the state and could not easily survive without it. Apart from force and interest, other more subtle ties assured cooperation and loyalty. Class and personal loyalties often drew together central administrators and local elites. The officials of the central government were drawn from the provincial notable families. Provincial landowning and notable families sent their sons to careers in the central government. Merchant families maintained branches in Baghdad, and facilitated financial contacts between the administrative center and the provinces.

Furthermore, the connections between high-ranking central officials and their country cousins were sometimes organized in the form of clienteles. Central administrators appointed their provincial representatives, and patronage, fortified by ethnic, religious, regional, and family affiliations, no doubt helped to smooth the operations of the ᶜAbbasid state. For example, a governor of Khurasan, Tahir (820–22), explained that only he could govern the province because all the notable families were allied to him by marriage and clientship. Clientele ties also crossed religious lines. Converts to Islam at the center dealt with provincial cousins who remained Christians or Zoroastrians. Conversion to the new religion did not necessarily disrupt family, clientele, and regional ties. Thus, the ᶜAbbasid policy of recruiting notables regardless of ethnic background not only soothed the conflicts which racked the Umayyad dynasty, but was essential if a centralized government was to be built at all. Insofar as effective administration was based upon sympathetic communication between central officials and local notables, the wider the recruitment, the greater the possibility for effective rule. The ᶜAbbasid empire, then, was formed by a coalition of provincial and capital city elites, who agreed on a common concept of the dynasty and the purposes of political power, and who were organized through bureaucratic and other political institutions to impose their rule on Middle Eastern peoples.

This regime did not impose itself in a single moment, but only after decades of political struggle. The process of empire-building was not smooth and uninterrupted, but depended on the forcible subjection of many dissident and unwilling populations. Mountainous provinces remote from Baghdad most easily resisted subordination. In the Caspian region the rulers of Tabaristan and Daylam, in Inner Asia, the semi-independent provinces of Kabul, Ushrusana and Farghana, refused tribute or allegiance, obliging the Caliphs to send military expeditions to recover their suzerainty. By the reign of al-Ma³mun (813–33), however, most of these places were incorporated into the empire and their rulers and officials converted to Islam. In North Africa the tendency after 800 was toward independence, although local ruling houses recognized the suzerainty of the Caliphate.

Arab opposition was also important. The old military caste, deprived of employment, salaries and prestige, and displaced by a single professional army, sporadically resisted the ᶜAbbasid settlement. Syrian Arabs rebelled in 760 and were defeated. In Egypt, the ᶜAbbasids established their own garrisons at al-Askar near Fustat, provoking Arab tribal fighting (785) and rebellions (793–4). Bedouins also rebelled against the consolidation of any government which might restrict their autonomy. Tribal raiding and resistance to state control occurred in Syria, Arabia, Sistan, Kirman, Fars, Khurasan, and most of all in Upper Mesopotamia where Arab and Kurdish outbreaks were virtually incessant. Until the beginning of the ninth century bedouin rebels adopted Kharijism to articulate their opposition to the empire. From then on Shiᶜism became the main expression of tribal opposition to centralized government.

In Iran, peasant villagers and mountaineers kept up their own staccato opposition to the ᶜAbbasid regime. Resistance to the Caliphate took the form of syncretistic sects, blending Shiᶜism and Mazdaism, "heresies" from both Islam and Zoroastrianism. The first of these Iranian rebellions was the rebellion of Bihafarid, a peasant leader near Nishapur, which spread widely in Khurasan in 747–50, advocating a combination of Muslim ideas and the ancient worship of Ahura Mazda. The rebellion was put down by the ᶜAbbasid governor Abu Muslim, significantly, at the request of the Zoroastrian mobads, for it was both a threat to the notables and to Islamic and Zoroastrian beliefs.

This same Abu Muslim later became the symbol of religious and social opposition. His role in the ᶜAbbasid revolution made him a precursor of the messiah in the popular imagination, and inspired Shiᶜi–Mazdaite syncretic heresies and rebellions in the name of Abu Muslim. The first of these broke out in the region of Nishapur under the leadership of a man named Sunpadh. Supported by the mountain peoples of Khurasan, it spread as far west as Rayy and Qum. Sunpadh preached that Abu Muslim was not dead, but lived on in the company of Mazdak and the mahdi and would return again. Similar outbreaks followed in Rayy, Herat, and Sistan. The most important of these was the movement led by a self-styled prophet called al-Muqanna, the veiled one. Al-Muqanna preached that he was God incarnate and that the spirit of God had passed from Muhammad to ᶜAli to Abu Muslim to him. He would, he said, die and return to rule the world. His emphasis on the passage of the spirit and his return as imam was parallel to extremist Shiᶜi views, and he was accused of advocating the Mazdaite social doctrines – communism of money and community of women. Most of his support came from peasant villages.

Insofar as the ᶜAbbasid regime in Iran depended upon the collaboration of a Muslim-imperial elite with local notables who were both Muslims and Zoroastrians, the empire presented itself as a kind of dual orthodoxy based upon a joint Muslim–Zoroastrian elite. Thus resistance to the consolidation of the empire was bound to cast itself in the form of syncretic religious hetero-doxy. The unusual degree of religious ferment was also due to the fact that in the wake of the Arab invasions and decades of warfare in Transoxania, the older religions, Zoroastrian and Christian, were severely disorganized and the new faith, Islam, not properly organized. The eighth century was a time of unique freedom for religious invention as part of social and political conflict.

Throughout the ᶜAbbasid empire the most profound opposition to the Caliphate took the form of Shiᶜism. The Shiᶜa had supported the ᶜAbbasid movement before it came to power, expecting that one of the legitimate heirs to the Caliphate would succeed the Umayyads, but the ᶜAbbasids disappointed these expectations by seizing the Caliphate for themselves. Thus in Basra, Kufa, Mecca, and Medina, the Shiᶜa provoked a succession of minor rebellions. A major Shiᶜi rebellion, backed by the bedouin tribes of Upper Mesopotamia, took place between 813 and 816. In the early tenth century, the Ismaᶜili movement, an offshoot of Shiᶜism, would provoke a new wave of anti-ᶜAbbasid provincial resistance.

Thus, the ᶜAbbasid empire as a political system has to be understood in terms of its organization, its social dynamics, its political concepts, and also in terms of its opponents. As an empire it was a regime governing a vast territory composed of small communities. Each community was headed by its notables: headmen, landowners, and other men of wealth and standing, who charac-teristically were allied to superiors and patrons with positions in the provincial or central governments. Government organization, communication and tax collection was bureaucratic in form, but the social mechanism which made the organization work was the contacts between central officials and provincial elites. The bureaucracy mobilized the skills and social influence of prominent persons throughout the empire and put these assets at the disposal of Baghdad. The bureaucracy bound together local and central elites to forge a coherent regime. This system of alliances was based on a concept of the empire as a product of God's will. By God's will the exalted person of the Caliph reigned in expectation of passive obedience from all his subjects. This political rationale, expressed both in Muslim and in pre-Islamic Middle Eastern terms, justified the coalition of elites by which the empire was governed.

Yet not all of the peoples and the provinces of the empire would submit to the imperial order. Mountain peoples, semi-sedentarized villagers, peasants, nomads, and segments of the town populations including strata of the upper as well as the lower classes refused to accept the system. They denied its legitimacy, and rebelled against it, though they could not overthrow it. Nor could they be altogether repressed. The ʿAbbasid regime was locked into constant struggle with its opponents.

CHAPTER 5

COSMOPOLITAN ISLAM: THE ISLAM OF THE IMPERIAL ELITE

The Arab conquests and settlement, century-long processes of economic and social change, and the formation of cosmopolitan urban societies and of a vast empire, governed not only political events but were the bases for the emergence of an Islamic civilization. New forms of Islamic religion and culture emerged as the expression of the communities and of the empire brought forth by the Arab conquests.

Islam, of course, goes back to the Prophet Muhammad, the revelation of the Quran, and the first Muslim community in Medina and Mecca, but the Islamic religion, as we now know it, was the amplification of these teachings, carried out in later centuries, not only in the original home of Islam in Arabia, but throughout the whole of the vast region from Spain to Inner Asia conquered by the Arab Muslims. The Islamic religion in this sense encompassed not only the Quran and the example of Muhammad, but a vastly expanded range of religious study and practices including law, theology, and mysticism, developed in numerous schools and sub-communities. Islam in this sense refers to the whole panoply of religious concepts and communities through which the original inspiration was later expressed. Furthermore, Islamic ideas permeated a vast culture of poetry and belles-lettres, arts and sciences which was also the cultural expression of the new Muslim empire and societies. In this larger body of literature, arts, and sciences, religious and non-religious influences intermingled.

In the Umayyad and early ʿAbbasid periods there were two foci of Islamic religious and cultural development: one was the court of the Caliphs and the political elite; the other was the heterogeneous urban communities. On the one hand, Islam expressed the political identity of the Caliphate and the political elites. On the other, Islam developed as the expression of the religious, moral, and social values of the Muslim urban populations. Out of the two milieus came two different forms of early Islamic civilization. The court milieus contributed especially to Islamic art, architecture, philosophy, science, and Iranian and Hellenistic forms of literature in Arabic. The city milieus contributed the literatures of Quran interpretation, law, mysticism, and theology in conjunction with an Arabic belles-lettres. Some subjects, such as poetry, theology, and history, were cultivated in both milieus.

To consolidate their regime the Umayyad and ᶜAbbasid dynasties attempted to give cultural legitimacy to the Arab-Muslim imperium and to weld the disparate elements of the governing class – the Caliph, his family and boon companions, Arab tribal chiefs and generals, Inner Asian soldiers, Iranian administrators, Christian ecclesiastics and Muslim religious scholars – into a cohesive imperial elite. While accepting an Islamic identity the court and imperial versions of Islamic culture stressed the aspects of poetry, philosophy, science, art, and architecture which could help define the authority of the regime and the legitimacy of the ruling classes. A common culture, shared values, symbols, and ideas were essential to the functioning of a political elite. A literary and philosophic culture was needed to present a vision of the universe as whole, of the role of the state and the ruler in the divine plan and in the functioning of human society, and a concept of the nature of human beings and their destiny in this world and the next. In the complex and heterogeneous society of the Umayyad and ᶜAbbasid empires this vision was expressed partly in Muslim terms, and partly in literary and artistic terms inherited from the ancient cultures of the Middle East.

In the Umayyad period, this imperial culture included Arabic poetry, derived from pre-Islamic conventions and oral traditions concerning the history of the Arabs, the life of the Prophet, the origins of Islam, and the deeds of the early Caliphs. It also incorporated Byzantine and Sasanian artistic and literary materials. Thus, Umayyad mosques and palaces fused Christian and Byzantine decorative and iconographic motifs with Muslim uses and concepts to create new modes of Islamic architecture. The Umayyads also sponsored formal debates among Muslims and Christians which led to the absorption of Hellenistic concepts into Muslim theology.

The ᶜAbbasid dynasty enlarged upon this repertoire, and patronized Arabic poetry (in both old bedouin and new courtly genres), the translation into Arabic of Iranian literary classics (including works of history, polite literature, fables, political precepts, and manuals of protocol and behavior for scribes), and the mythic and scientific lore of Persia and India. Similarly, Syriac and Greek classics were translated into Arabic. The Caliph al-Ma᾿mun established an academy and observatory, the *Bayt al-Hikma*, to stimulate the translation of logical, scientific, and philosophical works into Arabic.

ART, ARCHITECTURE AND THE CONCEPT OF THE CALIPHATE

The quintessential expression of this imperial program was court ceremony, art, and architecture. The court of the Umayyad Caliphs became a theater enacting the drama of royalty. The Caliph's residence was approached by ceremonial gates; its central feature was a longitudinal hall culminating in an absidal or domed room – a pattern found at Damascus, al-Wasit, Mushatta, and later Baghdad – derived from Hellenistic, Roman, Byzantine, and Sasanian patterns for the emperor's court. The Caliph held audience dressed in crown and royal robes, seated on a throne, and veiled from the rest of his audience by a curtain. His courtiers stood or sat on each side of the long hall. His day included consultations and receptions, prayer, and private entertainments – hunting, music, dancing girls, wine drinking, and poetry reading. A chamberlain controlled access to the royal person; everyone addressed him in submissive tones and with panegyric greetings.

The decorations of the court mirrored the royal way of life; representations of the Caliph depicted his majesty and power. In the desert palace at Qasr al-Khayr the Caliph appears in a formal, frontal pose; at Khirbat al-Mafjar he assumes a martial figure. Representations at Qusayr ᶜAmra portray the Caliph in a hieratic manner derived from Byzantine depictions of the Christ as Pantocrator. At Qusayr ᶜAmra his majesty also appears in its full triumph in a painting of the Shah of Iran, the Emperor of Byzantium, Roderic of Spain, the Negus of Abyssinia, the Emperor of China and the Emperor of the Turks greeting the Caliph as their master. The family of kings is portrayed as deriving its authority from its new suzerain, the Islamic Caliph, whose power embraces not only Islam, but the whole world. Other scenes depict hunting and gardens, birds and animals, banquets, attendants, and dancing girls. The court with its domed room was the center of the universe; its decorations signified the gathering of the living cosmos to glorify the Caliph. The Caliph is majestic; his reign universal; his court paradise. Art was the mirror of a narcissistic affirmation of royalty.

The array of court symbols conveyed the august majesty and unique rank of the Caliph among men. He was entitled to dress and furnishings, to ceremonies and amusements, and to gestures of respect which no other

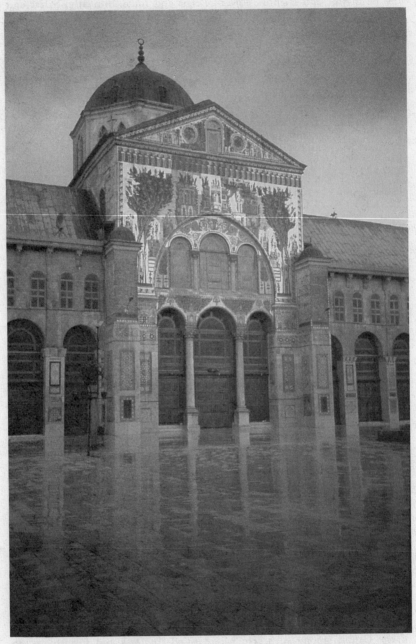

3 The Central Portico of the Umayyad Mosque of Damascus

humans enjoyed. Court poetry glorified the ruler and surrounded him with a divine aura. The court poets addressed the Caliph as *khalifat allah* (the deputy of God). The panegyrics sometimes imputed supernatural powers to the Caliph; his intercession brought rain. The *bayᶜa* or oath of allegiance became a gesture of the humble servitude of the courtier and subject before his overlord. Obedience and fidelity to an adored majestic personage was a leading theme in Umayyad court life.

By contrast, the public art of the Umayyad Caliphs emphasized Islamic themes. The reign of ᶜAbd al-Malik inaugurated public displays with the construction of the Dome of the Rock in Jerusalem. The Dome of the Rock was built on the legendary site of Abraham's intended sacrifice of Ishmael, the favored son in Muslim tradition, for the Muslims meant to forge a direct connection to the common ancestor of monotheism, whereby Islam became as venerable as the other religions. To appropriate and modify the Jewish temple area was to assert the primacy of Islam and its supersession of the previous monotheistic religions.

The Islamic triumph was further celebrated in the decoration of the building. Its ornamental motifs were borrowed from Byzantine and Persian forms, which expressed holiness and power, but were now used to show the sovereignty of Islam. Inscriptions proclaimed the mission of Islam, the truth of the new faith, and the surpassing of the old. The Dome of the Rock was built in the most sacred city of Judaism and Christianity in order to signify the political and religious appropriation of the past by a new faith embodied in a new empire. It asserted the sovereignty of the Caliph as the conqueror of old religions and empires and the benefactor of Islam.

The Umayyad Mosque of Damascus expressed different themes. The mosque itself was built by the absorption of a pagan sanctuary and Christian church, of classical, Roman, Hellenistic and Christian motifs into a new and distinctly Muslim architecture. The mosaics showed idyllic buildings and landscapes which may represent heaven itself or may imply the subjection of the whole world to the new Caliphs and the new faith. Moreover, in constructing the mosque and its decorations, the Umayyads employed Greek craftsmen whom they solicited from the emperor of Constantinople. To the Greeks this implied the cultural and political superiority of Byzantium; the Muslims, however, construed it as an appropriation of Byzantine culture and power, a submission of Greek vassals to Muslim masters, and an exhibit of the ambition, triumph, and supersession of Byzantium by a Muslim imperium.

Similarly, the Mosque of Medina bore witness to the victories of Islam. Umayyad Caliphs furnished this sacred place with the most exotic and lux-

4 A section of the mosaics of the Damascus mosque

urious spoils. They sent necklaces, ruby-encrusted crescents, cups and thrones to emphasize the submission of non-Muslim peoples to Islam, and their own piety in dedicating their victories to the faith. The very structure of the mosque evoked the Caliph's glory. It was built in Hellenistic royal architectural design, and contained a longitudinal hall, absidal niche, and a *minbar* (pulpit) from which the official Friday sermon recognizing the sovereignty of the Caliph and important political announcements were made. The mosque also contained a box (*maqsura*) to seclude the Caliph from his subjects, much as he was secluded at court. These architectural features identified the faith of Islam with the Caliph and made the mosque itself a symbol of the Caliph's prestige. In design, decoration, inscriptions, and ceremonial usage the mosque became a public version of the private court of the Caliph, witness to his triumphs and his primacy in Islam.

The Caliph as conqueror and endower treated religion as an intrinsic aspect of his own identity; the mosque as a symbol of the compact union of the political and religious aspects of his rule. Before entering the mosque the Caliph al-Walid changed from perfumed and multicolored clothes to pure white garments. On returning to the palace he put on the worldly and splendid garb of the court. While the Caliphate took Islam into its political majesty, Islam absorbed the Caliph into the service of religion.

The ʿAbbasid dynasty accepted this exalted position. Like its predecessors it adopted the panoply of court life which exalted the ruler, but refined, elaborated, and systematized Umayyad ideas. The Umayyads established the notion that the Caliph was not only selected by the community, but was appointed by God to follow in the ways of the Prophet and to lead the Muslim community along the path of Islam. The ʿAbbasid Caliphs, upon coming to power, reaffirmed the divine origin of their office and claimed to restore true guidance to the Muslim community. The ʿAbbasids had come to power on a current of messianic hopes, and their very titles stressed their role as saviors. Al-Mansur, al-Mahdi, al-Hadi, and al-Rashid claimed to be guided by God in righteous ways, to bring enlightenment, and to return the Muslims to the true path. They patronized scholars. They promoted the pilgrimage to Mecca by organizing the way stations, by providing military security in the desert, and by making gifts to the holy places. They themselves made the journey. The ʿAbbasid Caliphs also tried to draw Muslim religious leaders into public service as judges and administrators. They created a judicial hierarchy and tried to use the judges as intermediaries to organize cadres of scholars, teachers, and legists under the jurisdiction as well as the patronage of the state.

The ʿAbbasids also attempted to intervene in doctrinal matters. Beginning in the reign of al-Mahdi, the Caliphs made themselves responsible for the defense of what they held to be Islamic orthodoxy against free thinkers and heretics. Al-Mahdi began the persecution of the *zanadiqa*. The word means Manichaeans or dualists who believed in the existence of two divine powers, one for good and one for evil, as opposed to the unitary conception of Islam, but the term was used more generally to justify the suppression of Arab poets, theologians, scribes, and others. The ʿAbbasids really aimed at defining the boundaries of acceptable doctrine and unifying their cadres on common religious grounds. They had conceived the notion of a church hierarchy under state control as a foundation for political power.

This effort to bring Muslim religious life under state supervision descended from both Byzantine and Sasanian conceptions of the proper relationship between the state and religion. The Byzantine imperial view was that the emperor influenced the formulation of religious doctrines so that they were in accord with the political interests of the state. Byzantine emperors took the utmost interest in the regulation of church doctrine. They called and presided over church councils and suggested formulas for the creed. The emperors did not have the right to make doctrine – only the church itself as represented by the collectivity of the bishops could do that – but they saw that the decisions taken suited imperial political interests as well as the convictions of the bishops. The emperors also appointed the leading patriarchs, archbishops, and bishops.

The Sasanian system is less well known. However, we may take the early ʿAbbasid scribe and translator of Sasanian literature into Arabic, Ibn al-Muqaffaʿ, to represent the Sasanian view. He held that religious matters were of utmost importance to the state, and that uniformity in doctrine and control over religious organization were indispensable bases of power. He argued that the Caliphs could not afford doctrinal disputes in the administration and the army, and could not afford that the religious scholars and judges be outside state control. Ibn al-Muqaffaʿ urged that the Caliphs promulgate doctrine, organize a hierarchical judiciary, and appoint the leading judges.

At the same time the Caliphal court expressed its vision in non-Islamic terms. The Caliph was legitimated in terms of pre-Islamic Persian, Hellenistic, and other Middle Eastern concepts. He was the vice-regent of God on earth. By his magical powers he upheld the order of the cosmos, providing for the rain and the harvests, keeping all persons in their places and seeing to it that they fulfilled their functions in society. He was the symbol of civilization; agriculture, cities, arts, and learning depended on his blessings. The ʿAbbasids also expressed this concept of an august, semi-divine ruler in court ceremony, in protocol, in decorations depicting the majesty of the ruler, and in architectural monuments which expressed the cosmic and universal importance of his person. In the middle of the tenth century, a court chronicler reports that an unsophisticated provincial soldier, overcome by the splendor of the Caliph's appearance, momentarily thought he was in the presence of God. The poets approximated this awe as best they could. Court poets and court protocol elevated the Caliphs above angels and prophets, making them the chosen of God, God's shadow on earth, a refuge for all of his lesser creatures.

Palaces and palace cities also manifested the majesty of the Caliphate. Baghdad symbolized imperial authority. It incorporated materials taken from the ruins of Sasanian palaces as well as the iron gates of al-Wasit seized from a Sasanian village. The design of Baghdad also had symbolic implications. The Madinat al-Salam was a round city divided into four quadrants by axial streets running from east to west and north to south. The palace was situated in the very center. The structure of the city reproduced the symmetry and hierarchy of society and the central position of the Caliph within it. The design of the city also symbolized the cosmic and heavenly world; in this scheme the central placement of the Caliph signified his sovereignty over the four quarters of the world. Since ancient times the founding of a city had signified the creation of order out of chaos in the geographic, social, and cosmic levels of the universe. By the construction of a new city the Caliph became not only the upholder, but the creator of order in the otherwise formless, boundless, and threatening experience of mankind.

Thus, the ʿAbbasids fostered ideological or religious loyalty to the Caliphate on both Muslim and traditional Middle Eastern grounds. No longer Arab princes, they appealed to Muslim sentiment to recognize them as the legitimate successors to the Prophet, and as the protectors and organizers of the Muslim faith, which they sought to channel in directions consonant with the political needs of the dynasty. At the same time, they directed their appeal to non-Muslims and converts for recognition as divinely selected rulers, exalted princes sent by God for the right ordering of worldly affairs. Ceremony, art, and architecture thus expressed an imperial ideal.

THE ARABIC HUMANITIES

Literature as well as art served the imperial program. Almost inseparable from Islam as a religion was the development of an Arabic literature covering linguistic, poetic, and historical subjects. Arabic literature was cultivated in both court and popular circles. It was strongly influenced by the heritage of pre-Islamic bedouin Arabia, by the interest of Arabs in the glorification of the conquests, and by the interest of the Caliphate in using Arabic poetry as an expression of their affinity with the mass of Arabs and as glorification for imperial rule.

In urban religious circles Arabic literary interests were pursued as an essential adjunct of Quranic studies. In the century following the founding of Basra, Kufa, and other Arab cities, the Arabic language evolved away from the Quran. An Arabic lingua franca emerged for the diverse tribes. Persian and Aramaic speakers contributed to rapid changes in vocabulary, grammatical usages, style, and syntax. As the Arabic language changed, religious scholars feared that they would lose touch with the Arabic of the Quran and thus lose the meaning of God's revelations. To prevent this, it was necessary to recapture the pure Arabic of Mecca and of the desert tribes, and create a classic form of Arabic. In eighth-century Basra, philosophical, lexicographical, and grammatical studies were undertaken to stabilize the usage of Arabic. The roots of words had to be specified, vocabulary selected and explained, and proper speech given rules of grammar and syntax. This linguistic effort persisted over a century and produced what we know as classical Arabic. The great grammar of Sibawayh and the early dictionaries of Arabic were the products of this period.

The cultural ramifications of Quranic studies went beyond linguistic analysis. The basis of linguistic studies was the collection and gathering of all examples of old Arabic. Much in the manner of contemporary linguists or anthropologists, the scholars of Basra and Kufa sought out the bedouins and recorded their poems and sayings. Gradually, a tremendous body of lore was accumulated, and cast from oral into written form. This lore included information on the life of the Prophet and the revelations of the Quran, the early conquests, and the behavior of the early leaders of the Muslim community. Most of what is known about this early period was collected in the eighth century. Religious studies thus became a guiding motif in the elaboration of a general Arabic culture.

Other segments of the Arab milieu, inspired by a more secular orientation, also contributed to its enrichment. Apart from the classical poetry of the desert, a new sort of poetry, reflecting the interests, entertainments, and the imagery of the urban and court environments, came into being. Historical studies had a similar secular inspiration. Caliphal, ethnic, and tribal pride in the conquests, the desire to glorify their own past and therefore their present importance, and the desire to defend their status against the claims of non-Arab peoples to be culturally superior, motivated historical scholarship.

The totality of this literary and religious culture was gathered, compiled, edited, and criticized in several encyclopaedic collections of the eighth century. With the culmination of this literary effort, Islam as a religion was embedded in a general literary culture. Understanding the Quran depended on being versed in the Arabic language and its literary traditions. Conversely, Arab literary culture was itself shaped to reflect, elucidate, and be in conformity with the Quran. Arabic literary culture was not purely the heritage of the desert but was shaped in the early Islamic era out of Arabian elements, with a view toward the religious and historical concerns of the Umayyad and early ʿAbbasid period.

Thus there was a dialectical relationship of religion and literary culture, sometimes expressing alternate religious and ethnic identities, sometimes merging the two, which would ever after be the basis of Islamic civilization. Arabic culture, partly the product of the urban middle class and scholarly communities interested in Islam, partly the product of Arab tribal loyalties, and partly the product of the court and Caliphal patronage, had a crucial role to play in defining the identity of the political elite. Though Arab identity was subtly merged with Islamic identity, the development of Arabic literature preserved an ethnic and linguistic alternative to the Islamic orientations of the Umayyad and ʿAbbasid elites. Arabism could stand apart from Islam as the foundation of political and cultural supremacy.

PERSIAN LITERATURE

Within the court milieus there were literary and cultural alternatives to Islam and Arabism. In keeping with the recruitment of the late Umayyad and ʿAbbasid political elites from all parts of the empire, Persian influences made themselves felt in Umayyad times. In the reign of Caliph Hisham (724–43) Persian court procedures were adopted, and the first translations of Persian political documents were made. Under the ʿAbbasids Persian scribes, merchants, workers, and soldiers who made Baghdad their home saw to the translation of Persian manuals of behavior and protocol (*adab*) for scribes and administrators into Arabic. The manuals contained advice on how to conduct the affairs of state, carry out the duties of various offices, behave in the presence of rulers, and described the qualities required for different positions. This advice was embedded in tales and anecdotes about the great Persian rulers of the past.

With political advice came technical and scientific knowledge. Iran was an important transmitter of Indian and Hellenistic medical, mathematical, and astronomical ideas. Works on horsemanship and the care and use of weapons, practical knowledge about government, agricultural management, and irrigation were all translated into Arabic. So too were literary masterworks such as the fables of the *Kalila wa Dimna* and some of the tales of the *Arabian Nights*.

The intense interest in Persian culture and translations led to rivalry among Persian courtiers and scribes and their Arab counterparts. A literary movement, the Shuᶜubiya, was formed to assert the cultural superiority of the Persians to the Arabs, and to influence the official culture of the ᶜAbbasid Caliphate. Persians advanced concepts which differed profoundly from the prevailing sentiment in Arabic-Islamic circles. Persian ideas emphasized the absolute and unlimited authority of the monarch, his divine selection, and his superiority in matters of religion as well as state. Persian literature also espoused an hierarchical view of society in which each person – ruler, noble, warrior, scribe, priest, merchant, worker, or peasant – had a fixed place. The duty of government was to preserve everyone in his place, giving each class its due prerogatives. By contrast, Arab circles tended to deny the ruler authority in religious matters, and refused the notion that the ruler was a law unto himself. Arab sentiment still clung to the feeling that the ruler was the best man selected by the community and was responsible to the community and its religion. Arab-Muslim sentiment was also more egalitarian and less hierarchical. Also embedded in Persian literature was a religious challenge to Islam. While Iranian administrators were Muslims, many were still sympathetic to Zoroastrianism; others may have been Manichaeans, gnostics or even agnostics and atheists.

Arab scholars resisted Persian ideas and attempted to meet the temptations of Persian literary sophistication on its own grounds. In response to Persian literature, Islamic literary culture was pushed into new directions for the sake of defending its old essence. In the ninth century Arabic writers began to synthesize the Arabic humanities with Persian adab. Ibn Qutayba (828–89) compiled treatises on such themes as government, war, nobility, scholarship, asceticism, love, friendship, and women. His selections were done in the manner of Arabic literature and included quotations from the Quran and hadith, and from Arabic histories of the early Caliphs and the Arab empire, but also enough borrowings from Persian adab works, Indian tales, and Aristotle's philosophy to attract the Persian elites. A second ninth-century writer, al-Jahiz (d. 869), who is often regarded as the finest prose stylist in the history of Arabic letters, also synthesized the literary interests of Arab and Persian-minded elites. Out of the encyclopaedic works of his predecessors, he selected, adapted, edited, and made palatable a body of literature which would serve as a common culture for both Arabs and Arabic-speaking Persians. The flood of translations from Persian had been diverted and rechanneled into the stream of a literature bearing a Persian imprint in manner, style and subjects, but firmly wedded to Arabic and Islamic ideas. Arabic writers thus offered some of the fruits of Persian thought to Muslims, but obscured the elements which were in conflict with Islam and Arabic values.

Through the movement of translations and fusion with Arabic, elements of the Persian heritage became an integral part of Islamic civilization. Still, Iranian political and religious ideas survived outside the Islamic synthesis and were not deprived of their importance. Persian political ideas continued to influence the practice of Middle Eastern governments; Persian gnosticism would return to inspire later Islamic religious developments.

HELLENISM

While Persian literature was screened and absorbed by Arabic writers, the heritage of Greek thought had a more complex and varied role in the formation of Islamic civilization. Greek culture as it became known in court circles was not the thought of ancient Greece, but rather the thought of Greece as it had evolved and come to be understood in the Mediterranean world in the centuries immediately prior to Islam. Greek thought in the Islamic world was Greek thought as preserved, understood, and interpreted in the late Roman empire. This culture was immensely variegated. Plato's ideas were represented by his political works and some of his dialogues. Aristotle's logical and scientific works, ethics, and metaphysics were also known. However, most of the materials called the work of Aristotle and Plato had actually been written in the centuries following the deaths of the two master philosophers, when they were reinterpreted in neo-Platonic terms as teachers of a path to spiritual salvation. The Greek heritage also included the scientific and medical ideas of Galen, the pseudo-science of the Hellenistic world including alchemy and the semi-mystical, semi-scientific ideas of the neo-Pythagoreans and the Hermetics.

The transmission of Hellenistic literature depended on the survival of the pre-Muslim academies. The most important of these academies were originally located in Athens and Alexandria, but with the Christianization of the Roman empire in the fourth and fifth centuries, the pagan schools were dispersed. They found a haven in the Christian but non-Roman parts of the Middle East. The school of Athens was rescued by the Nestorian Church, which sponsored the translation of Greek works into Syriac in Edessa and Nasibin. In the sixth century, this school was transferred to Jundishapur, a Sasanian royal city in Fars. In the sixth and seventh centuries Hellenistic philosophic and scientific studies flourished under the influence of Persian and Indian religious and occult conceptions, though the Jundishapur school and its personnel were still mainly Nestorian Christians. The transfer of this school to Baghdad marks the beginning of its direct influence on Arab-Muslim thinkers.

Alexandrian Hellenistic thought also came into the mainstream of the emerging Islamic culture. The Alexandrian school was moved to Antioch in Syria and then to Marw in Khurasan and Harran in Mesopotamia. Some of the scholars were Nestorian Christians, but others, at Harran, were pagans. From Mesopotamia, this school also moved to Baghdad at the end of the ninth and the beginning of the tenth centuries. Thus Greek thought under church and royal patronage survived and was transferred to ʿAbbasid Baghdad.

Hellenistic thought first came to the attention of Muslims interested in theological questions. Debates between Muslims and Christians which took place in the tolerant court of the Umayyad Caliphs, instructed Muslim thinkers in Greco-Christian, or Hellenistic vocabularies, forms of rational argument, and literary methods. The early encounters at Damascus were followed by scientific research in Baghdad, and by the translation of Syriac and Greek works into Arabic. At the Bayt al-Hikma, Syriac and Greek logical, scientific, and technical works were translated into Arabic. These included Aristotle's logical treatises, and the works of Galen and Hippocrates. The Bayt al-Hikma also contained an astronomical observatory.

By the middle of the ninth century the Bayt al-Hikma was superseded by a school of translators under the guidance of Hunayn ibn Ishaq. Hunayn and his school translated other scientific works of Galen and the philosophic and metaphysical works of Aristotle and Plato. The output of the translators was prodigious, and the editors achieved excellence in the preparation of accurate and reliable editions. This school of philologically competent editors created a body of translations and a spirit of critical inquiry which made philosophical studies in the Islamic era rigorous and exacting. The translated works were then commented on and glossed by Muslim and Christian scholars, and lectures, compendiums, and texts were prepared to disseminate the ideas.

Greek culture had a profound impact upon the growth of Islamic civilization. Its various strands entered in a multitude of ways into the formation of Islamic thought. The most profound impact of Hellenistic culture was in the realm of philosophy. Philosophy was a movement with a great variety of positions united by a shared vocabulary and by commitment to a rational program of investigations, including logic, natural science, and metaphysics.

Philosophers in the Muslim era also dealt with theological issues such as the nature of God and his attributes, the theory of prophecy, ethics and questions of the relationship of philosophy to scriptural revelation.

Philosophy, however, was not a neutral form of analysis, but itself a kind of religion. Its ultimate goal was not only intellectual knowledge but the reabsorption of the human soul in the spiritual universe from which it had come. Philosophic teachings also differed from Islamic teachings on such questions as the resurrection and punishment of the body, the theory of the eternity or creation of the world, and God's knowledge of universals and particulars. Hellenistic philosophy thus represented a heritage of rational reflection upon metaphysical reality, the physical world, and human beings which posed a fundamental challenge to the Quranic revelation as a source of complete and infallible truth.

There were several responses to this challenge. One was the acceptance of philosophic teachings by a group of Muslim thinkers called *falasifa* (philosophers). One of the earliest Muslim specialists, the ninth-century philosopher, al-Kindi, believed in the primacy of the Quran, of faith over reason, as the way to discovery of religious truths. He believed that the teachings of the Quran required no philosophic justification. Though he held that reason could clarify and even extend faith into areas left vague by Quranic pronouncements, he was not prepared to accept Platonic and Aristotelian opinions such as belief in creation ex nihilo. He believed in the superiority of the Prophet to the philosophers as a knower of the divine world.

Later Muslim philosophers, however, gave primacy to philosophy as the means to the divine truth, and regarded Islam as no more than an acceptable approximation of philosophic truth. Al-Farabi (d. 950) established the broad outlines of philosophy and defined its relation to Muslim scripture. He believed in a supreme and eternal being who was the first cause of all existing things. He also believed that the supreme being was connected to the world by an hierarchical series of emanations, conceived as intelligences, which constituted the structure of the spiritual world and gave form to the material world. The successive levels of intellect mediated between God and the material world.

Al-Farabi's view of the human condition was logically related to his view of the universe. The human being, like all created beings, was itself formed by the intelligences of the spiritual world, while at the same time constituting an object in the material world. Implanted in the human being was the faculty of reason which is a counterpart of the spiritual intelligences. The destiny of humanity, then, is to cultivate rational intelligence to the utmost, and to use intellect and reason to control behavior and feeling so that the soul may be purified and returned thereby to its ultimate destiny – knowledge of, vision of, and reintegration into the spiritual world.

By contrast, religion for al-Farabi was an inferior and indirect way of symbolizing the truth, suitable for the masses of the people. The imagination of the Prophet, he believed, was inferior to the intelligence of the sage. To reconcile his stress on philosophy with Islam, al-Farabi held that Islam was a true religion, and that Muhammad was the perfect sage and philosopher as well as a Prophet who could express the truth in a fashion persuasive to ordinary people. Insofar as al-Farabi valued Muhammad, it was not as Prophet, but as philosopher. Thus, philosophers did not truly reconcile Greek thought to Islam; rather, they tried to rationalize their acceptance of Greek thought in terms of Islam. Their metaphysical and religious mentality was based on Greek opinions rather than Quranic tradition. Philosophy, they thought, was a higher vision, superior to the revealed but inferior version of truth known as Islam.

Other aspects of the Greek heritage remained the pursuits of a cosmopolitan-minded aristocracy and somewhat remote from the mainstream of Islamic religious and cultural trends. Muslim contributions to astronomy, mathematics, medicine, chemistry, zoology, mineralogy, and meteorology often surpassed the received heritage of Greek, Persian, and Indian ideas. Muslim natural science showed a great talent for direct observation and experiment. The occult sciences, however, had a spiritual objective and represented an alternative religious mentality. Alchemy, occult physics, optics, and occult neo-Pythagorean mathematics were not directed toward a scientific appraisal of the universe, but toward esoteric revelations. Neo-Pythagorean numbers, for example, were not mathematical entities but symbols of a higher and unseen reality which the occult scientist tried to conjure forth. In alchemy the object was not only to transform materials, but to discover the hidden relation of the material to the immaterial world. In place of Islam, which prescribed obedience to the law and devotion to the Quran, the occult sciences proposed another way to knowledge of the world beyond. Hellenistic thought in this mode introduced not an experimental endeavor or practical technology, but a non-theistic spiritual and religious conviction.

Persian and Greek thought were important in court circles because they introduced the human ideal of aristocratic self-cultivation, which served to define the moral and social quality of the imperial elite in terms which were partly consistent with Islam but were also derived from the non-Islamic heritage of the ancient world. This aristocratic ideal called upon the courtier, the administrator, and the servant of Caliphs to believe in God, and to be pious and conscious of the coming last judgment. Yet it also called upon him to be a refined, cultivated, learned, and worldly gentleman. The aristocrat had to be knowledgeable in all the sciences, literature, history, philosophy, and religion. He was to be gentlemanly in manners, gracious, and sensitive to the nuances of rank and honor. He should also be competent in finance, in letter writing, in horsemanship and in technical matters of administration. The aristocrat's cultivation included Islamic virtues, but its essential quality was a worldly refinement which set him apart from the lowly and justified his claim to power. Indirectly the cultivation of Persian and Greek letters implied a common culture for a heterogeneous elite based upon the presumption of inherent aristocratic superiority.

Furthermore all the court literatures served to propagate a pre-Islamic concept of the ruler and the empire. Interest in the secular aspects of Arabic literature, Persian adab, and Hellenistic philosophies and sciences signified the appropriation of a cultural heritage which could be used to legitimize Caliphal rule. They provided, in the Arabic case, an ethnic concept of political leadership; in the Persian case, a continuation of the heritage of ancient Middle Eastern kings; and in the Hellenistic case, a concept of the structure of the universe itself, in philosophic and scientific form, as the ultimate justification for imperial rule. The patronage of these several literatures implied ultimately that the Caliph, though a Muslim ruler, was legitimized in non-Islamic cultural terms going back to the heritage of the ancient Middle East.

CHAPTER 6

URBAN ISLAM:
THE ISLAM OF THE RELIGIOUS ELITES

While the Caliphal courts developed one version of early Islamic civilization, another version was the creation of the garrison cities and towns settled by the Arabs. From the very beginning the Caliphs had been considered the heirs of the Prophet's religious authority as well as his political leadership, but the politicization of the Caliphal regime provoked severe tension between its religious obligations and political needs. The Shiʿa, the Kharijis, and the Yemeni Arabs who brought the ʿAbbasids to power opposed the Umayyad dynasty in the name of religious principles. The ʿAbbasids, however, also built up a strong state apparatus, gave the ruler a ceremonial grandeur that bordered on divinity, and thus provoked Shiʿi rebellions and deep distrust even among their own followers. Moreover, though they were heads of state, the Caliphs did not inherit Muhammad's prophethood, nor were they a source of religious doctrine and law. At the core of their executive and symbolic primacy there was a void, for neither the office nor the Caliph himself held the authority from which Muslim religious conceptions and practices were derived. The Quran, the revealed book, stood apart from the authority of the Caliph, and was available to every believer.

Within the garrison city populations a new religious elite separate from and autonomous of the Caliphate took form. The settlements fused Arab and non-Arab peoples into new communities composed of a middle class of merchants, artisans, teachers, and scholars devoted to their newly defined Islamic identity. Some of these people were originally descended from Arab bedouins but after a century of sedentarization they were thoroughly urbanized. Others were non-Arabs, converts and clients of the Arabs, who spoke Arabic and assimilated themselves into the tribal, religious, and literary traditions of the conquering elite. Within this milieu private persons had given themselves to the study of the Quran and to the practice of Muslim rites. Private students of religion who were without office, without institutional means of support, and without priestly status including the *qurra*ʾ (the readers of the Quran), the ʿulamaʾ (religious scholars), and the Sufis (the ascetics) became the custodians of the Quran and the teaching of the Prophet. Officially, the Muslim community was headed by the Caliph and his governors, but in fact the learned and pious people who held no official position, but who had acquired a reputation for knowledge of and devotion to the faith, were accepted by ordinary Muslims as the true authorities on Islam. These devotees of Islam formed circles of disciples and students dedicated to the study of hadith (accounts of the sayings and deeds of the Prophet), law, theology, or mysticism. The Muslim masses turned to them rather than to the Caliphs for moral instruction and religious guidance. Thus the development of religious authorities independent of the Caliphate was coupled with the emergence of "sectarian" bodies within the Islamic umma. From a religious and communal point of view, the Caliphate and Islam were no longer wholly integrated.

The private religious scholars and their followers represented many different points of view. Some were supporters of the Caliphate; others were opponents. Some were concerned primarily with scripture, the study and explication of the Quran, the recollection of the sayings of the Prophet and the elaboration of law; others were committed to theology or mysticism. Urban Islamic religious culture was ultimately the combined product of all of these orientations, and the outcome of the struggles among them and the struggles between them and the court and Caliphal versions of Islam.

SUNNI SCRIPTURALISM

The Quran is the fulcrum of Muslim faith, for it embodies the Muslim vision of the world. Muslims believe in the Quran as a book of guidance. The Quran begins:

> In the Name of God, the Merciful, the Compassionate,
> Praise belongs to God, the Lord of all Being,
> the All-merciful, the All-compassionate,
> the Master of the Day of Doom.
> Thee only we serve; to Thee alone we pray for succour.
> Guide us in the straight path,
> the path of those whom Thou hast blessed,
> not of those against whom Thou art wrathful,
> nor of those who are astray.

5 A page of an illuminated Quran

At the center of the Quranic guidance is a vision of the reality of God's being. God is transcendent, eternal, utterly other, unfettered in will or action, almighty creator of the world and its creatures. He has placed human beings in the world to do his will as revealed in the holy scripture. God will judge human beings at the end of days and mete out eternal reward or eternal punishment. The reality of the world to come is presented with potent eschatological symbols whose influence continues to be a living force in Islamic culture.

The eschatological and religious vision – the reality of God's will – defines the place of human beings in the world. The Quran requires belief in God and submission to his will. Sent to convert men to Islam, it carries strong exhortations to believe, warnings, proofs, threats of judgment and appeals to gratitude to God.

As guidance, the Quran is a revelation of God's will, and teaches what men should believe about God, nature and history. It gives rules about what men should do and not do in religious rituals and in relation to their fellow men. It prescribes the basic beliefs of Islam and the five pillars: profession of faith, prayer, fasting, giving of alms, and pilgrimage. It sets out laws of marriage, divorce, inheritance, and business matters. It also presents the spiritual qualities which should infuse ritual, social, and legal obligations. These qualities include gratitude to God for one's existence, repentance, moral earnestness, fear of the Last Judgment, loyalty to the faith, sincerity and truthfulness. The Quran condemns arrogance, thanklessness, and pride.

Beyond precise specification is the moral spirit in which a man lives. The Quran leaves each man to judge what constitutes proper fulfillment of God's command. For example, the law defining the supererogatory night prayers are not given as a rule but as permission to adapt the injunction to pray to individual circumstances:

> Therefore recite of the Koran so much as is feasible.
> He knows that some of you are sick, and others
> journeying in the land, seeking the bounty of God,
> and others fighting in the way of God.
> So recite of it so much as is feasible.[1]

Because the guidance is open, the boundaries of human responsibility become problematic. The prospects of achieving eternal reward are uncertain. Some passages in the Quran stress the full measure of human responsibility. God is just and he will weigh every deed and thought at the day of judgment in the

[1] A. J. Arberry, *The Koran Interpreted*, London: Allen and Unwin, 1955, 1, p. 29, 11, pp. 309–10.

scales of eternal reward and punishment. Other passages, however, stress God's power, his predetermination of all events and man's helpless insufficiency before his majesty. The Quran speaks in several voices on this question because the problematics of the judgment are as much a part of the human condition as the openness of the guidance.

For early readers and commentators the Quran was more than a text. The scholars were eager to mold their own lives by the Quran and to infuse the lives of their contemporaries with the spirit and teachings of the holy book. They wanted the Quran to be the basis of a Muslim style of action and belief in personal behavior, ritual, family, and business matters, and also in political questions such as the selection of rulers, justice, and taxation. They aspired to cast the whole of life in the mold of the Quran.

This interest in the application of the Quran led first to the commentary, exegesis, and criticism called *tafsir*. It also led to the accumulation and study of accounts of the sayings and deeds of the Prophet. Everything which Muhammad said and did was of prime religious importance, because his deeds and actions were authoritative examples of how a proper Muslim life was led. From the beginning of the eighth century, hadith, kept alive in oral tradition, began to be collected, and in the ninth an authoritative canon was compiled that stands alongside the Quran as Muslim scripture.

In the classical manuals and compilations hadiths were organized by topics. In the *Sahih* of Bukhari they are organized under such headings as faith, purification, prayer, alms, fasting, pilgrimage, commerce, inheritance, wills, vows and oaths, crimes, murders, judicial procedure, war, hunting, and wine. In each chapter there are anecdotal descriptions of how the Prophet dealt with these matters.

Hadith are read by Muslim believers in close relationship with the Quran. They clarify, supplement, and expand the range of specific guidance. They also constitute an open rather than a prescriptive text. The range of specific issues and advice is so great that whatever a Muslim believes and does there are infinite aspects of the hadith that elude him. There is an endless tension among precepts fulfilled, precepts neglected, and precepts not understood.

A similar impulse to fashion a divinely guided way of life led to the development of Muslim law. Shariʿa was not strictly speaking the revealed word of God but it was widely taken by Muslims to be a divinely inspired extension of the teachings of the Quran and hadith. Muslim law had its origins in the efforts of seventh-century judges and scholars to reform existing legal practice and inspire it with Islamic ethical standards. This religio-judicial task was not the work of any single group, but was carried out in Basra, Kufa, Syria, Medina, and Mecca by men who formed in each place a "school of law."

Table 3. *Early schools of law*

Founding father	Region	School
al-Awza'i (d. 744)	Syria	Awza'i
Abu Hanifa (d. 767)	Iraq	Hanafi
Malik b. Anas (d. 795)	Medina	Maliki
al-Shafi'i (d. 820)	Egypt	Shafi'i
Ibn Hanbal (d. 855)	Iraq	Hanbali
Dawud b. Khalaf (d. 883)	Iraq	Zahiri

Note. The four surviving schools of law are the Hanafi, Maliki, Shafi'i, and Hanbali.

Beginning with actual practice in familial, commercial, and criminal law, administrative regulations, Sasanian, Byzantine, and Hellenistic popular maxims, the canon law of the Orthodox Church, Talmudic, Rabbinic and old Babylonian law, the scholars sought to bring everything into conformity with God's will. Their discussions did not generate cold statute law, but a discursive body of rules laced with ethical, moral, and theological precepts.

Muslim law was divided into three substantive categories: *'ibadat* (ritual regulations); *mu'amalat* (rules of social relations); and *imama* (theory of collective organization). Under these categories the law dealt with prayer, almsgiving and fasting, matters of marriage, divorce, slavery, partnerships, debts, wills and other legal and social concerns. In all these matters non-Islamic law and custom were reconciled to Islamic religious principles. The final corpus of the Shari'a thus represents custom and tradition transformed by Islamic ethical conviction.

Hadith and Shari'a represent different approaches to defining the will of God, but historically they evolved in intimate connection with each other. Toward the end of the eighth century the work of the legal scholars came under attack by the people of hadith. The people of hadith were those religious scholars, often minority members of the different law schools, who held the conviction that the only religiously valid opinions stemmed directly from the sayings of the Prophet, for these were of divine inspiration and a source of faith virtually as important as the Quran. The differences between the legal-minded and the hadith-minded were differences about specific issues, and also differences about the proper sources of legal judgments. Most scholars believed in the traditions of their school and in a certain amount of personal discretion. The hadith-minded could not conceive of any legitimate source of law or morals other than the Quran itself and the sayings of the Prophet. They objected to the arbitrary personal opinions of their opponents.

Inevitably, the position of the people of hadith gained ground. The logic of accepting the views of the Prophet as a higher authority than the personal opinion of the legists was irrefutable. Still, the legists were not prepared to yield, and defended their position against unreliable hadiths. Eventually, the jurist al-Shafiʿi (767–820) found a modus vivendi. He accepted the authority of hadiths as overriding, but sought to control hadiths by holding that only the *ijmaʿ*, or agreement of the qualified scholars, could decide which hadiths were authentic and which were not. Though the hadith-minded forced the legists to accept hadiths as a fundamental source of law and to modify some of the early legal doctrines, the legists, led by al-Shafiʿi, found means to reconcile the use of hadiths with their traditional methods of reasoning and discussion.

Reciprocally the people of hadith could not ignore the legists' criticisms of the reliability of hadiths. Under pressure of debate, the hadith supporters evolved their own internal criticism to guarantee the infallibility of hadiths. In a tradition-minded society, where the authority of the ancients counted for more than the opinions of contemporaries, no textual criticism or similar justification would do. One had to demonstrate simply and plainly that Muhammad's sayings were reported by a person of known probity, who in turn heard them from earlier holy men. Chains of authorities, called *isnad*, were built up to guarantee the authenticity of hadiths. The defense of the hadith-minded was to develop the logic of hadith to its utmost, without appeal or reference to external sources of appraisal or criticism. They relied only on whatever was dependably reported as having been said by the Prophet.

By the middle of the ninth century, the approach of the legists and the approach of the people of hadith were well consolidated. The outcome of the long struggle was to take two vaguely defined religious orientations, and by forcing the implicit conflicts between them to elaborate and systematize the law as a code of religious teaching based on Quran, hadith, the consensus of the learned, and analogical reasoning to assure the authenticity of hadith by some kind of external criticism. The long debate refined the shape of law and hadith, and persuaded Muslims that both corpuses of religious expression were scriptures of Islam.

Still, concealed within this consensus was a profound disagreement over the meaning of a truly religious life in Islam. The proponents of hadith thought of Islam as a completely revealed faith, a religion of submission to the word of God and literal acceptance of the words of Muhammad as an indirect expression of God's guidance. The proponents of consensus of the community and of individual judgment as the basis of law held that Islam was a religion based on scripture, but a religion which must be adapted to new or changing circumstances by the agreement of the community and by human judgment about how the scripture should be applied. Implicit in the agreement that Islam was a religiously sanctified way of life lived in accordance with God's will as set out in scripture was profound disagreement about the boundaries between revealed truth and human interpretation, the requirements of faith and the use of reason, the degree of man's submission to God or his autonomy in living a Muslim life. The same outer life, as embodied in Quran and hadith, could imply radically different forms of spirituality.

THEOLOGY

Other Sunni Muslims directed their attention toward the intellectual and spiritual dimensions of Islam and interested themselves in theology. Theological questions were first prompted by political disputes. The Kharijis had opposed ʿAli's reign as the Caliph on the grounds that a sinner could not be Caliph. Only sinless peoples, they held, were true Muslims. The supporters of Muʿawiya, however, did not want to open the personal religious qualifications of a Caliph to question and held that all persons who professed Islam were ipso facto true Muslims. Political neutrals called Muʿtazila held that sinners were neither true Muslims nor infidels, but fell within an intermediate classification, and continued to belong to the Muslim community. Other neutrals called Murjiʾa crystallized the truly theological issue. In the Murjiʾa view, neither good nor bad deeds made a man a true Muslim, but faith and intention. The Murjiʾa introduced the problem of faith and works.

The Kharijis also broached the problem of free will and predestination. The question came up over the issue of whether children were automatically Muslims or had they to elect membership in the community? The Kharijis held for election; it was consistent with their view that only a blameless person was a true Muslim, and by implication that every person had a choice and was responsible for his choices. The Murjiʾa and the Muʿtazila agreed and believed therefore in free will. Once this issue was broached, a host of theological subtleties followed. The question of free will or predestination raised the question of the meaning of God's attributes. What is to be understood by such Quranic phrases as "God's power" and "God's knowledge"? The question of attributes raised the further question of God's unity.

The theological problems raised in the Arab-Muslim milieu, however, were not solved wholly in the vocabulary of Arab-Muslim conceptions. Pious Muslims debating the importance of faith versus works, or free will and predestination, or the nature of God and how his seemingly contradictory qualities should be understood, discovered that Greek philosophers and Christian theologians had already devised a tradition of argumentation upon which Muslim thinkers could draw to refine their conceptions. Converts introduced this earlier tradition into Muslim circles, and debates between Muslims and Christians in Damascus, in the multi-religious and tolerant court of the Umayyad Caliphs, and the translation of Greek and Syriac literature into Arabic, led Muslim thinkers to adopt Hellenistic vocabulary and Greco-Christian forms of rational argument. Theology was thus in part the product of Islamic urban milieus and in part the product of the philosophic and religious interests of the Caliphal court.

In Muslim theological circles, the people most aggressively interested in Greek dialectics were the Mu'tazila. In the forefront of debate, competing with Christian trinitarianism, Manichaean dualism, pagan materialism, and even anthropomorphic conceptions widespread among Muslims, the Mu'tazila upheld God's unity and transcendence. They affirmed that there was but one God who is pure ultimate being. As pure being, God was not like any created matter, not like a human person, nor divided in any way. In the Aristotelian language adopted by the Mu'tazila, God's essence was his existence.

Other Mu'tazili doctrines were a corollary of their conception of God's transcendence and unity. For example, they held that the Quran was a created thing and not part of the essence of God, as opposed to the orthodox Christian view that Christ, the logos, the word of God, proceeds from God as part of his essence and is co-eternal with him. The Mu'tazila denied that the Muslim "logos," the Quran, was part of God or divine itself, but asserted that it was a created message inspired by God in Muhammad. Other Muslims refused to accept this, and the issue became a cause célèbre in Muslim theology and the most important issue in the religious politics of the 'Abbasid Caliphate.

A corollary of the Mu'tazili conception of God's transcendence and unity was the doctrine of man's moral freedom and responsibility: men choose their own acts; they are not created by or determined by God. In holding this view, the Mu'tazila upheld God's justice, for he rightly punishes and rewards men for their deeds. And they upheld God's goodness; not God, but men, were the authors of evil. If men were not morally free, they argued, God would by implication be the cause of evil.

The main tenets of the Mu'tazila, though presented in terms of Greek thought, were profoundly Islamic in inspiration. Though other Muslims might disagree, their stress on God's unity and man's responsibility seemed to be the essence of Islam itself. Yet the Mu'tazila went beyond strictly Islamic issues to develop, on the basis of Greek thought, a metaphysics of being, a theory of the origin of the universe, a physics of created things, and a psychology of man, based on the teachings of Aristotle, Democritus, Empedocles, and other Greek philosophers. The crucial tenet in their philosophy was that God's being, the universe and man's nature were all rationally ordered and knowable to human reason. God was defined by his essence, which is reason. The created world functions according to its own rational laws and, once created, is independent of God and not changeable by him. Similarly, in moral matters, good and evil have an intrinsic value. They are not dependent on, or changed by, divine will. God's justice is constrained by the laws of good and evil. A natural corollary of the Mu‘tazili position, though not necessarily drawn by all, was that revelation was of secondary importance, and could no more than amplify or make the teachings of reason more specific. Revelation could supply details, complete, confirm, or complement reason, but no truths unknown, unknowable, or inconsistent with the dictates of reason could be revealed.

Though the Mu‘tazila served Islam well in their defense of the unity of God and in their clarification of man's free will and responsibility, their larger philosophy, developed under the influence of Greek thought, betrayed the majority sentiment of the Arab-Muslim milieu about the nature of God and his creation. For other Muslims, Muhammad and the Quran, not reason, were the central experiences of Islam. The Quran contained God's will for men and the duties he had assigned them, and Muhammad was the last messenger of God, bringing the last revelation. For most Muslims, man must submit to God, not presume to know better than God. The people of hadith, who had so severely criticized the legists for the application of personal judgment to legal problems, were especially incensed that Muslim theologians were relying on reason for the discussion of religious matters. The hadith scholars rejected, without compromise, any accommodation with Greek methods of discussion. Reason had no place in religion at all, for the statements of the hadith were God's will, and not to be questioned. They rejected the siren song of Greek ideas as incompatible with complete and unassuming devotion to God and his revelations.

Thus, the hadith scholars opposed the Mu‘tazili conception of *tawhid*, or unity of God. They insisted that the attributes of God, whose independent existence was denied by the Mu‘tazila, must exist because they are mentioned in the Quran. To deny or explain them away would be to derogate from God's own revelation of his being. They rejected the Mu‘tazila notion of the createdness of the Quran, affirmed the contrary, its uncreatedness, and made this a fundamental tenet of faith, as a way of asserting the superiority of the

Quran to all human reasoning and knowledge. Finally, they held that man's acts were predetermined by God; he had no share in their genesis. For hadith scholars, God's omnipotent power and his untrammeled inscrutable will, not his rationality or his justice, were the heartfelt attributes.

Thus by the ninth century two basic positions had emerged in Muslim theology. One was a rationalist-oriented position that emphasized the centrality of reason as an ordering principle in God's being in the human understanding of the universe, and in the governance of human behavior. The rationalist position had, as its corollary, belief in free will and individual responsibility for moral choices. A contrary position stressed the absolute omnipotence and inscrutability of the divine being, who could be known only insofar as he had chosen to reveal himself through the Quran. This view denied the utility of reason in religious or moral choices. All human action was ultimately an expression of the power of the creator rather than an autonomous exercise of free judgment and will.

Dissatisfied with the excesses of Mu'tazili rationalism, and appalled by the constricting literalism of the people of hadith, ninth- and tenth-century Muslim theologians tried to find a middle ground consistent with emphasis on the importance of hadiths, but preserving some role for reasoning in the discussion of theological issues. Several such compromises were elaborated, but the most important in the history of Muslim theology was the work of al-Ash'ari (d. 935).

On doctrinal matters al-Ash'ari adopted the hadith scholars' views, but refined them to meet the higher standards of Mu'tazili reasoning. For example, on the problem of the createdness of the Quran, al-Ash'ari held that it was uncreated, but adducing a philosophic distinction between essence and existence, pointed out that any particular copy of the Quran was created. On the question of free will, al-Ash'ari held that all acts of man were decided or created by God, but that man, by *kasb* (acquisition), has a certain responsibility for them. God is the ultimate author of man's actions, but man is the instrument of or participant in these actions.

Thus, al-Ash'ari defended a theological viewpoint that stressed the overwhelming importance of the divine revelation and the humble quality of man's own will and rational faculties. However, to defend these positions adequately, to meet rather than withdraw from the theological objections, al-Ash'ari adopted rational techniques. He used Greek concepts to defend his position. Though he rejected rational metaphysics as a key to the nature of God and the universe, and established the primacy of the revelation, reason, he allowed, could spell out the meanings embodied in the Quran and hadith.

More important, reason could defend religious truth, could protect it against its adversaries, and could be used to persuade others of its validity. *Kalam* (theology) does not of itself discover truths, but reinforces by rational comprehension belief in God and his purposes as understood from revelation and obedience to God's will as expressed in hadith and law.

MYSTICS AND SUFISM

Alongside the scholars of hadith, law and theology, mystics and ascetics carried on another form of quest for religious fulfillment. While the legists and the theologians concentrated upon finding out the rules which God had commanded to govern everyday life and sought a rational understanding of their beliefs, the mystics attempted to acquire an immediate and personal experience of God's reality. They sought to order their lives, channel their thoughts and feelings, and hone a language which would make possible a direct experience of the presence of a God who was otherwise acknowledged to be a transcendent and inaccessible being. In this quest language was particularly important, because only right language could unify the soul of the individual, break down the barriers between human and divine discourse, and enable the mystic to symbolize the reality that he attempted to experience. In religious terms this is a quest for unity with the divine being; in humanistic terms it is an effort to overcome the divided self, to realize the truths by which life must be lived, and to attain wholeness of being.

Islamic mysticism originated in the spiritual aspirations and religious practices of the Prophet Muhammad, his companions, and their successors. While the Arab-Muslim elite was engaged in conquest and empire, other Muslims questioned the value of a worldly life. They discussed such issues as the value of celibacy versus marriage, poverty versus wealth, and retreat versus active engagement. Many of these questioners chose a piety which emphasized the memorization of the Quran, devotion to hadith and the law, and the fulfillment of their teachings in daily life. Others chose a more extreme asceticism. They renounced their attachment to this world, and concentrated upon religious devotions. For some this meant utmost poverty and isolation, constant watchfulness to avoid any sin, great or small, fear of the last judgment, and yearning for the paradise promised true believers. Their lives were marked by fear of heedlessness, fear of temptation or sin, and by sadness. They wept for their sins and the punishment to come; they wept for the misery of the world. They taught that the only proper life for a good Muslim was one of humility and poverty; the only proper expression, tears rather than laughter, but that silence was best of all. In silence one could concentrate on the recollection of God and on waiting for the last judgment. For others, however, the purgative way implied a more moderate asceticism and discipline of bodily desires. For still others, asceticism implied an attitude of emotional disinterest, of detachment, without requiring physical renunciation. Goodness in following the teachings of the Quran, avoidance of sin and a humble yearning attitude toward God was summed up in the word *zuhd* (renunciation). This form of piety, like Muhammad's own vision, echoes eastern Christian spirituality.

Hasan al-Basri (d. 728) has come down through Muslim history as the exemplar of ascetic engagement in the world. Hasan al-Basri wept for his unworthiness and feared death, the last judgment and the hellfire to come, but he also taught obedience to the commands of the Quran and the strict practice of the rules of religion reinforced by ascetic restrictions and devotions. Equally important was his attitude of patient acceptance of the trials of this world, submission to God's will and constant anticipation of the last judgment. For Hasan al-Basri, the cultivation of proper acts and attitudes was an individual responsibility. While accepting God's determination and guidance in all matters, he sought to reconcile the power of God with the responsibility of individuals through the mystical concept of *rida* (contentment), an attitude that brought the soul into harmony with God's will and thus reconciled freedom of choice with God's power to determine all things.

Furthermore, for Hasan al-Basri, moral responsibility extended from the life of the individual to the community as a whole. Hasan himself fought in the frontier wars to expand Islam and held public offices in Basra. He lived an active life devoted to *jihad* (holy war), teaching, preaching, and administration. It was the responsibility of good Muslims to give moral advice to rulers and to counsel ordinary believers on their obligations to God. However, Hasan was opposed to violence. Even when rulers were unjust, the proper response was moral counsel but not violent rebellion. For Hasan individual ascetic renunciation and self-restraint were the basis of responsibility and moral conduct in political affairs. Religious insight was the basis of political action. Paradoxically, renunciation of the world led back to the actual fulfillment of the divine law for both the individual and the community as a whole.

Sufism or Islamic mysticism emerged out of this early ascetic attitude as the ascetics also cultivated psychological, emotional, and spiritual awareness. Recitation of the Quran, *dhikr* (the remembrance of God and repetition of his name), litanies and meditation coupled with the struggle to subdue bad impulses and to suppress inner vices were thought to free the deepest capacities of the soul and to prepare it for the vision of God. The Quran provided the

Sufis with inspiration, guidance and a vocabulary for these experiences. Muqatil ibn Sulayman (d. 767) developed a form of commentary that allowed the
interpreter of the Quran to transcend its literal meaning and to arrive at its
spiritual meaning. Muqatil saw in each passage of the Quran a literal, a
historical, and an allegoric meaning that, when combined, liberated the imagination from the letter of the text and made possible mystical vision. Other
writers such as Ja⸋far al-Sadiq (d. 765) taught that every passage of the Quran
spoke on four levels of meaning that could be appreciated by people having
the requisite spiritual experience. These levels were ⸋ibara, the physical words
of the Quran, ishara, allusion to an outside object, latifa, the mysterious fruit
within the Quran, and finally haqiqa, the truth or reality of the Quran.

A new level was reached when mystics no longer interpreted the vocabulary
of the Quran directly but developed their own language to express the stages of
spiritual experience and ascent toward God. Shaqiq al-Balkhi (d. 810) was one
of the first Sufi writers to speak of four stages. The first was zuhd, renunciation
of the appetites of the body; the second was fear of God and constant humility;
the third was yearning for paradise; the fourth was love of God. Each stage
was partly a product of human effort and partly a gift of God's grace. Later
writers such as Abu Sa⸋id Kharraz (d. 890 or 899) described seven stages on
the way to God in which the term qurb, or nearness, was the central metaphor.
Other writers enlarged upon the concept of the soul's progress to include
numerous stages of moral elevation (maqam) which were the result of the Sufi's
own disciplined efforts and numerous temporary states of being (hal) which
were God's gift.

As the concept of stages of ascent became more elaborate, the Sufi repertoire
came to stress certain stages. One was sabr, patience in accepting God's will
and in renunciation of the world; others were shukr, gratitude; tawakkul, trust
in God, which implied utter reliance upon God and acceptance of his will
without recourse or hope in worldly things; rida, acceptance of the vicissitudes
of life and the reality of the divine decree with equanimity and even with joy
and love. Love implied yearning for God, obedience to God's will, complete
surrender, and dying to one's self in the hope of closeness to God. Rabi⸋a, a
woman mystic (d. 801), put into passionate poems her thirst, her desire to be
joined to God. Some Sufis saw love as yearning; others understood love as
union. Still others thought of love of God in terms of God's mercy and
forgiveness upon which sinful man was always dependent. Love of God
opened the way to a still higher stage, tawhid (unity), understood in this
context as loss of self and absorption in the divine being.

By the ninth century two broad but definable tendencies had emerged within the Sufi movement. These should not be thought of as schools, for they had no organizational coherence, but held together through the influence of the great masters and informal communication. The Khurasanian tendency was characterized by emphasis on tawakkul, resignation to God's will expressed through voluntary poverty and renunciation of work. This mysticism ruptured the ordinary pattern of Muslim religious activities and ignored obedience to Quranic commands and conformity to the law in search of a transcending religious self-realization.

Abu Yazid al-Bistami (d. 873) epitomized the quest for an intoxicated rapturous union with God. In al-Bistami's view, the mystic seeks annihilation of self and union with the divine names or attributes. The mystic's identification with God is expressed in *shath*, theopathic utterances, which are the voice of God speaking through his person. Al-Hallaj (d. 923), who lived as a preacher and missionary in Khurasan and Afghanistan, also sought loss of self and unity in God. As a manifestation of this union, al-Hallaj proclaimed, "I am the Truth," performed miracles, and claimed a religious authority greater than the authority of Caliphs and ʿulamaʾ because it was the authority of the divine presence. His claims to miracles, his usurpation of power, and his doctrine of divine love and union led to prosecution for heresy and his execution in 923.

Other mystics held back from the radical implications of ecstatic Sufism and the concept of annihilation of the self in God. The Baghdadi tendency placed heavy stress on asceticism and renunciation of worldly things combined with the cultivation of practical virtues such as patience, trust, gratitude, and love of God. The Baghdadi tendency, however, as opposed to the Khurasanian, believed in observance of the Quran and conformity with Muslim law. Practically and intellectually, the Baghdadis were more closely integrated with ordinary Muslim religious practice and belief.

Al-Harith al-Muhasabi (781–857) was the great ninth-century proponent of this position. His teachings combined the quest for interior moral perfection with observance of Muslim law and theological clarification of the principles of belief. Al-Muhasabi taught that every human action must be made in the name of God, that scrupulous observance of God's commands and prohibition was required. Service to God was the principal object of a human life. Love of God should be expressed in love of his commandments and acceptance of their sovereignty in daily life.

Al-Junayd (d. 911) continued this effort to integrate Sufism with other aspects of Islamic religious life. Al-Junayd laid stress upon renunciation, purification, and mental struggle in order to return to that preexistent state in which the human being is a concept in the mind of God. Al-Junayd professed the two-stage concept of Sufi union. Beyond *fana'* he found *baqa'*, or persistence in his own identity. Al-Junayd held that the mystic's goal was not loss of self as the final end but, through loss of self, a return to a daily life transformed by the vision of God and ever after conducted in the presence of God. As opposed to the Khurasanians, al-Junayd taught that beyond the ecstasy of loss of self there was sober persistence of self in the ordinary world in never-failing devotion to the fulfillment of God's will as expressed in the teachings of the Quran and the Prophet of Islam. For the Baghdadis, visionary insight into the reality of God's being was not an escape from but an intensification of the Sufi's commitment to the fulfillment of God's will in daily life. To Khurasanian intoxication al-Junayd opposed Baghdadi sobriety.

While mystics differed on the stages of the ascent toward God, they had by the end of the ninth century collectively articulated a theory of spiritual progress that combined the Quranic inspiration and vocabulary with the lived experience of generations of seekers. Later Sufis such as Niffari (d. 985) further perfected the language of Sufism. He employed symbols that came into being in the moment of mystic experience, and cultivated a language that condensed human experience with its transcendent reference. Through symbols, the mystic became familiar with the God who reveals himself in the language of men without compromising his transcendence. Symbolic language itself became a symbol of the mystic's absorption into the divine reality.

Sufism's pragmatic program of spiritual and moral developments was accompanied by a quest for intellectual insight. Sufis also cultivated a metaphysical, theosophical, and philosophical concept of the divine reality, the creation of the material world, the place of the human being in the universe created by God, and a theory of the correspondence of the essential reality of man's nature with that of the divine being. By the early tenth century several metaphysical theories of the relation of human beings to God had been put forth. All of them in one form or another posited a transcendent God but one whose spiritual radiance or emanation was implanted in human beings. This implantation, however, is obscured, overcome sometimes by the material and worldly side of human beings. A human being must overcome these bodily and animal forces, restore purity of will and intellect, and thus realize his inherently divine nature. Through this realization he returns to his origins in God.

One version of this was presented by Sahl al-Tustari (d. 896). In al-Tustari's view, God's essence is light which is a single and transcendent illumination, but it is a light which radiates from him to create spiritual prototypes of the material world. Enshrined in this light are the prototypes of the prophets and of ordinary human beings who exist before their worldly birth as particles of the divine light. In this preexistent state human beings recognize and testify to the oneness and the lordship of God, a primordial covenant. In the life of this world man attempts to reactualize this preexistent covenant. In prayer he contemplates God's existence; in dhikr or Sufi ceremony, he attempts to recollect God's primordial self-revelation. To do this, he must purify the heart and make it triumph over the forces of the bodily self, following Quran and hadith with sincerity and repentance, living according to God's commands and prohibitions. Penitence and inner struggle free him from his bodily self (nafs) and allow him to realize his spiritual self, qalb (heart), *aql* (reason), or ruh (spirit). By the resurrection of this preexisting reality the mystic prepares himself for the vision of God and life eternal in the presence of the divine being.

With the translation of the Syriac and Greek classics into Arabic, the intellectual mysticism that stemmed from the thought of Plotinus (d. 270) provided a similar theosophical concept of the mystic way. Neo-Platonism introduced the idea that the universe radiated from the divine being in successive stages of spiritual and then material manifestation. Man, who stood at the juncture of the spiritual and material world, was capable by inner knowledge or illumination of rising up in the hierarchy of being to the ultimate vision of God. By discovery of the inward truths of the heart which correspond to the cosmological structure of the universe, the mystic ascends from his material state toward ever higher levels of spiritual being and the ultimate illuminative knowledge of God.

Thus, in several forms, early Sufi metaphysics combined a transcendentalist with an immanentist view of God's existence. God is utterly different from any created reality; yet he is also the source of spiritual illuminations which make it possible for human beings, in whom there dwells some aspect of the reality of God, to return from their material exile to their spiritual home.

Finally, there was a miraculous and magical aspect to Sufism. The individual who had achieved knowledge of God's being through his daily behavior and visionary insight was considered more than human. In his person he was an epiphany, a manifestation, of the divine being, and the vehicle of communication between man and God. The mystic was considered a healer, a magician, a worker of miracles, and a pillar of the universe. For many Muslim believers the Sufi was not only a person of great moral and spiritual quality but was a living expression of God's power in the world. Al-Tirmidhi (d. 898) advanced the theory that the Sufi adept was a saint who by his spiritual achievements upheld the order of the universe. Standing in the hierarchy of

God's emanation, he was as a vessel of God's being capable of miraculous deeds. Al-Tirmidhi's doctrine of sainthood became the basis of an almost universal Muslim belief in saints as intercessors between ordinary human beings and God, and of a worshipful veneration of saints and the descendants, disciples and tombs of saints as repositories of the divine presence. In metaphysical doctrine and in magical practice, the Sufis represented the possibility of salvation by entry into the presence of God.

Sufism began in the seventh century as the quest for individual spiritual redemption, but became by the late eighth century a collective religious movement. By this period Sufis had developed a concept of themselves – the people of the coarse white wool garment – as initiates in a form of Muslim religious life which was different from the piety enshrined in scholarship and legal practice. Sufis gathered to recite the Quran and to sit in the presence of great masters. Collective retreats such as the *khanaqa* at Abadan helped give some coherence to Sufism as a movement.

Thus, by the early tenth century Sufism had developed from a quest of isolated individual ascetics into a religious movement. Combining ascetic renunciation with spiritual development leading toward union with God, Sufism was grounded in philosophical and metaphysical conceptions of God's being, and a doctrine of the venerable and miraculous nature of saints. At the same time Sufism had begun to develop the rudiments of both a social organization and a public mission. All of these trends would be consolidated and further developed in the centuries following the collapse of the ʿAbbasid empire.

SHIʿI ISLAM

While the Sunni communities elaborated their several concepts of Islam, the Shiʿa developed their own. For Shiʿi Muslims the critical issue was not law or mysticism but loyalty to the Caliph ʿAli and the conviction that the true Caliphate could only descend in his family. In the seventh and eighth centuries this had led to a political movement in opposition to the Umayyad and ʿAbbasid dynasties. Family loyalists tried again and again to seize the Caliphate. Defeat channeled many of the Shiʿa from political activity into religious reflection.

In the middle of the eighth century, two concerns governed the intensification of religious activity in Shiʿi circles. First, since the Shiʿa denied the legitimacy of the Sunni succession of Caliphs, Abu Bakr and ʿUmar, though companions of the Prophet, could no longer be accepted as authoritative sources of Muslim religious teaching. An independent hadith and law in which

Fig. 4. The Shiʿi Imams.

ʿAli was the prime authority was necessary. Thus the Shiʿa elaborated their own hadith and law, differing from the Sunni versions only in matters of detail and in chains of transmission. The hadiths of the imams, and especially the hadiths attributed to ʿAli and collected in the *Nahj al-Balagha* (Path of Eloquence) are central teachings of Shiʿism. The Shiʿa were also in close touch with political sympathizers such as Muʿtazili theologians, and by the end of the ninth century also debated the questions of free will and God's attributes.

Secondly, the claims of the Shiʿi imams to the Caliphate had to be defended. Jaʿfar al-Sadiq (d. 765), the sixth imam in the line of ʿAli, taught that the true

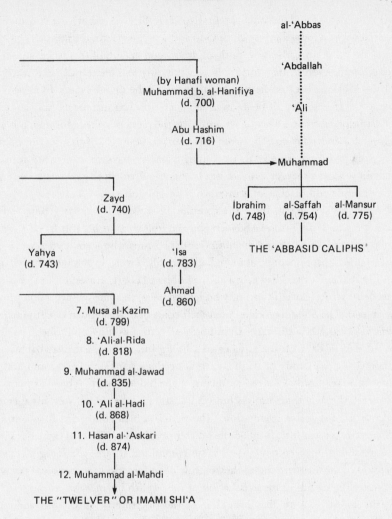

Caliph and ruler of the Muslim community descended in the family of ʿAli by virtue of *nass* – the designation by each incumbent imam of his successor. Through nass the imam inherited a secret knowledge and exclusive authority to interpret the Quran and hadith and therefore to elaborate the legal system of Islam. By the ninth century, Shiʿi concepts of the imam came to include the notion that he was *maʿsum*, a sinless and infallible guide to religious truth.

A still more exalted concept of the imam was proposed by Shiʿa who saw the imam not only as the foremost authority on the law of Islam, but also as the guide to esoteric comprehension of the truth. In the *ghulat* (extremist) view, which would become integral to later Shiʿi thought, the imam was vested with an indwelling spirit of God and was the mahdi, the messiah chosen by God to restore the true faith of Islam and to establish justice and the kingdom of God in the world. He was the only legitimate ruler and teacher of the Muslims because he was an epiphany of the divine being. In the Shiʿi view, the true source of belief in each generation was ultimately not the text of tradition, the consensus of the jurist, or the piety of other Muslims, but an imam descended from ʿAli. From this vantage point Shiʿism left a legacy of religious teachings similar to the Sunni types we have discussed but it also moved toward a merger with Sufism in that the divinely graced imam became the example and teacher of a mystical reunion with God.

After Jaʿfar's death, the Shiʿi community divided into two groups – the followers of Jaʿfar's son ʿAbdallah and the followers of his son Ismaʿil. The followers of ʿAbdallah and the ninth-century imams who were his descendants maintained a prominent position in Baghdad. Shiʿa were important in merchant and scribal circles and had access to the ʿAbbasid court. However, in 874 with the death of the eleventh imam, who left no heirs, this line of succession came to an end. The Shiʿa then elaborated their concept of the hidden twelfth imam, who is not dead, but in retreat until he shall return as the mahdi, the messiah, at the end of days. In the absence of a living imam, the Banu Nawbakht, an important Shiʿi family of Baghdad, took up the leadership of the community, and from 874 until 941 acted as agents of the hidden imam. This first period, in which the twelfth imam was hidden but still in direct touch with his agents, was called the lesser occultation. The period which followed, in which all direct contact was lost, is called the greater occultation. Thus, in these decades the Baghdad Shiʿi community became committed to an eschatological conception of the imamate and to the doctrine of an historical succession of twelve imams culminating in the occultation of the twelfth imam, who would return as the messiah. With the formation of the doctrine of succession and occultation, the *ithna ʿashari* ("twelver"), or Imami Shiʿi community, took its definitive historical form. In politics this implied that the "twelvers," though opposed to the ʿAbbasid regime in principle, were willing to postpone their expectations of a Shiʿi imam and reign of justice until the indefinite future.

The second branch of Shiʿa was the followers of Jaʿfar's son Ismaʿil. The early Ismaʿilis retained the doctrine of the sinless and infallible imam but differed from the others in recognizing Ismaʿil rather than ʿAbdallah as the true imam. However, a strong messianic orientation led to doctrinal changes and to political activism. In Ismaʿili doctrine, the Quran revealed two truths – the *zahir*, or the external, literal truth of the divine message, and the *batin*, the inner esoteric truth of the Quran, which could only be known by the proper exegesis of the Quranic text and by comprehension of the zahir as the symbol of an inner spiritual principle. For the Isma⁽ilis of the ninth century the doctrine implied a conception of the imam as the teacher and guide to the esoteric and inner meaning of the Quranic revelation.

Isma⁽ilis also generated a historical and eschatological concept of the imam. According to their doctrine, prophetic revelation was always complemented by the appearance of a *wasi*, who was the executor and interpreter of the inner meaning of the revelation. In history, there were to be seven prophets, each followed by a cycle of seven imams. Muhammad was the sixth prophet. His wasi was ⁽Ali, who was to be followed by a cycle of imams culminating in Muhammad the son of Isma⁽il, the mahdi, who would return as the seventh and final prophet to reveal the truth in its fullness and establish everlasting justice. Isma⁽ilism combined a historical cyclical concept of prophetology with eschatological messianism.

The Isma⁽ilis held further that the imams were figures in a universal hierarchy as well as participants in prophetic cycles. The prophet, the *natiq*, was superior to the imams, who in turn were superior to the *hujja*, the proof, who represented the imams in their absence and were in turn represented by *da⁽is* or missionaries. This structure of communal religious authority was at once a hierarchy of leadership and the mark of successive stages of spiritual initiation.

The Isma⁽ilis of the ninth century were active missionaries and political organizers. While the Shi⁽a of Baghdad maintained their position in ⁽Abbasid society and government, Isma⁽ilis set out to proselytize tribal and peasant peoples in Arabia, Syria, Iraq, North Africa, and in the towns of Iran, preaching equality and justice, the need for reform and the coming of the mahdi. Isma⁽ili da⁽is converted new peoples to their version of Islam and led extensive rebellions against the ⁽Abbasid Caliphate. Isma⁽ili dynasties were founded in North Africa, the Caspian region, Bahrain, Multan, and other places. While Imami Shi⁽ism was politically quietist, Isma⁽ili Shi⁽ism carried the banner of Islamic revolution.

In either form, Shi⁽ism was characterized by a religious mood which stressed messianic hopes and chiliastic expectations. The Shi⁽a believed in the return of the imam as a messiah, and that the historical world would come to an end with the fulfillment of successive cycles of prophets and imams in a cataclysmic era out of which would come a reborn mankind and the establishment of a kingdom of God on earth. While Sunni and Shi⁽i Muslims did not differ much in their orientation to daily life they differed profoundly in the emotional mood through which they saw worldly reality.

CHAPTER 7

ISLAMIC CULTURE AND THE SEPARATION OF STATE AND RELIGION

Islamic civilization, in both its courtly cosmopolitan and urban religious forms, represented the cultural expression of political and religious elites thrown up by the Arab conquests. Each version also represented a selection and synthesis of the heritage of Middle Eastern civilizations. The ancient world communicated Jewish, Christian, Hellenistic, Byzantine and Sasanian culture. Christian eschatology and theology, neo-Platonic and Hellenistic philosophy, became part of Islamic theology and mysticism. Jewish scriptural, prophetic, ritual, and legal precedents were absorbed into Islamic law. Hellenistic science was studied in a continuous tradition. Sasanian and Byzantine court ceremony, art and architecture, administrative precedents, and political concepts were assimilated by the Umayyad and ʿAbbasid empires.

The appropriation of the past was in part unconscious and in part deliberate. In the new era, the past was a living presence. The majority of Middle Eastern peoples remained Jews, Christians, or Zoroastrians. Presumably family, village, neighborhood, tribal, and other forms of small-scale community organization were not affected by the Arab conquests and the Muslim empires. Despite changes in economic activity the basic institutions of agricultural production and urban commerce remained unchanged. Byzantine and Sasanian imperial institutions, including the very concept of the ruler and his responsibility for religion, were directly taken over by the Arab-Muslim Caliphate. Monotheistic religious belief and congregational forms of religious organization became the template for the newly forming Muslim religious communities. Converts brought their previous education, cultural style and political identifications into the new faith. The vast reach of the Islamic empires, the broad recruitment of the imperial elite, and the cosmopolitan quality of Baghdad brought the whole of the ancient Middle Eastern heritage into the purview of Islam. The new elites were impelled to generate a unified culture to provide a coherent way of life in their melting-pot cities, to integrate the disparate elements of the new elite, and to articulate the triumph, the legitimacy and the permanence of the new order. These needs could only be fulfilled by the assimilation of the crucial elements of the ancient heritage.

In historical retrospect Islam appears as a new guise for a more ancient civilization. The Islamization of the Middle East did not involve the transformation of basic institutional structures, in the sense that it did not introduce new modes of economic production, or new forms of family, tribe, or empire; rather, Islam seems to have infused inherited institutional forms with a new vocabulary, concepts and value preferences, and a new definition of personal, social, and political identity. In certain respects the formation of Islamic societies was a recapitulation of earlier processes of Middle Eastern historical development and a redefinition of pre-Islamic institutional forms in Muslim cultural terms. Still this heritage was assimilated in a manner which is indisputably Islamic. No matter how deliberate the appropriation of Christian, Byzantine and Sasanian artistic motifs, the resulting configuration was original and unmistakably Islamic. So in literature, law, theology, mysticism, and philosophy, the materials of the past have been reshaped. Islamic civilization harbors strong tension between the tendency to incorporate the past and the tendency to assert a new identity; a tension between the ancient religions of the Book and the new dispensation; between the continuity of Middle Eastern imperial regimes and the novelty of the Muslim Caliphate.

The process of forming Islamic civilization was not a passive assimilation but an active struggle among the proponents of different views. Within court circles, representatives of Arabic, Persian, and Hellenistic literatures struggled to shape the identity of the Caliphate. The proponents of Arabic and Persian identities fought for a century until Arabic triumphed as the primary language of the empire and Persian and Hellenistic literatures were absorbed into Arabic literary forms.

Similarly, the Muslim urban communities embodied, not one but a number of conflicting orientations. The Sunni Muslims were divided among those who stressed the importance of good works and correct practice and those who were concerned with doctrine and true belief; still others urged the importance of direct experience of the being of God. Some Muslims emphasized the authority of the scholarly tradition; others the teaching of the imams, or the charismatic presence of the saints. The Sunnis tended to stress the revealed text itself and the line of commentary and interpretation going back through the generations directly to the Prophet. They were secure in the continuity of the tradition of scholarship and the collective authority of the learned men as the basis of Islamic belief and practice. In Shiʿi circles emphasis was placed on the teaching of the imams, the divinely given successors to Muhammad, and on personal loyalty to them. Expressed in one form or another were fundamentalist, conservative, puritanical, accommodationist, realist, and millenarian religious attitudes.

Each of these positions was itself formed by debate. We have seen how the scripturalists held different views about the authority of the Quran, hadith, and law, and differed over the boundaries of revelation and human judgment. The theologians disputed the nature of God's being and his attributes, free will, and predestination, and the role of reason and philosophy in the foundation of Islam. The mystics were divided by world-renouncing and world-accepting attitudes, and by ecstatic and sober practices. By the middle of the tenth century, however, certain problems had been resolved but others had not. Within the scriptural orientation, hadith and law had been integrated, though the integration posed new issues for later discussion. Within theology the balance between revelation and reason was defined in terms of a limited use of reason, and the more rationalistic Muʿtazili position was proscribed. However, the problems of the relation of law, theology, and mysticism had not been resolved. Just as there were intense debates within each orientation over the proper values of the religious life, there were intense conflicts among them. Scholars of law questioned the validity of mysticism. Theologians wrestled with the hadith-minded commitment to revelation rather than reason. Though sober Sufism posited obvious ways to reconcile the personal quest for religious salvation with adherence to law, proponents of law and proponents of mysticism were still at odds. Though a moderate position about the role of theology had been formulated, the debate over reason and revelation was not over and the place of philosophy in Muslim learning was not decided. The relations of scripture, theology, mysticism, and philosophy would have to be reconsidered in a later era.

The most fateful confrontations, however, were between the court and the urban versions of Islam. Islamic court culture was visual, literary, philosophic, and scientific. As opposed to the courtly concern for symbols to articulate a vision of the universe which justified the authority of the Caliph and the supremacy of the dominant elite, the urban version of Islam emphasized individual piety in pursuit of an Islamic way of life. The pious milieus opposed their concept of humbleness and devotion to aristocratic elegance and refinement. For the urban milieus Islam defined the good life. For the courtly milieu Islam was but an aspect of a cosmopolitan identity and worldview.

These differences led to conflict on several levels. The Shuʿubiya controversy over the supremacy of Arabic or Persian literary values was partly a court-centered dispute, but it also spilled over into a confrontation between court and urban milieus. While the proponents of Persian literature espoused political domination, social hierarchy, and aristocratic refinement, the urban ʿulamaʾ affirmed religious equality, political accountability, and personal values based upon the Quranic revelation and the Arabic identity of the town populations.

An equally important struggle was waged over the legitimacy of Hellenistic thought. Hellenism represented both a reinforcement of and a challenge to the urban ʿulamaʾ worldview. Without embracing the religious and metaphysical views of the philosophers, many Muslim thinkers were prepared to treat philosophy as a neutral science which provided valuable aids for clarifying theological and religious problems. Court and urban theologians welcomed logical methods of argument to clarify Muslim perspectives and defend them against philosophic attack. While Muslim theologians could accept its logical techniques, insofar as philosophy was conceived as an alternate source of divine truths, they had to reject the primacy of reason in religious matters. Similarly, neo-Platonism was on one level intrinsic to the philosophic vision and was therefore a court-sponsored alternative to urban Islam, but on another level it reinforced Sufi ascetic tendencies and gave them a rationale and even a method for the mystical quest. Neo-Platonism thus reinforced an already existing strand of Muslim mysticism, added to the richness of religious life in the Muslim communities, and was accepted by both Shiʿa and Sunnis. Other aspects of Hellenistic teaching such as science, philosophy, and occult metaphysics were acceptable intellectual interests in court milieus, but were rejected in the urban ʿulamaʾ versions of Islam. Like Persian adab, Hellenistic culture was screened, adapted, and utilized to reinforce the basic moral and religious positions of the urban ʿulamaʾ. Yet though rejected in one milieu it continued to be sponsored in court circles as an aspect of cosmopolitan and aristocratic cultivation. In this guise Hellenistic philosophy and science would be preserved for future confrontations and interaction with Islamic religious thought, and for eventual transmission to Christian Europe.

The conflict of worldviews also led to a struggle between the Caliphate and the urban ʿulamaʾ communities over the content of Islamic belief, religious authority and the role of the Caliphate in the governance of the Muslim community. From the very beginning the Caliphs had claimed to be the protectors of both the religious and the political interests of the Muslim umma. While the Umayyads defended the interests of an Islamic empire, the ʿAbbasid Caliph al-Mahdi (775–85) claimed to be the protector of Islam against heresy and arrogated the right to define acceptable doctrine. Later al-Maʾmun (813–33) tried to remake the religious foundations of the Caliphate in the wake of the disruptive civil war which brought him to power. He tried to win over his opponents by making a Shiʿi imam, ʿAli al-Rida, the eighth descendant of ʿAli, heir to the Caliphate. The rapprochement with Shiʿism implied that al-Maʾmun accepted the Shiʿi view of the Caliph as divinely chosen by God with the authority to define religious belief and law. By identifying with the Shiʿa, he sought to bolster the intrinsic authority of his office.

ʿAli al-Rida died within a year. Thwarted in his Shiʿi policy al-Maʾmun tried to accomplish the same objective by adopting the Muʿtazili thesis that the Quran was created and not of the divine essence. This doctrine served to emphasize the religious importance of the Caliph by implying that the Quran, as a created thing, was, like all created things, subject to authoritative Caliphal interpretation. These were not idle claims. Al-Maʾmun initiated an inquisition to force Muslim scholars to accept this doctrine and his right to proclaim it.

In fact, virtually all of the leading religious scholars capitulated. Among religious leaders, only Ahmad b. Hanbal refused to accept the Caliph's contentions. Ahmad, already reputed to be the greatest hadith scholar of his time, now emerged as the public leader of the urban ʿulamaʾ point of view. He denied that the Quran was created and affirmed the transcendent authority of the written word as opposed to human interpreters. Islamic religious obligations, he argued, were not derived from Caliphal pronouncements, but from the fundamental texts known to the leading scholars. The Caliph was merely the executor of the Islamic community, and not the source of its beliefs. A protracted struggle between the Caliphate and the ʿulamaʾ eventually ended with the victory of the latter. In 848–49 the Caliph al-Mutawakkil reversed the policy of his predecessors, abandoned the Muʿtazili thesis, and accepted the contention that the Quran was not the created word of God. The Caliph conceded both the point of doctrine and his claims to be the ultimate source of religious beliefs.

Despite the reversal, the damage done to Caliphal authority was irreparable. The claims of the Caliphate brought out a long-smoldering resentment against its corruption. As a political institution the Caliphate had become suspect to the ʿulamaʾ and other pious Muslims, who saw it as falling away from true religious principles. Insofar as the ᶜAbbasid empire had in part been built up on the effort to identify Islam and the Caliphate, this loss of support was politically catastrophic. Though the Caliphate remained head of the umma and a symbol of Muslim unity, a gulf had opened between the state and religious communities. Henceforth, the Caliph would represent the administrative and executive interests of Islam while the scholars and Sufis defined Islamic religious belief. Henceforth Islam would evolve in full autonomy of the state under the aegis of the religious teachers. The struggle over the "createdness of the Quran" confirmed the separateness of the two forms of early Islamic culture and community, the division of state and religious institutions, of court and urban ᶜulamaᵓ, and of cosmopolitan and religious forms of Islamic civilization. The further evolution of state institutions and cosmopolitan forms of culture, and the evolution of Muslim religious institutions, values, and practices would proceed along separate lines.

CHAPTER 8

THE FALL OF THE ᶜABBASID EMPIRE

The very processes which gave rise to the early Islamic empire, its elites and its cultural forms, led to its collapse and transformation. The decline of the ᶜAbbasid empire began even in the midst of consolidation. While the regime was strengthening its military and administrative institutions, and encouraging a flourishing economy and culture, other occurrences set in motion the forces which would eventually unravel the ᶜAbbasid empire.

As early as the reign of Harun al-Rashid (786–809) the problems of succession had become critical. Harun bequeathed his elder son, al-Amin, the Caliphate, and the younger, al-Maᵓmun, the governorship of Khurasan and the right to succeed his brother. With the death of Harun, al-Amin attempted to displace his brother in favor of his own son. Civil war resulted. Al-Amin was backed by the ᶜAbbasid army of Baghdad, while al-Maᵓmun was forced to turn for support to independent Khurasanian warlords. Al-Maᵓmun defeated his brother and assumed the Caliphate in 813 but not until a bitter civil war had alienated the defeated ᶜAbbasid armies and the populations of Iraq and other provinces.

Al-Maᵓmun attempted to deal with his unreconciled opponents and subjects by a double policy. One goal was to restore the legitimacy of the Caliphate by winning control over religious affairs. This policy, as we have seen, failed, and failing, deprived the Caliphate of an important measure of popular support. Al-Maᵓmun also adopted a new military policy. To win control of the Caliphate, al-Maᵓmun had depended on the support of a Khurasanian lord, Tahir, who in return was made governor of Khurasan (820–22) and general of ᶜAbbasid forces throughout the empire, with the promise that the offices would be inherited by his heirs. Despite the momentary usefulness of the arrangement, the concession of an hereditary governorship defeated the Caliphal objective of unifying the provincial notables into a political system focused on the central government. The effort at direct unification of elites under the aegis of the Caliph had been checked and in its place the empire was to be governed by an alliance of the Caliph with the most important provincial lord.

To offset the power of the Tahirids and regain direct control of the provinces, the Caliphs were eager to create new military forces. Thus, al-Maʾmun and al-Muᶜtasim (833–842) raised forces of two types. The first were *shakiriya*, intact units under the leadership of their local chiefs, from Transoxania, Armenia, and North Africa. Though the soldiers were not directly beholden to the Caliphs, they served as a counterweight to the Tahirids and created a balance of forces which relieved the dependence of the Caliphs on any one potentate. The second type of forces were Turkish slaves, called *ghilman* (pl.), who were purchased individually, but grouped into regiments. For the sake of efficiency and morale, and a balance of power between the regiments, each lived in its own neighborhood, had its own mosque and markets, and was trained, supplied, and paid by its commander. Thus slave regiments also became self-contained units which gave their primary loyalty to their officers rather than to the Caliphs.

The systematic recruitment, training, and employment of slave soldiers was a major innovation in Middle Eastern history, and the beginning of an institution which would characterize many later Muslim regimes. The pressing military and political need for loyal troops must have directed the attention of the Caliphs to long-established precedents for the employment of military forces from peripheral regions and marginal populations. Since Umayyad times the Caliphs and governors of the Arab-Muslim empire had raised supplementary troops in eastern Iran and had depended upon servile, client, and even slave troops, for their personal bodyguards. The employment of servile or client forces became the norm in later Umayyad and ᶜAbbasid armies especially with the retirement of Arab tribesmen. The new system of slave regiments was then a rationalization of earlier practices now made the centerpiece of ᶜAbbasid military organization.

These new regiments strengthened the hand of the Caliphs, but they were also a source of troubles. The Transoxanian and Turkish soldiers soon ran afoul of the Baghdadi populace and of the former Arab soldiers in the Baghdadi army, and bloody clashes ensued. Eventually, the Caliph al-Muᶜtasim decided to build a new capital to isolate the troops from the masses. Beginning in 836 the city of Samarra was built about 70 miles north of Baghdad. While Baghdad remained the cultural and commercial capital of the region, from 836 to 870 Samarra was the military and administrative headquarters of the Caliphate. However, the new city only created further difficulties. The Caliphs, who hoped to avoid clashes between the populace and the troops, instead became embroiled in rivalries among the various guard regiments. The officers took civilian bureaucrats into their patronage, won control of provincial governorships, and eventually attempted to control succession to the Caliphate itself. Regimental rivalries led to anarchy. Between 861 and 870 all the leading officers were killed, and the troops fell out of control and turned to banditry. Moreover, the employment of slave armies alienated the Caliphate from the populace it ruled. While the early ᶜAbbasid empire had depended upon the military support of its own subjects, the late empire tried to dominate its people with foreign troops.

In this same period, changes in administrative organization also reduced the capacity of the central government to control the empire. These changes in administration were partly due to the interference of the army, partly to the rise of independent provincial powers, but they were also due to overwhelming internal stresses inherent in the normal operation of the bureaucracy. In time the bureaucracy ceased to serve the interests of the ruler and the empire, and began to act on behalf of the personal and factional interests of the scribes. ᶜAbbasid bureaucracy came to be dominated by cliques and factions, formed among the functionaries, whose main interest was to exploit bureaucratic office for private gain. Such factions were endemic in ᶜAbbasid government because all high-ranking officers employed their personal followers to do their staff work. By the late ninth century, however, the numerous small cliques attached to many leading officials had become polarized into two great factions, called the Banu Furat and the Banu Jarrah.

Each of these two great late ninth-century factions was built around a wazir and his relatives and clients, who were appointed to apprenticeships and promoted to state offices. To learn the art of being an accountant or scribe a young man entered the service of a master, lived in his household, and was a dedicated personal servant. He owed his master respect and obedience for life, and the patron was obliged not only to train him but to protect him and advance his career. The families also had a larger following based on social and ideological affiliations. The Banu Jarrah faction was composed mainly, though not exclusively, of Nestorian Christians or Christian converts, often educated in the monastery of Dayr Qunna in southern Iraq. By the middle of the ninth century, this faction had already grown powerful enough to influence state policy. In 852 al-Mutawakkil (847–61) was persuaded to assure Christians freedom of religion, freedom from military service, and the right to construct churches, and to give the Nestorian Catholicos full jurisdiction over all Christians. The Caliph also conceded the right of converts to inherit the property of parents who were still Christians, though Muslim law did not permit such transfers. These concessions, however, were soon revoked. The other major faction, the Banu Furat, were mainly Baghdadi Shi⁽a.

The chiefs of these factions eventually gained control of the whole government service. In the reign of al-Mutawakkil the wazirs were put in charge of all the administrative bureaus. While they could be appointed and removed by the Caliph at will, the Caliphs rarely intervened in the routine operations of the bureaucracy. A wazir and his faction came to power by intrigues and by bribing the Caliph and other influential courtiers. Their main concern was to exploit their offices, earn back the bribes, and prepare for future hard times by various frauds, such as padded payrolls, false bookkeeping, illegal speculations, and taking bribes. The officials regarded their positions as a property which they bought, sold, and exploited for private gain. When a faction had been in power and was known to have become rich, the Caliph and the opposing faction were eager to seize the fortunes accumulated by the incumbents. The Caliph then appointed a new wazir, and a rival group came to power which confiscated the revenues seized by the defeated party. Some of the money went to the Caliph and back to the treasury, but some of it went into the pockets of the victorious faction. Special bureaus were set up to handle the reclaimed monies; the *diwan al-musadarat* for confiscated estates and the *diwan al-marafiq* for confiscated bribes. The Caliphate could maintain only a modicum of influence by rotating the leading factions in office and using each change of government as an occasion to extort the resources stolen by the faction last in power.

The cost, however, was extraordinary, and the central government was forced to look to new administrative devices to make up the political and financial losses occasioned by a corrupt bureaucracy. One method was to distribute iqta⁽s to soldiers, courtiers and officials, who collected the taxes ordinarily due from the peasants and paid a portion to the central government. While bringing in a short-term income, iqta⁽s reduced long-term revenues, and subverted the normal operation of provincial and local administration since the iqta⁽-holders paid their fees directly to the central treasury. In addition, the sale of iqta⁽s created a nucleus for the formation of large landed estates which eventually absorbed small landlords and free peasants. Peasants, under pressure from the tax bureaus, would appeal for protection to the powerful iqta^c-holders and sign over their lands. The practice was called *taljia* (commendation), or *himaya* (protection). Iqta^cs acted as crystals to collect and aggregate small holdings, and the growth of large estates further diminished the areas under routine administration. Large landowners were better able to resist the demands of the government. Instead of taxing peasants in a relatively direct way, the government found itself dealing more and more with powerful local landowning notables, who reduced the task of the administration to the collection of negotiated fees.

Other expedients to compensate for the corruption of the central bureaucracy were also costly. In addition to the sale of iqta^cs, the central government also came to rely upon tax-farming in Iraq and western Iran. To receive direct payments in advance, the government sold the right to collect revenues to tax-farmers. The state was guaranteed a fixed revenue a year in advance of when it could normally be collected, and the tax-farmers profited by collecting taxes in excess of what they had to pay the state. To make the arrangement work to the benefit of the central government, strict inspection was essential, and the government tried to put tax-farms up to annual auction, or at least to estimate the likely yields on the basis of past experience and lease the land at a fair price.

Tax-farming, however, was not merely a financial arrangement but a substitute form of administration. The tax-farmer not only paid a sum to collect taxes, but agreed to maintain local administration, meet all the government's local expenses, invest in irrigation, and support the local police. Though government inspectors supervised tax-farming operations and tried to protect the peasants from abuse, the basic apparatus of local administration was being displaced by private governments. Through the distribution of iqta^cs and through sale of tax-farms, the government, in effect, forfeited its control over the revenue-bearing countryside.

With the decline of the military and financial capacities of the central government, the provinces became increasingly independent. The peripheral provinces, governed by tributary rulers, freed themselves altogether from their subordination to the empire, and many of the core provinces, once directly administered by Baghdad, became peripheral provinces under the control of semi-independent governors. The devolution of provincial powers occurred in two main ways. In one case, Turkish guard officers usurped provincial governorships, denied the responsibilities of deputed administration, and made themselves independent of the central government. For example, Egypt between 868 and 905 came under the control of the Tulunid dynasty. The founder of the dynasty, Ahmad b. Tulun (868–84), was originally a sub-governor of Egypt who took advantage of the weakness of the central government to build up a private slave army, seize control of Egypt's finances, and establish his own dynasty, all the while protected by patrons at the Caliphal court. In other areas, governors chipped away at the prerogatives of the central government. Some ceased to remit tax revenues. Others negotiated a fixed payment in return for their assignments.

Secondly, the decline of central authority allowed for popular resistance to central control. Iraq was the scene of a prolonged revolt of the Zanj slave laborers. In the middle of the ninth century, there was a mass uprising of *ghazis* (frontier soldiers) in Sijistan (southeastern Iran) under the leadership of the Saffarids. The Saffarids took control of Sijistan, Kirman, and northern India, seized Khurasan from the Tahirids, and then took western Iran and invaded Iraq. Though defeated in Iraq, the Caliphate had to recognize their control of Khurasan and most of western Iran. The Saffarid victory displaced the older landowning and administrative elites with ghazi leadership.

Despite the loss of Egypt and Iran, the Caliphate was able to reassert itself. In 900, the Samanid rulers of Transoxania defeated the Saffarids. The Samanid victory was a great gain for the ʿAbbasids because the Samanids represented the same landowning and administrative notables as governed the ʿAbbasid empire, and because they restored cooperation between a major independent provincial dynasty and the ʿAbbasid central government. In 905, the Caliphs also managed to defeat the Tulunid dynasty in Egypt and Syria. The restoration of central authority, however, was only temporary. Since there was no way to stem the disintegration of the bureaucracy, it was impossible for the Caliphate to use its temporary military victories to reorganize the empire. These victories were but a lull in a downward course which became headlong between 905 and 945.

In the early decades of the tenth century, Shiʿism again became the leading form of popular resistance to the ʿAbbasid empire. Ismaʿilism was preached in southern Iraq, Bahrain, Syria, Mesopotamia, Yemen, Daylam, eastern Iran, and North Africa. The Ismaʿilis seem to have had a central directorate which the missionaries recognized as their supreme spiritual authority, but no consistent doctrine was taught. The Ismaʿili mission was adapted to the prior religious convictions and understanding of the persons being proselytized, and the Ismaʿilis initiated their converts step by step, so that the true teachings of the faith were not fully presented to everyone. Moreover, the movement addressed itself to all classes of the population whether peasants in Iraq and Syria, bedouins in Arabia, villagers in Iran, Berbers in North Africa, or the upper classes of eastern Iran.

Ismaᶜili religio-political agitation led to a series of peasant and bedouin rebellions in Iraq, Syria and Arabia, called the Qarmatian movement. Around 900 there were peasant jacqueries in Iraq, and bedouin revolts in Syria and northeastern Arabia which led to the formation of a Qarmatian state in Bahrain. In the 920s the Qarmatians attacked Basra and Kufa and threatened Baghdad, cut the pilgrimage routes, pillaged Mecca, and made off with the black stone of the Kaᶜba. In North Africa another offshoot of the Ismaᶜili movement founded the Fatimid dynasty (909) which conquered all of North Africa and Egypt by 969. The Fatimids claimed to be the rightful successors to the Prophet, not only for their own provinces, but for the whole of the Muslim world. They even adopted the title of Caliph, thus breaking the symbolic unity of the Muslim community. The Fatimids were followed in this respect by the Umayyad dynasty in Spain and by other North African states (see Part II) who thus debased the title, prestige, and legitimacy of the ᶜAbbasid dynasty. Fatimid pretensions challenged not only the political power of the Caliphs, but even the symbolic right of the ᶜAbbasid house to the leadership of the Muslim community.

Shiᶜism also inspired resistance to the ᶜAbbasids in Mesopotamia, where an independent Arab bedouin people under the leadership of the Hamdanid family extended their influence southward from Mosul to Baghdad, westward into northern Syria, and northward into Armenia. In the Caspian province of Daylam, Shiᶜi refugees fleeing ᶜAbbasid persecution converted the local people to Islam. In 864 the Daylam Shiᶜa declared their independence of the Caliphate, forced out the ᶜAbbasid governor, and established an independent state. In the early tenth century, a local Daylamite ruler named Mardawij ibn Ziyar conquered most of western Iran. When he was killed in 937, his empire was inherited by the Daylamite mercenaries in his service, led by the Buwayhid brothers, who established their dominion in the region.

﹐Other governors and warlords also seized extensive territories, and by 935 the Caliphate had lost control of virtually all of its provinces except the region around Baghdad. Administratively and militarily helpless, the Caliphs could only appeal for protection to one or another of the provincial forces, or play them off against each other. In 936, to stave off the enemies pressing in on Baghdad, the Caliphs created the post of *amir ul-umaraᵓ* (General-in-chief) and divested themselves of all actual power save the formal right to select the most powerful of their subjects as chief of state. After a complex many-sided struggle, the Buwayhids took control of Baghdad in 945. The Caliphs were allowed to continue in nominal authority; indeed, the ᶜAbbasid dynasty lasted until 1258, but they no longer ruled; the ʿAbbasid empire had ceased to exist.

The disintegration of the ʿAbbasid empire into a number of independent provincial regimes also implied vast changes in the organization of society. The emergence of a slave military elite and the new iqtaʿ form of administration assured not only the breakup of the empire but the transfer of power from old to new elites. The transformation of the ʿAbbasid social system had begun in the ninth century. Early ʿAbbasid government had been built upon a coalition of the central government staffs with provincial landowning and other notable families. The empire attracted into central government service the scions of provincial families whose contacts and goodwill served to unify the empire and make the central government effective in the provinces. Over time, however, the staffs of the central administration tended increasingly to be composed of the descendants of former scribes rather than be drawn from provincial families. As generations of scribes succeeded each other, Baghdad lost contact with the outlying districts. In time, the bureaucracy became a city-based organization, scarcely connected to the provinces. It ceased to represent the diverse populations of the empire. Moreover, the introduction of tax-farming, which required large investments, favored the interests of merchants grown wealthy in slave, grain and international trade. Bankers who could raise the necessary sums and channel them into state investments became politically ever more important. Thus, a merchant-elite, the product of the empire's fiscal centralization and tax-collecting methods, and a product of the opportunities it offered for worldwide trade, began to displace the scribal class, with its provincial contacts, as the political mainstay of the central government.

The decline of the central government also brought in its wake the destruction of the provincial landowning notability which had originally supported the ʿAbbasid empire. The rise of military warlords and a new capital-city financial and administrative elite, the development of new forms of land tenure including iqtaʿ assignments and tax-farms, brought to the countryside a new elite backed by the waning but still significant powers of the central government to compete with the old provincial notables. In many regions a new class of large land controllers and landowners foisted by central government policies upon the countryside displaced the traditional small-scale landholding notables of the villages.

These extensive political and social changes were accompanied by widespread economic regression. In the course of the late ninth and early tenth centuries, the economy of Iraq was ruined. For more than a century the

Table 4. *Middle Eastern provincial regimes:* ʿ*Abbasid empire and post-imperial era*

	Iraq	Western Iran	Khurasan	Mesopotamia (Mosul)	Egypt	Syria
700	ʿAbbasids 750–945	ʿAbbasids 750–934	ʿAbbasids 750–821	ʿAbbasids 750–905	ʿAbbasids 750–868	ʿAbbasids 750–945
800			Tahirids 821–73 Saffarids 873–900 Samanids 900–99		Tulunids 868–905	
900		Buwayhids 934 – c. 1040	Ghaznavids 999–1040 (in Afghanistan, 961–1186)	Hamdanids 905–91 ʿUqaylids (992–1096)	ʿAbbasids 905–35 Ikhshidids 935–69 Fatimids (969–1171)	Partitioned between Hamdanids in Aleppo 945–1004 and Fatimids in Damascus 978–1076
	Buwayhids 945–1055					

Saljuqs
1055–1194

Saljuqs
1055–1194

Saljuqs
1038–1157

Mirdasids
1023–79
in Aleppo

Saljuq conquest 1078;
Saljuqid states 1078–1183;
crusader states 1099–1291

Ayyubids
1183–1260

Mamluks
1260–1517

Ottomans
1517–1918

Conquest by
Saladin 1169
Ayyubids
1169–1250

Mamluks
1250–1517

Ottomans
1517–1805

Zangids
1127–1222

Nomadic invasions
culminating in
Mongols

Mongols
1258

1000

1100

1200

Caliphate had neglected investment in irrigation and reclamation projects in the most productive of its provinces. Irrigation works in the Tigris region were severely damaged by almost incessant warfare, and large districts became depopulated. The distribution of iqtaᶜs and the creation of tax-farms removed all incentives for maintaining rural productivity. In southern Iraq, the slave rebellions also led to agricultural losses. While the early Buwayhid rulers attempted to restore canals and to reclaim abandoned lands, political instability and fiscal exploitation ruined the countrysides. Iraq, once the most prosperous of Middle Eastern regions, now became one of the poorest, and would not recover its agricultural prosperity until the twentieth century.

Iraq also suffered from declining international trade. The Qarmatian rebellions hurt the trade of the Persian Gulf and the trade between Arabia and Iraq. The disruption of the Caliphate interfered with the international routes which brought goods from the Far East and South Asia to Baghdad for transhipment to the Mediterranean. In the late tenth century, the Fatimid regime helped to promote an alternative international route through the Red Sea and Cairo, which also damaged the commercial prosperity of Iraq.

Other provinces were similarly in decline. Mesopotamia, which had been settled in the seventh century by large numbers of bedouins, suffered economically from the encroachment of pastoralism upon agriculture. As early as the late eighth century, peasants suffering from bedouin raids and excessive taxation were abandoning the land. In the course of the ninth century, there was a general regression of sedentary life under nomadic pressure. The emergence of the Hamdanid dynasty ratified the dominance of pastoral over sedentary peoples. Egypt was also in decline, owing to the exploitation of the peasantry. Iran, however, maintained its high levels of urban and agricultural development well into the eleventh century.

Thus, the breakup of the ᶜAbbasid empire was at once a political, a social, and an economic transformation. It led to the substitution of small states for a single and unified empire. The bureaucratic and small landowning elites who favored centralized government were replaced by large-scale landowners and military lords who opposed centralized administration. The overall decline of the economy also contributed to the weakening of the empire and indeed to the ruin of the prospects for ever recreating a single Middle Eastern imperial regime. The transformation set in motion by the military, administrative, and cultural policies of the empire itself paved the way for its collapse, and the eventual formation of a new type of Middle Eastern state and society.

FROM ISLAMIC CULTURE TO ISLAMIC SOCIETY: IRAN AND IRAQ, 945 – c. 1200

CHAPTER 9

THE POST-ʿABBASID MIDDLE EASTERN STATE SYSTEM

With the breakup of the ʿAbbasid empire it is no longer possible to recount Middle Eastern history from a central point of view. The chaotic history of the period which follows is best understood by distinguishing the eastern parts of the Middle East including Transoxania, Iran, and Iraq, and the western parts consisting primarily of Syria and Egypt. In the east, the first generation of regimes which succeeded to the domains of the ʿAbbasid empire included the Buwayhids in Iraq and western Iran (945–1055), the Samanids in eastern Iran and Transoxania (to 999) and the Ghaznavids in Afghanistan and Khurasan (to 1040). These regimes gave way to a succession of nomadic empires. With the collapse of the ʿAbbasid empire the frontiers between the settled parts of the Middle East and Inner Asia broke down and Turkish nomadic peoples began to infiltrate the region. In the tenth century, the Qarakhanids invaded and took control of Transoxania. In the eleventh century, the Saljuqs seized Iran and Anatolia. Ghuzz and Nayman followed in the twelfth century; the Mongols conquered most of the region in the thirteenth.

In the west, the Fatimids succeeded to the former ʿAbbasid provinces of Egypt and parts of Syria, but the breakdown of political order in Syria permitted a succession of foreign invasions. In the tenth century, the Byzantine empire reoccupied the north and even attempted to conquer Jerusalem. Byzantine armies were followed by Latin crusaders, and finally by Saljuqs, who established a new series of governments. With the establishment of Saljuq-derived regimes the western parts of the Middle East rejoined the stream of eastern developments. Here we shall consider the eastern regimes and reserve discussion of Syria, Egypt, and North Africa for Part II.

Map 4. The post-imperial succession regimes: late tenth century.

Iran and Iraq were the crucial centers for the formation of new state, communal, and religious institutions. In this region, no matter how numerous and ephemeral, Middle Eastern states came to be built around similar elites and institutions. Everywhere the old landowning and bureaucratic elites lost their authority and were replaced by new military and political elites composed of nomadic chieftains and slave soldiers. Everywhere the cohesion of the state came to depend upon slave armies and a semi-feudal form of administration. Each state became the patron of a regional culture. In the Arab provinces poetry, manuscript illumination, architecture, and minor arts developed. In Iran a new regional type of Islamic civilization based on Persian language and arts emerged. At the same time, the ᶜulamaᵓ and the Sufis, who in the earlier imperial age had been the informal spokesmen of Islamic religious values, became the heads of communal organizations. They presided over the conversion of Middle Eastern peoples, organized schools of law, Sufi brotherhoods and Shiᶜi sects, standardized Islamic religious teachings and articulated an Islamic social and political ethic. Despite political fragmentation, a new form of Islamic state, community, and religion came into being.

The Buwayhids, who ruled western Iran, Iraq, and Mesopotamia, pioneered the new type of regime which would govern the Middle East from the tenth to the thirteenth centuries. The Buwayhids left the Caliphs in position as titular heads of state, recognized them as the chiefs of all Sunni Muslims, conceded their right to make appointments to religious offices, and accepted the idea that their own right to govern was based on Caliphal recognition. In practice the regime was based upon a family coalition in which each of the conquering brothers was assigned a province of Iran or Iraq as his appanage. The armies, composed partly of Daylamite infantry and partly of slave Turkish cavalry, were, like the forces of the latter-day Caliphate, organized into regiments loyal more to their own leaders and to their own ambitions for wealth and power than to the state itself. These regiments fought each other and encouraged conflicts among various Buwayhid princes. These conflicts further reduced the powers of the central government as the Buwayhids gave the soldiers the right to collect taxes from designated areas in lieu of salaries. To these new grants the old name iqtaᶜ was often applied. In Kirman, Fars, and Khuzistan, foreign Turkish and Daylamite mercenaries usurped ownership of the land, neglected investments in agriculture, and exploited the peasants for short-term gain. The result was further regression of the agricultural economy of Iraq and western Iran.

In eastern Iran and Transoxania, the Samanid dynasty maintained the ᶜAbbasid system for another half-century. The regime was administered by a

Map 1. The Middle East in the Ghaznavid era: early eleventh century.

FARGHANA

Kashgar

(Syr Darya)

Jaxartes R.

TRANSOXANIA

Samarqand

KHWARIZM

Bukhara

(Amu Darya)

Balkh

Oxus R.

Aral
Sea

OGHUZ

Caspian
Sea

Marw

Mashhad

Nishapur

KHURASAN

Herat

AFGHANISTAN

Kabul

Ghazna

Lahore

MULTAN

SISTAN

KIRMAN

Kirman

Arabian Sea

DAYLAM

TABARISTAN

(Rayy)

Qum

Isfahan

Shiraz

FARS

OMAN

Persian Gulf

BAHRAIN

HADHRAMAUT

Tabriz

Urmiya

AZARBAYJAN

Baghdad

JIBAL

AHWAZ

IRAQ

Mosul

Tigris R.

Euphrates R.

Karbala

ARMENIA

L.Van

Black Sea

Constantinople

ANATOLIA

Aleppo

Antioch

SYRIA

Damascus

Jerusalem

CYPRUS

Mediterranean Sea

Alexandria

Cairo

EGYPT

NUBIA

ARABIA

Medina

Mecca

HIJAZ

Red Sea

YEMEN

Aden

ABYSSINIA

Danube R.

500 km

500 miles

0

Ghaznavids and tributary
states

Qarakhanids

Buyids

Fatimids

Byzantine empire

bureaucratic elite which depended on the local notables and landlord families, while the attached provinces of Sijistan, Khwarizm and Afghanistan were governed by tributary lords or slave governors. Like the ᶜAbbasids, the Samanids were also the patrons of a fabulously creative Islamic culture. In the tenth century, Bukhara emerged as the center of a new Persian-Islamic literature and art as Arabic religious, legal, philosophic and literary ideas were recast into Persian. For the first time the religion and culture of Islam became available in a language other than Arabic.

However, the Samanid regime disintegrated in the tenth century, and their domains in Khurasan and Afghanistan fell to Alptigin, a slave governor whose capital was Ghazna (Afghanistan). Alptigin founded a regime of slave soldiers who conquered and ruled Khurasan from 999 to 1040, and Afghanistan until 1186. They attacked Transoxania and western Iran, plundered Lahore in 1030, and occupied parts of northern India until 1187. Everywhere they destroyed established elites and replaced them with slave soldiers. The Ghaznavids pioneered the first regime in which the slave soldiers dominated the state; the rulers were themselves former slaves. Like the Buwayhids they gave iqtaᶜs to their soldiers, but they also maintained the vestiges of Samanid bureaucratic administration to keep central control over the distribution of landed estates and to collect tributes, booty, and the revenues of crown estates. The Ghaznavids also started the policy of cultivating the support of Muslim religious leaders, by declaring allegiance to the Caliphate, and supporting Islamic education and a Persian literary revival. The slave army, decentralized administration, and patronage of Persian-Islamic culture were henceforth the defining features of Middle Eastern regimes.

By the middle of the eleventh century, Ghaznavid rule gave way to new forces which had their origin in Inner Asia. Inner Asia, between the borders of the Iranian and the Chinese empires, was inhabited by pastoral peoples who raised horses and sheep for their livelihood. These people generally lived in small bands, but they could form confederations to contest control of pasture lands and to attack settled areas. In the course of the seventh and eighth centuries, nomadic peoples on the eastern frontiers of China, prevented from entering China by the T'ang dynasty, began to push westward in search of pasturage. This started a wave of migrations pushing Inner Asian peoples into the region of the Aral Sea, Transoxania, Khwarizm and Afghanistan.

These peoples were organized under the leadership of royal families and other chiefs. They entered regular commercial and cultural relations with the settled areas. From the settled peoples the nomads purchased grain, spices, textiles, and weapons. In return they sold livestock, hides, wool, and slaves.

This lively exchange induced settled peoples to drive trading posts and towns out onto the steppes and involved Inner Asian nomads in the caravan traffic between Transoxania, the Volga and Siberian regions to the north, and China to the east.

Furthermore, nomadic peoples, in contact with Muslim merchants, scholars, and Sufis, were introduced to Islam. Originally they were pagans who believed that the world, animate and inanimate, was peopled by living and vital spirits; and Shamanists who believed that some of their members had the capacity to separate body and soul, and in ecstatic moments, rise up to heaven or descend to the underworld. Knowledge of the realms and powers beyond made the shamans healers and interpreters of dreams. Inner Asian peoples, however, were familiar with Nestorian Christianity, which had been preached on the steppes. Many were Buddhists; some were Manicheans. In the middle of the tenth century, the Qarluq peoples who were to make up the Qarakhanid empire, were converted to Islam. Shortly before the end of the century, Oghuz peoples associated with the Saljuq family were also converted to Islam. Thus, by the end of the tenth century, Turkish-Inner Asian peoples had developed the capacity for large-scale coalitions, had stratified elites and royal institutions, had experience in trade and had adopted the religious identity of the settled peoples. They would enter the Middle East with the political and cultural capacities to become a new imperial elite.

This leveling of political and cultural capacities opened the way for the breakdown of the frontier between steppe and sown. With the conversion of Inner Asian peoples, the settled frontier warriors or ghazis, who had hitherto resisted Turkish incursions on the grounds that they were defending their Muslim civilization against barbarians, gave up the jihad. With the conversion of the Turks, the whole rationale of the ghazi life was subverted and ghazis abandoned the eastern frontiers. Many made their way with the Ghaznavids into India; others moved to the Byzantine frontier. With the frontier defenses in disarray, Qarluq peoples, led by the Qarakhanid dynasty, took Bukhara in 992 and Samarqand in 999.

The Qarakhanid elites were quickly assimilated to the traditions of eastern Iranian-Islamic states. In Inner Asian fashion the new rulers divided their domains into a western Khanate which ruled Transoxania until 1211, and an eastern Khanate for Farghana and Kashgaria. The new rulers of Transoxania accepted the nominal authority of the ʿAbbasid Caliphs and directly or indirectly promoted the spread of Islam among the populace of Transoxania, Kashgar, and the Tarim basin. The Qarakhanids also patronized the formation of a new Turkish literature, based upon Arabic and Persian models, which

Map 6. The Saljuq empire in the late eleventh century.

Qarakhanids
Fatimids
Ghaznavids
Saljuqs
Byzantine empire

0   500 km.
0   500 miles

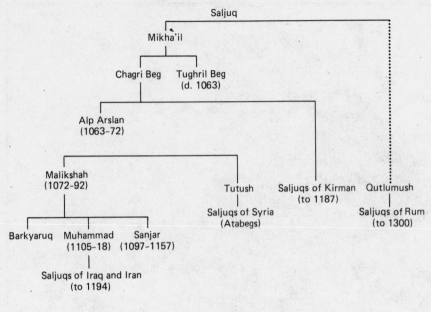

Atabeg dynasties

Damascus	Burids, 1103-54
Mosul-Aleppo	Zangids, 1127-1222
Irbil	Begtiginids, 1144-1232
Diyarbakr	Artuqids (1), 1098-1232
Mesopotamia, Mardin	Artuqids (2), 1104-1408
Armenia (Khilat)	Shah-Armans, 1100-1207
Azarbayjan	Ildegizids, 1137-1225
Fars	Salghurids, 1148-1270
Alamut	Isma'ilis, 1090-1256

Fig. 5. Saljuq period dynasties.

made it possible to recreate the religious and literary content of Islamic Middle
Eastern civilization in Turkish dress. Just as the Samanids had presided over
the formation of a Persian-Islamic culture, the Qarakhanids were the patrons
of a new Turkish-Islamic civilization.

While the Qarluq peoples occupied Transoxania, Oghuz peoples, under the
leadership of the Saljuq family, crossed the Oxus River in 1025. In 1037 they
took Nishapur; in 1040 they defeated the Ghaznavids and became the new
rulers of Khurasan. This was the beginning of a Saljuq empire. The Saljuq
chiefs, Tughril Beg and his brother Chagri Beg, led their followers into western
Iran, defeated the Buwayhids, seized control of Baghdad and the Caliphate in
1055, and were named *Sultans* and rulers of a new Middle Eastern empire from

Khurasan to Iraq. Nomadic bands pushed into Armenia, Azarbayjan, and Byzantine Anatolia, where in 1071, at the battle of Manzikert, they defeated the Byzantine army, captured the emperor, and opened the whole of Asia Minor to Turkish penetration. The advancing Turkish peoples also entered Iraq and Mesopotamia, and extended Saljuq domination as far as the Mediterranean.

Thus the Saljuqs reunited most of the former ᶜAbbasid empire and rekindled the dream of Muslim unity and universal empire. The Sultanate, backed by Persians who had served the Ghaznavids, aspired to recreate a centralized government and an imperial Sultanate. They sought to rebuild bureaucratic forms of administration, and to sponsor Muslim religious activity as the basis of their legitimacy. But while the Saljuqs aspired to a unified Middle Eastern empire, the organizational and institutional capacities needed to sustain a large empire were not available. The economy of Iraq could no longer support a centralized government; bureaucratic administration could not be effectively restored in a society dominated by the military landowners who had replaced the smallholding notables of the late Sasanian and ᶜAbbasid periods.

Moreover, the Saljuq heritage of nomadic concepts and institutions proved detrimental to their imperial ambitions. While nominally unified under the authority of a single Sultan, the Saljuqs had no fixed idea about legitimate succession, and considered the right to rule to inhere in the leading family as a whole. Thus members of the ruling house were entitled to share the family domains on behalf of the tribal subgroups whom they led. Furthermore, tribal tradition cherished the institution of the *atabeg*, who was a tutor or regent assigned to raise a minor prince and govern in his name. In case of the death of his ward, the atabeg was entitled to marry his ward's mother and become a governor in his own right. This was the start of many independent Saljuq-related principalities. Finally, tribal groups were entitled to regions for habitation and grazing. All these aspects of the nomadic heritage worked against imperial unity under the leadership of a single Sultan.

To overcome these inherent liabilities, the Saljuq Sultans adopted Buwayhid and Ghaznavid institutions. They tried to reduce their dependence on the Turkish peoples who had conquered the empire by creating slave armies of Turks, Greeks, Khurasanians, Kurds, Georgians and others. They adopted the Buwayhid practice of granting lands in payment of salaries for soldiers. Nonetheless the unified empire lasted only from 1055 until the death of Malik Shah in 1092. His sons then divided the provinces among themselves, establishing independent dynasties in Iraq, Anatolia, Azarbayjan, Mesopotamia, Syria, Khuzistan, Fars, Kirman, and Khurasan. These proved to be ephemeral regimes, unable to consolidate power or defend their frontiers. The result was renewed nomadic invasions. In the late twelfth century, the Qarakhitay, a Mongol people who had ruled northern China in the eleventh century, took control of Transoxania from the Qarakhanids. Ghuzz peoples, displaced by the Qarakhitay, invaded Khurasan, and in 1153 destroyed the last bulwark of Saljuq resistance to further nomadic incursion from Inner Asia. They were followed by the Naymans and the Mongols. These invasions had long-term demographic consequences. In the eleventh century, Armenia, Azarbayjan, and parts of Mesopotamia which had been Iranian or Kurdish became Turkish. The Greeks of Anatolia were in the process of being converted. Iran, however, experienced an almost complete breakdown of state authority, unremitting nomadic invasions and unprecedented destruction. The ultimate symbol of this chaotic era was the execution of the last ᶜAbbasid Caliph in 1258.

THE SLAVE STATES AND ADMINISTRATION

Despite the numerous and short-lived provincial regimes, between 950 and 1200 a region-wide pattern of governmental institutions took shape. These institutions had their origin in the late ᶜAbbasid concept of the Caliphate, in the use of slave military forces and the iqtaᶜ forms of tax administration, and in nomadic concepts of family and state authority. This new order first took shape in the eastern provinces of the former ᶜAbbasid empire under the aegis of the Buwayhids, the Ghaznavids, and the early Saljuqs.

With the demise of the ᶜAbbasid empire a new concept of governmental authority was devised to accommodate the changing political realities. Though the ᶜAbbasid dynasty continued in office until 1258, the Caliphs no longer possessed exclusive political authority. Other rulers in Egypt, North Africa, and Spain claimed their once privileged title, and they lost effective military and administrative power. They retained, however, a role in judicial and religious affairs in that the Caliph was considered the head of the religious establishment and could suspend the administration of justice and worship. The Caliphs also retained an important moral authority and were able to intervene to temper the policies of the secular lords. Above all, they retained their symbolic standing as heads of the Muslim community; all provincial authorities were considered delegates of the Caliphs and governed by virtue of their designation.

At the same time, however, the conquerors and reigning warlords sought to establish an independent basis for their authority. The Buwayhids, whose power was based upon personal loyalty and lifelong patronage in exchange for loyal service and sworn oaths and vows exchanged among warriors and officials, still sought to generate a public aura of legitimacy. They revived an ancient Iranian titulature including the title *Shah-en-shah* (King of Kings), adopted sonorous-sounding Muslim names, practiced ceremonies to display royal insignias such as the crown and the throne, and cultivated a mystique of kingship suggesting divine selection revealed in dreams, miracles and prophecies. The Buwayhids fabricated genealogies which connected them to ancient Iranian kings, and patronized public works, literature, and the arts as symbols of kingship. Similarly, the Ghaznavids sought recognition by the Caliphs, and implicitly assumed responsibility for the protection of Islam, but also glorified their reigns by the creation of splendid palace architecture and court ceremony, and by the erection of magnificent mosques and minarets as a sign of their service to the faith, to society, and to civilization. Like their predecessors, the Saljuqs professed to be the appointees of the Caliph, to serve Islam, and to support the institutions of religion. The first Saljuq ruler, Tughril Beg, adopted the title Sultan to assert supreme and exclusive power, though the title eventually became the ordinary name for Middle Eastern rulers.

The division of authority and power between Caliphs and Sultans was uncertain. As long as Saljuq Sultans were effective rulers, the Caliphs had a limited political position, but whenever the reigning Sultans were weak, the Caliphs were again tempted to assert their political authority in Baghdad and the surrounding regions. Sultans, though dependent upon Caliphs for recognition of their legitimate rule, sought religious prestige by the patronage of Islamic religious life and by claims, in the Iranian fashion, to hold their authority and responsibility for the protection of their subjects directly from God. Thus, in the course of the post-ᶜAbbasid era, the Islamic aspect of political authority came more and more to the fore. Appointment by the Caliph was considered essential to legitimacy. Responsibility for Islamic institutions became the main justification of political authority, though ancient Iranian and Turkish concepts of rulership did not disappear.

New institutional arrangements as well as new concepts of government authority characterized the post-imperial era. All post-ᶜAbbasid regimes were made up of an alien military elite. The Buwayhid, Ghaznavid, Qarakhanid, and Saljuq regimes were built by ethnic minorities, including mercenaries from the Caspian Sea and nomadic Turkish peoples from Inner Asia. These elites had no ethnic, cultural, linguistic, or historical connection with the peoples they ruled. While a single ruler became head of state it was common for the royal authority and the conquered territories to be divided among the leading families. These alien, commonly nomadic forces were combined with a praetorian guard of slave soldiers organized to offset the military and political influence of the nomadic elites. Slaves were commonly purchased in Inner Asia while still young and then raised at the court of their masters. Every regime followed a policy of pitting slave regiments against each other to maintain the authority of the ruler. Occasionally, as in the Ghaznavid case, the slaves themselves would seize control of the state and the leading generals would become Sultans.

Military slavery and slave states were "peculiar" institutions. However, the translation of the word *ghulam* or *mamaluk* into English as "slave" gives the concept inappropriate connotations. In its Arabic and Muslim sense the slave soldier was the personal property of a master and could be bought and sold. He was a servile retainer depending upon the master for security and support. However, the social position of the slave did not reflect his personal servitude, but rather the status of his master. The slave of the Sultan could be a general or minister of state; the slave of a general, an officer in the army or administration. The concept of ghulam or mamaluk designated a binding personal obedience but not necessarily a humble situation in society. Furthermore, military slaves were eventually manumitted and became freedmen, clients of their former master, which gave them limited legal rights to property, marriage, and personal security. In any case, in the operation of the slave army regiments, legal status was not crucial. Rather it was the exclusive personal loyalty of the slave or client-soldier to his master that was vital to the political supremacy of rulers and to the post-ʿAbbasid organization of states.

The system of state fiscal administration was closely related to military organization. ʿAbbasid government had been based on bureaucratic methods of taxation and disbursements to the court and the army. The central government staffs collected revenues from the countryside and made payments in cash and kind to the officials and soldiers who served the state. The decline of ʿAbbasid administration and of central government, however, meant the progressive substitution of iqtaʿs for bureaucratic methods of administration. With the advent of the Buwayhid dynasty in 945 soldiers for the first time were assigned iqtaʿs in payment for military service. The Ghaznavids adopted a similar system and the Saljuqs extended this means of paying the army from Iraq and western Iran to Khurasan. They also introduced the system into Syria and eventually, under the Ayyubid dynasty, to Egypt.

The terms of assignments varied considerably. In the Ghaznavid and early Saljuq cases a strong central government maintained control over the assigned lands. Assignees were held to their military responsibilities and rotated at the will of the ruler; hereditary succession was not permitted. Central government officials kept registers indicating the value of the tax assignment, the number of troops to be provided, and the terms of service.

In the later Saljuq period, however, the central government was not able to maintain control. Iqtaᶜs became hereditary, and the assignees usurped the land and turned their tax-collecting rights into private property. The assignees not only collected the taxes due, but obtained the rights of landlords over peasants. Hereditary control of rural districts in the hands of military assignees gave rise to virtually independent principalities in Mesopotamia and Syria. In general, Saljuq administrative practices led to a drastic fragmentation of political power, and to the substitution of small principalities for large-scale states. The Saljuq practice of giving appanages to the members of the ruling family, the encouragement to independence inherent in the institution of the atabeg, the decline of central checks on the authority of provincial governors, the widespread assignment of salary iqtaᶜs, and the usurpation of iqtaᶜs tended to disperse political power.

Many scholars have referred to this development as a period of Middle Eastern feudalism. The decline of the ᶜAbbasid empire may be seen as parallel to the breakup of the Roman empire, and the widespread distribution of iqtaᶜs in the Middle East as analogous to the widespread distribution of fiefs in Europe. In fact, however, the Middle Eastern development is different from the European. European feudalism also had its origin in the breakup of a centralized state – the Carolingian empire – and the distribution of land to a multitude of small lords in France in the late tenth and eleventh centuries. However, for the purposes of comparative history the essence of feudalism did not lie in the decentralization of power and in the multiplication of numerous and relatively small principalities, but in certain characteristic institutions governing the relationships between the peasant populations and their lords, and the relationships among the lords themselves.

The relationship of peasant and lord was defined by the manor, an agricultural estate made up of the residence of the lord and his private properties surrounded by the small plots of the peasants. The manor, when assigned to a lord by his overlord as a *benefice*, was a grant of the services of peasants, who became tenants of the lord and owed him economic dues for the use of the land. Benefices, however, were also conceded with immunity from central inspection. Then the lord was made judge and his tenants became his political subjects. Finally, and perhaps most important, they became his personal servitors as well. They could not leave the land and their heirs were automatically serfs. They had to work his lands; they were conveyable by him;

they had to ransom the right to marry and to pass on their property. The economic powers of the landlord and the fiscal and jurisdictional rights of the state were united with the power of the patriarch over his household. The combination of powers defined the manor as a *fief*.

In the twelfth century some hierarchical order was brought into the distribution of fiefs and they came to be considered a concession of a higher lord to one of his vassals in return for military service. All lords of fiefs were in principle the vassals of higher-ranking lords. The king, highest lord of all, was the source of everyone's tenures and jurisdictions. In the feudal system the relationships between lords were not governmental relations of superior to subordinate, but were relations of personal dependence. A vassal was a sworn client of his lord, exchanging service and devotion for protection and support. The relation between vassal and lord, moreover, was a contractual one, in which violation of the agreement on either side resulted in the termination of the contract, the dismissal or withdrawal of the vassal from service, and the return of the fief to the lord. One crucial aspect of this relationship was that disputes were judged in a court composed of other vassals. Every vassal, as part of his obligations and rights, had to attend his lord's court for the settlement of disputes between the vassals and the lord and the judgment of other matters.

Time and the weakness of lords in France favored the entrenchment of vassals in their fiefs. The fief ceased to be granted solely on condition of service but became an hereditary right. This reversed the old priorities. Vassals had formerly been given a fief because they were clients of their lord; but once the fief became an inherited right, it could not properly be taken from the vassal. Eventually all connection with military service and clientage was dissociated from the possession of a fief, which became simply an hereditary governmental jurisdiction and personal property.

As inheritable property, the possession of a fief also defined the social status of the warrior class. A fief meant not only economic rights, personal servants, and governmental jurisdiction, but also conferred the privileges of nobility. Feudalism thus became not only a system which confounded public and private powers, but also a kind of society in which function or occupation, social status, political power, styles of life and culture, and economic wealth were all tied to the possession of land.

The Middle Eastern case was not feudal in this European sense. The collapse of the ᶜAbbasid empire indeed led to a decentralization of political authority, to the emergence of many petty rulers, and to the distribution of land in iqtaᶜs, but the situation differed in several ways. In the Middle East the idea of public authority and the distinctions between governmental powers and personal possessions and rights were never abandoned. However decentralized the powers of government, a subordinate was never considered a vassal, but always a governor or delegate of the ruler. The ruler assigned a post to an official and he could unilaterally, at his pleasure, remove his agent from office. The ruler may have made a bargain with his delegates, but he made no contracts and assured them no right to be consulted in the way that the feudal vassal was entitled to be present in the lord's court. It was possible, of course, and common in the Middle East, for the governor to be a personal dependent of the Sultan, just as the vassal in Europe was a personal dependent, but still the relations were different. The vassal was a free man who contracted his dependency, while dependents in the Muslim world were slaves or freedmen. Also in the Middle East the personal relationship did not substitute for the political relationship but only supplemented it. When a man was appointed as a governor he performed certain duties on the instructions of his political chief. If he was a slave of the ruler, this was added assurance that the governor would serve his master loyally. Not the personal relationship as such, but the designation of the ruler conferred authority on a governor.

A second difference was the distinction between an iqtaᶜ and a fief. In principle, an iqtaᶜ was a grant of the right to collect taxes and to keep them in lieu of salary. The iqtaᶜ was simply a mechanism to decentralize the collection and disbursement of revenues due to the state. In principle, iqtaᶜs were conceded only on condition of military service being rendered, and were valid only for the lifetime of the incumbent. They could be increased or decreased, revoked or reassigned by the ruler. An iqtaᶜ was not a personal property. It could not be sold, leased, or willed. Nor was it a government jurisdiction. It brought no political, judicial, or personal powers over the peasants, who were considered subjects of the state, and not serfs or slaves of the iqtaᶜ-holder. Nor did the possession of an iqtaᶜ confer status privileges or legal rights. The status of the holder had nothing to do with the land, but was determined by his rank and duties as a soldier or administrator and his closeness to the ruler. Finally, iqtaᶜs were not fiefs, in that they could not be assigned to subordinates. All iqtaᶜs were direct concessions of the ruler to his officers. Officers were responsible for bringing men to service in proportion to the size of their iqtaᶜs, but in principle they did not pay their men by granting them iqtaᶜs in turn.

In practice certain powers not originally envisaged in the grants of an iqtaᶜ were usurped. Iqtaᶜs might be made hereditary; often an iqtaᶜ gave the holder enough local wealth to accumulate other properties and eventually, by con-

fusing his iqtaᶜ and other lands, to make the iqtaᶜ hereditary private property
as well. Furthermore, iqtaᶜ-holders might force the peasants to surrender their
land and to become personal dependents. In some cases iqtaᶜ-holders even
acquired governmental powers by usurpation or immunities. When coupled
with private power over land and peasants, this created a fief-like or "feudal"
condition. Such aberrations, even though widespread in the Saljuq period,
never became a recognized system of governmental relations. Muslim rulers
always maintained substantial slave bodyguards and the bureaucratic staffs and
records essential to the enforcement of obligations and the utilization of iqtaᶜs
as a component of state power. While some iqtaᶜs became fiefs, a feudal system
did not consolidate. In the Middle East, then, decentralization entailed no
fundamental institutional changes and could, in changed circumstances, be
reversed. Imperial governments could and would be reconstructed by the later
Mamluk, Ottoman and Safavid empires.

Thus, from 950 to 1200, the unity of the ᶜAbbasid age was lost, and the
successor states were short-lived and provincial in scale. Still, despite the
numerous different regimes, certain uniformities in the political concepts and
institutions of the period may be noted. The supremacy of the Caliphate and
of Islamic principles was universally accepted, while effective political power
was conceded to nomadic conquerors and slave warlords. Similar institutions
of nomadic family practice, military slavery, and iqtaᶜ administration were
developed, with variations, throughout the region. Everywhere the political
concepts and military and administrative institutions adumbrated in the ᶜAbbasid age were integrated with the institutions and concepts of the nomadic
conquerors and worked into a new system of government. In an era of
unprecedented fragmentation of power and instability, these institutions were
everywhere similar. They constituted, via numerous small experiments, an
enduring legacy in the experience of Islamic government.

LOCAL COURTS AND REGIONAL CULTURES: ISLAM IN PERSIAN GARB

The new system of Middle Eastern states also opened a new era in the
development of aristocratic and cosmopolitan Islamic culture. The post-
imperial era reveals two dominant trends. One was the continuation of ᶜAbbasid tendencies toward the bifurcation of Islamic cosmopolitan and Islamic
religious culture, though, in many respects, an intimate relationship was
maintained between the two. While art and architecture, poetry, science, and

certain forms of prose literature were expressions of court, regime, and governing elites, court patronage also extended to Islamic religious studies. Some genres such as history, political studies, and some forms of philosophy and theology were cultivated in both court and private urban milieus.

The second trend was toward regional diversity. While there were substantial continuities with the artistic, literary, and religious precedents of the ᶜAbbasid era, the numerous post-imperial regimes introduced important provincial variations into Islamic culture. As Baghdad dwindled, Samarqand and Bukhara, Nishapur and Isfahan, Cairo, Fez, and Cordova became the new capitals of Islamic civilization. Each had its own government and court, which brought new vitality into the propagation of Islamic culture. In place of the single cosmopolitan court culture each capital generated its own blend of Islamic motifs and a local heritage. Islamic architecture would now differ from region to region. Samanid brickwork, Ghaznavid minarets, Isfahan domes, and Fatimid shrines were emblematic of a new cultural diversity.

Within this diversity there was a tendency to divide the former regions of the ᶜAbbasid empire into two language and cultural zones – a sphere of Arabic and a sphere of Persian literary and artistic culture. In the western regions, including Iraq, Syria and Egypt, and the lands of the far Islamic West including North Africa and Spain, Arabic became the predominant language of both high literary culture and spoken discourse. In the eastern lands, including Iran and Transoxania, Persian became the predominant literary language. Now the poems and epics of the east would be composed in Persian while the odes and quatrains of Baghdad and Cordova would be written in Arabic. However, the two cultural regions would share a common system of religious values and institutions.

In the post-ᶜAbbasid era Baghdad maintained its position as a capital of Islamic religious and Arabic literary studies. In the tenth and eleventh centuries under the influence of Ibn Qutayba's compilations, anthologies of poetry, history, and other subjects were composed. Arabic letter writing and secretarial correspondence became an art of elaborate rhymed prose displaying great technical virtuosity. The *Maqamat* of al-Hariri (d. 1122), done in virtuoso prose and with philological subtlety, was perhaps the greatest achievement of this type. Historical writing also flourished. Histories of the Caliphate were superseded by new world histories, local histories, collections of biographies and historical anecdotes written to entertain and enlighten. Arabic prose literature, however, was profoundly influenced by a new literary criticism which insisted upon formal qualities in writing, manner of exposition, verbal skill and virtuosity and sharply deemphasized novelty or significance in content. Baghdadi poetry continued to follow ninth-century forms. The *qasida* or panegyric and the *ghazal* or lyric were the most important forms of poetic expression. Al-Mutanabbi (d. 965) and Abu al-ᶜAla al-Maᶜarri (d. 1057) were the most important poets. Sufi poetry celebrated ecstatic experiences in the imagery of the intoxication of wine and love.

Persian culture developed in a multitude of places over a period of many centuries but was nonetheless strikingly unified. It has its origins in eastern Iran. In the ninth century Sijistan, Khurasan, and Transoxania were the primary centers of the new Persian literary development. Only in the late tenth and the eleventh century did the new Persian language and literature created in eastern Iran become the literature of western Iran. At the courts of the Tahirids of Nishapur and Marw, the Samanids of Bukhara, and the Ghaznavids, the basis was laid for a new civilization. In later generations Saljuqs, Ghurids, Ilkhanids, and Timurids would produce their own contribution to the common culture. Persian culture not only became the characteristic style of Iran, but had an important influence upon the development of Muslim culture in Inner Asia, India, and Indonesia. Persian literary and artistic styles superseded Arabic as the crucial influence in the formation of the eastern Islamic world.

The development of new Persian was conditioned by two factors. One was the linguistic situation in eastern Iran just prior to the Arab conquests. In late Sasanian times, Parsi (Pahlavi) or Middle Persian, was the official religious and literary language of the empire. Dari was the dialect version of this language spoken throughout much of Iran. Alongside a formal Parsi and spoken Dari there existed a third level of Persian language and literature – a popular oral literature cultivated by poets and entertainers for the amusement of the common people and the local lords, also expressed in a version of Dari. All three levels of Persian would contribute to the formation of the new Persian language.

The second factor was the Arab conquest, which profoundly and unexpectedly changed the linguistic situation. Under Arab rule, Arabic became the principal language for administration and religion. Parsi declined and was maintained largely by the Zoroastrian priesthood in western Iran. The substitution of Arabic for Middle Persian was facilitated by the translation of Persian classics into Arabic. Arabic became the main vehicle of Persian high culture and remained such well into the eleventh century. The Arab conquests, however, helped make Dari rather than Arabic the common spoken language in Khurasan, Afghanistan, and the lands beyond the Oxus River. Paradoxically, Arab and Islamic domination created a Persian cultural region in areas never before unified by Persian speech.

A new Persian evolved out of this complex linguistic situation. In the ninth century the Tahirid governors of Khurasan (820–73) began to have the old Persian language written in Arabic script rather than in Pahlavi characters. At the same time eastern Iranian lords in the small principalities began to patronize a local court poetry in an elevated form of Dari. The new poetry was inspired by Arabic verse forms, so that Iranian patrons who did not understand Arabic could comprehend and enjoy the presentation of an elevated and dignified poetry in the manner of Baghdad. This new poetry flourished in regions where the influence of ʿAbbasid Arabic culture was attenuated and where it had no competition from the surviving tradition of Middle Persian literary classics cultivated for religious purposes as in western Iran.

The new poetry borrowed both from Arabic literary forms and from the tradition of oral Iranian literature. The qasida became the chief form of this new poetry. Based on Arabic rhythmic patterns and rhyming schemes, it was used mainly for panegyrics praising Iranian princes. Oral Persian poetry and the natural features of the Persian language, however, contributed a distinctive rhythmic pattern. The most important early poets in the new vein were the Samanid court poets, Rudaki (d. 940–41), who was considered the father of the new Persian poetry, and Daqiqi (d. *c.* 980), who was especially successful in conveying the qualities of daily life in his poems. Bilingual poets began to translate Arabic poems into Persian and to compose poems of their own in both Arabic and Persian.

The Persian literary heritage of stories, romances, fables, and dynastic histories also formed the basis of a new type of epic poetry. The Samanids revived Iranian interest in the ancient history of kings and in the literary collections of the Sasanian period. From the pen of Firdausi (d. 1020–21 or 1025–26) emerged an immense historical epic. His *Shah-name* or "Book of Kings" contains not only the court histories collected by the Sasanians, but also a cycle concerning the life of the great hero Rustam. For patrons who were attempting to legitimize their rule by virtue of their historic descent from ancient Iranian rulers and their emulation of ancient Iranian virtues, Firdausi composed a new epic preoccupied with problems of sovereignty and feudalism and the war of good and evil. The poem in new Persian language with a moderate influence of Arabic vocabulary became the literary standard of the new era.

Prose was equally important in the development of the new Persian language. The historical works of al-Tabari were translated, and a small number of geographical, philosophic, and scientific works were written in Persian. Commentaries on the Quran, mystical treatises, legal and other religious texts were translated from Arabic. Such works were generally written in a straightforward and utilitarian style without the elaborate literary pretensions of lyric and epic poetry. Still, under the influence of these translations and new compositions, Dari became more and more highly Arabized until the Persian language evolved into "new Persian" – Persian heavily influenced by Arabic vocabulary and syntax.

The new language and literature flourished at other regional courts. Mahmud of Ghazna (988–1030) sought the help of poets to legitimize and justify his regime. Mahmud patronized Unsuri (d. 1039–40), whose qasidas celebrated the court festivals, the changing of the seasons, the royal entertainments, and the pleasures of music and wine. Mahmud was also the patron of Firdausi, the scientist and geographer Biruni, and a host of historians who chronicled the events of the era. Poetry also flourished brilliantly in the Saljuq courts of the eleventh and twelfth centuries. The poets moved from court to court looking for patrons, thus giving continuity and unity to a literary activity carried on in numerous places throughout Iran.

Under Samanid and Ghaznavid patronage the new Persian literature favored several poetic and prose genres. Poetry was commonly composed in one of four metric forms. The qasida was largely the form of court panegyric poetry. The ghazal, a lyric poem of some seven to fifteen lines on the theme of love, expressed private sentiments but in standard images and symbols, such as the nightingale in love with the rose. The rubaᶜi or quatrain, was a variant form of lyric which used a strong verbal pattern to express a single idea, usually a theme of mystical or profane love. The *masnavi* or rhyming couplet was a loose form used for narratives such as tales, romances, legends, and histories. Persian literature was rich in such materials, including the tales of Sindbad, the heroic accounts of the life of Alexander the Great, the fables of *Kalila wa-Dimna*, and the lives of saints. The characteristic product of court poets was, of course, panegyric poems produced for money, sometimes in qasida, sometimes in masnavi form. Characteristically, the poems contained images of the king as ruler over cities, generous in gifts, noble in ancestry. The most important representative of this type of poetry was Anvari (1116–89) who lived at times in Marw, Nishapur, and Balkh. The Persian poets did not aim at self-expression, originality, creativity, or personal insight. Poetry was a public recitation, an adornment for court life, and the main value was virtuosity in

6 An old woman petitions Sultan Sanjar

handling familiar forms and content. Persian poetry was idealized and ab-
stracted – a poetry of masks which wandered, digressing from theme to theme,
so as to be a vehicle of sensuous appreciations or philosophical thoughts.

Other genres of poetry flourished too. In Azarbayjan romantic poetry was
favored. Courtly romances told the story of heroes consumed by physical
passion and heroes who sublimated their love into an idealization of a perfect
but inaccessible woman. Court poetry dwelt on the theme of the lover who
suffers for but a glance, while his only comfort is wine. These were love stories
based not on personal experience but on literary convention. Perhaps the most
important writer in this genre was Nizami (*c.* 1140–1209) who wrote the stories
of Alexander's quest for the water of life; the love story of Shirin and the
emperor Khusraw Parviz, and the story of Majnun, who became mad with
longing for Layla whom he could never attain. Nizami's poetry cultivated a
strong personal emphasis and brought into high Persian poetic tradition a local
and vernacular vocabulary.

Sufi poetry also became important from the twelfth century. Images of
wine, drinking, and love were adopted to express yearning for and love of
God. The most important writer of this genre was Farid al-Din ʿAttar
(1142–1221), who was famous for his histories of the Sufis, his books of
wisdom, the *Language of the Birds* and the *Book of God*, whose principal themes
were renunciation of worldly desires and the soul's journey toward
metaphysical vision. His works describe the forty stations of the visionary and
cosmic passage by which the traveler progressively leaves behind this world
in his quest for the world to come. Rumi (1207–73) was perhaps the greatest
of the Persian mystical poets seeking the identification of the human self with
the divine being. His *Mathnavi* combined impassioned lyrics with gentle story-
telling, merging profane and mystical themes.

The development of this new literature allowed for the translation and
recreation of Baghdadi-style Arabic-Islamic culture in the Persian language.
Thus for the first time Islam was relieved of its association with Arabic. Then,
under the auspices of the Qarakhanids, who succeeded the Samanids as the
rulers of Transoxania, Islamic culture was recreated in Turkish. A new Turkish
language, developed first by translation and then by scholarly and literary
recreation of Persian literature, became the bearer of Islamic civilization
throughout Inner Asia. Islam was becoming a universal religion and civilization in several linguistic media.

An Iranian artistic style also emerged in the Saljuq period. In the ninth
century, under the influence of Chinese wares, Nishapur and Samarqand

produced white pottery decorated with Kufic writing. Pottery decorated with animals, birds, and vegetal elements was made to please an urban middle-class taste, and silver and gold objects were produced in imitation of Sasanian models. Kashan and Rayy produced new types of ceramics. One type was a blue-black or turquoise floral or calligraphic design under glaze; another was a polychrome painting over glaze in which court scenes or historic legends were depicted. The court scenes included hunting, polo, music, and dancing. The objects were illustrated with astronomical signs. Another type of ceramic depicted one or two persons sitting together, sometimes playing a musical instrument, perhaps an illustration of love or meditation. Ceramics were often decorated with texts on the theme of love. Ceramic manufacture of this sort continued until the middle of the fourteenth century.

The history of Iranian architecture followed a similar rhythm. In Iran the most important buildings were the tombs of holy-men and rulers. These were covered by a dome and surrounded by a complex of buildings dedicated to worship and study. The most famous of these was the Samanid mausoleum at Bukhara built before 943 and the Gumbad-i Qabus dated 1006–07. Mosques with cupolas, round minarets, and monumental arcades derived from Iranian precedents were also built. By the middle of the eleventh century the characteristic features of Iranian architecture included brick construction, arcades, stalactite projections and the use of stucco decorated with geometric and vegetal designs to cover the surfaces of large buildings.

Most striking was the development of a new standard form of mosque which spread rapidly throughout Iran in the twelfth century and replaced the earlier Arab-inspired mosque built around a colonnaded courtyard. The new design grew out of elements used in earlier structures, and consisted of a large central courtyard surrounded by arcades, the largest being on the qibla or Mecca side of the mosque and surmounted by a large dome. The mosques were built mainly of brick and with pointed barreled vaults. They also had *muqarnas* (stalactite-like projections) at the junctions between the domes and the substructures. In addition to mosques, numerous tower tombs and mausoleums with cupolas were built in the twelfth and thirteenth century, especially in Azarbayjan and Transoxania.

Royal patronage for poetry, literature, architecture and art indicates a profound integration of the political and religious meaning of artistic composition. Courtly arts, architecture, and literature were intended to adorn, glorify, and justify the position of a ruler and a ruling elite and to inspire obedience. At the same time kingship was justified by the construction and

decoration of mosques, schools, tombs, minarets, and other religious buildings. Similarly the blending of profane and spiritual themes in Persian love
poetry also bespeaks the inseparability of art and literature from religion.

In the post-imperial era the whole concept of an aristocratic culture was
modified by the integration of secular and religious motifs and courtly arts.
Whereas in the early ʿAbbasid era, aristocratic culture maintained a certain
distance from Islam, in the Saljuq era the education of an aristocrat combined
literary or secular studies, be they poetry, belles-lettres, history, mathematics,
or philosophy, with Islam. The secular aspects of the training were designed
to develop the courtier as an elegant stylist, technician, and engineer who was
competent in finance and public works as well as a refined and graceful
adornment to the court of his king; the religious aspects were a moral and
spiritual initiation intended to provide the deeper qualities of soul essential for
the successful pursuit of a worldly career.

Yet from a strictly religious point of view, art remained suspect. Islamic
religious sentiment was iconophobic. Islamic sentiment was opposed to
magic, to the display of riches, to the stimulation of the senses, and to myths
which might rival the Quran. Islamic egalitarian and puritanical sentiment was
also opposed to indulgence in wine, silk, music, and other riches; it opposed
figural images which were a temptation to idolatry. The Shariʿa provided no
legitimation for the main forms of art. Thus, there was an ambiguity inherent
in the courtly and royal sponsorship of art. On the one hand, it was a
contribution to the adornment and glory of Islam, especially in its political and
communal aspect; on the other hand, it threatened Muslim religious beliefs.

This ambiguity informed the whole stylistic development of Islamic art.
While the arts served both a religious and a political purpose, the images and
motifs employed in Islamic art avoided cosmological or mythical meanings.
Sculpture was almost unknown; religious arts avoided the reproduction of
human and animal figures. Islamic arts concentrated on purely visual or verbal
demonstrations of richness, quality of craftsmanship, elaboration of invention
and compositional effects. The unifying element in Islamic art was the repetition of calligraphic motifs, arabesques, or geometric designs; when human
figures were used they appeared as an impersonal detached image rather than
a human presence or hieratic symbol.

By avoiding cosmic myths and minimizing visual forms, Islamic art con-
formed to a Muslim theological and philosophic view of the universe as being
without an overall pattern or even causal interconnectedness. This world,
created ex nihilo and maintained by continuous creation and recreation, is
governed by God's will; its apparent regularity is not intrinsic in nature but

is his bounty. This accords with a human ideal. Moral and spiritual qualities do not correspond to the ontological order of the world but derive from the fulfillment of God's will as expressed in the teachings of the Quran and the tradition. A human life is a sequence of actions correctly performed according to the divine command. Islamic art and literature, then, cultivated for the glory of the court, the ruler, and the elite were expressive of the universal aspects of Islamic religious culture. While they intruded the claims of the ruler upon Islamic religious sensibility, they were close enough to expressing that sensibility to be acceptable as an expression of the genius not only of regimes but of the whole civilization.

CHAPTER 10

MUSLIM COMMUNITIES AND MIDDLE EASTERN SOCIETIES

The transformation of state institutions in the centuries following the collapse of the ʿAbbasid empire was accompanied by an equally far-reaching transformation of local communal and religious life. The establishment of a political elite of nomadic and slave warlords, and the probable ruin of local landowners and other notables, paved the way for far-reaching changes in the organization of town and village communities. The crucial change in this period was the crystallization of new types of Muslim sectarian communities, under ʿulamaʾ leadership, taking the form of Shiʿi sects, Sunni schools of law and theology, and Sufi brotherhoods. Bitter rivalries among them and strong state support for both Shiʿi and Sunni movements hastened their diffusion and rapidly integrated them into the fabric of Middle Eastern town and village societies. At the same time the masses of Middle Eastern peoples were converted to Islam and absorbed into Muslim social bodies. In this era, Islam, originally the religion of a political and urban elite, became the religion and social identity of most Middle Eastern peoples. In the pages that follow we shall first discuss the Muslim socioreligious institutions of the post-imperial age, then the conversion of Middle Eastern peoples, and the emergence of a new form of Islamic society.

The creation of an Islamic communal and religious identity apart from the Caliphate had already begun in the seventh and eighth centuries. In his ideal and early form, the Caliph was the sole ruler of a single community and custodian of both its religious principles and its political interests. From the outset, however, pious believers were disenchanted with the worldliness of the early Caliphal regimes. This disenchantment first expressed itself in Khariji,

Shiⁱi and ⁱAbbasid movements to return the Caliphate to its ideal incumbents. With the victory of the ⁱAbbasids, and the defeat of both Khariji and Shiⁱi aspirations, the political opponents of the Caliphate began to evolve into religious sects.

THE SHIⁱI COMMUNITIES

The Shiⁱa were the earliest example of a new form of sectarian community. As we have seen, the early Shiⁱa were divided into different groups depending upon their theory of the true succession of imams. One of these was the Baghdadi "twelver" community which believed in the imamate of Jaⁱfar's son ⁱAbdallah and his descendants; another was the believers in the imamate of Jaⁱfar's son Ismaⁱil and his descendants. From the time of Jaⁱfar, the Baghdadi community denied in theory, but accepted in practice, the reign of the ⁱAbbasid Caliphs and concentrated more and more on religious teaching. In 873, however, the last of its living imams disappeared, and in 941, direct communication with the imam was lost altogether. The loss of direct divine guidance completely changed the religious and social character of the Baghdadi Shiⁱa. They began to codify their religious and cultural heritage and organize a new communal life to compensate for the missing imam. In the late decades of the tenth century they began the public ritual cursing of Muⁱawiya, the enemy of ⁱAli, made a public holiday of mourning for the death of Husayn at Karbala (*ⁱAshura*), and a day of celebration for Muhammad's adoption of ⁱAli as his successor (*Ghadir Khumm*). Now pilgrimage to the tombs of ⁱAli at Najaf, Husayn at Karbala, and ⁱAli al-Rida at Mashhad became important rituals. The passionate mourning for Husayn, identification with the suffering of the martyr, and the messianic hopes implicit in the commemoration of Karbala gave emotional and religious depth to "twelver" Shiⁱism.

At the same period, "twelver" teaching in hadith, law, and theology also took definitive form. The first formal compilation of Shiⁱi hadith, ritual, and law was made by al-Kulayni (d. 940). Later scholars debated whether their beliefs were based solely on the teachings of the imams or whether *ijtihad*, the exercise of individual judgment in matters of law, was permissible. The concept of the imam was reformulated in neo-Platonic and gnostic terms. The imam came to be understood as an emanation of the divine being, the *ⁱaql al-kull*, the universal intelligence, and thus a bearer of direct knowledge of the secret truths and states of spirituality which lead to the reunion of the soul of man with God. Neo-Platonic concepts put an earlier Shiⁱi understanding of the imams in a new metaphysical context and opened the way within imami Shiⁱism for gnostic as well as ritual forms of religious experience.

By the mid-eleventh century the imami Shiᶜa had created a worldly life lived in perpetual expectation of the world to come. In permanent opposition to the established political regimes, imamism had become a religion of salvation. This salvation might be attained by living in accord with the hadith of the Prophet and the imams, by emotional absorption into their martyrdom, or by gnostic vision and mystical identification with the emanations of the divine being. With the consolidation of their doctrinal beliefs in written form, the development of a public ritual life, and political recognition by the reigning authorities, the Baghdadi Shiᶜa emerged as a sectarian community within the body of Islam.

THE SCHOOLS OF LAW AND SUNNI SECTARIANISM

In the same period Muslim religious leaders, committed to but independent of the Caliphs, arose in Sunni circles. Scholars of Quran and hadith, students of law and theology, formed their own study groups, won popular recognition and established an autonomous authority in religious matters. These independent scholarly groups survived the tenth-century debacle of the imperial Caliphate with their religious authority and prestige intact. The consolidation of the Baghdadi Shiᶜi community and the success of the Ismaᶜilis' missions stimulated the Sunni ᶜulamaᵓ to further institutionalize their practice of Islam. Groups of teachers and disciples, including the schools of law and theology and Sufi brotherhoods, became the focus of important institutional and communal developments.

The schools of law had their origin in the late seventh century as groups of scholars committed to a common legal doctrine and method of legal analysis. By the ninth century the schools were well established as bodies of teachers and students and as agencies for legal administration. From their origins in Medina, Basra, Baghdad and Fustat, they spread throughout the ᶜAbbasid realm. The travels of scholars and students in search of hadith and the appointment of provincial judges with law school affiliations introduced the schools into new provinces. The Hanafi school began in Iraq and was soon established in western Iran and Transoxania. The Hanbali school, Baghdadi in origin, spread to northern Iraq and Syria. Hanbali judges (qadis) were appointed in Damascus and Homs. Hanbalism also had its followers in the important cities of Iran. The Shafiᶜi school first developed in Egypt but, by the tenth century, was established in Syria, Baghdad, and in all of the important towns of western Iran, Khurasan and Transoxania. The Maliki school was concentrated primarily in Egypt and North Africa. The schools were united by the travels of students, who came to study with great masters, and to obtain certificates certifying their knowledge of the books they had learned. Having acquired a wide range of learning from different teachers, a successful student eventually settled down with a single professor, whom he would eventually succeed. This international system of connections was informal but sufficient to maintain the identity of the major schools.

Though the law schools were most important, Muslim theological schools also acquired a coherent social identity. Though they did not have judicial and administrative functions, the Muᶜtazila and Ashᶜaris became important religious movements. The Karrami movement, which combined theological tenets and Sufi practices, appealing mainly to the lower classes, was influential in Khurasan, Transoxania, and Afghanistan.

In the course of the tenth and eleventh centuries, the early law schools found a new mode of organization. The *madrasa*, or college, came into being as a center for legal studies. A madrasa was a building used for study and as a residence for teachers and students, commonly provided with a library. Madrasas were also endowed with permanent sources of income, such as land, or rent-bearing urban property, set aside in perpetuity. These *waqf* paid the salaries of the faculty and stipends for students. By giving such gifts donors could preserve their property intact against fragmenting inheritance laws and appoint their heirs as administrators. Through salaries and the administration of endowments, the ᶜulamaᵓ rose to the position of a rentier class.

The madrasa, as a formally organized college, probably had its origins in Khurasan. Here Muslim law was originally taught in private homes, which were then converted into hostels for traveling scholars and students. In Baghdad, the madrasa was organized by combining the mosque in which the teaching was carried out, the *khan* or boarding house for students, private libraries, and the practice of community financial support. The madrasa thus consolidated informal legal instruction into an institution with a physical center and permanently endowed funds, and made possible professional full-time study of Muslim law and the expanded training of cadres of Muslim legal teachers and administrators.

In educational terms, the madrasa was an informal school. It did not have a program of specialized degrees or a graded curriculum. Rather, a madrasa was the preserve of its professor; the students were certified only to teach the texts they had studied with the master. The relationship of teacher and student was intensely personal, for the master communicated not only specialized learning but religious insight. The personal relation of master and disciple, which could be traced generation by generation back to the Prophet himself, was the primary vehicle for the communication of Muslim truths.

The curriculum of the madrasas was therefore variable. Most, however, were academies of law, teaching the particular version of the professor's own *madhhab* or school. Madrasas commonly taught the related subjects of Quran, hadith and Arabic grammar; some professors taught theology or Sufism. In all cases there was an intense consciousness of the importance of training Muslim scholars to combat Shiᶜism and Ismaᶜilism. Madrasas were not only colleges, but centers for religious propaganda and political action.

The madrasa soon became the standard Sunni Muslim way for the organization of religious and legal instruction. It spread from Iran throughout Samanid and Ghaznavid domains and then westward with the Saljuq conquests. Nizam al-Mulk, the leading vizier of the early Saljuq period (1063–92), endowed Hanafi and Shafiᶜi madrasas in all the major cities of the empire and made it the state's policy to support organized Muslim religious scholarship. The Hanbalis adopted the madrasa form of instruction early in the twelfth century.

As the madrasas became the centers of the schools of law, the schools themselves were becoming popular religious movements. Originally, each madhhab was built around a core of scholars and judges and their students, court functionaries, wealthy patrons and local followers. Progressively, the leadership of the schools was extended to the masses, beginning with charitable, educational and judicial services, and carrying on to informal social and political leadership.

The Hanbalis were the first to convert informal, popular influence and sympathy into a sectarian movement. As we have seen, the Hanbalis resisted the efforts of the ᶜAbbasid Caliphate to promulgate religious doctrine. They opposed al-Maᵓmun's claims to authority, and held that while obedience was due to the Caliph in matters of state, authority in religion rested with the scholars of Quran and hadith. Preaching to their followers among former ᶜAbbasid soldiers and residents of the Harbiya quarter of Baghdad, the scholars mobilized popular support. They asserted both a religious authority and a social leadership independent of the state. They created within the Sunni milieu the first Muslim community apart from the Caliphate.

The formation of Sunni as well as Shiᶜi sectarian movements contributed to the spread of religious factionalism. Throughout the ninth and tenth centuries, Hanbali preachers continued to arouse popular demonstrations for or against Caliphal policy. The Hanbalis emerged as a vociferous popular party determined to enforce their own religious views. They organized groups of vigilantes, who attacked their opponents, and suppressed such immoral activities as wine drinking and prostitution. While the Shiʿa organized public celebrations of their faith, the Sunnis similarly commemorated the reigns of the Rashidun Caliphs, Muʿawiya and other symbols of Sunni identity. Hanbali preachers led anti-Shiʿi riots, and opposed the Muʿtazili and the Ashʿari theological schools. Between 1068 and 1072 Baghdad was rocked by the affair of Ibn ʿAqil, a scholar who was forced by public demonstrations to give up his Muʿtazili colleagues and renounce his earlier religious views in favor of a strict Hanbali creed. For over a century Baghdad was frequently in turmoil because of the battles between the religious factions.

A similar evolution of schools of law into popular factions took place in eastern Iran. In the tenth and eleventh centuries, the Shafiʿis, Hanafis, and other religious schools became the basis of factions. Hanafi, Shafiʿi, Karrami, and Ismaʿili groups struggled for local social and political influence. The Hanbalis of Baghdad and the Shafiʿis or Hanafis of many Iranian towns had become ʿasabiyat, exclusive and mutually hostile small communities. In this guise, the schools resembled the neighborhood, lineage, or other parochial bodies into which Middle Eastern towns had always been divided. Religion now superseded tribal or quarter identifications.

The history of Nishapur in the eleventh and twelfth centuries is the best known example of the law schools as factions. In Nishapur the Hanafi school was built around leading merchant, official and ʿulamaʾ families who controlled the judiciary of the city, important waqf revenues, madrasas, and mosques. Their main opponents were the Shafiʿis, who controlled most of the teaching positions in the madrasas, and also the revenues of important endowments. The Shafiʿi following, however, was broader than the Hanafi, in that the Shafiʿis were united with Ashʿaris and Sufis and seemed to have had mass support. The antagonism of the two schools of law spread from disputes over control of teaching and judicial positions to competition for governmental support and to pitched battles in which large segments of the town and the surrounding rural populace were mobilized to fight for their group. As a result, Nishapur was physically and socially destroyed by the middle of the twelfth century.

Thus in many places the schools of law developed from scholarly groups and legal administrative agencies into communal movements. In permanently endowed madrasas the ʿulamaʾ as a body found institutional means to perpetuate their system of religious and legal training. The schools also mobilized popular support behind the leading judges and teachers.

SUFI BROTHERHOODS

The development of the Sufi movement in many respects paralleled the development of the schools of law. From the tenth to the fourteenth century Sufism reached maturity as a social movement, and completed the development of a Sufi metaphysics and the integration of Sufi thought and practice with other forms of Islamic belief and worship. From their origins until the middle of the tenth century, Sufis had attained coherent identity as one among the many Muslim groups pursuing the truth of Islam. While Sufism was highly individual, Sufi meeting-houses gave them a collective identity. *Ribats* were originally residences for Muslim warriors scattered along the frontiers of the Byzantine empire in North Africa; on the frontiers of eastern Iran they accommodated the volunteers for the holy war. On the model of frontier ribats similar meeting-houses were founded at Abadan, Damascus and Ramla in the course of the eighth century. In imitation of Christian monks, there were grottoes in Khurasan. Ordinarily Sufis met in private houses.

The term khanaqa appeared in the late ninth century and came to be widely used for Sufi residences in Khurasan and Transoxania. The word was applied to residences for migrant individuals without a shared affiliation to a particular master, but the khanaqa was adapted to more sectarian purposes by the mystic and theologian Muhammad ibn Karram (806–69), a student of hadith, and an ascetic preacher in southern and eastern Iran who taught a God-fearing way of life based on mortification of the flesh and pious devotion to God's will, and a theological doctrine emphasizing an anthropomorphic view of God, taking literally the Quranic usages which suggest that God has substance and a body. Ibn Karram won a large lower-class following in Transoxania, Afghanistan, and eastern Iran, and built khanaqas as centers of missionary activity.

Other Sufi masters followed his example. Shaykh Abu Ishaq Ibrahim al-Kazaruni (963–1033) cultivated a large following in his home district in western Iran, proselytized amongst the population of his area, and converted numerous Zoroastrians and Jews to Islam. His warriors also fought on the Byzantine frontier. They built some 65 khanaqas in southwestern Iran as centers for teaching, missionary activity and as places to distribute charity to the poor. His near contemporary Abu Saᶜid b. Abi Khayr (967-1049), who was born and died in the region of Nishapur, was the first Sufi master to set up rules for worship and a code of behavior and to regulate the communal life of the khanaqa. Thus, by the late eleventh century the khanaqa served the needs both of unorganized individuals and groups devoted to a particular master. By the end of the eleventh century, in addition to their devotional, instructional, and missionary functions, the khanaqas came to be used as tombs for venerated Sufi masters and became the object of pilgrimage by ordinary believers.

From the tenth to the thirteenth centuries important changes in Sufi concepts also reinforced the trend toward coherent religious groups. A changed concept of the relations between masters and disciples paved the way for a more formal type of organization. In the ninth and tenth centuries a Sufi novice was considered to be someone who took lessons from his master. By the eleventh century he was a disciple who owed total obedience, just as any man owes obedience to God. The authority of the master was vastly enhanced. In religious matters he was considered not only a teacher but a healer of souls, and a repository of God's blessing. These new and deeper bonds were the basis of a more lasting loyalty of disciple to master and the basis for the perpetuation of the authority of miraculous teachers over the generations.

New forms of Sufi ceremony emerged to symbolize the new relations. In the earlier era a student received an *ijaza* or license to teach the subject he had learned from his master. In the new era, the *khirqa* or cloak of the master was conferred upon him and ceremonies of initiation were instituted to induct disciples of the same master into shared vigils, litanies, devotions, and other forms of worship. With the elaboration of the master's authority the spiritual genealogy of masters and disciples also became important. In the course of the twelfth and thirteenth centuries, chains of authority or *silsilas* reaching from the present masters across the generations to ʿAli and to the Prophet were formulated. The authority of Sufi teaching in any given generation was guaranteed by a chain of contacts which led from the present to the moment of revelation. Initiation into Sufism bore with it a spiritual power derived directly from the original revelation of Islam.

Thus the conceptual basis was set for the formation of the Sufi *tariqat*, or religious brotherhoods. The origins of the tariqat are shadowy, but we may surmise that the concept crystallized in the thirteenth and fourteenth centuries in the minds of the disciples of the great twelfth- and thirteenth-century masters. These Sufis had defined their pious methods and collective organization, and attributed their practices and doctrine to a famous earlier shaykh or originating master, and recognized that all of the Sufis of a given generation who shared a common spiritual ancestor were in principle related to each other. The major Sufi orders were organized in the names of masters who were recognized as the intermediary transmitters of Sufi teaching and the founders of later families of Sufi brotherhoods. They were thought to have appointed the *khalifas* or delegates who established new chapters of the order and who would in turn appoint their lieutenants and successors to carry on the work of the tariqa.

Fig. 6. The early tariqat and their founders.

The known historical facts about the founding of these orders are few. The Suhrawardi order attributed to Abu Najib al-Suhrawardi was actually founded by his nephew ʿUmar al-Suhrawardi (1145–1234). ʿUmar was appointed by the Caliph al-Nasir (1180–1225) to be the head of a group of ribats founded in Baghdad. ʿUmar wrote a treatise on the behavior of Sufi novices and thus established a "monastic" rule. The Shadhili order, which was introduced into Egypt in the late thirteenth century, began in Morocco with the teachings of Abu Madyan (d. 1197). His student al-Shadhili (d. 1258) moved to Alexandria in 1244, gathered followers and disciples, and created the particular pattern of devotional activities, social life, and avoidance of close relations with government authorities that ever after characterized the order. The Qadiriya was at first a local chapter centered around the tomb of ʿAbd al-Qadir al-Jilani in Baghdad, but a hospice for Qadiriya was founded in Damascus at the end of the fourteenth century. Later the order spread throughout the Arab world and sub-Saharan Africa. The order named after Najm al-Din Kubra was in fact organized in Iran by al-Simnani (d. 1336) and spread widely in Khurasan, Khwarizm, and Transoxania. Al-Simnani was the founder of a movement which emphasized the unity of the Islamic community. His following embraced both Sunnis and Shiᶜas, venerated the family of the Prophet, including ᶜAli, along with the great Sunni masters, and appealed to Buddhists and pagans to convert to Islam. Sufism, in the view of this order, was an all-embracing form of the Muslim religion which transcended sectarian divisions.

By the end of the fourteenth century the Sufi tariqat were well established throughout the Middle East. In eastern Iran and Transoxania, the Kubrawiya was most important. In Iraq the Suhrawardiya was dominant. In Syria, the Qadiriya, and the Rifaᶜiya were well established. In Egypt the Rifaᶜiya, the Qadiriya, the Shadhiliya, and the Badawiya were widespread. Sufi orders in Egypt enjoyed government patronage, the attendance of Sultans at Sufi devotions, and a considerable popular following.

Thus from the tenth to the fourteenth centuries there had been a slow consolidation of organized Sufi institutions. Small discipleships had formed; the khanaqa became a focus of collective life; a concept of tariqa or brotherhood was enshrined. Everywhere, however, the individual Sufis with their followings of disciples and lay believers were the basic units of Sufism. The tariqat served only to bring some uniformity into the teachings of the myriad of local Sufi masters and saints. Sufism was the shared culture of individual teachers rather than a highly organized religious and social movement.

Nonetheless, the influence of Sufi teaching was considerable. In each community where Sufis penetrated they represented, in competition with the schools of law and theological sects, an alternative form of social affiliation. Sufism was much more important on the frontiers of Islamic expansion in North Africa, Inner Asia, and India. The alliance of Sufism with the ghazi commitment to holy war and its tradition of missionary activity made the new and peripheral rather than the historic regions of Islamic influence the centers of Sufi expansion. Still, Sufis were received at the court of rulers and were called upon to give their blessings and counsel, and were allowed to intercede on behalf of their constituents. Sufis also became integrated into the Shafiᶜi and the Hanbali schools of law, where they exerted a profound influence upon Islamic religious and legal ideals. Most important, they exerted a vast influence upon the common people. The Sufi khanaqa was a center of public preaching, of religious instruction, and of shared worship for lay followers. Insofar as the khanaqa was also the tomb of a venerated saint, Muslims made pilgrimages to worship, to be cured and to receive spiritual blessing and material aid. Worship at the tombs of saints, increasingly widespread in the thirteenth and fourteenth centuries, would become the main vehicle of the Sufi form of Islam.

MUSLIM RELIGIOUS MOVEMENTS AND THE STATE

The religious and social importance of the Sunni schools of law, theological sects, Shiʿi communities, and Sufi brotherhoods made them of utmost importance to Middle Eastern military regimes. They were not only of local political consequence, but they were tied into a Middle Eastern-wide political and cultural struggle between competing forms of Islam. In the course of the ninth and tenth centuries the rise of Shiʿism posed throughout the Middle East a challenge to Sunni dominance. Shiʿi regimes came to power everywhere. The Buwayhids, the Hamdanids, and the Qarmatians were officially Shiʿa. The Buwayhids authorized, patronized, and guided the organization of the imami community in Baghdad. The Fatimids were the sponsors of Ismaʿili missions that reached from North Africa to Khurasan, Afghanistan, and Transoxania. The triumph of the Shiʿi dynasties and general political and social turmoil also permitted a literary and cultural renaissance in which Hellenistic, philosophic, and secularist views flourished. In response to these challenges the Sunni ʿulamaʾ were led to strengthen their concept of Islam, in cultural terms by a more rigorous definition of its content, and in social terms by the organization of a more closely knit community life.

Baghdad in the tenth and eleventh centuries became the focus of Sunni-Shiʿi antagonism. The Caliph al-Qadir (991-1031) took the lead in the Sunni struggle against Shiʿism and tried to organize a Sunni religious mission to restore the true practice of the faith. He helped the Sunnis set up their own festivals to rival the Shiʿi celebrations; by official proclamation he made Hanbalism the official Muslim position. In an address of 1019 the Caliph condemned allegorical explanations of the Quran and the thesis that the Quran was created, and proclaimed the excellence of the first four Caliphs in order of historic access to their office. His successor, al-Qaim (1031-75), renewed the effort to define Islamic orthodoxy in Hanbali terms and to mobilize popular support for a restoration of Caliphal supremacy in religious and political affairs. In reaction to Shiʿism the Sunni revival of the eleventh century aspired not only to the definition of orthodoxy but to the restoration of the Caliphs as the heads of the Islamic community.

The advent of the Saljuqs in 1055 profoundly changed the relations between sectarian religious communities and the state. From the very beginning of their conquests in Khurasan, the Saljuqs became embroiled in religious controversy and soon devised their own policy of alliance with selected Islamic movements. The Saljuqs espoused an uncompromising anti-Shiʿi policy, and helped to suppress Shiʿi activities throughout their domains. Their hostility was motivated partly by rivalry with the Fatimids and partly by Sunni anxiety over subversion by underground Shiʿi movements. The virulence of Saljuq opposition to Shiʿism, however, cannot fully be explained by the magnitude of the Shiʿi threat. While many Middle Eastern regimes were officially committed to Shiʿism and many localities were under Ismaʿili control, Shiʿism never had sufficient popular support to be a real threat to the Saljuqs. Saljuq opposition to Shiʿism was nonetheless vigorously pressed to create a sense of Sunni solidarity and to promote the legitimacy of Saljuq states in the name of the true Islam.

Saljuq policy also evolved a position vis-à-vis the competing Sunni schools. First, the Saljuqs intervened in the Hanafi–Shafiʿi and Hanbali–Ashʿari struggles, favoring the Hanafi school of law and forcibly suppressing Shafiʿi and Ashʿari activity. In 1063, however, Nizam al-Mulk, newly appointed wazir, reversed his predecessor's policy in favor of moderate support for Shafiʿi and Ashʿari teaching without penalizing the other Sunni schools. Nizam al-Mulk proposed to calm Sunni religious quarrels and create a sense of unity among the Sunni groups by patronizing both the Hanafis and the Shafiʿis. The major instrument of this policy was the construction and endowment of madrasas in every major city of the Saljuq domain. Saljuq support for madrasas would create a broad base for the education of Sunni religious teachers and for Sunni missions to the general populace. Under state sponsorship a broad Sunni front to oppose Fatimid and Ismaʿili claims would be formed. At the same time Nizam al-Mulk probably aimed at state control over the Sunni movement, and meant to use the major legal and theological schools as a vehicle for political influence over the masses.

From the time of Nizam al-Mulk, state support for Sunni religious activity was a lasting part of Saljuq policy. After his death in 1092, Saljuq policy oscillated between patronizing the Hanafis and patronizing the Shafiʿis. Until the middle of the twelfth century the Hanafis were most in favor, but in the second part of the century the Hanbalis and the Shafiʿis recovered and were endowed with new colleges. The late twelfth century, however, brought a shift from sponsorship of individual schools to equal recognition of the four major schools of law. Alongside the madrasas which taught the legal doctrine of each of the four main schools a new type of college, called *Dar al-Hadith*, was created to teach the sayings of Muhammad. The Dar al-Hadith, however, was not assigned to a particular school of law but represented the common Muslim interest in the legacy of the Prophet. In 1234, as a further expression of a pan-Sunni policy, a new madrasa was founded in Baghdad to house all four of the law schools. In the course of the century and a half, government policy had moved from identifying itself with particular sectarian movements to an effort to define Islamic orthodoxy as including all of the major schools of law and the most prominent theological groups.

The Saljuqs also understood that the khanaqa was as important a center of religious instruction and popular influence as the madrasa and undertook to sponsor and endow khanaqas as well as colleges. They brought the institution to Baghdad, where these centers were known as ribats. Ribats housed scholars of hadith, legists, and theologians, and were, in particular, residences for preachers engaged in religious and political propaganda on behalf of the Saljuq Sultans.

Thus, by sponsorship of madrasas, schools of law, theological groups, and khanaqas, Nizam al-Mulk initiated a state policy of seeking legitimacy and political stability by patronage and sponsorship of Sunni religious institutions. State support and sponsorship of religious schools also helped overcome factional antagonisms and helped establish a uniform system of legal organization and education. The madrasas and khanaqas served as an organizational base for legal teaching, as a vehicle for providing financial support for Muslim religious scholarship, as centers for the training of religious and administrative cadres, and as bases for the conversion of Middle Eastern populations as well as for missionary activity to establish the universal acceptance of Sunnism as the commonly held form of Muslim belief and community. In return for Sunni support and legitimation of state policy, the Saljuq regimes helped to realize the Sunni ambition for a universal Muslim society.

ISLAMIC INSTITUTIONS AND A MASS ISLAMIC SOCIETY

The institutionalization of Shiʿi sects, Sunni schools of law, and Sufi brotherhoods was but one aspect of a larger process by which Middle Eastern communities were absorbed into an "Islamic" type of society. Equally important were broad historical developments which made Islamic religious leaders and organizations the basis of organized community life throughout the region.

The translation of Islamic institutions into an Islamic type of society depended upon the mass conversion of Middle Eastern peoples to Islam. Curiously, mass conversion was not achieved in the age of the ʿAbbasid empire. The empire which created the first forms of Islamic literary, religious, and court culture never succeeded in making Islam the religion of the majority of Middle Eastern peoples. Despite numerous conversions, substantial Christian populations remained in Iraq, Mesopotamia, Syria, and Egypt; substantial

Zoroastrian populations survived in Iran. While there were conversions among individuals who migrated to the Arab capitals and became Muslims, as late as two centuries after the Muslim conquest the Muslims remained an elite minority among non-Muslim peoples.

The first mass conversion of a Middle Eastern population took place in Egypt in the middle of the ninth century. A massive Coptic peasant rebellion was crushed in 832. In the wake of the rebellion bedouins attacked Christian villages; money was extorted from the church. Under pressure of communal defeat, bedouin attack, and the impotence of the church, Christian loyalties were subverted. In regions which had been partially settled by an Arab population, such as the eastern delta and parts of upper Egypt, mass conversions to Islam took place. Other parts of Egypt, however, especially the western delta region, remained Christian.

Only with the breakup of the ᶜAbbasid empire and the vast upheavals attendant upon the destruction of the established elites, did the masses of Middle Eastern people convert. Extensive warfare, rural insecurity, and the decline of the old elites and village communities, allowed large numbers of Persians to convert to Islam. Sufi missionaries seem to have played a crucial part. In western Iran Shaykh al-Kazaruni and his followers converted numerous villages. Islamic missionary activity also had substantial success in eastern Iran, where Muᶜtazili and Karrami missions were successful in making converts. The Caspian regions were converted by Shiᶜa fleeing from Baghdad. By the end of the tenth century Islam was the dominant religion in Iran. Sufis pushed out into Inner Asia where they converted Turkish peoples. By the eleventh century, as best we can tell from exceedingly fragmentary evidence, Islam was no longer the faith of a dominant minority, but was the majority faith of Middle Eastern peoples living in Iraq and Iran. In northern Mesopotamia and Syria, however, the bulk of the population remained Christian until the late thirteenth century.

In this era of upheavals, old Muslims and new converts found a basis for a reorganized communal life in the institutions of the Islamic religion. Just as Islam had served in the imperial era to define the identity of the political aristocracy and the dominant Arab-Muslim urban society, so in the new era it was progressively adapted to express the communal identity of masses of Middle Eastern peoples. In the course of the tenth to the thirteenth centuries Islamic communal groups and religious leaders were able to take charge of Middle Eastern communities, and infuse them with Islamic identifications. This was possible because old landowning and office-holding notables lost their power to new military regimes dominated by slave soldiers or migratory nomadic chiefs. The new military lords were clients and sometimes slaves, foreign in race and language, and had no historic ties to the societies they conquered. They could restore provincial government but they could not take the place of the old official and landowning classes, and offer, on a local level, the protection, advice, and assistance that the powerful traditionally offered the poor. Faced with military elites unfamiliar with local traditions, the ʿulamaʾ emerged, on the basis of religious prestige and educational and judicial authority as a new communal notability. The ʿulamaʾ married into established merchant, administrative, and landowning families, and merged with the older local elites to form a new upper class defined by religious qualifications.

The ʿulamaʾ assumed the functions as well as the status of the former elites. They took charge of local taxation, irrigation, judicial and police affairs, and often became scribes and officials in the Saljuq succession states. The ʿulamaʾ thus developed from a purely scholarly and religious elite with judicial functions into a broad social and political elite. In many instances, given the relative instability of military regimes, they became the effective representatives, and even governors, of their towns and territories. Like tribal chiefs, local landowners, princes and military governors, leading ʿulamaʾ families sometimes ruled their towns in de facto independence of the provincial military regimes. The families descended from Abu Burda governed Shiraz for centuries; the Mikalis family, as *ruʾasaʾ* of Nishapur, and the Burhan family of Bukhara provided local governors who collaborated with the various nomadic regimes which successively conquered eastern Iran and Transoxania. The acceptance of this new authority was, of course, a reversal of the earlier ʿulamaʾ resistance to involvement in politics and is explained by the dramatic breakdown of the Caliphate.

The position of the ʿulamaʾ notables was not based upon holding appointed office, though this was sometimes one of their prerogatives, nor upon representation of corporate interests. Their real authority was personal and was grounded in the relationship of individual religious teachers to their disciples and followers. In the case of a Shiʿi imam, the head of a school of law, or a Sufi shaykh, the personal relationship of layman to scholar, of worshiper to preacher, of sectarian to religious guide, of disciple to master, was crucial. Since authority derived essentially from achieved learning and reputation for sanctity, there was no central or church-like agency to ordain, license, or validate religious leadership. Religious authority was validated by the recognition of other scholars and ordinary people. The influence of the ʿulamaʾ notables with the general populace was further reinforced by the exercise of patronage, which bound ordinary people to the educated elite. The binding force in society was not a structure of offices and institutions, but the networks of personal ties assumed under general commitment to upholding family, religious community, and umma as the essential expressions of an Islamic social order.

At the same time the Shiʿi sects, Sunni schools of law, and Sufi brotherhoods served as a cadre for the exercise of communal and social authority. The schools of law were particularly important as channels of local political organization. The schools, made up of study groups, teachers and students, interested members of the community, and their patrons, and legal functionaries such as deputies, witnesses, orderlies, and clerks grouped around the important judges, formed an organized party or faction. The ʿulamaʾ had close ties to merchant families, bureaucrats, and officials. Their popular following was often found in the quarters where their mosques and schools were organized, among the people who sought their advice and protection. By the eleventh century, everyone was considered to be a member of one of the four schools of law on the basis of birth or the traditional membership of his quarter, city or region. The common people belonged in that they looked to one or another of the schools for authoritative opinions on what were the divinely commanded rules of behavior. They went to the scholars of the law for judgments on their duties in uncertain cases, and to the witnesses and judges for commercial and legal matters. Thus, the schools of law had ramified social contacts and were the focus of solidarity and the basis of ʿulamaʾ leadership.

While Muslim religious bodies became the usual organizing cadre for local communities, they were by no means exclusive. Other small-scale or primary groups maintained their political or social importance. Small primary groups including families, or villages and town quarters defined by family, ethnic, or sectarian homogeneity, or by shared employment in some craft or trade remained active forces. Young men's gangs, called *fityan*, *ʿayyarun* or ghazis, made up of unmarried men of working-class background, separate from family, tribal, or craft organizations, espoused an ethic of bravery in sports and fighting, and played a complex role in the social life of towns and villages. The ʿayyarun of Iraq and Iran were often gangs of criminals who sometimes served as strong-arm men for local notables, quarters or religious sects, sometimes acting as criminal predators, and sometimes defending their home communities. The ghazis of rural eastern Iran were also an important element in local resistance to nomadic invasions. Most likely an already venerable culture of masculine honor and social sanction for revenge helped reinforce the tendency to factionalism and feuds in Middle Eastern town and village communities.

The existence of well-organized solidarity groups made Middle Eastern towns factious and quarrelsome places, but also gave them a limited capacity for organized resistance to nomadic and slave regimes.

Towns and villages were thus segmentary societies made up of numerous groups, defined by neighborhood, or by religious sect, and sometimes by occupation, but never by economic class. This is not to deny that the notables formed an elite stratum or that lower-class groups could be independently organized. In Iranian towns the patriarchates, consisting of officials, professionals, landowners, and merchants, tended to dominate lower-class groups, but by and large, social and political groups were organized in communal rather than in class terms. As a consequence of these strong internal communal and parochial ties, villages and towns were rarely unitary corporate bodies.

In fragmented societies, the Muslim schools of law and Sufi brotherhoods were often parochial and factional bodies struggling for control of judicial offices and teaching positions, and often involved in pitched battles with rival schools over doctrine, prestige, and control of the streets. In other cases, the schools of law and the Sufi brotherhoods could serve to integrate disparate town populations and bring factional groups into a more embracing Muslim community. They often brought the residents of a town and the surrounding district into the same community; moreover, they transcended town, district, or local boundaries. The schools of law and tariqat were organized across the territories of states and empires; and beyond that they existed as Muslim worldwide fraternities of the students and scholars who adhered to the same body of law, and the same principles of legal theory. Transcending loyalties to any particular place, a sense of shared membership in a school of law or a Sufi brotherhood, and a sense of the umma as a whole, was an important part of social consciousness. United by the travels of ʿulamaʾ, Sufis, merchants, and students, as well as by the acceptance of common doctrine, the schools of law and Sufi tariqat were at once crucial in the formation of local community life and in linking each small locality to the worldwide brotherhood of Islam. Muslim communal loyalties were factional and parochial at the local level, but cosmopolitan and universal at the international level.

This pattern of social affiliations and identifications excluded one alternative pattern of communal organization – the corporation of citizens resident in a particular locality. The town or village from which a person hailed, however important in his consciousness, conveyed no sense of political citizenship, did not constitute a corporate body, and had no territorial administration. No institutions corresponded to the social or psychological facts of town or village life. In this type of society with its combination of parochial and cosmopolitan identifications and its weak geographic solidarity, people depended upon the informal authority and mediation of the ʿulamaʾ notables to cope with problems of shared concern. Informal consultation of respected notables and their networks of patronage ties allowed for mediation of local disputes, for mobilization across parochial group lines, and for the expression of shared religious and political interests. Town populations found what coordination they could on the basis of the personal authority of the ʿulamaʾ and informal negotiations.

Town and village societies of this type were not ordinarily self-governing. The ʿulamaʾ notables were neither a military nor a territorial elite. They did not have the skills for warfare; nor did they control land and revenues. Middle Eastern societies lacked the technical, the organizational, and the economic bases for political independence. They lacked the internal cohesion necessary for political autonomy and they feared the breakdown of internal order more than the heavy hand of alien regimes.

This is not to say that the lack of political autonomy was their fault. Conquest by nomadic peoples and slave warlords who militarily and economically dominated both town and country precluded the possibility of communal independence. Only in interregnum periods, in the absence of strong military regimes, could the combination of informal influence and mediation by ʿulamaʾ notables and parochial clienteles suffice to give local forces temporary independence. Urban resistance to abusive exploitation, revolts against unpopular governors, and protests against taxation were indeed common. When the ruling empires were weak, poorly established and under pressure from both internal contenders for the throne and outside enemies, town resistance based on religious leadership and ʿayyarun or ghazi forces could even settle the fate of empires. In 992 when the Samanids were faced with the advancing Qarakhanids, their last hope lay with the masses of Bukhara, whose religious spokesmen counseled neutrality. Similarly, the notables and the ʿulamaʾ of Nishapur determined the success of the Saljuq invasion. Deciding that the Ghaznavids could no longer defend Khurasan, they surrendered to the Saljuqs and offered the services of a socially and administratively skilled populace to the new regime. Otherwise, empires reigned.

Thus, in the period between 950 and 1200 local community structures and elites in Iran and Iraq had become Islamized. Through the schools of law, Sufi brotherhoods, and Shiʿi sects, Islamic religious leaders provided the cadres of communal organization not only for a small sectarian following, but, in the age of conversions, for the masses of Middle Eastern peoples. Under their leadership local community life was increasingly defined by Muslim leaders in terms of Muslim affiliations. Islam thus gave the post-imperial Middle East a new identity. While conquerors and regimes came and went, Islam became ever more firmly and widely entrenched as the basis of the social and political order.

CHAPTER 11

.THE COLLECTIVE IDEAL

The new realities of state, communal, and religious institutions were reflected in an abundant literature of political theory. This theory had three principal branches: a Sunni theory of the Caliphate, the work of the ʿulamaʾ, a Persian-inspired genre of mirrors for princes, mainly a court genre, and a philosophical theory of the ideal state composed by commentators on Plato and Aristotle. Each of them responded in part to the changing social universe, and in part to their own literary canons, but they also embodied a common perception of the ultimate significance of politics and community. The shared values and shared assumptions bring us to the core of the post-imperial conception of a Muslim society.

The Sunni–Shariʿa theory of the Caliphate was set forth in theological and juridical treatises. The Sunni writers tried to explain why there should be a Caliphate at all, what purposes the office served, what qualifications were required of its incumbents, how they were to be selected, and what determined the obligations of subjects. The underlying assumption of the Sunni literature was that rulers held office to implement the Shariʿa and maintain the existence of the Muslim community.

Before the middle of the tenth century Muslim political debate turned on the question of who was qualified to hold this office and what guaranteed the capacity of the Caliphs to fulfill their obligations. The Sunnis proposed certain personal qualifications combined with an electoral process to guarantee the legitimacy of a ruler. While Sunni authors discussed the formalities of assuming the office, including the formal act of designation, the consultation with the religious scholars, the oath of investiture, and the contract with the community, legal thinking in effect justified the actual pattern of succession and especially the designation by the incumbent of his heir.

By the tenth and eleventh centuries it was clear that the Caliphs could no longer fulfill their political and religious roles. The Sultanates had stripped the Caliphate of its actual powers; sectarian quarrels diminished its religious authority. Sunni theorists accommodated to these realities. Al-Mawardi (d. 1058), a Sunni jurist, wrote the *Ahkam al-Sultaniya* (Principles of Government), to show that the primary duties of the Caliph are to maintain religion according to early precedents, enforce judicial decisions, and protect the peoples of Islam. His traditional and legalistic account of the Caliph, however, was not merely a gesture of historical nostalgia. Insofar as the Caliphate continued to struggle for actual power, the assertion of its authority was of practical importance. Thus, al-Mawardi followed his theoretical affirmation with a discussion of the delegation of authority, the conditions of appointments and tenure for all classes of governmental officials, and the personal and moral qualities required of each office-holder. He described the organization of judicial administration, tax collection, government measures to stimulate agricultural production, and the application of legal penalties for criminal offenses. In effect he set out a comprehensive blueprint for the exercise of an Islamic government. Embedded in this elaborate literary exercise is a poignant mixture of scholarly devotion, religious idealism and political ambition. For al-Mawardi the Caliphate was both a religious commitment and a political actuality.

Al-Ghazzali (1058–1111) similarly combined allegiance to religious tradition with a pragmatic awareness of political realities. He too wanted to restore the Caliphate to its true function as the protector of the tradition of the Prophet and of Muslim law, to recapture the unity of Muslim peoples, and to restore their military and worldly might. To do this, he realized, it was necessary to assimilate the Turkish military aristocracy, subordinate them to the Caliphate, reform political administration, and above all to use the combined powers of Caliphs and reigning sultans to suppress the enemies of Islam, especially the Shiᶜa. Most important for al-Ghazzali was the need to inculcate in every individual Muslim true belief, true piety, and true practice of Muslim law. Despite the continuing commitment to the Caliphate, there were subtle accommodations to the rise to power of nomadic chieftains and slave warlords. Al-Ghazzali was realistic enough to recognize that military lords often appointed the Caliphs who in turn legitimized their powers. His theory conceived of Muslim government as a condominium of the authority of the Caliphs and the effective powers of the Sultans.

More important was the ever increasing emphasis upon the necessity of obedience. The sanction for this lies in the Quran and in hadiths which stressed the need for obedience to the state. The Hanbali theologian, Ibn Batta (d. 997), condemned armed revolt against an established government. Obedience was required of all subjects, he held, but this obedience was limited, in that the individual should refuse to disobey a command of God. Similarly, al-Ghazzali held that rulers should be obeyed because resistance, even to tyranny, was a worse alternative. For fear of civil war, any government had to be accepted as a matter of necessity.

Behind this total commitment to order lay a number of implicit assumptions about political and moral realities. Muslim jurists assumed that men must be forced to obey the law and desist from unjust actions. They also believed that in the absence of a strong government factional hostilities would lead to anarchy. These fears were not unrealistic. Under the pressure of political necessity Muslim jurists were led to accept any established government as legitimate and to put aside their insistence on the supremacy of the Caliphate.

With the demise of the Caliphate in 1258, Sunni political thinkers could finally articulate a concept of Islamic government based upon the collaboration of secular rulers and religious teachers. Political theorists assigned the ʿulamaʾ an ever larger role in the government of Muslim communities as advisers and counselors to reigning princes. As early as the ninth century the Hanbalis emphasized the importance of the Quranic injunction to "command the good and forbid the evil" as the basis of the responsibility of every scholar and of every Muslim to apply God's law in community affairs. With the rise to power of slave and nomadic chieftains, Hanbalis and other Muslim theologians also stressed the requirement for *nasiha*, or advising and admonishing the ruling elites to induce them to observe and implement Islam.

With the demise of the Caliphate the authority of the scholars and Sufis was widely accepted as representing the essence of Islamic religious and communal aspirations. Just as the authority of Caliphs was based upon succession to the Prophet and on the presumption that they had the knowledge, understanding, and moral qualities essential to implement the revealed law, so the authority of the ʿulamaʾ and Sufis was based on and combined with elements of hereditary and charismatic succession. The Sunni tradition has always emphasized the direct and personal transmission of texts from masters to students; the authority of hadith depended, in part, on the unbroken chain of oral communication going back to the Prophet. Similarly, the teaching of legal texts depended upon the personal communication from teacher to disciple in each generation. The authority of Sufi masters was also based upon a combination of personal achievements and the silsila or chain of initiations. Thus the followers of the Caliphate, the students of the ᶜulamaᵓ, and the devotees of the Sufis respected the same essential principle – the transmitted presence of the Prophet.

In practice and theory Ahmad b. Taymiya (1263–1328) represented the epitome of the trend to make the ᶜulamaᵓ the focus of Muslim religio-communal interests. Ahmad b. Taymiya was an outstanding Hanbali scholar of Quran and hadith and a prolific writer on a great variety of religious questions. Born in Harran, Mesopotamia, he fled from the Mongol invasions to Damascus. He first achieved notoriety in 1293 when he led a campaign to execute a Christian who was accused of insulting the Prophet. In sermons and speeches, legal responsa, and published creeds he violently denounced his religious enemies. He opposed the Ashᶜaris and speculative theology in all its forms; he opposed all forms of metaphysical Sufism; he denounced esoteric and antinomian religious views and the veneration of saints' tombs, and involved himself in violent controversies on legal matters such as the law of divorce. He took part in demonstrations to destroy cultic forms of worship, expeditions against the Ismaᶜilis in the mountains of the Lebanon, and led Muslim resistance to the Mongol invasions of Damascus. He insistently demanded that the Shariᶜa be a continuing and vital force in the everyday life of every Muslim.

In accord with his own political role, Ibn Taymiya held that the ᶜulamaᵓ were responsible for upholding the law by giving religious advice to rulers, teaching true principles to the community of Muslims, and "commanding the good and forbidding the evil." Ibn Taymiya set aside the traditional question of the Caliphate – true Caliphs have not ruled since the early days of Islam, he argued – and defined Muslim governments in terms of the actual ruling authorities, and the importance of their heeding the advice of the ᶜulamaᵓ. His political activism thus embodied a new concept of state and society in which the ᶜulamaᵓ rather than the Caliphs became the principal actors and laid claim to a role for local peoples in otherwise foreign military regimes. Sunni political theory had shifted slowly to deemphasize the Caliphate and to accept the reality of Sultan and scholar as the key figures in the Muslim political order.

While Sunni theory developed in Islamic religious circles, the mirror literature rose out of a Persian tradition of manuals of statecraft. The first works of this kind were translated into Arabic in the course of the eighth and ninth centuries to counsel the ᶜAbbasid Caliphs. The upheavals of the tenth and eleventh centuries led to a new wave of mirrors for princes, written by government officials and religious scholars, to define the rules of good government for their new Turkish overlords.

7 A youth prostrating himself before a ruler

The most important treatise of this kind was *The Book of Government* by Nizam al-Mulk (d. 1092). *The Book of Government* urges the Sultan to do justice and gives him specific advice on the techniques of rule. The work is devoted to explicating the proper role of soldiers, police, spies, and finance officials; it tells anecdotes about the great ancient rulers to illustrate its lessons. Another important work, the *Qabus-name* of Kai Ka'us (d. 1082) was a compendium of the wisdom of an old king written for his favorite son, containing advice on the proper conduct of a household, agriculture, the professions and government. The *Qabus-name* tries to teach a youth how to be a statesman, a gentleman, and a good Muslim. The *Book of Counsel for Kings* by al-Ghazzali is an altogether different kind of mirror. While Nizam al-Mulk concentrated upon pragmatic political questions, and Kai Ka'us was concerned with the education of an aristocrat, al-Ghazzali's *Book of Counsel* sets out the beliefs of Islam, the moral qualities and attitudes expected of a ruler, and his duty to uphold the true religion. The example of ancient Persian kings and the sayings of sages are quoted to illustrate these teachings, and to give a work with Muslim religious content a Persian literary flavor.

These works are strikingly diverse in tone and content, but they are all concerned with the ultimate ends of government and with the cultivation of rulers who have the vision, the character, and the technique to realize these ends. The purpose of government is to uphold justice. In the work of Nizam al-Mulk, the ruler is responsible for the welfare of his people. Justice means that each class of the population – soldiers, administrators, merchants, and peasants – shall have its due; the weak shall be protected, and the productivity of the population assured. In concrete circumstances justice is defined by custom and by Muslim law. It is the ruler's obligation to preserve the Islamic tradition as well as to maintain the productivity and stability of society. For these obligations a ruler is responsible to God. "Each of you is a shepherd and each one of you is answerable for his flock."

Al-Ghazzali's *Book of Counsel for Kings* also stresses the importance of justice. The ruler should understand that God loves a just Sultan and that God will judge him at the final day. The ruler should see that his officers, servants, and slaves are also disciplined. His most important responsibility is to shun heresy and evil actions, to keep to the tradition of the Prophet, and to reward virtuous people and condemn evil ones. For al-Ghazzali as well as for the secular writers, the principal function of kingship is to uphold order in society and the teachings of the true faith.

According to the implicit theory of the mirrors for princes the principal means for realizing justice is that the ruler be himself a just person. Though there are numerous pragmatic or political matters which must be managed, societies depend ultimately on the intellectual and moral qualities of their rulers. The good ruler must be a man of intelligence, knowledge, and experience, deliberate and circumspect, patient and self-restrained. This nobility must be expressed in a grave, dignified, and stern manner, for the ruler must inspire awe, loyalty, and good behavior in his subordinates. He must therefore avoid lying, avarice, anger, envy, and cowardice. If the ruler is a liar, men will have no fear; if he is avaricious, no hope. If he is angry, they will not confide in him. The most desirable trait is generosity. The ruler must reward his servants and spend his treasure on those who help him. His good character not only wins the support of his subordinates but serves as an example and induces them to be good to the subjects. Thus the moral qualities of the ruler are at the heart of his capacity to make justice reign. For al-Ghazzali this essential goodness is based upon religious humility. The virtues of princes come from fear of God; for we are temporary sojourners in this world and our ultimate destiny is in the world to come.

To achieve goodness the ruler must consult with the sages and the scholars. They will teach him what God requires; they will divert him from heresy and innovation; they will help make his soul into the image of a just ruler. The ʿulamaʾ thus define the goodness incumbent upon the ruler and help instill it in him. The literature of the mirror for princes, then, trusts to personal virtue as the basis of social justice.

From the Greek heritage stems a third literature: the Islamic commentators on Plato and Aristotle, al-Farabi (d. 950), Ibn Sina (Avicenna, 980–1037), Ibn Rushd (Averroes, 1126–1198), and others who examine the ideal state and the ideal ruler. The highest goal in philosophic political theory is the perfection of the human speculative intelligence and the attainment of happiness through the rational contemplation of the divine reality. For the realization of this blessed state, the cooperation of human beings is essential.

Al-Farabi was the premier political theorist in the philosophic tradition. In the *Madinat al-Fadila* (The Virtuous State), al-Farabi begins with a résumé of the principles covering the divine being, the emanation of the celestial intelligences, and the relation of human intelligence and imagination to the spiritual universe. His real purpose is to understand the nature of being and intellect and to attain a spiritual vision of reality; his principal concern is the person of the philosopher, who must know the truth and be responsible for actualizing it in human society. The philosopher who has attained a theoretical vision of the truth is the only person qualified to rule, instruct his people, form their character in accord with moral principles, teach them practical arts, and rouse them to do good acts so that they in turn reach their highest possible perfection.

In the *Aphorisms of the Statesmen*, al-Farabi explains that there are two levels of ideal state. One is the state ruled by the philosopher-prophet-prince, whose personal guiding presence is the inspiration for a virtuous society. The second type of state is the one ruled in accord with the law set down by the original philosopher-prophet. In this state the ruler must have knowledge of ancient laws, good judgment about how to apply them, initiative in coping with new situations, and practical wisdom to handle matters where tradition does not suffice. The second type of ideal state corresponds to the Islamic society governed by the revealed law under the guidance of a ruler who implements the law – it is akin to the ideal Caliphate of Sunni legal theory.

Later political philosophers hold much the same position. Ibn Rushd offered a comprehensive vision of the spiritual universe and the place of human society within it. This is presented in his commentary on Plato's *Republic*. The perfection of speculative intelligence is the highest goal of human existence; human society exists for the sake of this perfection. The ideal society requires a philosopher-king and lawgiver who will create an order in which each person fulfills the tasks appropriate to his nature. When the virtues of the soul – intellect, temperament, and appetite – receive proper expression, there is justice in the society and in each person. The ruler establishes this perfect order by teaching philosophy to the elect and theology and poetry to the others. He trains the people by providing laws which guide them toward proper actions. In Ibn Rushd, as in al-Farabi, there are two levels of ideal society. One is established by the philosopher-prophet, who combines wisdom, intelligence, and the imaginative capacity to directly communicate the truth to the masses of men. The other is based upon law, which is a way of implementing the speculative truth known to philosophers. Law, whether in the form of rational Greek *nomos* or revealed Muslim law promulgated by the prophetic lawgiver, is conducive to the perfection of the soul which depends upon right belief and right action. In either case the good ruler is essential to the realization of a good society.

All three forms of Muslim political theory are ultimately grounded in the premise that the goal of the social order is the formation of individuals who live rightly in this world in accord with the truth and are so prepared to achieve salvation in the world to come. Politics is but part of a larger quest for religious salvation. Nonetheless, in each theory the definition of that truth is somewhat different. In the Sunni theory the fulfillment of the law is the fulfillment of God's revealed will. In the mirror theory the substance of religious fulfillment is not discussed but it is assumed that justice corresponds to the realization of religious principles. In the philosophical theory knowledge of the world of intelligences and the purification of the soul frees the human intellect to regain its visionary attachment to the spiritual world.

The three genres of Muslim political theory are further agreed that political society is essential to the realization of this perfection. In the philosophical theory a properly ordered society is necessary to the cultivation of souls who may comprehend the structure of ultimate reality. In both philosophical and Sunni theory law is the essential device for instructing, educating, and forming the morals of human beings. In turn, the state is essential for the enforcement of laws and the protection of individuals from being harmed or doing harm. In the mirror for princes, literature, justice, the preservation of custom and the implementation of religious beliefs are the basic contributions of society toward the realization of ultimate ends. In all three theories society is necessary to enforce justice and order, sustain basic human needs, teach and instruct individuals in their moral duties and support their spiritual quests.

The three genres also agree that the proper social order requires a good ruler, be it a philosopher, Caliph, or Sultan. Happiness in society is made to depend upon the person of the ruler. In the Sunni theory the ruler is selected by God through election of the community in order to implement his commands. In the mirror literatures the good prince is the source of prosperity and security. The philosophers see him as the perfect soul implementing a perfect social order.

Furthermore, in all three forms of Muslim political literature the ruler symbolizes the integration or the orderly relation of human beings to the cosmos and to God. In the philosophical literature the ruler stands not only for personal religious fulfillment but for the harmony of the individual and society with the spiritual cosmos. The ruler who actualizes his rational potentials brings his own soul into contact with the active intellect and the spiritual intelligences. He symbolizes in mythic terms the integration of man and God. In Sunni and mirror theory the ruler does not have a mythic function: the Caliph is not divine, nor semi-divine, nor an incarnate savior, nor perfect man. He is, however, God's vice-regent, God's shadow, his vehicle for the maintenance of order in society, and for fulfilling the conditions essential to the implementation of the Muslim law. The Caliph is seen in the image of God as the upholder of order and justice. He is mighty, capricious, inscrutable, and deserving of loyalty regardless of his actual deeds. An ordered society is unimaginable without a ruler, just as an ordered universe is unimaginable without God.

The ruler not only symbolizes meaningful order, but also the inherent tension of order and disorder. The ideal ruler is presented as ethical, just and God-fearing, but the unspoken motive for the composition of these literatures is that actual rulers are capricious, willful, self-serving, and tyrannical. The unspoken contrast symbolizes the deep conflict which is experienced in the soul of every individual and in the body of society – the conflict of unbridled passion and unrestrained exercise of power, and moderation and self-control. It also symbolizes the ever-present conflict in society generated by family antagonisms, tribal wars, factional struggles, conquests, and the rise and fall of regimes, as opposed to the hope for peace. The ruler signifies not merely order but the quest for order in a society composed of self-seeking human beings and groups.

The person of the ruler is so important that all of these works neglect, with the partial exception of Nizam al-Mulk, actual political institutions. The philosophical writers give no concrete description of the ideal city. They regard natural and revealed systems of law as a means of social discipline but the content of social and ritual practice is never discussed. Society is described as organized into classes but the classes are merely metaphors for the virtues of the well-ordered soul. In the Sunni theory the emphasis is upon the person of the Caliph, and not upon the mechanisms which could bring religious principles into practice. The mirror literatures are similarly vague about the meaning of justice and hierarchy. There is no concrete description of the classes of society, their rights, and duties. In none of these literatures do economic issues have an important place.

There are several reasons for this emphasis upon the person of the ruler. One is that these literatures reflect the realities of their time. While modern political theory may focus upon institutions because of the highly bureaucratic and legalistic structure of modern societies, Muslim writers turned their attention to the ruler because authority was vested in patriarchal figures who depended upon the personal loyalty of their soldiers and officials to maintain their regimes. In a society which depended on men rather than institutions the only conceivable check upon the powers of rulers was their character as human beings.

Furthermore, the emphasis upon the ruler also reflects the weakness of organized institutions. Though ubiquitous in influence, the ʿulamaʾ and the Sufis had no central organization. Urban communities were divided into factional groups. Landowners and other economic elites were divided by region and faction and had no formal ways of generating solidarity. Apart from the small urban family or rural clans, lineages, and tribes, there was no organized political society. Even the state was often the household of the prince.

Finally, the person of the ruler is emphasized because the ruler symbolizes not only the aspiration for political justice, but the hope for individual religious perfection. In the philosophic literature the ultimate concern of political theory is the education of the philosopher. Analogously, the ultimate concern of Sunni writers is not politics but religious and moral perfection to be attained by adherence to the law. The Caliph is a symbol of that perfection. Similarly the mirror literature describes the ruler as a person in control of his own evil impulses and those of others. He is not an administrator but a model for how men should live. While addressing the question of the state, the underlying premise of Muslim "political literatures" is that the good state is the product of good human beings.

CHAPTER 12

THE PERSONAL ETHIC

Through the formation of state institutions, schools of law, theological sects, and Sufi brotherhoods, Islam became part of the fabric of Middle Eastern urban and village societies. This social consolidation was accompanied by the consolidation of Islamic religious literatures, beliefs and values and the crystallization of an Islamic way of life. As we have seen, from the origin of Islam until the tenth century the basic literatures of Quran commentary, hadith, law, theology, and mysticism had been formulated. From the tenth to the thirteenth centuries these literatures inculcated moral and spiritual goals for each individual and for the collective life of the Muslim community as a whole. Moreover, despite the absence of a centralized authority, the several literary genres and mentalities were merged into a number of religious constructs which in their whole and integrated forms were accepted as "Islam." One of these integrated religious visions – the Sunni scripturalist Sufi orientation – became the most commonly accepted version of Islam. Other religious visions – Shiʿism, philosophy, theosophy, and popular religion – stood as alternatives to the Sunni consensus. The post-imperial era crystallized both the normative form of Islamic religious belief and practice, and the alternatives, and thus defined the issues which would ever after constitute the *problématique* of Muslim religious discourse.

NORMATIVE ISLAM: SCRIPTURE, SUFISM AND THEOLOGY

Scripture was consolidated as central to the definition of Islam. The Quran continued to be the basic source of Muslim religious inspiration. In the post-imperial era the Quran was understood to present a vision of the human being as a person who does the good deeds commanded by God, as a moderate, humble person, acting kindly and justly, and as steadfast and tranquil in the face of his own passions. The true Muslim is the slave of God. He accepts his humble place in the world, takes no pride or consolation in human prowess, but recognizes the limited worth of all worldly things and the greater importance of pleasing God.

By the ninth century, hadith had also achieved a central place in Muslim religious life, and the basic canons had been codified. Young scholars maintained the practice of traveling from place to place to collect hadith in an unbroken tradition of oral recollection going back to the Prophet. Hadith studies in the post-canonical age tended to concentrate on the criticism of isnads, or chains of authority, and on the compilation of anthologies garnered out of the earlier canons. Sunni works of law, theology, and mysticism continued to quote proof-texts from the Quran and hadith, and the study of hadith was enshrined in the madrasa curriculum. By the twelfth century new colleges were dedicated to their study.

In addition to Quran and hadith, Muslim law was a component of Islamic scripture. By the middle of the tenth century the schools of law had already developed their basic jurisprudential procedures and had elaborated a considerable body of legal materials. By then it was widely agreed that there were four major schools of jurisprudence, though there were also numerous independent scholars and small personal schools. By 1300 only the four major schools, the Hanafi, Shafiꜥi, Maliki, and Hanbali, had survived. Despite the consolidation of the schools of law there was still considerable legal development after 950. While the Hanafi, Maliki and Shafiꜥi schools agreed that the "gate of ijtihad" or independent reasoning was closed and that scholars of later generations were not free to give personal or independent interpretations of the law, the Hanbalis and a minority of Shafi'i writers never accepted the principle of *taqlid*, or obedience to the traditional canon, and upheld the authority of every qualified legal scholar to use rational and independent judgment in legal questions. Even the more conservative schools allowed for flexible accommodation of legal principles to custom and tradition. The application of the law to practical situations and the procedure of consulting scholars for legal opinions also allowed for the further evolution of law.

From the tenth to the thirteenth centuries scholarly procedures also changed. Islamic law became more logical and systematic. Shariꜥa probably reached its definitive literary form when the *Hidaya* (Guide) of al-Marghinani (d. 1196) opened a new phase of compilation, repetition, and formalism in Islamic legal

Table 5. *Central concepts in law*

fiqh	understanding, law
usul al-fiqh	sources of law: Quran, *hadith* (sayings of the Prophet); *ijmaᶜ* (consensus of schools and community); *qiyas* (reasoning by analogy)
ᶜilm	knowledge, especially of law, the learning of the *ᶜalim* (pl. *ᶜulamaᵓ*)
taqlid	imitation; following the established teachings
ijtihad	independent judgment of qualified legal scholar (*mujtahid*)
Shariᶜa	the way, the total corpus of Muslim law and belief
fatwa	advisory opinion on a matter of law given by a *mufti* (jurisconsult)
qada	court judgment made by a *qadi* (judge) on the basis of Shariᶜa

scholarship. The standard of legal reasoning also declined and logical consistency broke down. In many cases the guiding principles of law were lost in favor of eclectic dependence on analogy from individual cases. The law took the form of a vast reservoir of case materials and precedents which could be used as the basis of judicial decisions but no longer offered a rigid cadre of rules for the regulation of social, familial, and commercial matters. The possibilities for individual interpretation and selection out of the repertoire of numerous jurists combined with the discretion of judges in the application of the law gave Islamic law almost boundless flexibility in practice.

Thus a peculiar contradiction arose. The authority of law was absolute but it was not adhered to in practice. In principle, the life of a good Muslim was taken to be the fulfillment of God's every command in the form of specific rules and the imitation of concrete examples. The literalist schools, such as the Hanbali, stressed the necessity of adhering to every detail of law. Yet most Muslims recognized that the law was not necessarily precise. Legal rules were mixed with moral injunctions and Muslim jurists distinguished several categories of legal norms. Some actions were required, others were recommended; some were forbidden, others discouraged. In some matters the law was neutral. In many categories the law did not provide sanctions and its application was left to conscience. Furthermore, custom often decided whether or not aspects of the law were applied. There were even legalistic devices (*hiyal*) to allow for exceptions to the principles of the law while keeping to its letter.

This flexibility in practice was acceptable because the law was not only legislation, but a symbol of the meaningfulness of the world in its connection to God. The problem of adherence points to a deep spiritual tension in Islam – a tension between ethical ideals and legal rules, between fulfillment in spirit and letter, and between law as a symbol of truth and as a system of rules. Furthermore, embedded in the problem of adherence to the law was the question of the sources of law. What role did divine authority in scripture, expert judgment, and communal values play in the formulation of the rules by which every Muslim was supposed to live? Was law based on assent to authority, rational judgment or allegiance to the tradition and consensus of the community? The effort to live according to the Shariᶜa posed for every believer the question of what role did reason, consensus, and tradition play in the formulation of his religious judgments. Acceptance of scripture, then, implied faith in revelation, commitment to a specific way of life, and a search for personal realization of the moral and spiritual as well as the behavioral qualities implied in the Muslim revelation. In Quran, hadith, and law, we find not only prescriptive rules but the vocabulary of an open religious quest.

Sufism attempted to bypass the uncertainties inherent in the practice of law by seeking the purification of the soul in preparation for an immediate experience of the reality of God's existence rather than a practical realization of his commands. Sufism devalued worldly things in the quest for an ecstatic self-realization through the direct visionary experience of God's being. Sufism also carried with it a theosophical view of the universe which explained the structure of the cosmos and the possibility of religious ascent toward union with God. Finally, it encompassed belief in the miraculous powers of saints as channels for God's action in the world. Sufism thus encompassed piety and ethical behavior, ascetic and ecstatic practices, theosophical metaphysics, and magical beliefs. It embraced at once a scripturalist, an agnostic, and a miraculous concept of Islam. Sufism thus led both toward and away from Islamic law and practice. Its ascetic and theosophical aspects were consistent with devoted practice of Islamic law; the veneration of the magical powers of Sufi saints led rather to religious practices which were expected to produce miracles or to induce ecstatic visions. Thus some forms of Sufism would be integrated with law; while others tended to gnosticism and the veneration of saints. Sufism was thus not one but several forms of religious inspiration united under the same name.

At the end of the tenth century, Sufism, once expressed through the aphorisms of numerous independent masters, began to consolidate. Sufi writers defined their movement as a science, parallel to that of law, capable of leading to true knowledge of God by virtue of correct doctrine, religious practices, and methods of mystical contemplation. Sufi writers worked out a technical vocabulary to define, defend, and standardize Sufi practice, integrate it with law and theology, and thus legitimize it within the framework of Islam.

In the tenth and eleventh centuries the emerging Sufi position was expressed and systematized in compilations of biographies of Sufis which linked the novices of any given time with a chain of teachers leading back through al-Junayd to Hasan al-Basri and the companions of the Prophet Muhammad. Other Sufi treatises set forth the main ideas derived from Sufi experience, and tried to communicate the actual experiences of the masters through anecdotes and sayings. They illustrated the great piety and scrupulousness of Sufis, their trust in God, their unconcern for the things of this world, and their qualities of heart and soul. Such works included the *Qut al-Qulub* (The Food of Hearts) of al-Makki (d. 998) which set out Sufi prayers and recitations, and the *Kitab al-Luma*ᶜ (Book of Radiances) of al-Sarraj (d. 988) which identified Sufis as a branch of the ʿulamaʾ and explained Sufi concepts, utterances, and miracles. The *Kashf al-Mahjub* (Unveiling of the Hidden) of al-Hujwiri (d. 1071) and the *Risala* (Epistle) of al-Qushayri (d. 1074) explained the meaning of key Sufi terms, discussed metaphysical and theological issues, reported the opinions of revered Sufis, and gave the biographies of famous masters.

The central motif of this literature is renunciation of individual will, of worldly concerns, and of everything except God. This renunciation, however, refers to an attitude of mind, a stance toward the things of this world, and an insight into one's true nature rather than a literal state of motionlessness, emptiness, or vacuum. The Sufi lives with material things, but does not care about them. He owns things but does not derive his esteem from them.

Further, the Sufis taught that the true Islam is the submission of man's will to God's will. Al-Hujwiri says:

> Divine grace is this – that God through His will should restrain a man from his own will and should overpower him with will-lessness, so that if he were thirsty and plunged into a river, the river would become dry.

And further:

> What we choose for ourselves is noxious to us. I desire only that God should desire for me, and therein preserve me from the evil thereof and save me from the wickedness of my soul...I have no choice beyond His choice.

The Sufi does not wish his own wishes, but makes his wish whatever God has commanded; he is satisfied with whatever God decrees for his life; indeed, he embraces God's choices, doing God's will joyfully.

This does not mean that the Sufi does not have a "will" in the ordinary sense; it means he has fused the chaotic wishes of every human into his authentic will, his willing acceptance of God's command. In this, Sufism is consistent with the Quran, which sees that the unbeliever is one who gives free reign to unchecked passions, to self-assertiveness, and who serves his apparent needs for wealth, honor, fame, power, or whatever. Controlling this false willfulness, obeying God's command, restraint, and modesty are the true Islam.

Sufism further teaches that the will is tamed by the love of God. The politicians would curb men by force; the moralists, by public opinion; the philosophers, by reason; the theologians, by faith. The Sufis teach that the true love of God is to love his will as one's own. They yearn to do God's will as a lover yearns to fulfill the wishes of his beloved.

"God's choice for His servant with His knowledge of His servant is better than His servant's choice for himself with his ignorance of his Lord," because love, as all agree, is the negation of the lover's choice by affirmation of the Beloved's choice.[1]

Love of God makes his every command the Sufi's own heartfelt wish. By this love of God, the Sufi transcends the letter to realize the spirit of the law.

The quest for love of God and submission to his will was wedded to a profound Sufi determination to fuse personal religious experience with the practice of Islam according to revealed law and tradition. Sufis of the tenth and eleventh centuries grappled with the tension between scripturalist Islam, a religion of external laws, rituals, moral and social norms required of all Muslims, and Sufism, a religion of the subjective being of Man inculcating purity of heart and intention, goodness of motive, dedication of the will, meditative, visionary knowledge, and love of God. Despite the efforts of generations of Sufis, including al-Junayd and al-Qushayri, and the growing rapprochement of law and Sufism in the tenth and eleventh centuries, the two forms of Islam continued to be taken as alternative paths to religious fulfillment pursued by different groups of religious scholars. Shari'a still meant the conformity of outer behavior to legal requirements. Sufism still meant the purification of the heart for the sake of the vision of God. Finally, al-Ghazzali was able to combine acceptance of the transcendence of God with the authority of the Prophet and the historical tradition of the community, with the personal experience and authority of the Sufi master. Al-Ghazzali, seizing upon currents in philosophy, theology, law, and Sufi practice, fused revealed truth, fulfillment of the law, and inner religious experience. His achievement was to integrate Sufism and the law in a way which has become definitive in Islamic civilization.

Al-Ghazzali came to his vocation in a crisis of which he told in a memoir whose immediacy and poignancy is vivid to the present day. Al-Ghazzali

[1] Al-Hujwiri, *The Kashf al-Mahjub*, tr. R. A. Nicolson, London: Luzac and Co., 1970, pp. 378–9.

studied law and theology in Tus and Nishapur. At the age of thirty-three he was appointed professor in the Nizamiya school of Baghdad, one of the most prestigious positions of the time. He wrote treatises on law and theology, mastered philosophy and esoteric subjects, gave authoritative legal decisions, and lectured to hundreds of students. He was widely regarded as living an exemplary Muslim life. Yet he was beset by doubts: "...as I drew near the age of adolescence the bonds of mere authority [taqlid] ceased to hold me and inherited beliefs lost their grip upon me." At the time of his greatest success, his doubts flowed into a deep sense of unworthiness.

> Next I considered the circumstances of my life, and realized that I was caught in a veritable thicket of attachments. I also considered my activities, of which the best was my teaching and lecturing, and realized that in them I was dealing with sciences that were unimportant and contributed nothing to the attainment of eternal life.
>
> After that I examined my motive in my work of teaching, and realized that it was not a pure desire for the things of God, but that the impulse moving me...was the desire for an influential position and public recognition.

Al-Ghazzali yearned to give up this false life, to sever the attachment to worldly things, leaving "wealth and position and fleeing from all-consuming entanglements." But he could not do it. The conflict absorbed his energies.

> One day I would form the resolution to quit Baghdad and get rid of these adverse circumstances; the next day I would abandon my resolution. I put one foot forward and drew the other back. If in the morning I had a genuine longing to seek eternal life, by the evening the attack of a whole host of desires had reduced it to impotence.

One voice cried, "To the road! To the road!" The other, "This is a passing mood...do not yield to it, for it will quickly disappear." It did not.

> For nearly six months beginning with Rajab 488 A.H. [July, A.D. 1095], I was continuously tossed about between the attractions of worldly desires and the impulses towards eternal life. In that month the matter ceased to be one of choice and became one of compulsion. God caused my tongue to dry up so that I was prevented from lecturing. One particular day I would make an effort to lecture in order to gratify the hearts of my following, but my tongue would not utter a single word nor could I accomplish anything at all.
>
> This impediment in my speech produced grief in my heart, and at the same time my power to digest and assimilate food and drink was impaired; I could hardly swallow or digest a single mouthful of food.

Al-Ghazzali had come to an emotional crisis. His doctors said wisely but helplessly:

> This trouble arises from the heart...and from there it has spread through the constitution; the only method of treatment is that the anxiety which has come over the heart should be allayed.

His decision was made. Al-Ghazzali took up the life of a wandering Sufi. For ten years he pursued the mysteries of Sufism. His retreat, however, was neither total nor permanent. It was really part of a larger life strategy which envisaged a return to worldly life to continue the work of religious teaching and religious reform. After ten years, al-Ghazzali took up his public career again, returned to a professorship at Nishapur, and wrote his major treatises. He had resolved the doubt in his heart; he had come to certain knowledge of the truth of God's existence and of the nature of his obligations to him. He saw his return as a return to his old work in a new way.

> In myself I know that, even if I went back to the work of disseminating knowledge, yet I did not go back. To go back is to return to the previous state of things. Previously, however, I had been disseminating the knowledge by which worldly success is attained; by word and deed I had called men to it; and that had been my aim and intention. But now I am calling men to the knowledge whereby worldly success is given up and its low position in the scale of real worth is recognized.[1]

Al-Ghazzali did not renounce the world; what he did was abandon false goals in worldly activity.

Sufism brought al-Ghazzali to certain knowledge of God and certain knowledge brought him back to Muslim beliefs, prayer, and teaching, to the Given Way of scripture and tradition. For a Muslim, maturity entailed a return to, and a fulfillment of, the fundamentals of the religion. His master of theology, al-Juwayni, had already said:

> I had read thousands of books; then I left the people of Islam with their religion and their manifest sciences in these books, and I embarked on the open sea, plunging into the literature the people of Islam rejected. All this was in quest of the truth. At an early age, I fled from the acceptance of others' opinions [taqlid]. But now I have returned from everything to the word of truth. "Hold to the religion of the old women."[2]

In the *Ihya᾿ ᶜUlum al-Din* (Revivification of the Religious Sciences), al-Ghazzali gives his mature conception of the relationship of the outer and inner life, of Shariᶜa and Sufism, of the two parts of his own long experience. His position was rooted in a philosophic concept of the nature of the human being. In his view, the essence of the human being is the soul, which is a divine, spiritual substance variously called qalb, ruh, nafs, or ᶜaql. In its original state, *al-fitra*, before it is joined to the body, it is a pure, angelic, eternal substance. In this state the soul possesses reason, the capacity to know the essence of things and

---

[1] W. M. Watt, *The Faith and Practice of al-Ghazali*, London: Allen and Unwin,1953, pp. 21, 56–76.

[2] W. M. Watt, *A Muslim Intellectual: A Study of al-Ghazali*, Edinburgh, 1963, pp. 23–4.

the capacity for the knowledge of God. The highest good is the actualization of this inherent potential.

For this to be achieved the soul is joined to the body, for the body is the vehicle which carries the soul on its journey to God, but here there is a dilemma. The body necessarily corrupts the pure state of the soul. In the combined constitution of man, desire, anger, and *shaytaniya* (the inclination to do evil) are joined to the purely spiritual elements. The human being thus comes to possess both an animal soul made up of the faculties of desire and anger (nafs), and a divine soul (*rabbaniya*) possessing the faculties of reason and justice. To perfect the soul, then, every person must subordinate the animal faculties to the higher faculties and perfect the virtues – temperance, courage, wisdom and justice – appropriate to each faculty. The overall process of purification and of acquiring good traits is variously called *tazqiyat al-qalb* and *tahdhib al-akhlaq*. The true goal of life is to perfect the soul so that the spiritual and the divine elements prevail over the material and the satanic. ʿAql has to prevail over nafs. This does not mean, however, the destruction or abandonment of the lesser parts of the soul but rather the dominance of reason over the other faculties. The proper channeling of the animal parts, and the achievement of some harmony of faculties is called justice in the soul. The goal is not to destroy, but to make use of nafs in the interest of ʿaql.

The Sufi quest is aimed at such purification. The Sufis seek it by detachment from the world, by retreat from the assaults of everyday life to the khanaqa, where the Sufi can concentrate on renunciation of worldly attachments, and by dhikr, repetition and remembrance of the name of God to empty the mind of all distracting passions. As al-Ghazzali explains, the Sufi path to knowledge of the spiritual world is to shut the gate on sense perception, sexual passion, and worldly ties; to shut the gate on the material side of the mind. To do this one does not need elaborate education, formal knowledge, or book learning – here is the quarrel of Sufism with the ʿulamaʾ. The certain knowledge of God does not come from learning but from piety.

Sufi detachment, however, is but an extreme tactic in a more broadly conceived reform of the heart. This reform has both an outer and an inner aspect. It involves the triad of good actions, virtues, and knowledge. According to the *Ihyaʾ*, actions come first. The first book of the *Ihyaʾ*, after the introduction on knowledge, is entirely devoted to ʿibadat, ritual actions. These include ablutions, prayer, alms, fasting, pilgrimage, reading the Quran, dhikr, and *wird* (the continual remembering of God). Book II of the *Ihyaʾ* is devoted to social actions – to table manners, marriage, earning a living, friendship, and journeys. These actions, ritual and social, are important precisely because they are God's revealed ways to cleanse the soul of passions and invoke the remembrance which is inherent in al-fitra – the original soul. The prescribed acts of themselves purify.

The second aspect of purification is a direct assault on the inner vices. The vices include the sins of speech – cursing, false promises, lying, slander, backbiting; they include anger, envy, greed, jealousy, gluttony, miserliness, ostentation, pride, love of wealth and power, and love of this world. These vices sully the heart and stand in the way of ultimate happiness, not to speak of ordinary well-being.

The elimination of these vices is a lifelong process. Children must be raised properly with praise and blame, reward and punishment, to discipline their desires, and habituate them to good acts. As children become adults, the discipline of society, the admonition of friends, the counsel of elders, and the imitation of good people is also helpful. In adulthood, however, the process of rooting out the vices becomes an individual responsibility. The individual must himself become aware that he is beset by vice, and self-awareness must be followed by inner struggle (*mujahada*), self-training (*riyada*), and habituation (*i'tiyad*), by sturdy resistance to any external expression of bad impulses in speech or action. Indeed, the individual must not only control his impulses, he must oppose his vices by deliberately acting contrary to them. He has to create in the soul a struggle between vices and their opposites so that the faculties are driven from extreme expression toward the virtuous mean.

The elimination of vices paves the way for a new level of inward achievement, the acquisition of the mystical virtues. Book IV is devoted to these virtues – the states and stations on the way to God. They include repentance, fear, asceticism, and patience, which are preliminary to gratitude, trust, love, and intimacy. In one sense, these virtues develop spontaneously. They flourish like flowers in a garden, when the garden is weeded. In another sense, they can only be won through God's guidance and grace (*rahma*). A good Muslim strives for ethical self-control, but the mystical virtues flourish only by passive acceptance of God's will.

Passive fulfillment is at the heart of al-Ghazzali's discussion of tawakkul – abandonment of self or trust in God. In the Revivification of the Religious Sciences, al-Ghazzali explains that trust in God means to leave everything to God and to have no will, initiative, or activity of one's own. There are three levels of this extraordinary state. One is akin to the trust of a man in the attorney who represents his interests. The man turns over his affairs to the management of another in whose honesty, energy, and ability he has confidence. This delegation, however, is limited to a particular case, and the subject does not surrender his awareness of what is going on, his judgment, or his ultimate right to make choices. This modest degree of trust may continue indefinitely.

The second degree of trust is akin to the dependence and confidence of a very small child in his mother. The infant cannot take care of himself; he knows only his mother, seeks refuge with her, and depends on her support. The infant has no capacity for initiative of his own, but he can cry, call for his mother, run after her, and tug her dress. At any distress, his first thought is of his mother; he has complete confidence that she will meet his needs. This is like the man who trusts entirely to God and has complete confidence that he will be nourished by the Almighty, to whom he addresses his prayers and petitions. This state of passivity may last a day or two, like a fever, before it passes and the mystic is returned to an everyday condition.

The third state is to be in the hands of God as a corpse in the hands of the washer. The mystic sees himself as dead, moved by God, certain that he does not move, or will, or know, save by God's decree. In this state, the mystic trusts completely that he will be sustained. He does not call out like a child nor pray like an adult. This third state, al-Ghazzali says, lasts no longer than the pallor produced by fear.

These images convey the state of being that al-Ghazzali has in mind. The trust of the child in his mother is a man's trust in his basic security, his confidence that his being will be sustained. The trust of the corpse in the washer, that passivity that can only be communicated by images of death, whose interval is the moment of fear, lies beyond the infant's trust. To know it, one passes through the helplessness of infancy, through the fear of death, through the terror of nonexistence. This trust is known by the abandonment of one's own efforts and resources, by the testing of one's capacity to endure a total surrender of one's own life to the very ground of all life. To know this trust is to know that one's existence is assured without striving, effort, or will of one's own. It is assured as such.

Renunciation of the will, of the self, abandonment to God, and trust in God do not represent detachment in a physical sense from the ongoing life of the world, but moments that come to pass and return as part of the flow of man's psychic reality. These moments of passive grounding in trust become the basis of an active Muslim life and of the active virtues that pervade the scriptural and traditional imagery.

The third aspect of purification is knowledge. Knowledge has the most complex implications. It is at once a means and a goal to be attained. It is also a metaphor for the whole of the process by which religious vision is achieved.

First, knowledge is basic. Knowledge of the principles of the faith, belief in God and his attributes, the angelic world, paradise, and the last judgment; knowledge of the character and actions of the Prophet, knowledge of which actions are commanded, which are prohibited; knowledge of the heart and how to cure evil impulses – all of this is essential. The scholar's knowledge, indeed, the knowledge contained in the volumes of the *Ihya*ᵓ, is important information.

In another sense, knowledge for al-Ghazzali is not what is learned but what is experienced. It is precisely the insights impressed upon the heart by the actions and the inner traits of the person. Every action of the heart or the limbs, or inner movement of the soul impresses itself as an image (*athar*) on the heart. Or, he sometimes says, the heart is like a mirror which reflects the *sura*, the form, the essence of the actions and dispositions it knows. Sometimes al-Ghazzali speaks of the heart as acquiring a hal, a condition, or a *sifa*, an attribute. In effect, every action implants a thought, an idea on the soul, for the essence of the soul is intellect. This knowledge of the heart is more than just information. This knowledge so impregnates the mind that all thinking runs by allusion from one passage of the Quran or sunna to another, controlling the will and the actions of the believer totally. Such knowledge is a "disposition deeply rooted in the soul from which actions flow naturally and easily without means of reflection or judgment." Such knowledge is not only what we know but what we feel. It is knowledge which is not only known but meant. The fusion of knowing, feeling, and doing integrates the outer and the inner man.

Finally, this maturation of the soul through good deeds and virtues leads to knowledge in yet another sense, to mystical vision and love of God. Purification brings *kashf*, the lifting of veils and a vision of God as real beyond doubt. How is this to be interpreted? In one sense, it seems to mean that the soul once purified is set free from the trammels of the body and rises up to a transcending vision of God, but in fact al-Ghazzali does not allow any direct contact, vision, or unity between man and God. The vision, *maᶜrifa*, means knowledge of the truths of religion known with utmost clarity without any intervening screen. In this sense, the vision of God is not another reality but a way of understanding reality, and the way of living life as a whole which results from the good deeds and virtues which impress themselves upon the heart as truth. Maᶜrifa, in this sense, is not an extra experience but insight into the meaning of reality which rises from intellect and conviction, from behavior in the world and conformity to the principles of one's culture.

Actions, virtues, and knowledge are provisions for the eternal happiness of the soul. The three factors, however, are not cultivated successively or independently. They are altogether interrelated. In al-Ghazzali's view, doing good deeds establishes inner virtues. In turn, the virtues of the heart govern the actions of the limbs. As each act, each thought, each deed presses itself as an image upon the heart or becomes an attribute of the heart, the acquired attributes become all the more continuous, deeply rooted, and seemingly natural. Moreover, since the heart is the seat of knowledge this maturation of the soul through good deeds and virtues leads to mystical vision and love of God. Reciprocally, mystical vision is the source of virtue and channels all action according to God's will. What al-Ghazzali tells us about the relation of inward and outward deeds, of acts and knowledge, of the struggle for virtue and the vision of God, is that they are aspects of a single progressive achievement in the course of which the believer becomes more wise, more just, and more obedient at each step, until he achieves a totality of being which entails at once mystical vision and ordinary piety. Thus al-Ghazzali gives expression to a cultural ideal, the integration of Shariᶜa and Sufism, the outer and the inner way – an ideal which seems to be manifest in his own life in the return from Sufi retreat to his old work as teacher, adviser, and reformer of Muslims. This kind of Sufism reinforces the everyday fulfillment of the Muslim law by providing the believer with a still deeper insight into the reality of God's existence. It is a way to realizing the wholeness of an active worldly life and the inner values which are the Muslim ideal. In these terms al-Ghazzali unified Shariᶜa and Sufism and made them the normative form of Sunni Islam. Alternative forms of mysticism we shall examine shortly.

Theology offered another option for the deepening of scriptural Islam. It rose out of the need to give rational expression to religious concerns. By the middle of the tenth century, after the early debates over the proper understanding of the divine revelation, three basic positions had been accepted. One was a rationalist position which emphasized the centrality of reason as an ordering principle in God's being, in the human understanding of the universe, and in the governing of human behavior. The rationalist position had as its corollary belief in free will and individual responsibility for moral choice. This position was advanced by the Muᶜtazila as well as by philosophers.

A contrary position stressed the absolute omnipotence and inscrutability of the divine being, who could be known only insofar as he had chosen to reveal himself through the Quran. Religious insight could only be attained by accepting the teachings of the Quran and hadith. By extension, all human action was ultimately an expression of the power of the creator rather than an autonomous exercise of free judgment and will, and reason was of no use for

Table 6. *The vocabulary of Sufism*

The anthropology of the soul	
al-fitra	pure state of being, before investment of soul in the body
qalb	heart, soul, seat of knowledge and conscience
ᶜaql	reasoning faculty, often equivalent of *qalb*
nafs	the passions and appetites to be subdued and ordered by reason
The spiritual path	
maqam	achieved status on the way to God
hal	state of rapture by grace of God
ᶜibadat and muᶜamalat	ritual and social obligations
zuhd	piety, asceticism, renunciation
sabr	patience in accepting God's will
shukr	gratitude
tawba	repentance
tawakkul	trust in God
rida	contentment; acceptance of the divine will
Islam	acceptance of God's will
ᶜishq	love, yearning for God
fanaʾ	annihilation of the self
baqaʾ	remaining in God
dhawq	tasting of divine reality
kashf	unveiling, revelation
maᶜrifa	immediate experience of truth
tawhid	unity of God and union in God

religious knowledge or moral choice. The Hanbalis who held this position rejected allegorical interpretation or rational speculation upon the text of the Quran or hadith.

An intermediate position was held by other theologians of the Ashᶜari and Maturidi schools. The Ashᶜaris, as we have seen, affirmed an intermediate position on the role of reason. Religious truths, according to the Ashᶜari position, can only be known through revelation, though reason may play a subordinate role in defending the truth and persuading others. In moral matters all human action is governed by God's power but human beings acquire or participate in their own actions. Al-Ashᶜari thus steered a middle course between Muᶜtazili rationalism and Hanbali literalism.

From the tenth to the twelfth centuries, the Ashᶜaris continued to hold the intermediate position, but they evolved away from the thought of the master in the direction of a more philosophical form of theology. As the foremost opponent of philosophy, Ashᶜarism absorbed the strategies of the opposition. While philosophy declined in influence, philosophic methods and reasoning became an integral part of a new type of philosophical kalam.

In the work of al-Ash⁢ari, kalam argumentation was not methodical, like philosophical proofs, but indicative, in the sense of persuading or demonstrating the validity of a proposition. The main point of kalam was to attack and denounce all false religious views. It was the science of partisan dispute. Thus al-Baqillani (d. 1013) refuted Manichean, Jewish, Christian and heretical Muslim views and advanced his own demonstrations of the existence of God.

Al-Juwayni (d. 1085) and al-Ghazzali were key figures in the development of a new form of Ash⁢ari theology. In the prevailing mode of dialectical argumentation, the theologian presented accepted positions and reasoned by analogy to draw conclusions about an unknown. Al-Juwayni supplemented this form of argumentation by using the Aristotelian syllogism to deduce conclusions from universal principles or logical premises. He also adopted a systematic form of literary exposition. In his *Irshad* (Guide) he discussed in order the principles of reason, the existence of God, God's attributes, possible acts of God, creation of human acts, the last judgment, prophetology, eschatology, and leadership of the community. Al-Juwayni shifted the meaning of kalam from rational argumentation toward systematic philosophical discussion of the principles of religion. Al-Ghazzali further advanced the use of Aristotelian logic to improve the quality of kalam, and organized his theological treatise (*Iqtisad*) in the new standard form. Fakhr al-Din Razi (1149–1209) completed the integration of theology and philosophy. His *Muhassal* begins with an elaborate discussion of ontology and logic. In later manuals of theology, virtually two-thirds of the text was devoted to logic, natural philosophy, and ontology.

The absorption of a philosophic format did not imply a reconciliation of kalam with the principal teachings of philosophy. On the contrary: Ash⁢ari kalam, revitalized by a more sophisticated method of argument, was all the more vigorous in its condemnation of philosophic teachings which were contrary to the scriptural revelation. Al-Ghazzali's *Incoherence of the Philosophers* exposed the contradictions among philosophical writers, and affirmed that a transcendent God could not be known by rational insight. From this vantage al-Ghazzali denied the philosophic concept of the eternity of the world in favor of the Quranic idea of its creation in time, defended the doctrine of the resurrection of the body and of rewards and punishments against the philosophic belief in the eternity of the soul, and affirmed God's knowledge of particulars against the philosophic belief which limited God's knowledge to universals. Al-Ghazzali employed Aristotelian logic and acknowledged the importance of philosophy in the study of nature and mathematics, but in religious matters he insisted on the Ashʿari position on revelation, divine will, and God's command over human acts.

Despite his effectiveness in theological debate, al-Ghazzali was skeptical about the role of kalam. Kalam was useful, he acknowledged, for the defense of religious truth against certain kinds of intellectual confusion, but it was not itself a way of confirming the reality of God's existence. Insight into religious truth, he came to hold, could be found neither in philosophy nor in theology, but only in the direct religious experience provided by Sufism.

Through the synthesis of philosophy and theology, rational inquiry found an integral place in Islamic religious culture, but important differences remained. Philosophy made use of reason without guidance of principles of faith, operating upon the natural order with the conviction that reason alone would suffice to reveal the reality of things. For most theologians, however, reason without support of revelation could not address ultimate realities. Muslim theologians remained acutely conscious of the limitations upon the use of reason. However important in theoretical matters, reason could not discover the truth. The content of what was believed could not be changed by rational speculation, nor could reason discover God's will in matters of good and evil, or serve to control moral behavior, though the knowledge which comes by divine revelation could be enlarged by rational insight and transformed from faith based on tradition to reasoned faith. In this important respect philosophy and theology continued to diverge despite the close alliance between them.

For Muslim theologians, faith as opposed to reason was the key to religious fulfillment. Muslim faith, called *iman*, means knowing the truth and believing in it. Faith begins in the intellect, knowing that God exists, knowing his attributes, his prophets, his will – and accepting this knowledge as the truth (*tasdiq*). Tasdiq is a conviction about what has been preached and recorded, that binds the heart and becomes the basis of a commitment to live one's life in accord with that reality. It is an emotion in the heart as well as a thought in the mind. It is a state of devotion; it entails trust in and submission to God, fear and love of God, and above all love of what God wants men to do and hatred for what he has forbidden. Iman issues in devoted worship; every deed of everyday life is carried out as an expression of God's will.

Ibn Khaldun, a North African scribe and historian (1332–1406) explained the theological tradition. For Ibn Khaldun faith (tasdiq) had several degrees. First, faith is simply genuine belief in the teachings of Islam as traditionally defined: "the affirmation by the heart of what the tongue says." Beyond simple faith there is a higher degree of faith, perfect faith. Calling on Sufi thought Ibn Khaldun defined perfect faith as knowledge of the oneness of

God. This knowledge, however, is not merely a knowledge known, but knowledge which has become a built-in attribute (sifa) modifying the very nature of a man's being. The difference, Ibn Khaldun explains, between

> "state" and knowledge in questions of dogma is the same as that between talking [about attributes] and having them.

It is the difference between knowing that mercy on orphans is recommended and gladly giving alms.

This quality of faith can only be acquired by repeated affirmation of belief and by acts of worship and good deeds. Faith like any habit arises from actions, is perfected by action, and governs all actions.

> The highest degree is the acquisition, from the belief of the heart and the resulting actions, of a quality that has complete control over the heart. It commands the actions of the limbs. Every activity takes place in submissiveness to it. Thus all actions, eventually, become subservient to this affirmation of faith, and this is the highest degree of faith. It is perfect faith. The believer who has it will commit neither a great nor a small sin.[1]

In the theological tradition the capacity for faith rather than reason sums up the human potential for religious salvation. Yet faith includes intellect, and devotion to scriptural truth implies acceptance of a rational dimension in human religiosity. Thus kalam transcended its purely apologetic functions and asserted an essential role for rational speculation in the elucidation of Islamic belief.

ALTERNATIVE ISLAM: PHILOSOPHY, GNOSTIC AND POPULAR SUFISM

Scripturalist Islam integrated with theology and Sufism defined the normative form of Islamic belief and practices. The supreme authority of scripture as revealed truth was integrated with rational judgment. Commitment to the fulfillment of God's command in everyday life was allied to the quest for spiritual insight. Normative Islam was thus a religion of living the life of this world in terms of its ultimate meaning. Within the purview of Islamic culture, however, there were alternative visions of human nature and religious salvation. They were embodied in intellectual form in philosophy and gnosticism; they were expressed in popular rituals and worship. These other forms of Islam overlapped with theology and Sufism, but they were at the same time profound challenges to Sunni–Sharic a–Sufi Islam.

[1] F. Rosenthal, *Ibn Khaldun, The Muqaddimah*, New York: Pantheon Books, 1958, III, pp. 31–3.

Islamic philosophy was the work of a small group of elite scholars committed to rational inquiry and to a specific Hellenistic literary tradition. Al-Farabi had defined philosophy as a comprehensive vision of the divine reality and the human condition. Ibn Sina (Avicenna), the great physician and metaphysician, continued this tradition and gave new vitality to philosophic thought. The son of a Persian official serving the Samanid regime near Bukhara, he studied logic, natural science, and medicine. By the age of 18, he was the master of all subjects. He became a minister of the Samanids but as a result of court intrigues was forced to flee from place to place. He lived for 14 years in Isfahan and died at Hamadhan in 1037. A man of action, he produced numerous scholarly works. He contributed to all the natural sciences including physics, chemistry, astronomy, mathematics, and natural history, and composed the monumental *Qanun fi al-Tibb* (Canon of Medicine). The Canon includes an introduction to the general study of medicine and volumes on pharmacology of herbs, pathology of organs, fevers, surgery, and other books. His most important philosophical work was the *Kitab al-Shifaʾ* (Book of Remedy). Like his philosophic predecessors, Ibn Sina wrote on neo-Platonic metaphysics, natural science, and mysticism.

The core of Ibn Sina's teaching was his ontology or doctrine of being. God is conceived as transcendent and prior to the universe. He stands utterly beyond all being. However, while distinct from him in essence, the universe is brought forth from God. Ibn Sina attempts to preserve the belief in the transcendence of God and yet to allow for a continuity between the necessary being and the contingent universe. He thus accommodates his basic concept of God's existence to scriptural tradition.

This doctrine is based on Ibn Sina's distinction of essence and existence. In Ibn Sina's view this is a distinction made by the mind. Reversing traditional philosophic views, he argued that essences are logical categories, except for the essence which is by definition inseparable from existence. This is the necessary being or God. All other beings are contingent, for their existence does not necessarily follow from their essence. All contingent beings are divided into two categories: necessary being, the eternal intellectual substances; and possible beings, impermanent material things.

The distinction of necessary and possible beings allowed Ibn Sina to conceive of God as utterly transcendent and yet to explain how the universe was brought into existence. Following the neo-Platonic tradition, Ibn Sina held that the process of self-contemplation brings the lower orders into existence. The first being brings forth the first intellect which, contemplating the essence of the necessary being and its own being, brings forth the second intellect. The process of contemplation proceeds until it brings forth the tenth intellect, which completes the celestial and spiritual universe. Thus, there are successive levels of heavenly being, each of which is an intellect emanating from the divine being, comprised of a substance generated by the next higher level of being; each level includes an angel, a soul and a heavenly sphere. The tenth or active intellect apprehends itself and forms ideas which bring into existence the concrete beings of the terrestrial realm. The tenth intellect also illuminates the minds of human beings and enables them to contemplate the universals existing in the angelic sphere.

This theory attempts to account for a necessary being who transcends all other reality and who yet remains the source of a contingent and created world. The theory of the creation also defines the ultimate relation of human beings to God. The human soul is an eternal substance whose destiny is to be reunited with the active intellect and through it with the heavenly world and God. In Ibn Sina's view, the human soul is composed of several faculties. The rational faculty is divided into the practical faculty, the source of all movement and activity, and the theoretical or speculative faculty. The theoretical faculty may be perfected through several stages until it reaches the level of intellect in which the human soul itself becomes an image of the intelligible and spiritual world receiving illumination from the active intellect. The active intelligence thus makes known to the human intellect the reality of the intelligible world. Religious vision is essentially an intellectual one, for God may be known only as pure intelligence; his first cause is manifest to reason but there is no suggestion of direct union between the human being and the necessary being. In Ibn Sina's view, the highest level of intellection belongs to prophets, who come to know all things perfectly and directly from the active intellect and who communicate their knowledge in imaginative images to ordinary human beings. Prophets teach the existence of God and the practical and ritual aspects of religion. Religion then is an imaginative presentation of truths which are known in a pure form to the purely rational soul.

The *Recital of Hayy*, the *Recital of the Bird* and the *Recital of Salmon and Absal*, three allegorized texts believed to have been written by Ibn Sina, develop the mystical aspects of his philosophical concepts. They recount how a beautiful stranger, an angel of initiation, leads the soul to the orient, to the source of light and the vision of God. In the visionary tales, the soul journeys through the cosmos with the help of angelic guides. This journey of the soul is at once an inward exploration of its own being and a progress through the cosmos. The consciousness which attains knowledge of itself attains knowledge of the successive levels of the divine emanation in the form of angels' souls and celestial spheres. This journey is motivated by love of the divine being and by the realization that the soul is a stranger in the world seeking to return to its origin. The method of this journey is *ta'wil*, interpretation of all existing things in a symbolic way so as to arrive at a new insight into reality. The study of the visionary recitals is then a psychic event leading the soul back to the experience which these texts symbolize.

This journey requires that the soul be detached from every worldly and corrupting influence. Like a steel mirror the soul must be polished to perfection to see the divine radiance reflected in itself. In this vision, the soul loses consciousness of itself as the medium of vision and retains consciousness only of the divine presence. This mode of union, however, is not a substantial union of the soul with God, but an intellectual vision of God as the necessary being who is the cause of the contingent world. By purifying imagination and by concentrating the intellect, the soul, driven by love of God, may lose itself in contemplation of the divine truth, but it has no prospect of merger with a transcendent God.

Ibn Sina's philosophy is thus a form of intellectual mysticism, which attempted to reconcile a Greek philosophic and theosophical point of view with the scriptural tradition. The doctrine of the necessary being is couched in a language which attempts to be consistent with the scripturalist view of the transcendence of God and the separation of the created world from him. The concept of human salvation, while allowing for human intellectual and philosophic comprehension of divine reality, is presented in a way which maintains the ultimate distance between man and God.

Ibn Sina's views were in many respects similar to Sufi theosophy and inspired later Sufi and gnostic mystics. His metaphysical universe corresponded to similar Sufi visions of the structure of the cosmos and the nature of the quest for salvation. Ibn Sina stands therefore not only as a central figure in philosophy, but as a precursor to Suhrawardi, Ibn al-ᶜArabi and later philosophers and mystics of the sixteenth- and seventeenth-century Iranian school of *hikma* (wisdom). His concepts stand at the center of a long tradition of philosophic speculation and gnostic experimentation – a tradition which continues to appeal to intellectual and religious minorities in Muslim countries to the present day.

While Ibn Sina tried to reconcile the scriptural vision of the transcending oneness and otherness of God, with the philosophical and mystical conviction that God and humans shared the same spiritual essence, that God was available to human knowledge, and that humans were capable of return to and salvation in the divine being, his effort was still out of tune with the scriptural tradition.

His images and vocabulary come from Greek philosophy rather than Quranic symbols. Moreover, some of his specific doctrines are actually heretical. Ibn Sina's doctrine of the eternity of the world and its creation as a form of emanation from the divine being contradicts the revelation that the world was created ex nihilo. His emphasis upon the inherent rationality contradicts the scripturalist conviction that all which exists is the product of God's inscrutable will. His views on the nature of the soul and the body also contradict the scripturalist position. For Ibn Sina, the soul survives by union with the spiritual order from which it is derived. This is contradictory to the Muslim view that man, constituted of both body and soul, will at the day of judgment be resurrected as an entity and rewarded or punished as such. Philosophy might attempt to define its positions in accord with scripture but its inspiration and religious vision remained profoundly alien to scripturalist Muslims.

While one stream of Sufism led to an effort to fulfill God's will and command as revealed in scripture, another stream of Sufism attempted to achieve a contemplative knowledge of God's being. The Shariʿa forms of Sufism stressed the fulfillment of God's command to the very deepest levels of man's being as the way to salvation; the gnostic forms of Sufism sought spiritual fulfillment by bringing the human soul into complete harmony with God. The former was an active fulfillment of God's commands; the latter a contemplative state of being. Sufi gnosticism was fed by strong currents in Islamic philosophy, neo-Platonism, Ismaʿili metaphysics, ancient Greek or Hermetic occult sciences, and other Middle Eastern religious ideas. In the post-imperial era two figures stood out as the spokesmen of a theosophical and gnostic form of Sufism oriented toward metaphysical comprehension and ecstatic contemplation.

Suhrawardi was born in 1153 and was executed for heresy in 1191. Suhrawardi combined the philosophical and theosophical aspects of Sufism with Ibn Sina's philosophy of emanations, and with ancient Zoroastrian, Platonic and Hermetic symbols, and synthesized them into a new form of Islamic mysticism. In Suhrawardi's view, he was reviving an ancient esoteric wisdom, revealed to Hermes Trismegistus and then communicated in two streams of tradition, via Greece, Persia and Egypt, to Islam. Suhrawardi believed himself to be the spokesman of a universal wisdom known to the ancient sages of Iran, Greece and India and now revealed once again in the Quran.

In his *Hikmat al-Ishraq* (Theosophy of the Orient of Lights) and other symbolic and mystical narratives, Suhrawardi taught that the divine essence was pure light, the source of all existence, and that the reality of all other

things was derived from the supreme light. Degrees of light were associated
with degrees of knowledge and self-awareness. For Suhrawardi, as for Ibn
Sina, the emanation of light from the primary being established a hierarchy of
angelic substances standing between God and this world. The angels were
limitless in number. In Suhrawardi's vision there were two orders of angels:
a vertical order in which each higher angel generated and dominated the lower
ones and each lower angel loved the higher – the vertical order of angels gave
rise to the celestial spheres; the horizontal order of angels constituted the
world of Platonic forms and archetypes, and gave rise to the angels who
governed human souls.

In this spiritual universe the human soul stood in a privileged position. The
soul was, in part, a heavenly body and, in part, it was imprisoned in an earthly
body. The imprisoned part sought to reunite with its angelic half and to escape
its material and pitiful state. The souls who succeeded in freeing themselves
would enjoy the proximity of the supreme light. In Suhrawardi's theosophy
the hierarchy of being was a ladder of illumination along which the purified
soul could return from the material world to the world of archetypes. In its
own symbols this vision resembles neo-Platonic, Sufi, and Avicennan ideas.

Ibn al-ʿArabi (1165–1240), born in Murcia, Spain and educated in Seville,
made the pilgrimage to Mecca, where he had a vision of the spiritual universe.
He saw the divine throne upheld by pillars of light. In the vision he was told
that he was the seal of sainthood, the supreme figure in the hierarchy of saints
who upheld the universe. As a result of these visions he wrote the *Meccan
Revelations*. From Mecca he moved to Konya (Turkey) and Damascus, where
he finally settled and where he died. In Damascus he wrote *The Bezels of Wisdom*,
dictated to him by God through the angel Gabriel. This book was the
masterpiece of esoteric sciences for it synthesized Hermetic, neo-Platonic,
Ismaʿili, and Sufi influences into a religious vision for which Ibn al-ʿArabi
claimed an authority equivalent to that of the Prophet.

In Ibn Al-ʿArabi's thought all reality is one. This is the doctrine of *wahdat
al-wujud*, the unity of being. Everything which exists is God. The divine reality
transcends all manifestations, but the manifestations are encompassed by and
plunged in God. While God is transcendent the manifested world is identical
with him in essence. A hadith says: "I was a hidden treasure and I longed to
be known so I created the world that I might be known." Yet all manifestations which reveal God are but the veils which conceal him.

The reality of the universe is manifested on several planes; the lower planes
being symbols of the higher. The highest is the absolute essence of God; there

follow in the hierarchy of being the attributes and names of God, the actions
and the presence of lordship, the world of spiritual existences, archetypes and
forms, and finally, the world of senses and sensible experience.

The existence of the hierarchy of being is understood in terms of theophanies
(*tajalliyat*) instead of the neo-Platonic emanations. Each level of reality is a
theophany of the divine names, which is brought into being by the self-
consciousness of a higher level which, becoming conscious, generates another
state of spiritual being. The process of creation is further imagined as the result
of the divine breath just as words are formed by human breath. The creation
is renewed at every breath of the Lord. Existence gushes out from the absolute
being whose mercy and love of his own fulfillment bestows existence.

Ibn al-ʿArabi's vision of the unfolding of the divine being and the creation
of the material world follows in broad outline the philosophic and neo-Platonic
theory. To these theories, he adds a rich and original vocabulary and corollary
symbols. For example, in Ibn al-ʿArabi's vision, the first intellect of the
philosophers, the primary manifestation of the divine being, is variously
symbolized as the attributes and names of God, the logos, the prototypes of
creation, the *insan al-kamil*, or perfect man, and the *haqiqa muhammadiya*, or
Muhammadan reality. The divine names symbolize at once the creation of the
world, the revelation and the appearance of prophets, and the spiritual capacities of human beings. The prophets and the saints symbolize the fact that
man himself is a manifestation of and ultimately an aspect of the absolute. The
person who understands the nature of reality and the unity of existence is the
perfect saint. Having discovered the truth he in turn becomes a guide for the
rest of mankind. The symbols of the perfect man and the Muhammadan reality
compress in a personified image the reality of the universe. Ibn al-ʿArabi unites
cosmic and human symbols of the same truth. This condensation of symbols
also links the gnostic and philosophic traditions to the Muslim revelation. The
gnostic concept of the spiritual reality is linked with the Muslim concept of the
historic actuality of Muhammad as Prophet.

Gnostic theosophy teaches that the world is one, and that all things participate in the chain of being, the continuous hierarchy of existence extending
from God to the spiritual world to the lowliest beings. In this hierarchy man
stands in a central position linked to both the world of spirit and the world
of matter. Because each thing in the world is an analog of the spiritual reality,
by understanding the symbolism of this reality we may pass from this world
to the spiritual world beyond. Because the spiritual world is a hierarchy of
intelligences, through our capacity for knowledge we may participate in the
divine reality. By contemplating the cosmos, we become one with the universe.

Thus human beings occupy a privileged place in the creation, for they are capable of rising above their place in the material world to return to their true home in the presence of God. For Ibn al-ʿArabi the sensible world is but a dream, and must be interpreted to reveal the reality to which it points. Everything in nature is a symbol of *haqq*, the divine reality.

This return to God is motivated by love; it is driven by prayer and worship. Its fulfillment is symbolized not by the concepts of fanaʾ and baqaʾ as in ordinary Sufism but by the symbols of intellect and the perfect man. In the vision of Ibn al-ʿArabi, God is the mirror in which man contemplates his own reality and man is the mirror in which God knows his essence. Man needs God to exist, and God needs the world to know him.

The concept of a heavenly world, a realm of being which is the counterpart of the actual world, the archetype, the idea, the cause, and the governor of the world in which all humans live, welds the reality of the world and of the human mind. The intellectual and spiritual task assumed by Muslim gnostics was to understand the nature of symbolic discourse and its relation to concrete reality and to integrate the two by making speech and thought correspond to the physical and social actuality of the world. They attempted to achieve wholeness of being, to attain the truth which seems always to elude us because of the paradoxical relation of thought to actuality. In gnostic thought the intangible reality of meaning carried in language and conveyed between persons is a realm of reality separate from the physical world; yet it is the model of the physical world, the image of it, and the guide of our actions in it. Thought and language in the theosophy of Ibn al-ʿArabi are ever the same and ever different from the actualities which they define.

The doctrine of Ibn al-ʿArabi was the culmination of centuries of Sufi gnostic and philosophical contemplation. His theoretical vision and his personal authority shaped for centuries to come the further development of Sufi theosophy and practice. Ever after, Sufi discourse turned upon the problem of understanding the unity of being and reconciling theosophy with Quranic concepts.

Furthermore, the thought of Ibn al-ʿArabi had a profound, though unintended implication for later Sufi practice and even for the daily life of Muslim believers. By implication theosophical metaphysics diminished the importance of observance of Shariʿa and Muslim ritual. For Sufis cosmic harmony became a justification for abandoning Muslim laws and for seeking states of intoxicated ecstasy. For many later Sufis it justified an antinomian morality. Such doctrines were also used to minimize the importance of communal loyalties, for truth is universal. Theosophical views increased the importance of dreams, visions and

ecstasy rather than ordinary Muslim devotions. In some cases it was allied to
the use of drugs and physical techniques to gain ecstatic vision.

The doctrines of the perfect man and the invisible hierarchy of saints, the
doctrine of the *qutb* or pole of the universe around which the cosmos revolves,
also enforced popular belief in Sufi miracles. Though consistent in principle
with the Shariᶜa–Sufi orientation, the theosophical doctrines of Ibn al-ᶜArabi
allowed for forms of religious practice and popular belief by which Muslims
sought to short-circuit the trying discipline of the Shariᶜa way of life and to
directly achieve spiritual redemption by contemplative, miraculous, and
magical means. For the Sufi masters Sufism was a devotional practice or
gnostic illumination. For ordinary believers it came to mean the veneration of
saints and the tombs of saints.

This veneration has its Muslim origin in the Quran and the hadith which
mention the Prophet, the angels, the scholars, and holy-men as potential
intercessors between the ordinary Muslim believers and God. The earliest
form of Muslim veneration of human intermediaries was the cult of the
Prophet. By the end of the eighth century the Prophet's burial place had
become an important place for prayer. The story of his *miᶜraj* or ascension to
heaven in Jerusalem became a focus of popular piety and Sufi inspiration. Al-
Bistami (d. 873) used the ascension as a model for his mystical journey, in
which the stages of the Prophet's ascent became equivalent to the stations of
the Sufis' progress toward God. Sufis wrote their own miᶜrajs, modeled on the
Prophet's, which organized the levels of heaven into stages corresponding to
the emotional levels of the journey toward unity. In the tenth and eleventh
centuries the site of the Prophet's ascension in Jerusalem became a popular
place for Muslim worship. Already theologians were explaining that the
Prophet was not of ordinary flesh and that he was immune from ordinary
sins.

The Shiᶜa were probably the first to revere the family of the Prophet. In the
early tenth century the Shiᶜi holy places were provided with elaborate tombs
and became centers of pilgrimage. Najaf, the burial place of ᶜAli, became a
hallowed cemetery; Mashhad, Karbala, and Qum became Shiᶜi shrines. The
Fatimid Caliphs marked the Prophet's birthday (*mawlid*) by ceremonies and a
procession of court dignitaries in the presence of the Caliph. The Fatimids also
built a number of monumental shrines on the graves of descendants of the
Prophet, which became the object of popular pilgrimage in the course of the
twelfth century. In 1154 and 1155 the head of Husayn, the martyred son of
ᶜAli, was transferred to Cairo, where it became the focus of a popular Sunni

8 A Sufi preaching

cult lasting to the present day. By the end of the eleventh century the mawlid
had also become a popular custom among Sunnis in Mesopotamia and Syria,
and Saladin brought it back to Egypt as a popular festival.

Sunni veneration of the Prophet, the family of the Prophet, and of later
Muslim martyrs and saints, developed either in parallel with, or in reaction to
Shiʿi pilgrimage and worship at the tombs of the family of ʿAli. In the eleventh
century a mausoleum and school in the memory of Abu Hanifa, the founder
of the Hanafi school of law, was reconstructed in Baghdad. In 1176 the
Ayyubid dynasty rebuilt the college and tomb of al-Shafiʿi in Cairo. It became
customary for pilgrims to visit the tombs of companions of the Prophet, and
to pray at the graves of holy-men who martyred themselves for Islam or
through whom miracles had been performed. By the beginning of the thirteenth century there were hundreds of sanctuaries all over the Muslim world.
Guides and manuals were written to tell the miracles of the saints and to

prescribe the rituals and prayers which would bring blessing upon the pilgrim. Early thirteenth-century guidebooks show shrines dispersed throughout Syria, Egypt, Turkey, Iraq, and Iran.

Formal theology and mystical writing gave support to popular belief. As early as the ninth century al-Tirmidhi (d. 893) developed a theory of sainthood as an explanation of the mysterious power of Sufis. Al-Baqillani (d. 1013) wrote that Sufi masters were friends of God who were capable of doing miracles and of interceding on behalf of ordinary Muslims. He elaborated a theological doctrine to distinguish saints from the Prophet and to define the nature of their miraculous powers. Al-Qushayri and al-Ghazzali accepted this doctrine and made it part of formal Muslim belief. Ibn al-ʿArabi elaborated this faith into a cosmological doctrine of the hierarchy of saints who upheld the order of the universe. These teachings gave support to popular faith in Sufi ceremonies, belief in the efficacy of prayers performed at the tombs of saints, and the quest for ecstatic experiences. The equation of holy-men and martyrs with the spiritual universe became an inherent aspect of Islamic religious culture. Whatever the legal, the intellectual or the doctrinal basis of Sufism, its power and appeal to the masses of everyday Muslim believers came from faith in the miraculous power of saints.

THE DIALOGUES WITHIN ISLAM

Sunni Islamic beliefs and practices, as expressed in a variety of literatures, fell into certain patterns. By the ninth century, Sunnis accepted the Quran, hadith, and law as the core of Islam; schools of law and madrasas became the central institutional expression of this conviction. In Sunni Islam the main organizational impulse focused on schools of law, each of which had its own version of the Shariʿa and its own jurisprudential methods for deriving the substance of the law. Though they varied in matters of detail there was widespread agreement upon basic religious issues.

With the consolidation of hadith and Shariʿa as the central expression of Islamic identity, the great debates of the tenth to the thirteenth century turned on the relation of hadith and law to theology and Sufism. The debate over law and theology was especially complex, for it involved a debate over the role of rationalism carried out at several levels. At one level there was a debate between philosophy and kalam over reason and revelation. At another level there was a general debate between kalam and scripturalism over the role which theology itself would have in Islamic belief. The result of these debates was the integration of theological rationalism into the Shariʿa religious men-

Table 7. *Muslim religious movements and sects*

Shiʿism	
ʿAlid imams	Claim to be sole rightful leaders of Muslim community
Zaydis	Followers of Zayd; establish dynasties in the Caspian region and Yemen
Ismaʿilis	Militant, establish Fatimid and Qarmatian movements
Ithna ʿashari	"Twelvers," Imamis, pacifist, primarily Iraq
Kharijism (calls for election of Caliphs)	
Azariqa (684 – *c.* 700)	Southwestern Iran. Sinners must be excluded from the Muslim community; declare war on all other Muslims
Ibadis	States founded in Oman, North Africa; sinners may remain Muslims with limited rights; permit political compromise
Theological Schools	
Qadaris	Hasan al-Basri (d. 728); discussed God's determination and human autonomy
Murjiʾa	Defined good Muslims by faith rather than works; refused to judge between ʿUthman and ʿAli
Muʿtazila	Neutral in the disputes over the proper succession to the Caliphate; affirm human free will and createdness of the Quran
Ashʿaris	al-Ashʿari (d. 935); compromise between Muʿtazila and Hanbali theological positions
Sufism	
School of Khurasan	al-Hallaj (d. 923), ecstatic
School of Baghdad	al-Junayd (d. 910), sober
Sunni Schools of Law	
Maliki	
Hanafi	
Shafiʿi	
Hanbali (ahl al-hadith)	
Falasifa	
Hunayn b. Ishaq	Translator of Greek texts
al-Kindi (d. *c.* 866)	Accepts Muʿtazili kalam
al-Farabi (d. 950)	Tradition of Alexandrian Hellenistic thought; superiority of reason to revelation
Ibn Sina (Avicenna, d. 1037)	Neo-Platonic philosophy and medicine
Ibn Rushd (Averroes, d. 1198)	Aristotelian, reconciliation with Shariʿa

tality. Theology (kalam) became an acceptable adjunct of Islamic belief. Some scholars even regarded theology as an exalted science which could prove the truth of revelation. Rational understanding of the truth, in their view, was essential to being a good Muslim. For many other scholars, however, theology was but a secondary concern limited to the defense of revealed truth, a kind of medicine for doubters. It was necessary that at least some members of the community pursue it but it was not essential for all believers.

The schools of theology became closely linked to the schools of law. The

Hanafi school of law harbored the Maturidi school of theology. The Shafiʿi law school was the home of Ashʿarism. However, not all legists in each school were committed to a theological position. While schools of theology found a home among the different groups of lawyers, a theological position was not necessarily part of the teaching of the law schools. The legists treated theology as an enrichment of their intellectual and religious life rather than as the center of their scriptural position.

The Hanbalis, however, neither harbored nor tolerated a school of theology. They rejected rational speculation in any form. The Hanbali school was thus simultaneously a school of jurisprudence specifying hadith as the source of law and a school of theology affirming the overriding importance of revelation in Islamic law. At the same time, Hanbalism represented a conservative Sunni political tradition insisting upon the legitimacy of all Caliphs, past and present. Thus by broad, but not quite complete consensus, theology in various forms was accepted as an important adjunct to Islamic religious faith and activity.

Sufism was similarly integrated with scripturalism. Sufis began with a religious community, leadership, and forms of worship separate from that of the schools of law. Progressively, however, there was a rapprochement between the legal and the Sufi approaches to Islam. The legists and the Sufis accepted each other. Sufis accepted hadith and law as the basis of Muslim belief and practice. Legists became Sufis and recognized the importance of the inner life to the full realization of the teachings of the law. As this rapprochement took place, the meaning of Shariʿa progressively changed. In the eighth century the term referred to the legal and moral norms for behavior specified in the Quran, hadith, and law. In the course of the tenth and eleventh centuries, a succession of Sufi lawyers and theologians, culminating in al-Ghazzali, redefined Shariʿa to include a moral aspect. Thus, Shariʿa came to be a comprehensive term implying not only legally correct behavior, but a rich intellectual, spiritual, and mystical life. While the term Shariʿa continued to be used in the narrow sense to mean revealed law as opposed to rational principles, or the law of external behavior as opposed to spiritual truths, the prevailing concept was all-inclusive.

By the thirteenth century the Sunni religious position included a spectrum of religious beliefs and practices built up around acceptance of the law, deepened by rational understanding and argument, and by Sufi interior piety. Law, theology, and Sufism shaped the Muslim consensus around belief in a transcendent God who had created the world and revealed his will to human beings through the agency of his prophets. Muslims believed in the authority of Muhammad and his Prophethood and in the tradition of the community. They accepted the priority of earlier generations, the goodness of the companions, the genius of the imams of the law schools, and the piety of Sufi masters as the sources of right guidance. They accepted the literatures of law, theology, and mysticism as setting forth the beliefs, practices, and ethical and moral attitudes required of a good Muslim. The integrated concept of Islam thus combined the scriptural revelation of required actions with philosophical, theosophical, and mystical views of the nature of the universe and the meaning of human action within it.

The Sunni consensus presented a Muslim ideal of an individual who lives in society according to the rules he has been brought up to respect, according to the norms and laws of the Quran, hadith, law and social custom, yet in harmony with his own inner knowledge, dispositions, choices, and feelings. This cultural ideal combined the practice of Shariᶜa and the cultivation of mystical knowledge. The Sunni–Shariᶜa–Sufi form of Islam sought salvation in the this-worldly conduct of the ritual and social prescriptions of Islam. Social relationships, friendships, earning a living, marriage, and family all came under the purview of religion. For Sunni Muslims, a religious life was an active life, consisting of everyday occupations in politics and business, of marriage and family, intermixed with the practice of ritual and other religious obligations. For the Muslim merchant or artisan in the marketplace, the scholar in school, the scribe at court, or the mystic at worship, worldly action and fulfillment of religious commands were the soil in which intellectual and moral skills could grow. Religious knowledge and virtue could only be achieved by engaging in worldly affairs, but worldly activity has no ultimate value unless it is infused by religious purposes. The Sunni–Shariᶜa–Sufi tradition rejected worldly values pursued for their own sake; the enjoyment of family, economic well-being, and power is of secondary importance. It turned its back upon the *aretē* of the warrior, the civic responsibility of the Greek citizen, the intellectualism of professionals and the aestheticism of aristocrats. Still it did not embrace other-worldly detachment, like the spirituality of the monk, the creativity of the romantic, or the abstract knowledge of the scientist. It was neither a surrender to the world nor an escape from the world. It was a way of living in the world without being absorbed by it or fleeing from it. The goal of the Sunni–Shariᶜa–Sufi view of life was devotion to God as the basis of an active worldly personality.

The existence of a normative concept of Islam did not mean the formation of a new orthodoxy. The complex of views contained in Sunni–Shariᶜa–Sufi Islam never became a formal system. Islam has no master science as Christianity has in theology, and no unified definition of itself. Within the Sunni complex there were numerous collections of hadith, several equally valid versions of the law, several acceptable theological positions, and different schools of mysticism. Within the Sunni consensus the range of theological viewpoints could vary from sophisticated philosophical reasoning in theology and law to complete exclusion of the use of reasoning and literal reliance on scripture. Muslim mystics varied from strict adherence to the law to complete antinomian lack of interest in convention, ritual, and morality.

While the Sunni–Shariʿa–Sufi consensus allowed considerable flexibility within itself, the Sunni community also permitted major religious positions to develop outside its framework. While devotional, rational Sufi positions were partly merged into the general position, philosophy, gnosticism, and popular religion maintained an independent stance challenging the normative form of Islam. Beyond the debates within the Sunni fold important religious alternatives were available. Their availability and the debate concerning their validity made up a more comprehensive program of Islamic religious discussions.

The most important religious alternative came from within Sufism. The gnostic and theosophical tradition influenced by philosophy, while partly accepted into the general Sunni consensus, represented an altogether different view of human religious goals. The gnostic vision was embodied in the Sufi movement, in Ismaʿili Shiʿism, and in philosophical literatures. While the scripturalist view insisted upon the fulfillment of God's command in worldly action, the gnostic view stressed knowledge of reality as the basis of the ultimate reunion of the human being with the basic structure of being. The goal of life was insight and contemplative union with the divine reality, to be achieved by purification of the soul and its detachment from bodily and material concerns.

The several forms of gnosticism, however, differed in their comprehension of the mechanism of this purification, vision, and union with God. Some gnostics stressed reason as the essential aspect of the human soul and the metaphysical structure of the universe. Others stressed emotional forms of illumination; still others stressed the authority of imams and spiritual guides in the process of liberation from the confines of the material world. The peripatetic philosophers stressed reason as the basis of knowledge of God and as the key to a total transformation of the soul which enabled the gnostic not only to comprehend but to enter into the divine presence. In all its variations, gnosticism was a quest for a direct contemplative realization of the divine for which scripturalist symbols, rational dialectics, ritual practices and ethical

Table 8. *Muslim worship*

Five pillars of Islam	
shahada	statement of faith. There is no God but God, and Muhammad is the Prophet of God
zakat	almsgiving
salat	prayer performed five times daily: before dawn, noon, mid-afternoon, before sunset, mid-evening
muezzin	stands in the minaret to summon worshipers to prayer
wuduʾ	ritual ablutions prior to prayer
qibla	prayer performed facing in the direction of Mecca
masjid	mosque; place of prayer furnished with a *mihrab* (niche to mark direction of Mecca); *minbar* (pulpit); *maqsura* (box for Caliph)
imam	leader of prayer
Friday midday prayer	performed in *jamiᶜ* (mosque for the whole community). Prayer followed by *khutba*, or sermon preached by *khatib* from the *minbar*, in which the authority of the ruler is acknowledged
Ramadan	ninth lunar month, dedicated to daytime fasting
laylat al-qadr	27th of Ramadan: Night of Majesty commemorating first revelation of the Quran
ᶜid al-fitr	lesser *ᶜid*: festival celebrating the end of Ramadan
hajj	pilgrimage to Mecca
ᶜid al-adha	greater *ᶜid*: celebration and animal sacrifices to mark end of the pilgrimage
Optional festivals	
mawlid al-nabi	birthday of the Prophet
laylat al-miᶜraj	night of Muhammad's ascent to heaven from Jerusalem
ᶜashura	10th of Muharram: Shiᶜi festival commemorating martyrdom of Husayn

behavior were all secondary considerations. It was a religion of the visionary soul rather than the active person.

Another religious alternative within the Sunni tradition was popular Islam. Though popular belief in the magical powers of saints and their capacity to intercede for men before God was sanctioned by Sufi theory, popular Muslim beliefs cultivated a magical attitude toward spiritual truth. Popular faith held that God's miraculous power could be transmitted into the world through the person of his saints and the physical things with which they had come into contact. Tombs of saints were considered especially potent. This magical faith in direct divine intervention in human affairs put aside the whole of the Sunni effort to build a morally disciplined worldly life upon the teachings of the scriptural tradition.

Outside of the Sunni fold there were also communal alternatives. For the Shiᶜa the critical issue was not law or mysticism but loyalty to the family of ᶜAli. The Shiᶜa held that the family of ᶜAli was entitled to the leadership because of the presence of a divine spirit in each successive generation. This divine grace both entitled the ᶜAlids to the Caliphate and made them an infallible source of knowledge of the divine will. Muhammad, in the Shiᶜi view, had revealed God's will in the Quran, but the interpretation of the Quran was vested in the infallible imams. In their view, the true source of belief in each generation was ultimately not the text of tradition, the consensus of the jurists, or the piety of other Muslims, but an imam descended from ᶜAli. From this vantage point Shiᶜism left a legacy of religious teachings similar to the Sunni types, but it also moved toward a merger with Sufism, in that the divinely graced imam became the example of a mystical reunion with God. Shiᶜism is also characterized by a religious mood which stresses messianic hope in the return of the imam as a messiah who will redeem Muslims from the burdens of the world. Shiᶜism is also chiliastic in believing that history will come to an end. The cycles of prophets and imams will issue in a cataclysm, out of which will emerge a reborn mankind and the kingdom of God on earth.

Shiᶜi Islam clusters in different ways from Sunni Islam. Instead of schools of law there are sects founded by the followers of the various imams. By the late ninth century the Shiᶜi movement had split into several branches. The "twelver" branch followed one line of succession; the Ismaᶜilis followed another. In time there would be more disagreements, each disagreement leading to the development of a new sect with varying religious principles. Shiᶜi communities, often at war with their Sunni neighbors, were established throughout the Middle East.

With all these variations what did it mean to be a Muslim? It meant that one believed in the truth of God's existence, in the revelation of the Quran, and that one adhered to at least some of the positions in a wide range of religious expression. Muslim believers clustered around one of several Sunni schools of law or one of several Shiᶜi sects. Islam, then, included a variety of religious positions sharing the same historical tradition. To be a Muslim meant to ponder these positions in the terms set down in the formative era of Islamic civilization.

CONCLUSION: THE MIDDLE EASTERN ISLAMIC PARADIGM

The process of forming a Middle Eastern Islamic civilization occupied six hundred years from the beginning of the seventh to the beginning of the thirteenth century. However innovative, Islamic civilization was constructed upon a framework of institutions and cultures inherited from the ancient Middle East. On the eve of the Islamic era Middle Eastern society was organized on several levels. At the base there were numerous local, parochial communities built around factional, lineage, tribal, and village groups. These communities were integrated by market exchanges, and by great religious associations – Jewish, Christian, or Zoroastrian. The larger-scale economic networks and religious associations were in turn under the rule of the Byzantine and Sasanian empires. On the cultural level the ancient heritage included the monotheistic religions, imperial arts and literatures, and philosophy and science. This complex institutional and cultural heritage was carried over into the Islamic era. Despite the rise and fall of empires and shifts in economic activity, the fundamental aspects of technology, modes of production, and the relation of human communities to the natural environment continued unaltered. Also, the basic modes of state organization and family and religious association remained the same. The characteristic changes of the Islamic era were the formation of new political and social identities, the organization of new religious communities, and the generation, out of the elements of the past, of a new cultural style.

The process of creating a new political and religious identity for Middle Eastern societies began in Arabia. While under the influence of Byzantine and Sasanian civilizations, Arabia was not fully integrated into the rest of the region. Arabia was basically a lineage type of society in which the conflicts of lineage and commercial communities, and the religious and cultural influences emanating from the rest of the Middle East made possible the emergence of a new Prophet, Muhammad, and the revelation of a new religion, Islam. To Muhammad God revealed a new monotheism, which differed in its specific teachings, eschatological consciousness, and literary qualities from Judaism and Christianity. The Prophet also organized a new community, the umma of the Muslims, parallel in form to Jewish and Christian religious associations. While the new society in principle resembled Middle Eastern forms of civilization, it differed in one crucial respect. Islam merged state and religious communal organizations, and did not, as did Byzantine-Christian and Sasanian-Zoroastrian/Christian societies, differentiate between the realm of Caesar and the realm of God.

The creation of a Muslim community in Mecca and Medina represented the formation of an overarching religiously defined community as an integrating force in a lineage society. The Prophet and his disciples transformed a segmentary society to make it serve the purposes of mediation among lineage groups, regulation of economy, state formation, and moral reform while maintaining its basic lineage structures. In Arabia the existence of two levels of segmentary and religious organization resulted in a complex system of values. In principle the Quran introduced a concept of transcendent reality which was opposed to the values of tribal culture. It was opposed to the aggrandizement of tribal groups and the aretē of the tyrannical, boastful, and hedonistic warrior, a community based on religious brotherhood and personal humility, modesty, and self-restraint. In practice, however, the family and lineage structures of Arabian peoples became part of Islamic society. Pagan virtues were preserved by being vested with new meaning as Islamic ethics, and bedouin identity persisted alongside of Islamic loyalties. The ethos, then, of the first Islamic society in Arabia was an amalgam of different levels of religious transcendence, modification of worldly reality, and acceptance of non-Islamic Arabian bedouin civilization. In its first guise the Islamic mission became a model for how radical religious values and sectarian impulses would actually function in lineage and tribal societies.

The next phase in the creation of a Middle Eastern Islamic society was the Arab conquests and migrations. They led to the creation of a new regime, the Caliphate, the settlement of new cities and towns, the formation of new urban communities, the rise of trade, and the growth of agriculture. In the garrison cities of the Middle East warrior-bedouin migrants were assimilated to non-Arab populations to form new mixed communities. The Arabs were transformed into an urban-dwelling, occupationally differentiated population which included workers, artisans, merchants, and a new religious elite of Quran readers, scholars of law and Arabic letters, and ascetic and charismatic preachers. The town populations were also stratified on the basis of political office holding, landownership, and tribal chieftainship, and organized into new religious sects and political movements.

The new urban societies generated both the resources and the conflicts which would shape the Caliphate and the imperial regime. From the towns the Caliphate could draw skilled manpower and economic resources. The ᶜAbbasids in particular based their regime upon the diverse populations which flocked to Baghdad as well as other Arab cities. The pressures of urban social change also created new interest groups and classes, new alliances, new forms of communal organizations, and therefore conflict over political interests and over the Caliphate. The first Muslim century witnessed a series of civil wars. In the first the problem was factional divisions in the Arab elite, the balance of central and local power, and the role of religious versus political factors in the concept and identity of the regime. The major struggle was between factions united by commitment to Islam and Arab tribal coalitions. The second civil war was motivated by sectarian Khariji and Shiᶜi communities and by continuing factionalism within the Arab elite. The third civil war, which brought the ᶜAbbasids to power, was the product of the division between Arabs assimilated into the general society and those active in the military, a struggle marked by strong ideological conflict over Arab versus Muslim identity.

Each of the civil wars forced the Caliphate to develop the institutional mechanisms to keep political power and to legitimize dynastic rule. To consolidate its position the Caliphate adopted Byzantine and Sasanian institutions and concepts of imperial rule while giving them a new Islamic definition. The Umayyads adopted the bureaucratic administration of the older empires, and patronized architectural works which integrated Byzantine, Sasanian, and Christian symbols into Muslim designs. The ᶜAbbasids continued the Umayyad trend toward consolidation of an imperial regime and its definition in transmuted Middle Eastern terms. Their regime was centered on a royal court; they governed the provinces through clients and servants of the rulers using a combination of bureaucratic tax-collecting methods and quasi-feudal forms of administration in which local princes and chieftains were confirmed in power and given status as servants of the Caliph. ᶜAbbasid administration depended upon a coalition of elites throughout the Middle East. The regime brought together Arab soldiers, Iraqi, Egyptian, and Iranian landlords, Nestorian scribes, Jewish merchants, Inner Asian warlords, and others to serve the central regime. These elites were united by loyalty to the Caliphate, by clientele and family ties linking the center and the provinces, and by common interests in the exploitation of the empire. These were the people made available by the extended period of economic change, social mobility and urbanization which followed the Arab conquests. They transformed the Arab conquest kingdom into a universal Middle Eastern empire.

To symbolize and legitimize their domination the ᶜAbbasids patronized cultural activities which made clear the historic roots of the regime and its cosmopolitan inclusiveness. The court culture signified the superiority of the Arab-Muslim imperium by borrowing the artistic and ceremonial themes of its ancestors and incorporating them into a new ritual of state. It signified its universality by patronizing the several Middle Eastern cultures: the poetic and historical traditions of the Arabs, the adab literature of Iran, and the Hellenistic philosophy and sciences of the Mediterranean. Imperial culture justified the exercise of power as a divine necessity, stressed the hierarchy of society, the responsibility of masters, and the subordination of the masses. The new culture gave the new elite a shared language, literary expression, and personal values based on the validation of worldly power and wealth. In the ancient debate over whether it was legitimate to enjoy the goods of this world the ᶜAbbasid imperial culture was resoundingly positive. Thus, as in the past, out of the formation of an empire came a new civilization. Again empire was a moral and cultural entity as well as a system of political exploitation.

However, the very social processes which had made it possible to construct an empire extending over all the Middle East – the new urban centers, economic growth and the formation of cosmopolitan communities – also created an independent urban population, led by religious chiefs and organized into sectarian communities, who would oppose the imperial vision with one of their own. The family or companions of the Prophet and their descendants, reciters of the Quran, scholars of Muslim law and history, and Sufi ascetics won over groups of disciples, students and followers and thus generated numerous Shiᶜi and Khariji associations, Sunni schools of law, and later, Sufi discipleships. Most of these groups were small, even esoteric, cults. Some of them acquired a mass following. In opposition to the Caliphs all of the groups claimed to embody the tradition of the Prophet and the true teachings of Islam. The Shiᶜa and the Kharijis at first violently opposed the Caliphate, but by the ninth century the "twelver" Shiᶜa and many Kharijis had renounced world-transforming political aspirations in favor of local community affairs and pious personal lives, and lived in an atmosphere of mourning for lost hopes and messianic dreams. They withdrew from transforming the world to a pious existence within the world. Even the Sunnis, who supported the Caliphate in principle, withdrew from public commitments and concentrated on small-scale community life and personal piety. In the urban milieu, the crucial question was: what is the proper way to live the life of this world in view of the eternity to come? Was a good Muslim a person of good deeds or of inner faith, one who fulfilled his obligations to the law or who cultivated a spiritual contact with God? Between the seventh and the tenth century the Muslim urban response to these questions was elaborated in Quran commentary, hadith, law, theology, and mystical discourses which incorporated into Islam the heritage of Greece and Iran as well as of Arabia and Muhammad, and recast the historic religions of the Middle East into a new high cultural monotheistic vision.

The imperial and urban versions of Islamic culture were closely related. The court accepted the religious supremacy of the Quran, the validity of hadith, and the Muslim historical tradition. Law had important political and regulatory as well as moral functions; many legists and jurists were employed by the state. Muʿtazili theology was as much a court as an urban science. Similarly urban ʿulamaʾ and Sufis accepted many aspects of court culture. The symbols of palace and mosque, the legitimacy of the Caliph's authority, the cultural primacy of the Arabic language, poetry and history, and aspects of philosophy, neo-Platonism, and theology were all accepted in urban circles. Still, despite the interpenetration of cultural interests, the two milieus were in conflict over basic values. The Hanbalis, in particular, defied the religious authority of the Caliphs, and opened a chasm between the state and the religious communities. As a result of the ninth-century struggles between Caliph and ʿulamaʾ it became clear that the Islamic mission was carried by two composite elites, Caliphate and court, ʿulamaʾ and Sufis, and two distinct concepts of Islam – one imperial and one urban, one political and one communal, one worldly and one pietistic. Ever after, Islamic societies have been characterized, in fact, if not in culturally recognized principle, by separate state and religious institutions.

At the end of the ninth century the Islamic elites and their cultural vision still represented only a limited population, including the state elites and the populace of the Arab-Muslim towns and converted rural districts. The translation of these elite influences and cultural paradigms into a mass Islamic society began only with the disintegration of the ʿAbbasid empire in the ninth and tenth centuries. The empire disintegrated not as the result of external shocks but as the outcome of the inherent evolution of its basic institutions. The Caliphate, caught in the dilemma of representing both worldly power and religious values, compromised its political authority and was forced to depend more and more upon military force at a time when the instruments of power proved insufficient. Both army and administration broke up into independent and self-serving factions; factional competition made it impossible for the Caliphate to maintain control over the central government and the provinces. The result was the rise to power of independent warlords and the outbreak of popular rebellions. By 945 the empire was no more. The process of disintegration, moreover, destroyed the bureaucratic and landowning classes who had controlled the empire and opened the way to power for nomadic elites, slave soldiers, local warlords, and others who had no interest in collaboration with the central government.

With the breakdown of the ʿAbbasid empire, the separation of state and religious elites and institutions became more marked. The successor states to the ʿAbbasid empire were even more secular regimes; Muslim religious associations independently took on the task of organizing the populace into a mass Islamic society. In the chaotic conditions of the tenth to the thirteenth centuries new regimes and new elites replaced the old empire. The Middle East was conquered by Turkish nomadic warriors and by slave warlords who ruled the several Middle Eastern provinces. In the post-imperial era, the ʿAbbasid Caliphs kept only nominal authority, while Buwayhid, Ghaznavid, and Saljuq Sultans organized the actual political regimes.

Under the Saljuqs a standard pattern of institutions developed, in which the power of the ruler was based upon a praetorian slave guard and the manipulation of nomadic tribal levies. Court bureaucrats and ʿulamaʾ helped maintain administrative services; in the provinces the Sultans were represented by governors, garrisons, and fiscal inspectors. Iqtaʿs were distributed widely to decentralize control over rural revenues. These institutions did not suffice to provide a lasting political order. Disputes among competing members of aristocratic lineages, tribal lords, and slave generals prevented the centralization of power. The iqtaʿ system of administration, in which tax-collecting privileges were parceled out among the military elite, also contributed to the fragmentation of power. Still the institution of the Sultanate, slave military forces, and iqtaʿ administration formed a pattern of government which would ever after constitute the norm.

The consolidation of these institutions was accompanied by the articulation of concepts to define, rationalize, and legitimize the exercise of power. Three concepts of government gained general currency. One was Muslim. In the Muslim view the Caliphate was the institution mandated by the Prophet to uphold Muslim law, fulfill God's command, protect the security of Muslim peoples, and wage jihad. All legitimate power was delegated from the Caliph to Sultans and from Sultans to their subordinates. Sultans, however, were expected to uphold Islamic justice and education, patronize the ʿulamaʾ, and suppress heresy. If he upheld the Shariʿa, a ruler was considered legitimate no matter how he had come to power. Secondly, government was legitimized in personal terms. All regimes were built upon the loyalties of slaves, clients, and retainers to their masters and patrons. A subordinate officer did not conceive of himself as a functionary of the state, but as an elevated servant of the ruler. Slavery was but the most forceful expression of the personal bonds which complemented concepts of delegated authority.

In yet another sense was government legitimized in personal terms. The state was identified with the person of the ruler. In all the political literatures of the time – Muslim, Persian, and Greek – the ruler was portrayed as the prototype of the perfected human being. He embodied wisdom and virtue, restrained the evil inclinations of his subordinates and inspired goodness in his subjects. Government functioned as a consequence of personal ties and was considered legitimate because it was conducive to the fulfillment of religious ideals.

On a third level government was legitimized in terms of historic descent from ancient empires and of the fulfillment of cosmic and divine purposes. Architecture, art, and poetry, in Arabic or Persian regional variants, symbolized the attachment of the political regimes to the divinely given order of the universe, the inherent glory of the ruler, the rightness of the pursuit and exercise of power, and the legitimacy of aesthetic refinement and luxury. The Sultanal regimes patronized historical writing to trace the genealogical descent and mythic connection of present rulers to ancient Persian and Turkish kings. As God's own servant the ruler was entrusted with the care of the world, and given authority over men whose fate was confided to him. The ruler ordered society, promoted the construction of civilization, and even had magical powers, which could affect the course of nature. Despite the arbitrary exercise of powers, states were an image of the cosmos. They were vital not only to daily life but to the mythic wholeness of the social order. However damaged the great empires, however many military lords became independent, however much control of the land was distributed in iqtaʿs, however much authority was conceded to local notables and local militias, the state continued to represent a commitment to a transcending, more than human, order. Thus while the Sultanates had Islamic functions and identities, their Islamic aspect was paralleled by a non-Islamic Persian and Turkish political ethos or concept of the purposes of government. An "Islamic" state was also an expression of a non-Islamic territorial and cultural identity.

As states became militarized and secularized, Islamic religious associations became the almost universal basis of Middle Eastern communal organization. Until the ninth century Islam was the religion of the Arab populations and assimilated urban groups, but from the tenth to the thirteenth centuries the mass of Middle Eastern peoples were converted to Islam. This was due in part to the dissolution of the ʿAbbasid empire, its replacement by foreign military elites, the ruin of the landowning and administrative classes, and their replacement by Muslim religious leaders who converted the uprooted masses, and provided them with leadership and forms of communal organization based on the religious associations created in the Caliphal period.

From the tenth to the thirteenth century the Middle Eastern masses came to be identified with the Sunni schools of law, Sufi brotherhoods, Shiʿi sects, and other Muslim groups. The schools of law were associations of scholars, teachers and students adhering to the law codes developed by discussion among legal scholars in the eighth and ninth centuries. Through the law schools, the ʿulamaʾ organized higher education, and trained teachers and judicial administrators; from the schools came consultants, notaries, and judges. Also the schools gathered a popular following. The students considered themselves personal disciples of their masters; the communities in which the schools were located provided patrons and supporters, especially from the merchant and artisan classes. The Sufi brotherhoods were based on the disciples of each master and upon the groups of Sufis who lived in common residences called khanaqas. Tariqats or brotherhoods were formed when Sufi masters in the twelfth and thirteenth centuries began to reckon themselves the descendants of earlier teachers. Those who descended from the same teacher regarded themselves as perpetuating a common spiritual discipline and as units of a much larger religious movement accepting the same higher authority. Such formations grew beyond their local origins and became regional and even worldwide brotherhoods.

In an urban context the schools of law and Sufi brotherhoods served as confessional collectivities which could recruit individuals across the lines of existing community structures and unify smaller-scale family, clan or residential collectivities into larger units. In such cases religious fellowships cut across the lines of existing communities. But Muslim religious associations could also operate wholly within the framework of existing collective units. Schools of law, Sufi brotherhoods, or Shiʿi sects were often identified with particular neighborhoods, or occupational and ethnic minorities, and gave previously existing collectivities an Islamic identity.

These Islamic religious associations represented a different ethos from that of the political elites. While Muslim religious associations varied on a spectrum ranging from other-worldly ecstatic, contemplative forms of Sufism to a very worldly family- and business-oriented ethos there was a broad synthetic middle ground – the Sunni–Shariᶜa–Sufi position. This position was represented by the Hanafi and Shafiᶜi schools of law, the Ashᶜari and Maturidi schools of theology, and the "sober" Sufi tradition of al-Junayd, al-Qushayri and al-Ghazzali. It attempted to integrate commitment to the principle of the Caliphate as the basis of the ideal Muslim community, devotion to the fulfillment of the teachings of the Shariᶜa, belief in the limited use of reason for understanding religious truths, and the practice of Sufi ethical and meditational exercises. This position attempted to combine the correct external forms of social and ritual behavior with internal emotional and spiritual awareness.

Sunnis with this orientation had a nuanced attitude to worldly actualities. They accepted existing regimes as legitimate by virtue of the inherent need for order in society and they worked out routine ways of collaborating with established states. Political obedience was highly emphasized. The ᶜulamaᵓ reserved for themselves a consultative role and the right to admonish, educate, and give moral advice to rulers, and they expected states to give them control over legal administration and patronize Muslim educational and charitable activities. Within this framework, however, Sunnis were not so much involved in politics as in community affairs. Their concern was to uphold public morality, to apply the Shariᶜa to family and commercial affairs, to educate, to heal, and to mediate local conflicts.

Sunni Islam accepted the given clan, lineage, tribal or clientele substructures of Middle Eastern societies, and with them inequalities of wealth and property. They regarded social and economic justice as matters of individual behavior. Sunni values were thus neutral with regard to different economic systems; there was no Muslim teaching on the proper structure of the economy, and no obvious correlation between Islamic beliefs and any particular economic organization. Furthermore, if we compare the Sunni attitude toward economic activity with later Protestant attitudes, we find that though Muslims were highly motivated in economic matters, they did not see such activity as a vehicle for the transformation of the world or of the individual. Sunni Islam did not try to mobilize people for economic ends, but called upon them to lead a pious life in the context of economic and other worldly activities.

World acceptance was modified, though, by an attitude of detachment and

refusal of commitment. While many ʿulamaʾ and Sufis accepted the responsibilities of political power, held office, accumulated land and property, and
served as spokesmen for the needs of their people, there was a deep strand of
feeling which opposed such engagements. The companions of princes were
regarded as morally corrupted. ʿUlamaʾ and Sufis characteristically refused
official positions and turned down royal gifts. Disengagement was taken as a
mark of piety and the highest moral virtue. The refusal to give moral assent
to the world as it is was accompanied by a nostalgia for the restoration of the
true Caliphate and a yearning for the coming of the mahdi. Nostalgia expressed
withdrawal from the actual world but it also served to ratify things as they
were.

The Hanbalis cultivated a more active stance. They took to vigilante action
to enforce morality, suppress alcohol and prostitution, and attack rival sects.
They rallied Muslim volunteers for holy war and on occasion attempted to
restore the political power of the Caliphate. This activism, however, was
channeled mainly into pressuring existing political regimes to uphold Muslim
morality rather than being aimed at changing the political order. Thus all
Sunnis accepted the world as it was, yet withheld their full assent by refusing
to be directly involved in politics, by actively campaigning to improve public
morals, and by nostalgic reflection and eschatological yearning.

The reasons for this complex orientation can be understood when we
consider that Muslim religious associations were partially but never fully
differentiated from other socio-political institutions. The Sunni position reflects a transcendent religious vision embedded in sectarian associations, but
these associations existed within the overall political framework of the Sultanal
regimes, and they were interlocked with parochial lineage, village and other
solidarities. Therefore the tension between religious and other commitments
could not be absolute and the complex relationships among them had to be
expressed in subtle modes of acceptance, detachment, and rejection.

Islamic organizations and identities were also institutionalized in rural
societies, though on different terms. Throughout the Middle East clans,
lineages, and village communities led by independent chieftains, legitimized in
terms of tribal tradition and by the acceptance of an age-old pattern of culture,
continued to be the backbone of the social order. The basic lineage and
factional structures were reinforced by the Arab and the Turkish migrations.
In these societies Muslim religious leadership and Muslim symbols were used
to unite factionalized peoples into more unified religious-political movements.
The Arab-Muslim movement is the prototypical case. In addition, Berbers in
North Africa were united under Kharijism, Shiʿism, Sunni reformism, and

later Sufism, into conquering religious movements such as the Fatimid, the Almoravid, and the Almohad. Kharijis in eastern Arabia, Qarmatis in the fertile crescent, and later the Safavids in western Iran are other examples of Muslim religious leaders and symbols becoming the basis of rural unification in the quest for the ever elusive just Islamic society.

There is also evidence for the beginnings of widespread acceptance of Islamic identity by rural collectivities in the form of the veneration of Sufis and the worship at shrines. Before the thirteenth century the doctrinal basis for the veneration of Sufis as intercessors between man and God had been established and pre-Islamic magical practices and superstitions were accepted as part of popular Islam. Sufis were commonly believed to be saints and were venerated as intermediaries between the material and the spiritual worlds, as miracle-workers, and dispensers of blessings. On this basis Sufis served to mediate disputes, facilitate the selection of chiefs, organize long-distance trade, teach the young, heal the sick, provide amulets, officiate at circumcisions, marriages, and funerals, celebrate festivals, do white magic, and otherwise uphold the tenuous connection of human beings with the world of the spirits and the divine. This type of Sufism also led to the veneration of the tomb, and the disciples and descendants of the holy-man, and to a religious life of sacrifices and festivals around the tombs. In such cases Islam did not necessarily lead to the formation of an organized association capable of collective action, but served as a shared identity among diverse peoples who preserved their own kinship, territorial, linguistic, ethnic, and other bases of non-Islamic culture.

By the thirteenth century Muslim societies were organized in terms of state regimes, urban religious associations and rural, religious groupings, each with its own version – courtly, Shariᶜa-Sufi, or shrine-Sufi – of Islam. Also by the late Saljuq period the different types of Islamic institutions had been integrated into a larger system defined by the interrelation of these various state, communal, and religious institutions. The crucial feature in the system of relations was the tacit collaboration of state military, local ᶜulamaᵓ, and Sufi elites.

On the one hand, the nomadic and slave military elites needed the collaboration of the ᶜulamaᵓ in order to govern. The Saljuqs were leaders of tribal groups with no experience in ruling an agriculturally based empire. Scribes, finance officials, estate managers, and other technicians were vital. Furthermore, the nomadic and slave elites needed the ᶜulamaᵓ, for both political and psychological reasons, to recognize the rightfulness of their regime. The ᶜulamaᵓ were the guardians of tradition, and to the Saljuqs, lacking in technical skills and literary and social knowledge, represented the epitome of a desired way of life. They looked to the ᶜulamaᵓ to be tutored, educated, and guided in socially and morally acceptable courses of action. Thus the conquerors were conquered by their subjects.

On the other hand, the ʿulamaʾ accepted the need for a military regime. Only a military regime could protect the trade routes, and the agricultural villages from bedouins and bandits. The ʿulamaʾ favored a strong state to repress factional strife and gang warfare and to act as an arbiter of disputes which the communities themselves could not regulate. Moreover, they were interested in an accommodation with military regimes because they could, by serving in the state administration, transform themselves from local elites into an imperial governing class. The state accorded them positions which could consolidate their local power. Finally, military elites could give valuable support to the Sunni social and educational mission.

To work out this tacit bargain the Ghaznavids and the Saljuqs restored mosques, built madrasas and khanaqas, endowed waqfs, and appointed members of the law schools to official positions. The Saljuqs suppressed Shiʿism and gave vigorous support to Sunni Islam. In return the ʿulamaʾ preached the legitimacy of established regimes, supported favored princes against their rivals, supplied cadres for the state administration, facilitated taxation, and accepted the nomadic and slave conquest states as part of the legitimate and necessary order of Islamic society. While the religious notables could mediate between military regimes and city populations, they lacked the ideological and economic bases to be fully independent. Thus, their inevitable collaboration with the state elites brought the rest of society under control.

In the post-imperial period, new forms of state organization, community life and culture were integrated into a new order. The post-imperial system of government and society was profoundly different from that of the earlier era. The earlier ʿAbbasid era was characterized by a universal empire built upon the support of Middle Eastern landowning, bureaucratic, and merchant elites who forged a common religious and cultural identity. In the post-imperial period, the unity of the Middle East was no longer to be found in empire, but in the almost universal diffusion of certain forms of social and political organization and of allegiance to common values and symbols. For the first time in Middle Eastern history, the peoples of Iran and Iraq belonged, if not to the same empire, to the same culture, religion, and type of political society. Islam had become a universal society without a universal empire.

The construction of this new form of Islamic society in Iran and Iraq marked the culmination of the formative period in the history of Islamic societies. In successive phases the historic societies of the Middle East had acquired an Islamic identity. An Islamic-tribal form of society had been created in Arabia under charismatic-prophetic leadership; conquest and urbanization gave rise to a universal empire and to the Caliphs, ʿulamaʾ, and Sufis who would be the bearers of Islamic high civilization. The disintegration of the empire allowed for a reconstruction of Middle Eastern societies into a post-imperial or Saljuq complex of state and socio-religious institutions and attendant Islamic identities.

This Middle Eastern Islamic society held a crucial place in the development of all later Islamic societies. It bequeathed a repertoire of cultural and religious ideas which remain operative in Islamic lands to the present day. From this era came the forms of Islamic orthopraxis contained in hadith and law, Sufi forms of ethical and spiritual self-cultivation, Shiʿi concepts of religious leadership, ideals of mystical and gnostic transcendence, popular saint worship and magical practices, and a socially active and reformist Islamic ideal. This period also gave rise to the basic elements of Islamic social organization: states, schools of law, and Sufi tariqat. Finally this era set the precedent for a separation between state institutions and Muslim religious communities. All the while, the persistence of non-Islamic modes of social and economic organization, and non-Islamic cultures, generated an endlessly rich variety of social and communal possibilities, and an abiding ambiguity as to what constituted an Islamic society. Wherever Islam would be established, these institutions and cultural concepts would be combined and recombined and merged with local traditions to form new types of Islamic societies. Each of them would bear profoundly the imprint of the Middle Eastern origins of Islam.

THE WORLDWIDE DIFFUSION OF ISLAMIC SOCIETIES FROM THE TENTH TO THE NINETEENTH CENTURY

9 A battle scene

INTRODUCTION: THE ISLAMIC WORLD AND THE RISE OF EUROPE

Between the seventh and the thirteenth centuries the historic institutions of Middle Eastern societies were recast in Islamic forms. New empires and states were organized under the aegis of Islamic concepts of authority and symbols of legitimacy. Muslim religious elites including ʿulamaʾ scholars and Sufi holy-men generated Islamic forms of worship, education, and legal administration. The majority of Middle Eastern peoples were converted to Islam, and Middle Eastern pastoral tribes, peasants, urban artisans and merchants, and state elites took on an Islamic identity. A new literary and artistic civilization, in part royal and artistic, in part urban and pietistic, came into being.

In subsequent eras, the Islamic system of institutions and its several cultures would continue to evolve in the already Islamized regions of the Middle East including Iran, Transoxania, and the Arab provinces. They also served as a paradigm for the establishment of Islamic societies in other parts of the world. From the seventh to the nineteenth century Islamic societies, based on the interaction of local institutions and cultures and Middle Eastern influences, were established in Anatolia and the Balkans, Inner Asia, South and Southeast Asia, and sub-Saharan Africa. The evolution of a world system of Islamic societies, however, was cut short in the eighteenth and nineteenth centuries by the growing political and economic power of Europe. The consolidation of European colonial rule in most of the Muslim world marks the end of the pre-modern era and the beginning of the modern transformation of Muslim societies.

To introduce the reader to this varied history, this chapter deals with the general themes common to the study of all pre-modern Islamic societies. It discusses the diffusion of Islam, the process of conversion, the characteristic types of Muslim religious elites and collectivities, and concludes with a discussion of the rise of Europe and its impact upon these Muslim societies. The introduction is followed by case studies of Islamic societies in Iran, the Ottoman empire, the Arab fertile crescent, North Africa, Inner Asia, South and Southeast Asia, and sub-Saharan Africa. Part II will conclude with a brief analysis of the variant types of Islamic societies on the eve of their modern transformation.

CONVERSION TO ISLAM

From the seventh to the tenth century, Islam was carried by the Arab conquests to North Africa, Spain, Sicily, and the Mediterranean coasts of Europe. Arab warriors and merchants brought it to Saharan and Sudanic Africa. Other Islamic societies were born from the conversion of Inner Asian Turkish peoples to Islam and their migrations, conquests, and empire building. From the tenth to the fourteenth century, Turkish peoples brought Islam westward into Anatolia, the Balkans, and southeastern Europe; eastward into Inner Asia and China, and southward into Afghanistan and the Indian subcontinent. They thus played a crucial historical role in the diffusion of Islam and in the founding of the Saljuq, Mongol, Timurid, Safavid, Ottoman, Uzbek, and Mughal empires. Finally, another cluster of Islamic societies originated from the expansion of Muslim merchants in the Indian Ocean. From Arabia Islam reached India and East Africa (tenth to twelfth century); from Arabia and India it reached the Malay peninsula and the Indonesian archipelago (thirteenth to fifteenth century); from the coastal zones it spread to the interior of the islands and continents.

The expansion of Islam involved different forces. In North Africa, Anatolia, the Balkans, and India, Islam was carried by nomadic Arab or Turkish conquerors. In the Indian Ocean and West Africa it spread by peaceful contacts among merchants or through the preaching of missionaries. In some cases the diffusion of Islam depended upon its adoption by local ruling families; in others, it appealed to urban classes of the population or tribal communities. Sometimes its appeal was couched in terms of political and economic benefits; sometimes in terms of social status; sometimes in terms of a sophisticated culture and religion. All of these factors were interwoven and each case must be examined to disentangle the predominant reasons for the diffusion of Islam in any given world area.

The question of why people convert to Islam has always generated intense feeling. Earlier generations of European scholars believed that conversions to

Map 7. The expansion of Muslim states and populations: 900–1700.

Pacific
Ocean

Peking
Yellow R.
Yangtze R.
Canton
Mekong R.
South
China
Sea
Java Sea
Jaxarta
Malacca

Bay of
Bengal

Indian Ocean

Kashgar
Lahore
Delhi
Ganges R.
Indus R.
Kabul
Samarqand
Balkhash L.
Syr Darya R.
Bukhara
Herat
Isfahan
Tabriz
Aral Sea
Caspian Sea

Arabian
Sea

Zanzibar

Baghdad
Jerusalem
Basra
Persian Gulf
Medina
Mecca
Red Sea
Damascus
Cairo
Nile R.

Kazan
Volga R.
Moscow
Don R.
Dnieper R.
Black Sea
Constantinople
Venice
Athens
Vienna
Danube R.
Genoa
Mediterranean Sea
Tunis
Granada
Cordova
Fez

North
Sea
Atlantic
Ocean

L. Chad
Kano
Timbuktu
Niger R.
Senegal R.

Muslim expansion to 900
Muslim expansion to 1300
Muslim expansion to 1500
Muslim expansion to 1700
Muslim lands lost by 1300
Muslim lands lost by 1500
Muslim lands lost by 1700

0   1000 miles
0   2000 km

Islam were made at the point of the sword and that conquered peoples were given the choice of conversion or death. It is now apparent that conversion by force, while not unknown in Muslim countries, was, in fact, rare. Muslim conquerors ordinarily wished to dominate rather than convert, and most conversions to Islam were voluntary.

Even voluntary conversions are suspect to European observers. Were they made out of true belief, or for opportunistic political or social reasons? Did people convert to Islam out of faith or as a result of the pressure of political, economic, and social circumstances? Surely there are innumerable cases of conversion to Islam by the illumination of faith or by virtue of the perceived sanctity of Muslim scholars and holy-men, as well as by calculation of political and economic advantage. It seems more realistic to recognize that in most cases worldly and spiritual motives for conversion blended and cannot be differentiated. Conversion to Islam meant the acceptance of Islamic beliefs and rituals and social and political loyalties on the basis of a range of considerations that included purely religious and purely pragmatic concerns. Moreover, conversion to Islam did not necessarily imply a complete turning from an old life to a totally new life. While it entailed the acceptance of new religious beliefs, including belief in God and the Prophet, and a sense of membership in a new religious community, the new beliefs, practices, and loyalties were not necessarily exclusive. Most converts retained a deep attachment to the cultures and communities from which they came. In the sections that follow, I will stress the historical circumstances that have induced large numbers of people to adhere to Islam rather than analyze the spiritual or material motives of individuals for becoming Muslims. This is not to diminish the centrality of belief and commitment in the subjective experience of individual converts, but to account on an historical basis for the responses of great numbers of human beings.

The first conversions to Islam occurred in the Middle East between the seventh and the thirteenth centuries. These conversions took place in two phases, the first being the conversion of animists and polytheists belonging to the tribal societies of the Arabian desert and the periphery of the fertile crescent; the second, the conversion of the monotheistic populations of the Middle Eastern agrarian, urbanized, and imperial societies. The process of Islamization among pastoral and tribal peoples has to be distinguished from the Islamization of agricultural and state-type civilizations. Similarly, the conversion of pagan peoples has to be distinguished from the conversion of Jews, Christians, Zoroastrians or Buddhists.

The conversion of Arabian populations was part of the process of transmitting the civilization of the sedentarized imperial societies to the nomadic periphery. Arabian peoples, standing on the margin of the agricultural and commercial zones of the Middle East, strongly influenced by Middle Eastern commerce and religious thought, found in Muhammad's teaching a way to formulate a form of Middle Eastern monotheistic religion parallel to but distinct from the established Christian and Zoroastrian religions. The conversion of Arabian pagan peoples to Islam represented the response of a tribal, pastoral population to the need for a larger framework for political and economic integration, a more stable state, and a more imaginative and encompassing moral vision to cope with the problems of a tumultuous society. Conversion, then, was the process of integrating Arabians into a new cultural and political order defined in monotheistic religious terms.

The conversion of sedentary Middle Eastern peoples to Islam was a different process. In this case Islam was substituted for Byzantine or Sasanian political identity and for Jewish, Christian or Zoroastrian religious affiliation. The transformation of identities among Middle Eastern peoples took place in two stages. In the first century of the Islamic imperium the Arab conquerors attempted to maintain themselves as an exclusive Muslim elite. They did not require the conversion, but rather the subordination of non-Muslim peoples. At the outset, they were hostile to conversions because new Muslims diluted the economic and status advantages of the Arabs. However, Muslim rule offered substantial incentives for conversion. It formed a protective umbrella over Muslim communities and conferred the prestige of the state on Muslim religious life. Political patronage allowed for the establishment of mosques, the organization of the pilgrimage, and the creation of Muslim judicial institutions. The establishment of an Arab empire made Islam attractive to elements of the former Byzantine and Sasanian aristocracies including soldiers, officials, landlords, and others. Arab garrison cities attracted non-Arab migrants who found careers in the army and administration open to converts. Merchants, artisans, workers and fugitive peasants seeking the patronage of the new elite were also tempted to accept Islam.

Despite these attractions, the mass of Middle Eastern peoples were not soon or easily converted. Only with the breakdown of the social and religious structures of non-Muslim communities in the tenth to the twelfth century did the weakening of churches, the awakening of Muslim hostility to non-Muslims, sporadic and localized persecution, and the destruction of the landed gentry of Iraq and Iran break the communal organization of non-Muslim peoples. Muslim teachers were then able to take the lead in the reconstruction of local communities on the basis of Islamic beliefs and identities. Large parts of Egypt and Iran were probably converted in the tenth and eleventh centuries. In northern Syria, however, Christian majorities survived through the twelfth century, but, compromised in the eyes of the Muslims by their sympathies with and assistance to the crusaders, were put under severe pressure. Most converted in the thirteenth and fourteenth centuries, but substantial Christian minorities remained. Similarly, most of the remaining Christian population of Egypt adopted Islam in the fourteenth century.

Conversions from Judaism, Christianity, and Zoroastrianism to Islam were accompanied by the formation of an urban and urbane high Islamic literary culture and popular forms of Sufi belief and worship which could be substituted for former religious cultures. To adherents of the monotheistic and communalist faiths, Islam offered the same variety of intellectual, legal, theological and mystical appeals. While Islam had a specific religious orientation toward the inscrutable and untrammeled will of Allah and the necessity for submission of spirit and actions to the will of God, its basic religious positions were fundamentally similar to those of the other monotheistic religions.

The conversion of North Africa also began with the Arab conquests, but was a different process because it involved primarily the adoption of Islam, notably in sectarian form, by the chiefs of Berber societies as the basis of tribal coalitions and state formation. Khariji states in Algeria and Morocco represented the adoption of Islam for the purposes of regulating tribal relations and long-distance trade. The process of Islamization of the masses of Christians and Jews is not known, but it may be related to the spread of ribats (forts manned by warriors for the faith), trade, and Sufis. In any case it seems to have been rapid compared with conversion in the Middle East.

The diffusion of Islam to regions beyond the Middle East involved analogous processes. The spread of Islam in Inner Asia, Anatolia, the Balkans, and India was closely tied to the conversion of pastoral Turkish, rather than Arab, peoples. The conversion of Turkish Inner Asian peoples began in the tenth century. Inner Asian peoples came into contact with Muslims through caravan trade and contacts with merchants who operated on the steppes as brokers between nomadic and settled populations. Muslim missionaries and Sufis also moved out to proselytize among the Turks. Political ambition prompted the Qarakhanid and Saljuq elites to take up the new religion. Later Inner Asian regimes, including the Mongols of the Golden Horde and the Chaghatay Khanates, also adopted Islam and brought it to the northern steppes and eastern Turkestan. In Inner Asia Islamization was important for the establishment of nomadic regimes over sedentary populations, for the creation of politically cohesive ethnic identities among Tatars, Uzbeks, Kazakhs, and other peoples, and for the organization of long-distance trade.

The spread of Islam into Anatolia and the Balkans paralleled the historical process of the spread of Islam in the Middle East. The Saljuq and Ottoman conquests of the eleventh to the fourteenth century led to the organization of Muslim regimes that favored the consolidation of an Islamic teaching and judicial establishment. The Turkish aristocracy assumed responsibility for patronizing Sunni law schools, Islamic judicial administration, and the construction of schools and colleges, and other religious and communal facilities. It gave protection to ʿulamaʾ and Sufis who founded centers for teaching and social services in the conquered territories. Furthermore, Islam was carried into the region by migrant Turkish warriors under the leadership of Muslim holy-men. The migration of a substantial Turkish population uprooted Anatolian agricultural communities and replaced them with Turkish Muslim peoples. Nomadic conquests and the hostility of the Saljuq government to the Byzantine and Greek church also led in Anatolia to the progressive reduction of church lands, administrative capacities, and authority. The weakening of the church deprived the Christian population of leadership and organization. In Anatolia, as in Inner Asia, India, and Africa, jihad-minded Sufi warriors and activist missionaries helped to establish Islam among a newly conquered peasant population. The assimilation of Anatolian peoples was facilitated on the cultural as well as the social level by the familiarity of Islamic religious concepts which were easily adapted to the religious beliefs of the Christians. In Anatolia, as in the rest of the Middle East, the conjunction of Muslim state power, the decline of organized Christian societies, and the social and cultural relevance of Islam facilitated mass conversions to the new religion.

In the Balkans the factors favoring Islamization and conversion of local peoples were similar to those in Anatolia: the establishment of a regime which favored Islam and the migration and settlement of a substantial Turkish population. Islamization under these pressures was especially pronounced in the towns. In the Balkans, however, the spread of Islam was limited by the vitality of the Christian churches. Coming at a later stage of Turkish conquests, at a time when Ottoman policy favored Christian nobles and churches as vehicles of Ottoman administration, the social structure of Balkan communities was maintained intact, and indeed, reinforced. Most Balkan peoples, buttressed by the continuity of organized Christian community life, remained loyal to their faith.

The history of Islam in India most closely resembles that of the Balkans.

Islam was brought into India by a conquering Afghan and Turkish military elite which established the Delhi Sultanate in the thirteenth century. Conversions were made as a result of the political attraction of the dominant regime to both non-Muslim elites and dependent peasants and workers. Also, as in the Middle East, the construction of new cities favored the conversion of mobile peoples attracted to the centers of Muslim administration and trade. In most of India, however, as in the Balkans, the appeal of Islam was relatively restricted. Only in the Northwest Frontier, the Punjab, Sind, and Bengal were the populations converted en masse. In these regions the transition from hunter–gatherer and pastoral activities to settled agriculture was the occasion for a total reconstruction of society under Muslim leadership and for the development of new Islamic loyalties and identifications. Conversion to Islam on a mass scale seems to have been most likely among disorganized populations.

In general, however, the assimilative capacity of Islam in the subcontinent was limited by the relative thinness of the Muslim elite. While Muslim rule in India attracted numerous warriors, administrators and religious teachers, the Muslim conquest was not accompanied by massive migrations as in the case of the Arab conquest of the Middle East or the Turkish conquest of Anatolia. Furthermore, the social structure of conquered peoples remained intact. Hindu Rajputs, for example, maintained their authority under Muslim suzerainty; nor were Brahmanic Hinduism and the caste system challenged by Muslim rule. Indeed, Hindu philosophy and popular religions were invigorated by Muslim competition. In the face of an ordered social and religious structure, conversions to Islam were inhibited.

When conversions did occur, Sufism played a considerable part. Following the scent of battle, Sufis streamed into India from Afghanistan, Iran, and Inner Asia. Many came as warriors to establish Muslim supremacy and convert the infidels. Some tied their fortunes to the state. Others fanned out in north India establishing their influence by personal merit. Here too, the adaptability of Sufism to traditional religious cultures was important in the transition from Hindu and Buddhist identities to Islam. In India the boundary between Hindu and Muslim beliefs, ritual practices, and social loyalties was thin. As in the Middle East and the Ottoman empire, Islam was established under the auspices both of a political elite and of independent religious teachers.

The conversion of Malaya, Indonesia, and sub-Saharan Africa to Islam followed a different pattern. In these regions, Islam was not established by conquest, by the imposition of a single centralized state, or by the settlement of a substantial foreign Muslim population; nor was it associated with massive social change. It was rather due to the diffusion of Muslim merchants and missionaries who founded small communities, and sometimes induced (or forced) local elites interested in state formation, trade, and political legitimation to accept their religion. Islam spread as the result of commercial contacts, political and commercial rivalries, and by the progressive acceptance of new symbols of identity by ongoing societies.

Islam was first introduced into Indonesia at the end of the thirteenth century by merchants and Sufis from India, Arabia, and perhaps China. It appealed to the rulers of small coastal and riverain principalities who had close trading contacts with the Muslims and intense rivalries with Indonesian and Chinese traders. Acceptance of Islam by local merchant princes won them social and administrative support and an entrée into extensive trading networks. The spread of Islam in coastal regions of Malaya and Indonesia was closely related to the formation of new small states based upon trade. Portuguese and later Dutch intervention in the Indies further stimulated the acceptance of Islam. The struggle against the Portuguese and the Dutch made it desirable for the merchants of coastal Indonesia and Malaya to accept Islam as a bond of solidarity in resistance to the efforts of Christian powers to establish trading monopolies. Local competition facilitated the further spread of Islam. The struggle of the coastal principalities with the interior states of Java led eventually to the establishment of Islam as the official religion of the whole of Java. As a result Indonesian state and elite culture was shaped, not by an aristocracy coming from the Middle East, but by a local elite which preserved its political and cultural continuity, and adopted Islam as an additional expression, or reinforcement, of its earlier legitimacy. Throughout Indonesia and Malaya, Islam was also integrated into popular culture. Sufi missionaries and village teachers settled widely and made Islam part of folk culture and folk identity. In Southeast Asia, as opposed to India and the Balkans where it reached only a minority, Islam became the religion of great majorities of the population.

In most of Africa, Islam was established by processes more closely resembling those of Southeast Asia than the Middle East and India. Muslim merchants and missionary colonies, rather than conquest and empire, were central to Islamization on the continent. Arab and Berber traders and settlers in the Saharan and Sudanic regions, Arab and Persian settlers on the East African coasts, and Dyula communities in West Africa, were the nuclei of Muslim influences. In Sudanic Africa, colonies of Muslim traders became allied with local political elites and induced the rulers of the states of Ghana, Mali, Kanem, Songhay, Hausaland, and Dogomba to accept Islam. It is possible that Muslims themselves seized kingships and created small states. Islam was adopted to consolidate political power, reinforce commercial contacts, recruit skilled personnel, and mobilize spiritual and magical powers in the interests of state elites. As in North Africa, acceptance of Islam provided an additional basis for legitimation of state regimes, coalition formation among disparate peoples, organization of trading networks, and employment of skilled personnel. Under the auspices of Muslim states, a small scholarly elite of qadis, ʿulamaʾ, and imams was established, but no evidence for conversion of the lower classes is available. Islam was primarily the religion of the political and commercial elites.

In other parts of West Africa, the Islamic presence was established by Dyula traders, landowners, missionaries, and teachers scattered throughout the region who created an Islamic presence without necessarily generating Islamic states and without attendant Islamization of the population. These family communities seem to have fitted into a highly stratified and subdivided society, whose internal divisions made it acceptable to have unassimilated communities, but were a barrier to the further diffusion of Islam.

Whereas in West Africa, Arab merchants inspired warrior elites to convert to Islam, in East Africa, Arab traders themselves took over the leadership of small states. In Somalia and Ethiopia, Arab merchants married into local lineages and assumed leadership of tribal coalitions which then adopted an Arab and Islamic identity. In the East African city-states, Arab settlers intermarried with local peoples and became the elites of the coastal Swahili society based on a new language and cultural style which symbolized the merger of populations. Muslim communities were consolidated by the integration of peoples and the formation of new cultural idioms.

As the religion of the state and trading classes, Islam in Africa appeared in highly syncretic forms. Since African elites were not conquered and replaced, but converted and maintained in power, they brought with them a strong component of traditional, non-Islamic African practices. African Islam, like Islam in Indonesia, was adopted by native elites and blended into a native culture. The relative continuity of political elites was an important factor in the syncretism of Islam with local regional cultures at the state level.

In some cases, the formation of African Muslim states was followed by the conversion of the masses. In Somalia, Mauritania and other Saharan regions, the large numbers of Arab migrants, the close identification of pastoral peoples with Arab nomads, and the utility of holy leadership for the regulation of relations among tribal communities may help to explain why Islam was so widely accepted. In the Funj and Darfur Sultanates, state elites adopted Islam as a result of trading contacts, and opened the way for a large influx of Sufi missionaries. Muslim holy-men, supported by state grants of land, established their authority and converted the common people to Islam. In the Sudan, the spread of Arabic language and Muslim identity, coupled with contacts with Egypt and the Middle East, helped to establish Islam among the common people.

By the eighteenth and nineteenth centuries, throughout West Africa, the spread of Muslim trading communities linked by lineage, trade, teaching, and Sufi affiliations had reached a critical mass which enabled Muslims to fight for power and work for larger-scale political regimes. Motivated by a tradition of hostility to rulers among both trading and pastoral peoples, African Muslim communities attempted to seize political power and to Islamize both state regimes and the masses of the African population. In Sudanic, savannah and forest West Africa, the jihads were the equivalent of Islamic conquests in other parts of the world, and led indeed to the Islamization of northern Nigeria, Senegambia, and parts of the upper Guinea coast. However, even when colonial conquest put an end to Muslim jihads, Islam, without state support, continued to be attractive to uprooted peoples in much of West Africa, Tanzania, and other parts of East Africa. In the twentieth century, Islam served to express anti-colonialism and to unite uprooted peoples into new communal structures. In Africa, then, the process of conversion was tied to a double mechanism of peaceful expansion of traders, settlers, and teachers, and to militant conquest. As in other parts of the world, the two could work either separately or in tandem.

If there is an underlying common factor in the worldwide diffusion of Islam it seems to be its capacity to generate religious fellowship, larger-order communities, and states among peoples otherwise living in highly factionalized or fragmented societies. Islam became the religion of tribal peoples and merchant groups seeking economic integration, and state elites seeking consolidated political power. In general, the spread of Islam seems to have been most effective when it gave a new social identity to peoples severed from their traditional social structures.

Throughout the old world the diffusion of Islam led to the formation of new communities and states or to the redefinition of existing communities and empires in Islamic terms. In many parts of Africa and Inner Asia the introduction of Islam was the basis for the first conversions from animistic to monotheistic religions and for the first construction of states in hitherto stateless societies. In most places, however, the advent of Islam inspired the reconstruction of societies which already had "higher" religions and state institutions.

In all these cases, the Middle Eastern experience served as a paradigm for the formation of the new societies. The Middle Eastern Islamic societies were built around three different types of collectivities: parochial groups, religious associations, and state regimes. Parochial groups were based upon family, clan, lineage, tribal, clientele, and neighborhood ties. At the level of religious associations ʿulamaʾ and Sufi elites were organized around schools of law, Sufi fraternities, and shrines. State regimes were characterized by such institutions as nomadic or ethnic elite armies, slave or other marginal military forces, a combination of bureaucratic and quasi-feudal forms of administration, and a Muslim terminology for taxation. These components of the Middle Eastern societies involved a combination of Islamic and non-Islamic institutions and concepts. While religious associations and certain aspects of state regimes were specifically Islamic, state bureaucratic, administrative, and feudal-like systems of taxation were not peculiarly Islamic. Furthermore, the prevailing concepts of legitimacy were formulated in patrimonial, ethnic, historic, or cosmopolitan cultural terms as well as Muslim symbols. Similarly, the social systems and cultural expressions of parochial communities owed little to Islam. Thus our template for "Islamic societies" by definition includes non-Islamic institutions and cultures.

In the diffusion of Islamic institutions and identities, Middle Eastern precedents were sometimes transmitted as a whole system, sometimes in parts, depending upon who were the bearers of Islam and what were the conditions of its diffusion and reception in different societies. For example, conquest by nomadic peoples as opposed to contact among small groups of merchants made a significant difference in the way in which Middle Eastern Islamic influences were transmitted and received. In all instances, however, the diffusion of Islam released tremendous artistic and cultural forces as each new Islamic state and society attempted to work out its own synthesis of Middle Eastern Islamic institutions and local traditions. The history of Islamic societies illustrates the originality of Muslim regimes the world over and yet reveals them to be variations upon an underlying pattern shaped by indigenous conditions in each part of the Muslim world.

MUSLIM ELITES AND ISLAMIC COMMUNITIES

The one common trait shared by all Islamic societies was the establishment of ʿulamaʾ and Sufis as the teachers and exemplars of Islam and the leaders of Muslim communities. The ʿulamaʾ were the scholars knowledgeable about Muslim hadith, law, and theology. Everywhere their primary function was instruction and judicial administration. In West Africa we find ʿulamaʾ under the local names of *mallam* or *karamoko* teaching in villages and town quarters. In Indonesia they were the teachers in pesantren, sometimes called *kiyayi*. In Iran, Inner Asia, and the Ottoman empire they were the mullahs, who taught in Quran schools and higher-level madrasas. Despite important distinctions of knowledge, lineage, and wealth between higher- and lower-ranking ʿulamaʾ, there were rarely formal distinctions among them. Only in Bukhara or West Africa were ʿulamaʾ graded by rank.

ʿUlamaʾ were commonly organized into schools of law, which were associations of scholars, teachers, and students adhering to the codes of law developed by discussion and debate among legal scholars in the eighth and ninth centuries. The principal Sunni schools were the Hanafi, Shafiʿi, Maliki, and Hanbali, though the Shiʿi ʿulamaʾ of Iran were organized in an analogous fashion. Through the law schools, the scholars organized higher education and trained teachers and judicial administrators. From the law schools came *muftis* or legal consultants, notaries, and judges.

These activities generated a popular or mass following for the scholars and their schools. The students usually considered themselves the personal disciples and loyal clients of their masters. In Africa and Indonesia they worked in the master's employ to pay their tuition. They commonly married into the master's family. As an organized following they could have a considerable local political importance. The students of Istanbul and Bukhara were ready to take to the streets to defend their collective interests. Apart from students, the communities in which the schools were located provided patrons and supporters, usually from the merchant and artisan classes. In eastern Iran and Transoxania, under Mongol and Timurid suzerainty, and in West African Dyula settlements, the ʿulamaʾ were the leaders of their communities.

The religious authority of the ʿulamaʾ, their expertise in law, and their social leadership made it important for state regimes to control them. The Ottoman, the Safavid, and the Mughal regimes, and the states of Tunisia and Bukhara all provide, in differing degrees, examples of bureaucratic organization of ʿulamaʾ. In other North and Sudanic African states the ʿulamaʾ were not bureaucratically organized but were still courtiers and clients of the political elites. By contrast, Hanbalis in Egypt and Syria, Malikis in North and West Africa, and Naqshbandis in India not only maintained their autonomy, but were the active opponents of state elites in the name of Islamic principles.

The ʿulamaʾ performed different political roles, depending upon their class level and the type of political system in which they were embedded. Higher-ranking ʿulamaʾ were commonly state functionaries, while lower-level ʿulamaʾ teachers were often spiritual counselors for the common people. In the Ottoman empire, ʿulamaʾ bureaucrats belonged to the state elites; lower-ranking students and teachers to the opposition. In Iran, the Shiʿi ʿulamaʾ evolved from a position of subordination to the state elite to autonomy and leadership of the common people.

The most striking socio-religious development of post-thirteenth century Islamic societies was the emergence of Sufism in innumerable variations as the principal expression of Islamic beliefs and communal identities. Sufism personified in scholar mystics, ardent reformers, ecstatic preachers, and miracle-working holy-men became the almost universal sign of the Muslim presence. Sufism is difficult to characterize briefly, since the word was used to apply to religious and social practices so diverse that they did not in fact constitute a single phenomenon. In general, Sufism is Muslim mysticism or the spiritual quest that leads to direct experience of the reality of God's being. With variations, the term covers two basic constellations of religious ideas. One kind of Sufism is a religious and ethical discipline built upon adherence to the teachings of the Quran, the hadith, and the law, supplemented by spiritual practices designed to cultivate an outward conformity to Muslim norms and an inner insight into the ultimate spiritual realities. Muslim holy-men of this type cultivate religious knowledge, ethical discipline, and spiritual insight, and are commonly integrated with the ʿulamaʾ. The ordinary Sufi of this type is at once a scholar and a spiritual master.

A second kind of Sufism emphasizes faith in Sufi saints, and seems to arise out of preexisting belief in the world of spirits and the magical powers of holy-men. To many ordinary Muslims, a Sufi is a person who has attained a quality of inner consciousness that makes him close to God, and therefore a person to be venerated as an intermediary between the material and the spiritual worlds. This is possible because of the inherent metaphysical connection between individual human spirituality and divine reality. The saint is directly connected to the cosmos because he participates in the essential forces of rational or spiritual power. The Sufi is considered by his followers as a spiritual teacher, a miracle worker, a dispenser of blessings, and a mediator between men and God. This type of Sufism led to veneration of the person of the holy-man, and the heirs of his *baraka* (power of blessing) be they his tomb or shrine, or his disciples and descendants. It led to a religious life of offerings, sacrifices, and communal festivals around the shrines of saints. Shrine-Sufism, then, is a religion of magical acquisition of divine powers rather than a religion of ethical or emotional self-cultivation. Though both types of Sufism are called Islam, they represent profoundly contrasting concepts of the religious life.

In either case, the social organization of Sufism followed from the authority of the Sufi masters. The ultimate social unit was the individual Sufi surrounded by his disciples. The individual holy-man and his disciples could also win lay followers among the people of his village, quarter, or camp. Such small communities might in turn be linked together in lineages or brotherhoods, sharing a common religious identity.

Holy lineages derived from a concept of Sufi authority built on a combination of knowledge of the Quran and mystical achievements and inherited powers transmitted by spiritual and/or genealogical descent from an earlier saint or from the Prophet himself. In many respects this concept is parallel to that of the Shiꜥi imams. Just as the silsila or chain of religious transmission went back to the companions of the Prophet, the genealogies of Sufis were commonly traced back to the Caliphs and the Prophet. Such was the case for the *mirs*, *khwajas*, and *sayyids* of Transoxania and the *sharifs* of Morocco. The fusion of spiritual and genealogical descent was easy to make, for the Sufi was indeed a child of the Prophet; one who imitated his ways, recreated his life, and concentrated within himself the noble qualities, or the sura – the image of the Prophet. Given the widespread Muslim veneration for the holiness of ancestors, it was natural to identify present holiness with descent from superior beings.

In turn, the personal authority of the master was transmitted by silsilas, baraka, and genealogical descent to his descendants, to his disciples, and to his tomb. The descendants of a famous saint would by definition be regarded as constituting a holy community based on their inheritance of his spiritual qualities and lineage ties. Descent from the Prophet became particularly important in many regions in the fourteenth century and later. Certain lineages in Egypt, the khwajas of Bukhara and Kashgar, the sharifs of Morocco, Jakhanke lineages in West Africa, *evliadi* groups among Turkmens, and Berber *zawaya* lineages in Mauritania were identified as holy communities, every male member of which was a descendant of a saint and heir to his spiritual qualities.

More common was the organization of a tariqa, or Sufi brotherhood. A tariqa was formed when several Sufi masters considered themselves the disciples of an earlier common teacher, perpetuating a common spiritual discipline. Although the tariqa cells were independent of each other, they recognized the same higher authority, and became units of a larger-order association. Some of these associations were regional in scale. In India the introduction of the tariqa structure was the basis of the subsequent organization of a region-wide Islamic society. In West Africa the consolidation of such brotherhoods in the eighteenth and nineteenth centuries was in part the basis of the effort to create a large-scale Muslim political order. Some of these brotherhoods such as the Naqshbandi, the Qadiri, and others, became worldwide Muslim religious orders.

Veneration of shrines also led to special forms of communal or political organization. Commonly the tomb of the original saint became a focus of worship, administered by his descendants. Shrines were endowed with agricultural estates to provide funds for their upkeep and for charitable activities. The tomb complex became the focus of the community composed of all the people who believed that the saint could perform miracles. In such cases a Sufi order came to include not only the descendants of the saint and the active disciples, but all of the people who believed in the saint and worshiped at his tomb. This fellowship of believers, however, remained highly diffuse, segmented, and little capable of organized group activity. Still, from the thirteenth to the end of the eighteenth century, the veneration of shrines and holy places became the most widespread form of Islamic religious life. The Sufis and shrines provided ritual and spiritual counsel, medical cures, and mediation among different groups and strata of the population. Sufis helped to integrate corporate bodies such as guilds and to form political organizations among diverse lineage groups.

Sufism, then, embodied a great variety of religious and social practices. The individual Sufi may have subscribed to a wide variety of religious or theosophical beliefs, may have come from any walk of life, may have had multiple affiliations (including simultaneous membership in different schools of law and Sufi brotherhoods), and may have coupled his mystical insights and practices with any of a number of worldly vocations, combining the roles of Sufi and scholar, merchant, artisan, or political chieftain. Similarly, the disciples and followers, while united by their adherence to the master and to the religious practices of their order, represented every conceivable social milieu. Given all this variation, Sufism cannot generally be defined, but may only be described case by case. The underlying common factor is the exercise of religious insight, discipline, or authority in worldly affairs and a reputation for sanctity.

By the nineteenth century, Islamic societies the world over had acquired similar types of Muslim elites, beliefs, religious practices, and social organ-

Table 9. *The social organization of Sufism*

The Sufi master	
shaykh	teacher
murshid, pir, ishan	guide
wali	friend of God, saint
^c*arif*	gnostic
khalifa	deputy, head of branch of Sufi order with authority to initiate new members
Sufi lineages	
ashraf, shurafaʾ, zawaya, insilimen, evliad	descendants of the Prophet, of companions of the Prophet and of saints
Tariqa	brotherhood
murshid – khalifa – murid	hierarchy of members
silsila	chain of transmission of blessing from the Prophet to a present master
khirqa	the patched cloak of the master transmitted to the disciple as a sign of initiation
khanaqa, zawiya, tekke, dargah	residences and facilities of an order
waqf	endowed financial support
Tombs and shrines	
baraka	blessing, God's power communicated through the saints
karamat	miracles of saints
ziyara	visit to venerate a saint's tomb and seek his intercession before God
^c*urs*	celebration of the anniversary of the death of a saint, his marriage to God

izations. In each Muslim region we find not one but several variant types of Islam. We find the ʿulamaʾ who represent formal scholastic learning, organized education, and judicial administration, affiliated through schools of law. We find the ʿulamaʾ-cum-Sufis who combine legal learning with mystical discipline and contemplation, in an effort to live their lives in imitation of the Prophet. Such religious teachers perpetuated a tradition of learning which combined law, theology, and Sufi wisdom representing Sunni–Shariʿa–Sufi Islam. We find ecstatic visionary Sufis in the tradition of Ibn al-ʿArabi and the gnostic forms of Islamic mysticism. We find the popular forms of Sufi Islam expressed in veneration of saints, faith in their charismatic powers, and belief in the magic of their shrines. Throughout the Muslim world, Sufism in all its forms became the most widespread and popular form of Islam.

In reaction to the consolidation of the several forms of ʿulamaʾ and Sufi Islam, the seventeenth and eighteenth centuries witnessed the rise of a reformist movement opposed to the rigidities of the schools of law and the cultic aspects of shrine Sufism. In principle, the reformist mentality goes back to the early Hanbali movement, which in religious terms emphasized commitment to the hadith of the Prophet, rather than law or cultic worship, and to social activism to improve the quality of Muslim political and communal life. By the seventeenth century this position had new adherents outside of Hanbali circles. Muslim scholars in the Ottoman empire and North Africa were again emphasizing the primacy of hadith. The Naqshbandi and Khalwati orders stressed the importance of combining hadith and law with Sufi asceticism and meditation in opposition to shrine worship and festivals. Social reformers were active in India. The reformers stressed a combination of hadith and Sufism because their religious goal was not union with God but identification with the spirit and active life of the Prophet.

The several proto-reformist tendencies came together in seventeenth- and eighteenth-century Mecca and Medina, where scholars representing the new trends in Morocco, Iraq, India and elsewhere came together to study the hadith and neo-Sufi doctrines. These groups stressed the importance of studying the earliest possible texts of hadith rather than the later standard collections. They made al-Ghazzali the premier teacher of Sufism and set the foundation for religious orders that would propagate the new devotional seriousness. They sought to eliminate religious practices that were not found in the Quran and in the teachings of the Prophet. In the holy cities North African hadith scholarship combined with Indian social activism to generate the reformist version of Islam.

The reformist position spread rapidly by informal contacts among Muslim scholars. Naqshbandi teachers brought the order from Yemen to Egypt, and from India to Syria. In Cairo al-Azhar emerged as an important center of the new tendency, communicating hadith scholarship and the teachings of al-Ghazzali while repudiating the tradition of Ibn al-ʿArabi. Cairo was also the place where visiting North African scholars taught their doctrine of imitation of and union with the spirit of the Prophet rather than pantheistic union with God.

The first political expression of the reformist tendency was the Wahhabi movement in Arabia, which rejected traditional forms of Sufism and the veneration of any human being. The religious goal of Wahhabi teaching was the purification of the heart from vices and sin. To accomplish this, any authority except the Prophet himself had to be rejected in favor of individual obedience and responsibility, and acknowledgement of the unity and transcendence of God. Wahhabism thus set an example of militant moral and social reform.

In India, which was in continuous interaction with Arabia through the travels of merchants, the movements of scholars, and the journeys of pilgrims, reform movements also took root in Delhi, the Northwest Frontier and Bengal. Reformism inspired the Padri movement in Minangkabau (Sumatra). It would also become extremely important in Africa, where it inspired the Sanusiya, the Tijaniya, the jihad of al-Hajj ʿUmar, and Sufi tariqat in the Sudan. As we shall see, the breakdown of the political system of Muslim countries and the rise of European imperialism would give reformed Sufism a new role in the mobilization of Muslim peoples for defense against European domination.

The diffusion of the several types of Muslim elites, beliefs, and associations gave Muslim societies a complex structure. On one level, Islam may be considered an international religion in which all Muslims were linked by a shared tradition of learning and belief, by travel and pilgrimage to common centers of learning and worship, and by membership in international schools of law and religious brotherhoods. For example, Istanbul was the religious capital, not only of the Ottoman empire and of many of the Arab provinces, but also of Inner Asia. Cairo drew students to al-Azhar from as far away as Indonesia and West Africa. Schools of law found their affiliates over broad regions. The Malikis were predominant in North and West Africa; the Hanafis in the Ottoman empire, Inner Asia, and India; and the Shafiʿis in India, Southeast Asia, and East Africa. Similarly, the Sufi brotherhoods generated regional and international loyalties. The Naqshbandis spread throughout India, Inner Asia, China, the Caucasus, and the Middle East. The Tijaniya in the eighteenth and nineteenth centuries became a North and West Africa-wide brotherhood with important branches in the Arab Middle East. The reform movement was centered upon Mecca and Medina, but radiated its influence to India, West Africa, Inner Asia, and China. Thus, individual Muslim teachers and holy-men affiliated through religious brotherhoods, schools of law, and informal patterns of study and travel constituted an international Muslim community. This universality enables us to speak of the Muslim world. Still, on another level, Islam remained intensely local in that scholars and Sufis were embedded in particular communities and represented concepts and practices which were a fusion of the universal forms of Islam with local customs, beliefs, and lifestyles. Islam, then, has to be understood both as a universal religion and in its numerous particular contexts.

Islamic religious leadership and beliefs had a profound effect upon the social organization of Muslim peoples. In general, Muslim religious leadership and loyalties could be integrated with existing collectivities formed on a non-Muslim basis, or Muslim associations, such as schools of law and Sufi brotherhoods, could cut across the lines of existing communities and integrate

Map 8. Muslim schools of law and Sufi brotherhoods: c. 1500.

believers into confessional rather than traditionally defined groups. To understand the social role of Muslim elites it is convenient to distinguish urban and rural settings.

In urban societies Islam played both roles. Urban communities in the Muslim world were commonly divided into strong family, clan, clientele, and residential groups which commonly assumed an Islamic identity. Islam could be the basis for the organization of neighborhood communities around a mosque, khanaqa, or college. Within the urban fabric there were schools of law, Sufi brotherhoods, or Shiʿi sects identified with particular neighborhoods, occupations, or ethnic minorities. For example, in eleventh- and twelfth-century Iranian cities, neighborhood communities were closely identified with schools of law. In India and East Africa, merchant groups sometimes had a sectarian Ismaʿili identity. Ismaʿilis formed *jamatbandis*, or collective associations, which provided political leadership, and organized worship and instruction for a self-contained small community. The jamatbandis thus formed organized Muslim enclaves within larger urban societies. Similarly, Dyula or Hausa merchant groups formed close-knit communities in West Africa. In these cases, the special trust and cohesion required for commercial activities came from religiously reinforced familial and ethnic loyalties.

Towns and cities, however, also provided a setting for social and political integration. This took place through markets, direct political negotiations among town notables, and the activities of ʿulamaʾ and Sufis. Schools of law and Sufi tariqat drew diverse elements of the population into common religious bodies, and Islamic collectivities formed a superordinate community. Their integrative function was expressed in terms of allegiance to Shariʿa and to Islamic high-culture norms of religious behavior. Through urban communities Islam also played an important role in creating regional and international trading networks, administrative organizations, and state regimes.

Islamic religious leadership was similarly integrated into village societies. In many village societies, Muslim identity was often superimposed upon pre-existing village identity. In Minangkabau (Sumatra) peasant villages were conceived in terms of a double social structure in which family and property were treated on matriarchal lines while trade and politics were symbolized in patriarchal Muslim terms. In other cases, the merger of Islamic and non-Islamic cultural identity was expressed through shrine worship, festivals, belief in spirits, and shamanistic or magical curing practices which blended faith in the miraculous powers of Islamic holy-men with pre-Islamic beliefs. Religious conviction was expressed through worship of shrines and holy places in an annual cycle of religious festivals, magical activities, and other rituals which

Table 10. *Muslim religious officials*

Caliph	head of Sunni Muslim *umma*
Mosques	
imam	leader of prayer
khatib	preacher of official sermon
muezzin	crier of calls to prayer
Schools	
faqih or *ᶜalim* (pl. *ᶜulamaᵓ*)	scholar of law
mudaris	professor of *madrasa*
Legal administrators	
qadi	judge
mufti	jurisconsult
Shaykh al-Islam	chief *mufti* and head of judicial establishment
muhtasib	market inspector and enforcer of morals
Sufi brotherhoods	
shaykh (*murshid*, etc.)	master and guide
khalifa	deputy
muqqadam	local headman in brotherhood
shaykh al-shuyukh	chief of Sufi shaykhs (Egypt)
sajjada nishin	successor, chief of shrine
Descendants of Prophet	
sayyid, sharif (pl. *ashraf, shurafaᵓ*)	
naqib al-ashraf	syndic of the descendants of the Prophet
Ithna ᶜashari Shi ᶜa	
mujtahid	scholar of law qualified to give independent legal judgment
Hujjatollah	proof of God: higher-ranking *mujtahid*
Ayatollah	sign of God: highest-ranking *mujtahid*
Marjaᶜ i-taqlid	religious teacher to whom obedience is due
Ismaᶜilis	
daᶜi	missionaries
hujja	proof-representative of imam
imams	successors to the Prophet and leaders of the Muslims

incorporated non- or pre-Islamic concepts and ceremonies. Islamic belief, then, did not necessarily lead to the formation of an organized body of believers, but could serve as a shared identity among diverse peoples who preserved their own kinship, territorial, linguistic, ethnic, and other bases of non-Islamic culture in group organization and social relations.

After the thirteenth century Sufism became central to the structure of lineage societies in many parts of the Muslim world. In lineage societies Muslim holymen appeared as individual charismatic teachers; sometimes the custodians of local shrines; sometimes affiliated with brotherhoods. They also appeared as members of holy lineages, living among other lineages or members of tribes. Sufi lineages in Algeria, Morocco, southern Somalia, Mauritania, and Turkmenistan are among the many examples of groups tracing their descent to the Prophet or the early Caliphs, who are organized as separate communities within the framework of the surrounding tribal society. Similarly, African Dyula communities were made up of lineages or specialized occupational castes operating as components of complex, usually non-Muslim, segmented societies. Such lineages came to be accepted as having a social authority in part based on descent and in part based upon Sufi qualities. In any case, whether as individuals or lineages, Sufis served to facilitate the selection of chiefs, mediate disputes, organize long-distance trade or other economic ventures requiring the coordination and cooperation of different groups, teach the young, heal the sick, provide amulets, officiate at circumcisions, marriages, and funerals, celebrate festivals, perform white magic, and uphold the tenuous connection of human beings with the world of the spirits and the divine.

Sufi leadership could also be the basis of organized political action, tribal conquests, and the formation of state regimes. Sufi holy-men could unite clans, lineages, and tribes into larger movements. In such cases, religious leadership and loyalties created a double structure of society in which religious elites represented the larger movement and secular tribal or group chieftains represented the smaller units. In these cases, the larger religious identity did not efface other aspects of ethnic, tribal, or clan loyalties, but rather was superimposed upon them. Movements created in this way were likely to fragment into their component parts.

The prime example of this type is the original Islam which integrated Arabian bedouins into a conquering movement. The unification of pastoral or tribal peoples under Islamic religious leadership was a recurring phenomenon. In Oman Arab tribesmen were united and governed by the Ibadi (Khariji) imams. In North Africa from the seventh to the thirteenth century, Berber peoples were united under Kharijism, Shiʿism, Sunni reformism, and Sufism to form the Fatimid, Almoravid, Almohad and other movements. After the twelfth century, Sufism played a particularly important role in tribal unification. Rural populations throughout North Africa came to be organized in Sufi-led communities. In Morocco, the Saʿdian and the Alawi dynasties were based on Sufi-led coalitions of pastoral and mountain peasant peoples. The Safavids united individuals, clientele and clan groups to conquer and govern Iran. The conquerors of Anatolia and the Balkans, while under overall dynastic direction, were at the local level led by Sufis. In Inner Asia, the khwajas served to mediate among and create coalitions of pastoral peoples. The tribes which occupied Somalia were united by allegiance to Sufis. So too the Fulani jihads of the eighteenth and nineteenth centuries were built on reform preaching.

Thus many of the great "tribal" movements that led to the formation of Islamic states were built upon Muslim religious leadership or the integration of Muslim religious and secular chieftainship. In such societies Muslim leadership inspired millenarian revolts and radical opposition to established regimes. Before the modern era this was the principal expression of the Islamic impulse to transform the world and fashion a new human order.

THE STATE REGIMES

Alongside of ʿulamaʾ and Sufi leadership a principal feature of all Muslim societies was the organization of state regimes. While there was no transferable model of an Islamic State, Muslim societies were often based upon similar concepts, institutions and vocabularies. Generally, for Muslims, a Muslim ruler was the symbol of a legitimate regime, the guarantor that Muslim laws would be enforced, and the representative of the historic continuity of Muslim communities and their attachment to the Prophet. Muslims regarded states and empires as the ultimate protectors of worship, education, and law. In times of war they expected protection againt infidel enemies; in times of peace, patronage for scholars and saints. The existence of a Muslim state assured its peoples that the civilized order of the world was being upheld.

Muslim states, however, differed greatly as to the nature of their religious legitimation. In many cases, this legitimation was attached to the person of the ruler. The Umayyads of Damascus, ʿAbbasids, Fatimids, Almoravids, Almohads, Umayyads in Spain, and the leaders of West African jihads in the nineteenth century all considered themselves hierocratic rulers. They were the heirs to the authority of the Prophet; they were at once teachers and rulers. Similarly, the khwajas of Kashgar, the Sufi masters of small Moroccan states, and the Safavids of Iran regarded themselves as the repository of religious as well as temporal authority. In Morocco, the legitimacy of the ruler depended upon his sharifian descent and Sufi qualities. The reform movements of the nineteenth century would bring a resurgence of the aspiration to unite religious and political leadership.

In other Muslim societies, legitimacy was attached directly to the state institutions. For example, the Ottoman empire had an institutionalized legitimacy based on its reputation as a warrior regime that expanded the frontiers of Islam and defended Muslim peoples against the infidels. Its authority became so deeply embedded that even in the nineteenth century, when the Ottoman state was in decline and overwhelmed by European powers, its importance to Muslim security remained unquestioned.

Furthermore, Muslim states tended to adopt similar political practices and to redefine local political precedents in Islamic terms. The militias of tribal-founded Muslim empires were commonly transformed into slave or client forces. This was especially important in the Middle East, where slave troops were recruited to supplement or to displace tribal levies, as in the cases of the ͨAbbasid, Ghaznavid, Saljuq, Mamluk, Ottoman, and Safavid empires. Slaves were also used in North and West Africa. Slaves were generally recruited in Inner Asia and the Caucasus, but were also taken from non-Muslim populations in the Balkans, Georgia, and sub-Saharan Africa. Slaves commonly retained an ethnic and cultural identity based on their non-Muslim past.

In administration Muslim states also shared similar practices. The ͨAbbasids inherited Byzantine and Sasanian practices in granting tax revenues for military services, and the Saljuqs molded the iqta ͨ institution of late ͨAbbasid times into a system of financial administration which, under various names, was later adapted by the Mongol, Timurid, Ottoman, Safavid, Uzbek and Mughal empires. The iqta ͨ, *timar*, *tuyul*, and *jagir* (all names for grants of tax revenues) represent a similar principle of decentralized financial support for the state military elite. Other examples of administrative uniformities among Muslim states are taxation on a kharaj-jizya or land and poll tax basis, and the endowment of waqfs for religious purposes. In many cases, as in Inner Asia and North Africa, these uniformities were due to the direct transfer of Middle Eastern institutions, but in many other cases, these widespread similarities in administration and fiscal practices were due to the independent inheritance of similar institutions from earlier non-Muslim regimes, and to the adoption of a common Muslim terminology for these separate precedents.

Alongside the several specifically Islamic practices and symbols, Islamic states were defined by their relationship to the ͨulama ͻ and the Sufis. The Ottoman, Safavid, and Bukhara monarchies were strongly supported by an organized ͨulama ͻ bureaucracy which was committed to the regime and looked upon the state as indispensable to Islam. These states built up a bureaucracy to control justice and education and diminished the religious prestige of the Sufis. They suppressed antagonistic brotherhoods, and appropriated the political functions of Sufis by endowing government officials with extensive powers to dispense justice, regulate economic matters, protect trade, and sponsor education. In these cases, ͨulama ͻ commonly held the view that even a corrupt and evil state had to be accepted and obeyed, for any regime was better than none. In their view, the alternative to state control was anarchy and communal violence. In some African kingdoms, the ͨulama ͻ, while not highly organized by the state, were still the source of the legitimation of regimes in the eyes of other states and in the eyes of their subjects who, while not Muslim, accepted the superior magic of literate Muslim courtiers. In India the Mughals drew limited support and much criticism from the ʿulamaʾ. In Indonesia, by contrast, organized Muslim elites had little or no role in the legitimation of the regimes and if anything were the leaders of peasant resistance.

While the relations of state regimes and ʿulamaʾ tended toward interdependence, relations between states and Sufis tended toward opposition. Some Sufi orders cooperated with central governments and transmitted governmental authority to the common people, as did the Suhrawardis of India and the Mevlevis of the Ottoman empire, but Sufism was more usually apolitical, as in the case of the Chistis in India. Many Sufi orders were not only independent of state regimes but opposed them, as in eighteenth-century Algeria and Morocco. In general, highly organized states regarded the ʿulamaʾ as politically compatible, but considered the Sufis as political competitors to be suppressed or coopted.

Even in cases where Sufis were independent, an intimate connection existed between them and the state authorities. Rulers patronized the Sufi masters in order to acquire some of the blessing and magic attributed to the saints. In India the same rituals and ceremonies were observed in both the court of the Sufi and the court of the ruler. Both courts were called by the same name – *dargah*. Such symbols transferred the legitimacy of the Sufis to the princes. Conversely, the authority of Sufi masters was built around worldly success, power, and efficacy in daily affairs.

Alongside the Muslim aspects of these states, there were shared non-Muslim factors. One of these was the incorporation of non-Muslim elites. "Muslim" state elites were often warrior peoples for whom tribal identity was more salient than Muslim identity. Moreover, such tribal military forces were frequently supplemented or replaced by avowedly non-Muslim levies. The Mughal regime, for example, absorbed Hindu lords; North African regimes depended upon Catalan or Aragonese forces. Also the subordinate vassal principalities of large Muslim empires included non-Muslim tribal chiefs, feudal lords, and other local notables. These subordinate regimes were ordinarily legitimized in patriarchal or patrimonial terms and not by recourse to Islamic symbols or ideology.

Legitimation, more generally, depended upon a combination of Muslim and non-Muslim patrimonial, cosmopolitan, or cosmological symbols. The ʿAbbasid regime and its Mamluk, Ottoman, Safavid, and Mughal successors appealed to genealogical descent from earlier Arab, Persian, or Turkish nobility to justify their rule. Each regime also patronized a cosmopolitan culture to define its political identity: the ʿAbbasids and Ottomans, architecture; the Mughals, painting and music. Through their patronage of philosophy and science, Muslim regimes appealed to universal symbols as the basis of the political order. Muslim statecraft was also conceived of as being regulated by rules derived entirely from secular monarchical traditions. Thus the state elites distanced themselves from Islamic commitments by cultivating artistic, literary, and scientific achievements that had little to do with Islam but were part of the historic political culture of the several Muslim regions. The multiple levels of legitimation responded to the need to win political support or acquiescence from the multi-ethnic, multi-religious populations who were commonly subjected to Muslim rule.

Furthermore, there were variations in the choice and degree of emphasis placed upon Islamic or non-Islamic symbols of legitimacy. Each regime showed characteristic originality in the selection of cultural and artistic styles, and in the degree of emphasis placed upon Islamic, cosmopolitan, cosmological, and patrimonial symbols. Thus the Arab regimes tended to be strongly Islamic, without noteworthy cosmopolitan symbols; the Indian Mughal empire was highly syncretic. Indonesian-Malayan regimes perpetuated a non-Islamic culture of imperium with little more than Islamic titles. By contrast, the nineteenth-century African jihads were dedicated to an Islamic utopia.

In any case Muslim regimes and empires were usually composite formations that embodied Islamic institutions in the matrix of a broader political culture. They carried an inherent ambiguity of identity. On one level, they were Muslim; on another, they were cosmopolitan patrons of a style of monarchical culture which, despite variations, gave a similar gestalt to Ottoman, Safavid, Mughal, and other Muslim state cultures. The production of illuminated manuscripts, the diffusion of Persian literary forms into Turkish and Urdu, the construction of domed architectural monuments, and many other features identify an imperial variant of Islamic civilization. On another level, the culture of Muslim regimes was also regional and derived from the pre-Islamic and non-Islamic substrates of the societies they ruled. Local languages, poetic traditions, literary forms, architectural motifs, musical motifs, and cultic practices made each Muslim regime an expression of a particular locality. The several interacting levels of universal Islamic, cosmopolitan imperial, and local cultural styles afforded each regime a distinctive identity.

CONFRONTATION WITH EUROPE

By the eighteenth century the worldwide system of Islamic societies had reached its apogee and begun its political decline. The Safavid state had been defeated by Afghan invaders and, deserted by its tribal vassals, disintegrated completely. The Ottoman empire went through a period of decentralization, though the concept of an imperial state was unimpaired. The Mughal empire disintegrated into numerous competing provincial and feudal regimes. In Southeast Asia, a centralized regime had never been established over the Indonesian archipelago or the Malay peninsula, and the largest Indonesian state, the Mataram empire of Java, came under direct Dutch economic and indirect Dutch political control. In North Africa, Muslim states were being subverted by their declining commercial position in the Mediterranean, and provincial, tribal, and Sufi resistance was on the increase. The Sudanic states had long passed the peak of their commercial prosperity, though Muslim communities were growing in influence in other parts of Africa. By this period much of the northern steppes of Inner Asia had come under Russian control and eastern Turkestan came under Chinese rule.

The crucial common factor in the decline of Muslim regimes was the rising power of Europe. On the far western fringe of the Eurasian land mass European peoples were making a revolution in world history. From the late Middle Ages to modern times, European societies were developing an unprecedented technological inventiveness and an unrivaled capacity to generate economic wealth and military power. These developments would profoundly change the conditions of life not only for Muslims, but for all the world's peoples. While we assess the impact of Europe upon Muslim societies, we should be aware that the encounter of European and Islamic civilizations was but one instance of a universal phenomenon.

European world power had its origins in a set of intertwined socio-economic and cultural conditions that led to the formation of a highly pluralistic society. From the outset, European societies were profoundly different from Islamic Middle Eastern societies, for they were not organized upon the threefold template of kinship, religious community, and empire. Medieval European family structure did not tend to the formation of closed lineage groups, but rather to the formation of open and interlocking social networks based on bilateral connections of both husband and wife. With the fall of Rome and the failures of the Carolingian and Holy Roman empires, European states no longer had the all-embracing political and mythic importance they held in the Middle East. In place of empires, feudal governments based on personal and contractual loyalties, governments by oath association, and communes or popular assemblies based on Roman or Germanic notions of popular sovereignty were accepted as legitimate.

Most important was the tendency toward separation of state and church. While in the Middle East Muslim symbols were becoming pervasive, European society was becoming secularized. The potentiality for secularization was already implicit in the nature of the Christian church. The fact that the church was a highly organized, corporate institution governed under laws and norms appropriate to itself but not to lay society made it possible in principle to define a profane realm – "the world" – outside of the church, a world governed by non-church or non-canonical laws. At the same time, European society had independent sources of secular civic and cultural values. Greek and Roman political and legal ideas, and German communal and feudal concepts, defined a realm of organized public life, legal authority and secular values which, though not Christian, were held to be legitimate. Not only were church and state separate institutions, but Christian and secular societies had separate foundations.

The historical trends of the twelfth and thirteenth centuries favored the enhancement of the pluralism implicit in European family, state, and religious organization. The growth of commerce, a money economy, and towns broke up village communities, favored the mobility of individuals, and promoted occupational specialization. New urban classes of land-owning and capital-investing patricians, merchants and bankers, entrepreneurs in manufacturing, ship-building, or commerce, artisans, journeymen, and workers grew in size. With the growth of secular learning in literature, philosophy, law, and medicine, a non-clerical intelligentsia of poets, writers, physicians, lawyers, professors, administrators, and judges came into being. Thus, European society was divided into numerous social strata and classes: nobles, knights, clergy, and a bourgeoisie, subdivided again among merchants, artisans, intellectuals, lawyers, and other groups.

The differentiation of late medieval European society stimulated the formation of corporate groups to advance the interests of their members. Some groups served the need for political security. Feudal fiefdoms, aristocratic factions, church governments, peace associations, and communes, all became active centers of political power. Within the church new monastic orders and confraternities were formed to express new religious orientations. Merchant and artisan guilds and commercial companies organized economic activities. Universities were founded to carry on secular learning.

This pluralism was expressed in values as well as social organization. While

Muslim societies maintained a holistic commitment to the law and umma, Europe recognized the legitimacy of several religious, ethical, or philosophic systems including feudal chivalry and romance, Roman law, philosophy, and bourgeois business ethics – each of which constituted a world of values independent of Christian beliefs. Each type of government, each stratum, each group operated in accord with its own laws and regulations, its own moral concepts, and its own implicit idea of the nature of the human being and of human fulfillment.

This differentiation of activities and values was accompanied and sustained by an increasing awareness of and commitment to the intrinsic worth of the human individual. Christianity, feudalism and urban humanism came together to give the individual a transcending importance. Basic Christian values stressed the importance of the salvation of the individual soul. Secular impulses sustained this individualism. Medieval society recognized the inherent honor of the warrior – his aretē, his prowess and his right to express that prowess in conquest, chivalric daring and courtesy, vendetta, and the quest for love. The inherent genius of the warrior and the rights of the warrior and other honorable men to compete for wealth, power, and love legitimized individual interests and self-expression. Similarly the new humanistic culture of the cities held the claims of the individual to be greater than those of society. Thirteenth-century Florentine society held the individual to be capable of personal refinement and redemption through Christian and chivalric love and through rhetorical and courtly instruction. Christian faith, chivalry and urban ideals combined to generate confidence in individual free expression.

In this complex and pluralistic society the relationship between the individual and society was different from that of the Middle East. Whereas in the Middle East individual obligations were defined in terms of religiously commanded participation in a religiously defined community, in Europe the individual was perceived on two levels. One was in terms of the specialized roles which individuals played in occupational, corporate, and office-holding situations; the other was in terms of an inherent spiritual identity. Society itself came to be conceived in terms of individuals fulfilling a function, a calling, a role in a corporate, pluralistic, and secular world.

The Renaissance and the Protestant Reformation seem to have exaggerated the underlying European tendency to pluralistic values and individual aggrandizement. In many parts of Europe the breakdown of agrarian feudal society, the growth of towns, and the ever-expanding system of commerce generated an extreme anxiety over personal security and ultimately over the worth of individuals and their capacity for salvation. Such forces were not uniform in their operation but they were potent in critical milieus in England, France, Germany, and Switzerland where new Protestant communities were organized in response to the aching need for order and communal association. In Protestant communities the anxieties of the age were reinforced by the doctrine of predestination, according to which it was impossible for a person either to know or to affect his prospects for salvation. Who were the sinners and who were the saved? Also Protestant puritanism closed off the ordinary emotional and ritual outlets for inner stress. Protestant hostility to art, to music and dance, to sensuality and sexuality, to religious pageantry and ritual, and to Catholic confession and absolution, left few channels for the satisfaction of inner emotional needs.

These combined socio-economic, theological, and psychological pressures drove individuals to seek worldly signs of their salvation through methodical and devoted labor in their calling so as to curb inherent human wickedness and eliminate public sins and moral faults. Self-controlled, self-disciplined activity in God's service was the antidote to anxiety and anomie. Anxiety, then, could be relieved by the systematic acquisition of wealth as a demonstration of God's favor. The emergence of this cast of mind in people uprooted from organic communities, who were striving to form new formal associations, and who were capable of systematic behavior and the subordination of all extraneous considerations – personal, emotional, aesthetic, and even ethical – to the demand for a patterned way of living, was what Max Weber called the spirit of capitalism. A similar systematic attitude could also be applied in politics, as in the English Puritan revolution, to the construction of a holy society. It could be applied to engineering, invention and scientific discovery, architectural and artistic design, and indeed to all realms of human endeavor. Weber saw that this capacity for impersonal unemotional commitment to the inherent norms of an enterprise, and for pursuing specialized goals to their ultimate implications was the defining characteristic of a new type of human culture and personality and the basis for modern European civilization.

This type of personality was only just emerging in the Renaissance period. While it would be centuries before the full implications of Renaissance urban and Protestant culture would be realized, the new orientation was already being applied to technical invention and to the pursuit of material well-being. By the thirteenth and fourteenth centuries the towns of Italy, Flanders, and the Baltic were already committed to commerce and industry, rather than agriculture, as sources of wealth. Out of these towns came novel techniques for investment, banking, and insurance, and other methods of economic organization and exchange. The pursuit of wealth and the sophisticated means to generate it led to a tremendous outward expansion of European city-states in search of exotic luxury products and also of new sources of food, fuel, and raw materials for their growing and ambitious populations.

The trading impulse led by stages to revolution in world commerce and politics. The first stage was the creation of a new worldwide pattern of trade. Venice and Genoa had already created extensive networks of colonies and trading posts in the eastern Mediterranean and the Black Sea where they could purchase spices, drugs, dyes, silk, and other exotic products of the East. When the rise of the Ottoman empire cut off the Italian city-states from their eastern sources, Genoa was forced to turn to the western Mediterranean and the Atlantic for its supplies of wool, sugar, alum, silk, cereals, dyes, and spices. The Portuguese undertook the search for a new route to the Indies which would bypass Middle Eastern routes and enable them to bring eastern products directly to Lisbon, and thus discovered an African route to the Indian Ocean. Spanish and Italian explorers discovered new continents. Portugal and Spain conquered empires in the southern seas and the new world, and brought home untold wealth.

The sixteenth century was occupied by the struggle to control the new world economy. The Ottomans and the French fought the Habsburgs in Italy, eastern Europe, and the Mediterranean, and the Ottomans fought the Portuguese in the Indian Ocean. By the end of the sixteenth century the Ottomans had consolidated their position in the Balkans and North Africa, but the Spanish empire had fallen apart, ruining in its collapse the great commercial and banking houses of Italy, Germany, and Castile. Their demise opened the way for a new phase in the struggle to control the world economy. New smaller states took the initiative. At the end of the sixteenth century, Holland, England, and France emerged as the dominant forces in world trade. Each of them would create a worldwide commercial empire based on bourgeois initiative, sophisticated trading, advanced gunnery and sailing techniques, and utter ruthlessness in the pursuit of gain. Portugal, England, and Holland were tiny countries whose power came from technological and economic advantages – better ships and guns, more productive business enterprises, and more efficient use of human resources. The capacity to mobilize and organize men with maximum military and economic efficiency would give them a decisive advantage.

This advantage led not only to a transfer of political and commercial dominance, but to the transformation of the basic structures of the world economy. While the discovery of new routes to the Orient did not close the traditional Middle Eastern international routes, they created a revolution in the distribution of wealth. Now Europe would prosper on the captured gold and silver, spices, and other products of the new world and the old. The Baltic and the Atlantic replaced the Mediterranean and the Indian Ocean as the most important centers of world trade. The shift of international trading routes from the Mediterranean to the Atlantic meant not only a change of routes but a change in the nature of the goods being exchanged. While the traditional trade was largely a trade in luxury goods, the modern trade was a trade in agricultural and industrial products – timber, grain, fish, salt – on a mass scale, and represented a new level of commodity production and division of labor in the world economy. The formation of the new commercial empires made possible a system of economic exploitation in which Europe became the principal beneficiary of a worldwide division of labor between colonies producing raw materials and metropoles producing high-value industrial goods and commercial services. European commercial dominance in the seventeenth and eighteenth centuries led ultimately to the emergence of a new form of capitalist industrial economy.

The rising power of Europe brought it into worldwide conflict with Muslim societies. While Islam was expanding from the Middle East into South and Southeast Asia, Africa, and Eastern Europe, the Atlantic and northern European powers began to assert their own ambitions, expanding on the northern and southern flanks of Islamic societies. While not strictly a society of the western European type, Russia in the sixteenth century began its expansion across Inner Asia and Siberia to the Pacific. Russian expansion was primarily territorial and involved the conquest and absorption of Muslim populations into a Russian empire. In the sixteenth century Russia absorbed the Tatar states in the Volga basin; by the nineteenth century most of the Kazakh population of the northern steppes was in Russian control. The Russian conquests culminated in the absorption of Transoxania and the Transcaspian regions in the late nineteenth century. At the same time China established its suzerainty in eastern Turkestan in the eighteenth century and made it a province of China in the late nineteenth. Between them Russia and China took control of most of the Muslim populations of Inner Asia.

On the southern flanks of Islam, European expansion began with Portuguese, Dutch, and British merchant adventurers who won naval and trading empires in the southern seas and ended by establishing colonial regimes. The Portuguese established a series of bases in the Indian Ocean and at Malacca in the early sixteenth century, but they were displaced by the Dutch, who took control of the Southeast Asian trade in the seventeenth century. The Dutch soon converted their commercial empire into a territorial one. They made

Map 9. European domination over Muslim and other lands: 1815.

themselves suzerains of Java by the middle of the eighteenth century and conquered the rest of the Indies in the course of the nineteenth century.

The British also began by establishing trading bases and ended by conquering an empire in India. After bitter rivalries with the French, the British took control of Bengal in the late eighteenth century and went on to dominate the Indian subcontinent in the early decades of the nineteenth century. At the same time the British also took full control of the Indian Ocean, with bases in Malaya, the Persian Gulf, the Red Sea, and East Africa. Europeans also established their commercial dominance in the Mediterranean and took territorial control of Egypt and North Africa. Africa was the last of the major regions with a large Muslim population to be subjected to colonial domination. Of the Muslim societies only the Ottoman empire and Iran maintained their political identity, without experiencing direct colonial rule.

By the eighteenth century the reorganization of the world economy and the consolidation of European commercial and political dominance subverted Muslim societies by depriving Muslim regimes of revenues from taxes and trade. The political consequence was to weaken the central governments, which depended on commercial revenues, and to promote factional strife and the exploitation of the peasantries. European ascendancy took a cultural as well as a political and economic form. By the nineteenth century, Europe was beginning to seize the imagination of Muslim peoples. The Ottomans, for example, were impressed with European military and technological efficiency, artistic style, and the morality of activism and individualism. European political, and especially nationalist, concepts and moral values began to influence Muslim populations. This influence opened a new era in the history of Muslim peoples. Part II concludes with the Muslim world on the eve of its modern transformation.

THE MIDDLE EASTERN
ISLAMIC SOCIETIES

CHAPTER 13

IRAN: THE MONGOL, TIMURID, AND
SAFAVID EMPIRES

The history of Iran from the thirteenth to the eighteenth century is our first case study of the later institutional and cultural development of Islamic societies. From an earlier age, Iran inherited an agricultural civilization and a monarchical regime. The Saljuq empire had bequeathed its particular pattern of slave military elites and iqtaᶜ forms of administration; mixed Islamic and Iranian royal culture; Muslim religious associations in the form of Sunni schools of law, Sufi brotherhoods, and Shiᶜi sects; and strong local urban factions and rural clan communities.

MONGOLS AND TIMURIDS

The Mongol invasions, however, dealt a devastating blow to Iranian-Muslim civilization. The Mongol invasions originated with the formation of a confederation of Inner Asian peoples under the leadership of Chinggis Khan. Believing in a God-given destiny, the Mongols set out to conquer the whole of the known world and brought East Asia, the Middle East, and the East European steppes under their rule. Within a few decades the Mongols ruled all of Eurasia from central Europe to the Pacific. This vast empire was divided among the four sons of Chinggis. The division of the empire was intended for administrative convenience, but it provoked struggles for power among the descendants of Chinggis as a result of an inherent ambiguity in the Mongol concept of the state. The Mongols regarded the conquered territories as the joint possession of the family of Chinggis, though they were divided among individual princes. Since there was neither a defined succession nor any way

276

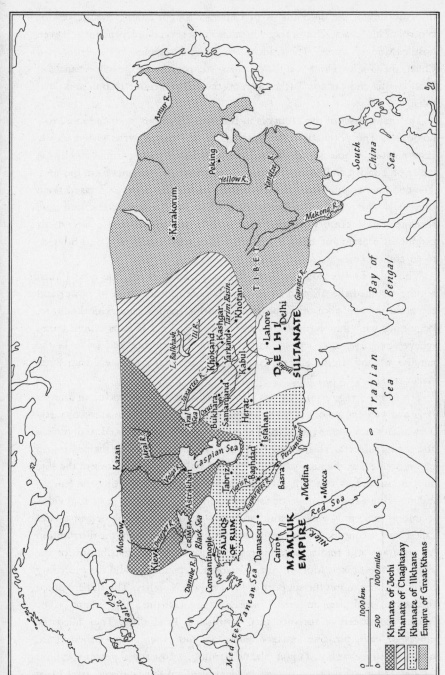

Map 10. The Mongol empires in the thirteenth century.

Khanate of Jochi
Khanate of Chaghatay
Khanate of Ilkhans
Empire of Great Khans

1000 km.

500   1000 miles

South
China
Sea

Bay of
Bengal

Arabian
Sea

TIBET

Peking

Yellow R.

Yangtze R.

Mekong R.

Karakorum

Amur R.

Ili R.

L.Balkhash

Kashgar
Yarkand Tarim Basin Khotan
Khokand

Kabul

Lahore

DELHI Delhi

SULTANATE

Ganges

Indus

Herat

Isfahan

Samarqand
Bukhara
Jaxartes R.
Oxus R.
Aral
Sea

Khiva

Ural R.

Kazan

Caspian Sea

Volga R.

Astrakhan

Moscow

Kiev
Dnieper R.
CRIMEA
Black Sea

Constantinople

Danube R.

SALJUQS
OF RUM

Damascus

Tabriz

Baghdad
Tigris R.
Euphrates R.
Basra
Persian Gulf

Medina
Mecca

Red Sea

Nile R.

Cairo

MAMLUK
EMPIRE

Mediterranean Sea

Baltic
Sea

to assure unity, the descendants of Chinggis fought among themselves for control of his legacy. Out of these disputes came several independent and even hostile Mongol states. These included Mongol regimes in Mongolia and China, the Golden Horde on the northern steppes, the Chaghatay Khanate in Transoxania and eastern Turkestan, and the Ilkhan regime in Iran and Anatolia.

The first impact of the Mongols in Iran was disastrous, and amounted to a holocaust. The populations of many cities and towns were systematically exterminated. Whole regions were depopulated by invading armies and by the influx of Turkish and Mongol nomads who drove the peasants from the land. The conquerors plundered their subjects, made them serfs, and taxed them ruinously. The result was a catastrophic fall in population, income, and state revenue. For a century or more fine pottery and metalwares ceased to be produced. A period of urban autonomy and cultural vitality was thus brought to an end.

While the first century of Mongol rule wreaked havoc, the later Ilkhan regime resumed the historic trend toward state centralization of power and recreated the brilliance of Saljuq period Turkic-Iranian monarchical culture. Beginning with the reign of Ghazan (1295–1304), the Ilkhans rebuilt cities, redeveloped irrigation works, and sponsored agriculture and trade in the familiar way of Middle Eastern empires. In particular they opened up Inner Asian trade routes to China.

The Mongol regime in Iran was a conquest state. It was made up of a single large army composed of a tribal military aristocracy allied to the ruling dynasty. This aristocracy conceived of itself as a privileged people entitled to dominate and tax its subjects. This sense of superiority was explained by the possession of a supreme law, the *yasa*, which defined the rights and obligations of the elite and legitimized its rule. The Mongols ruled Iran by distributing the land to military chiefs for pasturage or for tax revenues. The chiefs, in turn, divided it among their followers. Pasture and plow lands were combined in estates called *tuyul*, a concept which combined Mongolian ideas about the distribution of pasturage and Iranian administrative concepts of the distribution of the right to collect taxes. Mongol rule, moreover, depended, as did the preceding Saljuq regimes, upon the support of local notable families. The Ilkhans allied themselves with Iranian urban bureaucrats, merchants, and ʿulamaʾ. The ʿulamaʾ continued or resumed their position as local elites. They filled the offices of qadi, preacher, market inspector, and other posts. Urban elites, whose prestige was based upon Islamic learning, whose social power was built on ownership of urban quarters, gardens, and village land and control of waqfs, and whose functions included financial and judicial administration, provided continuity in local government and buffered the impact of changing military regimes. They also provided the administrative personnel for the construction of successive Mongol and Timurid governments.

Despite the self-conscious superiority, however, the Ilkhan state did not bring a new linguistic or religious identity to the Middle East. Unlike the Arabs, who changed both the language and the religion of the region, the Mongols were absorbed by Islam and Persian culture. However, they brought a new phase of creativity to that culture. In the reign of Ghazan, the Mongol and Turkish military elite was converted to Islam and drew its cultural legitimation from Mongolian traditions as well as from Iranian literary sources. Under Mongol sponsorship, history writing flourished, reflecting the Mongol sense of universal destiny. Al-Juvaini's (1226–83) *History of the World Conquerors* told the story of Chinggis Khan and the conquest of Iran. His near-contemporary, Rashid al-Din (1247–1318), a physician and vizier, wrote the *Compendium of Histories*, integrating Chinese, Indian, European, Muslim and Mongol history into a new cosmopolitan perspective on the fate of mankind. The Ilkhans, like other Turkish conquerors, were devoted to the construction of monumental tombs, and adapted older Iranian architectural forms for the monuments of Tabriz, Sultaniya, and Varamin. The most important of the Ilkhan constructions was the mausoleum of Oljeytu (1304–17) at Sultaniya, whose large central dome was a major technical achievement. Stucco, terracotta, and colored bricks or tiles were used to decorate the exterior surfaces.

The Mongol contribution to the revival of the glory of Iranian monarchy was most brilliantly expressed in the revival of painting and manuscript illustration. Tabriz became the center of a flourishing school. The historical works of Rashid al-Din were frequently copied and illustrated. So were the epic poems of the *Shah-name*, the *Life of Alexander*, and the fables of the *Kalila wa-Dimna*. Chinese influences were introduced by the travels of Mongol administrators, soldiers, and merchants across Inner Asia, and by the importation of Chinese silks and pottery. Chinese influences are evident in the artistic treatment of landscapes, birds, flowers, and clouds; in the composition of scenes that appear to be drawn on receding planes, and in new ways of grouping human figures. One type of human figure was aristocratic, elongated, motionless, with facial features precisely drawn, perhaps gesturing slightly with a movement of the head or finger; a second type was a caricature with highly exaggerated expressions of comedy or pain. Thus the Ilkhan regime continued the cosmopolitan aspect of Iranian monarchy, reinforced by Mongol concepts of authority and political destiny.

Table 11. *Iran: outline chronology*

Mongol conquests begin	1219
Ilkhanid dynasty	1256–1336
Iran partitioned among several local regimes	1336–
Conquest by Timur (Tamerlane)	1370–1405
Succession states	
Qara Qoyunlu, Azarbayjan	1380–1468
Aq Qoyunlu	1378–1508
Timurids of Herat	1407–1506
Safavids	
Sufi masters:	
Safi al-Din Ishaq	d. 1334
Sadr al-Din	d. 1391
Khwaja ʿAli	d. 1429
Ibrahim	d. 1447
Junayd	d. 1460
Haydar	d. 1488
Ismaʿil I	d. 1524
Safavid conquest of Iran	1501–1510
Safavid dynasty	1501–1722
Ismaʿil I	1501–1524
ʿAbbas I	1588–1629
Afsharids	1736–1795
Nadir Shah	1736–1747
Zands	1750–1794
Qajars	1779–1924
Pahlavis	1925–1979
Islamic republic	1979–

The Ilkhan regime lasted until 1336 when, like the Saljuq empire before it, it dissolved into competing provincial states. The small successor states were in turn absorbed into a new empire established by Timur (Tamerlane, 1370–1405) and his heirs who introduced a new phase in the development of Iranian monarchical culture. Timur was a military adventurer who came to power by building up loyal bands of followers and defeating other chieftains. In 1370 he made Samarqand his capital, and thus became a successor to the Chaghatay branch of Mongol rulers in Transoxania. Timur was also supported by the local Muslim elites including the *Shaykh al-Islam* (chief jurisconsult) of Samarqand and the Sufis who became his spiritual advisers. Muslim religious leaders later served him as qadis, diplomats, and tutors for young princes. They may have helped him rally support from both nomadic and town populations as well as to legitimize his new regime.

Once in power Timur began his extraordinary world-scale conquests. From 1379 to 1402, zigzagging between east and west, he conquered Iran, northern

India, Anatolia, and northern Syria. These conquests were made in the name of the Shariʿa, on the pretext that his enemies were traitors to Islam. To administer his empire, Timur appointed his sons and grandsons provincial governors, but he was careful to restrict their power by frequently rotating the gubernatorial assignments, appointing generals and tax collectors who were directly responsible to him, and assigning his personal representatives (*darughas*) to oversee their rule.

After Timur's death in 1405 his empire was divided into two realms, each of which became an important center of Iranian culture. Under Ulugh-beg (1404–49) Transoxania became a center of Muslim architectural, philosophic, and scientific achievement, and generated a new variant of Iranian-Islamic royal civilization. Great monuments were built at Samarqand, Bukhara, Herat and Balkh, including the tomb complex of the Shah-i Zindah at Samarqand and the mausoleum of Timur, the Gur-i Mire, which is famous for its blue and turquoise tile decorations and gorgeous dome. Ulugh-beg presided over a court of musicians, poets, and singers. He was himself an astronomer and had a large observatory built for his studies.

The religious point of view was represented in Samarqand by the Naqshbandi Sufis and their merchant and artisan followers. In Bukhara the Sufi leaders led revolts against the political authorities, and Ulugh-beg sought to pacify them by endowing madrasas in both Bukhara and Samarqand. He also built a khanaqa for Sufis and a great new mosque. After the death of Ulugh-beg, local political power was assumed by Khwaja Ahrar (1404–90), a Naqshbandi holy-man who denounced the life of the upper classes and had a strong influence on the army and the common people.

Herat was the second center of Muslim culture. Shah Rukh (1407–47) lived in an observant Muslim style, attended prayers, observed the fast of Ramadan, and heard readings from the Quran; he presided over a society in which the market inspectors were empowered to enter private houses and destroy wine. Sultan Husayn (1469–1506), however, made Herat a center of Turkish literary culture. The great figure of his time was Mir ʿAli Shir Navaʾi (1441–1501). Born in Herat of a bureaucratic family, he was a leading poet and patron of the arts and sciences. As a courtier he was an intermediary between the state and the town religious elites and was initiated into the Naqshbandi order. He was most famous as a translator of Persian literature into Chaghatay and as the poet who made Chaghatay Turkish the principal language of Turkish-Islamic high culture.

Under the Timurids, Herat and Bukhara also became centers of manuscript illustration. The school of Bihzad (d. 1535–36) at Herat, and later Tabriz, created a new style. Timurid-period paintings were composed in a way which broke up the surface of the painting into several scenes, each of which seemed to be independent of the others. Each wall, floor, or garden had its own self-contained pattern. Yet all the beautifully decorated objects within a painting – houses, gardens, tiles, carpets, animals, and human figures – were expected to form part of a larger ensemble. The ideal was not the single beautiful motif but the beauty of the whole.

In Timurid paintings everything was subordinated to design. Even human figures were presented in a way which stressed graceful lines rather than conveying the feeling of a human presence. Faces were expressionless. The Timurid painter, like the court poet, wanted to adorn, delight the spectator, perhaps convey the glory of a patron, but not reveal emotional depths.

Sufi influences also had a powerful effect upon late fifteenth-century Persian painting. Classic Persian love stories, such as the story of Majnun and Layla, were depicted to suggest a spiritual ideal. The final meeting of the two lovers, which causes them to lose consciousness before they can consummate their love, symbolizes that the Sufi can only attain the object of his devotion after death. Physical features took on a spiritual meaning. For example, doorways and gates imply the movement from outer to inner worlds, the passage from the physical to the spiritual plane.

While the Mongols and Timurids revived Iranian monarchy, their rule saw profound changes in the structure of Iranian society. The Mongol invasions brought lasting demographic, economic, and political changes. In the twelfth and thirteenth centuries, large numbers of Turkish and Mongol peoples settled in northwestern Iran and eastern Anatolia, and, by the fourteenth century, a large Turkish population was also established in eastern Iran and in the Oxus region. Ever since, Turkish peoples have constituted about one-fourth of the total population of Iran. The Turkish presence radically changed the economy of Iran. Substantial territories were turned from agriculture into pasturage. Villagers were induced to take up a migratory existence, farming in valley bottoms and pasturing sheep in adjacent mountain highlands. Only in the reign of Ghazan (1295–1304) did the Ilkhans attempt to develop a more balanced relationship between agricultural and pastoral activities, and a system of property organization which maintained the position of both agricultural and pastoral peoples. The Ilkhans began to stabilize the division of Iran into two economic and cultural worlds – one, the world of the sedentary village; the other, the world of the pastoral camp.

From Inner Asia also came new political institutions. To the Iranian legacy of monarchical and hierarchical institutions and Islamic community organization were added Turkish and Mongolian political traditions. While the Iranian tradition conceived of society as governed by a regular system of hereditary rule, the Turkish conception of society was based upon military competition. Rulership in Turkish society was achieved by victory in battle and was maintained by active struggle against rivals.

The crucial expression of chieftainship in the Turko-Mongolian societies was the *uymaq* or household state. An uymaq was an elite military formation organized as a great household under the leadership of its chief. The chief was supported by his family and by other lesser chiefs and their followers whose support was won by delicate negotiations and/or by success in war. The uymaq chief used his military support to collect taxes from townsmen and peasants, and to establish, in effect, a local territorial government commonly based in a citadel or fortress. The powers of an uymaq chieftain could be reinforced by royal appointment to a position that gave him the right to tax and to supervise the local bureaucracy.

The uymaq, however, was generally unstable owing to the fact that it was based on the personal prowess of chiefs and upon semi-independent warriors, clans, and vassal groups who constantly calculated their relative advantage, bitterly competed for leadership, and regularly rebelled against the dominance of the great chiefs. The authority of an uymaq lord was always challenged by lesser chieftains. Competition among all these groups made the uymaq extremely volatile and led to rapid rises and falls of fortune.

Under pressure of a Turko-Mongol population, the agricultural and political heritage of ancient and early Islamic Iran was compromised. As pastoralism expanded at the expense of agricultural production and reduced the capacity for capital accumulation from agriculture, a new type of uymaq chieftainship consolidated political forces opposed to a centralized state. All post-Saljuq Iranian states, therefore, acquired a dual heritage of an Iranian monarchical tradition and of Turkish uymaq polities. The Mongols, the Timurids, and the Safavids in succession had to struggle with the problems of maintaining a centralized monarchy and of coping with the tribal and military chiefs. Indeed, the later dynamic of Iranian history would turn on the relation of state and uymaqs.

The shattering impact of the Mongol invasions, the succession of unstable and ruinous regimes, and the intrusion of Turkish pastoralists also provoked new forms of socioreligious organization among the common people of Iran. With the widespread destruction of towns and the decline of state protection, Islamic leadership in western Anatolia, northeastern Iran, and northern Mesopotamia passed into the hands of Sufi preachers, shamans, and sorcerers.

These preachers performed miraculous cures, manipulated occult forces, and claimed a religious authority based upon an esoteric knowledge vouchsafed through direct revelation or the interpretation of magical texts. They taught their followers that a savior would come to redeem ordinary people from the traumatic political and economic circumstances of the time, and that the *qutb*, the pillar of the saintly world, would provide a haven for oppressed peoples. Responding to the need for political protection and spiritual reassurance, the Sufis organized a variety of local movements to unite rural populations and resist political oppression.

Several of these movements are noteworthy. In the thirteenth century the Kubrawi order in western Iran, named after Najm al-Din Kubra (1145/6-1221) but actually founded by al-Simnani (1261-1336), stood closest to high-culture Islam. Al-Simnani preached a doctrine which attempted to transcend sectarian divisions. The order appealed to both Sunnis and Shiʿa, by venerating the family of the Prophet, including ʿAli, along with the great Sunni masters. Kubrawi mysticism was also intended to win Buddhists and pagan converts to Islam. The Hurufiya, founded by Fadlallah Astarabadi (d. 1394), represented a more populist version of Islam. Astarabadi claimed to be a hidden imam, the beneficiary of a direct revelation of God's will. He taught that it was possible to gain knowledge of secret and spiritual matters through the interpretation of the alphabet and the understanding of its implicit numerical values, for the letters of the alphabet are the microcosm of the divine reality and therefore subject to esoteric interpretation. This secret knowledge would bring his followers salvation. Other millenarian movements looked forward to the ultimate confrontation between good and evil, the coming of a messiah and the redemption of mankind. The Sarbadar order, founded by Shaykh Khalifa (mid-fourteenth century) and his disciple Hasan Juri, taught that the hidden imam would soon appear to redeem the world from its decay, and allied itself to local lords in order to oppose Mongol rule. Nurbaksh (1393-1465), like many other militant Sufi preachers, held that the true messiah must carry out jihad in the name of Islam. He led a rebellion in Kurdistan against the local Timurid rulers.

The Safavid movement, founded by Shaykh Safi al-Din (1252-1334), a Sunni Sufi religious teacher descended from a Kurdish family in northwestern Iran, also represented a resurgence of popular Islam in opposition to chaotic and exploitative military domination. The Safavid movement, however, unlike the others, led to the conquest of Iran and the establishment of a new dynasty which would reign from 1501 to 1722. The founder began by preaching a purified and restored Islam. His son, Sadr al-Din, who headed the order from 1334 until 1391, made it into a hierarchical, politically sensitive, and propertied organization. He was the first head of the order to claim descent from the Prophet. He expanded the family compound in Ardabil, providing it with schools and residences, and broadened the movement's missionary activities. He organized the hierarchy of the *murshid* who was the head of the order, and the khalifas who were his direct agents, and supervised the missionaries, assistants, students, and novices.

In the fifteenth century, the Safavid movement became a powerful political force in northwestern Iran and eastern Anatolia. The Safavids took advantage of the breakup of the Timurid regime and of the bitter Turkish tribal conflicts to turn from preaching to militant action. Shaykh Junayd (Sufi master, 1447–60) was the first murshid to emphasize the importance of jihad and to gather followers from eastern Anatolia whom he led against Christian populations in Georgia and Trebizond. His wars against the Christians were soon turned against established Muslim states, which he denounced as infidel regimes.

The more militant Safavid policy depended upon the active recruitment of individuals and of uymaq and tribal chieftains. The Safavids' Anatolian followers were made up of small groups from Asia Minor and northern Syria, often identified by the name of the districts from which they came. This suggests that they were not lineage or kinship groups so much as individual soldiers and adventurers from specific regions given political organization by the Safavid order. The Iranian supporters were Turkish-, Kurdish- and Luri-speaking pastoralists, peasants, artisans, and middle-level lineage chiefs who joined the Safavids to oppose the more powerful tribal lords. In addition, Shaykh Junayd married into the families of local princes to form military alliances and to recruit whole tribes to his cause. His recruits were called *Qizilbash*, after their distinctive red headgear, which showed that they were the disciples and warriors of the Safavid house. In the Safavid movement individuals, uymaqs, and tribes found religious justification and political allies for the struggle against local regimes.

The reorientation toward militant political action was accompanied by doctrinal elaboration. The Safavids declared their Shiʿi allegiances and Shah Ismaʿil (1487–1524) proclaimed that he was the hidden imam, the reincarnation of ʿAli, and an epiphany of the divine being. Ismaʿil claimed to be descended from the seventh imam, and to be the seventh descendant in the Safavid line, each successive imam the bearer of the divine fire passed down from generation to generation. The Safavid emphasis upon hereditary descent had the important consequence of legitimizing a principle of succession which proved crucial to the stabilization of their empire in Iran. Isma͑il, leaning on the religious syncretisms of almost two centuries of Sufi movements in north-western Iran and Anatolia, and combining diverse religious influences including Shi͑ism, Sunni messianism, Buddhism and Zoroastrianism, also proclaimed himself the incarnation of Khidr, the bearer of ancient wisdom, and the spirit of Jesus. Illuminated by the divine pre-eternal fire, that fire which precedes the Quran and the creation of the universe, which has passed down in the family of the Prophet to its embodiment in Isma͑il, he was messiah and shah, possessor of both temporal power and mystical rulership. On the basis of these religious claims, the Safavid leaders called for absolute and unquestioning obedience from their Sufi and Qizilbash followers. To question the authority of the perfect master was tantamount to apostasy.

These far-reaching religious claims and political militancy made the Safavids a novel type of Iranian Sufi movement. While the earlier messianic movements were Sunni, or were devoted to the imams as an expression of pan-Islamic synthesis rather than a specifically Shi͑i commitment, the Safavids claimed to be incarnate imams. Also by the extensive recruitment of Turkish soldiers, tribal chiefs and warlords, the Safavids utilized their religious authority to create a coalition of uymaq chieftains and a religio-political movement on an unprecedented scale.

Thus, on the eve of the founding of the Safavid empire, the traditions of Persian monarchy had been reinforced by Turkish and Mongol concepts of rule and had been rendered visible in gorgeous manuscript illuminations and architectural designs. Yet, while monarchical concepts were being reinforced, the political and religious bases of centralized government were being challenged. The migration of a large Inner Asian population into Iran, and the instability of the successive Mongol and Timurid states, allowed for the strengthening of the tribal and pastoral elements of the Iranian population. Uymaq chieftainships became the dominant form of social organization. In reaction, abused and exploited peasant populations flocked to the Sufi brotherhoods to find leadership in their struggle for existence and to give expression to their hope for redemption. Out of these Sufi movements, the Safavids combined the forces of their religious devotees and uymaq clients to establish a dynasty and an empire representing a new constellation of imperial, religious, and tribal forces.

SAFAVID IRAN

In 1501 Isma⁏il occupied Tabriz and proclaimed himself Shah of Iran. Over the remainder of the decade he conquered the rest of Iran. While the rival Ottoman empire to the west seized eastern Anatolia and the Shaybanid empire to the east took control of Transoxania as far as the Oxus River, Isma⁏il established the borders that have defined Iran until the present day. These borders divided the Middle East into separate realms of Turkish Ottoman, Iranian, and Inner Asian Muslim cultures. Political rivalries cut off the Ottoman empire from Islamic culture in Iran, and reinforced a growing cultural divide between Iran and Inner Asia.

The problems of rebuilding the Iranian state and society were formidable. Centuries of political upheaval had worn away the infrastructure of centralized imperial government. Agricultural and urban production had been undermined by nomadic invasions. Economic regression reduced the resources essential for a centralized state. A declining peasant population also reduced the manpower reserves available to a centralized government.

The main problem of the Safavid state was to consolidate the religious authority of the Shah and the military and administrative power of the central government over the Qizilbash uymaqs which had actually conquered Iran. Beneath the level of the Safavid state, Iran was actually organized into uymaq chieftainships which ruled over subject clans, tribal affiliates, and towns and villages. For example, the Mausillus, who were originally regional rulers in northern Syria and eastern Anatolia, controlled vast territories in western Iran. The Ustajlu expanded into Azarbayjan and the Elburz mountains from their home base in Jilan. The chiefs held official positions in the Safavid government and received subsidies, allotments of infantry, soldiers, tax revenues, and economic rights which made them all the more powerful.

Moreover, the fluid uymaq and tribal groups were not the only contenders for political power. The uymaqs continued to be opposed by urban bourgeoisie and by peasants organized in secret religious societies. For example, in 1537 and 1538, there was a rebellion in Astarabad of local Persian peoples against the Turkish elites, led by Muhammad Salih Bitikchi, who preached an equalitarian doctrine and a deliverance of oppressed peoples from the hands of evil masters. There were similar peasant rebellions in Mazandaran, Jilan, Azarbayjan, Fars, and Afghanistan. Tribal-led, merchant-led, and Sufi-led peasant groups waged a multi-sided struggle for political and social power. Throughout the Safavid era, the reigning dynasty could only secure a limited

Map 11. Iran under the Safavids: seventeenth century.

Black Sea

OTTOMAN
EMPIRE

Red
Sea

Chaldiran
Lake Van
Mosul

Tigris River
Euphrates River

Baghdad

Karbala
Najaf

Basra

Tabriz
AZARBAIJAN
Ardabil
JILAN
Sultaniya
Qazvin
MAZANDARAN
Yaramin
Tehran

Baku

Caspian Sea

KHANATE
of KHIVA Khiva

Aral
Sea

ASTARABAD

Qum
Kashan

Isfahan

Yazd

Shiraz

FARS

Persian Gulf

Kirman

Bandar Abbas
Hurmuz

Arabian Sea

Mashhad

Herat

Qandahar

Balkh

Bukhara

Samarqand

KHANATE of
BUKHARA

Oxus River

Jaxartes River

AFGHANISTAN

Kabul

Indus R.

MUGHAL EMPIRE

500 km.
300 miles
0

Safavids
Ottoman Control 1514–1603
Area contested by Uzbeks in sixteenth century
Area contested by Mughals in seventeenth century

degree of control. The Shahs were but suzerains over a society dominated on the local level by uymaqs and other groups battling to enlarge their power.

To fight this inherent dispersion of power, the Safavids proposed to centralize the military and administrative powers of the state and to create a religious establishment that would bolster the authority of the Shah and offset the power of the local elites. First, Shah Isma°il attempted to bureaucratize the administration and enhance the powers of Persian central officials vis-à-vis the Turkish military elites. The government was organized under the authority of a viceroy (*wakil*) who was also commander of the armies and head of the religious order. The civil administration was headed by a *wazir*. The military officers (*amirs*) were given land grants from which they had to pay a sum of money to the central government and support a contingent of troops. Isma°il also tried to control the army by appointing as generals men of lesser uymaq standing in order to limit the power of the great Qizilbash lords. A chief religious bureaucrat (*sadr*) supervised judicial appointments and charitable endowments. In the tradition of earlier Islamic regimes, the Safavids built up Georgian, Circassian, Armenian, and Turkish slave forces to offset the power of Turkish warlords.

The struggle to centralize political power was set back by several ineffectual reigns in the late sixteenth century, but the state building program was resumed by Shah °Abbas (1588–1629). °Abbas attempted to transform the whole political system of Iran by reducing the power of the uymaqs through the consolidation of a slave army and a new centralized administration supported by a revived economy and by the reassertion of both the religious and the royal bases of monarchical legitimacy.

°Abbas began with the reconstruction of the army. He rallied loyal Qizilbash supporters, usually by favoring middling and lesser lords against the great chieftains, and organized them into the forces called *shah-seven* or lovers of the Shah. He supplemented these troops with Georgian and Armenian slaves commanded by a Georgian convert named Allahberdi Khan. Musket and artillery units were organized to give the Shah's armies modern fire power and to make them equal to the Ottoman janissaries. The combination of Caucasian slaves and Persian infantry and artillery gave °Abbas the military power to consolidate the frontiers of his realm and to fortify his internal authority. Thus, °Abbas returned to the centuries-old Islamic Middle Eastern methods of state military organization to combat the power of autonomous elites.

The administrative support for these new armies depended upon a reconstruction of Persian administration. The financial basis of the slave armies was secured by removing territory from Qizilbash control and turning it into crown lands. The wazirs were made responsible for putting crown lands into cultivation and for making loans to peasants and tenants. They were expected to invest in irrigation works, protect the peasants from oppression, and assure the collection of rents and taxes. Bureaucratic administration, however, was not completely centralized. In order to pay the salaries of the soldiers, ʿAbbas reverted to the basic Islamic and Iranian practice of assigning iqtaʿ or tuyul. Such lands were sometimes excused from central government inspection and often became the private properties of the assignees. Thus, ʿAbbas attempted to find some balance between the capacities of the central administration to directly control provincial revenues and the need to maintain an infrastructure of military and political support by the distribution of estates.

The effect upon the uymaq system was profound but not decisive. In some cases the program of state centralization led to the confiscation of estates administered by uymaq chiefs and the aggrandizement of slave soldiers (who in turn became uymaq chiefs) and Persian central administrators at the expense of the Turkish magnates. Generally, however, royal influence was used to tip the local balance of power against the great magnates in favor of lesser chieftains who would ally with the Shah. ʿAbbas often succeeded in reducing the power of the great magnates without changing the basic structure of the Turkish uymaq political system. Upon his death, the Iranian state continued to function by virtue of the shifting balance of power between the Safavid regime and the uymaq elites.

Shah ʿAbbas's military and administrative reforms were partly financed by an elaborate mercantilist venture. He stimulated silk production and marketed the product through state-controlled merchants. By bringing Armenian merchants to Isfahan and making them intermediaries between the Shah and foreign customers, the royal court gained a strong position in Iranian trade. ʿAbbas also established royal factories to produce luxury products for royal use and for international sale. Carpet-making, which began as a cottage industry, was centralized in great factories in Isfahan. Silk-making also became a royal industry, producing velvets, damasks, satins, and taffetas to be sold in Europe. Safavid ceramicists produced their own "china" based on Chinese porcelains with the help of Chinese workmen imported to establish the new industry. Throughout Iran, trade was stimulated by the construction of roads and caravansaries.

Iran's first opportunities to enter directly into international commerce came as a result of British initiative. Ever since the Portuguese seized control of the Indian Ocean trade in the early sixteenth century, the British had been looking for opportunities to bypass Lisbon and find direct access to eastern spices and

10 Shops in the Maydan-i Shah of Isfahan

luxury goods. The first Englishmen to make their way to Iran were Anthony and Robert Sherley, merchant adventurers who arrived in 1598. In 1616, the English East India Company acquired the right to trade freely in Iran. In return, the English helped ʿAbbas expel the Portuguese from the Persian Gulf port of Hurmuz and to create Bandar ʿAbbas as a new port for the Persian–Indian Ocean trade. The British–Iranian victory encouraged the Dutch to enter the Iranian trade, and by 1645 the English had been overrun by Dutch competition. The French East India Company entered the scene in 1664, but the first treaty between France and Iran was signed only in 1708, granting trading privileges and the protection of Christian religious orders in Iran. In the eighteenth and nineteenth centuries, the English reestablished their supremacy in the Indian Ocean and Persian Gulf.

Thus from the time of Shah ʿAbbas, Armenian merchants in alliance with the British, the French, and the Dutch, and supported by the Shah, were competing with the Ottomans and Portuguese in the silk, wool carpet, shawl, and porcelain trades. By the late seventeenth century, however, European merchants were substantially in control of Iranian trade and the economic benefits of international trade were probably lost to Iran.

The centerpiece of Shah ʿAbbas's administrative and economic program was the creation of a great new capital city, Isfahan. Isfahan was essential to

11 Persian court dress in the Safavid period: (*a*) male

the political and economic goal of a centralized Iranian state and to the symbolic legitimation of the Safavid dynasty. The Safavids built the new city around the Maydan-i Shah, a huge square which measures about 160 by 500 meters. The square served as market, carnival place, and polo ground. It was surrounded by two-storied rows of shops and by principal buildings or arches on each of the cardinal sides. To the east the Masjid-i Shaykh Lutfallah, begun in 1603 and completed in 1618, was an oratory designed for the Shah's private

11 Persian court dress in the Safavid period: (*b*) female

worship. To the south stood the royal mosque, begun in 1611 and completed in 1629. On the west stood the ᶜAli Qapu palace or Sublime Porte which was the headquarters of the government. On the north side of the Maydan was the monumental arch which marked the entrance to the royal bazaar and its innumerable shops, baths, caravansaries, mosques, and colleges. From the Maydan, the Chahar Bagh avenue ran two and a half miles to the summer palace in which the ruler gave audiences to ambassadors and held state ceremonies. On either side of the avenue were elaborate gardens, the Shah's harem, and residences for courtiers and foreign ambassadors. The whole ensemble was a masterpiece of Middle Eastern city planning.

Isfahan's bazaars were essential to the state economy, for they concentrated production and marketing activities and brought them under the taxing authority of the state, thus weakening the economic base of uymaq chieftains. The new capital was also essential as a reservoir for recruits to the imperial armies and administration. The capital was equally important to the vitality of Iranian Islam. In 1666, Isfahan, according to a European visitor, had 162 mosques, 48 colleges, 182 caravansaries, and 273 public baths, almost all of them erected by ʿAbbas I and his successor, ʿAbbas II (1642–66).

Isfahan symbolized the legitimacy of the dynasty. Its vast plazas and bazaars were a symbol of the ordering of the world by royal decree; its religious monuments signified royal sustenance for the faith; its gorgeous decoration was the universal sign of royal splendor. Thus, Safavid claims to legitimacy were broadened from their initial religious basis to include the traditional motifs of Iranian monarchical grandeur.

There were other signs of a new conception of monarchy. In 1510 the Timurid school of painting was transferred from Herat to Tabriz. Bahzad, the greatest painter of the time, was appointed Director of the Royal Library and supervisor of a workshop which produced illuminated manuscripts. Shah Tahmasp was also a great patron of the production of robes, silk hangings, and works in metal and ceramics. He kept these treasures as a private and courtly adornment, and devoted no attention to mosques, shrines, or colleges or other public expressions of imperial authority. Out of this school came an illuminated edition of the *Shah-name* (Book of Kings) which contains more than 250 paintings and is one of the great masterpieces of Iranian and Islamic illuminated manuscript art. ʿAbbas created the public style of royalty. Isfahan was his masterpiece, but he also patronized paintings of battles, hunting scenes and royal ceremonies. After his death artistic effort turned to emotional expression and themes of private daily life. The great themes of the royal tradition were put aside in favor of more realistic paintings of secular scenes, such as couples embracing, which may have appealed to an aristocracy of bureaucrats, landlords and soldiers. Single-page drawings and paintings were made for inclusion in albums. The later seventeenth-century style combined sensuality and realism.

Under ʿAbbas I the Safavid monarchy reached the height of its political power. His reign was a glorified household state with the ruler surrounded by his personal servitors, soldiers, and administrators. The ruler closely controlled the bureaucracy and tax collection, monopolized the manufacture and sale of important cloth goods and other products, built great cities, and maintained shrines and roads as an expression of his fatherly concern for the welfare of his people. Though his reign marked the apogee of the Iranian state, his achievement was flawed. ᶜAbbas never succeeded in establishing a fully centralized regime. The military and administrative policies that reduced the power of Turkish lords did not succeed in replacing them. His commercial policies had only a short-lived success; his religious and artistic efforts were eventually appropriated by others. Ultimately the rural elites proved too powerful, and urban merchant and rural landlord support too weak to sustain a centralized state.

THE CONVERSION OF IRAN TO SHIᶜISM

Parallel to the Safavid program of state formation was a Safavid determination to create a religious establishment which would lend its authority and administrative services to the support of the regime. The new regime, however, had come to power on the basis of a religious doctrine which posed grave complications for dynastic and imperial government. Safavid religious appeals were first addressed primarily to their Qizilbash and tribal supporters, to whom they promised messianic fulfillment. Shah Ismaᶜil claimed to be the manifestation of God, the divine fire of the hidden imam, and the mahdi. He titled himself the Shadow of God on Earth, in the manner of Persian emperors. As the descendant of the seventh imam, an infallible leader and an emanation of the divine being, his authority was absolute and unquestioned.

This absolute authority was communicated to his followers through his role as *murshid-i kamil* or perfect master. To the already magisterial and absolute claims of the Sufi master over his disciples, the Safavids added a divine dimension. The followers of Ismaᶜil were supposed to adhere strictly to a code of conduct called *sufigare*; disobedience was punished by expulsion from the order and probably by execution. The devotion of the Qizilbash, however, was a double-edged sword, for the millenarian impulses which had brought the Safavids to power could also be turned against them. The defeat by the Ottomans at the battle of Chaldiran in 1514 was a terrible religious shock because it shattered the Qizilbash belief in the invincibility of their leader.

Thus, to cope with the complications of Qizilbash enthusiasm and the tepid response of the Iranian population, the Safavids attempted to establish Shiᶜism in Iran in a form that would sustain the dynasty, broaden their base of support, and consolidate the authority of the Shahs. "Twelver" Shiᶜism was proclaimed the official religion of Iran and messianic Shiᶜi claims were set aside in favor of a more institutionalized form of Shiᶜism. Ismaᶜil, however, had little to build on; the majority of the population was Sunni, though there were pockets of Shiᶜa in Qum and Isfahan. To reinforce Iranian Shiᶜism, Ismaᶜil imported "twelver" Shiᶜi scholars from Syria, Bahrain, northeastern Arabia and Iraq. ᶜAli al-Karaki (1465–1534) founded the first Shiᶜi madrasa in Iran.

The Safavids then organized the ᶜulamaᵓ into a state-controlled bureaucracy. The sadr was the liaison between the Shah and the religious establishment. He was initially responsible for the ritual cursing of the first three Caliphs; his duties were gradually enlarged to the appointment of judges and teachers and to the administration of endowments. The office of *Divan Bagi* was created as a high court of appeal, and the incumbent raised to a status equal to that of army generals, thus bringing the administration of law under direct governmental control. The Shahs also dominated the religious establishment by the provision of land and endowments to support religious activities. The Safavids provided waqfs for the shrine of Imam Riza in Mashhad and for the shrine of his sister Fatima in Qum. Grants of land called *soyurghal* were also made to eminent religious families, and were allowed to pass from generation to generation immune from taxation. The religious elite became part of the Iranian landowning aristocracy.

The state powers were supplemented by the Shah's personal religious authority as descendant of the seventh imam, a master of the Safavid order, and an incarnation of the hidden imam. This personal authority was reinforced by the cult of the Safavid ancestors at Ardabil and by direct Safavid patronage of the major Iranian shrines. Shah ᶜAbbas I visited the tomb of his ancestors before a military campaign, and made a pilgrimage on foot from Isfahan to Mashhad which took 28 days. In the early period of Iranian Shiᶜism, the administrative and moral authority of the Shahs over the religious establishment was virtually complete. This disposed the Shiᶜi ᶜulamaᵓ to accept the state authority and to stress those elements of the Shiᶜi tradition which affirmed the state order as an historical necessity.

To sustain the official religion, the Safavids embarked on a bold program to eliminate all rival forms of Islam in a highly pluralistic – Sunni, Sufi, and Shiᶜi – religious society. "Twelver" Shiᶜism was imposed by a wave of persecutions which has little or no parallel in other Muslim regions. The first object of Safavid policy was to suppress the messianic and extremist Shiᶜi movements. Safavid Shahs were quick to dispose of the followers who seemed likely to turn their religious passion against them. Ismaᶜil and Tahmasp executed religious enthusiasts who proclaimed them as messiahs. ᶜAbbas I massacred their Sufi disciples, who were accused of collaborating with the

Ottomans and of failing to place the will of the master before all other concerns. Other chiliastic movements spawned in northwestern Iran – continuations of the religious fervor of the fifteenth century – were also suppressed.

The dominance of Shi'ism was also assured by the violent suppression of Sunnism. The Safavids ritually insulted the memory of the first three Caliphs and violated the tombs of Sunni scholars. Sufi shrines were destroyed; the pilgrimage to Mecca was deemphasized in favor of ritual visits to the shrines of Shi'i Imams. Isma'il desecrated Naqshbandi tombs, and suppressed the Khalwatiya, Dhahabiya, and Nurbakhshiya orders. 'Abbas I later seized the Nimatullahi khanaqas and turned them over to youth organizations. The persecution of Sunnis and Sufis continued sporadically throughout the sixteenth and seventeenth centuries until Muhammad Baqir al-Majlisi (d. 1699), the head of the Shi'i 'ulama', completed the suppression of Sunnism and expelled the remaining Sufis from Isfahan. However, despite persecution, individual Qalandaris, committed to a wandering life, rejecting all worldly connections, remained an important spiritual influence.

The Shahs were also hostile to non-Muslim communities. Decrees of 'Abbas I made it possible for a convert to Islam from Judaism or Christianity to claim the property of his relatives. In 1656, Shah 'Abbas II granted extensive powers to his wazirs to force Jews to become Muslims. Al-Majlisi, following on these precedents, persuaded Shah Husayn (1688–1726) to decree the forcible conversion of Zoroastrians. The Shi'i 'ulama', however, were less harsh in their treatment of Armenians. The Armenians maintained good relations with the Iranian regime because of their shared hostility to the Greek Orthodox church whose base was in the Ottoman empire. Also, Armenians and Georgians provided important recruits for the Shahs' military and commercial establishments.

The success of "twelver" Shi'ism depended not only upon the power of the state, but upon its intrinsic religious appeal. The suppression of Sufism led to the incorporation of gnostic and philosophic ideas within the "twelver" establishment, and to the absorption of the popular veneration of Husayn, 'Ali, and other Shi'i imams as an integral part of Iranian Islam. Iranian Shi'ism thus integrated the legal, gnostic and popular forms of Islam.

The integration of gnostic Sufism with Shi'i beliefs took place in the course of the sixteenth and seventeenth centuries. A new school of philosophy, under the leadership of Mir Damad (d. 1631) and his disciple, Mulla Sadra (d. 1640), combined Shi'i scripture, theology, and mystical reflection to create a Shi'i version of Sufism and give a philosophic basis to individual religious consciousness and to Shiᶜi loyalty to the imams. The new school combined the illuminationism of Suhrawardi (see Chapter 12) with the sayings of ᶜAli and the imams, elements of Greek philosophy, and the teachings of Ibn al-ᶜArabi. The new wisdom belonged to the neo-Platonic rather than the Aristotelian tradition of Greek and Muslim philosophy.

The central problem for Mir Damad was the creation of the universe and the place of the human being within it. He approached the classic issue of scholastic theology – whether the world is eternal or is created in time – by introducing an intermediary state. Mir Damad divided temporal reality into three categories – *dahr*, *sarmad* and *zaman*. Dahr means eternity and defines the divine essence, which is unitary and has no internal distinctions. The divine essence, however, is the source of the names and attributes which are integral to it and yet separate from it. The relation of essence and attributes is characterized as sarmad. In turn the names and attributes are the archetypes which generate the material and changeable world. The latter is characterized as zaman or temporality. While existing in time, the created world is not purely temporal in its origin, for it is brought into being by archetypes which exist before the creation of the world and are themselves eternal. Like the neo-Platonists, Mir Damad tried to close the gulf between God and the creation posited by scripture and to reconcile the absolute otherness and transcendence of God with his immanence in the created world.

For Mir Damad, as for the neo-Platonists and illuminationist philosophers, the human being stands in an intermediate position, as a bridge between the world of eternity and the world of time. Man possesses qualities of perception, imagination, and intellect which link the visible and the invisible worlds. The soul both receives sensible perceptions from the material world, and is illuminated by intelligible concepts from the spiritual world. The *alam al-mithal* or realm of archetypes, intermediate between material sense perception and intellectual abstraction, is the ontological basis for symbolic imagination, dream experience, and religious commitment. The emphasis upon this intermediary reality gave Shiᶜism a rationalistic explanation of revealed truth, and defined the metaphysical meaning of the individual's quest for spiritual salvation.

Similarly, popular veneration for sacred figures was made part of Iranian Shiᶜism. The great shrines of Mashhad and Qum were rebuilt in the reign of ᶜAbbas I, and endowed with extensive properties and made the focal points of Iranian Shiᶜism. *Imamzadas* in memory of people born or related to imams, and *imambaras*, shrines devoted to Husayn and Hasan, replaced popular village shrines. The pilgrimage to Karbala was substituted for the pilgrimage to

Mecca. *Ziyarat* or ceremonial visits to the shrines of imams and their families were promoted as an alternative to the veneration of Sufi shrines; imambaras replaced Sufi khanaqas as devotional centers, just as the hidden imam replaced the Sufi qutb as the object of religious veneration.

The festivals of the month of Muharram became the ceremonial center of the Shiᶜi religious calendar. Recitations of the heart-rending story of Husayn, processions which included public flagellation, passion plays, sermons, and recitations of elegies, marked a period of mourning and atonement for his death. Neighborhood groups, youth gangs, and religious factions competed in their veneration of Husayn and often ended up in bloody struggles. Thus, Shiᶜism seized hold of popular emotions in order to attach the Iranian populace to the religious establishment. By the late Safavid period, Shiᶜism had duplicated the whole complex of religious sensibility already found within Sunnism. It thus became a comprehensive alternative version of Islam.

THE DISSOLUTION OF THE SAFAVID EMPIRE

The Safavid pattern of state, tribal and religious institutions created by Shah ᶜAbbas I was profoundly altered in the late seventeenth and early eighteenth centuries. While the tendency of the sixteenth and early seventeenth centuries was to strengthen the hand of the state and of the Shiᶜi religious establishment, the later period brought a profound weakening of the Safavid regime, its eventual destruction at the hands of tribal forces, and the liberation of Shiᶜi Islam from state control.

The decline of the central government was already manifest after the death of ᶜAbbas I. In order to prevent violent struggle among potential successors to the throne, succeeding generations of Safavid princes were confined to the harem and palace precincts, and were raised with a narrow education and without any experience of public life. No ruler after ᶜAbbas I had his vision or authority. Furthermore, after the peace of 1639 with the Ottoman empire, the army was neglected and declined into a number of small and ill-disciplined regiments. By the end of the seventeenth century, the Safavid army was no longer a competent military machine. Central administration also fell apart, and the procedures for regulating taxation and distributing revenue were abandoned. The weakening of the central state permitted the revival of uymaq chieftainships and provincial revolts against Safavid authority. In the eighteenth century Iran fell into anarchy. The most important of the new competitors for political power were the Afghans, Afshars, Zands, and Qajars. Ghalzai Afghans took control of Isfahan, the Safavid capital, in 1722. Iran was then attacked by both its Ottoman and its Russian neighbors, who in 1724 agreed on a partition of Transcaucasia in which the Ottomans gained Armenia and parts of Azarbayjan and the Russians obtained the Caspian Sea provinces of Jilan, Mazandaran, and Astarabad.

With the Afghans in control of the south and the Russians and the Ottomans in control of the north, Nadir, an Afshar chieftain of Chaghatay descent, seized power. Nadir deposed the last of the Safavids and in 1736 named himself Shah of Iran. His effort was not merely a Bonapartist-like adventure but harks back to an eastern-Iranian frontier tradition of Turkish resistance to an Iranian central government and ethnic Persian rule. For centuries, a frontier population, closely resembling the Cossacks of the Russian steppes, maneuvered between the larger powers and kept alive its aspirations to establish a new khanate on the basis of a Chaghatay and Sunni identity.

In his short reign, Nadir restored the territory of the Iranian state and also attempted to promote a reconciliation of Sunni and Shiʿi Islam, in order to integrate more effectively Afghan and eastern Iranian tribal peoples into the regime and to legitimize his struggle with the Ottoman empire. He proposed to make Shiʿism a fifth school of law, called the Jaʿfari school, equal in status to the four Sunni schools. He also weakened the Shiʿi ʿulamaʾ by confiscating properties, abolishing clerical positions in the government, and canceling the jurisdiction of religious courts.

Nadir was succeeded by Karim Khan, the leader of a coalition of Zand tribal groups in western Iran, whose effective regime lasted from 1750 to 1779. In turn it gave way to the Qajars, who were originally Turkish lords in Safavid service, and local governors in Mazandaran and Astarabad. In 1779 the Qajars defeated the Zand and established a dynasty which would last until 1924.

The destruction of the Iranian state in the eighteenth century also had profound implications for the relations between state regimes and religious elites. It allowed latent Shiʿi claims to autonomy to come to the fore. The first steps were taken with the reaffirmation of the Shiʿi millenarian concept that the hidden imam would establish his personal rule only at the end of time. This worked against any definitive Shiʿi commitment to the state. Without directly challenging the authority of the state, the ʿulamaʾ withdrew from engagement in public affairs. Despite the establishment of Shiʿism as a state religion, and despite the proselytizing zeal with which the Shiʿis converted Iran, by the seventeenth century religious motivation for worldly action was being replaced by a pious disdain for involvement in worldly affairs. The early fusion of the religious and political aspects of Safavid society was superseded by a separation of religion and politics and a devaluation of political action.

Furthermore, by the late seventeenth century many Shiʿi scholars were no longer willing to concede that the Safavids represented the hidden imam. First, the ʿulamaʾ cast doubt upon the inherited authority of the Shah as the primary bearer of Shiʿi Islam. This authority depended upon descent from the seventh imam, and on the possession of hereditary infallibility (ʿisma). In Shiʿi theory, however, biological inheritance was not sufficient without testamentary designation (*nass*) to determine which of the descendants of a given imam had inherited his authority. The Safavid position was weak because they could not demonstrate designation by testament. Secondly, according to "twelver" Shiʿi belief, ever since the greater occultation of 941 the hidden imam was represented on earth by religious scholars. The ʿulamaʾ thus asserted that the *mujtahids* (scholars capable of independent religious judgments) bore the highest religious authority. Several schools of ʿulamaʾ elaborated upon the nature of that authority. The *usuli* school gave the mujtahids a wide latitude for it saw their authority as based on such complex factors as knowledge of the Quran, the tradition of ʿAli, and the consensus of the community. The *akhbari* school restricted the authority of individual scholars by stressing the importance of literal adherence to the letter of the tradition passed down by the Prophet and the imams. That such a debate could take place was itself a demonstration of the autonomy of the religious establishment. The monolithic and all-absorbing religious establishment created by the Shahs was disengaging itself from the embrace of the state. In the nineteenth century it would become the leading opponent of the Iranian regime.

From the Mongol invasions to the collapse of the Safavid empire the history of Iran was marked both by continuity and transformation of the basic patterns of state, religion, and society inherited from the Saljuq era. From the Saljuq era the Mongols, Timurids, and Safavids inherited a tradition of centralized monarchy and sought to strengthen the power of the central state by subordinating the tribal or uymaq conquerors to slave military forces and a quasi-centralized administration. Nonetheless, the Turkish and Mongol invasions had permanently consolidated the parochial uymaq or tribal forces in Iranian society, and all Iranian monarchs were obliged to rely on the political co-operation of uymaq and tribal chiefs and on iqtaʿ (or tuyul) forms of tax administration to effect their rule. Iranian states remained at best household or court regimes with limited powers in the countryside. Even when the state overcame the power of the uymaq lords and tribal chiefs, as in the reign of Shah ʿAbbas I, it could not change the political system of Iran. With the weakening of the state in the eighteenth century, the uymaq lords again partitioned Iran and brought new dynasties to power.

Iran also went through extraordinary changes in the relation of state and religion. In the Mongol and Timurid periods, rural Sufi movements organized popular opposition to brutal foreign regimes. Islam again served, as it had in the era of the Prophet, to unite disparate peoples into larger moral and political movements. The Safavids orginated as such a movement, but upon coming to power suppressed the millenarian forms of Sufi Islam in favor of a state-constructed ʿulamaʾ establishment. The Safavids made "twelver" Shiʿism the official religion of Iran, and eliminated their own Sufi followers as well as the Sunni ʿulamaʾ. Safavid-period Shiʿism absorbed philosophic and gnostic ideas and popular saint worship. Iran was virtually unique among Muslim societies in the degree to which the state controlled the religious establishment and in the extent to which it absorbed all religious tendencies found within the Muslim spectrum.

The eighteenth-century crisis brought to an end the pre-modern history of Iran. Whereas in most Muslim regions the pre-modern period ended with European intervention, conquest, and the establishment of colonial regimes, in this case the consolidation of European economic and political influence was preceded by the breakup of the Safavid empire and the liberation of the ʿulamaʾ. Thus the Safavid regime left as its legacy to modern Iran a Persian tradition of glorified monarchy, a regime based on powerful uymaq or tribal principalities, and a cohesive, monolithic, and partially autonomous Shiʿi religious establishment.

CHAPTER 14

THE TURKISH MIGRATIONS AND THE OTTOMAN EMPIRE

The migrations which gave rise to the Saljuq, Mongol, and Timurid empires in Iran also gave birth to a great western Muslim empire. In the late eleventh century, Turkish peoples began to conquer lands which had never before been Muslim. From these migrations came the Saljuq state in Anatolia and later the Ottoman empire in Anatolia and the Balkans. The Ottoman empire eventually absorbed the already Islamized lands of the Arab Middle East and North Africa (to be considered in subsequent chapters).

The Ottoman empire represented yet another type of Islamic society. From the Saljuq state of Rum (Anatolia, twelfth and thirteenth centuries), it inherited the Iranian-Saljuq pattern of society and gave it an innovative turn. The Ottomans made the state the dominant institution, and brought the religious elites, the Turkish nomadic populations of Anatolia, and the masses of its subjects under state control. The development of this particular state-centered variant of Islamic society took place in the course of a complex history which falls into several phases: the Turkish migrations and the establishment of the Saljuq-Turkish regime in Anatolia between 1071 and 1243; the subsequent Turkish conquest of the Byzantine empire and the formation of the Ottoman system from approximately 1280 to 1574; and the transformation and decentralization of the empire in the seventeenth and eighteenth centuries.

THE TURKISH MIGRATIONS AND TURKISH-ISLAMIC STATES
IN ANATOLIA (1071–1243)

The Oghuz peoples, who established the Saljuq empire in Iran and Iraq, also pushed their way into Georgia, Armenia, and Byzantine Anatolia, and established in these territories another Saljuq state and society. At the battle of Manzikert in 1071, the Turks captured the Byzantine emperor, Romanos I. In the next century, they spread across Asia Minor. The migrating peoples were organized into small bands of warriors called ghazis under the leadership of chieftains (*beys*) or Sufi holy-men (*babas*). Veneration of the chiefs and the desire to find rich pasturage, gather booty, and win victories against the infidels in the name of Islam, held them together. The migrants destroyed agricultural enterprises, depopulated large territories, and cut off cities from their hinterlands and trading connections. Only a few fortified Byzantine towns remained as isolated islands in a sea of nomadic peoples. Greek and Armenian Christian populations, already reduced by previous invasions, were further reduced by warfare and migration, and by conversion to Islam. Turks became the majority in much of Anatolia.

Turkish expansion in Anatolia was soon counterbalanced by the formation of states which attempted to gain control over the nomadic peoples and the territory they had conquered, check their predatory adventures, and restore agricultural production. The formation of Turkish states toward the end of the eleventh century introduced the governing motif of Turkish, Anatolian and Ottoman history for the next 500 years – the struggle between independent nomadic warriors and organized settled society. The history of Turkish Anatolia thus repeated the Saljuq experience in Iran and Iraq, in which state regimes attempted to subordinate pastoral conquerors in the interests of a sedentary society.

Of the several regimes established by the end of the eleventh century, the Saljuq state in central and southern Anatolia, with its capital at Konya, assiduously reconstructed the whole panoply of Turkish Saljuq Islamic government. To dominate the nomadic populations and the conquered Christian peoples, the Saljuqs built up a large standing army of Turkish and Christian slaves, and maintained detachments of Georgian and other Christian mercenaries. The administrative elite was composed of Iranian scribes. In the early thirteenth century a fiscal survey was made and state-controlled properties were distributed in the form of iqtaʿs. The Saljuq state maintained close administrative control over such assignments so as to extract the maximum of military service. It appointed provincial governors, made the chiefs subordinate officials of the regime, and even attempted to extract taxes from the pastoral population. Energetic efforts were made to sedentarize nomadic groups. The Saljuqs favored the sedentary economy by building caravan-saries. Ocean traffic was encouraged from Saljuq-controlled seaports on the Black Sea, the Aegean, and the Mediterranean.

The Saljuqs also built up the whole infrastructure of Sunni Islam. Scholars from Iran were invited to settle in Anatolia. Qadis were appointed, colleges were endowed with waqfs, and funds were provided for the education of converts. The money came primarily from levies on Christian villages and appropriated ecclesiastical properties. The Saljuq regime also attempted to bring independent Sufi fraternities under government influence by providing them with schools, hospices, and endowments. Sufis were particularly important in Anatolia. Members of the Qalandariya, Rifaʿiya and other Sufi brotherhoods migrated into Anatolia from Inner Asia and eastern Iran; others were driven westward by the Mongol invasions. The Sufi babas provided leadership for migrating Turkish peoples, and then established their residences in newly settled areas and helped to bring those areas into cultivation. They built hospices and mills, planted orchards, developed schools, provided for the safety of travelers and mediated disputes among tribes. Thus they brought order into a fragmented warrior society.

Rural Sufis also adopted a tolerant attitude toward Christians and facilitated the conversion of Greek and Armenian peoples to Islam. Haji Bektash (d. *c.* 1297) who was widely revered in Anatolia, preached a version of Islam which synthesized Sunni and Shiʿi beliefs and Muslim and Christian religious practices. He converted Tatar communities and arranged that they perform military service in return for assignments of land. Urban religious fraternities called *akhis* (groups of unmarried young men devoted to the futuwwa (youth) ethic of bravery and hospitality) were equally important in the formation of town society. The akhis were recruited from the artisan and merchant strata of the population. They protected local populace from abuse and gave charity to strangers and the poor. The akhis were closely allied to the Mevlevi order, whose Friday prayers and common meals were a focus of town life.

In the late twelfth and early thirteenth centuries Saljuq rulers built up an urban and sedentary society; the Mongol invasions destroyed their work. In 1242–3 the Mongols defeated the Saljuqs, made them vassals, and tipped the balance of power in Anatolia from the central state of the pastoral warrior populations and smaller principalities. The Mongols also opened the way to further Turkish migrations. Large numbers of new migrants entered Anatolia in the 1230s, settled in the mountainous country on the frontiers of the Byzantine empire, and founded new principalities.

The new states attracted nomads, refugees, adventurers, and bandits to their service. Small groups of warriors, eager to escape Mongol oppression, and motivated by pressure of population and by the desire for pasturage, booty, and glory in the holy war, resumed the struggle against the Byzantine empire. Successful local chiefs considered themselves heroes in the traditions of Inner Asian Turkish warrior culture. The most important of these new states was the Karaman beylik in Cilicia, which in 1335 made Konya its capital and claimed to inherit Saljuq authority, the dynasty of Dulgadir in the northern reaches of the Euphrates River and Menteshe and Germiyan in the region of Kutahya.

THE RISE OF THE OTTOMANS (*c.* 1280–1453)

Of these frontier warrior states, the one led by Ertugrul (d. *c.* 1280) and his son Osman was destined to attain greatness. The name of the Ottoman dynasty derived from Osman. Ertugrul had brought some 400 followers into Saljuq service. Struggling for control of pasturage, his son expanded onto the plains, and his grandson seized the important town of Bursa in 1326 and crossed the straits to Gallipoli (1345). Having established a foothold in Europe, the Ottomans invited masses of Turkish warriors into the Balkans, and occupied northern Greece, Macedonia, and Bulgaria. Ottoman control of the western Balkans was decisively established by their victory at the battle of Kosovo in 1389. On the basis of their European empire, the Ottomans began to annex rival Turkish principalities in western Anatolia and to plan for the conquest of Constantinople.

This ambitious plan was temporarily set back in 1402 by the invasion of Timur who, provoked by the eastward expansion of the Ottoman empire, made himself the defender of the Muslim principalities of Anatolia, defeated Bayazid I (1389–1402), and reduced the Ottoman state to vassalage. The Ottomans, however, survived this defeat, again annexed other Turkish principalities in Anatolia, and expanded Ottoman domains into Serbia.

The Ottoman conquests inspired a Europe-wide anxiety. To check Ottoman expansion, the European states mobilized latter-day crusades. In 1396 a coalition organized by the papacy and Venice was defeated at the battle of Nicopolis. In 1444, the papacy and a coalition of powers including the Kings of Hungary, Poland and Naples, and the rulers of Transylvania, Serbia, Venice and Genoa, launched another crusade, only to be defeated at the battle

Table 12. *The Ottoman dynasty*

Accession date	
1281	ʿUthman I (Osman)
1324	Orhan
1360	Murad I
1389	Bayazid I
1402	Interregnum
1413	Mehmed I
1421	Murad II
1444	Mehmed II the Conqueror
1446	Murad II (second reign)
1451	Mehmed II the Conqueror (second reign)
1481	Bayazid II
1512	Selim I
1520	Sulayman I ("the Law-giver" or "the Magnificent")
1566	Selim II
1574	Murad III
1594	Muhammad III
1603	Ahmad I
1617	Mustafa I (first reign)
1618	ʿUthman II
1622	Mustafa I (second reign)
1623	Murad IV
1640	Ibrahim
1648	Muhammad IV
1678	Sulayman II
1691	Ahmad II
1695	Mustafa II
1703	Ahmad III
1730	Mahmud I
1754	ʿUthman III
1757	Mustafa III
1774	ʿAbd al-Hamid I
1789	Selim III
1807	Mustafa IV
1808	Mahmud II
1839	ʿAbd al-Majid I
1861	ʿAbd al-Aziz
1876	Murad V
1876	ʿAbd al-Hamid II
1909	Muhammad V Rashid
1918	Muhammad VI Wahid al-Din
1922–24	ʿAbd al-Majid II (as Caliph only)

of Varna. Nothing could prevent the conquest of Constantinople in 1453, a triumph which fulfilled an age-old Muslim ambition to inherit the domains of the Roman empire.

From Constantinople, the Ottomans pushed on to complete the absorption of the Balkans as far as the Danube and the Aegean. Mehmed II, the conqueror of Constantinople, pushed the Serbian frontiers to the Danube by 1449. In the next half century the Ottomans absorbed Greece, Bosnia, Herzegovina, and Albania. The Turkish advance was reinforced by the capacity of the Ottomans to gather political support from former Byzantine civil servants and Christian nobles who were integrated into the Ottoman armies and administration. The Ottomans also protected the Greek Orthodox church in an effort to win the support of Balkan peoples.

The absorption of the former Byzantine empire by Turkish-Muslim conquerors led to the eventual conversion of Anatolia and thus added new territories to the domain of Islam. Before the Turkish migrations, the Greek, Armenian, Georgian, and Syrian population of Anatolia was in the vast majority Christian. By the fifteenth century more than 90 percent of the population was Muslim. Some of this change was due to the immigration of a large Muslim population, but in great part it was due to the conversion of Christians to Islam.

These conversions were basically due to the breakdown of Anatolian Christianity through the weakening of the Byzantine state and the Greek Orthodox church, and the collapse of Anatolian society in the face of Turkish migrations. In the late thirteenth and fourteenth centuries the Turks excluded bishops and metropolitans from their sees. Church revenues and properties were confiscated. Hospitals, schools, orphanages and monasteries were destroyed or abandoned, and the Anatolian Christian population was left without leadership and social services. The remaining Christian clerics had to turn to Turkish authorities to handle internal disputes on terms which only further weakened Christian institutions.

At the same time, an ordered Islamic society was being built up to replace the dying Byzantine state and church. The Saljuq state and the Turkish emirates built up their own infrastructure of social and charitable institutions. Palaces, mosques, colleges, caravansaries, and hospitals, supported by endowments and staffed with Persian and Arab scholars, were the focal points for the construction of an urban Muslim society after the initial and ruinous nomadic invasions. Such institutions were magnets for a disoriented Christian population.

Moreover, Muslim missionaries appealed to a demoralized Christian population which saw their defeat as a sign of punishment from God or even of the end of history. Muslim holy-men further appealed to Christians by presenting Islam as a syncretism of Muslim and Christian religious beliefs. Christian holy places were taken over; Jesus was venerated by Muslims. Byzantine princes, lords and administrators were tempted to convert to Islam in order to join the Ottoman aristocracy. By the end of the fifteenth century Anatolia was largely Muslim.

The Ottoman conquests in the Balkans also established Muslim hegemony over large Christian populations, but did not lead, as in Anatolia, to the substantial assimilation of the regional population to Islam. Several considerations seem to explain the difference. One is that the bulk of Turkish settlement took place in Anatolia rather than in the Balkans. The second is that Ottoman administrative policy in the Balkans favored the Christian churches. Until the conquest of Constantinople the churches in Anatolia which were identified with the rival Byzantine empire were harried and suppressed. After the conquest, the Orthodox church in the Balkans was reorganized, confirmed in its jurisdictions and properties, and allowed to protect Christian communities.

In the Balkans, the Turkish-Muslim presence was first established by Turkish migrants who entered Thrace, the Maritsa Valley, northern Bulgaria, and Albania in the course of the fourteenth and fifteenth centuries. Hundreds of new villages were founded, often around Sufi hospices (*tekkes*); the major towns were settled by Muslims. In the Balkans, as in Anatolia, conversion was facilitated by the preaching of the Sufi orders, such as the Bektashis and the Mevlevis, and most likely occurred in rural areas. Though there were some cases of forced conversion in Serbia, Albania, and Bulgaria, there was no systematic persecution. Converts to Islam often brought with them Christian beliefs and practices. Baptism, worship of saints, the celebration of Easter, and belief in the healing efficacy of churches were taken from Christianity into Islam. In the Balkans Islam was also influenced by pagan practices which had remained a strong aspect of Balkan folk Christianity.

A census of 1520–30 showed that about 19 percent of the Balkan population was Muslim and 81 percent was Christian, with a small Jewish minority. The Muslim population of Bosnia, one of the highest, was 45 percent. In general, Muslims were concentrated in towns. For example, Sofia had a Muslim majority of 66.4 percent, whereas the surrounding district was only 6 percent Muslim. The town of Edirne was 82 percent Muslim in a district which was otherwise 74 percent Christian. The Muslim element was most numerous in Thrace, Macedonia, Thessaly, Bosnia, Herzegovina and Silistria. A new wave of Islamization occurred between 1666 and 1690 in the Rhodope. Islam came to northern Albania and Montenegro in the seventeenth century. Greeks in southwestern Macedonia and Crete converted in the course of the seventeenth and eighteenth centuries.

THE OTTOMAN WORLD EMPIRE

The conquest of Constantinople and the Balkans was a turning-point in Ottoman history. Rather than satisfying Turkish, Ottoman, and Muslim ambitions, it made them boundless. The Ottomans became the greatest of Muslim warriors for the faith. Mehmed II the Conqueror (1444–46, 1451–81) fused the Turkish interest in victories over the infidels with the imperial ambitions of both the Muslim Caliphate and the Roman empire. He saw himself as a successor to the Byzantine emperors, constructed vast formal palaces, and legislated new codes of law. Art and policy were adapted to symbolize the ambition for a universal empire. This empire would sweep eastward to the borders of Iran, and subsume the Arab provinces of the Middle East and North Africa and the holy places of Arabia. With the conquest of the former lands of the ʿAbbasid Caliphate, the Ottomans would inherit Muslim world leadership. The absorption of Damascus, Cairo, Mecca and Medina would bring a great influx of Muslim scholars to Istanbul. In addition to the title of ghazi or Warrior for the Faith, the Ottoman rulers would take the titles of "Servitor of the Two Holy Sanctuaries" and "Defender of the Shariʿa." Muslims the world over would appeal to them for military and political support. The Mamluks of Egypt and the Muslims of Gujarat and Acheh would invoke their aid in the Indian Ocean struggle against the Portuguese. Muslims in Spain would appeal for Ottoman help against the Christian reconquista. Sunnis in Inner Asia would call to their Ottoman brothers to protect them against the Safavids and the Russians. From their dominant position in the Muslim East the Ottomans would also sweep northwards and westward over northern and central Europe and the Mediterranean. The sixteenth century was the period of the most aggressive expansion, the seventeenth century a period of maintenance; the eighteenth century would bring the first serious reversals to an expanding Ottoman empire.

The great eastern sweep began after the conquest of Constantinople. Ottoman successes in the Balkans were accompanied by campaigns to absorb the rival Turkish principalities in Anatolia. Ottoman expansion, exacerbated by Sunni–Shiʿi religious antagonism, brought them into rivalry with the Safavids for control of eastern Anatolia and western Iran. The decisive battle of Chaldiran (1514) enabled the Ottomans to annex eastern Anatolia and northern Mesopotamia, and to take control of the important trade routes leading from Tabriz to Aleppo and Bursa. From there the Ottomans pushed on in 1516 and 1517 to take over the Mamluk empire of Syria and Egypt and the Muslim holy places of Arabia.

As rulers of Egypt, the Ottomans became responsible for Muslim interests in the Indian Ocean. They inherited the leadership of the Muslim struggle against European efforts to divert the international spice trade from the Mediterranean to Atlantic routes. By 1507 the Portuguese had already established a series of bases in the Indian Ocean cutting off commerce to the Red Sea and the Mediterranean. After 1517 the Ottomans developed their position in the Indian Ocean by establishing bases in Arabia and East Africa including Sawakin, Aden, and Yemen. From these bases the Red Sea fleets under the leadership of Piri Re'is (1465–1554) managed to reopen the routes which led to Alexandria and Aleppo. In the Persian gulf region, they occupied Baghdad in 1534, Basra in 1538, and Bahrain in 1554.

In this epic struggle, the Portuguese and the Ottoman strategies were entirely different. The Portuguese relied upon maritime commerce for the support of the homeland and their primary reason for naval expansion was the control of trade. They concentrated on dominating naval bases and avoided pushing inland. The Ottomans, by contrast, depended on the revenues of their vast territorial empire, and had only a defensive interest in the seas because of the limited possibilities for systematic taxation. Thus, the Ottoman commitment to the Indian Ocean was limited to some 25 ships and 4,000 men – merely a holding operation – and the Portuguese and the Ottomans could establish a frontier in the Indian Ocean based upon their respective interests. The moment had not yet come for the ultimate confrontation between Ottoman territorial and European naval power.

For a time Ottoman interests were diverted to the Arab world and the Indian Ocean, but the Ottoman struggle with Iran resumed, and continued sporadically for more than a century, from the Ottoman conquest of Baghdad (1534) to the treaty of Qasr Shirin (1639) which gave Baghdad and Iraq to the Ottomans and the Caucasus to Iran. This treaty confirmed the modern boundaries between Iraq and Iran. The wars between Iran and the Ottoman empire divided the historic homelands of Islam. The Ottoman–Safavid rivalry cut the Ottoman empire off from the roots of Islamic culture in Iran and led to its Turkification. The schism between Iran and the Ottomans also reinforced Arab influence in the further development of Ottoman civilization.

The conquest of the Balkans opened the way for a two-centuries-long world war against the powers of Europe. In this war the Ottomans were primarily allied to France against their principal enemies, the Habsburg empire in Spain, the Netherlands, Austria and Hungary, and Tsarist Russia. The world war unfolded in three principal theaters. In central Europe the Ottomans pushed beyond the Danube and absorbed the Rumanian principalities by 1504. They

Map 12. Expansion of th

Legend:

- ■ Ottoman lands 1359
- ▨ Ottoman lands 1451
- ▦ Ottoman lands 1520
- ▧ Ottoman lands 1560
- ◨ Ottoman lands 1683
- ⠂ Territories restored to Safavid control 1603

0 — 500 — 1000 km

0 — 500 miles

oman empire: *c.* 1280–1683.

confirmed local princes in power, but maintained forts and garrisons and received a tribute of cereals, honey, hides, and cloth. The Hungarian monarchy, crippled by its dependence on an aristocracy divided by perpetual factional quarrels, and by unrest among the peasants, lost Belgrade in 1520, and was forced to accept Ottoman suzerainty in 1526. In 1529 the Ottomans besieged Vienna. Though the siege of Vienna failed, it assured the Ottomans control of Hungary. Still expanding, the Ottomans made Transylvania a vassal in 1559. Finally, the long war of 1593–1606 brought an end to Ottoman expansion. By the treaty of Zsitva Torok (1606), Ottoman rule over Rumania, Hungary, and Transylvania was confirmed, but the Ottoman Sultans had to recognize the Habsburg emperors as their equals. The treaty of 1606 also implicitly recognized that the Ottoman offensive was reduced to small-scale frontier raids. The Ottoman state could no longer muster large and disciplined armies, finance the cost of its world-scale empire, and maintain its frontiers. The Ottomans had come up against the highly organized societies of central Europe, and at vast distances from their capital, Istanbul, could no longer make significant advances. Still the struggle to break the stalemate went on and culminated in the last, and fruitless, Ottoman siege of Vienna in 1683.

The wars in central Europe were accompanied by an equally vast Ottoman–Habsburg struggle for control of the Mediterranean. In the early days of Ottoman expansion, the dominant naval powers in the Mediterranean were Venice and Genoa, both of whom had established a series of fortified trading posts along the Mediterranean and Aegean coasts in order to sustain their commerce. When the conquest of Constantinople and consolidation of Ottoman rule in the Balkans put Byzantine maritime resources into the hands of the conquerors, Mehmed built a new navy based on Italian designs and Greek seamanship. The Ottomans pushed Venice out of the eastern Mediterranean, and after the conquest of Egypt in 1517, encouraged Muslim privateers in the western Mediterranean. Khayr al-Din Barbarossa led privateering operations out of Tunis, took Algiers in 1529, and was made Grand Admiral of the Ottoman fleets in 1533 – a clear expression of Ottoman aspirations to control the western Mediterranean.

Crucial to this ambition was the control of the narrows between Sicily and Tunisia. The battles of Algiers (1529) and Tunis (1534–35) marked successful Ottoman advances. The Spanish Habsburgs counter-attacked by building a series of fortified posts along the coast of North Africa reaching as far as Tripoli in 1510 and La Goletta in 1535, but eventually the Ottomans seized Tripoli (1551), Bougie (1555), Jerba (1560), Malta (1565), and Cyprus (1570). This provoked the formation of a coalition among the papacy, Venice, and the Habsburgs, who defeated the Ottomans at the battle of Lepanto in 1571. Lepanto was celebrated as a triumph of Christian Europe over the Muslim Turks. The Europeans regained their confidence, quashed the fear of Turkish invincibility and aspired to reverse the Ottoman gains. In fact, however, the Ottomans restored their fleets and, in a resounding victory, seized Tunis in 1574. In 1580 the Mediterranean wars came to an end. Philip II, faced with revolts in Spain, negotiated peace between the Habsburgs and the Ottomans, both eager to cultivate other fields. The protagonists recognized that they could no longer change Mediterranean boundaries; the truce of 1580 confirmed the frontier between Christian and Muslim civilizations that has lasted to the present day.

In northern Europe, Russia and the Ottoman empire were rivals for control of the regions north of the Black Sea and between the Black and the Caspian seas. In the late fifteenth century the Ottomans established their suzerainty over Rumania and the Crimean Tatars, but the Russians seized Kazan (1552) and Astrakan (1556) and thus won control of the lower Volga. In response, the Ottomans determined on the bold strategy of building a channel between the Don and the Volga rivers which would enable them to transfer ships from the Black to the Caspian seas, block Russian expansion into the Caucasus, and keep open the trade and pilgrimage routes from Inner Asia. An Ottoman expedition of 1569–70, however, was defeated and the Ottomans were forced to renounce their ambitions. Ottoman defeat meant that the Russians could gradually increase their pressure on the Crimea and the Caucasus. Russian expansion led eventually to a three-way Polish, Russian, and Ottoman struggle for control of the Ukraine which culminated in 1676 with the Ottomans in control of the Black Sea and the right bank of the Ukraine. Thus the Ottomans reached the apogee of their expansion in northern Europe.

By the end of the seventeenth century the Ottomans had created a world-scale empire reaching from the western Mediterranean to Iran and from the Ukraine to Yemen. The dynamism for the world-wide expansion of Ottoman rule came from the characteristics of Turkish and Ottoman society. The spearhead of Ottoman conquests were ghazi-warrior adventurers, united under the leadership of popular military chieftains or venerated holy-men. Behind the holy war was an imperial state of exceptional organizational capacities, employing an advanced military technology based on cannons and massed infantry musket fire, tolerant and able to assimilate non-Muslim populations and reconcile them to Ottoman rule. This combination of qualities had no peer until the eighteenth century, when Europe generated the power to check and throw back the Ottoman advances.

Behind the conquests was a highly organized and efficient Ottoman state whose institutions were directly derived from the Saljuq state in Anatolia and indirectly from the Mamluk regime of Egypt and Syria. The Saljuqs had adopted a slave military corps and iqta^c type of administration, patronized the religious elites, protected trade and urban life, sponsored agricultural cultivation, and thus built up the infrastructure of a society which was capable of supporting an elaborate state apparatus and of suppressing predatory nomadic populations. The Ottoman empire was thus a continuation of earlier Islamic Middle Eastern states, and extended Middle Eastern forms of state organization into new regions. Certain features of the Ottoman state, however, which have no Middle Eastern antecedents, seem to derive from Byzantine examples. Administrative practices, architectural style, patronage of the Christian churches, the guild system and controls over the provincial economy seem to stem from Byzantine rather than Islamic precedents.

At the center of the Ottoman state was an elaborate court or palace apparatus. The Istanbul palace – the Topkapi Saray – was divided into an inner and an outer section. The inner section was the very heart of the empire. It included the residence of the Sultan and his harem, the privy chambers and treasury of the ruler, the royal kitchens, and the schools for the training of pages and slaves for the inner service. The outer service included the state offices for both military and civilian administration, the offices for palace religious scholars, kitchen staffs, artisans, and gardeners who maintained the palace grounds and performed military service.

Like previous Middle Eastern rulers, the Ottomans sought to replace their all-too-powerful and independent tribal followers with slave troops. Murad I (1360–89) created slave military units (*kapikullari*) organized either as infantry (the famous janissaries) or cavalry. The new troops were at first taken from prisoners and volunteers, but in 1395 the *devshirme* was instituted as a kind of "tax" in manpower taken on the Christian population of the Balkans to provide slaves for the Sultan's armies. While the mamluks of previous Middle Eastern regimes were ordinarily Turkish and Circassian slaves recruited from outside the territories of the empires they served, the Ottoman janissaries were Balkan Christians taken from the subject population. The Ottoman system of recruitment afforded a more regular supply of manpower and perhaps a cheaper source of slaves, but it entailed the eventual complication that the system was originally designed to avoid. Slaves recruited in the Balkans could resume family and social contacts in their home regions.

The most promising of the slave recruits were educated in the court and palace schools of the Sultan to be pages in the royal household, officers in the army or administrative officials, were given a Turkish, Arabic and Islamic education, and were cultivated as gentlemen in the Ottoman style. Other young recruits were apprenticed to Turkish officers in Anatolia, and were trained in modern techniques of war to operate as infantry in organized formations, using firearms. New infantry tactics were devised in combination with the battlefield use of artillery to make the janissaries the most effective of Middle Eastern and European armies.

The janissary corps was complemented by provincial cavalry. Some of the Ottoman cavalrymen were slaves, but most were recruited from the free Turkish population, supported by timars, the equivalent of the Middle Eastern iqta's – assignments of tax revenues in return for military service. In 1527 there were about 28,000 slave infantry and some 70 to 80,000 cavalry of whom 37,500 were timar holders. In addition, there were auxiliary garrison and frontier raiders who were financed by tax exemptions.

A bureaucratic administration was essential to the financing of the slave armies. Orhan (1324–60) appointed a wazir for the central administration and military and civil governors for the conquered provinces. The chief officials were united in an imperial council. As the Ottoman empire expanded, provinces that were initially tributaries were annexed and brought into a routine system of administration. The largest provincial units, called *beylerbeyliks*, were subdivided into *sanjak beyliks* and further divided into *timarliks* which were the districts assigned to military officers in lieu of salary. In the sixteenth century the term *vali* was substituted for *beylerbey* to mean governor and the term *eyalet* was introduced to mean province. The European provinces of Rumania and Transylvania, the Crimea, and certain Anatolian districts in the control of Kurdish and Turkish peoples continued to be quasi-independent tributary provinces (*hukumet*).

Local revenue collection was the essential aspect of provincial administration. Some provinces were administered by salaried officials who collected taxes and sent the surplus to Istanbul; others were administered by timar holders. For tax purposes cadastral surveys called *tahrirs* listed the villages, the households, the adult males who were responsible for the payment of taxes, and their crops and other resources.

The Ottoman state organization did not of course come into fullblown existence all at once, but evolved over 300 years. The driving force in the evolution of Ottoman administration was the conflict between the Turkish or ghazi party which was powerful in the provincial armies and the religious administration, and the slave or devshirme party which was powerful in the imperial service and in the janissary corps. The frontier soldiers and the Turkish aristocracy favored expansion against Christian countries in Europe; the slave advisers of the Sultan preferred expansion in Anatolia and in other Muslim regions. The ghazi warriors wanted decentralized, as opposed to a strong patrimonial and central government, and a Muslim and Turkish as opposed to a cosmopolitan and imperial cultural style.

Successive Sultans favored the policies of one party or another or manipulated them against each other. Bayazid I (1389–1402) consolidated the slave party by introducing the slave soldiers into administrative positions and by bringing the provinces under routine central control, but Mehmed I (1413–21), in the wake of defeat by Timur, gave full support to the Turkish and ghazi elements. He removed Byzantine advisers from the court and made Turkish and Persian, rather than Greek, the official languages of administration.

Mehmed II returned power to the slave soldiers. He removed the Turkish nobility and all competing members of the Ottoman family from power and reserved the most important positions in the central government for his own slaves. Still, to maintain some balance of power, a functional division was made between the offices of the Grand Vizier, the religious notables, the treasury administration and the chancery services, and some Turkish families were restored to favor and allowed to keep their properties. Mehmed also sought the support of the Greek Orthodox clergy by recognizing their civil as well as religious authority over the church laity. He centralized government controls by taking tax surveys and absorbing independent vassal territories into the timar system, and he promulgated the first systematic legal codes dealing with the organization of the state and the obligations of subjects. By the reign of Sulayman I (1520–66), the dominance of the janissaries was uncontested. Their final victory, however, upset the internal balance of power and stimulated factionalism and harem intrigues.

Like the rulers of the ᶜAbbasid and later Persian empires, the authority of the Ottoman Sultans combined patrimonial, Islamic, and imperial dimensions. The patrimonial authority of the Ottoman Sultans was foremost. The state was his household; his subjects his personal retainers. The soldiers were his slaves, loyal to him personally. The territory of the empire was his personal property, but much of it was given to members of the ruling class in the form of iqtaᶜs. The alienation of state revenues in any form, however, was not considered a derogation of the absolute ownership of the Sultan.

At the core of this system based on absolute authority was an ambiguity about the transmission of that authority which subverted the effectiveness of Sultanal government. According to Turkish practice, the authority of the Sultan was passed on within the royal family, but the line of succession was not specified. Thus, the death of a reigning Sultan led to a struggle for power, usually among the surviving sons, which was ordinarily resolved by a test of military strength and sometimes by fratricide. A reigning Sultan might favor one of his sons by giving him an administrative or military position which would benefit him in the eventual struggle for power, but after 1595 all male relatives of the Sultan were imprisoned in the harem. Palace and harem intrigue became the road to power.

From the Islamic point of view, the Sultan's authority was derived from his role as executor of Muslim law. In the Muslim theory of government, the Sultan was responsible to the Shariᶜa and in turn the subjects were responsible to him. Even a government which seized power by military force was regarded as legitimate as long as it recognized the sovereignty of the Shariᶜa and respected the basic interests of the Muslim community.

The Shariᶜa, however, did not cover all aspects of Ottoman political and social life. In order to regulate the relations of the Ottoman aristocracy and subjects, and to define the status, duties and dress codes of each, the Sultans were empowered to issue *firmans*. These decrees were gathered in codes called *kanun*, which were a form of secular and administrative law considered to be a valid extension of religious law as a result of the ruler's right to exercise legal judgment on behalf of the community. Mehmed II and Sulayman the Magnificent created new law codes dealing with administrative and criminal justice, the discipline of officials, military affairs, and the organization of the religious hierarchy. In a broad range of issues not covered directly by Shariᶜa, systematic codification of law was probably inspired by the Codes of Justinian.

The authority of Ottoman Sultans was also based upon a cosmopolitan culture comprising Arab, Persian, Byzantine and European elements. Mehmed II, a liberal patron of the arts, cultivated both Persian poetry and European painting. At his court, Arab and Persian literati, Italian painters, and Greek and Serbian poets were welcome. Later regimes, however, moved away from Christian and European influences toward a more Muslim and Turkish style.

As at the courts of Arab and Persian princes, poetry was the principal expression of royal style. Court poetry was based on the *aruz*, a prosodic meter derived from Arabic meters, and was heavily infused with Arabic and Persian words. The basic poetic forms were those already pioneered in Persian court poetry – the qasida, the ghazal, the masnavi and the rubaᶜi. The Ottoman poetic tradition began with Saljuq rulers who patronized Hoja Dehhani, a composer of panegyrics, and wine and love songs in the Persian manner. The greatest Ottoman poet of the classical period was Baki (1526–1600). Nefᶜi

(1582–1636), a panegyrist and satirist, composed poetry celebrating power and struggle. Yahya Efendi (1552–1644) developed an original subject matter based on direct observation of life and nature and expressing personal emotion.

Ottoman prose literature was strongly influenced by Ottoman imperial ambitions. Early Ottoman historical writing was composed in Arabic and then translated into Turkish to legitimize the origin of the dynasty and its rise to power and to chronicle everyday court and military events. In the course of the sixteenth century, Ottoman world ambitions were given expression in the composition of universal histories. Mustafa ʿAli's (1541–99) *Kunh al-Akhbar* contained a history of the world from Adam to Jesus, a history of early Islam, a history of Turkish peoples up to the rise of the Ottomans, and a concluding part on the Ottoman empire. In the seventeenth century historians were employed to compile daily court chronicles. Geographical writing was stimulated by the expansion of Ottoman naval power. Piri Reʾis, the Ottoman commander in the Indian Ocean, was the author of an important atlas. Evliya Chelebi's (1614–82) *Seyahat-name* (Book of Travels) contains a comprehensive description of journeys throughout the Ottoman empire and his observations of Ottoman society and economy.

Ottoman manuscript illustration also expressed the Ottoman sense of an imperial destiny. From the time of Mehmed II, the Ottoman regime maintained a court studio, or *nakkashhane*, which employed calligraphers, painters, illuminators, and bookbinders to produce manuscripts and to generate the designs for Ottoman ceramics, woodwork, metalwork, textiles, and carpets. Between 1451 and 1520, Persian precedents formed the basis of Ottoman manuscript art. Artists from Shiraz, Tabriz, and Herat were brought to Istanbul. The earliest works were illustrated copies of Persian classics such as ʿAttar's *Language of the Birds*, the *Love Story of Khosraw and Shirin*, the *Khamsa* of Amir Khosraw, and the fables of the *Kalila Wa-Dimna*. The history of Alexander's conquests and illustrated contemporary histories became staple products of the Ottoman workshop.

Sixteenth-century manuscripts turned from the illustration of classic literature to contemporary events such as the ceremonial reception of ambassadors, the collection of taxes, and the conquests of famous fortresses in the Balkans. Victories of kings, descriptions of festivals, accessions, royal processions, battles, sieges, banquets and celebrations were all the subject of manuscript illustrations. The *Shahinshah-name* of 1581 depicts the circumcision festivals held in Istanbul, athletic performances, guild parades, and other court events. Viziers, janissaries, cavalrymen, scholars, guildsmen, merchants and

12 Sultan Selim the First

Sultans appear in profusion. The *Shah-name-i Al-i Osman*, Book of Kings of the House of Osman, by Arifi (d. 1561/62) is one of the famous productions of this period. By the end of the sixteenth century, illustrated history, celebrating the splendor of the Ottoman state and its conquests, had become a special Turkish contribution to the tradition of Middle Eastern and Muslim manuscript illumination. Ottoman manuscript art celebrated the self-consciousness of the Ottoman elite as a world historical force.

The Ottoman imperial sensibility was similarly reflected in architecture. Ottoman mosques and colleges expressed the close Ottoman tie to Islam, but Ottoman design features, such as single large domes, tall minarets, and colonnaded courtyards, showed the strong influence of Aya Sophia, the greatest of Byzantine churches. Ottoman mosques thus mimic the great eastern Christian churches and express, like the Dome of the Rock in Jerusalem, the triumph of Islam over Christian rivals. Hoja Sinan (1490–1578) was the master of this style of architecture.

In sum, the Ottoman regime, in both concept and practice, was derived from Turkish, Saljuq, and Mamluk Middle Eastern precedents. Christian and European influences were relatively limited. Yet the Ottoman regime was innovative and distinctive because of the refinement of the slave military organization and the importance of jihad. The Turkish warriors, royal slaves, court historians and artists were all committed to an imperial vision of Islamic expansion; the Sultan was glorified as a warrior prince, as a Muslim Caliph, and as a conquering emperor.

RULERS AND SUBJECTS

As a patrimonial, Islamic, and cosmopolitan regime, the Ottoman empire had a powerful effect on the fate of all Middle Eastern and Balkan peoples. To an unusual degree, the Ottoman regime dominated, controlled and shaped the society it governed. A central Ottoman concept was the distinction between *askeri* and *reᶜaya*, rulers and ruled, elites and subjects, warriors and producers, tax-collectors and tax-payers. The chief attribute of the ruling elite was the right to exploit the wealth of the subjects. In addition, to be a member of the ruling class one had to be cultivated in the distinctive language and manners called "the Ottoman way." One could become an Ottoman either by birth or by education in the imperial, military, or Muslim religious schools.

The distinction of rulers and ruled was not the same as between Muslims and non-Muslims. The ruling elites and the subject populations included both. Alongside of Turkish soldiers and Arab and Persian scribes and scholars, the ruling elite included Balkan Christian lords and scribes. The patrician Greek families of the Phanar district of Istanbul, who became prominent merchants, bankers, government functionaries, and provincial rulers in Rumania, and the higher clergy of the Orthodox Church, may be considered part of the Ottoman elite. Jewish refugees from Spain also became important in Ottoman trade and banking in the fifteenth and sixteenth centuries. Joseph Nasi (1520–79), for example, a refugee descended from a Portuguese Jewish family which had moved to Antwerp and then to Italy after the expulsion of the Jews from Spain, came to Istanbul in 1554. Nasi had European business and diplomatic connections and soon became a close adviser to Sulayman, played an influential role in French–Ottoman diplomatic relations, and in 1566 was made Duke of Naxos and given a monopoly on customs revenues and the export of wine. Nasi was also a patron of Jewish community life and of Jewish settlement in Palestine. In the course of the sixteenth and seventeenth centuries, however, the Ottoman elite became more uniformly Muslim. Only the Phanar Greek financial aristocracy maintained its position, owing to its administrative and economic role in Rumania.

The subjects, the reᶜaya, were organized into innumerable small communities. Ottoman society was an elaborate mosaic of territorial associations, religious fraternities, and corporate economic groups. From the Ottoman point of view, the religious communities organized to administer the educational, judicial, and charitable affairs of the subject population were fundamental. Most of the non-Muslim population were considered members of the Eastern Orthodox church which included Greek, Rumanian, Slavic, Bulgarian, and Arab believers. The Armenian church was an administrative body, which included monophysites in Syria and Egypt, Assyrians, Bogomils, and Gypsies. Maronites, Uniate Armenians, and Latin Catholics in Hungary, Croatia and Albania had their own churches; Sephardi and Ashkenazi Jews their own synagogues.

The Ottomans, like previous Muslim regimes, considered the non-Muslim subjects autonomous but dependent peoples whose internal social, religious, and communal life was regulated by their own religious organizations, but whose leaders were appointed by, and responsible to, a Muslim state. Non-Muslim communities were called by the generic terms of *dhimmi* (protected peoples), *taᵓifa* (group), or *jamat* (religious community). In general the Ottomans seem to have made separate arrangements with local bodies of Christians and Jews which gave them a measure of local autonomy and administrative responsibility. Minority leaders, sometimes ecclesiastics, sometimes laymen, represented their communities to the authorities, and dealt with ecclesiastical matters, internal disputes, and fines and taxes on a local basis. However, recent research has cast doubt on the notion that these arrangements constituted an empire-wide "millet" system. The word "millet" was never applied to non-Muslim communities. Though the Greek Orthodox church had its own concept of ecumenical authority, and may have attempted to convert the local authority of the Patriarch of Constantinople into an empire-wide authority, it was resisted by the churches of Ohrid (Bulgaria) and Pech (Serbia). The authority of the Patriarch of Constantinople was never clearly defined.

The Muslim masses, as a subject or reʿaya population, were organized in a parallel way. The Muslim population was subdivided into numerous schools of law and Sufi brotherhoods, which the Ottomans were keen to bring under state control. They did this by extending their patronage to the ʿulamaʾ and Sufi elites. Ottoman patronage led to the organization of an elaborate system of madrasa education. The first Ottoman madrasa was established in Iznik in 1331, when scholars were invited from Iran and Egypt to augment Muslim instruction in the new territories. Later Sultans founded colleges in Bursa, Edirne and Istanbul. In the late fifteenth century these were arranged in a hierarchy which defined the career path for the promotion of leading scholars. The college built by Sulayman between 1550 and 1559 eventually became the highest-ranking. Beneath it were ranked the colleges founded by previous Sultans, and beneath these the colleges founded by state officials and religious scholars. The madrasas were not only organized by rank but also were distinguished by their educational functions. The lowest-level madrasa taught Arabic grammar and syntax, logic, theology, astronomy, geometry and rhetoric. The second-level stressed literature and rhetoric. The higher-level colleges taught law and theology.

A similar elaboration took place in judicial administration. The qadiships of Istanbul, Bursa, and Edirne were originally the most important appointments, but the hierarchy came to include judgeships in Damascus, Aleppo, Cairo, Baghdad, Medina, Izmir, and Konya. The judicial service was headed by two *qadi-askers*, one for the Balkans and one for Anatolia, and by the Shaykh al-Islam, the chief jurisconsult of Istanbul, who held the highest-ranking position in the system and had direct access to the Sultan. Ordinary *mullahs* or judges were also graded into several ranks, including qadis and their deputies who served as notaries public, registrars of deeds and administrators of the properties of orphans and minors. Qadis supervised the administration of colleges and had an important role in certification of taxes, overseeing harvests, inspection of military forces, and supervision of the urban economy, including government regulations for artisan guilds and markets. An organization of *muftis* or jurisconsults paralleled the organization of judges, but muftis received no official salaries. The educational and the judicial hierarchies were interlocked. Appointments to judgeships required the attainment of appropriate levels in the educational system. Through the interlocking educational and judicial hierarchies, the Ottoman state appointed all important judges, jurisconsults, and professors of law and thereby maintained a direct bureaucratic control over the religious establishment.

Sufis were also important to the Ottoman state because of their large role in Turkish rural society. Sufi babas mobilized bands of Turkish warriors and led them to holy war, protected travelers, mediated disputes, and otherwise helped to create social order in rural areas. Wandering dervishes, called Malamatiya or Qalandariya, who openly disregarded the Shariʿa and opposed contact with government authorities, were nonetheless venerated by rural people as bearers of God's blessings and of magical powers.

The rural Sufis were politically important because they could inspire resistance to the state. Eastern Anatolia, like northwestern Iran, was a breeding ground for Sufi revolts which espoused messianic beliefs and organized local opposition to state domination. For example, Bedreddin (d. 1416) denied the literal truth of heaven and hell, the day of judgment, the resurrection of the body, the creation of the world, and other basic tenets of Muslim belief. The Hurufiya (whose doctrine spread among both Muslims and Christians in Anatolia and Bulgaria at the end of the fourteenth century) preached that the only rightful income was that earned by manual work. Sufi-led rebellions also occurred in the late fifteenth century. In 1519 a preacher named Jelal took the name of Shah Ismaʿil, claimed to be the mahdi, and attracted Turkish cultivator and pastoralist opposition to the imposition of taxes. The early sixteenth-century wave of revolts was closely related to the Safavid agitation and the opposition of eastern Anatolian peoples to the Ottoman-Sunni regime. Jelal gave his name to a whole series of later sixteenth-century revolts, but these, as we shall see, represented a different social and political situation.

Anatolian resistance was fostered by Turkish folk culture. Itinerant minstrel poets (*saz shairi*) toured the villages singing of the struggles of the Turks with the Georgians, Circassians, and Byzantines and celebrating the virtues of Turkish peoples. Epic poetry was then translated into the Karagoz or shadow play theater, which became another vehicle for Turkish folk culture. Sufi poets, of whom the most important was Yunus Emre (1238–1329), also kept popular literary and religious culture alive. Poets traveled with the soldiers, sang in the camps, entertained people at fairs, and conducted contests which were the basis of an Anatolian folk consciousness. The heritage of nomadic populations, independent states, and Sufi brotherhoods separated the Anatolian provinces from the capital city elites.

The Bektashis were among the most influential of these Sufis. Haji Bektash, the founder of the order, probably lived toward the end of the thirteenth century. According to legend, he and some forty followers set up tekkes throughout eastern Anatolia and among Turkomans in Macedonia, Thessaly, and the Rhodope. Bektashis spread throughout Anatolia and the Balkans in the course of the fifteenth century. Around 1500, Balim Sultan organized the rituals of the order and perfected its system of tekkes.

The Bektashis were strongly influenced by both Shiʿism and Christianity. They took the sixth imam, Jaʿfar, as their patron saint, venerated the trinity of God, Muhammad, and ʿAli, offered bread and wine in initiation ceremonies, and required celibacy of their teachers. They taught that there were four levels of religious belief: Shariʿa, adherence to the law; tariqa, initiation in special ceremonies to the Sufi order; maʿrifa, understanding of the truth; and haqiqa, the direct experience of the divine reality. Initiates were introduced progressively to the secret knowledge and ceremonies of the group.

Alongside the rural Sufis, urban religious orders also flourished in Anatolia and the Balkans. The Mevlevi leaders were spiritually descended from Mawlana Jalal al-Din Rumi (1207–73) and have become universally known for their ceremonial dancing as the whirling dervishes. Apart from their ceremonial function, Mevlevi tekkes were also important for the study of Persian literature and Sufi thought, and for the education of the Ottoman bureaucratic elite. Naqshbandis and Khalwatis were also important.

In the course of the fifteenth and sixteenth centuries the Ottomans brought the Sufi orders under state control. The state coopted Sufi tekkes by providing them with permanent endowments and gifts for charitable purposes. The Bektashis, in particular, were taken under the wing of the Ottomans as chaplains to the janissaries. They lived and marched with the soldiers and provided them with magical protection in battle. This enabled the order to spread throughout eastern Anatolia and among Turkish migrants in Macedonia and Albania. At the beginning of the sixteenth century the head of the order, Balim Sultan, was appointed by the Ottoman Sultan. The Mevlevis were similarly tied to the Ottoman state; they acquired the right to gird a Sultan with a holy sword upon his accession. Thus the Ottomans succeeded in domesticating the major Sufi brotherhoods without entirely eliminating the independent influence of Sufi teachers.

The absorption of the Ottoman ʿulamaʾ and the Sufi brotherhoods into the state bureaucracy made religious controversies matters of state concern. Ottoman scholars assimilated the Arabic and Persian classics, including the madrasa curriculum, theology, and science. The translation of Arabic and Persian classics, including important works on literature, history, politics, astrology, medicine, the life of the Prophet and Sufi treatises, made the corpus of Muslim religious literature available to Turkish elites. In theology, al-Ghazzali and al-Razi were recognized as the master teachers, and the controversy between al-Ghazzali and Averroes was reopened. ʿUlamaʾ, committed to a narrow definition of Islamic religious studies focused on hadith and law, soon found themselves opposed to ʿulamaʾ interested in philosophy and science, and the Sufis who stressed personal religious experience rather than formal learning.

The narrow point of view progressively gained ground. As early as the 1540s theology and mathematics were losing popularity. In 1580 an observatory attached to the Sulaymaniya madrasa in Istanbul was destroyed. In the sixteenth and seventeenth centuries the more restrictive and puritanical forms of Islam asserted themselves against popular Sufi beliefs. Reform-minded religious scholars opposed popular ceremonies for the dead, Sufi dancing and singing, and the consumption of coffee and tobacco. Puritanical legalists, supported by madrasa students and tradesmen, won strong support for a more narrow definition of Islamic learning and practice. The supporters of Qadizade Mehmed Efendi (d. 1635) formed a party to control religious endowments and to persuade the authorities to enforce a Shariʿa-oriented form of Islamic practice. Under the influence of this party tekkes were closed and Sufis were imprisoned. Finally the quality of the religious elite declined. Intellectual discussion was suppressed. With the elaboration of a bureaucratic hierarchy, the biographies of scholars show that interest in careers outweighed genuine piety and learning. The influence of entrenched families enabled them to promote their children into the higher grades of the educational and judicial hierarchies without having reached the proper preliminary levels, while theological students who could not find patronage were excluded. In the course of the eighteenth century the ʿulamaʾ, entrenched in their bureaucratic positions, became a powerful conservative pressure group.

The bureaucratization of the ʿulamaʾ gave them enormous social power as teachers, preachers, controllers of endowments, judges, and provincial officials. These powers, however, were acquired at high cost. As servants of the state the ʿulamaʾ could no longer represent the communal and religious interests of the mass of Muslim believers, and protect the people from the abuses of political power. The ideological consequences were equally heavy. Traditionally, the ʿulamaʾ had maintained an ambivalent position toward

Muslim states, seeing them as indispensable adjuncts to Islamic communal life, but also as a major cause of harm to Muslim interests. In the Ottoman empire, however, the commitment of the ʿulamaʾ to the state regime was so complete that they could not effectively represent a transcendental Islamic ideal opposed to worldly corruption. Their dependency upon and integration into the Ottoman regime made them simply the spokesmen of Ottoman legitimacy.

THE OTTOMAN ECONOMY AND PROVINCIAL ADMINISTRATION

The subject population was further controlled by state regulation of economic activity. From the Ottoman point of view, the economic well-being of the subjects was essential to the viability of the regime, and the early Ottoman conquests were directed to the control of trade routes and productive resources. Ottoman expansion in the Black Sea, the Aegean, and the Mediterranean was intended to wrest control of trade and naval resources from the Venetians and the Genoese. In wars which lasted from 1463 to 1479 and from 1499 to 1503, Venetian possessions in Greece and the Aegean were conquered. Cyprus was taken in 1570; Crete in 1669. To bypass Venetian trade, the Ottomans also allied with the Adriatic port of Ragusa (Dubrovnic). After 1484 the Ottomans excluded foreigners from the Black Sea, with the exception of ships bringing wine from Crete or Chios. The Black Sea trade, in general, passed from the Genoese to Armenians, Jews, Greeks, Turks, and Rumanians in the course of the fifteenth century.

Ottoman conquests in Iran, the Arab provinces, Egypt and the Indian Ocean were also part of a program of channeling traffic in eastern goods through the Ottoman empire. Products from Iran, the Persian Gulf, and the Red Sea helped make the empire a flourishing center of international trade. Egypt imported silk, yarn, cotton, textiles, soap and dried fruit from Syria, and exported rice, beans, wheat, sugar, and hides. From Anatolia, textiles, dried fruit, and wood were exported to Egypt, the Sudan, and India. From Syria, pistachios, dates, spices, and slaves were returned to Anatolia. The pilgrimage routes brought people from all over the empire to Mecca and Medina. Mecca was an emporium for spices, pearls, pepper, and coffee, and almost every pilgrim financed his journey by bringing goods to sell in Mecca and returning with goods to sell at home. The provisioning of the pilgrimage caravans in Damascus, Cairo, and Baghdad was an important business. Through Egypt, the Ottomans traded with the Sudan and with North and West Africa. The Red Sea ports of Arabia and of East Africa gave the Ottomans access to the Indian Ocean trade. Baghdad and Basra traded with Iran and India.

In the course of the fifteenth and sixteenth centuries, Bursa became the most important commercial center in Anatolia and an important transfer town for goods en route from the East to Istanbul, Poland, and Russia. From Bursa, silks, spices, cotton, rice, iron, mohair, nuts, opium, vinegar, rugs, and other products were shipped across the Black Sea to the Crimea, whence they were carried into the Ukraine, Poland, and Russia. Bursa also had a large silk industry and a rich merchant elite whose fortunes were invested in specie, real estates, slaves, and cloth.

In general, the Ottoman conquests meant economic revival in Anatolia, the Middle East, and the Balkans. The Ottomans suppressed piracy and revived sea traffic in both the Mediterranean and the Indian Ocean. They stimulated land traffic by building bridges and caravansaries, digging wells, and garrisoning major road junctions. Population growth stimulated agricultural production in Anatolia, which in turn set free urban populations for the production of textiles. By the end of the sixteenth century, however, excessive population growth led to the cultivation of marginal lands, the substitution of barley for wheat, and a deterioration of security in the countryside.

The European market also stimulated Ottoman exports. Anatolian cottons and Salonica woolens were exported north of the Danube. The Balkan region flourished. Edirne had a "capitalist" population including money-changers, jewelers, long-distance traders, local landowners growing wheat or raisng cattle, and moneylenders who invested in textiles or milling. Soldiers and government officials were prominent among the wealthy. The riches of Edirne seem to have been based largely on the exploitation of the surrounding countryside and the export of raw materials.

Ottoman policy was important for the internal Ottoman economy because of the endowment of *imarets* and of rural tekkes. An imaret was a complex of buildings, including a mosque, a college, a hospital, and a hospice for travelers and students, endowed with properties such as markets, mills, or kitchens to support its charitable activities. Sufi tekkes became the centers of cultivation, trade and local administration as well as educational and charitable activities. Numerous villages founded by Sufis in Anatolia and the Balkans were thus backed by state support. Endowment funds for mosques, colleges, hospitals, bridges, convents, soup kitchens, libraries, and other institutions were invested in baths, bazaars, shops, tenements, workshops, mills, presses, slaughterhouses, tanneries, and tile factories, and were an important source of capital for commerce and agriculture.

The single greatest state project was the reconstruction of Istanbul to satisfy the glory of the Sultan and the needs of administration and trade. At the time of the conquest, Constantinople probably had a population of some 50,000 to 60,000 people. To repopulate it, the Ottoman government obliged Muslim merchants from Bursa, Konya, and other Anatolian places to move to Istanbul. Large numbers of Balkan peoples were similarly transferred. To stimulate settlement, the government gave land, houses, and tax concessions to the new migrants. Numerous villages in the vicinity of the city were laid out and settled with slaves, prisoners, and deportees from the Balkans. According to the census of 1478, there were about 9,000 Muslim, 3,100 Greek Christian, 1,650 Jewish, and about 1,000 Armenian and gypsy dwellings in Istanbul. Thus the population was about 60 percent Muslim, 30 percent Christian and 10 percent Jewish, and totalled less than 100,000. Within a century it would rise to over 700,000, more than twice the population of the largest European cities of the time.

The city was rebuilt by constructing public institutions such as schools, hospitals, baths, and caravansaries with attached bazaars, bakeries, mills, or factories in several districts. Each neighborhood was centered around an important religious and public institution and its attendant facilities. Between 1453 and 1481 alone, 209 mosques, 24 schools or seminaries, 32 public baths, and 12 inns or bazaars were built in Istanbul. Many thousands of houses and shops were constructed by waqf administrators in order to generate revenue.

Ottoman policies also attempted to regulate economic activity in the interests of the state. The primary concern of the empire was the provisioning of Istanbul. Istanbul's demand led to an increased output of grain and cotton for thread and fabric. Istanbul's requirements stimulated the creation of *chiftliks* or large estates because of the profits to be made by supplying the market. Adana, for example, became an important cotton-growing region. To provision Istanbul, however, the government did not rely solely upon market forces. Strong government controls assured that the surplus of Anatolia and of other regions was directed toward the capital. The government strictly regulated the trade in wheat, rice, salt, meat, oil, fish, honey and wax, requiring traders to guarantee delivery of supplies directly to the palace and the capital city at fixed prices. Merchants were thus made agents of the state to meet the fiscal and provisioning needs of the capital and the government establishment.

Guilds were the basic cadre for the control of the urban populations. Thus, Ottoman guilds were not the spontaneous expression of the interests of merchants and craftsmen, but were formed in the course of the fifteenth century to meet the needs of the state. Merchants, craftsmen, transport workers, and even entertainers and prostitutes were organized into corporate bodies to enforce economic discipline and facilitate administration. The authorities regulated entry into trades, opening of new shops, and types and quality of merchandise produced. Maximum prices designed to protect consumer interests were set by the state. Weights and measures were regulated by government inspection. Guilds were expected to supply workers to accompany military campaigns and provide labor services. Egyptian, but not Turkish, guilds were also obliged to collect taxes from their members. A somewhat greater degree of administrative autonomy, however, was accorded guilds in Balkan cities.

The administrative apparatus which supervised the activity of professional corporations was elaborate. The grand vizier and the Agha (chief) of the janissaries, qadis, and market inspectors supervised the enforcement of guild regulations. Shaykhs and other guild officials were appointed by the government in consultation with guild members in order to implement state rules. The chiefs of guilds acted through an informal body of guild elders, who were collectively responsible to the state.

Nevertheless, organized crafts did acquire functions of their own. Guilds arbitrated disputes among their members and collected funds for mutual aid, religious ceremonies, and charities. They staged picnics and celebrations. The guilds were also religious confraternities which held common prayers and pilgrimages and heard lectures on the value of sobriety and honesty. Though guilds commonly had a patron saint and initiation ceremonies modeled on Sufi lines, they were not primarily religious associations. They were essentially collectivities of workers formed for the purpose of facilitating state control which took on certain social and religious functions as an expression of the solidarity of the members. The internal solidarity of guilds was probably reinforced by the fact that they were confined to people of the same religious community. Only a minority of guilds had a mixed Muslim and Christian, or Muslim and Jewish membership.

Some sectors of the Ottoman economy escaped direct administrative control. Merchants engaged in money-changing and international trade were usually able to operate without close governmental supervision. Some merchants organized a putting-out system of manufacture in rural areas to compete with the monopolies of town guilds. Also, as janissaries penetrated into commerce and craft production in the seventeenth and eighteenth centuries, it became increasingly difficult for the government to regulate the artisan population.

Apart from the religious administrations and government regulation of the urban economy, control over the rural population was effected through provincial administration. All provinces were in principle subordinate to the central authority and subject to taxation. Western and central Anatolia and the eastern Balkans were the core provinces of the empire, where the central government could exercise relatively close administrative control and channel the surplus of the region to Istanbul. In peripheral areas, the state had to make compromises with local chieftains and tribes. The Arab provinces were virtually subsidiary regions organized around their own capital cities, Cairo, Damascus, Aleppo, and Baghdad.

Anatolia, the geographical, ethnic and religious core province of the Ottoman empire was, in principle, governed by an administrative hierarchy. From the outset, however, Anatolia was the home of a bellicose pastoral population whose chieftains were important local political figures. Small Turkish and Kurdish regimes formed in the course of the thirteenth and fourteenth centuries were regarded as legitimate Muslim states with as much claim to regional autonomy as the Ottoman state itself. The absorption of these states into the Ottoman empire in the course of the fourteenth and fifteenth centuries was, therefore, slow, piecemeal, and never fully complete. Sufi resistance, as we have seen, was almost endemic.

In the Balkans there was a similar tension between Ottoman control and local autonomy. In the early phases of the Ottoman conquest, Balkan lords were accepted as Ottoman vassals, but eventually the vassals were converted into timar holders. Fiscal surveys, supervised by central government officials, were the basis of a regular territorial administration with the ordinary apparatus for tax collection and police control. In the directly administered provinces, Ottoman rule tended to perpetuate the social structure of Balkan populations. The towns tended to be Turkish and Muslim with some Jews, Armenians, and Greeks. Urban communities were organized into quarters and bazaars. Imarets were the centers of settlement. The working population was organized into guilds with appointed guild chiefs supervised by the local judges and market inspectors. The rural population was Greek, Serbian, Bulgarian, and Albanian. Tribal groups, the Serbian *zadruga* or joint family, and independent churches such as the Serbian patriarchate at Pech (between 1557 and 1766) were all permitted a quasi-autonomous existence. The Orthodox church helped to preserve the ethnic and linguistic character of Greek and other Balkan peoples.

Internal autonomy was accorded Rumania, Transylvania, Albania, and Montenegro, where local non-Muslim aristocracies were allowed to consolidate their power under Muslim rule. The Greek aristocracy of Istanbul controlled church properties, tax farms, and the commerce of much of the region. In the eighteenth century, leading Phanariot merchants were appointed as rulers of Rumania. Thus the administrative and religious policies of the Ottomans helped to assure the survival of Balkan-Christian peoples. Ottoman administration of the Middle Eastern and North African Arab provinces will be considered in a subsequent chapter.

The Ottoman regime is thus striking for the degree of centralization of state control over the subject societies. The Ottomans controlled vast territories and extracted from each village and locality the surplus wealth which supported the central government and sustained the wars of expansion. The state resisted the formation of independent loci of authority such as ʿulamaʾ schools, Sufi brotherhoods, akhi fraternities or independent merchant and artisan associations. The empire was not only assured its dominance through force but also through its hold on the minds of men. It stood for Islam and the arts of civilization. It won the cooperation of local chiefs, landlords, village headmen, and religious leaders, all of whom had to respect the power of the central regime, and all of whom benefited from being its accomplices.

Only in rural administration did the absorptive and regulatory capacities of the regime reach its limits. Throughout rural Anatolia, tribal communities and mountain chiefs were able to maintain a degree of independence. In the Balkans this independence was underlined by the perpetuation of Christian identity. The power of the central government was always limited because the people who served the state had ambivalent purposes. The men who made up the armies and the central administration always looked for ways to advance their private, familial, and factional interests. The local notables who supported the regime also resisted an excessive encroachment on their prerogatives. Even at its apogee, Ottoman power had to contend with the forces of localism. Nevertheless the Ottoman regime was vastly more powerful than the Safavid, and autonomous chiefs played a much smaller role in its history.

THE OTTOMAN EMPIRE IN DISARRAY

In the seventeenth and eighteenth centuries there were profound alterations in the Ottoman system and a serious decentralization of power. With the end of Ottoman expansion, the state institutions lost their administrative and military capacities, and the empire was beset by popular revolts, economic regression, and eventually military defeats. The long-latent struggle between central and provincial elites for control of the revenues of the tax-producing population came into the open, and power was transferred from the central government to janissaries, ʿulamaʾ, and Ottoman families, who successfully established themselves in the provinces. From the point of view of the central government the devolution of power was regarded as a corruption of Ottoman institutions. From the point of view of provincial chieftains, officials, and merchants, it was a reduction of the exploitative capacities of the center and a gain in local autonomy. Elements of corruption and elements of beneficial change were mixed into the overall transformation of the empire.

These political changes were closely interwoven with changes in the Ottoman economy, with the position of the Ottoman empire in the world trading economy, and with the rise of European imperialism. Commercialization of the Ottoman economy due to demographic changes in Anatolia, the devolution of power to provincial elites, and above all to European commercial penetration, subverted Ottoman control of trade, fostered decentralization and over long periods of time permanently transferred political and economic power from the Ottoman state to provincial elites and to foreign commercial powers. In the transformation of the Ottoman empire demographic, economic, and political factors were thoroughly interwoven.

These changes have their origin in the decline of the central state apparatus. The removal of the Sultans from direct control of affairs of state, and the practice of confining young princes to the harem and preventing them from assuming active military and administrative positions deprived successive generations of Ottoman princes of adequate education and worldly experience. Seventeenth-century Ottoman Sultans had no exposure to the realities of the political world beyond harem intrigues. The result was incompetence and a drastic decline of authority.

A second factor in the decline of the central state apparatus was the breakdown in the discipline and loyalty of the janissaries. The demoralization of the janissaries was due in part to the monopoly of state power acquired by the slave establishment in the sixteenth century and in part to falling incomes. As it ceased to expand, the empire ceased to acquire booty. After 1580, inflation, due to the influx of American silver, also reduced the value of Ottoman incomes in a society which was not able to make compensatory adjustments. Inadequately paid soldiers and officials resorted to seizing provincial lands and diverting the revenues for their private benefit. Janissaries also entered commerce and the crafts to supplement their income, married and established families, and then promoted their own children into the military corps. Close ties developed among janissaries, artisans, and ʿulamaʾ which made it politically impossible to control the soldiers. Discipline in the army was reduced to the point that there were pay riots in 1622 and 1631, accompanied by the looting of Istanbul. The abandonment of the devshirme in 1637 made it impossible to redress these trends. By the middle of the eighteenth century the traditional army corps were no longer useful, and the Ottoman regime was dependent upon Crimean Tatars, provincial garrisons, and the private armies of provincial notables. The new troops were not as well disciplined, trained, and armed as the traditional Ottoman corps and were all the more ineffective against their European enemies.

Equally important was the gradual abandonment of the timar system. As firearms and organized infantry became ever more important, the Ottoman cavalry (*sipahis*) were no longer able to resist German riflemen. Also, as the state increasingly needed ready cash to meet the demands of the janissaries and other needs, it converted the timars into tax farms. This denuded rural areas of loyal troops and left a vacuum of administrative and police authority in the countryside.

The position of the Ottoman state was also undermined by the growing power of Europe. As early as the sixteenth century the Ottomans were competing with the Portuguese for control of the Indian Ocean trade. In the seventeenth and eighteenth centuries, however, the Dutch and the British supplanted the Portuguese as the dominant powers in the Indian Ocean and took control of the trade in Asia. The Black Sea trade was captured by Russia. There was some compensation to the Ottomans in the growth of trade in coffee which came from Yemen through Egypt to Istanbul and was then exported to Europe.

European control of the Asian trade helped them build up a strong position in the Mediterranean as well. The Ottoman–French alliance against the Habsburg empire disposed the Ottomans to give France a monopoly of Ottoman trade. For a time all European ships had to sail under the French flag. The English, however, entered the Levant trade in 1580. British Ambassador Harbourne succeeded in 1583 in negotiating a trade treaty with the Ottoman empire which reduced the taxes on English goods to 3 percent. The English formed the Levant Company to export cloth and tin, essential to make brass for cannon founding, in return for silk, mohair, cotton, wool, carpets, drugs, spices, and indigo.

In the seventeenth and eighteenth centuries competition in the Mediterranean among the French, English, and Dutch was fierce. The Dutch and the English organized convoys and heavily armed their merchant ships. Armenians and Jews operated through Smyrna and Livorno, and the Venetians and Genoese were also active. Each of the competitors experienced wide fluctuations in trading activity and profits, but the overall volume of Mediterranean trade was probably declining, on account of the competition of direct shipments from South and Southeast Asia to Europe. Spices from the Indies, cloth from India, and Persian goods were coming to Europe over Atlantic routes. The British East India Company, buying Far Eastern goods at their source and bringing them into the Mediterranean via London, actually became a competitor of the British Levant Company which depended on the Persian Gulf and Red Sea routes. Bursa ceased to be a leading trading city.

The decline of the eastern trade shifted European interest from Turkey and the Arab provinces to the Balkans. European traders, with the participation of Jewish and Greek intermediaries, distributed imported products to the interior and gathered goods for export. From Salonika, European trade reached Bosnia, Albania, Serbia, and Bulgaria. The English imported luxury cloth; the French, middle-quality cloth. Venice sold silk, satin, and taffeta. The Germans brought paper, tin, iron, copper, sugar, and indigo. European merchants exported wood, cotton, silk, leather, tobacco, beeswax, and hides by sea; cattle went overland from Rumania and Hungary into central Europe. Ordinarily the Ottomans prohibited the export of iron, lead, copper, and grain, but there was an active trade in contraband.

The evidence concerning the impact of this trade on the Ottoman economy in the seventeenth and eighteenth centuries is very scattered, but it seems that some regions suffered while others prospered. The production of Bursa silk cloth and Ankara mohair woolens fell when Europeans began to replace Turkish textiles with their own manufactures. The output of pottery and tiles at Iznik and Kutahya also declined. In Izmir, however, there may have been an increase in cotton production. While there is no proof of a general decline in the Ottoman economy, clearly the balance of trade was shifting. In general, the Ottoman empire was importing manufactured goods and exporting raw materials. Ottomans began to prefer European textiles, glass, clocks, flowers, architectural adornments, and home furnishings.

The declining political effectiveness of the central government and increasing economic weakness meant that it was losing power in the provinces to its own officials. Provincial governors, soldiers, and others seized local power. Judicial and financial administrators gained exceptional importance in the course of the seventeenth century, and transformed fiscal and administrative institutions in their interests. They converted tax farms into life tenures (*malikane*) and ultimately into private properties, usurped revenues, and built up private armies recruited among former janissaries, demobilized soldiers, and bandits. Janissaries serving in the retinue of provincial governors, assigned to garrison small towns, soon formed an exploitative class living off illegal tax revenues. Rival groups of janissaries, irregular soldiers, rebels, and bandits imposed their own illegal taxes.

To regain control, the central government started to rotate provincial governors more frequently, and began to assign provincial governorships to high courtiers in Istanbul. They appointed deputies (*mutesellim*) to administer the provinces on their behalf. Many of these deputies were notables (*aʿyan*) who derived from several strata of society. Some were descendants of slave army officers; some belonged to the families of important ʿulamaʾ; others were tax collectors, owners of large estates, or rich merchants who had the financial resources to buy deputy governorships and build up independent military retinues. Deputy governors also succeeded in the struggle for power by converting their tax farms into life tenures.

During the eighteenth century, councils of aʿyan played a large role in administration. They won control over the appointment of deputy governors and judges, enforced guild regulations, prevented food shortages, and maintained public buildings. By the laws of 1784 the procedures for appointment to councils and deputy governorships were regularized. In 1809 the aʿyan extracted from the Sultan formal recognition of their rights and prerogatives. This was the high point of aʿyan influence and political decentralization, and was followed in the nineteenth century by strong government efforts to reestablish central control over Anatolia.

The rise to power of independent local officials and notables was itself based on still more profound changes in Anatolian society. The growth of Anatolian population in the course of the sixteenth century promoted the growth of provincial towns and intensified the competition for control of revenues. Population growth led to a great surplus of peasant laborers, unemployed soldiers, and students who migrated to the towns looking for work. The end of Ottoman conquests in Hungary and Iran also forced would-be soldiers to return to their villages and towns as unemployed drifters who sought to earn a living as retainers for local notables, students with stipends, or even bandits. Provincial notables built up armies and administrative staffs, developed local markets, and thus retained for local use an increasing part of the provincial surplus. In turn the growth of town populations spurred the exploitation of the peasantry and an endless cycle of fugitivism, banditry, and increasing exploitation.

These political and demographic changes were interwoven with important economic changes. The decentralization of power and the rising influence of local officials contributed to the disruption of the traditional Ottoman economy. In an earlier era, the empire was able to channel the surplus produce of Anatolia to the benefit of the political elite and the populace of Istanbul. The state regulated the merchant classes and forced them to give priority to the provisioning of the capital city markets. In the sixteenth, seventeenth, and eighteenth centuries, new forces conspired to break the state hold on the economy. Independent tax farmers and local officials redirected the agricultural surpluses from the capital to provincial towns and markets controlled by the aᶜyan and their personal armies. Furthermore, increasing European demand for Ottoman products, fueled by the influx of American silver and the inflation of prices, gave local notables, merchants, and estate owners an incentive for avoiding state regulations and exporting surplus produce to Europe. The export of grain, cotton, silk, and other raw materials in turn stimulated inflation in the Ottoman empire. Parts of the Balkans, western Anatolia, and the Adana region went over to cash-crop farming. The combined Istanbul, provincial, and international markets also increased the incentives for provincial notables to convert tax farms into chiftliks or private estates. Commercialization thus reinforced decentralization.

The transformation of political and social power in the Balkans followed similar lines. The authority of the central government declined and the power of local officials correspondingly rose. In the Balkans, as in Anatolia, the janissary corps were corrupted, the rural cavalry evaded central control, and timar administration broke down. Tax farms replaced timars and Ottoman officials acquired lifetime tax-farm tenures and even private estates. In the course of the seventeenth and eighteenth centuries, a new landlord class made up of former Muslim governors and army officers, and rich non-Muslim merchants and other notables emerged. These landlords were aggressively interested in the commercial prospects of their estates. They raised new crops such as maize, rice, and animals for export despite the fact that this was illegal under Ottoman regulations. Increasing European demand for agricultural goods gave every incentive for the appropriation of tax farms and their transformation into private estates. In the Balkans, commercialization also stimulated the growth of towns. Absentee landlords, tax farmers, rich notables, and import–export merchants formed a new urban aristocracy whose wealth was based upon agricultural production and marketing. Janissary-workers and peasant migrants flocked to the towns looking for work. Town populations tended to become less Turkish and to take on the ethnicity of the people living in the surrounding countrysides.

These changes also increased the power of the common people. With the consolidation of private estates, peasants increasingly moved into villages clustered around fortified manor houses. This concentration strengthened local community ties and encouraged the emergence of a stronger peasant leadership. Changing social and economic conditions also led to the rise of banditry among unemployed soldiers and landless peasants. In many parts of the Balkans, the breakdown of Ottoman central authority led to a three-way struggle for power among provincial officeholding and landowning notables, janissaries and artisans, and peasant bandits.

Such massive changes did not occur all at once or once and for all, but evolved over a period of more than 200 years, marked by constant struggle between the central state and provincial elites and by constant changes in the balance of power between them. The seventeenth century was a period of open struggle for power marked by repeated "jelali" rebellions led by lower-ranking military and administrative officers seeking lucrative local positions. The new wave of revolts represented the ambitions of local contenders for power trying to force their way into the Ottoman elite. In the face of these pressures, the Ottoman empire repeatedly suppressed rebellions and attempted to reconsolidate its power. The Koprulu family of viziers attempted a complete reform. Mehmed Koprulu (1656–61), born of an Albanian Christian father, recruited through the devshirme, became a palace servant, then a timar holder in Anatolia, and from time to time held various court positions in Istanbul. When he was eighty years old he was appointed Grand Vizier with a reform mandate. Koprulu confiscated the properties of the chief qadis, and suppressed the religious orders and provincial rebellions. Nonetheless, by the end of the century Anatolia was again in the hands of rebellious local officials.

The first half of the eighteenth century was in general a period of consolidation. The vizierial and chancery services helped maintain effective discipline within the scribal corporation. In many provinces the Ottomans reorganized administration and appointed effective governors. Some semblance of order was also maintained by the self-interest of local officials and landowners, who wished to protect their estates and assure continued production.

By the end of the century, however, almost all of the Ottoman empire was again in the control of independent officials. The Karaosmanoglu dominated southwestern Anatolia, the Chapanoglu the central plateau, and the Pashaoglu the northeast. In the Balkans, ʿAli Pasha of Janina (1788–1822) had a small regional state in northern Albania and Greece; Osman Pasvanoglu (1799–1807) ruled western Bulgaria and parts of Serbia and Rumania. Other Balkan lords occupied eastern Bulgaria and Thrace. In the Arab provinces, as we shall see, the governors of Damascus, Mosul, Baghdad, and Basra were substantially independent. Egypt was governed by the Mamluks. North Africa was autonomous.

The decentralization of power occurred throughout the Ottoman empire, but it had very different implications in the different regions. Though Turkish and Arab society escaped close central government control, the identity of local elites remained bound up with the Ottoman empire and with Islam. The Sultans continued to be recognized as legitimate suzerains, and local officials continued to be Ottomans. Decentralization did not lead to the institutionalization of autonomy.

In the Balkan provinces, however, autonomy was a harbinger of revolutionary change. Balkan peoples, predominantly Christians, never fully assimilated into Ottoman society, began to conceive of national independence. In its heyday, the Ottoman system had won general acceptance, but the breakdown of rural security turned Balkan populations against the empire. Rural lords, peasant bandits and urban merchants released from Ottoman political control turned more and more to Europe. Also, the moral and social controls of the Orthodox church were on the wane. While the church continued to ally itself with the Ottoman regime as a bulwark against European, Latin, and Catholic influences, its influence among its own people was diminishing. Orthodox Slavs were dissatisfied with Greek leadership. Middle-class townsmen began to look westward not only for economic exchange but for intellectual stimulation.

Gradually, as a result of the loosening of traditional social controls, segments of the Balkan mercantile and landowning elites, prospering as exporters and middlemen in the trade with Europe, began to develop a new political consciousness. Advanced elements of the Christian urban middle classes in Greece sponsored secular schools to replace church schools and patronized literary and intellectual movements which fostered secular and nationalist ideas. In the Balkans, social change combined with the breakdown of church authority and increasing contacts with Europe led to a revolution in political consciousness and to the formation of movements for national independence. The decentralization of the Ottoman empire paved the way for the ultimate rejection of Ottoman rule.

While the Ottoman empire was becoming internally decentralized it was also falling behind the rising powers of Europe. For centuries the Ottomans and other Muslim powers had been competing with Europeans on a world-scale. For centuries the Ottomans held the initiative, but in the sixteenth century the Ottomans and the Portuguese in the Indian Ocean, and the Ottomans and the Habsburgs in the Mediterranean, came to a stalemate. In the seventeenth century the immediate threat was Russian expansion. The Russians were moving south across the steppes to the Black and Caspian seas. Though the Ottomans checked the Russian advance by their occupation of Podolia in 1676, Russia, under Peter the Great, with its armies newly modernized, took

Azov in the Crimea in 1696. The Habsburgs seized most of Hungary north of the Danube between 1684 and 1687 and took Serbia in 1689. The Venetians seized Dalmatia and the Morea. Poland invaded Podolia. For the first time the European powers had pushed back the frontiers of the Ottoman empire.

The Ottomans were able to restore their territorial position in the early decades of the eighteenth century. By the peace of Passarowitz in 1718, they regained the Morea. In 1739 the Sava–Danube frontier was restored by the Treaty of Belgrade. The Ottomans further consolidated their position in Rumania by replacing the Hospoders with Phanariot Greek merchants from Istanbul. By the late eighteenth century, however, Russian expansion resumed. Between 1768 and 1774 the Russians occupied Rumania and the Crimea, and by the treaty of Kuchuk Kaynarja (1774) achieved access to the Black Sea. In 1779 they won the right to take tribute from Rumania, though sovereignty was left in Ottoman hands. A new series of wars, culminating in the Peace of Jassy (1792), allowed the Russians to advance to the Dniester, to establish a protectorate over Georgia, and to consolidate their position in the Crimea.

These Russian advances caused consternation in Istanbul, for the Ottomans were forced to recognize their military inferiority and the threat of still further Russian advances. Until the eighteenth century they dealt with European powers as inferiors, and considered treaties concessions by the Ottoman Sultan to the infidels. Now Ottoman treaties were manifestly reciprocal, and often unfavorable arrangements. Military and diplomatic pressure combined with the commercial penetration and provincial decentralization had brought the empire to the nadir of its fortunes. Yet the Ottoman empire maintained its territorial domains, political resiliency, and cultural vitality. From an internal point of view, the decline of the central government and the decentralization of authority may be regarded as a transformation allowing for new political, economic, and cultural departures. From the international point of view, however, these changes can only be seen as a decline of power relative to the growing strength of Europe. Despite its considerable remaining powers, the empire was falling behind its European competitors.

Ottoman historians and court officials gave thoughtful attention to the problems of the regime, and wrote volumes of advice to rulers. Gradually, Ottoman opinion adjusted to the new realities. In the seventeenth century, they saw the issue in terms of a restoration of traditional Ottoman institutions. The *Risale* of Mustafa Kochu Bey, written in 1631, advised the Sultan to return to the direct management of the government, restore the authority of the Grand Vizier, reconstruct the timars, and suppress factions. He warned against the oppression of the peasantry. Katip Chelebi analyzed the decline in terms of the abuse of peasants, the loss of production and revenues, and the flight to the cities, and called for the restoration of just taxation and lawful order. Mustafa Naima (1665–1716), an official historian of the Ottoman court, advised the government to balance its income and expenditures, pay stipends to the military and purge the army of incompetent soldiers.

By the beginning of the eighteenth century, however, there was a reorientation of Ottoman perceptions. The Treaty of Karlowitz (1699), the first time that the Ottomans lost territory to a European power, made it seem no longer adequate to return to the past. European innovations in military technology, economic organization and cultural style had reached the level where they were a direct commercial and territorial threat to the Ottoman empire. For the first time the hitherto victorious empire had to consider the implications of the new situation; the Ottomans cautiously began to import European advisers to implement military reforms. Between 1734 and 1738 de Bonneval taught mathematics and artillery techniques to Ottoman soldiers. In 1773 Baron de Tott provided up-to-date instruction in artillery and naval warfare. An Ottoman printing press was established to print European technical works dealing with military subjects, engineering, geography, and history.

The new political consciousness was expressed in literary style and the emulation of European fashions. Turkish poetry turned to themes of everyday life and adopted a more vernacular language. Turkish proverbs, puns, and jokes became part of the poetry of such writers as Ahmed Nedim (1681–1730). Mehmed Emin Belig (d. 1758) described the life of the artisans, the bazaars, and the baths.

Ottomans also became enamored of European architectural decoration and furniture. Ottoman mosques were decorated in baroque fashion. Summer palaces and water fountains, built on traditional Ottoman architectural lines, were decorated in a French-inspired rococo manner. European painting influenced Ottoman wall paintings which in this period showed battle and hunting scenes, dancing girls, and musical instruments. Ottoman writers reported on French theater and opera, dress and decorations, garden design, and the freer style of relations among the people. The craze for tulips in the reign of Ahmed III (1703–30) has become the emblem of this new sensibility. Ottoman art lost its hieratic quality; the taste for naturalistic and floral design replaced the formality of traditional geometric and Arabesque decoration. These changes indicate a shift from a self-conscious imperial style of culture to a more personal sensibility much in parallel with the evolution of Safavid taste in an era of imperial decline.

Decentralization and the changing international balance of power had mixed implications for the survival of the Ottoman system. In most of the empire, decentralization did not change the classic Ottoman arrangements. The concept of a legitimate state, its importance as the representative of Islam, and its authority as the overlord of local notables in Anatolia and the Arab provinces was unimpaired. The state maintained its dominance over the ʿulamaʾ and the religious establishment despite the increased autonomy of tribal and other corporate groups. In the Balkans, however, European influence enhanced the autonomy of the Christian populations, and gave them new advantages in international trade that paved the way for the ultimate liberation of Balkan populations from Ottoman control.

Nevertheless, while other Muslim regimes succumbed to international pressures, or to European intervention, the Ottomans maintained dynastic continuity. At the end of the pre-modern era Ottoman-Islamic society was still built upon a strong state regime, legitimate in military, patrimonial, and cosmopolitan as well as Muslim terms, a well-organized and subordinate Muslim religious establishment, and an abiding acceptance of the concept of state control over parochial communities. These institutions would powerfully affect the modern development of Islamic societies in Turkey and other parts of the Middle East.

CHAPTER 15

THE ARAB MIDDLE EAST

From our present perspective, the Arab provinces of the Middle East and North Africa form a single cultural and ethnic unit. The region is interconnected by the Arabic language, by ethnic identity and by the shared experience of Ottoman rule from the sixteenth to the nineteenth century. For the sake of narrative convenience, however, we have grouped the history of the Arab world into two successive chapters. In this chapter we shall deal with the history of Egypt and Syria. The following chapter deals with North Africa and Spain. Our account of the Arabian peninsula, which generally stood outside the framework of general Middle Eastern developments, is reserved for Part III.

The history of each region will be divided into three time frames. The first corresponds to the Caliphal phase in the history of the Middle East. This was the period of the Arab conquests, the formation of Muslim regimes in which political and religious authority were combined, and the beginnings of Islam. This period includes the Fatimid Caliphate in Egypt and North Africa, the Umayyad Caliphate in Spain, and the Almoravid and Almohad regimes in Morocco. The second phase or middle period was the era in which the Arab Middle East and North Africa came under the influence of Saljuq institutions, and developed new frameworks for state and religious organization which were variations upon the emerging universal Islamic pattern. This was the period of the Ayyubids and Mamluks in Egypt and Syria, the Hafsids in Tunisia and the Marinids in Morocco. The third phase continues the history of the new institutions in the period of Ottoman domination from the sixteenth to the nineteenth century, and explores the Moroccan variant.

EGYPT AND SYRIA IN THE "CALIPHAL" AGE

Egypt and Syria were among the first Middle Eastern provinces to be absorbed into the Arab-Muslim Caliphate. They were both conquered in 641. Their populations rapidly adopted the Arabic language, though they were slow to accept Islam. Under the Umayyad and early ʿAbbasid Caliphates, Egypt was a subsidiary province of the Muslim empire, but from the middle of the ninth century Egypt showed the first signs of becoming an independent region. Slave soldiers appointed by the ʿAbbasids established short-lived dynasties. The Tulunids ruled Egypt from 868 to 905 and the Ikhshidids from 935 to 969. In 969 the Fatimids conquered the country and established a new Caliphate which lasted until 1171.

The Fatimid dynasty was not merely an independent governorship, but was a revolutionary regime which claimed universal authority. It had its origin in the Ismaʿili movement which had built up an extensive missionary organization and had inspired violent outbursts in Syria, Iraq, Arabia, and North Africa. The Qarmatians in the fertile crescent and Arabia had roused peasant and bedouin opposition around 900. Similarly, the Fatimids incited Kitama Berbers to overthrow the Aghlabid regime of Tunisia in 909, and established a new government based on the claim of ʿUbaydallah to be the living imam. Under the leadership of the Fatimid imams, the Berbers conquered North Africa, Egypt, and parts of Syria. With the shattering of the ʿAbbasid empire, Egypt emerged as a principal center of Arabic civilization.

The Fatimid dynasty (969–1171), like the ʿAbbasid, laid claim to being the true leader of Islam. This claim was advanced in the several vocabularies of Mediterranean civilization. The Fatimids presented an Ismaʿili, a philosophical, a Byzantine, and an ʿAbbasid symbolism of political authority. They proclaimed that they were the true imams, the descendants of ʿAli; thus they broke with the prevailing Shiʿi tradition that the imam was hidden and would return as the messiah. The declaration of a Fatimid imamate required a redefinition of the historic succession of imams and of the eschatological cycles of history. The Fatimids held that they were the continuation of the sixth cycle of imams and that the coming of the messiah and the closure of the historic cycles was postponed to the indefinite future.

Under the auspices of the new theory, neo-Platonic and gnostic concepts were incorporated into Ismaʿili thinking. At the beginning of the tenth century, al-Nasafi, an Ismaʿili missionary in eastern Iran, fused Quranic religious ideas with neo-Platonism to produce a new Ismaʿili cosmology and doctrine. According to this theory, the universe was brought into being by

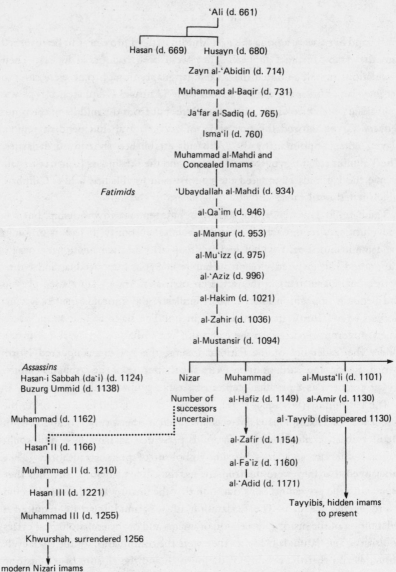

Fig. 7. The Ismaᶜili Imams.

divine emanations in the form of intellectual essences. The imams corresponded to these emanations and were thus the true interpreters, indeed the embodiment, of the revelation. Through the imams the believers would be initiated into spiritual truth; by gnostic illumination they would become the Truth.

The Fatimid concepts of ruler and imperium were also expressed in court ceremony, art, and architecture. Emulating the rival ᶜAbbasid and Byzantine empires, the palace of the ruler was decorated with extraordinary splendor. Gold rafters supported the ceiling; rare birds and animals decorated the walls and the furniture; fountains of cascading water cooled the air. The ruler himself sat on a gold throne protected by a curtain in a fashion inspired by the ᶜAbbasids and resembling Byzantine enthronement. He was entitled to a special crown, sword, scepter, parasol, weapons and other implements that were signs of his sovereignty. Court decorations, some the gift of foreign ambassadors, some of Byzantine manufacture, and some ᶜAbbasid relics, depicted his glory. A huge silk hanging with a map of all the lands of the world and their rulers expressed the Fatimid claim to belong to the family of kings. Fatimid paintings and illuminated manuscripts showed the influence of the ᶜAbbasids' court at Samarra. Fatimid ceramics were decorated with vegetal and animal themes, which were symbols of good luck, and with hunters, musicians, dancers, and human figures who depicted court life. Their intent was to magically recreate the splendor of Fatimid rule.

The court decorations and utensils were housed in royal treasuries, for they were considered not only useful ornamentations but rare and exotic objects reserved for the sole use of the sovereign and the court. In 1067, however, in the course of a civil war, the Fatimid treasury was looted, and royal objects became accessible for imitation. Fatimid ceramics, metalworks, and woodcraft thus inspired an Egyptian craft culture based upon international imperial motifs.

Equally important in the palace symbolism was Islam. The palace contained halls for the teaching of Ismaᶜili beliefs. Judges, missionaries, reciters of the Quran, and prayer leaders were regularly present for court ceremonies. Formal religious processions symbolized the sublime importance of the monarchy. Audiences with the Caliph, reviews of the soldiers, receptions of ambassadors, Ramadan and New Year processions, and formal openings of the Nile canals brought the Caliph and his entourage to the mosques of the city where he delivered the sermon, celebrated the festivals and displayed the magnificent and sacred objects of the Fatimid treasury. Thus the Caliph brought home to the populace the importance of the ruler both in the spheres of war and politics and in those of religion, nature, and magic.

The public architecture of the Fatimids was an extension of the ceremonial aspect of the royal court. The new Fatimid capital city, al-Qahira, Cairo, founded in 969, with its magnificent palaces and grand mosques, was an imperial city designed for imperial pageants. The principal mosques – al-

Azhar and al-Hakim – were constructed with minarets and cupolas which symbolized the preeminence of the imam and recalled the holy places of Mecca and Medina as a way of glorifying the ruler in the service of God and Islam.

The Fatimids further cultivated religious glory by sponsoring the cult of the family of ʿAli; the cult of the living imam was replaced by the cult of the deceased family of the Prophet. The Fatimids constructed numerous mausolea over the supposed graves of the family of ʿAli in order to encourage pilgrimage and to inculcate a popular enthusiasm for shrines and relics. Quranic inscriptions encouraged obedience to the imam and called upon people to accept his authority as an expression of God's will. In 1153 the head of the martyr Husayn was moved from Ascalon, and a new mausoleum, Sayyidna al-Husayn, was constructed to house it. Pilgrims circumambulated the tomb, kissed his final resting place, wept, and begged the favor of the imam. The graves of Caliphs were also considered holy, but they were buried in the palace precincts and could be venerated only by court personnel. These constructions introduced artistic motifs, such as the muqarnas or stalactite decoration, facades with decorated gates and minarets, and the use of figural representation, which would become staple features of later Islamic art.

In their secular aspect the Fatimids were simply a conquest regime based on Berber tribal forces and Turkish and Sudanese slave regiments. They controlled Eygpt by means of an efficient administration inherited from the ʿAbbasids, staffed by Jewish and Christian officials. While the new regime made Ismaʿilism the state religion, it made no effort to change the allegiances of the Egyptian population. The Muslim population of Egypt remained predominantly Sunni.

The rhythm of Fatimid history was similar to that of the ʿAbbasids. The period from 969 to 1021 was one of political and religious consolidation. The second phase from 1021 to 1073 saw a breakdown of political order, warfare between military factions, and the division of the country into iqtaʿs, controlled by the leading military officers. This decline was arrested by the administration of Badr al-Jamali and his son, al-Afdal, from 1073 to 1121, in which the military chiefs replaced the Caliphs as the effective heads of government.

The internal decline of the Fatimid Caliphate accentuated the contradiction between its revolutionary pretensions and the actualities of its Egyptian political base. The decline of Caliphal authority led to schisms as the missionary, messianic, eschatological, and politically radical branches of the Ismaʿili movement split off. Ismaʿilis again divided over the historic identity of the true imam. In the Lebanon was founded the Druze sect which believed that the Caliph al-Hakim (d. 1021) was the last imam and was indeed God himself. At the death of the Caliph al-Mustansir in 1036, his son al-Mustaᶜli succeeded him, but the missionary movement in Syria, Mesopotamia, and Iran, cut off from the Fatimids in Egypt, broke with the parent regime, recognized al-Mustansir's son Nizar as the true imam, and founded a new branch of Ismaᶜilism. The Nizari Ismaᶜilis later came to be known as the Assassins. They would carry on the Ismaᶜili challenge to Sunni Islam.

While the Fatimids ruled Egypt, Syria, a province characterized by numerous ecological and political zones – coastal, mountain, town, and desert – and exposed to multiple influences from Anatolia, the Mediterranean, Egypt, and Iraq, was divided into numerous small states. The Fatimids established their authority in southern Syria and took control of Damascus from 978 to 1076. Northern Syria, after a brief interlude of Hamdanid, Buwayhid, and Byzantine warfare, came under Byzantine control from 968 to 1086. The balance of power between the Byzantine and Fatimid empires allowed for a proliferation of bedouin principalities in Mesopotamia and northern Syria under the aegis of the ᶜUqaylid (990–1096), Marwanid (983–1085) and Mirdasid (1023–79) dynasties. Southern Syria was in the hands of Kalb tribes. Towns such as Tripoli became independent city-states. Mountain populations in the Lebanon preserved their autonomy. In this fragmented condition, Syria was overrun by the Saljuqs. The Saljuqs conquered Damascus in 1079, and took Antioch and Aleppo in 1085. Syria was then divided between two Saljuq succession regimes, one based in Aleppo and one based in Damascus.

Syria was then exposed to yet another wave of invasions, this time by western, Latin Crusaders. The Crusades had their origin in a general European counter-attack against Muslim powers in the Mediterranean. Italian towns were pushing back Muslim pirates. The reconquista had begun in Spain; by 1085 Toledo was in Christian hands. In 1087 Pisa and Genoa destroyed Mahdia, the political and commercial capital of Muslim North Africa. The Normans conquered Sicily between 1061 and 1091 and moved on to attack the Byzantine empire. Furthermore, the papacy was eager to reconcile the Greek and western churches, and to support the Byzantine empire against the Saljuq Turks. It was eager to establish new states under its auspices in the eastern Mediterranean in order to spread the influence of the Latin church among eastern Christian peoples.

Alongside the political currents ran a strong passion for pilgrimage. Eleventh-century Christian feeling stressed the importance of penance and the quest for remission of sins. Jerusalem, the heavenly city, symbolized salvation.

Map 13. Egypt and Syria, showing the crusader states in the twelfth century.

Thus the Saljuq invasions raised European anxieties about access to Jerusalem and generated a passionate desire to secure the holy city in Christian hands.

These trends came together in 1096 in the visit of Pope Urban II to France. Speaking to an audience of restive warriors at Claremont, conscious of papal policy needs, and influenced by the passionate pilgrimage sensibility, Urban broached the idea of an armed pilgrimage to capture the holy places from the infidels. To those who would undertake this mission, Urban offered protection of property at home, new lands in the east, plenary indulgences, and the total remission of all temporal punishments which might be imposed by the church for the commission of past sins. His audience probably heard this as a promise of absolution from sin and of salvation.

By sea and by land European warriors set out for the east. Between 1099 and 1109 they captured Edessa, Antioch, and Tripoli, and established the Latin Kingdom of Jerusalem. Baldwin was elected King, ruling as a feudal lord with the support of the Knights Templars and Hospitalers. Latin clergy took control of Christian administration in the holy land, but the eastern Christian sects were not eliminated.

The Muslim response to the Crusades was slow to develop, but when it did it led eventually to the unification of Syria and Egypt into a single Muslim state. The first Muslim reaction was, by and large, indifference. Syria was so fragmented as to preclude any unified opposition to the intruders; several more little states among many did not much disturb existing interests. The fact that these new states were Christian was not exceptional – the Byzantines had also ruled northern Syria, and there was a substantial, if not a majority, local Christian population.

Gradually, however, a Muslim counter-attack developed which may be described in three phases. From 1099 to 1146 was the phase of Mesopotamian leadership. The Saljuqid Atabegs of Mosul, who had nominal authority over Syria, wished to create their own small empire. Between 1109 and 1113, Mawdud campaigned in Syria, but lacking disciplined troops and meeting local Muslim, as well as Christian, resistance, he was unable to make his power effective. Only in 1128 did a new governor of Mosul, Zengi (*c.* 1127–46) seize Aleppo, and thus command a Syrian base for his goal of establishing a consolidated Muslim state in Mesopotamia and northern Syria. In 1144 he managed by chance to capture Edessa, which substantially weakened the Crusader presence and consolidated Zengi's communications between Mosul and Aleppo. When Zengi died in 1146, however, Mosul and Aleppo were severed from each other to make independent principalities for his surviving sons. Throughout this period, the Mosul campaigns were not primarily directed against the Crusaders, but were aimed at winning territory from either Muslim or Christian rulers whenever possible. There was little consciousness of Muslim–Christian antagonism per se. In fact, Christian and Muslim princelings often allied to resist Zengi's encroachments.

A second phase began with the succession of Nur al-Din (*c.* 1146–74), the son of Zengi, who inherited Aleppo. Nur al-Din made the capture of Damascus his main goal. In 1147, he helped relieve the siege of Damascus by the second Crusade. In 1154, a local rebellion expelled the ruling Saljuqid governors, and the populace of the city turned it over to him. This unexpected turn of events reveals the underground growth of a new Muslim communal and religious spirit, frankly anti-Christian and opposed to the Crusader presence.

By this time the Crusades had activated a latent Muslim veneration for Jerusalem. The Dome of the Rock had been built in Jerusalem by the Umayyad Caliphs to symbolize the Muslim appropriation of the sacred past of Judaism and Christianity. In the course of the eighth, ninth, and tenth centuries Jerusalem assumed a place in Muslim religious lore. Jewish and Christian ideas about Jerusalem were assimilated into Islamic teachings. Jerusalem, according to these views, was an axis of communication between this world and the next. It became venerable to Muslims as part of their own prophetic history because Muhammad was believed to have ascended to heaven from Jerusalem. These Muslim sensibilities were awakened by a literary and religious campaign, led by refugees, about the religious merit of Jerusalem and the importance of jihad. By the middle of the twelfth century this sentiment had become a popular force, and this helps to account for the surrender of Damascus to Nur al-Din. Nur al-Din, who opposed the Crusaders, symbolized the Muslim prince who would redeem Jerusalem.

In fact, the reign of Nur al-Din in Damascus from 1154 to 1174 did not concentrate upon the redemption of Jerusalem but upon the consolidation of his little kingdom in Syria. Nur al-Din made treaties with the Byzantines and the Latins, and concentrated upon the conquest of Mosul, which he took in 1170, thus fulfilling a family ambition to reunite Syria and Mesopotamia; he also entered into the struggle for control of Egypt. With the Fatimid regime in total disarray, and Amalric, the Latin king of Jerusalem, maneuvering to seize the country, Nur al-Din sent his General Shirkuh and Shirkuh's nephew Salah al-Din (Saladin) with Muslim forces to take control of Egypt in 1169. In 1171 they removed the last of the Fatimid Caliphs, and established a Sunni regime. Now the history of Egypt and Syria would be joined until the nineteenth century.

The advent of Saladin to the Sultanate of Egypt opened a third phase of the Muslim response to the Crusades. From Egypt, Saladin brought Syria and Mesopotamia into a unified Muslim state. In 1174 he took Damascus; in 1183, Aleppo; in 1186, Mosul. On the basis of this newly unified state, Saladin defeated the Crusaders at the battle of Hattin (1187) and brought an end to the Latin occupation of Jerusalem. At the siege of Acre (1192), however, Saladin made a truce with Richard the Lion-Heart which allowed the crusading principalities to maintain their foothold on the coasts of Palestine and Syria.

THE SALJUQ MODEL: STATE AND RELIGION

The conquest of Syria and then of Egypt by Turkish (and Kurdish) warriors and the establishment of Saljuqid regimes began a new era in the history of these regions. The Saljuqid era put an end to the legacy of Caliphal institutions and concepts, and introduced in the former western provinces of the ʿAbbasid empire the system of state and religious organization which was being worked out in the eastern provinces. Under Nur al-Din, the system of state patronage for Muslim legal scholarship that had been developed in the eastern Saljuq empire was transferred to Damascus. Under his patronage new colleges of law were founded in Damascus and endowed with permanent funds. Stimulated by scholars from Iran and Spain they re-created the tradition of legal learning already developed in other parts of the Muslim world. The influx of Hanafi and Shafiʿi scholars integrated the Syrian provinces into what was becoming the prevalent system of education in the Middle East.

The conquest of Egypt by Saladin in 1171 opened the way for the installation of the Sunni schools in Egypt. The Shafiʿi school had survived under Fatimid rule, but Saladin introduced the Hanafi school, endowed colleges of law, and recruited prominent teachers and judges from abroad. By the early thirteenth century state policy in Egypt also tried to promote a shared Sunni religious identity. The Dar al-Hadith al-Kamiliya was founded in 1222 to teach the points of law which were held in common among the schools. The madrasa al-Salihiya was founded in 1239 to house all four schools of law in the same building. The Ayyubid government in Egypt thus adopted a pan-Sunni policy of equal recognition and equal sponsorship of all schools of law.

Similarly, the Saljuq sponsorship of khanaqas and ribats helped spread these institutions from eastern Iran to Baghdad and to the western Arab provinces. The first Syrian khanaqa was built in Aleppo in 1115. Nur al-Din established the institution in Damascus after 1154. The conquest of Egypt by Saladin led to the founding of a khanaqa in 1173 as a hostel for foreign Sufis, but it was not intended for any particular brotherhood. Another khanaqa was founded by Saladin in Jerusalem in 1189.

Upon Saladin's death in 1193, his family, the Ayyubid house, succeeded to the rule of Egypt (to 1250) and Syria (to 1260). The family divided his empire into the smaller kingdoms of Egypt, Damascus, Aleppo, and Mosul in accord with the Saljuq idea that the state was the patrimony of the royal family. Though the state was divided among the leading members of the Ayyubid family, the Ayyubids did not revert to the fragmentation of earlier regimes. The Sultan of Egypt usually managed to assert his suzerainty over the rest of the family and to make use of family loyalties to integrate the regime. The Ayyubids ruled Egypt and Syria through a military aristocracy composed of Kurdish and Turkish troops and some slave forces. They administered Egypt by the age-old bureaucratic system which prevailed in that country, and Syria by the distribution of iqtaᶜs to the leading military officers.

The Ayyubids were notably reluctant to continue the struggle against the remaining Crusader principalities. Having achieved a tenuous unity, and a prosperous Mediterranean trade between Syria and Egypt and the ports of Italy and Europe, the Ayyubids drew back from the struggle for Palestine, and gave priority to the protection of Egypt. Having realized that Egypt was the key to the recovery of the Holy Land, the Christians attacked it in 1197, 1217, 1229, and 1249. In 1217, to divert the Crusaders from Egypt, al-Kamil (1218–38) offered concessions in Palestine. In 1229, the Ayyubids negotiated a treaty with Frederick II agreeing to return Jerusalem to Christian hands on the condition that the city should not be fortified and that the temple area should remain open to Muslim pilgrims. Thus the Ayyubids gave preference to political and economic over religious and symbolic considerations. However deep Muslim anti-Christian sentiment might be, its effective expression still required that religious feeling correspond to the interests of the political elite.

In 1250 the Ayyubid house was overthrown by a rebellion of one of its Mamluk or slave regiments, which killed the last Ayyubid ruler of Egypt and named one of its own officers, Aybeg, to be the new Sultan. The Mamluks defended Syria against the Mongols at the battle of ᶜAyn Jalut in 1260, crushed the last of the independent Syrian principalities, expelled the remaining Crusader states by 1291, and expanded the boundaries of their empire into the upper Euphrates valley and Armenia. Thus they were able to unify Egypt and Syria until the Ottoman conquest in 1517. This was the longest-lived Muslim state in the Middle East between the ᶜAbbasid and the Ottoman empires.

The Mamluk era was noted for the perfection of the post-ᶜAbbasid slave-military system. Before the Mamluk period, slave regiments had been employed in all Middle Eastern armies, but the Mamluks were the first Middle Eastern regime to be based entirely on the slave-military machine. The elite personnel of the regime, including the Sultan, were slaves or former slaves. In principle, though there were important exceptions, no one could be a member of the military elite unless he was of foreign origin, usually Turkish or Circassian, purchased and raised as a slave, and trained to be a soldier and administrator. No native of Egypt or Syria could ever belong to this elite, nor, in principle, could the sons of slaves and rulers. The raison d'être of this arrangement was that every man who served the regime belonged entirely to the state and was without any family or local ties to compromise his total dedication to his master and to the service of the military caste.

Mamluks were purchased from abroad at the age of ten or twelve, were converted to Islam and raised in barracks, where they not only learned military technique but were imbued with loyalty to their masters and to their comrades-in-arms. Upon graduating from the barracks schools, the fully trained Mamluks served either in the Sultan's Mamluk regiment, or as soldiers in the service of other leading officers. The officers possessed their own personal slaves, apart from the regiments of the Sultan. A Mamluk army, then, may be imagined as a grouping of slave regiments, made up of the Sultan's troops and of the regiments loyal to individual officers, who were in turn personally loyal to the Sultan. This army was not organized so much by hierarchy of rank as by personal allegiance.

To support the military elite, the bureaucratic tradition of Egypt and the iqtaᶜs of Syria were combined. The tax revenues of Egypt and Syria were assigned to pay the salaries of the Sultan and the Mamluk officers. In Egypt the amirs were assigned iqtaᶜ revenues, but the central bureaucracy kept close control over taxation. The bureaucracy made surveys to determine the available resources and to prevent the Mamluks from acquiring excessive revenues or other rights in the countryside. The iqtaᶜ parcels were frequently redistributed and every effort was made to keep Mamluks from acquiring governmental authority over their iqtaᶜs. With the decline of the Mamluk state in the late fourteenth century, central controls were less effective.

The need to legitimize the military regime led to a program of imperial and court ceremony and cultural patronage designed to glorify the rulers. The presence at court of the Caliph and the chief judges, the guardianship of the annual pilgrimage caravan to the holy places of Mecca and Medina, the formal presence of the Sultan in the Hall of Justice, and the celebration of Islamic religious feasts emphasized the religious importance of the regime. The magical as well as the religious aspects of royal power were also celebrated. The ruler was revered as someone who had in his control the powers of the cosmos. A good ruler could bring rain and abundant harvests; a bad ruler could bring ruin. The tomb of al-Mansur Qalaᵓun (1280–90) copied features of the Dome of the Rock in Jerusalem to signify the Mamluk pretension to be heirs to the glory of the first Islamic dynasty. In a similar spirit the royal libraries were provided with copies of Persian illuminated manuscripts telling of the conquests of Alexander the Great and the history of Persian kings. Late Mamluk era culture was rich in Persian and Ottoman influences. The cosmopolitan heritage of Mamluk Egypt was also reinforced by the migration of Iranian, Turkish, Spanish, and Mesopotamian craftsmen and scholars, who brought with them metalwork, textile, ceramic, and building crafts, which were adopted by the Mamluks to adorn the life of the court and the military aristocracy.

The religious and the cosmopolitan aspects of Mamluk court culture were tempered by a parochial ethnic and military emphasis. The Mamluk court listened to Turkish and Circassian poetry. The Mamluks also reveled in military reviews, tournaments, and displays of martial arts. They thus attempted to legitimize themselves by emphasizing their right to rule by virtue of military conquest, by cosmopolitan affiliation to Middle Eastern and ancient rulers, and by service to Islam. In the course of this effort to legitimize themselves, the Mamluks left a distinctive Egyptian-Islamic artistic legacy.

The Ayyubids and the Mamluks also continued the Saljuq policy of strong state support for and control of Islam. The decisive force behind Ayyubid and Mamluk era Egyptian culture was the commitment of the state to Sunni rather than Shiᶜi Islam. The early Mamluk period was dominated by intense Muslim religious feeling expressed in warfare against the Crusaders, the Mongols, and the Ismaᶜilis, and hostility to Christians and Jews, coupled with pressures for the conversion of non-Muslims to Islam. In addition, both the Ayyubids and the Mamluks sponsored a revival of Sunni Islamic religious activity. In the Ayyubid period (1193–1260) there were no fewer than 255 religious structures built in Damascus. This was followed by an equally intense period of construction in the first century of Mamluk rule, at the instance of governors, generals, judges, and rich merchants. The Ayyubids and Mamluks also followed Fatimid precedents by constructing tombs for venerated Muslim ancestors and for deceased rulers. One of the first Ayyubid projects was the construction of a madrasa near the grave of al-Shafiᶜi, the founder of the principal Egyptian school of law. Colleges and khanaqas came to be provided

13 The minarets of al-Azhar, Cairo

with a mausoleum for the remains of their founders. A tomb advertised the sanctity of the ruler, and his devotion to Islam.

A characteristic architectural design emerged for the religious architecture of this period. Mosques, madrasas, and khanaqas were often built with an open central courtyard surrounded by four galleries or *liwans* on the principal sides of the courtyard, with the intervening spaces filled in with rooms for students. The mausoleum itself was often topped by a dome and the whole structure provided with tall slender minarets. Such buildings, clustered along main streets or in the cemeteries, created a vast visual display, shaped the physical fabric of the city, and symbolized the integral relation of the state, Islam, and the urban society. With strong state support the schools of law became the foci for the spread of Islamic teaching among the common people. In Damascus, lawyers issued legal advice, preachers exhorted the general populace, and religious manuals instructed the people on the practical application of Muslim teachings.

Moreover, in Syria and Egypt, the Saljuq succession states converted the routine patronage of the ʿulamaʾ and Sufis into a system of state control. Nur al-Din selected the appointees to judicial and teaching offices and created a supervisory post for the administration of Sufi khanaqas. He pioneered a policy of making the ʿulamaʾ and Sufis directly dependent upon state patronage and state appointments. Saladin further developed the system of state control. He appointed a chief qadi and a chief shaykh for the Sufis. In 1263, Sultan Baybars (1260–77) adopted the policy of appointing a head qadi for each of the four major schools of law, a chief shaykh for the Sufis, and a syndic for the corporation of descendants of the Prophet (naqib al-ashraf). Under the Mamluks the state appointed judges, legal administrators, professors, Sufi shaykhs, prayer leaders, and other Muslim officials. They paid the salaries of religious personnel, endowed their school and thus brought the religious establishment into a state bureaucracy. Never did the state attempt to define the content of religious teaching. Thus, the Mamluks extended the Saljuq-Iranian pattern of organized religious life to Syria and Egypt, and created a standard form of Islamic religious teaching and organization throughout the Middle East. Owing to this strong support for Islam, Mamluk royal culture emphasized its Islamic rather than its cosmopolitan bases. It was thus typical of the tendency in the Arab provinces to legitimize states in Muslim rather than universalist terms.

THE OTTOMAN ERA

The Ottoman conquest of Egypt in 1517 perpetuated, with some modifications, the ongoing system of society. In many respects Egypt remained a separate political society. The Ottomans garrisoned Egypt with several corps of janissaries, once again centralized administration, and appointed military governors, inspectors, and finance officers to assure the collection of taxes and the remittance of the surpluses to Istanbul. The main functions of Ottoman administration were to pacify the country, protect agriculture, irrigation, and trade, control the bedouins, and thus assure the flow of tax revenues. In the course of the first century and a half of Ottoman rule, the irrigation system of Egypt was rebuilt, cultivation increased, and trade restored by reopening the routes between India and Egypt. Egypt was also important to Ottoman control of the Red Sea, the holy places in Arabia, Yemen, Nubia, and Abyssinia.

Beneath the top level of Ottoman administration, however, the old institutional structure remained intact. The local Mamluk households, built around a leading officer and their freedmen, secretaries, and clients, continued to be militarily important and were assigned taxable estates. The religious establishment remained a highly organized and important political and social force. While the Ottomans appointed a chief qadi and a chief syndic for the corporation of descendants of the Prophet from Istanbul, the rest of the ʿulamaʾ establishment was of local origin. The ʿulamaʾ were organized into the several schools of law, holy lineages, and tariqat. The muftis of the law schools, the chiefs of the holy lineages, and the rector of al-Azhar were the principal leaders of the religious establishment, and were responsible for the discipline of their followers. They managed the waqf revenues and, in the eighteenth century, the tax farms assigned for their personal upkeep and the maintenance of the religious function of their schools and fraternities.

Beginning in the fifteenth century, there were important changes in the character of Egyptian religious life. While in the early Mamluk period the schools of law and the madrasas had been the most important expression of Sunni Islam, now Sufism became increasingly important. The Khalwatiya, Shadhiliya, Ahmadiya, and other brotherhoods were organized under centralized leadership, and endowed with substantial properties. They were held in reverence by the military elites and the common people alike, and played a central role in the ceremonial and religious life of Egypt. The mawlids or birthdays of the Prophet and of famous Sufi saints were occasions for immense celebrations in which many thousands of people participated. Visits to the tombs or shrines of saints became a routine part of Egyptian religious life.

In Egypt, as in many other parts of the Muslim world, the consolidation of Sufism and shrine worship also precipitated a religious reaction. The influence of reformist circles in Mecca and Medina and of reformist Sufi orders made itself felt throughout the Ottoman empire in the eighteenth century. In Istanbul and Syria, the Naqshbandis and other reform-minded scholars opposed the shrine forms of Sufism and called for a restoration of Quran and hadith as the sole bases of Muslim religious practice. In Egypt, too, reform influences made themselves felt at al-Azhar, where hadith studies were revived. The Naqshbandis and the Khalwatis reinforced the trend. It is possible that reformism was especially appealing to, or indeed the expression of, the more scholarly, ethical, and puritanical spirit of merchant-ʿulamaʾ milieus with their wider range of commercial and intellectual contacts and their need for a more universal form of Islam as opposed to the parochial and localized forms of saint worship. In the late eighteenth century, Egypt seems to have maintained a variety of religious styles, including Shariʿa, Sufi-Shariʿa, shrine-Sufi, and reformist types of Islam.

Throughout this period, the ʿulamaʾ and the Sufi leaders also played an important political and social role. They were the intermediaries between the Mamluk elites and the common people. On the one hand, higher-ranking ʿulamaʾ were often the clients of Mamluk regiments from whom they received waqfs, gifts, salaries, and fees for teaching and religious services. In the eighteenth century these ties enabled the leading ʿulamaʾ to become extremely prosperous from the management of waqfs, control of tax farms (*iltizams*), and other incomes. They served the Mamluks as negotiators and mediators in disputes among the factions, acted as bankers and tax collectors, and communicated the demands of the regime to the common people. On the other hand the ʿulamaʾ were also closely connected to the commoners. They married into merchant families, commonly invested in trade and real estate, managed schools, hospitals, and charities, and served as patrons for the people of their quarters. A leading scholar or Sufi would arbitrate local disputes, feed the poor, and protect his people from abuse by the soldiers and the tax collectors. He could either organize or calm local resistance. Thus, in Egypt, the ʿulamaʾ and Sufis played a critical role as intermediaries in the functioning of their society.

The relations of Ottoman suzerains, Mamluk regiments, and ʿulamaʾ–Sufi intermediaries were considerably altered in the seventeenth and eighteenth centuries. As in many other parts of the Ottoman empire, the governors declined, the Mamluks gained control over military expenditures, appropriated tax farms, which they gradually converted into lifetime tenures, and seized control of waqf endowments. Once in power, the Mamluk households divided into factions. In the seventeenth and eighteenth centuries the Qasimiya and the Faqariya fought for political power. While the dominant faction controlled Cairo, the defeated faction usually retired to Upper Egypt, where it bided its time until it had another chance to return to the capital. Factional fighting ended in the late eighteenth century in the despotism of ʿAli Bey. Mamluk factionalism also enhanced the role of the religious leaders. As intermediaries, they became all the more important and all the more wealthy. By the end of the eighteenth century the ʿulamaʾ had reached the apogee of their political influence. In 1786–7 the Ottomans, however, finally defeated the Mamluk factions and restored central government control.

The late eighteenth century in Egypt was thus a period of violent warfare, exploitative taxation, decline of irrigation, and rising bedouin power. It was also a period of economic hardship due to inflation and decline in commerce. In the sixteenth and seventeenth centuries Egypt lost some of its trade to Portuguese and then Dutch competition, but gained partial compensations from the coffee trade with Yemen. The eighteenth century, however, brought more severe European competition. European textiles, ceramics, and glass beat down Egyptian industries. Even coffee was imported into the Ottoman empire from the Antilles. By the end of the eighteenth century, Egypt's economy had become vulnerable to European commercial and political pressure.

In the fertile crescent, the Ottomans also took over and perpetuated the organized political society of the region. Unlike Egypt, which was a single province, the Ottomans ruled this region through the major towns such as Damascus, Aleppo, Mosul, and Baghdad, which formed the territorial base for several Ottoman governorships. Ottoman administration had very limited means for centralizing political power. The primary concern in Istanbul was to make it difficult for its own appointees to defy central authority. Thus, the Ottomans aimed at the minimum of governmental power needed to prevent officials from becoming independent and still allow them to maintain order, collect taxes, and remit the surplus to Istanbul. Political authority was divided among military governors and independent civil and judicial officials. The army was divided into numerous units including regiments of janissaries and cavalry sent from Istanbul, the governor's private retainers, and local janissaries. Bedouin tribes served as auxiliary military units. The weakness of the state apparatus made it necessary to depend upon local notables, such as janissaries, office-holders, and religious functionaries. Their power was based upon control of taxation and waqfs, and upon the support they could rally from town quarters, artisan guilds, and local soldiers. In any case, control of the towns did not necessarily mean control of the countrysides. Bedouins, especially in southern Iraq and along the Syrian margins of the north Arabian desert, and hill peoples in Kurdistan, northern Syria, and the Lebanon, maintained freedom from central control.

The notables differed in composition from city to city. In Damascus the ʿulamaʾ were particularly important. Throughout the period of Ottoman rule a relatively small group of notable families controlled the posts of qadi, preacher, mufti, and teachers in the colleges and constituted a religious patriarchate. The leading families continued to be organized primarily through the schools of law. While Sufism was well established in Syria, it does not seem to have played so large a role as in Egypt. The ʿulamaʾ–Sufi synthesis was less complete and the Syrian ʿulamaʾ tended to be hostile to the less "orthodox" forms of Sufism. Sufi brotherhoods, khanaqas, shrines, and mawlids also seem to have had a smaller place in Syrian religious life. The major exception to this was the veneration of the shrine of Ibn al-ʿArabi in Damascus.

Throughout the sixteenth century the Ottomans maintained a dominant position, but by the end of the century the Ottoman position deteriorated. Janissary units, aggrieved by the declining value of their salaries, rebelled against the central government, seized tax farms, and turned them into life-tenure farms or private estates. Janissaries enrolled their children in the army corps and purchased their own slaves. To resist this loss of power, Ottoman governors were reduced to manipulating the competing military factions. Then, in the first half of the eighteenth century, the Ottomans regained control of Damascus and Syria. In 1708 the newly appointed governor of Damascus was relieved of military duties in other parts of the empire, was given direct authority over other administrative subdistricts of Syria, and was charged with responsibility for the organization and security of the pilgrimage. These positions had hitherto been assigned to other officials. His job was to maintain the goodwill of the urban notables, and to curb the bedouins by offering them bribes and offices, and by progressively sedentarizing the nomadic populations. For a period of some fifty years Ottoman rule in Syria was well consolidated, but after 1758 the central government was defeated by local forces and lost its grip on the province. In the latter part of the eighteenth century, the Ottomans could no longer control the notables or protect the pilgrimage.

In Syria and other parts of the fertile crescent, local centres of power were consolidated. Local governors established stable dynasties. The ʿAzm family ruled Damascus from 1724 to 1780; the heirs of Hasan Pasha governed Baghdad and Basra from 1704 until the 1830s; the Jalili family governed

Mosul from 1726 to 1834. In Palestine and the Lebanon, there were several small-scale regimes. Zahir al-ᶜUmar took control of Acre in 1750 and established a local despotism based on efficient economic management. He encouraged the production of cash crops, established monopolies over production and foreign trade, and wooed European advisers. This short-lived regime ended in 1775, when the territory reverted to the governorship of Damascus. After 1780, Ahmad al-Jazzar succeeded to the control of Acre and Sidon and also built up a personal domain based on a strong army, economic monopolies, and a lively European trade. This new type of despotism foreshadowed the nineteenth-century reform movement in Turkey and Egypt which led to a recentralization of power and to efficient government controls over the local economy.

While local governors continued to control the towns and the grain-producing countrysides, they often lost control of rural areas. In Palestine, though the Ottomans continued to control Jerusalem, the coastal ports and the revenue-producing districts of the north, they gave up many other parts of the country. As the regular administration declined, janissaries and other notables acquired control of tax farms and avoided military service. Bedouins began to evade their service obligations and prey on the sedentary population, and struggles between the Qays and Yemen factions grew more virulent.

The Lebanon posed special problems for Ottoman authority. In the north and in the Kisrawan region lived the Maronites. They had been Monothelite Christians until the period of the Crusades, when they accepted Catholic doctrine and Papal supremacy. Turkish Muslims also inhabited the north, but in the Gharb and the Shuf the population was largely Druze. Though the Lebanese peasants were affiliated with the religious communities, the local political order was not based on religion, but on allegiance to village and valley chiefs who were subordinate to feudal suzerains, in turn subordinate to the governor of Damascus and the Sultan in Istanbul. This hierarchy of authority was at best unstable and subject to fluctuations in the balance of central and local power. Between 1544 and 1697 the Maᶜn family was the most powerful. The great ruler of this era, Fakhr al-Din (1603–35), governed by means of a Maronite and Druze peasant coalition. Under him, the Maᶜn family expanded into northern Palestine. In 1697 the Maᶜn were succeeded by the Shihabi, who ruled from 1697 to 1840.

In other parts of the fertile crescent, Ottoman power was subverted by bedouin opposition. The parts of Syria east of Hama and Hims were occupied by the Arab bedouins, who threatened agricultural settlement and the security of the pilgrimage route. Turkmen and Kurdish tribes occupied the regions north of Damascus. The northern Euphrates region was taken over by the ʿAnaza confederation and the southern reaches of the river were occupied by the Shamar.

Thus, Egypt and the fertile crescent societies were governed by an Ottoman elite with the cooperation of local intermediaries. In Egypt, these were Mamluk households and ʿulamaʾ. In the fertile crescent, they were local janissaries, officials, ʿulamaʾ and mountain and bedouin chieftains. In the late eighteenth century, the balance of power between the central state and the provinces, and even between provincial capitals and their hinterlands, shifted in favor of the latter. Almost every local political body – Mamluk or janissary households, ʿulamaʾ, officeholders, tax farmers, guildsmen, town quarters, bedouin tribes, and mountain communities – managed to increase its autonomy. Still the basic institutional structures of these societies and the historic system of ever-changing balances of power among state military, religious, and parochial elites continued to function.

On the horizon, however, the clouds of new forms of highly centralized state regimes and of European commercial and political penetration were already visible. The whole structure of Muslim supremacy was being threatened by European trade and by the rising influence of Greek, Armenian, Maronite, and other Christian merchants who prospered under the protection of foreign powers while Muslim communities were in disarray. The decentralization of the late eighteenth century made it impossible to crystallize a regional political identity, or to protect the Muslims against the competition of local and foreign Christians. This political disarray would also make it extremely difficult, as we shall see, to form stable national states in the twentieth century.

CHAPTER 16

ISLAMIC NORTH AFRICA AND SPAIN TO THE NINETEENTH CENTURY

Islamic civilizations in North Africa and Spain were initiated by the Arab conquests in the seventh and eighth centuries. Between the conquests and the middle of the thirteenth century, the history of these regions paralleled the Caliphal phase in Middle Eastern development and were provincial variants of the Middle Eastern type of early Islamic civilization. In the twelfth and thirteenth centuries the Muslim states of North Africa began to take on an institutional configuration resembling that of the Saljuq empire in Iraq and Iran and the Mamluk empire of Egypt and Syria. In the sixteenth century, most of North Africa (with the exception of Morocco), like the Arab states of the Middle East, came under Ottoman dominion which extended Ottoman institutions to Algeria and helped consolidate the North African forms of Islamic societies. In the eighteenth and nineteenth centuries, these societies were undermined by European economic competition and brought under colonial rule.

STATE FORMATION IN THE "CALIPHAL" PHASE

Arab-Islamic civilization in North Africa was based on the integration of Arab conquerors with Berber peoples and Mediterranean cities. The Berbers, known under the names of Masmuda, Sanhaja, and Zenata, were a diverse population including camel-herding nomads, pastoralists, and peasants. While they shared a common culture, they had rarely, if ever, formed state regimes. The North African towns were the outposts of Punic and Roman-Byzantine civilization.

Table 13. *North Africa: outline chronology*

	Libya	Tunisia (Ifriqiya)	Algeria	Morocco	Spain
700	Arab conquests 643–				Arab conquest begins 711; the Umayyad dynasty, 756–1031
800		Aghlabids (Tunisia and eastern Algeria) (Qayrawan) 800–909	Rustamids (Tahert) 761–909	Idrisids (Fez) 789–926	
900		Fatimids 909–	Fatimids	Fatimids 921–	First Caliph ʿAbd al-Rahman III 912–961 Muluk al-Tawaif *c.* 1030 – *c.* 1090 the party kings in Malaga, Seville, Cordova, Toledo, Valencia, Saragossa, etc.
1000	Hilali migrations 1052	Zirids 972–1148	Hammadids 1015–1152	Almoravids (Marrakesh) 1056–1147	Christian conquest of Toledo, 1085 Almoravid conquest, 1086–1106 Almohad conquest, 1145
1100		Almohads 1160–	Almohads 1147–	Almohads 1130–1269	

1200	Defeat of Muslims, Las Navas de Tolosa, 1212 Christian conquest of Cordova, 1236, and Seville, 1248 Nasrids of Granada 1230–1492			Hafsids (Tunisia and eastern Algeria) 1228–1574	
1300		Marinids 1196–1549 (take Marrakesh in 1269)	ʿAbd al-Wadids (Tlemcen) 1236–1574		
1400		Portuguese take Ceuta 1415 Wattasid Regency and Sultanate 1428–1549			
1500		Saʿdians 1511–1659	Ottomans capture Algiers 1529, Tlemcen 1551	Ottomans capture Tunis 1574; Deys of Tunisia 1591–1705	Ottoman conquests Ottomans 1551–1711
1600		ʿAlawis 1631–present	Deys 1689–1830		
1700				Beys 1705–1957 French protectorate 1881	Qaramanlis 1711–1835
1800			French occupation begins 1830		Ottomans 1835–1912 Sanusiya 1837–1902 (Cyrenaica) Italian conquest 1911
1900		French protectorate 1912–56 Independence 1956	Independence 1962	Independence 1956	Independence 1951

The Arab conquest of both Berber peoples and Byzantine towns began with scattered raids from Egypt. Around 670, Tunisia was occupied and Qayrawan was founded as a base of Arab operations, and the Arabs reached Morocco and Spain (711). Even then the Arab presence was limited. Arab garrisons were established in Qayrawan, Tripoli, Tunis, Tobna and in numerous Byzantine forts or frontier ribats. The people who manned these ribats were committed to Muslim holy war and cultivated an ideology of piety and longing for martyrdom. While sedentarized Berbers at first remained Christians, nomadic Berbers enlisted in the Arab armies, and helped spread Islam into Algeria, Morocco, and Spain. While many Berbers threw in their lot with the Arabs, many others adopted Kharijism, which allowed them to accept the new religion but to oppose Arab domination. There was continuous Berber resistance.

The conquests led to the establishment of an Arab-Muslim regime in Tunisia and the adoption of Islam as the basis of tribal coalition regimes in much of the rest of North Africa. By the thirteenth century a new territorial state was consolidated in Morocco. Islamic religious elites and institutions were to be found throughout North Africa, and the populace was substantially converted to Islam. Thus the period from the seventh to the thirteenth centuries corresponds to the Caliphal period in the Middle East (to 945) which witnessed the simultaneous institutionalization of Muslim regimes and independent Muslim religious associations.

Tunisia was a natural center for an Arab-Islamic regime and society. While Middle Eastern societies had for several millennia experienced the rise and decline of empires, in the Carthaginian and Roman eras only Tunisia had developed the urban, agricultural, and commercial infrastructures essential for the existence of a centralized state. As a former center of Byzantine administration, only Tunisia had the professional cadres essential for a centralized regime. On this basis the Aghlabid dynasty provided Arab governors for Tripolitania, Tunisia, and eastern Algeria from 800 to 909. The Aghlabid state organization was basically derived from Tunisian precedents, Arab Middle Eastern practice, Byzantine monetary and fiscal techniques, and former Byzantine personnel. The Aghlabid elites were drawn from the descendants of Arab invaders, Islamized and Arabized Berbers, and black slave soldiers. The administrative staffs comprised dependent client Arab and Persian immigrants, bilingual natives, and some Christians and Jews.

Tunisia flourished under Arab rule. Extensive irrigation works were installed to supply towns with water, irrigate royal gardens, and promote olive production. In the Qayrawan region hundreds of basins were built to store water to support horse raising. Important trade routes linked Tunisia with the

Map 14. North Africa, Spain, and the Mediterranean in the ninth century.

Byzantine empire
'Abbasid empire
Aghlabids
Rustamids
Idrisids
Umayyads in Spain
Kharijis

Atlantic Ocean

Black Sea

Adriatic Sea

Mediterranean Sea

Sahara

500 km
300 miles

Poitiers

Toulouse
Marseilles
Genoa
Pisa
Venice
Naples

Constantinople

Aleppo
Damascus
Jerusalem
Fustat
Alexandria

CYPRUS

Barqa

E G Y P T
Nile R.

CRETE

SICILY
Palermo

SARDINIA

Tunis
Bone
Bougie
Constantine
Monastir
Mahdia
Sfax
Gabes
Tripoli
TRIPOLITANIA

Qayrawan
I.FR.

Aures Mts.

KABYLIA
Tahert
Wargala
Sijilmassa

ASTURIAS–
LEON
CASTILE
NAVARRE
ARAGON
CATALONIA
Barcelona
Valencia
Murcia
Granada
Saragossa
Segovia
Avila
Toledo
Cordova
Badajoz
Seville
Malaga
Ceuta
Tangiers
Volubilis
Fez
Tlemcen

Ebro
Duero
Tagus R.
Guadiana R.
Guadalquivir R.

Atlas Mts.
w. Sus

Sahara, the Sudan, and the Mediterranean. A flourishing economy permitted a refined and luxurious court life and the construction of the new palace cities of al-ʿAbbasiya (809) and Raqqada (877).

Tunisia's importance as a base of Arab rule was shaken, however, by the Fatimid movement and by the subsequent Hilali-Arab migrations. The Fatimid movement began as an offshoot of Ismaʿili missionary resistance to the ʿAbbasid dynasty. Ismaʿili proselytizing among Kitama Berbers of the Kabyle region won their belief in the Imam ʿUbaydallah. The Kitama conquered Sijilmassa, Tahert, and Qayrawan; ʿUbaydallah then declared himself Caliph and established a new capital at Mahdiya. The Fatimids went on to conquer much of the rest of North Africa and Egypt (969). Moving their capital to Cairo the Fatimids abandoned North Africa to local Zirid (972–1148) and Hammadid (1015–1152) vassals. A long period of political instability followed as North Africa was submerged in quarrels among the Zirids and Hammadids, Berber principalities, the Sunni religious leaders of Qayrawan, and the Umayyads of Spain who intervened to protect their clients.

Political instability may be connected with the decline of Tunisian trade and agriculture. The transfer of the Fatimid regime to Egypt favored Egyptian rather than Tunisian routes to the Sahara. Between 1000 and 1150 Spanish-patronized western routes also competed with eastern ones. A growing agricultural and urban population made excessive demands upon reserves of water, pasturage, and forest. Economic hardship and political turmoil in Tunisia were then furthered by European attacks upon Muslim North Africa. The Genoese and Pisans attacked Bone in 1034. The Normans conquered Sicily between 1061 and 1092, devastated Mahdiya in 1087, and between 1135 and 1153 raided and conquered the coastal strip from Tripoli to Cape Bon.

The economy of Tunisia was further disrupted by the stream of nomadic migrants from Arabia and Egypt who invaded North Africa in the eleventh and twelfth centuries. The reasons for this protracted migration are obscure, but the Hilali bedouins defeated the Zirid and Hammadid states and sacked Qayrawan (1057). As the invaders took control of the plains, sedentary peoples were forced to take refuge in the mountains. In central and northern Tunisia, farming gave way to pastoralism, a process which would later extend to Algeria and Morocco. Urban life declined as a result of the impoverishment of the countryside. Qayrawan and other cities, created by the first wave of Arab conquests, were ruined by the second. The decline of the Tunisian economy, then, was the result of a number of factors including Arab invasions, the internal weakness of local regimes, European assaults on coastal towns, and the shift of the Sahara trading economy to other routes.

The destruction, however, was not total. The coastal regions survived. Agriculture flourished in Monastir. Tripoli retained its palm, olive, fig, and other fruit plantations. Tunis became an important Mediterranean city for textiles, ceramics, glass, oil, soap, leather, and other urban manufactures. Moreover, not all of North Africa was in economic decline. Some of the factors which favored decline in the east favored economic development in the Moroccan far west. The revival of western trade routes favored the exchange of salt and luxury products from the north for gold, slaves, hides, ivory, and wood from the south.

While in Tunisia an urbanized agricultural society made possible the transplantation of a Middle Eastern type of state regime, elsewhere in North Africa smaller principalities were founded by Muslim chieftains with political support from the Berber population. These were tribal coalition regimes held together by religious symbols and the mediating function of religious leaders, for whom Khariji Islam became the basis of the religious identity in opposition to a very limited sphere of Arab conquest and domination. In the middle of the eighth century Berber-Khariji principalities were established at Tlemsen, Tahert, and Sijilmassa (Morocco). The Ibadi Khariji kingdom of Tahert (761–909) was founded by ʿAbd al-Rahman ibn Rustam. The imam was elected by the notables and lived an ascetic life interpreting laws, rendering justice, and leading his warriors in battle. Life at Tahert was conducted in a perpetual state of religious fervor. The theocratic community enforced a high standard of social behavior by physical punishment and imprisonment. The Rustamid regime did not have a regular army or centralized administration but was recognized by Kharijis in southern Tunisia and in the large region extending all across southern North Africa from Tripoli to Tlemsen. In the tenth century the Khariji dynasties were replaced by Zenata Berber princes of tribal origin.

These North African states maintained a flourishing economy. The countryside produced olives, grapes, and cereals; the towns had lively textile and ceramic industries. Trade with Europe, Egypt and sub-Saharan Africa was crucial to this economy. North African commerce with the Sudan, controlled by Qayrawan and by the Berber kingdoms, went from Qayrawan to Wargala, from Tripoli to the Fezzan, and through the Jerid to the Niger. Sijilmassa was linked to the Sudan and traded with Tahert, Tlemsen, and possibly Fez. On the Sudanic routes the principal products were slaves and gold.

Northern Morocco was the center of another cluster of Arab-Berber principalities. These showed a tendency toward the eventual consolidation of a unified Moroccan territorial state. The Idrisid regime was founded at the former Roman capital of Volubilis by a descendant of ʿAli and Fatima who escaped from Arabia after the failure of a Shiʿi revolt in 786. Idris formed a tribal coalition which quickly conquered northern Morocco. His son Idris II was the founder of Fez, built in 808. Despite its small size the Idrisid kingdom was the first Moroccan-Islamic state, and a center of active proselytization on behalf of Islam. The rest of Morocco was divided among a number of localized states including that of the Barghwata peoples, the followers of Salih b. Tarif, who declared himself a prophet, composed a "revealed book" in Berber, gave rules for fasting and prayer, and otherwise established a Berber version of Islam on the coastal plains of central Morocco. All of these regimes were islands of kingly rule in a sea of independent Berber peoples living in pre-state types of political community.

The rise of a unified Moroccan state was bound up with the Almoravid movement. Like the Fatimids, the Almoravids were a coalition of Berber peoples united by religious leadership and doctrine. The movement rose among Sanhaja peoples in the western Sahara who were being pushed out of their trading livelihood by Zenata Berbers who controlled the northern ends of the trans-Saharan trade routes, and by the Sudanic state of Ghana which deprived the Sanhajas of control over the southern outlets of the trans-Saharan trade. The Sanhaja were being squeezed between Zenata domination in the north, and an expanding Sudanese kingdom in the south.

Islam played an important role in the Sanhaja adaptation to these pressures. Islam was already important in the Sus region, where the populace was divided among Malikis and Shiʿas, and where there was a scattering of ribats devoted to Muslim piety and to war against Berber heretics. One Sanhaja chieftain, Yahya b. Ibrahim, on returning from his pilgrimage to Mecca, resolved to bring back religious teachers to spread the true practice of Islam. He returned with a Moroccan student, ʿAbdallah b. Yasin, who taught Quran, hadith, and law. Ibn Yasin called for repentance and warned of the coming last day. He insisted that sinners be punished according to Muslim legal penalties, and he imposed a strict moral and religious discipline upon his followers. The inner jihad – the purification of body and soul – had to precede the warriors' outer jihad. The name of the movement he founded, al-Murabitun, was derived from the Quranic root *r–b–t*, referring to the technique of fighting in closed ranks, with infantry in front and camels and horsemen in the rear, rather than in the long, loose lines common to Berber battles. Almoravid, then, refers to those who wage holy war in the Quranically prescribed fashion. In any case, ʿAbdallah provided the religious cement for a Sanhaja counter-attack, under

Map 15. North Africa, Spain, and the Mediterranean in the late eleventh century and the Almoravid conquests.

Map labels

Atlantic Ocean

Black Sea

Aleppo
Damascus
Jerusalem
Constantinople
CYPRUS
Cairo
Alexandria
EGYPT
Niger R.
Barqa
CRETE

Adriatic Sea
Mediterranean Sea
Sahara

Venice
Pisa
Genoa
Naples
SARDINIA
Palermo
SICILY
Tunis
Monastir
Mahdia
Sfax
IFRIQIYA
Qayrawan
Gabes
Tripoli
TRIPOLITANIA
Wargala

Poitiers
Toulouse
Marseilles
Barcelona
CATALONIA
Saragossa
ARAGON
NAVARRE
LEÓN
GALICIA
CASTILE
Valencia
Murcia
Granada
Málaga
Cordova
Seville
Badajoz
Avila
Segovia
Toledo
Ebro
Duero
Tagus R.
Guadiana R.
Guadalquivir R.

Ceuta
Tangiers
Volubilis
Fez
Tlemcen
Marrakesh
Sijilmassa
Wargala
Algiers
Bougie
Constantine
KABYLIA
Aures Mts
Tahert
Rif Mts
Atlas Mts
High Atlas

500 km
300 miles
0

Legend

Byzantine empire
Fatimids
Zirids
Hammadids
Almoravids
Party Kings

the leadership of the Lamtuna tribe, against pagan Sudanese kingdoms to the south and impious Zenata domination in the north.

The Almoravids went on to conquer Morocco, and founded Marrakesh as their capital around 1070. New evidence refutes the idea that they also conquered Ghana; rather, trade helped bring about the conversion of Ghana to Islam in 1076–77. Then, between 1086 and 1106, the Almoravids conquered southern Spain. The Almoravid conquests thus linked the Sahara, Morocco and Spain into a new trading zone. Morocco, benefiting from trade and empire, became in the course of the eleventh to the thirteenth century a commercial and urbanized society. These changes provided the foundation for a succession of unified Moroccan regimes until the present.

The Almoravid regime was built around the Lamtuna tribal aristocracy, but the Almoravids also used Christian mercenaries, recruited in Spain, and black slaves to form a cavalry bodyguard for the ruler, which gave him predominance over camel-riding Berber troops. The Almoravids in addition employed Spanish scribes. The legitimacy of the regime was based on claims to religious purity. ʿAbdallah b. Yasin closed taverns, destroyed musical instruments, abolished illegal taxes, and implemented Muslim laws for the distribution of booty. Later Almoravid rulers were titled *amir al-muslimin*, and recognized the suzerainty of the ʿAbbasids. Scholars of Maliki law sat in executive council with the ruler and gave legal advice. The legalists condemned Muslim theology and opposed Sufism. Despite their narrow religious position the Almoravids laid the foundation for a flourishing North African civilization. They aided the final triumph of Sunni Islam and the Maliki school of law over Shiʿi and Khariji rivals. North African rulers became patrons of Spanish scribes, philosophers, poets, and architects. The great mosque of Tlemsen, built in 1136, and the rebuilt Qarawiyin mosque of Fez were designed in the Andalusian manner.

By the middle of the twelfth century the Almoravid state began to unravel. In Spain local Muslim princes rejected its authority. In southern Morocco a new religious movement denied its legitimacy. The Almohad movement (*al-Muwahhidun*) was founded by Muhammad ibn ʿAbdallah ibn Tumart, a scholar of Islam who made the pilgrimage to Mecca and studied in Baghdad and Damascus. On his return he began to preach moral reform. Espousing the supremacy of Quran and hadith, he refused to accept the authority of the law schools. He also preached the transcendence and oneness of God. Grounding himself in the theology of al-Ashʿari, he rejected anthropomorphism and a physical interpretation of the attributes of God mentioned in the Quran. Ibn Tumart also denounced pagan Berber customs taken into Islamic practice and proscribed wine drinking, music, and the enjoyment of luxurious clothing. He regarded himself as the heir of the Prophet, his career as a duplication of the Prophet's career, and his teaching an effort to restore the Islamic community as it had existed in the Prophet's lifetime. At Tinmal in southern Morocco he received the support of a local chieftain, Abu Hafs ʿUmar, and declared himself mahdi, imam, and maʿsum or infallible leader sent by God. Under his authority a new government was organized under a council of ten disciples, who in turn was advised by an assembly of fifty tribal delegates. His followers joined the movement as collectivities under the leadership of their chiefs. Thus a religious hierarchy was superimposed upon a tribal society. After the death of Ibn Tumart, his successor ʿAbd al-Muʾmin (1130–63) took the title Caliph of Ibn Tumart. The new ruler put his family in power but attached to each of its youthful members an Almohad shaykh as a teacher. He thus converted a religious oligarchy into a family-based monarchy.

ʿAbd al-Muʾmin conquered Morocco, intervened in Spain, and invaded Algeria and Tunisia. His regime was organized in hierarchical fashion under the Council of Ten instituted by Ibn Tumart. It depended on a military aristocracy made up of the tribes which had originally supported the movement. The tribal aristocracy was backed up by slaves, Arab tribes, contingents of Turkish, Kurdish, and black soldiers and urban auxiliaries. An elaborate religious administration including a keeper of morals (*mizwar*), muezzins, and instructors in the Quran was also established. Among the duties of the mizwar were the destruction of musical instruments and the prohibition of alcohol. A civil bureaucracy of the Andalusian type was mobilized to support the government. Thus the Almohad regime was based on a combination of a royal household, a hierarchical religious organization, a tribal military elite with Berber and Arab tribal allies, and a Spanish-type administration.

Despite the power of the regime the Almohad doctrine was never successfully implemented. Alternative expressions of Islam, including that of the Maliki jurists, the popular cult of saints and Sufis, and the philosophy of Averroes, were always tolerated. Later rulers abandoned Almohad doctrine, objecting to the excessive emphasis upon the teachings of Ibn Tumart, and conflict within the ruling elite led in 1229 to the formal renunciation of the teachings of Ibn Tumart and a return to Maliki law.

The Almohad empire like its predecessors soon dissolved. In 1212 the Almohads were defeated in Spain, and southern Morocco was invaded by Arab tribes of Banu Maʿqil who ruined the villages and undermined the authority of the central government. By the middle of the thirteenth century the Almohads were replaced by a new regime. By then, Morocco had slowly evolved from a region divided among Arab and Berber principalities into a unified state with a lasting territorial identity. The collapse of the Almohad empire marked the conclusion of the "Caliphal" phase of state formation and Islamization in North Africa. In this era a succession of regimes – Rustamid, Idrisid, Fatimid, Almoravid, and Almohad – had used Islamic religious beliefs to legitimize new political elites and to unify Berber tribal peoples. Islam had become the basis of political solidarity among factious populations. The role of religion in the formation of these states, however, varied from case to case. The Idrisid, Fatimid, Almoravid, and Almohad rulers all claimed an unmediated, divine authority based on their personal qualifications, and their descent in the family of the Prophet. In some respects these regimes were the ideological equivalents of the Caliphate. The Khariji states of southern Tunisia and Algeria, however, stressed ideology rather than the person of the rulers. They were built upon an ascetic, equalitarian concept of the social order in which the imam was a representative of collective values rather than an embodiment of the divine mystery.

To build these states religious authority was joined to revenues from commerce and the support of a segmented tribal society. Yet the North African states were short-lived, subject to changing patterns of trade, the rise of new tribal movements, and the breakdown of coalitions. Moreover, they did not fully control the territories under their nominal domain, but were suzerainties over independent peoples. Sometimes the states were no more than islands in a sea of autonomous and unorganized Berber populations.

While Islamization was associated with state formation, as early as the eighth century religious elites separate from the state, and committed to Islamic values above state interests, had also come into being. Under Aghlabid patronage Qayrawan became the leading North Africa center of Sunni Islam and the Maliki school of law. The Maliki school was established by scholars from both the eastern Islamic provinces and from Andalusia and by the travels of North African scholars to Mecca, Medina, and Iraq. By the late ninth century the mosques of Qayrawan and Tunis already had a Muslim world importance as centers of learning. Despite the criticism that the Maliki school was rigid and literal-minded it was not monolithic. Theological issues were hotly debated. Such topics as the creation of the Quran, free will and predestination, and the meaning of the Caliphate were debated as much in Qayrawan as in Baghdad. In the course of the tenth century Ashʿarism was assimilated into the Maliki school, and was later transmitted to the Almohads. Maliki scholars were also students of grammar, philology, mathematics, astronomy, and medicine. Ibn al-Tabban (923–81) was a student of law, philology, grammar, mathematics, astronomy, medicine, and the interpretation of dreams. Al-Qabisi (935–1012) was a theologian who stressed hadith and mysticism, and an intensely pious religious practice. These men exemplified divergent orientations within the Maliki school parallel to those in the eastern Shafiᶜi school.

The schools of law were the vehicles for the mobilization of public opinion in the struggles among political regimes. In Qayrawan the Hanafis, representing an upper-class milieu, were favored by the Aghlabids and later collaborated with the Fatimids. The Malikis, by contrast, eschewed collaboration with the state and appointment to office and won popular support. Under Fatimid rule, the Malikis denounced Shiᶜism, provoked anti-Shiᶜi riots and massacres in Qayrawan, and in 1049 forced the Zirids to accept Sunni allegiance and to recognize the ᶜAbbasid Caliphs. While Qayrawan and Tunis were the main centers of Maliki teaching, the Maliki position was also strongly supported in the coastal ribats, and spread to southern Morocco and West Africa.

Alongside of the Maliki school of law, mysticism was an important religious force in the early Islamic period. Sufi ascetism, stressing sadness, silence, suffering, fear of God, attention to the coming of the last judgment, and the virtues of humility and charity, was being cultivated in Qayrawan in the ninth century. The ribats combined holy war with pious devotions. The common people believed in saints who had the power to heal, bring rain, perform miracles, communicate with spiritual forces, interpret dreams, and otherwise act as intermediaries between men and God. Sufism in North Africa, as in the Middle East, was not so much an organized religious movement as a religious sensibility.

In the eleventh and twelfth centuries, a new form of Sufism, based on both Spanish and eastern teachings, was introduced to North Africa, and spread in reaction to the Almoravid and Almohad conquests. Abu Madyan al-Andalusi (d. 1197) brought to Africa the Spanish form of Sufism which integrated ascetic mysticism with the study of law. His tomb became a venerated place of pilgrimage and his successors continued the tradition of combining the study of hadith and law with mystical practices. Sufi scholars were established in Tunisia at Tunis, Bone, Qayrawan, and were represented in Morocco at Aghmat, Marrakesh, and other places. The Maliki school, the early ribats, Khariji teachers and Sufis helped to diffuse Islam from its Tunisian base into southern Morocco. Traders and scholars also brought it to the Saharan region.

Unfortunately our knowledge of this early period is too scattered to give an assured account of the rhythm of the diffusion of Islam. Libya appears to have been relatively quickly converted in the wake of the early conquests. Large numbers of Berbers accepted Khariji Islam, but Qayrawan, Tunis, Tripoli, Sfax, Mahdiya, Bougie, Bone, and other cities still had Christian communities in the eleventh and twelfth centuries. However, the 200 bishoprics known in the seventh century had been reduced to five by 1053 and to three by 1076. The Almohads, however, effectively put an end to Christianity in North Africa; Christians survived only in isolated villages. Jews were drastically reduced in number, and the cultural vitality of the Jewish communities was destroyed.

Thus, by the middle of the thirteenth century, the Arab invasions and the introduction of Islam had inspired a centuries-long wave of state construction culminating in the integration of Morocco as well as Tunisia into a territorial state. Though the state institutions were much more highly developed in Tunisia than elsewhere, the rudiments of legitimacy and the military and administrative organization essential to historical states had also been consolidated in Morocco. At the same time Islam had been established as the dominant religion. Informal schools of legal instruction, theology, and mysticism emerged and Islamic religious teachers acquired a large popular following. With the Islamization of the region religious leadership and loyalties and informal communal ties were differentiated from state institutions. The culmination of this early phase of state formation, the defeat of the great tribal and religious movements which sought to unify North Africa, and the formation of an autonomous Islamic religious elite opened the way for a new historic phase of the relationships between state and Islam in North African societies.

SPANISH ISLAMIC CIVILIZATION

Muslim Spain from the Arab conquest to the liquidation of the last Muslim possessions in Granada in 1492 represents yet another variant of the Caliphal type of early Islamic civilization. This civilization was built upon the assimilation of the Spanish and Berber population to Arabic and Islamic culture and was fostered by extraordinary economic prosperity. Muslim Spain bears an aura of glory. The great mosque of Cordova, the gardens, fountains and courtyards of the Alhambra, the *muwashshahat* and *zajal* poetry with their Arabic verses and occasional romance language refrains, the irrigated gardens of Seville and Valencia, the wisdom of philosophy and science – these are the monuments of Spanish Islam. Spain was the focal point for the transmission of Greek philosophy from the Arab world to Europe. No less important was the drama of the defeat of this brilliant Muslim civilization by its European enemies, the expulsion of the Arabs, and the reabsorption of Spain into Christian Europe.

For all its brilliance Muslim Spain was a province of the Arab Caliphate. Already overrun by successive waves of Alaric and Vandal invasions from the north, Spain was conquered by Arab and Berber forces from North Africa led by Tariq, who defeated the Visigothic King Rodrigo at the River Barbate in 711. The Arab advance into France was checked finally by Charles Martel at the battle of Poitiers in 732.

The Arabs were not at first able to establish a strong regime. Whereas in the East, Arab conquerors were generally forced to settle in garrison towns and villages, leaving the land in the direct control of its pre-conquest landlord elite and a tax-collecting bureaucracy, in Spain large territories were parceled out among Arab and Berber clans. This immediately led to factional quarrels. In the very first decades of Muslim rule, Berbers, allocated poor mountain lands in Galicia and Cantabria, rebelled against Arab governors. The rebellions were put down by Syrian Arabs and the new forces were in turn given fiefs. The Arabs themselves were divided into tribal factions called Qays and Yemen, representing the first-generation settlers and later immigrants.

Dispersed settlement, however, contributed enormously to the Arabization and Islamization of Spain. The Arabs took clients, captured slaves, hired mercenaries, and married into local families. By the ninth century Arabic was widely used by the indigenous population and there were many converts (*muwalladun*). As converts multiplied, the distinction between original Arab elite and assimilated Arabs blurred, and a more homogeneous Hispano-Arab society came into being.

This development was abetted by extraordinary economic prosperity in the ninth and tenth centuries. The introduction of irrigation agriculture based on eastern models led to the cultivation of valuable new crops including cherries, apples, pears, almonds, pomegranates, figs, dates, sugarcane, bananas, cotton, flax, and silk. A Damascus type of irrigation assigned water to each cultivator in proportion to the size of his land. A Yemeni type of irrigation, used in the oasis-like *huertas* of Valencia, distributed water by a fixed time flow. Irrigation was administered either by a town authority under the control of the *sahib al-saqiya*, who policed the distribution of water and assured equity, or it was run by local communities who selected their own irrigation manager. At the same time, Spain entered a phase of commercial prosperity due to the breakdown of Byzantine naval control over the western Mediterranean. Cities such as Seville and Cordova prospered on the bases of rich agricultural production and international trade.

The result of these social and economic changes was political consolidation. After a succession of weak governors appointed from North Africa, three great rulers built up the Spanish-Muslim state. ʿAbd al-Rahman I (756–88), a grandson of the Umayyad Caliph Hisham, supported by Berbers from North Africa and by Syrian clients of the Umayyads, founded the Umayyad dynasty in Spain. The new regime followed the ʿAbbasid pattern. It suppressed local revolts, and built up a client army of soldiers coming from north of the Pyrenees. ʿAbd al-Rahman II (822–52) further centralized administration, brought into being a new secretarial class made up of merchants and clients, and created state monopolies and control of urban markets. ʿAbd al-Rahman III (912–61) completed the consolidation of the central government. He built his army upon captives from northern Spain, Germany, and the Slavic countries. These troops, known as *saqaliba*, were later reinforced with de-tribalized professional Berber soldiers and local levies. The administration was also strengthened. A *hajib*, equal in rank to a vizier, was in charge of administration and taxation. Provincial tax collectors were appointed to raise revenues and send the surplus to Cordova. While twenty-one provinces were governed by appointees of the central government, frontier districts were managed by local *qaʾids* and hereditary petty lords. A chief qadi supervised judicial administration and managed the properties endowed for religious and charitable purposes.

ʿAbd al-Rahman III also sought a new basis for the legitimation of his regime by adopting Baghdadi ʿAbbasid cultural forms. While Islamic culture in Spain assimilated some aspects of local culture, it was primarily an outpost of Middle Eastern Arabic-Islamic civilization. As in the East, court culture tried to integrate Muslim and cosmopolitan symbols. ʿAbd al-Rahman adopted the title Caliph or *amir al-muʾminin* in reaction to the claims of the Fatimids in North Africa. Thus the precious title signifying the unity of the Muslim community was claimed by no fewer than three rulers in the early tenth century. ʿAbd al-Rahman expanded the Cordova mosque, installed irrigation works, and waged jihad to check Christian attacks in northern Spain.

On the cosmopolitan side, poetry became the primary expression of Spanish civilization. Spanish poetry was originally based on Arabic models, which carried with them the warrior sentiments and factional interests of the Arab conquerors. The urbane Baghdadi style was introduced by bringing the poet and singer Ziryab (789–857) to Cordova. In early Hispano-Arabic poetry, the qasida, which praised the virtues of the ruler and served official purposes, was the dominant form.

New Spanish forms, however, came into being. The new poems had Arabic strophes, and sometimes an additional *kharja* or refrain in Romance dialect, and were a synthesis of Arabic and Romance verse forms. The Arabic part, usually a love poem, was courtly in theme, masculine in tone; the kharja was usually the voice of the lower classes, or of a Christian slave girl, and feminine in inspiration. While the poems were composed in Arabic, the metrical system, the syllabic prosody, and the rhyme scheme all indicate a Romance influence.

Other literary activities flourished under Caliphal patronage. Eastern scholars emigrated to Spain, and the royal libraries were enlarged. Grammar and philology came from Iraq. Adab, or belles-lettres in eastern style, was first composed in Spain by Ibn ʿAbd al-Rabbih (d. 940). Caliphal patronage broadened scientific learning. Aristotle's philosophy was introduced by the reception of the *Organon*; the *Republic*, the *Laws*, and the *Timaeus* of Plato were known. Galen became the standard medical author. A new translation of a classic work – Dioscorides' *Materia Medica* – was made in Spain. The earliest translations of astronomical and geometric works from Arabic into Latin were also made in the tenth century.

The architecture of the Caliphate, including mosques, palaces, and baths, was also eastern in inspiration. The mosque of Cordova was expanded and rebuilt by successive rulers. It was a vast hall divided by columns surmounted by horseshoe arches; a niche with a fluted shell-like vault and a horseshoe arch indicated the direction of prayer. Visigothic and Roman elements were built into the Muslim design. The mosque was redecorated between 961 and 966 by mosaic workers, who gave it a vivid and brilliant interior. The mosque of Cordova, like the mosque of Damascus, was a symbol of the incorporation of ancient values and their supersession by Islamic civilization. In the tenth century the Caliphs also built the royal city of Madinat al-Zahraʾ, a city of splendid palaces, fountains, and gardens which imitated the palace complexes of Baghdad.

Under the auspices of the Umayyad regime, a Muslim as well as an Arab civilization came into being. The Syrian school of law, founded by al-Awzaʿi, favored by Syrian-Arab military lords, was imported into Spain, but the town populations favored the Maliki school from North Africa. From the East came Shafiʿi's concepts. Hadith studies were introduced in the ninth century, and Muslim scholars were divided between the *shuyukh al-ʿilm* or students who favoured hadith and theology, and the *shuyukh al-fiqh* or scholars of law. This distinction may, as in Nishapur, represent the division between Arab elites and later converts. Shafiʿi scholars, however, had to accept Maliki law, and Malikism remained the primary religious identity of Muslim Spain. Muslim theology and Muʿtazilism were also introduced from Baghdad in the ninth century. Muhammad b. Masarra (883–931), whose father studied in Basra, amalgamated neo-Platonic, Shiʿi and Sufi thought. The legal scholars, however, restricted the public expression of mystical tendencies.

Arabic-Islamic culture in Spain was associated with different social milieus and sociopolitical movements. Monumental architecture, formal poetry, and philosophic interests characterized the royal style of culture in Spain as in Baghdad. The scribal class was identified with Arabic belles-lettres. As in the East, the secretarial class, composed of Spanish converts, generated an Arabic literature which was intended to prove their equality with the Arab warrior elites. The *Risala* of Abu ʿAmir b. Garcia provoked an avalanche of contemptuous Arabic poetry in response.

Important lower-class social movements were also connected with religious trends. In circumstances which still remain obscure, the ʿulamaʾ of the Rabad quarter of Cordova led local rebellions in 805 and 818. They denounced the regime for corruption, fiscal exploitation, use of foreign military forces, and chronic insecurity. Though the revolts were put down, the power of the religious leaders rose. ʿAbd al-Rahman II created a religious council to demonstrate that he ruled in accord with Islam. Thus the Umayyad princes sought to legitimize their rule by coopting the scholars of law. As in North Africa, Baghdad, and other parts of the Muslim world, the ʿulamaʾ assumed political responsibilities and a voice in the direction of society. Sufis led a lower-class movement opposed to the exploitative accumulation of wealth by the upper classes, and espoused an ascetic, mystical, and communalist doctrine.

Arab-Muslim rule also had profound effects on the Christians. Christians under Muslim rule rapidly adopted the Arabic language, Arab customs and manners, and assumed the style of life led by the political elites. Thus the *mozarab* identity came into being. This assimilation of Christians was opposed by a priest named Eulogius, who called for a more purely Christian culture stripped of Arab influences. Between 850 and 859 he led a revolt of the mozarabs of Cordova in which Christians made martyrs of themselves to protest against Arab-Muslim rule.

Like their ʿAbbasid model, the Spanish-Muslim state was subverted by intense internal conflicts. The hostilities between provincial and urban mercantile elites, between townsmen and Berber troops, converts and Arabs made it impossible to stabilize the regime. In the early eleventh century, the Caliphs lost control of the central government, provincial governors became independent, and Arab clans revolted. As in the history of the eastern Caliphate, a central imperial government was replaced by smaller provincial regimes. The Caliphate was abolished and Spain was divided into petty warring principalities, called the *muluk al-tawaᵓif*, or the party kings (1030–90). Arab, Slav, and Berber soldiers and local elites took power, and each province became an independent state with an army, court, and administration of its own. The Amirids – descendants of former Caliphal administrators – ruled the eastern coast of Andalus. The saqaliba settled Denia in the southeast. Regimes based on local Arab families were founded at Cordova, Seville, and Saragossa; Berber-dominated states were founded at Toledo, Badajoz, and Granada. In Granada the Berber ruling elite governed with the help of the Jewish Banu Naghrila family. This provoked intense Muslim hostility and a pogrom against Jews in 1066.

While the emergence of provincial regimes was a defeat for centralized government, Spanish society was not as fragmented as the political division of power would imply. Muslim law and a Muslim-Arab identity were universally accepted, and the ᶜulamaᵓ continued to represent the urban populations. Spanish-Muslim society was also integrated by a flourishing regional and international commerce. Andalusia traded with Morocco, importing wood, alum, antimony, and cloth, and exporting cloth and copper. It traded with Tunisia and through Tunisia with Egypt, importing the wool, flax, and dyes which came to Egypt from Iran, Arabia, India, and China. Spanish Muslims also traded with the Christian north, where growing wealth and the rising power of new states created ever larger markets.

Despite its great prosperity and cultivated urban life, the extreme degree of political fragmentation threatened the very existence of Spanish-Islamic civilization. For centuries the Christians had been preparing for the reconquest of Spain. The initial Muslim advance had left a small belt of northern territories along the Pyrenees in Christian hands. In the course of the eighth and ninth centuries new small kingdoms in this region began to reconquer and recolonize the Muslim areas of Spain. Christian sentiment was also expressed in the founding of Benedictine monasteries and the pilgrimage of Santiago de Compostela. Pope Gregory VII made the reconquest a religious duty of Christians as well as a territorial ambition of Spanish kings.

The disintegration of the Muslim states in the eleventh century allowed for the rapid expansion of the several Christian kingdoms. In 1085 Alfonso VI, on the strength of the unified kingdoms of Castile, Leon, and Galicia, conquered Toledo. This was a signal event in the struggle between Muslims and Christians, for a brilliant center of Muslim civilization, once the capital of Visigothic Spain, again fell into Christian hands. Christian migrants flocked to Toledo, but the Muslim and Mozarab populations were allowed to remain. In the meantime the Kingdom of Aragon captured Huesca (1096), Saragossa

(1118), Tortosa (1148), and Lerida (1149). In the second half of the twelfth century the reconquest became institutionalized. Religious-military fraternities, such as the orders of Calatrava and Santiago, financed by landed estates, conquered and colonized Muslim territories.

The Christian advance was countered by the Muslims. In 1082 a delegation of ʿulamaʾ urged the Almoravids to intervene on behalf of the Spanish-Muslim community. Thus in 1086 a Moroccan army crossed the straits and defeated Alfonso VI, and from 1090 to 1145 the North Africans conquered the Spanish-Muslim cities and governed Spain as a province of Marrakesh. Military commanders governed the cities in collaboration with the ʿulamaʾ. Almoravid rule, however, increasingly incurred the hostility of the local population. There were Sufi-led revolts in Silves and Niebla, and ʿulamaʾ-led revolts in Cordova and Valencia which eventually overthrew Almoravid rule. The Almoravid empire came apart under the pressure of local resistance and the rise of the Almohad movement. The Almohads who took Marrakesh in 1147 unhesitatingly accepted the concept of a Moroccan empire which included Spain. In turn, they took Seville and Cordova in 1149, and the rest of Muslim Spain by 1172.

A new Moroccan suzerainty was imposed upon Spain, but the Muslim position nonetheless continued to disintegrate under the combination of Christian pressures and regional anarchy. The Almohads were defeated in 1212 by the combined Christian forces of Leon, Castile, Navarre, and Aragon at the battle of Las Navas de Tolosa. With the defeat of the Almohads the Spanish-Muslim states again found themselves independent but helpless before the resumption of the Christian reconquest. The union of Castile and Leon in 1230 opened the way for the conquest of Cordova in 1236 and Seville in 1248. The Aragonese advanced along the coast to take Valencia in 1238 and Murcia in 1243. By 1249–50 the Portuguese had taken all of the lands west of the Guadiana River. By the middle of the thirteenth century only Granada remained in Muslim hands. It was protected by a large populace, a mountainous territory, and a productive economy which paid heavy tribute to the princes of Castile. Also Aragon turned its interests to the Mediterranean, Castile was embroiled in civil wars, and the military orders were disbanded. Christian rulers gave no priority to the conquest of Granada until the union of Castile and Aragon opened the way for the final conquest of the last Muslim possession in Spain in 1492.

The disintegration of the Caliphate and the centuries of struggles with the Christians did not disrupt Spanish-Muslim cultural life. With the decline of the Caliphate the patronage of art and culture shifted to the courts of the provincial rulers and merchant-elites. In place of grand mosques, private palaces became the characteristic locale of Hispano-Arabic civilization. In the late tenth century the muwashshahat poetry flourished, as city dwellers redis-covered the beauties of nature. Freed of religious restraints, qasidas devoted to descriptions of nature and gardens, wine and war, and love and passion were composed. Ibn Quzman (d. 1160) cultivated the zajal, a form of poetry in colloquial Arabic, whose themes were the life of towns and markets, the common people, and the underworld. This was a deliberately irreligious form of art. After a long period in which the Baghdadi style had dominated Arabic-Spanish literature, poetic interests were transferred from the political to the personal. Love and art for art's sake became the dominant themes.

Love was the central theme of the philosophy of Ibn Hazm (d. 1063). He taught that the attraction of two people was based on an eternal affinity, a timeless connection of souls. Ibn al-ʿArabi later explained that a man loves a woman because she is the mirror which reveals his innermost true being – the spiritual being which transcends his animal reality. The love of a woman is the love of the reminder of the original nature of the soul and therefore a reminder of God. Love stems, therefore, from the creation of man in the image of God, and sexual love is a symbol of the extinction of the separate natures in the divine reality.

With the breakdown of Spanish-Islamic society, Sufism also became im-portant. From Almeria came Abu al-ʿAbbas b. al-ʿArif (1088–1141), whose writings described the stages of mystical ascent to the realization that only God exists. Ibn al-ʿArabi, also from Spain, was probably the greatest Muslim mystical metaphysician.

The Almohads' rule also introduced theological and philosophic debates. While the Almoravids had favored strictly legal views, the Almohads were the patrons of Ibn Rushd (Averroes, 1126–98). Averroes took up the classic debate of theology and philosophy concerning human knowledge of spiritual realities. While al-Ghazzali held that direct apprehension was the basis for the knowledge of the divine being, and that the Quran was a direct expression of God's being, Averroes held that reason was the basis of human knowledge of the divine being, and that the Quran was an allegory requiring rational interpretation.

From Spain, Islamic scientific and philosophical thought was transmitted to Europe. With the conquest of Toledo in 1085 and Saragossa in 1118, Hispano-Islamic culture had a strong and immediate influence upon Christian style. Nobles and churchmen built their houses in the Moorish manner and borrowed Hispanic-Islamic motifs for their heraldry. They dressed in Arab fabrics, and had Jewish and Muslim literatures translated into Castilian and Latin. Alfonso X arranged for the translation of the Bible, the Talmud, and the Quran into Castilian. The story of the mi^craj or the ascent of the Prophet into heaven, was translated into Castilian and then into old French and Latin, where it may have become available to Dante. In Toledo, Petrus Alphonsi, a Jewish convert to Christianity, and other translators under the patronage of Archbishop Don Raimundo, rendered Arabic works on astrology and astronomy into Castilian and then into Latin. The works of Ptolemy were translated. The Muslim philosophers al-Kindi, al-Farabi, and Avicenna were also translated into Latin, making the thought of Aristotle available to Europeans. Between 1160 and 1187 Gerard of Cremona translated some 87 works, including the Quran, many books of Aristotle, and the *Qanun* of Avicenna, into Latin. Between 1220 and 1250 Averroes's commentaries on Aristotle and the works of Maimonides were rendered in Latin and were quoted by St Thomas Aquinas. Thus Greek philosophic thought came through the Arab world to Europe.

Not even the reconquista could extinguish the cultural vitality of Muslim Spain. Granada, the surviving Muslim enclave, maintained a sophisticated style of life. The city was adorned with patios, fountains, and pavements; Granada copied eastern styles in bronzes, ivories, ceramics, and furniture. In order to meet its huge burden of tribute, Granada developed an export trade in ceramics, porcelains, silks, and weapons.

The Alhambra was one of the great achievements of Islamic urban art. The Alhambra was first constructed as a fortress and royal residence in the eleventh century. By the thirteenth century it had been enlarged into a princely city. Like Baghdad and Cairo, it was a symbol of the power and aloofness of royalty. The Nasrid dynasty of Granada (1230–1492) built the famous Court of the Myrtles, the Court of the Lions, and innumerable gardens and pavilions.

The palace complex was decorated with Islamic symbols and water motifs. It was embellished with Quranic inscriptions, and provided with a large mosque, an open prayer field, and a "Gate of the Law." Pools and fountains symbolized refuge, repose, and paradise. Inscriptions bore allusions to the legend of the glass floor built by King Solomon to resemble a pool of water – the Solomonic story linked Granada with the royal art of the ancient Near East and its later Islamic versions. It was a last echo of the courtly cosmopolitan civilization of the Arab East in the Mediterranean far West.

The Christian reconquest did not extinguish the Muslim presence. In the eleventh and twelfth centuries Muslim populations were found under Christian rule in Toledo and Saragossa. In the thirteenth century Muslims under Christian domination survived in Valencia. Apart from the small crusading

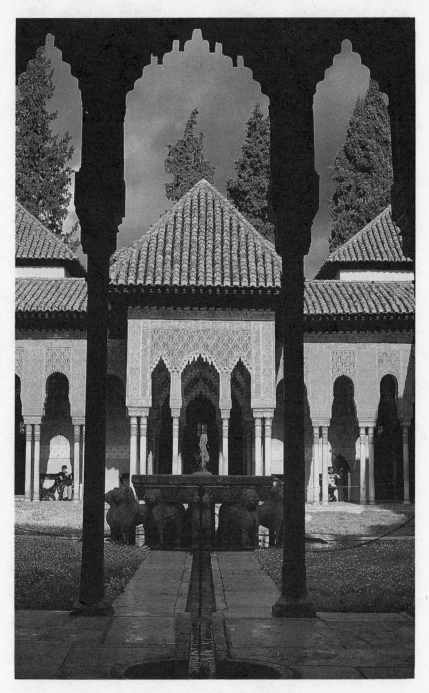

14 The Alhambra, Granada

principalities in Palestine, Lebanon, and Sicily, this was the first experience of Muslims under non-Muslim rule.

Valencia under the crown of Aragon is the best-known case. James I of Aragon who took Valencia in 1238, attempted to secure Christian hegemony by bringing in new settlers, establishing religious orders, giving lands to Christian landlords, and organizing a tax-collecting administration. Otherwise the Christians did not interfere with the Muslim population. Muslims kept their residences; merchants and artisans continued to flourish, and indeed took the lead in the overseas trade of Valencia. Small farmers, property owners and tenants kept their tenures.

There was also substantial continuity in the social and political organization of the Muslim population. The kings of Aragon at first maintained the authority of the Muslim elites by treating them as vassals of the crown. They required oaths of loyalty and military service. The old rural social structure, consisting of small village or castle-scale communities governed by a qaid, was maintained. In the cities, Muslims retained control of civil courts and of internal community matters. The qadi was the chief Muslim official, the *amin*, the main administrator and tax collector, and the *sahib al-madina* was in charge of the police. The organized Muslim communities could thus both cooperate with and ward off state interference. Organized as a self-regulating religious community the Muslims became, as the Christians had been, a protected population.

The terms of Muslim survival, however, would not always remain favorable. While the monarchy took a beneficent attitude Christian nobles and churchmen sought to exploit their new subjects. Christian settlement and competition for trade and land led to rioting between Christians and Muslims. In 1276 Christians attacked the Muslim quarters in Valencia and other towns, and Muslims rebelled. In retaliation, Muslim property was seized, Muslim quarters were looted, and many people were sold into slavery.

By the middle of the fourteenth century the Muslim position had sharply deteriorated. The Muslims acquired additional financial obligations; Muslim communities lost their internal autonomy and their right to select qadis and came to be directly controlled by the Aragonese crown and its nobles. Military orders were often granted Muslim serfs, pushing segments of the free Muslim population into servitude. Political control also led to a progressive restriction of Muslim religious liberties. In 1311 King James II prohibited the public call to prayer, though in 1357, in return for payment, it was permitted in a low voice. By the middle of the fourteenth century some 80 percent of judicial cases were heard in Christian rather than Muslim courts and were tried under

Christian rather than Muslim law. By the late fourteenth century the once organized and autonomous Muslim community had been subordinated to direct Christian rule.

Despite this deteriorating environment, the Valencian Muslim population maintained its identity. While Aragonese Muslims who had been conquered centuries earlier lost their knowledge of Arabic and were fully assimilated to Christian rule, Valencian Muslims continued to speak Arabic, refused to learn the Romance language of Valencia, did not feel any loyalty to the Aragonese crown, and did not interact with the Christian population. Valencia's Muslims continued to identify with Granada and North Africa.

However, by the late fourteenth century Christians became actively interested in the conversion of the Jews and Muslims and the creation of religious uniformity in Spain. In 1391 Jews were forced to accept baptism. In 1478 the inquisition was inaugurated and offered Jews a choice of baptism or exile. In 1492 virtually the entire Jewish population, once a flourishing commercial and cultural community, was expelled from Spain to other parts of Europe and the Ottoman empire.

The Christian conquest of Granada in 1492 marked the beginning of the end of Muslim population in Spain. While the treaty of surrender guaranteed Muslim religious liberty and property, in practice these rights were ignored. In 1501 Spanish law offered Muslims a choice between conversion or exile. Many Granadans became crypto-Muslims who tried to reconcile the secret practice of Islam with the outward profession of Christianity. Thus Arabic texts of the sixteenth century try to excuse Christian practices to Muslim consciences by claiming, for example, that the son-hood of Jesus was but a figure of speech, or that the mass was performed with water and not with wine. In 1556 Arab and Muslim dress was forbidden in Granada, and in 1566 Philip II decreed that the Arabic language could no longer be used. Thus there emerged the *aljamiado* literature composed in Romance language but written in Arabic script and translating Arabic texts. Finally, in 1609 Philip III expelled the Muslims from Spain. They took refuge in North Africa where Andalusian communities once again contributed to a flourishing Islamic civilization.

Thus the first major Muslim experience of Christian rule showed how in the multi-ethnic and multi-religious societies of the Mediterranean, Middle Eastern and Muslim concepts of autonomous religious community could serve for a time to accommodate Muslims into a Christian society just as they had accommodated Christians into a Muslim society. In the long run, however, the Christian demand for religious homogeneity led to the forced assimilation or expulsion of the Jewish and Muslim populations.

THE TRIPARTITE REGIME: TUNISIA, ALGERIA, AND MOROCCO
FROM THE THIRTEENTH TO THE NINETEENTH CENTURY

While the Muslim presence in Spain was being liquidated, Islamic societies in North Africa were entering a new stage of development. With the collapse of the Almohads, North Africa began to take on a new configuration of state and society. While older claims to a "Caliphal" type of religious authority were carried into the new era, North African states increasingly moved toward the Saljuq (and Egyptian Ayyubid-Mamluk) type of Middle Eastern Islamic institutional structure. The state regimes would be based upon political institutions inherited directly from their Almohad predecessor in that they would be supported by client, slave, or mercenary armies and a small household bureaucracy which was part of the entourage of the rulers, and would be dependent on a governing coalition of tribal forces. The degree of central state consolidation and the degree of dependence upon autonomous tribal coalitions would distinguish the several regimes from each other. Parallel to state consolidation was the spread of Sufism. Inspired by developments in the eastern Muslim world and in Spain, Sufism took root throughout North Africa in the twelfth and later centuries, and Sufi-led communities became an important form of social organization for rural populations. The state regimes of the post-Almohad era would have to develop a new relationship between the political elites and religious notables. Some of them would surrender their claims to direct religious authority; all would accept the ʿulamaʾ and Sufis as the bearers of Islamic legitimacy and as intermediaries in the government of their societies. In different forms they implemented the eastern patronage concept of a Muslim state.

The power of these states vis-à-vis internal tribal and other political powers depended upon the trade routes that linked North Africa, the Sahara, the Sudan, and Europe. All of them depended on revenues from European trade and sometimes on direct European military support. However, from the end of the fourteenth century, under pressure of tribal resistance and of Catalan, Portuguese, and Spanish expansion, centralized regimes broke down. The breakdown of these regimes shifted the balance of power in North Africa to Sufi-led tribal communities formed in opposition to both native states and Christian invaders. Sufi leadership united rural peoples to meet the needs of political order, defense, economic organization, mediation of disputes, and other essential functions. The growing importance of Muslim religious communities throughout North Africa linked the region to the wider Arab and Middle Eastern Islamic world.

Map 16. North Africa and Spain in the fifteenth and sixteenth centuries.

Marinids, Wattasids

Zayanids

Hafsids

Ottoman empire

Christian reconquest

Atlantic Ocean

Black Sea

Adriatic Sea

Mediterranean Sea

Crete Sea

S a h a r a

Poitiers
Toulouse
Marseilles
Venice
Genoa
Pisa
SARDINIA
Naples
Palermo
SICILY
Istanbul
Aleppo
Damascus
CYPRUS
Jerusalem
Cairo
Nile R.
Alexandria
Barqa
Tripoli
EGYPT

Lisbon
PORTUGAL
Badajoz
Cordova
Seville
Malaga
Granada
GRANADA
Murcia
Valencia
Barcelona
Saragossa
ARAGON
Madrid
Toledo
Avila
Segovia
Duero R.
Ebro R.
Tagus R.
Guadalquivir
CASTILE
Tangier
Ceuta
Tetuan
Melilla
Oran
Algiers
Bougie
Bone
Tunis
Constantine
Qayrawan
Monastir
Mahdia
Sfax
Gabes
Yerba
TRIPOLITANIA

Alqazar al-Quivir
Sale
Rabat
Meknes
Fez
Taza
Tlemcen
Tahert
KABYLIA
Aures Mts

Marrakesh
Agadir
Sijilmasa
al-Aghmat
Wargala

500 km
300 miles

The North African crisis attracted Ottoman intervention and opened a century-long struggle between the Ottoman and Habsburg empires for control of North Africa and the Mediterranean, a struggle that culminated in the imposition of Ottoman suzerainty on Libya, Tunisia, and Algeria, but confirmed the independence of Morocco. Ottoman suzerainty consolidated North African politico-religious institutions and identities as variations upon Middle Eastern Islamic themes. Each of the North African societies, however, constituted a separate variation upon the Islamic paradigm and affords revealing comparisons which highlight the basic organizational mechanisms of Islamic societies.

Tunisian society from the thirteenth to the nineteenth century was essentially a reconstruction of past forms of centralized state regimes based on an urbanized economy and relatively close political control over rural and pastoral populations. Such a regime had been consolidated in the eighth and ninth centuries and, though it had lapsed under the pressure of the Hilali invasions and economic decline, was rebuilt with significant innovations by the Hafsid dynasty (1228–1574). Hafsid power, however, was intermittent and its control over the whole of Tunisia sporadic. Tunisian regimes from the thirteenth to the nineteenth century went through repeated phases of consolidation and disintegration. Nonetheless they stood for an institutional complex which defined Tunisian society until the modern era.

In terms of political institutions the Hafsid regime grew directly out of the Almohad empire. The dynasty descended from an aristocratic Almohad family, and was built around the former Almohad elites. The Hafsid armies included Almohad tribes, Arab nomads, Berbers from the Constantine and Bougie regions, Turks and Kurds, black slaves, and a Christian militia whom the rulers of Aragon considered under their suzerain control. In the fifteenth century, the descendants of earlier generations of mercenaries continued to form a bodyguard for the rulers, though they had in the meantime become Arabized. The Hafsids also maintained a weak navy supplemented by privateers.

The civil administration was dominated by Andalusian scribes who provided the viziers of the army, finance, and chancery services. They were the principal officers for court affairs, governors of the royal palace, secretaries, chamberlains, and treasurers. The elites were supported by the distribution of iqtaˁs to government officials, Almohad shaykhs, and tribal chiefs. Nomadic tribes, however, were quasi-independent. The Hafsids tried to win influence with these groups by influencing the choice of the chiefs, by putting them under military pressure, by winning favor through fiscal or territorial concessions or by integrating tribal factions into the royal armies. Southern tribes were particularly likely to be independent.

The relative strength of the state was related to the revenues of international trade. While the Hilali invasions, European assaults, and the transfer of international trade routes to Egypt and Morocco had badly compromised the economic prosperity of Tunisia in the eleventh and twelfth centuries, a series of thirteenth-century treaties with Sicily, Venice, Marseilles, Genoa, and Florence helped revive Tunisian prosperity. At the end of the fourteenth century Tunis was exporting cereals, dried fruits, dates, olive oil, fish, salt, spices, sugar, wool, leather, cotton goods, coral, weapons, and slaves, and it was importing cereals, spices, wine, cloth goods, dyes, wood, metal, weapons, and jewelry. At the end of the fifteenth century the Portuguese discovery of a route to India and the aggressive expansion of Portugal and Spain along the coasts of North Africa undermined Tunisian trade, and ultimately reduced it to dependency upon the Ottoman empire.

Out of the broad possibilities afforded by the repertoire of Muslim, cosmopolitan, and patrimonial concepts of rule, the Hafsids chose to portray themselves as Muslim rulers. They took the titles of Caliph and amir al-muʾ-minin; the head of state was later called Malik al-Sultan in imitation of Mamluk Egyptian rulers. Succession was legitimized by the oath of allegiance and the recognition of the ruler in the Friday prayer. Solemn public processions accompanied by flags and drums were also prerogatives of the sovereign.

The rulers conducted state business in a formal court attended by tribal chiefs, soldiers, men of religion, intellectuals and other courtiers. Morning was reserved for military business; afternoon for civil administration; evening for entertainment. The households of the ruler were not only centers of political administration, but also of religious worship with mosques and academies of learning. Scholars from all over North Africa and Spain gathered to instruct the rulers, to minister to religious needs, and to symbolize the religious credentials of the Sultans. The Hafsid court produced studies of the Quran, hadith, law, Arabic grammar, biographies of the Prophet and of saints, dictionaries of famous scholars, histories, and works of theology. The architectural style of the Hafsid period was derived from Morocco and Egypt. However, science and medicine languished.

Like the Mamluks in Egypt, the Hafsids sponsored Muslim law and a Maliki restoration. They maintained an Islamic religious administration under the authority of the *qadi al-jamaᶜa*, a title which goes back to Umayyad Spain. Tunis had a second qadi who specialized in marriage law. A weekly council of qadis and muftis met to review important cases in the presence of the rulers.

In 1257 the Hafsids endowed the al-Mustansiriya madrasa and by the beginning of the fourteenth century were appointing Maliki scholars to all official religious posts. The feast of the end of Ramadan and the feast of the conclusion of the pilgrimage were celebrated by massive public prayers led by the sovereign. The birthday of the Prophet, marked first in Egypt in the thirteenth century, and declared an official festival in Morocco in 1292, was accepted as an official feast in Tunisia at the end of the fourteenth century. The Sultans also sponsored the daily reading of hadith and of the biography of the Prophet in the great mosque of Tunis.

Gradually, however, Sufism began to displace law as the most important expression of Tunisian Islam. Between the eleventh and the thirteenth centuries, Sufism spread from the towns into rural areas. Al-Shadhali, who was born in Morocco, educated in Egypt, and died in Tunis in 1258, left numerous disciples who combined formal scholarship with mystical exercises. As friends of God, they were believed to perform miracles, know what would happen at a distance, see or dream the future, transport themselves magically over time and space, cure the sick, and intercede before God for ordinary believers. They gathered groups of disciples, sworn to absolute obedience, to whom they taught the special techniques which had given them their mystical powers, and whom they initiated by transmitting the khirqa or cloak of the Sufi. The more puritanical of the Sufis deplored the common practices of visits to tombs and the use of music to achieve ecstasy.

From the late thirteenth century Sufi zawiyas began to assume social and political functions. Sufis organized tribal coalitions to safeguard the trade routes, suppress brigandage, promote religious piety, and oppose illegal taxation. In the course of the fourteenth century Sufism was sufficiently consolidated for the political authorities to seek the favor of the Sufis. Territorial or fiscal concessions were given to the *zawiyas*. In Tunis a combination zawiya–madrasa, founded in 1399, marked the integration of urban Sufism and Maliki Islam. Sufism was gradually becoming the basis of social organization for urban as well as rural peoples. The breakup of the Hafsid state in the fourteenth century, its subsequent reconstruction in the fifteenth, and final decline in the sixteenth century, allowed organized Sufi Islam to become the most powerful force in Tunisian society.

The Tunisian state was rebuilt by the imposition of Ottoman rule in the late sixteenth century. The great Ottoman–Habsburg wars of the sixteenth century led to the Ottoman conquest of Algiers in 1529 and to the capture of Tunis in 1574. The Ottomans made Tunisia a province of their empire, and garrisoned Tunis with 4,000 janissaries recruited in Anatolia, reinforced by renegade Christians from Italy, Spain, and Provence. In 1591 the local janissary officers replaced the Sultan's appointee with one of their own men, called the Dey. While the Dey dominated Tunis, a Corsican-born Tunisian tax collector (Bey) named Murad (d. 1640), and his descendants, dominated the rest of the country. The struggle for power made allies of the Dey, the janissaries, and bedouin tribes against the Beys, the towns, and the fertile regions of the countryside. The Muradid Beys eventually triumphed, and ruled until 1705, when Husayn b. ʿAli came to power and established a dynasty which would reign until 1957. In theory Tunisia continued to be a vassal of the Ottoman empire – the Friday prayer was pronounced in the name of the Ottoman Sultan, money was coined in his honour, and an annual ambassador brought gifts to Istanbul – but the Ottomans never again exacted obedience.

Under Ottoman suzerainty Tunisia resumed the system of political control over the religious elites developed under the Hafsids. Under the Husaynids there were both Hanafi and Maliki qadis, a qadi of the Bey's palace, a qadi of the army involved in tax collecting, a qadi of the treasury dealing in estates without male heirs, and other qadis. The leading qadis and muftis participated in the Bey's council. The Bey could appoint and dismiss the judges, juris-consults, teachers in madrasas, and Sufi shaykhs of zawiyas. While the religious establishment was highly integrated, and ʿulamaʾ and Sufis were closely identified, it was dependent upon the state. The central government also controlled the rural tribes. It broke the power of the great tribal chiefs and left only lesser chieftainships and smaller units intact. Tunisia was ruled by some 60 qaʾids (district governors) and some 2,000 local shaykhs. Much of the rural population, however, was quasi-independent on the basis of organized lineages, Sufi brotherhoods, and political alliances.

The migration of Spanish Muslims to North Africa reinforced the sedentary and commercial sectors of Tunisian society. Andalusian poets, scribes, schol-ars, and soldiers took refuge with the Hafsids. Many were incorporated into the Tunisian armies. After the fall of Granada in 1492, increasing Christian pressure on the Muslim population in Spain led to a steady emigration to North Africa, which reached its peak with the expulsion of the Moriscos at the beginning of the seventeenth century. Many newcomers settled in the Zuqaq al-Andalus and other suburbs of Tunis. Numerous Andalusian villages were founded and produced olives, silk, and grapes. As cultivators, the Andalusians introduced new irrigation systems, mills, gardens, and vineyards in the Spanish fashion. The migrants were accorded autonomy in tax collections; an official spokesman, the Shaykh al-Andalus, represented them to the government. A cultured community, they continued to speak their own languages and founded mosques and colleges.

Until the late eighteenth and early nineteenth centuries the Tunisian economy functioned in the traditional way. It was divided into a sector of self-sufficient nomads and cultivators, and a sector attached to international trade. Tunisia exported meat, wool, olive oil, hides, beeswax, dates, and sponges, and imported European cloth and paper. The Beys entered the trade, gathering taxes of wheat and wool in kind which they sold to European merchants. In the eighteenth century ʿAli (1759–1782) and Hammuda Pasha (1782–1813) followed a policy designed to maximize commercial advantages. They seized the opportunities provided by European wars to enlarge Tunisian trade, improve ports, and encourage Tunisian cloth production.

The felt cap industry, introduced by Andalusians, was one of the most important. The *shashiya* was the standard cap worn throughout the Mediterranean by Christians, Jews, Armenians, and Muslims, and was widely sold throughout the Ottoman empire, the Balkans, and Iran. The production of these caps also depended upon international trade. Wool came from Spain, vermilion from Portugal, and alum from Rome. The imports, however, were generally in the control of French merchants from Marseilles and Jewish merchants from Livorno. Hundreds of workshops were organized by merchant investors, and Tunisian production often reached 100,000 dozen hats per year. There were between 15,000 and 50,000 people engaged in the trade. Though Tunisians suffered from liabilities, such as the regulations imposed by the Bey of Tunis, European control of raw materials, a rigid corporate organization, and high costs of production, they had the advantage of understanding the market and producing an appropriate product.

In the late eighteenth century, however, the Tunisian economy went into decline. From 1784 to 1820 there were repeated crop failures and outbreaks of plague. One consequence was that olive oil replaced wheat as the major export. At the same time Europeans turned the terms of trade in the Mediterranean to the disadvantage of Tunisia. The shashiya was forced off the market by French competition. The industrial revolution and the tremendous increase of European production undermined the industry. By the middle decades of the nineteenth century the most highly capitalized and the most profitable Tunisian industry was in decline. At the same time the price of olive oil declined drastically, and Tunisia was left importing manufactured and luxury products in an unfavorable balance-of-payments situation.

In spite of economic decline, the government attempted to build up the army and the state apparatus. The government multiplied taxes and monopolies and forced producers to sell olive oil to the state at a discount. Ahmad Bey (1837–55) broke the power of local notables and centralized control of taxes. In 1856 the government proposed a consolidated tax called the *majba* which raised the effective level of taxation. Doubled in 1863 to repay Tunisian loans, it provoked a great peasant uprising in 1864. The revolt of 1864 spread throughout the country, but lack of coordination among the various resistance groups allowed it to be suppressed piecemeal.

Foreign economic and political influence interacted with a declining internal situation to bring Tunisia into complete dependence on the European powers. By the 1840s the Tunisian government no longer had adequate revenues to maintain the army. Borrowing from European banks led to bankruptcy in 1867. In 1869 Tunisia had to submit to a French, British, and Italian commission to collect tax revenues and repay the bondholders. The political barriers to complete foreign control were removed by the Congress of Berlin, where the European powers encouraged France to establish a protectorate over Tunisia to divert her from the loss of Alsace-Lorraine and to compensate her for Russian gains in the Balkans and the British occupation of Cyprus. The protectorate was declared in 1881. Thus while Tunisia shook off Ottoman rule, and maintained a centralized state structure, the decline of the Tunisian economy opened the way to European occupation.

While Tunisia had a long history of state regimes, the region we now know as Algeria had virtually none. Though there had been Khariji principalities and tribal dynasties, Algeria had no central state and no territorial identity. From the thirteenth to the fifteenth century it was generally under Hafsid suzerainty. In the course of the fifteenth century, however, the internal social structure was changing. Sufi teachers gathered followers, acquired large territories as gifts from local rulers or from their devotees and became landowners, patrons, and spiritual counselors for multitudes of small cultivators. Henceforth the political structure of Algeria would be based upon tribal or lineage groups, Sufi-led communities, and state regimes.

An Algerian state was first organized as a result of the Ottoman conquest. With the help of Ottoman guns and janissaries Khayr al-Din Barbarossa captured Algiers in 1529. From 1529 to 1587 Algiers was ruled by a beylerbey (provincial governor), supported by janissaries, directly appointed by the Sultan in Istanbul, who was responsible for Ottoman land and sea forces in the western Mediterranean. Against heavy odds the new Algiers regime carved out a North African empire. Tlemsen was taken in 1551, Bougie in 1555, and Turkish suzerainty was established in the rest of Algeria. Tunisia was taken under Ottoman control in 1574, but Ottoman efforts to impose suzerainty upon Morocco were defeated. The Ottoman advance into Morocco was checked by the emergence of a strong Moroccan state and the restored balance of power between Ottomans and the Habsburgs of Spain. The Habsburg–Ottoman peace of 1580 allowed Morocco to exist as a buffer state between the great Mediterranean empires. The century-long Ottoman–Spanish struggle left North Africa in Muslim control and most of it, from Egypt to the borders of Morocco, under Ottoman suzerainty.

With the termination of Ottoman campaigns in the western Mediterranean, direct Ottoman control of Algeria was allowed to lapse. The authority of the Ottoman-appointed governors was slowly undermined by the rising power of the *Agha*, the chief officer of the janissaries, and the raʾis, the captain of the fleets. In 1659 the Agha of the janissaries became the ruler of Algeria and in 1689 the head of state was titled Dey. From 1689 to 1830 Algeria was ruled by the Deys and the Turkish janissary military elite. While tribute was sent to Istanbul in exchange for the Sultan's political and ideological support and the right to recruit janissaries in Anatolia, the Algerian state was essentially independent.

The legitimacy of this regime was based on its warrior origins, its struggle against the infidels, and the prestige derived from allegiance to the Ottoman Sultans. The janissaries created a dual Muslim judicial system, one for the Hanafis, mainly the Turkish elite, and the other for Malikis or local people. Each had its muftis and qadis appointed by the Ottoman Sultans. In the case of disputes among the different law courts a tribunal composed of leading qadis, muftis and religious scholars held final jurisdiction. Apart from the judicial administration there is little evidence for a large ʿulamaʾ establishment or for state sponsorship of a Muslim educational system. There was no institution in Algeria comparable to the Qarawiyin college of Fez or the Zaytuna mosque of Tunis.

The real base of the regime was its military forces. A privileged body, entitled by conquest to collect taxes, the Turkish military corps or *ujaq* numbered approximately 15,000 men. The sons of Turkish soldiers and local women, called *kulughlis* were in principle excluded from the ujaq but served as subordinate militias. The Dey was elected by the officers to administer the city of Algiers and its agricultural environs. The rest of the country was divided into three regions, Constantine, Mascara and Titteri, governed by representatives of the Dey who were called Beys. The power of the Beys was built on the command of a janissary garrison, kulughli auxiliaries, and loyal tribes. To subdistricts within their jurisdiction the Beys named qaʾids who controlled the local tribal leaders, levied taxes, settled judicial disputes, and presided over the markets.

Apart from zones of direct administration, the population was organized under the authority of intermediary religious and tribal chieftains. The Ottoman–Turkish regime actually helped to create a tribal structure by consolidating small groups into tribes and appointing local chiefs. In some cases, they helped to transform a basically equalitarian lineage society into a hierarchical one linked to the central polity. In other cases independent tribal or religious chiefs were confirmed in their existing local power. Many of the local chiefs were Sufis. To win their support the Algerian regime accorded them respect, endowed mosques and tombs, appointed them to judicial positions and gave them land and tax revenues. The Sufi-organized tribal communities were particularly important on the Moroccan frontier but were much less important in the Constantine region and on the Tunisian frontier. Some districts, such as the Kabyle, Aurès, and the Sahara, remained fully autonomous.

Apart from their reliance on local religious and tribal chiefs the Turkish-Algerian regime also had considerable powers to manipulate rural populations by requiring that all persons wishing to trade or work in the marketplace have a permit issued by the Agha of the janissaries. The Kabyle region, in particular, was dependent on these permits because it was overpopulated and relied upon the export of olive oil, figs, craft products, and surplus labor for survival. Each year the notables of the Kabyle organized a large caravan carrying oil and figs, which returned with grain and animals. In southern Algeria the government controlled the movements of pastoralists by manipulating the price of grain and levying a tax on each camel load. To collect taxes the government also had recourse to a *mahalla* or military expedition to coerce the local population.

In the course of the sixteenth century privateering was a flourishing enterprise. Algerian corsairs seized European ships at sea, confiscated their goods, and sold their crews into slavery. Portions of the booty went to support the government and repay merchants who helped finance the ventures, but there was also a great increase in the number of mosques and pious foundations endowed by the earnings of the corsairs.

In the eighteenth century, however, the power of the central government declined. While the Dey was able to consolidate his personal power, the state suffered drastic losses in revenue from privateering and trade. As Algerian naval power declined the Dey himself had to resort to European shipowners to assure his vital military links with the Ottoman empire. After 1700 there was an increasing tendency to compensate for declining sea revenues by increased taxation of the countryside. The Deys were also obliged to rely on Jewish, French, and English merchants for financial support.

At the beginning of the nineteenth century the relationship between the Algerian-Turkish regime and the Sufi orders broke down. In the decades between 1800 and 1830 there were sporadic rebellions led by the Darqawa, the Qadiriya, and the Tijaniya. Since the various orders were confined to particular regions – the Rahmaniya to the Kabyle, the Tijaniya to the Sahara, and the Darqawa to the Oranie – the rebels were not able to unite. The small scale of many of the Sufi constituencies, the existence of large rival tribal formations, and the mutual hostility between the Tijaniya and the Darqawa, made it impossible to present the regime with a united opposition.

Nevertheless, in the period of its ascendancy, the Turkish regime had managed to define the territorial identity of Algeria and to create a centralized state in the region between Tunisia and Morocco. The state apparatus was highly institutionalized in the Ottoman manner, but its control over the country was limited by independent rural communities. The control of the periphery depended on the military supremacy of the janissaries. In the six-teenth and seventeenth centuries a small professional army could deal with dispersed tribal coalitions, but by the eighteenth century, as fewer recruits came from Anatolia and as modern weapons were more widely dispersed, the state's hegemony diminished. As the state depended increasingly upon foreign financial connections, its legitimacy was compromised. Turkish military force and economic controls were enough in some parts of Algeria to assure the continued subordination of religious and tribal chiefs, but in other regions the Sufis and their clienteles rebelled. The Algerian state had long been a "sectored" regime, a regime effective only in part of its nominal domains. In the early nineteenth century the balance of power between this limited central government and the rest of Algerian society was turning against the Turkish state. This was the moment for the French invasion of 1830.

In Morocco, as in Tunisia, the defeat of the Almohads was followed by the formation of a new type of Islamic state. The Almoravids and Almohads had created the bases for a Moroccan territorial state and centralized regime. Morocco would go through successive cycles of political consolidation and decline as the Marinid, Saᶜdian, and ᶜAlawi dynasties in turn captured the state and lost control to other forces.

The Marinids were the dominant group in a coalition of Zenata Berbers who overthrew the Almohads and conquered Morocco between 1244 and 1274. Their government was built around a court city and a small household administration. The Marinids built Fez Jadid in 1275 as a military and administrative residence for the ruler and his family, officials and troops. Here were quartered Castilian or Catalonian militias. The dynasty was supported by a coalition of Moroccan tribes which included the Banu Marin, the Banu Maᶜqil who controlled the territory south of the Atlas, and various Zenata-Berber chieftains in the Atlas region and Algeria. Government control was effective on the plains of central and northern Morocco but not in the mountain regions. To legitimize the regime, the Friday prayers were first said in the name of the Hafsid Caliphs; the Marinid princes claimed the title of amir al-muslimin. Gradually, however, they abandoned Almohad doctrine and simply claimed to be the protectors of Sunni Islam. They favored ᶜulamaᵓ and madrasa forms of religious instruction. In 1437 they attempted to coopt the legitimacy attached to descendants of the Prophet by their discovery of the tomb of Idris II and the creation of a Marinid-sponsored cult around his tomb.

The Marinid regime, however, was undermined by a variety of economic problems. In the course of the fourteenth century there were profound changes in the pattern of international trade which were detrimental to Moroccan prosperity. The kingdom of Mali entered into competition for the southern sectors of the Sahara–Sudan routes, and helped revitalize competing trade routes via Tlemsen, Bougie, Tunis, and Egypt which substantially cut into Morocco's share of the profitable traffic. Economic competition pitted Hafsids and Marinids against each other as rivals for the control of Tlemsen. Morocco's Mediterranean trade also declined even though, throughout the fourteenth and fifteenth centuries, ships from Venice, Genoa, Pisa, Marseilles, Catalonia, and Aragon regularly traded in Moroccan ports. Morocco imported metals, hardware, textiles, woolens, spices, and wine, and exported leather, hides, carpets, wool, coral, grain, slaves, and sugar.

From the beginning of the fifteenth century, Morocco was further damaged by Portuguese efforts to establish their political and commercial supremacy in the western Mediterranean. In 1415 the Portuguese seized Ceuta and in 1471 Tangiers. Between 1486 and 1550 they established themselves on the Atlantic coast of Morocco. The Portuguese did not attempt to use their forts for further inland conquests, though they made occasional raids to keep the local populations off balance. Rather, they moved along the African coast opening the way for direct trade with Sudanic Africa.

Even in the short run, the Portuguese threat brought about both a crisis of economy and a crisis of political legitimacy. Within Morocco the precarious balance between the state and tribal forces shifted in favor of the latter. Already Hilali Arabs had pushed their way into the Sus and Saharan regions of Morocco and done severe damage to agriculture. After a century of bedouin occupation, only the towns, the oases, and the mountain regions remained centers of agriculture. With the decline of the central government the Banu Maᶜqil created their own small empire south of the Atlas. Although they recognized Marinid suzerainty, they took control of Sijilmassa and made themselves an independent power. Marrakesh fell into the control of tribal chiefs. The Wattasids, originally tribal allies of the Marinids, became regents for the dynasty in 1428 and then assumed the Sultanate from 1472 to 1549. Under the Wattasids the weakness of the central state allowed nomadic peoples to make further gains at the expense of peasant cultivation and permitted the Portuguese to seize and fortify numerous coastal ports.

The economic and political regression of Morocco in the Marinid and Wattasid periods led to the rise of Sufism. Moroccan Sufis were generally religious scholars living in village communities. A typical Moroccan Sufi of the fourteenth century combined knowledge of mysticism and law, literate scholarship, and esoteric practices. In the Moroccan ideal of the time the perfected Sufi was a symbol of the religious qualities of the Prophet who was in turn a symbol of the reality of God. The Sufi was venerated not in his person but as a symbol of the *surat al-Muhammadiya* – the laudable qualities which belong to the spiritual universe and are concentrated in the person of the Prophet. Sufis were affiliated with zawiyas as centers of worship and teaching, but in this period they did not have political functions.

In the fifteenth century, however, the breakdown of the Moroccan state and the occupation of Moroccan territory by the Portuguese brought the dynasty contempt for failing to defend Islam. Sufism became crucial for organizing local self-defense and mobilizing popular resistance to the Portuguese. Sufis became the leaders of local tribal coalitions. Moreover, the scale of Sufi organization was greatly enlarged by the introduction of the tariqat. Under the inspiration of Abu ᶜAbdallah Muhammad al-Jazuli (d. 1465) the independent Sufi zawiyas were affiliated with larger organizations. This occurred when a master zawiya created satellite communities, or when existing zawiyas united into a single brotherhood based on a shared spiritual lineage. Loyalty to the shaykhs, shared dhikrs, and ceremonies of initiation bound together the members of the brotherhoods.

Sufi authority was also buttressed by the acceptance of a new concept of religious authority. In addition to authority based on the imitation of the Prophet, descent was taken to assure religious sanctity. The descendants of the Prophet (pl. *shurafaᵓ*) were already a privileged caste in local society, supported by religious endowments, and organized under the leadership of a *naqib*, who acted as judge, maintained records, and represented the interests of the group. With the decline of the Marinid state the shurafaᵓ managed to establish the idea that they had a moral right to oversee political affairs. Ever after, Moroccan Sufis and princes would claim sharifian descent.

With the formation of new Sufi brotherhoods and a new concept of authority, a profound change had taken place in the structure of Moroccan society. A new form of social organization based on the authority of the Sufis and the shurafaᵓ challenged both tribal and the state concepts of the political order and allowed for the creation of local coalitions on the basis of tribal allegiances to the Sufi orders. Henceforth, no Moroccan regime could come to power or maintain itself without integrating this new concept of authority and the organizational form in which it was embedded into its own political practice.

By the fifteenth century, then, Morocco, like Tunisia and Algeria, was a society with a central state regime and a Sufi-led rural population. In the course of the fifteenth and sixteenth centuries the central regime temporarily broke down and Sufi-led communities became the dominant force, but in the late sixteenth century the Moroccan state was seized by the Saᶜdians and restored to a precarious sovereignty. The Saᶜdians had their origins in a local jihad against the Portuguese fortress of Agadir led by Muhammad al-Mahdi. The holy war gathered the support of Sufi and tribal chiefs and Muhammad was elected amir of the Sus. The growing Saᶜdian principality financed itself by developing sugar plantations and by encouraging trade in gold with the Sudan. From the Sus the Saᶜdians moved on to conquer all of Morocco. At the same time both the Ottomans and the Portuguese intervened in Morocco, but the Portuguese were defeated at the battle of Alcazaralquivir (1578) and Morocco emerged as an independent state, protected by the balance of power between the Habsburgs and the Ottomans. The Saᶜdians ruled Morocco from 1554 to 1659.

While Algeria and Tunisia were shaped by Ottoman institutions, the Saᶜdians provided Morocco with another type of Islamic regime. Like the Ottomans, the authority of the new regime rested on its service to Islam in the holy war, but the Saᶜdians claimed descent from the Prophet Muhammad and thus linked themselves to a concept which had, in the course of the fifteenth century, become central to Moroccan notions of political authority. This descent was conceived partly in genealogical terms, partly in terms of devotion to the teachings of the Prophet, and partly in terms of the symbolic embodiment of divine virtues. The Saᶜdians linked themselves to the Sufis by moving the body of al-Jazuli to Marrakesh to symbolize the formation of a coalition of Sufi brotherhoods around the venerated tomb, and later made the birthday of the Prophet the premier Moroccan religious festival.

The celebration of the Prophet's birthday gave added import to the political claims of the dynasty. It appealed to the Sufi brotherhoods because they too claimed physical and spiritual closeness to Muhammad, and it gave the common people a worshipful closeness to the principal figure in their religion. Sultan al-Mansur (1578–1603) also tried to embellish the ritual paraphernalia of his office by introducing a more elaborate court ceremonial. In the absence of Ottoman institutions the Sultans ruled not only by administrative means but by the baraka (power of blessing) derived from sharifian descent, by dynastic inheritance, and by elective authority conferred by tribe, city, and the army. Thus the Saʿdian Sultanate represented Islamic religious unity and authority in a territory dominated by tribal and Sufi concepts of society. In this regard Moroccan authority resembled that of the Safavids rather than the Ottomans.

Al-Mansur emerged as the great organizer of the regime. He expanded the army from its Berber tribal base to include mercenaries from Spain, Turkey, and Africa who were competent in the use of firearms. In 1603 there were 4,000 European renegades, 4,000 Andalusians, and 1,500 Turks in an army of some 40,000. Modern artillery units were incorporated. Fortifications capable of mounting artillery were built at Taza, Fez, and Marrakesh. Both England and the Netherlands provided Morocco with ships, cannon, and powder in their shared enmity to Habsburg Spain. Loyal tribes enabled the regime to control the plains of northern Morocco and the Atlantic coastal regions.

The Saʿdians were able to consolidate their power with the help of economic resources gained from trade with Europe and the Sudan. For a time Moroccan sugar was an important source of royal revenues. The industry was owned by the Sultans, managed by Jews and European Christians, and operated by slave labor. As early as the late thirteenth century Moroccan sugar was being exported to Flanders, Venice, and later to Spain, but in the seventeenth century new plantations in Madeira, the Canary Islands, and the Americas squeezed Morocco out of the international market. The Saʿdians also attempted to increase their revenues by controlling the Saharan trade. They first captured the Portuguese along the Atlantic coast, and then, in 1591, seized Timbuktu, and took control of trans-Saharan trade.

Despite the favorable economic conditions, the Moroccan state broke down upon the death of al-Mansur. Saʿdian princes established separate regimes at Fez and Marrakesh; Sufi chiefs created independent principalities. In the ensuing struggle for power, the brothers Maulay Muhammad and Maulay Rashid, leaders of a sharifian faction in Tafilalt, triumphed over other factional forces, and established the dynasty which governs Morocco to the present day.

Despite the change of dynasty the ʿAlawi regime represented the same type of state and society as its Saʿdian predecessors.

Like the Saʿdians the ʿAlawis came to power on the basis of the religious legitimacy provided by descent from the Prophet and war against the infidels. Maulay Ismaʿil (1672–1727) was the first great ruler of the dynasty. He attempted once again to reconstruct the centralized state by building up a professional army of some 30,000 to 50,000 slaves. These slaves were most likely recruited from the existing Moroccan slave population and from the subordinate, client tribes called *haratin*. They are called blacks, but it is doubtful that they came from the Sudan. The slave army was supplemented by the tribes who furnished troops in return for tax exemptions and rights to land. Civil administration was based essentially on the royal palace household at Meknes. High government functionaries were recruited from the dominant tribes and from the town bourgeoisie, including the leading families of Fez and families of Andalusian descent. ʿUlamaʾ filled the offices of judge, market inspector, administrator of intestate properties, and other posts. In the provinces the government was represented by qaʾids who varied in power from subordinate functionaries to independent local lords.

Despite the ostensible strength of the central government apparatus it had limited power in the provinces. While rural peoples did not question the Sultan's authority, in practice defiance of his power was the norm. In principle the Sufi leaders were also subordinate to the authority of the central government, but in fact they remained independent. The ʿAlawis had come to power without the aid of rural Sufis and attempted to overcome their influence by using the authority of the Sultan over religious activities. The ʿAlawis built up cadres of ʿulamaʾ in Fez. They took over the right to ratify succession to the chieftainship of a zawiya and the control of its properties and conferred upon the Sufis both spiritual titles and control over land and revenues. In cases of dispute over succession to the chieftainship of a zawiya, the Sultan or his appointed delegate was the final arbiter. Still Sufi chiefs played an important role in trade, and their headquarters were commonly located along trade routes or along the boundaries between tribal groups, where they could facilitate traffic and negotiate disputes. The zawiyas were also centers of agriculture, and provided educational and judicial services. A zawiya was at once a hotel, a hospital, a school, a market, a mosque, a court of law, and a refuge.

Sufi influence continued to expand as new brotherhoods were founded throughout the seventeenth, eighteenth, and nineteenth centuries. These included the Nasiriya which claimed to represent the purest Islamic orthodoxy.

Its rituals consisted of supplementary prayers and the recitation of the expression "There is no God but God" a thousand times a day. Its chiefs refused to use the name of the ʿAlawi Sultan in the Friday prayers on the grounds that it was blasphemous to mention a human being in the course of divine supplication. The Darqawa, founded in the late eighteenth century, denounced the pointless repetition of prayers and sought to restore direct communication with the divine being through a prayer and dance designed to induce religious ecstasy. The relation of the Sufi orders to governments was a complicated combination of antagonism and cooperation. In some cases the Sufi orders helped the state consolidate its authority, in other cases they resisted. Moroccan rulers were forced to revert to bribes, gifts, and the manipulation of local interests.

The balance of royal and rural power was strongly affected by the trading economy. From the conquest of the Sudan in 1591 until the nineteenth century Morocco prospered from control over the Sudanese and Saharan trade. In the eighteenth century Morocco was importing large numbers of slaves in return for cloth, leather, silk, jewelry, iron, lead, and weapons, and European-derived tea, coffee, sugar, paper, tin, copper utensils, and Indian spices. Britain and France were Morocco's principal trading partners, but dyes came from Spain, and woolen goods, other textiles, spices, and metals came from Holland. Italy supplied alum and artisanal products. From the eastern Mediterranean came silk, cotton, and opium. Salé was the most frequented port, but Agadir and then Mogador were important for the contacts between Europe, the Sus, and the Sudan. Trade, however, did not necessarily benefit the central government, because it could be organized by tribal confederations under religious protection. Local sharifs played an important part in providing the liaisons and guarantees of security for caravans. For example, descendants of Maulay Ismaʿil, residing in the fortresses of Tafilalt, had a monopoly of guiding caravan traffic to Touat.

In the nineteenth century European trade led to the economic penetration of the country. In 1856 Morocco was forced by British pressure to conclude a treaty which opened the country to free trade on the basis of a 10 percent customs duty. Also, Moroccan exports declined after the opening of the Suez Canal (1869) and the introduction of steamships and railroads which made it possible for American, Russian, and Australian producers to provide wheat and wool to European markets in competition with Moroccan products. The Moroccan Saharan trade also dwindled owing to French expansion in West Africa that drew Sudanic and Saharan goods to Atlantic ports at the end of the century. Moreover, after the middle of the century the Europeans were no longer content to maintain a strictly commercial relationship and began to try to directly control the means of production. They began to purchase land, extend loans at high rates of interest, and take Moroccans under extraterritorial protection.

As a result certain elements of the Moroccan population prospered while others suffered. A new Moroccan bourgeoisie, including the large merchant intermediaries between the European and the local markets, and a host of petty traders and retailers, prospered. Customs officials and other functionaries also profited from trade, and acquired property and education. The merchants of Fez maintained their dominant position as Fassi families established colonies in Manchester, Marseilles, Genoa, and French West Africa. The Fez textile industry survived European competition by cultivating new Middle Eastern, African, and domestic markets. The production of straw mats, rugs, carpets and wool blankets, and the building trades, also continued to prosper. Other Moroccan crafts suffered from European competition. Imported products destroyed cotton farming and manufacturing and the Moroccan shoe industry. The Moroccan state was among the economic losers.

Faced with declining revenues, declining power, and declining territory, Sultan Hasan (1873 – 95) attempted to reform the army by means of military instructors and weapons obtained from Europe, and to reform the state bureaucracy by a reorganization of provincial administration. He also proposed to improve the economic infrastructure of the country by building bridges and railways and by establishing cotton and sugar plantations. These reforms had only a limited success. Most of the religious and political elite opposed them as infringements of tradition and law; the European powers were hostile to changes which might reduce their economic privileges.

As a result, in the course of the nineteenth century, Berbers pushed government forces out of the Middle and Central Atlas and moved down onto the plains toward Fez and Meknes. The High Atlas was in the hands of the quasi-independent great qaʾids. By the end of the century the central government controlled scarcely a third of the land and about half of the population, concentrated in the plains of eastern Morocco, the Rif, Fez, and the Atlantic zones from Tangiers to the Atlas. Even in these regions local chieftains were often paramount.

Rural tribes and chieftains continued to resist central taxation. To maintain his influence the ruler commonly had to move a small army into non-complying or rebellious territory, camp, live off the resources of the country, and require payment of taxes in arrears. The local people were thus under pressure to save their crops; the Sultan, however, was also under pressure to conclude an agreement so that he could move on to another rebellious district, and religious chieftains would mediate between the tribes and the ruler until some kind of deal was made.

This kind of polity was little able to resist European colonization. Between 1899 and 1912 the French occupied Morocco, abetted by diplomatic agreements with Italy, Spain, Britain, and eventually Germany. To consolidate their gains, the French manipulated the various players in the Moroccan political system. Thus in the region of Touat, faced with French intervention, local chiefs expected that the Sultan would defend them. They demanded that the Sultan wage jihad, but at the same time they resisted his efforts to collect taxes. The shortage of revenues made the Sultan dependent upon French financial support, and in turn he lost legitimacy in the eyes of local people, who then felt justified in yielding to French military superiority. The autonomy of local officials, religious leaders, and chiefs made it impossible for Morocco to put up a unified resistance to French aggression.

The Sultan's efforts to increase the power of the state only played into the hands of the French. From 1901 to 1903 Sultan ʿAbd al-ʿAziz tried to strengthen the central government by implementing a new tax on agriculture and livestock, and by the appointment of new officials to assure the collection of taxes. He proposed to tax tribes, religious leaders, government officials, and others hitherto exempt. The opposition of the rural notables and the ʿulamaʾ, however, was resolute, and ʿAbd al-ʿAziz was forced instead to mortgage the customs revenues and borrowed heavily from the French. For this he was greeted with widespread revolt and a revolution which deposed him in favor of his brother ʿAbd al-Hafiz.

The intervention of the ʿulamaʾ was a novelty in Moroccan history. Traditionally the Moroccan ʿulamaʾ were a group of officials but not an organized corporate body. The chief qadi of Fez named the professors of the major mosques and colleges and controlled their endowed properties. For more than half a century, however, the government had been gaining increasing control over the appointment of judges and professors and of madrasa graduates who entered the state bureaucracy. Nonetheless, after 1900 many ʿulamaʾ joined the opposition because they could not accept the collaboration of the Sultan with the French, his failure to protect Moroccan territory, and his tax reforms, loans, and European advisers. In all, the result of ʿulamaʾ and rural tribal opposition was the loss of independence and the declaration of French and Spanish protectorates in 1912.

STATES AND ISLAM: NORTH AFRICAN VARIATIONS

From the origins of the Islamic era to the nineteenth century, the history of North African society turned on two essential motifs: state formation and Islamization. Historically the small family, hamlet, or group of hamlets were the basic units of society. They were englobed in factional and tribal groups; class stratification, feudal dominance, and state power were generally weak. The economy was correspondingly based on small-scale grain, fruit, and olive gardening, stockraising by pastoral peoples and limited urban-based textile and other small-scale manufacturing activities. While trade was important, the merchant middle class was not highly developed. As opposed to the history of the Middle East, North Africa did not have a long experience of imperial organization, monotheistic religious communities, and sedentarized agricultural and urban commercial development. It had a veneer of imperial and urban Christian civilization set down by the Phoenicians and Romans and confined to relatively limited coastal territories.

The Arab conquest gave new impetus to state formation and to the organization of North African society into Muslim communities. Tunisia in the eighth century, Morocco in the eleventh, and Algeria in the sixteenth acquired territorial identity and state regimes. The conquests also led to the institutionalization of Islam for the masses of the population. Starting in the eighth century, the Maliki school of law became rooted throughout North Africa and remained the mainstay of legal administration, education, and state legitimation until the nineteenth century. From about the twelfth century, Sufism also became institutionalized and the primary basis for the organization of rural populations. Sufis became the chieftains of rural communities in Tunisia, Algeria, and Morocco and the leaders of tribal coalitions, in parallel to and in opposition to state regimes. Much of the history of North Africa from the thirteenth to the nineteenth century may be defined in terms of the relations of state and Sufi forces. Finally, the Arab conquests also gave North Africa an Arab identity due to successive waves of Arab migration, and Arab dominance of states. Large parts of southern Tunisia, Algeria, and Morocco, however, were primarily Berber. Only in the twentieth century would Arabic become the universal language of societies which had been Muslim since the Almohad era.

Each society, however, exhibited its own variations upon state, religious, and tribal institutions. At the time of the Arab conquests, Tunisia was already the center of a developed civilization and remained throughout its history a society marked by a highly developed agricultural and commercial economy governed by an aristocracy of landowners, merchants, and urban intellectuals. Islamic regimes and Islamic religious culture were introduced in successive phases from the East. Tunisia in the early Muslim era, like the Middle East, maintained its inherited institutional base but accepted an Islamic version of ancient civilization. Under the early Arab and Aghlabid governors a Caliphal type of administration and the Maliki school of law flourished. The Hafsid regime adopted the Sultanal type of administration and ʿulamaʾ and Sufi forms of Islam. With the Ottoman conquest at the end of the sixteenth century, Ottoman janissary and administrative institutions and the Ottoman type of ʿulamaʾ bureaucracy modified the structure of the Tunisian state. Throughout this era Tunisia maintained its state institutions, despite a large pastoral and tribal population in the southern parts of the country, and constant fluctuations in the balance of power between the state and the tribal parts of the society. Until the nineteenth century Tunisia was in all respects a provincial variant of the Middle Eastern Islamic world.

Algeria has a different history. Algeria as a whole remained without state organization well into the Islamic era though it supported a number of local dynasties, such as the Hammadids and the Zayyanids, on the basis of a share of Saharan and European trade. These local regimes, however, never controlled the whole of the territory and gave way readily to tribal opposition. A stable state regime was finally introduced by the Ottoman conquests. The Ottomans provided a ready-made military elite, administrative cadres who were supervised from Istanbul, and the rudiments of a religious bureaucracy. The concepts of jihad against Christians and of Sultanal authority served to legitimize this regime.

At first the Algerian regime was confined to the city-state of Algiers, and was based on privateering and on direct support from Istanbul, but progressively Algiers established its own administrative, tax collecting, and judicial authority throughout a large territory. Ottoman-Turkish authority came to be recognized throughout Algeria though it was not uniformly effective. Provincial, tribal, and Sufi resistance, however, grew in the eighteenth and nineteenth centuries. Thus the Algerian regime resembled Ottoman Syria and Iraq, where a centralized state governed a strongly segmented society. The Ottoman-Algerian regime succeeded in creating an Algerian territorial and administrative identity, while the spread of Sufism among rural populations gave it Islamic identity.

The history of Morocco shows yet a third variation on the theme of Islam and state formation in a highly fragmented society. Though Volubilis was the capital of a Roman province, Morocco on the eve of the Arab conquests had neither territorial identity nor a history of centralized regimes. A number of local principalities emerged in the wake of the Arab conquests, based upon personal religious authority of the rulers, but from the eighth to the eleventh century the process of state formation was inhibited by internal fragmentation and external Fatimid and Umayyad interventions. The Almoravid conquests began the process of creating the territorial base for a Moroccan state. It was the first of a series of conquests of Morocco by coalitions of tribal peoples from the south united on the basis of religious principles. The Almoravids were succeeded by the Almohads, the Marinids, the Saʿdians, and the ʿAlawis, each of whom was legitimized by an appeal to the charismatic authority of the ruler, although this authority was articulated in different ways. In the Almoravid and Almohad cases the leaders were heads of reform movements. Later Saʿdian and ʿAlawi rulers possessed the baraka of descent from the Prophet and were believed to have the charismatic powers of Sufi saints. They were also regarded as Caliphs, successors to the Prophet in the defense and administration of an Islamic society. The Sultan was at once Caliph, imam, sharif, wali and mujtahid. He had important ritual roles at the Muslim holidays and shared in the national veneration for religious leaders.

Moroccan Sultans, however, did not have a monopoly of religious legitimacy but shared sharifian descent and Sufi baraka with other religious leaders. This sharing of authority was both supportive and competitive. It was supportive in that the Sufis provided the Sultans with a cultural basis for their claims to worldly authority. It was competitive in the sense that the sources of moral judgment and political authority were independent of the state and dispersed among many individuals in the society. This dispersion meant that Morocco could not easily create a unified national regime.

The highly personal nature of the Moroccan monarchy assured its legitimacy and historical continuity but was also a source of weakness. Power was effected by means of personal contacts between the ruler and his clients. The highly personal nature of state relations implied weak institutions. The central regime was supported by household administration and by mercenary and slave soldiers, but the *makhzan* or coalition of independent, tribal, or Sufi power-holders supplying military forces to the regime, was crucial to its effectiveness. With the help of the makhzan the government could control the towns and the central plains, but not the mountains and the deserts. Morocco preserved a distinctive territorial and monarchical identity, based on the personal religious authority of the Sultans. This differed from Tunisia, which combined a

Muslim statist concept of political legitimacy with centralized political administration, and from Algeria, which had a highly developed central government but a weak sense of political identity.

The reasons for the failure to consolidate a central Moroccan state have been the subject of considerable discussion. One cluster of factors is the inherent structure of Moroccan economy and society. While Morocco was a relatively wealthy region, its agricultural and commercial sectors were relatively small in relation to its pastoral populations. Successive bedouin invasions destroyed peasant village life. From the sixteenth to the eighteenth century the weakness of the central government allowed a further expansion of pastoral groups. Only the towns, the oases, and the mountains remained zones of sedentary agriculture.

A related factor was the weakness of the urban bureaucratic, commercial, and intellectual elites. Andalusian minorities provided the cadres of administration. Without links to either the rural or urban masses, however, they could serve only as secretaries. The ʿulamaʾ, also, were merely a slim stratum of the population, dependent on the Sultans, restricted to the urban areas, and without politically potent ties to the common people. They also had to compete for religious prestige with the Sultans, the saintly lineages, and the Sufi brotherhoods. Not enough is known to estimate the strength of the commercial bourgeoisie, but all indications are that it did not have the means or the autonomy to exercise an important political role.

The corollary of the weakness of the sedentary society was the strength of autonomous tribal and Sufi groups. Their independence was enhanced in the seventeenth and eighteenth centuries by their access to European weapons, which made tribal communities even more effective opponents of government armies. The effort to control the tribes and Sufi coalitions was continually subverted by intra-elite struggles for power and by the need to make fiscal, territorial, and other concessions to pacify communities that could not be defeated.

In any case, Moroccan tribes were themselves unstable constellations. They used the patrilineal idiom but they did not have a firm hierarchy or permanent constituencies. Tribal chieftainships were temporary positions subject to a constant competition for power. Sufi lineages and coalitions were similarly unstable, for the power of Sufis was personal rather than organizational, and depended on the voluntary adherence of the tribes to the saints. In the rural social organization of Morocco, group integration depended heavily upon ritual and symbolic means.

The weakness of the state made it difficult to collect regular taxes. To supplement poor tax revenues the Sultans attempted to exploit long-distance trade. Trade incomes, however, were available to the Sultans only insofar as they controlled the trade routes and the ports. Rival Moroccan principalities, and Sudanese, Algerian, and European competitors, appropriated important shares. While Moroccan dynasties often came to power on the basis of control of trade, it proved impossible to monopolize trade revenues for extended periods.

The late eighteenth and nineteenth centuries were a period of protracted crisis for North African-Muslim societies. Their Ottoman suzerain could no longer protect them. Their state regimes were no longer capable of exerting close political control or of generating large revenues and strong armies. Their economies were increasingly in bondage to European ones. The decline of economic power altogether subverted the North African regimes and made them prey to French conquest and French protectorates.

ISLAM IN CENTRAL AND SOUTHERN ASIA

CHAPTER 17

INNER ASIA FROM THE MONGOL CONQUESTS TO THE NINETEENTH CENTURY

The development of an Islamic civilization in Inner Asia was closely related to that of Iran. Islam first spread in this region as a result of the Arab conquests of Iran and Transoxania and the movement of Muslim traders and Sufis from the towns to the steppes. The two regions were also linked by the Turkish migrations of the tenth to the fourteenth century which brought Inner Asian peoples into Iran, and Iranian monarchical culture and Islamic civilization into Inner Asia. In the tenth and eleventh centuries Qarluq and Oghuz peoples were converted and founded the Qarakhanid and Saljuq empires. Under the Qarakhanids, the Hanafi school of law and Maturidi school of theology were established in Transoxania, and a new Turkish literature inspired by Persian Islamic literature came into being. The Qarakhanids also favored the diffusion of Islam from Transoxania into the Tarim Basin and the northern steppes. Sufi preachers, especially Shaykh Ahmad al-Yasavi (d. 1166) helped to spread Islam among nomadic peoples.

The connections between Iran and Inner Asia were reinforced by the Mongol invasions. In the thirteenth century non-Muslim Mongolian peoples established their suzerainty over the whole of Inner Asia, much of the Middle East, and China. The Mongol conquests vastly enlarged the regions of Inner Asia in contact with the Middle East by bringing the steppe regions north of the Black, the Caspian, and Aral seas into contact with Muslim peoples in Transoxania and Iran, and by linking Muslim Transoxania with eastern Inner Asia and China.

The advent of Islam in this region led to the formation of three types of Islamic society. In some cases, as among the Kazakhs, to the best of our knowledge, Islam became part of popular identity and belief, but not the basis of social organization. In other cases, among tribal peoples, and in some oasis communities such as Kashgar, Sufi masters or Sufi lineages took on the role of mediating, organizing, and sometimes governing. In large-scale urbanized societies such as Transoxania, state-organized Islamic societies of the Middle Eastern type were developed.

For millennia the central theme in the history of this vast and varied region was the relationship of nomadic-pastoral and sedentary peoples. While the great civilizations of the Middle East and China were primarily imperial and agricultural, the region between them was a zone of steppe lands and scattered oases. The population was predominantly pastoral and lived by raising horses and sheep. It was also organized into clans and tribes which were sometimes assembled into great confederations. The settled peoples lived primarily in the oasis districts of Transoxania, Khwarizm, Farghana, and Kashgar, and in scattered towns along the trade routes which linked China, the Middle East and Europe. Settled and pastoral peoples had close relationships with each other, exchanging products, and participating in caravan trade. Pastoral peoples also infiltrated the settled areas and became farmers or townsmen. Sometimes they conquered the agricultural oases and became rulers and land-lords. Inner Asia was also the reservoir holding a sea of peoples who, organized into great confederations, from time to time conquered the Middle East and China. From the second millennium B.C. to the eighteenth century the history of the region may be told in terms of ever repeated nomadic conquests, the formation of empires over oasis and settled populations, and the constant tension between pastoral and agricultural peoples.

Eventually, however, all of Inner Asia was brought under Russian and Chinese rule. As early as the sixteenth century Russia absorbed the Tatar states of the Volga region. In the eighteenth and nineteenth centuries Russia took control of the Crimea, the northern steppes, Turkestan, and Transcaspia. The Chinese occupied eastern Turkestan in the eighteenth century. By the end of the nineteenth century Inner Asia was divided into spheres of Russian and Chinese rule. The rule of settled (and non-Muslim) empires brought to an end the ancient patterns of nomadic migration and empire formation and pro-foundly altered the further development of Inner Asian-Islamic societies.

The history of Islamic societies in Inner Asia from the Mongol period to the contemporary era may for convenience be divided into three parts. Here we shall review the western and northern steppes, the realm of the Golden Horde and their successors, the Kazakhs; Turkestan (the modern name for Trans-oxania and adjacent territories), which was the core of the Timurid and later

Table 14. *Inner Asia: outline chronology*

	Northern and western steppes			Turkestan		
	Volga	N. Steppes	Crimea	Khwarizm	Transoxania	Eastern Turkestan
1200		*Mongol conquests* Chinggis Khan (1206–1227)				
1300		Blue Horde, Batuids (1227–1341) unites with White Horde to form Golden Horde (1378–1502)			Chaghatays 1227–1370 Timurid empire 1370–1500	
1400	Partitioned into several khanates (fifteenth century)	Formation of Uzbek and Kazakh "nations" (fifteenth century)	Giray Khans 1426–1792			
1500	Kazan Khanate annexed by Moscow, 1552 Astrakhan Khanate, annexed 1556 Siberian Khanate, annexed 1598			Khans of Khiva 1515–1920	Shaybanids 1500–1598	Chaghatays continue as nominal suzerains until 1678

1600

1700

1800

1900

Astrakhanids
1599–1785

Kashgar, ruled by
khwajas 1678–1756

Khokand, ruled by
Khanate c. 1700–1876;
Russian annexation, 1876

Chinese conquest
of Sinkiang, 1759

Mangits 1785–
1920
Russian
protectorate,
1868

China annexes Sinkiang,
1884

Russian
protectorate,
1873

Annexed by
Russia, 1783

Russian annexation of
Kazakhstan completed
by 1868

Uzbek states; and eastern Turkestan, the region of oasis caravan cities, which became the Chinese province of Sinkiang at the end of the nineteenth century.

THE WESTERN AND NORTHERN STEPPES

The semi-arid steppe region north of a line drawn across the top of the Black, Caspian, and Aral seas and Lake Balkhash was inhabited predominantly by pastoral peoples whose livelihood depended upon raising cattle, horses, goats, sheep, camels, and yaks. The populace was divided into numerous communities who spoke Turkic-Altaic languages and shared a social system defined in patrilineal terms. Steppe peoples were organized into families, clans and confederations (hordes), with the clan being the basic unit of tax collection, military organization, adjudication of disputes, and other political activities. While small communities were based on lineage, a political or territorial concept was woven into the higher levels of organization.

The Mongol conquests gave this region a semblance of political unity. In 1236 under the leadership of Batu, Mongol and Turkish nomads conquered the regions north of the Aral and Caspian seas, and established their capital on the Volga River. In one of the most extraordinary campaigns in world history the Golden Horde also conquered Russia, the Ukraine, southern Poland, Hungary, and Bulgaria and created an empire which extended north to the forests of Russia, south to the Black Sea and the Caucasus, west to the Carpathians, and east to Khwarizm. Throughout this region local princes were left in power as vassals of the Golden Horde and were used to extract tribute from the population. Moscow was the principal vassal of the Golden Horde; other Russian principalities were responsible to Moscow for the payment of tribute.

The conquering Turkish and Mongol peoples soon acquired a new historical identity. Amalgamating with the conquered peoples, they evolved over time into the Turkic-speaking "Tatar" population, and were eventually converted to Islam. Khan Berke (1257–67) was the first Muslim ruler, but only from the time of Uzbek Khan (1313–40) were the rulers routinely Muslims. The Islamic loyalties of the royal family were probably reinforced by cultural and political contacts with the settled Muslim populations of Khwarizm and Transoxania and perhaps by the absorption of the Bulgars who had been Muslims since the tenth century. Culturally the Golden Horde was dependent upon Egypt and Syria, which provided artists and artisans to produce wall paintings, mosaics, lamps, tombstones, and other artistic objects. In the steppes of northern Asia, the Golden Horde acquired aspects of Mediterranean-Islamic culture.

The empire of the Golden Horde maintained its suzerainty from the middle of the thirteenth to the middle of the fifteenth century, but gradually disintegrated under the pressure of Ottoman expansion (which cut off the Golden Horde from the Mediterranean), and the rise of Moscow, Moldavia, and Lithuania. Also, in the course of the fourteenth to the sixteenth century, the Golden Horde broke up into smaller principalities and became differentiated into separate Crimean Tatar, Volga Tatar, Uzbek and Kazakh ethnic and political groups. The Khans of the Crimea, who claimed to be descendants of Chinggis Khan, declared themselves independent rulers in 1441. The Khans of Kazan, Astrakhan, and Siberia also established their autonomy. Each of these Khans had the right to conduct war and diplomacy and dispense justice, but their powers were checked by clan and tribal leaders who had a voice in their succession.

In the eastern steppes, from the Caspian–Ural region to the Tien-shan and Altai mountains, nomadic populations coalesced into two main ethnic groups. The Uzbeks probably originated as a coalition of warrior clans united under the leadership of the Shayban family and took their name from Uzbek Khan. The stability and political success of the Shaybanid confederation led gradually to the development of an Uzbek language and an Uzbek ethnic identity.

The Kazakhs formed a second confederation in the regions north of the Caspian and Aral seas. The term "Kazakh" probably means free (of Uzbek authority?) and referred at first to a warrior stratum, then to a political confederation, and finally to an ethnic population. Kazakhs were organized into extended families called *aul* whose size was governed by the availability of pasture, and ranged between 3 and 15 tents. Each aul had its own pasturage and migrated as a unit to exploit its grazing lands. The auls could also be grouped into larger units, called uymaqs, which were mixed groups of different clans. In the seventeenth century the Kazakhs formed the Great, Middle, and Little Hordes. A fourth horde, called the Bukey (Inner Horde), was formed at the beginning of the nineteenth century. These loosely organized hordes became politically united only when they required a Khan to unite them against a common enemy, or when larger states (such as Russia) built up the power of the Khans to facilitate control of the nomadic peoples.

In the fifteenth and sixteenth centuries Naqshbandi and the Yasavi missionaries began to make converts among the Kazakhs. Islam, however, probably made little impression upon them until the eighteenth century, when Tatar merchants, missionaries, secretaries, and teachers helped construct mosques and schools. Kazakh nomads accepted Muslim circumcision, marriage, and burial practices, and came to believe in the Muslim jinn as the equivalent of their spirit gods. They used Quranic amulets for protection and treated Muslim holy-men as a kind of supplementary shaman. They worshipped at saints' tombs and observed Muslim holidays. Alongside of Muslim festivals, however, the Kazakhs also maintained a folk culture in which wandering poets sang epic songs. Their style of Islam, like that of nomadic and rural peoples the world over, merged ancient folk beliefs and practices into the new religion.

Thus the new Uzbek and Kazakh polities came into being when warrior or political elites built their power upon a confederation of families and clans, who in time assumed a genealogical relatedness and ethnic identity reinforced by shared Muslim religious beliefs and by a common language. The emergence of new state elites and the acceptance of Islamic identity was the basis of new Inner Asian ethnicities. Still, language, ethnicity, and political loyalty were probably much less stable than we are wont to think, and small groups undoubtedly shifted from confederation to confederation with appropriate changes in identity.

The decline of the Golden Horde and the rise of new states opened the way for a multi-sided struggle for control of the western and northern steppes. In the fifteenth century, the Ottoman empire, Russia, Poland, Lithuania, and the Muslim states of Crimea, Kazan, and Astrakhan struggled for control of the Ural–Volga region. The ultimate outcome of these wars was that Russia freed itself from Tatar and Muslim domination and itself became master of the northern steppes and the Muslim populations. By 1535 Moscow claimed the right of investiture of Kazan rulers and began to regard Kazan, with its fertile territories and strategic trading position, as its ancient patrimony. Muscovy chroniclers developed a notion that Kazan was "Russian land" which had to be recovered to reunite Russia. Church writers stressed the perfidy of the Tatars and the bitterness of the Christian–Muslim conflict. Amidst a growing sense of religious superiority and national mission, Moscow conquered Kazan in 1552 and Astrakhan in 1556. This gave it control of the Volga River and the north shore of the Caspian Sea and paved the way for the submission of the Siberian Khanate in 1598.

Russian conquest of the Crimea, however, was delayed for almost two centuries. In the seventeenth century Moscow developed adequate frontier defenses against Ottoman and Crimean attack and began to colonize the southern steppes. Russian (and Polish) expansion led to a new series of Crimean, Ottoman, and Central European wars which resulted ultimately in the Russian occupation of Azov in 1699. Peter the Great had to cede Azov to the Ottoman empire in 1711, but in 1774 the Russians defeated the Ottomans, and took full control of the Crimea in 1783. The Ottomans recognized the new sovereign in 1792.

From their dominant position in the Volga region the Russians set out to conquer the Kazakh steppes. Under Peter the Great, the Russians established a string of forts across the northern steppes from the Ural to the Irtysh rivers, including Orenburg, Omsk, Barnaul, and Semipalatinsk. In 1723 the Kazakh Great Horde, and in 1730 the Kazakh Little Horde, were forced to accept Russian suzerainty. A century of slow consolidation was followed in 1822–24 by the abolition of the Kazakh Khanates and the submission of the Kazakhs to Russian political control. In 1864 the Russians took the Syr–Darya region and completed the occupation of Kazakh territories. This victory was not easily won. Between 1783 and 1797 Batyr Srym led a series of counter-attacks, followed by some 60 years of Kazakh resistance. The Bukey Horde revolted between 1836 and 1838; Khan Kenesary Kasimov led Kazakh resistance between 1837 and 1847. The last revolt, in the name of Islam, was crushed in 1868. Thus Russia became the heir of the Golden Horde in the Ural–Volga region and on the northern and eastern steppes.

The Russian conquests were a disaster for Muslim peoples. Upon the conquest of Kazan and Astrakhan the Russians expelled the Tatars from the important cities, redistributed the land to Russian nobles and monasteries, and colonized the region with Russian artisans and peasants. Muslim religious leaders were also undermined as mosques were destroyed, Quran schools closed, and waqfs seized by the Russian treasury. The Russians aimed at no less than the complete conversion of the Tatars to Christianity. The first Russian bishop of Kazan founded churches and monasteries, supported by native lands and serfs, as bases for an intensive effort to Christianize the Tatars. There was some success with Muslim nobles and their clients who were interested in collaboration with the Russians, but in general, Muslim resistance was fierce. From 1552 until 1610 there were repeated revolts by the Tatar nobility. Their defeat was followed by peasant uprisings from 1608 to 1615, and Tatar participation in Kazakh rebellions. Paradoxically, however, Russian conquest helped to spread Islam. Driven out of the major towns and deprived of land, Tatar nobles became merchants and established commercial colonies in rural areas. As merchants and religious leaders fled to the countryside, they established mosques and schools and propagated Islam among the nomads.

In the seventeenth century the Russians suspended their efforts at assimilation and worked mainly to prevent the apostasy of converts, but in 1710 Peter the Great began a new campaign which lasted until 1764. Converts were

Map 17. Russian expansion in Muslim Inner Asia to 1920.

MONGOLIA

SINKIANG

Hami
Turfan
Urumchi
Kucha
Yarkand
Kashgar
Khotan

JUNGARIA

TIBET

Bay of Bengal

Ganges R.

1000 km

500 miles

500

KASHMIR

LADAKH

Lahore
Delhi

Indus R.

Kabul
Balkh
Herat

GREAT KAZAKH HORDE

L. Balkhash

Ili R.

Semipalatinsk

Omsk

Sibir

Ufa

Orenburg

MIDDLE KAZAKH HORDE

LITTLE KAZAKH HORDE

Jaxartes R.

Yasi

Tashkent

Khokand

FARGHANA

TRANSOXANIA

Samarkand

Bukhara

KHWARIZM

Khiva

UZBEGS

Oxus R.

Aral Sea

Marw

Mashhad

TURKMENS

IRAN

Isfahan

Tehran

Kazan

Moscow

Volga R.

Astrakhan

Caspian Sea

Derbent

Baku

DAGHESTAN

GEORGIA

Tiflis

Erivan

Azov

CRIMEA

Kiev

Dnieper R.

Black Sea

Tigris R.

Euphrates R.

Mashhad

Persian Gulf

Arabian Sea

Red Sea

OTTOMAN EMPIRE

Nineteenth-century Khanates

Khiva
Bukhara
Khokand

Russian expansion

1584
1800
1881
1920

transferred to purely Russian villages. Muslim children were sent to schools and adults were forced to accept baptism. Churches were constructed in Muslim villages. Yet after half a century there were only a small number of Tatar converts; many of these joined Pugachev's rebellion (1773–75).

To calm her eastern provinces Catherine the Great adopted a new policy in 1773. Aware of the importance of Tatar trading communities and eager to avoid further rebellions, she adopted a number of measures intended to win the favor of the Muslims and make them loyal subjects of the empire. Catherine ended religious persecution, gave Tatar nobles equal rights with Russian nobles, and encouraged Tatar merchants to trade between Russia and Transoxania. Decrees of 1782 and 1784 authorized the construction of mosques; in 1788 an Islamic spiritual administration was organized at Ufa under the leadership of a mufti. Under Catherine's peace, Tatar merchants flourished and invested in tanneries, and paper and woolen mills. Peasants were also able to develop cottage industries. Commercial success opened the way to European education and eventually stimulated an intellectual enlightenment based on new schools and improved teaching of the Tatar and Russian languages.

In the Crimea, Catherine guaranteed the nobility possession of their lands and the Muslim ʿulamaʾ freedom of religion. A Muslim spiritual directorate for the Crimea was established in 1794; the mufti was nominated by the Tsar. In time, however, the Russians began to seize Tatar estates and waqfs for the benefit of the Russian aristocracy and European colonists who flocked to the country. Between 1783 and 1896 most of the Crimean Tatars were forced to migrate to the Ottoman empire; the remnant formed a minority in their own country.

TURKESTAN (TRANSOXANIA, KHWARIZM, AND FARGHANA)

While the northern steppes were the domain of the Golden Horde and later of settled Tatar and pastoral Kazakh peoples, Turkestan, the domain of the Chaghatays, was primarily agricultural and the site of numerous important oasis-cities such as Bukhara and Samarqand. The commerce of these cities reached from China to the Black Sea, linking Iran, Afghanistan, India, China, and Russia. They were also important centers of Muslim religious learning. While nomadic peoples from the surrounding steppes time and again conquered the region, they accepted its city tradition and became patrons of its culture.

Throughout the period of the Caliphate and the Turkish and Mongol invasions, the history of Turkestan was tied to that of eastern Iran. Turkestan was ruled in succession by the Qarakhanids, the Mongols, the Chaghatays, and the Timurids. The collapse of the Timurid empire, however, led to a permanent break in the ties between the two regions. Iran was conquered by the Safavids, and Transoxania (the principal part of Turkestan) was conquered by the Uzbeks. Rival regimes then separated the two regions. The trade routes which linked Transoxania to Iran were disrupted by Shaybanid–Safavid hostilities and Transoxania was cut off from the west. Iran under Safavid rule was converted to Shiᶜism; Transoxania under Shaybanid rule remained Sunni. While Persians held sway in Iran, Turkish peoples and Chaghatay literary culture grew stronger in the east. Though it preserved a rich component of its Middle Eastern Islamic heritage, Transoxania under Uzbek rule was integrated once again into Inner Asia, and became the urban and agricultural center of Inner Asian-Islamic civilization.

Uzbek domination of Transoxania began with the Shaybanid dynasty (1500–98), and endured through successive dynasties until the establishment of a Russian protectorate in 1868. Transoxania's Uzbek conquerors were substantially sedentarized in the course of the sixteenth and seventeenth centuries, and the Shaybanids were in many ways typical of Turkish conquest regimes in sedentary societies. The conquering elite was divided between the ruling dynasty and its administrative, religious, and merchant supporters, and uymaq or tribal chiefs and their clients and retainers. The two segments of the elite struggled for their share of the spoils of power. The surplus taken from the peasantry and the pastoralists was divided among the various segments of the political and religious elite according to a system inherited from the Timurid period. The Khan himself kept a portion of the territory as state lands and a portion as *khasa* or private revenue estates which he controlled absolutely. A considerable portion of these lands was assigned as waqfs to Muslim religious leaders, and the rest was assigned to the nobility. It was divided into provinces called *wilayat*, and each wilayat was further subdivided into iqtaᶜs distributed to the supporters of the regional governors. The estates controlled by the members of the ruling family and the tribal chiefs (*beg*) were rated by *tumen*, probably a measure of the number of troops to be provided in return for the grant of revenues. Such grants of land tended to become hereditary, depriving the rulers of control. Strong rulers would seek to reestablish their power by seizing the iqtaᶜs, reducing the size of land grants, confiscating the excess properties of religious leaders, and paying their retainers in cash. In this respect the Shaybanid Khanate resembled the Safavid regime of Iran; the central rulers struggled against the uymaq and tribal forces which dominated the localities.

15 The Registan of Samarqand

The Shaybanid Khanate, like earlier Muslim regimes, was legitimized by a combination of references to Sunni Islam and Persian literary culture. The Khans took the titles of *Khalifat al-Rahman* (lieutenant of the merciful God) and *Imam al-Zaman* (ruler of the times), quoted hadith to justify their rule, and became disciples of the Naqshbandi Sufi masters. At the same time court poets wrote panegyrics, portraits were commissioned, and literary activity was patronized to depict the Shaybanids as Turkish-Persian princes. The *Shah-name* was translated into Turkish and many Iranian scholars came to Transoxania, where they found generous Uzbek patronage. Thus the Shaybanids maintained their own version of the Timurid heritage and created an Uzbek-dominated Irano-Islamic state.

The religious elites played a large role in the legitimation of the regime. These elites included the qadis and the ʿulamaʾ who taught in the madrasas, but ever since the Timurid period the leading position was held by the Naqshbandis. The Naqshbandis had their origin in the *Tariqa-yi Khwajagan* or "way of the masters" founded by Yusuf Hamadani (1048–1143). His disciple, Ahmad al-Yasavi helped to spread Islam among Turkish peoples. Ahmad's tomb at Yasi was built by Timur as a gesture of obeisance to the Turkish Muslim Sufi tradition. His successor, ʿAbd al-Khaliq Ghujdavani (d. 1220), a principal teacher of the Bukharan populace, introduced the crucial spiritual and social principle which later defined the Naqshbandi position: solitude in society – inner devotion expressed in outward social and political activity. The order then received its name from Baha᾽ al-Din Naqshband (d. 1389). ῾Ubaydallah (*khwaja*) Ahrar (1404–90), a wealthy farmer and merchant, who acquired a reputation for mysticism and magical powers, was the dominant Sufi figure in the late fifteenth century. He was an adviser of princes, a teacher of famous poets, and a revered master to the common people. He and other Sufis played a large political role in protecting Muslim populations from oppression, winning over the souls of kings, and defending the Muslim way of life. Sufi leaders who had contacts in all reaches of society united the Inner Asian communities.

While Shaybanid rule constructed a variant form of Irano-Islamic state and society, larger historical forces were profoundly altering Inner Asia. For centuries the riches of Transoxania were built upon trade and manufactures. The upper merchant strata were engaged in long-distance international trade. Merchants, rich religious leaders, and government officials participated in the trade with China and Russia. Bukhara, Samarqand, Tashkent, Yasi, and other towns were also centers of lively silk, cotton, leather, rug, jewelry, wood-carving, metal, and paper industries. Craftworkers were organized into associations under the leadership of officials appointed by the rulers, but maintained a social and religious solidarity of their own based on the identification of guilds with patron saints, Sufi masters, and shared religious rituals.

In the course of the sixteenth century, however, the rise of the Safavids and the closure of Iranian routes to the Indian Ocean, the Russian conquest of the Volga region, and internal disorder and insecurity undermined the Inner Asian trade. The decline of Inner Asian routes was also hastened by the discovery of new sea routes between Europe and the Indies, and later by Russian expansion across Siberia to the Pacific which opened new routes to China. Inner Asia was cut off both from economic riches and from cultural stimulation. The roads which once brought Buddhist, Christian, and other religious and cultural influences into the region fell into disuse; once the links to the outside Muslim world were cut, provincialism, economic stagnation, and political fragmentation set in.

The decline of Inner Asian trade compromised Shaybanid efforts to maintain a centralized state. It deprived the Khans of tax revenues, the merchants of profits, and the religious elites of investment opportunities. Power drifted into the hands of tribal and uymaq chieftains. From the end of the Shaybanid dynasty (1598) to the nineteenth century, centralized political administration was the rare and precarious achievement of exceptionally able rulers.

The nineteenth century, however, brought a revival. Bukhara (Transoxania), Khiva (Khwarizm), and Khokand (Farghana) each became centers of a newly flourishing Muslim society. In Bukhara, the Shaybanid dynasty had been succeeded by the Astrakhanid dynasty (1599–1785), which maintained only the barest continuity with Shaybanid traditions. It was in turn succeeded by the Mangit dynasty (1785–1920). The Mangits had served for some decades as the principal advisers of the Astrakhanids, but they seized control of the sovereign office in 1785. Murad, the first ruler of the Mangit dynasty, ruled as Amir rather than Sultan, but also claimed an authority based on his conquests, his services as defender and executive of the Muslim community, and his personal charisma derived from being a descendant of the Prophet.

Under the Mangit dynasty Bukhara continued to follow the basic Islamic pattern exemplified by the Shaybanids. Mangit Bukhara was still governed by an aristocracy of tribal origin. The state was ruled by the Amir who was served by a *qush begi*, or chief minister, and by Persian administrative officials. The territory was subdivided into wilayats and tax-collecting districts consisting of a group of villages or hamlets under the authority of an *aqsakal* or elder. The territories and tax revenues were divided among the Amir and the leading notables. In the nineteenth century about 12 percent of the taxable land belonged to the ruler, 56 percent to the state, 24 percent to waqfs and 8 percent to the rest of the population. State lands could be taxed in both cash and kind, the rates being adjusted to the unit of surface, the amount of water, and the type of crop, in order to approximate the value of the produce. State lands were commonly granted to tribal notables in return for which they promised to supply troops to the regime. They could also be given away as permanent rather than conditional gifts.

In the nineteenth century the Mangit dynasty struggled successfully to reduce the power of the tribal and uymaq chiefs. Amir Nasrallah (1826–60) attempted to increase his authority by removing hostile Uzbek chieftains from office and replacing them with Persian, Turkmen, and Arab functionaries. He also confiscated landed properties, redistributed them to his supporters on a non-hereditary basis, and regulated the relations of the landholders to the peasants. This consolidation was aided by the sedentarization of Uzbek pastoralists, which brought both men and land under the authority of the Amir. Still the local chiefs kept their castles, their retainers, and at least part of their revenues.

As in Iran and the Ottoman empire, a religious administration was highly organized. Bukhara also had a state-controlled religious administration under the authority of a Shaykh al-Islam (chief jurisconsult) and a *qadi kalan*, who was in control of judicial administration, colleges, elementary schools, and mosques. The religious administration included the qadis and sub-qadis appointed to provincial districts, and muftis who recorded evidence, interpreted the law and sat in council to pass judgment on the conformity of state regulations to Muslim law. The scholars staffed more than 110 madrasas and taught in the elementary schools. They were organized in an hierarchy of three ranks under the titles *awraq, sudur,* and *sadr,* which were honorific distinctions given to scholars who had a madrasa education and who served as functionaries. People who held these ranks were entitled to *tankho* (rights to collect taxes) and gifts of land. A functionary called the raʾis served as the equivalent of the medieval muhtasib, enforcing honest market practices and good public morals. The raʾis could require delinquent Muslims to attend mosque or school in order to improve their religious practice and knowledge. Neighborhood religious life was under the direction of imams who presided over the recitation of prayers. The term "mullah" was applied to everyone who taught in schools, presided over prayers, and officiated at marriages, funerals, and other ceremonies. The whole of this elaborate religious organization was directly controlled by the Amir, who appointed the chief qadis and muftis, the professors in the madrasas, and other functionaries.

The social power of the ʿulamaʾ of Bukhara was enhanced by their corporate organization. The religious establishment included organized privileged groups such as the sayyids, or descendants of the Prophet, the mirs, or descendants of the first three Caliphs, and the khwajas, or descendants of the early Arab conquerors. These groups formed endogamous lineages which were accorded popular veneration and religious prestige. Though not formally organized, the teaching ʿulamaʾ also derived considerable political and social support from the mass of their students. Alongside of the lineages, there were organized Sufi brotherhoods including the Naqshbandiya, the Qadiriya, and the Kubrawiya. The Sufi masters had a considerable following including their immediate disciples and the lay brothers attached to the orders. Sufis lived in khanaqas and worshiped at the shrines of venerated teachers. Sufi beggars, called Qalandaris, had their own community. Sufism was also important among the rural and nomadic populations, where it was strongly oriented to saint worship, healing, and use of amulets. Together, the holy lineages, the Sufi brotherhoods, and the student clienteles made a considerable force in Bukharan society.

Religious influence was also pervasive in the mentality of the Bukharan population. This was most commonly expressed in the veneration of tombs of saints. The relics of Timur in Samarqand were the object of pilgrimage, as were the tombs of the famous Naqshbandi teachers. When a shrine began to acquire a wide reputation it was commonly taken over by a Sufi order, which received the gifts of the pilgrims. The cult of ꜤAli was widespread, even among Sunnis, for ꜤAli was the patron saint of the canal-diggers and soldiers. Bibi Seshambeh (Lady Tuesday) and "Lady Solver of Problems" were the patron saints of women. Craft guilds were also organized under patron saints and had collective rituals. Guild saints included Noah, the saint of carpenters, and David, the saint of metalworkers. Also the Muslim populace celebrated the *bayram* festivals (the ꜤIds of the sacrifice and of the end of Ramadan), and the birthday of the Prophet. Muslim spirituality, however, was tempered by a lively folk culture, which included secular entertainments by musicians, dancers, acrobats, jugglers, and gypsies. The populace also enjoyed tobacco, tea, and wine.

Despite the longevity of this form of state and society, important changes were taking place in the nineteenth century. First the number of landless peasants was increasing and the state had difficulty in collecting taxes. As formerly nomadic Uzbeks were sedentarized, irrigation lagged behind the pace of settlement, partly because of the lack of skill among first-generation farmers, and partly because of political struggles over the control of water. While there were adequate lands for pasturage, lands suitable for cultivation were over-populated.

The nineteenth-century consolidation of the Bukharan state also brought into being a new intermediary class between the ruling elites and the peasants and pastoralists. These included lower-ranking functionaries, scribes, secretaries, couriers, and policemen. Promoted by an active Bukharan commerce with Afghanistan, Iran, India, and Russia, the commercial bourgeoisie also became more important. Bukhara became important as a center for the redistribution of goods arriving by long-distance caravans. Bukhara also controlled the central Asian trade in raw silk and silk fabrics. Its merchants organized cotton industries and financed modest banking firms. With a growing merchant elite, private property and private land ownership became more important between 1840 and 1870.

The territories of Farghana and Khwarizm were also reorganized. Before the eighteenth century, Farghana had been divided into a number of small states governed by religious chiefs, but in the early eighteenth century migrant Uzbeks assumed power and forced surrounding Kazakh and Kirgiz tribes to submit to a new state with its capital at Khokand. The consolidation of the Khanate of Khokand was based on a flourishing economy in which irrigation agriculture, cotton and silk production, and trade with Kashgar, Bukhara, Khiva, and Russia were important sources of income. Khokand was the breakpoint where Russian and Chinese goods were sold and reshipped. The consolidation of state power, however, was inhibited by the struggle for control of land between the sedentary Persianized population and Qipchaq tribal peoples. Khwarizm went through a parallel phase of state consolidation and commercial development in the nineteenth century. However, the efforts of Muhammad Rahim I (1806–25) to centralize the Khwarizmian state were undermined by the constant struggle with the Turkmen nomadic population supported by Sufi holy-men.

Undermined by conflicts among the ruling dynasties, uymaq and tribal chiefs, and pastoral and sedentary populations, the Inner Asian societies became prey to Russian expansion. Motivated by the desire to secure its borders, control trade, and exploit rich agricultural lands, Russia had already absorbed the Tatar and Kazakh steppes. Further expansion would give Russia political and trading advantages in relations with Iran, India, and China and enable her to forestall potential British rivalry. The governing factor in Russian expansion, however, was the ambitions of its generals and the willingness of the Tsars to tolerate their initiative and benefit from their successes.

From their bases on the Kazakh steppes Russian generals effected the conquest of Turkestan. They occupied Tashkent in 1865, Samarqand in 1868, and forced Bukhara to pay indemnities and open up to Russian trade. Khokand was absorbed in 1876, the Transcaspian province in 1881, and the Pamirs were taken in 1895. Great Britain also took an interest in Inner Asia as a remote extension of its Indian sphere of influence. At the Congress of Berlin (1878) and by the Treaty of 1907 Central Asia, Afghanistan, and India were divided into Russian and British spheres of influence. Thus, by the late nineteenth century the Russians had rounded out their Inner Asian empire and had become the masters of Tatar, Kazakh, Uzbek, and other Inner Asian peoples. After a bitter and futile struggle to convert the Tatars, the Russian impact upon Muslim peoples would be made through new political arrangements, economic change, and educational influence. These forces would profoundly change Inner Asian Muslim societies in the late nineteenth and twentieth centuries.

EASTERN TURKESTAN AND CHINA

Eastern Turkestan was also a region of nomadic peoples and important agricultural and oasis cities. From the time of the Mongol conquests, eastern Turkestan, parts of the northern steppes, and parts of Transoxania were the nominal domain of the Chaghatay Khans, successors of Chinggis Khan. In the middle of the fourteenth century the Chaghatay empire was divided, and its domains restricted to eastern Turkestan (Moghulistan). Chaghatay suzerainty was rarely more than nominal. Nomadic chieftains and the rulers of the oasis towns generally maintained their autonomy.

Nevertheless, in the Chaghatay era, eastern Turkestan came into the domain of Turkish-Islamic culture. This was the result of a long, slow, and little-documented process in which Mongol peoples were converted to Islam and won over to the use of Turkish languages. Muslim rulers tried to use Islam as legitimation for warfare against non-Muslim peoples. By the time that Komul (Hami) came under Muslim rule in 1513, Sunni Islam was widely accepted in the Tarim basin and Chaghatay was spreading as a literary language. Mosques were appearing along the trade routes between Inner Asia and China. Muslim expansion, however, was checked by Oirats (Mongols) who accepted Buddhism at the end of the sixteenth century. By then, however, much of the populace of Inner Asia outside of Mongolia and Tibet was Muslim or under Muslim suzerainty.

The most striking manifestation of the influence of Islam was the role of khwajas, or Sufis who traced their biological as well as their spiritual lineage to the Prophet Muhammad or to the early Caliphs. The earliest of these figures were probably itinerant holy-men, faith healers, and miracle workers who in the fourteenth century acquired local prestige, gained a livelihood from gifts of tithes and landed estates, and married into prominent families. In many ways they resembled the sharifs of Morocco by combining Sufi qualities with descent from the Prophet. The khwajas gradually attained a spiritual ascendancy over secular rulers, all of whom became disciples of the Sufi masters. The descendants of Makhdum-i Aᶜzam (d. 1540), the spiritual master of Bukhara, became the principal advisers to local rulers in Kashgar and Yarkand and eventually the rulers of these cities. From 1678 to 1756 Kashgar was ruled by a dynasty of khwajas which claimed descent from Muhammad, headship of a Sufi order, and a family relation to Chinggis Khan. Thus the khwajas united spiritual and political authority. Nonetheless the elites of these oasis cities were divided into bitterly hostile factions. Factional wars eventually led the khwajas to appeal to nomadic peoples for political support – a measure which eventually cost the oases their independence.

While Chaghatay Khans, khwajas, and tribal chiefs ruled eastern Turkestan, a new Oirat–Mongol empire called the Dzungarian Confederation, the last of the great Inner Asian nomadic empires, was being formed. The Dzungarian Confederation had its origins between 1400 and 1550 when Mongolian peoples were cut off from the markets of China and were forced to move westward and northward into eastern Turkestan, the northern steppes, and Transoxania. By the early seventeenth century an Oirat Khanate had come into existence – its power based on trade and dominance of peasants – and its leaders adopted Tibetan Lamaism as the religion of the confederation. Buddhism helped, as did Islam, to foster political unity among pastoral peoples, and to join them to sedentary populations. Expanding westward the Oirats attacked the Kirgiz and the Uzbeks, their competitors for pasture and access to cattle markets in Transoxania, and conquered the Tarim basin. Allied with the religious factions of Kashgar and Yarkand the Oirats took control of the oasis cities and appointed the khwajas as their vassals.

Oirat expansion, however, provoked Chinese intervention. China had long regarded Inner Asia as part of its inherent domain, and was concerned for the protection of its frontiers against barbarian incursions. The Chinese considered Inner Asian rulers as their vassals. In the guise of tributes and exchanges of gifts, China imported horses, furs, metals, and jade in exchange for paper, textiles, drugs, tea, and porcelain. The Chinese pursued their commercial and diplomatic policy under the assumption that they possessed cultural and political supremacy and considered all exchanges as a form of tribute. By 1759 the Chinese defeated the Dzungarians, took control of the oasis cities, drove out the khwajas, and absorbed eastern Turkestan. In addition the Chinese made the eastern Kazakhs and Khokand their tributaries. With these new vassals the Chinese exchanged silk, tea, and porcelain for horses, cattle, and Russian products.

The conquest of eastern Turkestan brought a new Muslim population under Chinese control. The earliest Muslims in China were Arab troops coming from Inner Asia and Muslim merchants who settled in Canton in the eighth century. Though permanent residents, these Muslims were considered foreigners, subjects of far-off Muslim rulers, and enjoyed an extraterritorial jurisdiction under their own officials. The Mongol conquests and the formation of the Yuan dynasty (1271–1368) reinforced the Muslim population. The Mongols employed Muslim administrators and tax collectors, encouraged trade between China and Inner Asia, and sponsored the migration and settlement of Muslims not only in northwestern but also in southwestern China and Yunnan. In many cities, Muslims, living under the leadership of their own Shaykh al-Islam and qadis, occupied separate quarters provided with mosques and bazaars. Under the Ming dynasty (1368–1644) Muslims served the emperor as astronomers, diviners, translators, postal officials and caravaners.

In the Ming period the name Hui was applied to Chinese of Muslim faith, both to assimilated foreign Muslims and to Chinese converts to Islam. Muslims adopted the speech, names, manners, clothing, and other outward features of being Chinese. Muslim writers in this period attempted to show how Islam and Confucianism could be reconciled and how Chinese mythology and Islamic history were congruent. Still, Muslims retained an inner Muslim identity defined by their prayer rituals, Arabic names, and communal affiliations. Under the authority of an imam, Muslims had their own mosques, schools, charities, and endowments. Chinese Muslims, however, were not an organized group. There was no unity among the numerous different congregations, and the Hui were widely dispersed throughout territorial China. The Manchu dynasty dealt with the Hui by assurances of protection and threats of punishment, and a pragmatic policy of suppressing resistance and tolerating religious differences. As long as Muslim identity did not interfere with their outward conformity it was acceptable to the Chinese. This coexistence lasted until the great Muslim revolts of the nineteenth century.

The newly conquered Muslim population of eastern Turkestan was very different from the assimilated Hui. Turkestani Muslims were mainly Uighurs and Kazakhs and were not assimilated to the Chinese way of life. Under Chinese suzerainty, the Islamic identity of both the town and the nomadic populations was fully maintained. Colleges in Yarkand, for example, were endowed with land. Kashgar was the site of the much venerated tomb of Hazrat Afaq and his family. Beggars and dervishes lived in the cemeteries; religious colonies surrounded the tomb. Pre-Islamic survivals such as fluttering flags, yak tails, and heaps of horns marked the reverence in which this place was held. While the Muslims of China proper had become a Chinese religious minority, the Muslims of Inner Asia remained a politically subordinate non-Chinese population.

The Chinese administration of eastern Turkestan was based on a superstructure of Chinese garrisons and administrative officers in the oasis towns of Komul, Urumchi, Kashgar, Khotan, and other places, who governed through local Muslim chieftains (begs). The begs collected taxes, controlled water supplies, administered justice, and maintained order. They were granted land and serfs to pay the costs of their offices, and then tried to increase these holdings and to convert them into private properties. Chinese rule, however, introduced a period of security and commercial prosperity. By the 1820s the cultivated lands in the oasis district of Kashgar had doubled and Chinese peasants were being brought in to reclaim wastelands.

Inner Asian Muslims, however, never fully accepted Chinese rule. In the face of Chinese rule, a new Muslim religious movement, the so-called new teachings (Hsin-chiao), a variant of the Naqshbandi order, was introduced by Ma Ming-hsin, who came to China in 1761. He studied in Yarkand and Kashgar and propagated a form of Sufism expressed in loud chanting of the Quran, prayers with dance-like head-shaking and foot-stamping, belief in miracles and visions, and worship of saints. New sect members believed that faith was more important than family. They were reformers who were hostile to the old practices and to the political elites. Ma attracted a following in Kansu province, and, in 1781, rebelled against Chinese rule. The movement was soon repressed, but repression caused general resentment and later revolts by Kirgiz warriors. The political unrest in eastern Turkestan tempted the khwajas, the former rulers of Kashgar who had taken refuge in Khokand, to try to regain their former possession. Between the 1820s and 1862 they led a series of attacks on Chinese territory, supported by Kirgiz and local Uighurs. The rulers of Khokand also aspired to a larger sphere of influence in eastern Turkestan. Chafing at Chinese political and trading restrictions, Khokand demanded the right to control the caravan trade and to appoint tax collectors in Kashgar. Chinese concessions only led to an expansion of Khokand's trade and influence in eastern Turkestan, and to covert Khokandi support for the aspirations of the khwajas.

The weakness of the Ch'ing dynasty (1644–1911) in eastern Turkestan was only a symptom of the general breakdown of the Chinese empire. Beset by the Taiping and numerous provincial rebellions, the Ch'ing were forced to allow their subjects to organize local military forces and yet had to press them for increased taxes. Also with the breakdown of the Ch'ing, Chinese hostility to Muslims and demands for their assimilation increased. Ch'ing misrule provoked Muslim rebellions in Yunnan, Shensi, Kansu, and eastern Turkestan. Hanafi law, which legitimizes rebellion if non-Muslim law is enforced or if non-Muslim territory separates Muslims from each other, provided a legal basis for secret societies and revolts. Muslim religious and political consciousness was stimulated by an outpouring of Islamic literature stressing the importance of emulating the teachings of the Prophet, ritual purity, and fulfilling God's commands. This nineteenth-century literature stressed the superiority of Islam and attacked Chinese civilization rather than attempting to be reconciled to it. Chinese Muslim scholars no longer insisted on the similarities of Islam and Confucianism and urged Muslims to abide by Islamic law and to avoid Chinese customs. The nineteenth-century Muslim rebellions were also abetted by reformist Muslim influences coming from India or other parts of Inner Asia.

A series of Muslim rebellions in Yunnan culminated in the formation of an independent Muslim state from 1856 to 1873 under the leadership of Tu Wen-hsiu, who called himself Commander of the Faithful and Sultan. The principal Muslim rebellion in Shensi province was led by Ma Hua-lung, who represented the new teaching movement. Here Muslim secession took on a peculiarly Chinese quality. Ma Hua-lung adopted the name Tsung-ta A-hung or General Grand A-hung, which is a Muslim name but when written in Chinese characters means, "the horse became a dragon," and thus evoked Chinese as well as Muslim symbols. The new sect adopted Chinese popular symbols as the basis of a Muslim revivalism with separatist political implications. Under his leadership, Kucha and Ili rebelled, cutting off Chinese communications with Kashgar.

Taking advantage of Chinese embarrassment, the Khan of Khokand sent the surviving khwajas of Kashgar with a military subordinate named Ya⁽qub Beg to take control of local Kirgiz and Uighur peoples. Ya⁽qub quickly conquered most of eastern Turkestan and the oasis states. He ruled in the name of the Shari⁽a, enforced Muslim law, gave large gifts to mosques, and coined silver money in his own name. However, he was dependent on Khokandis, Afghans, and others for his army. In a direct affront to Chinese authority, he recognized Ottoman suzerainty; the Ottomans acknowledged him as Amir in 1873.

Ya⁽qub's fate and that of the Muslim rebellions was linked to Russian and British maneuvers. In the nineteenth century eastern Turkestan was the object of Russian and British rivalry; both of them were interested in trading advantages and the protection of their respective territories in Russia and India. Generally the British planned to cooperate with friendly local rulers to check Russian advances, but in the late 1860s they backed China's efforts to suppress local rebellions, for fear that the dismemberment of China would hamper British access to Inner Asia. Russian occupation of the Ili province in 1871 led the British to see Ya⁽qub Beg as a potential buffer against the possibility of further Russian penetration of Inner Asia. In 1874 they supplied him with a small number of rifles. A revival of Chinese power under the leadership of Governor Tso Tsung-t'ang (1812–85) put an end both to Ya⁽qub and to British concerns. Tso reorganized Chinese forces, reconquered Shensi and Kansu, took Aksu and Kashgar by 1878, and suppressed the new teaching.

In 1881 China and Russia negotiated a treaty which restored the Ili province to China and paved the way for the reorganization of eastern Turkestan as a province under civilian Chinese administration. Named Sinkiang, it became part of China in 1884. By then all of Inner Asia had come under either Russian or Chinese rule. It remained only to define the borders between Russia and China in 1892 and between Russia and Afghanistan in 1895. The expansion of the two great imperial powers brought an end to 3,000 years of nomadic migration and empires.

Inner Asian societies, until their conquest by Russia and China, exemplified several types of Muslim society. On the northern steppes and in eastern Turkestan Tatar, Uzbek, Kazakh, Kirgiz, Uighur, and other peoples were organized in family units and loose confederations. The uymaq or tribe, an alliance of family and clan units, was the effective political unit. Still larger-order Khanates and hordes were fragile coalitions.

Nevertheless, pastoral peoples conquered the sedentary areas. In the sedentarized districts of Transoxania, Farghana, Kashgaria, and other oases, they founded centralized state regimes, legitimized partly in Muslim and partly in cosmopolitan cultural terms. In urban areas Islamic organization was crucial to the viability of states. The Mangit dynasty was virtually the expression of the ʿulamaʾ of Bukhara, who controlled judicial administration and education and whose organized bodies of sayyids, khwajas, mirs, Sufis, students, and guilds made up the body politic. In Kashgar, dynasties of khwajas ruled directly. Muslim society in sedentary Inner Asia was built around the tripartite division of power and authority among tribal, state, and religious elites, but Russian and Chinese rule would, as colonial rule did everywhere in the Muslim world, profoundly change this historic configuration.

CHAPTER 18

THE INDIAN SUBCONTINENT: THE DELHI SULTANATES AND THE MUGHAL EMPIRE

In the Indian subcontinent Islam was introduced into an already developed civilization defined by agriculture, urbanization, organized higher religions, and complex political regimes. In India civilization was defined by the caste system, by Brahmanic Hinduism and Buddhist religions, and by dominant Rajput and other Hindu political elites. In the past there had been great empires, but on the eve of the Muslim invasion India was divided into numerous local states. The Muslim conquests brought a new elite and a new level of political integration, and began the process of generating a distinctive form of Muslim civilization. The culture of the state and the political elites became a blend of universal Muslim concepts and symbols of statecraft, cosmopolitan artistic pursuits such as architecture and painting, and regional motifs. Muslim religio-communal orientations encompassed all of the principal varieties of Islam – ʿulamaʾ scholasticism, Sufi–Shariʿa synthesis, shrine worship, and reformist Islam. In India, as opposed to Iran or the Ottoman empire, a pluralistic religious society escaped bureaucratization and state control. The special cultural qualities of Indian-Islamic civilization, and the autonomy and plurality of religious tendencies made it a distinctive variant of the universal Islamic pattern.

THE MUSLIM CONQUESTS AND THE DELHI SULTANATES

The history of Islamic societies in the subcontinent goes back to the chaotic era following the collapse of the ʿAbbasid empire in the middle of the tenth century. There had been previous Arab invasions, as in 711–13 when Muslim

437

Table 15. *Muslim India: outline chronology*

Ghaznavids (begin the Muslim conquest of India)	
Afghanistan	977–1186
Khurasan	999–1040
Ghurids	
Afghanistan	1186–1215
India	1173–1206
Delhi sultanates	
Dynasty of Aybeg	1206–1290
Khalji	1290–1320
Tughluq	1320–1413
Sayyid	1414–1451
Lodi	1451–1526
Independent Muslim regimes	
Bengal	1336–1576
Kashmir	1346–1589
Gujarat	1407–1572
Jawnpur	1394–1479
Malwa	1401–1531
Deccan (Bahmanids)	1347–1527
Deccan (Faruqis)	1370–1601
Mughal empire	1526–1858
Suri dynasty	1540–1555
Akbar I	1556–1605
Aurangzeb	1658–1707
British victory at Plassey	1757
Britain becomes paramount power	1818
British Raj	1858–1947

rule was established in Sind, but the definitive Muslim conquest came from the post-ᶜAbbasid military regimes in Afghanistan. The Ghaznavids captured Lahore in 1030 and plundered north India. In the late twelfth century, the Ghaznavids were replaced by local mountain chieftains under the leadership of the Ghurid dynasty, who began the systematic conquest of India. Between 1175 and 1192 they occupied Uch, Multan, Peshawar, Lahore, and Delhi. In 1206, one of the Ghurid generals, Qutb al-Din Aybeg, the conqueror of Delhi, made himself independent and founded the first of a succession of dynasties collectively known as the Delhi Sultanates (1206–1526). The Sultanates represent a single period in Muslim-Indian history because of the continuity of the ruling elite, composed of Afghan or Turkish Inner Asian military lords and their clients. Each dynasty represented a different segment of the Afghan-Turkish elite, the victors of the moment in the constant jockeying for power. The successive dynasties made continued efforts to centralize state power, but none of them achieved absolute political control; each was merely senior in a political society composed of numerous local Muslim and Hindu lords. Finally, each dealt with the problem of establishing an Islamic state in a region of profound Hindu and Buddhist culture. Out of their collective achievement came a distinct kind of Muslim civilization.

Under ʿAla al-Din Khalji (1296–1316), the Delhi regime reestablished its imperial status, and extended its power to Gujarat, Rajasthan, the Deccan and some parts of south India. ʿAla al-Din tried also to strengthen the state's agrarian administration. Before the Muslim conquest agrarian taxation was based on the principle that peasants had a duty to cultivate the land and to pay the ruler a share of the produce. The share exacted by the ruler could be assessed by measuring the land and taxing each measured unit by a fixed amount or dividing the actual crop. Much less common was a contract under which peasants paid a fixed tax regardless of the size of the crop. Before the Muslim conquests, local rulers generally dealt with the villages as a unit, and collected the taxes with the assistance of local headmen who would assess the individual peasants. The ruler commonly assigned his tax rights to pay the salaries of his soldiers or administrative employees. In 1300, in the core areas of northern India, ʿAla al-Din Khalji fixed a new standard of revenue demand at one-half the produce, abolished the perquisites of local chiefs, and confiscated all existing land grants in an effort to deprive local lords of their military and financial power. He also controlled the grain market in Delhi, where grain was distributed at controlled prices to the soldiers and the urban population.

The Khalji regime barely survived the death of its founder; it was succeeded in 1320 by the Tughluq dynasty (1320–1413). Muhammad b. Tughluq (1325–51) attempted to counterbalance the political influence of well-established Muslim families by cultivating the support of newly immigrant Turkish warriors. He was the first sultan to appoint non-Muslims to military and government offices, participate in local festivals, and permit the construction of Hindu temples. To maintain the Muslim credentials of his regime, Muhammad b. Tughluq followed a strong pro-Sunni policy. He stressed his credentials as a Muslim warrior by defending India against the Mongols. He gave formal adherence to the Shariʿa, accepted the ʿAbbasid Caliph in Cairo as head of the Muslim umma, appointed a chief judge, and imposed the head tax on non-Muslims. Muhammad b. Tughluq was generally favorable to the ʿulamaʾ. His was the first Muslim regime to integrate Turkish warlords, Hindu feudatories, and Muslim scholars in the political elite.

The Tughluq empire, however, disintegrated rapidly under pressure of

Map 18. The Delhi Sultanates.

revolts by governors, local resistance in the Deccan, and the formation of independent Hindu kingdoms. In the early sixteenth century, the struggles over the Delhi Sultanate led to the intervention of Babur (a descendant of Timur), a warrior adventurer and local lord in Farghana, who was for a short time ruler of Samarqand and then of Kabul, Herat, and Qandahar. In 1526 Babur defeated the Lodis at the battle of Panipat, and established himself as the ruler of Delhi. His son Humayun lost the throne to the Afghan lord, Sher Shah (1540–55), but then reestablished himself in Delhi and Agra and handed on his rule to Akbar. Akbar was the true founder of the Mughal empire.

For the Delhi Sultanate, an offshoot of Muslim expansion sustained by a small and factious military aristocracy, ruling over the vast Indian subcontinent, cultural and ideological cohesion was essential. To soothe the factional quarrels, maintain solidarity among the Muslims, and integrate the Hindu lords into their inevitable place in the governing elite, the Delhi Sultanate elaborated its own cultural and political identity. This was at once Muslim and cosmopolitan, built upon both Persian and Indic languages, literature and arts, brought together into a new Indian-Islamic civilization.

This cultural policy, however, took time to develop. At the outset the Delhi Sultanate was aggressively Muslim, exclusive, and hostile to the political participation of non-Muslims. The Delhi regimes stressed allegiance to the Caliph and support for the judicial establishment of the ʿulamaʾ. Some rulers like ʿAla al-Din sought Sufi rather than ʿulamaʾ support for the Sultans, since the Sufis shared a hierarchical concept of political society. Just as the Sufi saints stood at the apex of the universal spiritual order, the Sultans stood at the head of secular society.

The Muslim concept of kingship derived substantially from the Iranian Muslim tradition. Barani's (died c. 1360) treatise on kingship began with a section on the moral purpose of human existence as the realization of the true practice of Islam. Men are created, Barani argued, with a mixture of vices and virtues; to cause the good to prevail, the ruler must change the dispositions of his subjects and help them act as true Muslims. He must himself follow the teachings of the Prophet, enforce the Shariʿa, suppress rebellions, punish heretics, subordinate the unbelievers, and protect the weak against the strong. A Muslim king is responsible for order, for stability, and for the safety and prosperity of his subjects.

Barani's moral principles are followed by practical advice on the management of the army, the treasury, and the subordinate officials. The ruler, he says, must appoint to office people who have the requisite virtues; rank should be determined by moral qualifications, for the ruler and his servants set an example of good behavior for all the subjects and they create the conditions that make it possible for them to fulfill their religious duties. Thus, his political theory aims ultimately at the creation of a social order that brings men into accord with God's command by cultivating moral virtues in the governing authorities.

The Delhi regime also inherited pre-Islamic Persian concepts of kingship that allowed for the exaltation of rulers, and prompted them to demonstrate their authority in lavish public works. Sher Shah, for example, constructed forts, mosques, and caravansaries for travelers along the main highways where food and fodder were provided for troops and merchants. He also built splendid monumental tombs for his grandfather, his father, and himself to legitimize the reign of a parvenu. The tombs were placed in strategic locations as an assertion of legitimacy, and near the tombs of saints to give religious respectability.

The Delhi regime also had substantial appeal to Hindu lords. The Muslim emphasis upon loyalty to the ruler, patron–client relations, and the virtues of service and honor were consistent with Hindu political ideals. Muslim recognition of the hierarchy of ranks validated the organization of Hindu society. Both cultures accepted the dominance of kings, but the meaning of kingship was different. For Hindus, the ruler upholds the order of the world by virtue of who he is as *axis mundi*; for Muslims, he fulfills his role by virtue of what he does – implementing the Shariᶜa.

Despite the tacit agreement about political authority, the early Delhi Sultanate did not try to incorporate the local Hindu lords. Indeed the first gesture of the Muslim conquest was to destroy major Hindu temples and replace them with great mosques, whose size, design, and inscriptions were symbols of Muslim domination. The mosque of Quwwat al-Islam in Delhi incorporated stones and iron pillars from Hindu monuments in order to symbolize that an Islamic order had superseded a Hindu one. The Qutb Minar, a towering brick structure, signaled the presence of a Muslim community. Only in the fourteenth century did the Tughluq dynasty begin to absorb Hindu motifs into Muslim architecture as a symbol of the Muslim appropriation of Hindu political authority. Tughluqid architecture borrowed such design features as the Hindu *chatri* or kiosk, heavy stone balustrades, eaves, block pillars, and capitals.

The historic task of forming a shared cosmopolitan culture was furthered in the various provincial Muslim regimes. In Bengal, Sufi writers and Muslim rulers adopted the local languages. The Hindu classic, *Mahabharata*, and Arabic and Persian classics, including stories from the Arabian Nights, were translated into Bengali at the order of Muslim rulers. Muslim poets also wrote in Bengali about Hindu deities and myths, using Arabic and Persian loan words. This synthesis of languages and literatures was the basis for the emergence of a new literary Bengali language. Similarly, the independent Sultans of Gujarat (1407–1572) patronized the regional languages instead of Sanskrit or Persian.

In the Deccan, Bijapur and Golconda were important centers for the synthesis of Islam and local cultures. The Bahmanid regime in Bijapur (1347–1527) ruled a land that lay between Marathi-speaking peoples to the north and Kannada-speakers to the south. In each of these regions there were local devotional movements and strong attachments to local saints. In neither was the Hindu Sanskritic tradition strong. In this zone, where Indian high culture was relatively weak, a Muslim regime encouraged the reconciliation and integration of elements of Marathi and Kannada culture and the formation of a new regional language, Dakhni, strongly influenced by Persian. The local Muslim elites developed a shared culture for the diverse linguistic and religious elements of the Bijapur state, defined in opposition to the northern regimes.

In Golconda the synthesis of Muslim and Hindu aristocracies and cultures developed under the Qutb Shah dynasty (1491–1688). This regime helped to integrate a Muslim and a Telugu-speaking elite by patronizing the local warrior aristocracy, providing tax-free lands for Saivite Hindu temples, and sponsoring a regional culture based on the bilingual use of Telugu and Persian. Thus, while the Delhi Sultanate leaned to Muslim supremacy, the provincial Muslim regimes fostered the integration of Muslim and Hindu cultures and the formation of an Indian version of Islamic civilization.

CONVERSION AND THE MUSLIM COMMUNITIES

Under the cover of the conquest, Muslim scholars, scribes, Sufis, poets and intellectuals flocked to India, seeking the patronage of the new regimes, organizing colleges and khanaqas, and opening the way for the conversion of Indian peoples to Islam. Though we know little about early conversions, a few facts stand out. One is that conversion was relatively limited; it seems doubtful that more than 20 or 25 percent of the populace of the subcontinent ever became Muslim. Muslims were concentrated in the Indus Valley, northwest India, and Bengal. In the fourteenth century Islam spread across the Brahmaputra River into Assam, and was represented in the Deccan. While the aristocracy was composed of Muslims who came from Afghanistan, Iran, and Inner Asia, Indian converts were mostly from the lower classes. Conversions commonly occurred when Muslim lords endowed a mosque or khanaqa and invited scholars or Sufis to take up residence in the territories which they controlled. Around the lord and his sponsored religious teachers gathered peasants and service people who took on the religion of their masters. However, the Turkish and Afghan warrior elite was probably hostile to conversions of nobles lest they compete for political power. Their position was similar to that of the early Arab regimes in the Middle East, for whom Islam signified the suzerainty and the solidarity of an otherwise factious ruling caste.

Conversions were also affected by the growth of cities. Cities broke down caste and geographical barriers to social interaction. Peoples who had given up their social and political status, and who were ambitious to make careers under a new regime, such as itinerant merchants, workers and peddlers, fugitive peasants and vagabonds, found in Islam a unifying ideology. Sufi khanaqas may similarly have served as centers for converting rural Indians to Islam. Khanaqas were often established on the outskirts of towns and villages where they might appeal to lower-caste elements. In north India they were the centers for the birth of Urdu as the lingua franca among Muslims and between Muslims and non-Muslim populations.

In some cases conversions to Islam were correlated with important changes in regional societies. In the northwest provinces, where the Jats, a hunter–gatherer and pastoral population, was coming into contact with a state-based agricultural society and a literate form of civilization, Islam became the religion of peoples who were becoming peasants. In Bengal, conversion similarly represented the change of hunter–gatherer and pastoral peoples to a sedentary way of life. Before the advent of Islam, the transformation of hunter–gatherers into peasants was marked by incorporation into Hindu caste society, for Hinduism was well established in west Bengal, where rice culture supported a Brahmin religious aristocracy and Hindu temples. In east Bengal, Brahmin and caste influences were weaker, and Buddhism was the dominant religion. Under Muslim rule, east and west Bengal were integrated under a single regime and the new political environment was permeated by Islamic symbols. Under the leadership of Muslim landlords, warriors, and Sufis, the process of agricultural expansion continued into east Bengal making converts out of newly sedentarized peoples. New communities with Muslim allegiances were formed under the auspices of this new landlord aristocracy.

Whatever the social mechanisms for the spread of Islam, the influence of Sufis was crucial. The story of Farid al-Din Ganj-i Shakr (d. 1245), one of the early heads of the Chisti order is illuminating. Baba Farid, as he is called, settled in a place now called Pak-pattan, a village in the north Indian plain. A small dusty place of mud houses and a few shops, peopled by men reputed to be illiterate, superstitious, and quarrelsome, it had a reputation for robbing travelers. Baba Farid came to this village seeking escape from the distractions and temptations of the court in Delhi. He had for years practiced a rigorous asceticism, denying himself worldly satisfactions, and concentrating his attention upon devotion to God. At Pak-pattan he stopped at the edge of the village under a clump of trees, unfolded his prayer rug, and lived for days, weeks, and perhaps months in solitude, subsisting on small gifts of food which he did not acknowledge. He spent all his time in prayer.

After a time he began to acknowledge his visitors. People recognized him as a holy-man. The poor came for cures and amulets, and advice on family matters. They asked him to intercede with the landlords and the tax collectors. Officials, landowners, scholars, and the rich, weary of the emptiness of the world, went to consult him. Tribal chiefs visited to ask his help in negotiating feuds. Merchants sought his protection to pass through the town unmolested. Other holy-men, Muslim and non-Muslim, sat in his presence. As his reputation grew, Baba Farid acquired enough gifts to build a hospice. Disciples came to live with him. In the eyes of his followers, his personal discipline, devotion to prayer, and success as a healer and negotiator were miraculous. Stories circulated about his wisdom; he came to be venerated. In his name, people converted to Islam. Thus an other-worldly man acquired worldly power. Renunciation was the basis of his worldly success. Because he no longer cared for the ordinary things of life, he was able to see matters in context and measure their relative importance. Because he did not care for himself, he was a good judge of other people's motives and interests; he was, therefore, successful as a teacher, healer, and mediator.

His followers did not see this as ordinary wisdom. They saw his powers as a sign of God's blessings being channeled into this world. They believed that he possessed baraka, the capacity to know things unknown and to dispense blessings which are ultimately only in God's gift. When he died, his grave became the repository of his baraka. The people visited his tomb, touched and kissed the holy place, made gifts and sacrifices, and celebrated seasonal festivals and his birth and death days.

Behind the mystical and magical powers of individual saints like Baba Farid lay deep cultural sympathies which made the person of the Sufi and his teachings attractive to non-Muslims. The Sufi who renounced worldly gain, devoted himself to prayer and expressed himself through poetry, corresponded in the popular imagination to the Bhakti devotional preacher who had given up his past life and had access to higher wisdom. Sufism stood for detachment within the world rather than renunciation of the world. The Sufis married and raised children, cared for the community, and sought to bring justice and ethical values into human affairs. Similarly, Indic philosophies valued a detached style of life that permitted the believer to outwardly fulfill the complex requirements of the social and moral code, and yet inwardly be free for spiritual progress. The masses saw in the Sufis the kind of spiritual achievement which they had come to expect from the yogis.

Sufi teachings and practices also corresponded to the Hindu metaphysical concept of the universe. The monotheism of the Sufis was not a surprise to Hindus, because the Saivite and Vaisnavite traditions had monotheistic trends. At the same time the claims of the Sufi masters to be the concrete manifestation of the powers of God were compatible with Hindu polytheism. Moreover, the Sufis did not wholly exclude the worship of local gods within and alongside of Islam. Indeed the veneration of Sufi graves and their annual festivals corresponded in some cases with the Hindu calendar. In Bengal and the Punjab Muslims celebrated Hindu festivals, worshiped at Hindu shrines, offered gifts to Hindu gods and goddesses, and celebrated marriages in Hindu fashion. Hindus who converted to Islam retained many of their past beliefs and practices; many Hindus venerated Muslim saints without change of religious identity.

Thus, in popular religious culture, the boundaries between Islam and Hinduism were more flexible than in formal doctrine. Islam entered into the Indian environment sometimes by assimilating converts into a new communal identity and religious beliefs and sometimes by being assimilated into the indigenous culture. Conversion to Islam was a subtle matter in which Islamic elements might be added to an existing complex of Hindu religious beliefs, without change of worldview or social identity, or in which the convert could make a revolutionary change in both beliefs and allegiances.

Yet, despite considerable success in the conversion of Hindus to Islam, the great majority of the subcontinent's peoples remained Hindus. While the Middle East and Indonesia were almost totally converted, India like the Balkans, remained substantially non-Muslim. There are several reasons for this. First was the thin veneer of the Muslim conquest in India. The Muslims were small bands of warriors who were not, as in the case of the Arab or Turkish conquests of the Middle East, backed by large numbers of settlers. The Muslims established a political elite, but they could not colonize the country. Secondly, the pre-Islamic political structure of India remained intact. The previous regime was highly decentralized, composed of local lords and a Brahmin religious elite who retained local political power under Muslim suzerainty. The caste social structure under Brahmin leadership was also resistant to change. As in the Balkans, the thinness of the governing elite, the confirmation of local lords and the protection of the non-Muslim populations, all served to maintain a continuity of non-Muslim identity.

The combination of migrations from the Middle East and Inner Asia and local conversions gave the subcontinent all varieties of Islam. The ʿulamaʾ often became part of the state establishment. The Sultans appointed a chief sadr, a chief qadi, and a Shaykh al-Islam; the post of *Sadr-i Jahan* was created in 1248 to supervise most religious activities, including justice, prayer, markets, and endowed funds. The chief justice administered the court system, and qadis were appointed at provincial and district levels. Subordinate sadrs dealt with local land and registration matters and qadis dealt with civil and criminal cases. Preachers and prayer leaders were also state-appointed and state-paid officials. Madrasas were established and the teachers salaried by the government. The Muʿizzi and the Nasiriya madrasa curriculum included Arabic, hadith, law, logic, theology, literature, and mysticism. However, despite the formal Muslim establishment, the influence of the ʿulamaʾ on the general society was very limited. Rather, Sufism played the critical role in the creation of a Muslim community in India. Sufi warriors flocked to India looking for religious merit in the holy war. As on the Ottoman frontiers, they became the leaders of migrating Turkish warrior bands. The Kazaruniya order helped to establish Islam in Kashmir. Rural mystics spread the Sufi notion of the universal hierarchy of saints and the practices of veneration of tombs. Malamatis and Qalandaris, individual wandering dervishes, exemplified rejection of the worldly way of life.

The tariqat were represented by the Suhrawardiya, the Chistiya, and the Shattariya, who established extensive networks of khanaqas throughout north India. The disciples of ʿUmar al-Suhrawardi, under the leadership of Shaykh Bahaʾ al-Din Zakariya (d. 1267), brought the order to India. Multan was their main base, but the order was also important in Uch and Gujarat. The Chisti order was introduced into India by Muʿin al-Din Hasan Chist who, born in southeastern Iran in 1141, settled in India, and died at Ajmer in 1236. His order spread throughout Rajasthan, Bengal, and the Deccan, and was especially important in the northern Gangetic plain and the Punjab. The Chisti order accepted the doctrine of Ibn al-ʿArabi concerning the unity of being, and preached a non-political and non-violent philosophy.

The Shattari order was introduced into India by Shaykh ʿAbdallah Shattar (d. 1485) who toured the Ganges Valley dressed like a king with followers in military uniforms, carrying banners and beating drums, in order to propagate his beliefs. His followers regarded him as being in direct contact with the saints, the Prophet, and with God himself, a man possessed of both earthly and spiritual power and absolved by his detachment from the world from all ordinary legal and social norms. The Shattari order appealed to the rich and was closely identified with the state elites. It withered away when it lost the favor of the Mughal emperor Akbar.

The several orders represented variations on the system of Sufism which had developed in the Middle East. The distinctive feature of these movements was the organization of a brotherhood built around the total devotion and obedience of the disciples to the master. The central experience of the disciple was to be initiated into the discipline and spiritual technique taught by the master. Once the novice had been initiated there was a ceremonial passing on of the cloak or khirqa of the master to his disciple. The Sufis believed in the miraculous powers of their saints, and that the very order of the universe was upheld by a hierarchy of Sufi masters, the leading one of whom was called the qutb. Thus, Shaykh Nizam al-Din Auliya (d. 1325), one of the founding fathers of the Chisti order, was perceived by his followers to be the head of a spiritual hierarchy who ruled a kingdom parallel to that of temporal rulers. The great Sufi leaders held a court that rivaled that of temporal Sultans; the patched cloak, the prayer carpet, the wooden sandals and the rosary were the mystics' insignias of chieftainship. The head of the order dispatched his khalifas or lieutenants to various provinces, and they, in turn, appointed subordinates to bring the mission to towns and cities. The chief of the whole network of Sufis was often called the Shah or Sultan to symbolize the combination of a territorial and a spiritual sphere of influence. The khanaqa was the collective home of the Sufi community. A Chisti khanaqa consisted of a big hall called a *jamaʿat khana* in which the followers lived their communal life. The hall was usually a large room supported by pillars which marked the places where the Sufis prayed, studied, and slept. Some khanaqas had rooms attached for the private use of the shaykh and the senior members. Often there was a garden, a veranda, and a kitchen. The life of a khanaqa was organized like that of a royal court. The Sufi master took a central place; his disciples hung about waiting to be invited to sit near him. The Shah received the general public, listened to petitioners, gave amulets to heal the sick, mediated disputes, and dispensed spiritual counsel.

The people attached to the khanaqa were divided between permanent residents and visitors; the permanent residents were organized in a hierarchy depending upon their spiritual standing and the duties assigned them. The disciples did personal services for the master and his family and they organized the common housekeeping tasks of the khanaqa. The visitors were numerous; they included scholars, government officials and businessmen looking for some escape from worldly burdens. Poor people came for money, advice, recommendations, or intercessions with their superiors. They came for cures, sympathy, and blessings. The mystics taught them how to worship in the manner of Islam.

Apart from the Quran and hadith, the most important religious influence on Indian Islam was the teaching of Ibn al-ʿArabi and the doctrine of wahdat al-wujud, the unity of being. These teachings were spread both by the Chistis and the Shattaris, who believed that spiritual attitude was more important than specific religious laws or practices. They also saw that Islam and Hinduism shared spiritual insights and this led to an assimilation of Sufi and Hindu beliefs about the control of emotional life as a prerequisite to the control of external behavior. The Sufis adopted Hindu ceremonies, devotional songs, and yoga techniques. Popular religious culture became a mixture of Muslim and Hindu practices. Thus, the Sufis were divided among monist, pantheist, and syncretist religious tendencies, between commitment to individual spirituality and collective Shariʿa, and between universal Muslim practices and specific Indian forms of worship.

Sufism was closely connected to the vernacular languages; Sufis pioneered the absorption of Indian language, music, and poetic forms into Islamic practice. Hindi became their spoken language, and inspired the birth of Urdu, a literary version of Hindi, as a Muslim language. The earliest work in Urdu was a treatise on Sufism written in 1308. Dakhni was first used by Chistis in Golconda in the early fifteenth century and was developed further by Sufis in Bijapur and Gujarat. Mystical poetry in Sindhi and Punjabi dates back to the fifteenth century; Pashto mystical poetry to the late sixteenth century. Poetry in the vernacular languages took up the classical Persian themes of the yearning for and love of God. The love of the Prophet was also told and retold in poems, folk songs, riddles, and bridal songs. Hindu poets also wrote mystical poems using Muslim images and themes, including the honor of the Prophet and the mourning for Husayn.

Other Muslim movements veered away from the spiritualist and syncretic forms of Sufism. The Mahdawi movement was founded at the end of the fifteenth century by Sayyid Muhammad of Jawnpur. Sayyid Muhammad claimed to be the mahdi and traced his descent to Musa al-Kazim, the seventh in the "twelver" line of imams. He preached poverty, renunciation, and prayer, and sought to restore the purity of religious belief and practice, and to build a community based upon allegiance to Muslim law. His followers established *daira* or communities in which they lived an ascetic life, shared their earnings, and attempted to minimize their worldly involvement so as not to be distracted from their dependence upon God. Weekly the members met to confess their sins. The Mahdawi movement was important in Gujarat in the sixteenth century and was widely accepted in the reign of the great Mughal Sultan Akbar. With acceptance came a loss of missionary zeal, and with the passing of the millennium, the thousandth year of the Muslim era, the followers of Sayyid Muhammad lost their conviction of the imminent coming of the mahdi.

Yet another alternative was a "reformist" type of Islamic belief which stressed hadith as the basis of Muslim learning and pious practice. Opposed to the excesses both of legal studies and of Sufi spirituality, the hadith scholars found their master in Shaykh ʿAbd al-Haqq Dihlawi (d. 1642). The Suhrawardis were committed to Muslim law, taught the doctrine of *wahdat al-shuhud* (unity of witness), and insisted upon the superiority of prophecy to sainthood. These movements would inspire Sirhindi (1564–1624) and the reformers of the seventeenth and eighteenth centuries.

The relations among ʿulamaʾ, Sufis, and the state were varied. In principle, the ʿulamaʾ were servants of the state regime. They benefited from state protection of Islamic religious life, enforcement of Islamic religious law, and state employment as bureaucratic officials, judges, prayer leaders, and teachers. The ʿulamaʾ and the state had a symbiotic relationship because of the clear division of political and religious authority.

The Sufi relationship to state authority was more ambiguous. Sufi orders like the Suhrawardi and the Chisti were themselves quasi-political societies within the Delhi Sultanate. The Suhrawardis maintained a close and collaborative relationship with the Delhi regimes, facilitated by their geographical distribution. Concentrated in the border regions of Multan, Uch, and Gujarat, remote from the center of power, the Suhrawardis were able to enjoy state patronage, gifts of land, and other favors and still maintain their autonomy as provincial notables. Their role was to mediate between the Delhi Sultanate and provincial princes and tribes. Sufism thus played an important role in integrating tribal and frontier peoples into the Delhi regime. The ability of the Suhrawardis to fulfill these political functions was the basis of their spiritual authority. Wealthy state-supported khanaqas were the worldly symbol of the Suhrawardi claim to mediate in the world to come.

The Chistis lived by a different political philosophy. Their shaykhs rejected government service, refused endowments, and expected to earn their living by cultivating wastelands or receiving unsolicited gifts from the common people.

The shaykhs even refused interviews with Sultans. For ordinary disciples, however, earning a living in some simple productive way was considered meritorious. As part of their responsibility for improving the worldly condition of Muslims, they were permitted to take employment. For the order as a whole, charity and responsibility for the poor were primary values. The Chistis maintained their spiritual authority by detachment from rather than by mediation among worldly powers.

Though rejecting worldly concerns, the Chistis were after all in the midst of the world. They implicitly accepted the political cadre of the Sultanate and indirectly validated the authority of the Sultans by advocating a concept of universal hierarchy which Sultans could use to validate their claims to be the heads of a temporal world order. Only wandering Qalandaris and Malamatis denounced and wholly withdrew from the world.

The relations of ʿulamaʾ and Sufis to the state and to each other changed over time. In the course of the thirteenth century, ʿulamaʾ influence was ascendant, but under the Khalji dynasty (1290–1320) Sufis were promoted as a counterweight to the ʿulamaʾ. ʿAla al-Din used the latitude given him by Chisti ties to reduce the power of Turkish nobles and ʿulamaʾ and to bring Indian Muslims into the governing elite. Muhammad b. Tughluq, however, called upon the ʿulamaʾ and the Suhrawardis to condemn Chisti religious practices, such as *samaʿ* or musically accompanied religious ceremonies. Nizam al-Din Auliya, the head of the Chisti order, had to appear in person to defend himself. The Tughluqs succeeded in forcing the Chistis to abandon their headquarters in Delhi and to disperse all over India. The Chistis were also forced to serve in military campaigns in south India and to take up missionary activities under government sponsorship. Under political pressure, the Chistis split. Some collaborated with the government and others refused. The division within the order broke the power of its all-India organization.

The political power of the Suhrawardis was also eventually broken by the state authorities. Muhammad b. Tughluq gave them lands and villages, and then forbade anyone to visit their khanaqas without permission from the governors. Disputes over succession to the leadership of the order had to be brought to the Sultans for resolution. As the Suhrawardis became more dependent upon the state, their mediating powers declined. Only in Gujarat, which had an independent dynasty, did the Suhrawardis continue to be regarded as patron saints. In Gujarat they continued to receive gifts of landed estates and maintained their influence over public opinion. With the absorption of Gujarat into the Mughal empire in 1572, the Suhrawardis completely lost their political importance. Their decline allowed for the spread of the

Naqshbandi and Qadiri orders and the eventual resurgence of ʿulamaʾ and reformist types of Islam which demanded that state policy be based on allegiance to Shariʿa rather than upon Sufi principles.

The Delhi period thus set the basis for an Islamic society with its characteristic ambiguities of Islamic and non-Islamic aspects of state ideology and popular culture. Islam in India was marked by a pluralism of religious communities, Sunni and Shiʿa, ethnic groups, and ʿulamaʾ, Sufi, and reformist movements. The Delhi period passed this pluralism on to the Mughal empire.

THE MUGHAL EMPIRE

The Mughal empire was a continuation of the Delhi Sultanate, for it witnessed the culmination of the long struggle to create a centralized Indian empire, the culmination of the effort to create an Islamic culture based on a synthesis of the Persian and Indian heritages, and the culmination of the struggle between a Perso-Indian and an Islamic identity for state and society.

The empire was created by the victories of Babur and was consolidated by the reign of his grandson Akbar (1556–1605). Akbar expanded the empire from its original territories in Hindustan and the Punjab, Gujarat, Rajasthan, Bihar, and Bengal. In the north he took Kabul, Kashmir, Sind, and Baluchistan. The Deccan was absorbed in 1600. Not until the end of the seventeenth century did the empire expand further south and absorb Bijapur, Golconda, and other hitherto independent south Indian provinces. Nonetheless, large parts of India remained outside the direct control of the empire. Rajasthan remained in the hands of local Hindu lords and east central India was governed by tributary tribes.

Akbar established the institutional as well as the geographical basis of the empire. The government was controlled by a military and political elite which was primarily made up of Afghan, Iranian, and Turkish lords and native Indian Muslims. While the ruling elite was officially Muslim, Hindus – mostly Rajputs and Marathas – formed about 20 percent of the Mughal aristocracy. The Hindus were important as subordinate military lords, administrative officials, financiers, merchants, and landowners. Hindu officials commonly shared the Persian cultural style of their Muslim counterparts.

From the Mughal point of view, the ruling elite was held together by the loyalty and service of subordinate lineages to the dominant Mughal lineage. The aristocracy was organized into lineage groups called *biradari, jati* or *qawm*, which were defined by the marriage ties and linked by ceremonial loyalties, gifts, and concessions of property and office. The Mughals ruled India by

Map 19. The Mughal empire: 1605–1707.

making clients of the powerful Muslim and Hindu lineages and of the local lords who in turn made their clients the supporters of the Mughal state. From the Mughal point of view Indian society was a condominium of noble lineages bound to the emperor by territorial or political concessions, family ties, and ceremonial and cultural style. The aristocracy was defined in patrimonial as well as in Muslim terms.

This ruling elite was further organized according to the *mansabdar* system. This was a military hierarchy in which each office-holder had two ranks – a *zat* rank that defined his standing in the hierarchy and a *sawar* rank that defined the number of troops he was expected to bring to battle. The mansab officers were paid either in cash or by the grant of an estate called a jagir, which was the equivalent of a Middle Eastern iqta^c. The jagirs were awarded to the military officers of the emperor, local princes, Rajputs, and tribal leaders. About $\frac{7}{8}$ of the taxable land of the Mughal empire was distributed to military assignees and about $\frac{1}{8}$ was reserved as the personal estate of the ruler.

Mansabdars were responsible for the collection of revenues and the provision of soldiers, but other officials were partly responsible for local law and order. Each noble maintained an administration that included a military contingent, a financial and administrative staff, a household staff, a harem, and servants. The household of a noble imitated the household of the ruler. Mughal nobles also assumed responsibility for building mosques, bridges, and caravansaries and for patronizing scientific and literary activity.

A major administrative problem was to set the assignment of territories and revenues in proportion to the military obligation of the assignees. Changes in local conditions required constant redistribution of land in order to maintain a realistic correspondence between rated values, actual income, and military obligation. Lords were transferred from one jagir to another to prevent them from acquiring a vested interest in a particular region. The empire was also divided into provinces and districts staffed by central government officials to assure the collection of taxes and to prevent abuse of the peasantry.

Beneath the level of the mansabdars there were numerous local chieftains. These included *zamindars*, or local notables, who had a claim to a portion of the land revenues, but not, in principle, proprietary rights over the land. These claims had originated independently of imperial rights by virtue of local conquests or caste dominance. The zamindars, however, were subject to the authority of the emperor and could be expelled from office. Mughal rulers often tried to displace Rajput and other Hindu lords in favor of Muslim zamindars. Still, a local zamindar had a considerable advantage in the struggle to maintain his position. Every zamindar was backed by armed retainers, who helped him coerce the peasants and who protected his interests against central government intervention. His ability to dominate the peasantry and to mediate between them and the central government gave him a strong political and economic position.

Beneath the level of the zamindars there were several classes. Moneylenders and grain merchants, rich peasants, small peasant landowners, landless laborers and agricultural workers of various castes, and "untouchables" made up a structured society ranked by ritual purity. Each peasant village was headed by a local official, called the *muqaddam* or *patel*, whose position was likely to be hereditary, responsible to the authorities for payment of revenues and for the prevention of crimes. Peasants were guaranteed permanent and hereditary occupancy of the land, but they were also bound to it. The authorities brought fugitive peasants back to their villages by force. In an age when land was abundant, people scarce, and peasants prone to flee to uninhabited regions, physical force had to be used to keep them in place. (This is just the reverse of modern conditions, where landlords dominate an excessive number of human beings by threatening to evict them.)

The system for the collection of taxes which applied to the central provinces of the empire, including Multan, Lahore, Delhi, Agra, Oudh, and Allahabad, went back to Sher Shah, was continued by Akbar, and lasted until the end of the seventeenth century. Taxation was administered according to the *zabt* system. A fixed fee was assessed for each unit of land and paid in cash. The rate of assessment was based on the value of the crop raised and the average yield of the previous ten years. The calculation of the value of the crop was adjusted from empire-wide norms to local prices and then to estimates of cash value. The amount actually collected was ordinarily half of the total crop. Everything which could be taxed without depriving the peasants of their subsistence and their capacity to produce another crop was taken. The actual collection of taxes was entrusted to the *jagirdar*, but local functionaries representing the central administration had an important part in the tax collection. At the subdistrict level, the local administration was represented by a *qanungo*, who kept local accounts and who was supposed to supervise the agents of the jagirdar; and a *chaudhuri*, who collected funds from the zamindars.

Akbar also set the cultural style of the Mughal era on the basis of the combined legacy of Chaghatay Inner Asia (communicated through Babur) and the Delhi Sultanate. The Chaghatay heritage stressed the role of the ruler as a warrior lord and leader of jihad. Babur added to this the sedentary urban and Persian Islamic tradition which made the ʿulamaʾ advisers, tutors, diplomats, and administrative servants of the Chaghatay ruler. He sought to raise himself above the rank of an ordinary chief by winning control of a major city and territory which he would rule, not through a council of elders and equals, but through subordinate officials. Thus, Babur's heritage included a combination of Inner Asian, Turkish and Persian concepts of rulership. The Delhi Sultanate also contributed concepts of royal authority derived from the Persian monarchical tradition, and Islamic concepts of political responsibility. Akbar in addition sought to transcend the specifically Muslim aspect of this double tradition by integrating Hindus into the Mughal regime. The Mughals went beyond the indirect appeals of the Delhi Sultanate to the non-Muslim elites and supported a cultural policy that was intended to create a cosmopolitan Indian-Islamic rather than an exclusively Muslim culture.

Akbar set the new pattern on several levels of religious and cultural policy. While he appealed to Muslim scholars by the endowment of madrasas and libraries, he also sponsored a more universalistic culture. He supported the Chisti order which was tolerant of syntheses between Hinduism and Islam, and started a state cult called *Din-i Ilahi*, or divine religion, with the emperor himself considered to be the Sufi master of a new religious order. The *Akbarname* of Abu'l-Fazl ᶜAllami (1551–1602) is perhaps the best expression of the values of this reign. This book describes a court society in which the ruler is considered a philosopher-king, protector of all his subjects regardless of their religion, and a spiritual guide who brings reconciliation and love, and fosters well-being in the whole of his domain.

In supplement to religious policy, a broader cultural policy also sought to focus loyalty upon the ruler as the protector of a shared Hindu–Muslim elite culture in manners, dress, art, painting, architecture, poetry, and belles-lettres. The style of this culture can best be observed in architecture and painting. The architectural style patronized by Akbar and exhibited in the major palace and fort complexes of Ajmer, Agra, Allahabad, Lahore, and Fathepur Sikri was based upon motifs drawn from both Muslim and Hindu architecture. The combination of these elements goes back to earlier Indian structures. Post and lintel construction was widely used in the domestic architecture of the Delhi Sultanate period. Serpentine brackets to support eaves, zoomorphic forms, bell and chain motifs, and other devices were all used in earlier mosques and palaces. Similarly, Hindu palaces and temples commonly used abstract geometric decorations and domed roofs which derived from the Muslim tradition. Thus, already in the Delhi Sultanate period, Indian architecture had assimilated diverse forms in ways which no longer retained a specifically sectarian implication. A style transcending religious and regional origins was already part

16 The marriage of Akbar

of the vernacular of Indian architecture. Adopting this architectural style, Akbar fostered a common culture for a diverse elite.

Similarly, Indian painting was derived from Persian ways of figure drawing, illumination, and calligraphy, but it took on specifically Mughal qualities which emphasized line and form rather than color. While Mughal painting depicted court and hunting scenes, battles, animals, flowers, portraits and other motifs of Persian art, it also drew inspiration from Hindu subjects and landscapes. Paintings were used to illustrate both Persian and Hindu literary works, including the *Mahabharata* and the *Ramayana*, and were produced by artists of both religious backgrounds. Indian painting, like Indian architecture, was meant to transcend sectarian implications.

The Muslim communal-religious structures of the Mughal era were derived from the Delhi period. The great majority of the subcontinent's population was Hindu. The Muslims were a minority, but not all Muslims were part of the ruling elite. They did not constitute a single community but belonged to different ethnic groups, lineages, classes of population, and even castes. Muslims, like Hindus, were often identified with kinship and specialized occupational groups, ordered in a hierarchy which gave the highest status to warriors from Afghanistan and Inner Asia and religious families descended from the Prophet or from Iranian and Arab scholars. The craftsmen and service people were of lower status.

Indian Muslims formed numerous religious bodies divided by allegiance to schools of law, Sufi orders, and to the teaching of individual shaykhs, scholars, and saints. Some were Sunnis and some Shiᶜa, though this was not an absolute distinction, owing to the strong sympathies for the family of ᶜAli among Sunnis. Sunnis were themselves divided between those committed to scripturalist Islam – to the beliefs and laws set out in the Quran, the hadith of the Prophet, and the Shariᶜa – and those devoted to popular Sufism, a form of religion in which veneration of saints, living and dead, with associated ceremonies of remembrance, mourning, and ritual marriages and funerals, was the principal form of religious expression. One current in Indian Islam ran toward the disciplined, rational, and controlled practice of Islamic law; the other toward emotional faith and identification with the miraculous powers of saints. Each of these orientations was represented by numerous groups and individuals. Into the first camp fell such diverse groups as the ᶜulamaᵓ, the organized schools of law, and Shariᶜa-minded Sufi orders. In the second camp there were the Sufi saints, and their descendants who managed their tombs, shrines, and the brotherhoods founded in their name. The two orientations led to different views about the boundaries between Muslims and non-Muslims.

Popular saint worship blurred the religious distinctions among Muslims and Hindus; certain Sufi theories and cosmologies blended Hindu and Muslim concepts.

In the Mughal era, the ʿulamaʾ were those scholars in the service of the state. The Mughals continued the Delhi Sultanate system of bureaucratic religious administration. Full control over the judiciary was given to a chief qadi. The provincial sadr was in charge of local judges, muhtasibs, preachers, prayer leaders, muezzins and trust fund administrators. He was responsible also for the appointment of muftis and for liaison between the government and the ʿulamaʾ. His office provided stipends for scholars and sometimes included the power of making grants of landed property; waqfs were donated to provide income for shrines, tombs, and schools. He issued the daily allowances for religious persons and made payments out of the funds of charitable endowments. The sadr was also responsible for charities and for feeding the poor. In the course of the seventeenth century his power was checked by administrative arrangements which gave other officials control over land and by the creation of a more decentalized religious administration in the provinces. His judicial powers were also limited by rulers who involved themselves directly in religious affairs.

In the Mughal period, the influence of the Naqshbandis and the Qadiris replaced that of the Suhrawardis and Chistis. The Naqshbandis cultivated a spiritual discipline leading to the vision of God, but they also insisted upon the necessity for active engagement in worldly affairs. The Naqshbandi shaykhs sought to generate unity among Muslims by claiming to be heirs to the whole of the Sufi tradition.

The histories of two Naqshbandi shaykhs of the eighteenth century illustrate the religious and social principles espoused by the order. Mirza Mazhar (c. 1700–81), the founder of the Mujaddidiya branch of the order, came from a family of soldiers and administrators, and took up the Sufi life to avoid political conflicts and to control the violent impulses in himself. He turned to Sufism as a way of finding tranquility and security in an uncertain world. His teachings stressed the harmony of the several Sufi traditions. He minimized the differences between the theosophical and legalistic forms of Sufism. His whole life was lived in cautious efforts to protect himself from contamination by food, gifts, and other worldly things which were all scrutinized for their legality and appropriateness. He also recommended celibacy. Mirza Mazhar never claimed the power to do miracles but his followers believed it of him anyway.

His successor was Shah Ghulam ʿAli (1753–1824), who stressed the social and political roles of the Naqshbandi shaykh, organized the khanaqa, sent disciples to proselytize in Iran and Afghanistan, and distributed charity and spiritual and moral advice to supplicants. He used his moral influence with political figures whenever possible.

By contrast with this style of Sufism, the Sufi orders that stressed veneration of saints held that Shariʿa was only a preliminary step towards haqiqa, the realization of God that was attained only through ascetic exercises and emotional insight. Orders like the Chisti were originally built upon the personal religious insights of the founding teacher and the personal devotion of his disciples, but as time passed, the charisma of the saints was taken to reside in their tombs. Their descendants then served as the managers of their shrines and the organizers of the orders that flourished around them. The *pirzadas*, the hereditary descendants and managers of the saint's tombs, supervised the festivities commemorating the birth and death anniversaries of the saints, maintained public kitchens, led community prayers, and offered amulets along with spiritual and social advice. The growth of the shrines as centers of worship, led to the accumulation of properties granted and protected by the state authorities. The Mughals awarded landed properties to the Sufis, a practice which legitimized both donor and recipient and enabled the Mughals to intervene in succession disputes and to control the managers of the shrines. They converted the pirzadas into a petty gentry sensitive to the wishes of the political authorities.

In the sixteenth century the influence of Shiʿism was also very strong. Golconda and Kashmir were ruled by Shiʿi princes. The Mughals had Shiʿi wives and many Shiʿa held high offices. The Indian Shiʿi communities included not only the "twelvers," whose teachings we have examined in the chapter on Iran, but also the Nizaris and the Bohras. The Nizaris had their origin in a schism among the Fatimids. They were the "Assassins" of twelfth-century Iran; their mission in India began in the late twelfth or early thirteenth century in Sind and Gujarat. At first the Nizari communities in India acknowledged the supremacy of the imams in Iran, though they were essentially autonomous, but in the sixteenth century the movement split, and only some of the Nizaris maintained this connection. Eventually the imamate was transferred from Iran to India by Aga Khan I, Hasan ʿAli Shah, who moved to Bombay in 1845.

With the collapse of the Nizari state of Alamut in 1256, the mission had entered a new passive phase, concentrating on symbolic and religious rather than political expressions of its goals. Ismaʿili doctrine evolved through several stages. On the principle that God was utterly transcendent and unknowable and that he brought into existence the world of intelligences, religious salvation was seen to come from ascending the ladder of intelligences and returning to the first intelligence through which man achieved unification with God. The Nizaris believed that the cosmic order was represented in history by Prophets and imams who appeared in cyclical fashion. There were seven cycles of Prophets, each cycle consisting of seven imams; the final cycle ends with the resurrection.

The Bohras had their origin in the same schism that gave rise to the Nizaris. With the disappearance of their imam Musta'li in 1133, leadership of the community was turned over to the *da'i al-mutluq*. The da'i stands in a hierarchy that includes other missionaries, including the higher-ranking *hujja*, natiq, and the imams. When the imams and the higher authorities are concealed, the da'i becomes the highest functionary in the social world. He is empowered to teach the community, resolve internal disputes, and name his successor in accord with divine inspiration. He operates through agents called *amils* and shaykhs who are the equivalent of 'ulama'.

The Bohra branch of Isma'ili Shi'ism was first established in Yemen and the Bohras probably came to Gujarat in the early thirteenth century. A deputy called a wali ruled in India until 1539 when the first Indian da'i was appointed. In the long history of the Bohra community, there were several major schisms. In 1840, with the death of the last da'i of the Rajput line, the authority of the da'is was compromised. The nineteenth-century Bohras tended to regard them as administrative figures rather than spiritual teachers, and their leadership was challenged by the scholars.

The diversity of Muslim religious and social groups in India inspired conflicting concepts about the social meaning of Islamic religious belief. The Shari'a-minded conceived of Muslim society as cutting across lineage and class lines. They defined Muslims not by inherited lineage, position in the state, or occupation, but by individual belief in Islam which transcended all other social ties and made men equals and brothers in religion. While they recognized the importance of the Mughal empire, Islam in their view was still a universal community. By contrast popular Sufism took Islam to be an integral aspect of lineage, occupational, and neighborhood ties. Shari'a-minded Muslims also stood for state enforcement of Islamic law and state-mandated subordination of Hindus to Muslim rule by discriminatory taxes and restrictions.

These differences of religious orientation were an important political issue in the seventeenth and eighteenth centuries. While the state pursued a policy of conciliation among different Muslim groups and among Muslims and Hindus, it was opposed by the exponents of the Shari'a orientation. 'Ulama' critics of Akbar opposed his religious toleration, his openness to non-Shari'a religious ideas, and his assumption of the prerogatives of a Sufi. The most important opponent of imperial policies was Shaykh Ahmad Sirhindi. Sirhindi claimed to be the *mujaddid*, the renewer of Islam in his century, a man standing on the spiritual level of the early Caliphs. Initiated into the Naqshbandi order, he became the principal Indian spokesman of the Shariᶜa and reformist point of view. He affirmed the principle of obedience to the teachings of the Shariᶜa as the basis of realization of its inner meaning, and modified Ibn al-ᶜArabi's doctrine of the unity of being and the metaphysical basis of religious syn-cretism, in favor of the doctrine of unity of witness. He opposed the in-sinuation into Islam of Sufi and Hindu practices such as worship of saints, sacrifice of animals, and religious festivals. As a reformer of Islam he waged an unrelenting crusade to persuade the Mughal authorities to adopt policies befitting an Islamic state. He regarded Hinduism and Islam as mutually exclusive; it was the obligation of Muslims to subdue non-Muslims. Thus he urged rulers and nobles to impose the poll tax on non-Muslims, to permit cow slaughter, to remove non-Muslims from political office, and to enforce the Shariᶜa in every way.

Sirhindi's great follower was Shah Waliallah (1702–63), who pursued the tradition of reform in different circumstances. In the declining age of the Mughal empire, Shah Waliallah was concerned with securing the Muslim presence in the subcontinent. After visiting Mecca, the center of reformist teaching, he stressed the importance of returning to the Prophet's teachings and the need to purge Islam of saint worship, which was subsequent to and inconsistent with the true meaning of the Prophet's life. He translated the Quran into Persian and made an argument for the use of independent scholarly judgment in the adaptation of the law to local conditions. While supporting the supremacy of Quran and Sunna, he attempted to synthesize the different schools of law and reduce the legal divergences among Muslims.

Shah Waliallah believed that reform required a Muslim state, modeled on the early Caliphate, to enforce the Shariᶜa. He defined the Caliph as the religious leader who is closest to the example of the Prophet, a perfect man who strives for justice and tries to use administrative and judicial techniques to lead his people to religious virtue. In Shah Waliallah's view, the will of God radiates through the Caliph into the feelings and minds of his subjects. Even in the absence of this spiritual function, a Caliph provides for the political defense of Muslim peoples and the organization of Muslim law. His duty is to enforce Islamic religious practice, collect the alms tax, promote the pilgrimage, foster study and teaching, administer justice, and wage jihad. This was a program of religious consolidation in the struggle against popular Sufi Islam and in opposition to a lax Mughal regime.

As a consequence of this pluralism, there was no sense in India of a universal or unified Muslim identity. The relation of the Mughal empire to Muslim religious life was conditioned by this pluralism. While the state patronized the small ʿulamaʾ establishment, both ʿulamaʾ and Sufis were generally independent of state control. Reformist-minded ʿulamaʾ who represented the universalistic Islamic ideal were often critical of the Mughal state for its cosmopolitan and imperial culture, its Hindu elite, and its patrimonial loyalties. The Sufi religious leaders, by contrast, tended to be accommodationist and to accept state support and the legitimacy of the regime, or they withdrew altogether from political concepts. Thus the legacy of pre-modern Indian-Islamic organization was not state control of doctrine, teaching, or judicial administration, nor a history of well-established schools of law and ʿulamaʾ, but one of numerous autonomous and competitive Muslim religious movements.

THE DECLINE OF THE MUGHAL EMPIRE

The classic system of the Mughal empire lasted from the reign of Akbar until the reign of Aurangzeb (1658–1707). Aurangzeb was the first Mughal ruler to reverse the policy of conciliation of Hindus in favor of Islamic supremacy. In 1659 Aurangzeb forbade drinking, gambling, prostitution, the use of narcotics, and other vices. In 1664 he forbade *sati*, the Hindu sacrifice of widows, and abolished taxes which were not legal under Muslim law. In 1668 he banned music at court, imposed the poll tax on non-Muslims, ordered the destruction of Hindu temples, and sponsored the codification of Islamic laws called the *Fatawa-i Alangiri*. He also founded Muslim colleges to promote the study of Shariʿa. The religious climate of his reign reversed the tendency toward syncretism in favor of exclusivist Muslim policies. Aurangzeb's reforms antagonized Hindus but still fell short of Muslim reformist demands.

The reign of Aurangzeb also saw profound changes in the structure of the Mughal nobility. Aurangzeb was the first ruler since Akbar to expand the frontiers of the empire. He absorbed east Bengal, pacified the northwest frontier, took direct control of Rajasthan, and expanded the Mughal empire in the Deccan. The invasion of the Deccan involved the incorporation of a large number of Bijapuris, Hyderabadis, Marathas, and other Hindu lords into the imperial elite. As a result the proportion of Hindus in the mansabdar system rose from approximately 20 to 30 percent; Marathas came to outnumber Rajput lords. While the new lords could easily be assigned a place in the rank system, there was no way to provide estates for the enlarged military elite. The result was increased competition for scarce jagirs, factionalism, and the exploitation of the peasants. In the late seventeenth century taxes began to be collected before the harvest. The poll tax on non-Muslims also increased the fiscal burden of peasants.

The decentralization of power and of the tax-collecting system allowed for the rise of new social forces. As in the Ottoman empire, land grantees, village headmen, and tax farmers became landlords. By the eighteenth century village headmen were the key figures in the collection of village revenues and in negotiations with the government authorities. Zamindars became increasingly independent and refused payment of revenues. Mansabdars converted their jagirs into permanent zamindari tenures.

Furthermore a new urban commercial and merchant class came into being. The breakup of the centralized state and the decline of the capital encouraged the growth of provincial towns and local elites. Rich farmers, small-town and rural shopkeepers, coin changers, moneylenders, and landlords profited from the redistribution of fiscal authority. Small towns and markets throughout north India grew in commercial importance on the basis of wider market networks and rural enterprises. Sustained by aristocratic consumer demand in such growing cities as Lucknow and Benares, Hindu merchants and their clients and dependents prospered. Their commercial networks overlapped with religious sects as a rising elite sought communal solidarity and corporate protection. Similarly, decentralization of power favored the growth of small-town Muslim families composed of local qadis, government functionaries, landowners, urban rentiers, and religious leaders who controlled the revenues of mosques, tombs, and shrines. Muslim landlords and moneylenders acquired a corporate consciousness. In the *qasbahs* (small and medium-size towns) the leading Muslim families, sharing *ashraf* (noble Arab, Mughal, or Pathan) status, united by intermarriage, linked to the town madrasas and academies, and to Sufi tombs and shrines, emerged as a local elite. Peasants also organized to resist exploitation. Castes, religious sects, and the clienteles of zamindar chiefs provided the social basis for peasant action.

In these changing political circumstances, succession struggles after the death of Aurangzeb and a series of feeble rulers compromised the efficacy of the Mughal state and left it prey to internal rebellions and foreign invasions. In the early eighteenth century, several regions of the Mughal empire became independent states under the rule of local mansabdars now become *nawwabs*. The Nizam of Hyderabad became an independent ruler in 1723. In Bengal the change of regimes destroyed the jagir form of assignments, and the old Mughal aristocracy lost its position. Zamindars and bankers seized control of the tax system.

In other parts of India, regimes based on Hindu lordships and popular uprisings came to power. Hindu-governed principalities regained control of Rajasthan. In the Punjab, religious and ethnic groups such as the Sikhs and the Jats established local regimes. The Maratha movement, based on peasant resistance to taxation, Hindu revivalism, and vernacular languages, and led by Shah Shahji and his son Shivaji, defied Mughal authority. By the middle of the eighteenth century, the Marathas controlled most of south India, and had replaced the Mughals as the dominant power in Gujarat.

By the middle of the century, Marathas, Sikhs, and Afghan tribesmen from the north fought to control the remaining territories of the moribund Mughal empire. The Marathas consolidated their grip on central and western India and formed five independent and expanding states. In 1739 Nadir Shah, the conqueror of Iran, took control of Kabul and sacked Delhi. The helpless Mughal regime had to call upon Maratha support to resist the Afghans, but at the battle of Panipat (1761) the Marathas were defeated by Ahmad Shah Durrani. No Indian power proved capable of resisting the foreign invaders. As a result, the Sikhs were able to expand in the Punjab between 1750 and 1799 and establish a new state with its capital at Lahore. The way was also opened for the emergence of the British as the paramount power in India.

The British East India Company had been trading in India since 1600. British factories were founded at Surat in 1612, Madras in 1640, Bombay in 1674, and Calcutta in 1690. They exported Indian cotton and silk cloth, cotton yarn, raw silk, saltpeter, indigo, and spices, and imported silver bullion and other metals. Gradually the East India Company made itself into a local government. In a long series of eighteenth-century wars, the British defeated their French rivals. When the nawwab of Bengal attacked the British settlement at Calcutta, he was defeated at the battle of Plassey (1757) and again at the battle of Baksar (1764), and the British established themselves as the de facto rulers of Bengal. In 1772 Warren Hastings, the British governor of Bengal, took charge of the British factories of Madras and Bombay and created a unified regime for the several factories in India. Hastings' success marks the beginning of a British Indian empire.

The transformation of the British position in India received legal recognition in the mother country and in the subcontinent. By the India Act of 1784 the British parliament required that mercantile and administrative activities henceforth be separated and that all East India Company officials in India be responsible to Parliament. In Bengal, under Cornwallis (1786–93), the British established a new system of taxation and judicial administration. They took control of the courts, separated administrative and judicial jurisdictions, and established a British-officered police and army. By the so-called Permanent Settlement (1793), rural taxes were set at fixed rates, a measure which ruined the old Muslim elite and opened the way for the purchase of zamandari tenures by wealthy Hindu merchants and investors from Calcutta. At the same time British goods came to dominate the local economy. British power in Bengal was soon extended to other parts of India, and by 1818 the remaining Rajput and Maratha rulers acknowledged the British as the paramount power. The Punjab and the Northwest Frontier were absorbed at a later date. While the British in India continued to recognize the Mughal emperors as their suzerains, they had persistently and patiently acquired a new Indian empire.

Over the centuries a distinctive form of Islamic civilization had emerged in the Indian subcontinent. Like their Iranian and Middle Eastern predecessors, the Delhi Sultanates and the Mughal empire were committed to a concept of state culture which blended Islamic symbols with a royal heritage. In the Iranian case these were the symbols of ancient Iran as transmitted through the ʿAbbasid Caliphate. In India royalty meant the heritage of Iran combined with Mongol, Timurid, and Chaghatay concepts and with Indian and Hindu motifs which introduced new qualities into Islamic imperial culture. Thus in India the pursuit of a cosmopolitan state identity led to a distinctive civilization.

Similarly, Muslim religious life both resembled and departed from Middle Eastern norms. Islam in India replicated the basic forms of ʿulamaʾ and Sufi Islam. Whereas in Iran Shiʿism absorbed all levels of Islam into a monolithic establishment, in India the various forms of ʿulamaʾ scholarship, Sufi contemplation, worship of saints, and reformist tendencies remained in open competition with each other. In India Islamic belief and practice on the popular level was manifestly mixed with local Hindu and Buddhist forms of belief and worship. The formation of a popular Muslim subculture in India was not, however, a departure from Muslim norms, but an example of a process that was universal in the formation of Muslim societies. In the Middle East, Islam had been formed as a syncretism of popular Christian and Jewish religious practices with Muslim teachings, though the passage of time has concealed the syncretic nature of Middle Eastern Islam. Thus the Mughal era bequeathed to modern India a distinctive variant of Muslim institutions and culture.

CHAPTER 19

THE FORMATION OF ISLAMIC SOCIETIES
IN SOUTHEAST ASIA

Just as Islam spread from the Middle East to Inner Asia and from Afghanistan to India, it spread from various parts of India and Arabia to the Malay peninsula and the Indonesian archipelago in the late thirteenth, fourteenth, and fifteenth centuries. Islam was introduced into maritime Southeast Asia and flourished in conditions rather different from those of the Middle East and the Indian subcontinent. While Islam was established in other regions by Arab or Turkish conquests, it was introduced into Southeast Asia by traveling merchants and Sufis. Whereas in the Middle East and India, Muslim regimes were founded by new elites, in Southeast Asia existing regimes were consolidated by conversion to Islam. The continuity of elites gave strong expression to the pre-Islamic components of Southeast Asian-Islamic civilization. The royal culture of Java seems more local and less Muslim than the corresponding royal culture of the Mughal empire was Indian. The syncretisms of Islam and village cultures, however, were probably equally intense in the subcontinent and in Indonesia. Yet while Muslims remained a minority in India, in the regions of Indonesia and Malaya an overwhelming majority of the population eventually accepted an Islamic identity.

THE DIFFUSION OF ISLAM

Indigenous pre-Islamic Southeast Asian culture formed the basis of later Islamic civilization. By the beginning of the Christian era the diverse population of Southeast Asia had developed a civilization based upon irrigated rice cultivation, animal husbandry, and metallurgy. The native cultures had

467

their own religious beliefs and artistic accomplishments such as the wayang puppet theater and the gamelan orchestra recitals of Java and Bali. The early Southeast Asian societies were already state-ruled but there was no single polity. The interior of Java was a region of rice agriculture and the locus of small kingdoms. In the coastal regions of Sumatra and Java, the smaller islands, and the Malay peninsula, the populace earned its living by trade and was strongly influenced by contacts with Hindu cultures. From earliest times, there had been a tension between the agrarian hierarchical society of Java and the cultures of the coastal towns.

The Javanese kingdoms were important because they formed a lasting mold for the reception and expression of Islam. The first historic kingdoms on Java date from the fifth century A.D. From the fifth century to the fifteenth century, there were several important centers of culture and political power. Each kingdom was a suzerainty over petty lordships maintained by control of rice and by mythic, magical, and mystical means. Each was a center for the diffusion of high culture to the surrounding countryside. The first kingdom of importance was the Shailendra dynasty (*c.* 760–860). This regime had already blended indigenous Indonesian culture with Sanskrit literature and Brahmin and Saivite versions of Hinduism. Hinduism was probably established in Java by local princes who borrowed Indian and Hindu political concepts to help legitimize their rule. The Hindu concepts of a God King and of the terrestrial order as an analogue of the cosmic order sanctified temporal power as an expression of the spiritual universe. Great imperial palaces and Hindu and Buddhist monumental tombs were constructed by these early rulers. In the tenth century the center of culture and power in Java shifted to Mataram, which held sway from 929 to 1222. Mataram was succeeded by a number of other regional kingdoms, notably by Majapahit (1293–1389).

The most important maritime kingdom was Srivijaya, first centered at Palembang and then at Jambi (Sumatra). This kingdom controlled the Malacca Straits and established a commercial hegemony located between India and China. Its cosmopolitan trading connections helped establish a Hinduized culture just as it would later favor the introduction of Islam.

In the context of Hinduized Southeast Asian societies, the advent of Islam depended upon the previous establishment of Muslim peoples in Arabia and the Indian Ocean region and the close trading relationships between India and Southeast Asia. While the earliest contacts between Southeast Asia and the Muslim world may go back to Muslim merchants involved in the China trade, only after the consolidation of Islam on the subcontinent did Muslim merchants and Sufi missionaries begin to trade and proselytize extensively. By the thirteenth century, Southeast Asia was in contact with the Muslims of China, Bengal, Gujarat, Iran, Yemen, and south Arabia. The fact that Malayan and Indonesian Islam is Shafi'i points to south India as the major source of Islamic influences.

Three theories purport to explain the eventual acceptance of Islam. One stresses the role of merchants who established themselves in Indonesian ports, married into local ruling families, and provided important diplomatic skills, wealth, and international experience for the commercial enterprises of coastal rulers. The first converts were local rulers who sought to attract Muslim traffic and win allies in the struggle against Hindu traders from Java. Coastal chiefs used conversion to legitimize their resistance to the authority of Majapahit and to throw off the suzerainty of central Javan empires.

The second theory stresses the importance of missionaries from Gujarat, Bengal, and Arabia. The Sufis came not only as teachers but as traders and politicians who penetrated the courts of rulers, the quarters of merchants, and the villages of the countryside. They could communicate their religious vision in a form compatible with beliefs already held in Indonesia. Pantheistic doctrines were understood because of Hindu teachings. Saint worship and faith in the saint as a healer were common to both Muslims and Indonesians.

A third theory stresses the value of Islam to the common people rather than to the ruling elites. Islam provided an ideological basis for individual worth, for solidarity in peasant and merchant communities, and for the integration of small parochial groups into larger societies. In an era of expanded trade Islam may have helped to create an integrated community to replace the village-scale societies disrupted by commerce and political change. It seems likely that all three factors were at work, though circumstances undoubtedly differed from place to place. There was no single process or single source for the spread of Islam in Southeast Asia, but the travels of individual merchants and Sufis, the winning of apprentices and disciples, and the founding of schools, seems crucial.

The facts that signal the establishment of Islam are few. In 1282, the Hindu Malay ruler of Samudra (Sumatra) had Muslim advisers. A Muslim community in Pasai in north Sumatra was reported in 1292 by Marco Polo. The tomb of Sultan Malik al-Salih in Perlak dated 1297 indicates the conversion of a local ruler. In 1345-6, Ibn Battuta, on his world tour of Muslim communities, found Shafi'i scholars in Samudra.

At the beginning of the fifteenth century, Iskandar, the former ruler of the trading kingdom of Srivijaya, was defeated by Javanese rivals, and forced to flee Palembang. He founded Malacca and converted to Islam. Iskandar based his political claims upon genealogical descent from past rulers, Buddhist consecration, and Islam. By such syncretism Islam was added to the panoply of Southeast Asian cultures. Malacca built up a trading empire with extensive contacts in India, Java, and China. Ships from Malacca sailed to Gujarat, Bengal, and the smaller islands of the East Indies archipelago. Malacca also attempted to build up a Malay-Sumatran territorial empire with possessions on both sides of the straits.

With the consolidation of its political and commercial prosperity, Malacca became a base for the spread of Islamic influence throughout the region. By 1474 the Malay rulers of Pahang, Kedah, and Patani were converted to Islam; on Sumatra Islam reached Roken, Siak, Kampar, and Indragiri. While Javanese students were coming to Malacca and Pasai as early as 1414 to study with Muslim teachers, the coastal principalities of Java, Demak, Tuban, Madura, and Surabaya became Muslim in the middle of the fifteenth century. These conversions were probably stimulated by their rivalry with the interior kingdom of Majapahit. By the late fifteenth century, Islam was spreading into the interior.

From its bases in Sumatra and Java, Islam spread further eastward. Ternate was converted in 1495. The Moluccas became Muslim in 1498 as a result of contacts with Java, and the coastal towns of Borneo were converted by Javanese contacts before the arrival of the Portuguese in 1511. Islamic influences from Sumatra, Ternate, and Borneo reached the Philippines. Conversions were made in Luzon, Sulu, and Mindanao. On the basis of the intersecting interests of traders and local princes, and the migrations of merchants and missionaries, Islam became the common religion of the Indies.

THE PORTUGUESE, THE DUTCH, AND THE MUSLIM STATES

The Portuguese established themselves as an Indian Ocean power in the early sixteenth century. In 1509 they defeated a combined Egyptian and Indian fleet and took Goa. In 1511 they conquered Malacca, in 1515 Hormuz on the Persian Gulf, and in 1522 Ternate in an attempt to control the trade between China, Japan, Siam, the Moluccas, the Indian Ocean, and Europe. The Portuguese were expelled from Ternate in 1575, but they held on to other islands in the Moluccas.

Portuguese intervention paradoxically contributed to the further spread of Islam. With the fall of Malacca, Muslim teachers and missionaries migrated to northern Sumatra, Java, the Moluccas, and Borneo. After the fall of Malacca, three main centers of Muslim political and cultural life emerged. In Acheh, Sultan ʿAli Mughayat Shah rallied the opponents of the Portuguese, defeated them at Pidie in 1521 and at Pasai in 1524, conquered the north coast of Sumatra, and thus set the basis for an Achenese kingdom which would be the main rival of the Portuguese. Between 1529 and 1587 Acheh made continual efforts to recapture Malacca. Between 1618 and 1620, it took Pahang, Kedah, and Perak. The apogee of Achenese power was reached under Sultan Iskandar Muda (1607–36), who organized an efficient regime and established his dominance over the local lords (*uleebalang*) and village associations. Sultan Iskandar's ambition to control the whole peninsula, however, was defeated by other Malay states in 1629.

On the Malay peninsula a number of Muslim Sultanates were established in the fifteenth and sixteenth centuries. Of these Johore (1512–1812) was particularly important. The Johore Sultanate did not have a dynasty but was a chieftainship revived by different rulers. Johore struggled with Acheh and the Portuguese for control of Malacca.

Java became the third principal Muslim center of power. Between 1513 and 1528 a coalition of the Muslim kingdoms defeated Majapahit, and two new states emerged in central Java – Banten in central and western Java (founded in 1568), and Mataram in east central Java. Under Sultan Agung (1613–45) and Sultan Mangkurax (1646–77) Mataram reduced the independent princes of the island to vassals and ministers of the Mataram state, and became the ruling empire on Java.

The region-wide struggle between the Muslims and the Portuguese was complicated by the arrival of the Dutch. Like the Portuguese, the Dutch came to the East Indies in quest of pepper. While in the course of the sixteenth century European pepper imports tripled, in 1594 Holland won its war of independence from the Habsburg monarchy, and was excluded from access to pepper and spices in the Lisbon market. Thus, Dutch fleets sailed to the East Indies in 1595; in 1602 the United East India Company was chartered to control Dutch trading and to achieve a monopoly between the Cape of Good Hope and the Magellan Straits.

The Dutch pushed their way into the East Indies trade by naval warfare. The spice trade required naval bases; bases needed surrounding territory; trade required empire. The Dutch defeated the Portuguese and took Amboyna in 1605. They founded Batavia in 1619, Banda in 1621, and took Ceylon in 1640. With the help of Acheh and Johore they seized Malacca in 1641. From these fortress bases the Dutch eliminated the Portuguese and established their supremacy over the Muslim states of the region.

Map 20. Muslim states of Southeast Asia to 1800.

In the course of the seventeenth century the Dutch became the paramount power in the East Indies. With the defeat of Achenese forces in Malaya in 1629 and the Dutch conquest of Malacca in 1641, the Achenese kingdom dissolved into numerous small principalities led by uleebalang, Muslim imams, and former government officers. Acheh thus came under Dutch commercial control between 1629 and 1663. Fragmented Acheh could not resist a treaty of 1639 that allowed the Dutch to buy tin, and treaties of 1650 and 1659 that gave them half, and then two-thirds, of the kingdom's tin supplies. From Acheh Dutch economic power extended to the rest of Sumatra. They took Palembang in 1658, and in 1663 they obtained a monopoly of the pepper trade of Minangkabau. The Dutch defeated resistance in the Moluccas by 1658 and established a monopoly of cloves and nutmeg. In 1669 they forced Macassar to give them a monopoly of its trade, and subsequently established forts on Ternate, Macassar, and Borneo.

On Java the Dutch established themselves as territorial overlords. They consolidated their control of Batavia and the small territory around it by defeating the ruler of Mataram, Sultan Agung (1613–49), in 1629. In 1646 they forced Mataram to recognize their monopolies in the spice islands. Peace prevailed until 1675, when the rivalries of Mataram and Banten required Mataram to ask for Dutch help, for which she was obliged to give the Dutch a monopoly over the cloth and opium trades. Dutch help was purchased again and again by tributes and concessions of land until, in 1755, with the partition of Mataram into two kingdoms, Surakarta and Jogyakarta, the Dutch became suzerains of both.

By the middle of the eighteenth century the Dutch had acquired substantial control over the trade in pepper and spices by establishing forts and bases throughout the East Indies archipelago, and by forcing local rulers to grant them trading monopolies, sometimes by violence and sometimes in return for political help. With the establishment of territorial political power, Dutch interests turned from trade to a new system of economic exploitation requiring local rulers to deliver tributes. Agrarian Java replaced the spice islands as the most lucrative Dutch possession. In 1723 the Dutch required an annual quota of coffee, and native princes were expected to comply with Dutch demands for timber, cotton, and indigo. At first the local princes were autonomous intermediaries, but gradually Dutch overseers were appointed to see to the production of coffee, cloves, cinnamon, and pepper. The tributes in kind were supplemented by forced deliveries of spices at fixed prices. These goods the Dutch exported for resale in Europe.

ISLAMIC SOCIETIES IN SOUTHEAST ASIA

From the sixteenth to the nineteenth centuries, the East Indies and Malaya came under the control of the Portuguese and the Dutch. As in the Tatar steppes of Inner Asia, European economic and political supremacy did not prevent but actually stimulated the spread of Islam. While the Dutch established their commercial supremacy, Islamic loyalties, Muslim regimes, and Islamic institutions were being consolidated as the basic indigenous expression of cultural identity, political resistance, and economic competition. In each maritime Southeast Asian region, such as Acheh, Malaya, Minangkabau, and Java, a form of Islamic society developed which was at once characteristic of the particular region, reminiscent of Indonesian-Islamic societies in other areas, and recognizably Islamic in international terms.

Acheh was the homeland of Indonesian-Islamic societies. The earliest conversions go back to the thirteenth century, but the main period in the development of indigenous Islamic religious teaching and social organization was the late sixteenth and seventeenth centuries. This era was marked by Acheh's struggle against the Portuguese and the Dutch, contacts with the Ottoman empire, and the influx of Ottoman and Mughal scholars and Sufis.

The Sufi masters formed the backbone of Achenese Islam. The indigenous Sufi tradition goes back to Hamza Fansuri, who died around 1600. He founded the Qadari order in Indonesia, wrote mystical commentaries in Malay, and propagated the teachings of Ibn al-ʿArabi and the doctrine of the unity of being. Shams al-Din Pasai (d. 1630) represented the school of Junayd, with its stress upon worldly activity and fulfillment of the religious law. The early masters were followed by ʿAbd al-Raʾuf Singkeli, who returned at some time after 1661 to Acheh from Arabia, bringing with him the legal and mystical teachings of scholars in Medina, and established the Shattari order. Sufism in Acheh was inspired and sustained by the travels of teachers, students, and pilgrims to and from the sources of Islamic learning in Arabia and India. Correspondence, books, and diplomatic missions tied Acheh directly to the international world of Islamic learning. As a result of these contacts the primary form of Islamic thought to reach the Indies was the tradition of Ibn al-ʿArabi, with its emphasis on mystical unity and ecstatic experiences and its receptiveness to folk-culture versions of Islam. At the end of the eighteenth century, however, ʿAbd al-Samad of Palembang (1779–89) translated al-Ghazzali's work into Malay. Achenese Islam, then, came to encompass the ecstatic and the reformist tendencies characteristic of Islam in the Indian subcontinent and other regions.

Muslim teachings did not remain an isolated phenomenon but became part of Achenese identity. Though we know little of Achenese society before the middle of the nineteenth century, from late nineteenth- and early twentieth-century observations we can reconstruct the role of Islam in Acheh. In fact there was no single relationship of Islam to Acheh's highly compartmentalized society. The village communities, the schools of the ʿulamaʾ, and the Sultan and his regime, all had different relationships with Islamic ideas and institutions.

Achenese village society was built around lineages or *qawm*. The lineage units, however, were not organized by territory; people of different lineages lived in the same villages. In each village there were two types of authorities. One was the village headman who ruled in the name of customary law and represented the state. The other was the *tuanku*, the village religious leader, a combination of Muslim scholar and Sufi adept. Ordinarily the village tuanku organized prayers, taught religious law and performed feats of spirit healing. The two authorities represented two parallel cultural and social structures in village life: one based on kinship, custom, and political allegiance; the other based on Islamic belief and worship.

Outside of the villages, the ʿulamaʾ and Sufis maintained schools which were self-supporting agricultural communities; in these, the students not only studied but worked on the land belonging to the teachers. The schools taught ritual recitation of the Quran, Sufi beliefs, and magical formulae to students who would in turn become village teachers. These schools represented a very different world from that of the village – the world of purely Islamic social and religious obligations beyond the ties of kinship and territoriality. Islam, then, was integral to the village communities, and yet offered a radical alternative. In place of kinship, it offered brotherhood based on faith.

At a third level Islam was closely tied to the state. The state in Acheh was represented by the Sultan, originally the ruler of a small capital town and the surrounding territory. The Sultans of Acheh rose to power by controlling trade, unifying the country around them and defending Islam. An elaborate structure of titles, ceremonies and offices attached to their position. The ruler was considered a Muslim monarch and the court used Islamic symbols, ideas, and rituals to legitimize his regime. The ruler of Acheh waged jihad against the Portuguese and the Dutch and patronized the teaching of Islam in his domains. In the political realm, Islam was the principle which legitimized and defined the organization of the state.

Islam in the riverain states of Malaya was also closely integrated with both village life and the organization of the state. As in Achenese villages there were

17 The Ubadiah Mosque, Kuala Kangson, Malaysia

two parallel authorities. The village headman or *penghulu* was appointed by the higher authorities to keep the local peace, arbitrate disputes, collect taxes, organize labor, and act as a healer and spirit doctor. At the same time, the imam of the mosque, supported by a muezzin and a preacher, organized local worship and taught in the local school. The holy-man was often venerated for having made the pilgrimage to Mecca and for his magical powers. Islam made an important contribution to the rituals and festivals marking the solidarity of the village community, and to the commemoration of important events in the life cycle of individuals, such as birth, marriage, and death.

In both Achenese and Malay villages Islam was thoroughly merged into the existing community life. Achenese and Malay villagers followed both Muslim and non-Muslim religious practices, believed in holy spirits, holy places and saints who were venerated in both Muslim and non-Muslim guise. In the villages there were Muslim and non-Muslim holy-men to offer counsel and cures. There were both Muslim and non-Muslim festivals to mark the natural cycle of life and the agricultural year. Malay and Achenese villagers considered themselves Muslims but Islam did not thereby distinguish them as a group, as a community, or as a cult separate from the total fabric of the society.

Islam was also important for the Malay state. The Sultans of the several Malay states were the head of a group of aristocratic lineages who made up the political elite of the country and were the village overlords. The Malay Sultans traced their descent to the Sultan of Malacca. A ruler was called at once Sultan, *Raja*, and *Yang di-Pertuan*, He Who Was Made Lord. His titles were Muslim and Hindu, and he was believed to be descended from ancient and divine Hindu lords as well as Muslim ancestors. His regalia symbolized his sacred and mystical personality. Drums, weapons, clothing, food and adornments were reserved for him. While the ruler was believed to have supernatural powers, there was scarcely any public expression of his Islamic role. Apart from prayers at royal inaugurations and funerals, there were no Muslim public rituals. While Shariᶜa was known, it is not clear that there was a Muslim judicial administration. Religion, then, symbolized the legitimacy of the state, but did not define the operation of the political system or political practices. Compared with other Muslim states, Islam had a minimal impact. In a highly compartmentalized political system it symbolized the unity of the society based upon the allegiance of states and village communities to the same religious symbols.

Minangkabau, and its colony, Negri Sembilan in Malaya, is another example of how Islam operated on several levels in Malay-Indonesian societies. Minangkabau was a region of rice agriculture and of trade in pepper and gold.

Islam was introduced into Minangkabau in the sixteenth century by Sufi missionaries and Muslim traders. By the seventeenth century Islamic schools were established, and the Naqshbandiya, the Qadariya, and Shattariya were organized. In the eighteenth century the Shattariya became the leading Sufi order.

The society in which Islam established itself was built on two parallel principles, one matrilineal, the other patrilineal. On the village level, clan organization, laws of marriage, land ownership and property were defined in matrilineal terms. The village community, called *nagari*, was a grouping of a number of clans administered by chieftains called penghulus. The nagaris were integrated into still larger federations called *alaras*, under the authority of a prince or Raja. Islam represented the masculine principle. In the villages it was institutionalized in the *surau*, young men's houses, which became schools and centers of Sufi brotherhoods. In practice, however, there was a considerable overlap between matrilineal and patrilineal forms of organization. Marriage practices and inheritance laws were blends of Islamic and traditional Minangkabau norms. The two forms of law and social structure were integrated into a single society.

In the eighteenth century Minangkabau economy and society were radically changed. The gold and pepper trades collapsed, and coffee production expanded. In the economic upheaval some communities disintegrated while new entrepreneurs and peasants prospered. Rice and coffee producers came into conflict over land. Uprooted people sought their living in towns and markets. Traditional morality gave way to a new individualism.

In this context, the old order was challenged by a religious revival under the leadership of Tuanku Nan Tua, who militantly insisted that local religious and social practice be reformed to meet the demands of Islam. Tuanku Nan Tua taught that it was necessary to strictly observe the rules of the Shariᶜa, especially in inheritance and family matters, improve mosques and dwellings, celebrate the birthday of the Prophet, and in general, make the teachings of the Prophet, rather than custom, supreme. He also taught that Muslim religious law and mystical vision, Shariᶜa and haqiqa, should be integrated in religious life. His reform was not directed at the matrilineal village communities, but at the newly mobile merchant and peasant population to whom Shariᶜa was offered as guidance for the regulation of economic conflict and moral problems. In Minangkabau, as in India, the reformist version of Islam challenged local usages.

The reform movement led to bitter civil war. In 1803 the reformers were reinforced by pilgrims returning from Mecca who had imbibed the principles current in the holy cities of Arabia. The returned pilgrims, preaching in the coffee-producing villages, called for the purification of Islamic life, adherence to the Shariᶜa, regularity in prayer, and an end to gambling, cock fighting, opium consumption, drinking, smoking, robbery, and violence. They called for a Muslim way of life in strict accord with the teachings of the Prophet and opposed the magical practices which were part of the village concept of Islam. The reformist movement soon divided. While Nan Tua advocated a pacific preaching, one of his disciples, Tuanku Nan Rincheh, organized a military movement. His followers were pledged to dress in white, wear beards, and abstain from bodily satisfactions. They were also prepared to wage war against the nagari, kill the penghulus, confiscate their property and establish a new regime, headed by an imam and a qadi, dedicated to the enforcement of Islamic law. The reformers burned the Shattariya schools.

Some penghulus accepted the Shariᶜa peacefully and assisted in the reform. This was especially true in merchant communities which had extensive trading connections with other parts of Malaya and Sumatra. Most of the customary chiefs, however, refused to accept the reformist movement. To defend themselves they invited the Dutch to intercede. A bitter and protracted war followed (1819–39), until the Dutch finally defeated the reformers and conquered the province. By then the internal momentum of the reform movement was spent, the Muslim factions woke up to their fate, and sought to unite to overthrow Dutch rule. Their resistance (1839–45) was unsuccessful.

Despite the final compromise between traditional leaders and reformist Muslims, the reform movement had a profound effect on Minangkabau society. While Acheh and Malaya maintained the traditional balance among village, school, and state forms of Islam, in Minangkabau the conflict between traditional village and reformist versions of Islam strengthened the practice of Shariᶜa Islam and succeeded in Islamizing the village communities.

Islamic societies in Java were another variation upon the basic Malay-Indonesian way of synthesizing Islam with non-Islamic Southeast Asian traditions. Islamic societies in Java go back to the conversion of the coastal trading principalities, their victory over Majapahit, and the rise of Mataram. Before the consolidation of Mataram, Muslim holy-men, or walis, established independent kingdoms centered around important sanctuaries or tombs, as at Giri, Cheribon, Kadilangu, and Semarang. Muslim scholars, preachers, and holy-men established mosques and schools, and proselytized among Javanese. The Shattariya entered Java from Acheh in the late seventeenth century. Banten (eastern Java), already in contact with Mecca and Medina, received the Qadiriya. By the late seventeenth century the Islamic presence was institutionalized in the form of schools and shrine complexes, and had local political power alongside of and within the authority of the Mataram empire. A bitter struggle took place between the state and the Islamic religious centers in which Mataram progressively destroyed the political power of the Muslim lords, though not their local religious influence. The Muslim holy-men retained a charisma which could be used to rally opposition to the state. On Java Islam became both the banner of the state and the standard of the opposition.

The Mataram state combined Islamic and Hindu concepts of rule. The rulers of Mataram believed that they derived their authority directly from God – the ruler was God's representative on earth, *kalipatullah* – and indirectly from the tomb of Sunan Kalijaga, the saint and holy-man who represented the spiritual presence of Islam. Despite the new layer of Islamic titulature and legitimation, the Hindu cosmological conception of the state continued to be valued. In the pre-Islamic Javan conception the universe was taken to be a single and unified phenomenon; the cosmos harmoniously ordered; the world of human beings grounded in cosmic principles. The ruler had access to cosmic powers and transmitted them to his people. For each individual the ideal of life was to cultivate an inner tranquility which made the soul correspond to the order of society and the universe.

In the Mataram conception the ruler was a sacred and indeed divine figure; the repository of *wahyu* or divine radiance, or a luminous light which suffused his person and emanated from him. Wahyu was a concrete, tangible, creative energy which flows through the universe – a force which can be accumulated, concentrated, and preserved in individuals as a result of yogic practices and extreme self-denial. Heroes concentrate power, their adversaries diffuse it. Power is also concentrated by public rituals, including mass demonstrations, powerful slogans, and the presence of thousands of submissive persons. It is concentrated by the ownership of *pusaka*, heirlooms, including spears, musical instruments, and carriages, and control over extraordinary or deformed human beings. Power is manifest in wealth and sexual energy. Fertility, political unity, prosperity, stability, and glory of the kingdom are all considered expressions of power. However, possession of power is prior to legitimacy. Power is neither good nor evil; it is just real. Thus, in the Javanese conception of kingship the ruler was glorified by his descent from gods as well as human beings, by his possession of holy relics, and by court ceremonies where weapons and decorations symbolized his special powers. The ruler had the deepest knowledge of reality, sense of justice, and a flawless personality acquired by ritual and by observance of taboos. The king's actions were taken to be God's will.

Royal administration was conceived in terms of maintaining order and justice in the whole of the kingdom. The ruler's subordinates were fully responsible for their districts and personally accountable to him. They formed a social class called the *priyayi*, bound to their lord by *kawula-gusti*, the bond of lord and servant. The ruler must care for his officials as a father and the servants must give total love, submission, and gratitude to their lord. Officials were paid by benefices allotted to them by their patron. The central political problem for a ruler was to control the land granted to his supporters and not to allow it to become hereditary. When provincial notables built up an independent base of power, the ruler tried to use his household clients to offset their influence and to absorb or coopt them into the state system. The king and the nobility lived on the labor of the peasantry. The king was entitled to part of the produce of the land. The salaries for court workers and guards were paid for by taxes from designated districts. Peasants also labored to build water works and bridges, and provided transportation and personal services to the king and his officials.

The ideal of the Mataram aristocracy was based on individual self-cultivation. To be loyal to their lord and to fulfill their role in the cosmic order, the priyayi had to cultivate an inner life of refined feeling and an outer life of polite formality. The ruling elite was distinguished from the rest of the population by a quality called *halus*, which meant smoothness of spirit, beauty, elegance, politeness, and sensitivity. The opposite of halus was *kasar*, lack of control, coarseness, and the degradation that comes from indulging in purely selfish and personal desires. Control of emotion, equanimity, patience, acceptance of fate without protest, and detachment from the external world were the most highly regarded virtues.

This inner restraint was the basis of realistic behavior. In the outer world the priyayi would express themselves by conformity to etiquette and ethics, and by speaking in correct linguistic form. Language, dance, music, and art were all channeled outer expressions of a restrained inner being. The priyayi ethic of control over the outer world protected them against inner disturbance; a balanced inner world expressed itself in outward order. The cultivation of true feeling and of true expression, both called *rasa*, was a realization of the individual's true self and a recognition of the reality of God's existence; it was also a means to worldly power through concentration and mastery of spiritual capacities.

Thus, Mataram society was in name Islamic but the actual organization of state, including its concepts of rulership and the personal ideal of the priyayi elite, was based upon Hindu and Javanese mythical and cosmological conceptions. The strong emphasis upon the Javanese and Hindu basis of Mataram culture was due to the continuity of political elites. While Muslim regimes in India, the Ottoman empire, and many other parts of the world were established by conquerors who brought their Muslim identity from without, the Mataram regime was converted from within. Though Islam had been introduced by the wars between the coastal principalities and the rulers of the interior, Mataram eventually destroyed the coastal powers, suppressed the sea trade and made the aristocracy of the interior, rather than the commercial lords of the coast, the dominant elites on Java. Islamic identity then served to reinforce the legitimacy of the old order and allowed Javanese society to define its opposition to Dutch rule without disturbing the inherited structures of political order and personal values. The state continued its traditional, political and symbolic functions in Islamic guise. As compared with Safavid Iran and even Mughal India, which also combined universal Islamic norms with local regional culture, Mataram leaned strongly in the direction of the non-Islamic aspects of state culture.

Alongside the state the local communal form of Islam was built around a *pesantren*, which was part school and part religious brotherhood. The pupils lived in dormitories, worked in the fields or at some craft which helped support the school, studied chanting of the Quran and learned magical and mystical formulae. The influence of the ʿulamaʾ or *kiyayis* extended from the schools to the villages. In the villages they won a following of strict Muslim believers who looked to the teachers as their spiritual masters and who joined religious orders, ordinarily the Naqshbandiya and Qadiriya. The teachers, students and village followers who adhered to this Muslim way of life were called *santris*.

The mass of villagers, however, were Muslim in a different sense. (Generally little is known about Javanese village life in the pre-modern era. The observations I make here for the sake of completeness are a projection backwards, based on recently observed conditions.) For most Javanese villagers Islam was not a question of political legitimacy or doctrine but was simply part of their mentality – part of their attitude toward the world seen and the world unseen. Islam was not a religion or a sect in the sense of being an ideology and a defined social allegiance so much as a vocabulary by which people defined the sacred forces in everyday life.

Villagers called themselves Muslims, and the influence of the ʿulamaʾ who represented conventional Islamic beliefs and practices was considerable. However, village culture was in fact compounded of animist, Hindu, and Islamic elements. The *slametan* was the primary village ritual. A slametan was given to mark such important life events as birth, marriage, illness, and death, personal and business occasions, village ceremonies of purification and solidarity, and

Muslim holidays. The feast was meant to establish security and equanimity for the host, his family and his guests, to dispel hostility and aggression, and to defend against evil spirits. Its symbolic purpose was to organize society, regulate behavior and feeling, and ward off the forces which threatened to bring disorder and chaos into everyday life. The ceremonial itself was marked by a short speech given by the host, a prayer or Quranic passage chanted in Arabic, followed by a meal. The Arabic recitation, the participation of the village religious teacher, and the choice of Muslim occasions such as the birthday of the Prophet or the ending of the fast of Ramadan made this multi-purpose village ceremony an Islamic occasion. The curing of disease and the warding off of evil spirits was also the function of the *dukun*, or village sorcerer, who worked his magic by spells, amulets, and herbs, sometimes giving them a Muslim orientation by chanting Quranic verses.

Islam was thus assimilated to a village religious mentality which really focused on belief in a world of spirits, demons, and the powers of nature which beset human beings. Islam in the village context was not so much a meta-physical, ethical, or legal system, nor a form of social and political organ-ization, but another metaphor for an ongoing community life based on traditional religious and social conceptions.

Thus, Islam in Java was institutionalized on three levels: that of the state, the ʿulamaʾ community, and the village. Yet, despite the close integration of Islam with the established institutions of society, it maintained the capacity for organizing resistance and opposition to state policies. Between 1825 and 1830, Dipanegara, an aristocrat of royal lineage, rebelled in the name of Islam and with the support of Islamic teachers, against an abusive government and the growing Dutch power. Throughout the nineteenth century local kiyayis ap-pealed to the sentiments of jihad and Islamic justice to generate peasant uprisings against local and foreign oppression. Uprisings in Banten between 1880 and 1888 were led by local religious teachers linked with the major Sufi orders. Though Islam in Java had been assimilated to a Hindu cosmological concept of an ordered universe and society, it also symbolized a principle of truth and justice which transcended the given social order and legitimized resistance to oppression.

THE NEW IMPERIALISM

While the several Islamic societies of maritime Southeast Asia had grown up under the shadow of Portuguese and Dutch commercial empires, these empires did not shape the development of local societies and cultures. They were

Map 21. The Portuguese, Dutch, and British empires in Southeast Asia: 1500–1914.

primarily mechanisms to control trade, create monopolies, and extract tributes. In the nineteenth century, however, both the Dutch and the British went on to consolidate territorial colonial regimes, which would eventually disrupt the established societies and lead to new types of state and religious organizations.

At the end of the eighteenth century the Dutch commercial empire was destroyed, only to be reconstituted in the nineteenth century as an expanding territorial state. Two forces undermined the early Dutch empire. One was British competition. In 1786 the British made an agreement with the Sultan of Kedah to use Penang, an island off the coast of Malaya, to repair and equip fleets for the Indian Ocean, and as a base from which they could sell British goods to raise revenues for the purchase of silk and tea in China. In 1791 Penang, and in 1800 a strip of mainland called Province Wellesley, were ceded to them.

At the same time, the French revolution, the Napoleonic wars, and the conquest of Holland by France in 1795, undermined the Dutch empire. William V was deprived of his throne and a Dutch republic was formed under French auspices from 1795 to 1806. William turned Malacca and other Dutch colonies over to the British for use in the war against France. When, in 1810, Holland was absorbed into France, England took control of Java. At the end of the Napoleonic wars, Britain agreed to return Dutch possessions in order to restore Holland as a buffer between Britain and France and prevent the development of a French-Dutch alliance in the postwar period. However, the British retained control of the Malacca Straits, and established a new base at Singapore in 1819. In a treaty of 1824 the Dutch recognized India and Malaya as being in the British sphere of influence, and the British recognized Dutch predominance in Sumatra, Java, and the rest of the Indies. The British, however, still opposed Dutch government monopolies, and favored small local states and free trade.

The consolidation of Dutch control over Java led the way to the expansion of Dutch administration to other parts of the East Indies. While conservatives opposed the costs of military action, Dutch officials, soldiers, and traders pressed for expansion. Between 1824 and 1858, the Dutch acquired much of Sumatra. Dutch expansion was motivated by the interest in coffee, sugar, tobacco, pepper, and spice production, and, after 1870, in tin and rubber.

Commercial and military expansion brought the Dutch into direct conflict with Acheh for control of the pepper ports of northern and western Sumatra. A trade treaty with Britain in 1871 opened the way for a Dutch attack. After two campaigns in 1871 and 1874 the Dutch declared the annexation of Acheh and the abolition of the Sultanate, and demanded the unconditional surrender of the local district lords, the uleebalangs. The Dutch removed the Sultan and refused to deal with the local rulers; and the result was ᶜulamaᵓ-led guerrilla resistance. However, Dutch control of the trade of north Sumatra, aggressive military action, and a religious policy which called for the suppression of militant Muslim opposition but the acceptance of pacific Muslim religious interests enabled the Dutch to divide the uleebalangs from the ᶜulamaᵓ, suppress the guerrilla resistance, and dominate Acheh by 1908.

Dutch control was also extended to the outer islands. South and central Celebes, the Moluccas, Borneo, and other places were absorbed into the Dutch empire. The Dutch either made vassals of the local chiefs or pushed them aside altogether. By 1911 they had complete control of the Indies. For the first time in history one empire ruled over the island archipelago. Thus the Dutch laid the foundation for the modern nation state of Indonesia.

Similarly, the British were building up an empire in Malaya. The British took control of the Malacca Straits and the port of Singapore in 1819. As early as 1826 they agreed with Siam to divide Malaya into British and Siamese spheres of influence. From 1824 to 1867 they attempted to maintain their trading position without extending political or territorial controls. Nonetheless, the economic development of the region generated strong pressures for further British intervention. As Malaya's tin mines were opened to exploitation, large numbers of Chinese and Indian laborers flocked into the country. After a time Malays constituted little more than half of the total population, the Chinese 35 percent and the Indians 11 percent. While Malays controlled the government, the Chinese, entrenched in the economy, were regarded by the Malays as an alien, threatening intrusion; the Chinese were themselves divided into warring secret societies. The Malay states were too weak and power too dispersed among local district chieftains to cope with this complex situation. Thus Chinese and British companies based in Singapore clamored for a strong government to secure their trading interests, and urged the East India Company to take a more aggressive stance toward the Malay hinterland. The British colonial office also wanted British intervention because it feared Dutch expansion on Sumatra and the French occupation of Indo-China. Finally, in 1874 the British intervened in local wars and negotiated the so-called Pangkor engagement, by which the Sultanate of Perak accepted a British resident whose advice had to be asked on all revenue and finance questions, but not on matters of religion and local custom.

This was the beginning of colonial control. From 1877 to 1889 the British residents helped to create a centralized government in Perak, including a civil service, a police force, a court system, roads, railways, and new taxes. At the same time the British took several of the smaller Malay states under their protection. Finally, in 1896 they brought Perak, Selangor, Pahang, and Negri Sembilan into a Federation of Malay states. In 1909 the Federation established a council of British officers and Sultans to deal with the problems of tin and rubber development and the immigration of large numbers of Chinese and Indian workers. By World War I the Federated Malay states and the several unfederated Malay states, including Kedah, Perlis, Kelantan, Trengganu, and Johore, were each subordinate to a British adviser. The Straits settlements, Singapore and Malacca were crown colonies. The maritime Southeast Asian societies had thus come fully under Dutch and British colonial control.

Before the impact of colonial rule was felt these societies constituted a variant on the worldwide structure of Islamic societies. Islam in Southeast Asia was institutionalized in three separate compartments of social organization – the state, the ʿulamaʾ schools, and village communities. At the state and village levels, Islam was absorbed into the regional cultures and identities. Islam at the state level did not define political or judicial institutions but rather signified the adherence of the ruler to principles of justice and shared identity. While real political power was held by district and village chiefs, the Sultans served as symbolic overlords who arbitrated disputes and reaffirmed the existence of an overarching social order in a world of innumerable village communities. Though a qadi or chief judicial official was appointed at the Mataram court, there was no hierarchical organization of ʿulamaʾ or of other Muslim religious leaders and therefore no state control of religious affairs as was the case in the Ottoman, Safavid, and Mughal empires. Nor was there any effective organization among the ʿulamaʾ or the Sufis themselves. While Malay-Indonesian ʿulamaʾ adhered to the Shafiʿi code of law, the local schools were independent of each other. Similarly, while local traders belonged to the Sufi brotherhoods, there was no centralized leadership or overall organization through the tariqat. Individual ʿulamaʾ and Sufis were independent both of the state and of each other. Islam in Southeast Asia was organized only on a local village scale around individual teachers and holy-men.

At the village level Islam similarly specified a minimum of ritual and social practices but did not define cultural style, *mentalité*, or social affiliation. Islam for ordinary villagers was but another symbol in the complex repertoire of ideas by which they tried to protect themselves from the malevolent forces of an uncertain world. In some respects the different meaning of Islam in ʿulamaʾ and in village communities is reminiscent of Islam in village India. In both places adherence to Islam permitted a wide variation in religious identity and religious practices. While many Muslims adhered to the high tradition defined by ʿulamaʾ and Sufi teachings, many, if not most, lived in a mental world defined by the heritage of local cultures. For most Southeast Asian villagers, Islam was an element of a more complex social and religious identity and not the exclusive symbol of personal and collective life. Nonetheless, in all its manifestations, Islamic identity, however understood, was the one shared factor in Malay-Indonesian societies.

CHAPTER 20

ISLAM IN SUDANIC, SAVANNAH, AND FOREST WEST AFRICA

The formation of Islamic societies in sub-Saharan Africa was similar to Indonesia. Whereas Islamic societies in the Middle East and the Indian subcontinent were established by conquest and ordered by state regimes, Islam in Africa was diffused by the migration of Muslim merchants, teachers, and settlers. Linked together by trading networks, family connections, teacher–student and Sufi fellowship, Muslim communities were established within small-scale regional states and in stateless societies. The Muslims sometimes formed peaceful minorities in non-Muslim societies. Sometimes, they converted local rulers and established a joint elite of warrior rulers and Muslim merchants. In some cases they made war against local rulers and conquered them in the name of Islam. Here we can only highlight a few of the peoples, kingdoms, and empires, and the forces of war and politics, trade and migration which were crucial to the spread of Islam. For convenience I shall divide the area into three main regions and historical periods. The first is the central and western Sudanic belt, from the origins of Islam until the eighteenth century; this was the center of a succession of Muslim empires. The second is the Guinean savannah, Senegambia, and Mauritania. This region was a center of Muslim communal settlement from the thirteenth to the nineteenth century and of Muslim jihads and state formation in the eighteenth and nineteenth centuries. In the following chapter I shall discuss the eastern Sudan and East Africa, and the establishment of European colonial empires throughout Muslim sub-Saharan Africa.

THE KINGDOMS OF THE WESTERN AND CENTRAL SUDAN

Before the coming of Arab and Berber Muslim tribesmen, traders, and settlers, the Sudanic region was already an agricultural and state-centered society. Herding was carried on in the Sahil, the grassy steppelands which border the Sahara. The Sudan, a broad savannah belt to the south, produced millet, maize, yams, groundnuts, cotton, tobacco, indigo, and other crops. Sudanic societies were built around small agricultural villages or herding communities, sometimes, but not always, integrated into larger tribal and linguistic groups. The Sudan region traded with other parts of Africa and the Mediterranean, often through Berber intermediaries. The Sudan exported gold, slaves, hides, and ivory, and imported copper, silver beads, dried fruit, and cloth. Gold was found at Bambuk, at the confluence of the Senegal and Faleme rivers. For centuries the Sudan was the principal source of gold for North Africa, the Middle East, and Europe. Sudanese gold sustained the Aghlabid, Fatimid, and Spanish Umayyad regimes and later formed the economic basis of the Almoravid empire in Morocco and Spain. Trade also stimulated the growth of desert port cities such as Takrur, Kumbi (Ghana), and Gao and led eventually to the foundation of states.

The western and central Sudan was divided into a number of local states, but there were also large areas which were not under state control. The oldest of the Sudanic kingdoms was Ghana, probably founded between the second and the fourth centuries A.D. In the ninth and tenth centuries Ghana was both a partner and a rival of Berbers for the trans-Saharan trade. To the west of Ghana was Takrur on the Senegal River. To the east the kingdom of Kawkaw had its capital at Gao on the middle Niger River. To the south of Ghana there were no large kingdoms, but a number of small chieftainships.

Sudanic states had their origin in family groups led by patriarchs, councils of elders, or chiefs of villages. The state came into existence when a local elder, an immigrant warrior or perhaps a priestly ruler, established his control over other communities. The key political factor was not the control of territory but the relations which enabled the ruler to monopolize religious prestige, draw military support, and exact taxes or tributes from the subject communities. A Sudanic empire commonly had a core territory integrated by ethnic, linguistic, or similar ties and a larger sphere of power defined by the rule of a particular person, or lineage, over numerous subordinate families, castes, lineages, and village communities. The kings were believed to have divine powers and were considered sacred persons. They did not appear in public and were not to be seen carrying out ordinary bodily functions like eating. Around the kings were numerous office-holders who helped govern the realm, and provincial and district chiefs often recruited from the junior members of the noble families. The Sudanic states were conquest regimes governing disparate peoples.

These societies acquired an Islamic identity as a result of the conversion of the Sudanic kingdoms. The Arab conquest of North Africa intensified interest in the Saharan trade routes and multiplied contacts among Arab, Berber, Saharan, and Sudanese peoples. North African Berbers converted to Khariji Islam in the seventh century, and Mauritanian Berbers were converted in the ninth century. By the late tenth and eleventh centuries most of the Sudanese trading towns had a Muslim quarter, and Muslims were important as advisers and functionaries at the courts of local rulers. For the sake of administrative support, legitimation, and commercial contacts, the rulers of Kawkaw, Takrur, Ghana, and Bornu adopted Islam in the late tenth and eleventh centuries. While Islam became an imperial cult and the religion of state elites and trading peoples, the agricultural populations maintained their traditional beliefs.

From the eleventh to the sixteenth century several kingdoms, in different geographical locations, succeeded each other as the principal centers of political power, trade, and Islamization. Takrur was the leading state in the eleventh century. It exported gold and slaves to North Africa in return for wool, copper, and beads. Takrur was strongly committed to jihad against its non-Muslim neighbors, but came under the suzerainty of Mali in the thirteenth century and later disintegrated.

Takrur was replaced by Ghana as the preeminent center of Islam in the western Sudan. Before the conversion of its ruler the capital city of Ghana, Kumbi-Saleh, was a dual town with one district for Muslims and one for non-Muslims. The Muslim town was equipped with mosques and religious functionaries including imams, muezzins, Quran reciters, and scholars. The Muslims provided the ruler with interpreters and officials. These local influences, reinforced by Almoravid economic, diplomatic, and cultural penetration, and by the proselytizing activities of the Almoravid leader, Abu Bakr (d. 1087) and his colleague Imam al-Hadrami (d. 1096), prompted the acceptance of Islam. With the decline of the Almoravids in the twelfth century, Ghana became the richest kingdom in the Sudan, but in the thirteenth century its former tributaries freed themselves from central control and the kingdom disintegrated.

From the early thirteenth to the end of the sixteenth century, Mali became the dominant regime in the western Sudan and the principal center of Islam. Mali had its origin among Malinke peoples living between the Senegal and the Niger rivers. A local chieftain, Sunjata (1230–55), of the Keita dynasty, was

Map 22. Sub-Saharan Africa: eleventh to fourteenth century.

The map contains the following labels:

Atlantic Ocean
Indian Ocean
Mediterranean Sea
Red Sea

Fez
Sijilmassa
Tripoli
Cairo
Nile R.
Medina
Mecca
Sawakin
San'a'
Aden
Zayla
Berbera
Merka
Mogadishu
Brava
Harar
SOMALI
IFAT
SHOA
AMHARA
ETHIOPIA
L. Tana
TIGRE
Sinnar
Blue Nile
NUBIA
Dongola
KORDOFAN
DARFUR
BAHR-AL-GHAZAL
White Nile
L. Victoria
WADAI
L. Chad
KANEM
BORNU
FEZZAN
Tademekka
Agades
Takedda
GOBIR
Katsina Kano
Zaria
HAUSA STATES
Niger R.
Benue R.
YORUBA
MOSSI
AKAN
Volta R.
SONGHAY
KAW KAW
Gao
Timbuktu
Walata
Awdaghast
MALI
WANKORE
GHANA
Kumbi
Bambuk
Niani
Jenne
Niger R.
WANGARA
BURE
Bafing R.
Bani R.
Senegal R.
Gambia R.
TAKRUR
Cape Verde

State boundaries tenth–twelfth century
State boundaries thirteenth–fourteenth century
Desert
Savannah
Forest

500 km   1000 km
500 miles

able to unite the Malinke chieftains, and capture the former territories of Ghana and the region between the Senegal and the Niger rivers. The expanded territory included Bure, on the Upper Niger, the principal Sudanic gold field, and afforded wider trading connections. The Keita dynasty ruled, with some interruptions, from 1230 to 1390. The most famous of its rulers, Mansa Musa (1307–32), made a sensational pilgrimage to Cairo in 1324, which made his kingdom legendary for its wealth in gold. Mansa Musa returned to Mali with Arab and Berber adventurers who served in his administration. He built new mosques and palaces and introduced Arabic-style poetry to his court.

The empire he ruled may be taken as a typical West African Islamic regime. The basis of the political order was family and village units, the head of the family being both priest and chieftain. A group of villages in turn formed a *kafu* or a territorial unit ruled by a chief called the *mansa*. The power of the mansa was originally based on election by a group of clans, but the support of his own kinsmen, clients, and slaves sometimes allowed him to escape the control of other families, usurp power, and make himself a local monarch. Then a mansa could adopt the Ghanaian and Sudanic concepts of kingship to institutionalize his power. As a ruler, he surrounded himself with a bodyguard of armed men, often slaves, numerous servants, and elaborate ceremonies. A quasi-divine figure, the king was accepted as a symbol of the power of life and death.

The ruler and the royal clan were supported by a consortium of related clans. The descendants of the mansa supplied the principal functionaries of the empire. Client clans, castes of dependent craftsmen, and people allied by marriage or by past service, also supported the ruler. Slaves and serfs worked in agricultural settlements to provide produce for the court, the army, and the administration. The power of the ruler was basically built upon the service of various noble, serf, and slave groups, but taxes and tributes were exacted from dependent communities. For administrative purposes, there was a central core of territory directly ruled by governors, and peripheral tribute-paying territories ruled by vassal chieftains.

With the establishment of Islam as the royal cult, the king and the entire court took part in public prayers held on the great Islamic festivals. Sermons praised the king and called for obedience. Rulers acquired their Muslim credentials by building mosques, attending public prayers, appointing preachers, and celebrating the festivals. The rulers of Mali brought Muslim scholars from Cairo and Fez to help establish a West African tradition of Islamic learning. The religion of the commercial classes and portions of the political elite helped unify the kingdom and gave cultural support to the dynasty. Islam was a bond of empire.

Muslim festivals were also the occasion for the performance of pagan ceremonies and dances. A Muslim ruler in Mali, like Muslim rulers in many other parts of the world, cultivated an authority based partly on Islam and partly on the non-Muslim cultural heritage of his own society. This was especially important in segmented African societies where only portions of the ruling elite and the trading classes were Muslim and the mass of the agricultural population was still pagan.

By the end of the fourteenth century the Mali empire was in decline. Jenne, probably settled by Muslim traders in the thirteenth century, became the crucial link to the Akan forest region (modern Ghana and the Ivory Coast) and new supplies of gold. Timbuktu (an important Tuareg trade and religious center settled in the thirteenth century) replaced Walata as a terminus of the Saharan caravan traffic. As the trade routes changed, local chieftains became inde-pendent, and reduced Mali once again to a petty chieftaincy. The people of Mali remained identifiable as having a common dialect and customs, but the empire was no more.

With the breakup of Mali, the kingdom of Kawkaw which had come under Mali's hegemony regained its independence. This allowed a local leader named Sunni ʿAli (1464/65–1492) to found a new empire, Songhay, in the region of the middle Niger and the western Sudan and take control of the trans-Saharan trade. Sunni ʿAli seized Timbuktu in 1468 and Jenne in 1473, and built his regime on the revenues of their trade and the cooperation of Muslim mer-chants. Sunni ʿAli behaved as a Muslim in giving alms and fasting during Ramadan, but he also worshiped idols and practiced non-Muslim rites.

His successor Askiya Muhammad Ture (1493–1528), supported by Mande clans, defeated Sunni ʿAli's son, seized the state, and furthered the work of state formation by building a standing army to supplement village levies. He extended the empire into the former territories of Mali. Askiya Muhammad also tried to rally the support of Muslim religious leaders. He made Islam the official religion, built mosques, and brought Muslim scholars, including al-Maghili (d. 1504), the founder of an important tradition of Sudanic African Muslim scholarship, to Gao. The legitimation of his regime also depended upon his investiture by the Sharif of Mecca as Caliph of the lands of Takrur. Nonetheless Islam remained the religion of the governing elite while the mass of Songhay society continued to be pagan.

The empire of Songhay was destroyed in 1591 by a Moroccan invasion, and the *arma* or the descendants of the invading army became the ruling elite in the

Niger region. Internal warfare and the shift of trade routes from the Sahara to the Atlantic in the eighteenth century led to the decline of the regime. Tuaregs and Bambaras established new states. By the end of the eighteenth century the once great Muslim kingdoms of the western Sudan had disintegrated into a plethora of small states.

The central, like the western Sudan, was also the home of diverse ethnic and linguistic groups and a center of state formation. The earliest state in this region was founded by Saharan nomads at some time in the ninth century, with its capital in the region of Kanem. Trade routes from the Fezzan brought Khariji merchants into the region, and by the late eleventh century, Islam was accepted as the religion of the ruling elite, but not until the thirteenth century did the rulers of Kanem make the pilgrimage and build mosques. In 1240 a madrasa was established in Cairo for Kanuri students, marking the integration of the central Sudan into the international network of Muslim scholarship. However, in the fourteenth century, the dynasty, defeated by pagan peoples living east of Lake Chad, was forced to abandon Kanem and move to Bornu west of Lake Chad. By this time the state had progressively united the various peoples subject to them into the Kanuri nation.

ᶜAli b. Dunama (1476–1503) founded the new capital of Ngazargamo in Bornu, and Idris b. ᶜAli (1570–1602) completed the process of state formation. He developed a standing army including a cavalry corps made up of members of the ruler's household and other chiefs, and an auxiliary infantry. The elite troops were provided with firearms. Idris b. ᶜAli also furthered the Islamization of the country by reintroducing Muslim law and courts, and by building mosques and a hostel in Mecca for Kanuri pilgrims. In the seventeenth century Ngazargamo became the foremost center of Islamic education in the central Sudan. Ngazargamo had four Friday mosques, each with its own imam; the ᶜulamaᵓ engaged in learned disputations at the court of the rulers. Islam, however, did not have a substantial following outside of court circles and was not the religion of the majority population.

Bornu's dominant interest was the trade in gold, salt, slaves, and weapons between the central Sudan, Tripoli, and Cairo. Its major rivals were the Hausa city-states; its major ally, the Ottoman regime in Libya. In 1551 the Ottomans had seized Tripoli and in 1577 the Fezzan, which had been a vassal of the empire of Kanem-Bornu. Bornu maintained good relations with Tripoli throughout the seventeenth and eighteenth centuries. Ambassadors brought rich presents of Ottoman weapons and luxury goods in exchange for slaves and gold. Bornu also maintained close trading connections with Cairo. However, by the middle of the eighteenth century Bornu's hegemony broke down, and Bornu was transformed from a regional empire into a smaller relatively homogeneous Kanuri state.

Hausaland, which now makes up northern Nigeria, lay between the eastern kingdoms of Kanem-Bornu and the western empires of Ghana and Mali. As a cultural and political region Hausaland has taken shape only in the last millennium as a result of the westward expansion of Hausa peoples. Their expansion was marked by the conversion of woodlands into open savannah and the introduction of grain cultivation and a denser peasant population. The early Hausa peoples established numerous hamlets, villages, and town communities and formed a multi-centered society.

The earliest Hausa societies were confederacies of kinship groups led by a priest-chief. The groups in the confederacy specialized in fishing, hunting, agriculture, and crafts such as blacksmithing and salt digging. Sometimes, kingship emerged by the concentration of power and wealth in the hands of one priest-chief, who then expected the others to legitimize his rule. Such kings often turned to a universalistic religion, such as Islam, to acquire autonomous legitimation and to undermine the authority of their competitors. In other cases kingship was not an indigenous institution but grew out of the dominance of a foreign trading community. In the towns of Kano and Katsina monarchical rule was established by colonies of Muslim traders who either directly seized the state or converted a local ruler. Yaji (1348–85) was the first Muslim ruler of Kano. He appointed a qadi and an imam as part of the state administration. Muhammad Rumfa (1463–99) is credited with the advancement of Islam by building mosques and schools. He commissioned al-Maghili to write a treatise on Muslim government. Other scholars from Egypt, Tunis, and Morocco turned Kano into a center of Muslim scholarship. In the sixteenth century, the new ruling dynasty of Katsina, founded by Muhammad al-Korau (d. 1541/2?), formally adopted Islam, and invited Muslim scholars from North Africa and Egypt to reside in Katsina. By the early sixteenth century an ʿulamaʾ class had emerged under royal patronage. It seems probable that the new rulers tried to convert local peoples and subvert the authority of local chiefs, but were eventually obliged to compromise. Hausaland then remained divided between a Muslim cosmopolitan urban royal society and the local kinship animistic rural societies.

The city regimes were characterized by a centralized chieftainship with a fortified capital, an elaborate court, and a substantial officialdom. By the fourteenth century, Kano had acquired a powerful military machine. The *madawaki*, or chief cavalry officer, was the commander of a professional officers' corps. The Kano armies were equipped with iron helmets and coats of mail.

Map 23. Sub-Saharan Africa: sixteenth to eighteenth century.

By conquest, Kano acquired great numbers of slaves who were used as soldiers, officials, agricultural laborers, and porters on the trade routes. Colonies were created to produce agricultural revenues. The power of the state was also based on extensive trading networks. Kano became a base for the trans-Saharan trade in salt, cloth, leather, and grain, and for trade with the Ashanti and the Yorubas. Islamization generally facilitated the expansion of trade. It was the basis of an enlarged marketing network, and the ʿulamaʾ provided legal support, guarantees, safe conducts, introductions, and other services.

In the course of the fifteenth century, under the influences of expanding international trade, and intense economic and political competition with surrounding states, the Hausa system expanded to other cities and some Hausa city-states were transformed into little empires. From the time of their institutional consolidation in the fifteenth century to the end of the eighteenth century the Hausa states were at war with each other and with neighboring peoples. In the late eighteenth century the Hausa states, like those of Bornu and the western Sudan, were economically and politically exhausted. Out of their time of troubles, however, new Muslim movements would be born.

Thus between the tenth and the eighteenth centuries a succession of Sudanic kingdoms were converted or organized under the banner of Islam. These kingdoms owed their existence to Muslim trading communities. In some cases the traders provided the economic resources, weapons, and horses that enabled local adventurers to establish state regimes. In other cases they were themselves the conquerors. In still other cases, existing Sudanic states, based upon previous nomadic conquests or chieftainships, found economic support and legitimation in Islam. The prayer, rituals, amulets, and magical books of the Muslim traders were as important as their financial and administrative assistance.

The relationship between Muslim beliefs, rituals, and holy-men and African chiefs was variable. In some cases the chiefs remained pagans but employed Muslims as officials, traders, and advisers. In other cases the chiefs converted to Islam but maintained a cultural style which synthesized Muslim rituals and festivals with pagan customs and ceremonies. African rulers built mosques, instituted public prayer, patronized Muslim scholars, and celebrated Muslim holidays, but ceremonial dances, recitations of poets, and the drama of court life had non-Muslim sources. In the history of a dynasty, early rulers often stressed their pagan warrior virtues while later rulers stressed their Muslim ones. They maintained a double cultural orientation to express both their Islamic and their indigenous bases of authority. African kings were not retrograde Muslims but simply followed the universal tendency of Muslim regimes to blend Muslim and non-Muslim cultures. In cases such as Takrur and Bornu the chiefs became fully Muslim and active patrons of Muslim religious life. Whatever the degree of their attachments, when chiefs accepted Islam, their lands were regarded by Muslims as being part of the realm of Islam (*Dar al-Islam*).

Muslim regimes favored the work of Muslim ʿulamaʾ and holy-men. Only a small number of scholars held positions at court or as judges and prayer leaders but their influence was considerable. The Muslim clerics presided over prayers, sacrifices, and festivals, applied Muslim law, and established a Muslim tradition of culture. Arabic thus became important not only for the diffusion of religion but for communications and trade. It was used for official correspondence in the Ghana empire before the end of the twelfth century and in Mali in the mid-fourteenth century where the highly Islamized state of Mansa Musa had qadis and administrative departments. The earliest known Arabic texts, though, come from Bornu at the end of the fourteenth century; Arabic reached Hausaland at about the same time; fifteenth-century immigrants brought Arabic books on language and theology. Kano became a great center of Muslim learning when it was visited by al-Maghili and other North African and Egyptian scholars.

Timbuktu was probably the most important center of Arabic and Muslim studies. Its scholarly elite was drawn from a number of interelated families representing the numerous tribal and ethnic subgroups which made up the populace of the city. While the state regimes of Mali, Songhay, and the arma of Morocco rose and fell, the scholars sustained Timbuktu society. The qadi was generally the head of the community, the principal spokesman before military regimes, and the principal mediator of internal commercial and religious disputes. His influence was maintained by his connections with trading groups, and with the families who made up the *jamaʿas* or communities of the four main (and several lesser) mosques. Through the qadis and the scholars, Timbuktu remained an organized community and a center of Muslim scholarship regardless of the fortunes of political regimes.

The scholarly families were sustained by trade, investments in cloth, camels, cattle and urban property, contributions of rulers and state officials, and the donations of their students and disciples, who worked as traders and tailors. For centuries the ʿulamaʾ of Timbuktu maintained a rich and vital tradition of Quranic, hadith, and legal studies, supplemented by studies in theology, linguistics, history, mathematics, and astronomy. An important biographical dictionary of late sixteenth- and early seventeenth-century scholars, written by Ahmad Baba (1556–1627), indicates a high level of Arabic learning, close contact with Mecca and Egypt, and the activity of numerous Muslim learned men. In the seventeenth and eighteenth centuries Timbuktu became a center of regional historical scholarship as well.

MERCHANTS AND MISSIONARIES IN THE DESERT, FOREST, AND COASTAL REGIONS

Outside of the Sudanic region Muslim merchant, pastoralist and cultivator communities, groups of warriors, traders, and religious teachers lived as caste-like enclaves within the larger society. These were generally small and scattered settlements. In different regions they had different roles to play in relation to other African communities and in the expansion of Islamic identities.

The Saharan regions from Mauritania to Lake Chad formed one zone of Muslim communal and religious organization. After the breakup of the Songhay empire at the end of the sixteenth century, the Saharan societies, regardless of ethnic or linguistic identity, came to be hierarchically stratified into a dominant warrior elite, usually ruled by a single lineage, and subordinated peoples. The subordinated peoples included religious lineages and artisan and slave groups. The religious lineages called zawaya or *insilimen* lived by pastoralism and commerce but were renowned for their scholars and held in high esteem because they claimed Arab or sharifian descent. Each of the major caravan trading posts such as Walata, Timbuktu, and Agades was the base of a particular religious community and a center of its economic and religious network. The religious lineages also shared a common intellectual tradition which merged Islamic law and Sufism, a combination which gave technical competence and personal authority to religious leaders and made them important as political mediators.

The Kunta family is the best-known example of a scholarly lineage with widespread influence throughout Mauritania, Senegambia, and other parts of the western Sudan. The family's history goes back to Shaykh Sidi Ahmad al-Bakka'i (d. 1504) who established a Qadiri zawiya (Sufi residence) in Walata. In the sixteenth century the family spread across the Sahara to Timbuktu, Agades, Bornu, Hausaland and other places, and in the eighteenth century large numbers of Kunta moved to the region of the middle Niger where they established the village of Mabruk. Sidi al-Mukhtar al-Kunti (1728–1811) united the Kunta factions by successful arbitration and negotiation and established an extensive confederation. Under his influence the Maliki school of law was reinvigorated and the Qadiri order spread throughout Mauritania, the middle

Niger region, Guinea, the Ivory Coast, Futa Toro, and Futa Jallon. Kunta colonies in the Senegambian region became centers of Muslim teaching.

A student of Sidi al-Mukhtar, Shaykh Sidiya al-Kabir (1775–1868), established another Islamic network in Mauritania. Sidiya began his religious education by memorizing the Quran and then went on to studies of poetry, theology, grammar, and law. In 1809–10 he apprenticed himself to Sidi al-Mukhtar. As student, secretary, and adviser to a family that had a powerful part in the revival of the Qadiri order, extensive trading operations, and political authority in the southern Sahara, Sidiya was introduced into one of the most sophisticated of Saharan and West African societies. Sidiya studied both law and mysticism, including the works of al-Ghazzali and Ibn al-ʿArabi. Knowledge of law was the basis of judicial and political authority. The two subjects were complementary. Sufism was the basis of the personal capacity to adapt textbook law to real situations. The authority of the judge not only depended on his technical knowledge but on his personal insight, his religious qualities, and his reputation for being able to perform miracles.

After some 35 years Sidiya returned to his home community, established his residence at Boutilimit and eventually won a predominant influence among the tribes of the region on the basis of his reputation for generosity, fairness, and sympathy in dealing with conflicting interests. As a successful mediator he became wealthy from gifts of livestock, the revenues of gum and salt caravans, and the work of clients who cultivated his fields. The shaykh, then, became the head of an association of believers who looked to him for guidance in political, economic, legal, and moral matters. As a successful mediator and economic organizer, Sidiya acquired a reputation as a miracle-worker. After his death his eldest son Sidiya Baba (1862/3–1926) succeeded him. Even after France occupied Mauritania, Sidiya's family was able to maintain its political influence.

A similar kind of Muslim religious community and scholarly tradition was found in the forest and coastal regions south and west of the Sudanic states – in the Voltaic River basin, and the Guinean forests. In this region the Muslim communities were founded by merchants and cultivators often linked by family ties and trading networks. These merchants were generally known as *Wangara* or Dyula. Their communities grew up along the trade routes at the crossings of rivers, at toll posts, and at stopping-places for caravans where merchants settled down to trade with the local populace. The trading communities often developed agricultural interests, and in some cases Muslims became the custodians of specialized crafts such as weaving and dyeing. Their scholars and holy-men carried on the tradition of Islamic learning and offered their religious services to local chiefs.

As in the Sahara, these communities were established amidst a highly segmented society. Lineage systems, age-group associations, secret societies, and religious cults were the bases of political association. State regimes were of limited scope. Political units were not based upon ideology or a history of shared culture and ethnicity but rather upon sudden conquests by small minorities. They governed heterogeneous populations which did not necessarily share a common language or customs. Heterogeneity was reinforced by rapid fluctuations in state power, migrations, and conquests, and by the movements of roving bands of refugees needing protection, warriors looking for conquests, or traders seeking profits. Moreover, these African societies were divided into caste-like strata including distinct elite political lineages, occupational groups including iron and leather workers, musicians, and different types of free men and slaves. In this highly segmented world, Muslim communities were introduced as yet another set of specialized warrior, trading, and religious groups.

In each sub-region the circumstances of Muslim settlement were different. The Upper Volta region attracted Muslim merchants in the fifteenth century by the opening of the Akan gold fields, and the opportunity for trade in gold, kola nuts, and salt. Some of these merchants were Soninke-speaking peoples from Timbuktu and Jenne who later adopted Malinke dialect and became known as Dyula. They settled the towns of Bobo-Dyulasso, Kong, Bunduku and other places leading to the gold fields. Other traders came from Kanem, Bornu, and the Hausa city-states and moved into Gonja, Dagomba, and other parts of the Volta region. The most important merchant center in this area was Begho, on the edge of the Akan forest, crucially situated for the exchange of gold and kola nuts. Begho became the terminus for the trade routes connecting Buna, Kong, Bobo-Dyulasso, and Jenne.

In these regions Muslim traders were well integrated into the general population. Sometimes Muslims married local women and raised families which were tied to the Muslim community through the father and to the local pagan community throgh the mother. The offspring of such marriages often inherited local chieftainships and brought about the conversion of local peoples. They helped carry on local festivals, offered prayers and divination at local courts, distributed talismans and participated in anti-witchcraft rituals. As a result, Muslims in the Middle Volta region were not a distinct language group but regarded themselves as part of the Dagomba, Gonja, or Mossi kingdoms.

Because of assimilation, Muslim religious influence was strongest in the kingdoms of Gonja and Dagomba. The Gonja state had been established

Map 24. Trade, settlements, and the diffusion of Islam in West Africa: 1500–1900.

toward the end of the sixteenth century by Mande warriors with the help of Muslim advisers and courtiers. Though the chiefs came under Muslim influence they did not formally convert to Islam. Court ceremony and culture remained a mixture of Islamic and pagan practices. Children in the families of the chiefs were circumcised and took Muslim names but this was done in accord with pagan and not Muslim ceremonies. Festivals followed the Muslim calendar but had no obvious Muslim features. Thus the chiefs tried to maintain elements of both pagan and Muslim ritual in order to satisfy the cultural interests of their double constituencies.

Islamic influence among the political elite spread from Gonja to Dagomba. The first Dagomba rulers to convert to Islam had been defeated by the Gonja rulers and therefore turned to the Muslims for the magic that helped produce victories. Dagomba chiefs adopted circumcision, Muslim names, the Muslim calendar, and Muslim festivals and burial practices. Maliki law influenced customary law and pre-Islamic pagan festivals were merged into Muslim ones. The relatively centralized political system of the Dagomba also favoured the spread of Islam. Since the state was divided into territorial and village chieftainships each of which, in imitation of the royal court, sought the religious and magical support of Muslim clerics, a Muslim presence was established throughout the region. Sons of Dagomba chiefs who had no prospect of obtaining a ruling position commonly converted to Islam. The chiefs also gave their daughters in marriage to Muslims in order to draw the two estates closer together.

In Dagomba Muslims came to perform important functions such as circumcision, washing the dead, officiating over festivals, and slaughtering meat. By the early nineteenth century imams were widely appointed in Dagomba villages. The imam of Yendi, the capital city, held a position of particular importance as the head of the Muslim community. He was the leader of Friday prayers and the enforcer of Muslim law. By the end of the nineteenth century, though the political chiefs remained pagan, many Dagomba families had Muslim members and Muslims were considered part of the Dagomba people.

While Muslims of Gonja and Dagomba were assimilated into the general society, west of the Black Volta the Muslim trading communities remained isolated enclaves and kept their own languages and a separate ethnic identity. Muslims maintained isolated communities built around their neighborhoods, mosques, and schools. Here Muslims were important as traders, courtiers, and religious magicians, but they had little missionary spirit and did not try to convert local peoples to Islam.

The Muslims of the Ashanti capital of Kumasi were an example of this type. In the early nineteenth century Kumasi had a Muslim community of about 1,000, drawn mostly from neighboring Gonja and Dagomba, but also including Dyula from Senegal and Arabs from North Africa. The Muslims were headed by Muhammad al-Ghamba, who was imam and qadi, principal of a Quran school, possessor of a large library, and a well-educated man. The Kumasi Muslims acted as agents for the Ashanti princes in the gold, kola nut, slave, and salt trade, and served Ashanti rulers as diplomats, bureaucrats, courtiers, soldiers, and religious functionaries. They provided amulets and performed rituals. Despite the importance of Muslims, Ashanti culture was not notably influenced by Islam. Muslims were not integrated into the local society, and non-Muslims were not usually converted. However, in the late nineteenth century strong reformist influences stimulated poetical and historical writing and raised Muslim exclusivist consciousness and a sense of commitment to Islam. Classical Middle Eastern and North African Arabic works, and West African books produced outside the Ghana region were widely circulated.

Throughout the region, the Dyula communities maintained a high standard of Muslim education. A Dyula family enterprise based on the *lu*, a working unit consisting of a father, his sons, and other attached males, could afford to train some of its younger men in Muslim learning. Thus there emerged a ʿulamaʾ class known as *karamokos*, who were educated in Quran and commentary, hadith, and the life of the Prophet. A student read these works with a single teacher over a period varying from five to thirty years, and earned his living as a part-time farmer working on the lands of his teacher. Having completed his studies, a karamoko obtained a turban and an isnad, his license to teach, and set forth in search of further instruction or to start up his own school in a remote village. A highly educated karamoko could become an imam or a qadi. Certain families provided scholars generation after generation. The Saghanughu was a Dyula lineage living in the northern and western Ivory Coast and in parts of Upper Volta. The lineage may be traced back to Timbuktu, but its principal figure was Muhammad al-Mustafa Saghanughu, the imam of Bobo-Dyulasso, who died around 1776/7. He was the author of a system of education based on three canonical texts of Quran commentary and hadith. His sons continued his teachings and spread out through the towns of Ghana and the Ivory Coast founding Muslim schools and acting as imams and qadis.

To the west and north of Ghana and the Ivory Coast, throughout Guinea, Sierra Leone, and Senegambia, Muslims also had a complex role to play. In

Senegambia the legacy of the Takrur and Mali empires was faintly kept alive in a number of small-scale states. To this was added Muslim village communities and town quarters amidst, but politically independent of, non-Muslim peoples and states. By the eighteenth century there were important Muslim settlements in Kankan, the hinterlands of Sierra Leone, Gambia, Futa Jallon, and Futa Toro. Nineteenth-century Freetown, for example, originally a Christian settlement for liberated slaves, had colonies of Dyula migrants and Hausa and Yoruba Muslims taken from slave ships. The various ethnic groups were organized into jamats (communities) which had their own mosques and imams and which settled their disputes internally. Taxes were imposed on the communities to provide for religious services and to support the poor. A council of *almamis* (religious leaders) shared a Friday mosque and a joint Muslim government high school founded in 1891, and organized banquets and prayers to celebrate the birthday of the Prophet. The Muslims acquired land and political power but commonly lived under their own chiefs (*alkalis* and almamis) and pursued their own lifestyle.

Of particular importance in this region were the Muslim scholarly lineages. In Senegambia, the Jakhanke inhabited scattered towns and villages in Futa Jallon, Bundu, Dentilia, Bambuk, and other places. These peoples claimed to originate in Ja on the Niger River and Jahaba on the Bafing River from which they moved into Bundu, Futa Jallon, and Gambia. The Jakhanke were not merchants but were settlers of small agricultural communities supported by slave labor. The various Jakhanke villages were independent of each other and of the local chiefs. One of their deepest principles was withdrawal from politics. The Jakhanke were committed to peaceful coexistence and refused to become engaged in politics or war. When threatened they simply moved their villages into safer territory. Often their villages enjoyed the privileges of sanctuary, judicial independence, and freedom from military service.

The Jakhanke had a reputation for exceptional learning. They traced their spiritual ancestry to al-Hajj Salim Suwari, who probably lived in the late fifteenth century. They adhered to Maliki law although they were tolerant of customary practice. They stressed the importance of obedience to the murshid or Sufi master, and of stages of initiation into the teachings of the community. The Jakhanke interpreted dreams and gave amulets for protection. They celebrated the birthday of the Prophet and the feasts of the end of Ramadan and other Muslim holidays. Though saint worship was not common in West Africa, they believed that the spirit of dead saints kept guard over their followers and interceded for them before God. The graves of al-Hajj Salim and

Fig. 8. The Qadiriya and the Tijaniya in West Africa.

other great teachers were centers for pilgrimage. In all but name the Jakhanke extended family was a Sufi lineage.

As a result of the diffusion of these communities, by the end of the eighteenth century Islam in West Africa was the religion of scattered groups of Tokolors and Songhays, and Dyula trading colonies, some Hausa towns, and of the dominant classes of the central Sudanic states. Islam also had a foothold among the Wolof, the Yoruba, and the Mossi. These communities sometimes converted to Islam when traditional agricultural communities broke down and their populations were integrated into larger social, political, and cultural units. Slave trading and state formation therefore favored Islam. Reciprocally, communities without extensive trading connections or political centralization found it easier to preserve a non-Muslim identity. The durability of family and village institutions, the depth of African religious culture and the strength of traditional authorities helped to maintain a non-Islamic African majority.

The Muslim settlements were also centers for the diffusion of Islamic and Arabic culture. Towns like Timbuktu made the Quran, the sayings of the Prophet, and Islamic law familiar to local peoples. The translation of religious texts into vernacular Swahili, Wolof, Hausa, Somali, and Zenaga followed.

Arabic also had a strong influence upon non-Arabic African languages. Many of them have come to be written in Arabic script; there was a heavy borrowing of Arab and Muslim vocabulary into Fulbe, Wolof, and other languages. Arabic was also used to record family histories, dowries, debts, merchants' accounts, information about trading itineraries, and so on. It became increasingly important as an ordinary means of communication for government and merchant elites.

These lineages – the Kunta, the Saghanughu, and the Jakhanke and others – were closely linked by trading networks, by affiliation with the Qadiriya brotherhood, and by shared religious and intellectual traditions. Without a territorial identity or a state regime they constituted an Islamic society in West Africa. They are a principal illustration of the way in which small communities organized by religious and lineage ties make up, even in the absence of state regimes, a self-sufficient type of Islamic society. The structure of these communities would be an important precedent for the organization of Muslim religious associations in twentieth-century secularized African states and has numerous parallels in the organization of Muslim minorities all over the world.

THE WEST AFRICAN JIHADS

While the quietist tradition was important for the spread of Islam, militant action could grow out of the same social structures and intellectual traditions. Alongside of peaceful Muslim colonization there was a parallel tradition of militant determination to turn small colonies into Muslim states by defeating corrupt Muslim rulers, conquering the pagan populations, converting them to Islam, and ruling them according to Muslim law. The jihads of the eighteenth and nineteenth centuries were led by Muslim scholars and teachers, itinerant preachers and their student followers, and the religious leaders of trading and agricultural communities. They took their inspiration from the militant reformers of the fifteenth century such as al-Maghili, from Islamic literary influences, and from the pilgrimage to Mecca and Medina, which may have brought West African scholars into contact with reformist Sufi circles.

With the Almoravid movement as a shadowy precedent, the jihads began in the sixteenth century when, from Mauritania to Chad, there were reformist outbursts. At first the jihads rose in dispersed places, but gradually they influenced each other, and culminated in a region-wide struggle to establish Muslim states. The jihads were finally suppressed by the British and the French at the end of the nineteenth century.

The earliest well-known jihads occurred in Mauritania and Senegambia in

Map 25. The jihad states of the nineteenth century.

the late seventeenth and eighteenth centuries. The jihad in Mauritania had its origin in the resistance of Berber peoples to the dominance of the Arab Banu Maʿqil. Their leader, Nasir al-Din, denounced the rulers for failing to perform the prayers, consorting with musicians and jugglers, and pillaging the people. Nasir al-Din claimed to be sent by God to stop the oppression. He called himself almami (imam) and amir al-muʾminin, the traditional title of Muslim Caliphs, proclaimed the end of time and the coming of the mahdi, and demanded that his followers conform to the teachings of the Quran. His followers swept through southern Mauritania in 1673, but Nasir al-Din was killed in 1674 and the movement defeated by 1677. The outcome of the wars was the lasting military dominance of the Arab tribes over the Berbers, who were henceforth deprived of political power and relegated to purely economic and religious roles. Though paying tribute to the Arab Hassanis, the Berbers (called zawaya) took up the roles of qadis, teachers, and spiritual counselors, and were economically engaged in the mining and marketing of salt and gum Arabic, maintaining wells, organizing caravans, and raising livestock. The zawaya would continue the struggle for Islamic principles and later give rise to both peaceful missionary movements and jihads in Senegal.

In Senegambia, Muslim jihads had their origins in the efforts of small Muslim communities to overthrow local rulers and to establish states of their own. In this region the jihads were not simply Muslim rebellions against pagan overlords. Senegambian society was stratified into three main caste levels: the nobility whose power rested upon training in war, the Islamic communities, and commoners engaged in crafts and agriculture. These castes were forbidden to intermarry, though one could leave either the noble or peasant castes to be initiated into the Muslim community. The basic issue in these societies was the conflicting claims of the military nobles and the Muslim clerics to political leadership. The nobles based their claim on experience in war and the Muslims based theirs upon superior knowledge. The conflict between the warriors and the Muslims was symbolized by the use of alcohol by the former and its rejection by the latter.

Muslim leadership came from a stratum of society called the *torodbe* that was neither a class nor an ethnic group. The torodbe were Muslim ʿulamaʾ, scholars, teachers, and students. Though they spoke Fulbe as a common language, they had no ethnic or tribal identity. Some torodbe were supported by the work of students or slaves and the contributions of artisans, but many were wandering beggars. The ranks of the torodbe also attracted uprooted peoples, outlaws, vagrants, and runaway slaves.

The first torodbe-led jihad came in Bundu at the end of the seventeenth century, where Malik Dauda Sy founded a Muslim regime over a mixed population. In the 1690s he and his successors organized a state with the power to appoint and dismiss village chiefs. In the eighteenth century the rulership reverted for a time to pagans, but by then Bundu had become predominantly Muslim.

The Futa Jallon jihad was the work of the settled Muslim communities allied with Fulani pastoralists. Both the settlers and the Fulani had been migrating into the region since the thirteenth century, with an additional influx of Fulani in the seventeenth century. Both groups were subordinated to the dominant Jalonke landlords to whom they paid taxes on trade and cattle. In the eighteenth century both the Muslim settlers and the pastoralists improved their economic position as a result of a growing trade in cattle and hides with Europe, and allied against their Jalonke landlords. Islam became the banner of their solidarity and their resistance to the non-Muslim elites. In 1726 Ibrahim Musa, known as Karamoko Alfa (d. 1751), proclaimed a holy war and took the title of almami. He gathered the support of young men's gangs, renegades, and slaves and began a long struggle against the political elites. The Muslims finally prevailed in 1776, when Ibrahim Sori (1776–93) was named almami. The new state was divided into several provinces, which formed a council to elect a ruler. The almami was selected alternatively from among the descendants of Ibrahim Musa and Ibrahim Sori; the former tended to represent the more pacific tradition of Muslim learning, the latter the more aggressive tradition of jihad. Under the authority of the almamis the provinces were ruled by appointed governors, and the *misidi* or family hamlets were ruled by local chiefs and councils of elders. The most important state activity was jihad, which was the source of slaves for export and for use on agricultural plantations. The central power, however, was gravely weakened by the emergence of a landowning aristocracy who descended from the original jihad warriors and by succession disputes between the two families which provided the almamis. Futa Jallon eventually came under a French protectorate in 1881 and recognized French suzerainty in 1896/7.

In the Senegal river valley, Futa Toro was the center of another jihad. Closely related to Bundu the Muslim movement in Futa Toro was the work of the torodbe religious teachers and itinerant beggars who rebelled against the local dynasty in protest at fiscal oppression and lack of protection from Mauritanian raids. Under the leadership of Sulayman Bal (d. 1776) the torodbe established an independent territory. Sulayman was succeeded by ʿAbd al-Qadir (1776–1806), a highly educated teacher, judge, and mediator, who had studied in Cayor province and thus was closely related to the widespread

Senegambian and Guinean network of Muslim teachers. From his inauguration the torodbe became more militant. The new state encouraged the construction of mosques, and furthered settlement of the river frontiers with Mauritania. It invoked jihad to attack the Moors in 1786 and invaded Walo, Jolof, and Cayor by 1790. The Muslim state expanded into the upper Senegal as well. After a critical defeat in 1790, the almamate disintegrated. The torodbe intermarried with the former rulers, seized land, and became an elite of local chieftains who usurped the power of the central government. While almamis continued to be appointed throughout the nineteenth century, they no longer had any political power. However, memory of the early successes would again inspire jihads in the latter part of the nineteenth century.

The central Sudan was a second locus of jihad. Here, too, Muslim clerics and reformers dreamed of establishing an Islamic society on the model of the life of the Prophet and the early Caliphs. In the late eighteenth and nineteenth centuries itinerant Muslim teachers aspired to reform the lives of Muslims and to create a truly Islamic society. Such teachers as Jibril b. ʿUmar had traveled to Mecca and Medina, where they were influenced by the then prevailing reformist Sufi views. They returned to preach the principles of the Quran and the tradition of the Prophet, upheld the rule of Shariʿa, and encouraged individuals to seek personal sanctity. They also taught the doctrine of the double jihad; the inner jihad, the struggle against the corruption of the body, which must precede the outer jihad, the war against pagan rulers and corrupt Muslim governments and their hired ʿulamaʾ. Hijra, migration to a true Muslim community, and jihad, a war in the name of the faith, were the overriding obligations. Thus they introduced a universalistic and theocratic concept of Islam as the supreme arbiter of social life and as the transforming force in the lives of individuals. For them Islam was an exclusive religion incompatible with African cults. This new message was preached with messianic fervor. Throughout west and central Africa the thirteenth Muslim century (corresponding to the nineteenth century) was expected to mark the victory of Islam over the infidel world. This was to be the age of the mujaddid or renewer of Islam who comes once every century, and of the Caliph of Takrur, the twelfth Caliph, whose rule would be followed by the coming of the mahdi; this would be the age of the precursors of the mahdi and of the messiah himself.

ʿUthman Don Fodio (1754–1817) was the greatest of these new leaders. ʿUthman was a descendant of a torodbe family, well established in Hausaland, a student of Jibril b. ʿUmar, an uncompromising opponent of corrupt practices, and a proponent of jihad. He began his African preaching in 1774/5, wandering from place to place as an itinerant *mallam* (religious scholar). For a time he accepted the patronage of the Hausa state of Gobir. His position was like that of the Muslim scholars who for centuries had found in the Hausa courts attractive opportunities to establish their influence, but who chafed against the restrictions placed upon them. Publicly expressing his frustration with the failure of the rulers to put Islam into practice, ʿUthman broke with the royal court. Disillusioned, he returned to Degel to preach to his followers.

The tradition of reform in which ʿUthman preached also had African origins. In the fifteenth century al-Maghili had denounced the corrupt and un-Islamic practices of West African Muslim states. He condemned illegal taxation and the seizure of private property, and denounced pagan ceremonial practices and "venal" mallams who served rulers without adequate knowledge of Arabic or Islam. Al-Maghili called for the implementation of Muslim law by a strong and committed Muslim ruler, and introduced into West Africa the concept of the mujaddid. In this vein, ʿUthman criticized the Hausa rulers for unjust and illegal taxes, for confiscations of property, compulsory military service, bribery, gift-taking, and the enslavement of Muslims. He also criticized them for condoning polytheism, worshiping fetishes and believing in the power of talismans, divination, and conjuring. Another strand in his preaching derived from the tradition of Maliki law, communicated through Timbuktu and Bornu, and reinforced by reformist religious currents emanating from Mecca and Medina. ʿUthman denounced pagan customs, the free socializing of men and women, dancing at bridal feasts, and inheritance practices which were contrary to Muslim law. As in other Islamic societies, the autonomy of Muslim communities under ʿulamaʾ leadership made it possible to resist the state and the state version of Islam in the name of the Shariʿa and the ideal Caliphate.

ʿUthman's influence was based on deep knowledge of Muslim law, and his many compositions in Arabic and Fulbe. Later he began to have mystical visions. A vision in 1789 led him to believe he had the power to work miracles, and to teach his own mystical *wird* or litany. He later had visions of ʿAbd al-Qadir al-Jilani, the founder of the Qadiriya, and an experience of ascension to heaven where he was initiated into the silsila of the Qadiriya and the Prophet. Here, he was named the imam of the walis (saints) and presented with the sword of truth. In general, his theological writings were concerned with the concepts of the mujaddid, the hijra, the role of ʿulamaʾ in teaching the true faith, and the role of reason and consensus in the derivation of Muslim law. All of these concerns bear on the problem of the authority of an individual scholar to challenge the established political and religious elites. Out of these concerns, ᶜUthman produced numerous tracts on political theory, biographies, histories, and other contributions to African-Islamic literature. Many people regarded him as the mahdi come in fulfillment of popular prophecies.

ᶜUthman's appeal to justice and morality rallied the outcasts of Hausa society. He found his principal constituency among the Fulani, a racially diverse pastoral population. Primarily cattle pastoralists, they were dependent upon peasants for access to river beds and grazing lands, and were taxed accordingly. Hausa peasants, runaway slaves, itinerant preachers and others also responded to ᶜUthman's preaching.

In 1804, the conflict between ᶜUthman and the rulers of Gobir came into the open. The rulers forbade Muslims to wear turbans and veils, prohibited conversions, and ordered converts to return to their old religion. ᶜUthman declared the hijra and moved from Degel to Gudu where he was elected imam, amir al-muᵓminin, and *Sarkin Musulmi* – head of the Muslim community. There he declared the jihad. In the wars which followed, the Muslims rallied Fulani support, and by 1808 defeated the rulers of Gobir, Kano, Katsina, and other Hausa states. They expanded into the territory south of Lake Chad and into Nupe and Yorubaland as far as the forest zone. By 1830 the jihad engulfed most of what is now northern Nigeria and the northern Cameroons.

The regime founded by ᶜUthman is known as the Caliphate of Sokoto. ᶜUthman was Caliph; his brother ᶜAbdallah, based in Gwandu, and his son Muhammad Bello, based in Sokoto, were his viceroys. ᶜUthman retired to teaching and writing and in 1817 Muhammad Bello succeeded him.

Sokoto was a combination of an Islamic state and a modified Hausa monarchy. Bello introduced an Islamic administration. Muslim judges, market inspectors, and prayer leaders were appointed, and an Islamic tax and land system was instituted, with revenues on the land considered kharaj and the fees levied on individual subjects called jizya, as in classical Islamic times. The Fulani cattle-herding nomads were sedentarized and converted to sheep and goat raising as part of an effort to urbanize them and bring them under the rule of Muslim law. Mosques and schools were built to teach the populace Islam. The state patronized a large community of religious scholars (mallams), some of whom were tied to the government as administrators and advisers, while others rejected worldly power and lived among the common people. The jihad movement helped to fortify the practice of Islamic law in Hausaland and also generated a theological, legal, astrological, and vernacular poetic literature in the Hausa language. Sufism became widespread and Hausa society became fully part of the Muslim world. Kano became famous for law, Zaria for Arabic grammar, and Sokoto for mysticism. The Sokoto scholars were mainly affil-

18 Northern Nigerian horsemen

iated with the Qadiriya, but the Tijani order was introduced by al-Hajj ʿUmar during the 1830s.

Under the authority of the Caliphate, the territories were divided into emirates, ruled by emirs appointed by and responsible to the Caliphs. Many emirates corresponded to the former Hausa states, and accepted Hausa methods of administration and palace organization. The power of the emirs was based on military force, but they governed with the aid of the Fulani lineages and the advice of the mallams. For rural administration the emirates were divided into fiefs, some of which were controlled by the rulers and some by local Fulani chiefs. Village chiefs administered their subjects through appointed ward-heads and through the chiefs of organized craftsmen. The crafts were also the fiefs of officials who were responsible for the collection of taxes, observance of Muslim law, and maintenance of public property such as mosques, roads, and walls. The fact that the greater part of the territory nominally ruled by Sokoto remained in the hands of local fiefholders and chieftains meant that Islamic ideas were only occasionally applied in the provinces. Government by secular-minded Fulani chieftains led quickly away from Muslim norms, and many of the practices which had been criticized by the Muslims flourished again. Despite the claims of reform, it is arguable that the emirates were but a modified version of the older Hausa states.

The economy of the Sokoto Caliphate was based upon slave villages or plantations. First developed in the Sokoto region after 1760 (and again after the jihad of 1804–8), the plantations helped create an agricultural and industrial base for the Sokoto regime, producing cotton, indigo, grain, rice, tobacco, kola nuts, and other crops. The state also promoted indigo and textile industries. The plantation economy flourished until the late nineteenth century, when the imposition of colonial rule and the suppression of slavery allowed for a revitalization of the peasant economy.

The jihad of ʿUthman was not confined to the Sokoto state but spilled out from its homeland in northern Nigeria to Bornu, the Lake Chad region, and to southern Nigeria, and inspired other jihads in the western Sudan and Senegambia. In the seventeenth century Bornu was already a center of Muslim learning, but it also had a substantial Fulani population aggrieved by landlord domination. Inspired by ʿUthman, the Fulani rose up to attack the rulers of Bornu. Bornu, however, successfully resisted the jihad by revitalizing its own Muslim credentials. Al-Kanemi, a mallam living in Ngala, helped the rulers to defeat the Fulani, and became the most powerful chieftain in Bornu. In 1814 he built his own town, Kukawa, expanded the area of his hegemony, appointed his own officials and essentially displaced the rulers. Speaking for Bornu, he denied that the jihad was legitimate when waged against Muslim peoples regardless of whether they were good or bad Muslims.

When al-Kanemi died in 1837 he was succeeded by his son, ʿUmar, who took direct possession of the Bornu monarchy. Thus a new dynasty and a new Muslim state was founded as a reaction against the jihad. The new regime was built upon an aristocracy consisting of the royal family, courtiers, and nobles called *kogonas*. The regime appointed qadis and imams, and professed to be as genuinely Muslim as the rival Sokoto Caliphate. The regime had a double structure of administration. One system was applied to the control of territories and all the resident populations; the other was directed to the control of clans and ethnic and craft associations. The existence of both territorial and group administrations indicates a society in transition from clan-lineage to territorial forms of organization.

In the region south of Lake Chad, Modibbo Adama (d. 1847) received the flag of legitimacy from ʿUthman and established a Muslim state in Fombina. This was also based on the support of Fulani pastoralists united by Islam. His government was reinforced by invitations to Muslim scholars to settle the region and take official positions. Later rulers proclaimed the supremacy of Muslim law, and a judicial hierarchy was established in which cases could be appealed from local courts to the ruler of Fombina and from him to Sokoto.

The jihad inspired by ʿUthman also helped spread Islamic state power and religious influence in southern Nigeria. Muslim traders from Bornu, Songhay, and Hausaland had come to Yorubaland in the sixteenth and seventeenth centuries and converted the first Yorubas to Islam. With the help of the Sokoto Caliphate Muslims won control of Ilorin, which was the principal Muslim center in southern Nigeria until it was replaced by Ibadan. At the same time, by peaceful means, Muslim quarters were being formed in Abeokuta and other towns where they cooperated with existing elites. Liberated slaves from Sierra Leone and Brazil established a Muslim presence in Lagos. Their communities were organized under the leadership of imams, who led the prayers and festivals and mediated disputes.

In the region of Air, north of Sokoto, the Caliphate supported the jihad of Muhammad al-Jaylani (1777–1840), a reformer who had read al-Maghili and wanted to establish a Muslim state. ʿUthman's jihad had awakened the aspirations of the Tuareg insilimen (religious lineages) to create a Muslim society independent of the warrior chiefs – a society which would settle and urbanize the Tuareg and regulate their lives in accord with the Quran. The new order would bring about the equality of all tribes, require the seclusion of women, and prohibit singing and drumming.

In Masina, ʿUthman inspired Ahmad Lobbo, a Fulani scholar born in 1775, to dream of overthrowing animist chiefs. Supported by scholars from his own clan, by slaves, and by a local trading clan (the Marka), he formed a small community. The Fulani helped Ahmad overthrow Bambara rule in 1816 and form a Muslim state which lasted until 1862. The Masina state had its capital at Hamdallahi, founded in 1821. Ahmad took the title of amir al-muʾminin and appointed a governor and a judge in each province. The state was based on a highly organized army supported by a system of granaries created to provision the soldiers and spare the local population from abuse. A council of state was made up of religious teachers; the local administrative apparatus was filled with relatives and clients of the learning counselors. Ahmad Lobbo also tried to create an Islamic type of society. Pagan Fulani were required to convert to Islam. New legislation was introduced, including controls over women, and the suppression of fortune telling, tobacco smoking, and prostitution.

The jihads of the central Sudan indirectly inspired a revival of jihad in the Senegambian region. The tradition of Futa Toro and Sokoto were combined to inspire al-Hajj ʿUmar (1794?–1864), another great nineteenth-century leader of West African Muslim movements. Al-Hajj ʿUmar was born in Futo Toro, became one of the torodbe, and in 1826 made the pilgrimage to Mecca, where he was initiated into the Tijani order and returned as the order's khalifa for the Sudan. He stayed in Sokoto from 1831 to 1837 and married a daughter of Muhammad Bello. In 1840 ʿUmar settled in Jagunku on the frontiers of Futa Jallon, where he could preach to local peoples. Growing tension with the leaders of Futa Jallon forced him to move in 1851 to Dingiray, where he began the militant phase of his mission. There he organized his followers into a professional army equipped with French weapons, and in 1852 proclaimed a jihad against pagan peoples, lapsed Muslims, and European intruders.

ʿUmar claimed a transcendental personal authority. He denied the importance of adherence to a school of law and favored ijtihad, or personal religious judgment. He taught that a believer need not belong to a school but should follow the guidance of a Sufi shaykh who has immediate personal knowledge of the divine truth. The teachings of such a shaykh, he held, would be in full accordance with the law. ʿUmar claimed the titles of amir al-muʾminin, khalifa (the successor of the Prophet), mujaddid (renewer of Islam), qutb (pole of the universe), and wazir of the mahdi. He claimed to possess *istikhara* or divine guidance in time of difficulties. Thus he claimed virtually every form of

Muslim spiritual and temporal authority. His allegiance to the Tijaniya was the basis for a break with all established Muslim authorities and for a personal appeal as shaykh and savior.

His appeal in Futa Toro, the scene of an earlier and by then aborted effort to establish a Muslim state, was enormous. ʿUmar first appealed to the populace on the basis of local grievances against the military elites. His followers regarded him as their almami and reviver of the eighteenth-century revolutions. His community also appealed to rootless individuals of mixed ethnic background, who found new social identity and opportunities for conquest under the aegis of Islam. ʿUmar came to embody the torodbe ideal of religious revival and conquest of pagans.

His jihad began in 1852 with the conquest of Futa Toro. There he came into conflict with the French, who were attempting to establish their own commercial supremacy along the Senegal River. At Medina in 1857, they defeated ʿUmar, and closed off the Senegal valley. In 1860 ʿUmar made a treaty with the French which recognized their sphere of influence in Futa Toro and assigned him the Bambara states of Kaarta and Segu. In quest of new territory, ʿUmar and masses of followers from Futa Toro invaded Masina, thus carrying the war to Muslim peoples along the Niger bend. His enemies, led by Ahmad al-Kunta al-Bakkaʾi (of the Qadiri order), denounced this as an illegitimate war of Muslims upon Muslims and promoted a coalition of local states, including Masina and Timbuktu, to resist. His enemies defeated and killed him in 1864, but his followers captured Hamdallahi and established a state which lasted until 1893.

ʿUmar's state was officially Muslim and forbade dancing and the use of tobacco and charms, and prohibited pagan ceremonies and the worship of idols. ʿUmar was strongly influenced not only by West African reformist concepts but by the teachings of the Tijaniya and of other reformist movements which stressed the importance of strict obedience to Muslim practice. Apart from this, its Islamic content was limited, and the primary function of the state was predatory warfare, slaving, and the accumulation of booty. The conquest state was not linked to the productive economy. The decline of the central government only accentuated the tendency to warfare, since local chieftains took to raiding to support their troops. Muslim jihad shaded over into a purely military exploitation of the surrounding peoples. ʿUmar's state, in disarray, was finally overwhelmed and absorbed into a growing French West African empire in 1893.

After ʿUmar's death jihad flared again in other parts of Senegambia. In the middle and latter part of the nineteenth century the action shifted to the Wolof people of Senegal. Berber and Tukolor Muslim teachers had been active since the eighteenth century in the provinces of Walo and Cayor, where they were respected for their literacy and their magical amulets. In the nineteenth century Muslim influence increased further, owing to the suppression of the slave trade and the growth of the peanut, oil, and soap industries. The development of the new industries favored the economic and political power of Muslim peasants against the *tyeddo* slave military elites. In response to new economic and political conditions Islam provided the idiom for peasant resistance to tyeddo rule and for the integration of peasants and traders into a larger economy.

The great Senegambian jihad of this period was led by Ma Ba (1809–67), a Quran teacher and the founder of an independent settlement. Rebelling against tyeddo domination, his followers swept through Senegambia, burning villages, killing pagans, and enslaving their enemies. Ma Ba himself never actively participated in battle and retired whenever possible from political affairs, but his victories stimulated other Muslim rebellions. The region he had overrun was divided among the Muslim war leaders, who could not unite to establish a stable regime. Lat Dior, the ruler of Cayor from 1871 to 1883, took up the struggle to establish a Muslim state. He was defeated by the French and killed in 1886; despite defeat, the cumulative effect of the Senegambian jihads was the substantial conversion of the Wolof to Islam.

In the jihad period, Islam also spread in the stateless regions of the Upper Volta, the Ivory Coast, and Guinea. The most important campaigns in this region were launched in Guinea by Mori-Ule Sise, educated in Futa Jallon, who gathered bandits, vagrants, and other rootless peoples, built the city of Medina, and launched a jihad in 1835 in the region of Toron and Konyan. Defeated and killed in 1845, he was succeeded by a local adventurer named Samory Ture. Samory was born about 1830 of a Dyula family. He served the Medina state, engaged in various local struggles, sometimes on the pagan side, and worked relentlessly to enlarge his personal army. In 1871 he gained control over the Milo River valley, seized Kankan in 1881, and became the principal power holder on the upper Niger. By 1883 he had brought the local chieftains in the territory southwest of ʿUmar's state under his control, and founded the Kingdom of Wasulu.

This new state was governed by Samory and a council of kinsmen and clients who took on the management of the chancery, the treasury, and administered justice, religious affairs, and foreign relations. The army was the essential institution. Samory imported horses and weapons and modernized his army along European lines. At first the new state made local chieftains its vassals, but after 1878 the conquered territories were organized under military governors supported by tribute payments. In the 1880s Samory attempted to convert his regime into an Islamic state. In 1884 he took the title of almami, opened Muslim schools, forbade the use of alcohol, and required his followers to pray. He destroyed pagan sacred groves and cult symbols and forbade pagan worship. Muslim teachers and holy-men were posted as officials in non-Muslim areas to enforce the Shariᶜa, and defeated peoples were forced to convert to Islam. Dyula traders supported Samory because of his encouragement of commerce, though they did not play a central part in the creation of the state. His Muslim policy, however, eventually led in 1888 to revolts which forced him to tolerate pagan religious associations and cults.

Samory's would-be Muslim empire was undone by the French, who forced him to move eastward to Upper Volta and the Ivory Coast, where he conquered new territories and set up a new state between 1892 and 1896. In this eastern zone Samory came into conflict with both the French and the British. The French took Sikasso in 1898, and sent Samory into exile, where he died in 1900.

With the defeat of Samory the era of eighteenth- and nineteenth-century jihads came to an end. Beginning in the western territories of Mauritania and Senegambia in the seventeenth and eighteenth centuries, they had spread throughout Sudanic and Guinean Africa. These movements represented an uprising of Muslim religious teachers and their followers against the military elites. The uprisings, however, took various forms. Most common were the revolts of Fulani pastoral peoples against landowning elites in Bundu, Futa Jallon, Hausaland, Bornu, Fombina, and other places. In some cases Muslim Fulanis formed coalitions with non-Muslim Fulani clans or with Muslim communities formed of uprooted peoples, former slaves and oppressed peasants. In other cases the jihads represented peasant rebellions. Throughout Senegambia Muslims who opposed the tyeddo slave military elite overthrew their masters. In some of the Wolof-inhabited parts of Senegal the Muslim assault overthrew the old social structure and paved the way for massive conversions. In the Volta region, Ivory Coast, and Guinea, Dyula peoples established independent states.

Aroused Muslim populations also provided the support for the expansion of Islam into new regions. The jihad of ᶜUthman spilled over into the Chad region and southern Nigeria. Under the leadership of al-Hajj ᶜUmar torodbe elites and Tukolor peoples of Futa Toro carried jihad into the western Sudan. Similarly, Muslims supported the movement of Samory Ture in Guinea. The Muslim mission therefore involved not only local social struggles but wars of expansion and conquest. In certain cases, such as that of Samori in Guinea, revolts in the name of Islam were the work of military adventurers manipulating Muslim symbols for the sake of a tenuous legitimacy. While some Islamic movements aimed at reform and conversion, all aimed at territorial empire. Throughout West Africa Islam had come to be the almost universal language of political ambition and moral reform.

The use of this language varied. In many cases Islam provided for the unification of heterogeneous peoples and the creation of state regimes. Many Muslim leaders waged jihad simply in the name of Islam and of putative Muslim states, but in the case of ʿUthman, a sophisticated Sudanic African tradition of religious reform also prompted a creative literary and religious effort. Al-Hajj ʿUmar turned for his religious vision to the reformist teachings of Mecca and Medina and returned from the holy places with Sufi inspiration. Otherwise the West African religious movements were inspired by an indigenous tradition of Muslim efforts to generate Muslim states.

As a result of the jihads, the Sokoto Caliphate took control of Hausaland and conquered satellite regions in Bornu and Chad. Muslim populations were consolidated in much of what is now northern Nigeria, Chad and the Cameroons. New states were also founded in Masina, parts of Guinea, and Senegambia. The formation of these states led to the conversion of local peoples to Islam. Parts of Senegambia and Masina became Muslim. Converts were made among the Fulani, Soninke, and Wolof peoples. This widespread conversion of Sudanic farmers marks the breakdown of the traditional order of society under Muslim pressure and the emergence of Islam as a principal organizing force in the creation of new societies. While Islam had frequently been adopted as an imperial cult without being spread among the subjects, the nineteenth-century jihads created Islamic states which sought to include the whole population rather than a limited aristocracy, and to create a political people out of smaller groups of diverse racial, ethnic, and linguistic backgrounds.

Though great numbers of people were converted to Islam, the process of conversion was slow and the change in institutions and beliefs variable. The result was not the formation of a uniform Islamic culture but of a plethora of local variations upon Islamic practice. While we may speak about conversion and the syncretism of Islam and African practices, there was no single cultural expression of Islamic civilization in sub-Saharan Africa. Among western Sudanic peoples, Islam appeared in family festivals, spirit practices, and legends. Among central Sudanic peoples, Islam was the cult of the aristocracy and of specialized groups. African societies were the bearers of many different concepts and practices of Islam.

In the first stage of conversion African peoples accepted elements of Islamic culture and practice without forming a Muslim identity. Elements of Islamic material culture including ornaments, dress, food, amulets, and some religious and mythological concepts, became part of the African cultural repertoire. In the second stage formal conversion was achieved and ʿulamaʾ were recognized as the sole representatives of God's will. The power of communal cults waned and the worship of Allah became supreme. A third stage of Islamization involved changes in conduct and custom as Muslim communities took on Arabic Islamic norms. At this stage Muslims recognized the supremacy of Islamic law, worshiped according to the five pillars of Islam, and incorporated Islamic practices into the rituals of circumcision, marriage, and death. Older customs and institutions were reinterpreted in Islamic terms. There also may have been legal and social changes from matrilineal to patrilineal forms of family, and from communal to private ownership of property.

At the very moment when masses of Sudanese peoples were being converted to Islam, Muslim expansion was being checked by European intervention. In the late nineteenth century the French and the British began to assert their own domination. The French took possession of Senegal and of the state founded by ʿUmar in 1893. They then defeated Samori in 1898. The British defeated the Sokoto Caliphate in 1903. The great century of jihad came to an end with the defeat of all the Muslim states and their absorption into European colonial empires.

CHAPTER 21

ISLAM IN EAST AFRICA AND THE RISE OF EUROPEAN COLONIAL EMPIRES

Outside of Sudanic Africa and the Guinean regions, the third major zone of Muslim population in Africa is the region of the eastern Sudan, the East African coasts, and the hinterlands of Ethiopia, Somali, and Kenya. The principles behind the diffusion of Islam and the organization of Muslim societies in these regions were much the same as those of West Africa, but the sources of Islamic influences were primarily Egypt, Arabia, and the Indian Ocean region, rather than North Africa. Also the circumstances in which East African Islamic societies were organized were different. This chapter will conclude with an overview of the establishment of European colonial empires and the partition of Muslim Africa.

SUDAN

The history of the eastern Sudan (the modern state of Sudan) evolved separately from that of the central and western Sudan owing to the fact that Islam reached the eastern Sudan from Egypt rather than from North Africa. Also, in the eastern Sudan a mass Islamic society was established at a relatively early date.

The Arabs occupied Egypt as far as Aswan in 641, but it was many centuries before Arab and Muslim peoples penetrated Nubia and the Sudanic belt to the south. The first Arab influx occurred in the ninth century, when Egyptians swarmed south to the newly discovered Allaqi gold fields between the Nile and the Red Sea. In the twelfth and thirteenth centuries Arab bedouin migrations increased the Muslim presence. Arabs married into local families and

Map 26. East Africa.

through matrilineal succession their children inherited local chieftainships. Arab penetration was followed by the Mamluk conquest of Nubia. In 1317 the church of Dongola was rededicated as a mosque. Most of the country, however, was in the hands of local Arab tribal chiefs, who continued to push south.

While Arabs were pushing south, herding peoples from the region of the Blue Nile called Funj were pushing north. The first historically known Funj ruler, Amara Dunqas, defeated the Christian kingdom of Alwa in 1504, and founded Sinnar as the capital of a Funj kingdom which reached north to the third cataract, south to the foothills of Ethiopia and east to the desert of Kordofan. The new Funj state, bordering on Arab-Muslim populations to the north, had an interest in facilitating trade with Egypt; its rulers had been converted to Islam, and used Arabic as the lingua franca of trade, though the court at Sinnar continued to speak Funj. Only in the eighteenth century did state documents in Arabic appear.

The Funj monarchy was a patrimonial regime built upon a Sudanese concept of semi-divine kingship. The public appearance of the Sultans was accompanied by pomp and ceremony, but Funj rulers spent most of their reigns secluded from public view. The ruler was in principle absolute but in practice very much under the sway of his ministers, courtiers, and family. Provincial nobles lived in castles supported by their own slave retainers. A provincial lord placed each village in his jurisdiction under the supervision of an experienced slave in order to exact taxes. Provincial nobles, however, had to appear before the Sultan each year to perform obeisance, account for their behavior, and deliver tribute. Each lesser lord was also required to take a wife from the royal family so that every vassal was related to the ruler. The ruling community formed a caste-like group which avoided intermarriage with the local population.

The Funj kingdom depended for its economic viability on the gold trade. All gold mined within the kingdom belonged to the Sultan, who was also the organizer of long-distance commerce. As trade expanded and foreign merchant communities in Sinnar grew larger, it became increasingly difficult to enforce the Sultan's trading monopoly. By 1700, with the introduction of coinage, an unregulated market system took hold and royal control over commerce evaporated.

Islam spread in the Funj Sultanate not only as the result of its acceptance by the governing elite and the trading communities, but as the result of the migration of Muslim scholars and holy-men into the region. In the sixteenth century Funj patronage attracted scholars from Upper Egypt, North Africa, and Arabia. These holy-men, known locally as *faqis*, were scholars of the Quran and Muslim law and Sufi mystics and magicians. The faqis gained considerable influence because they could intercede with and even rebuke the rulers, and because they were venerated by the common people for their magical powers.

The faqis founded lineages, settled in villages, established schools, and won the populace over to Islam. Their zawiyas were residences and places of prayer in which the holy-men lived surrounded by their families, servants, and disciples. Their schools (*khalwas*) taught young boys the Quran, law, and Muslim theology. In time the zawiyas grew into colonies and villages in which leading descendants of the original holy-men maintained a spiritual or temporal authority. They administered Maliki law, arbitrated local disputes, and instructed the people in Islam. The eastern Sudanic faqis were also part of the Sufi brotherhoods. The Shadhiliya was brought into the Sudan in the fifteenth century, the Qadiriya in the middle of the sixteenth, and the Majdhubiya in the eighteenth century.

After a long and fitful history, the Funj kingdom disintegrated in the eighteenth century. The system of marriage alliances and princely hostages upon which the power of the state depended broke down; local dynasties became autonomous. The Sultans lost control of trade to a new merchant middle class. At the same time civil wars forced the peasants to look to the holy-men for protection and the Sultans lost the peasant population to the faqis. Together, the autonomy of provincial vassals, merchant communities, and faqis and their peasant clients subverted the power of the Funj Sultanate. The Funj kingdom was finally brought to an end by the Egyptian conquest of 1820–21, which introduced a new state administration and new Islamic religious tendencies. These will be considered in Part III.

The Arabization and Islamization of Funj was followed by the spread of Islam and the formation of kingdoms further south and west. In Darfur, the Keira lineage of the Fur peoples established a new dynasty in the late sixteenth century and a small multi-ethnic state. The Keira state inherited Sudanic concepts of divine kingship; the daily life of the ruler was circumscribed by rituals of pagan origin. Between 1660 and 1680 Sulayman made Islam the royal cult, built mosques, and added Shariᶜa principles to his claims to legitimacy. Arabic became the language of the chancery; Fur remained the spoken language of the court.

At the end of the eighteenth century ᶜAbd al-Rahman al-Rashid (1786/7–1800/1) consolidated the Darfur Sultanate around a palace complex called al-Fashir. Al-Fashir was the hub of administration, a training ground for officers and courtiers, a center for the redistribution of goods, a final court of justice, and a stage for festivals, ceremonies, and parades. The Keira dynasty ruled their Fur subjects through a centralized administrative hierarchy, but their non-Fur subjects, the majority of the population, were divided into five provinces ruled by local chieftains. In the late eighteenth century the central government attempted to replace the traditional territorial leaders with the Sultan's slaves and clients, including merchants and Muslim holy-men. The new elite progressively took control of outlying areas. The rulers also rewarded their retainers with landed estates (*hakura*) and slaves. The land grantees, however, made their holdings hereditary, married into the local elites, and emerged as a quasi-independent aristocracy. The Muslim holy-men were particularly successful in consolidating their local power.

The political consolidation of Darfur was accompanied by further Islamization. Through the protection and patronage of the Sultans, and under the stimulus of trade with Egypt, traders and Sufis from the northern Sudan, Egypt, Arabia, and West Africa settled in Darfur. In eastern Darfur Islamic holy-men married local women and opened khalwas and mosques. Young boys left home to study with the faqis and cultivate their fields; they then returned to their homes to further spread the teachings of the faith. These holy-men helped sustain the regime by creating non-tribal communities, and by providing it with legitimizing genealogies and proper Arabic documents. The Sultans did little, however, to create an Islamic judicial administration. Nineteenth-century Sultans also attempted to bring the holy-men under bureaucratic control. After 1898 the faqis were organized district by district under the administration of muqaddams who were responsible for their discipline.

The Islamization of the eastern Sudan to the end of the eighteenth century differed profoundly from that of the western and central Sudan. While Islam in the western Sudan was essentially a royal cult·and the religion of trading communities, in the eastern Sudan it was a popular religion.

THE COASTAL CITIES AND SWAHILI ISLAM

On the coasts of the Red Sea and the Indian Ocean another form of Islamic civilization came into being as a result of the impact of Muslim merchants, teachers, and other settlers upon the indigenous African society. An earlier generation of scholars regarded Swahili East African coastal Islamic society as a colonial society based on the settlement of Arab or Persian migrants amidst a primitive African population. In the old view the Muslim settlers created cities and absorbed local people into an Arab or Persian Muslim-based culture.

The Swahili language and cultural style was considered the product of the assimilation of Africans into a basically Arab- or Persian-Muslim society. More recent scholarship stresses the indigenous African basis of Swahili civilization. The archeological evidence seems to show an indigenous urban society inhabiting mud and thatched hut settlements with some stone buildings. Most of these settlements were agricultural, probably growing fruit, rice, millet, and cotton, and keeping livestock. A few, on the islands, were oriented to commerce. Some southern towns, like Kilwa, ruled by African chiefs, traded in the Indian Ocean. The rise of an East African Islamic civilization, then, was not so much due to migration, settlement, and the founding of new towns as to contacts among merchants, the transfer of ideas and concepts, and the eventual settlement of Muslim traders.

The first Muslim contacts and settlements occurred in the ninth and tenth centuries on the northern or Somali part of the East African coast. Mogadishu, Merka, and Brava had Muslim populations in this early period. Apart from individuals, there were no Muslim communities on the southern coast before 1100 and very few before 1300. After 1100 the Muslim presence began to expand, stimulated by intensified trade and by Muslim expansion into India and the Indian Ocean region, including the extension of an Egyptian sphere of influence to the Red Sea, Aden, and southwestern Arabia, the conquest of India by Muslims from Afghanistan and Inner Asia, and the conversion of Indonesian coastal peoples. In the twelfth century the first mosques were built; Zanzibar and Pemba became the most important Muslim settlements. Though the sequences are not clear, Muslim migrants came from the towns on the Somali coast, Oman, and Iran, but the early settlers were superseded in influence in the thirteenth century by migrants from Yemen and Hadhramaut. The successive waves of migrants probably brought variant versions of Islam, including the Ibadi and Shafiʿi, and Arab and Persian influences, which eventually became integrated into the East African Swahili culture.

By the thirteenth century there were some three dozen towns between Mogadishu and Kilwa, the most important of which were Malindi, Mombasa, Zanzibar, and Sofala. These towns carried on a trade with Arabia and the Persian Gulf and, via Indonesian intermediaries, with China. Kilwa exported copper; Malindi and Mombasa, iron; and Mogadishu, cloth. Tortoise shells, rhinoceros horns, amber, leopard skins, slaves, ivory, and gold were also traded. There were also extensive coconut palm, orange, sugar cane, rice, and sesame cultivations along the coast. In the thirteenth century Kilwa replaced Mogadishu as the pre-eminent trading city. As Kilwa prospered, stone palaces, city-walls, and a Friday mosque were constructed; copper coins were minted.

By the end of the century a stone mosque was built, with domes in the Indian style.

Little is known about the political system of these towns but it may be surmised that they were composed of lineages. Each town may have had a council of lineage heads, although such councils were probably superseded by a dominant lineage or by an outside Arab or Persian chief who became ruler and mediator among the local clans. A small state might then be a suzerainty over the councils and lineage heads in the surrounding territories. The rulers were legitimized in terms both of hereditary succession and of African symbols.

Islam was also well established, for Arab and Persian migrants had married into local families, stimulated local peoples to adopt an Islamic identity, and developed an Arabic-African culture in language, architecture, and dress. Ibn Battuta, who visited around 1332, saw the towns at the height of their prosperity and culture. He described Mogadishu as a Muslim community with a madrasa, scholars of Shafiᶜi law, and a community of descendants of the Prophet. It was ruled by officials called wazirs and amirs and showed South Arabian influences in court ceremony. Kilwa was similarly a Shafiᶜi community and possessed a school of law.

This prosperous East African society was destroyed by the Portuguese. Vasco da Gama discovered the region in 1498, and this discovery was followed by a vigorous campaign to control the Indian Ocean and the eastern spice trade. The Portuguese Admiral d'Almeida took Kilwa in 1505 and sacked Mombasa. By 1530 the Portuguese controlled the entire coast, basing themselves on the offshore islands of Zanzibar, Pemba, and other places. The Portuguese fought the Ottomans for control of the Indian Ocean and helped defend Ethiopia in 1542 against Muslim expansion. Portuguese domination lasted until Oman expelled them from the Persian Gulf region in 1650, attacked Pemba and Zanzibar in 1652, and finally took Mombasa in 1696. This conquest opened the way for a new wave of migrants from Oman and Hadhramaut, and for the restoration of Arab supremacy. The Omani presence occasioned a considerable trade in cloth, ivory, and slaves between East Africa, Oman, and India, but Omani political authority was short-lived. Many of the coastal towns became independent in the course of the eighteenth century and only Zanzibar continued to recognize the overlordship of Oman.

In the nineteenth century Omani influence in East Africa was revived by Imam Sayyid Saᶜid b. Sultan (1804–56). His authority was at first accepted in Zanzibar and Kilwa, but progressively he forced Lamu, Paté, and Mombasa to recognize his regime. The new rulers appointed a *liwali* to represent them, but allowed for local autonomy through the office of the *matimim*, who was probably nominated by the local lineages. After the death of Imam Sayyid Saʿid his sons divided Oman and Zanzibar into separate kingdoms.

In this period Zanzibar became a center for a thriving East African slave trade and a market for ivory, cloves, and gum copal, which were exchanged for cloth, beads, hardware, and weapons. Zanzibar trade with the interior expanded enormously as new routes and trading towns were established. The ruler of Zanzibar monopolized the ivory and gum copal trade, encouraged Indian immigrant merchants to invest, and also stimulated the development of a clove plantation economy based on slave labor.

The thriving slave and trading economy brought Islam to the East African interior. For centuries the Muslim presence had been confined to coastal ports, while the hinterland remained pagan, composed of self-sufficient farming communities, little involved in trade. From the eighteenth century, however, the growth of population and the formation of small states in the interior made it possible to organize caravans which brought Nyamwezi traders to the coast and Arab and Swahili traders to the interior. The trade was stimulated by the commercial interests of Sultan Saʿid of Zanzibar. By the 1820s and 1830s a handful of Arab and Swahili merchants and adventurers, responding to the increased demand for ivory and slaves, became active in the interior.

Islam was carried inland along two major trade routes. A southern route connected the coastal towns of Kilwa and Malindi with the Lake Malawi region. On this route ʿAbdallah b. Salim settled in Nkhota Kota, dominated its trade, and became a local chieftain. His successors instituted Arabic and religious instruction. Yao peoples living on the eastern side of Lake Malawi adopted the new religion. The first local chieftain converted in 1870; the arrival of Muslim missionaries in 1885 helped persuade other Yao of the cultural as well as the economic value of ties to the coast. Islam was appealing as a vehicle of modernization, which brought literacy, international commerce, social contacts, and administrative expertise into central Africa.

A second route was the trade network connecting Zanzibar and the coastal town of Dar-es-Salaam with the Manyema region and Buganda. On this route Tabora was the key town; from Tabora Arab traders reached Lake Tanganyika, where they established Ujiji, which in turn became the center of an Arab and Muslim community and a base for the further diffusion of Islamic influence in Zaire, Burundi, and Rwanda. In this region Arab and Swahili traders supplied local chieftains with firearms in exchange for slaves, and thus intensified the local struggle for power. Local adventurers, often supported by uprooted young men turned warriors, took advantage of the situation to conquer small kingdoms. Tippu Tip, a Swahili trader and warrior, set up a small Muslim state. Another local chief in Buganda, Mutesa, Islamized his regime by observing Ramadan, building mosques and introducing the Muslim calendar. The Islamic presence was also reinforced by the settlement of Nubians from an Egyptian military expedition.

In this region Islam spread as the result of individual conversions rather than by the conversion of tribes or lineages. In general local chiefs who cooperated with Arabs in trade adopted Islam. So too did slaves and porters rooted out of their home communities. Because Islam was accepted as a religion rather than a political or communal identification, Muslims, Christians, and pagans often lived in the same villages and even in the same families. Yet, by the late nineteenth century Islam had only a scattered representation in the East African interior.

ETHIOPIA AND SOMALIA

Islam also reached Ethiopia and Somalia from the coast. To this day, the history of this region has been shaped by the struggle between Muslim and Christian peoples. In the ninth century coastal Arabs reached Harar on the Ethiopian plateau and founded a number of principalities. Arab merchants propagated Islam among their servants, trading partners, and in market villages. The Muslim Sultanate of Shoa, a loose confederation of local peoples led by merchant princes, was organized by the Mahzum family in the late twelfth century. The Muslim kingdom of Ifat annexed Shoa in 1285. Other Muslim principalities and smaller chieftainships abounded on the southwestern periphery of Ethiopia. Arab traders married Somali women, and created a concept of Arab Muslim Somali lineage identity. Somali peoples were mainly pastoral nomads whose culture came to be marked by heavy borrowing from Islam and the Arabic language.

The Muslim principalities bordered on an ancient and powerful Christian Ethiopian civilization. The dominant population of Ethiopia was Amharic-speaking, Amharic being a Semitic language related to south Arabian, Arabic, and Hebrew. The ancient kingdom of Axum was converted to Christianity in the fourth century; from 451 Axum adhered to the monophysite doctrine. The head of the Ethiopian church was appointed by the Patriarch of Alexandria (until 1948). The Ethiopians were ruled by a Christian monarch bearing the title of Nejashi, who reigned over tributary local rulers. The church helped identify the Ethiopian Christian nation with the Israel of the Old Testament as a beleaguered state surrounded by hostile pagan and Muslim neighbors. By the mid-thirteenth century a revived Ethiopian monarchy had begun to challenge Muslim merchants for control of the caravan routes to the coast. Thus began a long, bitter, and still unresolved conflict among rival kingdoms, trading peoples, and religions for control of Ethiopia.

Victory in the first phase of this struggle went to the Christians, who subdued the Muslim kingdom of Ifat and the lesser principalities by 1415. While some Muslim groups accepted Christian rule, descendants of the former rulers of Ifat founded a new Muslim kingdom called Adal along the coast of Somalia. Supported by nomadic peoples from ᶜAfar and Somalia, Adal resumed the war with Christian Ethiopia, and moved its capital to Harar in 1520. Between 1516 and 1542 Muslim forces under the leadership of Imam Ahmad, supported by Ottoman troops and firearms, conquered much of southern Ethiopia, but in a decisive battle between Muslims and Christians in the north near Lake Tana in 1542, the Portuguese intervened to help Christian Ethiopia prevail over the Muslims.

The Christian victory shattered the Muslim regimes. Only the plains of ᶜAfar, Somalia, and parts of southwestern Ethiopia remained Muslim. Muslim Sultanates and chieftainships disintegrated into tribal and village communities, though Harar and the coastal towns survived as centers of Islamic trade and religious activity. From the sixteenth through the eighteenth century, Muslims managed to propagate Islam among Galla peoples, ᶜAfar tribes, and some Tigre-speaking peoples of southern and eastern Ethiopia; in the mid-seventeenth century ᶜAli b. Daud founded a new Sultanate of Harar. Prosperity in the Red Sea and on the Horn of Africa and trade with Zayla and the Funj Sultanate helped maintain the Harar kingdom until the middle of the nineteenth century.

The Galla peoples, pastoralists with a common language, culture, and sociopolitical organization, had begun to move into Ethiopia in the early sixteenth century. The Galla settled in the vicinity of Harar, slowly expanded in the Shoa and ᶜAfar regions, adopted Islam, and accepted the ruler of Harar as their nominal master. In practice they maintained their tribal system and an independent political hierarchy. By the early nineteenth century the Galla tribes effectively dominated the region. Only the need to maintain an open trading base prevented the town from being overrun. Harar remained a Muslim town with numerous shrines of saints. Its peoples made the pilgrimage to Mecca.

In the early nineteenth century Muslim influence began to spread again, owing to the revival of the highland trade to the Red Sea, the pilgrimage to Mecca, and the increased demand for slaves in Arabia and elsewhere. Gondar, the capital of Ethiopia, was revived by Sudanese and Ethiopian merchants, who brought European products and Maria Theresa gold thalers in exchange for coffee, wax, musk, and slaves. Merchant caravans also penetrated the Galla country of south and southwestern Ethiopia, importing copper, brass, knives, swords, spices, and cloth in exchange for coffee, skins, wax, and slaves. By the second quarter of the nineteenth century some 6,000 to 7,000 Ethiopian slaves, mostly pagans of Galla and Sidama origin, were being exported from Ethiopian ports. The trade benefited the Muslim elements of the population and the penetration of Muslim caravans furthered the Islamization of Galla peoples.

In northern Ethiopia Galla peoples expanded into the Sidama highlands and the Amhara provinces. Their growing influence gave Muslim merchants and scholars a foothold in these regions. In the southwest the Galla influence was even more important. New Galla kingdoms of Limmu-Innarya and Jimma-Kakka were established. The Innarya kingdom was founded by an adventurer named Bofo Abba Gomol, who adopted Islam soon after coming to power and employed the help of Muslim merchants and advisers. As in Sudanic Africa, a local ruler relied on Muslim officials, scribes, and financiers to consolidate his power. The capital of Innarya, Sakka, was a town of some 10,000 to 12,000 with several hundred ʿulamaʾ. Sakka traded in ivory, skins, and incense from Lake Rudolph, musk, gold, ivory, and spices from Kaffa, and thousands of slaves. Gold was a royal monopoly.

Muslim holy-men and Sufi tariqat were important to the establishment of Islam. The Qadiriya had been active in the Harar region in earlier times, and spread into Somalia and Eritrea in the nineteenth century. The reform Muslim orders also came into the region. The Salihiya were established in Ogaden after 1850. Their agricultural settlements attracted runaway slaves and detribalized individuals. The Ahmadiya were established among Somali peoples by ʿAli Maye Durogba and founded agricultural settlements. The Mirghaniya were established in Massawa and Eritrea between 1860 and 1899 by Sayyid Hashim al-Mirghani. Muslim holy-men settled among pagan peoples, married into the families of local chiefs, and reared children who succeeded to chieftainships and brought whole peoples over to Islam. These new Muslims venerated the shrines of local saints. At these shrines cultic practices showed a mixture of influences from the Meccan pilgrimage, Muslim saint worship, and pre-Islamic Galla and other local ceremonies. Thus, under the influence of trade, Muslim settlement, and Galla expansion, numerous Ethiopians converted to Islam in the troubled nineteenth century.

While Galla peoples occupied the Harar plateau, Somali peoples moving southward and westward from ʿAfar took over the Ogaden. By the eighteenth century they had pushed as far as the Juba River and controlled the coastal towns of Mogadishu, Zayla, and Berbera. In the nineteenth century they moved as far south as northern Kenya. In the course of this centuries-long migration, Somali peoples pushed out or assimilated the original Galla inhabitants of the region. The movement of Galla and Somali lineages thus established a Muslim block of peoples in southern Ethiopia and on the Horn of Africa. Thus, through tribal affiliation, a mass Islamic society comparable to that of Mauritania was created in these regions.

COLONIALISM AND THE DEFEAT OF MUSLIM EXPANSION

The spread of Islamic polities in both West and East Africa was checked at the beginning of the twentieth century by the sudden imposition of European colonial rule. While European domination was secured in a sudden burst of conquests, European involvement in Africa goes back to the fifteenth century. The Portuguese were the first Europeans to explore the African coast, establish trading stations, and open commerce between West Africa and Europe. They were eager to find gold, break the monopoly of the Muslims over the traffic of the Sudan, convert local peoples to Christianity, and make them allies in the struggle against Islam. In an extraordinary century of exploration, the Portuguese discovered Madeira, the Azores, the mouth of the Senegal River, and Cape Verde, visited the Gold Coast, and finally in 1482 built the fortress of Elmina as the headquarters of a garrison which enforced the Portuguese monopoly of the Gold Coast trade.

With the discovery of the Americas and the potential for growing sugar and other crops, slaves became more important than gold, and human beings became the principal African export. The French, the English, and the Dutch entered the African trade. By the middle of the seventeenth century the Dutch had seized all of the major Portuguese bases on the Gold Coast, but in the eighteenth century, the English won control of the Gold Coast and became the leading European commercial and slave trading nation. In the meantime, the French established themselves on the Senegal River in 1637 at St Louis and Gorée and developed a trade in gum, wax, ivory, hides, and slaves. Europeans were almost entirely involved in exporting slaves and had little impact on the technological or cultural development of African societies. The growth of the slave trade, however, stimulated local warfare, increased the power of African rulers over their subjects, and brought new states into being. Kings and

Map 27. Colonial expansion in Africa to c. 1900.

officials became the principal slavers, exchanging slaves for weapons and other goods. Thus, most of southwestern Nigeria came under the control of the Oyo empire, and much of Ghana was ruled by the Ashanti.

In the nineteenth century, the British took the lead in suppressing the Atlantic slave trade. In 1807, an act of the British Parliament made it illegal for Britons to engage in the slave trade, and in 1833 Parliament abolished slavery in the British empire. The British used their navy to enforce the anti-slave trade laws and forced other countries to join in the prohibition. Behind the British resolve to abolish the trade was a combination of humanitarian concerns and the interest of manufacturers in a growing African market. From Bathurst, Freetown, fortresses on the Gold Coast, and the coast of Nigeria, British traders promoted traffic in palm oil, timber, ivory, and beeswax.

The suppression of the slave trade was also accompanied by the first European efforts to influence African societies. European explorers, missionaries, and colonists sought to convert Africans to Christianity and to create a new class of Europeanized Africans. European trade stimulated the rise of a new class of liberated, Western-educated Africans who formed a proto-bourgeoisie which would later become the bearer of African nationalism. For much of the nineteenth century Europeans still held the notion that Africans could be equals once they had acquired a European education and become Christians. French and British colonies were supplied with legislative and executive councils to introduce Africans to European modes of government; Africans were prepared to hold the highest offices of state. By the end of the century, however, with the rise of the determination to conquer African peoples, Europeans came to consider them inherently inferior.

In the second part of the nineteenth century, the British began to expand from the coasts into the interior looking for new markets and new sources of supply. After 1857 British factories were established up-river on the Niger. Lagos, the main port for Yorubaland, was annexed in 1861. Britain's policy was to use sufficient military and political force to protect trading interests but not to seek commercial or political monopolies. As long as interior African states were well enough organized to hold up their end of the trade and as long as other European powers did not intervene, Britain was content with minimal political engagement. The British debated whether they should keep their settlements as small and inexpensive as possible or whether they should develop strong political controls to suppress the slave trade and to promote commerce and missionary work. British policies oscillated between the two alternatives, but after 1865, in general the British moved toward direct intervention and control. Traders, explorers, and missionaries, who cried out for increased political protection, won their cause. In 1874 the British made the Gold Coast a crown colony.

In parallel with the British, the French developed their colonial empire in Senegambia. After the defeat of Napoleon, St Louis and Gorée were returned to France and became the main bases of French expansion. Suppression of the slave trade and the growth of the gum Arabic and peanut trade prompted the French to establish inland fortified trading posts on territories rented from local rulers. In 1849 they obtained rights to open factories at Joal and Kaolack. After 1851 the French adopted a more aggressive expansionist policy. Under Louis Faidherbe, military governor from 1854 to 1865, the French annexed Dakar (1857) and pushed French trading posts into the African interior. They blocked the western expansion of al-Hajj ʿUmar and took control of the lower Senegal River. In 1859 Faidherbe forced Sine and Saloum to guarantee freedom of French commerce and to give the French a monopoly of trade and the right to buy land. A second phase of French expansion completed the absorption of the Senegambian region. After 1863 the French laid plans to establish a series of garrisons and a railway to link the Senegal and the Niger rivers. They occupied Bamako in 1883, Cayor in 1886, and Nioro in 1887. The telegraph, the railway, and the cannon assured French domination. Henceforth, the French would not only protect trade but try to assure their permanent authority by constructing roads, establishing formal administration, and introducing legal and educational policies.

Thus the European powers turned from trading interests to political annexation. As late as 1880, Britain's Lord Salisbury denied any British or European interest in African colonies, but by 1884 the expansion of the several powers, their mutual rivalries, and their competition for prestige stimulated a wave of chauvinistic nationalism in all the European countries. The winds of nationalism fanned the flames of trading interests and political rivalry into a scramble for African colonies. The French created protectorates in Senegal; the British seized Egypt in 1882; the Germans created protectorates over Togo and the Cameroons in 1884. In the Niger region, George Taubman Goldie had already amalgamated British trading companies into the United Africa Company in 1878; in 1886 Goldie's Niger Company was given a royal charter to administer law and customs in its territories. In 1897 the company took control of Nupe, Ilorin, and Bida, and the British built a railway from Lagos to Ibadan. Progressively, in 1885, 1891, and 1900 the British government took control of the Niger Company's territories and reorganized them under the colonial office as the Protectorate of Southern and Northern Nigeria. Between 1900 and 1906 Sir Frederick Lugard subordinated the northern

Muslim emirates, and brought the Sokoto Caliphate under his control. Elsewhere, the British assumed a protectorate over the hinterlands of Sierra Leone in 1891. Having defeated the Ashanti in 1874, they took control of Kumasi and declared a protectorate over Ghana in 1896.

While the British took Nigeria, Ghana, and Sierra Leone, the French went on to complete their West African empire. By a treaty of 1889 they delineated the boundaries between French and British possessions in Senegal, Gambia, Sierra Leone, Guinea, and the Ivory Coast. By 1893 they took Masina and eliminated the state established by al-Hajj ʿUmar. They pushed back Samori and established French colonies in Guinea and the Ivory Coast. From their bases in Senegal and the Ivory Coast, the French moved on to establish a protectorate over Futa Jallon in 1897, defeated Samori in 1898, and took control of the Upper Volta. By 1900 they had swept across the whole of the Sudan and conquered the Sahara as far as Lake Chad. Though fighting continued in the Ivory Coast until 1908 and in the Niger region until 1921 the French and British African empires were essentially established by 1900.

As in West Africa, European rivalries provoked a scramble for East Africa. British interests were inspired by the desire for trade, by opposition to slavery, and by Christian missionary zeal. Britain also had established interests in India, South Africa, Aden, and other Indian Ocean ports. In 1841, the British appointed a consul to Zanzibar, and by 1873 had sufficiently consolidated their influence to force the Sultan of Zanzibar to prohibit the slave trade. Britain began to look upon Zanzibar as its proxy for the penetration of explorers, missionaries, and traders. In 1890 Zanzibar became a British protectorate.

British expansion provoked Germany to seek compensation. In 1884 the Germans established protectorates in Southwest Africa, the Cameroons, and Togo, and between 1884 and 1888 they took control of Tanganyika, including the territories that are now Rwanda and Burundi. By agreement between the Germans and the British in 1886 and 1891, East Africa was partitioned. In 1888, the British East Africa Company acquired Kenya, which was ruled from Zanzibar until 1904 when the Kenya protectorate received its first commissioner. Britain also created a protectorate in Uganda in 1893 by treaty with the Kabaka Mwanga, the "Second" of Buganda, by the terms of which the slave trade was prohibited. By 1914 the British had extended their control over most of the local chiefs of the region.

The British also led the way to the partition of the Somali and Red Sea coasts, primarily because of their concern for the security of traffic to Aden and the Indian Ocean. First, they encouraged Egyptian and Italian interests as a barrier to French expansion. Then in 1887 they established a protectorate on the Harar–Somali coast, and by agreement with the French defined the boundaries between their respective territories as lying between the ports of Zayla and Djibouti. In 1891 the British and the Italians agreed on boundaries between British and Italian protectorates in Somaliland. Further treaties in 1897 among Ethiopia, Britain, France, and Italy regulated the Somali protectorates. Italy achieved only a nominal and disputed protectorate over Ethiopia. In the meantime, on another front, the British, who had occupied Egypt in 1882, conquered most of the Sudan in 1898 and Darfur in 1916. Thus all of Muslim Africa – indeed all of Africa except Liberia and Ethiopia – came under European rule by World War I.

CONCLUSION: THE VARIETIES OF ISLAMIC SOCIETY

Islamic societies from the tenth to the nineteenth century had a complex structure. In some cases Muslim communities were isolated pastoral, village, or urban minorities living within non-Islamic societies. Examples of this type are merchant communities in West Africa or China, and lineage groups united by shrine veneration in the northern steppes of Inner Asia or parts of the Sahara. More commonly we find the several types of collectivities bound together in a larger system governed by a state regime. Islamic states were generally made up of numerous religious collectivities, village and tribal segmentary societies, urban jamats, Sufi brotherhoods, schools of law, and feudal principalities. Such societies have to be understood as complex systems of interacting tribal, village, and urban communities, Muslim religious associations, and the state.

The state type of Islamic system was modeled upon the Saljuq-period form of Middle Eastern Islamic society. The early Islamic model, though modified, persisted in Iran, and Turkish migrations and conquests brought it directly to Inner Asia, India, and the Arab Middle East, and via Anatolia to the Ottoman empire in the Balkans and North Africa. Though based on the same model, in each case there were differences in state organization, religious institutions, concepts of legitimacy, and religious beliefs. In the Ottoman, Mughal, Egyptian Mamluk, and Hafsid states, the government was strongly centralized. In Iran, Algeria, Morocco, and parts of the Arab world, states were weak because they were opposed by strong tribal societies, sometimes under Sufi leadership. State control of religious elites was marked in the Ottoman empire, Safavid Iran, and the state of Bukhara, but ʿulamaʾ and Sufis in India, Algeria, and

Morocco were relatively independent. Similarly the bases of legitimacy varied considerably. The Ottoman and Safavid empires emphasized a combination of Islamic and cosmopolitan qualities. In the Arab provinces of the Middle East and North Africa, Islamic elements predominated. Other variations occurred in the prevailing religious orientation of Muslim societies. ʿUlamaʾ Islam was particularly strong in the Ottoman empire, Inner Asia, and Iran. Shrine Sufism was pronounced in India and North Africa. Everywhere Islamic culture was marked by strong local syncretisms. To fully understand the variations, however, each of the regional societies has to be compared not only with regard to specific features but as a whole system in which state, religious, and parochial collectivities and cultures interact. To conclude Part II I shall review the main regional variants and compare the overall systems with each other.

The Iranian type of Islamic society may be understood in terms of the relations among state, religious, and tribal (uymaq) populations. The forces that gave shape to Iran go back to the Safavid conquest in 1500. The Safavids were the religious leaders of uymaq and tribal peoples, but their empire was gradually rebuilt on the basis of slave forces and a bureaucratic administration. The Safavid regime became a suzerainty superimposed upon a society parceled out into uymaq kingdoms. Each region of Iran was under the suzerainty of the Shah but was actually ruled by a tribal lord and his warriors, descended often from Mongol Inner Asian families, who organized a local government and economy and taxed the local population. In Iran political power was from the outset divided between an imperial state and tribal societies.

The central government attempted to legitimize its reign in Muslim terms. Safavid authority was based on the claim that the rulers were descendants of the seventh imam and therefore were quasi-divine persons. As chiefs of the dominant Sufi movement, they claimed the absolute obedience of all their disciples. To bolster the prestige of the state, the Safavid dynasty sponsored an Iranian-Islamic style of culture concentrating on court poetry, painting, and monumental architecture that symbolized not only the Islamic credentials of the state but also the glory of the ancient Persian tradition. The symbolism of the regime was essentially Muslim, but included strong overtones of an independent Iranian cultural heritage.

In the course of Safavid rule, Iran was converted from Sunni to Shiʿi Islam. When the Safavids conquered Iran they made Shiʿism the official religion of the country, built up cadres of Shiʿi ʿulamaʾ (mainly imported from Iraq), and ruthlessly suppressed rival religious movements. Sunni ʿulamaʾ and Sufi movements, even including the Safavids' own supporters, were crushed or driven from the country. By the seventeenth century the Safavids had built up a virtually monolithic religious establishment, and eliminated rival forms of Islamic belief and organization.

Still, the relationship between the state and the Shiʿi ʿulamaʾ was ambiguous. Historically, the ʿulamaʾ of Iran depended upon state support, deferred to state authority, and benefited from state appointment to political and religious offices and from state endowment of religious shrines. They played the role of intermediaries and mediators between the regime and the general populace. Altogether subordinate to the Safavid state, the ʿulamaʾ served to legitimize and support the central regime against its tribal and religious rivals, and took the lead in the persecution of Sunnis and Sufis. There were some doctrinal and social indications, however, of an ʿulamaʾ claim to autonomy from state control and of religious doubts of the legitimacy of the Safavid regime. With the decline and eventual destruction of the Safavids, some ʿulamaʾ argued that not the ruler, but the scholars themselves – the mujtahids – were the true leaders of the Islamic community. They had the wisdom to give guidance on spiritual matters in the absence of the true imam, and the people were bound, according to their teaching, to follow their advice.

The Iranian Shiʿi ʿulamaʾ differed from Sunni ʿulamaʾ in several respects. One was that the ʿulamaʾ of Iran formed a relatively cohesive body, related through the spiritual and intellectual genealogies of teachers and students, geographically defined by the boundaries of the country, and in communication with each other. Moreover, they held a large degree of authority with the common people, and did not, as did the ʿulamaʾ of the Ottoman empire, India, or Indonesia, have important Sufi or reformist movements as competitors. Thus, Iranian society before the eighteenth century was characterized by a legitimate but not powerfully centralized monarchy, a distribution of power among tribal principalities, and a monolithic religious establishment patronized by the regime.

The Ottoman empire represented a different constellation of state, religious, and small community relations. The Ottoman regime was highly centralized. A slave military elite, bureaucratic financial administration, and Muslim religious administration gave the central government control over the subject population. As early as the fourteenth and fifteenth centuries, the Ottoman state had effectively subordinated the Turkish and Kurdish tribal populations of eastern Anatolia.

Within the Ottoman empire, however, there was considerable variation in the degree of centralization of power and in the distribution of power from province to province. While the central regime was powerful in the Balkans, most of Anatolia, the Nile Valley, Tunisia, and Algiers, much of Iraq, Upper Egypt, parts of Algeria, southern Tunisia, and Syria were dominated by segmentary populations. In these regions the authority of the central state was tenuous and the local populations were organized in tribal or Sufi-led coalitions. In Tunisia, itself a subordinate state within the Ottoman empire, the centralized state was based on a highly sedentarized and urbanized population, and tribal domains were limited to the south of the country. In Algeria, another vassal state based on a small janissary militia, the state governed some of the coastal regions, but most of the country was ruled by tribal and Sufi chiefs. The weakening of the Ottoman state in the seventeenth and eighteenth centuries allowed, in general, for a strengthening of local elites and communities.

Ottoman success in centralizing state power depended upon a number of factors. First was the power of the central regime and the relative weakness of the tribal populations. As opposed to Iran, which came under the control of the uymaqs, the Oghuz peoples who entered Anatolia in the eleventh and twelfth centuries did not bring Mongol and Chaghatay concepts of political authority, and were not organized under chiefs who controlled a large central household and smaller segmentary groups. They were dispersed peoples operating in small bands united by successful warrior lords or by charismatic Sufi leaders. Since these bands were relatively small it was easy for the Ottoman state to suppress them, absorb the chiefs into Ottoman administration, and deprive the Sufis of their military and political authority.

Equally important was the concept of Ottoman legitimacy. Unlike the Safavids, the legitimacy of the Ottoman regime was never questioned from a Muslim point of view. Ottoman authority was based on a Turkish tradition of patrimonial leadership, the legacy of previous Muslim states in Anatolia and the Middle East, and the conquest of the Byzantine empire. The Ottomans thus inherited the responsibilities of the historic Caliphates and the imperial aura of the ancient empires. Above all, their legitimacy was based on their success as a warrior state which fulfilled the Muslim duty of jihad, protected the Holy Cities of Arabia, and organized the pilgrimage. The doubts about royal authority raised in the Safavid empire by the Shiʿi ʿulamaʾ, and the doubts raised in the Mughal empire by the accommodation of non-Muslim culture, were minimal.

The organized religious life of Ottoman Muslims was also different from that of Iran. The Ottoman empire, like the Safavid, organized an ʿulamaʾ bureaucracy but unlike the Safavids the Ottomans kept the loyalty of the religious establishment. Government patronage and the creation of an elaborate bureaucracy absorbed the ʿulamaʾ into the state machine. A graded judicial and a professorial hierarchy, state salaries, and state endowments effectively committed the ʿulamaʾ to the Ottoman regime. Even the Sufi brotherhoods, despite their large followings, were attached to the state machine and were neutralized or suppressed. Religious leaders of the Ottoman empire looked upon the state as indispensable to Islam. The Sunni ʿulamaʾ were totally committed to the authority of the Sultan, and stressed the legacy of religious attitudes that legitimized the rule of the state. In Iran, by contrast, the ʿulamaʾ came to be independent of and hostile to the state.

Thus, by the eighteenth century the Ottoman empire had an institutional pattern that emphasized the centralized state regime, legitimized in Muslim terms, and a centralized and unified Sunni religious establishment that served virtually as a department of state. Only in bedouin-populated regions of the Arab world and North Africa was some degree of autonomy possible.

In the subcontinent the pattern of Islamic society goes back to the founding of the Mughal empire. The Mughal state, like the Ottoman and Safavid empires, was a patrimonial regime. The emperor ruled through a royal household supported by a quasi-feudal elite. The armies were composed of Muslim officers, mainly of Afghan and Inner Asian descent, who were assigned tax revenues from the land in return for supplying contingents for military service. Native Hindu vassals such as the Rajputs formed an important part of the military establishment. Muslims were the original conquering elite but the Hindus were important as subordinate lords, administrative officials, financiers, merchants, and landowners. The regime was also supported by a bureaucratic administration that served to tax the subject populace and to register landed incomes. The bureaucracy was staffed by both Muslim and Hindu officials.

The Mughal regime wove together Muslim and Indian social and cultural considerations. The identity of the Muslim elites was based not only on the virtue of being Muslim, but on noble lineage. All members of the elite were members of extended families linked by ceremonies, gifts, and concessions of property and office. Muslim peasants and pastoralists were as much subjects of the empire as Hindus.

While the Mughal empire was officially Muslim, it cultivated a complex identity. The empire defended Islam, patronized Muslim religious life, and appointed Muslim judicial and other religious officials. The Mughals, however, also claimed the loyalty of Hindu lords and subjects and elaborated a court culture in which painting, music, literature, philosophy, and architecture embodied aspects of the Hindu as well as the Muslim heritage and blended them into a single stylistic form. Mughal culture prescribed the styles of architecture, painting, and belles-lettres, and the fashions in manners and dress. By contrast to the Ottoman and Safavid regimes, the Mughal empire had a strong non-Islamic expression for its cultural and political identity.

In religious organization proper, Mughal India also differed from the Middle Eastern empires. The Muslims of the subcontinent, as opposed to Iranian Muslims, recognized no single dominant concept of Islam and no single Muslim community or religious establishment. Indian Muslims formed numerous religious bodies, divided by allegiance to points of doctrine, schools of law, Sufi brotherhoods, and to the teaching of individual shaykhs, scholars, and saints. Indian Muslims-qua-Muslims appeared as a congeries of religious groups rather than as a single communal body.

This pluralism governed the relation of the Muslim communities to the state. Despite state patronage of a small ʿulamaʾ establishment, both ʿulamaʾ and Sufis were generally independent and often critical of the cosmopolitan and imperial culture, the Hindu elites and the patrimonial loyalties of the Mughal regime. Many Sufis, however, accepted state support or simply withdrew from concern with public issues. Thus, Indian Islamic society was not organized in terms of an Ottoman type of state control or an Iranian type of uniformity, but in terms of numerous independent and competitive Muslim religious movements.

Indo-Malay societies were not strictly parallel in form to Middle Eastern and South Asian Islamic empires. Southeast Asia had a similar heritage of an agrarian and commercial economic base and a history of state regimes legitimized in terms of high religious culture, but in Southeast Asia, political fragmentation rather than imperial unity was the rule. Southeast Asia was never conquered by Muslim tribal peoples. Nor were indigenous regimes able to achieve political unity. Indo-Malay polities evolved from within. The coastal and regional states of Malaya, Sumatra, and the principalities of Java took on an Islamic identity, but were derived historically from pre-Islamic states. Characteristically, Indo-Malay Muslim states depended heavily upon symbolic and cultural attachments to implement their rule. While Islam was woven into the symbolism of state authority, legitimation still depended upon the heritage of Hindu and Buddhist concepts. Even as compared with Mughal India, the non-Islamic cultural aspect of the political system was strongly pronounced.

The Muslim religious communities of Southeast Asia also tended to be decentralized; religious life was built around individual teachers and holy-men; the Sufi brotherhoods and the ʿulamaʾ schools were institutionally weak, and there were no significant tribal communities. Scholars functioned independently, teaching through the pesantren. The village holy-men were also important influences. In Indonesia, the mass of villagers considered themselves Muslims but were not strongly influenced by Islamic rituals, concepts, laws, ethics, or institutions. They followed a customary religious and social life that had existed prior to the establishment of Islam and assimilated Islam into this preexisting culture. Islam in Indonesia was manifest as identity rather than as social organization. Some regions were exceptions to this Indo-Malay pattern. In Minangkabau the Sufi orders were strongly organized and there was intense religious conflict as religious reformers struggled to bring Minangkabau into accord with Muslim norms.

Thus, Southeast Asian Islamic societies differed from the Middle Eastern in that there was little state participation in the organization of Muslim religious life. The village ʿulamaʾ, Sufis, and other popular teachers were wholly independent. Indeed, deep in the history of the ʿulamaʾ of Java and the outer islands, there was a tradition of resistance to state authority. The common people believed that a savior or just ruler would eventually overthrow the state order to create a truly Islamic society. In India and Southeast Asia initiative passed to numerous independent Sufi and ʿulamaʾ reformers and charismatic leaders who would struggle among themselves and with foreign and non-Islamic forces to try to shape the Islamic destiny of the area in the modern era.

Thus the several types of imperial agrarian Islamic societies may be analyzed in terms of a pattern of institutional arrangements which involved state, parochial, and Muslim religious institutions. In each case the pattern of relations describes a variant form of Muslim society. These illustrations could be extended to other cases, but a few suffice to show how different Islamic societies can be analyzed in terms of their characteristic constellation of state, religious, and local communal institutions. As Muslim societies entered the modern era they would be drastically changed by internal reorganization and by the impact of European imperialism and the world commercial economy. Nevertheless, the inherited patterns would be a powerful force in the shaping of modern Islamic societies.

THE MODERN TRANSFORMATION: MUSLIM PEOPLES IN THE NINETEENTH AND TWENTIETH CENTURIES

19 Pakistani woman in purdah

INTRODUCTION: MODERNITY AND THE
TRANSFORMATION OF MUSLIM SOCIETIES

By the eighteenth century a worldwide system of Muslim societies had come into being. Each was built upon the interaction of Middle Eastern Islamic state, religious and communal institutions, and local social institutions and cultures, and in each case the interactions generated a different type of Islamic society. Though each society was unique, they resembled each other in form and were interconnected by political and religious contacts and shared cultural values. Thus they made up a world system of Islamic societies.

In the eighteenth and nineteenth centuries the evolution of these societies was diverted by European intervention. By the late eighteenth century the Russians, the Dutch, and the British had already established territorial suzerainty in parts of the northern steppes of Asia, Southeast Asia, and the Indian subcontinent, and European commercial and diplomatic intervention was well advanced in other regions. In the nineteenth and early twentieth centuries, European states, driven by the need of industrial economies for raw materials and markets, and by economic and political competition with each other, established worldwide territorial empires. The Dutch completed the conquest of Indonesia; the Russians (and the Chinese) absorbed Inner Asia; the British consolidated their empires in India and Malaya, and took control of parts of the Middle East, East Africa, Nigeria, and other parts of West Africa. France seized North Africa and much of West Africa, parts of the Middle East, and other territories. Small German and Italian colonies were also founded in Africa. By the beginning of the twentieth century, the European powers (and China) had completed their conquest of almost all of the Muslim world.

Now European intervention would profoundly transform the inner struc-

Map 28. European domination and the Muslim world: c. 1920.

Legend:
- Britain
- Netherlands
- Portugal
- France
- Spain
- Italy
- USSR
- Muslim concentrations in USSR
- Independent Muslim states
- Muslim concentrations in China

tures of these societies. In each case the European impact was different, and these differences, combined with the institutional and cultural variations among the Muslim societies, would generate the various types of contemporary Islamic societies. Just as each Islamic society was the product of the interaction of a regional society with Middle Eastern influences, modern Islamic societies are the product of the interaction of regional Islamic societies with Europe. In the chapters which follow we shall examine the principal Muslim societies, and try to assess the relative roles of European influences and of the historic institutional and cultural bases of these societies in their modern transformation. Such transformations, of course, are not peculiar to the Muslim world. In the nineteenth and twentieth centuries European influence reached all human civilizations, provoked profound changes, and inducted them into the modern era.

These modern transformations, moreover, are not strictly comparable to the historic influence of one civilization upon another, for Europe represented not only another civilization but one which was qualitatively different. In Part II we have seen how in the late Middle Ages, Renaissance, and Reformation periods, European peoples, possessed of a unique form of social and institutional pluralism, and a mentality which stressed innovation, individual worldly activity, aggressive dominance, and technical experimentation, generated the advances which gave them worldwide military and commercial supremacy. This supremacy was not absolute, for the Ottoman empire and other Muslim and non-Muslim societies still resisted European encroachment.

The eighteenth and nineteenth centuries brought still more striking advances in the organization of Europe and a still more striking disparity of wealth and power between Europe and the rest of the world. European economic capacities were transformed by the Industrial Revolution in Britain in the eighteenth century, and in France, Germany, and other countries in the nineteenth century. With the development of bureaucratic forms of economic organization, new technologies for the production of steam and electricity, and by the expansion of scientific knowledge, the economic dominance of European countries was further enhanced.

The American and French revolutions brought equally profound changes in the realm of politics and statecraft. They brought into being the modern nation state built upon the relative equality and participation of its citizens, close identification of populations with the state, and a merging of national, political, and cultural identities. They also pioneered in the creation of parliamentary institutions which allowed for widespread political representation, and state structures which diffused or moderated the exercise of power in the interests of the autonomy of the civil society and the political freedom of individual citizens.

Furthermore, the European and American enlightenments completed the historic process of secularization. Political and economic institutions were fully differentiated from religious norms. The cultivation of scientific and of humanistic mentalities relegated religion to a narrowed sphere of worship and communal activities. The scientific mentality "disenchanted," demystified the world of nature and of human relations. Nature, society, and even the human personality, became accessible to rational understanding and to the conviction that they could be modified by conscious human intervention.

Throughout the Muslim world European dominance has meant the imposition of these institutions and cultural features upon non-European peoples. European political intervention, or more usually control, led to the construction of centralized bureaucratic territorial states. European economic and capitalist penetration usually led to increased and often exploitative trade, and stimulated the production of raw materials, and decline of local industries. The European powers forced or induced others to create modern schools, and to inculcate the values of European civilization, blended as best they could be with indigenous cultures. These changes in non-European societies involved the creation of new patterns of economic production and exchange and new technologies. In turn the new state and economic structures were the bases for the rise of new elites. Political managers, soldiers, technocrats, comprador merchants, intelligentsia, intellectuals, commercial farmers, and industrial workers became important forces in Muslim societies. European influence also stimulated the acceptance of new value systems – an appreciation for national identity and political participation, economic engagement, moral activism, and a new scientific worldview. Modernization then involved changes in economy and technology and related changes in political institutions, social organization, and cultural values. All of these changes involved the adoption or re-creation of the basic features of European civilization in the matrix of older Islamic societies.

Europeans and Americans have understood "modernization" in several ways. First, it is considered to be a universal evolutionary process. Though initiated in Europe and America, it leads everywhere to the formation of similar kinds of societies. The logic of industrialism, it was believed, would shape the sociocultural qualities of all the world societies into a modern mold, and development everywhere would converge to approximate the features of the West. Societies differed, then, only insofar as they were more or less advanced on the evolutionary ladder. In the late nineteenth century, and until very recently, Europeans and Americans and many of their Third World clients and subjects, assumed that European modernity was the height of human development. European attributes became the image of Third World aspirations for modernity. In view of the actual variations in historical development and the apparent divergence of many societies from the European –American norm, this view is no longer widely held.

Two new approaches are replacing the outmoded concept of a universal modernity. One point of view sees the world capitalist economy as the source of induced economic, technological, and class change in non-European societies. This view defines economic and technological change as the crucial features of modernization and regards state organization and culture as derivative considerations. Thus all the world's societies approximate certain forms of economic transformation, though they differ in superstructural political and cultural qualities.

The second approach recognizes that whatever the universal elements in European political domination or the world capitalist system, in fact there is no single European model or form of modern society. While modernity originates in Europe, it does not spread by direct borrowing, adoption, or even imposition. The impact of Europe is different in every part of the world, and like the impact of the great empires, religions, and civilizations of the past, Europe challenges existing elites, institutions, and cultures and forces them to define their own version of modernity. Modernity is plural because it results from the efforts of Third World indigenous elites to reconstruct their own societies.

The role of indigenous elites, institutions, and cultures in determining the pattern of development must be emphasized because of some important differences between the structure of Muslim and European societies. European societies in the nineteenth and twentieth centuries were to a considerable extent organized in terms of economically derived social classes. In many European countries bourgeois elites were the principal forces behind economic development, state organization, and world conquest. Industrial working classes are a principal force in production. In Muslim societies economically defined social classes were relatively less significant. In these societies, the economy was embedded in and regulated by tribal, communal, associational, and state political structures. State elites, and tribal and religious notables, used political power to control land and trading resources and to extract the surplus product of peasants and other producers. Even under colonial domination these elites continued to govern the economic as well as the political and cultural responses of their societies to European intervention.

European economic penetration, therefore, did not necessarily evoke an economic response, but rather a broadly conceived response that blended the conjoined economic, political, and cultural interests of the Muslim elites.

From this point of view indigenous elites, institutions, and cultural codes are as important to the shape of modernity as European imperial and economic systems. The impact of Europe on Muslim societies is mediated by the collaboration or resistance of local elites. Thus the transformations which take place in Muslim societies are forged in terms of the interests, perceptions, and responses of internal elites to the pressures and incentives generated by European power and by their desire to exploit European influences in the struggle for power within their own societies. Whatever the economic forces which impinged from without, in Muslim countries these elites had primarily a political or cultural orientation and tended to define the problem of European intervention in sociocultural rather than economic terms. In Muslim societies economic influences commonly led to political and cultural responses.

In each Muslim country the universal features of economy and technology are expressed, organized, and interrelated in ways which yield different versions of modernity. Thus, in the chapters which follow I shall try to assess the impact of Europe upon, and the responses of, each Muslim society, stressing internal continuities and their role in modern transformations. At the risk of underestimating the importance of economic and technological change, I shall stress the continuity of historic elites, institutions, and cultures in the "modernization" of these societies. Also, in the chapters which follow, I do not attempt a full analysis of modernity but only of those aspects which are essential to understanding the role of Islam in modern Muslim societies.

In general the history of the modern transformation of Islamic societies falls into several phases and shows certain common features throughout the Muslim world. The first phase was the period from the late eighteenth to the early twentieth century, marked by the breakup of the Muslim state system and the imposition of European commercial and territorial domination. In this phase Muslim political, religious, and tribal elites attempted to define new ideological and religious approaches to the internal development of their own societies. Out of these responses came a second phase of development, the twentieth-century formation of national states through which the elites of Muslim countries tried to give a modern political identity to their societies and to promote economic development and social change. The phase of national state-building began after World War I and persists to the present. The consolidation of national states in turn introduced a third phase in the development of almost all Muslim countries: conflict over the direction of their current development and the ultimate role of Islam.

ISLAMIC MODERNISM AND ISLAMIC REFORMISM

The implications of European colonial and economic domination continue to unfold to the present day. Colonial rule upset the equilibrium of institutions which made up the pre-modern system of Muslim societies, and induced a worldwide decline of Muslim political power and a regression of the Muslim presence in certain regions. The Ottoman empire lost control of the Balkans, and Muslim peoples in Inner Asia came under lasting Russian and Chinese rule. In place of the Mughal empire, the Indian subcontinent was partitioned, with the bulk of the region falling to India. The Muslim jihad states in Africa were defeated. In many cases Muslim populations have become minority citizens and subjects in societies dominated by non-Muslim peoples.

In almost all Muslim regions colonial rule brought new elites to the fore. Political power was taken from the hands of old-regime elites and transferred to a new stratum of military, bureaucratic, or landowning intelligentsia, and in some countries, in a later generation, to upwardly mobile, modern-educated, middle- and lower-class intellectuals, technicians, and soldiers. In a limited number of cases the economic changes induced by European penetration promoted new strata of merchants, commercial farmers, and industrial workers. All of these new groups and classes, however, were at first very small in size, for European influences had not yet reached the masses. Nonetheless, the new elites were the vanguard of the modernization of their societies.

These elites generated two principal responses to European pressures. One was the response of the political elites and of newly formed intelligentsias trained in Western techniques and enamored of Western cultural values and accomplishments. They favored Islamic modernist or secular nationalist concepts of the future of Muslim societies, and tended to redefine Islam to make it consistent with European forms of the state and economy. The second response came from tribal leaders, merchants, and commercial farmers led by ʿulamaʾ and Sufis, who espoused a reorganization of Muslim communities and the reform of individual behavior in terms of fundamental religious principles. It is noteworthy that whatever the exact form of European economic and political penetration all the Muslim elites had a political or cultural orientation and tended to define the problems of European intervention in sociocultural rather than economic terms.

The Muslim response of course differed from place to place. In the Ottoman regions, Turkey, Egypt, the Arab fertile crescent, and Tunisia, the dominant and indeed almost exclusive indigenous response was that of the established political elites and the political, technical, and literary intelligentsia who rose out of the political classes. In these regions European influence was primarily diplomatic, commercial, and educational. The rivalry of the European powers in the nineteenth century allowed the Ottoman empire to survive, but made it dependent upon British and Russian diplomatic pressures and later upon German military advisers and investors. The empire was also exposed to European commercial penetration. European traders extracted raw materials, and introduced European manufactures in competition with indigenous merchants and artisans. Europeans stimulated the production of cash crops such as grain, dried fruit, and cotton in Anatolia, silk in the Lebanon, cotton in Egypt, and olive oil in Tunisia, and generally depressed the handicrafts and manufacturing industries. Europeans also commonly invested in railroads, mining, and agriculture. European states and banks lent large sums to the Ottoman empire, Egypt, and Tunisia, and in each country eventually established a foreign fiscal administration. In Egypt and Tunisia these proved to be the basis for the creation of European protectorates. One other common outcome was the promotion of Christian and Jewish middlemen in the trade between Europe and the Muslim countries and to depress the opportunities of Muslim merchants. In the Ottoman empire, European competition weakened the Muslim bourgeoisie and helped concentrate economic power in the hands of the state elites. In general, economic changes were limited to the level of production and the distribution of income, but did not induce structural changes in the economy or far-reaching changes in class structure.

In these regions the response of the political elites and intelligentsias went through a cycle of several generations. In late eighteenth-century Palestine, the early nineteenth-century Ottoman empire and Egypt, and mid-nineteenth-century Tunisia, the political elites sought to reorganize their military forces, centralize and rationalize bureaucratic administration, and promote economic activities which would increase state revenues. Political elites also recognized the need to create new schools to educate modern professional and administrative personnel. In the next "generation," Ottoman, Egyptian, and Tunisian reformers realized the connections between a strong state and a productive and socially integrated society, and introduced social, legal, and educational programs which undermined the traditional roles of the religious elites and created the prototypes of modern judicial and educational systems.

The formation of new intelligentsias was the direct result of the state reform programs, but the circumstances of their formation differed. In the Ottoman case, a new "generation" of Western-educated physicians, engineers, army and navy officers, and administrators was the product of Ottoman professional schools and of studies in Europe. This Western-educated elite was partially absorbed into state service, but many of them found careers in law, journalism, and literary activities, turned against the entrenched elites, and attempted to win control of the state.

In Egypt and the fertile crescent countries, the formation of the new intelligentsia took different paths. The reform program in Egypt was unusual in the degree to which the state attempted to control the Egyptian economy. Muhammad ʿAli (1805–48) improved irrigation, stimulated cotton production, created trading monopolies, and invested in factories to produce military supplies. In Egypt, extensive economic change created a new landowning and bureaucratic class whose scions become officials, lawyers, journalists, and politicians in the late nineteenth century. With the establishment of British rule in 1882, the domestic elites lost control of the state and were forced into lower bureaucratic functions, the liberal professions, and journalism, and from these positions formed a national movement opposed to British rule.

In the Arab fertile crescent, European political influence and commercial penetration did not lead to structural and political changes until after World War I, but educational and literary influences in the middle and latter part of the nineteenth century promoted an Arab cultural renaissance and the birth of Arab literary nationalism. In Lebanon and Syria the new intelligentsia was in part the direct product of European and modernized late Ottoman education. The formation of dependent colonial states in 1920 provoked the coalescence of an opposition intelligentsia which included Ottoman and Western-educated soldiers and officials, landowners, religious notables, and sometimes tribal chiefs and merchants. By the 1930s and 1940s further education and development created a new generation of soldiers, technocrats, and journalists coming from middle- and lower-middle-class backgrounds who would rival the first generation of national leaders.

Tunisia went through a similar developmental sequence. Before the establishment of the French protectorate in 1881 the principal reaction to European economic domination came from state officials who attempted to modernize and rationalize the Tunisian regime. After the establishment of the French protectorate successive generations of Western- and modern-Muslim-educated Tunisians took the lead in resisting European control and demanding political rights. From approximately 1890 to 1920 domestic leadership was provided by government officials, reformist ʿulamaʾ, and French-educated notables. In 1930s and after, a new generation of Arab-French-educated upwardly mobile intellectuals, coming largely from provincial small-town, middle- and lower-class milieus, took the lead in the movement for Tunisian independence.

In all of these cases, ʿulamaʾ and merchants played only a secondary role.

ᶜUlamaᵓ were auxiliaries or participants in the early phase of national movements in Egypt, Syria, and Tunisia but were soon superseded by the Western-educated intelligentsias. Not until the 1930s did structural changes in the economy or sufficiently far-reaching changes in class structure generate a politically significant merchant or working class which could play an important political role. In no case did the new milieus disturb the dominance of the political intelligentsias.

In other Muslim regions similar intelligentsias came into being without the mediation of the old-regime state elites and internal programs of reform, but as a result of direct European rule, the displacement of former political elites from their governing positions, and their subordination to colonial administrators. In India, British control deprived the Muslim elites of political power, generated economic changes that weakened the grip of Muslim landlords on rural revenues, and threatened to undermine Muslim culture. In response, the displaced Muslim political elite transformed itself into a modern intelligentsia. Under the leadership of Sayyid Ahmad Khan (1817–98), they founded the college at Aligarh and defined a modern Islamic education to train a new generation of officials, lawyers, and journalists. After the turn of the century Aligarh graduates became the leaders of Muslim resistance to British rule and ultimately the proponents of Pakistan.

In Indonesia, Dutch rule similarly transformed the historic ruling classes, the priyayi, into subordinate functionaries of Dutch administration. The Dutch themselves provided the former elites with a Western professional education in order to generate the Indonesian cadres who were needed to maintain Dutch administration. From Dutch-sponsored colleges and technical, legal, and medical schools came the officials and intellectuals who became the advocates of Indonesian national independence.

In almost all Muslim countries politicians, displaced politicians, would-be politicians, professionals, technicians, and intellectuals trained in Western techniques sought to define new political ideologies for the development of their societies. In successive generations the political elites and intelligentsias adopted Islamic modernist, secular nationalist, and sometimes socialist conceptions of national transformation.

Islamic modernism was the nineteenth-century doctrine of Muslim political elites and intelligentsias, and must be distinguished from Islamic reformism, which was a doctrine of the ᶜulamaᵓ. The essential principle of modernism was that the defeat of Muslims at the hands of European powers had revealed their vulnerability, and that the restoration of their political power required them to borrow European military techniques, centralize state power, modernize their economies and provide a modern education for their elites. It meant that the medieval forms of Islamic civilization had to be repudiated but not that Islam itself was to be denied. Rather Islam was to be reconstructed on its own inherent, but neglected, principles of rationality, ethical activism, and patriotism.

The modernist point of view was first espoused by the Young Ottomans in the 1860s and 1870s. While committed to the principles of Islam, they called upon the endangered Ottoman regime to transform itself into a constitutional government and to promote a new social morality and revived culture based on a simplified Turkish language. Similarly, in India Sayyid Ahmad Khan argued that the survival of Indian Muslims under British rule required the education of a new generation of Muslim leaders loyal to the principles of Islam but adapted to the political and scientific culture of the modern world. While the Ottoman and Indian intelligentsias were concerned with local situations, Jamal al-Din al-Afghani (1839–97), proselytized for an international union of Muslim peoples committed to the modernization of Islam and to political unity in the face of colonial oppression. Islamic modernism, then, was the ideology of elites who were concerned with the restoration of state power but who cared for the indigenous social and cultural bases of power.

The commitment of the intelligentsias to Islamic modernism was followed by a turn to secular nationalism. In the Ottoman empire the Young Turks succeeded the Young Ottomans. In reaction to the pan-Islamic policies of Sultan ʿAbd al-Hamid II (1876–1908) they turned from an Islamic modernist to a secular constitutionalist position. In Tunisia, the first-generation elites blended Islamic modernist and secular orientations, but were followed in the 1930s by a revived independence movement articulated mainly in secular nationalist terms. In the Arab countries, at the end of World War I, the Damascus notables changed their emphasis from an Islamic to an Arab orientation. In Egypt, the first generation of modernist intelligentsia was superseded by secular liberal political parties. In India the Aligarh graduates were secular and modernist in lifestyle and personal religious orientation, but for reasons peculiar to the subcontinent developed a commitment to the formation of a "Muslim" national state. Only in Indonesia did the priyayi elites bypass the Islamic modernist phase and enter directly into a secular nationalist literary and political opposition to Dutch rule. In Indonesia, the shallow integration of Islamic values into the historic cultural orientation of the political elite helps to explain the immediate adoption of secular nationalism. In general, Young Turks, Arab nationalists, pan-Turkish intellectuals, Malay aristocrats, and others set aside the Muslim dimension of their political and cultural heritage to espouse the formation of secular national types of modern society. In Algeria, whose migrant workers in France and rural migrants to Algerian towns formed the popular base of Algerian national movements, and in Indonesia where the workers' movement and the Communist party were particularly strong, nationalism was blended with socialist conceptions of state control of the economy.

Nationalism came to be the preferred doctrine of the political elites and modern-educated intelligentsias for several reasons. Foremost was a Western education. Though opposed to colonial rule the first- and second-generation intelligentsias were raised in the intense glow of self-confident European supremacy and absorbed the convictions of their colonial rulers and instructors. National and secular symbols were also particularly meaningful to a segment of society which had been uprooted from local affiliations and cast into a world of cosmopolitan education and state-centered political movements. An independent national state was the only potential homeland for people who no longer belonged to their old communities and for whom colonial political societies could only offer subordinate positions.

There were also tactical reasons for the adoption of secular nationalism as the ideology of political intelligentsias. The nationalist position helped differentiate the new segments of the intelligentsia from the established elites, and could serve as a mobilizing symbol in the competition for the support of other uprooted strata of society and as a claim to leadership of the masses. In the Ottoman empire Young Turks used the new ideology against the pan-Islamic claims of the Sultan and in opposition to more conservative and entrenched Ottoman officials. In Lebanon and Syria nationalism was the preferred position of Christians in a predominantly Muslim society. In Tunisia, Arab-French-educated intellectuals used nationalism against the established reformist-oriented elites of Tunis. In Indonesia, priyayi nationalism developed partially in opposition to Muslim merchant reformist movements. Nationalism also served better than Islamic modernism to symbolize the ambiguous relation of Muslim intelligentsias to colonial political domination. On the one hand, secularism and nationalism signified that the intelligentsias were the advanced elements of their society and justified their claims to participate in colonial regimes. On the other hand, nationalism also legitimized resistance to foreign rule in the eyes of Europeans as well as Muslim peoples.

While political elites and intelligentsias became committed to Islamic modernist, secularist, and nationalist concepts of society, an alternative set of responses came from the ʿulamaʾ and allied merchant, artisan, and tribal milieus. In many Muslim countries the ʿulamaʾ opposed both colonial influences and the state intelligentsias. In Iran and Indonesia the opposition came from the conventional scholars. In Iran, Russian territorial expansion and Russian and British economic penetration in the form of monopolies and concessions, investments in mining, irrigation, and banks and heavy loans to the Shah, met with a double response. While the state elites made attempts to modernize the military and administrative apparatus and, through new professional schools and the education of Iranians abroad, to create a small intelligentsia, the Shiᶜi ᶜulamaᵓ protested against Russian military expansion, foreign economic penetration, and the military, administrative, and educational reform programs of the monarchy. At the beginning of the twentieth century, a coalition of ᶜulamaᵓ, merchants, artisans, and intellectuals overthrew the monarchy and established a short-lived constitutional regime. In Iran the heritage of a weak state and the strength of ᶜulamaᵓ, tribal, and guild organization made possible a competition between alternative conceptions of an Iranian response to colonialism and an open struggle for control of the state.

In Java, where the political elites became subordinate collaborators in Dutch rule, anti-colonial resistance was led by rural ᶜulamaᵓ united by the Sufi brotherhoods. In Banten (western Java) they led peasant riots, protests, and rebellions against Dutch rule and their priyayi overlords. By contrast with the Ottoman empire, where conventional ᶜulamaᵓ were generally subordinate to state elites and did not play an important role in resistance or adaptation to colonial rule, in the Indies ᶜulamaᵓ-led resistance was widespread.

More commonly, ᶜulamaᵓ resistance was expressed in reformist terms. Islamic reformism had its origin in the seventeenth and eighteenth centuries and preceded European domination. In Arabia and Cairo informal ᶜulamaᵓ and Sufi study groups espoused a purified version of Islamic belief and practice based on the study of the Quran, hadith, and law combined with Sufi asceticism. The imitation of the Prophet Muhammad became the ideal of a Muslim life. These reformers, aided by the conviction that God was punishing Muslims for failure to heed his will, opposed the tolerant attitude of Muslim states toward non-Muslim peoples and cultures, sought to abolish saint worship and the more florid religious cults and ceremonies, and to dispel superstitious or magical beliefs and practices. The reformers espoused instead a religion of personal discipline, moral responsibility, and commitment to a universal Muslim society. They were committed, if need be, to militant action to destroy corrupt versions of Islam and to create a just and truly Islamic community.

From Arabia and Cairo, traveling scholars, students and Sufis, merchants and craftsmen carried the reformist doctrine to India, Indonesia, and North and West Africa. The reformist discourse appealed to two milieus. First, it appealed to fragmented lineage and village societies whom it offered Islamic authority and leadership for the unification of diverse groups in the struggle against local rivals and state regimes. Thus reformism could be used as an ideology of mobilization for conquests, the formation of new states, and for anti-colonial resistance.

The earliest example of a reformist movement in a pastoral and tribal society was the Wahhabi movement in Arabia. Born out of an alliance of a reform preacher with the Saʿudi family, the Wahhabis united diverse tribal groups into a movement which conquered most of Arabia. In West Africa, Islamic reform had both indigenous roots and international Muslim connections. While eighteenth- and nineteenth-century reformist movements in the Senegambian region represented a local tradition of Muslim resistance to non-Muslim political elites, the Fulani conquests, led by ʿUthman Don Fodio (1754–1817), who established the Caliphate of Sokoto (1809–1903) in the region between the Niger and Lake Chad, had mixed local and Arabian inspiration. International reformist influences introduced by the Tijani order spread in Algeria, Morocco, and West Africa, and interacting with local forces eventually inspired the formation of the regime of al-Hajj ʿUmar (1794?–1864) in the regions from the Niger to Senegal. In Libya, the Sanusi helped to unify tribal peoples and created a loosely organized confederation of tribes and oases which served to mediate disputes and to organize trade. Reformism also became the basis of the local struggle against colonialism in the Caucasus and Inner Asia, where the Naqshbandi order became the bearer of new religious inspiration and ultimately of political resistance to both Russian and Chinese expansion. In the Indian Northwest Frontier, Sayyid Ahmad Barelwi tried to organize the Pathans against the British and the Sikhs on the basis of reformist teaching.

Secondly, reformism took root in agricultural and urban merchant milieus, in direct response to European political intervention and to economic changes that promoted new economic classes. In Bengal the reformist Faraʾidi movement was associated with the introduction of British rule and the rise of Hindu and British landlords. In northern India, British rule and the collapse of the Mughal empire led to reform movements in urban and small-town middle-class milieus. Based at Deoband, reformed ʿulamaʾ created throughout northern India a network of colleges which trained cadres to proselytize, educate, and make true Muslims out of Indian believers. Deoband and subsequent reformist movements in India contributed heavily to the creation of a sense of Muslim identity throughout the subcontinent.

Map 29. Islamic reform and resistance movements: eighteenth and nineteenth centuries.

Table 16. *Muslim reform and renewal movements, eighteenth to twentieth century*

Arabia
Reform teaching in Mecca and Medina
Wahhabiya – founded by Muhammad b. ʿAbd. al-Wahhab (1703–92); allied with Ibn Saʿud to create Saʿudi state
Idrisiya – founded in Mecca by Ahmad b. Idris (d. 1837)

Caucasus
Naqshbandiya – 1785–present, anti-Russian resistance

Inner Asia
Naqshbandiya – reform-oriented Sufi tariqa leads Muslim resistance to Russia and China
New teaching, 1761–1877 – offshoot of Naqshbandiya, late eighteenth- and late nineteenth-century resistance to Chinese rule
Khwajas and Yaʿqub Beg – holy Muslim lineage, formerly rulers of Kashgar, attempt to establish a Muslim state, defeated by China in 1878
Yunnan, 1856–73 – rebellion against Chinese rule and effort to establish a Muslim state
usul-i jadid – Kazan, Crimean, and Bukharan intellectuals, notably Ismaʿil Gasprinskii (1851–1914), sponsor new schools, combined Muslim and Russian education; modernization of Muslim peoples

India

Shah Waliallah (1703–62)

Shah ʿAbd al-ʿAziz (1746–1824)

Muhammad Ismaʿil (1781–1831)

Sayyid Ahmad Barelwi (1785–1831)
unites Pathans to resist British and Sikhs
|
Patna-Maulana Walayat ʿAli
Maulana Karamat   ahl-i hadith
ʿAli
|
Delhi School
|
Deoband – founded 1876. Muslim
college combined hadith studies
and Sufism and spawned
satellite schools
|
Tablighi Islam – founded 1927 by
Mawlana Muhammad Ilyas

Titu Mir (Bengal)

Meccan influences
|
Faraʾidi (Bengal);
1818–45 anti-Hindu
and anti-British

Southeast Asia
Padri Movement – Sumatra 1803–37
Dipanegara leads revolt on Java, 1825–30
Banten, West Java revolts, nineteenth century
Kaum Muda – Sumatra and Malaya movement for reform and modernization
Acheh – 1873–1908 ʿulamaʾ-led resistance to Dutch occupation
Muhammadiya – 1912; educational and social reform

Egypt and North Africa
Salafiya – founded by Muhammad ʿAbduh (d. 1905), influenced islah and national movements in North Africa; Tunisia, Young Tunisians; Algeria, Ben Badis; Morocco, ʿAllal al-Fasi
ʿAbd al-Qadir – Qadiriya chieftain attempts to establish Algerian State, defeated by the French

Continued on next page

Table 16. — *Continued*

Rahmaniya – religious brotherhood uses networks of zawiyas in Algeria and Tunisia to resist French occupation

Tijaniya – reform Sufi order inspires West and North African jihad and resistance movements

Khalwatiya – reformist Sufi brotherhood

Sanusiya – reformist brotherhood creates "state" structure in Libya, founded by Muhammad b. ʿAli al-Sanusi (d. 1859); resists Italian occupation

East Africa

Idrisiya spawned Rashidiya in Algeria; Amirghania in Sudan and Nubia; Sanusiya in Libya

Sudan – Sammaniya gives rise to Muhammad b. Ahmad al-Mahdi (d. 1898)

Somalia – Muhammad ʿAbdallah Hasan leads resistance to British, 1899–1920

West Africa

Jihad of ʿUthman Don Fodio (1754–1817) – Northern Nigerian reformist opposition to Hausa states

Sokoto Caliphate (1809–1903) and related jihads in Adamawa and Masina

Al-Hajj ʿUmar (1794?–1864)–jihad state in region of Mali and Senegal

Bundu, Futa Jallon, and Futa Toro, reform Muslim states in the Senegambian region

Ma Ba–nineteenth-century jihad in Senegal

Samory (1860s–98)–Muslim adventurer founds West African State

In Southeast Asia there have been successive waves of reformism. The early nineteenth-century Padri movement in Sumatra was associated with the commercialization of coffee production. Coffee farmers were receptive to the influence of the reformist pilgrims and scholars returning to Sumatra from Mecca and Medina, who launched a movement to Islamize Muslim villages. At the end of the nineteenth century reformism became the creed of the Indo-Malay merchant communities of Singapore and other Southeast Asian ports. Enlarged world trade, pilgrimage, the creation of a capitalist plantation economy in Sumatra and Malaya producing rubber, coffee, tobacco, pepper, sugar, pineapples, and palm oil for export, the formation of a plantation and mining proletariat, commercialization, urbanization, and other forces of socio-economic change broke down traditional family and social structures, favored the growth of a Muslim merchant class in Singapore and other island ports, and of commercial planters in Sumatra and Malaya, and led to the adoption of Muslim reformism as the doctrine of new communities. These and similar milieus were the basis of the early twentieth-century Muhammadiya movement in Indonesia and the Kaum Muda (Young Group) in Malaya. In Inner Asia, merchants and intelligentsia adopted *usul-i jadid* (New Methods) in response to Russian domination, and the need to revitalize a threatened Muslim community.

Reformism could, of course, be blended with Muslim modernism. An

Egyptian scholar, Muhammad ʿAbduh (1849–1905), combined the reformist principles – return to the Quran and the sayings of the Prophet, the right of independent judgment in religious matters, abandonment of a stifling conformity to outmoded tradition, and opposition to cultic Sufi practices – with a modernist responsiveness to the political and cultural pressures of Europe. This blend of modernist and reformist thought inspired the Salafiya movement in Egypt, the Arab Middle East, and North Africa. In North Africa the Salafiya movement became the principal ideological expression of the merchant bourgeoisie of Fez and other Moroccan towns in the 1920s and appealed in Algeria to urban petite bourgeoisie and uprooted rural migrants. In Morocco and Algeria reformism transcended specific class milieus and became for a time the ideology of national identity and resistance to French rule. These movements were devoted to the reform of education as a correction to shrine and saint worship and magical religious practices, and were committed to the need for adjustment to modern economic and technological conditions. They were latently, and sometimes actively, political, in that they cultivated a consciousness of the need for autonomy from European powers if the vitality of Islamic states and societies was to be restored.

Reformism, then, was the political and moral response of ʿulamaʾ, tribal, and urban communities to the transformation of the traditional structures of Muslim societies and to the threat of European political, economic and cultural domination. It had its origin in the seventeenth and eighteenth centuries in response, not to European pressures, but to purely internal conditions, and it was later adapted to anti-colonial resistance. Reformism appealed to tribal societies seeking political unification and to merchant and farmer milieus undergoing commercialization and urbanization where reformist doctrine provided a cultural basis for larger-scale communities. Though often politically passive, reformism contributed to the psychological mobilization of colonized peoples and became the vehicle for the reconstruction of Muslim political identity among subnational populations in the Caucasus, Inner Asia, India, and Indonesia and the basis for national movements in Algeria and Morocco.

Thus the two principal responses to the breakdown of Muslim societies and to European penetration came from the political intelligentsias and the ʿulamaʾ, and represented, despite modifications, a striking continuity in the structures of Islamic societies. In societies with a strong heritage of state domination over the ʿulamaʾ, such as the Ottoman empire and Turkey, the political intelligentsia led the way, unopposed, to national independence; but in the more pluralist Muslim societies colonial rule precipitated a multi-sided struggle for power waged against the colonial rulers and amongst the several

Islamic modernist secularist, nationalist, socialist, and Muslim traditional and reformist elites. In societies with a more open political structure, such as Iran, foreign pressures promoted a limited modernization of the state and collusion between government elites and foreign business interests, but it damaged Iranian merchant and artisan interests and ʿulamaʾ cultural security, and provoked a coalition of ʿulamaʾ, merchant, and intellectual opposition to foreign encroachment. The result was direct conflict between state and religious elites over Iranian national identity, policies of economic development, and foreign relations.

Similarly, in India the loss of political power, economic dominance, and cultural supremacy to English and Christian rulers provoked a multiple Muslim response. From the displaced political elites, transformed by modern education into an intelligentsia, came a movement for the formation of a national Muslim state in the subcontinent. From reformist ʿulamaʾ came repeated efforts to define the identity of an Indian Muslim population in terms of personal religious values.

Indonesia was also the center of a complex struggle among forces who had different experiences of colonial rule, different class and status interests, different historic variants of Indonesian Islamic culture, and different responses to the problems of colonialism and economic change. In Indonesia, the priyayi were transformed by Dutch education into a secularized intelligentsia who took the lead in the Indonesian nationalist movement while reformism became the preferred ideology of merchants and commercial farmers. In the more traditional, less disrupted parts of Java, ʿulamaʾ (kiyayi) maintained their leadership in the countryside and led peasant resistance against Dutch rule. Indonesian politics before and since independence has been characterized by a struggle for political and ideological power among Indonesian nationalist, reformist Muslim, and conservative Muslim movements.

Algerian society similarly evinced a plural response to French occupation and colonization. In Algeria the French destroyed the traditional society, but in the 1920s and 1930s urbanization and migration to the towns was the basis for the formation of a new Algerian elite. This elite was divided into three segments: the highly assimilated, French-educated Algerians who favored cultural and political assimilation into France and the acceptance of Muslims as citizens of France; reformist ʿulamaʾ who appealed to the petite bourgeoisie of the towns and to certain rural populations and attempted to define an Algerian national identity in Arab and Muslim terms; populist leaders who organized Algerian workers, both at home and in France, into a radical political movement. By the late 1940s all of these movements had failed to make significant progress toward Algerian independence, and a new generation of revolutionary soldiers took the lead in throwing off French colonialism and establishing an independent Algerian state. The new Algerian state nonetheless came to be defined by past elements of Islamic reformism and populist socialism.

Thus, in most Muslim societies the struggle among political intelligentsias, ʿulamaʾ, and other elites has given political and cultural definition to modern Muslim national states. In the ensuing chapters I shall review the history of each major Muslim region to examine the impact of colonial rule, the course of economic and social change, the transformation of Islamic religious beliefs, institutions and collectivities, and the role of Islamic modernist, nationalist, and reformist movements in the formation of contemporary Muslim states. In the concluding chapter I shall examine the changing relations of state regimes, religious institutions, and Islamic cultural orientations.

NATIONALISM AND ISLAM IN THE MIDDLE EAST

CHAPTER 22

IRAN: STATE AND RELIGION IN THE MODERN ERA

Modern Iran inherited from the Safavid period (1501–1722) the pattern of state, religious, and tribal (uymaq) institutions which would shape its history to the present day. The Qajar dynasty which ruled Iran from 1779 to 1925 resembled its Safavid predecessors in that it was a weakly centralized regime faced with strong provincial tribal forces, and an increasingly independent religious establishment. In the nineteenth century, European conquests, cultural influence, and above all economic penetration polarized state and society and led to the constitutional revolution of 1905, in which a coalition of intellectuals, ʿulamaʾ, merchants, and artisans attempted to create a parliamentary regime. The Pahlavi period from 1925 to 1979 virtually repeated the earlier history. The Pahlavis sought to centralize state power, and modernize the Iranian economy and society, and again provoked ʿulamaʾ-led nationwide resistance in the name of Islam. For the last 200 years the struggle between the state and the ʿulamaʾ has been a principal feature of Iranian society.

The modern cycle began with the Qajar regime. The Qajars came to power after a period of anarchy and tribal (uymaq) struggles to control the Iranian state. Their regime was never consolidated. Their armies were composed of a small Turkoman bodyguard and Georgian slaves; the central administration was a court government too little developed to effectively tax the country. The provinces they ruled were fragmented into innumerable tribal, ethnic, and local factions headed by their own chieftains. Khans and Ilkhans governed their own tribes. A combination of formal governmental appointments, control of land, rights to collect taxes, and the power to administer justice and mediate disputes made tribal chiefs virtually independent of the state. The authority of Khans was by no means absolute since it also depended upon the ability to rally support from lesser chiefs who had to be coerced, cajoled, bought off, or otherwise made allies of the paramount Khans, but it was often sufficient to assure their autonomy. Town quarters and guilds also had a degree of political autonomy. The new regime, moreover, never captured the aura of legitimacy which had inspired Safavid rule and never managed to fully establish its control. Effective local power remained in the hands of tribal chiefs, officials, and landowners, while the Qajars maintained their suzerainty by exploiting the rivalries of lesser chiefs.

While the Qajar state maintained a precarious suzerainty, the power of the religious establishment was enhanced. In the course of the eighteenth and nineteenth centuries, the ʿulamaʾ of Iran achieved an unprecedented degree of autonomy, a strong leadership, and organizational coherence. The religious authority of the ʿulamaʾ, known as mujtahids or interpreters of the religious law, was vastly enhanced by the claim that they had the right to exercise independent judgment and to make new interpretations in religious matters based on their spiritual and intellectual attainments. The authority of the religious scholars was also enhanced by the claim that the most pious and spiritual leaders were, in the absence of the imam, the true leaders of the Muslim community and that it was a religious obligation of ordinary people to take them as their absolute spiritual guides (*marjaʿi-taqlid*). The Shiʿi shrines, ceremonies of *taʿziya*, the mourning of Husayn, and the passion plays which commemorated his martyrdom helped to capture the allegiance of the Iranian populace. Furthermore, these claims to an enhanced religious authority, wrested from a weak political regime, were backed up by the formation of a loose system of communications which bound together the ʿulamaʾ of Iran and the spiritual centers of Shiʿism in Iraq. The Iraqi shrines gave Iranian Shiʿism a centralized leadership outside of the physical and political control of the Qajar monarchy.

The ʿulamaʾ also consolidated their ties with the common people through the administration of justice, trust funds, and charities, and by presiding over the prayers and ceremonies marking birth, marriage, and death. Their ties with the bazaar population of artisans, workers, and merchants were especially important. A secure financial foundation was built up on the basis of both the contributions of their followers and the endowment of state lands. All of these factors were conducive to the construction of a relatively coherent and politically independent religious community in Iran. It was not quite a church, because it lacked a formal hierarchy and regular internal organization, but it was nonetheless a partially autonomous and nationwide body which was capable of cohesive religious and political action.

The relationship of the ʿulamaʾ to the Qajar regime was a subtle one. Despite the weakness of the regime, there was good historical precedent for the collaboration of state and ʿulamaʾ elites. The ʿulamaʾ were deeply affected by a long tradition of quietism and rejection of active involvement in political affairs. Their ethos called for concentration on theological and religious matters and deference to the state authority in all other respects, and they depended upon the state for appointments to office, salaries, grants of land, and endowments for shrines and schools. Fath ʿAli Shah (1797–1834), whose power was precariously based on tribal forces, reconstructed the shrines, appointed ʿulamaʾ to official positions, and respected them as mediators between the government and the populace. He tolerated the independence of leading ʿulamaʾ notables, such as Sayyid Muhammad Baqir of Isfahan, whose power was based on substantial landed wealth, the control of religious endowments, and the support of numerous strong-arm men. Fath ʿAli aided in the suppression of Sufism, and joined the ʿulamaʾ in opposition to "heretical" doctrines. Fath ʿAli's reign, lacking political confidence and effective power, was characterized by deference to the religious elites. His policy had the double effect of binding them to the regime and preparing the way for their later autonomy.

European intervention significantly modified the position of the Qajar regime and heightened the implicit tensions between the state and the ʿulamaʾ. European encroachment upon Iran came first in the form of conquest and the creation of spheres of influence by rival European powers. In the course of the eighteenth and nineteenth centuries the Russians seized control of northwestern Iran. The treaty of Gulistan (1813) confirmed the loss to Russia of Georgia, Darband, Baku, Shirvan, and other parts of Armenia. In 1826 the Russians seized Tabriz. By the treaty of Turkmanchai (1828) Russia obtained Armenia, control of the Caspian Sea, and a favored position in Iranian trade. Between 1864 and 1885 a new wave of Russian expansion culminated in the seizure of Iran's central Asian provinces. Russian conquests were counterbalanced by the British, who assumed control over Afghanistan to protect their Indian empire. Iran, which itself aspired to Afghanistan, was defeated in 1856 at Herat and was forced to recognize the independence of Afghanistan and to make other political and commercial concessions. The net result of British policy was to create a Russian sphere of domination in Inner Asia and the Caucasus and a British sphere in Afghanistan. Significantly, the powers did not take Iran under direct colonial rule.

After 1857 the primary form of British and Russian penetration was economic. In 1872 the Iranian government gave extensive concessions to Baron de Reuter. De Reuter was given control of customs revenues for 24 years, a monopoly of rail and tramway construction, exclusive rights to mine numerous minerals and metals, to construct canals and irrigation works, and rights of first refusal for a national bank, roads, telegraphs, and mills in return for royalties and a share of profits for the Shahs. In 1889 an Imperial Bank of Persia was founded under British auspices, and in 1890, a British firm was conceded a monopoly of the Iranian tobacco industry including both domestic sales and exports. Russia made compensating economic gains. Caspian fisheries were turned over to Russia (1888), and a discount Bank of Persia was formed under Russian sponsorship (1891). In the course of the 1890s Russia became the primary investor in loans to the Shahs. Finally in 1907 an Anglo-Russian Agreement divided the country into two spheres of influence – a northern and a southeastern zone – with a neutral buffer between. In order to calm their own disputes in anticipation of a general European war, the powers allowed Iran to remain nominally independent and its monarchy intact, but effectively assumed control of the country.

As in the Ottoman empire, European political and economic intervention stimulated the Qajars to modernize and strengthen the state apparatus. Western influence created a vogue in upper-class government circles for reform of Iran's military and governmental institutions along Western lines. A new military corps was proposed in 1826, but was defeated by the opposition of the ʿulamaʾ. Nasir al-Din (1848–96) organized a military system that required each town or village to supply a quota of soldiers or to pay the equivalent of their salaries. He also tried to break the dependence of the regime on local governors, tribal chiefs, and landlords and to formalize a government administration along Russian lines. In 1851 the *Dar al-Funun*, or technical college, was created to train army and civil officers. In the latter part of the century missionary schools brought in Western techniques. Between 1878 and 1880 Austrian and Russian advisers helped the Iranians reorganize the cavalry and form the Cossack Brigade.

The reforms also brought into being a new stratum of Islamic modernist thinkers and Westernized intellectuals who favored the modernization of Iran as the only effective way to resist foreign control and improve the conditions of life for the mass of its people. This stratum included people educated in Europe, high-ranking government officials in contact with foreign powers, and various religious minorities influenced by radical movements in Russian-occupied Transcaucasia. European commercial activities also generated a small Iranian bourgeoisie which prospered from the roles of middlemen in the exchanges between Europe and Iran.

Both the governmental and intellectual reformers, however, had little

impact on the country as a whole. Government reorganization in a decentralized country was not adequate to make up for the inherent barriers to a
strong central state. Intellectual reforms reached a small milieu of court officials
and Western-educated Iranian journalists but did not touch the mass of the
population. The reform program faltered because the rulers were themselves
afraid that they might compromise their authority. Dependent on British and
Russian help to maintain their regime, they had little incentive to strike out on
their own. They found it difficult to raise money, and when they could raise
it, being used to thinking of state revenues as a form of private property, were
unable to use it in the public interest. Furthermore, tribal groups resisted
centralization of military power. The ʿulamaʾ opposed secularization. The
Russians hindered railway construction. In the face of such pressures, Qajar
reforms were inadequate for the centralization of state power and insufficient
to oppose foreign encroachment.

At the same time European intervention provoked resistance. Westernized
intellectuals objected to the corruption of the regime and to their exclusion
from power. Merchants and artisans, hurt by European competition and state-
sponsored monopolies, and ʿulamaʾ, anxious over the rise of alien influences,
were pushed into outright opposition to Qajar policies. The ʿulamaʾ became
the leading opponents of foreign influence and of the state itself as a collaborator with foreign powers. As early as 1826, the effort to establish a
Western-type army regiment along Ottoman lines provoked ʿulamaʾ opposition, and in 1828 the Russian occupation of the Caucasus led to a nationwide
agitation in favor of jihad. Muhammad Shah (1834–48) exacerbated the tension between the state and the ʿulamaʾ by pursuing a deliberately anti-ʿulamaʾ
religious policy, and by continuing the effort to adopt Western methods of
government and warfare. In 1840 he broke the power of Sayyid Muhammad
Baqir in Isfahan. The centralization of state power threatened the ʿulamaʾ both
as provincial notables and as religious leaders.

The tension between the state and the ʿulamaʾ rose higher in the reign of
Nasir al-Din Shah under the ministry of Mirza Taqi Khan, Amir Kabir. The
government tried to strengthen the state by limiting the jurisdiction of the
ʿulamaʾ and by establishing new courts. It restricted the right of sanctuary in
mosques and shrines, introduced measures to control endowments, reduced
allowances, and sponsored the formation of secular schools in competition
with ʿulamaʾ schools. The state also tried to abolish the taʿziya.

By the middle decades of the nineteenth century, the ʿulamaʾ found themselves beset not only by the toughened attitude of the state, but by the rise
of new religious movements. The yearning for religious certainty, inherent in

Shi'ism, broke out again in the preaching of Sayyid 'Ali Muhammad, who proclaimed that the believers were not in fact cut off from the hidden imam, but that there was always a human representative interpreting his will. In 1844 he declared himself to be that man, the *Bab* (gateway), and later proclaimed himself the true imam. This claim swept away the authority of the 'ulama', whom he denounced as venal and corrupt servants of the state. Sayyid 'Ali Muhammad further announced a new scripture, the Bayan, which superseded the Quran. His teachings included a powerful social message calling for justice, protection of property against taxes and confiscation, and freedom of trade and profit. He inspired rebellions in several Iranian provinces, but his movement was defeated and Sayyid 'Ali Muhammad himself was killed in 1852. His followers divided into two groups. One group, called the Azalis, maintained their intense hostility to the Qajars and were active in the 1905 revolution. The second group followed Baha'ollah who in 1863 declared himself a prophet and founded the Baha'i religion. From Baha'ism came a pacifist liberal outlook which would later appeal to elements of the Westernized business classes. The declaration of new religious authority was thus a way to generate "modernized" versions of Islam. For the 'ulama', the only compensating development was the emergence of Shaykh Murtada Ansari as the sole marja'i-taqlid, or spiritual leader who requires the obedience of all Shi'a. For the first time the religious leadership was concentrated in a single person.

The tension between the state and the 'ulama' came to a head over the De Reuter concessions. The concessions were bitterly opposed by the 'ulama' as a sellout of Iranian interests to foreigners, and by the Russians as a sellout of Iran to the British. Under pressure they were canceled in 1873. The Reuter agitation foreshadowed the struggle over the tobacco monopoly conceded to a British company in 1890. In 1891 and 1892 a coalition of 'ulama', merchants, liberal intellectuals, and officers led popular demonstrations and organized a national boycott of the tobacco monopoly. 'Ulama'-led demonstrations were held in Shiraz, Isfahan, Tabriz, and Mashhad. A fatwa, or judicial opinion, issued by Mirza Husayn Shirazi, who had succeeded Shaykh Murtada, led to a nationwide boycott of tobacco products and the eventual dissolution of the monopoly. This opposition was motivated by financial concerns, ideological hostility to foreign intervention, and political interest in resisting the strengthening of the Qajar regime. The 'ulama' were primarily opposed to the intrusion of foreigners, while the merchants were being reduced to the role of intermediary agents and brokers between foreign firms and the Iranian populace. The livelihood of Iranian artisans, cotton cloth makers, and weavers suffered drastically from foreign imports.

The opposition of ʿulamaʾ, merchants, and artisans was reinforced by the small stratum of Westernized intellectuals and Islamic modernist thinkers. Through secret societies, publications, and an extensive campaign of letter writing, they helped provoke and coordinate the resistance to the tobacco monopoly. This coalition merged the century-old hostility of the religious establishment with the opposition of middle-class merchants, artisans, officials, and intellectuals to create the first "national" resistance to the Qajar monarchy.

Peasant resistance, however, was minimal. In Iran, the middle-sized land-owning peasantry, which in many societies has been the basis of resistance to government oppression, was scarcely to be found. Most peasants were tenants and sharecroppers dependent upon their landlords. The isolation of the villages also prevented the development of class consciousness. The peasants of Iran were both too poor and too divided to participate in the insurrectionary movement.

The years between 1892 and 1905 were years of preparation for the culminating struggle between the state and the ʿulamaʾ – the constitutional crisis of 1905–11. While many ʿulamaʾ resumed collaboration with the Qajar monarchy, secret societies formed of intelligentsia, ʿulamaʾ, and merchants carried on an underground agitation. In these years, the traditional religious and economic objections to government policies were merged with constitutional ideas. The existence of European parliamentary states, the formation of the Russian Diet in 1905, and above all, the modernization of the Ottoman empire and Egypt inspired Iranians to rethink the political structure of their country. Liberal and revolutionary newspapers from Russian-held Transcaucasia, circulating in Iran, also helped to promote a new climate of opinion. Popular sovereignty, rule of law, and patriotism were advanced as the principles for a modernized Persian society. Akhund-Zadah (1812–78) proposed a liberal secular society. Malkum Khan (1833–1908), an Armenian converted to Islam and educated in Paris, who served most of his diplomatic and political career as an ambassador in Europe, published the newspaper *Qanun* in London to espouse a modernized Iranian society. Malkum Khan advocated a strong monarchy with an advisory assembly to undertake a program of Westernization and the introduction of a new system of education. He argued that reform was compatible with Islam. ʿAbd al-Rahim Talibov (1834–1911), a merchant who lived much of his life in Russia, also propagandized for a constitutional government and civil freedoms.

The constitutionalist and modernizing reformers were joined by pan-Islamic agitators. Pan-Islamic thinkers presented their views in religious terms though their long-term goal was in fact to modernize Iran. Jamal al-Din al-Afghani and Mirza Aqa Khan Kermani emphasized the political side of Islam as an anti-imperialist doctrine which would help revive national pride and mobilize Muslim peoples to resist Western interference. Liberal ᶜulamaᵓ such as Sayyid Muhammad Tabaᵓtabaᵓi also embraced a Western and secular concept of government.

The treatise called *Admonition and Refinement of the People*, written by Mirza Muhammad Husayn Naᵓini, embodied the position of the liberal ᶜulamaᵓ. Limitations on the authority of the ruler, he argued, are essential to prevent despotism; the best mechanism for controlling rulers would be a national consultative assembly. However, the possible conflicts between Islamic views and Western concepts of constitutional political organization, secular law and Muslim law, equality of citizens and Muslim supremacy over non-Muslims, freedom of speech and the propagation of religious truth, were not explored. Liberal ᶜulamaᵓ adopted constitutionalism partly out of misunderstanding and partly for tactical reasons. Some of them confused the concept of constitutional assembly with the traditional Islamic notion of a court of justice. Others saw constitutionalism as a form of government which limited the power of the state and thereby reduced the prospects for oppression and tyranny. Some ᶜulamaᵓ saw in a constitutional form of government a way of institutionalizing their own authority and hoped to use parliament to gain a voice in the administration of the country. The confusion between constitutional government and traditional forms of consultation, and between institutions to enforce Islamic law and institutions of representative government, allowed the ᶜulamaᵓ to form a coalition with liberals and merchants opposed to the monarchy.

The constitutional agitation came to a head in 1905 and 1906. Tension due to the increasing indebtedness of the Shah to the Russians, Russian support for the Bahaᵓis, and the appointment of a Belgian to the position of Minister of Post and Telegraph, led to protests in the bazaars. Public demands led in 1906 to the convening of a constituent national assembly. Of its members 26 percent were artisan leaders, 15 percent were merchants and 20 percent were ᶜulamaᵓ. The assembly, representing a coalition of ᶜulamaᵓ, merchants and Westernized liberals, created the constitution which remained officially in force until 1979. The new constitution subordinated the Shah to a parliamentary government, but declared Islam to be the official religion of Iran. It committed the government to the enforcement of the Shariᶜa, and created a committee of ᶜulamaᵓ to evaluate the conformity of new legislation with Muslim law.

The promulgation of a new constitution was only the beginning of a protracted struggle. The constitutionalist side was backed by many ᶜulamaᵓ, merchants, artisans, and Bakhtiyari tribesmen and had strong popular support in Tabriz and Isfahan. It was opposed by the Shah, conservative ʿulamaʾ, and wealthy landowners and their clienteles. Bitter battles were fought. In 1907 and 1908 the Shah used the Cossack Brigade to close parliament; the constitutionalists resumed power from 1909 to 1911. In the second constitutional period, the coalition between liberal reformers and ʿulamaʾ began to break up. When the reformers wanted to disestablish Islam, adopt far-reaching programs for redistribution of land, and introduce a new system of secular education, the ʿulamaʾ became disillusioned. In any case, the Russians intervened in 1911 to destroy the new regime and to restore the government of the Shah.

The constitutional crisis of 1905 to 1911 brought into relief some of the fundamental aspects of Iranian Islamic society in the nineteenth century. Throughout the century, many ʿulamaʾ supported the state authority, accepted state pensions, gifts, positions at court or in government service, owned land, and identified with the ruling elites. Others adopted a quietist position out of religious and doctrinal considerations, turned their backs on the corrupt affairs of the world and tried to preserve a measure of religious purity while waiting for the return of the hidden imam. They withdrew from political affairs to concentrate on teaching and worship, judicial administration, and charities. Their primary responsibility was to maintain by teaching, example, and admonition the best possible course of action. However, foreign influences, economic concessions, centralization of power, and state policies which restricted ʿulamaʾ judicial and educational prerogatives provoked their opposition. This opposition was generally directed against specific policies, to compel the regime to fulfill the responsibility of the state for defense of a Muslim way of life. The ʿulamaʾ were not in principle antimonarchical, but were simply concerned that state policies be consistent with Islamic religious norms.

The development of active resistance to state policies was based upon the potential of forming a coalition with other elements of society. The historical weakness of the state and the high degree of organization among ʿulamaʾ, tribes, guilds, and local communities made it possible for many strata in the society to articulate, organize, and carry out revolutionary activities. The emergence of active resistance also depended upon the changing relations between the state and religious leaders. The state position was weakened by non-Muslim tribal and other local competition and by the intervention of Russia and Britain. The ʿulamaʾ position, on the other hand, was strengthened by internal consolidation, by the resolution of questions of authority, and by the assumption of leadership; it led to direct confrontation with the state.

The twentieth century brought a new phase of historical change but one which repeated and sharpened the basic conflict between the state and the religious establishment. While the power of the state was finally consolidated on the basis of internal reforms and even closer dependence upon European and American support, the ʿulamaʾ continued to be the leading element in coalitions opposing state power, foreign influence, and policies contrary to Iranian Islamic values. In the twentieth century the long-term conflict between the state and the ʿulamaʾ was renewed in new ideological, economic, and political conditions.

The modern Iranian state rose out of a period of near-anarchy from 1911 to 1925. During this period foreign intervention reached its peak. In World War I Russian troops were garrisoned in the northern provinces and British troops occupied the south. With the collapse of the Tsarist regime in 1917, all of Iran fell into British hands; the Anglo-Persian treaty of 1919 made Iran a virtual protectorate of Britain. Under the terms of this treaty Britain would train an Iranian army, finance the economic development of the country, and provide technical and managerial advisers. At the same time the Soviet Union supported separatist movements in Jilan and Azarbayjan and communist parties in Tabriz and Tehran. In 1921, however, Iran and the Soviet Union concluded a treaty of friendship on terms very favorable to Iran. The Soviets agreed to withdraw from Jilan and cancel Iranian debts and concessions, and surrendered the special legal privileges afforded foreigners in Iran. The Soviets reserved the Caspian Sea fisheries and the right to intervene if Iran was threatened by another foreign power. Strengthened by the new treaty, Iran denounced the humiliating 1919 treaty with Britain.

Internally Iran was governed by a succession of ineffectual cabinets until Reza Khan, an officer in the Cossack Brigade, came to power as Head of the Army and Minister of Defense. He consolidated his control over the army and the police, defeated tribal and provincial forces, brought most of the country under military control, and in 1925 made himself the Shah of Iran, at once a constitutional monarch and the founder of the Pahlavi dynasty, which lasted from 1925 to 1979.

Under the rule of the Pahlavis a strong centralized government was created for the first time in Iranian history. The state was defined in nationalist ideological terms, and was committed to the implementation, under authoritarian rule, of an ambitious program of economic modernization and cultural Westernization. The centralized state gained control over the tribal societies, and even, for periods of time, over the ʿulamaʾ.

Reza Shah's first accomplishment was to build a modern army. While the

Qajars had attempted military reforms along Western lines, they maintained the traditional pattern of an army made up of competitive regiments rather than unified corps. Reza Shah set about training a new officer corps in France and introduced compulsory conscription. Some 33 percent of the annual government budget was spent for military purposes and further monies were spent out of a special oil revenues budget as well. He built up a Westernized army which could dominate the country politically, but proved unable to prevent Russia and Britain from occupying Iran in 1941.

Bolstered by its army and an expanded administration, the new regime overcame the opposition of religious, merchant, and tribal elites. It outlawed the communist party and the trade unions, reduced the parliament to a rubber stamp, and censored the press. For political support it looked to the land-owning classes. New laws in 1928 and 1929 recognized the de facto possession of land as proof of ownership, and required registration which was favorable to wealthy landowners rather than to poor tenants. The state also suppressed tribal forces. For the first time in history an Iranian state won complete control over the country as a whole by breaking the power of tribal communities and Khans. The tribes were forced to sedentarize, and the political power of the Khans was coopted by the state.

Though Reza Shah had come to power with the support of many ʿulamaʾ who desired to see a restoration of the monarchy and expected a strong government to resist foreign influence, once established the Pahlavi regime also diminished the power of the ʿulamaʾ. Through the creation of a secular education system, government supervision of religious schools, reduction of funds, and other measures the Pahlavis sought to bring the ʿulamaʾ under state control. In 1934 the Teacher Training Act provided for new colleges, and the Ministry of Education introduced its own curriculum for theological schools. Furthermore, as an alternative to religious education, technical schools were founded by the Ministries of Education, Industry, Health, Agriculture, War, and Finance. The University of Tehran was founded in 1935 and operated with a European-educated faculty under the close supervision of the government. Many students were educated abroad and returned to spread technical knowledge and Western ideas of social relations.

A second and equally damaging blow to the ʿulamaʾ was the reorganization of judicial administration. Though civil and criminal courts had been set up in the constitution of 1906, and new civil commercial codes promulgated in 1911 and 1915, judicial administration remained in the hands of the ʿulamaʾ. Reza Shah, however, introduced new law codes in 1928 which replaced the Shariʿa. In 1932 the parliament enacted a new law which turned registration of legal documents over to secular courts, and at a single stroke removed the most lucrative functions of the religious courts. A law of 1936 required all judges to hold a degree from the Tehran faculty of law or a foreign university, making it impossible for the ʿulamaʾ to sit in courts of law. During the 1930s a new court system was organized, following French models, to administer a haphazard mixture of Western and Muslim legal norms. Regardless of the adequacy of the legal system, in political terms it established the supremacy of the state. Other measures were taken to ban the presentation of passion plays, pilgrimages, and sermons and to legislate modern dress codes.

The secularization of legal administration and education was part of a still larger program of state-controlled economic modernization. The infrastructure of a modern economy was developed in the 1920s and 1930s. A new customs office was established, staffed by Belgian officials. American financial missions helped organize tax collection; an Iranian national bank was founded in 1927 under the management of German financial experts. An Iranian railway was constructed between 1926 and 1938, running from Bandar Shahpur on the Persian Gulf to Bandar Shah on the Caspian Sea. Designed in response to strategic needs, however, the railway neglected international connections, major cities, and links between the major economic areas of the country. Similarly, postal and telegraph communications and air transportation were introduced to facilitate economic development and help extend the authority of the central government to the provinces.

After 1930, owing to lack of sufficient capital in the private economy and lack of motivation among landowners to make long-term investments in industry, the state sponsored numerous industrial projects. Priority was given to consumer substitution industries (i.e., those replacing imports with domestic products), including cotton, woolen and silk factories, sugar refining and food processing plants such as bakeries, canneries and breweries. By 1941 soap, glass, paper, matches, and cigarettes were all produced in state-owned factories. The state also controlled trade and foreign exchange. In 1925 the government established a monopoly on imports of tea and sugar. It sought to regulate foreign interests. In the 1920s and 1930s, Russian and British influence remained relatively balanced. Russia was an important trading partner; Britain controlled the production of oil. To offset the influence of these two powers Iranian trade was reorientated toward Germany. German capital and technical assistance became important for Iranian projects, and Germany maintained a strong presence by the establishment of research and cultural institutes and espionage and political networks. In the 1930s the Russian share of Iranian exports fell from 34 percent to 1 percent and the German share rose from 20 percent to 42 percent. The state controlled approximately 33–40 percent of Iranian imports and exports.

Oil was an important but not a crucial source of government revenues. Oil was first found at Masjid-i Sulayman in 1908, and in 1909 the Anglo-Persian Oil Company was founded to exploit the discovery. The British government acquired a controlling interest in 1914. The refineries at Abadan were constructed in 1915. Oil production was profitable for Iran, but was a source of bitter resentment against foreign companies for their manipulation of royalties and the absence of Iranians in managerial and administrative positions. Iran was also dissatisfied with its share of the income. In 1933 it demanded a reduction in the territories conceded for foreign exploration and a fixed income. In return, Iran extended the existing concessions to 1993 and exempted the oil company from taxation. These arrangements cushioned Iran in the depression years but proved contrary to Iranian interests when prosperity was restored during and after World War II.

The modernized Iranian state defined its legitimacy in nationalist and secularist terms. A revival of interest in Persian history and themes of ancient kingship were used to legitimize the modernization of the army, the government, and the economy. The political program of the Pahlavi regime, however, was also strikingly dependent upon foreign support and on cadres of Western advisers and Western-educated Iranian administrators and intelligentsia. This phase of development created a small modern sector in an otherwise backward economy and society. Manufacturing was concentrated in cities and benefited only a small portion of the population. Agriculture remained unproductive. State centralization, economic modernization, and a new educational system helped to create an elite of army officers, bureaucrats, merchants, contractors, doctors, lawyers, engineers, teachers, and writers, who adopted Western values and a Western style of life. This new elite, allied to an older generation of ʿulamaʾ and tribal Khans, dominated an unproductive and impoverished peasant population.

World War II put an end to this phase of the Iranian experiment in centralization of state power and economic development. Britain and Russia, concerned to keep open the supply routes across Iran to Russia, and to assure the control of Iranian oil, first demanded the expulsion of Germans from the country. They then seized control of Iran, forced the Shah to resign, and made his minor son, Muhammad Reza Pahlavi, the nominal suzerain of the country. Between 1941 and 1953, Iran passed through a period of open political struggle among its several would-be foreign protectors and its several internal political parties. The United States gradually replaced both Russian and British influence and emerged as the principal patron of the postwar Iranian regime. The United States advised the Iranian government on economic management, organized Iran's police and military forces and supplied it with military aid. With American backing, Iran successfully resisted Soviet occupation of the northern provinces, Soviet demands for oil concessions, and Soviet sponsorship of separatist movements in Azarbayjan and Kurdistan.

In the late 1940s and early 1950s Iran also struggled to win control of the Anglo-Iranian Oil Company. In 1951, Muhammad Mosaddeq, the leader of the National Front, supported by a coalition of landowners, tribal leaders, leftist intelligentsia, merchants, and ʿulamaʾ, pushed through parliament a bill to nationalize the oil company. A bitter three-year struggle followed, in which the United States refused to support Iran. The Western powers boycotted Iranian oil. The Iranian economy collapsed and the Mosaddeq coalition broke up. In the ensuing struggle for power the C.I.A. helped the army and the Shah to seize power, dismiss Mosaddeq, and reestablish an authoritarian regime. The dispute with the oil companies was settled in 1954 by the formation of a National Iranian Oil Company and a consortium of foreign oil companies including the Anglo-Iranian Oil Company (renamed British Petroleum) and several American firms. The consortium would produce and market oil and divide the profits with the National Iranian Oil Company. Thus the foreign companies avoided nationalization and maintained control of oil pricing and marketing.

The 1953 coup also put an end to the period of open struggle for political power and restored a centralized and authoritarian regime based on foreign support, and committed to economic and social modernization. The restored regime of Muhammad Reza Shah was technically a constitutional monarchy, but the Shah ruled with virtually absolute powers. He controlled the army and *Savak*, the secret intelligence and police agency, appointed the ministers, selected half of the senate, and manipulated parliamentary elections. A small elite of officers, administrators, landowners, and some wealthy merchants and religious leaders dominated Iranian political life. The Shah's regime was closely allied to the United States and was dependent upon American military and financial support. Having been brought to power with American assistance, Iran joined the Baghdad Pact (1955) and the Central Treaty Organization (1959). Iran maintained close relations with Israel. In the 1970s it assisted the Sultan of Oman in suppressing opposition, and in 1975 forced Iraq to settle disputed boundaries in the lower reaches of the Euphrates River. Close ties with the United States and even the strong build-up of military forces in the 1970s, however, did not prevent Iran from maintaining good relations with the Soviet Union to balance American influence and political pressure.

The resumption of state-sponsored modernization led to the far-reaching economic and political changes which lie behind the Iranian revolution. The Pahlavi program called for the construction of a centralized secular and nationalist regime and the further modernization of society along Western lines. Between 1960 and 1977 the government undertook a program to consolidate its autocratic rule, reform the structure of landowning, modernize the industrial economy, build up military forces which would assure its regional supremacy, and reform the social structure of the country. In conjunction with the agricultural reforms the Shah proposed the formation of a literacy and a health corps intended to bring the direct influence of the state into the countryside. Other reforms included the extension of voting rights to women and their employment in government offices.

A crucial aspect of the "white revolution" was land reform. In Iran the ownership of land was highly concentrated in the hands of a small number of families, mainly absentee landlords. The peasants were rarely owners. Most were sharecroppers and laborers. Then, in 1962–64 and 1968, landowners were required by law to sell excess land to smallholders and tenants, but because of widespread evasion not as much was distributed as was officially proposed. The new owners, moreover, lacked the capital, the technology, the cooperative organizations, and the government extension services necessary to maintain and increase productivity. Landless laborers, lacking the resources to farm or to pay for the land, received nothing, and, having lost their employment, had to migrate to the cities. Subsequent redistributions were even more conservative. While giving peasants benefits in ownership and tenancy rights, the reforms did not give them lands adequate for subsistence.

In fact the major thrust of the Shah's agricultural programs was the creation of large-scale units in the form of state-sponsored farm corporations and private agribusinesses. Farm corporations required peasants to pool their lands and take shares in the larger enterprise, often with the result that farms were mechanized and cultivators driven from the land. Private agribusinesses with heavy foreign investment also favored capital-intensive mechanized farming and forced peasants from the land. Thus, the state favored capital-intensive agriculture in a country with surplus labor. Similarly, nomads were forced to sedentarize, and pastoral livestock herding was replaced with mechanized meat and dairy farms. These farms commonly failed, and the result was not increasing but falling per capita production and a large-scale movement of rural people to the big cities, especially Tehran.

As per capita agricultural production declined in the 1960s and 1970s, Iran became more dependent upon industrial development. For the first time since the initial and limited industrialization of the 1930s, Iran experienced an industrial boom. State investments provided the infrastructure and roughly half of the capital invested in industry. The state also supported industrial growth by high tariffs, tax credits, licenses, and other devices and promoted a boom in steel, rubber, chemicals, building materials, and automobile assembly. The huge growth of oil revenues after 1973 also helped enhance the gross national product. Iranian industry, however, was too inefficient to compete in international markets, and suffered from lack of skilled management and labor. The combination of falling per capita agricultural output, inefficient industry, heavy purchases of foreign manufactured goods and weapons, with a booming oil economy led to severe inflation and probably to a lower standard of living for all Iranians not directly involved in the modern sector of the economy.

The Shah's regime also attempted modest reforms of the position of women. As early as the 1920s a few leading intellectuals, men and women, were working for improvements in women's education, social position, and legal rights. Women, in small numbers, began to enter into teaching, nursing and factory work. In 1936 wearing of the veil was forbidden and women of the urban upper and middle classes began to wear modern dress. While emancipation from traditional norms had begun, in the crucial areas of family law and political rights little was changed. Divorce remained easy for men. Guardianship of children remained the legal right of males. Polygamy and temporary marriage were still permitted. Only with the family protection laws of 1967 and 1975 were the male prerogatives partially circumscribed by legislation which required divorces to be reviewed in court and wives' consent for polygamous marriages. The government also prepared to give women the right to vote.

The program of modernization had profound effects on Iranian society. It expanded the cadres of Western and modern-educated intelligentsia, officials, soldiers, business managers, and skilled workers and created a modernized sector in the Iranian economy. It also provoked first the anxieties and then the active hostility of the ʿulamaʾ, the merchants and artisans of the bazaar, and leftist intellectuals who opposed the consolidation of the Shah's power, his dependence upon foreign support, and the policies which brought economic hardship to the peasantry and to the lower middle classes. Above all, the opposition was opposed to the highly authoritarian nature of the regime.

Opposition in the 1960s and 1970s was widespread but scattered and easily defeated. The Tudeh and National parties were crushed by *Savak*. Kurdish, Arab, and Baluchi minorities were defeated in their bids for regional autonomy. Militant guerrilla groups, such as the Marxist *Fedaʾiyan-i Khalq*, and the Islamic leftist *Mojahedin-i Khalq*, in the name of Shiʿism opposed

despotism, imperialism, and capitalism. The resistance provoked further repression but did not shake the grip of the Shah's regime.

Throughout this period the position of the ⁽ulama⁾ was ambiguous. The
politically open 1940s had encouraged ⁽ulama⁾ activism in political affairs.
From 1948 to 1953 Ayatollah Kashani, supported by street preachers and
lower-ranking ⁽ulama⁾, carried on an anti-British and anti-imperialist campaign
in favor of the nationalization of the oil industry and the termination of foreign
influence in Iran. For a time he supported the Mosaddeq government but later
turned against it and assisted in the restoration of the Shah.

The defeat of Mosaddeq, however, introduced a period of religious quietism
and tacit collaboration with the state. The government supported ⁽ulama⁾
interests through appointments at court, opportunities for enrichment through
landowning, and marriage into prominent families. It increased the amount of
religious instruction in public schools and periodically closed down movie
houses, liquor stores and public musical entertainments. In return, the ⁽ulama⁾
accepted the Baghdad Pact and tolerated the government's policy of cooperation with foreign companies. Under the leadership of Ayatollah Buru-
jirdi, the ⁽ulama⁾ remained politically quiet but also consolidated their internal
strength. In the 1950s and early 1960s, a national network of communications
developed, with Qum as the center of Shi⁽i religious instruction and
organization.

In the 1960s the government's economic and social policies generated
intense ⁽ulama⁾ opposition. The ⁽ulama⁾ opposed the new land laws. Scanty
evidence indicates that many ⁽ulama⁾ were wealthy landowners or controlled
extensive waqf properties. They opposed the extension of suffrage to women;
and they opposed Iran's close ties with the United States and Israel. They were
also threatened by the government's proposal to establish a literacy corps
which would give the state its own cadres to rival ⁽ulama⁾ influence in rural
areas. The quarrel between the government and the ⁽ulama⁾ came to blows in
1963 when the Shah decided to call a national referendum on land reform. The
proposed referendum and the police crackdown on ⁽ulama⁾ activities in Qum
provoked demonstrations, led by Ayatollah Khomayni, who was exiled to Iraq
in 1964.

As important as renewed ⁽ulama⁾ resistance to the state was the development
of a religious reform movement. The reformist view was crystallized in a
speech by Mehdi Bazargan in 1962 in which he went back to the Quran and
to Shi⁽i religious traditions to justify an active political role for the ⁽ulama⁾.
Political organization and collective struggle for a better society was the
responsibility of the custodians of Islam. No longer should the ⁽ulama⁾ wait

passively for a return of the imam, but actively prepare the way. The reformers further proposed the formation of a council of ʿulamaʾ to collectively fulfill the functions of giving authoritative religious advice, and the creation of a centralized financial organization to assure their autonomy from both government influence and popular pressure. Between 1967 and 1973 the reform movement took a new direction under the leadership of Dr ʿAli Shariʿati, who formed the Husayniyah Irshad. This was an informal "university" which was intended to revitalize Shiʿism by reconciling Islamic teachings with European social sciences and thereby generate the commitment to overthrow a repressive government. For Shariʿati, Shiʿism was a religion of protest.

Ayatollah Khomayni, from his sanctuary in Iraq, became the main spokesman of opposition to the monarchy. In 1961 Khomayni stood for a parliamentary form of government, but by 1971, in his book, *Islamic Government*, on the basis of the principles of jihad and "commanding the good," he argued that the clergy had to rebel against despotic governments. He declared the monarchy an un-Islamic institution and called for a total reform of political society in which the ʿulamaʾ would take a direct and active role. While based on a long tradition of ʿulamaʾ opposition to the abuse of monarchical powers, this was, in fact, a profound innovation. Khomayni's position was the most radical statement of ʿulamaʾ responsibilities.

These religious claims became the basis of a mass movement in opposition to the Shah. In the course of the 1970s the Pahlavi regime became all the more oppressive. The army and the secret police were widely feared and hated for numerous investigations, intimidations, imprisonments, torture, and assassinations of potential enemies of the regime. The regime was widely perceived as being based upon American political and military support and as benefiting only a very narrow elite consisting of the Shah and his family, the army, and a cadre of prominent supporters. The government was not only hated for being a dictatorship but was resented for mismanaging the economy. Great fortunes were being earned from oil income and were being spent on weapons and for the benefit of a small elite, while inflation was undermining the standard of living of bazaar merchants, artisans, and industrial workers. The bazaar population suffered particularly from confiscations, fines, and imprisonments, as the Shah sought to contain inflation by intimidating them. At the same time, the 1970s were disastrous times for masses of Iranian peasants. Millions fled the land for the cities, where they formed a huge mass of unemployed and underemployed people. By the late 1970s, Iran was importing most of its food from abroad.

In these deeply disturbed political and economic conditions, the spark for

20 Iranian women demonstrate against the Shah

revolution was a demonstration by religious students in Qum against an alleged assassination by Savak. The police shot a number of demonstrators, and provoked a new demonstration, mourning the martyrs of the last. Every forty days the protests were repeated and grew in scale until the month of Muharram (fall of 1978), when millions of people demonstrated against the regime. The Fedaʾiyan-i Khalq and Mojahedin-i Khalq were revived. The oil workers refused to produce, the bazaar merchants closed their shops, and the army either would not or could not suppress the revolt. The Shah fled the country and a new regime came to power. Masses of Iranians had been mobilized by a coalition of religious and liberal leaders under the guidance of the highest Iranian religious authority, Ayatollah Khomayni.

The victory of the revolution abolished the monarchy and established an Islamic government in Iran. The new regime was built upon the charismatic authority of Ayatollah – now Imam – Khomayni, the cadres of younger ʿulamaʾ, graduate and student activists, town and village militias, and the Islamic Republican Party – the party of the ʿulamaʾ. The dominant ʿulamaʾ eliminated their liberal, nationalist, and radical Marxist allies and now govern Iran in the name of Islam.

The Iranian Islamic revolution arose out of the particular configuration of Iranian state and religious institutions, but is nonetheless a signal event in the history of all Islamic societies. The revolution marks the culmination of an almost 200-year struggle between the Iranian state and the organized ʿulamaʾ. In the nineteenth century, the weaknesses of the state, partly due to the strength of non-state tribal and ethnic communities, allowed for the consolidation of a religious establishment capable of opposing the regime, and capable of mobilizing large-scale popular support. State efforts at modernization and European penetration of the Iranian economy led to the tobacco monopoly protests of 1891–92 and to the Constitutional Revolution of 1906. Again, in the twentieth century, the effort to centralize and modernize state power led to a crisis in which ʿulamaʾ, intellectuals, students, and large segments of the artisan and working population mobilized to oppose the government. The defeat of tribalism as a third force in Iranian society led to a polarization between the state and the ʿulamaʾ, and to an Islamic revolution.

Nonetheless, the history of ʿulamaʾ–state relations in nineteenth- and twentieth-century Iran was ambiguous. Resistance to the state was in fact sporadic, and at different times the ʿulamaʾ have espoused both revolutionary activism and religious quietism. Within Shiʿism there is justification for both. The activist position is justified by the doctrine of "commanding the good and forbidding the evil," and by the claims of the mujtahids to be spiritual advisers to all Iranians and the only legitimate authorities in the absence of the hidden imam. The example of Husayn stands as a paradigm of the obligation to confront and resist tyranny in the name of justice and Islam. Equally important, however, are the cultural traditions tending toward political pacifism. The Shiʿi expectation of worldly injustice and the hope for messianic redemption works against involvement in public life.

The Iranian revolution, therefore, cannot be said to be due to an inherent religious opposition to state authority, but has to be treated as a response to specific conditions. The Russian invasion of 1826, the Reuter concessions, the tobacco monopoly of 1891, the land reform acts of 1960 to 1963, and the economic tensions of the late 1970s impelled the ʿulamaʾ to adopt the active rather than the passive side of their complex tradition. The Constitutional Revolution of 1906 and the Iranian Revolution of 1979 are not expressions of a constant hostility between state and religion but the expression of a recurring possibility of confrontation between them. In Iran the weakness of the state, the organizational strength of the religious establishment, and the latent cultural permission for ʿulamaʾ resistance have all allowed for, though they have not mandated, revolutionary struggle in the name of Islam.

The revolution has worldwide importance. For the first time in the modern era religious leaders have been able to successfully oppose a modernized regime, and have taken control of the state. For the first time the revolutionary implications of Islam, hitherto manifest in lineage or tribal societies, have been realized in a modernizing industrializing society. Revolution has come, not primarily from the left, but from the religious establishment; not in the name of socialism, but in the name of Islam. The event has shaken the relations between state regimes and religious movements and opened doubts as to the future, not only of Iran, but of all Islamic societies.

CHAPTER 23

THE DISSOLUTION OF THE OTTOMAN EMPIRE
AND THE MODERNIZATION OF TURKEY

The dissolution of the Ottoman empire was one of the more complex cases in the transition from eighteenth-century Islamic imperial societies to modern national states. The Ottoman regime was suzerain over a vast territory, including the Balkans, Turkey, the Arab Middle East, Egypt, and North Africa. Its influence reached Inner Asia, the Red Sea, and the Sahara. While the empire had gone through a period of decentralization in the seventeenth and eighteenth centuries and had begun to give ground to its European political and commercial competitors, it retained its political legitimacy and its basic institutional structure. In the nineteenth century, the Ottomans substantially restored the power of the central state, consolidated control over the provinces, and generated the economic, social, and cultural reforms which they hoped would make them effective competitors in the modern world.

While the Ottomans struggled to reform state and society, the empire was slowly being dismembered. The European powers had consolidated their early military, economic, and technological advantages and were by the nineteenth century more powerful than the Ottoman regime. For survival the Ottomans depended increasingly upon the European balance of power. Until 1878 the British and the Russians offset each other and generally protected the Ottoman regime from direct encroachment. Between 1878 and 1914, however, most of the Balkans became independent and Russia, Britain, and Austria-Hungary all acquired direct control of Ottoman territories. The dismemberment of the Ottoman empire culminated at the end of World War I in the creation of a plethora of new states in Turkey and the Arab Middle East. Here we shall first examine the impact of the European powers, the dissolution of the Ottoman empire, and the political circumstances behind the formation of a new system of Middle Eastern national states. Then we shall consider the international transformation of the Ottoman empire in the nineteenth century and the subsequent development of the Turkish, Egyptian, and Arab states formed at the end of World War I. As in the case of Iran, the effects of European intervention would mingle with the Ottoman institutional and cultural heritage to generate a number of different modern Middle Eastern societies.

THE PARTITION OF THE OTTOMAN EMPIRE

By the end of the eighteenth century the Ottoman empire could no longer defend itself against the growing military power of Europe, nor ward off European commercial penetration. Russia had absorbed the Crimea and established itself on the Black Sea, while Britain, after helping defeat Napoleon's invasion of Egypt in 1798, became the paramount military and commercial power in the Mediterranean. Russia wanted to absorb Ottoman territories in the Balkans and win access to the Mediterranean; Britain wanted to shore up the empire as a bulwark against Russian expansion and protect its commercial and imperial interests in the Mediterranean, the Middle East, and India. Thus, the Ottoman empire was precariously protected by the balance of European power. The stage was set for the century-long struggle over the "sick man" of Europe.

The first test of the balance of power came with the invasion of Syria in 1831 by Muhammad ʿAli, the independent Ottoman governor of Egypt (1805–48). In response the Ottomans concluded the Treaty of Unkiar Skelessi (July, 1833) in which they agreed to close the Dardanelles and the Bosphorus to foreign warships in return for Russian support. Britain, threatened by the specter of a Russian protectorate over the Ottomans and possible Russian intervention in the Mediterranean, declared for the territorial integrity of the Ottoman empire and the restoration of Syria to Ottoman control. In 1840, Russia, Britain, and Austria agreed that Muhammad ʿAli would have to retreat from Syria and framed a new convention regulating passage through the straits. The powers agreed that no warships were to pass the Bosphorus and the Dardanelles in time of peace. Both Russia and Britain would be protected in their spheres of influence. By a supplementary agreement in 1841, the powers allowed Muhammad ʿAli to establish a hereditary regime in Egypt. Thus, the internal crisis of the empire led to a concert of European powers to regulate Ottoman affairs. The Ottoman empire had become a protectorate of Europe and a pawn of the great powers.

Map 30. Territorial losses and the partition of the Ottoman empire: 1683–1923.

The balance of power and the durability of the Ottoman empire were again tested in the Crimean war, 1854–56. Provoked by Russian demands for influence in Jerusalem and a protectorate over all Ottoman Christian subjects, British, French, and Ottoman forces entered the Black Sea and took Sebastapol in 1855. By the Treaty of Paris (1856) the Russians were forced to dismantle their naval forces on the Black Sea, but they were compensated by an agreement to make Rumania an autonomous province under Ottoman suzerainty.

The next crisis was the revolt of Bosnia and Herzegovina in 1876 against Ottoman rule. Nationalist resistance to Ottoman rule in the Balkans had begun with the Serbian revolt of 1804–13. Between 1821 and 1829, Greece gained its independence. Serbians, Rumanians, and Bulgarians also demanded autonomy. The Balkan campaigns for independence culminated in 1876 with Russian intervention. By the Treaty of San Stefano (1877), the Ottomans were forced to concede the independence of Bulgaria, Serbia, Rumania, and Montenegro. The huge Russian gains provoked the other European powers to call a Congress of European States at Berlin in 1878. At the Congress of Berlin a new settlement was imposed. Bessarabia was ceded by the Ottomans to Russia, but in compensation for Russian gains, Austria "temporarily" occupied Bosnia and Herzegovina, and Britain obtained the use of Cyprus as a base of operations. Bulgaria was reduced to a small size and Ottoman suzerainty was restored. Then, in 1882, to protect her interests in the Suez Canal and in the Egyptian debt to British and other European bond holders, Britain occupied Egypt. Britain had changed from a policy of defense of the territorial integrity of the empire to a policy of partition in order to maintain the European balance of power. Henceforth, the Eastern Question would be handled by the further dismemberment of the Ottoman state.

Between 1878 and 1908, the partition of the empire was postponed only by the rivalries of the European powers. Britain maintained its position in Cyprus and Egypt. Germany established its influence by investing in Ottoman railways and by supplying advisers and technicians to the Ottoman army. Big-power rivalry, however, centered on the Balkans. Austria managed to establish its diplomatic ascendancy over Serbia and good relations with Rumania and Greece; Russia remained the patron of Bulgaria. Serbia, Greece, and Bulgaria, however, fought for control of Macedonia.

In 1908 an internal Ottoman political crisis upset the balance of power. Taking advantage of the upheaval in the Ottoman empire, Austria annexed Bosnia and Herzegovina. Serbia, backed by Russia, protested against the Austrian annexation, but Germany supported Austria unconditionally. The Serbians and Russians were forced to back down. The crisis, however, re-

opened bitter competition between Austria and Russia and prompted the
Balkan states to form their own alliances. In 1912, Serbia and Bulgaria, then
Greece and Bulgaria, and finally Montenegro and Bulgaria, negotiated treaties,
ostensibly to keep Austria in check, but with secret clauses to attack the
Ottoman empire. In October 1912, the combined Balkan armies defeated the
Ottomans and took all of their remaining European territories except for a
small strip around the city of Istanbul. Then in 1913 the Balkan states went to
war with each other over the division of the spoils, allowing the Ottomans to
regain a small part of Thrace. Within a year the rivalries of Austria and Serbia
precipitated a general European war.

The first World War completed the process of dismemberment. In De-
cember 1914 the Ottomans entered the war on the side of Germany and Austria.
German military and economic assistance, the traditional Ottoman fear of
Russia, and perhaps an ambition to restore Ottoman control over lost provinces prompted the Ottomans to join the central powers. In response, the
British, the French, the Russians, and the Italians agreed to partition the
Ottoman provinces. By the Sykes–Picot agreement (1916), France was to
obtain a sphere of influence in Lebanon, southwestern Turkey, northern Syria,
and northern Iraq, and Britain would acquire Iraq, the Arabian side of the
Persian gulf, and Transjordan. Palestine would be subject to an international
regime. Russia was to obtain Istanbul and parts of eastern Anatolia. Italy was
promised southern Anatolia. To promote her ambition to be the paramount
power in the Near East, Britain also entered other, often contradictory,
agreements. In return for Arab support against their Ottoman overlords, the
British promised Sharif Husayn of Mecca that Britain would recognize an
independent Arab state, with reservations for Lebanon and British and French
interests. In 1917, the Balfour Declaration promised that Britain would also
support the formation of a Jewish National Home in Palestine.

By 1918 the European allies had defeated Germany, Austria, and the Ottoman empire; Britain conquered Palestine, Syria, and Iraq and the allies took
control of Istanbul and the straits. Britain and France agreed to divide the
Middle East into a number of new states, including Lebanon and Syria in the
French sphere of influence, and Palestine, Jordan, and Iraq in the British
sphere. Italy was conceded southwestern Anatolia. Greece was allowed to
occupy Thrace, Izmir, and the Aegean islands. Armenia was to be an independent state and Kurdistan an autonomous province. Istanbul and the straits
were put under joint allied occupation. Thus, between 1912 and 1920, the
Ottomans lost all of their former empire in the Balkans. New states were set
up in Lebanon, Syria, Palestine, Transjordan, and Iraq. Egypt became, under

a British protectorate, fully independent of Ottoman suzerainty. The political process, begun more than two centuries before, of reducing and dismembering the Ottoman empire, had reached its term in the formation of a new system of national states.

OTTOMAN REFORM

While the European powers divided the Ottoman empire into a number of national states, the institutional organization and ideological identity of these states was shaped by the interaction of European influence and the historical legacy of the several Middle Eastern societies. In the late nineteenth-century Ottoman empire, and in the formation of modern Turkey, the primary consideration was the continuity of historical institutional and cultural forms. While European powers exerted a tremendous influence, their impact upon the internal evolution of late Ottoman and early modern Turkish societies was mediated by Ottoman and Turkish elites. Unlike other Muslim empires, the Ottomans maintained their sovereignty and were able to implement their own program of modernization and reform.

As early as the seventeenth century, Ottomans debated the problem of how to restore the political integrity and military effectiveness of the regime. Two main positions emerged. The restorationists called for a return to the laws (kanuns) of Sulayman the Magnificent, and opposed any change which threatened to give Europeans and Christians, or European and Christian concepts and techniques, supremacy over Muslims. The modernists called for the adoption of European methods for military training, organization, and administration, and for the civil, economic, and educational changes which would be needed to support a modern state. Throughout the eighteenth and much of the nineteenth century these two points of view were in vigorous competition, but the dominant view came to be the one which favored modernization along European lines.

Already in the eighteenth century, European military advisers were employed to provide technical training for army officers, and a printing press was set up to publish translations of European technical, military, and geographical works. Selim III (1789–1807) introduced the first comprehensive reform program, called the *Nizam-i Jedid* or New Organization. This program called for the formation of a modern army corps, increased taxation, and technical schools to train cadres for the new regime. Selim's program, however, was defeated by the opposition of the ʿulamaʾ and the janissaries, and he was deposed in 1807.

In the decades which followed, Russian advances in the Caucasus, the rise to power of Muhammad ᶜAli in Egypt, and the Greek war for independence again made the need for reform urgent. Under Mahmud II (1807–39) the reform program was revived. While Mahmud's program of military, administrative, and educational projects began on the base pioneered by Selim III, the new effort to improve military capabilities, rationalize administration, subordinate the provinces, raise revenues, and establish schools was guided by a strong Western orientation and a more radical concept of a centralized state, governed by an absolute monarch. The reforms were intended to revive the absolute authority of the Ottoman rulers supported by new elites who were technically proficient and entirely devoted to the authority of the regime. Conservative resistance was utterly crushed. In 1826 the entire janissary corps was destroyed and feudal tenures were partially abolished. The ᶜulamaᵓ were weakened by the absorption of many waqf endowments, courts, and schools into new state-controlled ministries. The Bektashi religious order, associated with the janissaries, was dissolved. There would henceforth be little opposition to reform and even considerable support from the higher-ranking ᶜulamaᵓ.

This first phase of reform was followed by the *Tanzimat* or Reorganization period lasting from 1839 to 1876. In this period the reform program was extended from military and administrative matters to economic, social, and religious affairs. As the Ottomans realized that radical changes in society were needed to support a centralized state, they built factories to manufacture cloth, paper, and guns. Coal, iron, lead and copper mining were encouraged. To stimulate agriculture, the government undertook reclamation and resettlement. Technical modernization included the introduction of a postal system (1834), telegraph (1855), steamships, and the beginning of railway construction in 1866. Government monopolies were ended in 1838 and international commerce was stimulated by low tariffs. Though reforms in trade and banking enabled European traders and investors to achieve a dominant position in the Ottoman economy, the principle that a more productive economy was essential for state finances was established.

Important legal reforms were also undertaken. New law codes were promulgated to meet the demands of a new administration and economy and to respond to the political pressure generated by Ottoman subjects and foreign powers. Western types of law courts and law codes were introduced as early as 1840, when new commercial and penal codes regulating landowning and commerce were promulgated to supplement Shariᶜa legal principles. Laws of 1858 established private ownership of land. In 1870 the Ottoman government issued a new civil code, the *Mejelle*, which in substance followed the Shariᶜa, but nonetheless dramatically departed from tradition because it contained changes made on the personal authority of the Sultan and was administered in state rather than in Shariʿa courts. The family law of 1917, by adopting a European system of personal law, made a complete break with the Muslim past.

While Ottoman educational reform had begun with the establishment of professional schools, a new educational system including elementary and secondary schools was created to prepare students for higher technical education. Until the middle of the century, primary and secondary education was religious in content, but in 1847 the Ministry of Education undertook to organize middle schools (*Rushdiye*), and the army created a parallel system of secondary schools. After the Crimean war, the Ministry of Education and the army began experiments in elementary education, introducing arithmetic, geography, and Ottoman history. In 1870 the first efforts were made to create a university to integrate professional, humanistic, and religious studies. Much of the program, however, remained a paper system.

Similarly, extensive reforms were made in the administration of the non-Muslim populations. While Christians and Jews formed autonomous religious communities which administered their own civil laws, the nationalist revolts made it imperative to further integrate the Christian populations and win their loyalty for the Ottoman regime. The first Ottoman response to these pressures was the Noble Rescript (*Hatt-i Sherif*) of Gülhane (1839), a declaration of principles of government, recognizing the rights of life, property, and honor, and the equality of all religious groups before the law. In 1856 the *Hatt-i Humayun* (Imperial Rescript) promised equality for non-Muslims and guaranteed their right to serve in the army. In 1867 Christians began to be appointed to state councils.

The non-Muslim communities were also reorganized to shift power from clergy to laymen. In 1850 the newly formed Protestant "millet" was governed by an assembly of lay members rather than by clergy. In 1863, the Gregorian Armenians were granted the right to form a national assembly having a lay majority and to elect patriarchs and councils. The Ottoman government forced the Greek clergy to form a lay assembly and then separated the Bulgarian from the Greek Orthodox church. Behind the reorganization of the Christian communities under lay leadership was the goal of integrating the Muslim and non-Muslim populations into an Ottoman nation. No longer would religious differences be a barrier to Ottoman loyalty.

Transcending the statism of the first reforms, the Tanzimat amounted to a change in the very concept of Ottoman society. It repudiated the autonomous functioning of Islamic educational and judicial institutions, and challenged the very concept of Muslim supremacy. In the interest of a strong state, and the integration of its several religious and ethnic populations, the Ottoman authorities were tampering with the fundamental structures of Muslim society and replacing traditional educational, legal, and religious systems with secular organizations. The restoration of the empire was beginning to have revolutionary implications.

The state reforms proved revolutionary because they brought into being a new elite committed to still further change. While the Tanzimat did not deeply penetrate Ottoman society, or affect the masses of people whose lives, beliefs, and loyalties were still bound up with Islam, it created a "new class." With the destruction of the janissaries, the weakening of the ʿulamaʾ, and the adoption of the reform programs, political power in Ottoman society shifted to the *memurs* or bureaucrats, and within that elite to the Westernized and Westernizing element – the servants of the translation bureaus and the war office who were educated in secular schools and traveled in Europe. This group of bureaucrats was led by Mustafa Reshid Pasha (1800–58), the son of a waqf administrator who began his career in religious schools but entered the newly reorganized administrative service of Mahmud II and became a grand vizier; and his protégés, Mehmet ʿAli Pasha (1815–71), the son of an Istanbul shopkeeper, and Mehmed Fuad Pasha (1815–69), a former medical student.

By the 1860s, moreover, Tanzimat also generated its own opposition. While the "new class" occupied government offices, graduates of the middle and professional schools, middle-level bureaucrats, and sons of poor families who found their careers blocked by the entrenched older generation, turned their energies to literature, becoming poets, writers, journalists, and editors of opposition newspapers. Resentful of the established bureaucrats, they sought allies among lower-ranking military officers, liberal ʿulamaʾ, and theological students opposed to the Tanzimat program but interested in a different program of reforms.

The new intelligentsia was represented in the 1860s by the Young Ottoman society. In the name of a synthesis of Ottoman tradition and Ottoman reform, Young Ottomans such as Namik Kemal (1840–88), Ibrahim Shinasi (1826–71), and Ziya Pasha (1825–80), were committed at once to the continuity of the Ottoman regime, to the revitalization of Islam, and to modernization along European lines. First, the Young Ottomans, dazzled by the successes of Britain, favored a constitutional regime. They believed that the ultimate value of the empire was measured by its contribution to the inherent rights of its citizens, to the security of life and property, to justice, and to the reconciliation of Christians and Muslims. In their view, the empire could not survive unless it became rooted in the masses. Moreover, a constitutional regime was the natural expression of the political and moral values which they held to be inherent both in Islam and in European culture. Thus the Young Ottoman thinkers were, without the name, modernist Muslims. They held that Islam, properly understood, was compatible with a modern organization of society and a constitutional government. They stressed the aspects of the Islamic heritage which encouraged scientific and technical learning, the value of reason above blind faith, and the importance of an active striving for individual and social improvement. Along with their commitment to Islam, the Young Ottomans also espoused the use of a simplified version of the Turkish language to bridge the gap between the Ottoman elite and the mass of their subjects, a reform which must have been particularly appealing to upwardly mobile intelligentsia. Thus, they attempted to reconcile the Muslim-Ottoman identity with the technical, political, and moral demands of modernization. While criticizing the program of Tanzimat as religiously and socially insensitive, they were nonetheless committed to a modernized Ottoman society.

In 1876, taking advantage of Ottoman defeat by Russia, the constitution-alists staged a coup d'état and brought to power ʿAbd al-Hamid II (1876–1908) who was forced to accept a constitution limiting the powers of the Sultan, establishing a representative government, decentralizing administra-tion, and mandating equality for all religious groups. ʿAbd al-Hamid, however, was unwilling to surrender 500 years of Ottoman authority. Turning the tables on his constitutionalist supporters, he suspended Parliament and established an authoritarian and religiously conservative regime.

The Young Ottoman period of the 1860s and 1870s was followed by a reaction and by the dominance of an authoritarian and dictatorial regime opposed to Young Ottoman constitutional and modernist principles. The regime was based on the absolute power of the Sultan, the bureaucracy, and the police. The Sultan was considered the head of Islam, and laid claim to a worldwide authority over Muslims. The new regime, however, combined conservative Islamic loyalties with the continuation of technical Tanzimat reforms. New schools, legal codes, railroads, and military techniques were introduced.

The generation of Turkish intelligentsia raised in the 1880s and 1890s took shape in reaction to the conservative regime. Continued economic and edu-cational development swelled the ranks of the intelligentsia. The number of white-collar, technical, railway, and telegraph workers increased. Poor and middling families were made occupationally mobile. The opportunities for communication were enlarged despite government controls and censorship.

The press disseminated European ideas about science and politics and pop-ularized Western attitudes. Ideas spread from the capital to the provinces as students brought home a larger vision of the universe.

In Paris exiled journalists, writers, publishers, and agitators formed in 1889 the Ottoman Society for Union and Progress. The "Young Turks," as they were now called, maintained their allegiance to the Ottoman dynasty, but agitated for the restoration of a parliamentary and constitutional regime. Internally, the Young Turks were divided into a group led by Ahmad Riza, who favored a strong Sultan, centralization of power, and the predominance of the Turkish-Muslim elements of the Ottoman population; and a group led by Prince Sabaheddin, who emphasized decentralized forms of Ottoman rule. The latter gave less emphasis to the Turkish and Islamic peoples of the empire, and stood for a federated society with autonomy for Christians and other minorities.

Within the empire, army officers, bureaucrats, and physicians, outraged by the inefficiency of the government, by defeats suffered at the hands of European and Balkan powers, and by their exclusion from participation in power, formed revolutionary cells in Damascus, Salonika, and elsewhere. As these cells proliferated, the Fatherland Society was founded in 1905 by Mustafa Kemal, an Ottoman army officer later to be president of Turkey; a Young Turk congress created the Committee for Union and Progress in 1907. In 1908 the C.U.P. cell in Monastir mutinied and forced the Sultan to restore the con-stitution of 1876. The military coup established a facade of parliamentary government, but the new government was actually run by the C.U.P. and by the army and proved to be authoritarian and highly centralized. Between 1908 and 1912, a three-way struggle for power among the army, the C.U.P. liberals, and Muslim conservatives ended with the army in control. From 1912 to 1918 the C.U.P. ruled by decree.

In bitter reaction to the Islamic veneer of the reign of ʿAbd al-Hamid, the C.U.P. was resolutely secular. Between 1913 and 1918 it adopted a program of aggressive secularization of schools, courts, and law codes and passed the first measures for the emancipation of women. In 1916 the C.U.P. government reduced the powers of the Shaykh al-Islam, transferred jurisdiction over Muslim courts to the Ministry of Justice, and control of Muslim colleges to the Ministry of Education. In 1917 a new family code based on European principles was promulgated. While the regime of ʿAbd al-Hamid had been bolstered by appeals to Islam, the opposition intelligentsia moved from the Young Ottoman position, which synthesized Islam and constitutionalism, to a more radically secular position. The struggle for power among the various segments of the Ottoman governing elite and intelligentsia had led to a radicalization of the reform program along secularist lines.

The C.U.P. program was Ottoman and secularist, but it was also increasingly Turkish-oriented. Between 1908 and 1918 the idea of Ottoman reform was overtaken by a new concept. C.U.P. leaders began to conceive of the Ottoman empire in terms of Turkish nationality. For more than a century, Christians had pursued national goals and demanded that peoples who shared an ethnic, linguistic, and religious heritage have a territorial state of their own. By the late nineteenth century there were already several Christian nations – Greece, Serbia, Rumania, Bulgaria, and Montenegro – in what had once been the domains of the Ottoman empire. Albania was soon to revolt and Armenians were claiming territorial autonomy. For the Christians, it was easy to form a national identity in opposition to Muslim and Ottoman domination and in frank emulation of the Christian nations in the West. For the Muslims, however, it was difficult to disentangle nationalism from Islam and from the Ottoman empire. For the Muslims there was no ready distinction between Muslim interests and Ottoman authority. Furthermore, the peoples we now call Turks had no concept of themselves as an ethnic group. They thought of themselves either as Muslims or as subjects of the Sultan. The word "Turk" only meant peasant, nomad, or rural bumpkin – someone without education.

Still, the idea of a Turkish nation began to take shape in the late Ottoman era. Loyalty to Islam and to the Ottoman empire came to be considered a kind of patriotism described by the word *watan* or fatherland. Pan-Islamic identifications also inspired a sense of political unity. Muslim and Ottoman vocabularies could thus express a political concept akin to, but not identical with, the national ideal. A Turkish cultural consciousness also began to take shape. Young Ottoman writers were concerned with the reform of the Turkish language and the adaptation of the high-cultural style of Ottoman-Turkish for mass use. In the 1890s, under the stimulus of European students of Turkish language and culture, and of Crimean and Inner Asian intellectuals who were refugees or students in Istanbul, the Ottomans were introduced to the idea of the "Turkish people."

By the turn of the century, the press was glorifying Anatolia as the homeland of Turks, and peasants as the backbone of a Turkish nation. The Turkish idea was being propagated by literary clubs such as the Turkish Homeland Society and the Turkish Hearth. These organizations waged a "national" campaign to simplify the Turkish language, make it more accessible to the masses, and persuade the populace of its own Turkish nationality. Ziya Gokalp (1875/6–1924) emerged as the spokesman of Turkish nationalism. Without regrets for the declining Ottoman empire, he celebrated the folk culture of the Turkish people, and called for the reform of Islam to make it expressive of the Turkish ethos. ʿAbdallah Jevdet (1869–1932) presented a secular basis for Turkish nationalism. The Turkish national idea reinforced the tendencies toward secularism and modernity, for it made it possible for Turks to separate themselves from Islam without compromising their non-Western identity. The Turkish concept made it possible to define a new civilization which embodied the historic identity of the Turkish people but was not Muslim and which was modern but not Western.

Between 1908 and 1918 political events put an end to the possibility of a multi-national, multi-religious Ottoman empire, and made the Turkish idea more relevant. By 1908 the majority of the Christian population was already independent. Albania revolted in 1910 and its autonomy was conceded in 1912. The Balkan wars then stripped the Ottoman empire of virtually all of its European possessions, and during World War I, the Armenian population of eastern Anatolia was decimated by the hardships of war, deportation, and Turkish and Kurdish massacres. Even among Muslims, Kurdish and Arab national feeling was growing, and there were Arab conspiracies against the empire. By the end of World War I all that was left of the Ottoman empire was Anatolia, with its majority Turkish population and small Greek, Kurdish, and Armenian minorities. The realities of Ottoman political life now corresponded to the nationalist concept of a Turkish people. The war had cut the Gordian knot of Ottoman loyalties by stripping away most of the non-Muslim and non-Turkish populations.

By 1918 the Ottoman empire was destroyed, but military and bureaucratic elites had already shifted their commitments from a multi-national and multi-religious Ottoman regime to a Turkish national and secular state. After the war Mustafa Kemal carried the principles of the Young Turk generation into action. Under Kemal's leadership, the national elite was able to mobilize the Turkish masses to fight against foreign occupation and to support the national idea. Kemal organized the movement for the Defense of the Rights of Anatolia and Rumelia, established a Grand National Assembly at Ankara (1920), promulgated a new constitution (1921), and established a republican regime in most of Anatolia. The new regime defeated the Armenian republic in the Caucasus, the French in Cilicia, and the Greeks in central Anatolia, and in 1923 the European powers agreed, by the Treaty of Lausanne, to recognize the independence of Turkey in its present boundaries. Turkey alone of the Muslim-populated regions of the Middle East emerged from the First World War as a fully independent country. Already provided with a national intelligentsia of army officers, experienced administrators, politicians, lawyers, and intellectuals, and a unified national movement, modern Turkey came into being with a coherent state structure, a unified elite, and a strong sense of its cultural and political identity.

The dominance of Ottoman military and bureaucratic elites, their turn toward nationalism, and their absolute leadership in the creation of the Turkish Republic may be better understood in terms of the historical weakness of alternative national elites. First, the turn toward a concept of a secular national state was abetted by the inability of Ottoman religious leaders to articulate an effective Muslim opposition. The destruction of the janissaries and the weakening of the ʿulamaʾ in 1826 proved decisive. The ʿulamaʾ continued to support the state. For them, the Ottoman state maintained its power, its charismatic authority, and its appeal as a conquering warrior state and defender of Islam. The Sultan was still considered the religious chief of Muslim peoples. Selim III and Mahmud II built mosques and tombs, attended mosque prayers and Sufi ceremonies and appointed religious teachers for the soldiers. ʿAbd al-Hamid revived the identification of Sultan and Caliph, and based his authority on the claim that he was the *Padishah* of the Ottomans and the Caliph of all Muslims. The Ottoman state was able to persuade Muslim opinion that the empire, despite its apparent assault on Islamic educational and legal institutions and its willingness to grant political and economic equality to non-Muslims, was still a quintessentially Muslim regime.

Furthermore, many leading ʿulamaʾ were sympathetic to the need to make Islam effective in the modern world. Spokesmen for an Islamic modernism continued to believe in the validity of their faith, but felt it had to be revised to make it compatible with changing conditions. On one side, they opposed the traditionalists who failed to recognize the importance of the new military, economic, and technical civilization of the West. On the other side, they opposed the secularists who did not value the religious and communal inspiration of Islam. The Islamic modernists wished to persuade the traditionalists to accept modernization as consistent with Islam, and persuade the modernists to accept Islam as a moral force. The Ottoman reform program, then, was presented in a framework of loyalty to Islam and of shared concern for the adaptation of Islamic values to the modern world.

Moreover, the ʿulamaʾ remained committed to the Ottoman regime because they were the servants of the state and were committed to an ideology of obedience and acceptance of state authority. Leading ʿulamaʾ were also personal friends of the Sultan, enjoyed his financial favors, and were connected by family ties to the military and bureaucratic elites. Through the middle decades of the nineteenth century the only religious opposition came from lower-ranking functionaries, theological students, and rural Sufis. At the end of the century when the initiative passed to the radical secularists, Muslim religious leaders were not in a position to resist. The tradition of subservience to state initiative, and the ambivalent recognition of the need for modernizing reforms, made it impossible for them to oppose the powerful forces, national and international, which led toward the dissolution of the Ottoman empire.

Secondly, the Ottoman military and bureaucratic elites did not have to contend with a rival Muslim bourgeoisie or commercial middle class. In part this was due to the legacy of state domination of the society and in part to European economic penetration of the Ottoman empire. The Anglo-Ottoman treaty of 1838, which led to the removal of Ottoman monopolies and high tariffs, marked the full integration of the Ottoman empire into the international economy. Entry into world markets stimulated the production of cash crops such as grain, wool, raisins, tobacco, and opium, though cotton declined owing to American competition. By 1913 Anatolian agriculture provided 55 percent of the agricultural income of the Ottoman empire and 48 percent of the gross domestic product. Some 80 to 85 percent of exports were agricultural products.

Manufacturing also prospered. Though the trade treaty of 1838 is usually taken to be the beginning of a disaster for Turkish handicrafts, in fact Turkish cloth-weaving and carpet-making flourished in the nineteenth century, partly owing to investments by Austrian and British firms in a putting-out system of production. Industries, however, were very little developed except for state-owned factories which produced guns, clothing, and footwear for the soldiers, and sold the surplus to the general public. Ottoman efforts to create their own industries for cotton, textiles, iron, and weapons had limited prospects in the face of the high cost of imported raw materials and technicians. Nevertheless, Ottoman industrial output grew at a rate of 1.85 percent a year, about twice the rate of growth of the gross domestic product. In all, Ottoman engagement in the world economy led to intensified production for export, but generally to the failure of domestic industries and crafts in competition with Europe.

Ottoman engagement in the world economy also led to state indebtedness and financial dependency. The first Ottoman loans were contracted in 1854, and henceforth, Ottoman economic development depended upon European loans for the construction of railroads, mining, and public utilities. Foreign capital also financed military expenditures and the formation of Ottoman banks. By 1882 the Ottoman state could no longer pay the interest on its debts and was forced to accept a foreign debt administration. Henceforth foreign bankers controlled the Ottoman economy. However, from 1880 to 1914 there was increased prosperity in the Ottoman empire owing to the centralization of state power, security in the provinces, and the foreign stimulus to internal investment and trade.

This foreign-stimulated and foreign-regulated economy had important consequences for the social structure of Ottoman society. It favored the prosperity of Greek, Armenian, Jewish, and other minority groups involved in international trade, but the dependency of the Ottoman empire on the world economy did not proceed so far as to change the distribution of political power within Ottoman society. These groups could not challenge the dominance of the state elites. Control of taxation, major investments, and ideological and military power remained the prerogative of the Ottoman establishment. On the eve of the formation of the Turkish Republic, the military and administrative elites alone determined the destiny of the regime.

REPUBLICAN TURKEY

Thus, the Ottoman tradition of a strong centralized state and military leadership was transmitted to the Turkish republic. The history of modern Turkey can be divided into two phases. The period from 1921 to 1950 was the era of presidential dictatorship, religious reform, and the first stages of industrialization. From 1950 to the present is the era of a multi-party political system, of increasing social differentiation, rapid economic change, and resumed ideological conflict. The Kemalist period began in 1921 with the Law of Fundamental Organization which declared the sovereignty of the Turkish people. In 1923 Mustafa Kemal Ataturk was named president of the Republic for life. He was head of government, and head of the Republican People's Party. Despite brief experiments with an organized political opposition – the Progressive Party of 1924, and the Liberal Party in 1929 and 1930 – the regime was intolerant of opposition. The party was the main instrument of the regime in the countryside, and its offices disseminated information about agricultural improvements, organized educational programs, and taught the secular and national ideology to the country people. The regime thus continued the Ottoman system in which a highly educated, urban, bureaucratic, and military elite dominated the rest of the country. ʿUlamaʾ and local notables were excluded from political power but landlords were allowed to retain and consolidate their economic position. It was a regime in the name of the Turkish people, but without close connections with them.

The primary goals of Kemalist Turkey were economic development and cultural modernization. In the course of the nineteenth century, European competition forced Muslim elites out of commerce and into reliance on the state as the main vehicle of economic activity. Between 1908 and 1918, however, foreign capital was withdrawn, Greek and Armenian merchants were pushed out, and the way was opened for the growth of a new Turkish commercial elite. However, in the 1920s foreigners controlled Turkish banks and the import–export trade.

In the 1920s, the Kemalist regime resumed state sponsorship of economic development. It promoted agricultural production by reducing taxes and by investing in roads and railways. Exports of cotton, tobacco, and dried fruit rose. The Turkish Republic also took the lead in pioneering further industrial development. With Soviet loans and expertise, textile factories were built in the 1920s. Traditional crafts, however, floundered. With the collapse of the export market in 1929, Turkey turned to more energetic state control of the economy and planned economic development. The inspiration was at once Ottoman and Soviet. In the 1930s the state nationalized the railroads, utilities, ports, and mines. The first five-year plan (1929–33) promoted consumer substitution industries. The Sumer Bank was founded to finance textile, paper, glass, and sugar enterprises. Great Britain helped finance the construction of iron and steel works. In the 1920s and 1930s, the foundations were set for the emergence of a modern industrial economy.

The most important policy of the Kemalist regime was the cultural revolution. Mustafa Kemal sought to absorb the masses of the people into the ideological and cultural framework of the Republican regime, break the attachment of ordinary people to Islam, and win them to a Western and secular style of life. The new regime abolished the organized institutions of Islam. The Ottoman Sultanate was abolished in 1923 and the Caliphate in 1924. Waqf endowments and ʿulamaʾ were put under the control of a new office of religious affairs. In 1925 the Sufi orders were declared illegal and were disbanded. In 1927 the wearing of a fez was forbidden. In 1928 a new Latin script was introduced to replace the Arabic script, and an effort was begun to purify the Turkish language of its Arabic and Persian content. In 1935 all Turks were required to take surnames in the Western fashion. In the course of this period, a new family law based upon Swiss legal codes replaced the Shariʿa. Thus, Islam was "disestablished" and deprived of a role in public life, and the ordinary symbols of Turkish attachment to the traditional culture were replaced by new legal, linguistic, and other signs of modern identity.

Part of these changes was the transformation in the status of women. The nineteenth-century Tanzimat program had already provided elementary education for women, but at the turn of the century the secular nationalists made

21 Mustapha Kemal Ataturk with Rajep Pasha and his staff

the women's question a crucial concern. Ziya Gokalp theorized that equality of women was essential for the development of a modern Turkish society. He advocated equality in education, employment, and family life, allowing women equal rights in divorce and inheritance. In the first decade of the century urban women began to dress in European fashion. The first lycée for women was established in 1911, and schools for teachers, nurses, midwives, and secretaries expanded rapidly. The war years, which drained the Turkish male population, brought women into new professions and factory labor. Family legislation in 1916 and 1917 broke with the Shariᶜa, restricted polygamy and allowed women to obtain divorces in specified conditions. Thus the first steps were taken toward the legal and social equality of women, but they were only modest advances. Women still remained segregated in public places, including transportation. Theatrical entertainments, education, and many other activities were still carried on separately for men and women or in partitioned rooms.

The reforms of the 1920s and 1930s brought still more radical changes. Family laws of 1924 abolished polygamy, made the sexes substantially equal in rights to divorce, and required that divorce henceforth be subject to court rulings on specified conditions rather than a male prerogative. The constitution guaranteed the right of women to equality in education and employment, and in 1934 women were accorded the right to vote in national elections. In 1935 women deputies were elected to the Turkish parliament. The changes in attitude and legal principle have been the basis of an ever-expanding participation of women in Turkish public life.

Radical as were the economic and cultural policies, the Kemalist regime was not revolutionary. The dominant elites and organizations retained their authority. No effort was made to mobilize the peasantry. The cultural revolution, imposed from the top, had relatively slight penetration. It served to divide the country into an urban, modernized elite, and rural peasant masses oriented toward Islam. The combination of a radical cultural policy with conservative statist political and social policies made Turkey one of the first of a new type of modern Asian nation – an authoritarian regime attempting to carry out radical economic and cultural reforms.

Mustafa Kemal died in 1938, but the regime continued under his loyal colleague, Ismet Inonu. The period between Kemal's death and the end of the Inonu regime, however, prepared the way for a new political system. Economic development generated new groups of businessmen, factory managers, rural landowners, prosperous peasants, and a new generation of intellectuals who wanted political recognition. Also, Turkish legislation after World War II relaxed government controls over commerce and the universities and increased the expectation of political participation. The United States, which after World War II was becoming the main patron of Turkish political security and economic development, also favored a less paternalistic and more democratic multi-party system. Thus, in 1946 the Inonu government allowed the formation of the Democrat Party.

The Democrat Party mobilized a new coalition of small businessmen, landowners and their peasant dependents and clients, and middling and rich peasants, in opposition to the entrenched military and bureaucratic elites, and proposed a new economic orientation and religious policy. The Democrat Party promised to curtail state intervention in the economy, transfer enterprises to private control, increase marketing opportunities for peasants, and remove restrictions on the practice of Islam. The elections of 1950 exposed the conflict between a centralized authoritarian and secular regime, and the provincial demand for a liberal government tolerant of Islam.

The new party, led by Jelal Bayar and Adnan Menderes, ruled for a decade. It attempted to stimulate rapid economic development by relaxing state controls over the economy, encouraging private enterprise, and by relying upon extensive American aid and foreign investments. Turkish–American military collaboration led to the construction of roads, railways, airfields, ports and communications. In the course of the 1950s agriculture was modernized; production of sugar, cotton, and tobacco was increased. The villages were transformed by the introduction of roads, electricity, tractors, bus transportation, and schools. Hectic and chaotic growth, however, was marked by inflation, trade deficits, and an enlarged public debt. In 1958 the International Monetary Fund forced Turkey to cut back social services and wages, and to devalue the currency.

In response to its rural supporters the new regime also permitted religious instruction in Turkish schools. Mosques again received state support. The Sufi orders, however, were held in check and waqf endowments were not restored. The Democrat Party thus compromised the Kemalist dogma that only by secularization could Turkey become a modern country. It favored both economic modernization and tolerance of Islam.

Upon the collapse of the economy, a military coup on May 27, 1960, overthrew the Menderes government. The army, representing the Westernized elite and defending Kemalist secularist policies, aligned with bureaucrats and students against the rural, small-town business, and Islamic interest groups, took control of the government. The army regime, and the National Unity Committee which it spawned, stayed in power, however, only a year. This was long enough to abolish the Democrat Party and to promulgate a new constitution and parliamentary regime.

Under the new constitution, Turkey maintained a mixed economy. Industrial production and the industrial working force, spurred by state investment in infrastructure and by foreign trade, grew considerably. Economic expansion was based upon agricultural exports and the remittances of Turkish workers in Europe, but these earnings failed to pay for the heavy capital, raw materials, and other imports needed to maintain Turkey's consumer substitution industries. This led to economic unrest and another crisis of foreign exchange in 1971. In the 1970s the Turkish economy faltered badly. Rising oil prices and a general slowdown in the European economy led to inflation, unemployment, foreign debts, and exchange problems, and eventually to a new International Monetary Fund program of wage freezes and imposed deflation in 1979–80. Thus the Turkish economy grew in an irregular and highly vulnerable way, dependent upon foreign loans, and provoking conflicts of interest among large and small domestic capitalists, workers, and peasants.

In the 1960s Turkey returned to multi-party conflict. This was abetted not only by uneven economic development, but by increased social and economic differentiation, and an increased tendency toward political awareness and activism. In the 1960s, a new technical elite composed of engineers and industrial workers, a large worker movement, and militant ideological groups on both the right and the left, entered the political arena. The Republican People's Party under Ecevit came to represent the bureaucratic, intellectual, and technical elite of the country, including industrial workers and other urban groups. The party of Mustafa Kemal maintained its statist orientation, but became, in effect, a democratic socialist party appealing to a professional civil service and industrial clientele. The Justice Party, led by Demirel, was heir to the legacy of the Democrat Party. It was oriented to large-scale private enterprise and rural development. Alongside the two major parties, small but important socialist and Islamic parties came into being.

The parliamentary system failed to mediate among these conflicting interests and in 1971 the army temporarily took control of the state, but again restored a civilian government. The 1970s brought an intensification of the conflicts of the 1960s. New parties formed on both right and left, including the Agrarian Capitalists' Democratic Party, the small-town petit bourgeois National Salvation Party, the elitist and fascist National Movement Party, and the Turkish Workers Party and other left-wing worker, Maoist, and Soviet-oriented groups. By the late 1970s the right wing was openly at war with leftist groups. In 1980 the army again intervened to restore political order. In effect, economic and cultural development has made Turkey a highly pluralistic society which lacks effective political means to give coherent economic and ideological direction to the development of the country. Though Turkish society, built on a large smallholding peasant population, competing business interests, and a growing professional and working class, remains democratic, there is a grave risk of a lasting military regime.

The Islamic issue in Turkey has to be understood in terms of this pluralistic social change and political competition. In contemporary Turkey, the urban ʿulamaʾ tradition has been largely destroyed and has no influence upon public life. The ideology of the republic is secular and the upper classes are committed to it. For the Turkish urban educated upper classes, Islam remains the symbol of backwardness. However, the rural-Sufi tradition survived and the Islamic loyalties of ordinary people have never been seriously disturbed. The Turkish populace continued to identify itself as Muslim, and, throughout the Kemalist period, continued to carry on worship in mosques and at the tombs of saints.

Moreover, the economic and political stresses of the postwar era have led to the rise of movements and parties committed to the re-Islamization of state and society. One of the most important is the Said Nursi movement, founded by a religious preacher and writer, the author of the *Risale-i Nur* (Epistle of Light), which achieved a wide underground distribution in Turkey despite government opposition and the prosecution of Said Nursi for religious agitation. The *Risale-i Nur* has cultivated a revived devotion to Islam. Integrating science, tradition, theosophy, and mysticism, it especially appeals to technically educated people and to a less well-educated public nonetheless familiar with Western scientific ideas. While Said Nursi was himself concerned about politics the movement currently postpones political involvement in favor of religious self-cultivation.

Another aspect of Islamic revival is represented by the National Salvation Party, which also formed in the 1960s. The National Salvation Party favors not only a religious but a political re-establishment of an Islamic state in Turkey. It is hostile to capitalism and big business and calls upon the state to work for a moral and just society. Puritanical in moral tone, the party appeals to provincial small-town bazaar traders and artisans, especially in central and eastern Anatolia. It represents both an effort to protect Anatolia's petite bourgeoisie from the encroachment of the state and large-scale economic enterprises and an effort to increase its constituencies' share of economic development. The National Salvation Party won a small percentage of the vote in Turkish elections in the 1970s.

Islamic movements in Turkey also appeal to rural or small-town populations who have migrated to the larger cities and who preserve in the new environment a small-community orientation and old values. Finally they appeal to students, especially in technical and medical subjects, as an expression of alienation from an authoritarian state, of concern over economic prospects, and of moral doubt which stems from social and educational mobility. Striking in contemporary Turkey is the relative weakness of the traditional forms of

Islam. The two generations in which traditional ʿulamaʾ and Sufi forms of Islam were suppressed have channeled latent Islamic sentiment into new forms of Islamic organization.

While the revival of Islamic activism is of great contemporary importance, it remains so far a minority interest within contemporary Turkey. The complex social and political development of the country and the creation of a differentiated social structure has led to political and ideological crosscurrents which have submerged the traditional polarization between a secular state and Islamic religious values. To the traditional question of the role of Islam in political society have been added questions of central and provincial interests, management versus worker interests, and army and bureaucratic administration as opposed to private entrepreneurship. In Turkey the Islamic revival is only one of several ideological developments, including socialism, capitalism, communism, Maoism, and others, fighting for power in a very pluralistic and changing society. The issue of secularism versus Islam is only one of the many issues which occupy a modernizing Turkish society.

Thus the formation of the Turkish republic was prepared by the eighteenth- and nineteenth-century Ottoman empire. The Republican bureaucratic and military elite committed to the secular modernization of the country was a direct outgrowth of the late Ottoman elite. The complete defeat of Islamic interests and their subordination to state control was similarly the result of the subordination of the religious establishment and the acceptance by the ʿulamaʾ of the intrinsic legitimacy of the political regime. Furthermore, European intervention worked to strip away the Balkan Christian populations, and World War I led to the partition of the Ottoman empire in a way that substantially resolved the historic tensions between tribal and ethnic minorities and the Ottoman government. In the twentieth century, Turkish economic and social change has led to a highly pluralistic, secularized, and national society in which Islam continues to have profound religious meaning for much of the Turkish population, but finds only a restricted outlet in public life.

CHAPTER 24

EGYPT: SECULARISM AND ISLAMIC MODERNITY

Egyptian history in the nineteenth and twentieth centuries resembles that of Turkey but differs in important ways. Egypt also developed from an Ottoman and Islamic to a national and secular form of society. Its evolution also began with a period of state-managed reform, but its development was diverted by British occupation from 1882 to 1952. British rule cut off the consolidation of an Egyptian military and administrative elite and made a secondary elite of landowners, officials, merchants, and intelligentsia the spokesmen for national independence. These elites, still hampered by British occupation, came to power in 1922 and ruled until 1952. Unable to surmount the dilemmas of governing under foreign rule, divided by nationalist and Islamic political orientations, the liberal elites were removed from power and replaced by a new generation of Arab nationalist military officers who instituted the military and socialist regime which governs Egypt to the present day.

Though part of the Ottoman empire, Egypt retained a separate political and cultural identity. Under Ottoman suzerainty, Egypt was actually ruled by local Mamluk military factions. Like the rest of the Ottoman empire, Egypt had a strong ᶜulamaᵓ establishment and Sufi brotherhoods. In the course of the eighteenth century, as Ottoman control weakened, fighting among the Mamluk factions led to the decline of irrigation, excessive taxation, and increasing pastoralism and tribal autonomy. The weakness of the Ottomans led to profound changes in the whole system of Egyptian society. First, it exposed Egypt to invasion by Napoleon in 1798, to British counter-intervention, and finally to the appointment of Muhammad ᶜAli as governor in 1805. Muhammad ᶜAli determined to make himself an independent potentate, and founded a dynasty which ruled Egypt until 1952. Muhammad ʿAli had ambitious foreign projects. He defeated the Wahhabis and established Egyptian control over western Arabia and the holy places of Mecca and Medina. He expanded Egyptian power in the Sudan, and helped the Ottomans in the Greek war of independence. In 1831 Muhammad ʿAli invaded Syria and threatened the viability of the Ottoman empire.

This aggressive military regime was sustained by a far-reaching reorganization of the Egyptian state and society. Muhammad ʿAli tried to create a centralized dictatorship based upon an army of Turks, Kurds, Circassians, and other foreigners who were part of his personal household. With the help of Italian and French military advisers, he built a new army, for the first time recruiting Egyptian peasant soldiers. He devised a new tax system, employing salaried officials, to replace the old tax-farming arrangements. Coptic scribes were employed in subordinate administrative positions. All other political forces were broken; the old Mamluk households were destroyed. The power of the ʿulamaʾ, who had risen to financial and political eminence in the late eighteenth century, was broken as Muhammad ʿAli confiscated their tax farms and waqfs.

To support the state apparatus, the economy was totally reorganized. Muhammad ʿAli promoted sugar and cotton because they were cash crops with an international market. Major irrigation projects were undertaken to make it possible to cultivate the land all the year round. State control of agriculture and trade allowed Muhammad ʿAli to buy cotton from peasants at low prices and resell it to exporters at a profit. Machinery and technicians were imported to build factories to produce cotton, wool, and linen textiles, sugar, paper, glass, leather, and weapons. A new school system was founded to train technicians and army officers. For the sake of building an effective military machine, the administration and economy of the country were totally reorganized.

Muhammad ʿAli's descendant Ismaʿil (1863–79) carried the development of the country still further. He continued the program of economic and technical growth, extended the railroads and telegraph, and constructed the Suez Canal and a new harbor for Alexandria. He also gave Egypt European-type law-courts, secular schools and colleges, libraries, theaters, an opera house, and a Western-type press. Egypt, like the Ottoman empire, acquired the infrastructure of cultural modernity.

The effect of this reorganization was to destroy the old order of society in an upheaval even more profound than that which took place in the rest of the Ottoman empire. The whole balance of social power in Egyptian society was altered. Egyptians and Turko-Egyptian families became powerful in the army and administration. ʿUlamaʾ and Sufis lost their fiscal privileges. Muhammad ʿAli's economic and administrative policies promoted the development of a new landed elite. Members of the ruling family were awarded estates called *jifliks*, and tax-free lands were granted to village shaykhs who took control of taxes and corvées. The abolition of collective village responsibility made individuals responsible for paying taxes for whole villages. These measures led to the concentration of land in the hands of merchants, moneylenders, village headmen, and government officials. Further concentration was aided by changes in land law which abolished restrictions in private ownership of land and made it possible to buy, sell, or mortgage land, and in particular opened land to purchase by foreigners. By 1901 foreigners or Egyptians with foreign passports owned 23 percent of all estates of more than 50 acres (*faddan*). Finally, exports of cotton and sugar benefited landowners, merchants, and officials, and helped increase privately owned lands. From the new class of large-scale landowners came bureaucrats and army officers, who formed a new dominant elite. While its base was in landowning, the new elite had its commercial wing, including Egyptian, Jewish, and Syrian merchants, who prospered as middlemen in the growing trade with Europe. Out of this class came the lawyers, journalists, and intellectuals who would give voice to the aspirations of the new elite.

At the same time, the new economic system destroyed the village economies. Government controls and private ownership replaced village collectivities. The disruption led to peasant indebtedness, fugitivism, and to a series of peasant rebellions which swept Egypt in 1798 and 1812, throughout the 1820s, from 1846 to 1854 and from 1863 to 1865. Popular preachers who called themselves saints (*wilaya*) or mahdis appealed to the peasants' Sufi conceptions and eschatological hopes. Also the traditional guilds dissolved, and state controls replaced internal collective organization. A new economy promoted state control and individualism in place of the corporate structures of pre-nineteenth-century Egyptian society.

The position of the religious elites was equally transformed. In the eighteenth century, the ʿulamaʾ of Egypt, like the ʿulamaʾ of Istanbul were an integral element of the ruling elite and represented the interests of the regime, acting as intermediaries between the government and the common people. In the wake of the French invasion of Egypt and the struggle for power between Muhammad ʿAli and the local Mamluks, the ʿulamaʾ reached their maximum power. Muhammad ʿAli, in return for their support, agreed to consult them in political matters, and allowed them to grow wealthy by acquiring tax farms and by converting endowed funds to personal uses. After Muhammad ʿAli had consolidated power, however, he subordinated the ʿulamaʾ to the regime, banished their leading spokesmen, abolished the tax farms and waqfs, and made them dependent upon the ruler for their income. In the course of the nineteenth century, the ʿulamaʾ lost their influence on public policy. They were displaced by the new elites, and withdrew from public affairs to protect a narrow sphere of educational and judicial interests. The lack of an autonomous basis of power and a tradition of compliance operated in Egypt, as in the Ottoman empire, to confine the ʿulamaʾ to the defense of a narrow range of traditional prerogatives.

In the course of the nineteenth and early twentieth century, al-Azhar became the principal ʿulamaʾ institution, as confiscation of waqfs destroyed rival colleges, and made others administratively subordinate to the shaykh of al-Azhar. Laws of 1908 and 1911 legislated curriculum and administrative reforms which increased the authority of the shaykh over both ʿulamaʾ and students. In a more limited sphere he became principal spokesman of ʿulamaʾ Islam and the conduit of government influence among the religious elite.

The powers of Sufis were similarly circumscribed. Whereas the Sufi orders, families, shrines, and zawiyas of the eighteenth century were independent, Muhammad ʿAli brought them under state control. In 1812 he appointed the shaykh of the Bakri lineage as chief shaykh, and made the chiefs of Sufi lineages, shrines, and brotherhoods beholden to the new chief shaykh for the payment of their stipends and waqf revenues. After 1855 the state imposed a system of licensing that gave the chief shaykh and the government the authority to define the territories in which each order could stage ceremonies and mawlids (commemorations of their revered masters), and proselytize for new members. State regulations also suppressed the most dramatic of Sufi deviances from ʿulamaʾ religious norms. In 1881 a circular issued by the new chief of Sufis prohibited music and dance performances and such spectacles as flagellation and swallowing hot coals. The appointment of the chief Sufi shaykh also weakened the ʿulamaʾ, as religious authority was divided between the shaykh of the Sufis and the shaykh of al-Azhar. The government was then able to manipulate the two wings of Islam against each other, and could widen the gap between legal scholarship and Sufism. In 1903 and 1905 regulation of Sufis became the function of a government ministry. In general, both ʿulamaʾ and Sufis had been made subordinate to state control.

The subordination of the ʿulamaʾ and the emergence of a new landed commercial and intellectual elite opened the way for further radical change in Egyptian society. Before these new elites could make their influence felt, however, Egypt fell under direct British rule. British interest in Egypt derived ultimately from the consolidation of the British empire in India. Napoleon's invasion of 1798, Muhammad ʿAli's attack on Syria in 1831–39, and the construction of the Suez Canal between 1859 and 1869 underlined the fact that Egypt lay on the route to India and was essential to the defense of the empire. Furthermore, Britain had acquired a major interest in the Egyptian economy. The reforms of Muhammad ʿAli made Egypt an exporter of cotton and dependent for her earnings on the world market. Reciprocally Egypt had become an importer of British cloth. Heavy Egyptian borrowing to purchase consumer luxuries, military equipment, manufacturing machinery, and capital equipment for railroads and the Suez Canal put her into debt to European banks and governments. Egypt's economic dependence led eventually to bankruptcy, and to the imposition of a foreign-managed debt administration under Anglo-French control (1875).

The debt administration was the beginning of colonial rule. It led to open conflict between foreign interests and the new Egyptian elites. ʿUlamaʾ, land-owners, journalists, and native Egyptian army officers provoked demonstrations in 1879; in 1881, led by an army officer named ʿUrabi, they seized control of the war ministry and formed a parliamentary government. Britain refused to compromise with the nationalists, bombarded Alexandria, landed troops, defeated ʿUrabi, and in 1882 took complete control of the country in the name of the bond-holders. Thus, the crisis of 1879–82 not only gave political shape to the new Egyptian elite of army officers, officials, journalists, land-owners, and ʿulamaʾ who opposed domestic misrule and foreign intervention, but also culminated in British occupation of Egypt. In 1898 the British took the Sudan under joint Anglo-Egyptian rule.

From 1882 until World War I the British managed the Egyptian economy efficiently but in the imperial interest. The British improved agricultural productivity by investments in railroads and irrigation. They built a Delta barrage and the first Aswan dam (1906), and the cropped area grew from 5.7 million faddans in 1882 to 7.7 million in 1911. This is not to say that the peasantry was notably more prosperous. The population of the country grew from 6.8 million in 1882 to 11.3 million in 1917. Also, economic development encouraged the concentration of surplus wealth in the hands of large landlords. The British improved tax collection, consolidated private property ownership, and raised adequate revenues to pay for the Egyptian budget and the foreign debt. As a result of these policies, Egypt became ever more dependent upon cotton for export. Industrialization was prevented by a combination of British lack of interest in encouraging competition, landowners' unwillingness to invest, and lack of natural resources.

While British administration was in some respects favorable to Egyptian interests, there was deep resentment over the imposition of British rule by force, unbalanced economic policies, the displacement of Egyptian officials by British ones, neglect of education, and the exploitation of Egypt to expand the British empire in the Sudan. Under British rule the new Egyptian landowning elite and intelligentsia continued its resistance. This elite expressed itself through two related ideological positions – Islamic modernism and Egyptian nationalism. Like the Ottoman intelligentsia, the Egyptians defined first a modernist Islamic and then a secular concept of an independent Egyptian society.

The most influential spokesmen for nineteenth-century Egyptian Islamic modernism were Jamal al-Din al-Afghani (1839–97) and his Egyptian disciple, Muhammad ʿAbduh (1849–1905). Al-Afghani was an Iranian who later claimed to be an Afghan in order to ensure a favorable reception among Sunni Muslims. Educated as a Shiʿa, he was deeply versed in Muslim philosophy. Al-Afghani sought to awaken Muslims to the threat of European domination and to oppose Muslim rulers who abetted Christian intervention. His political career took him to India, Afghanistan, Egypt, France, England, Iran, and finally to Istanbul, where he died. A dramatic and passionate political intriguer, an inspiring lecturer, a man of novel and imaginative ideas, he devoted his life to persuading rulers to modernize Islam. He lectured widely on theology, natural science, philosophy, and mysticism. Everywhere he was mistrusted but used and then discarded by heads of state. He inspired suspicion and fear as much as confidence and hope.

Al-Afghani's primary objective was to encourage resistance to the European powers. He dreamed of restoring the ancient and true glory of Islam triumphant. In al-Afghani's view, the struggle for independence required solidarity. Also, Muslims had to become a scientific and technically competent modern people. To restore the glory of Islam, it was essential to reform corrupt Muslim societies.

For al-Afghani, the reform of Islam was essential because religion was the moral basis of technical and scientific achievement, and of political solidarity and power. For al-Afghani, Islam was quintessentially suited to serve as the basis of a modern society. Islam was a religion of reason and the free use of the mind. The Quran, he argued, should be interpreted by reason and was open to reinterpretation by individuals in every era of history. By stressing the rational interpretation of the Quran, al-Afghani believed that Islam could be made the basis of a modern scientific society, as it had once been the basis of a medieval society built upon faith.

Islam, properly understood, he also argued, was a dynamic faith, for it encouraged an active, responsible approach to worldly affairs. The passivity and resignation which he saw in medieval Muslims were a corruption of its true teachings. Further, Islam was the basis of patriotism and loyalty to one's people. As a religion of rationality, science, activism, and patriotism, Islam embodied precisely those virtues which had made the European countries world powers. Al-Afghani saw Islam as a religion which could be the well-spring of a rationally guided, active, responsible life, compatible with modern science, dedicated to the restoration of the autonomy of Muslim nations and to the revival of the political and cultural glory of Muslim peoples. He believed that it was essential to modernize Islam, but also that faith in Islam was essential to modernity. Al-Afghani's modernism was thus akin to that of the Young Ottomans and the Aligarh school in India.

In Egypt, Islamic modernism took a different turn in the hands of al-Afghani's disciple, Muhammad ʿAbduh. ʿAbduh was born of an educated village family and was schooled at al-Azhar. He participated in the ʿUrabi revolt of 1881, was exiled in 1882, and returned to Egypt in 1888, where he was appointed judge and later mufti, or chief of Islamic law, from 1889 to 1905. ʿAbduh's endeavors as mufti were directed toward modernizing Islamic law, and revising the curriculum of al-Azhar to include modern history and geography. Like al-Afghani, he was concerned with the defense of Muslim peoples against Europeans, but for ʿAbduh the central problem was not political but religious: how, when Muslims were adopting Western ways and Western values, could they maintain the vitality of Islam in the modern world?

ʿAbduh set about, therefore, to reformulate Islam, distinguish the essential from the non-essential, preserve the fundamentals and discard the accidental aspects of the historic legacy. He accepted the Quran and hadith as God's guidance, but in matters not expressly treated in the Quran and hadith he argued that individual reason and judgment were essential. While the Quran and hadith always applied to matters of worship, individual judgment, ijtihad, was essential to regulate social relations which were governed only by very general rational ideas and humane ethical considerations. In Islam he found general guidelines which had to be reinterpreted in each age, rather than an eternal, detailed blueprint for social and political organization. Thus, he denounced the slavish acceptance of past authority which, he held, had led Muslims to believe that the political and social arrangements of the past were a religious requirement for all ages.

Behind ʿAbduh's concepts lay the international movement of Islamic reform, and the eighteenth- and nineteenth-century revival of Egyptian interest in the Quran and hadith. The reform movement was associated with the diffusion of the Naqshbandi order in Syria and other parts of the Ottoman empire, and may also have been associated with the commercialization of Egypt's economy and increasing Egyptian contacts abroad. Thus hadith-oriented reformist Sufism made itself felt in the thought of ͨAbduh. In turn, ͨAbduh's Islamic reformism inspired the Salafiya movement in the Arab fertile crescent, in North Africa, and as far away as Indonesia.

Islamic modernism and Islamic religious reform were the ideological programs of the Egyptian intelligentsia in the decades between the ͨUrabi revolt and the turn of the century. The primary purpose of the Islamic movement was political revival. While al-Afghani emphasized the pragmatic need for Islamic solidarity, ͨAbduh pursued the same goals by emphasizing educational, legal, and spiritual reform.

In Egypt, however, as in Turkey, the Islamic modernism and reformism taught by al-Afghani and ͨAbduh gave way to a more secular nationalist concept of Egyptian identity and politics. The nationalist intelligentsia stemmed from the classes of landowners, officials, and Western-educated journalists and lawyers generated by earlier reforms. The leaders included Mustafa Kamil (1874–1908) who held a French law degree, Lutfi al-Sayyid (1872–1963) who came from an Egyptian village notable family and was educated in Quran schools and later in law, and Saͨd Zaghlul (1860–1928), the son of a village headman who began his career with a religious education and then turned to secular nationalism. Other nationalists were Jewish or Christian journalists and writers who became proponents of a secular society in which minority groups could be full citizens.

National feeling seems to have come easily in Egypt. Even before nationalism became a self-conscious doctrine, Egyptian writers spontaneously identified Egypt as the *watan*, the motherland. The homogeneity and isolation of the country, its long history of central government, and its distinctive cultural past encouraged a consciousness of Egyptian identity. In Egypt, more than in any other Middle Eastern country, the modern national state is based on the historic existence of an Egyptian people and an Egyptian state.

In the late nineteenth century, Egyptian patriotic sentiment was blended with the idea of modernizing reform. Nationalist writers like Mustafa Kamil propounded the idea of a unified nation, patriotic in spirit, passionate in its hatred of foreign rule, but also dedicated to a constitutional form of government and Western-type education. Lutfi al-Sayyid became the philosopher of a secular and constitutional society. Freedom, he argued, was the basis of society. Freedom from foreign rule, freedom from state control, and recognition of the inherent civil and political rights of citizens were its essential principles. For Lutfi al-Sayyid nationalism meant independence and also a new social and political system for Egypt.

The national movement began with speeches and journals, but it took political form with the formation of the Hizb al-Watani, or National Party, led by Mustafa Kamil, in the 1890s. This party and others took on formal identity in 1907. The Dinshaway episode conveyed the nationalist idea from its original middle-class milieu to students and even to the masses. In 1906 a group of British officers on a pigeon hunt got into a fight with local people. One of the officers was killed and in retaliation the British publicly executed four peasants and flogged numerous others. The outrage awakened widespread Egyptian hostility to British rule.

World War I crystallized the determination to be independent. The declaration of a British protectorate, martial law, requisitions of Egyptian labor and manufacturing capacity, heavy migration to Cairo, and widespread hardship stiffened Egyptian opposition to British rule. At the end of the war, a delegation (*wafd*) led by Sa'd Zaghlul, inspired with hope by Woodrow Wilson's proclamations, demanded complete independence. Zaghlul was able to mobilize mass support, and in the course of the three-year struggle from 1919 to 1922 forced the British to dissolve the protectorate. In 1922 Egypt emerged as a semi-independent state under British tutelage. An Egyptian king of the dynasty established by Muhammad 'Ali, and a parliament, governed Egyptian affairs. But foreign policy, the army, the attached region of the Sudan, and jurisdiction over all foreigners in the country was under British rather than Egyptian control.

Egypt like Turkey, came out of World War I with a secular national regime, but unlike Turkey, it remained partially dependent. The difference was due partly to the fact of foreign occupation and partly to the class composition of the Egyptian elite. The Turkish elite, composed essentially of army officers, deeply rooted in a statist tradition, was capable of mobilizing the political and military potential of the Turkish nation. The Egyptian elite, composed of landowners, journalists, and politicians, was capable of organizing a political, but not an effective military, resistance in the struggle for independence.

Egypt entered its era of semi-independence with all the makings of a national state. It had a unified population and a history of centralized government. Egypt also had a Westernized intelligentsia committed to liberal constitutional regime. The main problems which faced the country were those of achieving full independence, coping with the low standard of living and the need for economic development, and creating a modern cultural and ideological identity. In most respects, the liberal regime failed. It failed to win full independence and achieve adequate and equitable economic development or provide an abiding cultural identity, though it did give lasting importance to the concept of a free political and intellectual life. It was overthrown in 1952 by army officers who were to attempt the same objectives along new political and ideological lines.

The problem of achieving independence was complicated by a tripartite division of power between the King, the political parties, and the British. The British controlled the military and used their power at critical junctures to play off the rivalries of the King and the parties with each other; similarly, the King and the party leaders did not try to unite against the British but were only too glad to use British help to best their rivals.

Egyptian politics between 1922 and 1952 thus fell into a pattern. The Wafd Party, which had emerged from the struggle for independence as the most popular, would win national elections. The British and the King would conspire against the Wafd government and force it to resign. The King would, if necessary, suspend and dissolve Parliament and govern through his personal Cabinet, until new elections eventually returned the Wafd Party to power. The game would then begin again. The King and the British were generally united against the majority party until in 1942, when the King drew too close to German and Italian interests, the British – backed by tanks in the streets of Cairo – conspired with the Wafd to outmaneuver the monarchy. This maneuvering made it impossible for the liberal regime to achieve independence. The British were in any case content to let the issue ride. The King was not eager to have a treaty removing the British forces which maintained his power. The Wafd was unwilling to have any treaty negotiated by another party.

Despite these complications in 1936 a treaty was worked out which gave Egypt "independence" subject to certain reservations. The treaty provided for a twenty-year military alliance and British evacuation, except for the Canal Zone. It committed Britain to the defense of Egypt, committed Egypt and Britain to the joint defense of the Sudan, ended the special legal privileges of foreigners (such as mixed courts), and proposed that Egypt enter the League of Nations as an independent state. After the treaty, Egypt gained a greater degree of internal sovereignty, but Britain kept her predominant military position. World War II made Britain still more reluctant to withdraw. Postwar negotiations foundered over the control of the Sudan, until finally in 1950, Egypt abrogated the treaty of 1936 and the 1899 Sudan Convention. Guerrilla war against British occupation of the Canal Zone followed, and led to riots in January, and a military coup in July 1952, which ended the reign of the

Egyptian monarchy and the parliamentary system. Britain agreed finally to the evacuation of the Canal Zone.

The liberal regime also failed between 1922 and 1952 to cope with the problems of economic development. The per capita standard of living declined in the 1930s owing to rapid population growth and the decline of world markets for cotton. Per capita food production in the late 1920s, 1930s, and World War II actually declined below the level of 1886. However, important gains were made in the development of Egyptian consumer industries to produce processed foods, textiles, cement, paper, sugar, and other products. The Misr Bank was founded with ownership deliberately restricted to Egyptians in order to compete with foreign companies. In the 1920s and 1930s Egyptians began to take control of their economy out of the hands of foreigners.

However, the benefits of economic progress fell to a very limited part of the population. Businessmen, skilled workers, and white-collar bureaucrats prospered to a degree, but the general standard of living declined. While the parliamentary regime had come to power in 1922 owing to peasant uprisings, once in power the nationalist parties proved to represent landowner, bourgeois, industrial, and professional class interests, rather than the general need for economic growth.

Similarly, the liberal regime also left deep ambiguities about Egyptian cultural and political identity. In the 1920s Egyptian political and intellectual leaders were outspokenly secular and modernist. Many Egyptian intellectuals defended a Western orientation and liberal and national political principles. ʿAli ʿAbd al-Raziq defended the idea that Islam represented a purely spiritual community, and a code of individual behavior which had nothing to do with politics. Other writers tried to reinterpret Egyptian history in Pharaonic, but not in Muslim terms. Taha Husyan even called Quranic and biblical history into question, espousing a thoroughgoing rationalism. Others writers attacked custom, rejected ethical ideas based on revelation and other-worldly sanctions, and espoused Western humanistic values.

However, whereas the rulers of Turkey went on to implement a program of cultural modernization, Egyptian leaders could not. They lacked the absolute political power and unity essential for such a program. They were also overtaken by a growing disillusion with Europe. World War I, the political strife of the inter-war years, the Great Depression, and, finally, World War II exposed Egyptians to the failings of the constitutional and liberal governments of Europe, the ruthlessness of the powers, their indifference to principle in manipulating non-European peoples, and their contempt for their subjects.

These events shook the confidence of many Egyptians that the future belonged to the West, and left others disappointed and alienated. Furthermore, the failure of the liberal regime to win full independence and to deal equitably with the country's political and economic problems also undermined faith in parliamentary regimes and in the value of individualism.

Most important in the retreat from secularism and Westernism was the revival of popular commitment to Islam. The Islamic revival in Egypt in the 1930s and 1940s owed little to the traditional ʿulamaʾ or Sufi brotherhoods whose political and ideological position left them unable to resist the state authorities. Rather, a new generation of Muslim preachers and teachers representing Islamic youth associations, worked to teach Islamic morals and ethics, strengthen the ties of brotherhood among Muslims, and restore religious law and the supremacy of Islam in public life. They appealed to people with a traditional Muslim education such as clerks, lower civil servants, shopkeepers, students, and others who had been hurt by foreign occupation and by the change from Muslim to Western education or who had been uprooted from their position in the old order of society. Similarly, the movement appealed to a new generation of students and industrial workers who were dissatisfied with the dominance of a landowning elite committed to a foreign ideology.

The most important of the reform movements of this era was the Muslim Brotherhood founded by Hasan al-Banna in 1928. Hasan al-Banna preached the restoration of Islamic principles, and a return to the Quran and Islamic piety. He built up an extensive following divided into cells or chapters, which organized mosques, schools, clinics, and even cooperative work opportunities for their members. The movement became politically active in the 1930s, adding athletic and paramilitary groups to the other cells. Muslim brother volunteers went to support the Arab uprising in Palestine in 1936–39. In Egypt the Brotherhood allied with other Islamic youth movements to oppose British rule, the corruption of the Egyptian regime, and its defeat in the Palestine–Israel war. The Brotherhood supplied guerrilla fighters for the struggle in Suez, and sponsored violent demonstrations and strikes. By 1948–49, it had become the standard-bearer of Egyptian mass grievances against British rule and the failure of the liberal political system. It called for the establishment of an Islamic government based on consultation with the ʿulamaʾ and devoted to the application of the Shariʿa, proposed to regulate the economy in accord with a combination of Islamic and socialist principles, and to see to a more equitable distribution of income. Committed to the fundamental scriptures of Islam, to the assertion of an Islamic social and political identity, and to the adaptation of Islamic principles to the needs of a modern society, the Muslim Brotherhood was devoted to the reform of morals, education, economic projects, and the creation of a Muslim state. Islam in their minds was the blueprint for a total modern society and presented itself as an ideological and political alternative to liberalism or to communism.

In the face of this tide of public opinion Egyptian secularists had to give way. Such leaders as Muhammad Haykal did not so much change their views as seek for ways to make rationalism and scientific and secular attitudes meaningful to a mass Egyptian audience. His biography of the Prophet, and his attacks on materialism in Western culture, became the public framework of an effort to insinuate modern rational and ethical values within Islam. Thus, in the cultural atmosphere of the 1930s and 1940s, the secular intelligentsia lost the initiative, accepted an Islamic framework, and attempted to compromise between Islam and modernity. The net effect was not so much to rescue secularism as to legitimize the Muslim revival. In Egypt, as opposed to Turkey, the political elite was unable to control the national cultural agenda.

World War II and its aftermath brought the Egyptian regime to a crisis. The war further discredited British rule and intensified economic distress. Cotton prices fell, living standards declined, strikes were suppressed. Migrants from rural areas to Cairo could not find work. After the war the corruption of the Egyptian state was exposed by its failure to stop the formation of a Jewish state in Palestine. Egypt's army intervened in 1948 but was disgraced in battle, and government mismanagement and profiteering in the supply of military hardware was exposed. Soldiers returned embittered and denounced the regime for their defeat.

For a time it seemed as if the Muslim Brotherhood would seize power, but they were forstalled by the Free Officers. A new force had come into being in the persons of students and army officers with professional and technical educations, the sons of small-scale landowners, traders, or clerks, not implicated in the old regime. Shocked by its failure to defeat the British and by the corruption which undermined the Egyptian army in Palestine, they conspired to seize power. In 1952 the Free Officers, led by Muhammad Naguib, Jamal ʿAbd al-Nasser and Anwar Sadat, overthrew the King and brought the parliamentary regime to an end. In the three-way struggle among the liberal, secularized older generation, the Islamic and lower-class reformers, and the new generation of technically educated army intelligentsia, the army conspirators were victorious. Egyptian development would thus continue in a national and secular direction, albeit in new modes.

The regime established by the Free Officers in 1952 set Egypt on the course which by and large persists to the present day. The new regime transformed the domestic and international political identity of the country. The monarchy and Parliament were abolished and replaced by a presidential regime and one-party system which rested on a new political elite of army officers and bu-reaucrats of middle-class origin and not on the landowning and professional classes which had governed Egypt until the middle of the century. Ideologi-cally the Free Officers' government turned from liberalism to socialism, from collaboration to anti-imperialism, and from nationalism to Pan-Arabism to define the objectives of Egyptian national development.

The international crisis of the 1950s was crucial for the direction of Egypt's development. Nasser's regime came to power without a clear conception of its future; its position evolved in response to the international circumstances and domestic problems of the 1950s. In the course of the 1950s Eygpt became a leading spokesman for the independence of Third World nations and for neutrality in the Cold War, and a leader in the struggle of Arab countries against imperialism and Zionism. In 1955, under pressure to take sides in the Cold War, Egypt refused to accept the Baghdad Pact and negotiated Russian security guarantees and an arms deal with Czechoslovakia. In return, in March 1956, U.S. Secretary of State John Foster Dulles withdrew from promises to fund the construction of an Aswan dam and Nasser retaliated by nationalizing the Suez Canal. In October, Britain, France, and Israel attacked Egypt to regain control of the Canal, but were forced to withdraw because of united Russian and American opposition.

The Suez crisis, Nasser's espousal of neutralism, his defiance of the United States and Britain, his arms deal with Czechoslovakia, and his survival of the British–French–Israeli assault, made him the supreme leader of the Arab world. Arabs in Syria, Jordan, Iraq, Lebanon, and Palestine looked to him for leadership in the struggle against Israel. Nasserite parties were founded in several Arab countries. In 1958 a union was formed between Egypt and Syria which, it was hoped, would be the basis for a single Arab state. Though the union broke up in 1961, mainly because of Egyptian domination of Syria, Egypt maintained its position as the leader of the Arab world in its struggle against Israel. Egypt was committed to redressing the injustice in Palestine, prevailing in the struggle with Israel, and achieving Arab unity. Thus the defeat in the 1967 war with Israel discredited Nasser's claims to Arab world leadership, again labeled a secular Egyptian state as a failure, and opened the way to a revival of Muslim loyalties. Only the relatively good performance of Egyptian armies in the 1973 war allowed Egypt to remove the Palestine problem from the top of the government's agenda. After the war the "sacred

22 President Nasser's car is mobbed by townspeople

struggle" was put aside and Egypt turned to Sa'udi Arabia and the United States for economic and political support. The turning to the United States was tantamount to a renewed courting of Western culture. Sadat revived an earlier twentieth-century Egyptian desire to be accepted as a Western country.

In domestic affairs the president was the dominant figure, basing his power on the army, on the bureaucracy, and upon his talents for political manipulation and mobilizing public support. In political administration the major innovation of the regime was the one-party system to encourage new forms of political participation and economic cooperation for the mass of Egyptians. The Liberation Rally was formed in 1952, and succeeded in 1955 by the National Union. The single political party helped to keep the masses responsive to decisions at the top, helped keep the upper echelons of the government in touch with the needs of the society, and served as a channel for mobility. In 1962 a national congress created the Arab Socialist Union. The Arab Socialist Union established a local party organization to influence municipal administration, to train youth cadres for eventual leadership in the party and the government, and to inculcate a socialist ideology among peasants and workers. In 1965 'Ali Sabri reorganized the party to stress a militant youth organization, training camps, and a more aggressive party role in local affairs. After 1971 Sadat significantly reduced the importance of the A.S.U. in political management. The one-party system, however, was not so important in the government of the country as was Nasser's ability to balance powerful officers and officials who controlled the army, the ministries, and the major industries against each other.

From the late 1950s the Free Officers Regime also began to organize a socialist economy. This was not done out of ideological commitment, but as a result of pragmatic efforts to find a solution to Egypt's economic problems. The basic economic problem was to check the decline in the Egyptian standard of living. From 1882 to 1960 the population of the country had risen from 6.8 million to 26 million. In the same period the cropped area had risen from 5.7 million to 10.2 million faddans. The per capita standard of living had probably declined. Since it was impossible to increase agricultural production to keep pace with rising population, the development of industry was essential.

In the 1950s a new strategy, based on industrialization financed by increased agricultural productivity and appropriation of the agricultural surplus, was adopted to break the cycle of impoverishment. To carry out this policy Nasser's regime first destroyed the old political elite. The Wafd party was eliminated, the Muslim Brotherhood was crushed, and the old landowning aristocrats were damaged by land reform laws passed in 1953, 1961, and 1969. By the laws of 1953 the maximum acreage which could be held by any individual was 200 faddans. This was progressively reduced to fifty faddans. Thus, land was redistributed, large estates were eliminated and small ones favored, though there was not sufficient land to provide territory for all landless laborers. The government maintained private ownership of land but introduced state-controlled cooperatives in order to assure its goals. Productivity was to be increased by government provision of credits, fertilizers, and seeds, but the government requisitioned goods for export. Peasants were to be politically mobilized on the local level by opportunities to participate in local government. The state also provided vastly increased rural services in the form of roads, schools, health centers, cottage industries, and so on.

In agriculture, however, Nasser's regime hedged its commitments. In the 1950s the regime began a program of reclamation of desert land in Tahrir (Liberation) province. Faced with the choice of distributing the new lands to individual peasants or creating state-run collective farms on the Soviet model, Sayyid Marei, Minister of Agriculture, favored the former policy, and army officers administering the Tahrir development favored the latter. Nasser kept the issue open rather than allow either faction or either policy to win the upper hand. The result was a pragmatic and mixed economy in agriculture.

Egypt's industrial policy changed rapidly. Between 1952 and 1956 the Free Officers encouraged private entrepreneurs; but, discouraged by the hostility of the regime to large-scale private ownership in agriculture and handicapped by lack of capital and expertise, Egypt's business leaders could not make the transition from consumer to capital-goods industries. The Egyptian government believed that the policy of laissez faire had failed; its international orientation to the Third World and to the Soviet bloc made some kind of government control of the economy seem essential. Thus, between 1957 and 1960 the government took control of the major banks, sequestered British, French, and Jewish property, and developed plans for agricultural reform and for the construction of the Aswan dam. Still it lacked the means to realize its objectives. In 1960 and 1961, therefore, banks and major industries were nationalized and direct government control of important sectors of the economy – banking, insurance, foreign trade, transportation, construction, textile, and other manufactures – was instituted. Only retail trade and housing were left to the private sector. Both foreign and Egyptian bourgeoisies were dispossessed, and the economy was nationalized and Egyptianized. In all the new regime was dominated by the army, which became prominent in government administration and in management of industries. A second echelon consisted of officials, engineers, teachers, journalists, and lawyers. As the new elite became entrenched in power, it constituted a "state" bourgeoisie.

The socialized economy was expected to meet the needs of Egyptian economic development by freeing Egypt from foreign economic control, and by generating employment, higher-value products, and exports. By 1965 the public sector provided 45 percent of the output, 45 percent of the savings and 90 percent of the capital formation for the Egyptian economy as a whole. Still, the economy was faltering. Excessively ambitious planning, unwillingness to sacrifice welfare to investment goals, inefficiency, and corruption took their toll. Heavy defense expenditure and finally defeat in the 1967 war with Israel ruined the socialist experiment and seemed to demand a new sense of direction.

In the 1970s under the presidency of Sadat, the Egyptian regime returned to a mixed economy and to a policy of encouraging private investment. By 1974 this had become the policy of *infitah*, or open door to foreign investment. This new policy was correlated with alliances with the United States and with conservative Arab states. Despite foreign investments, however, Egyptian prosperity continued to depend upon petroleum exports, tourism, Suez Canal tolls, and remittances of Egyptian workers abroad. In fact, the Egyptian foreign debt grew enormously.

In agriculture, Sadat's policy was to compromise with the numerous interests involved. Some land was given to the syndicate of agricultural engineers. Some land was distributed to peasants who were enrolled in agricultural cooperatives. Other land was sold at auction to the highest bidder, which enabled wealthy industrialists to consolidate agribusiness holdings. In general, Egypt maintained a state-dominated economy sensitive to pragmatic political considerations.

The socialized and semi-socialized Egyptian economy has promoted a new distribution of power in Egyptian society. The old landowning elites have been replaced by a new generation of army officers, bureaucrats, and technocrats, but the orientation to infitah in the 1970s has encouraged foreign banks and joint venture companies and has generated a new elite of import–exporters, contractors, and speculators in housing. With the change in economic orientation Egypt has also retreated from the welfare and social service goals of the 1960s and accepted a less equitable distribution of income.

The emergence of a new state elite has also had important effects on the distribution of power in the countryside. Political power has been transferred from large landowning families to middle-size village notables and even to the peasant leaders of agricultural cooperatives. The rural middle class consists of a relatively small population of middle-size landowners (10–50 faddans) who, although only 3 percent of the population, own 40 percent of the land. This class, however, does not participate in national political power and is a subordinate clientele of the central state elites. An overcentralized and unresponsive municipal and agricultural cooperative administration still weighs heavily on Egyptian rural society.

Apart from class, elite, and pragmatic considerations, the continuing importance of Islam qualifies Egypt's commitments to socialism. Ninety percent of the Egyptian population is Muslim. In the 1950s and 1960s Nasser's regime attempted to bring Islamic religious activity under government control. Opposition movements like the Muslim Brotherhood were outlawed and the autonomy of other religious institutions was curtailed. Waqf land was taken under government control in 1960 and 1973, and private mosques were brought under government ministries. In 1961 al-Azhar was made a state university with a reformed curriculum. In the crucial field of legal administration, Egypt had already adapted new criminal and civil law codes in the nineteenth century. A new civil code based on French models was introduced in 1873; a double court system was established in 1875 to restrict the competence of Shariᶜa courts and to establish an alternative system of law. Yet another civil law code was introduced in 1949, and in 1955 the Egyptian government consolidated Shariᶜa courts and civil courts dealing with matters of personal status. Though the Shariᶜa continues to be applied, Muslim legal codes have been brought under governmental jurisdiction. In general the government has tried to control religious life, to use the ʿulamaʾ to support government policy, and to identify Islam with national and socialist programs.

This effort to create an apparent identity of Islam and the state is only partially successful. Muslim sentiment in the country remains powerful and independent of state control. Just as the 1930s brought a revival of Islamic sentiments in intellectual and political circles, the 1970s has witnessed a revival of Islam appealing to middle-class students and young professional people. There are several reasons for this. First is the background of deep-felt Islamic loyalties which have not been eradicated, but only held in abeyance among Western-educated professional and governmental elites; they have not really been supplanted by new national, secular, or socialist loyalties. Secondly, while the ʿulamaʾ and the official Islamic establishment remain under government control, independent preachers, missionaries, and teachers actively promote a revived commitment to Islam. Finally, the political and social atmosphere of the late 1960s and 1970s has given a new cachet to religious loyalties. The defeat in the 1967 war with Israel, the failure to solve the Palestinian problem, and the failure to develop economically have led to condemnation of Egypt's secular and socialist policies. As Egyptians returned to their faith for consolation, Sadat also took up the rhetoric of Islam and thereby lent added respectability to the new sentiment.

The problems of particular milieus have made these national issues increasingly relevant to important groups. The rapid urbanization of Cairo has attracted people from small towns and villages to a difficult environment. Expansion of the educational system has created a large and growing class of students and university graduates without prospect of employment. Finally, the failure of the nationalist, socialist, and secular regime contrasts with the success of a Saʿudi Arabian government that is dedicated to Islam. This inspires, especially among students and youth, a return to Islamic religious commitments in place of the secularist and socialist views of their parents' generation.

The new sentiment is the basis for the proliferation of Islamic revivalist groups. Generally speaking, these groups hold the same religious and social views as the Muslim Brotherhood. They believe that the Quran and Sunna must be the basis of individual morality, and stress the application of the Shariʿa in all relevant matters. In social policy they hold that the primary role of women should be the care of the family. They avoid ideological positions in economic matters, but stress the importance of minimizing the differences in wealth between rich and poor. For them, social justice is more important than technological, economic, or administrative issues. In general, these groups believe that their society has been corrupted by secular values and that only a return to Islamic principles will restore morality, economic well-being, and political power.

The more radical groups have adopted a doctrine of direct combat against the state. They are inspired by the teaching of Sayyid Qutb (d. 1966) whose *Signs of the Road* has become an influential manifesto. The central view of this book is that sovereignty belongs to God and all human authority derives from God's sovereignty. In human societies there is no middle ground between Islam and *jahiliya*, between an Islamic and a pagan way of life. Egypt in his view had become a jahiliya society and the primary tasks of good Muslims must be retreat (hijra), excommunication (*takfir*) of the false Muslims, the waging of jihad, and the reconversion of Egypt to Islam. This is an uncompromising revolutionary point of view.

In the 1970s Shukri Mustafa, the head of the Jamaᶜat al-Muslimin (called by others *al-takfir wa-al-hijra*) took up the same doctrine. He denounced reformist and collaborating points of view and excommunicated the jahiliya society led by Sadat. He formed a small group of followers who retreated from the mosques under the control of the authorities, refused all collaboration with Egyptian institutions, including the courts and schools, and even introduced a special form of marriage for the members of his community. This group, and similar ones, did not attempt to preach to the Egyptian masses but rather expected to seize power by first destroying the corrupt leadership. Such groups attempted assassinations of Egyptian political leaders in 1973 and 1977. In 1981 one of them succeeded in killing Sadat.

The assassins of Sadat seem typical of the radical Islamic groups. They denounced the Egyptian government as illegitimate because it did not apply Muslim law, because it was ruled by apostates and tyrants, and because it was allied to Zionists, communists, and imperialists. They denounced the ᶜulamaᵓ and Muslim charitable and religious associations who cooperated with the government as collaborators with a corrupt regime. They held that the state could be changed only by direct combat. After the assassination of Sadat the movement was not able to arouse sufficient public support and its uprisings in Asyut and other places were put down by the army.

More broadly based and reformist in orientation were the Jamaᶜat al-Islamiya, which were student associations dedicated to Islamization. These associations grew up after the defeat of 1967, and their objective was to recreate an Islamic society on the basis of a restored Caliphate. The student jamaᶜat began by forming poetry, painting, lecture, Quran reading, and other clubs. They were covertly aided by the police to break the power of the communists in the student movement. Apart from politics they served student interests by making copies of course syllabuses and distributing them at low cost, organizing bus services for women in Islamic dress, and providing subsidies for pilgrimage. Through independent mosques they began to preach to the common people in Cairo and the villages. They adopted the veil for women, the unshaven beard and the white dress for men, and favored public prayer demonstrations. In 1979 the jamaᶜat became involved in hostilities with the Copts. Muslim propaganda was circulated to denounce alleged Christian aggressions, proselytizing among Muslims, and cooperation between the state and the Coptic community. There were Muslim–Christian riots, and in 1981 the government dissolved the jamaᶜat, and removed church officials in a bid for popular support. The masses were generally quiet. The student radicals had overestimated the appeal of Islam over Egyptian nationalism, and had underestimated the power of the state to keep control of the population.

Alongside of politics a primary concern of the jamaᶜat was personal morality, family values, and cultural authenticity. The 1970s revival appealed especially to students and professional people – engineers, schoolteachers, and white-collar workers – often from rural backgrounds and from upwardly and geographically mobile, but socially conservative, families. Student enrollment in the universities had grown from less than 200,000 in 1970 to more than half a million in 1977. The students had almost no direct instruction and lived in extremely poor and crowded conditions. Intellectually they had become slaves of mimeographed course manuals; socially they felt oppressed and frustrated. Many young professional people also came from rural backgrounds and acquired a technical or professional skill without going through a deep process of social or cultural adjustment. In Cairo they found themselves, despite their high professional qualifications, without a place in society, living in marginal districts, alienated by inadequate salaries and distressed by the moral corruption of a big city. They were beset by sexual tensions and were concerned about finding proper spouses. In particular, young women professional students began to wear Islamic dress, which does not reveal the figure or expose hair or limbs. This new commitment to Islamic modesty came precisely at a time when women were increasingly entering professional schools and public life. Between 1952 and 1976 the ratio of female to male students in the universities rose from 1:12 to 1:2. For women who were entering the public world dominated by men, the veil and the profession of an Islamic modesty were ways of re-creating the traditional separation among young people who were otherwise – through education, travel and public transport, enjoyment of public entertainment, and political activities – thrown together. The adoption of Islamic dress implies unavailability and asexuality, and for young women from conservative rural families it serves as a way of controlling sexual confusion and protecting family values and marriage possibilities. Thus, while the Islamic revival in Egypt has important political aspects, it is also a mechanism for the adjustment of Muslim students to the complexities of an urban environment.

While Egypt has been committed to modernization and secular development since the early nineteenth century, the place of Islam in Egyptian national development remains an issue for political struggle. The regimes of Nasser and Sadat were committed to a moderate form of authoritarian and centralized rule, to socialized management of the economy, and to a socialist ideology modified to stress respect for Islam. As in the 1930s, government policy again allowed Islam to become the rallying call of opposition to the failures of the state. The consequence of a political elite which dominates the ʿulamaʾ without being able to dominate the cultural life of the country is permanent Islamic revival. In the 1930s and 1940s the Muslim Brotherhood stressed the anti-imperialist aspects of Islam because it saw the main enemy to be the British. In the 1950s and 1960s it stressed solidarity and justice in opposition to the corruption of the military regime. In the 1970s the Islamic reform movements emphasized personal morality and family values in response to the stresses of a changing social order. In Egypt, as opposed to Turkey, Islam remains the main vehicle of resistance to the state and its policies. The basic structures of Egyptian society are similar to those of Turkish society, but because of the more limited powers of the Egyptian political elite and the more limited degree of social and economic differentiation, there is a standing conflict between the secularized state elite and their Islamic petit bourgeois and student opponents.

CHAPTER 25

THE ARAB MIDDLE EAST: ARABISM, MILITARY STATES, AND ISLAM

Though Turkey, Egypt, and the Arab fertile crescent all had their origins in the Ottoman empire, the Arab fertile crescent had a different internal pattern of state, religious, and social institutions, and a different experience of European influence and colonial rule. Whereas in Turkey, an established state could absorb European influences, assume control of the reconstruction of Turkish society after World War I, and thus maintain the continuity of its historical institutional pattern, in the Arab fertile crescent there was no history of independent state regimes until after World War II, and no unified and continuing governing elite. In this region, Europeans defined the structure of Arab states. While an Arab national identity took form in the twentieth century it was replete with contradictions among cultural and ideological identities, and majority and minority interests. Arab nationalism, Islam, and the actual political structures of the region continue to present no settled relationship to each other.

NOTABLES AND THE RISE OF ARAB NATIONALISM

The modern Arab state system and the Arab national movement had its origins in the nineteenth century Ottoman system and the pattern of European influences on the fertile crescent. The Ottomans had ruled the fertile crescent as a number of separate small provinces. There were no units of territorial government corresponding to the Ottoman sub-states in Egypt, Tunisia, or Algeria. The principal cities of the region, such as Damascus, Aleppo, Mosul, and Baghdad, were the main centers of government. Rural districts were often autonomous. The variety of local jurisdictions would lead to different patterns of economic change and political consciousness.

Arab nationalism had its first home in Lebanon. In Lebanon "modernization" and the formation of a new political consciousness was directly influenced by European commercial, political, and educational penetration. In Lebanon and its Syrian hinterland, a growing volume of trade stimulated the production of cash crops such as silk, cotton, and cereals wherever they could easily be transported to the coast. Owing to rising population and greater economic specialization, some producers, such as silk weavers, were able to enhance their position. Other products, such as Syrian cloths woven with silver and gold threads, that could not be imitated in Europe, maintained their hold on a specialized market. After 1860 Beirut flourished as an exporting center. Lebanese–European trade in silk, soap, and leather expanded. Palestinian output and exports of cereals, fruits, olives, soap, textiles, and leather also increased owing to increased political control over bedouins, and to new lands brought into cultivation. However, many craftsmen succumbed to European competition. Christian merchants active in the import–export trade became the protégés of Europeans and gained an advantage over Muslims.

By the middle of the century the European powers also became the guarantors of the security of Lebanon. By this time Lebanon was in a state of sporadic civil war precipitated by growing European intervention, Ottoman efforts to centralize control, the breakdown of local principalities, and other factors. The origins of these wars were changes in the Maronite church. Until the middle of the eighteenth century, the church had been in the control of lay Maronite landlords who appointed the Patriarch and the bishops. Eighteenth-century reformers, led by churchmen educated in Rome, attempted to free the church from lay control. The reformers established a system of church schools and attempted to propagandize the populace in favor of a church-led Maronite government.

The political consequences of the Maronite revival were formidable. In 1820 there was a peasant revolt against the feudal landlords. The Maronite movement led also to increasing tension with the Druzes, who, in response to Maronite pressure, became more organized and unified. The policies of Bashir II (1788–1840), overlord of Lebanon, polarized the situation. Bashir tried to centralize power and eliminate his rivals, mainly Druze chieftains. He defeated the Druzes in 1825, and cooperated with the Egyptian invasion of Syria and Lebanon in 1831. In 1840, however, Britain and France intervened to evict the Egyptians, and encouraged Maronite opposition to Bashir and to

23 The oil refinery at Abadan

Egyptian authority. Bashir was removed from power, but the Maronites and Druzes remained divided and the country ungovernable. There were Maronite–Druze wars in 1838, 1841–42, and 1845.

The Ottoman authorities established a new government in 1843: one district in the north with a Maronite governor and one in the south with a Druze governor, and mixed councils for the country as a whole. This government lasted until 1858, when the Maronite populace again rebelled against its feudal lords. This was followed by a Druze–Muslim attack on the Maronites in 1859 and 1860; communal war superseded class war. The European powers again intervened and forced the Ottoman government to promulgate the Regulations of 1861. These regulations recognized Christian predominance. The head of government, or *Mutasarrif*, was to be a Christian, while a governing council represented the other religious communities. Lebanon became a privileged province within the Ottoman empire with the European powers guaranteeing its security.

European influence in regional commerce and politics was accompanied by direct educational efforts. Since the eighteenth century Lebanon's Maronite clergy was educated in Rome. France sponsored a vigorous educational program. French Jesuits established a school at Aintura in 1728 and Maronite colleges were established at Zigharta (1735) and Ayn Warqa (1789). The Syrian Protestant College, which eventually became the American University of Beirut, was founded in 1866. Zahleh, Damascus, and Aleppo acquired new schools between 1839 and 1873. The French-sponsored University of St Joseph was established in 1875.

In this case, foreign commercial, educational, and religious influences, rather than internal political and economic reforms, led to the formation of a new literary intelligentsia. What Tanzimat had done in Turkey and what economic change did in Egypt, Western education did in Lebanon. A small vanguard took the lead in formulating a cultural renaissance. Educated Arabs became aware, not only of the West, but of their own literary heritage. The early figures in the literary revival, such as Nasif Yaziji and Butrus Bustani, were Christian-Arab writers. Bustani, for example, was a Maronite, educated at the seminar of Ayn Warqa; he taught in American schools and authored a dictionary to revive interest in the Arabic language and the beauty of Arabic literature. These early publicists disseminated their views through cultural and national associations, such as the Society of Arts and Sciences founded in 1847 and the Syrian Scientific Society founded in 1857, to foster the study of Arabic literature and the recollection of the glory of the Arab past. The early Arab literary thinkers also stressed modernization and reform. Their newspapers and journals presented Western European scientific and political ideas as well as the history, language, and literature of the Arabs. Government, they preached, should be conducted in the interest of the governed, and provide for just and regular taxation, education and legal reform.

By the turn of the century the intellectual revival had turned into political unrest, based upon strong anti-Turkish feeling and a strong sense of the superiority of Arab to Turkish peoples. Al-Kawakibi (1849–1903) was one of the first Arab writers to say that Arabs must take over the leadership of the Muslim world from the corrupted Turks. The new literary attitude may have been promoted by a conspiracy to agitate for the restoration of the Caliphate in the person of the Sharif of Mecca, the custodian of the holy places, but behind this revival of Arab sensibility also lay Islamic religious feelings channeled into pro-Arab sentiments. Arabs, after all, were the first people of Islam. The Quran was revealed in Arabic, and the glorious days of the Islamic empire were Arab glories. Finally, Christian-Arab writers put forward the idea of secession from the Ottoman empire and the formation of a new Arab state. Negib Azoury called for the formation of a secular Arab state in which Christians and Muslims would be equal citizens under a constitutional regime.

For very different reasons, and at a later date, Arab nationalism also took root among the Muslim notables of Damascus. Here the primary factors were not political autonomy and commercial penetration, but the very operation of the Ottoman system and a Muslim reaction against growing European (and local Christian) commercial success. Before 1860 the Damascus notables were primarily ʿulamaʾ descended from prominent eighteenth-century families who supplied the officials for the religious posts of mufti, khatib (preacher), and Syndic of the Descendants of the Prophet. They also managed the waqfs and had strong support from merchants, artisans, janissaries, and the town quarters. In the late eighteenth and nineteenth centuries these families were joined by military chieftains (*aghawat*) whose power was based on janissary clienteles, and on control of suburban quarters and the grain trade which went through them. By the late nineteenth century ʿulamaʾ and aghawat families had merged into a combined religious and landowning elite. Rich merchants and Ottoman office holders were also part of this elite. By this time many families were sending their sons to Ottoman professional schools and were competing for places in the Ottoman government service. The notables, however, were not a unified body, but were divided into competing families and factions.

The position of the notables was challenged but not overturned by state programs of centralization or "Tanzimat." The Egyptian occupation of Syria (1831–39) attempted to overcome local independence, establish a centralized government, and promote economic development. Ibrahim, the son of Muhammad ʿAli, attempted to disarm the local population, and introduced conscription, corvée, and a new head tax. He established monopolies for the production of silk, cotton, and tobacco, and began mining for coal.

When Syria was returned to Ottoman suzerainty in 1841, the Ottomans intended to centralize power, eliminate the intermediary notables, and mobilize mass support for the state. They proposed to secularize the judicial system and introduce formal equality of Muslims and non-Muslims. Yet, to offset the power of local governors, they created local councils (*majlis*) and gave the notables important fiscal and administrative powers. Already threatened by European commercial competition, the growing role of Christians and Jews as intermediaries in trade with Europe, and the beginning of Christian and Jewish money-lending in rural areas, the Damascus notables were hostile to Ottoman reforms, and used their position to maintain the basic structure of Syrian society.

The rise of the Ottoman Committee of Union and Progress in 1908 pushed some of the Damascus notables into adopting the Arabist intellectual and political currents of the day. The new Ottoman government first inspired great hopes but C.U.P. efforts to centralize Ottoman power in the hands of Turks disappointed Arab leaders. In Damascus the imposition of Turkish as the language of schools and courts, Turkish controls over waqfs, and the dismissal of local officials led to the adoption of Arabism as the expression of opposition to secularization and Turkish rule. Just before and during World War I Arabism became the ideology of Damascus notables, military officers, lawyers, and those ʿulamaʾ who were out of government favor. Arabism before 1918, however, still meant change in the Ottoman system and not political independence. Arab leaders generally favored continuation of the Ottoman empire and an Arab–Turkish ruling condominium on the model of the Austro-Hungarian empire, and other schemes for decentralization and Arab equality.

A third current in the formation of Arabism came from Arabia. In 1915, Husayn, the Sharif of Mecca, entered secret negotiations with the British to promote an Arab revolt against Ottoman rule in Syria and Arabia. Husayn hoped, with British help, to overthrow the Ottomans and become king of an Arab state. His ambition was based upon his religious prestige as Sharif, or descendant of the Prophet, and as custodian of the holy places, and upon some earlier conspiracies to make him the new Caliph of the Islamic world. Husayn carefully tried to rally Arab national and literary sentiment to his side by cultivating *al-Fatat*, a secret society in Damascus, which had approached him to sound out his interest in an independent Arab state allied with Britain. Britain in return saw that Husayn could be helpful militarily and politically. Thus in a famous letter of October 1915, Sir Henry MacMahon, the British High Commissioner in Egypt, implied that the British would recognize an independent Arab state, except for Lebanon and unspecified French interests. In June 1916, Husayn was declared King and attempted to seize the Hijaz. He waged guerrilla warfare against the Turks with the help of British agents and military advisers, including T. E. Lawrence. His forces took ʿAqaba in July 1917. Together the British and the Arabs took Damascus. By the end of the war, the British were in control of most of the Near East, while Faysal, the son of Husayn, established himself as governor of Damascus under British auspices. Faysal, supported by Syrian notables, demanded that the British recognize him as the monarch of an independent Arab state.

The Arab wish to establish an independent state was aborted by the European powers. The British were not really committed to Husayn. By the Sykes–Picot agreement with France (1916), they promised to partition the Arab Near East into two zones of direct colonial rule and two spheres of influence, and in 1917 they promised to establish a Jewish National Home in Palestine. In response to Husayn's protests, Great Britain assured him that the political as well as the civil and religious rights of Arabs would be protected, and in other declarations promised to assist in the formation of independent states based on the consent of the governed. At the conference of San Remo in April 1920, Britain and France nonetheless decided to divide the Arab world in accord with the Sykes–Picot agreement. The allies created four dependent states. France took control of Lebanon and Syria and ousted Faysal from Damascus; Britain took control of Iraq and Palestine. In 1922 Palestine was divided to create a fifth state – Transjordan. The new colonies were legitimized as Mandates of the League of Nations, though they had been established without the participation of local peoples.

Thus, as opposed to Turkey and Egypt, the British and the French, rather than local elites, held complete sway over the formation of the Arab fertile crescent states. Arab resistance was scarcely conceivable. The Arab national movement was too weak and divided to affect the fortunes of the region. Its literary wing was barely coming to political consciousness; the Arab revolt led by Sharif Husayn did not represent the modernist aspirations of the intellectuals in Lebanon and Syria. The Damascus notables were divided by faction, party, and competition for power. While Arab ethnic and linguistic pride, and claims for autonomy or an equal place in the Ottoman empire had been expressed, no Arab leader had a clear image of the political future. Rather there were competing tendencies toward decentralization, toward a single Arab state, and toward regional states. In a society which had virtually no history of independent states and no history of internal institutional or economic reform, a national political movement could not but be immature. Thus the British and the French created the Arab states, gave them territorial boundaries and central regimes, and bequeathed to the future the dilemma of a cultural region partitioned into numerous small states.

ARABISM IN THE COLONIAL PERIOD

From the 1920s to the 1950s each of these states (apart from Palestine, which had special problems, to be considered shortly) was caught up in a double political struggle. Each attempted to win independence from its French or British colonial overlord, and within each there was a growing struggle for power between a dominant older-generation conservative elite and rising social forces. Out of these struggles came political independence in the late 1940s and a conjoined domestic and international crisis over political leadership and ideological identity in the 1950s.

In the mandate period each country was in the control of a foreign power allied to a conservative domestic political elite. In Iraq, a monarch, Ottoman and Sharifian army officers in the service of Faysal, and landowners and tribal chiefs composed the political elite. In Syria the elite included landowners, merchants, and religious leaders. In Transjordan the palace household of the Amir and the local bedouin chiefs governed the country. Lebanon was governed by the traditional landowning and sectarian bosses. The Arab population of Palestine had its clan and religious spokesmen. In each country the political elites accepted the mandate system. Their proximate goal was the consolidation of central governments, despite the inherent fragmentation of the population into numerous tribal, ethnic, or sectarian communities; their long-term goal was independence from Britain and France.

In the mandate period Arab nationalism became the principal expression of the demand for independence. Arab nationalism was by then a complex concept. In the minds of Damascus ʿulamaʾ and other notables it combined religious and nationalist objectives. The idea of Arabism was at first closely associated with autonomy within the Ottoman empire and with the revival of Arab leadership for the formation of a new Caliphate and a revitalized Islamic society. Under the pressure of the secular orientation of the elite graduates of Ottoman professional schools, the influence of Christian nationalist allies, and the unavoidable realities of the dissolution of the Ottoman empire, and the abolition of the Caliphate, Arabism became a more secular doctrine. In the 1920s and 1930s Arab nationalist thinkers tried to demonstrate, on the theoretical and philosophical level, the existence of an Arab nation. This nation they defined in terms of a shared language, history, and culture which could overcome the division of Arab peoples into tribes, regions, religions, and states. Sati al-Husri, an Iraqi Arab nationalist and educator, preached the need for unity and willingness to sacrifice parochial interests to the cause of the nation as a whole.

Map 31. The Middle East between the World Wars.

Michel Aflaq, the founder of the Baʿth party, gave the most romantic expression to this idea. He defined nationalism by the Arab word *qawmiya*, which means "belonging to a group," and implies a total absorption of the individual in the nation. Only through the nation can the individual achieve true freedom and a higher mode of existence. Through solidarity and love of the nation, Arab peoples would not only realize their political objectives but attain the highest spiritual fulfillment:

> The nationalism for which we call is love before everything else. It is the very same feeling that binds the individual to his family, because the fatherland is only a large household, and the nation a large family. Nationalism, like every kind of love, fills the heart with joy and spreads hope in the soul; he who feels it would wish to share with all the people this joy which raises him above narrow egotism, draws him nearer to goodness and perfection...It is, then, the best way to a true humanity.[1]

Arab nationalism served ideological as well as spiritual purposes. Given the facts of British and French rule and the consolidation of a number of separate Arab states, Arab nationalism became in practice a doctrine of legitimation for conservative national elites and a doctrine of the struggle of each of these states for freedom from their French or British colonial overlords. In the background, however, there remained a lingering yearning for Arab unity and a lingering religious meaning to a secular doctrine. Especially in the minds of the common people, Islam and Arab identity could not be differentiated.

In each country the conservative national elite was opposed by a younger generation of newly educated intelligentsia, including soldiers, technocrats, and intellectuals. As in the case of the Ottoman empire and Egypt in the nineteenth century, the reorganization and centralization of state authority, the provision of modern education, and a small degree of economic and social change led to mobility from villages to cities and from rural to urban occupations. Western-type colleges and military academies trained a new generation of technicians, bureaucrats, army officers, and intellectuals, uprooted from the old conditions of life, but not yet absorbed into the ruling elites. The military would prove to be particularly important. As in the nineteenth-century Ottoman empire, the combination of educational achievement, technical sophistication, political awareness, and social grievances against the ruling elites, and strong ambitions for personal and national glory, gave the military a dominant position. To these advantages of motivation and abilities, they added control of organized violence. This new generation also adopted the national ideology, for nationalism gave identity to people uprooted from local

---

[1] Quoted in S. Haim, ed., *Arab Nationalism: An Anthology*, Berkeley, 1976, p. 242.

communities and legitimized the struggle against foreign rule in terms recognized as valid by the colonial powers themselves. The new elite generation determined to seize control of the state in the name of domestic reform, anti-colonialism, and Arab nationalism.

Syria is a principal example of the generational and ideological conflict within Arab societies. In Syria the French secured public order, built roads and communications networks, and established the administrative infrastructure of a modern state. The French accelerated the sedentarization of the bedouins, which began in the late nineteenth century under the Ottomans, expanded cultivated territories at the expense of pastoralism, and converted bedouins into peasants and chiefs into landlords. After World War I the bedouins were further hemmed in by states, settlers, and roads and by heavy investment by city merchants and tribal shaykhs in land reclamation and cultivation.

In order to maintain effective administration, and to inhibit the development of a movement for independence, the French also divided Syria into ethnic and religious districts. Lebanon was made into a separate state. Latakia, which was predominantly populated by poverty-stricken ʿAlawi peasants dominated by Sunni landlords, was made into a separate administrative district. The Druze areas of southern Syria, and the Jazira, the plains of northern Syria and the Euphrates region, were given regional autonomy. Alexandretta received special status because of its substantial Turkish minority, and was annexed by Turkey in 1939. Thus, France established the framework of a modern Syrian state but then reinforced the ethnic and religious divisions of the country to prolong the difficulties of forming a socially cohesive national society capable of managing an independent regime. While the Syrian domestic elite struggled to form a parliamentary regime and to take a share in the government of the country, their struggle for independence was thwarted by ever-changing French governments and French policies.

Starting in the 1930s and continuing into the period of independence, the conservative elites were opposed by young army officers of middle-class backgrounds, educated in the military academy of Homs, and by Western-educated intellectuals and politicians. The most important expression of the younger generation was the Baʿth party. The Baʿth was founded in the 1940s by Michel Aflaq and Salah al-Din Bitar, two Syrian school-teachers educated in Paris in the 1930s. They developed a doctrine of Arab unity, social justice, democracy, and freedom. They were anti-colonialist in international orientation and socialist in domestic programs. They espoused not only a political doctrine but a mystical feeling for the rejuvenation of the Arab nation through national unity. In 1949 they were joined by Akram al-Hawrani, a socialist agitator and organizer of revolts in Homs, and a conspirator with close contacts in the army.

The conflict of the older generation and the new elite of army officers and intelligentsia began in earnest in the late 1940s after the defeat of France in World War II finally allowed for the formation of an independent Syrian regime in 1947. This regime was immediately beset by a series of military coups which progressively transferred power from the old generation to the new. The process of forming a new political regime, however, would not be completed without a protracted domestic and international crisis in the mid-1950s and early 1960s.

Iraq was carved out of the Ottoman empire and had a similar generational and national history. During the Ottoman period nomadism and pastoralism had displaced sedentary agriculture, especially in the upper Euphrates region, the Diyala region, and in southern Iraq. In the nineteenth century the Ottoman state started the process of reducing the power of tribal chiefs and developing private property in land. The land code of 1858 created a system which assured persons in possession of title deeds ownership of the land. These title deeds were acquired by city-dwelling merchants, tax farmers, and tribal leaders, who thus wrested control of the land from the tribesmen.

When the British conquered Iraq in 1917, they ruled it as a colony on the Indian model. In 1920, a revolt of Ottoman officials and landlords, Sunni and Shiᶜi religious leaders, and tribal groups forced them to include the Iraqi elites. The British helped set up a constitutional monarchy under King Faysal, to whom they felt obligated because of his help in the war. An Anglo-Iraqi treaty of 1922 gave the British control of military, financial, judicial, and foreign affairs. In 1930, a new treaty made Iraq legally independent but allowed Britain continued control over foreign and military affairs.

British administrators helped create the infrastructure of a modern state. The British consolidated the late Ottoman land system by using rural and tribal shaykhs to take charge of tax collection and labor organization. Under the monarchy, Iraq was run by a small coalition of rural landowners, tribal chiefs, ᶜulamaᵓ, Shiᶜi religious leaders, and army officers, the latter including Ottoman officers educated in Istanbul, Sharifian officers in the service of Faysal before coming to Iraq, and Iraqis educated in the Baghdad Military Academy. This elite, however, was deeply divided. Between 1936 and 1941 there were a number of military coups, and World War II brought bitter struggles between pro-British and pro-German factions. In 1941 Rashid ᶜAli al-Gaylani took control of the government in the interest of a pro-German policy, but British troops seized the country. From then until 1958 the King governed, often with the collaboration of his principal minister, Nuri al-Saᶜid, and a small minority of landowners, 2 percent of whom owned 66 percent of the land. In the name of Arab nationalism, this elite, predominantly of Sunni background, governed a populace which was half Shiᶜa and one-fourth Kurdish.

The dominance of the old elite was challenged by a new generation of soldiers, intellectuals, and workers thrown up by a changed economy. The appropriation of land by the shaykhs and the breakup of tribal communities drove large numbers of people to the cities. A new urban generation of lower-ranking officials, junior army officers, textile workers, and displaced peasants hostile to the entrenched regime took form. The army became the effective center of the opposition. Until 1958, the regime contained this growing opposition by proposals for extensive development programs but it did not survive to carry them out. An army coup brought an end to the monarchy in 1958.

Transjordan was, even more than Iraq, a British creation. It was the most "unnatural" of the new states, corresponding to no historic province or local community. Originally it was meant to be part of Palestine, but in 1922 the British allowed Amir ᶜAbdallah, a brother of Faysal, to establish a government. They built up the Arab Legion and provided subsidies. Thus, the British honored their commitment to the Hashimite family and also reduced their commitment to the Zionists by removing Transjordan from the area included in the Balfour Declaration's promise of a Jewish National Home. A 1928 treaty established a constitutional monarchy, a legislature, and political parties, but reserved for Britain control over foreign policy and the army. In 1946 Transjordan became independent, though a treaty of 1948 reserved for Britain the right to maintain bases. Between 1948 and 1950, as a result of the Arab–Israeli war, Transjordan absorbed parts of Palestine and was reorganized as the Kingdom of Jordan. By 1950, the state of Jordan comprised two totally different populations – the bedouins and farmers on the east bank of the Jordan, and the Palestinian population including refugees and inhabitants of the west bank. In order to establish an effective state, the constitution of 1952 gave representation to both elements in a new parliament. A National Guard was formed, comprised of Palestinian villagers, and was later integrated into the Arab Legion.

Throughout this period Jordan was governed by a king, an elite of British army officers, Palestinian-Arab officials, Circassian palace servants, and Muslim religious leaders. In Jordan, as opposed to Iraq, the influence of tribal chiefs was rapidly reduced. While the traditional society of Transjordan was based on kinship and tribal groups, the development of the centralized state power reduced the functions of the tribal chiefs and deprived them of their clienteles and military power. By 1950, they had ceased to be a threat to the authority of the state and the army. Other changes in Jordanian society also tended to subvert the tribes. Bureaucratic administration and the creation, through schools and colleges, of a new middle class of government officials, clerks, teachers, and merchants, helped to break down their influence. However, in Jordan, as elsewhere, the educated middle class became a source of opposition to the governing elite. While the army remained loyal to the state, the opposition was built on the intelligentsia and the Palestinians.

Lebanon has a somewhat different history. Here the struggle was not so much between generations or between military landowning elites and intelligentsia, as between confessional communities. Lebanon, like Syria, was a French creation. Though France had a long history of close relations with the Maronite population, the French did not create a purely Christian state. To the old province of Lebanon, new districts, including Tripoli, Sidon, the Biqaᶜ, and south Lebanon, were added to increase the total size of the country and the proportion of Muslims. Lebanon was initially governed by a French High Commissioner, but in 1926 a new constitution divided political power among the major religious communities. It provided for a president, a ministerial government, and a bicameral legislature, in which seats were distributed in a ratio of 6:5 for Christians and Muslims. By agreement, the president would always be a Maronite, the prime minister a Sunni, and the head of parliament a Shiᶜa. Foreign affairs would be in the hands of a Christian minister; the army would be headed by Maronites, with Muslim or Druze subalterns. Furthermore, the state institutions were designed to reinforce sectarian divisions rather than integrate Lebanese society. Government agencies did not build national services but rather subsidized sectarian religious schools, courts, and charities. Political parties in Lebanon were expressions of the *zaᵓims* or bosses, who were usually local landlords and religious leaders who developed patronage networks as the basis of their political power. They did not represent mass movements. Popular loyalties were channeled to the leaders of clienteles rather than to the state as such.

From 1920 to 1945 Lebanon was governed on the basis of compromise among sectarian and communal bosses. In the mandate period the bosses were linked up in two main political parties: the National Bloc was substantially Maronite Christian and favored independence but resisted ties with other Arab nationalists. The Constitutional Bloc favored close relations with Syria. In 1943 the Lebanese factions were able to agree on a national pact in which the

Christians and Muslims agreed to de-emphasize outside political ties, whether French or Arab, for the sake of greater internal cooperation. Thus the way was prepared for the formation of an independent regime in 1945. The postwar regime continued to be based upon the allocation of government powers and resources among the bosses and confessional groups. The state existed to maintain the balance of power among them, and from 1947 to 1958 the country was ruled by a succession of coalition governments.

THE STRUGGLE FOR ARAB UNITY AND THE CONTEMPORARY FERTILE CRESCENT STATES

The fertile crescent Arab states achieved independence in the years following World War II. Independence led to a political and ideological crisis out of which the contemporary form of Middle Eastern Arab societies has emerged. The problems of the Arab states were manifold. In each of them, the older generation military, landowning, and merchant elites, and younger generation military and technical intelligentsia struggled for power. The struggles were complicated by the Palestine-Israel War of 1948, the victory of the Jews, and the establishment of the State of Israel. They were also complicated by the maneuverings of the Great Powers and the advent of the Cold War, and by the movement for Arab national unity. As a result of these tensions, Syria underwent a series of military coups between 1947 and 1963. Iraq had a coup d'état in 1958 which led to the overthrow of the monarchy and the installation of a military regime. Jordan and Lebanon went through brief civil wars which resulted, due to foreign intervention, in the restoration of the status quo.

The movement for Arab unity had its origins in the pre-World War I Arab nationalist movement and in the brief and abortive effort of Faysal to establish an Arab kingdom in Damascus. With the formation of the Arab state system after World War I, the concept of a single Arab nation and state went into abeyance. It was revived in the late 1930s by the outbreak of the Arab revolt in Palestine. Between 1936 and 1939 Palestinian peasants carried on a double struggle against Jewish colonization and British rule which mobilized widespread support in Egypt and the fertile crescent countries for an Arab cause. Also, on the eve of World War II, Britain renewed its efforts to win Arab support by declaring itself in favor of a union of Arab countries. Egypt took up pan-Arabism as a vehicle for the assertion of Egyptian leadership in the Arab-speaking Middle East. In 1945 the League of Arab States was founded under Egyptian patronage, with an Egyptian secretary-general and headquarters in Cairo. However, the Hashimite rulers of Iraq and Transjordan had their own schemes for Arab unification and resisted Egyptian hegemony. For all practical purposes the League foundered over its failure to prevent the formation of the State of Israel in 1948.

The cause of Arab unity, however, was revived in the 1950s. By then it had been taken up by Nasser in Egypt, by the Baᶜth party in Syria, and by other elements of the new postwar Arab intelligentsia as the banner of united opposition to Israel, to colonial and post-colonial domination by foreign powers, and to conservative domestic elites who stood in the way of social reform and economic development. Inspired by Nasser's leadership, the struggle for power in each of the fertile crescent countries was now waged in the name of Arab unity.

The domestic struggles were also entangled in big-power rivalries. At the end of World War II Britain and France were no longer able to maintain their Middle Eastern positions and had to concede the independence of the fertile crescent states. The United States and the Soviet Union emerged as the principal competitors for regional influence. In the late 1940s Turkey and Iran were brought into the American sphere of influence, and in the 1950s the United States attempted to align the Arab countries in an American-sponsored treaty organization. The United States was supported by Nuri al-Saᶜid, the Prime Minister of Iraq, who proposed to link Iraq, Turkey, and Britain, and then bring the other Arab states into line. In January 1955 Adnan Menderes of Turkey and Nuri al-Saᶜid proclaimed the Baghdad Pact. Egypt and Syria, however, opposed the Iraqi initiative, and did not want to accept American aid. After the Israeli attack on the Sinai in February 1955, Egypt and Syria obtained Russian guarantees for their security. Nasser emerged as the leader of the Arab struggle against imperialism and Zionism. All the Arab countries were swept by a wave of sentiment in favor of Arab unity. In Egypt Nasser and the Free Officers came to power in 1952 and launched their socialist policies in the late 1950s. In Syria the Baᶜth party took power in the late 1950s and 1960s. In Iraq a coup d'état overthrew the monarchy and brought a military regime to power in 1958. In Lebanon and Jordan, however, American and British intervention helped defeat the opposition and kept the established regimes intact.

The crisis of the 1950s, then, led to the formation of new regimes in Egypt, Syria, and Iraq and gave them their political and ideological identity. In each country the new dominant force was a military elite legitimized by its formal commitments to Arab national independence, and state-guided modernization of the economy. The political consciousness of these elites, formed in the

1950s and 1960s, was anti-imperialist, anti-Israel, and neutralist in international politics. The post-World War II international struggle also prompted Egypt, Iraq, and Syria to adopt socialist regimes which were in accord with the rejection of Western imperialism, with the support given to underdeveloped countries by the Soviet Union and its allies, and with the need to reject the previous generation that had failed to make national economic and social progress. Nevertheless, the crisis did not lead to Arab unity. Throughout the late 1950s and 1960s, despite their common interest, the rivalries among Egypt, Syria, and Iraq prevented Arab unification. With the defeat of the Arab states in the 1967 war against Israel, Nasser's leadership was discredited, the Arab states were condemned as ineffectual, and the idea of Arab unity lost its political appeal.

Since the upheavals of the 1950s, the fortunes of Syria have been shaped by the Baʿth party and military regime. Throughout the 1950s, through elections and coup d'états, the Baʿth advanced toward the control of Syria. In the mid-1950s it promoted union with Egypt (1958–61), a disastrous move which destroyed the civilian leadership of the party and allowed the army to take power in 1963. Despite changes of personnel, since 1963 Syria has been governed by a regime of army officers. The leading officers are ʿAlawis, though other minority groups and the majority Sunni population are also represented. The regime attempts to overcome the inherent familial, ethnic, and religious factionalism of the country by a policy of centralized political control and socialized development of agriculture and industry. The Baʿth has also attempted to revolutionize Syrian society by creating a mass political machine based on middle- and lower-middle-class youths, often from rural areas, recruited from minority ʿAlawis, Ismaʿilis, and Christians. The party cadres have taken control of army officer posts, government jobs, agricultural and village cooperatives, and youth organizations. There are indications that the Baʿth is building a mass movement in Syria, effecting a major redistribution of national power, creating institutions that will spread nationalist and socialist ideals, and overcoming the factionalism and parochialism of the country.

In two respects, however, the revolutionary implications of this program are compromised by the Baʿth leaders, whose values reflect the traditional divisions of Syrian society rather than their aspirations for a unified future. Factionalism within the party remains a serious problem. Since coming to power in 1970, Hafiz al-Asad has attempted to diminish the importance of the party apparatus and to open new channels to political power through the army, through the police, and through professional and technical positions directly controlled by himself. More important is the dominance of the ʿAlawis, who represent only 10 percent of the population, but who control the army and the party. The ᶜAlawis were predominantly a poor peasant community living in northern Syria. Most of them were farmers indentured to wealthy Sunni, Christian, or ᶜAlawi landowners who lived in the towns and collected rents in the villages. Many ᶜAlawis became involved in revolutionary movements in the interwar years and others entered the Syrian army when the French promoted the minorities as a mechanism for controlling the majority Muslim population. ᶜAlawis were thus important in the Baᶜth and in the army circles which came to power in the 1960s and used their power to further benefit the minorities. Eventually non-ᶜAlawi army officers were purged and largely replaced by ᶜAlawis. The Syrian regime has a highly personal, factional, and sectarian quality.

In the management of the economy the Baᶜth party has pursued a socialist program. Agrarian reform began in 1958 with dismantling large estates and limiting ownership to a maximum of 50 hectares of irrigated and 300 hectares of unirrigated land. In 1961 lands were expropriated and redistributed to peasants. In 1966, the socialization of agriculture began in earnest, with the formation of agricultural collectives, a state monopoly of cotton production, and the beginning of the Tebke dam project which is expected to bring 640,000 hectares of reclaimed land in the Euphrates basin into cultivation. In 1973, however, Hafiz al-Asad began to dismantle state farms, and allow the resumption of private ownership in order to liberalize the economy and encourage agricultural growth.

In this centralized, secular, and socialist Arab state dominated by an ᶜAlawi minority, the majority of the population is Sunni Muslim. Islam is not mentioned in the constitutions of 1950 or 1973 and President Asad has refused to declare officially Islam the religion of the state. However, it is acknowledged that the head of state must be a Muslim, and the Shariᶜa is embodied in the 1953 Syrian law of personal status. Religiously defined Sunni opposition has surfaced in the form of the Muslim Brotherhood, founded in Aleppo and Damascus in the 1930s. As in Egypt, the Muslim Brotherhood appeals to the "old bazaar" shopkeepers, artisans, craftsmen, and their modern-educated student and intelligentsia offspring. Operating as a political party in the Syrian elections of 1961, the Muslim Brotherhood won 5.8 percent of the national vote and 17.6 percent of the Damascus vote. However, when Baᶜth party rule was consolidated in the 1960s and 1970s, the Muslim Brotherhood turned from electoral politics to civil disobedience and armed resistance. From mid-1979 to late 1981, in response to the Syrian government's intervention against the Palestinians in Lebanon, rising inflation, and the general decline of Sunni political influence, the Brotherhood launched guerrilla attacks and then large-scale uprisings in Aleppo and Hama. Thus the Islamic movement in Syria was essentially an urban reaction against a rural-based regime, an expression of Sunni hostility to ʿAlawis and a rebellion of the governed against the governing elite. It was supported by merchants and artisans, ʿulamaʾ, landowners, and other notables dispossessed by the Baʿth. However, the Muslim Brotherhood revolts were crushed. It is too early to assess how well the Brotherhood will succeed in mobilizing Sunni support and in sustaining its opposition.

In Iraq the old regime was also overthrown in the name of pan-Arab nationalism and domestic reform. In July 1958 a group of young army officers led by ʿAbd al-Krim Qassim, representing the generation of soldiers, administrators, intellectuals, and ideologues schooled in the nationalist ideals of the 1930s and 1940s, seized power. Their hatred of Iraq's dependence on Great Britain, the Baghdad Pact, and the 1958 effort to form a conservative alliance between Iraq and Jordan precipitated a coup d'état, the execution of the King, and the formation of a Revolutionary Council.

The new regime at first favored conservative reforms in land ownership, free enterprise in industry, and strong state policies to promote health care and education. Its immediate hopes, however, were disappointed. Under Qassim's leadership, it quickly turned into a military dictatorship based on strong Communist Party support. The Baʿth party, the Muslim Brotherhood, and other opposition groups were suppressed. The Qassim regime was in turn overthrown by a Baʿth party coup in 1963, also launched in the name of Arab unity, which set Iraq on its present course of socialist government. The Baʿth nationalized the major banks and industries. In 1968 another military coup brought Ahmad Hassan al-Bakr and Saddam Husayn to power in the name of Baʿth party principles. A new constitution declared Iraq part of the Arab nation, an Islamic state, and a socialist society. The regime established in 1968 under Saddam Husayn rules to the present.

As in Egypt the Iraqi regime is based on the army and on the support of bureaucrats and technocrats. A small cadre of army officers dominates the government and the ambassadorial corps and manages the major industries. Independent lawyers, landowners, and businessmen no longer have a significant part to play in public policy. The new elite comes from middle- and lower-middle class, and often conservative Islamic, backgrounds, but it is basically a state elite dependent upon the centralization of military, economic, and educational activities under state control.

This elite, however, represents only a narrow segment of the general population. The Baʿth regime is supported by a small group of families from the town of Takrit and by army officers who are graduates of the Baghdad Military Academy. The governing elite represents essentially the Sunni Muslim population of northwestern Iraq, and governs in the name of Arab nationalist ideals. It does not, however, represent the majority Shiʿi and substantial Kurdish populations of the country. Supported by the army and by revenues from oil production which are fully in its control, it has little incentive for compromise and negotiation, and little prospect for bringing about the political integration of Iraq. The regime is especially hostile to the Kurds, who demand regional autonomy, a share in economic development, and the promotion of the Kurdish language in Kurdish schools.

The Baʿth regime closely controls the economy. Government controls are exercised over unions, businesses, the universities, and the civil service. Agriculture is regulated by the state. With the establishment of the new military regime in 1958, a program of land reform on the Egyptian model was implemented. Laws were passed to limit ownership of land to 1,000 dunums (250 hectares) of irrigated or 2,000 dunums of unirrigated land and to organize the peasantry into agricultural cooperatives to assure efficient utilization of redistributed lands. This program was successful in expropriating the old landed elite, but, owing to lack of follow-up in distribution of lands and the organization of cooperatives, it was a disaster in terms of utilizing the productive capacity of the country. Only after 1970 were substantial acreages redistributed and peasant cooperatives, later collectives, organized. In the 1970s, however, the main emphasis was shifted to capital-intensive irrigation and the development of mechanized farms financed by the state. The government thus adopted an agricultural policy to bypass the peasant sector of the society. To consolidate its control of agriculture the state resisted tribal ownership of land, peasant unions, or other political forms of rural organization.

Nationalization and government controls have been applied in oil and industrial production. Oil was discovered in Iraq before World War I and was first exploited by the Turkish Petroleum Company, founded in 1912 with German, Dutch, and British participation. In 1929 the company was re-organized as the Iraqi Petroleum Company. In the course of the 1930s new concessions were granted to extend oil exploration, and in 1938 the several companies exploring for oil were merged into a single Iraqi Petroleum Company. In 1952 Iraq obtained an agreement from the international oil companies for a 50–50 share of oil profits. The new military regime took a more radical line. In 1961 Iraq revoked the oil concessions and in 1972 finally nationalized the Iraqi Petroleum Company. Oil production was maintained with Soviet and

French help but Iraq suffered considerable losses as a result of curtailed production.

The Iraqi economy has also suffered from the war with Iran. In 1980 Iraq attacked Iran. Iraq hoped, among its possible objectives, to reverse diplomatic losses of the 1970s, forestall the spread of Iranian revolutionary influences to its own Shiʿi population, capture valuable oil-producing territories, topple the Iranian revolutionary regime, and establish Iraqi supremacy in the Gulf region, if not in the Arab world. Iran, however, proved able to defend itself and the war, as of 1986, is stalemated at enormous cost to both countries.

Islam, in these circumstances, while retaining the strong allegiance of the population, plays little part in public life. Militant opposition to the Baʿth regime, however, has emerged. In the 1960s Shiʿi ʿulamaʾ formed the *Daʿwa al-Islamiya* (Islamic Mission) to work for an Islamic state and social justice. The more militant *Mujahidin* or Muslim Warriors was founded in 1979. The relatively strong Iraqi regime, however, has reduced this opposition to sporadic terrorism.

Thus, while Egypt, Syria, and Iraq are each governed by a military elite committed to Arab nationalism and a socialist economy, they have evolved in very different ways. Egypt, with the longest history of central government and a strong sense of political identity, has developed a relatively flexible regime. Socialism was adopted in Egypt as a pragmatic rather than a doctrinaire policy; it was never totally implemented and important sectors of the economy remained in private hands. The tendency of the 1970s has been to revert to private forms of economic organization. Only Islamic organizations pose a challenge to these pragmatic policies. In Syria a military and ʿAlawi sectarian elite has implemented a highly ideological socialist regime which, despite its military, organizational, and economic power, is not fully legitimized among the Sunni Muslim majority. Iraq has a narrowly based, authoritarian, and ideological government. Iraq lacks a history of national unity and the present regime represents the dominance of a minority. The regime clings all the more to military power, to oil wealth, and to a highly centralized economy, while it resists the integration of the Kurdish and Shiʿi populations.

While military-socialist regimes came to power in Egypt, Syria, and Iraq, in Jordan the opposition was defeated in 1958 with the help of British para-troopers. King Husayn retains his throne to the present. Jordan remains a conservative state, dependent upon Britain, the United States, and conservative Arab states. The regime is also based on military and bureaucratic elites who continue to dominate both the Jordanian and Palestinian parts of the population.

While state regimes have been consolidated in Syria, Iraq, and Jordan, Lebanon has disintegrated into civil war. The Lebanese balance of power first broke down in the 1950s under the pressure of the struggle for Arab unity. American intervention in 1958 helped to maintain the status quo for a time, but in the 1960s the status quo broke down. Though Lebanon was dominated by the Christians, the Muslims became the demographic majority and demanded an increased share of political power and economic opportunities. These internal problems were exacerbated by the Palestinian question. Lebanon was divided between those who would allow the Palestinians to use Lebanon as a base for the struggle against Israel and those who wanted to restrict Palestinian activities and avoid a Lebanese confrontation with Israel. The crosscurrents of domestic disagreements and foreign pressures made it impossible to find compromise positions, and in 1975 Lebanon was engulfed in civil war. On one side were the Phalange, other Maronite groups, and some Shiʿa who favored an independent Lebanon, a free enterprise economy, and non-involvement in the struggle against Israel. A second major coalition included the Progressive Socialist Party, primarily Druze, led by the Jumblatt family, which supported the Palestinians, a program of socialist development within Lebanon, and neutralism in world affairs. It also included the Syrian Social Nationalist Party which was largely Greek Orthodox and conservative, and opposed to the separatism espoused by the Maronites. Finally, this coalition embraced the Communist Party, and Baʿth, Nasserite, and Palestinian groups. All of these groups were united by their opposition to the status quo, to the predominance of Christians, and to the restriction of Palestinian activities.

With Lebanon divided, both Syria and Israel have intervened to manipulate the internal struggle. In January 1976 Syria invaded Lebanon to prevent a Palestinian victory that might have compromised Syria's relations with Israel. In 1978 Israel intervened in the southern part of the country to support Christian and separatist groups and to prevent the consolidation of the Palestinians on its borders. Israel invaded again in 1982 in an attempt to destroy the political base of the Palestinian movement in Lebanon and to establish a favorable Lebanese Christian regime in Beirut and the south. The Israeli invasion seriously damaged the Palestinian movement, but otherwise it has only served to confirm Syrian influence. Lebanon, manipulated by outside forces, has not been able to create a concept of state and society which transcends the factional and sectarian divisions of the country. Lebanon lives with the legacy of nineteenth-century factionalism, exaggerated by twentieth-century ideological splits, national wars, foreign intervention, and devastating weaponry.

Palestine is the only part of the fertile crescent not to become an Arab state. This was precluded by British support for the Zionist movement and the formation of the state of Israel. The Zionist movement was sparked by the publication of Theodore Herzl's *The Jewish State* in 1896. Inspired by the ideal of a revitalized Jewish national culture, and an egalitarian and socialist society in a democratic polity, Zionism represented the transformation of a religious community into a nation conceived in terms of a shared history and culture and requiring a territorial home. The development of Jewish nationalism thus paralleled the emergence of other nationalist movements in the Balkans and the Middle East at the end of the nineteenth century. The Jewish case was complicated, however, in that the Jews wished to establish the national home in a territory where they were a tiny minority amidst an Arab-Palestinian population. Nevertheless, in 1917 the British issued the Balfour Declaration and promised to favor a Jewish National Home in Palestine. The British imagined that a Jewish National Home would serve as a pretext for British claims to administer the country. They also thought that they could rally the support of Russian and American Jews for their war effort and forestall similar German initiatives. In doing this they neglected their conflicting commitments to the Arabs. After the war the League of Nations ratified a British mandate with the express purpose of developing a Jewish National Home.

The British, at the outset, committed to the Jews, allowed immigration and purchase of land, defended the Jewish community from riots, and permitted the organization of Jewish political institutions and the formation of a Jewish army. The British also suppressed the Arab-Palestinian opposition. Under British rule, the Jewish community in Palestine grew rapidly. By 1939 there were almost a half million Jews in some 250 settlements. The Jews were highly organized through the Zionist Organization, the Jewish Agency, the *Vad Leumi* or representative body of the *Yishuv* (the Jewish community in Palestine), Jewish political parties and a Jewish labor movement.

The Palestinian movement developed in opposition to the occupation of Palestine by the British and the Jews. In 1920 most Palestinian Arabs were peasants. The middle class of doctors, lawyers, journalists, and government officials was very small. The Arab community was deeply divided by numerous clans and groups of affiliated clans, by strong class distinction between landlords, tenants, and sharecroppers, and by religious divisions among Muslims and Christians. With a strong clan and religious consciousness the Palestinian Arabs had little sense of a national community and little potential for organizing a national movement.

However, in the course of the struggle against the British and the Zionists, parochial ties began to give way to a sense of regional identity. Palestinian political awareness in the 1920s was cultivated by an Arab elite which tried to build a mass resistance of Palestinians to Zionism. This elite was divided into two segments. The first were the nationalists, who formed in 1918 the first Muslim–Christian associations to protest against the Jewish National Home. They were at first allied to the Syrian national movement and envisioned a single greater Syrian-Arab state, but by 1920 Palestinian political activity separated itself from the general movement. The third Palestine Arab Congress set up the Arab Executive, which would until the 1930s be the principal spokesman of Palestinian Arab interests.

The second Palestinian elite was Muslim. In 1922 the British established a Supreme Muslim Council to control endowed funds and the appointment of Muslim functionaries, and appointed al-Hajj Muhammad Amin al-Husayni to be the head of the council and Mufti of Jerusalem. Husayni was also Syndic of the Descendants of the Prophet, patron of the popular Nabi Musa festival, and guardian of the mosque, and he came to control both the Arab Executive and the Muslim Council. From these platforms he attempted to arouse mass Arab support by protesting the danger of Zionism to the holy places in Jerusalem. Husayn and other religious notables organized their opposition in terms of Islam – the only idiom which was meaningful to the Palestinian population – and actively sponsored a number of demonstrations: the Nabi Musa riots of 1920, a boycott of the legislative council campaigns, the anti-land-sale campaign, and the 1929 Wailing Wall riots. They tried to make Palestine a pan-Islamic cause. In the 1920s, however, Arab leadership was highly fragmented. While Husayni and his followers controlled the Arab Executive and the Muslim Council, their rivals, led by the Nashashibi family, allied with mayors, landowners, and merchants, formed the National Party (1923) to contest leadership of Arab Palestine. The factional divisions led to bitter rivalries and destroyed the possibility of coordinated action.

The Palestinian movement was also beset in its early years by Muslim–Christian tensions. Christians had taken a large role in the development of Arab nationalism and in the formation of the Muslim–Christian associations, and had a heavy stake in the resistance to Jewish colonization. Also Christians were important for their abilities to negotiate with and perhaps obtain support from the West. Still unity was hard to achieve. Muslims found it threatening to see Christians taking an independent role, and Christians remained suspicious of the emphasis placed on Muslim symbols. Christians did not participate in the 1929 anti-British and anti-Jewish riots.

Despite these handicaps, considerable progress was made in the 1920s in creating a Palestinian identity and a Palestinian national movement. An ideology was formulated which defined the Arab nature of and the Arab right to Palestine. Islamic symbols of resistance to Zionism were mobilized. The Jerusalem notables emerged as leaders of the rural population, and despite religious tensions, Greek Orthodox Christians came to see themselves as part of the Palestinian Arab people.

The 1930s witnessed the beginnings of a mass movement. While the factional struggle between the Husaynis and the Nashashibis smoldered, the concept of direct mass action was being fostered by militant youth groups like the Young Men's Muslim Association under the leadership of Shaykh ʿIzz al-Din al-Qassam. Al-Qassam preached against British imperialism and Jewish settlement, and organized the Haifa Muslim Youth Association. He organized armed resistance cells to whom he preached a reformed Islam opposed to drinking, gambling, and prostitution. He also opposed popular religious practices such as mourning and grave visitation, and the mingling of sexes. A proponent both of militant action and of puritanical self-discipline, al-Qassam created the notion of mass militant action or jihad. His was a populist, activist notion of Islam concentrating on the appeal to save the holy land. The concepts of *mujahid* (warrior for the faith) and *shahid* (martyr) were used to generate popular participation. In the 1930s when factional and kinship ties were all-powerful, and before the symbols of national ethnic identity had widespread appeal, only Muslim symbols could mobilize the Palestinian masses.

Al-Qassam and his followers played a large part in stimulating the great Arab revolts of 1936–38. Teachers, health officers, and officials propagandized the villagers. In 1935 and 1936 a national strike begun by the Higher Arab Committee spread to the countryside. Throughout Palestine, Arab militants, villagers, bandits, and volunteers from Syria and Egypt, operating without central direction, attacked government installations and Jewish settlements, attempting to overthrow British rule and stop Zionist colonization. The sporadic revolts were suppressed by the British in 1938. The Husaynis were removed from the Supreme Muslim Council; the Higher Arab Committee was declared illegal and a British military administration was imposed.

The Arab revolt of 1936–38 was a climax in the development of the Palestinian movement. From the outset the Arabs had struggled to fend off Jewish immigration, to prevent the formation of a Jewish National Home or state, and to form an Arab state in Palestine. Their major tactic was to refuse cooperation with British administration and to press the Arab cause by demonstrations, riots, and eventually guerrilla warfare. By the late 1930s the

Palestinian movement had been able to partially mobilize the masses but the internal divisions in the leadership and the lack of a fully-developed national political consciousness made it impossible to create a coordinated opposition to British rule and Zionist colonization.

The decade from 1938 to 1948 brought the conflict to a crisis that proved disastrous for the Arab communities of Palestine. From the late 1930s Britain began to change her policy in Palestine in order to win Arab support in the impending war against Germany. In the White Paper of 1939, the British decided to restrict Jewish immigration and land purchases. At the conclusion of World War II Britain refused all but a very limited immigration of Jewish refugees, despite American and Zionist pressures, and favored a renewed British trusteeship. The Jewish reaction to this change of British policy was bitter. The rise of Nazism and the destruction of European Jews in World War II made the Zionists determined to establish a Jewish state as a refuge for the survivors. The Jews launched their own military struggle against the British mandate.

The Palestinians also regrouped. At the end of World War II Husayni returned from wartime exile in Europe to resume leadership of the Palestinian movement, and the League of Arab States, founded in 1945, took the initiative in defending the Palestinian cause. By 1947 a surface appearance of Arab unity was restored but beneath the surface Palestinian Arabs were at loggerheads, and the several Arab states pursued their separate interests. In 1947 Britain resigned the mandate and the United Nations determined to partition Palestine into a Jewish and an Arab state. The Arab League decided to forcibly resist the formation of a Jewish state, but in the war which followed, the Jews defeated the Arab states, and established their own state of Israel. Transjordan absorbed the portions of Palestine west of the Jordan River and Egypt took control of Gaza. A substantial portion of the Arab population of Palestine, over 700,000 people, was forced into exile. The Palestinians were scattered on the west bank of the Jordan and exiled to Transjordan, Lebanon, Syria, and other Arab states.

In the post-1948 exile the central issue for Palestinians has become the alienation from the land, which deprives them of existence as a people, and creates the need to assert a national identity. This identity is primarily defined in nationalist and secular terms. While Islam is no longer central to the mobilization and definition of the Palestinian population, it penetrates Palestinian discourse and self-image through the use of such terms as jihad, shahid, mujahid, and holy land. These concepts have a specifically religious meaning but merge into the secular nationalist vocabulary. Concepts such as *thawrah*

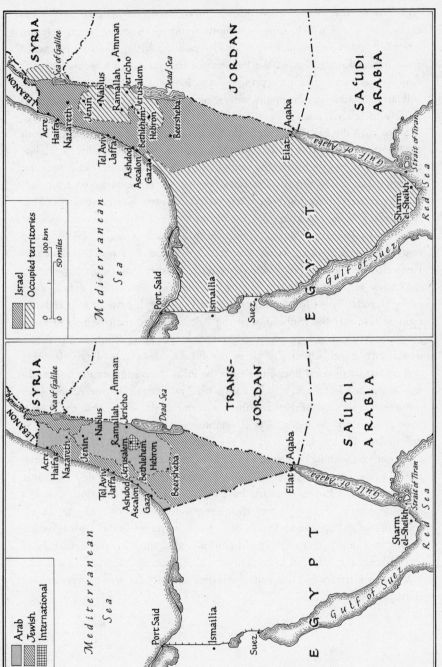

Map 32. Arab–Israeli conflict: (a) U.N. Partition Plan, 1947 (b) Israel and the occupied territories, 1967.

(revolution) and *fidaʾi* (self-sacrificing guerrilla) define national rights and dignity in words which imply redemption and resurrection. Islam helps to articulate and mobilize the Palestinians for political struggle. As in the case of Arab nationalism generally, the Palestinians have acquired a secular identity while at the same time preserving Islamic loyalties as the basis of political solidarity. Islamic sentiments, however, have not revived Islamic institutions or defined Islamic goals.

Since 1948 the Palestinian struggle has gone through several phases. From 1948 until 1967 the Arab states took the lead in the struggle against Israel, but their defeat in 1967 returned the struggle to Palestinian hands. Since 1967 the Palestine Liberation Organization has become the representative of the Palestinian cause. Founded in 1964 as a front for President Nasser's control of the Palestinians, it became after 1967 the bearer not only of Palestinian hopes for a return to Palestine, but of radical Arab aspirations for a revolutionary rejuvenation of Arab societies. The P.L.O. is a coalition which includes al-Fatah, led by Yassir Arafat, representing the Muslim Palestinian population, the largest segment of the movement. Smaller and more radical groups such as the Popular Front for the Liberation of Palestine, led by George Habash, espouse not only the restoration of the Palestinians to their homeland but a revolutionary transformation of all Arab countries as a prelude to the showdown with Israel. Other groups in the P.L.O. adopted a Marxist-Leninist and secular ideological line. Since 1967 the P.L.O. has engaged in commando attacks against Israel and also in wars with Arab states. Despite strong Arab sentiment in support of the Palestinian movement, the activities of the P.L.O. have threatened the legitimacy of established states. In 1970 al-Fatah was defeated in Jordan and forced to evacuate to Lebanon. When the P.L.O. threatened to become dominant in Lebanon, it was again defeated by an Arab state – Syria. With the Israeli invasion of Lebanon in 1982 the Palestinians lost their main base of operations and have become increasingly factionalized and dependent upon the support of their several Arab patrons. Despite the vicissitudes of the movement the Palestinians have succeeded to a considerable degree in winning international recognition and support for the legitimacy of establishing a Palestinian state. However, the conflict between Israeli and Palestinian interests and demands for justice and security seems as far as ever from peaceful resolution.

ARAB NATIONALISM AND ISLAM

In the Arab countries the relationships among state organizations, Arabism, and Islam have been particularly ambiguous and changing. In the Arab fertile crescent the quest for national identity and the struggle for political power has for over a century been conducted in terms of Arab nationalism. Arab nationalism was born before World War I in the literary revival of the Arabic language, the revival of Arab identification with the glories of the Islamic past, and the anti-Turkish political ambitions of Arab intellectuals. Arab nationalism in the prewar era shifted from an implied Islamic to a nationalist vocabulary in the course of the struggle to win autonomy within the Ottoman empire, and then in the effort to create an independent Arab state. Arabism rather than Islam became the dominant discourse, displacing the traditional vocabulary of political affiliation and political action.

In the colonial period Arab nationalism became the shared ideology of both the political elites and the intelligentsia opposition. The coalescence of ideologies was based on the shared desire for independence, the need to integrate non-Muslim minorities into the political system, and the awareness of the need for a modern national form of political identity corresponding to the actual state structures. After World War II, Arab identity became the basis of political goals such as anti-imperialism, struggle against Israel, and the formation of political regimes. From the 1950s to the 1970s the two crucial themes in Arab nationalist thinking were the struggle for unity and socio-economic development. At this stage some form of socialism generally became a part of Arab nationalist ideologies.

Arab nationalism, moreover, has always stood in an ambivalent relation to state nationalisms. In the 1950s pan-Arabism became the banner of opposition to the elites of Syria, Iraq, and Jordan. The Baᶜth party, which rules in both Syria and Iraq, espouses Arab unity, but separate wings of the party govern the two states and are deeply hostile to each other. Each regime in practice identifies Arab nationalism with the fulfillment of the socialist goals of its own state. A similar ambiguity characterizes the nationalism of the Palestinian movement. At one level it is a regional nationalism, yet it appeals to pan-Arab loyalties for political support. Some branches of the Palestinian movement see the ultimate solution to the Palestinian problem as the absorption of Palestine into a united Arab socialist society. Since the defeat of the Arab states in 1967 and the sudden great increase of oil wealth in the 1970s, the political climate has turned against pan-Arabism and in favor of national state regimes. The current tendency strongly identifies "Arab" interests with those of particular states.

While important, Islamic modernism and reformism have been subsidiary currents. In Syria, the Salafiya movement was interpreted in a conservative sense by Rashid Rida (1865–1935), the foremost of ᶜAbduh's disciples. Rida, like ᶜAbduh, held that the Quran and the teachings of Muhammad were the sole bases of Islam, but rather than stress the implications of this view for modernizing reforms, he emphasized opposition to Shiᶜism and to Sufi shrines. In Rida's view the crucial goal of an Islamic restoration was a polity, headed by a Caliph, advised by the ᶜulamaᵓ, which would revise the law of Islam in accord with contemporary needs. Rida stressed the importance of jihad, moral striving for purity and self-perfection, as the basis of loyalty and sacrifice for the common good. Other disciples of ᶜAbduh stressed the modernist implications of his teachings. They emphasized the importance of science and the legitimacy of social change. For the modernist writers, Islam was accepted as a true religion, but not as a touchstone for the development of a scientific civilization.

The trend toward secularism and nationalism goes back to the weaknesses of the ᶜulamaᵓ in the nineteenth century. In the Arab world, as in Egypt and Turkey, ᶜulamaᵓ resistance to secular trends generally came from lower-ranking religious functionaries such as prayer leaders, preachers in the smaller mosques, court clerks, notaries, Quran school teachers, and above all students in the religious colleges. In rural areas, leadership sometimes came from Sufi shaykhs or independent preachers. This opposition proved ineffective. In general secular legal and judicial institutions have replaced Muslim law. New penal and civil codes have been introduced, and a dual court system of state and Islamic courts has been established in Syria and Iraq.

Even when Shariᶜa principles continue to be accepted they have been profoundly modified by new legal procedures. Eclectic combinations of Shariᶜa law codes with Western criteria for evidence, cross-examination, and appellate jurisdiction have changed the actual administration of Shariᶜa law. The effect of legal reform is to accept the modernist view that the law is not eternally fixed and that it is subject to reformulation in terms of contemporary circumstances and state interests. The dilution of Muslim legal principles and the substitution of new law codes and court systems is perhaps the single most important index of the disestablishment of Islam in the public life of Arab countries.

Despite the disestablishment of religion and the dominance of Arab nationalist sentiment, Islam still plays a substantial role in the identity of Arab peoples. Arab national consciousness is still bound up with Islam. Arab nationalist thinkers of the 1920s and 1930s stressed the virtual identity of Arabism and Islam. The vocabulary of Arab nationalism is infused with words such as umma (community of Muslims) and milla (religious community) which have strong religious overtones but are used to express national solidarity. Furthermore, they equated the ideals of Islam with the ideals of Arab nationalism; Muhammad was regarded as the founding father. Even Christian writers considered Arabism and Islam to be two expressions of the same ideal. They stressed the glory of Muhammad as an heroic leader and praised his contribution to Arab nationality, but they maintained that national ties should transcend religious ties and advocated the formation of secular states.

The common people follow the nationalist thinkers in identifying the Arab nation with Islam. For them, to be an Arab is still primarily to be a Muslim, to share in the revelation of the Quran and the glory of the Arab conquests. In this loyalty there is a strong instinct to defend Islam against Christianity and also a strong apologetic tendency to insist that Islam is a modern religion and a practical basis for a modern society. The rhetoric may be nationalist, but the emotional identifications are Islamic.

Islam continues to be important in presumably secular Arab movements. It was crucial in the mobilization of Palestinians in the 1920s and 1930s to resist British rule and Zionism, and the Muslim attachment to Jerusalem remains important in Arab and Muslim world support for the Palestinian movement. Saʿudi support for the Palestinian cause does not distinguish Arab and Muslim interests. In the postwar era Arab constitutions often declared Islam the official religion of the state or required the head of state to be a Muslim.

Since 1967 Islam seems to be increasingly important in Arab political consciousness. Whereas secular economic ideologies and pan-Arabism have failed, the protest against political stagnation, economic injustice, and cultural alienation has taken the shape of a return to Islamic authenticity. In Egypt, the Islamic revival is virtually a national movement. In Syria and Iraq there has been intense opposition from militant guerrilla groups, but in neither country has Islam taken hold as a major expression of political and economic discontent. Islam has been substantially disestablished in the public life of the fertile crescent countries and plays only a limited political role. However, it maintains a latent cultural significance. Despite a century-old commitment to secular forms of Arab nationalism, Islam remains an integral part of Arab identity.

THE ARABIAN PENINSULA

For almost a millennium, the Arabian peninsula stood outside the mainstream of Middle Eastern developments. While the Arab conquests began a new era in Middle Eastern civilization, they left Arabia drained of much of its population, and relegated the peninsula to a marginal role in Middle Eastern history. In the Ottoman era, Egypt and the Arab fertile crescent became provinces of the Ottoman empire, but with the partial exception of peripheral areas, Arabia did not. Unlike Egypt and the fertile crescent states, the peninsula was governed by small tribal and family elites. The peninsula states generally rose from religiously legitimized tribal movements. Islam was a crucial factor in the unification of disparate clan and tribal groups into regional confederations and kingdoms. In the Imamate of Yemen, the Sultanates of Oman, and Saʿudi Arabia, religion and state remained closely identified. The rulers were and are considered the heads of the religion, responsible for the implementation of Islamic values. While the shaykhs of the Persian Gulf region did not formally claim charismatic religious authority, the religious nature of their societies was passively accepted. Throughout the peninsula the ʿulamaʾ, whether Zaydi, Shafiʿi, Ibadi, or Wahhabi, also played an important role as political advisers to rulers, administrators of judicial and educational institutions, and a source of moral advice and political authority.

Until the last decade or two, the peninsula was little affected by nationalism and secular modernism, and remained suspicious of and hostile to the social and ideological changes which were affecting the rest of the Arab world. Only since World War II has the peninsula become subject to the forces which have strongly shaped the rest of the Middle East. Modern means of government organization and revolutionary political concepts have been introduced. The discovery of oil has opened the way to technical and economic modernization and the transformation of traditional values. In the last several decades Yemen has been most subjected to revolutionary nationalism and political change, but Saʿudi Arabia and the Gulf states maintain the traditional bases of political order and legitimacy in the midst of extensive economic and social transformation. As in the fertile crescent states, so in the Arabian peninsula Arabism has become the basis of social and political identity.

Yemen has an exceptional position in the history of the peninsula because it has been, since ancient times, the center of an agricultural and state-organized society. Its history has been governed by the struggle between the states of the south and the pastoral, tribal population of the north. After Yemen was converted to Islam during the lifetime of the Prophet, it was absorbed into the early Umayyad and ʿAbbasid empires. In the late ninth century, like other regions far removed from Baghdad, Yemen became a center of Shiʿism. In northern Yemen, the local Arab tribes invited a Zaydi leader, named Yahya, to be imam and arbitrator of tribal disputes. Zaydi rule helped make peace among the tribal peoples and reinforced Islamic religious values. Thus began a dynasty which would, with interruptions, reign from 893 to 1962. Southern Yemen came under the influence of Egypt. First the Fatimids and then the Ayyubids established satellite states. The Rasulid dynasty (1229–1454) organized a strong central government and won the south over to Sunni Islam. This marks the origin of the lasting division of Yemen into a Sunni agricultural population in the south and a Zaydi tribal and pastoral population in the north. After the Ottomans conquered Egypt, they occupied southern Yemen from 1539 to 1635, but the Qasimid branch of the Zaydi dynasty eventually expelled them and restored Zaydi rule.

In the nineteenth century Yemen was divided between an Ottoman sphere of influence in the north and a British protectorate in the south. In the north, a treaty of 1911 confirmed Ottoman suzerainty but divided administrative control between the imam in the highlands and the Ottomans on the coast. This corresponded to the division into Sunni and Zaydi spheres of influence. With the defeat of the Ottomans in World War I, Imam Yahya won control over the whole of the country. He governed in conjunction with the sayyids, a landed aristocracy of descendants of the Prophet. The state was also supported by the Zaydi ʿulamaʾ, who were drawn from both the aristocracy and educated commoners, and were important in judicial administration and education. In the Sunni parts of the country, the Shafiʿi ʿulamaʾ held a similar position. Yemen in this period was thoroughly isolated from the outside world; there were few secular schools and few contacts with the rest of the Middle East. Every effort was made to preserve the traditional society.

Despite the efforts of Imam Yahya, social and ideological influences from the Arab Middle East began to penetrate Yemen in the 1940s. Diplomatic, military, and economic contacts with other Arab states multiplied. In 1948 Egyptian instructors were teaching in Sanʿaʾ, and after 1954 Yemeni army officers received training in Egypt. Yemeni merchants, workers, and students also went abroad. New ideas about constitutional authority and economic enterprise began to penetrate, and Yemen went through the same process of political and ideological modernization experienced by Ottoman elites in the nineteenth century and Arab elites in the early twentieth.

These political and ideological changes led to the formation of rival cliques within governing circles who used ideological distinctions to justify their

Table 17. Regimes of the Arabian peninsula

Persian Gulf		Oman	Central Arabia	Yemen
Bahrain	Kuwait			
Qaramita (Qarmatians) 894 to end of eleventh century	al-Sabah 1752 to present	Ibadi imams 796 to end of ninth century	Saʿudis	Zaydi imams (Sanʿaʾ) Rassid line ninth century to c. 1281
		Ibadi imams eleventh century	1746 Muhammad b. Saʿud	Sulayhids 1047–1138
		Bu-Saʿidis 1741 to present	1765 ʿAbd al-ʿAziz	Rasulids 1229–1454
			1803 Saʿud b. ʿAbd al-ʿAziz	Ottomans (South Yemen) 1539–1635
			1814 ʿAbdallah I b. Saʿud	Zaydi imams (Qasimid line) c. 1592–1962
			1818–22 Ottoman occupation	
			1823 Turki	

1834	Faysal I (first reign)
1837	Khalid b. Saʿud
1841	ʿAbdallah II (as vassal of Muhammad ʿAli of Egypt)
1843	Faysal I (second reign)
1865	ʿAbdallah III b. Faysal (first reign)
1871	Saʿud b. Faysal
1874	ʿAbdallah III (second reign)
1887	conquest by Rashidis of Hail, ʿAbdallah remains as governor of Riyadh until 1889
1889	ʿAbd al-Rahman b. Faysal, vassal governor
1891	Muhammad b. Faysal, vassal governor
1902	ʿAbd al-ʿAziz II
1953	Saʿud
1964	Faysal II
1975	Khalid
1982	Fahd

Republic of Yemen 1962 to present and People's Republic of South Yemen 1967; People's Democratic Republic of Yemen 1969 to present competition for power. In 1948 and 1955 factions of aristocratic families and army officers attempted to establish a Republican government, but failed. Growing Yemeni involvement in Arab world politics, however, led eventually to a more far-reaching revolution. The international struggles of the 1950s drew Yemen into Egypt's orbit and into the Arab nationalist movement. In 1956 Yemen established relations with the Soviet Union and in 1958 a federal union between the United Arab Republic and Yemen was declared. This was dissolved in 1961, but in 1962 a coalition of Zaydi army officers, Shafiꜥi merchants, and tribal chiefs led by ꜥAbdallah Sallal at last overthrew the Zaydi regime. The Republican regime was supported by an Egyptian army and was opposed by tribal groups defending the prerogatives of the Imamate, backed by Saꜥudi Arabia. The Egyptians and the Saꜥudis both withdrew from the conflict in 1967 and a new broadly based government under the leadership of Qadi ꜥAbd al-Rahman al-Iryani was formed. The new government steered a middle course between Egyptian and Saꜥudi influences and promulgated a constitution for a regime based on tribal military forces and religious elites. The constitution made Islam the official religion of the country, and allowed the sayyids (descendants of the Prophet), the Zaydis, and Sunni ꜥulamaꜣ to remain part of the governing elite. In January of 1974 Colonel Ibrahim Muhammad al-Hamdi overthrew the Iryani regime but continued the policy of balance among modernists, Islamic, and tribal forces. Thus the Republic of Yemen has upset the traditional regime without extensive changes in the basic political and social order of the country.

South Yemen came under British rule in 1839; in 1937 it was made a crown colony. The British protectorate included some 23 Sultanates, Emirates and tribal regimes which accepted British suzerainty and gave Britain control of foreign affairs. Under British control the traditional Arabian tribal and religious societies remained intact. These societies were composed of numerous clan groups organized in a highly stratified system. The Sultans dominated the towns; the sayyids owned the land and served as mediators among the clans. Plebeian clans were organized into specialized agricultural, craft, and servant groups.

Radical nationalism in Aden began as a reaction against British rule, and collaborator Sultanates and sayyid clans. In the name of Arab nationalism and socialism a local resistance movement was founded by George Habash. In 1959 the National Liberation Front took up the opposition cause. From 1962 to 1967 demonstrations, riots, and then guerrilla warfare forced the British to withdraw. The National Liberation Front, supported by the South Arabian Federation Army, came to power and proclaimed the People's Republic of

South Yemen. In 1969 the left wing of the National Liberation Front led by ᶜAbd al-Fattah Ismaᶜil took control of the government and changed its name to the People's Democratic Republic of Yemen. The new government replaced the traditional elite of tribal chiefs and Muslim religious teachers with a new generation of army officers and political activists. The new elite espouses a Marxist-Leninist ideology and has organized a single party, the National Front, to control all other organizations in the country. Industry has been nationalized, land ownership reformed, and feudalism and tribalism condemned. Significantly, Islam remains the state religion. South Yemen seems to be going through the first phases of the development of a secular national identity and the partial subordination of Islam and Islamic elites, similar to other Arab Middle Eastern states.

Central Arabia has become the domain of the Saᶜudi kingdom and the Wahhabi movement. In 1745 Ibn Saᶜud, the chief of a small tribal principality in north central Arabia, took up the cause of a Hanbali preacher, Muhammad b. ᶜAbd al-Wahhab (1703–87). Ibn ᶜAbd al-Wahhab had studied in Mecca, Medina, Damascus, and Basra, and began to preach the reform principles. He proposed to abolish the medieval accretions to the pure faith and to return to the fundamental principles embodied in Muslim scripture. He was therefore opposed to the customary practices of Arabian Islam, which included magical rituals, faith in holy-men, and the worship of saints. Wahhabi reformism took the extreme position of totally rejecting belief in and veneration of saints or of any human being as a form of *shirk* or polytheism. It also rejected the common pantheistic types of Sufi theology. Ibn ᶜAbd al-Wahhab and his followers insisted that the Quran and the Prophet were the only valid Muslim authorities. His preaching was the first political expression of a reform tendency which had developed in Mecca and would soon manifest itself throughout Islamic India, Indonesia, and North Africa.

With the conversion of Ibn Saᶜud to the Wahhabi cause, Wahhabism became the religious ideology of tribal unification. Echoing the life of the Prophet, Ibn Saᶜud and his successors waged war against the surrounding tribes, and converted them to the reformed version of Islam. As imams of the Wahhabi movement, they became the spiritual as well as the temporal chiefs of central Arabia. In 1773 they took Riyadh and made it their capital; in 1803 they captured Mecca, but Muhammad ᶜAli of Egypt defeated the Saᶜudis and took control of Mecca and Medina in 1812, and destroyed the Saᶜudi state in 1818. During much of the nineteenth century, the Saᶜudi house survived as a small tribal principality in the interior of Arabia, but in 1902, ᶜAbd al-ᶜAziz b. Saᶜud again took control of Riyadh, proclaimed himself imam of the

Wahhabis, and restored the Saᶜudi kingdom. The principal instrument of his power was the *Ikhwan* – a non-tribal military corps, settled in agricultural villages, which fought and proselytized for the Wahhabi movement. ᶜAbd al-ᶜAziz succeeded in unifying the tribes of central and eastern Arabia, declared himself Sultan of the Najd (1921) and proceeded to round out the boundaries of modern Saᶜudi Arabia by treaties with Iraq (1922), Jordan (1925), and Yemen (1934). In 1925 he took control of the Hijaz and the holy places.

The Saᶜudi regime was based on a subtle combination of political and religious powers. The Saᶜudi kings were first of all tribal chiefs who ruled by maintaining alliances and marriage ties with the families of other chiefs. The army was made up of loyal tribes. At the same time they were religious rulers, committed to upholding the laws of Islam and protecting the pilgrimage and the holy places. The ᶜulamaᵓ of the country, largely the descendants of ᶜAbd al-Wahhab, married into the royal family, were financially supported by the state, and had considerable influence in government circles.

The contemporary transformation of Saᶜudi Arabia began with the issuing of exploration concessions to the Standard Oil Company in 1933 and 1939, and the discovery of oil. Oil production in Saᶜudi Arabia began in earnest after World War II. However, only in 1973 did the price revolution in oil set the basis for an extensive development program. The Saᶜudi development budget reached 40 billion dollars in 1977 and 70 billion dollars in 1980. The program has led to the growth of cities, the construction of an industrial infrastructure, and a tremendous influx of foreign workers. In 1975, an estimated 43 percent of the population consisted of foreign workers from Yemen, Oman, Egypt, and Pakistan. Equally important is the revolution in education. By 1980 there were approximately one million children in schools, including large numbers of girls, some 40,000 students in Saᶜudi colleges, and some 15,000 students abroad. Increasing numbers of Saᶜudis are being trained for technical work in the petroleum industry, commerce, agriculture, finance, communications, and the military. Numerous members of the royal family have been educated in Western universities.

In the midst of these extensive educational, economic, and social changes the Saᶜudi state maintains its traditional political and religious authority. Kinship remains a crucial factor in the governing of Arabia. The government is run by a family council, or majlis, which operates by consensus. The Saᶜudis maintain close family relations with important regional and tribal chieftains, and they appoint family members and loyal tribal chiefs to ministerial and administrative offices.

Equally important is the continuing commitment to Islam. Saᶜudi society has been little affected by nationalism and secularism, and the Saʿudis cultivate their domestic legitimacy by close attention to Islamic religious affairs and the enforcement of Islamic morals. The organization for "commanding the good and forbidding the evil" enforces Wahhabi concepts of morality. The successful organization of the pilgrimage is another important sign of Saʿudi legitimacy. Internationally, the Saʿudis have cultivated an Islamic rather than an Arab national identity. They support Islamic institutes in numerous Muslim countries, oppose the Israeli occupation of Jerusalem, and defend the Palestinian cause. Saʿudi publications and conferences attempt to demonstrate the superiority of Islam and to promote its revival and diffusion in numerous countries.

The parallel tendencies toward economic modernization and religious conservatism have led to factional divisions within the royal family. The Sudayri faction, which includes many princes with a Western education, takes a modernizing orientation. Other factions represent traditional religious convictions, ʿulamaʾ influences, and resistance to cultural change. Arab nationalism made some impact on the royal family in the 1960s, when proposals for constitutional reform were advanced. These more radical suggestions were defeated, but the royal majlis was broadened to take a wider variety of opinions into account.

Forces outside the royal family have thus far achieved little political expression. Potential opposition exists among groups of merchants, businessmen, skilled technicians, and workers who are crucial to the emerging modern economy but who stand outside the status and political structure of the country. Religious opposition may come from groups which are disrupted by the breakdown of tribal society and the growth of individualism attendant upon urbanization, and economic and industrial change. The 1979 attack upon the Haram of Mecca may be an expression of this type of resistance. Nonetheless, the Saʿudi family seems to have absorbed massive economic, social and educational changes within the political and cultural framework of tribal and Islamic legitimacy. The traditional forms of polity even seem to be strengthened by the revival of Muslim self-confidence.

The history of the Persian Gulf region, like that of Yemen and central Arabia, is based upon the persisting identification of political and religious authority as the basis of tribal unification. In pre-Islamic times Oman was part of a Sasanian commercial network which reached from the Persian Gulf to Sind. Commercial profits were invested in an Iranian type of *qanat* irrigation, and Oman became a highly agricultural society. The Arab conquests, however, introduced a large pastoral population. In 796 Oman came under the rule of

Map 33. Arabia and the Persian Gulf: c. 1974.

Ibadi Imams, who managed to contain tribal rivalries, defend agriculture, and integrate the nomadic and settled populations. Under Ibadi leadership, Omanis founded commercial colonies in Basra, Siraf, Aden, and India, and traded on the east coast of Africa. At the end of the ninth century the Ibadi state and Omani commerce collapsed, and Egyptian-sponsored Red Sea routes took over the bulk of the Indian Ocean traffic. Oman, however, revived in the middle of the eleventh century when a second Imamate was founded, and a social system created which lasts to the present day. Cultivators accepted a tribal concept of social organization, and thus were integrated with pastoralists into a single society. Ibadism became a full-fledged Muslim school of law regulating personal and family behavior and political institutions. In the Ibadi system the imam is nominated by the elders of the community, and holds power insofar as he upholds the divine law and maintains the confidence of his electors. The Imamate was thus a tribal state, integrated by religious authority. The government did little to encourage investment in land. Village communities, which did not have adequate resources or organizational capacities to care for the irrigation system, were left on their own.

Oman remained one of the most conservative of the Persian Gulf states. Oman's prosperity, however, was revived in the seventeenth and eighteenth centuries when Omanis drove the Portuguese out of East Africa and the Sultans of the Bu Sa'id dynasty established their own trading network. Oman renewed its control over Zanzibar and other East African towns. While Zanzibar became a separate regime in 1856, the dynasty continues to rule Oman (and Muscat) to the present day. In 1955 Sa'id b. Taymur (1932–70), with British help, brought the whole country under his control. His narrow and tyrannical rule prompted several opposition movements. The Popular Front for the Liberation of Oman was formed in 1965 by embittered students; the Dhofar Liberation Front organized resistance in the personal estates of the Sultan. Until 1970, however, Sa'id b. Taymur was able to maintain complete control of the country owing to his British-officered army and the complete isolation of Oman from the outside world. In 1970 his son Qabus b. Sa'id took power to institute a more modernized regime. With Iranian help he crushed the resistance in Dhofar.

In other parts of the Persian Gulf a new political system took shape at the beginning of the eighteenth century. In a region of fragmented lineages, the Banu Khalid became the principal tribal power, and a number of local families established their preeminence. In 1752 Sabah b. Jabr of the Banu 'Utub became the first ruler of Kuwait and established the dynasty which rules Kuwait today. Kuwait has been a tribal state, a commercial entrepôt at the head of the Persian Gulf, and an important rival of Basra and other Persian Gulf ports. The al-Sabah family also assisted in the establishment of another branch of the ʿUtub, the al-Khalifa, in Bahrain.

By the end of the eighteenth century Britain had become the dominant power in the Gulf region and paramount over the small tribal regimes. In 1798 the British made the first of a series of treaties to protect British shipping in the Gulf and to install British political agents. British treaties with Kuwait, Bahrain, Oman, and the smaller "Trucial" states helped to strengthen the tribal rulers. British influence remained predominant until 1961, when Kuwait became fully independent. In 1970 and 1971, when Britain left the Gulf region, the Trucial states were severally reconstituted as members of the United Arab Emirates.

The modern transformation of the Persian Gulf region began with the discovery of oil in Bahrain in 1932, though production did not get underway in Bahrain, Kuwait, and Qatar until after World War II. In 1958 oil was found in Abu Dhabi and in 1973 in Sharja. The vast increase in oil revenues after 1973 has had the same effects in the Gulf as it has had in Saʿudi Arabia. The Gulf has become a highly urbanized area. More than half of the population, including a large number of Palestinians, Jordanians, Egyptians, Yemenis, and Pakistanis lives in cities. In some of the countries foreign labor accounts for between 70 and 85 percent of the labor force. Thus, the Gulf states remain small tribal principalities in which the superstructure of modern industry and development is carried by foreign laborers and administrators.

In each of the Gulf states the conditions of development are somewhat different. For example, Kuwait continues to be ruled by the al-Sabah family as a tribal state. Kinship and religious culture remain the bases of legitimacy. The secular and national aspects of Arabism are strongly present but Islam remains the basis of law and there is no pressure for secularization. A parliamentary and constitutional regime was introduced between 1962 and 1967 but it has since been suspended. The great wealth of the country – in 1976 the per capita income was equivalent to almost $16,000 per year – has been used to establish an extensive welfare system, including free health care and education. The population of Kuwait is almost entirely urban, with 76 percent of the total population living in Kuwait City alone.

Bahrain is also a traditional chieftainship, ruled since 1782 by the al-Khalifa family. Here the ruling family represents commercial and pearl fishing interests but not pastoral peoples. Thus when Bahrain became independent in 1971 it had an historical basis for a fairly sophisticated political system. A constitutional assembly was convened in 1973, granted by the ruling al-Khalifa family to its subjects in accord with the Muslim principle of consultation. The assembly, however, was suspended in 1975 when it threatened the dominance of the ruling Emir. The political elite of Bahrain includes not only the ruling family but also merchants and religious leaders. The distinctive feature of Bahrain political life is its numerous political clubs and professional societies which meet to discuss current issues. Also, owing to the early discovery of oil, Bahrain has a fairly strong union movement. As in Kuwait, the position of the ruling family is precariously balanced against the interests of a sophisticated and varied population.

The United Arab Emirates was formed from the small Trucial states. Abu Dhabi is the principal state in the federation with Dubai, Sharja, Ajnan, Umm al-Qaywayn, Fujayra, and Ras al-Khayma. These states were governed by local tribal chiefs who ruled a population divided between seafaring coastal residents and inland nomadic peoples. Upon the British withdrawal in 1971, Abu Dhabi and Dubai formed a federation with the smaller states. State authority rested on military prowess and control of oil revenues and patronage. The United Arab Emirates has built up an administrative apparatus for finance, justice, police, and public services. There is a federal council, cabinet, and defense forces.

Throughout the Gulf region the process of modernization remains in the hands of traditional monarchs and tribal chieftains. Nationalism has relatively little impact in this area, and there are only sporadic pressures for inclusion of larger elements of the population in the political process. In Kuwait and Bahrain the range of political consultation has been broadened. Arab nationalism as well as Islamic identities are stressed as the basis of social cohesion and political legitimacy. Considerable technical and economic change, a high degree of urbanization, and large numbers of foreign workers have thus far been absorbed without affecting the basic political and cultural quality of the Gulf regimes. Just as the Saʿudi regime has maintained its traditional position in the face of extensive changes, the Gulf states also show a surprising continuity of political leadership and Islamic loyalty. In these Arab countries, whose institutional heritage is tribal rather than Ottoman, secular national elites and ideologies have barely taken hold.

CHAPTER 26

NORTH AFRICA IN THE NINETEENTH AND TWENTIETH CENTURIES

The modern history of Arab North Africa parallels in important ways the history of the Arab Middle East. By the nineteenth century North Africa was substantially Muslim. Sufism played a large part in the organization of rural communities and state regimes tended to be legitimized in Muslim, rather than patrimonial, cosmopolitan, or ethnic terms. The urban populations were Arabic in speech and culture though in the southern, Saharan, and mountain regions, Berber was the common language and the basis of cultural identity.

In the course of the late eighteenth and early nineteenth centuries, the North African states were becoming more centralized and more rigorous in exacting taxes, but increased taxation provoked widespread local tribal and Sufi-led resistance. European economic competition further weakened the already tenuous hold of the North African states over their rural populations and intensified the internal struggles between states and tribal and sufi-led communities. These weakened North African states all succumbed to European domination. The French invaded Algeria in 1830, and established a protectorate in Tunisia in 1881 and in Morocco in 1912. Libya was invaded by Italy in 1911. The imposition of foreign rule on the several North African societies led, as in the Middle East, to profound changes in the structure of those societies, and to the emergence of independent national states.

ALGERIA

Algeria on the eve of the French conquest was governed by a regime which in many ways resembled that of Iraq and Syria. From the sixteenth century, a small force of janissaries organized the state institutions and gave Algeria its territorial identity, but most of the country was ruled with the collaboration of local tribal chiefs and Sufis who gathered their supporters on the basis of kinship affiliation or religious loyalty. By the early decades of the nineteenth century, the Algerian regime was in decline and the major Sufi brotherhoods, in reaction to fiscal burdens imposed by the central government, were in sporadic revolt.

In 1830, the government of Charles X, prompted by the need for a military victory to restore its political prestige after setbacks in the Greek War for Independence, and supported by Marseille's commercial interests, invaded Algeria. The French occupied Algiers and other coastal towns but the defeat of the Turkish administration allowed the subordinate tribes to rise up against the makhzan tribes and plunged much of rural Algeria into chaos. Out of this unrest a new Muslim state emerged in western Algeria. ʿAbd al-Qadir, whose father was head of the Qadiriya order, attempted to establish a Muslim state. In 1832 he declared himself Commander of the Faithful and Sultan of the Arabs and made himself responsible for applying Muslim holy law in his territories and for waging war against the French. He maintained the image of an ascetic Sufi; abstaining from alcohol, modest in dress and manner, he emulated the Prophet. However, he was careful to limit his claims so as not to offend his patron, the Sultan of Morocco. He did not have the Friday sermon delivered or the coinage minted in his name. On the basis of his religious prestige, his efforts to model himself on the life of the Prophet, and the propaganda of the Qadiriya order, most of the regional tribes accepted his authority.

ʿAbd al-Qadir developed a hierarchical administration for his state. He appointed subordinate khalifas with combined military, financial, and judicial authority. Beneath the khalifas were aghas, whose duty was to collect taxes. Below them were the qaʾids, who were chiefs of the tribes. ʿAbd al-Qadir chose his officials from important religious families and avoided using the people who had cooperated with the Turks. Alongside the state administration he organized a standing army.

From 1832 to 1841, ʿAbd al-Qadir alternately waged war and made peace with the French as part of a complex struggle for the loyalty of the Algerian tribes. In 1841, however, a new French general, Bugeaud, determined to win absolute domination of Algeria and open it to French colonization. The Moroccans intervened to protect their client, but at the battle of Isly in 1844 they were defeated, and in 1847, ʿAbd al-Qadir was deported to France and then to Damascus. The way was open to complete French control of Algeria.

Between 1851 and 1857 the French occupied Kabylia, and moved into the Sahara. In 1853 Wargala and the Mzab came under French suzerainty; the Mzab was annexed in 1882. In 1890 a treaty with Great Britain gave European political recognition to an expanded French Algerian empire.

The French began their reign in Algeria by adopting the Turkish and makhzan system. They combined a regional government modeled on that of the Turks with the mobilization of support from privileged tribes. After 1843, however, the French felt sufficiently in control to supervise the population directly through the Bureaux Arabes, some fifty units which combined military and civil administration. Also by the early 1840s the French had embarked upon the total occupation and substantial destruction of Algerian society to make way for French colonization. General Bugeaud adopted the strategy of massive raids in which he cut down orchards, burned crops, and destroyed peoples and villages. In this way the French subdued the Algerian population.

In the face of the destruction of their society, Algerian resistance was bitter but local in scale. In this resistance Muslim beliefs and loyalties played an important part. In northern Algeria there was a series of millennarian uprisings. In 1849 Bu Zian of Zaatsha, a local shaykh who had supported ʿAbd al-Qadir, was impelled by a dream, in which the Prophet Muhammad named him the representative of the mahdi, to resist taxation and to rebel against French control. In 1858 Sidi Sadok b. al-Hajj, a leader of a Rahmaniya zawiya who had been an ally of Bu Zian in 1849, resumed the jihad, but he and 88 followers were arrested. In 1860 Bu Khentash, a member of a pious and highly regarded warrior lineage, promised his followers miraculous protection against French bullets. He was killed in the same year. In 1879 Muhammad Amzian who had fought a generation earlier on the side of Sidi Sadok declared himself the mahdi and attacked the local officials. In southern Algeria there were also rebellions between 1851 and 1855 and 1871 and 1872, by camel-herding peoples who were attempting to protect the passages from the northern oases and to resist French officials. Sheep-herding nomads also rebelled to protect their access to markets and avoid complete economic dependence.

The organization of local resistance drew on the political mechanisms for generating unity in a factious Algerian rural society. The insurrections were sometimes prepared by secret societies called *shartiya*, which formed within each tribe to keep watch on officials, prepare horses and weapons, and mobilize the people to fight. Ecstatic preachers and Sufis, who claimed to be forerunners of the mahdi, created an atmosphere of ecstatic fervor, and played an important role in mobilizing revolts. Sufi brotherhoods were also important. From his base in Tunisia, Shaykh Mustafa b. ʿAzzuz (d. 1866) used his contacts in the

Rahmaniya order, religious prestige, kinship ties, and his central position in the munitions trade, to support anti-French propaganda and resistance in the Constantine region. For a time, however, the shaykh also made peace with the French. His policy was not to carry on an ideological or religious war but to make the best of the political realities.

In 1870–71 scattered local resistance finally crystallized into a massive Algerian uprising. Impelled by years of hardship and famine, by hopes that the defeat of Napoleon III in the Franco-Prussian war would make independence possible, and by fears that the rise of a Republican government in France would remove all restraints upon French colonization and lead to the seizure of Algerian lands, there were revolts throughout Algeria. These rebellions were given leadership and coordination by an Algerian tribal chief named al-Muqrani, supported by the Rahmaniya brotherhood. Al-Muqrani's family had been allies of the French since the 1830s, but in 1870 their position was threatened by French efforts to replace the dominant stratum with newer, more malleable administrative cadres, and to open the way for the settlement of French colons in the Mejana and the Kabyle. Al-Muqrani was defeated. The French extracted an enormous indemnity, amounting to ten times the usual tribute, and confiscated or held for ransom hundreds of thousands of hectares of land. In historical retrospect the resistance movements were signs of Algerian determination not to accept French rule, but they were also the last phase in the defeat of Algerian society by the European imperial power.

Thus the economic and political backbone of Algerian society was broken and the way prepared for 80 years of complete French domination and for an effort to assimilate Algeria to a European identity. Great numbers of people were killed as a result of war and famine. Algerian tribes were confined to specific districts or removed and resettled in the south to make way for French colons. Crucial to the reduction of Algerian society was the subordination of its elites. Between 1843 and 1870 the French undermined the tribal and religious chieftains in favor of a new generation of officials who lacked authority and were more amenable to French control. From 1874 the Muslim population was subject to the *code de l'indigénat* which made Muslims punishable for a long list of treasonable or illegal acts. These laws permitted confinement and confiscation of property.

The disorganization of Algerian society left it vulnerable to economic exploitation. Vast areas of land were confiscated. A few Muslim landowners were able to move from subsistence to a market economy, but the bulk of the population was forced into ownership of uneconomically small plots, sharecropping, labor, and destitution. While the French often argued that the poverty of the Muslims was inherent in their social and cultural limitations, or that not enough incentives had been provided to overcome a pre-market mentality, or that capitalism did not go far enough in Algeria to absorb the Muslim population, the major cause was the devastation wrought by the French invasion and the seizure of Algerian lands.

Muslim culture also suffered. Before the French conquest there were numerous schools and extensive properties endowed to support religious instruction. Constantine and Tlemcen, for example, had numerous primary schools, madrasas, and zawiyas with hundreds of advanced students. The colleges had provided a higher education stressing grammar, law, interpretation of the Quran, arithmetic, and astronomy. French occupation, however, led to the seizure of the revenues and the destruction of many schools. In principle they were supposed to be replaced by French schools to assimilate Algerian children into European civilization, but the new school system, introduced between 1883 and 1898, reached only a small minority and essentially trained native Algerian functionaries to cooperate with the French in the control of the Muslim population. While many Algerian middle-class families from the Kabyle, the Aurès, and Mzab enrolled in the new schools, the absolute numbers were small. In 1890 students enrolled in French schools amounted to 2 percent of the population; in 1930 almost 9 percent of Algerian children received some education; and in 1945 approximately 15 percent. In 1954 only three-quarters of a percent of Muslims of secondary school age were being educated. The system, minimal as it was, was resisted by the colons and by many Muslims. It was no remedy for the low political and economic status of Muslims.

The destruction of Algerian society was accompanied by massive French colonization. This began almost immediately after the French conquest as societies were formed in France to speculate in Algerian land, and would-be settlers seized abandoned properties. The French government soon decided to expropriate Algerian lands on a large scale. It began by sequestering the lands of the Dey and the Beys. After 1839 lands were seized from the followers of ʿAbd al-Qadir. A decree of 1843 ended the inalienability of religious endowments and allowed them to be bought and sold under European law. The French also forced tribal groups to move out of their traditional domains or to occupy smaller spaces within them so that the "surplus" land could be converted into colonial farms. Further regulations culminating in a law of 1873 broke down Algerian communal properties by allowing individual

Muslims to sell their portion of collective tribal lands as well as family property. The result was to make vast tracts available to French settlers.

Confiscation of land and new land laws allowed for the development of a large French and European colony. In 1847 the European population of Algeria reached 109,000, including 47,000 French and numerous Italians, Spaniards, Germans, Swiss, and Maltese. The foreign population rose to 376,000 in 1881. By 1900 Europeans held 1,700,000 hectares and by 1940 2,700,000 hectares, about 35 to 40 percent of the arable land of Algeria. European settlers were nonetheless extremely dependent upon government help. Before 1870 efforts to grow grain, sugar cane, cotton, tobacco, linen, tea, and mulberry all failed. Only after a series of grape crop failures in France did wine become the dominant European industry in Algeria.

The large European and French colony in Algeria demanded that Algeria be assimilated as an integral part of France. For decades French colonists fought for and finally won control of the government of Algeria and the substantial integration of Algeria into the French political system. This outcome was opposed by the French army, which itself wanted to govern Algeria through the Bureaux Arabes and which tried to restrain the appropriation of Muslim lands and the establishment of a civilian government for the colonial population. In 1860 Napoleon III visited Algeria and was convinced that his first obligation was to protect his 3,000,000 Arab subjects. Military administration was again strengthened, but between 1864 and 1870 famines, epidemics, and tribal insurrections discredited the military administration, and the defeat of the great Muslim revolt of 1870–71 finally allowed for the establishment of a regime committed to ruling Algeria entirely in the interests of the colons. The defeat of Napoleon forced the French government to give in to settler demands. Algeria was administratively incorporated into France and reorganized as three French departments, except that the country as a whole remained under the authority of a civil governor-general for all three departments. The colonists were given the right to municipal government and could elect deputies to the French assembly. For local administration Algeria was divided into European and "mixed" communes. European communes were full municipalities with elected councils and mayors. Mixed communes were administrative districts run by civil servants advised by town or village councils called *jamaʿat*, which were closely controlled by French administrative officers and were hardly institutions of self-government. In 1896 the system of direct control by French ministries in Paris was ended, and in 1898 an elected assembly, with vast European preponderance, was created. French settlers controlled local councils and the Algerian assembly and manipulated the French parliament so that the system operated to vest control of Algeria in the hands of the colons.

French domination of Algerian society was virtually complete but, paradoxically, colonial rule generated the conditions for the emergence of a renewed Algerian resistance and demands for independence. The vast but disorganized and impoverished Algerian population, confined to marginal lands, its tribal leadership demolished, its religious elites co-opted, its military resistance defeated, was nonetheless to be reborn. The very economic changes induced by the French led to the formation of new classes and a changing Algerian consciousness. As the French colonized the countryside they upset the village economies, forced rural peoples to migrate to the cities, and brought new elites into being as a result of the very effort to destroy the old. As the older generation of marabouts, tribal chiefs, and qaʾids was displaced from power, a new generation of Western- or Muslim-reform-educated men arose. They were often state employees such as teachers, postmen, pharmacists, and railway workers; sometimes they were returned war veterans. The new elites became the backbone of new organizations, including cultural associations, trade unions, and political parties. On a psychological level, French penetration came up against a hidden core of national feeling which was mobilized in symbolic ways until it eventually took political form. Popular poems and epics celebrated the past glory of Islam, destined to once again overcome the unbelievers. Disillusionment and anger were manifested in demonstrations, strikes, and sporadic violence. These were expressions of a refusal, however inarticulate and however limited, to accept the permanence of French power.

After World War I French policy indirectly encouraged Algerian resistance. In the flush of victory and gratitude for Algerian support in the war, there were several attempts to liberalize the administration of the Muslim population. France offered Muslims French citizenship if they would give up Muslim civil law. Other legislation enlarged the representation of native peoples in local assemblies and gave suffrage to property owners, officials, and veterans. Algerian settler pressure forced the French government to renege on many of these concessions, but not before French concepts of justice, equality, and citizenship had taken hold among Muslim intellectuals.

The indigenous Algerian elite had three main components. One was the graduates of French-Arab schools who expected to be fully integrated into French society, while retaining their social and legal identity as Muslims. After the turn of the century, a small group of French-educated Muslim intellectuals

organized the "Young Algerians" to press their demands. In 1927 the Fédération des Élus Indigènes d'Algérie was founded by liberal lawyers and
teachers who had been elected to municipal councils. This was followed in
1930 by the organization of the federation of Muslim representatives in the
department of Constantine, led by Dr Ben Jellul. The federation became the
spokesman for those Algerians who demanded equality in the army, in education, and in appointment to public office, and the abolition of all measures
which discriminated against the Muslim population. The French-educated
elite, however, did not demand Algerian independence. Farhat ᶜAbbas made
the famous statement: "I have questioned history; I have questioned the living
and the dead; I have visited the cemeteries. The empires of the Arabs and
Islam are in the past; our future is decisively linked to that of France."

A second Algerian elite of the 1920s and 1930s was more radical and
nationalist in orientation and grew up among Algerian émigrés in Paris. In
1926 L'Étoile Nord Africaine was established by the French Communist
Party; it communicated to Algerians the aspiration to establish an Algerian
parliament as a preliminary to an independent nation. The E.N.A. languished
until 1933, when Messali Hajj reactivated the movement. In its new version
the E.N.A. stressed Algerian independence but it played down the concept of
class struggle within Algeria in the interest of generating Algerian solidarity
against foreign rule. Messali Hajj thus tried to win the support of middle-class
moderate Algerians. In 1936 he was converted to pan-Arab ideals espoused by
Shakib Arslan, a Lebanese journalist living in Geneva, who called for an
independent Algeria rooted in Islamic values and allied to fellow Arabs. In
1937 the E.N.A. was transformed into the Parti du Peuple Algérien (P.P.A.).

The P.P.A. called for the creation of an Algerian parliament, universal
suffrage, admission of Algerians to all public functions on an equal basis, and
obligatory instruction in Arabic. It called for the total political independence
of Algeria, the removal of all occupying troops, the control by the new
Algerian state over banks, mines, railways, ports, and public facilities. The
organization also called on Algerians to conform to the principles of Islam.
The P.P.A. was essentially a populist movement whose social base widened
from its original migrant worker supporters to artisans, small merchants, and
workers. During World War II it was joined by students and graduates.

The third section of the new Algerian elite was the leaders of the Islamic
reformist movement, who adapted Islamic scripturalism to Algerian nationalist needs. Muslim reformism reached Algeria as a result of contacts with
Muhammad ᶜAbduh and with Muslim reformers in Tunisia, but did not take
hold until after World War I. The war undermined the position of rural

Sufis. The migration of workers to the cities reduced their clientele in the countryside, and collaboration with the French reduced their prestige. The growth of an urban petite bourgeoisie and working class subverted the appeal of the magical, thaumaturgic, and mystical authority of the marabouts. The rise of the reformers in turn pushed the marabouts into cooperation with the French and thus further subverted their position. At the same time French political generosity in the aftermath of World War I provoked fears that close relations with France might tempt Muslims to assimilate. Muslims felt more acutely the need for a Muslim press and religious associations to compete with Catholic organizations and French schools.

ᶜAbd al-Hamid b. Badis, educated at the Zaytuna in Tunis, became the principal leader of the reform ((*islah*) movement and of the postwar revival of Arab cultural identity in Algeria. He took his inspiration from Muhammad ᶜAbduh, Rashid Rida, and the Salafiya movement, and emphasized the importance of returning to the Quran and hadith as the basic sources of Muslim belief and practice. He stressed belief in the unity of God, denounced polytheism, and emphasized the revealed sources of Muslim knowledge, without diminishing the importance of reason. From the Quran Ben Badis extracted the general principles of the reform: belief in the unity of God, filial piety, respect for the rights of others, proper use of worldly fortunes, honesty in commercial transactions, and purity of moral intentions. A good Muslim should emulate the virtues of the Prophet.

The emphasis on divine unity was used as the basis of a bitter critique of Sufi beliefs and practices. The reformers denounced the veneration of saints and beliefs in miracles and attempted to use rational arguments to demystify rural Sufism. Maraboutism, they argued, was a reprehensible novelty introduced into Islam – neither prescribed in the Quran, recommended by the Prophet, nor practiced by the early Caliphs. Thus, they tried to change the way in which the birthday of the Prophet was celebrated. In schools, clubs and theaters, as well as mosques and zawiyas, the reformers, less ecstatic, less ritualistic and more austere, emphasized Muhammad's historical role and gave sermons on topics of current interest.

The reformers were particularly concerned with social and economic issues but conceived these issues in religious and moral terms. Thus they spoke a great deal about zakat (alms) as a source of income for the movement, and as an expression of the responsibility of the rich for the poor, but they had little to say about the conditions of urban workers and rural peasants, or about the problems of economic development and the use of capital. Following Rashid Rida they rejected feminism, favored the use of the veil, and opposed the social interaction of men and women. They opposed giving women equality in inheritance or the right to initiate divorce. In the classical sources they found nothing to contradict modern science and technology, but while they saw Islam as compatible with the modern world, they were not principally concerned with the modernization of society. What moved them was the defeat of Muslim countries by Europeans. Only a return to the purity and vigor of early Islam would enable Muslims to assimilate modern science and remedy their cultural and political situation. The reformer's journal combatted the social ills of modern societies, including alcoholism, gambling, and all other immoral activities forbidden by religion.

The reform movement intended not only to define a new doctrine but to create a social movement through which the new ideas could be passed on to the young. They organized conferences and discussion groups to propagandize for Muslim principles and Arabic culture. They sponsored a strong scout movement, and founded schools which combined teaching of the Quran, Arabic, Algerian history, and patriotic songs, plus some French, arithmetic, and geography, to inculcate the concept of an Algerian fatherland. Most of the reform schools were elementary schools but students could move on to the mosque at Constantine or the Zaytuna in Tunis for an advanced education. Only a small portion of the students actually earned an elementary certificate; few went on to higher education. The school movement reached its peak in 1954, when it had about 110 schools and 20,000 students. By then the schools were training militants for the nationalist movement, and were important in creating a sense of an Algerian national identity.

In 1931 Ben Badis also founded the Association of Muslim ʿUlamaʾ of Algeria to sponsor preaching, publications, and schools. The strengthening of the reform movement provoked resistance from the Sufis, who founded their own Association of ʿUlamaʾ in 1932. In 1933 the French forbade the use of mosques to reformist preachers and claimed control over journals published in Arabic as well as those published in French. French opposition put the reformers in the position of being the only outspoken indigenous opponents of French rule. Ben Badis defended religious liberty, and the right to teach Arabic and maintain a Muslim press. After 1935 the reform movement began to slide into a more overtly political role. A joint congress of the Association of Muslim ʿUlamaʾ and the Fédération des Élus Indigènes was held in 1936, at which Ben Badis emerged as the leading spokesman of opposition to French assimilation.

Behind the reform, then, was a political concept: though part of the French empire, Algeria was an Arab-Muslim entity. Arabism was meant not only to combat assimilation but to resist French efforts to divide Arabs and Berbers. Arabism implied social unity, national consciousness, and solidarity with the Arab peoples in the east in their common quest for religious and cultural identity in the face of foreign rule.

This concept was further elaborated in Ben Badis' position on the Caliphate. Ben Badis accepted the abolition of the Caliphate by the Turkish Republic on the grounds that the Turks had abolished an illusory symbol, and a tool in the hand of European powers. Muslims should govern themselves through a jamaᶜ, or permanent council, separate from and independent of states, though Muslims could also at the same time be citizens or subjects of states. His thinking distinguished cultural from political nationality, and thus allowed for a conception of a Muslim community as universal in principle and yet divided into politically and culturally distinct regional or national groups. By distinguishing religion from political nationality the reformers allowed for Algerian identity under French domination. In response to the famous declaration of Farhat ᶜAbbas, Ben Badis affirmed that "this Muslim nation is not France, it is not possible for it to be France. It does not want to become France, and even if it wanted to, it could not." The religious reformers thus popularized the notion that religiously, linguistically, and culturally, Algerians were a distinct people whose ultimate destiny was political independence.

The reform movement had strong appeal to the petite bourgeoisie of the coastal towns such as Constantine, Oran, and Algiers, and to areas in the countryside which felt the vacuum of authority and initiative left by the decline of tribal and Sufi elites. The adoption of reform teaching in rural contexts revealed the integration of rural areas into the national market economy and the development of a new stratification of society. For example, the descendants of Sidi al-Hashami, the rebel of 1879, used the islah idiom to attack their conventional Rahmaniya opponents. The reformers in this region established the Free Islamic Institute at Batna, the largest such school in Algeria. Reformism, then, adapted itself to local circumstances in both urban and rural areas to become the most energetic and widespread cultural force in Algeria. By the late 1930s the reformers had successfully resisted French efforts at assimilation. They had forced both the liberal bourgeois and the more radical worker movements to take on an Islamic aura and to legitimize themselves in Islamic terms. The death of Ben Badis in 1940 deprived the reform of its dynamism but its contribution to the creation of an Algerian national identity was lasting.

By the mid-1930s, the cultural preparations were made, and the struggle for Algerian independence began in earnest. Algerian demands grew ever more insistent, French responses ever more contradictory. By 1936 the several Algerian elites had coalesced in an Algerian Muslim congress which made demands for reform – maintenance of Muslim civil law, improvement in instruction and education, equality in salary and other economic matters, universal suffrage and representation in parliament – but not independence. The French were divided as to how to respond. Some favored a conciliatory, liberal policy, but French politics made it impossible to carry this out consistently. Threatened by the new elites, the French turned to repression, closed down reformist schools and journals, and broke with the Muslim liberal bourgeoisie. For two generations the French had cultivated a small Muslim elite by holding forth the expectation that educated Muslims could become French citizens, but in 1938 the Blum-Viollette proposal to grant French citizenship to Algerians without requiring them to renounce Muslim civil law was abandoned. Algerian liberals lost their hope for reform and assimilation.

From the outbreak of World War II until the beginning of the Algerian revolution, nationalist groups increased their demands upon the French, who responded alternately with belated reforms and continued obstruction and repression. Throughout the war years moderate Algerian opinion backed France, but in 1943 Farhat ʿAbbas issued his Manifesto of the Algerian People, which called for an end to colonial rule and the formation of an Algerian constitution that allowed for the participation of Muslims in the government of their own country. The Manifesto further advocated the recognition of the Arabic language as equal to French, freedom of press and association, universal school instruction, and other liberal measures. In 1946 the new Union Démocratique du Manifeste Algérien (U.D.M.A.) was founded as the voice of Algerian bourgeois opinion. This was followed by Messali's Mouvement pour le Triomphe des Libertés Démocratiques (M.T.L.D.). In 1947 the Algerians presented the French Assembly with a plan for an Algerian Republic as part of a North African Union federated with France. The French government rejected these proposals and instead passed the Statut d'Algérie in September 1947. The Statut defined Algeria as a group of departments within the French Republic administered by a Governor-General, though they were provided with an elected assembly and accorded limited financial and administrative autonomy. The Statut also provided for equality of citizenship and for recognition of the Islamic religious and Arabic language interests of the Algerian population. This plan not only fell far short of Muslim proposals, but the French government manipulated Algerian elections to exclude the major Muslim parties, and otherwise postponed the implementation of the reforms. The idea of gradual and non-violent emancipation and the concept of an

Algeria allied with France completely lost its value to Algerian Muslim public opinion.

Behind the maneuvering of the political elites, a new Algerian mass consciousness and political movement was in the making. In May 1945 Algerian demonstrations at Setif led to attacks on French colons and to terrible massacres of Muslims by the French. These events marked the beginning of a mass or popular nationalist sentiment. Also, within the M.T.L.D. some activists and militants concluded that armed insurrection was the only way to achieve Algerian independence. A more radical younger generation, from small towns and lower-middle-class families who had little opportunity for higher education and little contact with Europeans, but instead were stronger in their Arabic and Islamic identity – who bore a sharp sense of the misery of rural life and the injustice and indignity of French domination and a strong will to resist and to exercise power in the name of the Algerian nation – came to the fore. Within the M.T.L.D. an Organization Spéciale (O.S.), led by Ait Ahmed and Ben Bella, gave the Algerian resistance a paramilitary capability. By 1949 the cadres of a military resistance were ready, but until 1954 the various Algerian liberal, radical and revolutionary groups remained unable to agree upon such action.

Finally in 1954, the O.S. re-formed as the Comité Revolutionnaire de L'Unité d'Action (C.R.U.A.), split with M.T.L.D., organized the Front de Libération Nationale (F.L.N.) and launched the Algerian revolution by a nationwide campaign of guerrilla attacks on November 1, 1954. The revolutionaries organized Algeria into six provinces (*wilayat*); in Tunisia and Morocco they built up a strong Algerian army (A.L.N.), commanded eventually (1959) by Houari Boumedienne. The F.L.N. denounced the previous Algerian movements for their political failure and declared itself in favor of an independent, sovereign, democratic, and socialist Algerian state within Islamic principles – a state which could only be created by armed struggle.

The war itself brought a new generation of soldier–leaders to power. While the older Algerian elites had been committed either to assimilation to France or to a reformed Muslim social identity, the revolutionary generation was more pragmatic. While the F.L.N. was not officially Islamic, its supporters held strong Islamic sentiments and puritanical attitudes. The leaders of the revolution considered alcohol and tobacco symbols of betrayal. While they were anti-French, they were convinced that the revolution would open up for the masses the modernity which French domination had denied them. In the war itself, they were motivated by attachments to their wilayat and army units, and by a strong sense of personal mission and responsibility. The F.L.N.

rapidly gained the political support of the U.D.M.A., led by Farhat ʿAbbas, the centrists in the M.T.L.D., the ʿulamaʾ, and the Union Générale des Travailleurs Algériens (U.G.T.A.). In 1956 all groups were agreed on the goal of full Algerian independence. With the emergence of the F.L.N., armed resistance to the French was based on the support of the petite bourgeoisie, urban workers, and peasant activists. Students and intellectuals in both Algeria and France later supplied the administrative cadres for the Algerian state.

At the congress of Summam in August 1956 the revolutionaries resolved that theirs was a struggle to destroy an anachronistic colonization but not a war of religion, and proposed the formation of a social and democratic Algerian republic. From this point of view, the only issues to be negotiated with France were the transfer of administrative power, and subsequent co-operation in economic, social, and cultural activities. In 1958 a Gouvernement Provisionnel de la République Algérienne (G.P.R.A.) was formed to win international recognition, and was supported by Egypt and other Arab countries, the Communist states, and, to some degree, by American anti-colonialist sentiment. This international support was crucial to its eventual victory.

In response, the French reaffirmed the permanent presence of France in Algeria. The French won the military advantage, captured Ben Bella and his companions by kidnapping an airplane on which they were travelling, and under the leadership of General Massu launched the battle for Algiers. This was an urban anti-guerrilla operation which led in the middle of 1957 to the liquidation of the F.L.N. apparatus in Algiers. The French also blocked the flow of weapons and manpower into the country from Tunisia and Morocco, and defeated the F.L.N. in the Sahara. French tactics included massive military action and the resettlement of the Algerian population.

Though the French were winning the military victories, they could not sustain the war. On May 13, 1958, the French population of Algeria organized its own demonstrations which toppled the government of Algeria, undermined the Fourth Republic and, in June 1958, brought General de Gaulle to power. De Gaulle, however, disappointed the expectations of the colons by proposing a reconciliation of France and the F.L.N. He called for a referendum on a proposed new French constitution in which all residents of France and Algeria would have equal voting rights. After the referendum he proposed the Plan of Constantine for economic development, employment of Muslims, equalization of salaries, distribution of arable land to Muslim peasants, development of the school system for two-thirds of school-age children, and the construction of 200,000 housing units. This was to be financed by petroleum and gas development. Then in September 1959 de Gaulle spoke of a self-determined Algerian future, with Algerians given the right to choose among independence, autonomy in association with France, or assimilation. Thus the French government resigned its determination to maintain Algeria as part of France. Direct negotiations with the F.L.N. were begun in 1960, and in March 1962, at Evian, Algerian sovereignty was recognized, with France reserving bases for airplane and naval operations and for atomic testing. Future economic cooperation was agreed, and French colons were allowed to choose between French or Algerian citizenship.

Thus, after bitter struggle, terrible destruction, and massive sacrifice of human life – in spite of enormous political and administrative resources and the presence of a large European population, in spite of the passionate aspiration to assimilate its colony – France lost control of its Algerian empire. Both the French right and the French left believed that the existence of France as a nation depended on its empire. France was determined to hold on to Algeria at all costs, but this determination proved hollow. Caught between leftist liberalism and rightist authoritarianism, French policy allowed Muslim dissent to crystallize, and, by repressing its manifestations, prompted further resistance. The French position was further subverted by colons, who led the French government to excesses of policy and then themselves resisted central control. The divisions in France, the numerical predominance of the Muslim population, and the growth of its national consciousness made Algerian liberation irresistible.

The problems of organizing a regime, defining an economic policy, and creating a cultural identity for the new state were enormous. While Tunisia won its independence on the basis of a profound continuity of cultural and political leadership, Algeria came to independence after the whole fabric of Algerian society had been ripped asunder. There was no unified political elite and no clear ideological direction. The Algerian elite was assembled from among liberal bourgeois professionals, reformist ʿulamaʾ, petit bourgeois radicals, and revolutionary soldiers, and was divided among the F.L.N., the A.L.N., and G.P.R.A., and other groups. After several generations of assimilated French, reformist Muslim, and activist military leadership, the basic problem was the divisions within the political elite.

The outcome of the ensuing struggle for power was military dictatorship and a state bureaucratic regime. The Tripoli Congress of June 1962 formed a Political Bureau led by Ben Bella, which in turn created a national constituent assembly to draft a constitution. Ben Bella was named president and himself promulgated a socialist constitution; the F.L.N. became the only political

party. In the struggle for power the assembly dissolved into ineffectual opposition. Ben Bella and the army eliminated the wilaya commanders, and
purged the F.L.N. of his opponents. Older-generation leaders were eliminated
and replaced by younger trusted associates; all power was centralized in the
hands of the president. Only the Algerian union of workers (U.G.T.A.), a
militant force in organizing railroad, post office, petroleum, municipal construction, and other workers, kept some political autonomy. All other major
political bodies, the National Union of Algerian Women, the National Liberation Front Youth Movement, and the National Union of Algerian Students,
were poorly organized and had little potential for political action. Control
of the party and the administration, however, was not enough to save Ben
Bella from a coup in June 1965 led by General Houari Boumedienne, who
became President of the Republic. By 1967 the professional army officers
had eliminated their rivals and taken control of the state.

The new regime concentrated on the development of the urban and industrial sectors of the economy by using petroleum revenues to finance an
industrial revolution. State-owned steel, textile, glass, and insurance companies
were founded in 1967. Algeria nationalized its gas industry in 1971; investments have been made in export-oriented petrochemicals, steel, electricity,
fertilizer, chemical, and plastics industries.

Agricultural development has been subordinated to the needs of industrial
policy. Under the socialist-military regime, abandoned French estates were
nationalized and consolidated into some 2,300 farms. State decrees provided
that they would be run by worker-committees, with the profits to be shared
between workers and national employment and investment funds, but later
measures deprived the self-managed farms of control over their own financing
and marketing and made them dependent on government ministries. Little
was done, however, for the mass of the rural populace, which needed to rebuild
the villages and required capital and technical assistance; nothing was done for
600,000 landless rural workers. While a small portion of the rural society was
better off, the peasantry suffered from fragmentation of land ownership,
absentee landlordism, waqf and communal constraints on the ownership of
land, sharecropping, and inequitable distribution of income.

By 1971 demands for social justice, the need to reduce imports of food, to
create a more balanced production of dairy products and grain, and to check
the impoverishment of the rural population required a new agricultural policy.
The new policy was supposed to consist of a redistribution of land and
livestock from large to small holders, the organization of cooperatives, and the
coordination of cooperatives into a larger marketing system. The results have

not been encouraging. Land redistribution has been very limited. Many private owners have retained lands owing to exceptions in the law, and many of the potential beneficiaries of confiscated land have refused to accept it because of complications or misunderstanding of the cooperative system. The reform program has extended the state-controlled sector of the economy but has left the private sector with the continuing burden of an underemployed peasantry. Further planning calls for the reform of livestock production in steppe regions and envisages the formation of communes, concentrated village centers, investment in forest and soil improvement, and a decentralization of agricultural decision making.

By the late 1970s, the failures of these policies were borne in upon the regime. A large percentage of Algeria's food supplies had to be imported. Industrial projects were often uneconomical and dependent upon foreign technicians. Housing and welfare had been neglected; unemployment was high. Since the death of Boumedienne in 1978, his successor President Chadli b. Jadid, also a military officer has reversed the policies of the previous regime, slowed down industrial growth, tightened financial controls over industrial projects, increased consumption, and favored a greater participation of private entrepreneurs in the national economy. By and large, however, the Algerian government (resembling that of Iraq) governs through the army and a socialized economy. It has encouraged the capital-intensive sectors of the economy that are under state control at the expense of the economic needs of the rural population. The revolution has ended in state capitalism.

The ideological orientation of the Algerian regime embraces apparent contradictions. The new elites were divided in their ideological position. Ben Bella led the cadres who favored the modernization of the country and the creation of a socialist economy. They kept French as the language of government, business, and even of ideological discussion. Boumedienne became the chief spokesman for a Muslim and Arab identity and for close ties between Algeria, Tunisia, Morocco, and the Arab east. For many of the uprooted soldiers of the revolution, migrant workers returned from France, peasants residing in the towns, and mobile petite bourgeoisie, Arabism and Islam are the only common bases of social and national identity.

In Algeria, as in other Muslim countries the prevailing attitude toward women has become a test of cultural orientation. French rule and colonization created a certain precedent for the education of women and their employment in public positions, but this scarcely had any effect on the masses. The revolution, however, made some women militant fighters, whose contribution for a time freed them from control of fathers, husbands, and brothers. With independence, women generally remained veiled and stayed away from public places. European mores were seen as incompatible with Muslim traditions.

The Algerian constitution attempts to combine both orientations by declaring Algeria an Arab-Islamic country and a popular and democratic republic. Reformist Islam has been accepted as a legitimizing principle and its discourse has infiltrated all political language. The state, moreover, has been careful to absorb the independent Quran schools, control appointments to religious offices, and sponsor Islamic propaganda. The new generation of leaders, then, wants both to modernize Algeria and to deepen the religious-cultural basis of national identity. Nonetheless, the state has not entirely captured Islam. Unofficial mosques and schools harbor an independent-minded and potentially hostile Muslim community life. As in other Muslim countries, Islam in Algeria eludes state control and retains the capacity for articulating opposition to state policies.

TUNISIA

In the middle of the nineteenth century, Tunisia shared the problems of the Ottoman empire and Egypt. Faced with rising European economic power and a declining internal economy, the Beys of Tunisia attempted to modernize their regime. Ahmad Bey (1837–55) founded a polytechnic school in 1838 and invited Europeans to train a new infantry corps. In 1857 Muhammad Bey (1855–59) promulgated a constitution which guaranteed security for the Tunisian population, equality in taxation, freedom of religion, and mixed European–Tunisian courts. A liberal constitution of 1861 created an oligarchic senate recruited by cooptation. These efforts at reform, however, could not be fully institutionalized, for there were never sufficiently numerous well-trained troops or administrators.

A last attempt at strengthening the state came in the administration of Khayr al-Din between 1873 and 1877. Khayr al-Din tried to limit public spending, to eliminate tax collecting abuses, and to reform the administration of religious affairs. He helped to found the Sadiqi College in 1875 to train future government officials, and appointed new supervisors for the Zaytuna mosque. Under his leadership the government created new offices for the administration of waqfs and reorganized Muslim justice, especially to meet European demands for equity. Finally, the reform program included the creation of a government printing press to produce textbooks for the Sadiqi students and to reproduce classic Islamic legal treatises.

The reform program as a whole was based on the principle that good government is the foundation of economic and social vitality. It found in Europe the model of efficient administration and public security. Khayr al-Din's reforms called for political justice as the basis of progress, and made a special argument for equality among Europeans and Muslims. The power of the Bey, he argued, should be limited by the ʿulamaʾ, who should function as a parliament. Government, he believed, should promote science, industry, agriculture, and commerce.

Politically, the reform effort depended upon the support of ʿulamaʾ, whom Khayr al-Din tried to persuade to accept European methods of government. His arguments for reform were couched in the classic Islamic political terms of the responsibility of governments for their subjects. While the ʿulamaʾ had a limited capacity to initiate change or exercise political power, they held an important place in Tunisian society because they were the educated graduates of the principal mosques, and served as teachers and magistrates. Until the foundation of the Sadiqi College, they controlled all secondary education. Until the founding of modern newspapers they monopolized political opinion. Their social connections reinforced their influence. The ʿulamaʾ pushed their sons into government service and were tied by marriage to official and merchant families, who commonly educated their children as religious scholars. The ʿulamaʾ were also closely tied to the rural Sufis, who sent their children to the Zaytuna and who shared the same religious principles. In Tunisia there was little or no tension between the ʿulamaʾ and Sufi branches of the religious establishment. The high social influence of the religious leaders, however, was not accompanied by political power, for the Beys insisted on loyalty and passivity in return for appointments to office. In general the ʿulamaʾ did not oppose the technical aspects of the reform program, such as the telegraph, but otherwise they dissociated themselves from it. In 1877 Khayr al-Din was dismissed from office. Reforms in Tunisia followed in general the patterns established in Egypt and the Ottoman empire, but they did not go far enough to consolidate the power of the state.

At the same time Tunisia could no longer resist international economic and political pressures. The French, who had occupied Algeria since 1830, used border disputes as a pretext to impose French domination in 1881. The French progressively assumed the most responsible administrative positions, and by 1884 supervised all Tunisian government bureaus dealing with finance, post, education, telegraph, public works, and agriculture. They abolished the international finance commission and guaranteed the Tunisian debt, established a new judicial system for Europeans while keeping the Shariʿa courts for cases involving Tunisians, and developed roads, ports, railroads, and mines. In rural areas they strengthened the local officials (qaʾids) and weakened independent tribes.

Most important was the opening of Tunisia to French colonization and the introduction of modern agriculture and education. The French encouraged colonization by selling collective lands and waqfs. Changes in land law generated increasing state revenues by bringing land into cultivation and by guaranteeing title to European purchasers. The number of French colonists grew from 34,000 in 1906 to 144,000 in 1945, and the French occupied approximately one-fifth of the cultivable land. A French system of education was fostered by the Alliance Française and by the Catholic church. Between 1885 and 1912 some 3,000 Tunisians sent their children to Paris. The French also intervened in Muslim education. In 1898 they tried to reform the Zaytuna by adding modern subjects and pedagogical methods, but the ʿulamaʾ resisted this interference with the teaching of Muslim law. Nonetheless, some Tunisian ʿulamaʾ and French officials cooperated in the reform of public instruction, the administration of waqfs, and the management of Sadiqi College. Rural-born and socially mobile Malikis were more willing to cooperate with the French than their better established Hanafi colleagues. Splits among the ʿulamaʾ therefore allowed for an alliance between the government and some segments of the Muslim religious establishment. Thus Tunisian elites accepted French rule without great difficulty. Tunisians were pacified by the employment of Tunisian officials and ʿulamaʾ, and by French respect for Muslim institutions. The French saw to it that nothing would disturb the collection of taxes.

Still, despite the relative political quiet, Tunisian officials, intellectuals, and some ʿulamaʾ awoke to the costs of French rule. A new generation of Tunisian national leaders emerged, like the Ottoman, out of the modern-educated bureaucratic elite. From the 1880s until the 1930s Tunisian leaders came from administrative and ʿulamaʾ backgrounds; some were educated in French schools, others were oriented culturally to reformist Islam. From the 1880s to about 1905 these elites largely accepted French rule and concentrated on educational and cultural concerns. In 1888 graduates of the Zaytuna and the Sadiqi College created the weekly newspaper *al-Hadira* to comment on European and world events, and to discuss political, economic, and literary issues. This elite also sponsored the founding of the Khalduniya school in 1896 to supplement the Zaytuna education with modern subjects. From both the reformed Muslim schools and French schools emerged the self-styled "Young Tunisians." Fueled by eastern Arab influences, especially the teachings of al-Afghani, Muhammad ʿAbduh, and the Egyptian National Party, they espoused the modernization and Westernization of Tunisian society, and a revival of

Arabic culture, poetry, history, geography, law, and social theory. Inspired by Salafiya values they called for reform of Muslim legal, educational, and waqf administration. "Young Tunisians" also sponsored a reformed Quran school in which students were taught the Quran, Arabic, and the basics of arithmetic, geography, history, and French. This generation was still deeply concerned with the reform of Muslim legal administration and Arabic literary education.

The first political expression of the "Young Tunisians" came with the founding in 1907 of the journal, *The Tunisian*. Secular-minded liberals and Salafiya reformers developed a national political feeling under the impetus of the Russian revolution, Woodrow Wilson's principles of self-determination, the Wafd movement in Egypt, and the formation of a popularly elected parliament in Tripolitania. Until around 1920 the nationalists demanded equal opportunity and pay in administration, and liberal freedoms of press and association, but in 1920 ᶜAbd al-ᶜAziz al-Thaᶜalibi, a leading Arab journalist and reformer, became the chief spokesman of the Destour (Constitution) party. Its principal demand was the reinstatement of the constitution of 1861. In the 1920s, Tunisian efforts to organize political resistance became more vigorous. In 1922 the Bey gave the French resident-general an ultimatum, but a show of French military force suppressed the Tunisian resistance. The agitation was resumed in 1924 by workers returned from France, who formed the first Tunisian economic cooperative society and the first Tunisian trade union, the General Confederation of Tunisian Workers, but Tunisian strikes were broken, and the government jailed the leaders, closed down the newspapers and suppressed political activity.

In the 1930s a new generation of Tunisian nationalists came to the fore. For over a decade the Destour party had been led by conservative families, often Zaytuna-educated, with a strong Muslim and Arab identity. Now representatives of small and middling provincial cities, with a combined Arabic and French education and secular socialist ideas of Tunisian society, rose to challenge the old elites. The new leaders found support among townsmen and peasant migrants and an enlarged urban population. Led by Habib Bourguiba, born at Monastir in 1903 and educated in Paris in the 1920s, and Mahmud Materi, the new leaders demanded a broadened participation in the Destour, and a more militant, organized, and ideologically coherent resistance to the French. At a Destour congress in 1932 Bourguiba demanded independence for Tunisia and offered a treaty of friendship to guarantee French interests. In 1934 the radicals took over the Destour and created the neo-Destour party with Materi as president and Bourguiba as secretary-general. The new party promptly called for a boycott of French products and for the establishment of a democratic parliamentary regime. While basically secular in orientation, the neo-Destour leaders had Muslim roots and appealed to Muslim sentiment by meeting in mosques and zawiyas. They symbolized their Muslim identity by agitating against Muslim burial rights for Tunisians who had renounced Islam by taking French citizenship. Thus, the new party broke out of the limited social cadre of the original Destour and attempted to generate a mass movement. Yet by taking over the old party they assured continuity and national cohesion.

The neo-Destour movement began the twenty-year struggles which eventuated in Tunisian independence. At first Tunisians had high hopes of the popular front government in France, but Tunisian demonstrations in April 1938 led to violence. The French suppressed the demonstrations, dissolved the political parties, and imprisoned Bourguiba. The political pressure on the French, however, did not cease. While Bourguiba remained in forced exile, Munsif Bey (1942–43) the Tunisian head of state, took the lead in the effort to win greater autonomy. To the French resident-general he presented Tunisian demands for the formation of a new assembly, instruction in the schools in Arabic, and expropriation by the state of large utilities and transport enterprises. In 1943 he tried to form a new ministry without the consent of the resident-general and was removed by the French, thus becoming a national hero. In 1949 a new group of Destouriens, including supporters of Munsif, issued a declaration demanding self-government for Tunisia. Agricultural groups, students, feminists, and labor unions also supported the national demand. Bourguiba returned to lead the collaboration of the neo-Destour with labor unions and other groups. Despite Bourguiba's great patience and willingness to compromise, by late 1952 Tunisians were beginning to resort to urban terrorism. Finally defeated in Indochina, under diplomatic pressure in the United Nations, and faced with rising violence in Tunis, the French agreed in the spring of 1955 to a settlement recognizing Tunisian internal autonomy. A French–Tunisian protocol of March 1956 abolished the protectorate of 1881. For Tunisia independence was relatively easy to attain. Tunisia had maintained its political identity under the Husaynid Beys; it had considerable continuity of elites, and relative national unity. Moreover, it had not suffered as severely as Algeria from French colonization. As opposed to the *colons* in Algeria, the French settlers in Tunisia did not put up a powerful resistance to Tunisian independence.

The formation of an independent Tunisian government was followed by the rapid consolidation of Bourguiba's power. The 1957 constituent assembly stripped the Bey of his budget, his title, and his power; Bourguiba was made chief-of-state. A constitution of 1959 gave all power to the president. The new government progressively removed French officials and replaced them with party militants, though over 2,500 Frenchmen remained in Tunisian service.

In response to political pressures and economic need, the independent Tunisian regime has followed a number of different economic strategies. From 1956 until 1961, it generally pursued a liberal economic policy. In 1956 and 1957 the government purchased former French lands, put waqf land under government control, and opened the way for individual ownership of collective lands. These policies, however, failed to attract capital and meet Tunisia's investment goals. Under the pressure of union and student criticism, and the examples of socialist Algeria and Egypt, in 1962 Tunisia adopted a socialist orientation. European land was nationalized in 1964 and turned over to state financial cooperatives. A system of agricultural cooperatives and state-managed farms was set up. Heavy public investments and heavy borrowing from foreign sources was to be the basis of economic development. By 1969 this policy had also failed and Tunisia reverted to mixing the private, co-operative, and public sectors and encouraging renewed private foreign investment. The state elites did not have sufficient ideological clarity or sufficient control over the society to implement a state-centered program of investment in the face of competing demands for employment and welfare.

Alongside its efforts to build up the economy, the Tunisian regime committed itself to a drastic secularization of Tunisian society, akin to the program of Ataturk. The Zaytuna mosque was taken under the control of the Ministry of Education and religious schools were absorbed into the public school system. The new regime created a secular judiciary; the personal status code adopted in 1956 forbade polygamy and made marriage and divorce civil matters. It also favored equal rights for women. In 1960 the fast of Ramadan was denounced as a barrier to production. The neo-Destour party (renamed the Parti Socialiste Destourien) had thus become the manager of a socialist economy, the sponsor of a massive school program, the supporter of emancipation of women, the vehicle of mass political education, and the vanguard of secularization.

These modernizing and secularizing policies, however, have not fully taken hold of Tunisian society. Disillusioned by lack of economic opportunity and by lack of trust in the political elites, since the 1960s, Tunisian students and intellectuals have stressed their Arab and Muslim rather than their French-Tunisian identity. The younger intelligentsia places greater emphasis upon socialism and democracy as opposed to capitalism, foreign enterprise, and

European influence. It is also more strongly supportive of the Palestinian cause.

In the late 1960s and early 1970s, moreover, the change from a socialist to a mixed economy increased the influence of relatively conservative groups. The new political elite slackened the pace of reform. Conservatives now identified themselves with Islamic values, expressed in growing attendance at worship, the emergence of religious associations, and expressions of devotion to religious leaders. The new Islamic movement sponsored a newspaper called *al-Ma^rifa* and an association for the protection of the Quran. This movement has come into being as a reaction to the failure to maintain an active modernist propaganda and to the real costs of modernization. Also Tunisians were responding to forces similar to those which have favored Islamic revival in other Arab countries, especially the defeat of the Arab states in the 1967 war with Israel, and the growing influence of the Gulf states and Sa^udi Arabia. Among older people and small-town dwellers there was also opposition to equalization of the rights of women. Tunisia today remains a secular-oriented society, but harbours a strong Muslim sentiment and potential opposition to the secular state elites.

Tunisia's historical trajectory resembles in many ways that of Egypt. A highly statist Muslim society, it had come under foreign rule in the late nineteenth century. New generations of educated Tunisians responded to the loss of independence by turning to Islamic reformism and to secular nationalism for the salvation of their society. Under the aegis of a secularized nationalist elite, independence was achieved in 1956. Under their leadership, Tunisia attempted to develop a mixed economy and a secular society. As in Egypt and Turkey, the limitations and failures of the new regime promote opposition voiced in terms of Muslim values and Muslim allegiances.

MOROCCO

Morocco represents a third variation of North African Muslim society. Morocco resembled Algeria, Upper Egypt, the Syrian desert regions, and eastern Anatolia in the strength of its pastoral and tribal populations, but it was different because it was organized as an independent state and not as a dependency of the Ottoman empire. Morocco maintained a regime whose authority was founded on a combination of Caliphal and Sufi attributes, but it was difficult for the regime to make its authority felt in the countryside. The intermediary political classes, such as the landed notables, who in other Middle

Eastern societies favored centralized state controls, were in Morocco relatively weak while tribal populations were relatively strong. The authority of the Sultans was unquestioned, but their power was always rivalled by tribal and Sufi chiefs.

European economic penetration of Morocco in the late nineteenth century subverted the Moroccan state and led to the establishment of French and Spanish protectorates in 1912. The first French resident-general, Marshal Lyautey, ruled through the Sultan and the qaʾids. The government brought the tribes under control, intimidating them by show of military force, cutting them off from their pasture lands, and threatening to reduce them to starvation. The tribes were disarmed and forced to pay taxes. The French installed military posts, and appointed an officer to collect taxes, organize markets, and build roads, hospitals, and schools. The officers did not administer directly but controlled the qaʾids. The key to their success was a confidential relationship. Under French tutelage, the qaʾids took on new duties, including traffic control, licensing of weapons, settlement of disputes, and regulation of prices.

The territories south of the Atlas remained outside direct French control and under the jurisdiction of subordinate chieftains. The great tribal magnates, the Mtouggi, the Gundafa, and the Glawis, controlled the agricultural surplus, the passes over the Atlas Mountains, and the profits of the caravan traffic. Before 1912 the great qaʾids were able to purchase modern weapons, hire mercenaries, and build fortresses to control their districts. They were all vulnerable, however, to factionalism and personal rivalries. The French, fearing that anarchy would result from any effort to defeat the Glawis, restored their predominance and left all territories south of Marrakesh in their hands. After World War II they needed the Glawis to help resist the nationalist movement.

The French also brought the Muslim religious elites under their control. Most of the Sufi zawiyas accepted French authority, helped subordinate tribal regions to the central government, and kept the peace between migratory pastoral populations in the Atlas mountains. Sufi prestige, however, diminished as their political utility declined, and they were replaced by government administrators. The Sherqawa, the Sufis of Boujad, for example, lost their intermediary roles because secular disputes could be brought to the French, and Sherqawa decisions could be appealed to French officials. They were no longer needed to protect commerce, for the protectorate gave patents for local trade. After World War II, as new economic opportunities in commerce and real estate led rural people to migrate to the cities, the Sufi clientele further diminished. Furthermore, the French also brought the ʿulamaʾ and the administration of justice under their control. A minister of justice was appointed to supervise the qadis; in 1914 rules for procedures and maintenance of documents were promulgated. The French also created competing administrative tribunals, transferred penal justice to French courts, promoted Berber customary courts, and took other measures to restrict the jurisdiction of Shariᶜa.

Lyautey's social and educational policies were also intended to facilitate French control. The sons of notables were to be assimilated through new schools created in Fez and other places. In 1945 a Moroccan school of administration was created. Also, rural primary schools, technical schools, and Muslim colleges were founded in Rabat and Fez. Indirectly the French also patronized the traditional madrasas. French policy concentrated on the education of a small elite, and by the 1950s only 6 percent of the eligible age groups were in school. Though French educational efforts were intended to produce Moroccan collaborators, they seemed only to create a generation of hostile intelligentsia.

French policy toward the Berbers was also directed at finding support for French rule. The French viewed the Berbers as non-Arabs who could be separated from the general Moroccan population and allied to France. The French attempted to create a French-educated Berber elite and keep out Arabic and Islamic influences. The Berber *dahir*, or decree, of 1930 proposed to organize a system of Berber courts operating under customary law (except that criminal justice was transferred to French courts), as a deterrent to the use of Islamic law and as an encouragement of Berber culture. Muslims saw in it an effort to pave the way for the conversion of Berbers to Christianity, and, by an attack on the administration of Muslim justice, to divide the Moroccan people. There was not much chance of French success. Berber communities themselves resisted the French effort to establish customary law courts and demanded the application of the Shariᶜa. Berber students learned Arabic rather than French and adopted nationalist rather than separatist sympathies. Also, improved communications, migration to the towns, and the installation of Arabic-speaking administrative officers all worked to identify Berbers with Arab Islam. The notion of an independent Moroccan Berber society allied to France proved to be a myth.

French economic policy strongly favored the interests of French colonists. Extensive properties controlled by the Sultan and the tribes were made available for distribution. While the French held that roads and rivers, beaches, and forests were inalienable, all other properties could be bought and sold. In 1914 makhzan land was made available for sale to European colonists, and lands assigned to tribes in payment of military service were confiscated. The dahir of 1919 established that collective lands were the property of occupying groups, but that excess lands could be sold. Collectively owned tribal properties tended under French administration to become the private property of Europeans and tribal chiefs. As French administration increased the availability of collective lands for sale, European holdings grew enormously. In 1913 there were approximately 73,000 hectares cultivated by Europeans; by 1953 Europeans controlled approximately 1,000,000 hectares of land. Though Europeans were barely more than 1 percent of the rural population, they controlled 10 percent of the crop land and almost 25 percent of orchards and vineyards. French taxation also favored French over Moroccan interests. The *tartib*, a tax on revenue, was introduced in 1913, but rebates were given for European-type farming methods. European farmers were further advantaged by producing citrus fruits, vegetables, wine, and wheat which could be sold for export while Moroccans concentrated on less remunerative crops. French investment in irrigation and dams also favored Europeans. Nonetheless, the French benefited Morocco by bringing peace to the countryside and opening new markets. The French also helped Moroccan farmers by introducing new seeds, crops, and breeds of livestock, and by investing in irrigation.

In industry the French favored phosphate mining and the development of flour mills, sugar refining, cement manufacture, and textile production. Moroccan workers flocked to the towns looking for employment, but wages were low and unions were proscribed by the government. French policy, on balance, created a dual economy with a European sector favored by the administration and a relatively neglected Moroccan sector.

As in Tunisia and Algeria, French domination seemed economically and politically secure but it nonetheless generated the social and cultural conditions for the formation of an opposition movement. French rule helped to break down the traditional structure of Moroccan society. Changes in administration reduced the power of the tribal and religious chiefs. Seizure of Moroccan lands, recruitment of Moroccans into the French army, and new urban enterprises drew a substantial number of rural peoples to the towns and cities. The spread of European dress, movie theaters, and sports teams broke down local customs in favor of a more unified society. Large numbers of Moroccan workers in France also developed a Western lifestyle and political consciousness. Berber-speakers were integrated into the Arab population as a result of mixing in the towns, and by the spread of the Arabic language and Arabic and Islamic education. Thus the conditions were set for a revival of Moroccan political identity and for hostility to French rule.

Moroccan opposition received early expression in the rebellion of ᶜAbd al-Krim in the Spanish-occupied zone. ᶜAbd al-Krim was an intellectual, a qadi in his early career, a teacher, and the editor of a newspaper called *Telegrama*. He was familiar with Spanish culture and had numerous European contacts. His father, a tribal leader, had been involved with German mining interests and the son studied engineering in Spain. In 1923 ᶜAbd al-Krim declared the Rif a republican state. The state was made up of a federation of independent local tribes united by a nationalist ideology. ᶜAbd al-Krim denied that he was religiously inclined but nonetheless advocated the Salafiya teaching and opposed saint worship. His independent republic expanded to the point where it brought France into the war on the side of Spain and resulted in his defeat in 1926. Despite this defeat, ᶜAbd al-Krim remained a hero to young Moroccans who aspired to resist French rule.

A more lasting Moroccan resistance to French rule came from the religious reform movement. From the 1920s to the 1960s there was a subtle shift in the practice of Islam in Morocco. Both rural Sufis and urban ᶜulamaᵓ were discredited by French control, and Moroccan religious concerns flowed into reformism. As in Egypt, Algeria, and many other places in the Muslim world, foreign rule, centralization of state power, and Muslim awareness of the need for a higher degree of communal cooperation took the form of reform. Moroccan reformers, inspired by Muhammad ᶜAbduh, began an educational movement in Fez, Rabat, Salé, and other towns, founding schools to teach Arabic grammar, ethics, logic, Islamic history, and arithmetic, but not modern sciences. The Salafiya stressed the purification of Islam, opposition to saint worship, and defense against Western cultural encroachment.

Reformism took hold wherever the changes generated by French rule hurt the established bourgeoisie and propelled them toward national consciousness. Fez suffered a long depression from 1925 to 1940, as a result of European competition and the rise of Casablanca as a port and business center. While their material situation was compromised, the ambitions of Fassis remained unimpaired. Fassis continued to think of themselves as the elite of Moroccan society, and therefore denounced French rule, sponsored religious reform movements, trade union activities, secret cultural societies, and nationalist newspapers. Wounded in pocket and pride, Fassis were driven into political action.

Around 1925 and 1926 political groups began to form around the students and educators in the new schools, and in 1927 an association of Muslim North African students was born. It took the Berber dahir of 1930 to unite Moroccan sentiment behind the reformers. The French Berber program made preservation of Islam, and therefore of Moroccan society, a crucial issue. Communal prayers were organized, a press campaign launched, and new cells of reformist- and nationalist-minded people founded. The Moroccan proto-nationalists published in Paris a review in French called *Maghreb*, and in Fez, *L'Action du peuple*. In 1933 they proposed an annual festival in honor of the Sultan as a demonstration of Moroccan national loyalty. A year later a plan was presented to the Sultan and the French administration calling for the removal of direct French rule, appointment of Moroccan ministers, and the formation of an elected national council. The plan also called for a single judicial system based on government courts and the Shariᶜa. It called for the nationalization of the major industries, including mining, railroads, transport, electric power, and banks. This was the first political statement laying claim to Moroccan autonomy, if not to full independence from France. The emphasis upon Islamic reform in education was being replaced with interest in administrative and legal issues, problems of land, taxation, free speech, and free press. The French rejected the reform plan, and in 1936 and 1937 some of the nationalists moved to a new stage of resistance – organizing popular demonstrations against French rule. Taking advantage of the depression, the nationalists managed to arouse popular consciousness about the importance of defending Islam.

Here as elsewhere, World War II severely damaged the French and allowed the *Istiqlal* (Independence) Party, created in 1943, to come to the fore and attempt to rally mass support for Moroccan independence. After World War II Moroccan opposition leadership was transferred from the Salafiya to the Istiqlal Party in tacit alliance with the Sultan. The new party absorbed former ᶜulamaᵓ, administrators, and other elite persons and brought together a national elite recruited from the big cities. Its primary effort was to organize demonstrations in honor of Sultan Muhammad, who now committed himself to an autonomous Morocco. In a speech in Tangier in April 1947, he declared Morocco an Arab state attached to the Arab League and deliberately omitted the obligatory compliments to France. Sultan Muhammad defended Istiqlal sympathizers, and in 1949 refused to sign French-proposed legislative and administrative measures. The crisis came in 1953, when the French attempted to force the Sultan to agree to a dual sovereignty, suppress the Istiqlal Party, and rally provincial leaders to the French cause. Al-Glawi mustered large numbers of Berber tribesmen to converge on Fez and the French forced the Sultan to resign and leave the country. Istiqlal leaders were also imprisoned or exiled.

The exile of the Sultan made him a martyr and created a mass national sentiment. In his absence, many Moroccans ceased to attend the Friday prayers as a protest against an illegitimate regime. With the leading politicians in prison or exile, terrorism began in late 1953. By October 1955 al-Glawi had to yield and request the return of the Sultan. Muhammad, returned to his throne, declared that Morocco would become a constitutional monarchy and that he would conduct negotiations with France leading to independence and to a treaty of alliance. Under the leadership of Pierre Mendes-France, the French accepted Moroccan independence and signed a formal accord on March 7, 1956.

The Moroccan independence movement was strikingly different from that of Tunisia or Algeria. While in Algeria resistance was substantially the work of new elites, in Morocco the Sultan, the historic leader of the country, became the titular leader of the opposition and the embodiment of national identity. Thus he carried the old regime into the modern state. Muhammad was personally popular because of his outright obstruction of French rule; his deposition in 1953 only confirmed his authority. Also, as in Tunisia and Algeria, Moroccan resistance was first associated with the Salafiya reform movement, but while secular leaders took over in Tunisia and Algeria, Morocco was not easily secularized. Relatively few Moroccans had a French education.

With the restoration of independence, the Sultan remained the dominant political figure. While the Sufi brotherhoods were discredited by their collaboration with the French, Sultan Muhammad (d. 1961) and his successor, Hassan, have claimed the veneration usually accorded the Sufis by sponsoring saints' festivals. They have counterbalanced this, however, by building up the authority of the ʿulamaʾ and denouncing Sufi excesses in order to find a more institutionalized form of legitimation for state authority. Also, the Sultan judiciously appeals to the Western-educated intelligentsia and workers by using liberal and democratic rhetoric.

The protectorate also left the Sultan in an enhanced political and administrative position. The French had strengthened the bureaucracy and weakened independent rural chiefs. They left the Sultan in control of the army, the police, the Department of the Interior, the banks, and the newspapers. The Sultan also triumphed over the political parties. The hopes of Istiqlal to share in power were dashed, and the party split in 1959 into an Istiqlal wing and a new Union Nationale des Forces Populaires (U.N.F.P.). Each party has created its own trade union ally. In 1962 a new constitution and parliament were created but parliament was dissolved in 1965. Since then the Sultan has governed by emergency powers.

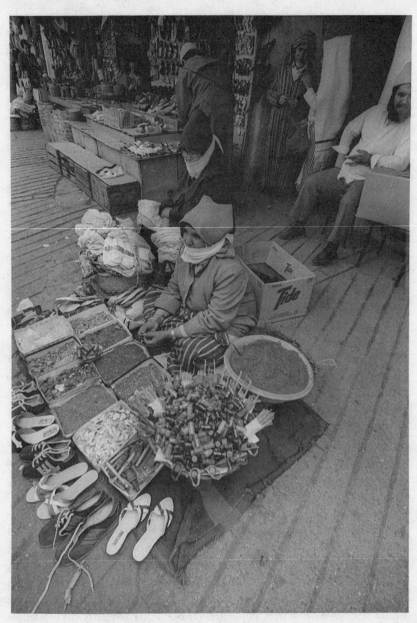

24 A Berber woman in the market of Tetuan, Morocco

The Sultan governs Morocco by a thoughtful manipulation of its myriad of factions, clienteles, interest groups, and tribes. The political elite includes the bourgeoisie of Fez, which provides officials, scholars, and merchants. Elites of rural background are important in the ministries of interior, education, and justice. Small-town and rural areas conserve traditional cultural values, and lineage structures remain powerful. Many communities continue to be integrated by the religious prestige of Sufi leaders and other intermediaries, and the tribes of the Rif and the middle and central Atlas are hostile to the regime. Nonetheless, the central government is more strongly in control of the countryside than ever. Leftist groups, however, are weak, the trade unions are dependent on the state, and the students are readily manipulated. The leading families tend to be organized into clientele groups which constantly maneuver for political influence. The Sultan stands outside of the political groupings as a kind of arbitrator. While he can muster national ideological support, he rules by holding the balance of power among the different groups and by his control over the army, the ministry of the interior and other key positions.

Since Morocco continues to be a segmented society built around personal ties to the King and fluid coalitions, it has a kind of dynamic stability but has not proved capable of defining new directions for economic and social change. Since independence, Morocco has suffered from the flight of capital, though French professional and technical workers are still important. Development plans in the 1960s failed, in part, for lack of reforms in land ownership. The government still has limited capacity to collect taxes – it collects about 15 percent of the gross domestic product as opposed to nearly twice as much in Algeria and Tunisia. In Morocco the political system maintains stability at the price of economic development and reform.

Morocco remains the most highly integrated and conservative of the Middle Eastern and North African Arab countries. In Morocco, Islam is still so closely identified with the monarchy and the state that it constitutes the Moroccan national identity. This is not to say, however, that Islamic values could not be used against the regime.

LIBYA

Ottoman rule also established the first state regime in the territories of Tripolitania, Cyrenaica, and the Fezzan which make up modern Libya. Until the Ottoman occupation, Libya was a territory without a history. The invasions of the seventh century helped to Arabize and Islamize the population but did not establish a central regime. Almohad authority was nominal; the Mamluks of Egypt had alliances with tribes in Cyrenaica which allowed them to claim that they were suzerains of the country. This claim was inherited by the Ottomans, who conquered Egypt in 1517 and Tripoli in 1551. From 1551 until 1711 Tripoli was governed by Ottoman pashas and janissary soldiers. In 1711 Ahmad Qaramanli, a local janissary officer, seized power and founded a dynasty under Ottoman suzerainty which lasted until 1835. In the early nineteenth century Qaramanli power waned as a result of the suppression of piracy and of growing British and French influence. In 1835 the Ottomans again intervened in Libya, and brought the Qaramanli dynasty to an end. Ottoman governors ruled Tripolitania and were suzerains of Cyrenaica until the Italian occupation of 1911 and Ottoman withdrawal in 1912.

From 1835 to 1911 the Ottomans made extensive changes in Tripolitania. By 1858 they had defeated local resistance, established their government throughout the region, and introduced Tanzimat reforms to Libya. The Ottoman governors strengthened the central authority, encouraged the sedentarization of the bedouins, developed towns and agriculture, and helped revive the trans-Saharan trade which flourished in Libya as the abolition of the slave traffic closed down Saharan routes going through Tunisia and Algeria. Ottoman rule encouraged local education and the formation of an intelligentsia inspired by the political and cultural life of Istanbul. In this phase of Ottoman administration, Tripolitanian officials, intellectuals, and tribal and village shaykhs attained some sense of identity as part of a larger provincial, Ottoman, Arab, and Muslim universe.

Cyrenaica remained a separate province under Ottoman suzerainty and went through a similar phase of development owing to Ottoman cooperation with the Sanusiya order. The Sanusiya was founded in 1837 by Muhammad b. ʿAli al-Sanusi (1787–1859), who was born in Algeria and educated in Fez and Mecca. Al-Sanusi, under the influence of reform currents, declared that his purpose was to return to the basic precepts of the Quran and hadith, and affirmed the right of believers to use ijtihad to deduce the principles by which a Muslim life should be conducted. The Sanusiya wished to unite all of the Muslim brotherhoods, and to contribute to the spread and revitalization of Islam.

His missionary intention led al-Sanusi to Cyrenaica, where he established a number of zawiyas before his death in 1859. The Sanusi zawiyas became centers of religious mission and teaching, but also of agricultural settlement and trade. The zawiyas, strung out along the trade routes which linked Cyrenaica with Kufra and Wadai, helped organize caravans and trade. The brotherhood progressively acquired a quasi-political authority among the bedouins of the region by negotiating cooperation in trade, by mediating disputes, and by providing urban services such as religious instruction, exchange of products, charity, and political representation. By the end of the century the Sanusi networks of zawiyas had built up a large tribal coalition in the regions west of Egypt and the Sudan. Under Sanusi leadership this tribal coalition resisted both French expansion in the region of Lake Chad and the Italian invasion of Libya.

Since the congress of 1878 the Italians had considered Tripolitania part of their imperial sphere of influence, and had attempted to establish their economic presence in the province. Franco-German diplomatic tensions afforded an opportunity, and Ottoman resistance to Italian economic penetration a pretext, for an Italian invasion in 1911. The Italians occupied the towns and forced the Ottomans to concede their suzerainty over Tripolitania and Cyrenaica, but the Sanusiya also claimed to be the heirs of Ottoman authority in Libya. Only after World War I was Italy able to defeat local opposition in Tripolitania and not until a protracted and destructive war which lasted from 1923 to 1932 were the Italians able to defeat the bedouins of Cyrenaica, seize the majority of their lands, and colonize the country. The Sanusi leaders were forced into exile, and while they retained a spiritual authority, they were obliged to accept Italian suzerainty. In 1934 the Italians completed the conquest of Cyrenaica and Tripolitania and united the two into modern Libya.

The Italians were defeated in World War II and Libya came under the control of Britain and France, but the United Nations decided to make it an independent country in 1951. The Sanusi leader, Amir Idris, became King, and governed the country on the basis of the religious legitimacy of his family and its services in the struggle against foreign rule. He ruled with the help of urban-based officials, with the support of the bedouins rallied through the Sanusi network of zawiyas, and with the assistance of client tribal chiefs. His regime was opposed as corrupt and dependent upon foreign support by a radical younger generation of nationalist- and socialist-minded students, technicians, petroleum and dock workers, and younger army officers inspired by the pan-Arab and socialist ideologies of Nasserism and the Baʿth party. In 1969, Libya's own Free Officers movement, comprised of middling officers and N.C.O.s, schooled at the Baghdad Military Academy, but drawn from the poorer and weaker of Libyan tribes, led by Muʿammar al-Qadhdhafi, seized power. The officers set up a Revolutionary Command Council and rapidly established an all-powerful military regime. Foreign bases were dismantled. Foreign banks and businesses were nationalized. Political parties and labor unions were outlawed. In 1973 the Revolution took a still more radical turn, with the arrest of officials, professionals and potential political opponents, and the creation of populist committees to take control of the government ministries, the schools, and the major enterprises. By the late 1970s the state had taken control of all important economic functions, had ruined the small middle class, and had substantially redistributed the country's wealth. The political effect of populism was to abolish all independent centers of wealth, and to create a system of checks on all public functionaries, thereby minimizing the prospect of opposition to Qadhdhafi.

Qadhdhafi is best known as the proponent of a radical Arab and Islamic ideology. His earliest revolutionary doctrine was a copy of Nasserite and Baʿthist ideologies and stressed Arab unity, opposition to colonialism and Zionism, and Libyan leadership in the quest for unity and in the Arab struggle against Israel. In the course of his rule Qadhdhafi has negotiated unions between Libya and Egypt, Libya and Syria, and Libya, Sudan, and Tunisia, none of which have come to fruition. In the early 1970s Qadhdhafi added a new dimension to his theory, in which he proposed an Arabic-Islamic mission as a Third Universal Alternative to capitalism and communism. Qadhdhafi has proclaimed an extreme form of Islamic scripturalism in which the Quran, but not the teachings of the Prophet (Sunna), is taken as the only source of authority for the reconstruction of society. Islamic scripturalism linked with populism destroys the authority of the ʿulamaʾ, Sufi shaykhs, bureaucrats, and technocrats, and makes Qadhdhafi himself the central figure in this version of Islamic modernism. Also in Libya a Quranic morality forbidding gambling, alcohol, and other "Western" vices is enforced. In the international arena, the Third Universal Alternative calls for jihad or struggle against imperialism and Zionism in the Middle East, Muslim Africa, and even in the Philippines, where there are Muslim separatist movements. Implied in this theory is an un-articulated identification of domestic socialism, Arabism, and Islam. In more extreme form, and with more emphatic international implications, it represents a version of the identification of Arabism and Islam common throughout the Middle East and North Africa.

ISLAM IN STATE IDEOLOGIES AND OPPOSITION MOVEMENTS

The North African Arab countries are grouped together not only because of geography but because of similarities in their historical development. In the pre-modern era, there were considerable variations in the social and political structure of each region and state, but in each one, lineage communities were the basis of society and pastoralists were an important social and political force. Effective state regimes in Tunisia and Algeria did not extend to the whole of each country. Morocco maintained a centralized state partly by institutional means but largely by emphasizing the legitimacy of its Sultans. Islam played a crucial political role both in the integration of tribal communities and the legitimation of state regimes.

French rule led to the introduction of elements of a modern economy and education, but the continuities in the structure of state regimes and in the role of Islam are striking. Morocco shows the greatest degree of historical continuity. French control, introduced only in 1912, seems to have had a limited impact on the Moroccan political system. The monarchy has retained, with transformed meaning, its Islamic legitimacy and its political centrality. The Sultans have kept their charismatic personal authority and their Islamic institutional authority. They benefited by taking symbolic leadership of the reform movement, and captured the emergent awareness of Moroccan nationality by leading resistance to the French. The Sultans actually increased their administrative power by effective use of a French-consolidated apparatus and by skillful manipulation of political factions and interest groups. With independence, Moroccan state and society are defined in the combined terms of protectorate-influenced monarchy and Islam. Morocco, more than almost any other Muslim state, retains the impress of its historic identity.

Algeria, by contrast, is the most radically reorganized North African society. The French occupation altogether destroyed Algerian society, and the Algerian elites who emerged after World War I were a narrow and fragile stratum divided among secularists with a strong French orientation, Muslim reformers, populist leaders, and military revolutionaries with inchoate ideological leanings. The ferocity of the struggle for independence has created a regime which is hostile to colonialism and has strong revolutionary, socialist, and equalitarian tendencies. The war for independence has also given power to a military elite in an otherwise disorganized society. The Algerian regime thus tends to pursue the development of an "enclave" state based on military power and the control of petroleum and gas resources and the industries financed by them. It has pursued a policy of state-centered development to the neglect of the agricultural population, but it seeks to bridge the gap between the elites and the masses by appeals to reformist Islam. With the destruction of the historic forms of tribal and religious organization, Islamic reformism – the religious language of national as opposed to parochial identities and the language of disciplined worldly activity – has become the basis of Algerian national identity.

Libya has shown a similar tendency to transform the historic structures of the society. As in Algeria, an Ottoman state regime provided the rudiments of territorial organization while Sufism was the basis for the organization of a predominantly bedouin population. In nineteenth-century Cyrenaica, moreover, Sufism was the preserve of the reformist Sanusi movement, which used its influence to organize trade, resist French and Italian colonization, and create a Libyan monarchy after World War II. The Free Officer revolutionaries, who seized power in 1969, inherited neither a strong state, nor a secular concept of monarchy, nor an integrated society. In Libya there was virtually no historical basis for a national regime. Thus the Qadhdhafi regime tends to be pan-Arab, Islamic, and international-revolutionary in ideological orientation, finding support for a radical reconstruction of Libyan society in universalistic terms. The Qadhdhafi regime is a unique combination of personal power and universalist pan-Arab and Islamic symbols.

Tunisia seems to be the exception to the North African pattern of strong Islamic identity based on the reformist movements of the late nineteenth century and the interwar years. While state-sponsored modernism had its origins in the pre-protectorate regimes, and reformism was introduced by the Salafiya during the Young Tunisian and Destour party eras, the leadership of independent Tunisia has, by and large, been seized by a secular-oriented elite. In Tunisia, the shift from Islamic reformist to secular nationalist ideologies was, in part, due to the struggle between the old and neo-Destour leaders in the 1930s. While the older generation had a Muslim education, the younger generation was French–Arabic in education. While the older generation represented a condominium of official and ʿulamaʾ families, the younger generation represented the upwardly mobile bourgeoisie of the coastal towns. The domestic struggle for power between the two elites, combined with the struggle against the French, turned the Bourguiba generation to nationalism, though Muslim loyalties were still latent in the appeal for mass support. Also, in Tunisia, there was a deep historical basis for a mass acceptance of a national identity. Tunisia thus seems to stand as an exception to the North African tendency for the political regimes to represent Islamic continuity, though beneath the surface of secular national identity, Tunisians are still Muslim in sentiment, and Islam retains its potential for expressing political opposition.

In general, throughout the Arab Middle East and North Africa, the official ideology of state regimes has been built upon varying combinations of nationalist, pan-Arab, and Islamic symbols. Such states as Syria, Iraq, and Tunisia stress the secular-national and sometimes the socialist basis of state identity, despite such exceptions as constitutional recognition of the Islamic character of the state or latent appeals to the Muslim sentiments of the populace. The institutionally more fragile states such as Syria, Iraq, and Libya, also heavily emphasize their pan-Arab loyalties. In these states, the Ottoman heritage of state-controlled religious establishments, and the social dominance of upwardly mobile military elites or of minority groups, has favored secular nationalism.

The Islamic element is much more pronounced in the official ideologies of Egypt, Algeria, and Libya. Since the turn of the twentieth century, Egypt has cultivated a strong nationalist, state-oriented self-concept with strong obeisance to Islam. The Arab and pan-Arab basis of Egyptian identity became more marked after World War II, but with the defeat of Egypt in the 1967 war with Israel, Egypt has returned to a more national state- and Islamic-centered concept of political identity. The religious loyalties of the populace and well-organized Islamic movements have made Islamic symbols a recurring part of Egypt's official ideology. Algeria and Libya are instances of a still more integral association of nationalist, pan-Arab, and Islamic symbols. In Morocco, the continuity of the monarchy and its close identification with both the Salafiya movement and Sufism make Islam central to both official ideology and national identity. In all these countries Islam is particularly important in popular political identity and in the ideologies of both conservative and revolutionary regimes, just as in the past it was the basis of both Sufi-organized rural societies and anti-colonial movements.

At the same time Islam has come to play an important role in the articulation of opposition to these same regimes. Since the 1967 war with Israel, and especially since the 1979 revolution in Iran, Islam has become an ideology of political opposition and revolutionary aspirations. The Muslim Brotherhood in Egypt and Syria, and jamaᶜat associations in Egypt and Tunisia, and independent religious leaders everywhere maintain the historic role of Islam as a communal and religious system apart from, and in opposition to, the state. Throughout the Arab east and Arab North Africa there are profound ambiguities in the uses of Islam as an element of political identity. State regimes are organized upon the basis of fluid combinations of national, pan-Arab, and Islamic identity; opposition movements are couched in terms of radical secular ideologies or of Islamic aspirations. Islam, then, is an element both of state ideologies and of revolutionary utopias. It is the shared medium of political discourse grounded in the ambiguity of mass culture in which state, ethnic, national, and Islamic identities are imperfectly fused.

SECULARISM AND ISLAM IN CENTRAL AND SOUTHERN ASIA

CHAPTER 27

THE INDIAN SUBCONTINENT: INDIA, PAKISTAN, AND BANGLADESH

The contemporary history of Muslim peoples in the Indian subcontinent has its origins in the breakup of the Mughal empire and the imposition of British rule in India. The change of regimes set in motion forces that would change the religious practices and sociopolitical structures of Muslim peoples of the subcontinent and lead eventually to the formation of three national states, two predominantly Muslim, and one in which there is a substantial Muslim minority.

On the eve of its modern transformation, the Mughal empire was, like the Ottoman and Safavid empires, a patrimonial regime which strongly emphasized its Persianate cosmopolitan and Indian identity. Muslim religious life in the subcontinent was highly pluralistic and not under state control. The long century of Mughal decline, from 1730 to 1857, favored the consolidation of a provincial Muslim gentry. Literate Muslim culture, similar religious practices, and noble (ashraf) status defined the Muslim communities, clustered around the mosques, schools, tombs, and gentry residences, of the Muslim quarters and small towns (qasbahs) of north India.

The position of this Muslim gentry and office-holding elite was gravely threatened by the rising power of the British. The decline of the Mughal regime had both symbolic and practical costs. The very existence of a Muslim regime was a charismatic guarantee of the well-being of Muslim societies. Now this assurance was gone. In many regions, such as Bengal, the concrete financial and political losses were substantial. With the reorganization of revenue and judicial administration, Europeans replaced Muslims in the top political positions, though Muslims kept their employment in subordinate posts. The Permanent Settlement in Bengal helped transfer control over landed property from Muslims to Hindus, though in the northwestern provinces, Muslim landlords were able to maintain their position relative to the Hindus. Soldiers who once served sovereign regimes were reduced to being the strong-arm men of the East India Company or of some British magistrate or zamindar. In Bengal, Muslim peasants subjected to Hindu landlords were deprived of customary rights, and Muslim weavers suffered from the competition of Lancashire cloth.

These early losses were compounded by general economic regression between 1830 and 1857. As the British consolidated their power they began to eliminate the incomes of the great zamindars. Nobles were deprived of taxes and mint revenues, tolls, and bazaar fees. The pensions paid to princely families came to be subdivided among numerous heirs and pledged to moneylenders. As aristocratic incomes declined, luxury consumption fell; soldiers, service people, and artisans were unemployed. While some landowners and grain merchants continued to do well, and while some districts continued to flourish, many gentry, minor officials, petty merchants, artisans, and laborers fared badly.

Furthermore, the new regime brought cultural as well as economic and political losses. At first the British sympathized with traditional Muslim education and the classical culture of India. By the 1830s, however, British missionaries became more active, and British officials began to suppress religious practices which they judged barbaric. English became the language of administration and instruction. In 1835 the new school budgets reserved government funds for English instruction; in 1837 Persian was abolished as the official language of the Mughal court. Changes in the court system, and the establishment of new rules for evidence and new definitions of offenses and penalties, struck at the heart of Muslim religious law. Progressively Muslims became aware that the tide of economic and political power, generated by Hindu merchant and British official competition, was running against them. By the 1850s the qasbah communities were in disarray. The need to come to terms with the loss of a Muslim state, with the consequences of foreign rule, and with the rising influence of Sikhs and Hindus, had become acute. The failure of the Mughal empire made Muslims question whether a Muslim way of life could continue in the subcontinent, and if so, what were the practical and symbolic alternatives to the Mughal system. What kind of political institutions would be needed? What attitude should they take toward British rule? What personal religious practices would be meaningful? In what way should Muslims practice the Shariʿa? Was it proper to venerate saints' shrines?

To these questions, there were three clusters of responses. The position of some religious groups such as the Barelwis and the ʿulamaʾ of Farangi Mahall was that little new need be done, but accept British rule, and transmit the traditional beliefs and practices of Islam, including respect for the Shariʿa and veneration of saints. The reformers, in the tradition of Shah Waliallah and the international movement of Muslim reform, proposed to refuse collaboration with British rule and to strengthen Muslim religious life by improving the practice of Islam and preventing the veneration of shrines. The third response was radically different. The former political elites aimed not at the revival of Muslim tradition but at the absorption of Western science and the creation of a modern Muslim political identity. This response was represented by Aligarh and the Muslim League, and led ultimately to the formation of Pakistan. While some leaders stressed personal religion, and others political issues, the Indian Muslim response to foreign rule was characterized – not as in the Ottoman empire by the evolution of a state policy of secularization, nor as in the Iranian case by the struggle between the state and the religious establishment – by a multi-sided struggle among Muslims, as well as between Muslims and Hindus, and Muslims and the British, over the cultural and political future of India. Out of these struggles would come new forms of Muslim political identity and religious practice.

MUSLIM MILITANCY FROM PLASSEY TO 1857

While the Muslim political and lineage elites were slow to adapt to the decline of the Mughal state, Muslim religious leaders were immediately shocked and galvanized into action. The Sufi leaders and managers of shrines felt the need to compensate for the loss of Mughal authority and Mughal support by reaffirming Muslim values. The Chisti order undertook internal reforms, and Sufi shrines became more active. The reformist ʿulamaʾ also reaffirmed their longstanding position. Their view of the need for strict adherence to the universal principles of Islam struck a chord among Indian Muslims, who felt that the true cause of the Mughal defeat was moral and religious corruption. Muslims had fallen from God's favor for their failure to observe Islam. Without the protection of the state, exposed to infidel rule, they felt that religious and communal self-discipline and active struggle were the only answers to their plight. Thus, in 1803, a son of Shah Waliallah, Shah ʿAbd al-ʿAziz (1746–1824) issued a fatwa or judicial opinion, declaring that India was *dar al-harb*. The unbelievers, he pointed out, administered taxation and criminal law at their discretion; India was no longer ruled by the Shariʿa. The proper response to British rule, he concluded, was that Indian Muslims must rise up in holy war.

His disciple, Sayyid Ahmad Barelwi (1786–1831), took up the cause. Sayyid Ahmad began his career as a missionary preacher in Uttar Pradesh, Bihar, and Bengal, seeking to reform religious practices. He made the pilgrimage to Mecca in 1821–24, and returned to India, settling finally in the Northwest Frontier province. He preached the reform program: belief in the unity of God and the elimination of polytheism and innovation in the form of shrine Sufism and Shiʿism. He sought to restore the true Islam by repudiating ordinary Indian Muslim mystical and ritual practices, and by basing the true faith on the Quran and Sunna alone. His preaching was accompanied by a determined effort to arouse Indian Muslims to throw off the yoke of foreign rule. In the Northwest Frontier province he rallied the Yusufzai Pathans. The Pathans, hard pressed on the north by their Afghan enemies and on the south by the expanding Sikh state in the Punjab, were a disunited tribal society which Sayyid Ahmad sought to unify under a single leadership to defend their political interests and the holy cause. In 1827 he claimed the title Imam, supreme religious leader, and led his people to war. Sayyid Ahmad, with a small group of followers, was killed at Balakot in 1831. The task of imposing unity and discipline on the Pathans was beyond reach. His religious legacy, however, remained in the form of the Way of Muhammad (Tariqa-i Muhammadi) movement which would, as we shall see, revitalize Indian Islam and give impetus to communal and religious reforms which survive to the present day.

Bengal was a second arena of Muslim reform and revival movements. Here the doctrinal position was similar, but the social and economic context was very different. In West Bengal, Titu Mir began his career as a disciple of the Tariqa-i Muhammadi. He had been converted to the new movement in Mecca and considered himself a khalifa of Sayyid Ahmad. He preached the primacy of the Quran and hadith and opposed the ceremonies at Sufi shrines. Titu Mir's reform became a political cause in 1830 when the local zamindars and indigo planters tried to resist the spread of his teachings by imposing a tax on his peasant followers. In reaction, Titu Mir and his followers defiled a Hindu temple. The authorities were called in and Titu Mir was killed by the police in 1831.

The Faraʾidi were a similar but unconnected movement under the leadership of Hajji Shariʿatallah (1781–1840). Hajji Shariʿatallah was born in Bengal, but lived for 18 years in Mecca, absorbed in the study of Hanafi law. He was initiated into the Qadiri order and was influenced by Meccan reformist views. In 1818 he returned to Bengal to preach *tawba* (repentance) and fulfillment of *fara°id* (religious duties). Islam was to be practiced as prescribed in the Quran, the Sunna of the Prophet, and the Hanafi codes of law. The Fara°idi were not in principle opposed to mysticism, but they strenuously opposed veneration of saints, seasonal festivals, celebration of the birthday of the Prophet and of saints' "birthdays," the ta°ziya procession in mourning for Husayn, and other practices which they regarded as Hindu, Buddhist, Shi°i, or Sufi perversions of the true faith.

Between 1818 and 1838 the Fara°idi won a large following in the villages of east Bengal. The movement appealed to Bengali peasants and workers, such as weavers and oil pressers who were being oppressed by Hindu zamindars and British indigo planters. At the death of Hajji Shari°atallah, his son, Dudu Mian, transformed the Fara°idi from a purely religious movement into a movement of peasant resistance to Hindu and British exploitation. From 1838 to 1846 he organized a communal government; a khalifa was appointed for each Fara°idi village with responsibility to set up schools, teach the proper performance of Islamic rituals, dispense justice, and organize armed gangs to defend peasant interests. Every ten villages were the responsibility of a higher official, who in turn reported to the leader of the movement.

FROM THE MUTINY TO WORLD WAR I

Thus, the first Muslim response to the imposition of British rule was characterized by the effort of religious reformers to fuse religious reform and political militancy, and to rally tribal and peasant populations to the defense of their interests and their religion. The Mutiny of 1857 turned Muslim activities into new directions. It began as an explosion of pent-up resentment against the accumulated insults of British rule. Hindu and Muslim recruits in British forces, the sepoys of Meerut, refused to use the newly issued Enfield rifles and cartridges because, it was rumored, the cartridges were greased with pigs' and cows' fat, an insult to men of either religion. The cartridges, however, were but a symbol of deeper cultural and political antagonisms. The Mutiny concerned not only Indian soldiers in the service of the British East India Company, but the Muslim and Hindu upper classes of central and northern India. For these classes the cost of British rule had grown heavier. The British continued to annex Indian principalities, and threatened the old Indian aristocracy, Hindu and Muslim, with replacement by British officials. British policies also led to heavy taxation and the confiscation of estates. Equally important was the threat to Indian cultural and social values. The British had introduced the English language and Western education. British ideas about polygamy, slavery, and the freedom of women; British opposition to suttee, the caste system, and other Hindu and Muslim religious practices; British interference with the operation of Muslim law; and, finally, the ever more widespread preaching, by English missionaries, of Christianity – all these threatened the self-esteem, the hallowed lifestyle, and the economic and political interests of the hitherto privileged Indian elites. As the economic and cultural price of political inferiority bore down upon Mughal India, it took only the pig fat incident to provoke a widespread Hindu–Muslim revolt against British rule.

The revolt was bitterly suppressed and not easily forgotten. In its wake, the British reorganized the government of India. They formally abolished the Mughal empire and the East India Company in favor of direct crown government, and proceeded to consolidate their Indian regime. The British completed the introduction of legal codes, such as the Penal Code of 1860, and the Law of Criminal and Civil Procedure of 1861, and reorganized the system of judicial administration. Between 1871 and 1882 they created a new financial system, making the provinces responsible for their own revenues and expenditures. The army was reorganized with the proportion of English to Indian troops raised from one-fifth to one-half. A closely-knit and professional officer corps was developed. In the half-century which followed the mutiny, the British created the largest imperial bureaucracy in Indian history. In the same period, they began the economic modernization of India. Agricultural production was increased; trade expanded under free trade laws introduced between 1882 and 1894, and industrial activities began. The British introduced railroads, coal mining, and mechanized textile production.

The new policies rested upon a revised set of attitudes. On the one hand, the British developed an ever-increasing aloofness, superciliousness, and condescending attitude toward Indians. The late nineteenth century was the heyday of confidence in the racial superiority of Europeans and in the God-given right to bring European order to less developed peoples. An unbridgeable gulf of political, racial, and caste supremacy divided British rulers from their Indian subjects. On the other hand, some of the lessons of the mutiny were learned. The British came to understand the limits of political centralization and to appreciate that British rule depended on the support and cooperation of Indian princes and landlords. They maintained in existence some 560 Indian princely states, restored loyalist Hindu and Muslim zamindars to their lands, and began to organize Indian municipal and advisory councils. The British also adopted a policy of non-intervention in religious matters and withdrew from efforts to reform Hindu caste or Muslim legal practices, but they continued to sponsor English education and to favor the Westernization of the Indian upper classes.

The British relationship with the Muslim population was particularly delicate. While many Britons were aware of how limited was Muslim involvement in the Mutiny of 1857, and how much it was a joint rebellion of the Muslim–Hindu upper classes, the British generally tended to stereotype the opposition in terms of Muslim resistance to British rule. They saw the Muslims as an entity, once the dominant elite of India, that was bound to be rebellious and had therefore to be suppressed. But the British also recognized the Muslims as a political interest entitled to special educational and electoral privileges. Until the end of the century the British continued to favor the appointment of Muslims to minor and middling government positions. By dealing with Muslims as an entity with a collective claim to political power on the basis of religious identity, they helped generate Muslim solidarity. Having defined a Muslim interest in their own mind, the British helped confirm it in the minds of Indian Muslims.

The Muslim reaction to the events of 1857 was equally consequential. At the time, qasbah political and religious elites did not think of themselves as a single political body, but all of them recognized that jihad was a failure and British rule was enduring. They agreed that their best interests lay in the cultivation of educational, religious, and cultural affairs, and in strengthening the Muslim community from within. While agreed in overall assessment, they were divided in practical matters. Some embraced the new regime in the hope of forming a British–Muslim condominium to govern India. Others maintained silent but deep anti-British and pan-Islamic sentiments; still others turned their backs on political issues altogether.

As the century moved on, three main strands may be distinguished in the post-Mutiny position of the qasbah elites. The first was the position of the conservative religious leaders who recognized the futility of jihad, the need for adjustment to British rule, and the importance of preserving the traditions of Islamic religious belief and practice. The Sufi leaders and *sajjada nishins*, or heads of shrines, wanted to maintain the panoply of saint worship and festivals and the loyalty of the Muslim masses. However, Mughal decline had deprived the shrines of economic and political support; British rule had subverted their worldly political influence. To maintain their position many Sufis associated themselves with British rule and had recourse to British courts to settle land tenure and succession disputes. The sajjada nishins often delegated their religious functions to subordinates while they saw to their political interests. Other Sufis attempted to adapt theory and practice to their declining worldly authority and stressed the purely contemplative and spiritual aspect of Sufism. They tried to preserve the inner meanings of Sufi tradition, and adopted more sober and Shariᶜa-oriented religious practices in the face of declining worldly authority. Conservative ᶜulamaᵓ similarly attempted to maintain their traditional position. The scholars of the Farangi Mahall quarter of Lucknow and the Barelwis continued to combine ᶜulamaᵓ scholarship and Sufi shrines.

The second response within ᶜulamaᵓ circles, however, was the resurgence of reformism in north India and Bengal. In north India, the pre-Mutiny program of religious reform survived political defeat. Its most important expression in the post-Mutiny period was the founding in 1867 of the reform college of Deoband, by Maulana Muhammad Qasim Nanautawi. Deoband's curriculum combined the study of the revealed sciences (Quran, hadith and law) with rational subjects (logic, philosophy, and science). At the same time it was Sufi in orientation and affiliated with the Chisti order. Its Sufism, however, was closely integrated with hadith scholarship and the proper legal practice of Islam.

The reform college served as an organizational focus for a Muslim community. Deoband trained its students for a public mission – to instruct the community in the true practice of Islam. Deobandis poured out, in Urdu vernacular, legal opinions on proper Islamic practice. The spread of printing made it possible for the first time to reach a mass audience. To the degree that reformism represents a long-term trend toward the adoption of normative Islamic practices, the modern era has increased the facilities for standardization. The publication, transportation, and communication facilities to reach ever-larger numbers of people have made it possible for the ᶜulamaᵓ to teach the common people a high-culture version of Islam. Deoband's reach was India-wide. Many students came from Afghanistan, Central Asia, Yemen, and Arabia. Within 30 years of its founding, its graduates established some 40 branch schools, making Deoband the center of the new *maslak* – a distinctive "way" in Indian Islam.

One of the crucial principles of the school was that it be detached from the private, familial, and local affiliations of its teachers and supporters. Deoband, unlike previous colleges in India, was organized as an independent institution, not as part of the household of the leading teachers, nor as a function of the local mosque. Deliberately, it avoided both the support of rich local landowners and other Muslim nobles, and the traditional system of waqf endowments, and sought annual contributions from a wide public. Through its system of annual pledges and regular publications, Deoband cultivated widespread middle- and lower-middle-class support. By the reform and standardization of Islamic belief and practice, a program of public education, and a system of affiliated schools and public contributions, Deoband sought to unite Indian Muslims around the leadership of the ʿulamaʾ and the schools.

The Deoband program represented a careful balance between innovative responsiveness to the new era and allegiance to traditional Muslim ideas. Many of the features of the Deoband school – the school as a physical institution with a distinct building and central library, the fixed professional staff, the ordered curriculum of study, examinations and public awards, affiliated colleges, public contributions, and missionary activities – were suggested by British practices. Deoband was thus a response to new forms of bureaucratic organization, the introduction of new secular ideals, and the competition of new elites. At the same time, Deoband was thoroughly Muslim in terms of education, worship, and withdrawal from politics. Deoband was founded at the very moment that the British Raj had deprived the Muslim community of the expected protection of a Muslim state, and it represented a concept of a Muslim community without a state as a community of religious practice under the leadership of the ʿulamaʾ whose primary institution was a system of schools. The Deobandi ʿulamaʾ had elected to preserve and reform the personal religious practice of Muslims at the cost of giving up the political aspect of Muslim communal organization.

In Bengal the reform movement went back to the pre-Mutiny efforts of Titu Mir and the Faraʾidi. Despite the impact of the earlier reform movement, most Bengali villages maintained an identity based on local dialects and a syncretic form of Muslim Hindu folk culture. While the village mullahs, prayer leaders, and teachers were spokesmen for Islam they had little in common with the educated urban ʿulamaʾ, the ashraf who claimed Arab or Persian ethnic origin, spoke Urdu, and were separated by wealth, status, and cultural style from the *atrap*, or common people. After 1870, however, reformism began to spread again in the Bengali countryside. Though there was no focal educational institution like Deoband, public debates and revivalist meetings fostered a heightened Muslim consciousness. *Anjumans* (religious associations) were formed to link town and countryside, urban and rural ʿulamaʾ, and to teach correct Islamic practice. Most importantly, a large volume of pamphlets was published to give advice on Muslim rituals, to counsel parents on how to raise children, and to censure gambling, drinking, and smoking. The typical pamphlet, called *Nasihat-nama* (Book of Advice), tried to purge rural Islam of its basis in Bengali folk culture and to bring it into closer accord with urban high-culture Islam. The reform movement, however, weakened by the conflict of urban and rural values, had only a limited impact in rural Bengal. Instead, it was to be the 1905–11 struggle over the partition of the province by the British that would truly awaken Muslim political consciousness.

The third strand in the post-Mutiny Muslim adjustment to British rule was that of the landowning and office-holding interests. Though the British had replaced the Mughals, it was still conceivable to the political elite that they could maintain their landed, official, and status interests, but it was obvious that to do so no longer depended on the traditional kinship networks and loyalties, but upon British laws and administrative regulations. British suspicion of Muslim ambitions had to be allayed, and Muslims had to accommodate to the English langugage and the superiority of British military, economic, and administrative technology.

For two generations, the response of the political elites was formulated by Sir Sayyid Ahmad Khan. Ahmad Khan was himself descended from a prominent family of Mughal administrators, and throughout his life continued to be posted as an officer of British administration. In his view the only adequate response to the realities of post-Mutiny India was to accept British rule. In Sayyid Ahmad Khan's view, British rule was lawful. Under British government Muslims could live in peace; the Shariᶜa was in fact applied, and in any case, Muslims were dependent upon British favor. In the course of his long public life he opposed pan-Islamic sentiments and Muslim participation in the Indian National Congress, which was aimed at wresting political power from, rather than simply collaborating with, the British.

His principal concern and that of his cohort was the need for Western-type education, under Muslim auspices, to train a new generation for political responsibility. The effort at cultural and educational reform began with the founding of the National Mohammadan Association in 1856 and the Mohammadan Literary Society in 1863. This was followed by the Anjuman-i Islam of Bombay and the establishment of new madrasas in Dacca and Chittagong. Sayyid Ahmad Khan himself sponsored the translation of English scientific works into Urdu, founded the Ghazipur Scientific Society in 1864, and encouraged instruction in Urdu at Calcutta University. After a visit to England in 1869–70 he published the journal *Tahdhib al-Akhlaq* (Purification of Morals) to educate Indian Muslims in the ways of modernism. The culmination of his efforts came in 1875 with the foundation of the Mohammadan Anglo-Oriental College at Aligarh, which became the training ground of the Muslim political leaders of the twentieth century.

The college at Aligarh was devoted to a combination of Islamic and English language studies. Sayyid Ahmad Khan would have preferred a modernized version of Islam, after his own fashion, but the school, for fear of scandal and loss of public support, eschewed his radical views and maintained a more conservative position. The real achievement of the school, however, lay not in the curriculum nor in the preparation of scholars, but in the social and moral values which it communicated to its students. Aligarh was meant to be the Eton of India; its playing fields as much as its classrooms were the training ground of a new generation of Muslim political leaders. Aligarh encouraged verbal skill, self-confidence, manly solidarity and competition, and the values of duty, loyalty, and leadership, exercised in games and in school clubs and societies, to produce young men capable of cooperation with each other in giving leadership to Indian Muslims in the context of British rule. Aligarh was intended to communicate moral and social virtues through the mechanism of a new curriculum and a new form of school community. Thus, the Muslim elites attempted to fortify the claim of the old ruling class to continued eminence under British rule, to provide themselves with the educational and cultural style appropriate to the new era, and to train a new generation in the moral and political, as well as the intellectual, qualities needed for participation in the British Raj.

Finally Sayyid Ahmad Khan favored the modernization of the Islamic religion so as to make it consistent with the new technical, cultural, and political order of modern times. Behind his political and educational program lay a philosophic and cultural concept of the role of Indian Muslims in the modern world. Sayyid Ahmad was a leading supporter of the modernization of Islam. To adapt Muslims to British rule, he had to persuade them that Western scientific thought was not antithetical to Islam. To demonstrate this, he and his contemporaries undertook the reinterpretation of the Quran. The Quran was God's revelation, and the passages which seemed difficult to understand in a modern context had to be interpreted symbolically, allegorically, or analytically to uncover their true meaning, which would always be consistent with reason and never contrary to nature. Stripping away the irrelevant details in favor of the main principles, stripping away the later accretions of Muslim tradition and exegesis and going back to fundamentals, Muslims have in the Quran, he argued, the source of a rational religion attuned to modern man's scientific interests.

While Sayyid Ahmad tried to persuade Muslims that the Quran allowed for scientific developments, he tried to persuade Europeans that Islam was a reasonable religion worthy of respect. He and his contemporaries attempted to explain the meaning of polygamy, slavery, and the place of non-Muslims and of women in Muslim societies in ways which would make Muslim social institutions acceptable to Westerners. He hoped thus to establish the worthiness of Islam in the eyes both of Muslims and of Westerners and to prepare the way for the collaboration of Muslims and non-Muslims in the government of India. Cultural and religious reform was tied to the educational and political tasks of maintaining the position of the Muslim elite in the British era.

Thus in the course of the late nineteenth century the qasbah elites of north India attempted to cope with their deteriorating social and political position and with the realities of British domination by developing new religious and cultural orientations. One wing of the qasbah elite stressed the importance of preserving the Islamic identity of Muslims, reform of religious practice, and the consolidation of larger-scale, more homogeneous Muslim communities on the bases of reformed Islam. A second wing stressed the importance of adopting the cultural style of their British overlords and thereby preserving a privileged position in the Indian state. For the time being both segments of the Muslim elite accepted the inevitability of British rule.

FROM ELITE TO MASS POLITICS

In the latter part of the century, however, the policies of loyalism and of political reform, whether of the religious reformist or the modernist variety, were challenged and eventually overthrown. The ambiguities in the British attitude toward the Muslims, increasing Hindu self-assertion, and the beginnings of the Indian national independence movement drove Muslim political and religious leaders toward a more aggressive anti-British policy, and brought into the open profound differences among Muslims as to their conception of the Muslim community and the goals of Muslim political action.

The British attitude toward the Muslim elites was a major factor in the eventual subversion of the loyalist policies of Sayyid Ahmad. The British considered that the Muslims, as former masters of India, harbored lingering ambitions to political power, and that they had therefore to be conciliated to win their favor but repressed lest they become too powerful. They accepted the idea that the former political elite was entitled to governmental appointments and to seats on councils in proportion to their political weight rather than their absolute numbers. At the same time the British tried to reduce the proportion of Muslims employed in government. British governors sometimes deliberately favored Hindu over Muslim appointees. The administrative position of Muslims, though still substantial, deteriorated steadily.

The introduction of municipal self-government and municipal councils by the Ripon Local Council Act of 1882 and the Indian Councils Act of 1892 also tended to the disadvantage of Muslims. The electoral system favored Hindus, who were the majority of the population, and made it possible for wealthy Hindu merchants and moneylenders to compete for office and to challenge the authority of the Muslim (and Hindu) landed and administrative families. While in eastern United Provinces and Oudh the old elite maintained its position, in western United Provinces and Doab the advantage went to aggressive Hindu newcomers.

Another factor which weakened the Muslim position was Hindu self-assertion in various forms. Religious revivalism went back to the founding in 1828 of the Brahmo Samaj in Calcutta to promote theism and social reform among Hindus. In 1875 the Arya Samaj was founded to modernize Hinduism and make it a suitable faith for Western-educated Hindu merchants, officials, and intellectuals – a faith able to compete with Christianity. Among Hindus, as well as Muslims, modernizing reform was accompanied by traditionalist and orthodox revival, and was changed from an elite to a mass movement. The first cow protection associations were founded in 1882; the first communal riots among Hindus and Muslims took place in 1893.

Of particular concern to educated Muslims was the campaign to make Hindi an official language. Hindu revivalism led to a literary renaissance, increasing numbers of newspapers with ever-wider circulation, and ultimately a Hindu crusade against the dominant place of Urdu in government affairs. Hindus campaigned to have Devanagari recognized as an official script for court and government use. The new script, they argued, would allow Hindus who did not know Persian to compete equally for government posts. The British were responsive to these demands. A British governor rejected a civil service candidates' list on the grounds that there were too many Muslims; Persian was removed from the curriculum of Allahabad University, and in 1900 the British accepted the use of Devanagari script for official purposes in the Northwest Frontier provinces and Oudh.

The formation of the Indian National Congress in 1885 was also a sign of the changing balance of power. Congress, though open to Muslims, was formed by Brahmin lawyers, professionals, and middle-class intellectuals. It expressed resentment of British attitudes toward Indians, called for increased participation of Indians in the civil service and increased political representation, and opposed British economic policies which damaged Indian industries. The beginning of the movement toward Indian national independence brought into question the generation-old Muslim policy of loyalty to British rule. However, no event was more important for the change in Muslim elite opinion than the partition of Bengal. In 1905 the British, largely for administrative reasons, partitioned Bengal in a way which created an eastern province with a substantial Muslim majority; but under intense Hindu pressure Britain reversed the partition in 1911. In the eyes of many Muslims this reversal utterly discredited the policy of collaboration, and lent force to the conviction that the British were basically hostile to Muslim interests.

The first Muslim response to these challenges was to continue the policies set down in the aftermath of the great mutiny. Sayyid Ahmad Khan reaffirmed his policy of collaboration and of using educational organizations as the spearhead of Muslim interests, but the younger generation of educated Muslim officials, lawyers, and journalists, especially those having difficulty finding suitable government employment, refused to accept the passivity of their elders. While the landowning and office-controlling elders pursued a policy of appeasement, the younger generation clamored for more direct political action. In 1900 the Urdu Defense Association was formed. In 1906 a delegation of Muslim leaders from Aligarh petitioned the British viceroy for a separate Muslim electorate, and Lord Minto acknowledged the Muslim right to representation in government in proportion to their assumed political importance. In 1909 the Indian Councils Act allowed for partially separate electorates. For the British this was a convenient way to satisfy the Muslim claim to political privilege; it was also a way to confirm the division of Indians into Muslim and Hindu interests and to make the British the arbiter among hostile communities.

The most important expressions of the new Muslim militancy were the founding of the All-India Muslim League in 1906, and the beginnings of political journalism. In 1908 a young journalist, Abu 'l-Kalam Azad (1888–1958) began to publish *al-Hilal* (The Crescent). *Al-Hilal* preached that Muslims the world over were a single people by virtue of common religion and that the Ottoman Caliph was their leader. Moreover, it was the duty of Muslims to work for home rule in India, and form an active political body to support the Caliphate. Another journalist, Muhammad ʿAli, a graduate of Aligarh, preached a similar creed in his paper, *Comrade*.

The new-found militancy of the Muslim political elite was paralleled by revived political activism among the reformist ʿulamaʾ. In this political reassertion the ʿulamaʾ of Deoband and Farangi Mahall played a large part. Farangi Mahall was the name given to a prominent ʿulamaʾ lineage, derived from the quarter of Lucknow which they had inhabited since the end of the seventeenth century. The quarter was renowned as one of the oldest centers of Indian madrasa education and Sufism, and the family scholars had wide networks of disciples. The Farangi Mahalli maintained a moderate version of Shariʿa–Sufi Islam, combining Quranic and legal studies with mysticism. They venerated the shrines of Sufi ancestors and kept up a festival calendar of "birthday" celebrations for the saints and the Prophet, but they were careful to emphasize that they did not worship the saints but rather came to the tombs in order to be closer to God. While Deobandis and other reformers criticized their Sufi practices, the Farangi Mahalli believed that their synthesis of Shariʿa and Sufism was a true representation of the life and teachings of the Prophet.

One crucial principle of the school was avoidance of contact with or dependence upon government. While the Farangis had accepted Mughal gifts in the seventeenth century, by the nineteenth they had withdrawn from politics to avoid contamination by the Shiʿi rulers of Lucknow and their British overlords. This apolitical stance, however, changed in the late nineteenth century. Beneath the acquiescent surface of apolitical religious activities was a smoldering resentment of infidel rule. This resentment was expressed in terms of sympathy with Muslims all over the world who were struggling against British, European, and Christian imperialism. The leaders of the Farangi Mahall played a large role in the formation of Muslim associations to support the Ottoman empire and protect the holy places in Arabia, and they were instrumental, after World War I, in launching the *Khilafat* movement and in the foundation of the *Jamiʿat al-ʿUlamaʾ-i Hind* (Association of the ʿUlamaʾ of India).

Between 1876 and 1878, the years of the Russo-Turkish war and the Congress of Berlin, which witnessed the first British, as well as Russian, participation in the partition of the Ottoman empire, Indian Muslims agitated for a pro-Turkish policy. Jamal al-Din al-Afghani propagated the doctrine of pan-Islamic solidarity as the only way for Muslim peoples to throw off the yoke of European rule. In 1888 Muslim religious opposition to British rule took a new turn when the rector of Deoband issued a fatwa in favor of a Muslim alliance with the Congress party to further the struggle against imperialism. The ʿulamaʾ considered foreign rule as a greater danger to Islam than domestic Hindu competition. These strong anti-colonial, anti-British, and pro-Ottoman sensibilities were stimulated in the years before the First World War by the Anglo-Russian Treaty of 1907 to create spheres of influence in Iran, the Italian invasion of Tripolitania, the establishment of the French protectorate over Morocco, and finally by the outbreak of the Balkan wars in 1912.

The Western-educated and the religious-educated leaders joined hands in open political action. In 1909 Mahmud al-Hasan, rector of Deoband, founded the *Jamiʿat al-Ansar*, Society of Helpers (of the Prophet), whose ultimate objective was an alliance of Turkey, Iran, and Afghanistan to expel the British from India. In 1912–13 Maulana ʿAbd al-Bari, the head of Farangi Mahall, and

Shaukat ʿAli, a brother of Muhammad ʿAli, and also a graduate of Aligarh, founded the *Anjuman-i Khuddam-i Kaʿba*, Association of the Servants of the Kaʿba, to oppose British rule and defend the Ottoman empire. During the war Mahmud al-Hasan made the pilgrimage to Mecca, where he contacted Ottoman leaders and tried to promote the cause of a pan-Islamic Caliphate. Maulana ʿUbaydallah Sindhi traveled to the Northwest Frontier provinces and Afghanistan to explore arms manufacturers, promote unrest among the tribal peoples, and eventually set up a provisional government of India in exile. During the war, hostility to the British mushroomed into pan-Islamic, pro-Caliphal political agitation and conspiracies to weaken British rule and promote the international cause of Islam.

These years were marked not only by the change from passivity to active political opposition, but also by a change from elite political and educational activities to efforts to rally mass Muslim support and to weld the disparate masses of Indian Muslims into a cohesive communal and political body. The crucial reason for this change was simply the anachronism of elite self-cultivation in an era of rising Hindu political action, and the weakness of small elite groups pleading for special privileges from a powerful British state. Mass support had become essential to protect and legitimize the claims of the Muslim elite.

However, the whole concept of a mass Muslim society in India had only the most tenuous basis. It was perhaps stronger in the minds of the British than in the minds of the Muslims. The British stressed the importance of religious ties, and the free exercise of religion as a cardinal principle of a liberal society, and reinforced the collective identity of religious groups by giving them the right to petition for relief of grievances and to elect their own representatives. The British identified the Muslims as a religious community; then they provided the political machinery to translate that identity into concerted group action. By the Indian Councils Act of 1909 they confirmed the existence of two separate communal electorates, Hindu and Muslim, and thus gave legal and political substance to the underlying differences of language and religion.

Among Muslims the concept of a Muslim Indian society had its basis in the inherent Muslim sense of communal and political solidarity. It also had some basis in the cultural unity of the qasbah elites, who shared a Persian and Urdu literary education and a relatively standardized religious practice. Nevertheless, the problems of creating a mass Muslim identity were profound. The culturally unified Muslim elites were divided into innumerable local family, quarter, or factional segments and were not at all unified for political purposes. They could not, as a group, provide political leadership for the mass of Indian

Muslims. Moreover, despite the partial successes of the reform movement in propagating a standardized Islamic religious practice, the masses were far from sharing a common identity. Among Indian Muslims parochial family, lineage, caste, regional, and class interests commonly overrode Muslim identity. In the late nineteenth century, there was not the organizational basis nor were there the unifying symbols for a mass Indian Muslim movement. Nonetheless, the Muslim elites, motivated by political necessity, in opposition to Hindu movements and in collaboration with British notions of politics, would attempt to bring into being a new political body – the Muslims of India. This task would never be attempted in a unified way, nor fully accomplished, yet the several parallel efforts to create a shared Indian Muslim identity and an Indian Muslim political organization would utterly change the position of Muslim peoples in the subcontinent.

The first sign of the new orientation to mass politics was the changing character of local demonstrations and riots. Through the nineteenth century, religious festivals had served to solidify local community consciousness and to mobilize Muslims as opposed to Hindus. By the end of the century, the formation of Islamic educational and defense associations, and increasing public debate gave national importance to local events. The Kanpur mosque episode of 1913 became the first symbol of national Muslim politics. The British wished to move the mosque washing facilities in order to put in a new road. In other times this might have been inconsequential, but now it was seen as a threat to the safety of the mosque and, almost literally, to Islam. The desecration of the mosque crystallized a feeling of mourning, martyrdom, and defeat among Muslims. Local committees were formed to defend the mosque; Delhi- or Lucknow-based Muslim leaders took up the Kanpur cause. The defense of the mosque condemned the policy of cooperation with the government, enshrined religious symbols as the basic way of articulating Muslim identity, and crystallized a larger-scale Indian Muslim consciousness.

The Kanpur riots were followed by Muslim riots in Calcutta in 1918, in Bombay in 1929, and again in Kanpur in 1931. These outbursts showed that an overarching Muslim identity was taking form in the minds of the urban common people, but that this symbolic identity outstripped the political structures available to organize and articulate Muslim interests. In these incidents local leadership was highly factionalized, inadequately integrated into municipal institutions, and thus unable either to direct or control popular feeling. Muslim symbols could spark large-scale demonstrations, but the factionalism among Muslim leaders prevented an organized political movement.

The closest approach to mass Muslim political action came from the Khilafat movement. In 1919 Gandhi and the Indian National Congress were about to launch the first great campaign of non-cooperation for establishing Indian home rule and independence; Muslim leaders formed two new associations with similar goals. Muhammad ʿAli founded the Khilafat Conference to press for the restoration of the Ottoman empire, and the ʿulamaʾ of Farangi Mahall and Deoband founded the Jamiʿat al-ʿUlamaʾ-i Hind to fight for Muslim religious interests and for the preservation of the Caliphate. But for a world-wide movement to succeed, it was necessary first to use familiar pan-Islamic symbols to make Indian Muslims aware of themselves as a people.

The primary strategy of the Khilafat movement was to ally with Congress to further their joint interest in overthrowing British rule and winning political independence for India. Congress, under the leadership of Gandhi, embraced the cause of the Caliphate; Muslims pledged themselves to non-cooperation. For the first time Hindus and Muslims participated in a broad-based national movement to compel the British to return India to Indian hands.

The joint movement soon collapsed. Muslim interests were divided. Some Muslims concentrated on non-cooperation. Others gave their attention to an abortive effort to move the Muslim masses to Afghanistan to set the basis for a jihad against British rule. Then, in 1923 and 1924, the independent Turkish state abolished the Sultanate and Caliphate, removing the external rationale of the movement. At the same time, the alliance with Congress foundered. The collapse of Gandhi's authority and liberal–conservative divisions within Congress compromised its commitment to a joint Muslim–Hindu movement. Hindu and Muslim extremists revived the latent antagonism between the two communities, and communal riots ensued. By 1924, the non-cooperation movement, the Khilafat movement, and Hindu–Muslim collaboration were finished.

Despite its defeat, the Khilafat movement had important consequences. It greatly enlarged the vocabulary and the shared culture of newspaper reading, poetry recitation, and public debates which conveyed anti-British and shared Muslim feeling. It created organizational cadres such as volunteers to escort leaders, enforce boycotts, and maintain order at public meetings. It brought secular and religious leaders together in a common cause. Thus the movement transformed Indian Muslim politics from the maneuvers of elites to the struggle of the masses for political identity.

With the breakdown of the Khilafat movement, Muslim communal activities were directed primarily into three channels. First, spontaneous riots over Muslim issues continued to express the rallying power of Muslim symbols, and the weakness of Muslim political organization. Second and more important was the revival of reformist movements and the effort to base Muslim identity upon personal religious practice. After the failure of the Khilafat effort the great mass movements of the 1920s and 1930s were the Tabligh and Tanzim.

In 1927 the Tablighi Islam movement was founded by Maulana Muhammad Ilyas, a spiritual descendant of Shah Waliallah, a graduate of Deoband, and a member of the Sabiri branch of the Chisti order. Ilyas began his career as a scholar and Sufi teacher, but gave it up to reconvert the Mewatis, a peasant community living near Delhi, to the true practice of Islam based on the Quran and hadith, observance of the Shariʿa, and pious worship and meditation according to Chisti principles. He eschewed political involvement and held that only by the practice of Islam could Muslims demonstrate their stewardship of worldly affairs. His movement began by preaching to villagers, and spread throughout north India by recruiting peasant disciples to preach his basic message in still other villages and towns. The Tanzim movement also flourished in north India as a call for the reform of personal religious practices, and for the defense of an endangered Islam and an abused Muslim minority. Like the Tabligh movement it concentrated on the religious rather than the political aspects of the Muslim problem, and had dramatic religious and emotional appeal but no overall political organization.

THE PAKISTAN MOVEMENT

It was left to a third Muslim movement to reverse the priority of personal religious reform over political unification, stress the importance of Muslim political solidarity rather than religious practice, and create the first mass political movement based on Islamic identity. While Tanzim and Tabligh had widespread local appeal, India-wide political initiative reverted to the Western-educated Muslim political elite. The secularized Muslim elite built upon the work of the Khilafat, the Tanzim, and similar movements in generating a consciousness of Muslim communal solidarity throughout the subcontinent, but turned that solidarity into a political and nationalist form. With the breakup of the Khilafat movement, separatist Muslim political demands were revived. In 1924 the Muslim League called for safeguards for the religious and civil rights of the Muslim populations, and for autonomy and political predominance in Bengal, the Punjab, and the Northwest Frontier provinces. In response, the Nehru Report of 1928 favored a unified Indian state without separate electorates and without Muslim majority provinces, though it conceded that Muslims should be provided with representation in excess of proportion to population. Muslims were confirmed in their fears of Hindu domination. Muhammad ᶜAli Jinnah, speaking for the Muslim League in 1929, reiterated the demand for a federal Indian state, with autonomous Muslim provinces, separate electorates and safeguards for Muslims in law, education, and religion. Muslim–Hindu conferences in the early 1930s did nothing to bridge the gap. British measures to find a compromise – the Simon report of 1930 favoring a federal government for India, the White Paper of 1932 upholding separate electorates but depriving Muslims of parliamentary majorities in Bengal and the Punjab, and the Government of India Act of 1935 which gave British guarantees for minority rights but enlarged the franchise to the advantage of Hindu majorities – were all rejected as inadequate to the demands of one side or the other and as unacceptable because these proposals assumed continued British rule of India. Much as the Muslims and Hindus disagreed, they were no longer willing to continue British rule as the solution to their conflict.

The elections of 1937 marked the turning of Muslim demands for separate electorates and constitutional guarantees to demands for a separate territorial nation. These elections were a defeat for the Muslim League, and after the elections, Congress refused to share ministries and control of the government with Muslim League politicians. Gandhi and Nehru also attempted to appeal directly to the Muslim masses over the heads of the League politicians. Class interests, they believed, were stronger than communal ties. Instead Congress only reinforced Muslim fears of Hindu domination, and stimulated Muslim support for the League. In 1938, to recoup the Muslim League position, Jinnah advanced the "two nations" theory and made the first formal demand for a separate Muslim homeland. In a 1940 resolution the Muslim League called for the formation of Pakistan.

The idea of a Muslim homeland went back only a decade to a 1930 speech by Muhammad Iqbal which called for the amalgamation of the Punjab, North-west Frontier province, Sind, and Baluchistan into a single state. Muhammad Iqbal (1876–1938) was the preeminent spokesman of Indian Muslims in the twentieth century. His philosophic integration of Sufi Islam with Western thought, his understanding of Islam in universal religious terms, his commitment to the reinterpretation of Muslim principles in light of contemporary conditions, and his passionate religious and moral poetry made him the spiritual leader of Indian modernism. Iqbal denied in this famous speech that Muslims and Hindus constituted a single Indian nation and called for the formation of a Muslim state, based on (unspecified) Islamic principles, to be part of a multinational system of Muslim states. Iqbal's vision revived the basic idea of the Khilafat movement – regional Muslim populations as elements of a universal pan-Islamic community – taking the two basic lessons of the movement to heart: its successes as defining an international system of Muslim communities; its failures as indicating the need to form a separate Muslim state or states in the subcontinent.

Chaudhari Rahmat ʿAli and Cambridge student friends also advanced the idea of an independent Muslim state. In their conception, the new state would be a commonwealth of Indian Muslim states including regions which had majority Muslim populations, provinces ruled by Muslim princes, and areas sacred to Muslims – the conglomeration of the whole to be called Pakistan. In Jinnah's conception, the commonwealth and international aspects were subordinated to the idea of the single Muslim state in the provinces of the Punjab, Northwest Frontier province, and Bengal. The idea of Pakistan was a revolution in Muslim thought, for this concept of a Muslim nation did not have a specifically religious content. The Pakistan program was the program of secularized elites who were forced by disunity of the Muslim population and by competition with the Hindu majorities to call their political society "Islamic."

Muslim public opinion was not prepared for such a development. In the United Provinces, there was indeed a relatively cohesive Muslim elite and a strong sense of religious community. Here the Muslim League leaders were able to separate Islam as a symbol of political community from its traditional religious implications and to manipulate this symbol as the basis of a new political identity. In other regions, however, the process of communal political identification was not so far advanced. In the Punjab, Islamic ideological ties had developed in urban areas but not in rural districts. In the rural areas, traditional identifications with the Sufi shrines and dependency on rural landlords remained the basic modes of social organization. Bengal had its own history of active Muslim religious movements which had stimulated the development of a Bengali Muslim consciousness, but these movements were directed to the reform of religious practice and to agrarian social and political issues. While Muslim consciousness was highly developed in Bengal, it was not directed to the kind of territorial political identity favored by the Muslim League.

From 1938 to 1945 an energetic propaganda campaign was launched to rally Muslims to the newly defined cause. The middle classes – Muslim businessmen, landlords, government officials, professionals, and university students – were easily won over. The ʿulamaʾ were generally won over by their fear of Hindu competition, the perceived need for Muslim political power, and the powerful appeal of an "Islamic" state. Most important for the League cause was the support of the sajjada nishins – the Sufi elite – in the important provinces of Uttar Pradesh and the Punjab. Under British rule they had been confirmed in their ownership of land, protected from competing Hindu financial interests, and even granted additional lands. The Sufis were further allied to landowners, from whom they received financial support. They married into their families, and had common interests. By 1945 the Muslim League had persuaded the religious leaders that whatever their local interests, a Muslim state, run by Muslims, to defend the principles of a Muslim way of life, was essential. The League had succeeded in capturing the symbolic attachment to Islam for the purposes of a national political movement. Yet behind the purely political use of the term, there lay a profound and utopian hope, evoked by the very name "Islam," for a society in which a secure Muslim community could live in justice committed to the realization of Muslim social and personal ideals. Appealing to these deep yearnings, the Muslim League won an overwhelming victory in the elections of 1945 and became the sole representative of Muslim political interests in India.

Throughout the period from 1924 to 1947 the ʿulamaʾ of the Jamiʿat al-ʿUlamaʾ-i Hind continued to resist Muslim League leadership and to advance an alternative conception of the Muslim community in India. Though very much a minority view, this conception had a profound effect upon the ideology and political situation of the millions of Muslims who remained citizens of India after the partition. The Jamiʿat al-ʿUlamaʾ-i Hind was founded in 1919 to guide the Muslim community, defend the principles of the Shariʿa, protect the holy places of the Hijaz, and help win the freedom of Muslim peoples from colonial rule. The Jamiʿat leaders were among the important sponsors of the Khilafat movement. With the collapse of the movement they turned their attention to the formation of Shariʿa courts and to a political program demanding assurances that Muslims could continue to live according to their law and faith.

Throughout its history the Jamiʿat supported the concept of a united India. It opposed British rule, called for jihad, and was prepared to enter into a joint struggle with the Congress party to expel the foreigners and to establish a united national state for both Muslims and Hindus. According to the theorists of the Jamiʿat, Muslims could be at once Muslims and members of the same nation with non-Muslims. In their view, a united Indian nation formed with Muslim cooperation would best protect Muslim religious and communal interests. The ʿulamaʾ imagined that this united India would provide full safeguards for Muslim law and custom. Their Saharanpur proposal of 1931 thus called for a federal state, autonomous provinces, and self-governing religious groups within the framework of a single state and constitution. According to some Muslim thinkers, the Muslim community would be headed by an Amir-i Hind, who would be a scholar of religious law and a delegate of the Caliph. The Amir would enforce Muslim law within the community, and would be selected by and bound to heed the advice of a consultative assembly of ʿulamaʾ. The Amir would in effect be the head of a Muslim state within an Indian union.

The Jamiʿat, however, was hostile to the program of the Muslim League, for it viewed the League as collaborating in a British plot to divide Indian peoples and forestall Indian independence. The ʿulamaʾ were also hostile to the secularism of the League's leading intellectuals. They feared that a new state, even though called Muslim, would not in fact be accountable to the ʿulamaʾ or to the principles of Islam, and would be all the more dangerous because of its appeal to the sentiments of the populace. They also feared that the division of the subcontinent into separate states would compromise the substantial Muslim populations that were bound to remain in the majority Hindu state, and would inhibit Muslim missionary work among non-Muslim Indians. They believed that the best interests of the Muslim community would be served by maintaining the unity of the Indian Muslim population inside a single state, where weight of numbers would protect their interests and enable them to influence the policy of the Indian state on behalf of Muslim brothers elsewhere in the world. The ʿulamaʾ of the Jamiʿat would rather have taken their chances in a unified Indian state than be left to the mercies of partition and secularization. In effect they favored a powerful diaspora in India to a weak homeland in Pakistan.

The positions of the Muslim League and the Jamiʿat reflect the dilemmas of Indian Islam. In fact, with the growth of communal consciousness the differences between them were narrower than is apparent. The concept of a communal society, whether formed in traditional religious terms or in modern political terms, had won over all segments of the Muslim elites. Both the League and the Jamiʿat called for a separate Muslim identity. Both agreed on the need for separate electorates, for decentralized and federal forms of government, for provincial autonomy, and for guarantees for Muslim religious interests. They differed only on the question of forming a national state for Muslims. For the Muslim League, the political security of Indian Muslims was the primary consideration and questions of religious concepts and practices were secondary. Their concept of a Muslim nation was built upon the purely political aspect of Muslim identity, which, contrary to the past history of the

Muslim community, was now severed from its religious components. The Jami‵at, by contrast, clung to fundamental Muslim religious ideas, but they were forced to give up the traditional idea of a Muslim state as the necessary protector of the Muslim community and as the obligatory policeman of the Shari‵a. They were also forced to accept cooperation with infidels, and indeed a state which would make Muslims merely a tolerated minority in a non-Muslim state. Under the pressure of twentieth-century imperialism and nationalist reaction, traditional Islamic concepts were transformed to save what men of conscience held to be essential and to sacrifice what they thought most expendable in the great tradition.

In the end, the tendency toward Muslim nationalism won out. It was based, despite fragmentation, upon a deep latent sense of community among the Muslims of the subcontinent. The anxieties of the Muslim upper classes threatened with political extinction, British insistence on an electoral system which divided Indians into Muslim and Hindu communities, the revivalist movements among both Muslims and Hindus which raised religious consciousness and stressed the antagonism between the two communities, and rising Muslim religious self-awareness – these forces consolidated a consciousness of Muslim-ness based on abstract symbols, such as the very name "Islam." The force of this symbolic consciousness overcame Muslim attachments to the larger Indian society. The constant efforts to reconcile Muslim and Hindu interests and to create a joint Indian political movement were frustrated by the barrier of deep incomprehension and suspicion. Muslim leaders felt that the Hindus would exploit their dominant numerical position to subordinate Muslims, and Hindu leaders felt that the Muslims were angling for an opportunity to reassert Muslim supremacy. In the course of the 1920s and 1930s, every effort to form a united Hindu–Muslim political front was defeated by incompatible demands and fears which could not be allayed. In these circumstances the Muslim position evolved from a demand for protection of communal rights to the demand for a separate territorial state, regardless of the consequences for the Muslims or the peoples of the subcontinent.

After the elections of 1945 the movement toward a Muslim national state was irresistible: if there were no partition, there would be civil war. In the end there was both. In 1946 both Congress and the Muslim League rejected a British plan for a federated government; by 1947 Congress was also ready to accept partition and only the question of boundaries remained. On August 14, 1947, Pakistan came into being, and on August 15 India became an independent state. The new nations were born in the throes of one of the most terrible civil and communal wars of modern history. Millions of people were forced to leave their homes; Hindus fled Pakistan, Muslims left Hindu areas. Hundreds of thousands of people were killed in communal riots. The two nations promptly went to war over Kashmir, which was seized by India on the grounds that its ruler was Hindu, despite the claim that by virtue of its Muslim population, Kashmir should be part of Pakistan. The partition of the sub-continent thus parallels the emergence of numerous Balkan, Arab, and Turkish states in the Middle East. In each case the violence unleashed by the trans-mutation of religious into political-national consciousness destroyed forever the civilization shared among peoples of different religious persuasions.

PAKISTAN, BANGLADESH, AND THE MUSLIMS OF INDIA

Thus Pakistan was founded on the idea that the Muslims of India formed a nation and were entitled to a territorial homeland of their own. Pakistan was made up of the territories of Sind, Baluchistan, Northwest Frontier province, and parts of the Punjab and Bengal – encompassing peoples who had never before formed a nation and among whom there were tremendous ethnic and linguistic differences – a nation of some 80 million people in two great ter-ritorial blocks divided by a thousand miles of intervening India. Some 50 million Muslims remained within India. In the western part of Pakistan, more than half of the people were Punjabis, but some 20 percent were Sindhis, 13 percent Pathans, and 3–4 percent Baluchis. Bengal was virtually a nation within the nation. The western region was without industrial infrastructure; the eastern region had been cut off from Calcutta, its main port and processing center for jute and other agricultural products.

The main problem of Pakistan was to create a national identity to suit the reality of the new political boundaries and to create an acceptable and stable regime for a populace divided by sharp ethnic, linguistic, ideological, and even religious differences. As in Turkey a secularized political elite descended from the older imperial elites took control of the political destinies of the country, but unlike Turkey, where the elites were avowedly secular and nationalist, the competition of Muslims with a majority Hindu population and the deep particularistic, ethnic, tribal, and local divisions shared among Muslims in a pluralistic society, forced the political elite to espouse an Islamic form of nationalism as a unifying symbol for the state of Pakistan. The appeal to their shared Muslim heritage was enough to overcome the immediate differences but not enough to suppress the contradictions of Muslim religious feeling, regional nationalisms, and class antagonisms within the new state. Pakistan

Map 34. India, Pakistan, and Bangladesh.

was born as an Islamic state to differentiate it from the rest of the subcontinent, but Muslim identity has not proved adequate to unite the country internally.

Pakistan came into being with at least two different concepts of what it meant to be an Islamic state. The political elite considered Islam a communal, political, and national identity stripped of its religious content. Yet a large segment of the populace, led by the ʿulamaʾ and other religious leaders, expected a state whose constitution, institutions, and routines of daily life would be governed by the Shariʿa and Islamic norms. The assembly called to devise a constitution, established a Board of Islamic Teaching which recommended that the state be governed by pious Muslim leaders in accord with the advice of the ʿulamaʾ. The *Jamaʿat-i Islami*, led by Abul ʿAla Mawdudi, a Muslim reformer, fundamentalist, and political organizer, called for the formation of a truly Islamic state with Islamic government, banking, and economic institutions – a state in which the Shariʿa would define the values of both public and personal life. Mawdudi appealed for a return to the Quran and Sunna and the use of rational judgment in religious matters so as to apply the principles of Islam to a modern society. The Jamaʿat demanded that governing officials be advised by religious councils and that non-Muslims be barred from high political posts.

The struggle over the role of Islam led to a long series of constitutional compromises. A constitution of 1956 declared Pakistan an Islamic state and made all parliamentary legislation subject to review by an Islamic Research Institute. In 1958 this constitution was abolished and a Republic of Pakistan declared, which tried to curb the power of the religious leaders. In 1963 the Islamic provisions of 1956 were by and large restored. In 1973 Prime Minister Bhutto declared Pakistan an Islamic Socialist Republic, and the present ruler, General Zia ul-Haq, has again declared it an Islamic state.

While the debates over the constitution went on, the real government of Pakistan was a Punjabi elite of soldiers, administrators, and landowners. After 10 years of chaotic civilian rule, the question of the role of Islam and the ethnic and regional rivalries between west Pakistan and Bengal had not been resolved. In 1958 the army, led by General Ayyub Khan, took control of the country. Under the Ayyub regime Pakistan continued to be ruled by its Punjabi elite. The government was highly centralized and strongly supported by landlords, business interests, officials, and also by the Sufi leaders. The Ayyub government centralized power but did not integrate a divided country. Defeat in war with India in 1965 allowed demands for a reopening of the electoral system, and for provincial autonomy for Bengal. Demonstrations and riots led in 1969 to the succession of General Yahya Khan, who imposed martial law and precipitated a struggle for power which culminated in civil war, war with India, and the transformation of east Pakistan into the independent state of Bangladesh in 1971.

In neither state has the question of the relationship of the religious and political aspects of Islam been resolved. From 1970 to 1977 west Pakistan was under the leadership of Zulfiqar ʿAli Bhutto and the Pakistan People's Party. The Pakistan People's Party espoused an Islamic socialism compounded of agricultural and industrial reforms and the promulgation of a new constitution which defined Pakistan as an Islamic Republic. The President and Prime Minister were to be Muslims and all laws were to be in conformity with Islam as determined by a council of ʿulamaʾ. As Pakistan became increasingly dependent on oil-rich Arab states for loans, commerce, and employment of labor, Bhutto made further concessions to Islamic morality such as prohibiting alcohol and gambling. However, to maintain itself in power, the Pakistan People's Party eventually succumbed to the influence of administrative and landlord groups, roused popular opposition, resorted to rigged elections, and was defeated in July 1977 by mass demonstrations and the intervention of the army.

The present military regime in Pakistan, led by General Zia ul-Haq, influenced by the Jamaʿat-i Islami, once again attempts to base its authority on a strong pro-Islamic stance. The government has reintroduced traditional Islamic punishments, prohibited gambling and alcohol consumption, and created a new judicial review system. While Islamic reform movements are usually concerned with the moral behavior of individuals, in Pakistan the emphasis is upon a total Islamic system or *nizam-i mustafa* which implies an Islamic government and economy. Pakistani planners have sought to eliminate interest by the creation of profit-sharing institutions such as the National Investment Trust, which issues profit-sharing bonds; the House Building Finance Corporation, which lends money to builders and shares in rental incomes; the Small Business Finance Corporation, which buys, sells, and leases goods; and other similar institutions. Profit- and loss-sharing accounts have been established at the nationalized banks. In their first year of operation these showed a return of between 8 and 15 percent. Thus an Islamic banking system proves profitable at least in the short run, though it faces the problems of limited capital and severe competition from institutions which use interest calculations.

The role of women has become a significant issue. On one side are those who favor limiting women to the household sphere and on the other those who wish to preserve women's freedom in public life. Proposed changes in

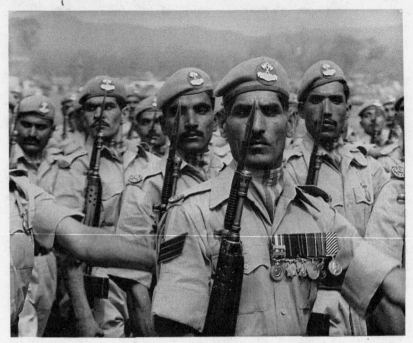

25 Pakistani soldiers

family law that give women certain rights in relation to divorce and in inheritance, and proposed modifications in the law of evidence which make two women the equivalent of a single male witness have been hotly debated. In general, the demand for Islamization seems to come from the military elites supported by some segments of the activist, urban population, and is closely tied to the ambitions of an authoritarian regime to maintain itself in power. Once again, Islam is being used to generate national solidarity. However, the tensions among Punjabi, Pathan, and Sindhi interests, and the divisions of Sunnis and Shiᶜa are not resolved by the reassertion of Islamic values.

Pakistan was formed out of a deep conviction that Muslims in India required a state of their own to assure their political security and their opportunities to cultivate a Muslim style of life; but since the founding of the state, appeals to Islam of themselves have not been able to resolve the question of what kind of institutions Pakistan should have. There have been a number of constitutions, a number of civilian, and a number of military regimes. The country holds together by military coercion, by strong administration, and by bargaining among various groups, but not by any deep sense of national identity.

By contrast with west Pakistan, Bangladesh has evolved in a national rather than in an Islamic direction. The immediate reaction to independence was to stress the national rather than the religious aspect of Bangladeshi identity. The constitution of 1972 proclaimed secularism a basic principle and outlawed political action by religious groups; a Bengali literary revival also stressed the Bengali rather than the Islamic aspects of national identity. Bangladesh had come into being with strong Indian support, had a large Hindu minority, and thus reacted against Pakistani insistence on a Muslim identity, and against the preference of religious groups for continued union. In 1977, however, the new military regime of General Zia ul-Rahman relaxed the constitutional proscription of Muslim activities and replaced the principle of secularism with a reference to trust in God. Still, the governing Bangladesh Nationalist Party overwhelmingly defeated the Islamic parties in the elections of 1979 and maintains a secular program of development combined with a generalized sense of Islamic religious affiliations. The Bengali emphasis, however, has not resolved the problem of distinguishing Bangladesh from Indian Bengal, and there are recent indications of a renewed emphasis upon Islam. Bengali identity has both an ethnic-national and a Muslim aspect, and one or the other may be emphasized depending upon changing political conditions.

The position of the Muslims who remain citizens of India is very different. Under the leadership of Abul Kalam Azad and the Jamiꜥat al-ꜤUlamaꜣ-i Hind, Indian Muslims accepted a composite nationality, considering themselves at once Muslim and Indian. Nonetheless, the problems of their place in India are considerable. Despite cooperation with Congress and the promotion of Indian Muslims into important national positions, the Muslims of India consider themselves an embattled minority. Except on the official level, Hindu–Muslim communal hostilities remain intense. Muslims are threatened by communal riots, and feel discrimination in employment and education. Muslims also fear the prospect of state intervention in Muslim personal law, and are doubtful of their political and cultural future. The Muslim position has become defensive as they seek to protect their cultural and political interests, including Muslim personal law, the use of the Urdu language, special employment and other economic opportunities, and proportional representation in legislatures and government bureaucracies. Physical protection against intercommunal violence is not the least of their concerns. Hindus, however, see Muslim demands as an assertion of social superiority, an insistence upon special privileges and a refusal to be integrated into the general society. Behind this refusal, some believe, is a lingering unwillingness to accept the role of citizens within the Indian national state and a lingering hope for a return to Muslim domination.

The trauma of the partition hangs over Muslim–Hindu relations. In practice, however, there has been considerable accommodation. The Indian state gives Muslims considerable latitude in cultural matters. Muslims in turn tend to support the Congress party. Many have been successful in business and avoid ideological or communal issues. The realities of the political situation allow a greater degree of accommodation than principled formulations would imply.

In their embattled situation, the Muslims of India have tended to remain socially and religiously conservative. They oppose the emphasis of the Pakistani Jamaʿat on the state as the critical force in Muslim life. Indian Muslim religious leaders stress individual religious commitment and present Islam in devotional rather than collective terms. They also cling more closely to traditional Muslim values and have resisted Indian state efforts to modify legal and educational institutions as unwarranted interference with religious rights. Indian Muslims, therefore, remain more conservative and tradition-minded than Pakistanis. Because the Pakistani state is officially Muslim it has had a more radical effect on Islamic practices. Whereas in Pakistan Muslims face the dilemmas of responsibility for the integration of Islam with a modern state and economy, in India Muslims face the dilemma of how to live a Muslim life without the protection of a Muslim regime.

The formation of the three Indian Muslim societies, then, can be understood in terms of the complex legacy of a Mughal state whose legitimacy was defined in Muslim, cosmopolitan, and Indian terms, and of a Muslim religious establishment which was both independent of the state and disunified. The pluralistic structure of Mughal society allowed for alternatives to Muslim identity expressed in tribal, caste, occupational, or ethnic terms. When this society faced the great shocks of European domination in the nineteenth and twentieth centuries, its pluralistic political and religious elites were divided over whether to define their interests in terms of ethnic, national, or religious identity; and, when they chose religious terms, whether to emphasize the communal-political or the personal-ethical aspects of Islam. In the subcontinent the complexity of the Muslim institutional and cultural heritage has allowed, according to circumstances, for all possible variations.

CHAPTER 28

ISLAM IN INDONESIA AND MALAYSIA

By the middle of the nineteenth century, Holland and Britain had established their empires in the regions of Indonesia and Malaya. The Muslim peoples of this region were not yet part of a unified culture or empire, but were divided into many ethnic and linguistic populations and numerous states. Only in the late nineteenth century did Dutch and British domination lead to profound transformations in political and economic life and provoke both nationalist and Muslim reactions to foreign intervention. As in South Asia, the fact that foreigners controlled the state meant that the dominant response to changing political and social conditions came not from government institutions, but from autonomous sectors of society. The traditional ʿulamaʾ and Sufi teachers, the former political elites, new strata of Indonesian administrators and intellectuals, Muslim reformers, and eventually radical military leaders rose up to lay claim to the future of Indonesian and Malayan societies. Secular nationalist, Communist, Islamic traditionalist, and reformist Islamic movements were pitted against Dutch and British rule, and against each other, in the struggle to define the shape of Malay–Indonesian societies in the twentieth century.

DUTCH RULE AND THE CAPITALIST SYSTEM

The reconstruction of the Dutch empire after the Napoleonic wars was the occasion for important changes in Dutch economic policy on Java. Between 1795 and 1815 the Dutch and the English experimented with various systems of state control and compulsory cultivation, and with free peasant agriculture, capitalist agriculture, and different policies of free and controlled trade. By

1830, however, the period of confusion was over and new policies were adopted which would set the course of Dutch colonial administration and Indonesian economic development for the rest of the nineteenth century.

Before 1795 the Dutch extracted produce, such as coffee and pepper, by forced deliveries for sale in Europe, but the defeat of Holland by France in 1795 and the collapse of the Dutch East India Company in 1799 led the Dutch Republic to seek new means for exploiting the colonial economy. The Dutch turned to centralized political control to maximize the extraction of tributes. In 1806 Governor Daendels was sent to subordinate local lords, reduce former rulers to the position of Dutch administrators, and encourage cotton and coffee production. When the British took control of Java in 1811, Sir Stamford Raffles introduced a capitalist type of economic development, conferred private ownership of land upon Indonesians, and devised a new tax system which substituted a cash tax, equivalent to two-fifths of the value of the produce, for forced deliveries. The produce was left to Javanese landlords and peasants who could dispose of it on the market. Raffles also tried to introduce wages instead of forced labor, and, in general, to promote a monetary economy, and build up the consuming power of the natives so that British goods could be sold in the Indies. When the Dutch returned in 1816 they reverted to direct controls. In 1825 they established the Nederlandsche Handel Maatschappij (N.H.M.), a monopoly company to organize trade between the East Indies and Holland. In 1830 Governor Van Den Bosch centralized political and economic controls. He divided Java into administrative districts called "residences" and further subdivided the residences into regencies. A Dutch controller supervised the local princes, or regents, whose position was made hereditary but reduced in actual effectiveness. In the course of the century the regents were deprived of their share of tax revenues. In 1867 their lands were confiscated, and in 1882 they were deprived of the labor and personal services once owed them by the peasants. The regents were reduced from independent princes to salaried local officials.

The economy was organized under "the culture system." This was a form of taxation which required the peasants to devote one-fifth of their land to government-assigned crops, usually sugar, indigo, coffee, tea, tobacco, cinnamon, and cotton, and to deliver the produce as a tribute in kind, in lieu of other rents or taxes. In addition, the peasants were required to contribute their labor, build irrigation canals, roads, and bridges, clear wastelands, and otherwise build up the economic infrastructure of the island. Though the system was supposed to assure the peasants a fixed obligation, in fact, they were subject to further extortion, rents and corvées. The goods delivered by the culture system were sold to the N.H.M. at contract prices and were shipped to Europe in Dutch bottoms. Imports to Java also came primarily from Holland. By 1848, however, the culture system was failing to produce adequate revenues. During the 1840s, it was overexploited, peasant welfare declined, and the Indies suffered from famines. The Dutch did not prosper, because of competition from English and Chinese merchants.

Furthermore, in Holland the revolution of 1848 brought to power a new merchant class with a liberal capitalist ideology, and led to the formation of a parliamentary government and a system of ministerial responsibility. In 1864 parliament assumed control of the Indies budget and thus brought the colonies under direct Dutch government control. Also, in the course of the 1850s and 1860s, Dutch public opinion underwent important changes. The publication of Dekker's *Max Havelaar*, and sugar contract scandals, discredited the culture system and brought a demand for a new colonial administration based on liberal principles. The liberals wanted to abolish state controls in favor of free enterprise and eliminate the system of forced deliveries in favor of direct taxation. In the course of the 1860s, state cultivation of pepper, cloves, nutmeg, indigo, tea, cinnamon, and tobacco was abolished, and the sugar law of 1870 mandated the progressive establishment of a free market in place of the traditional system of consignments. To bolster the new system of private enterprise, state lands were leased on a long-term basis, and new laws permitted long-term leasing of small holdings and of village lands to capitalist entrepreneurs. Corvée labor was abolished and wage labor implemented in 1882. The new policy stimulated capitalist forms of development, the expansion of the sugar industry, irrigation, and railway construction. By the end of the nineteenth century control of the Javanese economy had substantially shifted from Dutch government officers to private capitalist entrepreneurs.

These policies had profound economic consequences. On Java the culture system led to the cycle of development called "agricultural involution." The primary crops, sugar for export and rice for subsistence, were complementary. They could be grown in adjacent fields or alternated in the same fields when seasonally appropriate, and be maintained by the same labor of terracing and irrigation. This complementarity made it possible to provide at once for exports, government revenues, and food production. Moreover, since both sugar and rice output could both be increased by ever more intensive investments of labor, a cycle of development was entrained in which increased food production could sustain a larger population that could in turn increase both food and sugar production and thereby sustain further population increases. As population rose and rice production reached its limits, the system

26 Dawn prayer to celebrate the end of Ramadan, Jogyakarta, Indonesia

could be kept going by growing maize, soybeans, and other foods on lands unsuitable for rice and sugar. As a result of the culture system, Java entered a cycle of growth that led to ever higher populations and more intensive agricultural exploitation – a cycle which increased Dutch revenues from sugar output and also kept the native population at a subsistence level. As the population of Java rose from approximately 7 million in 1830 to 28.4 million in 1900, the system produced ever-increasing levels of output with no rise in the per capita standard of living. Thus an equalitarian labor-intensive society was meshed into a capitalistic and machine-intensive colonial economy, and still left village communities socially undisturbed.

Whereas in Java the capitalist economy could be superimposed upon and integrated with a peasant society, on Sumatra the introduction of a capitalist economy led to profound social changes. In the early nineteenth century, Sumatra was an important source of agricultural and forest commodities for export, and a market for textiles, hardware, and other foreign goods. However, Dutch control led to the introduction of tobacco, palm, tea, rubber plantations, and tin mining enterprises. Tobacco and food crops could be intertwined because tobacco was believed to require a long fallow period and because food crops were cultivated by very simple methods. The tobacco entrepreneurs leased extensive tracts of land from the Sultans, but allowed the peasants to use fallow lands to grow subsistence crops. However, when rubber, palm, tea, and similar plantations were introduced, they proved to be incompatible with rice and corn, and peasants were driven off the land. Capitalist development created a smallholder class of farmers who changed from slash-and-burn agriculture to fixed gardening operations, producing part of the rubber and coffee crop for export.

The new economic developments also led to an extensive commercialization of the Sumatran economy. New towns were founded for new settlers. Dutch schools were introduced. A network of village banks called the People's Credit System was established. Newspapers were printed. As opposed to Java, capitalism entered into the fabric of the traditional society to create new classes of population. The plantation and mining economy in Sumatra (and Malaya) created a laboring proletariat. A new middle class of merchants and commercial farmers producing coffee, rubber, and other products for the international market grew up with a vested interest in commercial and social change. Also in the outer islands, and in Malaya, the expansion of private land ownership led to important changes in village communities. While the Javanese village collectivity was protected by the peculiarities of wet rice ecology, in the outer islands traditional collective and family controls over land were weakened.

The values which regulated the communal economy broke down in the face of commercialization.

The Dutch conquest of the outer islands, the formation of the capitalist economy, the involution of agriculture on Java, and the growth of a capitalist and commercial economy on the outer islands led to an important redirection of Dutch administrative policy at the turn of the twentieth century. Despite the premises of liberal theory, the expansion of capitalist agriculture and industrial enterprises required state intervention. Even though Dutch capitalists and settlers were opposed to central government controls, they favored military expansion and investments in police, schools, irrigation, railroads, agricultural experimentation, and other services. Also, Dutch surveys of 1888 and 1891 uncovered abuses such as extortion, arbitrary demands on peasant labor services, and excessive appropriation of land by village officials. By 1900 it was clear that the liberal capitalist policy had favored individual capitalists, but had harmed native welfare, reduced government revenues, and injured Dutch manufacturers' interests in a prosperous Indonesian economy.

Humanitarians, liberals, and missionaries joined in the call for economic reform, protection of native interests, and the education and employment of Javanese officials in government service. Liberals held that it was Holland's duty to take responsibility for the welfare of the native population and even to repay Indonesia for centuries of economic exploitation. Some imagined that Dutch rule would be built upon the cooperation of Dutch and local peoples; others called for the assimilation of Indonesians into European culture and the creation of a unified Dutch–Indonesian elite to govern the country. The critics of government policy called for a revolution in the government of the Indies, and for the creation of a welfare state with Indonesian participation. This was called the Ethical Policy. Though well intentioned, it was entirely Euro-centered, and presupposed Dutch domination. The Ethical Policy was a Dutch version of the white man's burden.

By 1900, the combination of capitalist needs and humanitarian concerns reversed the laissez-faire policy of the previous generation in favor of state stimulation and management of economic development. State enterprises were to build up the agricultural, mineral, and industrial resources of the country. Railroads, roads, and shipping lines were to be developed; irrigation was to be extended. The state worked tin and coal mines, laid out rubber plantations, and established agricultural credit banks. It contributed agricultural, medical, and veterinary specialists to help in economic enterprises. Native welfare was promoted through education, public health, and protection of peasants and workers from capitalist exploitation. The Ethical Policy thus entailed extensive government involvement in village affairs. Throughout Java and the outer islands, the new policy meant a more direct involvement of Dutch officials in the daily routines of Indonesian communities, and a tremendous expansion of the civil service.

The Dutch were especially active in the creation of new schools for Indonesians. Dutch education of Indonesians went back to the early nineteenth century when Indonesian aristocrats were educated in the homes of Dutch settlers. The first Dutch school to train Indonesians for civil service jobs was founded in 1848. By 1851 there were schools for clerks and health officers which trained low-ranking priyayi for government services. Then, between 1902 and 1908, numerous technical schools were established to train Indonesian officials. An agricultural school was opened in 1903; medical and veterinary schools were in place by 1907; a law school was opened in 1908. By 1914 Western-type education was extended to the high school and elementary school levels, where Indonesians were introduced to a curriculum including study of Dutch, English, science, mathematics, and drawing. In the 1920s schools for law, engineering, and specialized administrative jobs were introduced.

Finally the new policy meant the centralization of Dutch political control over the whole of the archipelago and the formation, in 1914, of a single government for all of the Indies. The Dutch took the view that without central control other reforms would be impossible. Thus, they devised a new short contract to define the obligations of native princes to comply with Dutch rule, and eliminated the earlier long contract which specified native rights. Mixed European and Indonesian local councils were formed; in 1916 the Dutch introduced a new representative assembly, the Volksraad. This was an advisory assembly which included both elected and appointed Dutch and native representatives. In 1922 a new fundamental law gave the government of the Indies greater autonomy from Holland and made the Volksraad a legislative body for the colonial region. However, the new freedoms were offset by increasing the proportion of European representatives.

Dutch administrators also introduced new law codes. A code for foreign orientals was introduced in 1848 and a criminal code for native Indonesians in 1872. Between 1904 and 1927 the Dutch attempted to bring all customary native law into accord with European norms and to establish a unified system of legal administration. However, after 1927 Dutch policy reverted to a dualistic law system which attempted to maintain the customary Indonesian legal systems alongside European codes and procedures. Despite the policy of preserving customary or *adat* law, considerable inroads were made by statutory enactments. The Dutch gave Indonesia a legal system compounded of adat, Muslim, and Dutch statute law.

After centuries in which the Dutch had merely skimmed the profits of the Indies without touching the underlying structure of society, they began the modern transformation of Indonesia. The historical balance among the state elites, the ʿulamaʾ, and the peasantry was deeply disturbed. Dutch rule sapped the authority of the priyayi, and brought into being new classes to compete with the established elites for political and social power. On Java Dutch policies created medical, engineering, legal, and teaching professionals, and technically trained civil servants in the forestry, mining, agricultural, railway, telegraph, and health administrations. The new professionals and administrators were drawn from the lesser-ranking priyayi families, the scions of the newly rich in Minangkabau and the outer islands, the children of provincial chieftains, and Ambonese and Menadonese ·Christians. These newly educated professionals and administrators interposed themselves between the old aristocracy and the peasantry, competed with the village ʿulamaʾ and headmen, and laid claim to an enlarged political role.

These new classes were hostile to the Dutch government which had spawned them. The new administrators, though benefiting from Dutch educational and administrative policies which attempted to integrate Indonesians into Western culture and Dutch administration, were opposed to European domination. The new priyayi clamored for increased educational opportunities and for more political power. For their part, the merchants, landowners, and religious leaders of the outer islands opposed Dutch restrictions on trade and pilgrimage, and the competition of Christian missionaries. The merchants of Sumatra, Singapore, and Malaya, tied to a Muslim system of international economic and cultural exchanges, opposed Dutch rule as a threat both to their commercial and to their religious interests.

The emergence of these new and frustrated strata of Malay–Indonesian populations was the basis of an ideological and political renaissance in the early twentieth century. Out of these several milieus came new programs for secular nationalism, socialism, and Islamic revival, all of which aspired to an independent and modern form of Malayan and Indonesian civilization. Nationalism was the position of the new priyayi bureaucrats and intellectuals and it also appealed to Javanese peasants. The Communists represented lesser priyayi, student, and worker interests. Islamic reformism spread most widely in urban and middle-class milieus, and in many villages, especially in the outer islands. Islamic conservativism was the creed of rural kiyayi (ʿulamaʾ) and their peasant followers. Much as all of these movements were devoted to Indonesian independence, they were profoundly at odds with each other. Muslim middle-class leaders fought priyayi elites; intellectuals opposed the old aristocracy; reformers opposed customary community leadership; left-wing intellectuals and workers fought bourgeois interests. From 1912 until the achievements of independence, these movements struggled as much with each other as against the Dutch.

INDONESIAN TRADITIONALISM, NATIONALISM, AND ISLAMIC REFORM

The earliest reaction to consolidated Dutch rule and the decline of the aristocracies came from Muslim milieus. The changing balance of power allowed for resurgence of ʿulamaʾ challenges to the authority of the priyayi elites. Ever since the consolidation of Mataram in the early seventeenth century, the Javanese aristocracy had been divided into two groups – the priyayi, conditioned by Javanese values, who governed, and the kiyayi, who represented Islamic religious faith and community loyalty. With the absorption of the priyayi aristocracy into the Dutch colonial administration, the kiyayi became the only independent representatives of Javanese society. Their authority, numbers, and influence were vastly enhanced. Moreover, pilgrimage to Mecca and extensive journeys for religious study in Arabia brought Malay–Indonesian Muslims into contact with reformist teachings, heightened their consciousness of Muslim identity, and made them aware of Muslim worldwide opposition to European colonialism. The hajjis brought back a commitment to the improvement and intensification of Muslim religious life, a desire to arouse their people from torpor and misguidance to a proper Muslim worship, and a commitment to political autonomy.

ʿUlamaʾ-led peasant resistance began with the Java wars of 1825 to 1830. In Djokjakarta the Dutch had alienated both the nobility and the common people by a land policy which canceled leases instigated by previous Dutch administrations, and forced the rulers to pay compensation to the lessees. These same rulers also had to lease lands to the Dutch government, which were then turned over to European cultivators. In 1825 local resentment burst into civil war led by Prince Dipanegara, a member of the ruling family who had been passed over for succession and had devoted himself to religious studies. The corruption of the court and its subservience to the Dutch made him a spokesman for Muslim religious virtues. It became his mission to oppose the corruption of the aristocracy and purify Islam. Prince Dipanegara allied with religious leaders to lead a peasant revolt that lasted for five years. Though it was eventually put down, Dipanegara became a symbol of national resistance to foreign rule.

In the Banten region of Java, kiyayi and peasant resistance was virtually endemic. Banten had been conquered in the fifteenth and early sixteenth centuries by Muslims who set out the system of wet rice cultivation and established a system of feudal rule. The rice fields were cultivated by peasants on condition that they paid a tribute, and performed labor services, such as constructing roads. Some categories, called *abdis*, were obliged to perform personal services in the household of the sovereign or the lords as well. The lords' rights to personal services led to frequent abuses as people were commandeered to clean gardens, collect firewood, gather fodder for horses, and do other household tasks.

The Dutch annexed this stratified society in 1808 and retained the Sultans until 1832. To compensate for the loss of political autonomy, the old nobility began to take service in the colonial administration. There, they had to compete with civil servants of non-noble origin. Then in 1856 and 1882 the Dutch passed new laws to reduce, and then abolish, personal services and to replace them with a capitation tax, but the peasants were nonetheless obliged to serve. As a result, all elements of the population resented Dutch rule. Deprived noble families, religious leaders, village elders and chiefs, and abused peasants all had reason to revolt in the name of the old Sultanate or in the name of Islam. There were insurrections in 1820, 1822, 1825, 1827, 1831, 1833, 1836, and 1839. In 1845 peasant rebels put on white clothes to indicate that they were fighting a holy war. There were further revolts in 1850, 1851, 1862, 1866, and 1869.

In the 1840s and 1850s, Banten was swept by a religious revival. This included increased observance of Muslim rituals and pilgrimage, the establishment of schools, and enrollment in the religious brotherhoods. The Qadiri order in particular enlisted the independent kiyayis into a unified movement and strengthened the ties between the religious leaders and their followers. The orders preached a reformed version of Islam with insistence upon strict observance of Quranic rules, and combined religious revivalism with strong hostility to foreign rule. Equally important were expectations of the coming of the mahdi. Letters were circulated purporting to bear signs of the end of the world and the last days. Wandering preachers stimulated the fervor. Many kiyayis came to be venerated as miracle workers who could foretell the future and heal the sick. Religious hopes turned upon the conviction that the territory of Islam would be freed from foreign subjugation and that an independent Muslim state would come into being.

This religious revival built up to the Great Insurrection of 1888. In an atmosphere of bitter hostility to foreign rule, resentment against the corrupt aristocracy, and passionate hopes for the founding of an Islamic state, peasant gangs attacked Dutch officials and Javanese administrators. The government managed to suppress the rebellions. Elsewhere in the Indies, the Padri movement in Minangkabau, the Banjermasin war of 1859, and the Acheh wars of 1871–1908 all involved ʿulamaʾ-led peasant resistance to the expansion of Dutch authority and the authority of the local political elites.

The Dutch reaction to these developments only served to encourage them. By 1825 the Dutch had already identified the Muslim kiyayi as their main opponents. To counteract their influence, they attempted to ally with the local priyayi and customary chiefs, and curtail the pilgrimage, which they recognized as a principal stimulus to Indonesian resistance. The protracted Acheh wars and the massive Banten revolt finally forced a reexamination of Dutch policy. Upon the recommendation of Snouck Hurgronje, the Dutch distinguished Islam as a religion and Islam as political militancy. They decided to allow greater freedom to make the pilgrimage to Muslims who accepted Dutch rule. At the same they maintained their surveillance. Anti-Dutch political action was ruthlessly suppressed. Thus, while Islamic religious opposition did not shake Dutch rule, Islam became more deeply rooted in Indonesian rural society.

While Islamic kiyayi and peasant resistance was rooted in the traditional structures of Indonesian society, Indonesian nationalism had its origins in the late nineteenth-century reaction of the priyayi aristocracy to the consolidation of Dutch rule. The first priyayi response to the stripping away of royal authority and aristocratic privileges was a backward-looking revival of local court cultures. However, the Dutch-educated priyayi were not entirely prepared to enter passively into Dutch service. Stimulated by the Russo-Japanese war and by the Indian and Chinese nationalist movements, and threatened at home by Chinese political competition, Western-educated Indonesians banded together to promote an Indonesian cultural and political awareness.

Budi Utomo (Noble Endeavor), founded in 1908, was the first Javanese cultural association dedicated to education and the revival of the Hindu–Buddhist culture of old Java in the hope of recreating the refinement and stability which had been lost through excessive Westernization. Budi Utomo at first accepted the Dutch Ethical Policy and was loyal to the government, but in 1917 it moved from culture to politics by calling for autonomy and a parliamentary regime. A more radical Indische Partij was formed by Efi Douwes-Deckker in 1911 to represent the interests of the "Indos" of mixed

European and Indonesian descent and to present their claim for equality with Europeans. This was the first party to claim political independence for a united Indonesia. *Taman Siswa* (Garden of Learning), founded in 1922, was devoted to an educational program to restore Javanese arts and culture. The association founded some 250 schools and tried to create a community of students and teachers, a nationalist brotherhood, to symbolize the maturation of the Indonesian nation and its aspirations to independence. *Pudjangga Baru* (New Poet), founded in the 1930s, was a literary journal whose writers and readers attempted to deal with the problems of integrating Indonesian and Western values. Their ideal was to generate a national language which could express the Western content of their education.

Progressively, these cultural and educational groups became politicized, but only in the late 1920s and early 1930s did national political parties come into being. In 1927 the Indonesian Nationalist Party (P.N.I.), was formed out of a study group led by Sukarno, and was followed by other parties opposed to Dutch rule and in favor of Indonesian independence. In 1939 the federation of Indonesian political parties, G.A.P.I., was formed to give cohesion to the nationalist movement. These study clubs, educational associations and political parties represented the claims of Western-educated Indonesians to political power and Indonesian independence.

While the nationalist groups continued to operate within the framework of Dutch rule, more radical opponents to colonialism emerged. The labor union movement was established soon after the turn of the century. In 1905 a government railway workers' union was founded, followed by unions of tramway workers, customs officers, teachers, pawnshop employees, and public works and treasury officials. Radical political leadership was supplied first by the Indische Sociaal Democratische Vereeniging, founded in 1914, which introduced socialist and Communist ideas into Indonesian politics. The Communist Party of Indonesia was established in 1920. In 1925 and 1926 the Communists provoked a series of strikes in Semarang and revolts in Jakarta and other parts of Java and Sumatra. These revolts were easily crushed, and the Communist Party was declared illegal and forced underground.

Thus, the nationalist movement developed in two wings – one representing the interests of the Western-educated priyayi civil service and professional milieus and the other representing worker and radical intelligentsia ambitions for the formation of an independent socialist society. In both wings the national movement stressed secular values and the combination of the Indonesian heritage with international and Western ideals.

In the same period new forms of Islamic religious, social, and political action were born in the major ports of Sumatra, Java, and Malaya among Muslim merchants sensitive both to the pressures of the expanding colonial powers and to the currents of reformist thinking emanating from Mecca and Cairo. Singapore, a melting pot of Southeast Asian peoples, became the principal center of Islamic reformism and modernism. It harbored a large Malay population, immigrants from Minangkabau, Javanese laborers in transit to and from the rubber plantations of Malaya, and other Indonesians who passed through in the course of their pilgrimage to Mecca. Dutch restrictions on the hajj made British-ruled Singapore the major port for Indonesian pilgrims. Singapore also had significant Arab and Indian Muslim communities.

The Arab settlement was especially important. Many Arabs worked in Singapore as brokers arranging the pilgrimage traffic. Shaykhs and sayyids from Hadhramaut had a high prestige, and were respected for their religious probity. They formed a commercial elite, owned land and houses, invested in plantations and trade and had control of the batik, tobacco, and spice trades. This group built mosques, organized festivals, and worked to cultivate Arabic and Muslim cultural sophistication. The Jawi Peranakan, the offspring of Malabari Indian traders and Malay women, were also among the leaders of the cultural life of Malaya and helped generate a revival of the Malay language and an incipient Malay national consciousness. They worked as clerks, interpreters, schoolteachers, and merchants, and ranked after the Arab community in prestige and authority. In 1876 the Jawi Peranakan began to publish a Malay newspaper which was used as a teaching device in Malay schools. They sponsored the publication of Malay romances, poetry, tales, and translations of Arabic religious literature. The society for linguistic knowledge worked out Malay equivalents for English terms and absorbed Arabic words into Malay usage. Out of these efforts came a shared language and a new Malay consciousness transcending specific localities.

The Arabs, Jawi Peranakan, and Malays also sponsored the diffusion of Islamic reformism and of the Naqshbandi and Qadiri orders from Mecca and Cairo. They contributed to the development of a cosmopolitan Muslim religious consciousness no longer tied to particular localities but to a larger regional and Muslim worldwide community. In the port towns, Islam was not the religion of a village community but of mobile individuals united in an international association. From Singapore reform Islam spread throughout Southeast Asia by trade, pilgrimage, and by the movement of students, teachers, and Sufis.

Reformism was stimulated elsewhere by commerce, urbanization, and education. On Java, several Islamic movements were founded between 1905 and

1912. The most important of these educational and religious associations was Muhammadiya, which was founded in 1912 by Hajji Ahmad Dahlan for the reform of the practice of Islam and the betterment of the Muslim community. Dahlan was the son of a religious official, a pilgrim to Mecca, a mosque officer, and a trader in batik. His movement appealed to poor and middling traders operating in new economic contexts outside of the traditional social structures.

Muhammadiya espoused a pious religious life based on the duties described in the Quran and the sayings of the Prophet, but rejected the medieval Muslim legal and philosophic systems and the authority of Muslim saints in favor of ijtihad or individual reasoning in religious matters. Muhammadiya discouraged elaborate birth, circumcision, wedding, and funeral rituals, and opposed the worship of shrines, but not Sufism as such. It stressed the importance of ethics, purification of the soul, controlling base desires, and the deepening of wisdom and moral understanding. While Muhammadiya has sometimes been considered a modernist form of Islam, its primary concerns place it in the tradition of Muslim religious reform.

Muhammadiya taught also that personal virtue had to be expressed in social action. The primary effort of Muhammadiya was the creation of modern-type religious schools. While the pesantren were devoted to recitation of sacred scriptures and mystical formulae, the Muhammadiya schools taught basic Muslim religious principles, the Arabic language, Dutch, and secular subjects. They introduced a graded program of study, rationalized methods of instruction, and emphasized comprehension and reasoning rather than memorization. Muhammadiya sponsored a variety of schools, some primarily religious and some primarily secular, and attempted to adjust Muslim values to contemporary educational and social needs. By 1929 Muhammadiya had founded 64 village schools and several teacher training colleges. It also organized libraries, clinics, orphanages, hospitals, poor houses, and numerous related associations. Attached to Muhammadiya was a women's movement, and youth and scouting groups. The main function of the several Muhammadiya-related societies was *tabligh*, or evangelical teaching of the reformed Muslim faith.

Persatuan Islam, founded in west Java in 1923 by merchants led by Hajji Zamzam and Hajji Muhammad Yunus, was also dedicated to religious studies, the proper practice of Muslim rituals, and the observance of Muslim law. For this movement too the Quran and hadith were the only bases of Muslim belief and behavior, but the Quran and hadith could be adapted to new conditions by the independent judgment of qualified persons. Persatuan Islam opposed popular Indonesian religious practices such as the use of amulets and recourse to magic for healing. It opposed Sufism wherever Sufism encouraged improper rituals, saint worship, or belief in the intercession of holy-men with God. Persatuan Islam also denounced traditional Indonesian performances such as the wayang puppet theater because they represented Hindu values and encouraged the freedom of women. Though it was reformist in religious orientation, Persatuan Islam denied the need for adaptation to contemporary developments and held that Islam was inherently progressive. It also opposed secular nationalism because it represented a deification of the nation; priority belonged to the universal Muslim community. In its view, only by a return to true Muslim principles could the political power and the freedom of Indonesian and other Muslim peoples be restored. The movement founded colleges to train missionaries and published the journal *Pembela Islam*. Numerous tracts were published in standard Indonesian, and study groups were formed to educate Muslims in their religious responsibilities.

The Islamic religious and educational revival also took on political dimensions. In response to Chinese commercial competition, and Christian missionary activities in central Java, Hajji Samanhudi in 1911 formed an Islamic training association. With the aid of ʿUmar Saʿid Tjokroaminoto, he transformed his group into the *Sarekat Islam* in 1912. Tjokroaminoto soon turned the party into the premier political movement in Indonesia. The Sarekat Islam congress of 1917 declared that Islam required Indonesians to exert themselves in the faith and to avoid resignation to poverty. It made demands for the improvement of agriculture, government subsidies for education, the abolition of feudal privileges, and the extension of electoral rights to Indonesians. This combination of Islamic and political appeals made Sarekat Islam the first mass Indonesian political party. Not only middle-class and urban people but also ʿulamaʾ, villagers, and peasants supported the movement. Many peasants believed that Sarekat Islam was a harbinger of the coming of the *ratu adil*, the just prince, and the mahdi.

Minangkabau was another center for revitalized Islamic religious and social action. Minangkabau's history of Islamic reform began early in the nineteenth century with the Padri movement, which attempted to bring custom into accord with Shariʿa. The first phase in that struggle ended in Dutch rule and in compromises which redefined adat (customary law) and Shariʿa to bring them into conformity with each other. However, the issue was not put to rest. Reformist Sufis, especially of the Naqshbandi order, continued to denounce customary practices and to insist on the reform of Islam.

By the turn of the century, the economic and political impact of Dutch capitalism and the intrusion of new ideas from Singapore, Mecca, and Cairo generated renewed debate. The bearers of new ideas were called the Kaum

Muda, or Young Group. Some Kaum Muda groups concentrated on the modernization of customary law along Western and secular lines. The young Malay group (1906), Usaha (Association of Endeavor, 1912), and the Young Sumatran Union (1918) were founded to introduce modern education and to incorporate Western ideas into the old adat. Other Kaum Muda groups were oriented to Islamic reformism. Shaykh Ahmad Khatib (1855–1916) studied in Mecca, was introduced to the ideas of Muhammad ʿAbduh, and returned to raise a new generation of young Sumatran and Malayan scholars who in turn founded new schools, publications, and religious missionary movements. Shaykh Muhammad Tahir (1867–1957) also studied in Mecca, absorbed the ideas of Muhammad ʿAbduh, and founded the newspaper *al-Imam* in Singapore. *Al-Imam* tried to awaken Muslims to the need for education. It taught that the decline of Islam was due to neglect of the divine law and that submission to the Quran and hadith would uplift the lives of individual Muslims and help bring about a renaissance in the Muslim community. *Al-Imam* stressed the importance of using reason in religious matters and challenged customary beliefs and practices. It brought into public debate such religious questions as whether *talkin* prayers should be recited over graves, whether the correct procedure in prayer was to recite the *niyah* (intention) aloud or silently, and whether savings banks and cooperatives were legitimate. In the 1920s Penang became the center of reformist thought, owing to the work of Sayyid Shaykh al-Hadi, who founded the Madrasa al-Mashhor in 1919 and the Jelutong Press in 1927 to publish books on the subject of the emancipation of women and other reform issues.

The reformist schools combined a religious curriculum with a secular program of studies in history, geography, mathematics, and other modern subjects. By the 1920s there were 39 such schools and 17,000 students on Sumatra. These reformers opposed, as did their counterparts in Java and Singapore, popular Sufi practices such as celebrations of the death day of the saint, challenged adat marriage, funeral, and holy day ceremonies, and denounced the practices both of the traditional ʿulamaʾ and of the village penghulus (customary chiefs).

The movement for religious reform eventually became a challenge to the Dutch as well. Between 1918 and 1923 several efforts were made to unify the various Kaum Muda groups and channel them into political action. Radical intellectuals penetrated the Sumatran student movement to preach against capitalism and imperialism, oppose government taxes and forest policy, and call for independence both from the feudal rule of local notables and from the imperialistic rule of the Dutch. The Sumatran student groups appealed to petty traders and to smallholding peasants, and eventually provoked scattered rebellions which were put down by the Dutch in 1926 and early 1927. Thus, the Islamic movement on Minangkabau began with a religious and reformist orientation focused on correct belief and practice of Islam, and through educational and social action cultivated a political consciousness in opposition to Dutch rule and the authority of the traditional aristocracies.

The formation of several Muslim movements which emphasized religious reform, educational modernism, and political action provoked a counter-movement among the traditional ʿulamaʾ. In 1921 a Union of ʿUlamaʾ of Minangkabau was formed, and it was followed in 1926 by the Nahdatul ʿUlamaʾ (Union of ʿUlamaʾ) of Java. Nahdatul ʿUlamaʾ was built around a network of religious notables centered on the pesantren of Jombang in East Java. N.U. defended traditional religious principles, and reaffirmed the Shariʿa, the schools of law, and the Sufi practices that were at the core of their spirituality. They rejected the reformist emphasis upon the Quran and Sunna in favor of the traditional practice of Islam. The new association, however, marked an important change in the organization of traditional Javanese Islamic society. The adoption of organizational techniques borrowed from Muslim reform and nationalist movements meant the adoption of modern forms of political action. The kiyayi, who in the nineteenth century had organized through the Sufi tariqat to resist Dutch rule and priyayi administration, in the twentieth century entered the struggle over the shape of Indonesian society as a contemporary political party.

The differences between the old and new forms of Islam were manifold. The traditionalists viewed the world as unchanging; the reformers saw it as ever-changing in history. The traditionalists viewed religion as a mystical and magical disposition of mind. Prayer, fasting, and recitation were intended to create inner peace and bring about harmony between the believer and the truth. Traditional religion was oriented to ritual, to states of feeling, and to passive acceptance of reality. By contrast, the reformist position stressed active mastery of the self. The reformers defined religion in terms of individual responsibility for moral reform and for bringing into being a Muslim community adapted to contemporary conditions. Their religion was inner-directed, ethical, and intellectual. Whereas traditional religion maintained its commitment to a concept of the harmony of the individual with his community, the community with the state, and the state with the universe, reformist religion sought actively to transform the individual in society to bring about a Muslim utopia. To achieve these goals, the reformers adopted Western organizational and educational methods, accepted scientific ideas and the use of vernacular languages, and waged a vigorous campaign in the press to insinuate Islam into the social fabric. Scout movements, schools, orphanages, and hospitals were essential to making Islam an active force in society.

Ever since the 1920s, the several nationalist and Muslim parties provided ideological and political direction for Indonesian town and village communities. In parts of Java in the 1920s and 1930s the rapid growth of the sugar industry attracted Muslim and Chinese entrepreneurs, petty traders, and workers to growing towns. Muslim traders married into local landowning families and began to invest in small-scale cigarette, furniture, and other manufacturing industries. Batik merchants and itinerant peddlers, including women, also prospered. The depression of the 1930s, however, broke the economic back of these new groups. The Chinese took over the remnants of available business, and unemployed workers went into petty trade, bringing an end to middle-class economic development.

The urban administrative, commercial, and working population tended to regroup into new social units (*aliran*) built around the major religious and political movements and parties. The parties provided a basis for solidarity among uprooted middle-class and working groups. In the villages they not only provided ideological and cultural clarification, but organized such services as schools, charities, youth and women's groups, and social clubs. While many villages remained the preserve of one or another movement, others were polarized among the competing forces. Nationalist, Communist, and Muslim movements generated their own parochial followings tied to an array of social and religious activities. From the local point of view, national parties were more than ideologies. They were a new form of community which channeled everything from entertainment to political action into a single movement.

COMPROMISE AND COMPETITION: 1900–55

From 1900 to approximately 1920 Dutch policy indirectly favored the rise of the nationalist and Islamic movements. The Dutch supported education; Indonesians were employed in administration; political parties were legalized; freedom of the press was allowed. By 1917 Sarekat Islam emerged as a mass political movement and the main force in Indonesian opposition to Dutch rule, but in the course of the next decade and a half, it broke up over differences of ideology and political orientation. The rise of a socialist wing polarized the party. In 1923 the movement split; the leftists were forced out, and with them Sarekat Islam lost the mass of its followers. Sarekat Islam also lost its ascendancy over Indonesian peasants when it was challenged by Nahdatul ʿUlama². In the 1920s Sarekat Islam adopted the non-cooperation policy – a militant Islamic, anti-Communist, and anti-Dutch orientation. By the late 1920s, however, the pan-Islamic idea had failed to rally significant support, and Sarekat Islam turned to a nationalist line, changing its name to Partai Sarekat Islam Indonesia. This politically activist position led to a falling out with Muhammadiya. Muhammadiya, primarily concerned with educational and missionary activities, was willing to cooperate with the government, and its members were forced by a party decision in 1929 to choose between the two movements. In the 1930s, the Muslim movement remained divided among activist, reformist, and conservative religious wings, but the apolitical reformist Muslim position remained the most important. A single mass movement was still not possible, given the ideological and cultural divisions within Indonesian society. Nonetheless, the parallel activities of the several Muslim groups generated widespread support and created a broad base for their ultimate claim to form an independent and Muslim Indonesian state.

With the political decline of the Muslim movements, the initiative shifted to the nationalist clubs and parties. With the founding of the P.N.I. in 1927, Sukarno became the leading spokesman of Indonesian unity, independence from Holland, and the separation of state and religion. Sukarno wrote extensively on the question of Islam and the state and urged a solution resembling Ataturk's Turkey, in which Islam would be permitted as a private religion but would not be allowed to influence national politics. He thus presented a vision of Islam as a personal religion in the context of a secularized national state.

In response to the growing nationalist and Muslim opposition, the Dutch retreated from the ethical program and turned to repression and renewed centralization of power. The Dutch tried to hamper the Muslim movements by establishing state control of education, through the so-called "guru" ordinances (1905 and 1925) which required that Muslim instruction be licensed by the regents. A law of 1932 required government permission for non-state schools. Priyayi were given control over the legal administration of marriages, to the chagrin of the Muslims. Christian missionaries were supported by state subsidy for travel and schools. In 1935 the Dutch assumed the right to proscribe political parties; finally, in 1940, they banned political meetings.

In the face of nationalist competition and Dutch policies, the Muslims generated a new wave of political activism which was to last through the war years until 1955. While Muhammadiya gave priority to moral and educational reform, the Persatuan Muslimin Indonesia, founded in 1930, campaigned against imperialism and capitalism and called for Indonesian independence as an essential condition for both Islamic reform and economic prosperity. The

Partai Islam Indonesia similarly combined Muslim, anti-imperialist, and anti-capitalist slogans. This party called for reform of Islam, independence from Holland, the formation of a unified Indonesian parliamentary state, and state control of vital economic enterprises. Indonesian Muslim parties formulated new demands for a parliamentary regime which would include a ministry of Islamic affairs and in which two-thirds of the ministers would be Muslim.

The Japanese occupation (1942–45) gave tremendous encouragement to the Muslims. The Japanese undermined the old domestic aristocracy, and rapidly brought the Muslim movement under their control. While they suspended many of the political parties, they allowed Muhammadiya and Nahdatul ʿUlamaʾ to function. They established a religious affairs and propaganda office to take control of all Muslim education above the primary level. They also formed Muslim militias with the flag of crescent and rising sun to signify the identification of jihad with Japan's war against the West. Special training courses for intellectuals and kiyayis were established. In November 1943 the Japanese founded *Masjumi* to unify and coordinate the whole of the Muslim movement. Under the aegis of Masjumi the Japanese created a religious bureaucracy staffed by Muslims to connect the central administration with the villages. A Muslim coalition of middle-class merchants, rich peasants, and village ʿulamaʾ was thus mobilized to cooperate with the Japanese.

The administrative and military functions assigned to the Muslims greatly enhanced their political power and enlarged the clientele for later Muslim political action. The formation of labor and military battalions created new military and religious leaders from proletarian backgrounds. Thus, the Japanese gave the Muslims important advantages in the forthcoming struggle to determine the political and cultural principles of an independent Indonesian state.

Having destroyed the Dutch, the Japanese were in turn defeated in 1945, opening the way to Indonesian independence. On August 17, 1945, Sukarno proclaimed Indonesian independence, but the struggle to make that independence actual took five years more. With Australian and British help the Dutch attempted to regain control of the Indies; only in August 1950, under Indonesian military and United Nations political pressures, were the Dutch finally obliged to recognize an independent republic.

The government of the new republic was formed by a coalition of Muslim and nationalist parties including Masjumi, Nahdatul ʿUlamaʾ, P.N.I., and the Communist party (P.K.I.). Despite the great organizational gains made by the Muslims in the war years, they were still not in a position to wrest full control of Indonesia from the nationalists. The Muslim demands for the constitution and institutions of the new republic were only partially met. The Muslims first demanded the formation of a *Negara Islam*, a Muslim state. To Muslim conservatives this meant that most ministers would be Muslims and that a parliament of kiyayis would be formed to review legislation and pronounce on its conformity to Islamic law. To Muslim reformers it meant a general proclamation of the principle that the state was in accord with Islamic law. The Muslims were able to insert into the Jakarta charter the stipulation that it was "an obligation for the Muslims to carry out the Shariʿa." The nationalists, however, were in favor of the *pancasila*, or five principles, which included belief in God, nationalism, humanitarianism, democracy, and social justice. The nationalist program pointedly omitted any direct reference to Muslim symbols and emphasized instead secular concepts of society. In the subsequent constitution of the Republic, the pancasila was enshrined as the symbol of the new order and the phrases identifying the new state as Muslim were omitted.

To satisfy the Muslim interests, the constitution provided for the formation of a Ministry of Religion. The ministry was commissioned to protect religious freedom and to maintain harmonious relations among the different religious communities, but its primary purpose was to administer Muslim religious affairs, including marriage and divorce, endowments, mosques, and the pilgrimage. Its Bureau of Religious Education managed government-sponsored religious schools; the Bureau of Religious Propaganda distributed books and pamphlets and otherwise promoted Islamic missionary efforts. The Bureau of Religious Justice regulated Shariʿa courts. The new ministry was a vast bureaucracy apparatus which linked the central government to the villages and provided an important source of patronage and influence for the Muslim political parties. It satisfied Muslim interests in having state support for Islam and encouraged hopes for the eventual realization of a Muslim state.

On the outer islands, however, various Muslim groups refused to accept the compromise and determined to fight for the immediate realization of an Islamic state. During World War II Sumatra had gone through a revolution which destroyed the power of the feudal chiefs in Acheh, Minangkabau and the East Coast residency. In Acheh the ʿulamaʾ defeated the local uleebalang aristocracy and consolidated its own political position. Muslim groups in the Celebes and Kalimantan also insisted on the immediate formation of an Islamic state. In some of these cases, the concern for an Islamic state may have been a front to win the autonomy of outer islands from the central government on Java.

The most important of these rebel Islamic movements was the Dar ul-Islam, founded by a former Sarekat Islam activist named Kartosuwirjo. In 1940 Kartosuwirjo founded the Suffah Institute as a propaganda and training center to produce cadres for Muslim missionary work and for the Muslim military unit, *Hizbullah*, organized by the Japanese under Masjumi auspices. In 1945 he was put in charge of Masjumi military units in western Java. He fought against the Dutch in 1947 and in 1948 he refused to accept the Renville Agreement truce between Indonesian and Dutch forces, resigned from the party, determined to continue the military struggle on his own, and declared himself imam of an Islamic provisional government, Negara Islam Indonesia. The Islamic state was declared to be based upon the Quran, and was in constitutional form a republic with an elected parliament. The imam, elected by the parliament, was the head of state. The new state proclaimed that it would guarantee equality before the law, the right to a decent standard of living, and freedom of worship, speech, and assembly for all citizens. All important civil and military positions were reserved to Muslims. Armed struggle against the Dutch and later against the Indonesian Republic continued until it was finally suppressed in 1962.

The defeat of Dar ul-Islam transferred the struggle over the political identity of Indonesia to the political sphere. From 1950 to 1955 the P.N.I. and Masjumi quarreled over the role of Islam and of the Communists. But the Muslims were also divided. In 1952 Nahdatul ʿUlamaʾ withdrew from Masjumi and became a separate political party. There were divisions between Kaum Muda and Kaum Tua and Muhammadiya and Nahdatul ʿUlamaʾ religious orientations. The unresolved struggles among the political parties led to a national election in 1955, which proved a decisive event in Indonesian history. The political campaign led to an intense struggle for power as each party attempted to secure the support of influential officials, wealthy peasants, and village chiefs for its cause. In some cases, whole villages went to a single party, but in most cases the competition divided the villages between factions led by the traditional headman and those led by the kiyayi. The P.N.I. and P.K.I. appealed mainly to villages led by former aristocrats, landowners, and spirit healers. The Muslim parties appealed to different traditionalist and reformist village constituencies. Thus, village communities were transformed into politically organized aliran. The elections of 1955 consolidated a new form of Indonesian ideological and social organization, and yet preserved a profound continuity with the Indonesian past.

More immediately the election results were a decisive check to the campaign for the formation of an Islamic state. On Java the vote was split among P.N.I., Masjumi, N.U., and P.K.I. On the outer islands, in the strong Muslim areas of Sumatra, south Kalimantan, and north Sulawesi, the vote was substantially Muslim but it was divided between the reformers and the conservatives. In the national tally as a whole, however, the Muslim parties combined polled only 42.5 percent of the vote, and fell short of the majority essential to form a parliamentary Islamic state. From 1955 to the present the Muslim parties have struggled to adjust to the fact that though Indonesia is overwhelmingly a Muslim society, the Muslim parties are a political minority.

INDONESIA FROM 1955 TO THE PRESENT

With the defeat of Muslim aspirations to create an Islamic state, control of the state was taken over by President Sukarno and the army. In 1957 Sukarno attempted to bypass the parliamentary system by creating a Guided Democracy. He proposed the formation of a cabinet including the Communists and a national council to represent worker, peasant, youth, and regional interest groups. The shift in power created widespread apprehension of Communist influence, provoked fears of Javanese domination of the outer islands, and frustrated Muslim ambitions for regional autonomy. Army leaders on Sumatra and Sulawesi and Muslim spokesmen representing Masjumi, including Muhammad Natsir, the leader of the party, opposed the new program and formed a revolutionary government of the Republic of Indonesia. The revolutionary government was defeated, and in July 1959 Sukarno dissolved the constituent assembly and declared a return to the constitution of 1945, which provided for a strong presidential regime.

With the defeat of the Muslim and outer island opposition, President Sukarno devised new institutions which gave a leading role to the army and the civil service. Major sections of the economy were nationalized and the army took control of important industries. Authoritarian controls were set up over political parties, labor unions, and newspapers. The new regime was buttressed by a new ideological program called *Nasakom*, in which Sukarno attempted to synthesize nationalism, religion, and Communism as the symbols of a highly centralized regime and centrally planned economy. In 1960 Masjumi was disbanded, and its leaders arrested and imprisoned. Nahdatul ʿUlamaʾ, however, maintained close ties with Sukarno. While Masjumi represented outer island reformist, urban, and commercial interests, Nahdatul ʿUlamaʾ represented a Javanese peasant constituency. It was willing to accept Sukarno's authority, with its strong overtones of traditional Javanese statecraft, and suspend the ultimate goal of an Islamic state in return for control over the Ministry of Religion and for the protection of its political position in the Javanese countryside. While Masjumi was broken because of its ideological demands, Nahdatul ʿUlamaʾ was able to retain political and tactical flexibility.

The new regime soon alienated important forces in the society. Sukarno alienated the intellectual and artistic elites by the suppression of cultural and political expression. He furthermore brought the country to virtual economic ruin as a result of excessive spending and the accumulation of staggering foreign debts. The new regime also gave the Communists an important opportunity to consolidate their political position. The Communists threatened army control of the corporations nationalized in 1957 and 1958, and embarrassed the army in its relations with its main supplier, the United States. The party succeeded in bringing about a land reform program in 1963, and then attempted by direct action to expropriate the estates of large landowners, mostly belonging to P.N.I. and to N.U. The Communist challenge, however, provoked an alliance between the conservative Muslim parties and the army. In 1964 and 1965 there were direct clashes between Communist and Muslim youth gangs. In late 1965 an attempted Communist coup triggered off massive civil war in east and central Java and the slaughter of innumerable Communists.

With the defeat of the Communists, General Suharto established a new military regime at the end of 1965, edged Sukarno out of power, and assumed the presidency in 1966. General Suharto came to power on the basis of a coalition of Indonesian army officers, Islamic community organizations, and Protestant and Catholic minorities, with the support of the professional and bureaucratic middle class and the Westernized academic intelligentsia. Upon coming to power he undertook to reorganize the army and to develop a coherent national economic policy with the help of advisers educated in the United States. He adopted a free-enterprise program of development and brought inflation under control. He also allowed academic and artistic freedom of expression. The Suharto regime has taken a strong secular cultural line, with emphasis upon the pancasila as the basic principles of state and society.

However, the Suharto regime moved further and further toward coercion. The government political party, called Golkar, manipulated the national elections of 1971 and won 63 percent of the vote. Golkar drew its support from former Communist, P.N.I., and Masjumi supporters. Only the Nahdatul ʿUlamaʾ maintained its strength in east Java. The 1977 elections confirmed the continuing dominance of Golkar, but still more coercive tactics were necessary to maintain the government position.

Throughout this period, the Suharto regime kept close control over the Muslim movements and parties. The army resisted the effort to rehabilitate Masjumi and refused to forgive Masjumi for its role in the revolutionary government of 1958. It remained suspicious of Masjumi's insistence on an Islamic ideological program. The army believed that militant Islam introduced religious concerns into politics, divided the nation, and distracted it from the problems of modernization. Muslim insistence on the readoption of the Jakarta Charter of 1945, which gave Islam a larger place in public life, and Muslim insistence that the state enforce Islamic religious laws kept alive army fears that Muslims would use their mass support to control the state. Nonetheless, in 1968 President Suharto permitted the formation of the Partai Muslimin Indonesia on condition that all former Masjumi leaders were excluded from the executive of the new party. In 1969 the government also established its own center for Indonesian-Islamic *daʿwah*, or Muslim missionary activities, to take away the fire of the independent Muslim missions. The government generally succeeded in suppressing militant and reformist Islamic groups.

Nahdatul ʿUlamaʾ, by contrast, made the transition to the new order with relative ease. N.U. is still basically concerned with religious practice rather than political opposition, and has always cooperated with the government through the Ministry of Religion and through ʿulamaʾ councils in Acheh, west Java, and west Sumatra. In the elections of 1971, Nahdatul ʿUlamaʾ obtained 21 percent of the vote. However, the position of N.U. was weakened in 1972 and 1973 by the appointment of a reformist Muslim as the Minister of Religion and by the creation of a new Muslim party to be called the United Development Party. P.N.I., N.U. and other smaller Muslim parties were subsumed in the new organization, which was deprived of an Islamic name and of an Islamic identifying symbol. For a time young N.U. activists expressed opposition to the government, but N.U. congresses have accepted the pancasila, without reference to Islam, as the basic principles of Indonesian society. At the local level, however, the ʿulamaʾ remain a prominent political force.

The policy of the Sukarno and Suharto governments toward the Muslim movements was an echo of the policies introduced by the Dutch toward the end of the nineteenth century. The Dutch distinguished between the religious and the political aspects of Islam, tolerating the former and repressing the latter. Following the same line of thought, the Javanese military and bureaucratic elite has broken the political power of the Muslim parties; only Nahdatul ʿUlamaʾ, which is willing to cooperate with secular regimes, has maintained its influence.

Not only have Muslim political ambitions been checked, but Muslim cultural and political identity has been challenged by nationalist secular ideologies and by the revival of traditional Javanese mysticism. The pancasila principles stand for an Indonesian and Javanese alternative to Islam. Under the banner of secularism the Indonesian state began to encroach upon the areas reserved to Islamic law. The marriage reform bill of 1974 proposed secular inheritance and adoption laws in competition with Shariᶜa. In reaction Muslim courts have resisted internal modernization and have not gone through their own process of reform, as have Muslim courts in Middle Eastern countries. In Indonesia, as in India, Muslims have been more concerned with resisting state interference than in making legal reforms. In the absence of a strong internal push for reforms, Muslim judges are poorly trained, lack authority, and suffer from the competition of civil courts.

A second challenge came from the rising importance of Kebatinan or Javanese mystical groups. The 1965 anti-Communist civil war helped revive religious activity in Java, since religious affiliation became necessary to avoid the suspicion of belonging to the Communist party. Kebatinan groups began to claim that their practices constituted a religion in the same sense as Christianity, Hinduism, or Islam. Kebatinan supporters also tried to identify Javanese mysticism with the pancasila. The mystical groups were attempting to become a new national religion. Equally important was the threat of Christian proselytizing. The government allowed Catholics and the World Council of Churches to build schools and hospitals, though Indonesian law forbids direct missionary activities among people who already adhere to Hinduism, Buddhism, or Islam. Thus, the exclusion of Islamic groups from political power has legitimized the drift away from Muslim identity.

Despite these political and cultural setbacks, the basic strength of the Muslim movements remains considerable. The Ministry of Education supervises a nationwide bureaucracy and has had considerable success in promoting Muslim education and publications. Under the direction of Mahmud Yunus, the Ministry devised a comprehensive Islamic school program including six-year elementary, four-year intermediate, and four-year senior high school education. Religious instruction was added to the curriculum of all government schools. An Islamic State University, founded in 1951, was consolidated into the State Institute of Islamic Religion in 1960, with faculties of theology, law, education, and humanities. Since 1960 religion has been a compulsory subject at college and university levels. The Ministry of Religion supervises innumerable madrasas and pesantrens and has helped them reform their curricula.

The second feature of Islamic strength in Indonesia is the continuing importance of the rural ᶜulamaᵓ. In west Java and Sumatra, the kiyayi exert substantial influence upon family, agricultural, and other village affairs, apart from strictly religious matters. Through ʿulamaʾ and school networks, regional councils, national religious parties, and the Ministry of Religion the kiyayi exert considerable influence on the government. The rural ʿulamaʾ are at once religious scholars and national politicians.

A third factor in Islamic strength is the continuing vitality of the reformist and modernist movements. Muhammadiya remains an important force in providing a concept of community and a model of an ongoing Islamic society. Muhammadiya gives clear and simple guides to personal conduct and espouses an ideal of rational, efficient, and puritanical behavior. As of 1970 Muhammadiya claimed over 2,000 branches and an active membership numbered in millions. This basic strength, however, was not sufficient to give the several Muslim movements control of the Indonesian polity.

The Muslim activists have responded to this dilemma in a variety of ways. Frustrated since 1955 in their ideological objectives, frustrated in their economic interests owing to government controls over the economy, and frustrated by the high degree of centralization of power on Java and the lack of autonomy for the outer islands, many Muslims have intensified their demand for the formation of an Islamic state. A sense of urgent threat stimulates militant Muslim concerns with such symbolic issues as a declaration of commitment to Islamic principles. There is always the latent possibility of serious political or guerrilla action.

Another Muslim response to the Sukarno and Suharto regimes has been to avoid political action, and to attempt to bring an Islamic society into being by moral, religious, and social action. With the defeat of political hopes, Muhammadiya and other Muslim groups have turned from political action to religious reform, publication, education, and training for leadership. In 1963 the first of a series of new organizations was formed to organize Muslim daʿwah or missionary activities. In 1967 the *Dewan Daʿwah Islamiyah Indonesia* was sponsored by Muhammadiya and former members of Masjumi to distribute literature, to preach to public meetings, to organize mosque and library construction, and to sponsor irrigation and forestry projects. The Congress of ʿUlamaʾ of Acheh was formed to see that Muslims worshiped properly and maintained Islamic precepts in family and business matters. The general goal of these movements is to imbue Indonesians with Islamic values, strengthen the brotherhood of Muslims, and progressively convert nominal Muslims into dedicated and active participants in a Muslim community. For Muslims with this orientation, political activity has declined in favor of an upsurge of prayer, fasting, and other religious practices.

Other Muslims have responded to political and cultural pressures, however, by accommodating to the secularization of state and society. Muslim politicians are willing to put aside ideological objectives and operate in a pluralistic political system as one group among many. For these politicians, who have wide business, regional, or professional contacts, Islam is only one element of identity. Intellectuals have taken a similar approach by espousing withdrawal from competition for political influence and distinguishing worldly from spiritual values. This new form of Islamic modernism was represented in student groups such as the Indonesian Students' Association (H.M.I.) whose 1971 charter accepts the secularization of society and the concept of Islam as a personal religion. Its main spokesman was Nurcholis Majid, who argued that worldly matters are not regulated by divine law. For thinkers in this vein, the Quran serves to inspire and motivate behavior, but does not provide precise rules for the organization of daily life. Thus, Majid saw Islam as a private belief system rather than a communal and political one, and stressed cooperation with non-Islamic groups. Similar views have been expressed by other youth movement leaders. The younger generation may have begun to accommodate to political realities by making religion a matter of personal conviction, but in 1981 the military regime alienated the students' association. To express its dissent from authoritarian rule and the pancasila ideology, the students' association reaffirmed a concept of Islam both as a personal religion and as the basis of the sociopolitical order.

Muslim religious groups, then, are very diverse. Some maintain their primary interest in religious reform, the primacy of the Quran, and obedience to Islamic law. Some are also committed to the creation of an Islamic state. Others stress accommodation to modern science, technology, business, and even political administration. Still others are prepared to distinguish private religious standards from public life. Some are militant; others accept the political reality of a governing regime. The majority remain committed to the educational, economic, and social consolidation of Muslim community life and maintain flexibility in their pursuit of political goals. For the Islamic reformist movements generally, the several levels of religious, social, and political life should ideally be integrated in an Islamic state, but each level may be pursued independently when others are frustrated.

BRITISH MALAYA AND INDEPENDENT MALAYSIA

The consolidation of the British empire in Malaya at the turn of the twentieth century also entailed the creation of centralized states and a capitalist economy

concentrating upon agricultural and extractive industries. Sugar was introduced in the 1830s, coffee in the 1880s, and rubber at the end of the century.
Pineapples and oil palm became important in the first decade of the twentieth
century. Tin mining was important in Perak and Selangor. Gold and iron were
also mined. The mining industry was generally owned by Chinese and worked
by Chinese labor. Penang and Singapore became the main ports for the export
of Malayan tin and the import of Chinese and other foreign laborers. By 1910,
Malaya like India, was exporting raw materials to Britain and Europe.

These developments had profound effects upon the organization of religious
life and the relationship between Malay states and Muslim communities. In the
traditional era, the Sultans were the foremost religious and political functionaries, and symbolized the Muslim nature of Malayan society. They had,
however, a very limited role in the actual administration of Muslim law,
education, and worship. The village ʿulamaʾ were the principal representatives
of Islam. They maintained worship, taught Islamic lore, presided over ceremonies of marriage and death, arbitrated disputes, healed the sick, controlled
communal property, and collected Islamic taxes. Their influence was consolidated by marriages with other ʿulamaʾ and wealthy landlord families. Despite the occasional appointment of a qadi to the central administration, the
ʿulamaʾ were basically individual functionaries not subject to state control.
Though they belonged to the Shafiʿi law school, and often to a mystic order,
there was no central religious organization. The Sufi orders may have facilitated some standardization of religious views and education, but they did
not actually create an organized or collective body of religious teachers.

British domination drastically changed this system. When British residents
consolidated the apparatus of centralized government, they deprived Malay
Sultans of their effective authority in all matters except those bearing on
religion and custom. The Sultans, therefore, tried to strengthen their influence
in these areas as the only likely expression of their authority, and tried to
centralize Islamic religious organization and extend state control over village
religious life. As early as 1880, a state *kathi* was appointed in Perak. Between
1884 and 1904, Raja Muda Sulayman, the ruler of Selangor, codified marriage
and divorce laws, appointed qadis, and enacted Muslim penalties in civil and
criminal matters. In Kelantan there was similarly an official reorganization of
Islamic religious life due to local fears for the safety of Muslim tradition.
Under the combined pressures of Britain and Siam, between 1888 and 1894,
an official, styled *Maha Menteri*, insisted on the universal observance of Shariʿa,
required Muslims to attend the Friday prayers, provided for public readings
of hadith, and centralized control of the state over local imams. Under his

administration the government began to take a portion of the charity taxes and a constabulary was created to enforce religious norms. Between 1905 and 1909, however, the British strengthened the central government of Kelantan, favored civil courts at the expense of Shariᶜa courts, and removed the imams from revenue administration. The mufti, however, was given control of the village mosques and revenues. He was made a salaried member of the government and head of the Muslim religious court system.

In 1915 a *Majlis Ugama* (Religious Council) was created to take full authority over religious courts and village mosques. The Majlis also took control of three-fifths of the zakat revenues and four-fifths of the head tax ordinarily collected by village religious leaders. In later years the Majlis sponsored education in English, Arabic, and Malay, prepared texts and translations, and otherwise provided state leadership for the reform of Islamic religious life. Throughout the Malay peninsula, centralized administration of religious affairs and the creation of chief qadis, councils, and Shariᶜa committees brought Islamic legal, educational, ritual and financial affairs under state control. State control gave a strong conservative bias to Islamic affairs but proved to be a factor for political stability until the 1950s.

The changes introduced by British imperial controls and by the development of the Malayan economy further stimulated the Kaum Muda or reformist and modernist Muslim movement. The rise of the Kaum Muda was a grave challenge to both state and village Muslim elites. Traveled merchants and students came back to their villages to challenge the authority of local imams and Sufis and the state administration of Islam. In the late 1920s journals produced by students in Cairo broached the issues of pan-Islamic and pan-Malayan unity and anti-colonialism. In the 1930s the Kaum Muda became politically militant; the very name came to imply nationalist opposition to foreign rule. In response to this challenge several Malay states censored or banned publications and forbade the teaching of Islam without the permission of the Sultans. Religious officials condemned the new views.

In the 1920s and 1930s the initiative passed to secular nationalists. The English-educated scions of the dominant Malay aristocracy, motivated by fear of rising Chinese influence, formed Malay associations. Many of these associations did not necessarily challenge the authority of the Sultans or of the British, but called upon them to protect Malay privileges against Chinese competition; they laid claim to future leadership in Malayan politics. Other intelligentsia, however, began to speak against British rule and against the established aristocracy. The graduates of the Sultan Idris Training College, often of lower-class origin, strongly influenced by left-wing Indian nationalism, formed the *Kesatu Melayu Muda* in 1938 as the vehicle of their anti-British and anti-aristocratic program.

The nationalist movement was relatively little developed in the inter-war years, in part because the Malay aristocracy was relatively content with and dependent upon British control, and in part becase the 1920s were relatively prosperous. The availability of jobs for educated Malays in the Civil Service inhibited the formation of nationalist parties. The hostilities among Malays, Chinese, and Indians also made it difficult to crystallize a Malayan national movement conceived in territorial rather than in communal terms. In the 1920s and 1930s, the absence of basic economic and political changes affecting the mass of the population and weaknesses in political organization made it impossible to crystallize mass support for opposition to British and aristocratic Malay rule. Thus, opposition was limited to very small groups of modernist Muslims and modern-educated Malays.

The years following World War II brought profound changes to Malayan political life, as a result not of nationalist opposition to British rule, but of the devolution of British authority to the Malay aristocracy and the formation of an independent Malayan state governed by its traditional elites. Independent Malaya had its origins in 1946, with British proposals to create a Malayan union of the federated and unfederated Malay states, Singapore, Malacca, and Penang. The British proposed to bypass the Sultanates, set up a central government for the whole of the region, and give immigrant Chinese and Indian communities access to political power. These proposals were bitterly opposed by the Malay aristocracy, who in 1946 formed the United Malay National Organization. The strong resistance led the British to modify their proposals in 1948 in favor of a Federation of Malaya which preserved the separate existence of the several Malay states and guaranteed the supremacy of Malay interests.

This federation, however, was attacked by the Malayan Communist party, largely supported by Chinese workers. The Malayan Communist party had organized anti-Japanese resistance in the 1940s; after the war it launched a guerrilla movement against the new federation and the continued British influence which it implied. In reaction the United Malay National Organization, the Malayan Chinese Association, and the Malayan Indian Association allied. In 1957 an independent Malayan state was formed with the support of Malay officials, Chinese merchants, and Indian intellectuals under the leadership of Tunku ʿAbd al-Rahman. Under the new constitution, the dominance of Malays in education and the state bureaucracy and the dominance of non-Malays in the economy was confirmed. Islam was declared the official religion of Malaya, but freedom of worship was guaranteed. A ten-year grace period was given before Malay was to replace English, Chinese, and Tamil in state schools. In 1963 the federation of Malaya was reorganized to include North Borneo and Singapore (though Singapore withdrew in 1965) and the extended federation was officially renamed Malaysia.

In independent Malaysia, Islam continued to be an important issue for state policy. In the Federation period religion was a local concern, and most Malay states maintained a department of religious affairs involved in mosque construction, enforcement of moral and criminal codes, and the collection of alms taxes. Teaching heretical doctrines was punishable, and laws were passed to penalize individuals for failure to attend Friday prayers or keep the fasts. In 1957 independence gave the Federal Government some role in religious matters. Islam was made the official religion of the Federation. Malays received preferential treatment in the distribution of scholarships, licenses in certain businesses, and positions in public service. Schools were required to give Muslim religious instruction when there was a minimum number of Muslim students.

Despite the close association of the Malay states with Islam, an Islamic opposition developed in Kelantan and Trengganu. The Pan-Malayan Islamic party became the chief spokesman for Muslim communal hostility to the Chinese and Indians, and for an Islamic state to implement Islamic law. In Kelantan, P.M.I.P. rallied strong support from a coalition of village imams and religious leaders who were resisting centralized administration and the loss of tax authority, and young nationalist radicals and small peasant landowners who were hurt by increasing rents, falling prices, and the threat of losing their land. For these peasants and local elites, P.M.I.P.'s Islamic orientation symbolized not only economic concerns but anxiety over losing an Islamic way of life that depended upon a combination of ownership of land and Muslim religious authority. The appeal to Islam legitimized the defense of worldly interests by invoking collective solidarity and moral principles; it dignified the struggle to protect the peasant way of life by invoking a moral vision of a society grounded in justice – justice identified with peasant and village interests. The rhetoric of P.M.I.P. thus fused class interests with higher moral and social concerns.

P.M.I.P.'s success was telling. In 1959, it defeated the Alliance coalition in Kelantan and Trengganu, and built up the apparatus of Islamic administration under its own control. It strengthened the offices of qadi and mufti and suppressed immoral activities and competing religious sects. In response to the growth of P.M.I.P., the United Malay National Organization tried to bolster its own religious position. U.M.N.O. attempted to recruit religious leaders and pledged itself to promote Islamic interests. Using the powers of the state it offered, or threatened to withhold, support for Muslim projects such as new mosques. However, this tactic was turned against U.M.N.O. and was criticized as a misuse of Islam for self-interested political purposes.

Still more important were the implications of the struggle for Malayan national politics. P.M.I.P. represented a claim for Malay dominance over non-Malay minorities; U.M.N.O.'s movement toward an Islamic position threatened to undermine the coalition with Chinese and Indian groups. Also, throughout the 1960s, Malays reinforced their position in education and the Civil Service and began to demand a larger role in the national economy. Young Malay leaders claimed support for Malay state capitalism, and raised the question of whether Malayan society would be Muslim or pluralistic in ideological orientation. The elections of 1969 increased the pressures on the dominant parties. The P.M.I.P. gained in strength, and Chinese radicals attacked the complacent attitude of the Malayan Chinese Association toward their deteriorating situation and demanded equality for Chinese. The balance of power broke down into communal riots in 1969.

In reaction an emergency regime was installed. The new national front included much the same conservative forces. Again it attempted to maintain some balance among the communities, and yet to satisfy Malay economic grievances. A new economic policy, focused on the expansion of government investment and public enterprises, and financed by foreign capital and export earnings from petroleum, rubber, timber, and palm oil, was instituted in the 1970s; it aimed at promoting Malay involvement in the economy. Its goal was 30 percent Malay ownership and employment in Malaysian businesses, and the formation of a state-capitalist Malay economic elite.

These policies sparked renewed Muslim opposition. In 1972 P.M.I.P., under the new name of Partai Islam, was drawn into the national front and was politically domesticated. The decline of P.M.I.P. as a spokesman for a radical Islamic position led to the rise of *dakwah* (missionary and educational movements). White-collar workers, teachers and students, usually of secular educational background, became increasingly conscious of the corruption of their society and the need for Muslim reforms. Attending lectures, adopting Muslim dress, calling for a return to the guidance of the Quran and personal morality, they denounced the West as the principal source of evil. They also appealed to Malay ethnic chauvinism. The Islamic revival sentiment spawned three major groups. The Malay Muslim Youth League (A.B.I.M.), founded in 1971, led by Anwar Ibrahim, espoused reform on the individual level to bring practice into accord with the Quran, and reform on the social level to bring about a just Muslim collective order. The League was dedicated to the Islamization of the individual, the family, the umma, and the state, and the education of a God-fearing Malaysian youth. A second dakwah group is Darul Arqam, which sponsors cooperatives, workshops, clinics, and schools and stresses independence through economic activity such as agriculture and small-scale manufacturing. Darul Arqam is dedicated to living by Quranic and Arabic customs, including the segregation of the sexes. The Tabligh, which has its origin in India, is a preaching movement which appeals in Malaysia to well-educated people. These activist groups, fundamentalist in religious orientation, reformist in political affairs, operate in a context in which the assertion of Islamic religious and communal interests threatens to upset the delicate balances which preserve the cohesion of the Malaysian state.

The U.M.N.O.-led Malaysian government has responded to dakwah by attempting to coopt it. In 1982 Anwar Ibrahim accepted a place in the party, and the government declared its desire to absorb Islamic values. It competes for Muslim support through the Muslim Welfare League, which stresses the importance of economic modernization. The government also lends its support to a purely secular a-religious Malay nationalist movement, *Bumiputera* (Indigenous Sons of the Earth), which attempts to cultivate an ethnic Malay consciousness committed to technical and economic modernization. Some Muslim groups accept the government's response as reasonably favorable to Islamic interests, but others call for a rejection of government gestures of good will and for the total implementation of an Islamic order. In their view the conflict between an Islamic, and a secular, capitalist, and nationalist system is fundamental.

Thus, in the present political situation, the regime hovers between the need to cultivate Malay support and the need to maintain the collaboration of the Chinese. The more it stresses Islam the more it coopts the Malay-Muslim opposition, but the more it threatens the substantial non-Malay populations. Correspondingly, the dakwah movement hovers between challenge and collaboration. Its religious ideology does not represent a radical opposition to the established elites, but rather a debate over guiding values and symbols. As the Islamic discourse is adopted by politicians, ʿulamaʾ, Muslim activists, and others, it becomes more diffused as the basis of Malay political identity, but less specific as a political program.

In sum, the structures of contemporary Southeast Asian societies represent a coming together of the historic institutional and cultural patterns of the region and the influences generated by Dutch and British colonial rule. In the nineteenth century the Dutch and the British introduced radical economic and political changes. These changes, in the long run, awakened the conflict, in modern versions, between Southeast Asian secular and Muslim identities. Dutch rule provoked rural Muslim religious opposition. Dutch economic and trade policies stimulated Muslim merchants to create the Islamic modernist movements. Dutch educational and administrative measures were conducive to the formation of priyayi-led nationalist and Communist movements. The division of Indonesian forces reflected the historic divisions between those people who saw the world in Javanese and Indonesian cultural terms and those who viewed it in Muslim terms. The twentieth-century history of Indonesia is the history of the revived struggle of Islam against other forms of Indonesian culture.

In this struggle, the Muslims have, for the time being, lost their bid to determine the religious and ideological direction of Indonesian society. While the mass of the Indonesian population is nominally Muslim, the majority is not prepared to make Islamic norms the guiding rule of daily existence or to give political power to the committed Muslims. In Malaysia, as in Indonesia, the Muslim political challenge has also for the time being been checked and Islamic missionary reformist and political action has been turned into dakwah movements to raise Muslim consciousness and to consolidate Muslim religious practice. In Indonesia and Malaysia Muslims form the great majority of the population, but the commitment to an ideal Islamic state remains a minority aspiration.

CHAPTER 29

INNER ASIA UNDER RUSSIAN AND CHINESE RULE

By the end of the nineteenth century the Muslim populations of Inner Asia had come under Russian and Chinese rule. Like the Portuguese, the British, the French, the Germans, and the Dutch, the Russians and the Chinese became rulers of Muslim peoples. In their cases, however, colonial expansion took place on territories contiguous with the imperial homelands and were not regarded as foreign domains which would eventually win their independence but as integral parts of conquering empires. From the Russian and Chinese points of view the "colonial" problem took the form of a "minority" problem. How best could Inner Asian peoples be governed and eventually assimilated into the body politic of imperial and then Soviet Russian, and Chinese, societies? From the Muslim point of view the problem became how to define Muslim identity in the face of pressures for assimilation into a foreign civilization. Nowhere in the Muslim world has colonialism had a more profound and lasting effect.

TSARIST RULE AND JADID

The first stages of Russian rule in the nineteenth century paralleled other colonial situations. The Russian conquests gave Inner Asia a new territorial and administrative organization. The Russians dismantled the Muslim states and divided the region into two large governorates – one for the Kazakh steppes and one for the territory which would henceforth be known as Central Asia or Russian Turkestan. Autonomous vassal states remained at Bukhara and Khiva.

The Russians were at first favorable to Muslim religious organizations. In Bukhara, a highly organized, state-supported religious establishment retained its economic and social cohesion. Muslim education continued to be the preserve of the *maktab* (elementary Quran school) and the madrasa. The supervisors and teachers were appointed by the local rulers. The Shaykh al-Islam and the qadis were responsible for the supervision of the schools. Students and faculty received stipends from waqfs, and graduates usually went on to take positions as teachers, imams, muftis, and judges. Muslim holy-men continued to function among tribal and rural peoples. The veneration and visitation of shrines remained a central aspect of Inner Asian Muslim worship.

In territories under direct Russian rule, the Tsars actually promoted Muslim religious organizations in order to bring them under their control. In 1788 Catherine established the first Muslim religious administration at Ufa for European and Siberian Muslims. Another "muftiat" was organized in the Crimea in 1794. In 1872 separate Sunni and Shiʿi Boards were established in Transcaucasia. The Russian authorities appointed the Shiʿi Shaykh al-Islam and Sunni mufti, the qadis, and the heads of religious assemblies. The Tsar's administration regulated the appointment of muftis to local mosques (leaving many of them vacant), paid their salaries, supervised their activities, and required them to be politically loyal. The regime also supervised Muslim publications. Thus the Tsars encouraged the formation of a Muslim administrative hierarchy, and in principle brought it under state control. The Tsarist policy was similar to that of the Muslim rulers of Bukhara and the Ottoman empire, save that it was carried out under the auspices of a non-Muslim regime.

However, the jurisdiction of the state-ʿulamaʾ establishments was limited. In rural and nomadic areas qadis were appointed by the Khans but they had only a limited impact on the application of the Shariʿa to inheritance, land, water, and family problems. ʿUlamaʾ and schools were of secondary importance. Independent Sufi holy-men, called *ishans*, held the allegiance of the populace, and espoused a form of Muslim belief centered upon veneration of saints expressed in pilgrimages and festivals which combined Muslim and shamanistic practices. In Turkmenistan, for example, the people were organized by lineage and tribal affiliation; and venerated Sufis acted as intermediaries among the warring tribes and between the Khans and the tribes. Sometimes Sufis were the leaders of Turkmen rebellions against Iranian or Khivan authority. Sufis also served as caretakers of holy places, teachers, cemetery directors, intermediaries with dead saints, and practitioners of folk medicine. The ishans did not own property in land or water rights, but earned their living by selling talismans and amulets and by receiving payments for religious performances.

Most striking in Turkmen society were the evliads or holy lineages believed to descend from the Prophet and the first four Caliphs. The descendants of Muhammad and of the Caliphs ʿUthman and ʿAli by Muhammad's daughters, called sayyids, and the descendants of Abu Bakr and ʿUmar, called khwajas, were believed to have inherited the religious powers of their holy ancestors. The lineages in fact descended from intermediary Sufi masters. For example, Gezli Ata, the likely founder of the Ata lineage, was a fourteenth-century Sufi connected with the Yasavi order. In Turkmenistan, as in Egypt, Morocco, and many other places in the Muslim world, Sufi allegiance and prophetic lineage were combined. These holy lineages were considered inviolable; they could not be plundered. They were believed to possess shamanistic powers capable of driving out evil spirits. Their dhikr ceremonies effected spirit cures and were marked by trances and frenzies. Veneration for the holy lineages by ordinary Turkmens was similar to the pre-Islamic cult of ancestors.

In general, the creation of a Russian imperial administration, the settlement of Russian garrisons, the opening of the region to Russian trade, and the introduction of Russian education and cultural policies led to profound changes. The implications of Russian rule, however, were different in each of the regions they controlled, depending upon the local objectives of Russian policy, and the nature of the local Muslim societies.

In Turkmenistan Russian occupation led to important changes in the religious structure. The Russians pacified Turkmen feuds, encouraged private property in land, promoted a shift to sedentary life, and thus undermined the need for tribal solidarity and religious mediation. At the same time mosques, qadi courts, schools, and pilgrimage became more common. With sedentarization and the centralization of political power, even under infidel auspices, there was a shift from the mediating role of Sufis to an organized leadership of the ʿulamaʾ type. This was similar to the changes in Morocco and India, where the introduction of European rule reduced the authority of rural Sufis in favor of the ʿulamaʾ.

In the Kazakh regions, the Russians attempted to break up the old social structure and to implant a colonial society. The introduction of a market economy and taxation in cash undermined the Kazakh nobility by exposing it to both Russian rule and competition from Tatar merchants and clerks. The nomadic populations were forced to sedentarize and Russian colonists began to occupy "unused" fertile lands. The introduction of the scythe made it possible to cut hay for winter fodder and reduced the need to nomadize;

Russian laws made communal lands and collective rights to hay and fodder into private properties. Russian rule improved security for nomadic peoples, and allowed them to expand into new areas and survive on less extensive territories.

With the potentiality for restricting the nomads to smaller territories, Russian colonists were able to settle the steppes. Before 1868 the Russian government favored only the settlement of Cossacks or farmer-soldiers, but after the conquest of Turkestan Russia permitted peasant colonization as well. The emancipation of the serfs in 1861 allowed, and overcrowding in European Russia encouraged, Russian occupation. Between 1868 and 1880 some 4,000 Russian families settled in the Semirech'e and additional Tatar and Uzbek colonists came from Turkestan. Until 1889, the Russian government attempted to restrain colonization, but the establishment of a Russian settlement administration in 1896, the construction of the trans-Siberian railroad, and government support for the seizure of unoccupied or surplus Kazakh lands led to great waves of Russian immigration, especially after 1905. By 1912 more than $1\frac{1}{2}$ million Russians made up 40 percent of the population of the Kazakh steppes. In a continuing cycle, the ever-growing Russian population forced the Kazakhs into smaller spaces and the contraction of the Kazakhs encouraged still further Russian colonization. From the Russian point of view, colonization made it possible to convert the fertile steppe region from pastoral to agricultural uses, to secure it against possible revolts, and to reduce population pressure in western and central Russia. From the Kazakh point of view it meant the destruction of their society. The Kazakhs were forced into daily conflict with Russian settlers and were deprived of their migration routes, water, and land.

In Turkestan, by contrast, the Russians adopted a minimalist policy to assure military control and dominance in trade, and otherwise did not interfere with local economies, social organization, education and cultural life. While the Russians administered all the higher levels of territorial government, they allowed some measure of self-government at local levels. They instituted a three-year term for village elders and required district headmen to be elected by the natives though they could be dismissed by Russian officials. Muslim and customary law courts continued to function. Though limited at the local level, Russian administration still made village and religious chiefs subordinate to central control.

The Russian impact on the economy of Turkestan, however, was the critical lever for the changes which were to follow. While the Krasnovodsk–Caspian–Samarqand (1881–88)–Tashkent (1898) Railway was mainly of military importance, the Tashkent–Orenburg line, completed in 1906, opened the way for the immigration of Russian administrators and skilled workers and for the construction of modern Russian cities adjacent to old Muslim ones. Tashkent, the capital of Turkestan, was provided with schools, museums, libraries, newspapers, an observatory, and other institutions – a model of Russian modernity in Inner Asia. Other towns in Transcaspia and Semirech'e also acquired a large Russian population. Russian colonization in rural areas, by contrast with the Kazakh steppes, was limited by the fact that Turkestan was already densely occupied by a native peasant population.

Railway construction also led to a tremendous increase in cotton production. With railways, northern wheat could be brought from the Ukraine and western Siberia to make up for Central Asian lands turned over to cotton. As a result cotton acreage in Farghana rose from 14 percent of cultivated lands in 1885 to 44 percent in 1915, displacing wheat, sorghum, alfalfa, and rice. For Turkestan as a whole, however, only 13 percent of arable land was committed to cotton, owing to lack of adequate irrigation and drainage, the use of land by nomads, and large tracts of undeveloped land owned by the ruler of Bukhara. In 1912 Turkestani cotton accounted for 63.6 percent of all Russian cotton supplies and was vital to the industrialization of Russia. Thus under Russian control, Turkestan came to have a one-crop economy supplemented by silk, dried fruit, grapes, wine, and sugarbeets. Industrialization in Central Asia before 1917 was largely limited to cotton-processing industries in which all the skilled workers were Russians. Thus Turkestan was treated as a colonial economy whose raw materials were extracted for the benefit of the imperial power and whose industrialization was subordinate to export interests.

Russian land policies also had important long-run implications. In 1886 the Tsarist regime made waqf lands the property of their tenants, and required that new waqfs have official approval. In 1913 it declared all occupied lands the property of tenant producers, and all grazing and unused lands state property. By 1913 about 90 percent of irrigated land in Turkestan had become the property of small owners. While the changes in land law made peasants proprietors, it also made them vulnerable to the money economy and to the vagaries of the world market. Peasants had to find capital for tools, oxen, and seed and funds to tide over bad years in the cotton market. As a result many went into debt, lost their land to moneylenders, and reverted to the status of sharecroppers. The overall result of changes in the land law was a reconcentration of ownership in the hands of a new class of landlords, merchants, usurers, and, occasionally, successful older gentry. Concentration of land in Turkestan led to the consolidation of a new bourgeois landowning elite, and was not in the long run beneficial to the peasantry.

In the protectorate of Bukhara, Russian intervention had similar effects. The construction of railways opened Bukhara to Russian capital and closely linked it to the Russian economy. Permanent settlements of Russian railway workers were founded in Bukhara, Tirmidh, and other towns, and Russian business firms and banks were opened. Russia displaced Iran and India as Bukhara's principal trading partner. Bukhara exported cotton, lambskins, wool, silk, hides, dried fruits, and carpets, and imported Russian textiles, metals, sugar, and chinaware. Russia assumed control of Bukharan customs, and introduced Russian coinage. The reorientation of trade benefited Bukharan merchants and peddlers, but penalized local artisans and textile producers. Carpet and silk production was henceforth restricted to the luxury trades. Russian capital also undermined the Bukharan peasantry. To survive in the world cotton market, Bukharan peasants had to take out loans at high rates of interest, and sell the cotton crop in advance at low prices. Many would lose their land. While the bourgeoisie prospered in trade, as an intermediary between the Russians and the native population or as agents of Russian commercial firms, and acquired land, the artisans and peasants suffered.

The common people and the new bourgeoisie had different responses to Russian rule. By and large, the common people suffered passively. Despite the sedentarization and impoverishment of the nomads, there was virtually no military resistance in the Kazakh steppes between 1869 and 1916, and none in Transcaspia between 1881 and 1916. Only in Transoxania and Farghana was there scattered Sufi-led opposition and peasant banditry. There were riots in Tashkent in 1892 provoked by medical measures taken to resist a cholera epidemic which included inspection of women and restrictions on burials in Muslim cemeteries. In 1898 Ishan Muhammad al-Khalifa Kabir (1856-98), called Ishan Madali, led about 2,000 rebels to almost instant defeat. Madali had acquired a local reputation, first as a simpleton and then as a holy-man. He made the pilgrimage to Mecca in 1884 and returned to organize charities for the poor. With the help of his followers he built a school, a mosque, a great house, warehouses, kitchens, and rooms for his wives clustered in a big compound. Disgruntled 'ulama' and former officeholders became part of his following. In 1898 his people attacked several Russian garrisons, planning to evict the Russians and reestablish the Khokand Khanate. They were quickly dispersed and Madali was executed. Resistance in Turkestan, however, was not entirely quelled. Between 1906 and 1910 sporadic banditry in the countryside increased as peasants pushed off the land by usurers attacked Russian settlers.

World War I precipitated the first widespread Muslim rebellions. In 1916 at the height of the cotton harvesting season, the Russians attempted to mobilize

240,000 Muslim workers to serve in labor battalions. The resistance was strongest in regions which had large numbers of Russian colonists and where there had been forced sedentarization and seizure of lands. No doubt, long-suffered economic misery fueled the outburst. Kazakhs attacked government buildings, schools, post offices, rail and telegraph lines, Russian civilians, and other symbols of the Russian presence, but Russian peasants retaliated by seizing the property of natives and forcing them to flee. There were terrible communal massacres on both sides. Kirgiz peoples rebelled and many moved to China. The other Muslim regions were generally quiet.

Rather than resist, the middle classes became the bearers of a new cultural and political consciousness. Since the early nineteenth century the University of Kazan had been the principal center for the communication of Russian culture to Tatars and Kazakhs, and after the middle of the century the Russians vastly expanded their educational effort. Nicholas Il'minskii created schools which would give Tatars a Russian and European education, imparted by native instructors using native languages. While some Tatars resisted this program because they feared forced Russification, and some Russians were concerned about an education which would encourage national languages and separatism, many Tatars welcomed the new education as a means of spreading modernism and of entering into the life of the Russian state.

In Turkestan, Russian education came to Muslims as a result of different policies. Here Governor-General von Kaufman decided to create schools for Russian settlers (1876) which had no religious or confessional bias, and wait for Muslims to voluntarily enroll and adopt a superior Russian civilization. In 1884 the first Russian native school to teach Russian language, arithmetic, geography, history, literature, and other secular subjects in the morning, and Muslim religion and local languages in the afternoon, was founded. A small number of schools sufficed to create a cadre of Muslim translators, teachers, and intellectuals. Generally, however, Muslims found them unsatisfactory because of their poor teaching of Muslim subjects and the fear that their children would be weaned away from Islam. By 1917 Muslim education was still mostly in the hands of the ʿulamaʾ.

However, Russian conquests and colonization led to the development of a native bourgeoisie, and Russian education favored, as in colonial situations the Muslim world over, the emergence of a small intelligentsia. Under the influence of Russian education, and of new ideas from Turkey and Iran, this intelligentsia began to demand reform of Muslim practices, self-improvement, cultural enlightenment, and eventually, political autonomy. Some of the new intelligentsia stressed national development, some religious reform. After the turn of the century there would be advocates of socialism as well.

The most significant of the new cultural tendencies was the *usul-i jadid*, or New Method, a program of educational reform that gradually developed into a political movement. The usul-i jadid had its origin among wealthy and highly Europeanized Kazan and Crimean Tatars, often educated at the University of Kazan, who had not only become assimilated to Russian culture but sensitive to their own Turkish and Muslim heritage and aware of their backwardness. The Volga and Crimean Tatar bourgeoisie carried the new concept into Kazakhstan, Turkestan, and Bukhara, where it influenced other Muslim intellectuals. In the latter regions, however, the impact of jadid was slight and the preponderance of educational and religious influence remained with the old-fashioned Muslim ʿulamaʾ.

The Tatar intellectual revival began early in the nineteenth century under the leadership of Abu Nasr al-Kursavi (1783–1814), a young Tatar theologian and teacher in a madrasa in Bukhara, who proclaimed the primacy of reason over dogma. He was exiled, but his views were taken up by Shihab al-Din Marjani (1818–89), who called for freedom of reasoning and of independent judgment in religious matters, the abandonment of the fixed dogmas of the past, a new education based on the teaching of the Quran, hadith, and the history of Islam, and instruction in Russian language and modern science. His program was oriented toward a reform of Islamic belief and teaching and to a modernization and integration of Islam with Russian culture. Marjani thus represented a combination of the reformist and the modernist orientations.

A principal contributor to the creation of a Muslim literature which could communicate modern ideas was ʿAbd al-Qayyim Nasiri (1824–1904), the son of a village religious teacher, educated in the madrasas of Kazan and Bukhara, learned in Arabic, Persian, and Chaghatay, who taught himself Russian and taught for a time in a Russian theological seminary. In 1871 he left the seminary and opened his own school. Basing his work on his own pedagogical concepts, he taught not only Muslim subjects, but Russian language, arithmetic, geography, history, music, and drawing. For this enterprise Nasiri created his own texts, including a syntax for Tatars trying to learn Russian, and a Tatar–Russian dictionary. He also wrote on European sciences and published material on trade and industry. A folklorist who accumulated Tatar songs and legends, he preserved the knowledge of pre-Islamic beliefs. Though he was opposed to the conservative religious leaders and their concept of education, he was in fact a devout Muslim and published numerous religious works including studies of the life of the Prophet and stories of Muslim saints. In his own lifetime he was largely ignored, but as an encyclopedist and vulgarizer he was a pioneer in joining Muslim reform to Muslim modernism.

The most famous jadid leader was Ismaʿil Gasprinskii (1851–1914), a Crimean Tatar who had a European education and worked as a journalist in Istanbul and Paris. In 1883 he began to publish *Tarjuman*, which became the principal expression of the jadid campaign for the modernization and unification of Muslim peoples. Gasprinskii became a proponent of the modernist rather than the reformist orientation. He argued that Muslims must borrow from the West to revitalize their intellectual and social life. While Islam could remain a philosophic and theological system, Muslim peoples had to become part of modern technical civilization. He held up the positive example of the small Tatar community in Poland which was Muslim in religion but otherwise wholly assimilated, and the negative example of Bukhara as a benighted and backward Muslim society.

Gasprinskii pioneered in sponsoring jadid schools. By 1905 Kazan, Orenburg, Bagtchesaray, and Baku had become important centers of jadid education. He also tried to develop a standard Turkish literary language based on Ottoman to replace the traditional use of Arabic, Persian, and Chaghatay. Gasprinskii's ultimate object was to transmit European culture to Muslim peoples and to unify them on the basis of a common language, a rational form of religion, and a shared modern civilization.

Tatar merchants and intellectuals introduced the jadid schools to Tashkent and Bukhara where they were taken up by local cotton merchants and money lenders who had a Russian education or had been exposed to Russian ideas. Tashkent schools and the *Turkestan Native Gazette*, an official government publication produced in literary Uzbek with a Russian translation, were the main vehicles for the spread of interest in modernization. Stimulated by the Iranian revolution of 1906 and the Young Turk coup of 1908, Bukharans themselves founded additional schools which emphasized religion and provided supplementary studies of Russian language, arithmetic, geography, physics, and chemistry. These contrasted with the reformist schools in Crimea and Kazan, which stressed secular rather than religious instruction. In 1910 a new society called the Union of Noble Bukhara was founded to print a journal and distribute literary materials. These *Yeni Bukharlar* (Young Bukharans) included intellectuals of merchant and ʿulamaʾ background, many of whom were educated in Istanbul. They combined Young Turk-type reformism, Tatar jadidism, pan-Islamic, anti-Russian, and anti-feudal sentiments.

The leading ideologue of the Bukharan reform was ʿAbd al-Rauf Fitrat. He argued that Muslim civilization in Bukhara was in decline and that the conservative ʿulamaʾ were responsible. The ʿulamaʾ, he argued, had distorted the teaching of the Prophet, put Islam at the service of the privileged classes and made it hostile to progress. He was equally opposed to popular religious practices and the worship of saints. He argued that the regeneration of the Muslim community would depend upon a new understanding of Islam which rejected ignorant leadership and blind fidelity. Fitrat believed that the regeneration of the Muslim community could only be realized by a spiritual renovation of individuals, based on a reformed education, and by a social and political revolution which would bring an end to foreign domination and to a corrupt political elite. He was the first Bukharan thinker to emphasize political action and to propound an Islamic identity based on the concept of *vatan* (fatherland) and *millet* (nation).

The jadid movement in Tsarist Russia was similar to reformist movements in other parts of the Muslim world. In social origin it was a movement of intelligentsia drawn from bourgeois and merchant strata of society, a movement not of a displaced but of an aspiring political elite. While it echoed ⁽ulama⁾ reformism by its emphasis upon the Quran, Sunna, and ijtihad, jadid appears primarily as a modernist movement which attempted to transform Islam into another version of modern technical and national civilization. In this respect it seems closer to the modernism of the Ottoman empire and Sayyid Ahmad Khan in India than to the reformism of the Sufis.

Cultural concerns, moreover, soon led to politics. Within the jadid movement, and alongside of it, the Tatars began to discuss their political identity and to debate whether Tatars were Turks or a separate nation. Emigrés in Turkey took the pan-Turanian view that Tatar, Turkish, Mongolian, and Finno-Ugaric peoples formed a single nation glorified by the conquests of Attila, Chinggis Khan, and Tamerlane. Tatars within Russia generally held that Tatars formed a distinct nation (millet), and aspired to assimilation into Russian society. They demanded individual equality of Muslims with Russians and imagined a future of cooperation between the two peoples. Rashid Ibragimov imagined a Russian–Muslim federation on the Austro-Hungarian model. Socialist ideas also began to spread among Muslim intellectuals in Kazan, Kiev, Tiflis, and Orenburg. Being a dispersed population without much hope of territorial separation from Russia, Tatars were most likely to affirm pan-Islamic or pan-Turkish causes.

Kazakhs had equally advanced nationalist and assimilationist conceptions. A small number of Kazakhs served in the Russian army and administration and went to Russian schools. Hostile to Tatar merchants and cultural influences, they were willing to collaborate with Russian educators. Il'minskii and his student Ibragim Altynsarin (1841–89) collaborated in introducing a Russian-type education in the Kazakh language and in opening teacher training schools which used the Cyrillic alphabet. Altynsarin founded four Kazakh schools between 1879 and 1883, followed by a Kazakh teachers' college to train a native vanguard. This period of Kazakh-Russian collaboration ended with the first great wave of Russian colonization between 1896 and 1910. From then on Kazakh intellectuals began to cultivate a separate national consciousness. *Alash Orda* (named after a mythic Kazakh horde) was founded in 1905, though it did not become politically active until 1917. In 1907 the first newspapers were published. Kazakh intellectuals continued to favor European and modern education but opposed cultural Russification and Russian colonization. Among the radicals the first murmurs about Kazakh liberation and political autonomy were to be heard.

The Russian revolutionary years of 1904–05, the formation of a *Duma* or legislature in 1906, and temporary freedom of organization, press, and assembly stimulated a burst of Muslim newspapers, political parties, and congresses. A number of Muslim and socialist parties were created, primarily by Tatars and Azarbayjanis. In 1904 the Tatar students of the Muhammadiya madrasa founded *al-Islah* (Reform) to press the concepts of cultural jadid into the struggle for political rights. In 1905 a Marxist-nationalist party, *Berek* (Unity), was organized by graduates of the teachers' school. Berek combined with al-Islah to create the *Tangchylar* (Morning Star) which had a populist or socialist revolutionary orientation. Al-Islah people created a Kazan branch of the Russian Social Democratic party. Other Tatars founded the Tatar Social Democratic Group in 1907. A Crimean party, *Milli Firqa* (National Party), was formed about the same time.

In 1905 Kazan Tatars, Crimeans, and Azarbayjanis held an illegal all-Russian Muslim congress in Nizhnii Novgorod, which led to the founding of the Russian General Muslim Party (*Ittifaq al-Muslimin*). At three Muslim Congresses of 1905 and 1906 Tatar leaders attempted to create a union of the Muslims of Russia to work for a constitutional monarchy, equality and cooperation between Russians and Muslims, freedom of Muslim instruction, press, and publications, and respect for private property. Despite the superficial unity of the Congresses, the delegates were in fact deeply divided. Gasprinskii and older Tatar leaders opposed political action and wanted to concentrate on religious and cultural affairs. Muslims close to the Russian socialists opposed a religious party. The majority favored Muslim political action on a national religious basis and a platform calling for civil rights, toleration of minorities, equality of peoples, and cultural autonomy, but not territorial independence.

In Azarbayjan, Armenian and Russian influence combined with the conservatism of the Shiʿi ʿulamaʾ to promote a radical and anti-religious intelligentsia. *Hummet* (Endeavor), founded in Baku in 1904, was affiliated with the

Bolsheviks. Baku was the ideal location for a Muslim proletarian party since it had an industrial working class employed in the oil industry, a liberal Muslim tradition, and abundant contacts with radical political currents in the outside Muslim world.

By 1907, however, Russia's brief liberal period was succeeded by a reaction, and the Muslim intelligentsia was left politically isolated. Its efforts to ally with Russian liberals broke down and it had no support from the Muslim masses. Despite the traumas suffered by Kazakh herdsmen displaced by Russian colonists, and Turkestan peasants impoverished by Russian land administration and cotton policies, the mass of the people continued to live in lineage and village communities under the authority of tribal and religious chiefs. On the eve of the 1917 revolution the Muslim intelligentsia remained miniscule in size, divided by religious, socialist, and nationalist ideologies, and without popular support.

THE REVOLUTIONARY ERA

The outbreak of the Russian revolution in 1917 meant the sudden lifting of the Tsarist regime and the opening of the struggle for power among Russians and between Russians and Muslims. The Russian provisional government established in February 1917 gave way in October to a Soviet regime. Officially, Communist party doctrine proclaimed the right of all colonized peoples to self-determination and assured them the right of secession. When they established the Commissariat for Nationality Affairs in 1917 (with Stalin as chairman), the Soviets were prepared to think in terms of cultural or political autonomy, but by 1919 the party was determined to assert its rule over Muslim populations. The Communists found themselves heir to regions inhabited by numerous Russians and to territories and peoples of great strategic and economic importance which they were loathe to surrender. Russian populations in Inner Asia, regardless of political views, were also ready to fight to maintain Russian ethnic predominance.

While Russian Reds and Whites were embroiled in civil war, the Muslim intelligentsia and other regional and local leaders sought to take advantage of the breakdown of the Russian state. From 1917 to 1920 Muslims of Bashkiria, Kazakhstan, Azarbayjan, and the Caucasus struggled for regional independence. In the Urals the Bashkirs, a people closely related to the Tatars, who earned a living from stockraising, forestry, and some agriculture, fought for political autonomy in order to stop Russian colonization and return Russian-occupied lands to Bashkir owners. In 1917 they formed the Bashkir National Council and withdrew from the all-Russian Muslim Congress. Stalin at first favored the formation of a Bashkir Republic as an example of how the Soviets would support Muslim peoples; but local Tatars who dreamed of a unified Tatar state opposed Bashkir autonomy. The Bashkirs, too weak to win on their own, allied first with White and then Red Russians, but in 1920, supported by the Red Army, local Russians and Tatars destroyed the short-lived republic.

In Kazakhstan, the third all-Kazakh Congress in December 1917 proclaimed an autonomous region with capitals at Semipalatinsk and Jambeyty, and organized an independent Kazakh Muslim spiritual administration. Kazakhs demanded a halt to Russian colonization and the return of colonized lands. They came under attack from both the Bolsheviks and from Turkestani pan-Islamic critics, and found themselves involved in a complex civil war involving both White and Red Russians. In the end Alash Orda was defeated and an Autonomous Soviet Socialist Republic was declared in 1920. In Azarbayjan and the Caucasus local autonomy movements came to a similar end.

In other regions the Muslims strove not for full independence, but for cultural and partial political autonomy within a Russian-Soviet framework. In the Volga region Muslims formed moderate bourgeois and socialist parties which were often the outgrowth of associations that had developed after the 1905 revolution. Muslim congresses were held at Moscow and Kazan in May, July, and November 1917 to debate whether they should seek cultural autonomy within a Russian state or form a federation of Muslim states. The delegates were divided but the successive congresses took bolder steps to organize Muslim forces. The first created a National Council (*Milli Shura*) and an Executive Committee. The second formed a Military Council under Tatar and Bashkir leadership, and called the third congress, or Constituent Assembly, which declared the formation of an Idel-Ural Tatar state. This would-be state was dissolved by the Bolsheviks in 1918. Through the Central Commissariat for Muslim Affairs, Stalin succeeded in absorbing the Tatar socialists and national Communists into the Russian party, and in 1920 the Soviets organized a Tatar Autonomous Soviet Socialist Republic. In the Crimea Soviet rule was similarly established as a result of a coalition between the Russian Communist Party and the Milli Firqa party. A Democratic Tatar Republic, founded in 1917, came under Soviet control and was reorganized in 1921 as the Soviet Republic of the Crimea.

In Turkestan, the path to Soviet rule was tortuous. The revolution of February 1917 led to the formation of an entirely Russian provisional government. In response, Muslim intellectual leaders called a congress in April 1917, in an atmosphere governed by the brutal suppression of the 1916 insurrections, famine, and open conflict between Muslims and Russians for control of the land, to debate their political future. Most of the participants were Russian-educated intellectuals and Tatar merchants who favored cultural autonomy rather than political independence. Bolder delegates wanted territorial autonomy within a federated Russian state. All the delegates took a conciliatory attitude in the hope of future alliances with liberal and radical Russians. They also feared the strength of conservative religious leaders who might well control any independent Muslim movement and defeat the reformist intellectuals. As a result, the congress split into two groups. One formed an Islamic Council which represented the jadid orientation and was committed to the formation of a modern state federated on an equal basis with the Russian state; the other organized an association of ʿulamaʾ which was primarily concerned with the supremacy of the Shariʿa.

In October 1917 the Soviets took power in Turkestan and rejected Muslim participation in the government on the grounds that the Muslims did not represent the proletariat. In reaction, in November 1917 Muslims proclaimed an Autonomous Republic of Turkestan with its capital at Khokand – a republic based on the Shariʿa, to be federated with Russia. The Khokand government, in its brief lifetime, opened new schools, created a militia, returned land to the peasants, redistributed waqfs, and gave grain to the poor, but in February 1918 it was overthrown by Russian forces. Thus of the two revolutions in Turkestan, the European proletarian and the Muslim bourgeois, the superior military power won out. Turkestan was declared an Autonomous Soviet Socialist Republic.

In 1919, concerned about Russian chauvinism and the hostility of Muslims to the narrowly Russian regime, Moscow sent a special commission to centralize power and to create some basis for cooperation with local people. In order to win jadid support the Russians now guaranteed religious freedom, and appointed a commissariat for Turkestani self-administration. Jadid leaders flocked to join the Communist Party, and worked to modify Russian policies to meet the needs of the Muslim population. Their first interest was to cope with famine and disease.

While jadid intelligentsia tried to penetrate the regime from within, rural bandit-like resistance took hold in the countryside. Embittered former Khokand military units, landowners, merchants, village and clan notables, tribal chiefs, Sufis, unemployed tenant farmers, and workers were behind the so-called *Basmachi* or rural bandit resistance in the name of the Shariʿa, the Prophet Muhammad, and the Muslim obligation of jihad. By 1920 the numerous independent and uncooperative Basmachi groups were driven by the Russians into the most remote rural areas. Basmachi resistance, however, was not crushed. The introduction of anti-Muslim religious policies spurred renewed resistance. In 1921 and 1922 Enver Pasha, the former Ottoman minister of war, attempted to unify the movement. Enver, however, was killed in August 1922 and the opportunity was lost. In the meantime the Russians realized that military measures would not suffice to suppress the Basmachis and decided to make political concessions. Waqf lands were restored, madrasas were re-opened, and Shariᶜa courts were allowed to sit. Requisitions of cotton and other crops were suspended. Weakened by their own internal divisions, subverted by Soviet concessions, and overwhelmed by Russian military power, the Basmachis were crushed. Sporadic resistance flared up again in the late 1920s and early 1930s, but by 1924 Turkestan was effectively in Soviet control.

Bukhara and Khiva went through similar experiences of Soviet–Muslim collaboration and eventual reorganization and absorption into the Soviet state. The struggle in Bukhara began with the long-standing opposition between the Amir, the conservative Muslim administrative and religious elites, and the jadid reformers. The February revolution emboldened moderate jadidists to seek the formation of a salaried civil service, the separation of the treasury and the privy purse, and the removal of the chief qadi, who was a barrier to constructive reforms. The Young Bukharan radicals demanded the establishment of a parliament to limit the powers of the sovereign, freedom of teaching and publication, and exclusion of reactionary ministers from the cabinet. Allied with the Tashkent Soviet they tried to force the adoption of their program, but were defeated by a massive counterdemonstration led by conservative mullahs. However, in 1920, with Russian military help, the Bukharan radicals established a Bukharan Peoples' Soviet Republic supported by wealthy merchant families. The new regime was declared a popular democracy committed to Islam and the Shariᶜa. It guaranteed rights of property, and liberty of association, publication, and religious conscience, and made promises of political reform, distribution of land, and enfranchisement of women. These promises, however, proved impossible to implement since the new regime lacked the personnel to replace the old elite.

The Russian–Bukharan coalition was soon superseded by full Communist rule. The consolidation of Soviet power began with the penetration of Russians and Tatars into the army, school system, customs services, militias, police, and administrative services. Trade treaties gave the Soviets a virtual monopoly of Bukharan commerce. In 1923 a Central Asiatic Economic Council was formed to integrate Bukharan territories into the monetary, transport, and communications networks of the Soviet Union. The Russian Communist party accused the Bukharan party of bourgeois nationalist, pan-Islamic, and pan-Turkish tendencies, arrested Bukharan government officials, purged the party, and organized a new proletarian party hostile to Islam and to bourgeois influences. The Bukharan reformers were easily defeated because they did not represent a cohesive class interest and were not able to mobilize mass support from a population still committed to conservative Islamic concepts. Incorporation into the Soviet Union as a Soviet Socialist Republic followed in 1924. Khiva had already been assimilated in 1923.

In most of these cases, the Muslim intelligentsias had to collaborate with the Russian Communist Party, for the Muslims lacked the political power to independently realize their cultural and ideological goals. They were deeply divided among themselves, lacked organizational strength, had no military power, and no direct contact with the masses. Besides they were at odds with local chiefs and notables and with the conservative religious leaders. While some were hostile to the Russians, many were fully assimilated and imagined a cooperative future in the relations of Muslims and Russians. Lenin's promises of self-determination, the diplomatic skills of Stalin, who held open the hope of a federal Russian system, and the hope that the Communists would give equality to Muslims, brought them into the party. Some mistakenly identified the Russian revolution with jadid reform. Thus many former feudal nobles, rich merchants, reformed ʿulamaʾ, and intellectuals joined the Bolshevik party with the expectation that they would achieve equality with Russians and national liberation. Among the most important leaders to cooperate with the regime were Mir Said Sultan Galiev (1880–1928?), a Volga Tatar; Ahmad Baytursun (1873–1937), a Kazakh writer and founder of Alash Orda; ʿAbd al-Rauf Fitrat (d. 1938), one of the ideological leaders of the Young Bukhara movement; Fayzullah Khojaev (1896–1938), a young Bukharan; and Nariman Narimanov (1870–1933), an Azari social democrat and founder of Hummet.

Most of the Muslim Communists were pragmatic politicians pursuing immediate economic and political goals. They accepted Russian rule as inevitable and had little idea of what a Muslim political order would be in post-revolutionary conditions. Still, Muslim aspirations received some ideological articulation between 1919 and 1923. Sultan Galiev and other Muslim Communists understood Communism not as a theory of proletarian revolution but as a practical doctrine which explained how to organize an underground movement, agitate, educate the masses, gain political support, and articulate national rights. They set aside the Marxist emphasis upon class struggle and the centrality of the proletariat to argue that colonial peoples, regardless of internal divisions, were proletarian nations and that their principal task was to win their independence. National revolution had to precede class struggle. The revolution, in their view, would be led by peasants rather than workers and would center on the countryside rather than on the cities. Their first priority was national liberation, which would enable Muslim countries to bypass the capitalist stage of historical development and enter directly into socialism. Sultan Galiev, expressing the almost universal mistrust of Russians, was skeptical of the Russian claim that socialism would put an end to colonialism and held that a former capitalist oppressor nation, under socialism, would be a socialist oppressor nation. Emphasizing the national component of his political views, he believed that socialism and Islam were compatible and that Islam should be secularized and integrated into national Muslim societies.

This doctrine of international revolution and liberation of colonized peoples had important implications within the Soviet system. The national Muslim version of Communism enabled Muslim leaders to resist Russian interference in local affairs and to oppose policies promoting class struggle on the grounds that Islam minimized class antagonism and that national liberation from colonial rule had priority. It also articulated the desire to expel Russian colonists and be free of Russian political control. Some Muslim nationalists also harbored ambitions to infiltrate Muslims into the Communist Party, win control of education, and promote pan-Islamic and pan-Turkish ideals.

The Russian Communist Party vigorously opposed the Muslim national orientation. To counteract the Muslim Communists Stalin worked assiduously to build up organizations which would assimilate the Muslim groups. Stalin's view – that there could be only one Communist Party in the Soviet Union, that class struggle was intrinsic to or prior to national struggle, and that revolution would have to be pursued first in Europe rather than in Asia – prevailed. In 1923 the twelfth congress of the Russian Communist Party denounced the Georgian national Communists and demanded the subordination of regional parties to central interests. Sultan Galiev was vilified and expelled from the party as an opponent of centralized political power, a danger to Soviet security in the border regions, and a promoter of local nationalisms. In 1928 he was sent to prison camp and disappeared.

Thus, in regions where Soviet and Muslim nationalists had formed an alliance, Russians ousted their Muslim rivals, and defeated armed resistance. While Muslim nationalist and reformist leaders in most Third World countries had generations to consolidate their position, mobilize mass support, achieve independence, and generate a national identity on their own terms, in the Soviet Union, Muslim leaders were defeated, and Russian state control was established. By 1920 the Soviets had established Tatar, Crimean, Kazakh,

Map 35. Soviet and Chinese Inner Asia.

Turkestani, and Azarbayjani Soviet Socialist Republics, and two peoples' republics in Khiva and Bukhara. The latter were changed into Soviet Socialist Republics in 1923 and 1924. In 1924 Turkestan, Bukhara, and Khwarizm were territorially regrouped, and four Inner Asian republics – Uzbekistan, Turkmenistan, Kazakhstan, and Kirgizia – were organized. The republics were founded on the basis of ethnic and linguistic similarities among the populations, but part of the plan was to divide the Muslims and forestall the development of a pan-Turkish national movement. The republics all belong to the Union of Soviet Socialist Republics. In principle they are independent states federated for the purposes of defense, foreign policy, and economic management, but according to the Soviet constitution Soviet law prevails over local law, and all territories are considered the sovereign domain of the Soviet Union. In practice the republics are closely controlled by the Communist Party and the central state administration.

The system of "autonomous" national regimes was extended to other Muslim groups. According to Soviet classifications, Muslim nations (*natsii*), peoples who share a common history, language, cultural identity, and political-territorial organization, comprising more than 300,000 members, include Uzbeks, Tatars, Kazakhs, Azaris, Tajiks, Turkmens, Kirgiz, Bashkirs, Chechens, Ossets, Avars, Lezghins, Kabardes, and Karakalpaks. Other smaller groups, based on the unification of tribal people by shared language, but not having all of the characteristics of nations, are classified as nationalities (*narodnosti*). Since 1936 the various nations and nationalities have been organized into six Union Soviet Socialist Republics (Uzbekistan, Azarbayjan, Kazakhstan, Turkmenistan, Tajikistan, and Kirgizia) and eight Autonomous Soviet Socialist Republics including Tataristan, Bashkiria, Daghestan, and other Caucasian units. There are also four lesser-scale autonomous provinces in the Caucasus.

SOVIET MODERNIZATION

With the organization of a system of Soviet Socialist Republics in Inner Asia the further development of Muslim societies would take place on Soviet terms. The Soviet victory opened the way for a radical effort to modernize the conditions of life and the consciousness of Inner Asian peoples, and to integrate them into a socialist and Soviet society. To achieve these goals the Soviets subordinated Inner Asian peoples to Russian bureaucratic and political machinery, and undertook the economic transformation of native societies. Soviet political and economic policies were accompanied by direct efforts to subvert religious and family culture in order to promote instead Soviet-oriented "national" cultures as the basis of the incorporation of Muslims into a modern Soviet industrial and socialist society.

The 1920s and 1930s were the crucial first phase in this process. In this period the Soviets worked out a system of governmental and party controls to assure the dominance of the central regime. As we have seen, starting in 1922 and 1923 the Soviets began to remove the Muslim old guard and bourgeois nationalists in the Communist parties of Turkestan, Bukhara, Khiva, and other regions, and replace them with more dedicated Russian and local "proletarian" cadres. By 1928 the Communist parties of Tataristan and the Crimea were also purged. All of the literary, cultural, and scientific institutions of the Volga region were brought under Soviet control. In the 1930s the Communist parties of Kazakhstan, Uzbekistan, Kirgizia, Tajikistan, and the Crimea were systematically purged. By 1937 and 1938 the older generation of Muslim national Communists was totally destroyed. Despite lip service to the rights of national minorities, the Soviets asserted the absolute primacy of the central party and the subordination of regional units. "The right to self-determination cannot and must not serve as an obstacle to the exercise by the working class of its right to dictatorship" was the policy implemented by Stalin. In addition the bulk of administrative power was reserved for the central government ministries.

Communist party purges in the 1920s and 1930s raised the problem of finding politically loyal and technically proficient cadres. In Uzbekistan and other republics the Russians oscillated between efforts to promote native cadres in the interest of "affirmative action" and the employment of Russian experts. In the late 1920s and early 1930s the Communist Party encouraged the use of both Russian and local languages, improvements in education, and the employment of native cadres. By the middle and late 1930s, however, the Party had to acknowledge the educational deficiencies which hampered the training and employment of local peoples, and switched to a policy stressing Russian experts and the use of Russian as an international language. The lack of an adequately educated local population, and the desire of Europeans to command the government institutions meant that, in varying degrees, Russian personnel dominated the government and party apparatuses of the Inner Asian republics.

Economic development in Inner Asia had to begin virtually from scratch. From 1914 to 1920, civil war, famine, brigandage, and government confiscations had taken a tremendous toll. Untold numbers of people died in the revolutionary years. Agricultural and manufacturing output fell to miniscule levels. To restore the economy to pre-revolutionary levels the Soviets had to go back on their initial proposals to institute collective farming and adopted the New Economic Policy (N.E.P.). They returned confiscated lands to their Muslim owners, and encouraged the reconstruction of irrigation works, replacement of draft animals and other measures to repair the damages of the civil war period. The Soviets de-nationalized many enterprises and dropped forced requisitions. For a long time the government gave up trying to settle nomads but assigned them fixed pastures, a measure which was conducive to partial sedentarization. In March 1923 the Central Asiatic Economic Council took responsibility for restoring agricultural production, monetary systems, foreign trade, and transportation. The greatest efforts were made to increase cotton production at the expense of rice and other crops. By 1928 the New Economic Policy aided the recovery of agricultural and industrial production to about 70 percent of 1913 levels.

With the mending of the Inner Asian economies the Soviets launched their program of land reform. In Turkestan they began by seizing the land and water rights of landlords and waqfs. In 1924 they determined to eliminate "feudal and tribal survivals," seize all large properties and the "excess" properties of middle and small landowners, and redistribute the land among the poor and landless peasants. The goal was to increase the well-being of the poorest stratum of peasants, to break the political backbone of both the secular and religious rural elites, and to open the society to the more drastic reorganizations to follow. Land reform was carefully prepared by the organization of an agricultural workers' propaganda movement called *Koshchi*, which tried to undermine respect for traditional authority, encourage the peasants to drive out landowners, and promote class warfare. This was difficult because the economic and social gap between large and small owners was not in fact clearly demarcated and because of the close cultural and religious ties between the larger owners and the poorer peasants. Cooperatives and unions were also intended to accustom peasants to collective organization.

The great drive for collectivization of agriculture and the industrialization of the Inner Asian republics (and the whole of the Soviet Union) began in 1928. State farms and collectives were introduced that year. Between 1929 and 1934 a new trade union of agricultural and forestry workers was organized. In 1934 Machine Tractor Stations were introduced to centralize state control over agricultural production and generate more efficient utilization of mechanized resources. Peasants on collective farms were closely regimented. A new elite of collective farm administrators and a new proletariat of agricultural workers came into being. By 1937 collectivization was about 95 percent complete.

Tajikistan, for example, was transformed from a subsistence area to a producer of cotton, grain, fruit, and livestock for export.

Kazakhstan was a special case. Here land reform began in 1921 and 1922 with the distribution of water rights among the poor settlers; in 1926 and 1927 some 2,000,000 acres were taken from wealthy landowners and given to the poor. This was followed in 1928 by a redistribution of herds, forced sedentarization, and forced collectivization that squeezed the nomads into livestock collectives and state farms. By 1932 the sedentarization of Kazakhs was considered complete, but the costs were enormous. The Kazakh population declined by some 900,000 in the 1930s owing to executions and emigration to China, and there was a catastrophic collapse in the size of animal herds.

Industrial development in Inner Asia was of primary importance in long-term Soviet plans but of limited impact in the 1920s and 1930s. From 1917 to 1922, civil war and nationalizations led to the collapse of the cotton processing industry, but these industries were restored, and from 1928 to 1941 the Soviets introduced mechanized textile production and engineering industries, and increased the production of coal and electric power which served as a basis for further industrialization. Industrial development in Kazakhstan was limited to the restoration of agricultural processing, meat packing, wool, and canning industries.

While economic development was limited, the Soviets achieved an educational miracle by providing mass education in Inner Asia to the same standards that prevailed throughout the Soviet Union. The scope and success of this effort is unrivaled in any colonial regime or any independent Muslim country. In 1930 primary education was made universal and compulsory, and a literacy campaign to educate adults between the ages of 16 and 30 was launched. Local languages were used for instruction, though in 1938 Russian was made obligatory in minority schools. Until the 1940s the main objective was to make the population literate and to promote the acceptance of Soviet society. After that, emphasis was placed upon occupational training.

The literacy campaign was accompanied by an intensive effort to promote national cultures as the vehicle for the inculcation of a socialist mentality. The concept of nation had scarcely any precedent in pre-Soviet Muslim political culture. Most Muslims considered themselves members of a particular tribe, town, or village; probably only the elites identified themselves with territorial states such as Khokand or Bukhara. The jadid movement introduced the notion of a pan-Turkish or pan-Islamic political identity. To combat the threat of a unified Muslim population the Soviet regime divided the Muslims into a number of national states in an attempt to break down both sub-national tribal loyalties and supra-national religious or ethnic consciousness, and to encourage national identities which could be integrated into the Soviet political order. In the framework of the national republics an intense socialization and indoctrination program was carried out through schools, political meetings, theaters, clubs, newspapers, lectures, folk art, and parades led by a new generation of party activists, writers, and teachers. In the cultural field the Soviets attempted to blend regional culture into Soviet culture, using local history, languages, epics, folklore, and arts to carry the socialist message.

The most important changes were the reform of languages and literatures. In 1926 the Soviets decided at a Turkological congress held in Baku to eliminate Arabic script and introduce the Latin alphabet for all Turkic languages. The new alphabet had complex political implications. While it cut Muslim peoples off from the literatures of the past, it could also put Inner Asian Muslims in contact with Turkey, which also used the Latin alphabet. The Latin alphabet, furthermore, made it difficult to learn Russian. Thus in 1939 and 1940 the Soviets introduced a new Cyrillic script and attempted to modernize Inner Asian languages by promoting an ever-increasing use of Russian terms, some of which are international technical and scientific words modified to conform to Inner Asian phonemes and grammar. In any case, from 1938 Russian was required in minority schools.

The Soviets also made intensive efforts to modernize literature. In 1925 they called for the formation of national, as opposed to pan-Turkish or pan-Islamic, cultures. In 1934 they created a writers' union to define new criteria for writing and publication, and to oblige writers to follow the party line. The introduction of political controls over nationality literatures led to a tortuous struggle between the writers and the censors. In the 1920s and 1930s minority nationality writers responded to Soviet pressures by generating a new form of Soviet socialist realism in local languages, but Inner Asian writers also attempted to preserve the traditional and classical cultures while acknowledging only the most important Soviet themes. The purges of the late 1930s, however, destroyed the nationalist poets and intellectual groups.

At the same time that the Soviet regime helped promote national cultures, it made strenuous efforts to undermine Islam as an organized religion and as an influence in social and cultural affairs. Religion is considered a barrier to the full assimilation of citizens into Soviet society. The Soviet Union is officially secularist and refuses to recognize the corporate organizations and rights to property ownership of churches or other religious organizations. Soviet policy toward Islam is inherently antagonistic and favors the "dying out" or eradication of religious belief. Soviet propaganda, however, was extremely cautious, piecemeal, and compromising because of the tremendous sensitivities aroused by religious antagonisms.

In the civil war period from 1918 to 1920, the Soviets attempted to destroy all of the public aspects of Islam including Muslim judicial administration, religious properties, and schools, but their decrees were not effectively implemented. The ʿulamaʾ opposed revolutionary concepts as atheistic, and stirred popular resistance to Soviet policies. The Basmachi resistance and pressure from local elites forced the Soviets to restore Muslim schools, colleges, mosques and endowments. A *Makhama-i Shariʿa* or Muslim Directorate was established in Tashkent to supervise the administration of schools, the training of teachers, and the appointment of mosque functionaries. The Soviets had to concede that Islam had retained its hold on the beliefs and identity of the people. Nonetheless, from their point of view some progress had been made, as the influence of ʿulamaʾ decreased in urban areas and as Muslims began to rely more and more upon secular schools and courts.

The creation of the national republics in 1924 opened the way for a new Soviet effort at secularization, this time with lasting effect. In 1923 the separation of church and state was again proclaimed. Between 1923 and 1928 new laws were passed to deny religious organizations the right to exist as corporate bodies or own property, forbid religious instruction of children, confiscate large religious endowments, abolish religious courts, and eliminate religious education. A government agency took over complete control of waqfs, progressively restricted the types of property which could be used as waqfs, and by 1930 effectively legislated them out of existence. This was similar to most Muslim countries. While qadi and customary courts continued for a time to apply Muslim law concerning polygamy, bride price, and legal procedures, even in contradiction to Soviet law, progressively portions of Shariʿa which contradicted Soviet law were declared invalid, and in practice Muslims were obliged to turn to Russian courts. In 1926 the Shariʿa courts were reduced to voluntary agencies and by 1927 they had virtually disappeared. By about this time most Muslim schools were also forced to close. These measures were accompanied by intense anti-religious propaganda by the League of Militant Atheists, including attacks on belief in God, the Quran, and upon prayer and fasting. In 1929 Muslim religious leaders were arrested. Many were killed, and the Muslim religious administration was suppressed.

A major part of the Soviet anti-religious campaign was directed toward family law. Between 1924 and 1926 a new family law was promulgated which provided for equality of women's rights in divorce and property. The new law made the legal age of marriage 16 for females and 18 for males, abolished the bride price, prohibited polygamy and abduction, and gave women full rights to participate in the labor force. The practice of wearing the veil or *paranja*, which totally covers face and body, was denounced. Social pressures within the Muslim community, however, prevented women from changing traditional practices and asserting their legal rights. While stressing women's proper role in the labor force, by 1936 the Soviets conceded the importance of the "socialist" family and the importance of the roles of wife and mother. By this time, however, the whole institutional structure of Islamic worship, education, justice, and property had been destroyed.

Since World War II, the Soviet Union has continued its basic program of political and economic assimilation of the Muslim populations, but its religious and cultural policies have been significantly modified, especially after the death of Stalin in 1953. In recent times, Russians have continued to dominate the key administrative and party positions in the political police, the army, planning, communications, local industry, irrigation, transport, finance, and banking, but certain "representative" posts such as first Communist Party secretary, chairman of the council of ministers, or membership in the presidium of the supreme soviet are reserved for native Inner Asians. Control functions within the bureaucracy and the party are vested in Russian hands. Power positions in both governmental and party organizations are staffed by Russians or by Muslim functionaries with Russian (or other European) "doubles." One common arrangement was the appointment of nationals as first secretaries and Russians as second secretaries to control the party functionaries. Russian domination is partly a question of political reliability and partly a problem of the recruitment of adequately trained native cadres. Russians are suspicious of the technical and educational qualifications of local people and of their social and cultural style.

There has been a similar long-term continuity in policies of economic development. During World War II the Soviet government further built up Uzbekistan, Kazakhstan, and the Urals in order to create an industrial base behind the battle lines. After World War II fertilizer, steel, electric power, coal, oil, and natural gas were developed. Substantial irrigation programs added millions of hectares to the arable land of Turkestan, but backward methods of agriculture, and lack of fertilizer and machinery inhibited the development of the cotton industries. By the end of the 1960s the substitution of machines for hand labor in cotton harvesting made it possible to cultivate newly irrigated land and increased the productivity of labor. Khrushchev's virgin lands program in Kazakhstan has completed the process of turning the region from nomadic pastoralism to agriculture.

While there has been considerable industrialization in Inner Asia, most of it is concerned in cotton and textile production, food processing, hydroelectric development, copper mining in Kazakhstan, and oil extraction in Baku. Moscow subsidizes industrial and agricultural investments, and large numbers of Russian and Ukrainian workers provide the managerial and skilled working cadres. Economic changes have generated new institutions such as factories, collective farms, and unions, and have brought a large number of workers into a modern economy. Under Soviet rule Inner Asia has achieved a higher standard of living than almost any other Asian-Muslim country. By the 1950s diet was adequate and in the 1960s housing was improved. The Soviet government tolerates private initiative in food production, marketing, contracted services, and housing. The regime tries to reconcile economic egalitarianism, social welfare policies, and tolerance for Muslim economic preferences. In return Moscow extracts valuable raw materials including cotton, metals, and fuels from its still relatively underdeveloped Inner Asian regions.

Recent demographic developments may have reinforced the importance of the Muslim population. The Muslim population declined in the bitter revolutionary and civil war years and stagnated between 1917 and 1959 but then began to grow rapidly. It rose from 24,000,000 in 1959 to 47,000,000 in 1970. The Muslim population is growing four to five times as fast as the Slavic population owing to a large increase in fertility, which does not seem to be checked by rising incomes, education, or urbanization.

The maturation of the Soviet educational system has led to an ever increasing employment of Muslims in government, party, and technical positions, diminishing the role of Russians, Jews, and other Europeans. Local participation has been vigorously promoted, and native cadres are being rapidly integrated into the Soviet state and party organizations. By 1975 Muslim technicians formed 57.6 percent of the workforce in Uzbekistan. Educationally and socially less developed regions, like Tajikistan, have proportionally smaller native cadres. Despite this rapid integration, however, Muslims neither aspire to social integration nor suffer from discrimination. They have a status structure of their own, looking down upon lower classes of Russian settlers as uneducated and uncultivated people.

Since Stalin's death, political and economic assimilation has been accompanied by a greater acceptance of non-Russian cultures. While Khrushchev advocated an internationalist and unitary Soviet society, he recognized that the fusion of nations was not likely to be soon accomplished. After Brezhnev assumed power, official pronouncements and speeches tended to stress the shared values of Soviet peoples, but not the assimilation of nationalities. Ideology and similar socio-economic principles define the Soviet people, but national and ethnic differences are accepted as part of political reality. In practice this means that the minorities are accorded a measure of cultural autonomy in return for the acceptance of the primacy of Russian language and culture.

Since Stalin's death, a revival and re-creation of national cultures has been underway. Inner Asian oral literatures survive in the forms of songs for weddings and funerals, tales, legends, and epic poems and continue to be published and discussed. Historical novels and epic poems dealing with the glories of the past are being published, and literary and anthropological studies again recognize the eastern heritage of Uzbeks, Kazakhs, and other Asian peoples. The schools teach a modified form of their literary and historical past. Periodicals are published in Kazakh, Uzbek, Azeri, Tatar, Turkmen, Kirgiz, Tajik, Bashkir, and other languages. *Mirasism*, or "rediscovery of the pre-revolutionary national patrimony," has become an important cultural trend. Despite this liberalization, a vast number of books printed in Turkish and Inner Asian languages have primarily a Russian and European content, and novels and other literary works are still constrained by Soviet political supervision.

The overall effect has been to consolidate a new sense of nationality. While Uzbeks become politically loyal citizens of the Soviet Union, integral members of the administrative and technical workforce, fluent speakers of Russian, and European in public dress and manners, they still identify as Uzbeks and condemn the effort to "pass" or assimilate completely into a Russian identity. Similarly, Kazakh intellectuals try to reconcile political loyalty and ethnic identity and to reinterpret their national past in ways consistent with their Soviet present. Soviet Muslims are highly acculturated but not assimilated into Russian society.

In the postwar era, Soviet policy toward Islam has also moderated, but the official position is still hostile to religious belief and practice. From 1941 to 1953, in order to pacify Muslim opinion and win support for the war effort, the Soviet regime allowed the ʿulamaʾ to rebuild Islamic religious organizations under state control. In 1943 the muftiat or Directorate of Muslim Peoples was reestablished in Tashkent with jurisdiction over Uzbekistan, Kazakhstan, Kirgizia, Tajikistan, and Turkmenistan. Separate departments of religious affairs were recognized at Baku for Azarbayjan, at Ufa for Russian

27 ʿUlamaʾ study the Quran in Tashkent

and Siberian Tatars, and at Makhachkala (Daghestan) for the north Caucasus. Each of these boards is headed by an elected mufti, but the north Caucasus has two chiefs, a Sunni mufti and a Shiʿi Shaykh al-Islam. Councils of ʿulamaʾ and mosque representatives are called to give fatwas or legal decrees concerning religious and ritual matters, such as laws of marriage, divorce, and circumcision. Local mosque congregations are administered by an elected *mutawalliyat* or administrative committee, which controls the mosque's buildings and other property, and by an elected auditing commission. Elected lay members of the congregation have thus taken over the authority of the imams. These administrations report to the Council for the Affairs of Religious Cults established in 1944, and religious activity outside the control of these organizations is deemed illegal.

The Muslim Board for Central Asia and Kazakhstan is the most important and its influence and authority extend throughout the Soviet Union. It manages a number of mosques. The board also administers the only two madrasas in the Soviet Union which train students to be religious functionaries, the Mir-i Arab Madrasa of Bukhara and the more advanced Imam al-Bukhari Islamic Institute in Tashkent. Apart from the two colleges there are no Muslim schools, no Shariʿa courts, and no endowed waqfs.

The Tashkent Board is an active publisher of religious materials. Its publications include collections of hadith, classical texts, and the only Muslim periodical published in the Soviet Union, *Muslims of the Soviet East*. This journal is published in English, French, Russian, Arabic, Persian, Dari, and Uzbek. The journal publishes historical and literary notes, reviews of religious texts, and discussions of preservation of monuments. It gives religious advice on such questions as observance of Ramadan and the birthday of the Prophet and visits to saints' shrines. Alongside of the purely religious themes, it praises Soviet society for its economic achievements and publishes photographs of power plants next to those of mosques. It also defends the Soviet Union against its Western critics and strongly supports Soviet foreign policy with articles on fraternal delegations from Muslim countries, reports on disarmament and anti-nuclear conferences, and strong advocacy of the Palestinian struggle against Israel. ʿUlamaʾ play an important part in Soviet foreign affairs by receiving delegations, making official visits abroad and propagandizing for the advantages of Islam under socialism.

The maintenance of an official religious establishment indicates a tacit collaboration between the government and the ʿulamaʾ. The government sponsors Muslim administration in the hope of winning Muslim support, and for fear that disestablishment would reinforce underground Islamic movements. The leaders of official Islam lend their support to the Soviet regime in return for the opportunity to maintain a Muslim organization. Alongside of official or state-administered religion, there is a flourishing "parallel Islam" or unofficial Muslim religious activity which is especially strong in rural areas. Sufi brotherhoods, highly decentralized, are still important in the tribal regions of Turkmenistan, Kirgizia, Kazakhstan, and the Caucasus. Pilgrimage to shrines and saints' graves plays an important part in preserving an unofficial Muslim religious life.

Among less educated people animistic practices still survive under the guise of Islam. Amulets are used to ward off spirits, exorcise demons and heal injuries. The cult of ancestors, sometimes inherited from pre-Islamic sanctuaries, and shamanism continue to be practiced. Alongside of the Sufis there are numerous healers, wandering shamans, and other holy-men. In family affairs there are strong survivals of pre-Islamic rituals marking the birth of a child, and magical ceremonies on the occasion of marriages and funerals. In these cases, the persistence of traditional beliefs may be related to the persistence of communities which have not been absorbed into the mainstream of Soviet economic and political life.

In urban areas Muslim identity, belief, and practice are also important. Groups which are supported by strong kinship and neighborhood ties, living in isolated areas and lacking education, show higher levels of religiosity. Old-fashioned craft workers keep "professional cults." Wherever traditional family life is strong, pilgrimages, festivals, and family ceremonies continue to be observed. Rural migration to cities may actually increase Muslim identifications as a compensation for the stresses of adjusting to a new environment, and as a basis for the integration of heterogeneous populations in the new physical setting. Islam still serves as a shared culture for people of different parochial backgrounds.

In general, however, urbanization associated with industrialization, higher levels of formal education, and the incorporation of women into the work force has tended to secularize Soviet-Muslim populations. This secularization, especially among professionals and skilled workers, means a declining attention to prayer, fasting, mourning, and other religious ceremonies. The conflict between religious and modern Soviet norms for social behavior tends to reduce engagement in religious activities.

Still, even the educated intelligentsia remains strongly attached to its native language, ethnic identity, and religious customs. They do not intermarry with Russians. They resist assimilation by practicing traditional customs in relation to women, Ramadan observances and festivals, and Muslim rituals in birth, circumcision, marriage and burial ceremonies. Muslims seem to hold a modulated concept of political identity involving Soviet citizenship, minority nationality, and an Islamic heritage.

The question of Soviet, national, and religious identities is the subject of intense discussion. Despite the organization of Muslim administration, the Soviet regime remains hostile in principle to religious belief and worship. A strong anti-religious campaign was carried out under Khrushchev from 1954 to 1964; it involved the "deregistration" of Muslim clerics and the suppression of mosques. After Khrushchev's demise the Soviet regime adopted educational and persuasive methods, instead of administrative or police measures, to restrict religious activity. An elaborate anti-religious propaganda campaign, including publications, films, radio broadcasts, and reports of research institutes, continues to assail Islam. Soviet academic writers treat Islam as an archaic residue of an outmoded society and refute the pretensions of Muslim believers. In the 1970s there was a fresh anti-Islamic campaign directed at Sufism in the Caucasus. The campaign stressed the incompatibility of religion and modern science and the superiority of Communist to Muslim morals. It opposed the organization of a "parallel Islam." Since 1980 there has been a new wave of anti-Islamic propaganda.

In response, Muslim religious leaders attempt to demonstrate the compatibility of Islam, modernity, and socialism. Their very position requires them to support the Soviet system and to adapt Islam to the requirements of a socialist society. They are also sensitive to the needs of a secular, technically trained Muslim population for whom religious belief has to be justified and made meaningful in contemporary terms. Moreover, the Muslim religious leaders are themselves Soviet-educated citizens, participating in a Soviet society through part-time employment in the workforce and through marriage and family ties. Their own identity depends upon a blending of Soviet modernity and Islam.

Thus, contemporary Soviet-Muslim thought stresses the inherent compatibility of socialist and Muslim values such as equality, social justice, friendship of peoples, and education. Socialism and nationalization of the means of production are taken to be a modern extension of Islamic social justice. Muslim practices such as payment of zakat signify justice; pilgrimage and prayer symbolize equality. Islam is said to be compatible with modern science and religious justifications are found for scientific truths. They see the Quran as the embodiment of general principles, but recognize that it was revealed in a particular era and that changing historical conditions have made it obsolete in many respects. They also excuse Muslims from rituals involving animal sacrifices, from fasting – which is an excessive hardship in modern working conditions – and from other traditional observances. Muslim religious leaders thus attempt to justify Islam as a valid component of a modern society.

This trend in Soviet-Muslim thought may be evaluated from different points of view. Many Western writers see it as a necessary accommodation to the power of the Soviet regime. Some Soviet writers see it as a manipulative effort to win an audience in an increasingly agnostic society. "National" authors see it as the perpetuation of an important component of national identity. Muslim writers claim they are clarifying basic religious principles and reanimating Islam in the context of a modernizing society. Their views represent a Muslim jadid or modernism similar to that in other Muslim societies.

Scholars differ as to how to evaluate the degree of tension between Soviet citizenship and national separateness. Some insist that there is a "Homo Islamicus" who cannot be integrated and who is basically opposed to the Soviet system. Others believe that the Muslim elites have been entirely co-opted, or that the party elites are coopted and the mass of the people unassimilated. All seem to agree that there is a strong sense of opposition between Russian and Muslim nationalities and little sense of a Soviet people. Muslims have a distrustful sense of separateness, an identity based on multiple and sometimes conflicting loyalties directed to clan and tribe, national republics, the universal Muslim community, and the Soviet federal regime. Muslim identity in Soviet society is thus a subtle blend of political loyalty, national consciousness, and Muslim heritage.

Still the cultivation of separate national identities and even of Muslim loyalties is not inconsistent with the integration of these populations into the Soviet state and economy. Soviet modernization has acculturated Muslims to a socialist type of political society. Like their Tsarist predecessors, the Soviets have had to abandon the goal of complete assimilation in favor of a multi-ethnic society in which there is considerable latitude for variations in sub-political ethnic identities that are consistent with functional integration into the larger society. Muslim forms of identity, then, may be considered a variant type of Soviet culture rather than being antagonistic to it. The Soviet regime in practice must control local nationalisms, make appropriate economic and social concessions, and tolerate lifestyles which include national customs and Islamic religious practices.

THE CAUCASUS

The Caucasus region lies outside of Inner Asia, but it too was absorbed by Russia in the late eighteenth and nineteenth centuries, and its Muslim populations, once attached to those of the Ottoman and Safavid empires, have become linked to those of Inner Asia. Caucasian peoples were ruled by nobles who dominated free peasants and various categories of serfs and slaves. Some population groups were organized purely in lineages or small confederations of clans. Islam was first introduced to Azarbayjan and other areas south of the Caucasus by the Arab conquests in the seventh century. It was reinforced by the Saljuq migrations in the eleventh century. In the twelfth and thirteenth centuries the Golden Horde introduced Islam to the northern Caucasus, and the influence of the Crimean Khans and the Ottoman empire helped spread Islam among Caucasian peoples in the sixteenth and seventeenth centuries. Naqshbandi Sufis probably appeared in Daghestan in the eighteenth century. Studying in Mecca and Medina, teaching in Damascus and Aleppo, local scholars were connected to the international community of ʿulamaʾ and Sufis. Yet on the eve of Russian domination, only part of the Caucasian population of about $1\frac{1}{2}$ million, divided into some 20 different Turkish, Iranian, and Caucasian language groups, was Muslim. In many cases the elites were Muslim while the common people remained animists.

The Russians began to penetrate the region in the early eighteenth century. With the breakup of the Safavid empire the Russians took northern Daghestan in 1723 while the Ottomans occupied eastern Georgia and southern Daghestan.

Russia annexed Georgia in 1801–04. In response to Ottoman and Russian imperialism a local peasant movement emerged, led by a man called Shaykh Mansur, who may have been a Naqshbandi. After having visions of horsemen sent to him by the Prophet Muhammad, he proclaimed himself imam. He wore a veil to conceal his radiant holiness, and forbade drinking of wine or smoking of tobacco. Four main principles inspired his movement: the return to a purified Islam, the struggle against non-Islamic religious practices, the rule of Shariᶜa, and holy war against the infidels. Mansur raised a coalition of free peasants and local notables, but, deserted by the nobles, was defeated in 1787. Despite this defeat his efforts deepened the hold of Islam on local peoples and prepared the way for later Sufi preachers who would make the Caucasus a bastion of Islamic resistance to the Russians.

In the nineteenth century, Sufism spread in the villages as the basis of resistance to Russian rule. A succession of Naqshbandi imams, of whom the foremost was Shamil (active 1834–59), led the resistance of free peasant landowners who opposed the Russians and the local lords allied to them. By 1844 Shamil had annihilated most of the noble families in Daghestan. He proclaimed the reign of the Shariᶜa, and prohibited dancing, music, and smoking. He was defeated in 1859, but in spite, or perhaps because, of defeat, Sufism continued to flourish. The conviction that Sufis could communicate with supernatural beings, ward off evil spirits, and serve as guardian intermediaries between men and God grew stronger. The cult of saints flourished. The graves of saints – and other holy places such as crossroads, hills, caves, and stones which commemorated battles fought against the Russians – were visited by pilgrims seeking cures, aid in pregnancy, and other worldly good fortune. Alongside of the Naqshbandiya, the Qadiriya gained adherents and introduced their own dhikr based on loud recitation, dancing, music, and drumming. The two orders joined in a great revolt in 1877–78, but this also was crushed by the Russians. During the revolution the Muslims of the Caucasus again made a vigorous effort to expel the Russians and to establish an autonomous state. In 1917 a congress of ᶜulamaᵓ elected an imam, who led resistance from 1920 to 1925. The Russians defeated this resistance, arrested the religious leaders, disarmed the people, and liquidated Muslim institutions and Shariᶜa courts. Nonetheless, there were new revolts between 1928 and 1936 and from 1940 to 1944. During World War II the whole population of Chechen-Ingushia was deported to Kazakhstan and Siberia and the territory was jurisdictionally divided among the Russian and Georgian Soviet Republics. (Also in 1944 on the basis of allegations that the Tatars had collaborated with the Germans, the Russians deported the entire Tatar population of the Crimea to Inner Asia and incorporated the region into the Ukraine.) The Caucasian peoples have since been "rehabilitated," and the region reorganized as an autonomous republic. Caucasus populations remain closely attached to Islam, observe the fast of Ramadan, and make pilgrimages to tombs of saints. There are still numerous Quran schools and Sufi teachers officiating over prayers and family rituals.

The survival of the Sufi brotherhoods under intensive pressure is partly due to the discipline exerted by the leaders over their followers, and partly due to the identification of the Sufi brotherhoods with families and clans (*taip*). In some cases a group of families living in a village consider themselves both the members of a Sufi brotherhood and the descendants of a common ancestor. The double loyalty toward clan and brotherhood makes for intense solidarity. As recently as 1979 a Soviet journal told of a dhikr in which all the members of a clan, including the president of the local collective farm and the Soviet party secretary, participated.

THE MUSLIMS OF CHINA

China's Muslim populations fall into two main groups. The Hui are those Muslims spread throughout the regions of Han population who in physical appearance and language are Chinese but consider themselves a separate people because they do not eat pork, worship ancestors, gamble, drink or smoke opium. The other Muslims are non-assimilated Inner Asian peoples including Uighurs, Kazakhs, Kirgiz, and other minority groups most of whom speak Turkic languages and are not assimilated to a Chinese cultural style. These peoples were absorbed into the Chinese state in the late nineteenth century when the Chinese defeated the revolts of Chinese-speaking Muslims resident in Yunnan, Shensi, and Kansu provinces, and the revolts of Uighurs and Kazakhs in Sinkiang. In the Republican period (1911–49) China's relations with its Muslim minorities were based on the expectation that they would be totally assimilated and incorporated into Chinese society.

Sinkiang, however, preserved a considerable autonomy, and was ruled by a succession of independent warlords. Yang Tseng-hsin became the first governor (1911–28) under the Republican regime. To support his administration he mobilized both Chinese and Muslim soldiers to maintain a local balance of power, counteract Chinese secret societies, and forestall the possibility of Muslim forces being used to create an independent state. Yang gave the local chieftains autonomy, spared the province heavy economic burdens, and thus managed to maintain Chinese suzerainty and his personal control. In

1924 he signed a treaty with the Soviet Union which exchanged Chinese consulates in Soviet Central Asia for Soviet consulates in eastern Turkestan, and thus bolstered the autonomy of the region from central government control. Yang was assassinated in 1928 and in 1933 Sinkiang was taken over by Sheng Shih-ts'ai. Sheng also followed a policy of maintaining close ties with Russia and of rallying local non-Chinese support. He encouraged newspapers in local languages, stabilized the currency, and, with Russian investments, improved communications, built factories, and set up an oil refinery. The German invasion of Russia, however, cut off Russian support and obliged Sheng to restore Sinkiang to the control of the Chinese government.

World War II and the defeat of the regime of Chiang Kai-shek allowed for Kazakh and Uighur rebellions in 1944. The Soviet Union helped to negotiate the return of the province to China in 1946, and the rebel groups agreed to subordination to China in return for local autonomy and a reformed administration. The nationalist Chinese regime, however, forfeited its opportunity to win local goodwill, the Muslims failed to unite to maintain their independence, and the Chinese Communists were able to absorb the province in 1949 by cooperating with local elites.

Under Communist rule, China's Muslim minorities receive a great deal of political attention owing to the fact that they are concentrated on China's borders and because Muslim populated territories contain a great part of China's mineral resources, as well as its meat, milk, and wool supplies. For reasons of defense and economy, as well as national pride, the Chinese government is eager to win their loyalty, but there have been frequent changes in Chinese policy. The long-term Chinese goal is the disappearance of ethnic and nationality differences in a Chinese proletarian culture. The mechanisms for reaching that goal have been the subject of much dispute. One approach has been to tolerate the old elites and minority customs and to attempt to integrate the minorities into the Chinese political system by granting regional autonomy in the hope that political attachments would create a basis for greater homogeneity. Muslims were encouraged to cultivate traditional customs and beliefs, and yet to participate in the Chinese Communist party, state bureaucracies, and other mass organizations. It was expected that Han characteristics would thus be voluntarily accepted.

In the 1920s and 1930s the party followed the Russian line in promising self-determination to minorities. In 1938 Mao abandoned his support for self-determination in favor of a policy of autonomy within a unified Chinese state. Mao declared that minorities would receive equal rights with Chinese. Hui were taken into the party and the Red Army, and Muslims were promised that their religious interests would be protected.

Upon coming to power the Chinese Communists continued their policy of accommodation with Muslim communities. They ordered that Muslim customs be accepted in work places and government agencies. Muslim circumcision and marriage practices were permitted. A Chinese Islamic Association was founded in 1953 and a Chinese Institute of Islamic Theology, which trained religious scholars, was founded in 1955. Leading Muslims were confirmed in regional political positions and autonomous political areas were set up in Sinkiang and other provinces. Medical and educational work was begun. Scientific agricultural and stockbreeding techniques were introduced, and strenuous efforts were made to promote production with the help of Chinese workers who assisted local peoples. From 1949 until 1955 the Chinese government concentrated on integration of its minority regions.

By 1956 party leaders were convinced that it was time to move to a new stage of development and to speed up the socialization of the minority populations. Muslim leaders were encouraged by the Hundred Flowers Campaign to express their criticisms of the Communist Chinese regime. This revealed strong separatist tendencies, desires to be unified with fellow Muslims inside the Soviet Union, hopes for an Islamic state, and criticisms of Chinese control. Muslims had grievances due to food shortages, confiscation of mosques, and dissemination of Marxist education and propaganda. While they were not persecuted, Muslims felt a narrowing of the boundaries of their autonomy.

These revelations brought a severe Chinese reaction. In 1957 the Chinese Communists began more aggressive efforts to assimilate the minority populations. This included emphasis upon class struggle, the promotion of new activists, the abolition of special customs, limitations on autonomy, and other policies designed to promote more rapid assimilation. Local nationalisms were denounced as a form of ingratitude, and the Chinese decided to replace the traditional elites by cadres with an acceptable class background, to create cooperatives, to socialize production, and to eliminate bureaucracy. Minority languages, festivals, and customs were attacked, and pressure was put on the Hui to eat in common dining halls and intermarry with Chinese. Special Muslim restaurants and bathing facilities were closed. Women were obliged to put aside traditional clothing and go to work, and mosque properties were confiscated. Mixed-nationality communes were formed, and Han youth were sent to colonize minority areas. The Chinese Islamic Association was disbanded in 1958.

These measures provoked military resistance in Ninghsia province with the objective of establishing a Muslim republic. Kazakhs emigrated across the border into the Soviet Union. Thus it was evident that the campaign for assimilation had gone too rapidly and had to be repudiated. Resistance made the Chinese elites aware of the extent to which they had been misled by lower-level cadres and how cultural pressures which had no economic relevance could be counterproductive. Also the concern of the Chinese regime to protect its borders with the Soviet Union and to win the diplomatic support of Muslim Middle Eastern, African, and Asian states counseled an end to the Great Leap Forward. Some communes were dissolved, the Hui were permitted independent dining halls, and the special characteristics of minority populations were recognized as acceptable. The national problem was understood to be a long rather than a short-term concern.

In 1966, however, a new cultural revolution and the mobilization of the Red Guards reopened the struggle against the special privileges of minorities. The Red Guards demanded that mosques be closed, Quran study prohibited, and Muslim circumcision and marriage practices forbidden. Despite these pressures, by 1969 Hui schools were again functioning and religious festivals were being observed. A new constitution of 1970 recognized minority languages and customs but did not give particularly warm assurances about their protection. While policy toward the minorities was moderated for tactical reasons, many party activists continued to favor assimilation.

After 1975 the Chinese government reaffirmed the right of minorities to develop their own culture within the framework of the Chinese state. With the death of Mao and the overthrow of the Gang of Four in 1976, Muslims were more fully rehabilitated and allowed to rebuild schools, operate restaurants, and pursue religious activities. In 1980 the Chinese Islamic Association held its first meeting since 1963. Nonetheless, the Chinese government continues to pursue policies that would integrate Muslims into local administration, and tries to dilute Muslim power in the provinces by resettling large numbers of Chinese peasants in northwestern Muslim regions. The Chinese government also threatens to destroy counter-revolutionaries operating under the cover of religion. Frequent changes of direction indicate that the Chinese leadership itself is divided over what policies would lead ultimately to a homogeneous proletarian culture and a fusion of national minorities in Chinese society.

Sinkiang province, which harbors a substantial portion of the non-Han Muslim population, remains a special case. Chinese Communist authority was established in Sinkiang in 1949 and separate administrative regimes were set up for Kazakhs and Uighurs. The Chinese formed the Ili-Kazakh Autonomous Chou and the Sinkiang Uighur Autonomous Chou in 1955 for a population of some 3,500,000 people living in the Tarim basin and in the vicinity of Kashgar, Aksu, and Khotan. Nonetheless the Chinese made important changes. They

destroyed the traditional elites, collectivized agriculture and herding, introduced new schools, and favored economic development. They invested in
irrigation and reclamation projects and increased the output of wheat, cotton,
corn, and rice. In Kazakh districts the Chinese have developed coal, iron, and
petroleum. The government has also tried to sedentarize the nomads by
persuading them of the advantages of sedentary livestock herding. Large
numbers of Chinese settlers were moved into the region with the completion
of the Hami Railway in 1959.

In sum, Russian and Chinese control of Inner Asian peoples differs from
that of European imperial regimes in other parts of the Muslim world. These
imperialisms were a direct expansion of the Russian and Chinese states onto
contiguous territories and allowed for the migration and settlement of Europeans and Chinese in the conquered territories without either the colonial or
conquered peoples regarding the newcomers as temporary residents. In Soviet
Inner Asia the presence of a large European population has led to an unprecedented integration between the colonizing and the colonized societies.
Probably no other Muslim region is as highly modernized. This does not of
course mean a full equalization of Russians and Muslims. Muslim populations
remain subordinate to de facto Russian controls both in the government and
the party apparatus. While not a colonized population in the usual sense they
are still politically subordinate.

To a somewhat greater degree, elements of the Muslim population of China,
while integrated into Chinese society, continue to habor distinct cultural and
religious identities and separatist political ambitions. While some sectors of the
Muslim population have been assimilated for centuries, Hui do not lose their
identity or become fully absorbed into the Chinese polity. Muslim populations
in Inner Asia are still less assimilated than the Hui and separatist tendencies are
more marked. Neither Chinese nor Muslims have resolved these ambiguities;
they seem to be an inherent aspect of the place of Muslims in China.

From the point of view of Muslim peoples, these adaptations to Soviet and
Chinese conditions represent variations upon the repertoire of Muslim adaptations to non-Muslim regimes and to minority status found in many other
parts of the world. Muslims in China, India, and Africa have adapted to
minority status by accepting the sectarian aspects of Islamic community organization. The "millet" arrangement in India, "nationality" Muslim identity
in the Soviet Union, the emphasis of Hui Chinese upon exclusive practices, the
proliferation of religious clubs, associations, and communities in Africa –
these are all aspects of Muslim communal consolidation in the face of non-
Muslim regimes. The Soviet Union differs in that the state has made intensive

efforts to assimilate Muslims into the economy and the political system and suppresses or controls the social organization of Muslim believers. In the Soviet Union the organizational aspects of Muslim communal life are either coopted or forbidden, and Muslim communalism is channeled into ritual, symbolic, and other cultural expressions. More often it is fused with officially promoted forms of national culture. In this extreme case of modernization Islam remains the basis of subjective identity.

ISLAM IN TWENTIETH-CENTURY AFRICA

CHAPTER 30

ISLAM IN WEST AFRICA

To the end of the nineteenth century Islam had spread in Sudanic, savannah, and forest Africa by virtue of a combination of forces. Migrant trading communities and missionary teachers had established scattered Muslim communities throughout these regions. In parts of the Sudan and East Africa these communities converted local rulers and helped establish Muslim states. In other cases Muslim ʿulamaʾ and holy-men waged jihad to form their own territorial regimes. At the very end of the century European invaders brought a halt to these processes, defeated, subordinated, and broke up existing states and imposed their own regimes. Muslim state formation was checked and Muslim peoples became subject to new political and economic pressures.

In the following chapters we shall review the impact of European regimes upon several selected African societies and discuss Muslim responses to the sociopolitical and economic circumstances established by colonialism and by the formation of independent African national states. In this chapter we shall briefly review the impact of colonialism in West Africa and give case studies of post-independent Mauritania, Senegal, Nigeria, and Ghana to illustrate the principal forms of state and Muslim communal organization. In the following chapter we shall review Muslim states and communal structures in the Sudan, Ethiopia, Somalia, and Swahili-speaking East Africa. Though we have divided the region by geography, similar patterns of organization and state–communal relations are found in both East and West Africa. In many respects Mauritania and Somalia, Senegal and Tanzania, resemble each other more closely than other states in their immediate region. A conclusion to both chapters comes at the end of the discussion of East African Islam. Our purpose is not to give a comprehensive history of African societies, but to indicate the forces which have set the context for Muslim values, institutions, and regimes in contemporary Africa.

COLONIALISM AND INDEPENDENCE: AFRICAN STATES AND ISLAM

Colonial rule had almost paradoxical implications for the Muslim population of West Africa. On the one hand, colonial rule overthrew established Muslim African states and disrupted the patterns of development set in the earlier era. The colonial powers drew the new territorial boundaries that define African states to the present day. They helped inspire secular and national political identities. On the other hand, colonial rule also facilitated the spread of Islam and helped make it the majority religion in many African countries.

The French and the British empires between them largely determined the political configuration of modern African societies. By 1900 the French empire comprised a vast region including the Atlantic coastal territories of Senegal, Guinea, the Ivory Coast, and Dahomey. Between 1899 and 1922 the interior was organized into the large colonies of French Sudan, Niger, and Mauritania. Upper Volta was formed in 1919 but in 1932 it was divided among the Ivory Coast, Niger, and the Sudan, and then reconstituted in 1947. The French central African empire included Muslim populations in Chad. The British organized protectorates for Gambia, Sierra Leone, Ghana, and the northern and southern regions of Nigeria. The Nigerian protectorates were united as the colony and protectorate of Nigeria in 1914.

In the government of both British and French territories one basic principle applied. The local populations were ruled through intermediary local chiefs supervised by foreign officials. This principle was implemented in different ways. The French favored highly centralized and authoritarian means of control. In Senegambia and the Sudanic regions the French broke the potential for Muslim resistance, dissolved the larger states and paramount chieftainships, displaced the older aristocracies, and favored local-level district chiefs who were easy to subordinate to the central administration. These local chiefs were not men of traditional importance but rather newcomers promoted by the French to collect taxes, organize corvée, and administer the French judicial code. While local chieftains were used as intermediaries, the centralization of French administration destroyed their authority and paved the way for the rise of new elites.

The British pursued the goals of political control by the policy of "indirect rule." This meant that the British accepted a much larger scale of native administration than the French, and guaranteed the authority of the dominant elites. In northern Nigeria they bypassed the Sokoto Caliphate, and made the emirs, advised by British residents or divisional officers, responsible for administration, tax collection, and justice. British officers supervised the emirs but did not intervene between them and their subjects. However, the British helped replace feudal tenures by direct administration, reorganized the judicial system, established a territorial system of native courts, and greatly strengthened the Muslim judiciary. Thus the British rationalized local administration in northern Nigeria. They also protected it from the direct impact of European rule by laws which forbade Europeans to purchase lands and prohibited Christian missionaries from entering the predominantly Muslim regions.

Throughout West Africa the establishment of colonial regimes led to profound economic and social change. The principal interest of the colonial powers was to stimulate exports of cash crops such as peanuts from Senegal, timber from the Ivory Coast, and palm oil from Dahomey. The French collected taxes in cash to force increases in agricultural production, and used forced labor on banana, cocoa, and coffee plantations. The British developed cocoa, timber, rubber, manganese, aluminum and gold exports from the Gold Coast. Nigeria, which exported palm oil, cocoa, rubber, and peanuts, had high gross export earnings but a low per capita income.

Railway construction was essential to the colonial economic scheme, and the colonial powers built railways to link the interior with international markets. The French built railways from St Louis to Dakar and from Dakar to Bamako, linking the Niger River and the Atlantic. Railways in Guinea, Ivory Coast, Dahomey, Sierra Leone, and Nigeria tied the producing regions of the interior to the ports, but did not link the interior territories with each other. The railways destroyed the trans-Saharan traffic and ended the long struggle begun by the Atlantic slave trade, between Saharan and European peoples, for control of the commerce of Africa. Henceforth international trade would move by rail to the coast rather than by camel across the desert.

Trade, moreover, was controlled in the interest of the European companies. Currency, banking, navigation, customs, and legal arrangements ensured the domination of a few large colonial banks, shipping lines, and other firms. French restrictions on the domestic economy of their African colonies made prices in French West Africa higher than world levels, and French West Africa ran a consistently unfavorable balance of trade. Africans were eliminated from the export business and ruined by European competition. Arabs, Greeks, and Indians migrated to the French colonies and often took local retail trade out of African hands. Up until the 1930s neither the British nor the French invested in the colonies, but expected them to pay the costs of their administration. Only in reaction to the depression did the colonial powers begin to regard it in their interest to finance economic development. After World War II the British and the French began to invest more heavily.

Political and economic change in the West African colonies was accompanied, as elsewhere in the Muslim world, by the formation of new economic classes and social and political groups. Changes in the economy helped break down lineage bonds, generated mobility, brought individuals into large-scale market arrangements, upset old values, and generated a demand for individual as opposed to collectively shared wealth. It broke down the equilibrium of village communities, promoted seasonal or migrant labor and wage employment, and encouraged the growth of urban centers with their relative freedom from traditional authority and concepts. Changing patterns of trade and administration brought Africans to capital and port towns. Out of these uprooted populations new elites and new communities came into being.

In the cities an African bourgeoisie of professional men and women took form as Western education trained small minorities to serve as doctors, teachers, lawyers, journalists, interpreters, and government officials. Education, however, was very limited. In the French empire only about 3 percent of African students were enabled to go to school. In Nigeria, British education generated a small Western-educated elite which was mostly southern in origin. In the decade before 1942 some 300,000 students went to primary schools but only 2,000 to secondary schools. Almost all of these schools were in the south and a large proportion were Christian missionary schools. With a few exceptions Christian missionaries and Western schools were excluded from northern Nigeria.

Colonial administration and education also generated a subordinate elite of mechanics, transport workers, bricklayers, clerks, cash-crop farmers, and others. Clerks had a particularly close acquaintance with the workings of a modern administration and economy, and were important as liaisons between the sub-elites and higher-level government officials. Clerks and school teachers became important spokesmen and leaders in clubs, tribal, trade union, and political movements.

The new elites asserted themselves through a myriad of new associations. Tribal, ethnic, mutual aid, trade union, and debating societies, and ultimately political clubs, were the product of migration and urbanization and the basis for the emergence of political parties. Student and youth associations were particularly important for the ultimate formation of African nationalist movements.

The depression and World War II gave these new elites an opportunity to press their demands. The war fatally damaged the political power and moral authority of the European powers and allowed African leaders to claim self-determination and political independence. Though French administration was assisted by local councils with advisory powers and local chambers of commerce, high-ranking African chieftains, rich traders, property owners, and war veterans were the only people eligible for political participation. In time, however, the existence of an African-educated elite, however small, made it necessary to broaden the base of participation. In Nigeria the British also favored older elites and excluded the small Western-educated elite from the higher branches of government administration. However, encouraged by their education to believe that they would ultimately control the society, the new elites became anti-colonial nationalists and claimed the right to speak for the mass of the people. On behalf of the sub-elites of clerks, technicians, traders, and landowning farmers, they demanded equality in wages with European workers, equality in participation in the colonial regimes and ultimately independence.

The French fought a long rearguard action to moderate African demands and to maintain the subordination of the colonies. At the Brazzaville conference in 1944 they acknowledged their obligation to invest in African economic development, to build bridges, ports, and agricultural facilities, and to improve health services and education. The conference also adopted a new political goal. In place of the French concept of the assimilation of individual Africans to French citizenship, it proposed an association of African societies within a French union, and the formation of territorial assemblies which would be entitled to send representatives to the French parliament. In 1946 a new French constitution redefined the French republic to include French West Africa.

The formation of territorial assemblies led to the formation of political parties. Some of these were personal factions, or coalitions of smaller associations, but some were mass parties with a wide base of support. The most important was the Rassemblement Démocratique Africain, formed in 1946 as an anti-imperial congress-type movement, uniting professional elites, trade union leaders, and youth organizations under the leadership of Félix Houphouet-Boigny. Under French rule the R.D.A. was the principal party in the Ivory Coast, Sudan, Niger, and Guinea. Only in Senegal was it displaced by the African branch of the French Socialist Party and the Bloc Démocratique Sénégalais (B.D.S.), founded in 1949, led by Léopold Senghor and renamed Union Progressiste Sénégalaise in 1951. To forestall the movement toward independence the French decided in 1956 on a scheme to give the territorial assemblies full control over agriculture, health, law, civil administration, and other internal matters. Then in 1958 General de Gaulle proposed a referendum which offered African states a choice between immediate independence and self-government within the French community. Most of the West African states, obliged by economic dependence, voted to remain attached to France. Only Guinea voted for immediate independence without linkage to France. In 1959, however, despite its initial opposition, France agreed to accept the (temporary) Federated Republic of Mali (Senegal and Sudan) as independent within the French community. This lessening of French terms precipitated the demand for independence by Ivory Coast, Dahomey, Niger, and Upper Volta, which was conceded in 1960. In 1958 the Islamic Republic of Mauritania also became an independent state.

In British West Africa, Ghana, under the leadership of Nkrumah and the Convention People's Party, was the first country to achieve independence. In Nigeria, the movements which led to independence had their origin among Western-educated Africans in the aftermath of World War I. In the 1930s trade unions, worker associations, occupational and professional groups, and kinship and tribal unions were formed in great numbers and became channels for political agitation. In Nigeria the combined pressures of student and nationalist leaders and British change of heart about colonial rule led to the first Nigerian constitution in 1946. The Richards Constitution provided for a Nigerian legislative council and four provincial units – the Lagos Colony, and the Western, the Eastern, and the Northern provinces – each with a house of assembly recruited from the existing native authorities. The constitution promoted regional and ethnic rivalries among Yorubas and Ibos, northern Muslims and southerners, and between the dominant and minority groups in each region, over the distribution of regional and central authority. The Muslim north in particular feared subordination within a Nigerian state dominated by the south. Only in 1957 was self-government attained by the eastern and western regions; in 1959 the north finally announced that it was ready for independence. The federation as a whole finally became independent in 1960. The former British possessions of Sierra Leone and Gambia became independent in 1961 and 1965.

In the newly independent states, territorial boundaries, administrative structures, dominant elites, and ideological conceptions were all the products of the colonial era. While African and Muslim communities below the level of state regimes continued to embody very different principles of social organization and religious values, the new states were formed under the aegis

of nationalist and secular concepts. Most Sudanic and West African peoples
were and are ruled by a narrow, often military elite, in the name of interests
and ideologies which do not, with some exceptions, reflect the values and
identities of the masses. The new elites were commonly non-Muslims and were
primarily concerned with political and economic modernization. For most of
them Islam was a religion for private worship, but not an influence in public
affairs. They accepted Islam as a "personal religion" on a par with Christianity
and not necessarily as relevant to the political order.

Nonetheless, while European rule promoted secular elites, it aided the
peaceful spread of Islam. In both the colonial and independence periods there
were significant conversions to Islam among pagan peoples. In the region of
Mali, 3 percent of the Bambaras were Muslims in 1912. French pacification
opened new trading opportunities and led to widespread conversion, until
some 70 percent of the Bambara are now Muslims. In northern Nigeria, where
the British recognized Islam as the religion of the state, Hausas converted in
large numbers. For example the Bauchi emirate, which was 50 percent Muslim
in 1920, was 75 percent Muslim in 1952. Ilorin was 43 percent Muslim in 1931
and 63 percent Muslim in 1952. Islam was spread south by Hausa migrants and
by the large-scale conversion of Yorubas. According to the Nigerian census
of 1963 over 40 percent of the population of Lagos and the western region was
Muslim. By 1970 Nigeria as a whole was more than half Muslim.

Islam also made new converts in the Guinean and coastal regions. In Upper
Volta at the end of the nineteenth century there were only some 30,000
Muslims, but by 1959 there were 800,000, approximately 20 percent of the
population. In the Ivory Coast the Muslims formed 7 percent of the populace
in 1921, 22 percent in 1960 and 33 percent in 1970. Ghana is 25 percent and
Sierra Leone approximately 35 percent Muslim. Muslims are a majority in
Senegal, Mali, Nigeria, Gambia, Guinea, Niger, and Chad and a substantial
minority in Ghana, the Cameroons, Sierra Leone, Upper Volta, and other
countries. Between 1900 and 1960 the Muslim population of West Africa
approximately doubled, and continues to grow substantially.

Colonial administration indirectly favored the spread of Islam by creating
peace and order and by stimulating trade. Just as colonial rule led to the
formation of a modernized African elite in response to economic change, so
it favored Islam as a religion of uprooted peoples. Europeans broke down the
traditional structures of society, introduced new educational and social ideas,
opened markets, attracted migrant Africans to growing cities, and thereby
indirectly promoted Islam as a form of authority and as an expression of
cohesion among displaced peoples. The colonial powers also regarded Muslims

as being on a higher cultural and educational level than non-Muslim Africans and appointed Muslim chiefs and clerks as administrators in non-Muslim areas. They subsidized Muslim religious teachers, who were allowed to pursue their missionary, community organizing, and instructional activity. In some cases colonial authorities helped organize Islamic law courts.

Colonial rule not only favored the spread of Islam but created the conditions which shaped the social character, religious practices and communal identity of Muslims. European rule forced the Muslims to abandon their eighteenth- and nineteenth-century political aspirations and to accept foreign domination. In many cases Muslims not only accepted but collaborated with foreign or secular rulers. Muslim leaders, such as the emirs of northern Nigeria or the Sufis of Senegal, became the foremost participants in colonial and post-independence regimes. Muslim religious leaders commonly preached acceptance of these regimes and helped recruit manpower for European armies, collect taxes, and even suppress Muslim dissidents. As in India they saw themselves as an elite, the natural allies and the likely beneficiaries of cooperation with the state. Whereas in North Africa, the Arab Middle East, India, and Indonesia, Muslim associations were transformed into political movements, in Sudanic, Savannah, and forest West Africa this was not usually the case.

Many Muslims, however, refused cooperation and withdrew from contact with Europeans. While Muslim resistance to colonial expansion in the nine-teenth century was militant, after the consolidation of the European empires there was little armed resistance. Mahdists in Nigeria, Tuaregs in Niger, and Sufi-led warriors in Mauritania and Somalia were the only major exceptions. Muslim opposition to foreign rule could generally be expressed only indirectly through schools, reform movements, and Sufi-led brotherhoods. The Bam-idele movement in Ibadan (Nigeria), for example, insisted on preserving Arabic usage, Muslim dress, and reformed Islamic practices.

The Hamalliya similarly expressed opposition to foreign rule by symbolic means. The Hamalliya, founded by Shaykh Hamallah (1883–1943), was a Sufi brotherhood based in Nioro; it was an offshoot of the Tijani brotherhood, and it condemned the parent order for having corrupted the true teachings of the founder. Shaykh Hamallah himself lived in seclusion, taught only in his own mosque, and never solicited gifts, though he accepted contributions from people who visited him. His followers held up his humility and gentleness against the greed and pride of the regular Tijaniya. His very withdrawal, however, had important political implications. Though Muslim religious lead-ers under foreign rule turned to religious self-cultivation, they remained

Map 36. African states with large Muslim populations: *c.* 1980.

important to local people as a source of inspiration, blessing, protection, and guidance, and in unsettled conditions could attract a large following. Their disciples as well as their enemies could see in their retreat tacit gestures of political opposition. While Shaykh Hamallah refused to speak of political matters, he also refused to publicly acknowledge French authority. His followers took his refusal to be a tacit blessing for hostility to French rule. The French for their part ruled through a small number of administrators who had little understanding of African languages or peoples and operated through clerks, interpreters, informers, and spies. Their isolation led to an almost paranoid suspicion of what the natives were doing. The French were eager to control the activity of Muslim religious leaders and put them all under close surveillance. Outraged at the refusal of Shaykh Hamallah to give them political recognition, they deported him in 1925. In response he began to use an abbreviated prayer, and his followers turned to pray in the direction of his internment rather than Mecca. This symbolized the absence of a legitimate government.

The movement taught the social equality of all castes and appealed strongly to runaway slaves, youth, and people without tribal or social standing. In the 1940s the Hamallists divided into two wings. One refused to recognize the local religious authorities and was constantly involved in hostilities with the regular Tijaniya. A second wing, led by Tyerno Bokar Salif Tall (d. 1940), stressed the intellectual and mystical teachings of the master, egalitarianism, and rejection of foreign rule. Only after Hamallah's death did his followers begin to organize politically and to clash with the French.

As in other parts of the Muslim world, colonial rule channeled Muslims into community, educational, and social action. The Sufi tariqat spread throughout Nigeria, Senegal, and other places. Muslim ethnic groups such as the Hausas and Yorubas were organized to protect Muslim identity. Educational associations were formed among urban and "modernized" Muslims.

Muslim education and religious associations had a complex relationship to the larger African societies. In colonial Africa there was generally a split between the secular or Western-educated leaders who took over African regimes, and the leaders of Muslim communities who were not engaged in national but rather in small-group leadership. In many African states Muslims formed ethnic or religious minorities which were not fully assimilated into the political system. Here we examine several African-Muslim societies, to explore some of the major variations in the structure of national and Muslim political and communal organization, and in the Muslim adaptation to the larger African civilization.

MAURITANIA

Among African states, Mauritania shows the closest integration of state, national, and ethnic identities. The population of Mauritania is wholly Muslim, and the state identifies itself as Islamic. Mauritania is thus closest to Somalia or northern Sudan in the blending of popular Arab and Muslim identity and closest to Algeria and Libya in the integration of state and Islamic identity.

Modern Mauritania was born out of French rule. By the Treaty of Paris (1814) the European powers recognized French suzerainty over Senegal and the Atlantic Saharan regions, including the territories now part of Mauritania. The French strongly influenced the Mauritanian political system. They considered the Hassani tribes as the political elite, paid them subsidies, and institutionalized their authority as intermediaries between the French government and the general populace. The French also suppressed the traditional raiding activities and thus obliged the Hassanis to take up stockraising and commerce. Thus they deprived the zawaya (religious) tribes of their traditional functions – especially political mediation, economic negotiation, and the organization of production. While believing they were preserving the traditional order of society, the French broke down the symbiosis among the Mauritanian tribes and created a new hierarchical relationship. A French protectorate was declared in 1904, but between 1902 and 1934 Mauritania resisted absorption into the French empire. Local rebellions, however, were defeated and eventually most of the Muslim religious leaders gave up their faith in military resistance and accepted collaboration with the French to protect their religious and economic interests.

In 1946 the French Fourth Republic separated Mauritania from Senegal and attempted to create a new political structure for the country. A local assembly was created in 1947 and the first Mauritanian political party, the Entente Mouritanienne, was formed in 1948. The Entente was opposed by the Union Progressiste Mouritanienne. A splinter party from the U.P.M. created, in 1951–52, the Association de la Jeunesse Mouritanienne, which was more vociferous in its demands for independence. The parties represented a split in Mauritanian society between the traditional elites and the modern type of politician. A major issue in the 1950s was how to preserve Mauritanian identity by avoiding absorption into the Arab Moroccan north or the Senegalese and Sudanese south. In 1958 the Islamic Republic of Mauritania was proclaimed an independent state.

Independent Mauritania also has an apparently unified national elite ruling over a highly segmentary society. Upon achieving independence in 1958 the major Mauritanian political parties, the Entente and the U.P.M., formed a new Parti du Regroupement Mouritanien which was renamed the Mauritanian Peoples Party in 1961. In 1964 it became the only legitimate party. The ruling party represents the traditional political elites, is drawn mainly from the zawaya tribes and can be traced back to the factions of the nineteenth century. Thus the traditional segmentary communities of Mauritanian society have been united under a single regime. In the new structure some non-tribal associations such as trade unions, women's organizations, and schools have been introduced; changing patterns of economic activity have allowed a new class of entrepreneurs to rise in influence. The traditional divisions of the society are thus slowly being overcome by the formation of a more highly integrated community under a single regime speaking a metropolitan language and subscribing to an Islamic national identity. The degree to which the new national unity has in fact overcome the inherent factional and tribal divisions of the society is debatable.

SENEGAL

Senegal represents a different type of Muslim society. The Senegalese state, until 1980, was essentially a non-Muslim secular regime ruling over a largely Muslim population. While the regime was organized in accord with European political institutions and political culture and led by a non-Muslim elite, the bulk of the population was encadred in Sufi brotherhoods. Senegal held together by the collaboration of state and Sufi elites. Senegal represents a recreation of the classic pattern of supportive relations between Muslim states and Muslim communal organizations.

The pattern has its origins in the late nineteenth century, when the Muslim jihads and the French conquest transformed the traditional bases of Senegalese society. In the wars of the late nineteenth century, the tyeddo slave military elite and the ruling pagan families were eliminated. Soldiers, peasants, artisans dependent on the chiefs, and liberated slaves turned for leadership to Muslim holy-men. Many old families maintained their position by producing a Sufi master or by marrying into Muslim families. A changing economy, which made peanut production rather than slave-owning the basis of social power, assisted the transition. Thus a large portion of the Wolofs, the principal language group in Senegal, accepted Islam. For example, by 1913 close to half of western Saloum and three-quarters of lower Saloum was Muslim. By 1960 about half of the Serers had also converted to Islam.

French rule also helped to promote the spread of Islam. The French took a pragmatic attitude toward the Muslims and saw them as advanced in civilization, productive in economic life, and skilled in administration. The French used Muslim clerks and chiefs as intermediaries and allowed them to administer Muslim law. Under French rule Muslim holy-men traveled from place to place, teaching, founding schools, and building Muslim communities. The French, however, also feared the Muslims as potential political rivals and attempted to keep them disorganized and under control. A law of 1903 required schoolteachers to be licensed and to be capable of teaching French. In 1908 the French forbade the circulation of Arabic newspapers and tried to promote ethnic and territorial organizations to divide Muslim communities. In 1911 French was made mandatory for use in Muslim courts and Muslim holy-men were forbidden to collect alms.

These policies, however, were never consistently applied, and after World War I the French switched to a policy of selective support for and manipulation of Muslim leaders. In turn, the Sufis helped the French keep peace, raise troops, collect taxes, and encourage agricultural production. The Muslim elites adapted to the reality of French rule by giving up political militancy in favor of worship, education, and economic enterprise, and built up a new structure of Muslim brotherhoods under French rule. The Fadiliya were organized by Saᶜad Bouh (1850–1917), the Qadiriya by al-Hajj Malik Sy, and the Tijaniya by Ibrahim Niass (1900–78?), the scion of a Senegalese Tijani family, who founded his own branch of the order and claimed in the 1930s to be the "savior of the age." He was particularly attractive to Muslims attempting to adjust to migration and urban settlement.

The most important and well-known of the Senegalese brotherhoods is the Muridiya, founded in 1886 by Ahmad Bamba (1850–1927), a holy-man of Wolof and Tukulor descent, whose reputation was based on asceticism, piety, and lack of self-interest. He recognized that war against the French was futile, and took charge of the former followers of Ma Ba, Lat-dior, and others, urging them to turn from war to work. This reclusive and peaceful mystic was supported by Shaykh Ibra Fall (1858–1930), a former warrior who gave his allegiance to Ahmad in 1886, and worked to recruit his military followers into the Murid movement. Ibra Fall's submission marks the acceptance by the tyeddo of colonial domination and of Muslim leadership as the necessary conditions for the survival of Wolof society. The complementarity of marabout and warrior, of spiritual and worldly power, helped make the new order persuasive to numerous Senegalese. Ahmad Bamba was for a long time feared by the French as having territorial and political aspirations. He was exiled between 1895 and 1902 and again until 1907, but in 1912 the French accepted him as a spiritual and economic leader and allowed him to return to Diourbel.

The Murids became deeply involved in politics and integrated themselves into the French-dominated regime. Successive leaders of the order came to their position with French support, and became clients of the French government. Agricultural colonies and labor teams were organized to move into new lands along the edge of the deserts and reclaim them for peanut cultivation. Work was a form of withdrawal from politics and at the same time a form of adaptation to modern life. By turning to economic activity, a defeated people found new dignity.

Most of the Murids are peasants. The order also attracts landless, unemployed young men who often serve an apprenticeship from the age of 9 to 25 in *dara* or farming groups. Thus the leaders of the order own the fields and the villagers work on them either in work teams or on a weekly contributory basis. The Murids have become extremely popular. By 1912 they had 68,000 and by 1960 some 400,000 followers. By that time, one of every three Wolofs and one of every eight Senegalese was a member.

In religious terms the Murids give themselves – body, soul, and property – to the master, who then protects them and intercedes for them before God. The khalifa embodies the unity of the group and is the custodian of the founder's tomb. Beneath him are some 300 to 400 shaykhs who arbitrate disputes but do not usually teach or officiate in prayers. Their position depends upon public recognition as being persons with magical powers. The order stresses total obedience and regular payments of labor. It is extremely hierarchical, with lesser leaders owing allegiance to the higher.

Traditional Islamic practices are not emphasized. Though Ramadan is observed, ordinary prayers and fasts are not scrupulously attended. Wolofs in general know little about the theological or mystical teachings of Islam, do not follow the Muslim law of divorce, and continue to employ a system of justice emphasizing family responsibility in marriage and property matters. The Fall branch of the Murids is ostentatiously unorthodox and nonconformist. The descendants of Ibra Fall do not observe prayer or other Islamic rituals, but believe that through submission and work, charms and magical practices, they may attain religious blessing.

At the same time that Senegalese society was organized by Sufi brotherhoods, an urban non-Muslim professional and political elite took the lead in the struggle for independence. Senegal had a history of politically sophisticated elites going back to the middle of the nineteenth century, when the French extended citizenship to the residents of St Louis, Dakar, Gorée, and Rufisque. Senegalese elites participated in French administration, worked for European businesses, and eventually inherited control of the state. With the coming of independence in 1960 Senegal came to be ruled by a non-Muslim French-educated elite led by Léopold Senghor and the Union Progressiste Sénégalaise. Senegal, however, is a relatively unified African society because the Wolof language is spoken by about 80 percent of the people and because most Senegalese are Muslims.

The independent Senegalese government was modeled on the French Fifth Republic, headed by an elected president who selected the ministers. There was also an independent judicial system. Behind the institutional facade Senegal was governed by an alliance of national politicians and the local chieftains and religious leaders. The U.P.S. relied on the support of the clans or clienteles of important local chiefs. After the achievement of independence in 1960 Senghor dominated the country until he retired in 1980. By 1964 he had consolidated power, eliminated his rivals, and in 1966 he declared Senegal a one-party socialist state. From 1966 to 1976 the U.P.S. was the sole legal party and the brotherhoods aligned themselves as factions within the ruling party. From 1976 to 1980, possibly anticipating his retirement, Senghor permitted the creation of a multi-party system and national elections. The Socialist Party, the successor of the U.P.S., continued to win the overwhelming majority of the votes. After Senghor's retirement, for the first time a Muslim, Abdu Diouf, was elected president.

Thus post-independence Senegal resembles many other Muslim societies. A secular state governed by a foreign or non-Muslim elite dominates a Muslim populace. This populace is organized into Sufi brotherhoods which are the bases of rural economic organization. The state regime governs by collaboration with Muslim religious leaders who are intermediaries between them and the masses. The state supports its clients with honors and gifts of land and money and helps maintain the authority of the religious leaders over their followers. The Sufi orders organize the productive peanut economy and give political support to officials in rural areas. Muslim brotherhoods, then, have become an integral aspect of the Senegalese political system.

However, there are tensions between the state and the Sufi orders. While the Socialist Party depends upon the Sufis, it is committed to secularization and the modernization of Senegalese society. Since 1959 the government has attempted to create peasant cooperatives in order to improve agricultural techniques and to win control of the peanut industry. The farming practices of the Murid order are criticized for overcultivation of peanuts, neglect of rotation with other crops, deforestation, and exhaustion of the soil. The Murids, however, continue to open up new territories without regard to soil conservation, the use of machinery, or modern agricultural methods.

At the same time, urbanization in Senegal has led to the growth of populations which question the magical authority of the rural leaders. In the towns there has been a resurgence of interest in Arabic language and the kind of Islamic beliefs that stress regular prayer, pilgrimage, ethical deportment, and intellectual interests coupled with the repression of religious emotion. Dyula traders and other migrants from the countryside to the towns created in 1953 the Muslim Cultural Union, which sponsored Arabic and Muslim school instruction and opposed colonialism, capitalism, and the power of the rural Sufis. A Muslim Association of African students was founded in 1954; a movement for the teaching of Arabic in Senegal in 1957. The National Federation of Muslim Cultural Associations, founded in 1962, lobbies for educational improvements, expansion of teaching of Arabic and the Quran, scholarships, and other such matters. In response, the Murids have also created *daʾiras* or urban associations to maintain their hold over the followers as they migrate to the cities. These associations are devoted to meetings, collective singing, mutual aid, and collection of money. In the 1970s the growth of Arabic economic and cultural influences has stimulated calls for an Islamic constitution. Muslims oppose the family code of 1972, and press demands for compulsory religious education. With strong support from Arab states there is increased demand for the Islamization of state and society. Thus far, however, despite a Muslim president and the strength of Islamic feeling, the country is too divided among religious brotherhoods, urban and rural peoples, and traditionalists and modernists to generate a broad movement to turn Senegal into a Muslim state.

NIGERIA

The unification of northern and southern Nigeria under British rule added new dimensions to the role of Islam in an ethnically and religiously pluralistic society. Islam in northern Nigeria has been established as the religion of the state elites since the fifteenth century. The Sokoto Caliphate consolidated the Muslim identity of the political elites and brought Islam to a large proportion of the population. The emirs were responsible for the implementation of justice. They appointed mallams to lead the prayers, preside over festivals, and advise them on Muslim law. The mallams involved in government activity and judicial affairs were organized under the authority of supervisory officials. Unofficially, they arbitrated local disputes.

British rule tended to protect and consolidate this organized Muslim society. In 1931 the British set up a conference of emirs and chiefs of northern Nigeria; the MacPherson Constitution of 1951 provided northern Nigeria with an elected house of assembly. The traditional elites were also protected from Christian missionaries and from modern education. The British were in control of local budgets and repeatedly refused local requests for expansion of education because of lack of money and trained staff. The emirs, however, were eager to have English rather than Arabic taught in the schools. As a result they repeatedly insisted on educational expansion, sent their own children to the few schools that were established, and were not fearful that they would lose their children to Christianity.

There were no modern secondary schools until Katsina College was founded in 1922. English was made a compulsory subject in middle schools in 1930–31, and Arabic became part of the curriculum in 1932. Quranic instruction was provided by government-paid mallams. The Kano Law School had a fully Islamic curriculum. By the 1940s the British changed their policy and sought to provide the modern kind of education given in the south, but by the time of independence only a miniscule number of northerners had been exposed to Western and secular values.

British rule, while politically conservative, stimulated important economic and social changes. The introduction of roads and railways, and the promotion of export crops such as peanuts and cotton, brought the northern Nigeria peasantry into the international market economy. Vulnerable to changing world prices and excessive debt, many peasants lost their land and were forced to migrate to the cities.

This may have been one reason for the conversion of many Hausa peasants to Islam. The overall rate of conversion is not known, but studies of individual and communal experiences show that many converts were attracted by commercial opportunities. Successful trade depended on networks of relatives, friends, creditors, and customers. Traders therefore converted to Islam when their business enterprises had outgrown local markets and required the support of the larger-scale Muslim networks. Converts often moved from village to city levels of trade, and broke off ties with their village kin and the land. When a pagan Hausa converted he appeared before a Muslim judge and went through a ceremonial ablution. He was then given a gown, a turban, and a jug to hold the ablution water. This transition was fraught with dangers, which were conceptualized in terms of fear of evil charms and attack by spirits. Converts attempted to safeguard themselves by giving alms, having discussions with mallams, taking medicines, and so on. Converted Hausas abandoned their traditional village life and kinship relations. Women ceased farm work, entered into seclusion, and became the financial responsibility of their husbands, though many earned an income from crafts or trade. Though they became Muslims, Hausa converts often continued to believe in spirits, which they equated with the Muslim jinn.

The development of a commercial economy also led to important changes in the social structure of northern Nigeria's principal city, Kano. Since the 1920s there has been a dramatic increase in population as a result of the introduction of a railway, of peanuts as a cash crop, and of international air travel – developments which have made Kano the principal market of northern Nigeria, and the center of a flourishing merchant class. The large influx of population and the increasing importance of commerce required new mechanisms for social integration. At the turn of the century about 77 percent of the population of Kano city was Hausa, but in rural areas the population was about two-thirds Hausa and one-third Fulani. There was an Arab minority. The populace was thus divided along linguistic, ethnic, and class lines. The class structure consisted of a ruling-class Fulani elite, rich Hausa merchants, senior civil servants, middle-class traders, and the common people or *talakawa*. Occupational groups were organized into communities which were a combination of labor unions, welfare societies, and family councils. Throughout the nineteenth century religious activity was organized under the aegis of separate Hausa, Fulani, and Arab clans. By 1950 Kano was almost altogether Muslim, although non-Muslim ethnic minorities from other parts of Nigeria dominated modern industries and government administration.

The integration of this populace took place on the basis of a shared Hausa language and shared Muslim religious affiliations. Common economic interests drew together Hausa merchants and Fulani administrators, and Hausa and Fulani crafts-people in similar trades. Hausa language and customs have become common to the populace as a whole. A further mechanism for integration was the revival of Muslim brotherhoods, which served to bring Hausas, Fulanis, and Arabs into trans-ethnic religious associations, marking the change from a more fragmented to an integrated local identity. The most important sign of these changes was the spread of the reformed Tijani order in the 1930s. The Tijaniya were introduced into northern Nigeria in the nineteenth century by al-Hajj ʿUmar, who married the daughter of Ahmad Bello, but there were few Tijani emirs or mallams until the conversion of Emir ʿAbbas (1903–19). Muhammad Salga then became the imam of the first Tijani mosque in Kano. The allegiance of his following was later given to Ibrahim Niass, a Wolof residing in Kaolack (Senegal), who was regarded as the khalifa, the seal of saints and the mujaddid or reformer of the century. Some of his followers believed that he was also the mahdi or messiah. They believed that Ibrahim succeeded al-Hajj ʿUmar, the reformer of the thirteenth Muslim century, and ʿUthman Don Fodio, the reformer of the twelfth. Ibrahim had a strong following among women because of his reputation for *baraka* and conferral of blessings. He appealed to the Kano mallams with a reformed doctrine that called for purification and return to the true Islam but also had overtones of modernization as well. Muhammad Sanusi, Emir of Kano from 1953 to 1963, used his position to appoint reformed Tijaniya to administrative offices. The reformed order was further reinforced by the formation of the Youth of Islam and the Society of Young Muslims as the expression of younger-generation activists. By the 1960s about 60 percent of the mallams of Kano belonged to the reformed Tijaniya. Kano in turn became the base for the further expansion of the reformed order to other northern Nigerian cities such as Katsina and Kaduna and to rural areas.

Throughout Nigeria and West Africa the order functioned to organize religious ceremonies, such as the recitation of dhikr and the birthday of the Prophet, and to provide protection for its members against physical and spiritual dangers. The order sponsored numerous schools and contributed to a revival of Arabic and Muslim education in opposition to Western schools. Schools and zawiyas served as centers for teaching and worship and as residences for traveling pilgrims and merchants. The Tijaniya network made it possible for traders and travelers to find housing, jobs, and other assistance. The Qadiriya similarly became a mass organization, including Hausas as well as Arab and Fulani scholars, and emphasizing collective prayers and celebrations. The spread of the Tijaniya and the Qadiriya helped to integrate the new Kano commercial classes into a single community. The Hausa, Fulani, and Arab middle class became part of a larger social and cultural entity that became a principal patron of Muslim mosques, schools, and religious activities.

The emergence of a Kano-Muslim identity based on the Sufi brotherhoods was also tied to the integration of northern Nigeria into a larger Muslim universe. The Tijaniya were part of an international network. Kaolack was the center for the education of a new generation of Tijani leaders in Niger, Ghana, Chad, Mali, Mauritania, and Nigeria. The transnational affiliations of the Sufi brotherhoods, pilgrimages to Mecca, and studies in Cairo linked Kano to the outside Muslim world. Kano, as a hub of international travel and Muslim religious contacts, thus combined an integrated local identity with universal affiliations, a combination which superseded earlier, more parochial, ethnic and class concepts of social identity.

Just as Muslim brotherhoods became the expression of the middle classes, new Islamic political movements emerged to consolidate petit-bourgeois and lower-class opposition to the state and merchant elites. The Nigerian movement toward political independence prompted in 1948 the formation of the Nigerian Peoples Congress to represent the interests of the northern political establishment. Younger members of aristocratic families, newly prosperous merchants, and others founded the Northern Elements Progressive Union (1947–50). The N.E.P.U. was led by mallams who had a Western as well as an Arabic education. Aminu Kano, who studied Quran interpretation, wrote Hausa plays criticizing the abuses of the ruling elite. His criticism was directed not only against Britain but against the native establishment. The N.E.P.U. attempted, moreover, to maintain an Islamic sense of legitimacy. The party rallied teachers, clerks, servants, petty traders, craftsmen, workers, and lesser ʿulamaʾ to oppose colonial-autocratic rule. Thus in northern Nigeria, state, merchant and populist opposition were all committed to Muslim symbols, interpreted in varying ways.

By the time of independence, northern Nigerian and Kano identity, in particular, had several interrelated levels. On one level there were still the remnants of the nineteenth-century concepts of community. The Fulani elite had perpetuated its power, and Fulani, Hausa, and other ethnic identities remained strong among the common people. At the same time there was a shift toward Islamic affiliations among both elite and commoners and a tendency to redefine social identity in Muslim terms. The emirs stressed their Islamic functions; the Sufi brotherhoods and political parties stressed the Muslim aspirations of the merchants and the common people.

While in northern Nigeria Islam was the pervasive idiom of social organization and political conflict, in southern Nigeria, which until recently was predominantly non-Muslim, it did not define the system of society as a whole but was the religion of specific minority communities. In southern Nigeria the first Yoruba converts were made by Muslim traders from Bornu, Songhay, and Hausaland. In the nineteenth century liberated slaves from Sierra Leone and Brazil established colonies in Lagos, and Muslims from the north settled in Ilorin, Ibadan, and other towns. Muslim communal life in the southern towns tended to take shape on the basis of ethnic or other local affiliations.

Lagos has for more than a century been the center of important Muslim communities and Muslim movements. In 1861 it became a British colony. The British helped to resolve disputes among Muslims and acquired a reputation for being impartial in internal Muslim affairs. British officials even patronized Muslim mosques. The British also posed a great challenge to the Muslim community by introducing Western and Christian education. Christian schools had great appeal since Western education was a key to commercial, professional, and career advancement, but many Muslims were afraid they would subvert family beliefs. Thus, when in 1896 the British created a government-subsidized Muslim school with a mixed Western and Muslim curriculum, the Muslims responded to this as a Christian and Western cultural threat and formed their own educational societies. The *Egbe killa* society of Lagos was founded in the 1880s. The Ahmadiya, a missionary Muslim association from India, began their proselytizing during World War I; the *Ansar ud-deen* was founded in 1923. By 1960 it had some 50,000 members, teacher training colleges, high schools, and primary schools. Other associations were founded to serve the need for the education of women. Thus Lagos became a center of Muslim modernism.

Ibadan illustrates a different type of Muslim structure. Before Nigerian independence, Ibadan had two Muslim communities, one Yoruba and one Hausa. The Yoruba-Muslim community was organized under the authority of a chief imam and his subordinates. A council of ten scholars, who inherited their positions and were supported by alms and contributions, ran the affairs of the mosques and the community. The community supported a Quran school and a higher Muslim academy. Yoruba Muslims, however, did not live in an exclusive setting but had close social relationships with non-Muslim Yoruba, including sharing of churches, mosques, and ceremonies.

Alongside of the Yoruba there was also a Hausa-Muslim community. The Hausas came to Ibadan as migrant traders, teachers, beggars, porters, and workers. They were primarily engaged in long-distance trade in which they imported peanut oil, dried meat, fish, milk, and cattle from the north, and exported kola nuts, sugar, iron, salt, and manufactured goods from the south. The trade was conducted in a traditional framework without banks, insurance companies, civil courts, or even legal documents. Success depended upon the trust developed within a close-knit minority community. Hausa migrants thus had a critical interest in preserving a distinct community identity. At the beginning of the twentieth century Hausa businessmen living in Ibadan formed a quarter of their own, inhabited by migrant northerners and their wives and prostitutes. The British and the majority Yoruba favored the formation of such a quarter under the control of a Hausa chief as a way of regulating a restless migrant community which included not only peddlers and merchants, but beggars, thieves, and other troublemakers.

The chief of the quarter played an indispensable part in the life of the Ibadan community. The chief acted as judge, officiated at marriages, mediated inheritance and custody disputes, appointed the chiefs for occupational sub-groups, maintained public services, and policed the activity of strangers. He was an essential reference for creditworthiness. He was also essential for the legitimation of land and property ownership. Every man owed the chief direct personal allegiance which was signified by kneeling down in front of his office. There were also sub-chiefs to regulate the cattle market, the butchers, and the guilds of beggars. The beggars were organized into three sub-groups under a chief of the blind, a chief of the lame, and a chief of the lepers. Begging was a regular occupation, to which no stigma was attached. Each beggar was assigned a work place and paid his Friday earnings to the chief.

Landlords had a crucial economic function, for they were hotel and rooming-house keepers for itinerant workers. The landlords acted as inter-mediaries for their guests, arranging deals, advancing capital, holding deposits, and advising on business conditions. A wealthy landlord had a clientele of workers including his sons, foster-sons, and others who carried on the business of his firm. He helped generate the personal contacts which facilitated trade.

In the late 1940s and 1950s this society of chiefs and landlords was subverted by the rise of the nationalist movements. The disintegration of British control forced the Hausa to seek the sponsorship of the Nigerian political parties. In turn this threatened to subvert Hausa solidarity and Hausa trading monopolies. Faced with competition from the Yoruba and the rise of Nigerian nation-alism, the Hausas had to identify their own group interest in ways that would both exclude the Yoruba and be consistent with the new emphasis on national solidarity. Thus between 1950 and 1952 after an inspiring visit by Ibrahim Niass, virtually the whole of the Hausa community joined the Tijaniya. The revival of Hausa Muslim religious identity drew the residents of the quarter away from the Ibadan central mosque.

The new religious awareness also changed the nature of authority within the Hausa community. Now the mallams became important as teachers of correct Muslim practice. They provided for education; they advised the chiefs and the merchants as to whether it was propitious to undertake particular activities, and were believed to know the right religious and magical formulae to achieve practical results. They were also believed to have the purity of heart which was essential to mystical power. Members of the Tijaniya were attached to their ritual masters, looked to them for protection against evil spirits, and consulted them on all matters of family, business, and daily behavior. Anxious landlords, particularly sensitive to changing market conditions, looked to the mallams for social and moral support. The chiefs and the landlords signified their acceptance of this new religious authority by making the pilgrimage to Mecca and earning the title hajji. They became more sensitive to public pressures, especially those due to the practice of "public scandalizing," or denunciation of individuals for unacceptable behavior. The political elite now includes not only the chiefs and the landlords, but the leading mallams. Community organization, community authority, and community identity have been restructured in Muslim terms.

The formation of a Nigerian national state bringing north and south into the same political framework has profoundly altered the political meaning of Islam. The Nigerian state itself has had a tumultuous history. Owing to intense ethnic, religious, and regional differences the union of north and south into an independent Nigerian state was difficult to achieve. Nigeria became independent in 1960, but by the end of 1965 the failures of the government and the corruption of the politicians had generated an almost universal hostility. The crucial problem was the growing antagonism between the northern Muslim regions, the Yoruba west, and the Ibo east. These political pressures have resulted in a series of military coups. In 1966 disturbances throughout the country, and resistance to the federal government in the west, led General Ironsi to seize control of the government. He attempted to unify the civil services of the several regions, a move which was seen as an effort to give Ibos control of the country. Further riots and another coup led to the seizure of power by Colonel Gowon, who promulgated a new constitution which divided Nigeria into 12 smaller states in order to satisfy minority interests and reduce the power of the northern and southern blocs. The Ibos, however, refused incorporation into the new regime and in May 1967 proclaimed the Republic of Biafra. A bitter civil war was fought until 1970, resulting in the defeat of the eastern regions.

Then between 1970 and 1975 southern fears of northern domination, revived by cooperation among the northern states and a census which showed that the north had a majority of the population, contributed to a new uprising. In 1976 the Gowon regime was overthrown and replaced by a new military government which promised a return to civilian rule. After years of oscillation between a unitary and a federal concept of the Nigerian state, a constitutional commission tried to create a truly national party system, a strong presidency, and a multiplicity of small local states which could not rival the center. In the elections of 1979 most of the parties were committed to combining private enterprise and state support for education and development. The National Party of Nigeria, representing the Muslim elites of the north, won the elections. The north, having accepted integration into the national political system, became the predominant power. Their only class opposition came from the People's Revolutionary Party, which had the support of workers, craftsmen, and traders in Kano and Kaduna. Al-Hajji Shehu Shagari became the president of Nigeria's second republic. In 1984, however, a new coup restored power to the military. Nigeria has yet to find a stable form of either military or civilian rule.

Despite this instability, the post-1966 military regimes progressively strengthened the Nigerian state. The exploitation of Nigeria's oil reserves gave the federal government vastly increased revenues. The federal state also had major investments in the petrochemical, gas, fertilizer, cement, automobile, paper, and sugar industries, and the government took a major role in the regulation of the banks and the economy. State policies also favored the formation of an indigenous economic elite. In 1972 an indigenization decree reserved large areas of the economy for native Nigerians and prohibited foreign firms without a minimum Nigerian participation. Government banks began to allocate a substantial part of their loans to Nigerian businessmen and civil servants who were able to become entrepreneurs. Clientage relations between capitalists and clerks, artisans, and agents also enabled the common people to prosper.

The ever-changing political context has profoundly altered the role of Islam in northern Nigeria and in the nation as a whole. Throughout the 1950s and 1960s the conservative Muslim north remained suspicious of the federal regime, but the changes in the political situation helped cultivate a sense of Islamic identity blended with national identity. With the formation of a military regime in 1966 the political power of the emirs was reduced. The federal military governors appointed local military governors and civilian commissioners. Authority over the courts and the police was taken out of the hands of the emirs. Thus, their ceremonial and religious functions became correspondingly more important, and they became patrons of Muslim religious groups, helped to sponsor the translation of the Quran into Hausa, and diffused Islamic reform attitudes in order to integrate Arabic- and Hausa-speaking Muslims. Internal differences among Muslims were de-emphasized in favor of a shared Islamic identity. Kano became the leader of a newly emerging northern Muslim identity which was no longer based on the conservative emirates but upon the Hausa language and cultural pride.

Then, in the 1970s, the northern Muslim elites had to ally with non-Muslim southerners to maintain their political position. The close economic ties between the Hausa north and the Yoruba south, the economic interdependency of Kano and Lagos for transportation and the marketing of agricultural products, and the importance of federal subsidies, laid the foundation for interregional cooperation. Thus in the 1970s there was an increasing emphasis upon national Nigerian identity, as opposed to religious and regional ties. The emphasis on national unity in the media also helped create a sense of Nigerian identity.

Muslim identity has also become more important nationwide. In the post-independence era there has been ever-increasing Muslim educational and missionary activity. Since 1973 Muslim societies have been organized under the aegis of the Islamic Council for Nigeria. Muslims are increasingly assertive of their views in national social questions. Under Muslim influence the national education system provides for the teaching of Islam and for the use of the Hausa language. Many Muslims lobbied for the creation of a national Shariᶜa court of appeals as a necessary expression of Muslim interests, but this inspired bitter opposition as a symbol of northern and Muslim dominance. Yoruba Muslims and Christians were the main proponents of an eventual compromise. Three judges versed in Islamic law were appointed to the Federal Court of Appeals, but a separate Muslim court was not established. As Muslims are better integrated into national life, Muslim activists propound Islam as a blueprint for the social order as well as for personal religious behavior.

While Islam was becoming a national religion it also became the religion of lower- and middle-class opposition to the dominant elites. In the 1950s the Northern Elements Progressive Union opposed the emirate system and the established aristocracy in the name of the middle-class intelligentsia, the common people, and Islamic values. With the consolidation of state economic and political elites in the 1970s, Islam was revived as the banner of the opposition. In Kano, for example, petty traders and craftsmen dependent upon loyalty among Muslims for their custom, laborers and factory workers, many of whom are itinerant Quran students and downwardly mobile mallams, find in Muslim identity and Muslim values an outlet for their concerns about wage exploitation, inflation, and a declining standard of living for the common people. The mallams are particularly important, for they are themselves workers, permeate the working elements of the population, and provide interpretive and social leadership. In working-class milieus the mallams and the students teach the Quran, behave in the exemplary Hausa-Muslim manner, cultivate courtesy, modesty, patience, and honesty, advocate social solidarity and Muslim justice, and articulate the resentment of the poor at low wages, the excesses of consumption by the rich, and political oppression. In Muslim terms they express a lower-class demand for justice. As the political elites have adopted a national (and Muslim) identity, the petite bourgeoisie and workers of Kano have become Muslim in orientation. Similarly students have turned to Islamic revival movements. Homeless and unemployed Quran students have resorted to millenarian violence. Each finds in Islam symbols and vocabularies to oppose the political order.

At the same time that Islam symbolizes the fusion of Hausa and Fulani ethnicity and the complex interweaving of local Kano, northern regional, and Nigerian national identity, it also symbolizes the class conflict between the dispossessed and the elites. All parties find in Muslim identity the symbols and the organizational basis for the struggle for political power. As in other Muslim countries, Islam in northern Nigeria has become a universal idiom, an encompassing basis for social identity with sufficient internal differentiation to articulate conflicting interests in a complex society.

MUSLIM MINORITIES

In other parts of West Africa, Muslims form communal minorities and have not generally influenced the character of state regimes. While many West African states, such as Ivory Coast, Mali, Upper Volta, Niger, and Guinea, have been ruled by one-party systems, military regimes, and similar concentrated governments, often based on personal charisma, Muslim minorities are organized into small communities, Sufi brotherhoods, and modernist movements. In parts of West Africa where Muslim populations were established in the late nineteenth and early twentieth centuries, organized Muslim communal life continues to be built around schools and scholars, clerical lineages such as the Jakhanka and the Saghanuglu, Sufi brotherhoods, and minority ethnic communities. Rather than survey the whole region, here we shall consider two examples of Muslim religious organization and activities. One is the Muslim communal-ethnic minority in Kumasi (Ghana). The other is the Wahhabiya, an example of a modernist movement.

In the nineteenth century, Kumasi already had a strong Muslim community, which provided the Ashanti government with scribes, ambassadors, political advisers, soldiers, and religious magicians. The Muslims had a considerable influence because of the value attached to their amulets, and intermarried with the Ashanti elite. In addition to the local Muslims there were Hausa and Mossi traders who brought cattle, leather, and cloth to Kumasi in return for gold dust, salt, and kola nuts.

The British conquest of the Ashanti empire opened the way to unrestricted northern immigration to the south. In 1896 the British took Kumasi and in 1900–01 declared a protectorate over northern Ghana. The British developed the gold mines and cocoa plantations on the Gold Coast and attracted hundreds of thousands of workers from northern Ghana, Hausaland, Upper Volta, Togo, Dahomey, Niger, and Mali. Many of the migrants were not Muslims, but soon adopted Islam and the Hausa language. Ethnic differences were perpetuated through lineages, which appointed their own headmen. The headmen were vital because they helped the sick and poor, provided food and lodging, took care of orphans, supervised inheritances, performed marriages and burials, and adjudicated disputes on the basis of Islamic and customary law. This populace was concentrated in the Zongo or Muslim quarter of Kumasi. To rule the migrant population the British recognized the community headmen, allowed them to organize courts, and appointed a *sarkin* or chief of the Zongo. In the era of independence the state continued to be important to the community of the Zongo. With the coming of independence, the Muslim community was reorganized to meet the demands of the new situation. In 1957 Nkrumah removed the headmen from office and created a direct link between the government and the communities by the appointment, under the authority of the Minister of the Interior, of a man named Mutawakilu as sarkin Zongo. The Muslim Council was created as an instrument of government control. With the removal of Nkrumah in 1966 the Muslim communities again set up their own headmen.

Since 1966 the community structure of the Zongo has evolved to emphasize the common Muslim identity. Ethnic ties were generally strong among first-generation immigrants, but second- and third-generation residents identify with wider Islamic rather than with more parochial groups. The Hausa version of Islam has become standard. Marriage and naming ceremonies tend to follow the Hausa pattern. Neighborhood, school, and youth groups are formed on a multi-ethnic basis. Festivals, funerals, ceremonial days, and worship in the common mosque also serve to reinforce a trans-ethnic solidarity. The old ethnic lineage headmen were challenged by a younger generation of urban-born, highly educated leaders who speak for the Muslim community as a whole. Since 1966 tension in the Muslim community has developed between the Muslim mission, a modernizing group supported by the government, and the more traditional communities. Also after 1966, Muslims have become the scapegoat for Ghana's economic problems, and hostility between Ghanaians and alien Muslims has increased.

Alongside of the traditional kin-based and ethnic groups there are numerous reformist and modernist Muslim associations. They have become widespread in the post-independence period as an expression of Muslim communal interests in the context of non-Muslim national politics. In Ghana these include the Ahmadiya, the Ghana Muslim Mission, the Islamic Research and Re-

28 The Friday Mosque at Mopti, Mali

formation Center, the Islamic Solidarity Association of West Africa, the Supreme Council for Islamic Affairs in Ghana, and the Ghana Muslim Representative Council – all of which sponsor English–Arabic schools and missionary activities. Outside Ghana a Muslim community association was formed in Upper Volta in 1958–60 to work for the spread of modern Muslim education. In Gambia there were numerous reformist associations, including the Young Muslim Society (1936), the Muslim Association (1965), the Gambian Islamic Solidarity Association (1970), and other groups, operating schools, mosques, and dispensaries.

Modernist movements, moreover, are not localized in particular countries, but spread across national boundaries. The pressures of city life under colonial rule led to new educational and religious needs, and brought out a conflict of interest between well-established elders, who wanted to appropriate family wealth, and younger family members and workers, who protested at unfair discrimination and turned to modernist and educational reform movements as an expression of protest. The Wahhabiya, active throughout Guinea, Ivory Coast, and Upper Volta, is a good example. This movement was centered in Bamako, at the junction of the trade routes between Senegal, Guinea, Ivory Coast, Upper Volta, and the Niger region. Here there were no strong Tijani or Qadiri communities. The Wahhabiya was introduced by students who had gone to al-Azhar and Cairo University where they came into contact with the Muslim Brotherhood and other neo-Muslim movements. Pilgrimage to Mecca and Medina was also an important source of reformed religious ideas, and of a vision of a unified Islamic society. The name signifies their reformist intentions – not a connection with the Saʿudi Arabian movement.

One of these pilgrims, al-Hajj ʿAbdallah Mahmud, returned to Bamako imbued with reform ideas. He called on his fellow Muslims to study the Quran and the sayings of the Prophet, to adhere to the Maliki school of law and ascetic forms of Sufism, and to eschew saint worship and animistic religious practices. He attacked the local mallams for cultic rituals and for collaboration with colonial rulers. Al-Hajj ʿAbdallah founded a school in 1949, and organized the *Subbanu al-Muslimin* (Society of Young Muslims) in 1951. The prime function of this association was the education of children to prevent their assimilation of French values and to inculcate a knowledge of and commitment to Islam.

The movement spread rapidly over the trade routes of West Africa. The association developed branches in Kankan, Bo, Buake and other towns in Mali, Guinea, Sierra Leone, and the Ivory Coast. Most of the members were small and middling traders and petty functionaries. The group attracted young men from prominent families who were not dependent upon traditional authorities but whose futures were unpromising. The development of the reformist groups led to conflicts with other Muslims, disputes over the control of local mosques and commonly to the formation of separatist mosques in each town.

The rise of the reform movement was also closely associated with the R.D.A. political party in Sudan, Guinea, and the Ivory Coast. The reformers and R.D.A. shared a common opposition to French colonial rule, and to forced labor and other forms of taxation. Both were opposed to the conservative rural chiefs and religious leaders, and both were supported by modernized commercial groups. They shared principles of social justice and equality which could be expressed in either secular or Muslim terms. The R.D.A. politicians often used the Muslim vocabulary and readings from the Quran to appeal for Muslim support. Thus, the cultivation of reform Islamic religious principles was a way of raising political consciousness; conversely, nationalism was motivated by Muslim feeling. Since independence the Wahhabiya have continued to be active, and have spawned other reform movements. Wherever Muslims are minorities, reformist groups like the Wahhabiya and ethnic-based community groups remain the principal alternative forms of Muslim communal organization.

CHAPTER 31

ISLAM IN EAST AFRICA

The East African states are here grouped together for convenience, but the experience of each country is in fact very different. The history of the Sudan resembles that of North Africa and the Middle Eastern Arab countries. For a century and a half, the Sudan has been consolidating a modern state organization. The northern part of the country has an Arabic-speaking population, a Muslim identity, and strong Islamic movements, but the southern part of the country encompasses a non-Muslim African population which resists assimilation on Arab, Muslim, and central-state terms. Somalia also resembles the Sudan, the Arab Middle Eastern and North African countries, and Mauritania in that tribal, Muslim, and Arab identity have become part of Somali national identity. The situation of Muslims in Ethiopia is very different. Ethiopia also has a long history of state consolidation, but this has taken place under Christian rather than Muslim leadership. In Ethiopia the Muslim populace resists incorporation into a non-Muslim state, but Muslim resistance is expressed in secular rather than in religious terms. The histories of Kenya, Tanzania, Uganda, and other East African countries, by contrast, follow a West African pattern in which the dominant consideration in the twentieth century has been the formation of colonial regimes and their replacement by secular national states. In these countries Islam is the basis of local communal and social organization but not of state power or national identity.

SUDAN

By the nineteenth century the regions which comprise the modern state of Sudan already had a long history of Muslim Sultanates, substantial Muslim populations, and developed Muslim religious institutions. In the nineteenth and twentieth centuries the process of territorial unification and consolidation of state power proceeded relentlessly. It began with the Egyptian conquest of the Sudan by Muhammad ʿAli, nominally the Ottoman governor of Egypt, but already an independent ruler, who conquered the Funj Sultanate in 1820, and founded Khartoum as a new capital in 1830. Later Egyptian rulers expanded their territory to include the Upper Nile and equatorial provinces in 1871, Bahr al-Ghazal in 1873, and Darfur in 1874.

The new regime set out to administer the Sudan in accordance with the Tanzimat or modernization principles already being applied in Egypt. A local army was recruited from the southern population and the country was divided into administrative districts whose officials collected taxes from village headmen. The Egyptians organized a state trading monopoly, and slave raiding also became a state business. When the state trading monopolies were ended in the reign of Muhammad Saʿid (1854–63), Europeans flocked to the Sudan to take over the gum arabic, ostrich feather, and ivory trade. In 1863 Khedive Ismaʿil formed the Sudan, later the Egyptian, Trading and Commission Company to build and operate the railroads, steamships, and telegraph. A prosperous economy was the basis of large state revenues and the centralization of administration.

Egypt also attempted to subordinate the Muslim religious elites. The Egyptians canceled the special financial privileges of the local faqis, and suppressed some of the Sufi tariqat. Instead they encouraged an ʿulamaʾ establishment primarily staffed by Egyptians, though it incorporated local Sudanese students who were graduates of al-Azhar. The Egyptian religio-legal administration applied Hanafi law even though most of the local religious leaders were Malikis. The Egyptians also created a court (*majlis mahalli*) in the major towns and a court of appeals (*majlis al-ahdan*) in Khartoum.

Egyptian administration opened the way for the spread of the reformed Sufi orders. The weakening of local holy-men and tribal chiefs by a foreign regime led to the spread of the reformed tariqat. Already in the late eighteenth century reformist brotherhoods, inspired by pilgrims returning from Mecca and Medina, were making headway. The Sammaniya order was introduced by Shaykh Ahmad al-Tayyib b. al-Bashir, who returned around 1800. The reform teaching of Ahmad b. Idris al-Fasi (d. 1837) was introduced into the Sudan by

Muhammad al-Majdhub (1796–1833), a descendant of an established holy family, who remade the order according to new principles. The Khatmiya was introduced through the teaching of Muhammad ʿUthman al-Mirghani (1793–1853). These orders represented a new concept of Islamic religiosity, committed to formal Islamic law and hostile to the traditional veneration of the faqis as miracle workers and holy-men. The tariqat quickly became politically important. The Khatmiya established a nationwide organization and cooperated with the Egyptian regime. The Sammaniya also established a widespread network, but held aloof from the rulers and took the side of the local population. The Majdhubiya offered militant resistance. Thus, despite Egyptian efforts to impose a state form of Islamic administration, Sufism remained the basis of local organization and opposition to Egyptian rule.

A half-century of Egyptian rule eventually provoked violent resistance to oppressive Turkish officials, when Shaykh Muhammad Ahmad (1848–85), a pious member of the Sammaniya order, declared himself the Mahdi, the expected savior, and called for a restoration of the true Islam. By divine inspiration he gave instructions on such matters as seclusion of women and distribution of land, and attempted to modify customary Sudanese religious practices in accord with the teachings of the Shariʿa. He was opposed to the wearing of amulets, consumption of tobacco and alcohol, wailing of women at funerals, music in religious processions, and visiting of saints' tombs. In imitation of the migration of the Prophet, he and his followers retreated to the mountains of Kordofan, called themselves the ansar (Helpers of the Prophet), and created a revolutionary state with an organized army, treasury, and legal administration. The early supporters of the Mahdist revolt included an immediate circle of pious disciples and various organized tribal communities. Baqqara nomads made up the bulk of the army.

The Mahdists came into the open in 1881, and in 1885 they defeated General Gordon and took Khartoum. Upon the death of the Mahdi, ʿAbdallah b. Muhammad, his khalifa or designated lieutenant, assumed the task of building a state regime. His succession marked the transformation of the charismatic revolutionary movement into a conventional state. The Mahdists, who began by rebelling against Egyptian rule, continued the movement toward centralization of state power. The new ruler concentrated on building up military power, adopting the Turko-Egyptian fiscal system, and restoring the government's authority over rural areas. This meant in practice a return to the state bureaucracy and corruptions of the past. The Madhists also sought to reform Islamic practice in accord with international standards, suppressed local faqis and local forms of the veneration of saints. Thus they provoked local re-

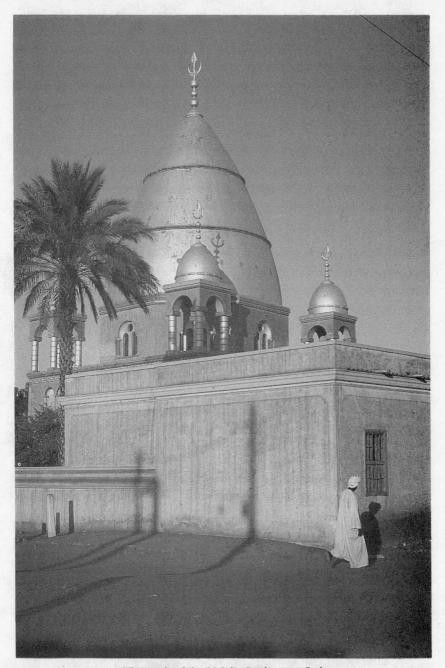

29 The tomb of the Mahdi, Omdurman, Sudan

sistance. In Darfur, where tribal chiefs had already been defeated, a local Muslim holy-man or faqi named Abu Jummayza attempted to revive the influence of the local faqis and tribal peoples against the encroachment of the consolidated central state and the international reformist religious brotherhoods. The Mahdist state, like its predecessor, both claimed to be Muslim and had to contend with Muslim resistance.

The Mahdist state had also to deal with expanding Italian, French, and British power. In 1898 an Anglo-Egyptian army defeated the Mahdists at the battle of Omdurman. The conquest led to the Anglo-Egyptian Condominium (1899–1955), or joint Anglo-Egyptian sovereignty. Egypt financed the army and the administration of the country but left a British governor-general in full military and civil control. Under Lord Kitchener and his successor, Sir Reginald Wingate (1900–16), the British defeated the remaining opposition and in 1916 incorporated the Darfur province into the Sudan. They set up a provincial administration with British officials at the head and Egyptians and Sudanese in the lower offices. Despite their defeat, however, the Mahdists retained wide support. They had helped overcome tribal particularism and would later be an important base for the development of Sudanese nationalism and an independent Sudanese state.

Though non-Muslims, the British reverted to the religious policy of the previous Egyptian regime. In the north they attempted to rebuild the ʿulamaʾ establishment by creating a board of ʿulamaʾ in 1901. They financed mosques and pilgrimages and encouraged the application of Muslim law in Muslim courts, staffed by Egyptian judges and some Sudanese trained at al-Azhar. Sudanese legal scholars graduated from Gordon College and from the Institute of Learning in Omdurman (founded in 1912). The Condominium government, while favorable to the ʿulamaʾ, was hostile to Sufism. Where the Mahdists had destroyed local shrines, the British refused to permit them to be rebuilt. However, they were unable to enforce their anti-Sufi policies and the tariqat set up new mosques and schools.

By World War I the British relented and began to promote the Khatmiya to win more political support. Despite the vacillations in British policy, the Mahdists accepted and even supported British rule and tried to increase their influence over that of the conventional faqis and Sufis within the status quo. The Ansar broadened their appeal from rural to town populations and began to publish a newspaper and urge a peaceful jihad. By 1924 the Khatmiya were sufficiently disturbed by the success of their rivals to declare that they would prefer continued British rule to a restoration of the Mahdist state. At the same time a secular nationalist movement was born. The Sudan Union Society was formed in 1920, calling for self-determination; the White Flag League supported by army officers followed, and there were nationalist demonstrations in 1924. The intelligentsia, however, was split between the two religious movements, and by the 1940s had failed to become an independent third force.

Disturbed by the increasing influence of the religious leaders and the nationalist ferment, the British adopted in 1924 a new administrative policy to counterbalance the urban and religious elites by increasing political reliance on tribal and rural chiefs. The British reduced the size of the bureaucracy in order to avoid educating and employing an urban elite, and encouraged English education in the south to foster regional separatism. By 1936, however, the British realized that indirect rule could not work. There was not in fact a strong tribal organization in rural areas to serve as the basis of indirect administration, though in some areas the British were able to create it. Having failed to cultivate adequate rural support, the British had to return to the urban intelligentsia, and again increased the opportunities for national and religious resistance. In the late 1930s Sudanese nationalist and religious leaders began to organize. In 1938 the Graduates General Congress was formed to give Sudanese officials a voice in administration, but by 1943 it had been taken over by the Mahdists. The first political party, the Ashiqqa, an offshoot of the Khatmiya, was formed in 1943. In 1944 the leader of the Mahdists, Sayyid ʿAbd al-Rahman, the son of the Madhi, formed the Umma Party, which favored independence, but was nonetheless friendly with the British. Thus as the problem of Islamic localism receded and the problem of national independence became central, the Islamic religious movements became the basis of nationalist political parties. The Muslim religious leaders were the only ones who could mobilize mass support.

The path to independence, however, remained tortuous. Britain was reluctant to concede its colonial powers, but to cope with the increasing Sudanese demand for autonomy, in 1947 it proposed the formation of a national legislative assembly and executive council, but reserved a veto for the British Governor-General. Southern leaders were doubtful about their place in a national union but at the Juba Conference of 1947 accepted the idea of national unity. Northern Sudanese religious and national groups were bitterly divided over the question of union with Egypt. The Ansar favored immediate independence and opposed a union of Egypt and the Sudan; their opponents feared a Mahdist restoration and favored an Egyptian alliance. The elections of 1953 showed that the country was completely divided. The National Union Party, representing the Khatmiya and the urban and riverain areas, dominated the Sudanese parliament, but the Umma Party (Mahdists) was strong in the Darfur, Kordofan, Blue Nile, and southern provinces. The Umma, who were violently against union with Egypt, made it clear by massive public demonstrations that the pursuit of this possibility would lead to civil war. The National Union Party in turn grew disillusioned with Nasser and suspicious of Egyptian intentions. Thus in January 1954 the British transferred power to the Sudanese, and in 1956 Sudan became officially independent.

Independent Sudan has had considerable difficulty in establishing a stable national regime. The religious and factional divisions within the country, the deep splits between those movements committed to an Arabic-Islamic conception of Sudanese identity and the military elites committed to a secular concept of Sudanese nationhood have made it difficult to stabilize the political regime. The differences of national concept are compounded by the split between the Arab-Muslim north and the non-Muslim south. About 40 percent of the Sudanese population is Arab, but Nilotic, Nilo-Cushitic peoples, including the Dinka, Nuer, Shilluk, and others, make up more than half the population. The problem of defining the relations of south and north complicates the effort to define a Sudanese regime and a Sudanese national identity. Northerners virtually excluded southerners from pre-independence politics and from the negotiations with Egypt and Britain. Thus the non-Arab southerners formed political parties, such as the Sudan African National Union (S.A.N.U.), which called for regional autonomy and even independence.

The parliamentary regime formed in 1954 was soon overtaken by a military coup led by General Ibrahim ʿAbbud. In 1958 a council of the armed forces seized control of the government, abolished the political parties and the trade unions, and, with the blessing of the Khatmiya and the tolerance of the Ansar, set out to impose central control and Arabic and Islamic identity on the southern regions. The military regime provoked southern, Communist, Muslim brotherhood, and student resistance, which led to guerrilla activity in the south and student demonstrations and railway strikes in the north. In 1964 ʿAbbud was forced to resign and was replaced by a civilian coalition government. This new government ruled from 1964 to 1969, but it too failed to cope with the problems of religious and secular identity and of north and south, and succumbed to a military coup led by Jaʿfar Numayri. Numayri dissolved the parliament, formed a revolutionary command council, and renamed the country the Democratic Republic of the Sudan. Between 1970 and 1972, he disbanded the Communists, crushed the Khatmiya and the Ansar parties, and determined to deal with the south by recognizing its African identity and autonomy. Numayri allowed the Bahr al-Ghazal, Equatorial, and

Upper Nile provinces to become a self-governing region, though the national government maintained control of defense, foreign policy, and currency. From 1976 the Numayri regime went through several phases. For a time it became Western-oriented. It rebuilt its ties with the Mahdists, maintained good relations with Egypt, and sponsored large-scale agricultural development along the Nile. In 1983 and 1984, however, it began to assert its Islamic identity and resumed efforts to bring the south under more direct control.

The two issues of Islamic reform and the unification of north and south are closely related. In the north, while the old Islamic parties and movements diminish in their capacity to express Islamic identity, new groups and programs have emerged. These groups are supported mainly by students and the educated elite and they reflect the particular concerns of student and university-educated milieus. These groups try to Islamicize the state and society and to increase the Islamic "content" of the national identity. They have prompted the formation of a legal commission to revise existing laws to bring them into closer conformity with the Shariᶜa. Discussions have been held on the nature of an Islamic constitution and efforts have been made to improve Islamic education. The new emphasis on reform and Islamic identity represents a shift in style in a population which has continuously been organized and identified in Muslim terms.

The growth of Islamic sentiment in the north intensifies the pressure for the integration and Islamicization of the south. Though more pragmatic military leaders have attempted to work out a settlement to integrate the south and the north, many northerners cannot imagine the Sudan as a secular, pluralist society. Many southerners still think in regional and local terms. The difficulty of conceiving a pluralistic state and reconciling the divisions among Sudanese, Arab nationalist, Islamic, and southern concepts of identity is a continuing problem.

SOMALIA

Somalia is reminiscent of Mauritania in that a state regime overlies an Arab-Muslim tribal society. By the eighteenth century the tribes of Somalia were largely Muslim and Arab. Somalia began to acquire the shape of a modern state in 1891, when it was divided between Britain and Italy. The Italian Protectorate was administered in a highly bureaucratic way and favored the development of irrigation, railroads, roads, and schools. With the outbreak of World War II, however, the British conquered Italian Somaliland and assumed control over the whole of what was to be the future Somali state. The first Somali opposition to colonial rule was expressed by the formation in 1935 of the Somaliland National Society, which was devoted to a modern education to overcome the Somali particularisms and to unify the population. A Somali Officials' Union was formed in 1937 and a Somali Youth League in 1943. In 1950 Somaliland was returned to Italy as a United Nations Trusteeship, and the northern and southern regions were unified in 1960, when Somaliland became an independent country. The new government managed to integrate the former British and Italian sectors with great rapidity.

The Somali people were a single cultural and linguistic nation but did not form a political entity. They are all Muslims but were divided into two lineage groups – the Somali and the Sab – who are further subdivided by a complex segmentary system into numerous confederacies, subconfederacies, tribes, and tribal sections. The tribe is the most common form of political organization; it has a chief who is both warrior and rainmaker and is believed to have religious and magical powers. The tribes have a strong Muslim identity and trace their descent to Muhammad, without being ethnic Arabs. The political parties formed in both Italian and British Somalia in the 1950s were thus clan-based. The Somaliland National Society was based on the Isaq group, and the United Somali Party was based on the Dir and the Darod. However, the development of a new script for the Somali language helped create a symbolic focus for national identity.

The Somalis are also adherents of three main Sufi brotherhoods – the Qadiriya, the Ahmadiya, and the Salihiya. The Qadiriya was introduced into Harar as early as the fifteenth century. One of its branches, the Uwaysiya, is active throughout East Africa. The Ahmadiya was founded by Ahmad b. Idris al-Fasi (1760–1837) and was brought to Somalia by ʿAli Maye Durogba. The Salihiya, founded by Muhammad b. Salih in 1887, had settlements between the Juba and the Sheballe rivers. This is the order which gave rise to Muhammad b. ʿAbdallah (Abdille Hassan), who returned from Mecca to preach the purification of Islam. He declared war against Christians and against British rule, but in 1908 concluded a temporary peace which allowed him to run a small quasi-autonomous state within Somalia. The British finally defeated his movement in 1920.

In general, the Sufi orders were closely allied with the Somali tribes. The Sufis served the tribes as teachers and judges, administering Muslim law in matrimonial, property, and contract matters. They also acted as mediators and arbitrators. When a local Sufi saint died, his tomb often became a venerated place, the object of pilgrimages, and was sanctified by his reputation for baraka. Besides the Sufi brotherhoods and the shrines, there were innumerable holy-men, who provided religious services and were the objects of veneration. The religious leaders were bridges between otherwise competing tribes and allowed some degree of unification across clan and tribal lines.

There were differences, however, between the role of Sufism in the north and in the south. Among northern peoples, who tend to be pastoralists, the Sufis were accepted as client tribes and were supplied with territory for cultivation. They were adopted into the lineages of the dominant tribes, who regard their ancestors as Sufi saints. In these cases the Sufi communities were commonly established on the boundaries between tribal groups where they could serve as mediators. In the southern parts of Somaliland, where there was more farming and less pastoralism, tribe structure was weaker and state organization stronger. Since lineage is less important, Sufis played a larger role in giving cohesion to the agricultural society and had a relatively more secure political position vis-à-vis the tribes.

The Somali government tried to integrate all of the major factions and local kinship units into the national state structure. The fluidity of the tribal structure allowed for flexible political bargaining and coalition-making. Despite the hostilities among them, all major groups considered themselves as belonging to the larger Somali state and culture. Thus segmentation could be made to operate not only as a force of factionalism but as a force for unification.

In 1966 General Siyad Barre staged a coup d'état, and the army took control of the government. He proclaimed Somalia's commitment to scientific socialism and turned to the Soviet Union for support. The government attempted to suppress lineage and tribal affiliations and appealed for nationalistic Somali cooperation. A national cult was created around the person of the head of state. Muslim religious leaders were executed in 1975, and women were given equal legal rights with men. Vigorous efforts were made to promote literacy, to sedentarize the nomads, and to resettle them on state farms or collectives. However, lineage loyalties endure, and the government considers itself both socialist and Muslim.

The most difficult political issue for Somalia was the claim to include Somalian peoples in Kenya, Djibouti, and Ethiopia in Somalia. These claims were resisted by the neighboring states, and the Organization of African States was loath to recognize any demands for border changes. With the withdrawal of the French from Djibouti and the outbreak of the Ethiopian revolution, Somalian guerrillas in Eritrea, Bale, and the Ogaden tried to wrest these provinces from Ethiopian control. In the regional and international struggle which followed, the Soviet Union abandoned Somalia in favor of Ethiopia, and Ethiopia, with Russian and Cuban support, was able to throw back the Somalian attack. The war with Ethiopia has intensified the emphasis upon the Islamic identity of Somalia.

ETHIOPIA

Like the Sudan, Ethiopia is an example of a state sharply divided between Muslim and non-Muslim populations. In this case the different religious groups have been in conflict since the thirteenth century. The territorial expansion of Islam and the rising power of Muslim principalities in the late eighteenth and early nineteenth centuries threatened to undermine Christian control of Ethiopia, but in 1831 Teodros came to the Ethiopian throne with a program of reuniting the Christians, conquering Jerusalem, Mecca, and Medina, abolishing Islam, and bringing the kingdom of peace. After his death (1867) Teodros was succeeded by Menelik II (1867–1913), the ruler of Showa, who became in 1889 king of kings. A consolidated Christian-Ethiopian kingdom set out again to absorb the Muslim minorities in Harar, Sidamo, Arussi, Bale, and Eritrea. The revived Ethiopian kingdom also managed to check the threat of European colonialism. In 1885 the Italians occupied Massawa on the Red Sea coast, but by the Treaty of Uccialli in 1896 Menelik achieved effective independence, though Italy regarded it as a Treaty of Protectorate.

After Menelik's death in 1913, there was a long interregnum until Haile Selassie ascended the throne in 1930 and resumed the effort to centralize the Ethiopian state. He attempted to bypass the power of the nobility by building up cadres of educated commoners. His work was interrupted by the Italian invasion of 1934 and 1935, which forced the Emperor to flee and led to the creation of an Italian East African empire, including Ethiopia, Eritrea, and Somalia. In 1941 the British helped to organize an Ethiopian resistance and returned Haile Selassie to the throne. The process of centralization resumed as Selassie defeated provincial rivals, curbed the power of the church, made the clergy subordinate to the Emperor, and deprived the nobility of its position as a military and tax-collecting elite. Despite this centralization, however, the state did not fully reach to local levels, and local ruling families commonly remained powerful.

As in many Third World countries, political centralization led to social change. Selassie had brought to power a new class of officials drawn out of the old nobility. In the 1950s these were superseded by a younger generation of army officers, secondary school and university graduates, labor union leaders, and others. The post-1950s elites, moreover, were impatient with the corruption of the older generation. There was a threat of a coup in 1960, and in 1974 a mutiny of soldiers, followed by widespread strikes and riots, led to a new regime run by the Coordinating Committee of the Army, or *Derg*, which dismantled the imperial government and deposed the Emperor. In 1975 the Derg was taken over by radicals who announced a Marxist-Leninist ideology, nationalization of property, and land reform. The breakup of the state opened the way for chaotic local fighting. Peasants and workers created their own political associations, and ethnic communities battled for power.

In this confused situation Muslim minorities seized the opportunity to resume their resistance to incorporation into the Ethiopian state. Since the nineteenth century, Muslims under Ethiopian rule had been excluded from public posts, though the 1931 constitution established equal rights and allowed Muslims to acquire land, hold official positions and receive official recognition for Muslim festivals. Muslim dissatisfaction, however, came into the open in the Bale province, where Somali and Galla peoples revolted. Backed by Saʿudi Arabia, the Sultan of the Afars rebelled in Ogaden. The Western Somalia Liberation Front opened its drive for autonomy. The Ethiopians defeated much of the opposition, and threw back a Somalian invasion.

Eritrea has become the main focus of continuing Muslim opposition. The borders of Eritrea were first defined by the Italians, and the Muslim population, consisting mainly of Tigray tribes, began to acquire political consciousness only in the 1940s. In 1952 Eritrea was federated with Ethiopia on the basis of regional autonomy, but Selassie worked to integrate it into Ethiopia. In 1957 Arabic and Tigriniya were abolished as official languages. This led to the formation of an Eritrean Liberation Front composed of students, workers, and intellectuals. By 1962 this movement had been suppressed and Eritrea was formally annexed by Ethiopia. In response the Eritrean Liberation Front was reorganized by exiled leaders in Cairo and by local soldiers supported by tribal and religious leaders. The new movement had no social or ideological platform but represented the resistance of Muslim groups without an Islamic or other ideological character. In 1970, however, dissatisfied Eritrean Liberation Front factions with a more radical ideological bent formed the Eritrean People's Liberation Front, and, on the basis of radical ideology rather than Muslim identity, created a coalition with Eritrean Christians hostile to the domination of the Amharic Ethiopian elite. The Eritrean People's Liberation Front called for a national democratic revolution, a people's war, and the revolutionary transformation of society. In 1977 E.P.L.F. and E.L.F. agreed on independence as a common goal, but in the following year Ethiopia defeated the E.L.F., seized the towns of Eritrea, and reduced the E.P.L.F. to a marginal though continuing resistance. In Ethiopia the war between the Christian-dominated state and its primarily Muslim opposition continues.

SWAHILI EAST AFRICA

By the nineteenth century the East African coast was the home of a Swahili Muslim civilization. The principal center of Muslim culture was Zanzibar. Zanzibar was conquered by Sayyid Saʿid b. Sultan, the ruler of Oman (1804–56) and was the capital of the only Muslim state in the region. The Muslim population was concentrated in the coastal towns and on the offshore islands, and consisted primarily of Swahili-speaking peoples, and enclaves of Indian Muslims who formed their own communities (jamatbandis). Zanzibar had the most highly organized system of Muslim administration and teaching. Zanzibar had qadis and muftis, most of them South Arabian in origin. Only Zanzibar and Lamu had madrasas and served as centers of higher education. In the interior the Somalis had been converted to Islam, but otherwise there were only occasional Muslim enclaves along the trade routes leading to the Lake region and the Congo. The Muslims of the interior were mainly Bantu-speakers under Swahili influence.

European protectorates were established at the end of the nineteenth century over Zanzibar, Tanganyika, Kenya, Uganda, and other territories, and gave new direction to the political history of the region. As in West Africa, colonial regimes gave rise to secular national states in which Muslim populations were a substantial minority and did not determine the ideological and political character of the regimes. As in West Africa, colonial administration, and even partial white settler colonization and Christian missionary influence, did not prevent the spread of Islam. Indeed, European rule actually hastened its diffusion. Trade brought interior peoples to the coastal towns, where they were converted to Islam and from where they returned to proselytize in their home country. European administration also favored the spread of Islam because the British and the Germans employed Muslims as government officials, policemen, soldiers, and schoolteachers. During World War I the Germans, who were allied with the Ottoman empire, made a point of being friendly to the Muslims and acting as patrons of Muslim interests. After World War I the proportion of Muslims in Tanganyika increased to 25 percent of the total population. It seems likely that the spread of Islam was facilitated by political instability, by the need for a common identity for heterogeneous peoples, and by the need for new bases of social and political organization. The spread of Islam was also favored by the use of Swahili as a lingua franca in Kenya,

Tanganyika, Uganda, Northern Rhodesia, Madagascar, the eastern Congo, and other East African regions.

The spread of Muslim allegiances was accompanied by the spread of Sufi orders. The Shadhiliya led by Muhammad Maʿruf (1853–1905) established missionary centers along the coast and introduced reformed Islamic practice. The Qadiriya, represented by the sub-order of the Uwaysiya, founded by Shaykh ʿUmar Uways al-Barawi (1847–1909), was based in Zanzibar but carried on active missionary activity in Tanganyika and Kenya and as far as the eastern Congo. The Uwaysiya were active among Swahili and Bantu-speaking peoples, winning Muslims to the brotherhood and converting pagans to Islam. They also led Muslim anti-German resistance in southern Tanganyika. Shaykh Uways became famous for his polemic with the Salihiya brotherhood over the question of whether it was legitimate to visit saints' tombs and whether deceased saints could be mediators between men and God. Uways took a conservative tolerant view of these practices in opposition to reformist teachings. For these views he was assassinated in 1909. In the course of the colonial period, then, the large Muslim minorities of East Africa were organized into Sufi-led brotherhoods.

The situation of Muslim populations differed in each colonial territory. Zanzibar was dominated by the Arab population, which owned most of the arable land, filled the civil service, and controlled the government and police. An Indo-Pakistani community controlled commerce and trade. The indigenous African majority were mainly craftsmen, fishermen, and workers, and called themselves Shirazis, though they were divided into numerous tribal groups. Migrants from mainland East Africa were concentrated in Zanzibar town and developed a strong sense of political unity. The Arabs resisted any attempts by the Africans to raise their status or political influence and formed a closed aristocratic and mercantile society.

While the British intended to rule through the established Sultanate and the Arab elites, they nonetheless promoted far-reaching changes in the structure of society and the balance of power within it. The British reduced the power of the Sultan and destroyed the economic base of the Arab elites by the abolition of slavery. At the same time, they tried not to disrupt the clove plantations. Slaves were made into semi-servile peasants owing labor service, and Nyamwezi workers were imported. The Arabs, however, lost control of the plantations to Indian moneylenders and merchants. The freeing of the slaves allowed a new African elite and community to take shape. Africans began to obtain ownership of land. In the 1930s political associations for Arabs, Indians, Shirazis, and migrant mainland Africans were formed.

World War II brought a movement toward independence and open political struggle among the different segments of Zanzibari society. At the end of World War II the island Arab and African populations became increasingly politically conscious as a result of the return of soldiers from the war and the news of events in Egypt and Palestine. British political reforms and the dock workers' strike of 1948 also had a mobilizing effect. The Arab minority united on the basis of shared language and culture, Muslim piety, ethnic pride, and former political dominance to attempt to expel the British and to create an Arab-Islamic state. The Zanzibar National Party, founded in 1956, became the principal proponent of the Arab interest. The Afro-Shirazi Union founded in 1957 became the expression of both native peasants and migrant mainland workers.

With the creation of a party political system in the 1950s, the Arabs struggled to win at least enough African support to control the government. They tried to create a national sentiment for a multinational state and stressed common solidarity based on Islam. In the elections of 1957 anti-Arab sentiment was not sufficient to unite all of the African factions. While the Arabs stood for immediate independence, the Afro-Shirazi party was portrayed as allowing racial animosity to inhibit the united drive for independence. By 1961 the Afro-Shirazi party was demoralized and divided. The Arab parties won the 1961 and the 1963 elections. However, in 1963 the government party weakened itself by attempting to dismiss the African police force and to replace it with Arabs and Asians. It also began to rule in a repressive way which left violence as the only recourse for the opposition. The Arab position was also weakened because it was no longer based on a military and land-owning elite but on a younger generation of civil servants, journalists, and politicians.

This rigid regime was attacked immediately after independence (December 1963) by African revolutionaries who seized the government, nationalized the land and the major businesses, opened foreign ties with eastern bloc countries, distributed confiscated Arab lands, decimated the Arab community, and proposed a new merger with Tanganyika. A small revolutionary cadre was able to seize control of Zanzibar and eliminate the Arab elite. The coup led to the merger of Zanzibar and Tanganyika into a greater Tanzania in 1964. Zanzibar as a province of Tanzania, however, maintains an Islamic if not an Arab identity. Quran schools and an Islamic Institute perpetuate Muslim and Arabic language instruction.

Tanganyika was given its first territorial government by the Germans, who declared a protectorate in 1885. German rule was established in the face of intense local resistance. The Bushiri revolt was led by slave traders attempting to protect their interests against German taxation and control. The resistance of the Yao peoples of the Makonde plateau lasted until 1889. The Unyanyembe of Tabora fought the Germans until 1893; the Hehe kingdom battled with the Germans for control of the trade routes until 1898. With the defeat of the Hehe kingdom the Germans were able to begin systematic administration and taxation. They established a government consisting of a central governor and twenty-two provincial districts with their own police and judicial services. *Akidas*, or officials of Arab and Swahili origin, were appointed where there were no local chiefs. The Germans favored economic development and experimented with plantations producing coffee, sisal, rubber, and cotton. Africans were forced to grow cash crops so that they could pay taxes. In some districts German settlement was encouraged and the whites used forced African labor. Economic exploitation led to new rebellions. The Maji Maji revolt in southeastern Tanganyika began in 1905 and attracted widespread support. This revolt was savagely repressed but later German governors tried to mitigate African hostility by forbidding corporal punishment and by instituting educational and health reforms.

After defeating the Germans in World War I the British took control of most of Tanganyika as a League of Nations mandate in 1919. Rwanda and Burundi were given to Belgium, and Kiyunga was annexed to Mozambique. They also encountered active African resistance, though in more peaceful form. British agricultural and educational policies helped form a new elite, and African welfare organizations were formed by civil servants, rich peasants, and educated youths in rivalry with traditional chiefs. In the 1920s and 1930s they evolved into nationalist political organizations. The Tanganyika African Association (founded in the 1920s), supported by farmers concerned about state agriculture and marketing policies, was in 1954 renamed the Tanganyika African National Union and reorganized, on the model of Ghana's Convention People's Party, as a national political coalition. It took the lead in creating a mass movement to win self-government on the basis of Tanganyikan unity, ignoring ethnic, racial, and religious divisions. T.A.N.U. won national elections in 1958 and 1959, and Tanganyika became independent in 1961.

Under the leadership of Julius Nyerere, Tanzania has been one of the most successful African states in creating a concept of a national society dedicated to the welfare and dignity of its citizens. Tanzania adopted the values of equality, democracy, decentralized administration, socialism, and full communal participation in the political society. The doctrinal concept is summed up in the term *ujamaa* or community. However, there is constant tension between these ideals and the tendency of T.A.N.U. to centralize power, create a strong civil service, and attempt a disciplined control of the masses. In the Arusha Declaration of 1967, Nyerere reaffirmed his vision of a democratic political society. He tried to define a truly African orientation for Tanzania in terms of decentralization of the economy and popular participation in political power. He tried to curtail the bureaucratic elite and to encourage labor-intensive agricultural development and independence of foreign loans and influence. New programs of village development were undertaken in the 1970s but the results have been meager.

As opposed to those in Zanzibar, Muslim communities in Tanganyika were not organized under state auspices but remained diverse religious minorities within the framework of a non-Muslim state. Though the British cut Tanganyika off from the official Islamic establishment of Zanzibar, Sufi Islam spread throughout the region as a form of native reaction to foreign rule. The tariqat became the principal Muslim organizing institutions, though the rivalries among the brotherhoods also spread dissension among the Muslims. The Muslim brotherhoods were then progressively linked to a national political movement. In 1934 the Muslim Association of Tanganyika (M.A.T.) was formed, in response to the need for better education and Muslim unity, by many of the same people who had participated in the formation of the Tanganyika African Association in 1929. Through the M.A.T., Sufi leaders became active supporters of T.A.N.U. In 1957 an All-Muslim National Union of Tanganyika was founded to give expression to purely Muslim interests, but the majority of the Muslim population continued to back the national party.

The case of Shaykh Ramiya of Bangamoyo is illustrative of both the local role of Sufism and its integration into national politics. Shaykh Ramiya was a former slave who became a merchant and landowner, pursued religious studies, and won great local respect. He collaborated with the British and was appointed a *liwali* or district officer. From his combined economic, religious, and political position Shaykh Ramiya established a branch of the Qadiriya order. Most of his followers were Africans who benefited from the social solidarity of the brotherhood and from their allegiance to a powerful patron. In 1938 his son and successor Shaykh Muhammad declared that the Prophet was not an Arab but a man of all races – an expression of the African identity of this Muslim community. Shaykh Muhammad encouraged his followers to join the national political party and himself became a local representative. After independence Nyerere appointed him *hakim* or local governor. Shaykh Muhammad was thus an African-Muslim religious leader who displaced the political power of older Shirazi lineages and became part of the Tanzanian national political elite. By organizing his followers into a religious brother-hood, he linked local communal structures to the national political regime. The Tanzanian state shows its recognition of this Muslim political support by appointments to the Ministry of Justice and to local judgeships. Swahili is also the national language.

While Tanganyika developed as an African society, Kenya became a white settler society. Kenya was acquired by the British East Africa Company in 1888, made a separate protectorate in 1904, and declared a crown colony in 1918. Between 1900 and 1919 the country was subjugated by force and organized for European settlement. Whites from South Africa, Britain, New Zealand, Australia, and Canada were settled in the highland territories and Africans were moved into native reserves. From 1923 to 1952 the British pursued a policy of segregated development, and favored the whites by manipulating African reserves to secure the best lands and mineral resources for white exploitation. It also favored the whites in medical, educational, and economic services. Separate local councils were set up for whites and Africans. Despite discrimination, an African elite emerged from British missionary schools and military service, and formed the East African Association, the Cavirondo Taxpayers' and Welfare Association, and, in 1944, the Kenya African Union under the leadership of Jomo Kenyatta. Africans demanded adequate employment, educational opportunities, and access to land. In 1952 the Mau Mau revolt broke out, as blacks carried on a guerrilla war against whites and white rule. The struggle led in 1959 to the removal of internal racial and territorial boundaries and to the formation in 1963 of an independent Kenyan state under the leadership of the Kenya Africa National Union Party.

The Muslim population of Kenya is relatively smaller than that of Tanzania but it is also very diverse, representing numerous African, Asian, and Arab communities. In the coastal regions the Muslim population is closely related to Zanzibar. The interior population includes Kikuyu, Masai, and Maru peoples, who converted to Islam after World War I as a result of trading contacts with the coast. There are numerous Muslim associations, such as the Kenya Muslim Welfare Society, which sponsors schools and clinics, but Kenya's Muslim population is not involved in national politics as an organized group.

In Uganda the organization of a colonial state also set the terms for the eventual emergence of an independent Uganda. Buganda became a British protectorate in 1893, and the Uganda agreement of 1900 brought the whole country under British rule. By 1914 the British had brought the remaining local chiefs under their control. In the struggle for power the British were closely allied with the Protestants and encouraged the spread of Christianity as a barrier to Islam. Under British rule, a Ugandan education system was set up, divided along religious lines. Catholics and Protestants were favored by government grants of land, but the Muslims were discriminated against in appointments to offices and in government support of mosques and schools. As opposed to Kenya, the British kept white settlers out of the region and favored a peasant economy based on cotton and coffee production. A small urban population, however, largely foreign in origin, included Indians, Europeans, and Arabs, who had come to trade.

African protest developed early. The young Baganda association called in the 1920s for African participation in government. A Uganda African Farmers Association was organized to protect African peasants' interests against Indian and European merchants. The development of nationalism and militant resistance to the British, however, was limited, since in Uganda Africans did not suffer from large-scale alienation of land and were buffered from foreign interference by the British system of indirect rule. However, in 1952 the Uganda National Congress was formed to call for independence. The Kabaka of Buganda, the most prominent local ruler, and the Protestant elites, emerged as the most powerful forces in the country. In 1960 the Uganda Peoples' Congress was formed to represent the interests of other chieftains and population groups in the struggle over the political complexion of the forthcoming independent state. The 1962 elections brought Sir Edward Mutesa, the hereditary ruler of Buganda to power but in the next few years the Uganda Peoples' Congress consolidated its grip on the civil service, subverted the trade unions, and built up the army. In 1966, on the strength of the army, Milton Obote seized power, abrogated the 1962 constitution, and assumed the office of executive president. While Uganda still had a civilian administration, from 1966 to 1971 it was in fact under military rule. In January 1971 an army coup d'état brought General Idi Amin to power. Idi Amin's power was built on the support of the Nubian forces in the Ugandan army who originally came from the Sudan in the 1880s. They have come to consider themselves a tribal group, superior to, separate from, and resentful of the rest of the population.

While British administrative policy in Uganda was inimical to Islam, Islam still spread as the result of the influence of Arab traders, Sudanese soldiers, and Swahili contacts. By 1930 there were approximately 122,000 Muslims. Mbogo, former Kabaka of Buganda, became the patron chief of the Muslim community. He had relatively little success, however, in promoting Muslim interests and failed to acquire government land for the support of mosques. After he died in 1921 the Muslims split up into two sects, the Kibuli and the Butambla, divided over competition for leadership and over the doctrinal question of whether it was necessary to say the noon prayers in addition to the congregational prayers on Friday. Also at issue was the authority of marriage registrars and teachers. The sectarian split inhibited the reform of Muslim education and the overall development of the Muslim community. By World War II strong efforts were being made to pacify the dispute. In 1944 the Ugandan Muslim Education Association was founded to overcome factionalism, and unify educational programs, and the parties were reconciled in 1948. The East African Muslim Welfare Society also constructed schools and mosques and provided fellowships for Muslim students. With development of the independence movement in the 1950s, Muslims were accorded a larger role in government, but by 1965 they still had little political influence. Some Muslims served as intermediaries between the state and the Muslim population, but these politicians did not have any deep legitimacy in the Muslim community. Thus the state could not control the Muslims any more than the Muslims could influence the state. In general the state acted as arbitrator in disputes among Muslim groups and as patron for particular Muslim demands such as funds for education, appointment of ministers, or symbolic recognition.

Under the regime of Idi Amin, himself a Muslim, Muslims enjoyed government support. The Uganda Muslim Students Association and the Uganda Muslim Supreme Council were formed as vehicles for the organization of the Muslim community under state tutelage. Amin had no more success than previous governments in mobilizing the Muslim community. They were neither united nor subordinated to the state apparatus. Amin also expelled Indians and Pakistanis. However, upon his defeat many Muslims fled the country and many mosques and schools were destroyed by their opponents.

In the 1960s other former colonial territories in East Africa such as Rwanda, Burundi, Malawi, and the Congo also emerged as independent states. Small Muslim populations also reside in these states. Muslim minorities have been established under the influence of Arab and Swahili traders, East African missionaries, and post-World War II Pakistani merchants. In these countries the Muslim populations are small, poor, ill-educated, and play little role in national politics.

The East African-Muslim population also includes small but important communities of Indian origin, including Ismaᶜilis, Bohras, Ithna-ᶜashari Shiᶜa and Ahmadis. Indian Muslims were first attracted to Zanzibar by Sayyid al-Saᶜid (1804–56), who appointed Indians as customs collectors and financial advisers, and encouraged them to trade. The British similarly encouraged trade and migration of Indians from Gujarat and other Indian provinces. Indians commonly came to work as laborers or shop assistants, learned Swahili, saved a little money, opened a shop, returned to India to marry, and brought back relatives to help in the business. With the opening of the interior by British and German railways many Ismaᶜilis migrated inland. Between 1900 and the 1960s they became a highly modernized community. Their secularly educated women are free from purdah, and the community has substantial educational and health facilities and collective investments in modern enterprises. It maintains clinics, sports clubs, libraries, meeting halls, hospitals, schools, and other facilities. The community has also formed investment trusts for insurance, agriculture, and housing projects. The Aga Khan governs the community through a hierarchy of councils. In principle, his authority is absolute and his approval is required for all appointments, but the Ismaᶜili community and its agencies are actually run by a small wealthy elite. A new generation of educated doctors, engineers, and professionals is gradually replacing the older commercial aristocracy. A constitution of 1954 created agencies for secular and religious affairs, education, health, property, alms and tax collection, and industrial development. The constitution also included a personal law which dealt with family and marriage matters. As revised in 1964 it explicitly prohibited polygamy, set a minimum marriage age of 16 years for females and 18 years for males, and granted substantial equality to women in divorce. Matters such as guardianship, adoption, and legitimacy were adjusted to correspond with territorial law in East Africa.

The Bohra Shiᶜa are a similar sectarian community. Highly active in trade, they include metalworkers, watchmakers, and merchants. The Bohra community is organized in an hierarchical way. The high chief for all of East Africa resides in Mombasa; local *amils* supervise the mullahs who teach school and perform local religious services. Between 1951 and 1955, a new congregation was formed, called the Daʾudi Bohra Jamat Corporation, which consists of all males over 18 years old, and elects a managing council which administers community property including mosques, assembly houses, schools, clubs, clinics, and real estate. The community is supported by endowments, gifts, and taxes on the membership.

The Ithna-ᶜashari Shiᶜi community also has a strong organization. Local congregations are organized as jamats, with an executive council, a board of trustees, and committees to administer the various communal properties and activities. There is a supreme council for East Africa representing the local jamats. The Ahmadis, a Muslim sect founded in northern India at the end of the nineteenth century, also have a small but active following in East Africa and are strongly interested in missionary activity. They are the first to have translated the Quran into Swahili. While the Asian communities are highly modernized, they are also close-knit and sectarian, and have not been integrated into the general African society.

Thus the Muslim communities in East Africa are highly diverse and fragmented by ethnic origins, religious belief, and sectarian organization. Throughout East Africa, excluding Sudan and Somalia, the Muslim population is a political minority in the sense that Muslims do not control state power. Nor do East African regimes identify themselves as Islamic. In Tanzania the Muslim population is held under strict political control. In Uganda it has been defeated in the recent struggle for power. As a political minority, Muslims concentrate on internal and religious matters and have formed numerous associations for educational and welfare purposes. Nonetheless, apart from the prosperous Asian and some of the coastal Swahili merchant communities, the Muslims remain a poor population and out of touch with developments in the rest of the Muslim world.

UNIVERSAL ISLAM AND AFRICAN DIVERSITY

The twentieth century has brought complex changes to Muslim peoples in sub-Saharan Africa. Throughout the nineteenth century, Muslims had been expanding the region as traders, missionaries, and warriors. In the Sudanic region, Muslim regimes were consolidated and new populations converted to Islam. From the Sudan Muslims penetrated the Guinean forest and coastal territories of West Africa. Large numbers of people in Nigeria and Senegal were Islamized. In East Africa Gallas, Somalis, and other peoples were converted to Islam.

The militant expansion of Islam was brought to a halt by European conquest between 1882 and 1900. The establishment of colonial rule, however, did not stop the spread of Islam by peaceful means. In fact, colonial rule facilitated the diffusion of Islam by providing political security and expanded commercial opportunities, and by stimulating urbanization and the migration of merchants and workers. At present Muslims constitute the overwhelming part of the population in such states as Mauritania, Senegal, Guinea, Mali, Niger, and Somalia. They are the majority in Nigeria, Sudan, and possibly Tanzania; and are substantial minorities in such states as Ivory Coast, Ghana, and Sierra Leone.

The rapid diffusion of Islam has had important consequences for the character of Muslim beliefs, for communal organization, and for the relation of

Muslim populations to state regimes and national societies. While the principal goal of many nineteenth-century Muslim movements was to establish Muslim states and a comprehensive Islamic society, colonial rule has led rather to the consolidation of secular or non-Muslim national states. Almost all the independent African regimes have adopted a secular national identity based on non-religious ideologies. Only where there are substantial Arab populations or claims to Arab identity – as in Mauritania, northern Sudan, and Somalia – is national identity expressed in Islamic terms. In Nigeria Muslim identity has been integrated into the national political system, and Muslim communal organizations and Muslim concepts of justice play an important role in the internal national struggle for political and social power. Elsewhere, secular elites treat their Muslim populations, however large or small, as communal constituencies. Reciprocally, twentieth-century developments have in general shifted the emphasis in Muslim affairs toward "sub-political" educational, religious, and economic activities. All African-Muslim populations are organized as communal groups seeking state protection and patronage for their economic, educational, and foreign policy interests.

Muslim communities vary considerably in organization. The traditional forms of ʿulamaʾ and law-school organization are found only in the Sudan. Elsewhere, Sufi brotherhoods are the principal form of Muslim association. In Mauritania, Senegal, Guinea, Mali, Nigeria, Somalia, Tanzania, and other parts of sub-Saharan Africa, they serve on a local basis to integrate diverse ethnic populations, as in Kano, or diverse tribes as in Somalia. They also serve to organize their members for worship and spiritual comfort, for economic competition, as in the case of the Murids of Senegal or the Hausa of Ibadan, or for political administration as in the case of the Tijaniya of Senegal and Nigeria, the Qadiriya in Tanzania, the Khatmiya in the Sudan, and the Sanusiya in Libya.

Apart from the organized brotherhoods, Sufi families, lineages, and individual holy-men also play an important social role. In Somalia, Sufi lineages serve as a link between tribal groups. In Guinean and coastal West Africa educated missionary families are the basis of Muslim settlements and Muslim education. In many parts of Guinean West Africa, Sudan, and Tanzania, Muslim communities are built around individual holy-men and revered local shrines.

In African cities and towns there has been an extraordinary proliferation of Muslim associations, fraternities, and clubs. Some are the expression of minority groups, such as the Ismaʿili or Bohra communities in East Africa, which form jamatbandis with a high degree of internal diversification for religious, welfare, educational, and economic activities. Other associations are the expression of ethnic minorities, such as northern migrants in southern Nigeria, Ghana, and Sierra Leone. Such associations, however, are not separated from but are merged into family, tribal, and ethnic groups. For the Dyula communities and Muslim-led missionary settlements in West Africa, Islam is part and parcel of a familial, occupational, and linguistic identity which distinguishes Muslim merchant groups from the peoples among whom they settle. Similarly, Islam is coupled with Hausa ethnicity to define Muslim communities in southern Nigeria. Among Arab peoples of Mauritania, Somalia, and the Sudan, Islam is fused with tribal, ethnic, and linguistic traits. To be Arab-Somali or zawaya Berber is by definition to be a Muslim. In these cases, too, Islam is fused not only with ethnicity but with nationality insofar as the Mauritanian and Somali regimes define themselves as Islamic.

Not all Muslim urban associations, however, are ethnic in quality. Many are small clubs built around the leadership of a particular teacher who organizes study groups, discussions and communal activities which may be as serious as managing a school or as playful as café conversation. The most striking type of urban association are the modernist groups devoted to Muslim reform and education. The Wahhabiya in Sudanic Africa and various Nigerian modernist groups are principal examples, but such associations are found throughout the region and form the backbone of Muslim efforts to combine modern education with religious commitments. In many areas where Muslims are minorities, as in Uganda or the Congo, educational associations have become the principal forms of Muslim communal organization. Muslim leaders try to bypass national and political institutions to carry on communal work.

Muslim communal structures, then, range from traditional forms of local kinship and village groups, to Sufi lineages, brotherhoods, educational associations and modernist reformist congregations. Islamic communal organization both reinforces minority ethnic identity and serves to link together different tribal and ethnic groups. It serves political purposes varying from collaboration with state authorities to passive withdrawal, passive resistance, active engagement, and even revolutionary action. Muslim belief and identity is highly adaptive to social context, and particularly responsive to the realities of political power.

Only in the last decade has the relationship between Muslim communities and state regimes been called into question. In the 1970s Muslims in Nigeria, Senegal, Guinea, Somalia, and elsewhere began to demand that the state systematically promote Muslim education, apply Muslim law, and assume a Muslim identity. Guinea, for example, which was ruled by Sekou Toure and the Parti Démocratique and had a long history of efforts to modernize the country and improve the position of women, began to organize Muslim festivals and invoke the militant Muslim legacy of Futa Jallon. In Nigeria and Senegal there is considerable tension between state regimes and Muslim communal leaders who demand that the state represent a Muslim ideal. In the Sudan Numayri attempted in 1985 to impose an Islamic identity on the southern parts of the country. In Ethiopia and Chad Muslim minorities are fighting for political autonomy or control of the state. Despite these major exceptions, however, for almost a century Muslims have accepted non-Muslim state regimes as the political cadre for their communal organizations.

Muslim religious orientations are as diverse as the forms of social organization. Some forms of popular Islam are highly syncretic and merged with African animist and spirit worship. In these mergers the Muslim calendar and festivals and rituals to celebrate births, circumcision, marriage, and death tend to be adopted outright. Otherwise, though Islam in principle challenges African belief systems, in practice it seems to rationalize and Islamicize existing beliefs rather than totally change the mentality of African peoples. While Islam emphasizes the absoluteness of God, it is also host to a variety of subsidiary powers and accepts the reality of divination, magic, witchcraft, and sorcery. African spirits are identified as jinn and spirit cults, such as the Holey of the Songhay, the Bori cult of the Hausa, and the Zar cult in Ethiopia, Somalia, and Sudan, have special appeal to Muslims. They supply catharsis and spiritual consolation for women in particular. Muslim belief sanctions magical practices directed toward the cure of disease and seeking of prosperity. Pagan ceremonies and artistic representations also serve to provide emotional comfort. Muslim religious leaders recognize the necessity of balancing strict religious principles with the practical needs of the common people for magical sustenance. Still, it is striking that popular Islam in Africa, by comparison with other parts of the Muslim world, does not generally cultivate saint worship, pilgrimage to shrines, and veneration of the burial places of Muslim holymen.

Alongside of accommodationist, assimilationist, or syncretic forms of Islam, there is the standard Shariᶜa-based Muslim practice and belief. Shariᶜa has had important effects, for example, in criminal law and in dealing with problems of injury and death. It has tended to reinforce patriarchal and patrilineal family organization and inheritance. Because it favors individual over communal interests, Shariᶜa is preferred by new converts who wish to extract themselves and their wealth from family control. However, where there is a strong corporate interest in land or livestock, as among the Somali, the Fulani, and others, Shariᶜa considerations tend to be ignored. The spread of Shariᶜa, then, depends upon local social structures, and the interests of individuals and contending parties. In some cases, for example, it is possible to gain an advantage in commercial or property matters by applying Shariᶜa rather than customary law.

Shariᶜa has had a strong influence on marriage practices. It defines marriage as a voluntary contract between individuals and assigns basic responsibilities to each. It also simplifies divorce for men. The Muslim marriage gift or *mahr* has been adopted by various African peoples as a gift, or promise of a gift, payable upon divorce or death of the husband directly to the bride. It supplements the ordinary payment of a brideprice to the bride's kin and guardians. Despite Shariᶜa, however, widow inheritance and replacement by sisters continue to be important wherever marriage is primarily conceived as an alliance among kinship groups.

Reformist Islam is another important version of Islamic belief and practice. While accommodationist and Shariᶜa-oriented Islam both seek to penetrate and transform African social ideals and behavior, the reformist trend stands altogether outside of the African tradition. Relying wholly on the Quran and Sunna, hostile to African spirit worship and belief in amulets, the reformers bring to Africa an international standard Muslim belief and practice. Reformism, moreover, blends into modernism. The educational associations of Freetown, Lagos, and Dakar are committed to the adaptation of Muslim identity, to modern and Western civilization, and to the integration of Muslims into secularized national African societies.

Finally, there are the sectarian forms of Islam – those minority groups of Muslims committed to particular doctrines. These include the Asian Ismaᶜili, Bohra, and other minority communities. From a pan-African perspective, Islam is not a single religion but a constellation of religious communities which share, however remotely, a sense of allied identity.

The diversity of sub-Saharan African Islam exposes the varied implications of Muslim belief for political and social behavior. While Muslim believers in the nineteenth century strove primarily to create Muslim states in Sudanic and West Africa, only where Muslim populations were relatively homogeneous (and Arab), as in Mauritania or Somalia, do avowedly Muslim states exist today. Whereas Islam in principle is committed to a comprehensive political order, the traditional Islamic ideal has been adapted to political actuality. Muslim communities in Africa are in the main associations for worship, education, and welfare. Whereas Islam is in principle a religion which shatters all lesser loyalties, in Africa it is an integral part of Hausa, Berber-Somali,

Arab, Mossi, Dyula, and other linguistic and ethnic affiliations. Whereas in principle Islam is a universal religion based on a revealed scripture, in Africa it takes on an infinite variety of local forms. Islam, then, is a symbol of identity which is adapted to various economic, social, and political circumstances and in which principles of religious belief, communal organization, and state power can be combined and recombined in different ways.

CONCLUSION: SECULARIZED ISLAM AND ISLAMIC REVIVAL

For nearly 5,000 years Middle Eastern and Islamic societies have been based upon the constellation of lineage, tribal, religious, and political institutions first evident in the ancient cities of Mesopotamia in the third millennium B.C. This configuration of institutions was the basis of pre-Islamic Middle Eastern societies and was the template upon which Middle Eastern Islamic societies were constructed. In Mecca 1,400 years ago the Prophet Muhammad received the revelations that would infuse the ancient patterns of society with new meaning. The new religion was institutionalized in Arabian tribal communities. After the Arab conquest of the Middle East, it was embedded in the ruling political institutions such as the Caliphates and Sultanates, and in Islamic religious communities such as Sunni schools of law, Sufi brotherhoods, and Shiʿi sects. It was also embedded in both literary culture and popular concepts and mores. The institutionalization of Islam gave rise to a new civilization.

The religious basis of this new civilization was faith in Islam as revealed in scripture and law, as understood in theology, and as practiced in mysticism. Islam provided a concept of the universe, ethical rules, legal norms for daily behavior, ritual prescriptions for mediating the relation of human beings and God, mystical methods of self-cultivation, and symbols of self-identity. In fact, Islam embodied, not one, but several religious ideals. Sunni-Sufis cultivated ethical and spiritual living within the world. The Shiʿa looked to the imams for guidance and salvation. By veneration of saints, Muslims sought to win divine blessing through the intercession of holy-men. Gnostic-philosophers and mystics sought escape from worldly actualities through rational and spiritual concepts of religious salvation.

Conquering tribesmen, traveling merchants, and wandering Sufis brought Islam to peoples outside of the Middle East. The diffusion of Islam and the conversion of new peoples brought Islamic societies into being in Inner Asia, India, Southeast Asia, Turkey, the Balkans, North and West Africa, and other regions. These societies were formed by the integration of the local pre-Islamic civilizations with the universal aspects of Islam to create a new family of human communities. The religious way of life and identity borne by the ʿulamaʾ and the Sufis again became articulated in parochial associations such as lineage, tribal, and village communities, urban communities, and state regimes. By the seventeenth century Islamic societies were fully institutionalized throughout much of Asia, Africa, and Eastern Europe. Each had a distinctive *gestalt* but each was intelligible as a variation upon an earlier Middle Eastern pattern of concepts and institutions.

Whatever the variations, Islam was never the sole or total organizing principle of pre-modern Islamic societies. Each inherited and maintained a cultural identity, a social organization, political institutions, and a system of economy defined in non-Islamic terms. The economies of Muslim peoples were almost never organized or conceived in Muslim terms except for certain modifying ethical concepts such as opposition to usury and demands for fairness, justice, and charity. The military and bureaucratic institutions, systems of taxation, and cultural legitimations of "Muslim" states always had a non-Islamic dimension inherited from the pre-Islamic culture of each region. The social organization, ethnic identity, and elite leadership of parochial communities were also commonly not Islamic. In all Muslim societies the prevailing culture was a mixture of Islamic concepts and symbols and non-Islamic institutions and identities. However important, Islam was still but one aspect of a more complex society.

THE INSTITUTIONAL AND CULTURAL FEATURES OF PRE-MODERN ISLAMIC SOCIETIES

A central feature of these societies was the structure of state and religious organization. We commonly say that in Muslim societies state and religion are unified and that Islam is a total way of life which defines political, as well as social and familial matters. This, of course, is the common Muslim view embodied in the ideal of the Prophet and the early Caliphs who were rulers and teachers, repositories of both temporal and religious authority, and whose mission was to lead the community in war and morality. This ideal continued to inspire the efforts of reformist, revivalist, and "Caliphal" movements to create an integrated Muslim state and society. Such movements were common in lineage communities, in which adherence to Islam led to tribal unification, conquest, and the formation of new empires as in the case of the Fatimid, Almoravid, and Almohad movements in North Africa, the Safavid movement in Iran, and others. In the eighteenth and nineteenth centuries reformist movements with a similar intention led to conquests and state formation in such cases as the Sokoto Caliphate in what is now Nigeria and the Mahdist state in Sudan. In different terms the ideal is invoked by contemporary neo-Muslim movements.

Most Muslim societies did not and do not conform to this ideal, and were and are built around separate state and religious institutions. By the eighth and ninth centuries, the early Caliphate was already evolving into an imperial and secular political regime, while Muslim populations were being organized into a multitude of religiously defined and religiously led associations or communal groups. These included schools of law, reformist movements, Sufi lineages, brotherhoods, shrine communities, Shiʿi sects, and ethnic associations. Such groups were or became independent of state regimes; most withdrew from participation in government, and were primarily concerned with solidarity, worship, education, law, personal morality, and upholding the public symbols of Islam. The separation on an institutional level of state institutions and religious associations became the norm for the late ʿAbbasid Caliphate, the Saljuq and Mamluk Sultanates, the Ottoman, Safavid, and Mughal empires, and other Muslim regimes.

This separation, however, was neither clear-cut nor complete. While the separation was clear on an institutional level and in terms of organizations, personnel, and ethos, in cultural concept there was a deep ambiguity about both state and religio-communal associations. Muslim states, on the one hand, were considered instruments of worldly secular power and were legitimized in terms of patrimonial claims to superior ancestry, state-patronized artistic and literary cultures, and appeals to universal cosmological or philosophical concepts. Their culture derived from the pre-Islamic and non-Islamic substrates of the societies they ruled. On the other hand, secular though they were, these states also had a Muslim religious value derived from historic continuity with the early Caliphate, or based on their role as defenders, patrons, and supporters of Muslim worship, education, law, and jihad. They also had an inherent sacred value, for in many Muslim societies the state was conceived as the direct expression of God's will for the ordering of human affairs. Their religious worth was derived both from service to Islam and directly from divine decree.

Similarly, Muslim religious associations, though basically committed to small communal and individual religious pursuits, were involved in politics. While Muslim religious leaders were in fact committed to an apolitical form of religiosity, in concept they could not imagine their associations as entirely independent of an all-embracing Islamic political order. In concept a Muslim state was necessary for a complete Muslim way of life.

These ambiguities in the concept of Muslim states and Muslim religious associations were translated into a variety of institutional patterns in the relation of state and religious associations. In some cases, such as the Ottoman and Safavid empires, the states themselves directly organized or controlled Muslim judicial, educational, and social functions. The Ottoman and Safavid monarchies were strongly supported by an organized ʿulamaʾ bureaucracy which was committed to the regime and looked upon the state as indispensable to Islam. In these empires Muslim religious associations became virtual departments of state, though in Iran the religious elites were eventually able to assert their autonomy. In other cases such as Mughal India, or Mataram Java, Muslim religious leaders, associations, and activities were largely autonomous, and often critical of state policies and state-patronized culture.

Thus in the pre-modern era there were two alternative concepts of Islamic society. One was the "Caliphate," which integrated the state and the community, the realms of politics and religion, into an inseparable whole. The second was the "Sultanate," or secular state, which ruled over the quasi-independent religious associations that were the true bearers of Muslim religious life. In one image the state was the all-encompassing expression of an Islamic society; in the other, an Islamic society was divided into separate state and religious institutions. The relationship of Muslim communities to state regimes was variable and ambiguous. They were sometimes subordinate and committed, sometimes independent and hostile. Sometimes they accepted the inherent legitimacy of ruling regimes as Muslim; sometimes they rejected them as antithetical to a truly Muslim society. Most often they regarded state regimes with detachment. While accepting the necessity of political order, they disdained political involvement and withdrew into communal and personal religious affairs. While accepting political realities, they were nostalgic for the better days of the true Caliphate and yearned for the era of justice. The legacy of pre-modern societies to the modern era, then, was not a defined structure of state and society, but a spectrum of variation and an inherent ambiguity about the relations between the two.

This legacy was transmitted through nineteenth-century changes into the twentieth-century structure of Muslim societies. In response to the impact of

European imperialism and commercial domination, Muslim political and religious elites proposed alternative concepts for the reconstruction of their societies, each a variation upon past orientations toward the relationship of state and religion. As we have seen, the political elites, transformed into intelligentsias, adopted first Islamic modernist, then secular nationalist, and sometimes socialist conceptions, of national transformation, and became committed to secular or even Western concepts of state and society. In one sense these concepts were a profound departure from the historic political culture, but in another sense they were consistent with aspects of the historical culture that conceived of the state in secular terms as possessed of an inherent legitimacy regardless of its relation to Islam. The interests of the transformed political elites intensified the indigenous concept of a state that was supreme in the society, autonomous of religious values, and legitimate in its own terms. In the nineteenth and twentieth centuries, the state intelligentsias did not so much change their fundamental position as shift from traditional to modern expressions of political identity. The adoption of Western ideologies and of Western political methods was for the political elites a continuation of the tradition in which domination was symbolized in non-Muslim cosmopolitan terms.

Alongside the political intelligentsias, the religious elites had their own response to the breakdown of the Muslim state system and to European domination. The most important religious response in this period was Islamic reformism or Islamic renewal, which became important, for different reasons, in different milieus. With the decline of Muslim states, the rise of European influence, and a changing balance of forces in Muslim societies, reformism gave lineage, village, and tribal communities new opportunities to resist state control, and helped village, artisan, and merchant milieus undergoing economic and commercial change to define new identities.

The reformist movements adopted the ambiguous attitude of the historic religious associations toward political actualities. Some of the movements tended to be apolitical and to concentrate upon educational and religious practices. This was true of the commercial middle classes and of such movements as Deoband, Tanzim, and Tabligh in India, and Muhammadiya in Indonesia. Some movements, however, tended to turn the energies generated by religious reform into political efforts to reconstruct an integral Islamic society encadred in a Muslim state. This was true in tribal milieus and anti-colonial movements such as the Sanusiya and the West African jihads.

NATIONS, NATIONALISM, AND ISLAM

The struggle against colonial domination, and the conflict among the several Muslim elites, each bearing within itself a variant version of the historic Muslim political culture, has given shape to modern Muslim societies. In most Muslim countries, the outcome of these struggles is a threefold structure of society. This includes a secularized state regime, a correspondingly differentiated body of non-political Muslim religious associations, and opposition movements that favor the reconstruction of an integrated Muslim state and society.

The most striking trend in most Muslim regions is the consolidation of centralized national states under the auspices of the political intelligentsia and their legitimation in secular terms. Some of these states came into being after World War I, the majority after World War II. Some derived from the transformation of early regimes such as the Ottoman empire, the Iranian monarchy, and Tunisian, Moroccan, Egyptian, and other Sultanates. Some are due to the construction of new territorial entities such as Syria, Iraq, Jordan, Indonesia, Malaysia, Nigeria, and Senegal, where colonial rulers commonly crushed local feudal, tribal, and religious opposition, and brought varied territories under state control. In the Soviet Union and the People's Republic of China, the conquerors absorbed Muslim populations into large non-Muslim empires. The new states are commonly based on military elites in Syria, Iraq, Egypt, Jordan, Algeria, Pakistan, Indonesia, Nigeria, Sudan, Libya, and many smaller African states. In almost all cases the central state is strengthened by the manipulation of economic development. Military elites, as in Syria, Iraq, and Algeria, and bureaucratic elites, as in Egypt and Malaysia, generate a state capitalism or socialism in the interest of the new dominant class. In Algeria, Libya, Iraq, Saʿudi Arabia, the Gulf States, Indonesia, Malaysia, and Nigeria, the elites are supported by state-controlled petroleum revenues.

In most countries the state elites have favored a secular ideological identity. With the notable exceptions of Saʿudi Arabia, Morocco, and the anomalous cases of Iran and Pakistan, states have become more fully differentiated from Muslim religious concepts and institutions, and Islam has been disestablished from its historic roles in the identification and legitimation of state regimes. Some states have attempted to neutralize Muslim activities by bringing them under official control. Government ministries in Egypt, Indonesia, Tanzania, and the Soviet Union coopt Muslim leaders and use them as intermediaries to control Muslim populations. In general, law and education have passed out of religious hands into state control or are left as parallel but secondary systems

Map 37. Contemporary distribution of Muslim populations.

of private adjudication and instruction. Sufism as a system of organizing tribal peoples for political purposes has virtually disappeared or is reduced to healing and ceremonial functions. Centralization of state power has also destroyed or neutralized tribal communities in Turkey, Iran, Inner Asia, Egypt, Syria, Algeria, and other places.

This transformation of relations between state and society is accompanied by new nationalist, liberal, and socialist ideologies and symbols of legitimation. In part this is due to the fact that the elites who took the lead in the struggle for independence were disposed, by experience of colonial rule, education, and acquaintance with Europe, and by the struggle against older feudal and religious elites, to define their concept of an independent society in national and ethnic rather than traditional imperial or religious terms. Even modernist and re-formist Muslim leaders, as in the Ottoman empire or Algeria, blended their hopes for Islamic reform with the realities of political struggle to give them a national definition. In areas where movements toward independence were cut off, as in Inner Asia, Muslim modernism has been redirected toward the cultivation of ethnic and national identity and to integration into state-dominated societies. In part, however, the ideological orientation of modern Muslim states derives from the historical practice of Muslim imperial regimes in the Middle East, South and Southeast Asia, and Africa which were legit-imized by a combination of Islamic and non-Islamic, of secular and religious, concepts and symbols. By maintaining a non-Islamic identity, political elites still try to distance themselves from the embrace of Islam and Islamic religious authority. By regulating state affairs in accord with secular norms and sym-bolizing them in "secular" cultural terms, the state elites shield themselves from Islamic religious precepts.

Similarly the identity of the masses is also reinterpreted in nationalist terms. In pre-modern Muslim societies political and social identities were formed on several levels. Each individual had at once political loyalties to a governing elite, a local familial, lineage, tribal, or village membership, and an Islamic religious identity. Linguistic and ethnic consciousness were usually subsidiary features of social self-awareness. Modern nationalisms, however, emphasize the hitherto subordinate factors. In the case of Turks, Arabs, Iranians, Malays, Uzbeks, Tajiks, Kazakhs, Bengalis, Pathans, and others, national identity is commonly built upon a merger of historic lineage, ethnic, linguistic, and Islamic symbols, recast in national terms.

This emphasis upon nationality rather than other aspects of traditional identity is due to a combination of factors. The national factor was first accepted by Western-educated elites, but became the identity of the masses wherever tribal and religious structures broke down. In many cases national identities have been fashioned by the struggle for independence from colonial regimes or from competing states. For example, the early stages of Arab nationalism in the Middle East were fashioned in opposition to the Ottoman empire and then to British and French rule. Furthermore, state formation is itself a source of national consciousness. Strong Tunisian, Egyptian, Algerian, Bengali, Indonesian, Uzbek, Kazakh, and Tajik identities have all been shaped by state organizations and policies.

National identity in Muslim countries, however, has an important and subtle intermixture of Islam. In many cases the emotive force behind nationalism is the tacit assumption that Islam is the basis of Turkish, Arab, Malay, or other nationalities. The capacity of Islam to symbolize social identity has been merged into national feeling. In such cases there can be shifts of emphasis from national to Muslim self-awareness. For example, in the post-1967 war period, Egyptians began to stress the Islamic aspect of their nationality. Malay elites, having cultivated an ethnic concept of Malay identity, have in recent years yielded to Islamic revival pressures to declare the Muslim character of the Malay people. Though Muslim identity is not in principle territorial, it has become the basis of state formation in Algeria, the Sudan, and Pakistan.

Muslim reformism has also helped to create national political movements, especially in North Africa, by calling for allegiance on the basis of Muslim principles which transcend purely local identifications. By turning Muslims from local sects, shrines, and mediators to the abstract principles of the faith, reformism set the foundations for the unification of large populations in national political struggles. Reformism provides the cultural standards and educational and egalitarian sentiments, which can serve, like nationalism, as the basis of modern political regimes. Only in Algeria, however, has reformism expressly become part of the national concept.

The secularization of Muslim states has had a double effect on Muslim religious associations. First, it often reinforces the reciprocal tendency, already inherent in the orientation of Islamic religious associations, to concentrate on local, communal, and individual religious needs. While older forms of tribal and Sufi organizations disappear in West Africa, Egypt, Indonesia, and Malaysia, ethnic associations, modernist religious congregations, and clubs multiply to meet the need for collective worship, education, charity, and for simple sociability and discussion. In many cases the local cells are independent, but in some they are linked up in larger movements, like the Tijaniya in West Africa, or such national movements as the Muslim Brotherhood in Egypt, Muhammadiya in Indonesia, and others. These associations have a strong appeal to students, intellectuals, technicians, professionals, and merchants.

Many of the modern associations are reformist in orientation and play an important role in the adaptation of Muslim populations to national states and economies. Reformist principles favor delayed emotional gratification and stress self-control and obedience to abstract rules and abstract authorities as the basis of religious fulfillment. Thus they direct pent-up emotions into a sense of individual responsibility to remake the world in accord with Islam. They facilitate the transfer of popular loyalties from tribal and parochial communities and from saintly religious authority to national regimes. They are also congruent with modern industrial societies because of their egalitarianism and emphasis upon universal education, and with urbanized societies, for they favor disciplined behavior. Muslim reform movements are not merely an accommodation to the secularization of Muslim societies but a creative adaptation to the development of a more complex and highly integrated type of social system.

Though reformism disposes believers to worldly activity, it is not necessarily a Muslim equivalent of the Protestant ethic. The doctrinal basis of radical Protestantism – the radically evil nature of human beings and predestination – is not found among Muslims; the psychological tension over the sinfulness of human beings is muted, and Muslim reformism does not necessarily lead to systematic and rationalized behavior directed to single economic and political goals.

Furthermore, in increasingly secularized societies there are strong tendencies for Islam to become less a religion of customary collective practice and more a religion of individual quest and commitment. As religion plays a smaller role in the public world or in explaining the universe of nature, it serves ethical and psychological needs. The decline of Sufi ceremonials and shrine worship has also favored a more generalized intellectual and ethical type of religion. The development of personal religion in Indonesia, Turkey, the Soviet Union, and other highly secularized societies illustrates the development of Islam as a quest without political implications. Finally, in some respects, Islam has been subsumed as an aspect of national identity without having a religious meaning. Many people are "Muslims" without being believers. They are Muslim by virtue of patriotism of community rather than personal piety. Islam as private belief and as social identity has become dissociated from the communal and political institutions in which such belief and identity were once embedded.

By contrast, the secularization of Muslim states and societies has also generated a contemporary reaction and new tendencies to reabsorb religion into politics. In many Muslim countries there is a renewal of religious and political reform movements that espouse Islam as a comprehensive blueprint for a modern way of life and call for the formation of Islamic states to enforce an Islamic morality. These include such groups as the Muslim Brotherhood and its contemporary successors in Egypt, the Jamaᶜat-i Islami in Pakistan, and similar associations in Nigeria, Tunisia, Malaysia, and Indonesia. Such movements are advanced as an alternative to nationalism, capitalism, or socialism and look to the formation of a totalistic Islamic society which will bring fulfillment in terms both of personal piety and of collective life. For the neo-Muslim movements, Islam is the design of a total and exalted way of life in which is contained all individual and social good. The neo-Muslim movements want to derive from Islam a position on every issue of private and public concern – women, education, economy, social structure, and government – to demonstrate that all modern needs can be met by the central symbols of their own tradition. Disillusion with secularism and the quest for indigenous rather than foreign values have led to efforts to define a post-modern concept of Muslim society.

The utopian aspirations of the neo-Muslim movements evoke the Muslim ideal of the Caliphate, but in many respects they are an altogether novel adaptation of Islamic concepts to modern conditions. The new Islamic movements have little of the traditional scriptural, legal, theological, or mystical content. While they may derive from previous reform tendencies, they are led by preachers such as Hasan al-Banna of the Muslim Brotherhood, or Mawdudi, or the Jamaᶜat-i Islami, who are not themselves ᶜulamaᵓ or Sufis. No longer based on schools of law or Sufi brotherhoods, they are organized through study groups, scout groups, women's auxiliaries, athletic clubs, economic enterprises, political parties, and paramilitary units.

Also they differ in their concept of the relation of Islam and politics. In the past, states and empires were legitimized in religious terms and were supposed to defend the religious interests of Muslims and uphold religious law, but religious aspirations were partially detached from political expectations. Religious leaders distanced themselves from politics. By contrast the neo-Muslim movements channel religious belief and solidarity, into politics. In the contemporary era religious feeling becomes the basis of total commitment to political causes. The merger of religion and politics may be a classic Islamic ideal, but only in the recent era have they actually been brought together.

These movements also appeal to new and varied clienteles. In Nigeria they appeal to peasant migrants in Kano, who organize Islamic groups under the leadership of rural religious teachers to press their economic interests as laborers. In Malaysia small-scale peasant landowners have organized under the banner of Islam to resist the pressures that deprive them of ownership of land. In Egypt they appeal to the old strata of artisan and merchant classes, and to the lower level of Muslim-educated teachers and clerks who are threatened by competition from new enterprises and with displacement by Western-educated elites. The neo-Islamic movements also appeal to the new intelligentsia of socially mobile but economically and professionally insecure students, intellectuals, technicians, middling bureaucrats, and professionals. In Turkey Islamic student groups and parties are strongest in the technical faculties while socialist groups predominate in the arts faculties. In Egypt Islamic radicalism won its strongest support among students in medicine, engineering, pharmacy, and other highly professional clienteles. In Iran student leadership was crucial in the internal revival until the revolution. The new classes of socially mobile and educated intelligentsia are successful but unsatisfied people. Separated by their education from traditional communities, they are not part of the political elites. Like uprooted peasants and bazaaris, these strata turn to Islam to symbolize their anxieties, their hostilities to the powers, domestic and foreign, that thwart them, and their dreams of a more perfect future.

Thus, while Muslims on one level keep alive the tradition of a political religious commitment, on another they revive the tradition which integrates religion and politics. Now, that tradition has become the discourse of urban working- and middle-class populations rather than rural lineage and tribal communities. In contemporary politics Islam has become the language of opposition to national states and their policy failures.

THE ROLE OF WOMEN IN MUSLIM SOCIETIES

One of the most difficult issues in the contemporary transformation of Muslim societies is the role of women. Important changes are taking place in the concept of male and female identity, in family roles and in the relations of men and women, and in the place of women in public life. But our understanding of women's roles, of family, and especially of subjective factors, is still extremely limited and the issues are clouded by intense and often ideological debate. For outsiders it is difficult to separate their own values from the conceptions of dignity, security, and love which prevail in Muslim societies. Here we shall attempt only a tentative summary of some of the principal considerations in the contemporary discussion of the role of women in Muslim societies. Also, these remarks are based primarily on the situation of Muslim peoples in the Middle East; other regions differ considerably.

The pre-modern structures of Middle Eastern Muslim families, women's roles, and the concept of women's identity are very little known, but there are a number of guiding considerations. In ideology and theory, and to a large degree in behavior, Middle Eastern Muslim societies made a relatively sharp division between men's and women's roles. The public sphere was almost always reserved for men; the family and household was the domain of women. Though women were commonly employed in domestic crafts, agriculture, and stock herding, the middle-class ideal was isolation from the marketplace, the bazaar, politics, and social life with men. Women were commonly segregated from men outside their immediate families. The pre-modern societies also assumed the dominance of men over women and public deference of women to the authority of men. In extended families and lineages women were subject to the authority of fathers, brothers, husbands, and husbands' male kin.

Male dominance was strongly supported by legal and social structures. Marriages were commonly arranged by families; the bride's male guardians were ultimately responsible for her welfare. A bride would ordinarily move to the house of her husband and reside with his kin. Laws as well as circumstances gave men considerable power over women. In Muslim law men had vast prerogatives to initiate divorce while women had few. In case of divorce, children beyond a certain age belonged to the husband and his family. Men had greater scope to threaten divorce, and to discipline and control their offspring. In Muslim law women had important economic rights, but social practice often restricted their opportunities to accumulate or to inherit properties. Inheritance practices were often contrary to Muslim law; families refused to permit women to inherit their legal share of the properties of husbands or other relatives.

The ideological and conceptual world of pre-modern Middle Eastern Muslim societies also required and legitimized male dominance. The prevailing ideologies held that men, who were physically stronger, more intelligent, and more suited to action, must rule over women, who were more subject to their emotions. Women were identified with the undisciplined forces of nature; men with the order imposed by culture. The rule of men should, of course, be gracious and protective. This basic attitude was reinforced by the belief that the honor of a man and his family, lineage, or tribe depended upon the honorable conduct of the women. As a consequence of these attitudes, in men's eyes women's sexuality was the essential aspect of their femininity.

However, this concept of the relations of men and women has to be modified to take into account important economic and social realities. The relations of men and women were more complicated than is implied in the simple concepts of male dominance and social segregation. While it may be true that women had a lesser role in the "public" sphere, it must be recognized that the "public" domain was much more restricted in pre-modern than in modern societies and that families played a much larger part in economic life and politics. The putative domain of women was thus more consequential than it would seem today. Women have always played a significant economic role in animal husbandry, agriculture, home crafts, and cottage industries. Women's lending and marketing networks were a source of income. Women also owned property or had access through family contacts to income from land and other assets. While there were important variations by region and class, the economic contributions of women's incomes and assets, and their control over the distribution of family food and other resources, gave them a considerable familial and social power. Other factors could also give women considerable autonomy and even dominance in domestic affairs. Women were commonly the custodians of the family social status, and they had the principal roles to play in arranging marriages and maintaining reciprocal relations with other families. In the direct relations between husbands and wives, wives' personal influence, manipulation of husbands, women's conspiracies and intrigues, threats to humiliate husbands by denouncing them for neglect or impotence, and setting sons against fathers – all worked to subvert the domestic power of the males. The dependence of men upon domestic life and the opinion of their neighbors and kin also helped to equalize the relationship between husbands and wives. Furthermore, women had their own bases of social and personal autonomy in women's friendships and social gatherings. The world of women was full of symbols and rituals that belittled and excluded men.

Thus the personal relations and attitudes of men and women toward each other must have had several dimensions corresponding to the complexity of their social and economic roles. Women were not only erotic objects, but must to some degree have been partners in earning a living and in family relations. While, from an outside point of view, men were dominant, women cannot be thought of as an oppressed class. They did not see themselves as forming a collectivity with interests opposed to those of men. It seems most likely that they saw themselves as playing a valued, legitimate, and important role in family and social life, one which differed from but was complementary to that of men.

The veil is usually taken as a symbol of the domination of women by men, but in fact it symbolizes the complexities of their relationships. Wearing of the veil was not, and is not, universal among Middle Eastern and Muslim women. It is most commonly worn by urban and middle-class women but not by working, peasant, and nomadic women. Indeed upward social mobility and urbanization has in some cases stimulated the wearing of the veil. Moreover, the veil is an ambiguous form of social communication. It is understood as a shield, protecting women against men, and society against the danger of temptation represented by women, but while it secludes and conceals women, it also creates mystery and attractiveness, and gives women freedom of move-ment. Thus it has an ambivalent significance in terms of purity and passion, autonomy and subordination, and dependence and independence.

The late nineteenth and twentieth century brought major changes in the historic position of women. As Westernized intelligentsias in Muslim countries sought political and social reforms, the more radical ones proposed the eman-cipation of women and their integration into the society as full equals of men. They held that the education of women was necessary to save them from idle and empty lives, fit them for employment, and train them for harmonious marriages and the raising of children. Only through a modern education, they argued, could women fulfill their domestic roles as mothers and educators of modern youth. Some argued further that the freedom of women was essential to the freedom of the whole society and that their emancipation was necessary for the creation of modern national states.

Intelligentsias took up the cause of women for several reasons. First it was part of their attempt to secularize Muslim societies, separate state and religion, reduce the domain of Islamic law and repudiate Ottoman authority. The condition of women was used to highlight the backwardness of the society; the demands of the intelligentsias for a change in women's place was a symbol of their demands for a change in the whole social order. Intelligentsias desired, by playing up the condition of women, to show their own emancipation and modernity, and to affirm the value of individuality expressed through personal achievement.

In nineteenth-century Ottoman society, the first demands for the modern-ization of the position of women called for monogamy in the royal household, the elimination of concubinage, and greater freedom for women in marriage and social activity. Education became the central concern of Turkish nation-alists. During World War I, women had to work in factories, banks, the postal service, municipal offices, and hospitals, and their experience opened the way for later reforms. In Iran, the education of women became common in upper middle-class circles, though women continued to lead segregated lives. The first public school for girls was opened in 1918 as a result of pressure from feminist advocates.

In the decades after World War I newly independent states such as Turkey and Iran became the most powerful force in changing the condition of women. States and ruling elites used the family issue to help consolidate their power, mobilize women for the labor force, undermine tribal communities, and create a symbolic identity for new nations. Ever after, Middle Eastern states have commonly favored the emancipation of women as a way of breaking down lineage and tribal organizations, and as a means of expanding the labor force and enhancing economic development. The nuclear family is seen as more compatible with industrialization and centralization of state power than the extended family. Under the auspices of the Turkish state, the University of Istanbul was made coeducational in 1921; women were given the same legal rights as women in Europe by the adoption of the Swiss civil code in 1926. The new family law enshrined the principle of monogamy, the right of women to obtain a divorce, and their formal equality in inheritance matters. They were given the right to vote in municipal elections in 1930 and in national elections in 1934.

In Iran, Reza Shah similarly promulgated measures to modernize the status of women. In the 1930s education and public entertainments were opened to women. The veil and the *chador* were outlawed. While men retained important legal privileges in family matters, the age of marriage was standardized, marriages had to be registered in court, and child marriages and temporary marriages were made more difficult. However, less was accomplished in fact than on paper, and after the Shah's abdication in 1941 a reaction destroyed almost all of the gains made in the previous two decades. In the 1950s and 1960s, however, women again benefited from the authoritarian Pahlavi regime. New family laws were promulgated in 1967 and 1973; these discouraged polygamy and made it harder for men to obtain unilateral divorces. Women were also entering the work force in larger numbers. By 1977 they made up more than a quarter of the civil service and of secondary school staffs, and more than half of elementary school staffs.

In other Middle Eastern countries women have been integrated into the labor force in varying degrees. In Arab countries such as Egypt, Iraq, Lebanon, and Tunisia women are employed in industrial labor. Iraq, for example, has facilitated the employment of women by providing state-subsidized housing and child care. Women workers are enrolled in unions and federations, but these organizations are closely controlled by the state. In politics women have been important in the revolutionary struggles of Iran, Algeria, and Yemen, and in the Palestinian movement, but the post-revolutionary period in several of these countries has brought a reaction and a withdrawal of women from active politics.

In legal matters, the tendency in Muslim countries has been to ameliorate the position of women, but change comes slowly. No Arab country has followed the example of Turkey and completely eliminated Muslim religious law as the basis of modern civil law (Tunisia is the closest approximation). Some countries still have Shariᶜa as the basis of the legal system; others combine religious and secular law. Arab countries reinterpret Shariᶜa in order to accommodate it to contemporary needs rather than reject it altogether in favor of foreign legal systems.

Most Middle Eastern countries have introduced a minimum age for marriage, to avoid child marriage and to minimize parental domination. Some countries, such as Tunisia, require the consent of both potential spouses for a valid marriage, but in Morocco a guardian may still speak for a woman. Polygamy has been restricted, but only Turkey, Tunisia, and such states as Israel and the Soviet Union forbid it to their Muslim populations. Morocco and Lebanon have not directly restricted polygamy, but in these countries it is possible for women to insert restrictive clauses into marriage contracts. Divorce regulations have been changed to increase the power of women, and most countries curtail the freedom of husbands to repudiate a marriage. In many cases divorce has been taken out of the hands of husbands by laws that require a court to issue a decree of dissolution of marriage, but only Iran (before the revolution) and South Yemen have abolished unilateral repudiation completely.

The only major changes in inheritance laws are those which have been made to allow orphaned grandchildren to become legal heirs. In Egypt this is done by permitting grandfathers to mandate inheritance in their wills; in Pakistan it is done by assigning a direct share to orphaned grandchildren. Similarly there are tendencies to consider the welfare of children in custody provisions. Many countries give the courts the right to grant custody of a child at their discretion, though Islamic law specifies that after a certain age the children come into the possession of the husband.

Middle Eastern states have thus developed new legal codes for family relations and have opened the way for female education and employment. Moreover, they promote the expectation of citizen equality by allowing women the right to vote, by providing for unveiling, and by the social and economic integration of women into the general society. The modern state has not only changed the legal position of women, but by the promotion of educational, health, and other social welfare programs, has usurped traditional family roles. Women have become clients of the public sector; state employees are substituted for the male members of the family as the principal source of important services. Women increasingly deal with men who are not kin as employers, teachers, bureaucrats, and colleagues.

Alongside of state formation, economic development, urbanization, and modern bureaucratic and industrial organizations have helped break down traditional families, promoted nuclear households, and favored the incorporation of women into the work force. Women in schools, hospitals, and workplaces then create new relationships outside of the home, based on specified roles and non-sexual friendly contacts with men. Women in modern roles add new forms of sociability to the traditional forms of women's sociability, devote less time to domestic activities, and find that kinship plays a reduced role in their lives. Such women in turn introduce new concepts to the rest of society. At the same time the mass media generate new values, tastes, fashions, and fads, and above all the awareness of Western lifestyles. Middle Eastern and Muslim women begin to value individual autonomy, choice in marriage, independent households, and self-fulfillment through love and work.

The degree of change differs in different Middle Eastern countries. In most countries the trends toward emancipation of women from the household and toward increased education and employment affect the upper classes and urban middle classes. Rural women are less affected. The picture of actual legal, family, social, and educational changes is very varied. In Turkey, for example, there is virtually complete legal equality but only upper-class and middle-class women in urban areas in fact receive secondary or higher education and are professionally employed. Turkish women make up a substantial percentage of the medical, legal, and other professional work forces. The position of lower-class women is also changed, but in less attractive ways. Women migrants to the cities sometimes become laborers. Lower-class women in rural areas are engaged in agriculture; when men leave home to work in Europe, women often become heads of households. Nonetheless, throughout Turkish society there is still a very strong bias toward male superiority.

In the Arab countries compulsory education has been established for both boys and girls, but women still lag behind men in education and literacy. Many people still feel that education for girls comes at the expense of needed household labor and child care or that it will ruin a girl's morals and her chances for a good marriage. There are also strong objections to integrated schools, but schools for girls are insufficient in number. In such countries as the Sudan, Iraq, and Egypt, however, there is a very high proportion of women students in higher education, though educated elite women are only a tiny percentage of the total female population. While there have been important gains in the employment of women, women in Arab countries seem to participate less in the work force than women in other less developed countries such as those of Latin America. Women are commonly found in scientific and technical professions, especially in teaching and nursing, and in agriculture and home industries. In general, family and social attitudes and low educational attainment still depress the absorption of women into the work force.

In the Arab East family practices are also changing, but only to a limited extent. The impulse for this adjustment is not so much economic and industrial change but Western cultural influences, the spread of egalitarian concepts, and nationalist ambitions for a larger contribution from women to the general society. In Lebanon, Jordan, and other Arab countries the extended family which was once the ideal is much diminished in practice. Marriages are less commonly arranged by parents; daughters are more usually consulted. The age of marriage for women is rising. There are still, however, strong preferences for endogamy, and for marriages among cousins or within a neighborhood or village. Even where families are fully nucleated there are strong social and residential ties to extended families. Polygamy is declining, but it is still found in rural areas and among the well-to-do classes.

In general, the barriers to change are formidable. The traditional status of women works against further change. Limited education, illiteracy, economic dependency, lack of employment opportunities, social segregation and male hostility to the social or political involvement of women inhibit contemporary trends. Some of the deepest barriers to change are the cultural values with which both men and women are imbued from childhood. In most Middle Eastern societies the traditional concepts of male superiority and family honor remain potent. Correspondingly, the highest values in regard to women stress the blessing of fertility and motherhood, and imbue women with the expectation of security, protection, and esteem in the family context, values that do, in fact, bring emotional and social gratification. Furthermore, deep within Middle Eastern cultures is the fear of uncontrolled sexuality. These attitudes reinforce the political and economic forces which inhibit further change.

The present situation is thus marked by conflicting trends. There are no widely accepted models for women's roles in society and no widely accepted values to legitimize one system of practices or another. Change therefore generates doubt, anxiety, and conflict. There is conflict between generations over the right to choose a spouse, conflict between mothers-in-law and wives for the allegiance of sons and husbands, and conflict between men and women over educational and employment opportunities. In many countries men find themselves economically and socially oppressed, often humiliated by political helplessness in their own societies, and they want to be compensated by control over women, precisely at a moment when women are asserting their own right to a fuller public life.

In this uncertain situation a central issue is the teachings of Islam. The major debate has been between traditionalist interpreters of the Quran, modernist interpreters of the Quran, and more radical feminist critics, who all differ on questions of polygamy, veiling, the economic rights of women, inheritance, and employment. The traditionalists argue that the Quranic texts are normative and specify eternally valid rules. They believe the Quran requires that women be lodged in the home and have no public role; they should be subordinate to men in order to protect their modesty. The neo-Muslim movements, in particular, espouse these values. The modernists argue that the Quranic norms concerning women's status in the family have to be treated as ethical injunctions rather than legal requirements. They argue that the Quran is descriptive of a given time and place and that with changes in historical and social conditions new adaptations are necessary. The modernists see the Quran as being supportive of the integration of women in society now that this has become essential to the fulfillment of family functions.

Feminist critics of the Muslim positions have taken several points of view. Among them there is almost universal agreement that female segregation and subordination is at least in part the product of patriarchal authority, male-based kinship organization, and class structure, though they note that Middle Eastern Muslim societies do not from this point of view much differ from Mediterranean European or Latin American societies. Many feminist critics see Islam as reinforcing this subordination. They argue that the Quran, Islamic law, and the moral attitudes carried by the ʿulamaʾ have favored a moral and social climate leading to subordination. Islam requires male control over females because of the perceived threat of uncontrolled sexuality and because of the potential for women to create allegiances that compete with man's obligation to God. The highest demand in Islam is subordination of human beings to God and avoidance of any life experience in politics, art, or love which competes with this ultimate religious demand. From this point of view Islam is thus intrinsically hostile to the equality of women and to the development of a full person-to-person love relationship between men and women. Also, the Islamic concept of man as the slave or servant of God, the humble, unassuming devotee of the divine being, has itself become the model for the relations between males and females.

There are, however, feminists who hold that Islam is in principle favorable to women. They believe that early Islam enhanced the position of women in Arabian society, and hold that not Islam itself, but the historical conditions of Middle Eastern societies, are to blame for the subordination and segregation of women. Other proponents of Islam point to the fact that Islam inculcates and defends a high standard of sexual and marital morality, provides for the protection and security of women, and guarantees many legal and property rights. In its historic context, and in the present, Islam has had an uplifting and civilizing effect upon the actual relations of men and women in Middle Eastern societies.

This debate is highly politicized and all the positions reflect political, ideological, and religious agendas. The debate over women has become the battleground for the broader issues of secularization versus Islamization, state power versus communal autonomy, and Westernization versus cultural authenticity that concern contemporary Muslim societies.

COMTEMPORARY PATTERNS IN THE RELATIONS OF STATES AND ISLAM: THE SECULARIZED MUSLIM SOCIETIES

The precise relationships and relative strengths of state regimes, apolitical Muslim religious associations, and politically active Islamic movements vary from country to country. These variations strikingly correspond to the historic configurations of state and religious institutions in each society, and seem to derive from the conflicts among political and religious elites and intelligentsias in the nineteenth and early twentieth centuries. Here we shall review a few cases to explore these variations and their relation to historic institutional and cultural structures.

The most common type of modern Muslim society is one which has a highly secularized regime, strong apolitical forms of Islamic communal life, relatively weak neo-Islamic movements, and a relatively weak penetration of Islam into national political identity. Turkey is prototypical of these secularized Muslim societies. Turkey has substantially disestablished Islam in public life and has created a pluralistic political system, but in many ways the modern form of development depends upon the institutions of the Ottoman empire. By the eighteenth century the Ottoman empire had a centralized state regime, legitimized in both Muslim and non-Muslim terms, and a centralized and unified

Sunni religious establishment. Through bureaucratic administration, the mil-let system, and guilds, the Ottoman regime controlled its subjects to a degree unparalleled among pre-modern Muslim societies. The eighteenth and nine-teenth centuries brought important changes to Ottoman society, but these changes served to carry the pattern of state domination into the twentieth century. As we have seen, foreign and domestic pressures provoked the Ottoman elites to modernize along Western lines – by improving military capabilities, rationalizing administration, restoring the authority of the central government, and making the social and cultural changes necessary to support a centralized state. These reforms brought into being a new intelligentsia – the graduates of military, medical, engineering, and diplomatic schools – each successive generation of which espoused a still more radical program of reform. By World War I the ruling "Young Turks" were committed to secularization in place of Ottomanism and Islam. The parts of this elite that survived the defeats of World War I, under the leadership of Mustafa Kemal, undertook the creation of the Turkish Republic.

The Ottoman religious elites could offer no effective response either to European intervention or to the determination of the state elites to create a secular national state. The religious elites were in effect subordinate func-tionaries of the state committed to the authority of a regime which for centuries had been a warrior state and protector of Muslim peoples. Nor were Ottoman commercial classes sufficiently developed to be a rival for political power. Whatever the opinion of the ʿulamaʾ, and whatever the shock to the feelings of masses of Turkish Muslims, the voice of the Westernized political estab-lishment was the only one heard at the foundation of the Turkish Republic.

The Republic thus inherited the Ottoman tradition of centralized govern-ment and competent military leadership, a long history of nineteenth-century reform and modernization, and an intelligentsia of army officers, adminis-trators, engineers, technical experts, and intellectuals. Modern Turkey came into being with a coherent state structure and a strong commitment to a state-directed society. The new regime transformed Turkish society and culture in ways which submerged the traditional religious organizations and Islamic identity. In the 1920s and 1930s Turkey set the foundations for a modern industrial economy, and sought to absorb the masses of the people into the cultural framework of the republican regime. It attempted to break the at-tachment of ordinary people to Islam and to win them to a Western and secular style of life. Economic development generated a more differentiated social structure including new groups of businessmen, factory managers, rural land-owners, prosperous peasants, engineers, industrial workers, and intellectuals.

However, the cultural changes imposed from the top had relatively slight penetration. They divided the country into a modernized urban elite and rural peasant masses whose Islamic loyalties had never been seriously disturbed. While the state is secular, the Turkish populace has continued to identify itself as Muslim and throughout the Republican era carried on worship in mosques and at the tombs of saints in the traditional way. While Islam remains officially disestablished, in the 1960s and 1970s movements and parties committed to the re-Islamization of state and society grew stronger. The Said Nursi movement, Naqshbandi Sufi groups, and the National Salvation Party, which favored the reestablishment of an Islamic state, grew increasingly active. Nonetheless the complex social and political development of the country has undermined the centrality of Islamic issues in the political system. In a largely secularized and pluralistic society Islam plays the role of private religion inherent in the national identity of the majority but is only faintly able to lay claim to the control of public life. Thus the secularization of Turkey derives from an historic tradition of state domination transmuted into modern national terms and reinforced by the cultivation of an economically and socially pluralistic society.

Tunisia also has an Ottoman heritage and shows similar tendencies to secular national identity. Like Turkey, Tunisia in the nineteenth century had a strong central state and a state-controlled ʿulamaʾ establishment. The breakdown of the commercial economy and foreign debt allowed for the establishment of a French protectorate in 1881. French rule discredited the officials and ʿulamaʾ, who became instruments of foreign rule. The French- and Muslim-educated bureaucrats and intelligentsia, who opposed French rule in terms of Islamic reform and proposals for the formation of a constitutional regime, failed to achieve their political goals. Therefore, in the 1930s, a younger generation representing the upwardly mobile French and Arab intellectuals of the Sahel region seized control of the Destour party. In opposition to the old elite and in the name of independence, nationalist rhetoric superseded Islamic reformism. In 1956 the Destour, led by Bourguiba, came to power, maintained its nationalist orientation, and generated first a socialist and then a mixed economy. Tunisia, however, like the Middle Eastern countries, retained Islam as part of the identity of the common people. This persisting Islamic identity has allowed for an Islamic revival in the 1970s in reaction to the failures of the state and a lagging economy. Thus Tunisia, like Turkey, has a history of centralized state power which allows for the formation of a modern state and a history of colonial occupation which has given the state elites a secular identity. However, though popular identities have been changed from Islamic to national forms, Islam remains inherent in the self-image of the masses and a potential source of reaction against the state regime.

Senegal affords the striking counterpoint of a highly secular, indeed non-Islamic, regime, which rules over an avowedly Muslim society. Pre-modern Senegal was divided into numerous non-Muslim kingdoms within which Muslim communities formed segregated enclaves. In the late eighteenth and nineteenth centuries the Muslims fought to win control of the Senegambian region, establish Muslim states and convert the populace to Islam. Senegal was the scene of the great jihads of Futa Toro, al-Hajj ʿUmar, Ma Ba, and others. These last Senegalese echoes of the "Caliphal" tradition of a unified Islamic state and society were defeated by the French conquest at the end of the nineteenth century.

The French created an entirely new political structure – a Senegalese territorial state in which the Muslim communities were reorganized as Sufi brotherhoods. In place of the quest for political power the Tijaniya, the Murids, and other Sufis organized the populace into Muslim brotherhoods, which provided social leadership, spiritual meaning, and organized economic activity. As organized communities, the Muslims assumed a non-state associational position, and worked out a pattern of cooperative relations with the French. When Senegal became independent in 1960, the state was taken over by a Western-educated Senegalese political elite who resumed the collaborative relationship with Senegalese religious notables. Thus the modern structure of Senegalese society is based on the historic division between state and religious elites and on the collaboration between them, but the mass of the population has retained a Muslim identity. Only recently has there been pressure for the Islamization of the state.

The Muslim societies of Southeast Asia have also developed secular national regimes, but these regimes are coupled with active and competing Islamic movements. The Southeast Asian combination of secular state and Islamic challenge has its origins in the historic structures of Indonesian societies as modified by the Dutch. Whereas in the territories of the former Ottoman empire, modern secular states were built upon an historical legacy of strong state regimes which dominated the religous elites – a legacy which could be transformed into legitimate secular state domination in the twentieth century – in Southeast Asia the historic states were weak and decentralized but were firmly legitimized in non-Muslim cultural terms. Their non-Islamic cultural identity, rather than their political strength, formed the basis for the secularization of Indonesian twentieth-century national society. Similarly the historic segmentation of Indonesian and Malaysian societies into separate state, religious, and village milieus permitted autonomous religious movements based on non-state communal structures.

The Dutch empire generated the transition from the old to the new forms of state and society. It set the geographical and administrative foundations for the modern state of Indonesia. Under Dutch tutelage, the Indonesian priyayi received a modern education and adopted secularist concepts. Thus they combined the non-Muslim aspects of priyayi culture with a Western orientation to become leaders of the nationalist movements. In reaction to the nationalism of the aristocrats, the Communist party organized Indonesian intellectuals and workers to fight for a secular but socialist society.

At the same time extensive economic changes throughout the Indonesian archipelago and the Malay peninsula brought forth competing elites. In the Indonesian outer islands, Singapore, and the Malayan ports, economic change stimulated the rise of merchant groups and independent landowners who expressed their cultural and political interests in terms of reformed and modernized Islam. In Indonesia the reformist sensibility led in two directions. One was toward religious and educational reform as typified by the Muhammadiya movement. The other was political action as exemplified by the Sarekat Islam party. In response to the modernist movement, the rural ʿulamaʾ organized their own political parties to defend village Islamic culture. Each of these movements built up a national following based on the aliran or integrated community. By the time of independence Indonesian society was divided into several ideologically defined and competing communities.

The Indonesian movements waged a successful war to free Indonesia from Dutch rule, and then a post-independence struggle to define the identity of the independent Indonesian state. The nationalist and Communist politicians, supported by the army, sought to define the Indonesian nation in accord with the pancasila principles. The several Muslim movements wished to have Indonesia declared an Islamic state. In the decisive elections of 1955 the Muslims failed to win a majority, and between 1955 and 1960 were driven from political power. The Communists were virtually annihilated in the massacres of 1965, and a secular-oriented military elite took power.

The military regime has coopted Nahdatul ʿUlamaʾ, the party of the religious leaders, which accommodates to secular rule in return for the protection of its interests in the Ministry of Religion and the villages, and has brought other Muslim political groups under close government supervision. The accommodationist position of the rural ʿulamaʾ returns to their pre-modern position – that personal and local-communal, rather than state, affairs are the principal terrain of Muslim life.

The reform Muslim movements in turn have adopted a modern version of their traditional orientation. While some Muslim groups remain active opponents of the regime and aspire to the formation of an Islamic state, many reformist associations have turned from politics to daʿwah, or educational preaching, and religious reform. They have accepted the dominance of the military secular state and define Islam as a communal-religious rather than political movement. In student and youth circles there is increasing talk of Islam as a personal belief system rather than a public institution.

A variant group of states resembles the more secularized societies in many ways but tends to merge national and Islamic identity. The basic structures of Egyptian society also derive from the eighteenth- and nineteenth-century Ottoman model, but differ in the degree to which Islam remained part of the Egyptian political process. In the early nineteenth century Egypt went through a phase of centralization of power and economic development which created new landowning elites and made the ʿulamaʾ and Sufis subordinate to the state administration. Egypt, however, unlike the central provinces of the Ottoman empire, came under direct British rule in 1882. British occupation provoked the formation of a new intelligentsia, committed first to Islamic reform and modernism and then to secular nationalism as the ideological basis for independence. In 1922 native Egyptian landowners, officials, journalists, and lawyers won partial autonomy and established a constitutional monarchy based on liberal principles. The liberal regime, however, failed to win full independence from Britain, and failed to cope with the grave problems of economic inequality. Nor could the Egyptian elites, who lacked direct continuity with the Ottoman heritage and the military capability, self-confidence, and authority of the Turks, carry through the kind of drastic secularization achieved in Turkey. Instead, in the 1930s and 1940s, the authority of the political elites was challenged by the Muslim Brotherhood, which proposed the establishment of an Islamic government based on consultation with the ʿulamaʾ and devoted to the application of Muslim law in public life, a regulated economy in accord with a combination of Islamic and socialist principles, and the adoption of Islam as an ideological and political alternative to liberalism or Communism. Under popular pressure, Islam again became part of the nation's political identity.

The failed monarchy and liberal regime was overthrown in 1952 by the Free Officers' coup led by Naguib, Nasser, and Sadat. The new Egyptian regime was committed to a moderate form of authoritarian rule, centralized management of the economy, and a socialist ideology. In the 1950s and 1960s it attempted, as did the liberal regime of the 1920s, 1930s, and 1940s, to bypass the influence of Islam and pursue a secular policy of development. Strong efforts were made to bring Islamic religious activity under government control. Opposition movements like the Muslim Brotherhood were outlawed and the autonomy of religious institutions was curtailed. Though Muslim law continued to be applied in Egypt, Muslim legal codes were brought under government jurisdiction. In general, the government tried to control religious life, to use the ʿulamaʾ to support its policies, and to identify Islam with national and socialist programs.

This effort to create an apparent identity of Islam and the state was only partially successful. Just as the 1930s brought a revival of Islamic sentiments in intellectual and political circles, the 1970s have witnessed a revival of Islam appealing to middle-class students and young professional people. While the ʿulamaʾ and the Islamic establishment remained under government control, independent preachers, missionaries, and teachers actively promoted a revived commitment to Islam. Also the 1967 defeat in the war with Israel, the failure to resolve the Palestinian problem, and the failure to develop economically have led to the condemnation of Egypt's secular and socialist policies. The result has been a return, especially among students and youth, to Islamic religious commitments in place of the socialist and secularist views of their parents' generation. The government has been obliged to express its loyalty to and respect for Islam. Thus while the basic structures of Egyptian society are similar to those of Turkish society, the more limited powers of the Egyptian political elite, and the more limited degree of social and economic differentiation, have left a standing conflict between the secularized state elites and their Islamic opponents.

Algeria, also a former province of the Ottoman empire, has evolved in a manner closer to Egypt than to Turkey or Tunisia. The historical Algerian state and its core of ʿulamaʾ controlled only a small part of Algerian society, while organized tribal and Sufi-led communities dominated the rest. The Islamic social order was diffused throughout the rural areas. Moreover, in Algeria, French colonialism had a more drastic impact than in any other part of the Middle East or North Africa. French occupation and massive European colonization led to the total destruction of the old society and its elites, seizure of the land, impoverishment of the people, and the ruin of its educational facilities and culture. Only after World War I did a new intelligentsia take shape, consisting of a small elite of French-educated intellectuals, Communist-led worker radicals, and Muslim reformist educators.

Whereas the national elites in Turkey, Egypt, and Tunisia were relatively unified, in Algeria none of the subgroups was able to give political and ideological leadership to the country as a whole, or to achieve political independence by peaceful means. In the course of the Algerian struggle for independence, militant revolutionary soldiers took charge. The soldiers who won Algerian independence then established a highly centralized military-bureaucratic regime and socialized economy in a shattered society. In Algeria the military and technocratic elite has concentrated upon the development of large petrochemical and associated industries and has neglected agricultural development and the peasant population. In a society shattered by colonialism and war, the political elite appeals to the one enduring aspect of the Algerian heritage. Insofar as popular identity has successively been shaped by rural Sufism and by Islamic reformism, the political elite tries to integrate reformist Islam with socialism.

THE NEO-ISLAMIC STATES

While the majority of modern national states in regions with substantial Muslim populations have adopted a secular national identity, certain states are avowedly Muslim. These include revolutionary Iran, Pakistan, and the conservative monarchies of Saʿudi Arabia and Morocco. Though all these states are nominally Muslim, they are Muslim in very different senses and for very different reasons.

Iran and Pakistan are best understood as variations upon the national-state–Muslim-society pattern we have already discussed. These societies both derive from earlier Muslim empires and are heirs to the classic ambiguity of relations between state and religious institutions. They have become Muslim as the result of particular variations in their institutional pattern and in the circumstances in which modern states have been formed.

Iran has a deep historical basis for the conflict of state and religious elites which has led to the present revolutionary regime. Unlike the Ottoman empire, where the state dominated the ʿulamaʾ and controlled modern development, in Iran there has been a steady conflict between a relatively weak state and a relatively strong ʿulamaʾ establishment. With the decline of the Safavid regime, and the succession of the Qajars, who ruled Iran for 150 years but were never able to control the country effectively, the power of the religious establishment was enhanced. By the end of the nineteenth century the state and religious establishments were in conflict over the increasing penetration of Russian and British interests. The ʿulamaʾ and other intelligentsia organized mass protests against the government's surrender to foreign pressures. These confrontations culminated in 1891–92 in protests against the tobacco monopoly granted to

British financiers and in 1905–11 in the Constitutional Revolution that led to the creation of a short-lived parliamentary regime. The historical weakness of the state and the autonomy of religious, tribal, and other local communities made it possible to organize a revolutionary movement under Islamic auspices.

Iranian history in the twentieth century repeated the conflict of state and religion but changed the role of tribal and ethnic communities. The modern Iranian state was created by Reza Khan (later Shah) who came to power in 1925 and established a regime in the name of secular modernity and Persian nationalism. He built up a centralized army and administration, and laid the foundations for an industrial economy and for Western-type educational and legal systems. Above all he broke the power of Iran's tribal communities. Reza Shah was forced to abdicate in 1941 and was replaced by his son, Muhammad Reza Shah, who reigned until 1979. The restored regime was technically constitutional but the Shah ruled with virtually absolute powers. In 1960 he launched the "white revolution," for land reform, for the construction of a centralized secular national regime, and for the modernization of economic, educational, and social life along Western lines.

The Pahlavi regime diminished the power of the ʿulamaʾ, but not decisively. Secular education, government supervision of religious schools, new legal codes, reductions of funds, and other measures brought the ʿulamaʾ for a time under state control. In the 1950s there was even a period of cooperation as the government lent tacit support to ʿulamaʾ interests, including appointments at court and opportunities for enrichment through landowning and marriage into prominent families. In return the ʿulamaʾ accepted the Baghdad Pact and tolerated the government's policy of cooperation with foreign oil companies. The white revolution caused a break in this cooperative relationship, for it aroused ʿulamaʾ concerns about the strengthening of state authority and provoked their hostility to the particular measures proposed. As important as renewed ʿulamaʾ resistance was the development of a reform movement which urged the ʿulamaʾ to take collective responsibility for a better society. From Iraq, Ayatollah Khomayni became the main spokesman of the opposition to the monarchy.

The revival of Islamic religious and political consciousness centered around ʿulamaʾ, intellectuals, students, and politicians soon became a movement of mass opposition to the Shah. The deterioration of the Iranian economy in the 1970s, the provocation of government imprisonments, torture, and intimidation, and the scandal of its overt dependence on American support led to the formation of a coalition of radical guerrilla groups, liberal politicians, and ʿulamaʾ, who were able to mobilize mass support for a series of demonstrations that eventually brought down the Shah's regime. The revolution abolished the monarchy and established an Islamic government in Iran. Thus the long conflict between the state and the religious institution has led to the formation of an Islamic state.

The history of Iran thus differs from that of the Ottoman empire, where the state elites, committed by nineteenth-century changes to a secular concept of society, did not have to contend after World War I with serious tribal or ethnic opposition, could dominate the religious elites, and could create a modern Turkish state in their ideological image. In Iran, by contrast, the weakened state, weak partly because of the strength of tribal communities, could not prevent the consolidation of a religious establishment capable of opposing it. In the twentieth century the elimination of tribalism as a crucial third force led to a polarization between the state and the general society led by the ʿulamaʾ. Thus in the Ottoman empire the historical strength of the state and the subordination of the religious establishment allowed the state elites to govern the direction of twentieth-century development, while in Iran the historic weaknesses of the state and the autonomy of the religious establishment allowed for national revolutionary struggle in the name of Islam. Owing to its peculiar historic balance of institutional powers Iran has yielded an Islamic variant of a modern national state.

While Iran has developed as an Islamic revolutionary state, Pakistan is dominated by a conservative military regime. The evolution of modern Pakistan also has its origins in the interaction of state, religious, tribal, and ethnic institutions embedded in the Mughal empire. The Mughals presided over a highly autonomous and pluralistic society organized into Muslim, ethnic, or tribal groups. When the empire was finally destroyed by the British there was no continuing Muslim state in the subcontinent to channel the further development of the society and no organized religious establishment to speak for its values.

The Muslims took several positions reflecting the pluralistic class, religious, and ethnic structure of Mughal society. The Muslim bureaucratic and landowning lineages accommodated to the reality of British rule and tried to maintain their class position. The former Mughal political elite adopted a Western-type education and espoused the modernization of Islam to make it consistent with the technical, cultural, and political order of the times. Out of this milieu came Aligarh, the Muslim League, and the Pakistan movement. This was the program of a secularized elite of landowners, officeholders, politicians, and journalists, who were not necessarily committed to the religious tradition but were forced by competition with the majority Hindu population, combined with the deep-set ethnic, tribal, and local differences among Muslims, to espouse an Islamic form of nationalism as a unifying symbol. Similarly, because the British had held India together rather than allowing it to break into particularistic states as in the Ottoman empire, the secularized Muslim political elites were obliged to use an Islamic ideology to rally the support of co-religionists throughout the subcontinent in their struggle with the British and with non-Muslim elites and communities.

The Muslim religious leaders had their own program. They attempted to reconstruct Muslim society, stressing the rational disciplined practice of Islam based on the Quran and the teaching of the Prophet. While many of the religious leaders were hostile to the secularism of the League's leading politicians, the reform movement helped to create a sentiment of Muslim identity throughout the subcontinent. The political elites sought to define an essentially secular position in terms of Muslim political symbols – the only symbols capable of rallying the fragmented Muslim society confronted with Hindu opposition – while the religious elites concentrated upon moral and communal reform.

Despite its Muslim identity Pakistan was divided by profound ethnic and regional differences. Created out of the territories of Sind, Baluchistan, Northwest Frontier provinces, West Punjab, and Bengal, it had an ethnic population consisting of Punjabis, Bengalis, Pathans, Sindhis, Baluchis, and others. The main problem of the state was to create a national identity to match the reality of new political boundaries and to generate an acceptable regime for a populace divided by a myriad of ethnic, linguistic, and ideological distinctions. With the fissure of Pakistan and Bangladesh, Bengali identity has already prevailed over national unity. Furthermore, Pakistan came into being with widely divergent concepts of what was meant by an Islamic state. The political elite considered Islam a communal and national identification, but a large segment of the populace, led by the ʿulamaʾ and other religious leaders, believed that the new state should be dedicated to the formation of a society whose constitution, institutions, and routines of daily life were governed by Islamic law. Through several changes of regime this problem has never been fully resolved, though the present regime of General Zia ul-Haq calls for the creation of an Islamic political system, Islamic banking, and Islamic taxation.

Pakistan, then, is the product of a history different from that of Turkey and Iran. Unlike the Ottoman empire and Turkey, the state lacked power; unlike Iran, the religious elites lacked unity; unlike both, the ethnic minorities were much too powerful. In Pakistan no coherent national identity has emerged. The state continues as in 1947 to appeal to Islam to overcome the pluralistic heritage of the subcontinent. In Pakistan, in contrast to Iran, the Islamic revival has politically conservative implications.

The conservative monarchical Muslim states such as Saᶜudi Arabia and Morocco represent yet other types of historical development. The Saᶜudi regime has its origins in an eighteenth-century movement of religious reform which enabled the family of Ibn Saᶜud to create a coalition of tribes which would fitfully dominate the Arabian peninsula. The Wahhabi movement was analogous in its political impact to Sufism in other tribal societies. In this case it created a chieftainship based on the integration of lineage and religious authority. Though the Saᶜudi state disintegrated in the nineteenth century, it was reconstructed and expanded in the twentieth on similar social and ideological lines. The continuity of functions and religious legitimation was reinforced by the Saᶜudi seizure of Mecca and Medina in 1926 and the assumption of custodianship for the holy places. Their great oil revenues have allowed the Saᶜudis to assume patronage for Muslim teaching and religious activities all over the world. Despite the extraordinary economic transformation, the Saᶜudi state continues to be governed as the property of the ruling family, which identifies family interests with Islam. In Saᶜudi Arabia a tribal state originally given political cohesion by appeal to Islamic reform, transformed by its extraordinary oil revenues (still considerable though declining in the 1980s), renews emphasis upon Islam to legitimize the ruling family.

Morocco, like Saᶜudi Arabia, continues to be defined as an Islamic society. Like Saᶜudi Arabia, its Islamic identity depends upon the continuity of the Moroccan monarchy from the pre-colonial era to the present. As early as the fifteenth and sixteenth centuries the Sultans of Morocco emerged as religious leaders venerated for their blessed descent from the Prophet and their Sufi achievements. For centuries they maintained the identity of a weakly centralized territorial state against powerful tribal–Sufi coalitions which dominated the countryside. In the nineteenth century European commercial penetration and finally French occupation subverted the state and led to the imposition of a foreign protectorate in 1912. The French, however, kept the Sultan as a facade for their rule, and behind this facade actually strengthened the state apparatus and undermined the political power of the tribal coalitions and the Sufi brotherhoods.

Moroccan resistance and the Moroccan struggle for independence were led by the younger sons of established bourgeois families. This elite made Islamic reform the banner of Moroccan national identity. The reformers gradually mobilized intellectuals and urban workers for the struggle against the French, and by the 1940s the Sultan himself had become the titular head of the national resistance. To his traditional Sufi charisma the Sultan added the role of patron of Islam and the nation. With the coming of independence in 1956, his authority, reinforced by his role in the struggle for independence, made him as never before the principal political figure in a reorganized Moroccan society. Islam, nationality, and monarchy became fully identified. While the Sultans also depended on the French centralization of state powers, Morocco bypassed the development of a powerful secular intelligentsia and the transformations of regime and economy which have broken the historic continuity of other North African and Muslim societies. The Moroccan state may then be considered a modified traditional Islamic state like the Saʿudi, rather than a national-Islamic state like Iran and Pakistan.

MUSLIMS AS POLITICAL MINORITIES

A number of Muslim societies, however, have not been encadred under indigenous state regimes but remain political minorities within state frameworks created by outside forces. This is the case for Muslim peoples in the Soviet Union, China, India, and much of Africa, where Muslims are a demographic and political minority.

These cases also fall into several types. In some cases the central issue is whether the Muslim populations will be able to define the political identity of mixed Muslim and non-Muslim societies on their own terms. In Sudan, Ethiopia, and Nigeria the principal problem has not been competition within the Muslim elites, but the struggle for control or unification of territorial states which were divided between Muslim and substantial non-Muslim populations. In the Sudan there has been repeated warfare between the north and south as the Arab-Muslim north attempts to extend its identity and political control to other regions.

Nigeria is also divided between a Muslim north and a non-Muslim south. The northern emirates became committed to an Islamic identity in the nineteenth century, and British rule preserved the political and cultural integrity of the Sokoto emirates. The commercialization of the northern economy and its new links to international markets further assisted the spread of Islam as a religion of traders, merchants, workers, and other mobile people. In the 1930s and 1940s Sufi brotherhoods helped integrate the various northern Nigerian ethnic and occupational groups into a more embracing society. The British, however, also made the old Sokoto region part of a larger Nigerian state. With the coming of independence in 1960, the northern Muslim regions joined a secular national state in which Muslims formed a near majority. For two decades there was intense regional and ethnic conflict in Nigeria, but the 1970s brought a consolidation of the Nigerian federal state on the basis of military rule and the control of oil revenues.

In the complex struggle for power, Nigerian and Islamic identities have become ideological alternatives. Vis-à-vis the south, the north defines itself as Muslim. Northern elites, however, accept Nigerian nationality in order to collaborate with the non-Muslim southerners with whom they share control of the central government. To the extent that the elites stress Nigerian identity, the common people and student groups adopt Islam as the banner of resistance to military rule, economic injustice, and cultural confusion. In northern Nigeria Islam is now part of the political identity of all classes, but it has a different significance for each class or milieu, and is used both to legitimize the state and to motivate the opposition.

In other situations, the problem for Muslim communities within non-Muslim societies is how to maintain their identity. The case of India, where Muslims form a minority of some 80,000,000 people in the midst of a cultural and political Hindu majority, is particularly important. Constant conflict between Hindus and Muslims has greatly increased Indian-Muslim awareness of their minority status. Indian Muslims respond by consolidating a separate communal identity stressing the maintenance of Shariᶜa, the endowment of Muslim schools, and their distinctive religious practices. Muslim parties have been formed to defend Muslim political interests, and Muslims bargain with the major political parties to gain support for special privileges in employment, schooling, and cultural affairs. Though Indian society is highly pluralistic and state control over population groups very limited, the tendency has been to increase communal separateness rather than enhance the assimilation of Muslims.

The Soviet Union and China represent yet another type of Muslim minority situation. While Muslim populations the world over have become politically independent, the peoples of Inner Asia have become subjects and citizens of the colonial states who conquered them in the nineteenth century. In these cases the crucial issue is not separateness, but the political and economic acculturation or assimilation of the Muslim populations and the meaning of Muslim identity in multinational societies.

In Russia, a Muslim reformist, modernist, and nationalist intelligentsia took shape under Tsarist domination but was defeated in the revolutionary era struggle for power. Muslim populations remained, then, under Russian control and are being integrated into Soviet political society. They have undergone intensive economic and social modernization and the inculcation of new values through Soviet scholastic and political education. In the Soviet Union traditional social structures have been broken down, traditional elites eliminated, and traditional religious educational, legal, and ritual practices constrained or abolished. The ʿulamaʾ establishment is closely dependent upon state control. Independent religious associations or Sufi brotherhoods can exist only as clandestine organizations and probably have a limited following, except in parts of the Caucasus. Even on the level of personal belief, Islam has been diminished, as the worldview of Muslim citizens of the Soviet Union comes to be formed by Soviet political and scientific concepts. At the same time the Soviets have helped cultivate a secularized national identity as a bridge to their integration into a multinational Soviet political society.

Though Islam has been disestablished on a political level and is barely organized in a communal associational sense, Muslim belief and identity remain important. Even the Muslims who have been assimilated at a political level and consider themselves Soviet citizens, who are loyal to the state and accept its socialist political and economic values, who in public behavior speak Russian, wear European dress, assume European manners, and who are competent in modern technical and administrative skills, maintain a separate identity on the level of ethnic and family culture and self-image. Cultivated by language and ethnic consciousness, Islam continues to have a subjective hold on Soviet populations of Muslim background. In rural areas, among rural migrants to cities, and among the older persons not affected by the process of social and economic change, Muslim belief remains in full force. Though there is a strong continuity of regime in Turkey, and the greatest possible break with the historic past in the Soviet Union, in both cases modern secular states press Islam into a religion of personal faith and social identity.

In the People's Republic of China the Muslim population falls into two main categories. The Muslim populations of Sinkiang province and other areas maintain a separate non-Chinese ethnic and communal identity under Chinese rule. They are enclave minorities. The Hui, however, have for centuries been fully assimilated into the larger Han Chinese society to the extent of being physically and in public manners indistinguishable from Han Chinese. Yet the Hui maintain a persisting consciousness of separateness through their particular food customs, family rituals, and religious identity. In the nineteenth century, this consciousness of religious and ethnic difference was sufficient to fuel great rebellions against the authority of the Ch'ing dynasty. Under Communist rule it suffices to maintain the religious identity of the Chinese-Muslim population. As in the Soviet Union, full occupational and political assimilation is accompanied by separate family, religious, and personal identity.

Table 18. *Twentieth-century world distribution of Muslims*

Areas	Number of Muslims*	Proportion of Muslims to total population	Chief languages spoken by Muslims
Arab countries Arabia, the fertile crescent, Egypt, Sudan, Maghrib (Libya to Morocco)	c. 165,000,000	Great majority Muslims; Christian minorities in many countries	*Arabic* (in various vernaculars), some Berber
Iranian highlands Iran (and Azarbayjan), Afghanistan, Tajikistan	c. 58,000,000	Almost entirely Muslim; some Christian, Jewish, and Zoroastrian minorities	*Persian*, Pashto, Baluchi, Kurdish, Turkish
Turkey and Southeast Europe Turkey (Anatolia), the Balkans, Crimea	c. 55,000,000	Muslim majority in Turkey; otherwise majority is Christian; Jewish minority	*Turkish*, Slavic, Albanian, some Greek
Inner Asia Volga Basin, Siberia; Kazakhstan, Uzbekistan, Turkmenistan, Kirgizistan, etc.	c. 50,000,000	Muslims are a minority along Volga and in Kazakhstans; republics are largely Muslim but recent Russian influx	*Turkish* in various forms
Indian subcontinent Pakistan, Bangladesh, Indus Valley, Ganges plain, Deccan, south India, Ceylon	c. 274,000,000	Majority in those areas which became Pakistan and Bangladesh; minority elsewhere among Hindus, Christians, Sikhs; Muslims about 1/4 of all Indic population	*Urdu*, Punjabi, Kashmiri, Bengali, Gujarati, Sindhi, Telegu, Tamil, Malayalam
Malaysia and Indonesia From Burma to Indonesia and the Philippines	c. 155,000,000	Great majority in most islands; minorities in Indochinese lands divided among Buddhists and some Hindus and Christians	*Malay* (Indonesian), Sudanese, Javanese
China All provinces but especially Kansu, Yunnan, Sinkiang	c. 15,000,000	Minority among Buddhist-Taoists	Chinese, Turkish
Sub-Saharan Africa East coast, western and central Sudan, and scattered	c. 111,000,000	Almost entirely Muslim in large parts, shading to a minority divided among animists and Christians	Swahili, Hausa, Somali, etc.
Elsewhere The Americas, the South Seas, western Europe	c. 15,000,000	Minorities, usually very small	Various

* Based on M. G. S. Hodgson, *Venture of Islam*, Chicago, 1974. and R. V. Weeks, *A World Ethnographic Survey*, Westport, Conn., 1984.

Here, too, Islam is not a symbol of the political order but a personal and family religion.

In many respects the changes which have taken place in the nineteenth and twentieth centuries have profoundly modified the historic pattern of Islamic societies. The old tripartite structure of state, religious, and parochial institutions has been transformed by the destruction of independent lineage and tribal communities and the increasing integration of territorial populations into national state regimes. The identity of Muslim peoples has been redefined in reformist Islamic or national terms, and this facilitates their assimilation into modern state societies. The contemporary era has also witnessed the transformation of the historic structures of state and religious institutions. State regimes tend to be more highly secularized; religious associations tend to be reoriented to communal and personal interests. At the same time there is a strong reaction against the trend to secularization and a resurgence of neo-Muslim religious and political movements which aspire to a utopian reintegration of all levels of personal, communal, and political life.

The ambiguities of secularization and Islamization and the conflict between secular and Islamic concepts of political and moral order reveal a profound continuity in the institutional structures of Islamic societies. The contemporary patterns of relations between state and religious institutions in Turkey, the Arab world, North Africa, Pakistan, Indonesia, Malaysia, Senegal, and other countries are recognizable variations upon the historic relationships of state and religious institutions in those societies. While the political elite preserves the syncretism between cosmopolitan and Islamic forms of culture, the Islamic revival evokes the heritage of personal religious identity and communal responsibility. This conflict reflects a similar nineteenth-century struggle between secularized and religious elites, and echoes the eighteenth-century premodern structures of Muslim societies. It may be traced back as far as the ninth-century differentiation of state and religious institutions within the early Islamic empire, which in turn was based on a still more ancient distinction between political and religious life characteristic of almost all Middle Eastern and Mediterranean societies since ancient times. Even the earliest civilization of Mesopotamia in the third millennium B.C. had differentiated temple and state institutions.

Apart from social institutions, Islam remains in the hearts and minds of individual Muslims an essential component of personal and political identity. To be a Muslim, after all, is not only a matter of state office, ʿulamaʾ colleges and Sufi hospices, but of individual morality, belief, and personal and social identity. Islam is the name of the primordial sentiment that defines for the individual believer both personal existence and the existence of a truly human community. Thus the neo-Muslim movements are not only grounded in institutions but in the cultural and symbolic meaning of Islam.

These reflections suggest that the structures of lineage, religious, and state institutions derived from the ancient Near East and Islamic religious culture are enduring, though modified, templates for the contemporary evolution of Islamic societies. This raises an important and indeed central historiographical question. In the history of these societies I have played down the material, technological, economic, and ecological factors, and have considered them as embedded in pre-modern state, ʿulamaʾ, Sufi, and tribal institutions and collectivities, and in the formation of contemporary social classes, ideologies, and states. I have not treated material and economic change as causal historical forces. My basic position has been, as indicated in the preface, that ancient agricultural, artisanal, and commercial technologies and economies had already shaped the institutional structures of human societies before the advent of the Islamic era, and that despite the rise and fall of human fortunes the basic "modes of production and exchange" in Muslim countries did not fundamentally change until the impact of European colonialism and industrial capitalism made itself felt in the nineteenth and twentieth centuries. The new technical and economic factors have a decisive influence upon political and cultural development, but in each country they are articulated and channeled by indigenous elites, institutions, and cultures. Economic and material considerations are taken into the human imagination and articulated in terms of the modes of thinking and the cultural vocabularies which have for a millennium governed Muslim thought and social organization.

However, even if we give priority to such institutional and cultural considerations, the course of nineteenth- and twentieth-century developments inevitably raises the question as to whether the forces of technology and economy associated with the development of industrial capitalism or socialism, and the creation of an integrated world economy will not in the end break down the historic political and religious institutions and the traditional modes of cultural discourse. For example, in Turkey changes in industrial development, land tenure, and production, and the emergence of a proletariat and new strata of bourgeois entrepreneurs seem to have broken down the historic structures of state and religious organization. In the Soviet Union radical political and cultural change has transformed Islam into a religion of private belief and national identities. Everywhere the forces of secularization and the forces of neo-Muslim integration represent important departures from historical templates. In many Muslim regions an active struggle is being waged to create a post-modern form of Islamic society. With these changes it has become open to question whether the Islamic institutional and cultural heritage may not in some cases be giving way to modern political, technological, and economic forces, and in others to new forms of Islam, and whether Muslim peoples still constitute, and will continue to constitute, Islamic societies.

GLOSSARY

ʿabd: slave; property rights in a person, regulated by law and Quranic ethics. In Muslim countries slaves were commonly employed as household servants and soldiers. *See also ghulam, mamluk.*

ada: (in Indonesia and Malaysia, *adat*); custom or customary law as opposed to Shariʿa or Muslim law.

adab: habit, upbringing, behavior, refinement of manners, literary cultivation, urbanity; the ideal behavior of a scribe or spiritual cultivation of a Sufi.

ʿadl: justice; in law, the quality required to be a legal witness; in religion, the state of personal perfection of one who fulfills God's teaching; in philosophy, the harmony among the faculties of the soul.

agha: Turkish word for elder brother, chief, or master; in Ottoman usage the title of a high-ranking military official; in Algeria, the head of the janissary corps.

ahl: people who occupy a tent; family or community.

ahl al-bayt: people of the house, family of the Prophet.

ahl al-dhimma: the people of the covenant; Jews, Christians, and others accepted as subjects under Muslim rule and entitled to legal protection in return for payment of taxes; also called *ahl al-kitab*, or people of the book.

ahl al-hadith: partisans of hadith as a principal source of Muslim law and morals; a term for the supporters of the Hanbali school of law.

ahl-i hadith: a community in India and Pakistan who profess to follow only the Quran and hadith as sources of Muslim law and do not accept the traditional schools of law.

akhi: member of fourteenth-century Anatolian groups of young men who held to the ideals of *futuwwa (q.v.)*; generally urban, artisan, and middle class.

918

akhlaq: ethics; Greek ethics conveyed into Islamic thought by the translation of Aristotle and Galen and incorporated into the writings of Miskawayh, al-Ghazzali and others.

ᶜ*Alids*: descendants of the Prophet's cousin ᶜAli; the family which claims to be the heirs of the Prophet's religious and political legacy and the rightful heads of the Muslim community.

ᶜ*alim* (pl. ᶜ*ulama*ᵓ): a learned man, particularly in Muslim legal and religious studies; occurs in varying forms such as *mallam, mullah, molla,* etc.

amin: trustworthy; title for the holder of an official position such as the head of a guild.

amir: title of a military commander, governor or prince; commonly transliterated "emir"; equivalent of the Turkish *bey* or *beg.*

*amir al-mu*ᵓ*minin*: Commander of the Believers, the proper title of the Caliph or successor to the Prophet.

*amir al-umara*ᵓ: supreme commander; title used for the military rulers who took over ᶜAbbasid government.

amsar: *see misr.*

anjuman: assembly; refers to religious educational and political associations of Muslims, especially in Iran, India, Pakistan, and Turkey.

ansar: "helpers" of Muhammad at Medina; later used as designation for members of Muslim religious and political associations.

ᶜ*aqida*: creed, article of faith.

ᶜ*aql*: reason, reasoning, intelligence; the rational faculty as opposed to the lower faculties of body and soul.

ᶜ*arud*: Arabic metrics.

ᶜ*asabiya*: spirit of kinship or faction; the tribal solidarity that enables a small pastoral community to conquer city-dwellers and create new empires; the political solidarity of ruling elites.

ashraf: people who trace their lineage to the Prophet or his companions; in India, the Mughal classes; *see sharif.*

ᶜ*ashura*: supererogatory fast day on the tenth of Muharram, the first month in the Muslim calendar; commemoration of the martyrdom of Husayn.

atabeg: the tutor of a Saljuq prince, his principal military adviser; later, independent governors.

*a*ᶜ*yan*: local notables; in late Ottoman times, holders of officially recognized political power.

ayatollah: miraculous sign of God, the highest-ranking scholar of law in the "twelver" Shiᶜi religious hierarchy.

ᶜ*ayyarun*: vagabonds; tenth- to twelfth-century urban gangs who subscribed to *futuwwa* (*q.v.*) ideals and often appeared as military opponents of state regimes.

baba: Turkish for father, old man, Sufi leader.

*baqa*ᵓ: survival in God, the divinely granted attribute of the mystic, who experiences the unity of God but returns to the world of daily activity.

baraka: blessing; the divine power emanating from a holy-man.

batin: the inner, esoteric meaning of a text.

bay^ca: contract; oath of allegiance recognizing the authority of a Caliph.

bayram: *see ^cid.*

bey: Turkish title for army officer, official or ruler of small principality; also transliterated *beg*; *see amir*.

Bohras: a Muslim community in India, mainly Isma^cilis. Most are merchants but many are Sunnis and peasants.

Caliph: *see khalifa.*

da^ci: "summoner"; propagandist or missionary for Shi^ci movements; usually the lowest-ranking figure in a Shi^ci hierarchy.

dakwah: *see da^cwa.*

dar al-harb: the land of war, territory not under Islamic law and subject to conquest by Muslims; contrasts with *dar al-Islam*, the lands in which Islamic law prevails.

dargah: royal court or residence; shrine and tomb of a Sufi master.

darwish: Persian for Sufi; *see Sufi.*

da^cwa: the summons to acknowledge religious truth and join a religious community; missionary movement; used in the variant forms *da^cwah* and *dakwah* in Southeast Asia.

da^cwah: *see da^cwa.*

dawla: dynasty; by extension, government or state.

devshirme: Ottoman levy of Christian youths to be trained as janissaries and court officers.

dhikr: reminding the self; continuous and rhythmic repetition of the name of God, a Sufi form of prayer which varies with the different Sufi orders.

dhimma: contract of hospitality and protection for peoples of the revealed religions; *see ahl al-dhimma.*

dihqan: landowner, village chief, the local notables of the late Sasanian and early Muslim empires.

diwan: a collection of poetry or prose; a register, the name applied to government bureaus which keep tax, military, and other records.

evliad: used in Inner Asia to refer to the Sufis who descend from the Prophet and the early Caliphs.

falasifa: wise men, philosophers, the Muslim proponents of Greek philosophy.

fana^>: in Sufi usage, annihilation of the self, the state that precedes the experience of the unity of God.

faqih (pl. *fuqaha^>*): scholar of Islamic law, jurist; *see ^calim.*

faqir: poverty-stricken mendicant who lives only for God; *see Sufi.*

fata (pl. *fityan*): young man, member of a group or gang devoted to the ideals of *futuwwa* (q.v.).

fatwa (pl. *fatawa*): an opinion on Islamic law given by a *mufti*; collected legal opinions form a corpus which modifies the application of the early codes of Islamic law.

fiqh: understanding, jurisprudence, Islamic religious law.

firman: command, edict of a ruler.

fitra: inherent original state of the soul before it is vested in the body.

fityan: *see fata.*

futuwwa: virtues or qualities of young men, including bravery and nobility; the ideology of fraternities and young men's street gangs; *see ᶜayyarun, akhi.*

ghazal: love song; an Arabic poetic form which passes with variations into Persian, Turkish, and Urdu poetry.

ghazi: a frontier warrior for the faith.

ghulam: a young male slave in military or palace service; *see ᶜabd, mamluk.*

ghulat: Shiᶜa who hold "extreme" views of the spiritual qualities of the imam.

hadith: a report of the sayings or deeds of the Prophet transmitted by his companions; collections of hadith are second in authority to the Quran as a source of Muslim belief and practice.

hajib: chamberlain, chief of palace administration and sometimes head of government.

hajj: the annual pilgrimage to Mecca required of every Muslim at least once in his lifetime.

hakim: one skilled in medical, philosophic or scientific learning.

hal: a Sufi term for spiritual state received by the grace of God; opposed to *makam*, a station on the way toward mystical union achieved by the Sufi's own effort.

hanif: an Arabian believer in the unity of God before the revelation of Islam.

haqiqa: in Sufism, truth or reality which is experienced through union with God; ultimate reality.

haram: the portion of a house reserved for the women, from which males are excluded.

hijra: the emigration of the Prophet from Mecca to Medina in 622, the base year of the Muslim era.

hikma: the wisdom attained through philosophy, science, or occult knowledge.

hila (pl. *hiyal*): legal stratagem.

hilm: forbearance, moderation, tranquility in the face of passion.

himaya: commendation or protection given by nomads to settlers, landlords to peasants, the powerful to the weak, in return for payment; the protection of European consuls for local clients.

hujja: proof; the person through whom God's presence becomes accessible; a rank in the hierarchy of Shiᶜi missionaries; *see daᶜi.*

ᶜibada (pl. *ᶜibadat*): obedience to ritual religious practices, including ablutions, prayer, fasting, pilgrimage, etc.

ᶜid: the Muslim festivals; *ᶜid al-fitr*, the breaking of the fast of Ramadan, and *ᶜid al-adha*, the sacrificial festival of the tenth of Dhu al-hijja; in Turkish called *bayram*.

ihsan: beneficence, charity, doing good deeds.

ijaza: a certificate given by a teacher to a student certifying his capacity to transmit a particular text.

ijma^c: consensus of legal scholars or of the community as a whole; a basis of Muslim law.

ijtihad: "exerting oneself" in Islamic law; reasoning by analogy, free from received opinions, in order to reinterpret Islamic law; *see mujtahid*.

^cilm: knowledge, especially of religious truths; the knowledge which guides behavior.

iltizam: a form of tax farm in the Ottoman empire and Egypt.

imam: the supreme leader of the Muslim community; the successor to the Prophet, used commonly by the Shi^ca for ^cAli and his descendants.

imamzada: a descendant of a Shi^ci imam; the shrines of sanctified descendants of ^cAli revered by pilgrims, who believe they have miraculous qualities.

iman: faith, fidelity, belief.

imaret: in Ottoman usage, an endowed complex of religious and charitable facilities, commonly including a place for prayer, a college, library, soup kitchens, etc.

insilimen: a term used in the Sahara for religious scholars and venerated holy lineages; *see zawaya*.

iqta^c: a grant of the rights to collect taxes from land conceded in return for development or administrative and military service; *see jagir, timar*.

ishan: an honorific used in Inner Asia as the equivalent of a Sufi shaykh or spiritual leader.

islah: reform, purification, and revitalization of the Muslim community based on a return to the first principles of the Quran and hadith; *see tajdid*.

Islam: submission, unconditional surrender to God, the name of the religion of Muslims, the institutions and cultural style of states and societies formed by the Islamic religion.

^cisma: immunity from error or sin; a quality of the Prophet attributed by the Shi^ca to the imams.

Isma^cilis: a branch of the Shi^ca who look to the leadership of Isma^cil, a son of Ja^cfar and his descendants; this branch includes the Fatimids; later divided into several branches, including the Nizariya who spread from Syria and Iran into India; subcommunities include the Khojas, Bohras, and others.

isnad: a chain of authorities, the series of transmitters of hadith whose names guarantee their validity.

ithna-^cashari: the branch of the Shi^ca who believe in the twelve imams descended from ^cAli, the last of whom disappeared and went into hiding in 873 and will return as the messiah; the branch of Shi^cism to which the majority of the populace of Iran adheres.

jagir: an assignment of revenues in Mughal India in lieu of payment of salary; *see iqta^c, timar*.

jama^ca: meeting, assembly, the community of believers, the umma.

jamatbandi: a collectivity or small community; used especially of the Shiʿi sects.

jamiʿ: mosque for Friday prayers.

janissary: member of the Ottoman infantry corps, the elite regiments of the Ottoman regime.

jihad: striving; effort directed toward inner religious perfection and toward holy war of the Muslims against the infidels.

jinn: spirit beings, composed of vapors or flames, who are imperceptible but malevolent influences.

jizya: the poll tax levied on non-Muslims in a Muslim-ruled society.

kaʿba: the central sanctuary of Islam, located in Mecca, the principal object of the hajj.

kafir: an unbeliever, one who is ungrateful to God for his gifts.

kalam: theology, the subject which attempts to give rational proofs for religious beliefs; deals with the problems of the divine unity, attributes, human free will, self-determination, etc.

kanun: state-promulgated administrative regulations or codes of law, usually dealing with financial and criminal matters; in contemporary usage, all codes of law promulgated by governments.

karamoko: a West African title for scholar and teacher; *see ʿalim*.

kasb: economic gain; in theology, the technical term for acquisition of responsibility and of reward or punishment for good or bad deeds.

kashf: lifting of the veils, the realization or vision of God as ultimate reality.

khalifa: successor of the Prophet and head of the Muslim community; the Caliph; in Sufism the disciple of the master authorized to transmit prayers, initiate new members, and act as a deputy or head of the Sufi order.

Khan: a Turkish title, originally the ruler of state but then applied to subordinate chiefs and nobles; also a caravansary.

khanaqa: a building for Sufi activities where the shaykh may live, instruct his disciples, and carry on Sufi worship. *See also ribat, tekke, zawiya*.

kharaj: the tax on land.

kharijism: early religio-political movements whose followers held that the Caliph should be elected by the community.

kharja: see *muwashshah*.

khatib: official preacher who presents the Friday sermon; in principle, the representative of the ruler.

khirqa: the patched cloak worn by Sufis and passed from master to initiate as a symbol of the communication of the blessings inherited from the Prophet.

Khojas: a sect of Nizari Ismaʿilis in India.

khwaja: a title variously used by merchants, scholars, and officials; in modern Turkish, *hoja*, a professional man of religion.

madhhab: a Muslim school of law; the four principal schools are the Hanafi, Maliki, Shafiʿi, and Hanbali.

madrasa: a college whose primary function is the teaching of law and related religious subjects.

mahalla: a town quarter.

mahdi: the "guided" one, the person who will appear on the last day and establish Islam and the reign of justice.

mahr: in Muslim law, the gift which the bridegroom gives the bride and which becomes her personal property.

majlis: a gathering, assembly, or council.

makhzan: Moroccan central government administration; royal court, army, and provincial officials.

maktab: an elementary school for teaching children recitation of the Quran and the basics of reading and writing.

mallam: the term used in West Africa for a religious scholar; *see ᶜalim*.

mamluk: a slave or freedman in military service.

maqam: a station on the Sufi path to unity with God acquired by the Sufi's own efforts.

marjaᶜi-taqlid: source of imitation; in Iran, just and learned scholars of law qualified to give authoritative legal opinions; common people are obliged to accept them as absolute religious authorities.

masjid: a mosque or place of prostration and prayer; a center for Muslim communal affairs.

masnavi: an epic poem in Persian and related literatures.

maᶜsum: a person who possesses *ᶜisma*, infallibility, freedom from committing sins.

mawali: *see mawla*.

mawla (pl. *mawali*): client or freedman, servant; the word also applies to the patron or master.

mawlid: the celebration of the birth of the Prophet; also applies to celebrations at saints' shrines.

mihrab: the ornamented niche in the wall of a mosque which indicates the direction of prayer.

millet: religion or religious communities; in contemporary usage, nation.

minaret: the tower of a mosque from which the call to prayer is proclaimed.

minbar: the high seat or chair in a mosque from which the preacher delivers the sermon.

miᶜraj: the ascent of the Prophet to heaven in Jerusalem after the miraculous night journey from Medina.

misr (pl. *amsar*): the military camps and garrisons constructed in the early Islamic conquests; administrative capitals for the conquered provinces.

mobad: a Zoroastrian clergyman.

muᶜamalat: Muslim laws pertaining to social relations.

mufti: an expert in Muslim law qualified to give authoritative legal opinions.

muhajirun: the emigrants who accompanied the Prophet on the hijra from Mecca to Medina.

muhtasib: an official who supervises fair market practices and public morals.

mujaddid: "the renewer"; the scholar or holy-man who comes once every century to restore the true knowledge and practice of Islam.

mujtahid: a person qualified to exercise *ijtihad* and give authoritative opinions on Islamic law.

mullah: a learned man; often used in the Indian subcontinent; the equivalent of ʿalim.

murshid: guide; a Sufi master and teacher; *see Sufi.*

muwashshah: love poem; form of Arabic verse popular in Spain, commonly ending in a *kharja*, or refrain of Romance origin.

nafs: soul; the animal faculties as opposed to the rational or angelic faculties.

naqib: a syndic or headman.

naqib al-ashraf: the syndic or headman of the groups of descendants of the Prophet found in many Muslim countries.

nasiha: faithful advice to a ruler; exhortation to do good.

nass: in Shiʿi usage, the explicit designation of a successor to the imamate, which confers upon him knowledge and power appropriate to the office.

niya: intention, necessary state of mind for the validity of religious actions.

padishah: a nineteenth-century title for the Ottoman Sultans.

pancasila: the five principles of Indonesian independence.

penghulu: headman, used in Indonesia as a title of a village administrator.

pesantren: in Indonesia, a school or seminary for Muslim students.

pir: a title for a Sufi shaykh.

pirzada: *see pir.*

priyayi: the governing and scribal class; the elite of pre-modern Indonesian society.

qadi: judge, the Caliph's designated representative to adjudicate disputes on the basis of Shariʿa.

qaʾid: a tribal, district or military chief; term widely used in North Africa.

qalb: in Sufism, the heart, the soul, the seat of conscience and knowledge.

qanat: an underground irrigation canal, commonly used in Iran.

qasaba: a fortified castle, residence of government officials; a chief town; in India, *qasbah*.

qasbah: *see qasaba.*

qasida: the classical Arabic ode which often eulogizes the tribe of the poet or a great man; the Persian *qasida* is a lyric poem.

qawm: lineage, tribe, religious community, nation.

qibla: the direction of the *kaʿba* in Mecca, which Muslims face during prayers.

Quran: Muslim scripture, the book containing the revelations of God to Muhammad.

qutb: the pivot around which something revolves; the head of the invisible hierarchy of saints upon whom the order of the universe depends.

ra'is (pl. *ru'asa'*): a person of high rank, a headman or chief.

Ramadan: the ninth month of the Muslim calendar, the month of annual fasting.

rashidun: the rightly guided, a title applied to the first four Caliphs.

ribat: a frontier fortress and residence for Muslim warriors and mystics.

ruh: soul, sometimes the equivalent of *qalb*.

rustaq: an administrative district comprising a town and subordinate villages.

sabr: steadfastness, patience, endurance in fulfillment of religious obligations.

sadaqa: voluntary alms, sometimes a synonym for *zakat*.

sajjada nishin: "one who sits on the prayer carpet"; the successor to the leadership of a *khanaqa* or the custodian of a Sufi shrine.

salat: Muslim ritual prayer performed five times daily; in Persian called *namaz*.

sama': Sufi musical session intended to inculcate states of ecstasy.

santri: in Indonesia, a student of Islam; devout and correct Muslim.

sarkin: a Hausa title for headman, ruler.

sawafi: crown estates seized by the Umayyad dynasty from former Sasanian royal and noble landowners.

sayyid: prince, lord, chief; a descendant of Husayn, the son of 'Ali.

shahada: "witnessing"; the Muslim profession of faith.

shah-en-shah: king of kings, a Persian title of the emperor.

shahid: witness; martyr.

Shari'a: the path to be followed; Muslim law, the totality of the Islamic way of life.

sharif (pl. *ashraf* or *shurafa'*): noble; a descendant of the Prophet.

shaykh: an elder, head, chief, respected man of religion, Sufi leader, teacher.

Shaykh al-Islam: a chief jurisconsult or *mufti*; the head of the religious establishment in the Ottoman empire.

Shi'a: the group of Muslims who regard 'Ali and his heirs as the only legitimate successors to the Prophet, divided into sects according to allegiance to different lines of 'Alid descent.

shirk: polytheism, associating other beings with God, the ultimate blasphemy.

shura: council; specifically the council established by the Caliph 'Umar to choose his successor.

shurafa': pl. of *sharif*.

silsila: the sequence of Sufi masters reaching back to the Prophet through whom a particular Sufi acquires his knowledge.

sipahi: a cavalry soldier in the Ottoman empire; appears in India as *sepoy*.

Sufi: a Muslim mystic; named after the early ascetics who wore garments of coarse wool; *see also ishan, murshid, pir, shaykh*.

Sultan: "power," authority, the title of a Muslim monarch.

Sunna: "the trodden path," custom, the practice of the Prophet and the early community which becomes for all Muslims an authoritative example of the correct way to live a Muslim life.

Sunnis: those who accept the *Sunna* and the historic succession of Caliphs, as opposed to the ʿAlids; the majority of the Muslim community.

sura: a group of Quranic verses collected in a single chapter.

tafsir: commentary and interpretation, the exegesis of the Quran.

tajdid: renewal, applied to the post-eighteenth-century movement to revive the true practice of Islam based on the Quran and hadith; *see islah*.

talakawa: a Hausa term for the peasants and working poor.

taljiʾa: commendation; see *himaya*.

Tanzimat: reorganization, the name for the Ottoman reforms of the nineteenth century.

taqlid: "imitation," the principle of following the established doctrines of the Muslim schools of law; the opposite of *ijtihad*.

tariqa: a way, the Sufi path; the system of beliefs and training transmitted by particular schools of Sufis; a brotherhood of Sufis.

tasawwuf: the practice of Sufism.

tasdiq: faith, affirmation of the truth of God's existence.

tawakkul: trust in God.

tawba: repentance, turning to God.

tawhid: unity, the oneness of God's being and the unity of the mystic with the divine being.

taʾwil: allegorical exegesis of the Quran.

taʿziya: the lamentation for a martyr, the mourning for Husayn displayed in processions and mystery plays in the month of Muharram; also refers to a model of Husayn's tomb at Karbala kept in imamzadas.

tekke: the Turkish name for a Sufi residence; *see khanaqa*.

timar: Turkish and Ottoman usage for a grant of tax revenues to support a military retainer of the Sultan.

tyeddo: the name of the warrior elite in Senegambia.

ʿ*ulamaʾ*: the collective term for the scholars or learned men of Islam; *see* ʿ*alim*.

uleebalang: an intermediary administrative official in the Malayan Sultanates.

umma: people or community; the whole of the brotherhood of Muslims.

ʿ*urs*: marriage, especially of a saint with God; the celebration of his death date marked by ceremonies at his shrine.

ʿ*ushr*: the tenth of the produce levied on Muslim-owned lands.

ustadh: a name for a Sufi master or other learned teacher.

uymaq: in Iran and Inner Asia a chieftaincy under the authority of a headman supported by military retainers and allied lineages.

wahdat al-shuhud: unity of witness.

wahdat al-wujud: unity of being, existential monism.

wali: a protector, a benefactor, a companion, a governor; a friend of God, a saint or a Sufi whose tomb is visited for its blessing; the legal guardian of a minor, woman, or incapacitated person.

waqf: an endowment, an irrevocable grant of the income of property set aside in perpetuity for a religious or charitable purpose.

watan: country, motherland.

wazir: "a helper," the chief secretary of a ruler; head of the bureaucracy; prime minister.

wilayat: a legal competence; power delegated to a governor or *wali*; in Ottoman usage, a term for an administrative district.

wird: a litany or patterned devotion chanted by Sufis.

yasa: Mongol law.

zahir: the external, literal meaning of a text as opposed to *batin*, its inner significance.

zakat: a legal alms tax raised from Muslims.

zamindar: a landowner; under the Mughals, a person who has a right to collect revenues from the land.

zanadaqa: a body of dualistic or heretical beliefs.

zawaya: Berber North African religious lineages.

zawiya: a building which functions as a Sufi residence, place of prayer, school, and the tomb of a saint; *see khanaqa*.

ziyara: a visit to the tomb of a saint or holy-man to pray for intercession before God.

BIBLIOGRAPHY

INTRODUCTION

This bibliography is intended as a guide to further reading and includes the most important translations and scholarly works. Most of the citations are to English language works, but important materials in French, German, and other languages are suggested. Readers will find further bibliographical references in many of the cited works. J. D. Pearson, *Index Islamicus*, Cambridge, 1958–, covers the periodical literature of all Islamic regions from 1906 to the present and book literature from 1976 to the present.

The following abbreviations are used in the bibliography:

AIÉO	*Annales de l'institut des études orientales*
BÉO	*Bulletin d'études orientales*
BSOAS	*Bulletin of the School of Oriental and African Studies*
CMRS	*Cahiers du monde russe et soviétique*
IJAHS	*International Journal of African Historial Studies*
IJMES	*International Journal of Middle East Studies*
JAH	*Journal of African History*
JAOS	*Journal of the American Oriental Society*
JESHO	*Journal of the Economic and Social History of the Orient*
JRAS	*Journal of the Royal Asiatic Society*
RÉI	*Revue des études islamiques*
ROMM	*Revue de l'Occident musulman et de la Méditerranée*
RSO	*Revista degli studi orientali*
SI	*Studia Islamica*
ZDMG	*Zeitschrift der deutschen morganländischen Gesellschaft*

PART I

Introduction

On Islamic history as a whole see M. G. S. Hodgson, *The Venture of Islam*, 3 vols., Chicago, 1974. Hodgson is particularly sensitive to religious and literary issues and to the existential meaning of Islamic discourses. The *Encyclopaedia of Islam*, new edn, eds. H. A. R. Gibb *et al.*, Leiden, 1960, is an inexhaustible reference work on all topics related to this volume. The following atlases are useful reference works: R. Roolvink, *Historical Atlas of the Muslim Peoples*, Amsterdam, 1957; F. Robinson, *Atlas of the Islamic World since 1500*, Oxford, 1982; J. L. Bacharach, *A Middle East Studies Handbook*, Seattle, Wash., 1984; C. F. Beckingham, *Atlas of the Arab World and the Middle East*, New York, 1960; D. E. Pitcher, *An Historical Geography of the Ottoman Empire*, Leiden, 1972; J. E. Schwartzberg, *A Historical Atlas of South Asia*, Chicago, 1978; G. S. P. Freeman-Grenville, *A Modern Atlas of African History*, London, 1976; and J. D. Fage, *An Atlas of African History*, New York, 1978.

On early Islamic history and civilization see J. J. Saunders, *A History of Medieval Islam*, London, 1965; H. A. R. Gibb, *Mohammedanism*, 2nd edn, London, 1969; F. Rahman, *Islam*, 2nd edn, Chicago, 1979; G. E. von Grunebaum, *Medieval Islam*, 2nd edn, Chicago, 1956. In French there is L. Gardet, *L'Islam, religion et communauté*, Paris, 1967; R. Mantran, *L'Expansion musulmane, VIIe–IXe siècles*, 2nd edn, Paris, 1979; C. Cahen, *Les Peuples musulmans dans l'histoire médiévale*, Paris, 1977.

Chapter 1

The most useful introduction to pre-Islamic Arabia is I. Shahid, "Pre-Islamic Arabia," *Cambridge History of Islam*, I, eds. P. M. Holt, A. K. S. Lambton, and B. Lewis, Cambridge, 1970, pp. 3–29. The pre-Islamic kingdoms of Yemen may be studied in J. Ryckmans, *L'Institution monarchique en Arabie méridionale avant l'Islam*, Louvain, 1951. On Arabian bedouin society see H. Lammens, *Le Berceau de l'Islam*, Rome, 1914, and *L'Arabie occidentale avant l'hégire*, Beirut, 1928; A. Musil, *Arabia Deserta*, New York, 1927; F. Gabrieli, *L'antica società beduina*, Rome, 1959. On the bedouinization of Arabia: W. Caskel, *Die Bedeutung der Beduinen in der Geschichte der Araber*, Cologne, 1953, and "The Bedouinization of Arabia," *American Anthropologist*, Memoirs, LXXVI (1954), pp. 36–46.

Pre-Islamic Arabian poetry is the principal literary source of our knowledge of Arabian peoples: C. Lyall, tr. and ed., *Translations of Ancient Arabian Poetry*, London, 1885; *The Mufaddaliyyat*, 2 vols., Oxford, 1918–21, and *The Poems of ʿAmr son of Qamiʾah*, Cambridge, 1919.

On pre-Islamic Arabian religion see B. Farès, *L'Honneur chez les Arabes avant l'Islam*, Paris, 1932; G. Ryckmans, *Les Religions arabes préislamiques*, 2nd edn, Louvain, 1951; J. Chelhod, *Le Sacrifice chez les Arabes*, Paris, 1955; *Introduction à la sociologie de l'Islam: De l'animisme a l'universalisme*, Paris, 1958, which gives an important evolutionary theory, and *Les Structures du sacré chez les Arabes*, Paris, 1964; T. Fahd, *La Divination arabe*, Leiden, 1966, and *Le Panthéon de l'Arabie centrale à la veille de l'hégire*, Paris, 1968; M. M. Bravmann, *The Spiritual Background of Early Islam*, Leiden, 1972.

Arabian family and social institutions are the subject of W. R. Smith, *Kinship and*

Marriage in Early Arabia, New York, 1979; G. H. Stern, *Marriage in Early Islam*, London, 1939; W. M. Watt, *Muhammad at Medina*, Oxford, 1956, pp. 261–302.

Mecca is the subject of H. Lammens, *Le Mecque à la veille de l'hégire*, Beirut, 1924, which develops the theory of the importance of Mecca as a trading center. On Meccan society and commerce: M. J. Kister, *Studies on Jahiliyya and Early Islam*, London, 1980.

Chapter 2

The most important source for the rise of Islam is the Quran itself. A vivid but not always literal translation is A. J. Arberry, tr., *The Koran Interpreted*, New York, 1955. More literal translations include J. M. Rodwell, tr., *The Koran*, London, 1939; E. H. Palmer, tr., *The Koran*, London, 1951. Introductions to the Quran include R. Bell, *Introduction to the Qurʾan*, Edinburgh, 1953; A. Jeffries, *The Qurʾan as Scripture*, New York, 1952; R. Blachère, *Introduction au Coran*, 2nd edn, Paris, 1959. R. Roberts, *The Social Laws of the Quran*, London, 1971 is a convenient compilation of all the texts dealing with social issues.

The earliest and authoritative Muslim biography of the Prophet is made up of the traditions collected in the second century after his death by Ibn Ishaq, and edited by Ibn Hisham, *Life of Muhammad*, tr. A. Guillaume, Lahore, 1955. The most important contemporary Western biography is W. M. Watt, *Muhammad at Mecca*, Oxford, 1953 and *Muhammad at Medina*, Oxford, 1956. See also M. Rodinson, *Mohammed*, tr. A. Carter, London, 1971.

The relationship of the Quran to the Bible and of Muhammad to Jewish and Christian tradition is the subject of Tor Andrae, *Les Origines de l'Islam et le Christianisme*, tr. Jules Roche, Paris, 1955, summarized in English, *Mohammed: The Man and His Faith*, tr. T. Menzel, London, 1956; R. Bell, *The Origins of Islam in Its Christian Environment*, London, 1968; H. Speyer, *Die biblischen Erzählungen im Qoran*, Hildesheim, 1961; C. C. Torrey, *The Jewish Foundation of Islam*, New York, 1933. The most important contributions to understanding the Quran in its Arabian context are T. Izutsu, *Ethico-Religious Concepts in the Qurʾan*, Montreal, 1966; and *God and Man in the Koran*, Tokyo, 1964.

Chapters 3 and 4

On the Arab conquests and settlement see al-Baladhuri, *Futah al-Buldan*, Leiden, 1866; P. K. Hitti and E. C. Murgotten, tr., *The Origins of the Islamic State*, 2 vols., New York, 1916–24; Fred M. Donner, *The Early Islamic Conquests*, Princeton, 1981; E. Shoufany, *Al-Riddah and the Muslim Conquest of Arabia*, Toronto, 1972. The classic history of the Umayyad period is J. Wellhausen, *The Arab Kingdom and Its Fall*, Calcutta, 1927. A good recent general history is M. A. Shaban, *Islamic History*, 1, Cambridge, 1971 with fresh but sometimes controversial interpretations. A useful recent collective work is G. H. A. Juynboll, ed., *Studies on the First Century of Islamic Society*, Carbondale, Ill., 1982. On the transition from ancient to Islamic times see M. Morony, *Iraq after the Muslim Conquest*, Princeton, 1983. E. L. Peterson, ʿ*Ali and Muʿawiya in Early Arabic Tradition*, Copenhagen, 1964 is of exceptional historiographical importance.

On the Umayyad Caliphs see G. Rotter, *Die Umayyaden und der zweite Burgerkreig, 680–692*, Wiesbaden, 1982; F. Gabrieli, "Il califfato di Hisham," *Mémoires de la Société royale d'archéologie d'Alexandrie*, VII, Alexandria, 1935. Fiscal administration is the subject of D. B. Dennett, *Conversion and the Poll Tax in Early Islam*, Cambridge, Mass., 1950.

Art and architecture: K. A. C. Creswell, *Early Muslim Architecture*, Oxford, 1969; J. Sauvaget, *La Mosquée omeyyade de Médine*, Paris, 1947; O. Grabar, *The Formation of Islamic Art*, New Haven, 1973; *City in the Desert: Qasr al-Hayr East*, 2 vols., Cambridge, Mass., 1978. See also Grabar's dissertation, *Ceremonies and Art at the Umayyad Court*, Princeton, 1954, and his collected papers, *Studies in Medieval Islamic Art*, London, 1972.

On Umayyad urbanism see Salih al-ʿAli, *Al-Tanẓīmāt al-ijtimāʿiya wa'l-iqtiṣādīya fīl-Baṣra*, Baghdad, 1953; and I. M. Lapidus, "Arab Settlement and Economic Development of Iraq and Iran in the Age of the Umayyad and Early ʿAbbasid Caliphs," *The Islamic Middle East, 700–1900: Studies in Economic and Social History*, ed. A. L. Udovitch, Princeton, 1981, pp. 177–208, with further references.

The anti-Umayyad movements to 750: S. M. Jafri, *Origins and Early Developments of Shīʿa Islam*, London, 1979; W. M. Watt, "Shiism under the Umayyads," *JRAS* (1960), pp. 158–72; W. M. Watt, "Kharijite Thought in the Umayyad Period," *Der Islam*, XXXVI (1961), pp. 215–31. The messianic movements of the late Umayyad era may be studied in G. Van Vloten, *Recherches sur la dominion arabe, le chiitisme et les croyances messianiques sous le khalifat des Omayades*, Amsterdam, 1894; B. Lewis, "An Apocalyptic Vision of Islamic History," *BSOAS*, XIII (1950), pp. 308–38. The ʿAbbasid Revolution is the subject of M. Shaban, *The ʿAbbasid Revolution*, Cambridge, 1970; F. Omar, *The ʿAbbasid Caliphate*, Baghdad, 1969; C. Cahen, "Points de vue sur la révolution ʿabbaside," *Revue historique*, CCXXX (1963), pp. 295–338.

The first century of the ʿAbbasid empire is covered by H. Kennedy, *The Early ʿAbbasid Caliphate*, London, 1981; and J. Lassner, *The Shaping of ʿAbbasid Rule*, Princeton, 1980.

ʿAbbasid urbanism is treated in I. M. Lapidus, "The Evolution of Muslim Urban Society," *Comparative Studies in Society and History*, XV (1973), pp. 21–50; J. Lassner, *The Topography of Baghdad in the Early Middle Ages*, Detroit, 1970. For ʿAbbasid military institutions see P. Crone, *Slaves on Horses*, Cambridge, 1980; D. Pipes, *Slaves, Soldiers and Islam*, New Haven, 1981. ʿAbbasid administration: the legal sources are translated by A. Ben Shemesh, *Taxation in Islam*, 3 vols., Leiden, 1958–69; D. Sourdel, *Le Vizirat ʿabbaside*, 2 vols., Damascus, 1959–60; S. D. Goitein, "The Origin of the Vizierate and Its True Character," *Islamic Culture*, XVI (1942), pp. 255–392; E. Tyan, *Histoire de l'organisation judiciaire en pays d'Islam*, Leiden, 1960 and his summary, "Judicial Organization," *Law in the Middle East*, eds. M. Khadduri and H. Liebesny, Washington, D.C., 1955, pp. 236–78. For provincial tax administration see F. Hussein, *Das Steuersystem in Ägypten, 639–868*, Frankfurt am Main, 1982; A. K. S. Lambton, *Landlord and Peasant in Persia*, London, 1953; C. Cahen, "L'Évolution de l'iqtaʿ du IXe au XIIIe siècle," *Annales E.S.C.*, VIII (1953), pp. 25–52.

Provincial histories: for Iran see R. N. Frye, ed., *Cambridge History of Iran*, IV, Cambridge, 1975; W. Barthold, *Turkestan Down to the Mongol Invasion*, London, 1968; G. H. Sadiqi, *Les Mouvements religieux Iraniens au IIe et au IIIe siècle de l'hégire*, Paris, 1938; C. E. Bosworth, *Sistan under the Arabs: From the Islamic Conquest to the Rise of the*

Saffarids, Rome, 1968, and the relevant articles in his collected *Medieval History of Iran, Afghanistan and Central Asia*, London, 1977. For Egypt see G. Wiet, *L'Egypte arabe*, Paris, 1937; Z. M. Hassan, *Les Tulunides*, Paris, 1933.

Chapter 5

The theory of the Caliphate is reviewed by T. Arnold, *The Caliphate*, London, 1965; E. Tyan, *Institutions du droit public musulman*, 1, Paris, 1954; L. Gardet, *La Cité musulmane*, Paris, 1954; H. A. R. Gibb, "Constitutional Organization," *Law in the Middle East*, eds. M. Khadduri and H. Liebesny, Washington, D.C., 1955, pp. 3–28; D. Sourdel, "Questions de cérémonial ʿabbaside," *RÉI*, xxvii (1960), pp. 121–48.

Several recent overviews of the development of Arabic literature include R. Blachère, *Histoire de la littérature arabe des origines à la fin du XVᵉ siècle de J.-C.*, 3 vols., Paris, 1952–66; A. F. L. Beeston *et al.*, eds., *Arabic Literature to the End of the Umayyad Period*, Cambridge, 1983; H. A. R. Gibb, *Arabic Literature: An Introduction*, 2nd edn, Oxford, 1963; G. E. von Grunebaum, *Themes in Medieval Arabic Literature*, London, 1981. A. Hamori, *On the Art of Medieval Arabic Literature*, Princeton, 1974; M. Zwettler, *The Oral Tradition of Classical Arabic Poetry: Its Character and Implications*, Columbus, Ohio, 1978. For Arabic literary criticism see V. Cantarino, *Arabic Poetics in the Golden Age*, Leiden, 1975; K. Abu Deeb, *Al-Jurjani's Theory of Poetic Imagery*, Warminster, 1979.

On Persian literature see G. Morrison, J. Baldick, and S. Kadkani, *History of Persian Literature from the Beginning of the Islamic Period to the Present Day*, Leiden and Cologne, 1981. J. Rypka, *History of Iranian Literature*, Dordrecht, 1968 is the classic work in the field. See also G. Lazard, ed. and tr., *Les Premiers Poètes persans*, Tehran, 1964.

Adab or courtly literatures of the ʿAbbasid era are treated in F. Rosenthal, *Knowledge Triumphant: The Concept of Knowledge in Medieval Islam*, Leiden, 1970; G. E. von Grunebaum, *Medieval Islam*, Chicago, 1946; J. C. Vadet, *L'Esprit courtois en Orient dans les cinq premiers siècles de l'hégire*, Paris, 1968; V. Monteil, *Abu-Nuwās: Le vin, le vent, la vie*, Paris, 1979.

For Ibn al-Muqaffaʿ, see D. Sourdel, "La Biographie d'Ibn al-Muqaffaʿ d'après les sources anciennes," *Arabica*, I (1954), pp. 307–23. Ibn Qutayba (d. 889) is the subject of G. Lecomte, *Ibn Qutayba: L'Homme, son oeuvre, ses idées*, Damascus, 1965. A partial translation of Ibn Qutayba's major work is provided by J. Horovitz, "Ibn Quteiba's ʿUyun al-Akhbar," *Islamic Culture*, IV (1930), pp. 171–98, 331–62, 488–530; V (1931), pp. 1–27, 194–224. For Jahiz: C. Pellat, ed. and tr., *The Life and Works of Jahiz*, Berkeley, Calif., 1969; *Le Milieu Basrien et la formation de Jahiz*, Paris, 1953.

A brief overview of Islamic philosophy may be found in W. M. Watt, *Islamic Philosophy and Theology*, Edinburgh, 1962; R. Walzer, *Greek into Arabic*, Oxford, 1962. On Shiʿi philosophy see H. Corbin, *Histoire de la philosophie islamique*, Paris, 1964. The transmission of Greek thought into Arabic is discussed in D. L. E. O'Leary, *How Greek Science Passed to the Arabs*, London, 1949; F. E. Peters, *Aristotle and the Arabs*, New York, 1968.

For the major Arab philosophers: G. N. Atiyeh, *Al-Kindi: The Philosopher of the Arabs*, Rawalpindi, 1966; *Al-Kindi's Metaphysics: A Translation of "On First Philosophy,"* tr. A. L. Ivry, Albany, N.Y., 1974; J. Jolivet, *L'Intellect selon Kindi*, Leiden, 1971;

al-Farabi, *Idées des habitants de la cité vertueuse*, tr. R. P. Jaussen, Cairo, 1949; *Fuṣūl al-Madanī: Aphorisms of the Statesman*, tr. D. M. Dunlop, Cambridge, 1961; *Philosophy of Plato and Aristotle*, tr. M. Mahdi, New York, 1962.

Chapter 6

Hadith and Law: al-Bukhari, *Al-Sahih: Les Traditions islamiques*, 4 vols., tr. O. Houdas, Paris, 1903–14. A convenient later collection of hadith is al-Khatib al-Tibrizi, *Mishkat al-Masabih*, 4 vols., tr. J. Robson, Lahore, 1960–65. Important studies on hadith include W. Graham, *Divine Word and Prophetic Word in Early Islam*, The Hague, 1977; G. H. A. Juynboll, *Muslim Tradition: Studies in Chronology, Provenance and Authorship of Early Hadith*, Cambridge, 1983. The classic studies in the field are I. Goldziher, *Muslim Studies*, 2 vols., tr. C. R. Barber and S. M. Stern, London, 1968–71; *Le Dogme et la loi de l'Islam*, Paris, 1973; *Introduction to Islamic Theology and Law*, tr. A. Hamori and R. Hamori, Princeton, 1980; J. Schacht, *The Origins of Muhammadan Jurisprudence*, Oxford, 1959. Good summary reviews of these findings are found in J. Schacht, *An Introduction to Islamic Law*, Oxford, 1964; N. J. Coulson, *A History of Islamic Law*, Edinburgh, 1964. Two important texts in the development of Muslim legal theory are M. Khadduri, tr., *Islamic Jurisprudence: Shafiʿi's Risala*, Baltimore, 1961; Malik b. Anas, *Al-Muwattaʾ*, trs. A. A. Tarjumana and Y. Johnson, Norwich, 1982. Important collections of articles on Islamic law include N. J. Coulson, *Conflicts and Tensions in Islamic Jurisprudence*, Chicago, 1969. For commercial law, see A. L. Udovitch, *Partnership and Profit in Medieval Islam*, Princeton, 1970. For law of war and peace: M. Khadduri, *War and Peace in the Law of Islam*, Baltimore, Md., 1955; al-Shaybani, *The Islamic Law of Nations*, tr. M. Khadduri, Baltimore, Md., 1966.

On theology (*kalam*): L. Gardet and M. Anawati, *Introduction à la théologie musulmane: Essai de théologie comparée*, Paris, 1948; P. Morewedge, *Islamic Philosophical Theology*, Albany, N.Y., 1979; L. Gardet, *Dieu et la destinée de l'homme*, Paris, 1967. For the origins and first century of Muslim theology see W. M. Watt, *The Formative Period of Islamic Thought*, Edinburgh, 1973; J. van Ess, *Zwischen Hadit und Theologie*, Berlin and New York, 1975; *Anfänge muslimischer Theologie*, Beirut, 1977; M. Cook, *Early Muslim Dogma: A Source-Critical Study*, Cambridge, 1981; A. J. Wensinck, *The Muslim Creed: Its Genesis and Historical Development*, London, 1965. On Muʿtazilism see J. van Ess, *Frühe Muʿtazilitische Haresiographie*, Beirut, 1971; A. Nader, *Le Système philosophique des Muʿtazila*, Beirut, 1956. For al-Ashʿari see M. Allard, *Le Problème des attributs divins dans la doctrine d'al-Asʿari et de ses premiers grands disciples*, Beirut, 1965; *The Theology of al-Ashʿari*, tr. R. J. McCarthy, Beirut, 1953.

Important works on special problems in Muslim theology include T. Izutsu, *The Concept of Belief in Islamic Theology*, Tokyo, 1965; L. Gardet, "Les Noms et les statuts: Le Problème de la foi et des oeuvres en Islam," *SI*, v (1956), pp. 61–123.

Sufism: M. G. S. Hodgson, *The Venture of Islam*, I, Chicago, 1974, pp. 359–409 gives a good general introduction. For a Muslim convert's point of view, see T. Burckhardt, *An Introduction to Sufi Doctrine*, tr. D. M. Matheson, Lahore, 1959. On early Sufism the pathbreaking work of L. Massignon, *Essai sur les origines du lexique technique de la mystique musulmane*, 2nd edn, Paris, 1954, *La Passion d'al-Husayn ibn Mansour al-Hallaj*, 2 vols., Paris, 1922, tr. H. Mason, *The Passion of al-Hallaj*, 4 vols., Princeton, 1982, and P.

Nwyia, *Exégèse coranique et language mystique*, Beirut, 1970 are indispensable. For other good general histories see A. Schimmel, *The Mystical Dimensions of Islam*, Chapel Hill, N.C., 1975; G. C. Anawati and L. Gardet, *La Mystique musulmane*, Paris, 1961. On the relation of Sufism to other mysticisms see L. Gardet, *Expériences mystiques en terres non-chrétiennes*, Paris, 1953; R. C. Zaehner, *Hindu and Muslim Mysticism*, New York, 1969; *Mysticism, Sacred and Profane*, Oxford, 1957.

Translations and works dealing with the principal early Sufi masters include H. Ritter, "Studien zur Geschichte der islamischen Frömmigkeit; Hasan el-Basri," *Der Islam*, xxi (1933), pp. 1–83; J. van Ess, *Die Gedankenwelt des Harit al-Muḥāsibi*, Bonn, 1961; M. Smith, *An Early Mystic of Baghdad. A Study of the Life, Teaching and Writings of al-Muḥasibi*, London, 1935; *Rabiᶜa the Mystic*, Cambridge, 1928; al-Kharraz, *The Book of Truthfulness [Kitāb al-sidq]*, tr. A. J. Arberry, London, 1937; A. H. Abdel-Kader, *The Life, Personality and Writings of al-Junayd*, London, 1962; al-Niffari, *Kitāb al-mawāqif wa-l-mukhaṭabat*, ed. and tr. A. J. Arberry, London, 1935; M. I. el-Geyoushi, "Al-Tirmidhī's Theory of Saints and Sainthood," *Islamic Quarterly*, xv (1971), pp. 17–61.

For ᶜAbbasid Period Shiᶜism, see H. Laoust, *Les Schismes dans l'Islam*, Paris, 1965. For Ismaᶜilism see B. Lewis, *The Origins of Ismaᶜilism*, Cambridge, 1940; T. Nagel, *Frühe Ismailiya und Fatimiden*, Bonn, 1972; W. Madelung, "Das Imamat in der frühen ismailitischen Lehre," *Der Islam*, xxxvii (1961), pp. 43–135.

Chapter 7

On the political and religious struggles of the reign of al-Maʾmun, see I. M. Lapidus, "The Separation of State and Religion," *IJMES*, vi (1975), pp. 363–85, where references may be found to earlier literature.

Chapter 8

On the century of ᶜAbbasid decline see H. Bowen, *The Life and Times of ᶜAli ibn ᶜIsa, the Good Vizier*, Cambridge, 1928; M. Forstner, *Das Kalifat des Abbasiden al-Musta ᶜin*, Mainz, 1968; W. Hellige, *Die Regentschaft al-Muwaffaqs*, Berlin, 1936; A. Popović, *La Révolte des esclaves en Iraq*, Paris, 1976.

Chapter 9

For the history of Iran in the late ᶜAbbasid, Saljuq, and Mongol eras see *Cambridge History of Iran*, iv, *The Period from the Arab Invasion to the Saljuqs*, ed. R. N. Frye, Cambridge, 1975, and v, *The Saljuq and Mongol Periods*, ed. J. A. Boyle, Cambridge, 1968. See also R. Frye, *Islamic Iran and Central Asia (7th–12th centuries)*, London, 1979; A. K. S. Lambton, *Theory and Practice in Medieval Persian Government*, London, 1980; D. S. Richards, ed., *Islamic Civilization 950–1150*, Oxford, 1973.

For the Buwayhids see M. Kabir, *The Buwayhid Dynasty of Baghdad*, Calcutta, 1964; H. Busse, *Chalif und Grosskönig, die Buyiden im Iraq*, Beirut, 1969; R. Mottahedeh, *Loyalty and Leadership in an Early Islamic Society*, Princeton, 1980 deals with the concepts which underlay Buwayhid social and political practices. On the Ghaznavids see C. E.

Bosworth, *The Ghaznavids*, Edinburgh, 1963. A regional history of the Caspian area is the V. Minorsky, *A History of Sharvan and Darband in the 10th–11th Century*, Cambridge, 1958.

On the Saljuq period see also C. Cahen, "The Turkish Invasion: The Selchukids," *A History of the Crusades*, 1, ed. M. W. Baldwin, Philadelphia, 1958, pp. 135–76, and "The Historiography of the Seljuqid Period," *Historians of the Middle East*, eds. B. Lewis and P. Holt, London, 1962, pp. 59–78; E. Tyan, *Institutions du droit public musulman: Sultanat et califat*, 11, Paris, 1957; Nizam al-Mulk, *Siyasat-Nama: The Book of Government*, tr. H. Darke, London, 1960. On the Khwarazmshahs see H. Horst, *Die Staatsverwaltung der Grosselgüqen und Hōrazmšāhs, 1038–1231*, Wiesbaden, 1964.

Political and cultural geography is the subject of X. de Planhol, *Le Monde islamique: Essai de géographie religieuse*, Paris, 1957, and *Les Fondements géographiques de l'histoire de l'Islam*, Paris, 1968; A. Miquel, *La Géographie humaine du monde musulman jusqu'au milieu du XIe siècle*, Paris, 1967. On economy and technology see R. Bulliet, *The Camel and the Wheel*, Cambridge, Mass., 1975; A. M. Watson, *Agricultural Innovation in the Early Islamic World: The Diffusion of Crops and Farming Techniques, 700–1100*, Cambridge, 1983; M. Lombard, *Les Textiles dans le monde musulman du VIIe au XIIe siècle*, Paris, 1978.

On the economic history of the Middle East from the origins of Islam to the thirteenth century see A. L. Udovitch, ed., *The Islamic Middle East, 700–1900: Studies in Economic and Social History*, Princeton, 1981; E. Ashtor, *A Social and Economic History of the Near East*, London, 1976; D. S. Richards, *Islam and the Trade of Asia*, Oxford, 1970.

The principal history of Mediterranean trade through the late Middle Ages is W. von Heyd, *Histoire du commerce du levant au moyen âge*, 2 vols., tr. F. Reynaud, Amsterdam, 1959. The study of Mediterranean trade in the early Middle Ages was for decades dominated by H. Pirenne, *Mohammed and Charlemagne*, New York, 1958. The controversy which followed is summed up in a pamphlet by A. F. Havighurst, *The Pirenne Thesis*, 3rd edn, Lexington, Mass., 1976. Important revisions include A. R. Lewis, *Naval Power and Trade in the Mediterranean*, Princeton, 1951; E. Eickhoff, *Seekrieg und Seepolitik zwischen Islam und Abendland. Das Mittelmeer unter byzantinischer und arabischer Hegemonie (650–1040)*, Berlin, 1966. For the period of the Crusades see E. H. Byrne, *Genoese Shipping in the Twelfth and Thirteenth Centuries*, Cambridge, Mass., 1930.

Chapter 10

For the social organization of the ʿulamaʾ see R. P. Mottahedeh, *Loyalty and Leadership in an Early Islamic Society*, Princeton, 1980; R. W. Bulliet, *The Patricians of Nishapur*, Cambridge, 1972; J. Gilbert, "Institutionalization of Muslim Scholarship and Professionalization of the ʿUlamaʾ in Medieval Damascus," *SI*, LII (1980), pp. 105–34. For the madrasa see G. Makdisi, "Muslim Institutions of Learning in Eleventh-century Baghdad," *BSOAS*, XXIV (1961), pp. 1–56; A. L. Tibawi, "Origin and Character of al-Madrasah," *BSOAS*, XXV (1962), pp. 225–38 is a rebuttal of Makdisi's views. Also important are D. Sourdel, "Reflexions sur la diffusion de la madrasa en Orient du XIe au XIIIe siècle," *RÉI*, XLIV (1976), pp. 165–84; G. Makdisi, "Ashʿari and the Ashʿarites in Islamic Religious History," *SI*, XVII (1962), pp. 37–80, XVIII (1962), pp. 19–39.

For religion and politics in the Saljuq era see H. Laoust, "La Pensée et l'action politiques d'Al-Mawardi, *RÉI*, xxxvi (1968), pp. 11–92; *La Politique de Gazālī*, Paris, 1970. On Hanbalism see G. Makdisi, *Ibn ᶜAqil et la résurgence de l'Islam traditionaliste au XIᵉ siècle*, Damascus, 1963, and "Hanbalite Islam," *Studies on Islam*, ed. M. L. Swartz, New York, 1981, pp. 216–74.

On the social history of Sufism see J. S. Trimingham, *The Sufi Orders in Islam*, Oxford, 1971. On veneration of saints see I. Goldziher, "Veneration of Saints in Islam," *Muslim Studies*, ii, London, 1971, pp. 253–341; J. Sourdel-Thomine, "Les Anciens Lieux de pèlerinage damascains," *BÉO*, xiv (1952–54), pp. 65–85.

On urbanism see I. M. Lapidus, "The Early Evolution of Muslim Urban Society," *Comparative Studies in Society and History*, xv (1973), pp. 21–50, "Muslim Cities and Islamic Societies," *Middle Eastern Cities*, ed. I. M. Lapidus, Berkeley, Calif., 1969, pp. 47–79, and *Muslim Cities in the Later Middle Ages*, Cambridge, 1984. Collective works devoted to cities include A. Hourani and S. M. Stern, *The Islamic City*, Oxford, 1970; L. C. Brown, *From Madina to Metropolis*, Princeton, 1973.

S. D. Goitein, *A Mediterranean Society: The Jewish Communities of the Arab World as Portrayed in the Documents of the Cairo Geniza*, 4 vols., Berkeley, Calif., 1967–78 portrays the Jewish communities of the Mediterranean but throws light on Muslim societies as well. On the Muslim merchant classes see S. D. Goitein, "The Rise of the Near-Eastern Bourgeoisie," *Journal of World History*, iii (1956), pp. 583–604; M. Rodinson, "Le Marchand musulman," *Islam and the Trade of Asia*, ed. D. S. Richards, Oxford, 1970, pp. 21–36; *Islam and Capitalism*, tr. B. Pearce, Austin, Texas, 1978. For guilds and working classes see R. Brunschvig, "Métiers vils en Islam," *SI*, xvi (1962), pp. 41–60; S. D. Goitein, "Artisans en Méditerranée orientale au haut moyen âge," *Annales E.S.C.*, xix (1964), pp. 847–68.

Futuwwa, ᶜayyarun, and urban young men's gangs: C. Cahen, "Mouvements populaires et autonomisme urbain dans l'Asie musulmane du moyen âge," *Arabica*, v (1958), pp. 225–50, vi (1959), pp. 25–56, 233–65; F. Taeschner, "Das Futuwwa-Rittertum des islamischen Mittelalters," *Beiträge zur Arabistik, Semitistik und Islamwissenschaft*, 1944, pp. 340–85.

Non-Muslim peoples under Muslim rule: A. Fattal, *Le Statut légal des non-musulmans en pays d'Islam*, Beirut, 1958; A. S. Tritton, *The Caliphs and Their Non-Muslim Subjects*, London, 1970; S. D. Goitein, *Jews and Arabs: Their Contacts through the Ages*, New York, 1964; N. A. Stillman, *The Jews of Arab Lands*, Philadelphia, 1979; A. S. Atiya, *A History of Eastern Christianity*, 2 vols., London, 1968–69; P. Rondot, *Les Chrétiens d'Orient*, Paris, 1955; M. Morony, "Religious Communities in Late Sassanian and Early Muslim Iraq," *JESHO*, xvii (1974), pp. 113–35.

Conversion to Islam has been little studied. See N. Levtzion, ed., *Conversion to Islam*, New York, 1979; R. Bulliet, *Conversion to Islam in the Medieval Period*, Cambridge, Mass., 1979; I. M. Lapidus, "The Conversion of Egypt to Islam," *In Memoriam S. M. Stern (Israel Oriental Studies)*, ii (1972), pp. 248–62.

Chapter 11

The best overviews of the literature are E. I. J. Rosenthal, *Political Thought in Medieval Islam*, Cambridge, 1958; W. M. Watt, *Islamic Political Thought*, Edinburgh, 1968. On juristic political theory see A. K. S. Lambton, *State and Government in Medieval Islam*, Oxford, 1981; Y. Ibish, *The Political Doctrine of al-Baqillani*, Beirut, 1968; al-Mawardi, *Les Statuts gouvernementaux*, tr. E. Fagnan, Algiers, 1915; Ibn Taymiya, *Ibn Taymiyah on Public and Private Law in Islam*, Beirut, 1968; H. Laoust, *Essai sur les doctrines sociales et politiques de Takī-d-Dīn Ahmad b. Taimīya*, Cairo, 1939.

Translations of the works of al-Farabi on political theory include *Idées des habitants de la cité vertueuse*, tr. R. P. Jaussen, Y. Karam, and J. Chlala, Cairo, 1949; *Fuṣūl al-Madanī: Aphorisms of the Statesman*, ed. and tr. D. M. Dunlop, Cambridge, 1961; *Philosophy of Plato and Aristotle*, tr. M. Mahdi, New York, 1962. Averroes' principal political work is the *Commentary on Plato's Republic*, ed. and tr. E. I. J. Rosenthal, Cambridge, 1966.

Translations of Mirrors for Princes include al-Jahiz, *Le Livre de la couronne*, tr. C. Pellat, Paris, 1954; Nizam al-Mulk, *The Book of Government or Rules for Kings*, tr. H. Darke, 2nd edn, London, 1978; al-Ghazzali, *Book of Counsel for Kings*, tr. F. Bagley, London, 1964; Kai Kaʾus b. Iskandar, *A Mirror for Princes: The Qābūs Nāma*, tr. R. Levy, New York, 1951; see also G. Richter, *Studien zur Geschichte der älteran arabischen Fürstenspiegel*, Leipzig, 1932.

The *Muqaddima* or Prolegomena of Ibn Khaldun is translated by W. M. de Slane, *Les Prolégomènes d'Ibn Khaldoun*, 3 vols., Paris, 1934–38; F. Rosenthal, *Ibn Khaldun, The Muqaddimah*, 3 vols., New York, 1958. Among recent scholarly works on Ibn Khaldun see M. Mahdi, *Ibn Khaldun's Philosophy of History*, London, 1957; W. J. Fischel, *Ibn Khaldun in Egypt*, Berkeley, 1967; Y. Lacoste, *Ibn Khaldoun: Naissance de l'histoire passé du Tiers-Monde*, Paris, 1966; M. M. Rabi, *The Political Theory of Ibn Khaldun*, Leiden, 1967; P. von Sivers, *Khalifat, Königtum und Verfall: Die Politische Theorie Ibn Khaldūns*, Munich, 1968; A. al-Azmeh, *Ibn Khaldūn in Modern Scholarship: A Study in Orientalism*, London, 1981, and *Ibn Khaldun: An Essay in Reinterpretation*, London, 1982.

Chapter 12

On ethics see M. Arkoun, "L'Éthique musulmane d'après Māwardī," *RÉI*, xxxi (1963), pp. 1–31; *Contribution à l'étude de l'humanisme arabe au IVᵉ/Xᵉ siècle: Miskawayh (320/325–421 – 932/936–1030), philosophe et historien*, Paris, 1970; Ibn Miskawayh, *Traité d'éthique*, tr. M. Arkoun, Damascus, 1969; Muhammad Abul Qassem, *The Ethics of al-Ghazali*, Petaling Jaya, 1975.

The post-945 development of Sufism is represented by al-Kalabadhi, *The Doctrine of the Ṣūfīs*, tr. A. J. Arberry, Cambridge, 1935; al-Sarraj, *The Kitab al-Lumaʿ fiʾl-Taṣawwuf of Abū Naṣr*, tr. R. A. Nicholson, London, 1963; al-Hujwīrī, *The Kashf al-Mahjūb*, tr. R. A. Nicholson, London, 1911; S. de Laugier de Beaurecueil, *Khwādja ʿAbdullāh Anṣārī mystique hanbalite*, Beirut, 1965.

For al-Ghazzali, see M. Bouyges, *Essai de chronologie des oeuvres d' al-Ghazali*, Beirut, 1959; H. Laoust, *La Politique de Gazzali*, Paris, 1970; H. Lazarus-Yafeh, *Studies in al-Ghazzali*, Jerusalem, 1975. The works of F. Jabré explore al-Ghazzali's conceptual vocabulary: *La Notion de certitude selon Ghazali*, Paris, 1958; *La Notion de la maʿrifa chez Ghazali*, Beirut, 1958; *Essai sur la lexique de Ghazali*, Beirut, 1970.

Translations of al-Ghazzali include W. M. Watt, *The Faith and Practice of al-Ghazali*, London, 1953, a translation of the autobiography, *Deliverance from Error: The Book of Knowledge*, tr. N. A. Faris, Lahore, 1962; *The Alchemy of Happiness*, tr. C. Field, London, 1980; *Al-Ghazali's Book of Fear and Hope*, tr. W. McKane, Leiden, 1965. G. H. Bousquet, *Ihyaʿ: ou Vivication des sciences de la foi, analyse et index*, Paris, 1955 – a résumé of al-Ghazzali's principal work; *Tahafut al-Falasifah* [Incoherence of the Philosophers], tr. S. A. Kamali, Lahore, 1958. On Suhrawardi al-Maqtul (d. 1191) see S. H. Nasr, *Three Muslim Sages*, Cambridge, Mass., 1964; H. Corbin, *Les Motifs zoroastriens dans la philosophie de Suhrawardi*, Tehran, 1946, and *Suhrawardi d'Alep*, Paris, 1939. Translations include *Opera metaphysica et mystica*, tr. H. Corbin, I, Istanbul, 1945, II, Tehran, 1952.

On Ibn al-ʿArabi (d. 1240) see A. E. Affifi, "Ibn ʿArabi," *History of Muslim Philosophy*, I, ed. M. M. Sharif, Wiesbaden, 1963, pp. 398–420, and *The Mystical Philosophy of Muhyid Dīn Ibnul-ʿArabi*, Cambridge, 1939; H. Corbin, *Creative Imagination in the Sufism of Ibn ʿArabi*, tr. R. Manheim, Princeton, N.J., 1969; T. Izutsu, *A Comparative Study of the Key Philosophical Concepts in Sufism and Taoism*, Berkeley, Calif., 1984.

Translations of Ibn al-ʿArabi's works include *Sufis of Andalusia. The Rūh al-quds and al-Durrat al-fākhirah of Ibn ʿArabī*, tr. R. W. J. Austin, Berkeley, Calif., 1977; *La Profession de foi*, tr. R. Deladrière, Paris, 1978; *The Bezels of Wisdom*, tr. R. W. J. Austin, New York, 1980; *The Seals of Wisdom*, tr. A. al-Tarjumana, Norwich, Eng., 1980; *Journey to the Lord of Power: A Sufi Manual on Retreat*, tr. T. Harris, New York, 1981.

On the philosophy of Ibn Sina see L. Gardet, *La Pensée religieuse d'Avicenne (Ibn Sīnā)*, Paris, 1951; A. M. Goichon, *La Philosophie d'Avicenne et son influence en Europe médiévale*, 2nd edn, Paris, 1951; A. Afnan, *Avicenna: His Life and Works*, London, 1958; H. Corbin, *Avicenna and the Visionary Recital*, tr. W. Trask, New York, 1960. Translations include *Avicenna on Theology*, tr. A. J. Arberry, London, 1951; *Livre des directives et remarques*, tr. A. M. Goichon, Beirut, 1951; *Avicenna's Psychology*, tr. F. Rahman, London, 1952; *The Metaphysica of Avicenna*, tr. P. Morewedge, New York, 1973. Translations of Averroes include *Tahafut al-Tahafut* [The Incoherence of the Incoherence], 2 vols., tr. S. van den Bergh, London, 1954; *On the Harmony of Religion and Philosophy*, tr. G. Hourani, London, 1961; *Averroes' Three Short Commentaries on Aristotle's "Topics," "Rhetoric," and "Poetics,"* tr. C. E. Butterworth, Albany, N.Y., 1977.

For special topics in Islamic philosophy see M. Fakhry, *Islamic Occasionalism and Its Critique by Averroes and Aquinas*, London, 1958; A. J. Arberry, *Revelation and Reason in Islam*, London, 1957; F. Rahman, *Prophecy in Islam*, London, 1958; S. H. Nasr, *An Introduction to Islamic Cosmological Doctrines*, Cambridge, Mass., 1964; I. R. Netton, *Muslim Neoplatonists: An Introduction to the Thought of the Brethren of Purity*, London, 1982.

The transmission of Arabic and Hebrew philosophy to Europe and the development of Christian scholasticism are the subjects of F. van Steenberghen, *Aristotle in the West: The Origins of Latin Aristotelianism*, tr. L. Johnston, Louvain, 1955, and *The Philosophical Movement in the Thirteenth Century*, Edinburgh, 1955; E. Gilson, "Les Sources gréco-arabes de l'Augustinisme avicennisant," *Archives d'histoire doctrinale et littéraire du Moyen*

Âge, xiv (1929), pp. 5–149; M. Steinschneider, *Die europäischen Übersetzungen aus dem Arabischen bis mitte des 17, Jahrhunderts*, Graz, 1956. For relations between Islam and the West more generally see R. W. Southern, *Western Views of Islam in the Middle Ages*, Cambridge, Mass., 1978; N. Daniel, *Islam and the West: The Making of an Image*, Edinburgh, 1960, and *The Arabs and Medieval Europe*, 2nd edn, London, 1979; J. Kritzech, *Peter the Venerable and Islam*, Princeton, 1964; K. I. Semaan, ed., *Islam and the Medieval West*, Albany, N.Y., 1980.

PART II

Chapter 13

For Iran under the Mongols see the relevant chapters of the *Cambridge History of Iran*, v, ed. J. A. Boyle, Cambridge, 1968; C. Cahen, "The Turks in Iran and Anatolia before the Mongol Invasions," *History of the Crusades*, ii, eds. R. L. Wolff and H. W. Hazard, Madison, Wis., 1969, pp. 661–92, and "The Mongols and the Near East," *ibid.*, pp. 715–34; B. Spuler, *Die Mongolen in Iran: Politik, Verwaltung und Kultur der Ilchanzeit, 1220–1350*, Berlin, 1968. On Mongol art see D. N. Wilber, *The Architecture of Islamic Iran*, Princeton, 1955; O. Grabar and S. Blair, *Epic Images and Contemporary History: The Illustrations of the Great Mongol Shahnama*, Chicago, 1980. See bibliography for Chapter 17 for further references to Mongols and Inner Asia.

For the political system of Iran in the fifteenth century see J. E. Woods, *The Aqquyunlu: Clan, Confederation, Empire*, Minneapolis, Minn., 1976. On the rise of the Safavid dynasty see M. Mazzaoui, *The Origins of the Safawids*, Wiesbaden, 1972. The only general history of the Safavid period in English is R. Savory, *Iran under the Safavids*, Cambridge, 1980. L. L. Bellan, *Chah ʿAbbas*, i, Paris, 1932 covers the principal reign of the dynasty. For Safavid and later Iranian relations with Europe see R. K. Ramazani, *The Foreign Policy of Iran: 1500–1941*, Charlottesville, Va., 1966.

Safavid state organization: A. K. S. Lambton, *Landlord and Peasant in Persia*, London, 1953. For the theory of Iranian monarchy see A. K. S. Lambton, "Quis custodiet custodes? Some Reflections on the Persian Theory of Government," *SI*, v (1956), pp. 125–48, vi (1956), pp. 125–46. For Safavid art and architecture see S. C. Welch, *A King's Book of Kings: The Shah-nameh of Shah Tahmasp*, London, 1972, and *Persian Painting: Five Royal Safavid Manuscripts of the Sixteenth Century*, New York, 1976.

The relations of state and religion in Safavid Iran are the subject of a number of important studies: J. Aubin, "Études safavides: i, Šāh Ismāʿīl et les notables de l'Iraq persan," *JESHO*, ii (1959), pp. 37–81, and "La Politique religieuse des Safavides," *Le Shīʿisme imāmite*, Paris, 1970, pp. 235–44; S. Arjomand, "Religion, Political Action and Legitimate Domination in Shiʿite Iran: 14th to 18th Centuries," *European Journal of Sociology*, xx (1979), pp. 59–109, and "Religious Extremism (Ghuluww), Sufism and Sunnism in Safavid Iran: 1501–1722," *Journal of Asian History*, xv (1981), pp. 1–35.

Iranian illuminationist philosophy has been examined by S. H. Nasr, "The School of Isfahan," *A History of Muslim Philosophy*, ii, ed. M. M. Sharif, Wiesbaden, 1966, pp. 904–31; H. Corbin, *En Islam iranien*, 3 vols., Paris, 1974, and *La Philosophie iranienne islamique aux XVIIᵉ et XVIIIᵉ siècles*, Paris, 1981. See also F. Rahman, *The Philosophy of Mulla Sadra (Sadr al-Din al-Shirazi)*, Albany, N.Y., 1976.

The recent work of James Reid on uymaq and tribal structures has contributed heavily to my interpretation of the dynamics of Iranian history. See *Tribalism and Society in Islamic Iran, 1500–1629*, Malibu, Calif., 1983, "The Qajar Uymaq in the Safavid Period, 1500–1722," *Iranian Studies*, XI (1978), pp. 117–143, and "Rebellion and Social Change in Astarabad, 1537–1744," *IJMES*, XIII (1981), pp. 35–53.

On the Iranian economy see R. Quiring-Zoche, *Isfahan im funfzehnten und sechzehnten Jahrhundert*, Freiburg, 1980; M. Keyvani, *Artisans and Guild Life in the Later Safavid Period*, Berlin, 1982.

For the eighteenth-century collapse of the Safavid regime see L. Lockhart, *The Fall of the Safavi Dynasty and the Afghan Occupation of Persia*, Cambridge, 1958, and *Nadir Shah: A Critical Study*, London, 1938; and J. R. Perry, *Karim Khan Zand: A History of Iran, 1747–1779*, Chicago, 1979. Other studies of Turko-Iranian tribal societies in the eighteenth and nineteenth centuries include G. Garthwaite, "Pastoral Nomadism and Tribal Power," *Iranian Studies*, XI (1978), pp. 173–97; R. Loeffler, "Tribal Order and the State: The Political Organization of the Boir Ahmad," *Iranian Studies*, XI (1978), pp. 144–71.

Chapter 14

The best general history of the Ottoman empire is H. Inalcik, *The Ottoman Empire: The Classical Age, 1300–1600*, tr. N. Itzkowitz and C. Imber, London, 1973. H. A. R. Gibb and H. Bowen, *Islamic Society and the West*, 2 parts, Oxford, 1950, 1957, despite out-of-date sections, is still an indispensable introduction. See also N. Itzkowitz, *The Ottoman Empire and Islamic Tradition*, New York, 1972; S. J. Shaw, *History of the Ottoman Empire and Modern Turkey*, 2 vols., Cambridge, 1976.

On pre-Ottoman Turkey see C. Cahen, *Pre-Ottoman Turkey, 1071–1330*, tr. J. Jones-Williams, London, 1968. Important studies of the Turkish principalities include B. Flemming, *Landschaftsgeschichte von Pamphylien, Pisidien und Lykien im Spätmittelalter*, Wiesbaden, 1964; P. Lemerle, *L'Émirat d'Aydin: Byzance et l'Occident. Recherches sur "La Geste d'Umur Pacha,"* Paris, 1957; P. Wittek, *Das fürstentum Mentesche*, Amsterdam, 1967; S. Vryonis, Jr., *The Decline of Medieval Hellenism in Asia Minor*, Berkeley, 1971, and "Nomadization and Islamization in Asia Minor," *Dumbarton Oaks Papers*, XXIX (1975), pp. 41–71.

On Ottoman conquests see P. Wittek, *Rise of the Ottoman Empire*, London, 1938; F. Babinger, *Mahomet II, le Conquérant, et son temps*, Paris, 1954; S. Runciman, *The Fall of Constantinople*, Cambridge, 1965. Ottoman wars with the Austro-Hungarian empire: D. Vaughan, *Europe and the Turk: A Pattern of Alliances, 1350–1700*, Liverpool, 1954; C. M. Kortepeter, *Ottoman Imperialism During the Reformation: Europe and the Caucasus*, New York, 1972; S. A. Fischer-Galati, *Ottoman Imperialism and German Protestantism*, Cambridge, Mass., 1959. For Ottoman expansion in the Crimea see H. Inalcik, "The Origin of the Ottoman–Russian Rivalry and the Don–Volga Canal (1569)," *Annales de l'Université d'Ankara*, I (1946–47), pp. 47–106; W. E. D. Allen, *Problems of Turkish Power in the Sixteenth Century*, London, 1963.

On Ottoman expansion in the Mediterranean see F. Braudel, *The Mediterranean and the Mediterranean World*, 2 vols., tr. S. Reynolds, New York, 1972; A. Hess, *The Forgotten Frontier: A History of the Sixteenth-century Ibero-African Frontier*, Chicago, 1978. For Ottoman–Safavid wars see E. Eberhard, *Osmanische Polemik gegen die Safawiden im 16. Jahr. nach arabischen Handschriften*, Freiburg, 1970. A useful collection of documents is

J. C. Hurewitz, *Diplomacy in the Near and Middle East: A Documentary Record, 1535–1914*, I, New York, 1956.

The principal account of Ottoman rule in the Balkans is P. F. Sugar, *Southeastern Europe under Ottoman Rule, 1354–1804*, Seattle, Wash., 1977. See also N. Beldiceanu, *Le Monde ottomen des Balkans (1402–1566)*, London, 1976.

For the institutions of the Ottoman State see A. D. Alderson, *The Structure of the Ottoman Dynasty*, Oxford, 1956; I. M. Kunt, *The Sultan's Servants: The Transformation of Ottoman Provincial Government, 1550–1650*, New York, 1983; H. Inalcik, "Military and Fiscal Transformation in the Ottoman Empire, 1600–1700," *Archivum Ottomanicum*, VI (1980), pp. 283–337. B. Miller, *The Palace School of Muhammad the Conqueror*, Cambridge, Mass., 1941 depicts the education of the janissaries.

For Islamic religious elites see H. A. R. Gibb and H. Bowen, *Islamic Society and the West*, Oxford, 1950–57, I, pp. 19–38, II, pp. 70–261; J. Birge, *The Bektashi Order of Dervishes*, London, 1937.

On the non-Muslim populations: F. W. Hasluck, *Christianity and Islam under the Sultans*, 2 vols., Oxford, 1929; T. Ware, *Eustratios Argenti: A Study of the Greek Church under Turkish Rule*, Oxford, 1964; N. J. Pantazopoulos, *Church and Law in the Balkan Peninsula during the Ottoman Rule*, Thessaloniki, 1967; S. Runciman, *The Great Church in Captivity*, London, 1968; L. Arpee, *A History of Armenian Christianity from the Beginning to Our Own Time*, New York, 1946. On the Jewish communities see M. A. Epstein, *The Ottoman Jewish Communities and Their Role in the Fifteenth and Sixteenth Centuries*, Freiburg, 1980; C. Roth, *The House of Nasi: The Duke of Naxos*, New York, 1948. The relations of Ottomans and Europeans is discussed in B. Homsy, *Les Capitulations et la protection des chrétiens au Proche-Orient aux XVIᵉ, XVIIᵉ et XVIIIᵉ siècles*, Paris, 1956; C. A. Frazee, *Catholics and Sultans: The Church and the Ottoman Empire, 1453–1923*, Cambridge, 1983. A major reinterpretation of the "millet" system is advanced by B. Braude, "Foundation Myths of the Millet System," *Christians and Jews in the Ottoman Empire*, I, ed. B. Braude and B. Lewis, New York, 1982, pp. 69–88.

For the development of Istanbul see B. Lewis, *Istanbul and the Civilization of the Ottoman Empire*, Norman, Okla., 1963; R. Mantran, *La Vie quotidienne à Constantinople au temps de Soliman le Magnifique et de ses successeurs*, Paris, 1965. Balkan cities are the subject of N. Todorov, ed., *La Ville balkanique sous les Ottomans, XVᵉ–XIXᵉ siècles*, London, 1977. On the small towns of Anatolia see S. Faroqhi, *Towns and Townsmen of Ottoman Anatolia*, Cambridge, 1984.

The demographic and economic development of Anatolia is treated by M. A. Cook, *Population Pressure in Rural Anatolia, 1450–1600*, London, 1972. See also H. Islamoglu and S. Faroqhi, "Crop Patterns and Agricultural Production Trends in Sixteenth-Century Anatolia," *Review*, (New York), II (1979), pp. 401–36. Ottoman trade: H. Inalcik, "Bursa and the Commerce of the Levant," *JESHO*, III (1960), pp. 131–47, and "Capital Formation in the Ottoman Empire," *Journal of Economic History*, XXIX (1969), pp. 97–140.

The struggle for control of the international spice trade is the subject of S. Y. Labib, *Handelsgeschichte Ägyptens im Spätmittelalter (1171–1517)*, Wiesbaden, 1965. For the rise of Europe and the transformation of the world economy see I. Wallerstein, *The Modern World System*, 2 vols., New York, 1974–80; P. Pachi, "The Shifting of International Trade Routes in the 15th–17th Centuries," *Acta Historica*, XIV (1968), pp. 287–321;

R. Mantran, "Transformation du commerce dans l'Empire Ottoman au dix-huitième siècle," *Studies in Eighteenth-Century Islamic History*, eds. T. Naff and R. Owen, Carbondale, Ill., 1977, pp. 217–35.

The growth of European commerce in the seventeenth and eighteenth centuries is studied in P. Masson, *Histoire du commerce français dans le Levant au XVIIe siècle*, Paris, 1896, and *Histoire du commerce français dans le Levant au XVIIIe siècle*, Paris, 1911; N. G. Svoronos, *Le Commerce de Salonique au XVIIIe siècle*, Paris, 1956; A. C. Wood, *A History of the Levant Company*, London, 1935.

On Turkish Art and Literature see E. Atil, ed., *Turkish Art*, Washington, D.C., 1980; G. Goodwin, *A History of Ottoman Architecture*, Baltimore, Md., 1971; O. Aslanapa, *Turkish Art and Architecture*, London, 1971; M. And, *A History of Theatre and Popular Entertainment in Turkey*, Ankara, 1963–4, and *Turkish Miniature Painting*, Ankara, 1974; E. Atil, *Turkish Miniature Painting*, Tokyo, 1960.

On the seventeenth and eighteenth centuries see S. J. Shaw, *Between Old and New: The Ottoman Empire under Sultan Selim III, 1789–1807*, Cambridge, Mass., 1971; T. Naff and R. Owen, eds., *Studies in Eighteenth Century Islamic History*, London, 1977. Specialized studies on the internal condition of the Ottoman empire include W. J. Griswold, *The Great Anatolian Rebellion: 1000–1020/1591–1611*, Berlin, 1983.

Ottoman military and political relations with Europe in the eighteenth century are treated in M. S. Anderson, *The Eastern Question, 1774–1923*, London, 1966; L. Cassels, *The Struggle for the Ottoman Empire, 1717–1740*, London, 1966; A. W. Fisher, *The Russian Annexation of the Crimea, 1772–1783*, Cambridge, 1970; B. H. Sumner, *Peter the Great and the Ottoman Empire*, Oxford, 1949; G. S. Thomson, *Catherine the Great and the Expansion of Russia*, London, 1947.

Chapter 15

For Fatimid art see K. A. C. Creswell, *The Muslim Architecture of Egypt*, 2 vols., Oxford, 1952–59; O. Grabar, "Imperial and Urban Art in Islam: The Subject Matter of Fatimid Art," *Colloque international sur l'histoire du Caire*, Cairo, 1973, pp. 173–89; J. M. Bloom, "The Mosque of al-Hakim in Cairo," *Muqarnas*, I (1983), pp. 15–36; C. Williams, "The Cult of Alid Saints in the Fatimid Monuments of Cairo," *Muqarnas*, I (1983), pp. 37–52; M. Canard, "Le Cérémonie fatimite et le cérémonie Byzantin," *Byzantion*, XXI (1951), pp. 355–420, and "La Procession du nouvel an chez les Fatimides," *AIÉO*, x (1952), pp. 364–98.

For Syria in the early Islamic era see K. S. Salibi, *Syria under Islam: Empire on Trial, 634–1097*, Delmar, N.Y., 1976; M. Canard, *Histoire de la dynastie des Hamdanides de Jazīra et de Syrie*, Paris, 1953. Histories of the crusades include S. Runciman, *A History of the Crusades*, 3 vols., Cambridge, 1951–54; H. E. Mayer, *The Crusades*, tr. J. Gillingham, London, 1972; J. Prawers, *Crusader Institutions*, Oxford, 1980; H. W. Hazard, *The Art and Architecture of the Crusader States*, Madison, Wis., 1977.

For the history of Muslim Syria in the crusading era the fundamental work is C. Cahen, *La Syrie du Nord à l'époque des Croisades*, Paris, 1940. Good general accounts may be found in K. M. Setton, ed., *A History of the Crusades*, 2nd edn, 4 vols., Madison, Wis., 1969–77. See also N. Elisseeff, *Nūr ad-Dīn: Un grand prince musulman de Syrie au temps des Croisades (511–569H. / 1118–1174)*, 3 vols., Damascus, 1967; E. Sivan, *L'Islam et la Croisade*, Paris, 1968.

Useful translations of Arabic sources include F. Gabrieli, ed., *Arab Historians of the Crusades*, Berkeley, 1969; *Recueil des historiens des Croisades*, Académie des inscriptions et belles-lettres, 14 vols., Paris, 1966–67; Ibn al-Qalānisī, *The Damascus Chronicle of the Crusades*, tr. H. A. R. Gibb., London, 1932; Usāmah ibn Munqidh, *An Arab-Syrian Gentleman and Warrior in the Period of the Crusades*, tr. P. K. Hitti, New York, 1929.

Ismaʿilism in the crusade period is the subject of M. G. S. Hodgson, *The Order of Assassins*, The Hague, 1955; B. Lewis, *The Assassins*, London, 1967. See especially M. G. S. Hodgson, "The Ismaʿili State," *Cambridge History of Iran*, v, pp. 422–82.

For Egypt and Syria under Saladin and the Ayyubids see A. Ehrenkreutz, *Saladin*, Albany, N.Y., 1972; R. S. Humphreys, *From Saladin to the Mongols*, Albany, N.Y., 1972. Ayyubid military organization is treated by S. Elbeheiry, *Les Institutions de l'Égypte au temps des Ayyūbides. L'organisation de l'armée et des institutions militaires*, Paris, 1971; R. S. Humphreys, "The Emergence of the Mamluk Army," *SI*, XLV (1977), pp. 67–100, XLVI (1977), pp. 147–82. Ayyubid administration has been extensively studied by C. Cahen, *Makhzūmiyyāt: Études sur l'histoire économique et financière de l'Égypte médiévale*, Leiden, 1977.

For Syrian Muslim towns see E. Ashtor-Strauss, "L'Administration urbaine en Syrie médiévale," *RSO*, XXXI (1956), pp. 73–128; C. Cahen, "Mouvements populaires et autonomisme urbain dans l'Asie musulmane du moyen âge," *Arabica*, v (1958), pp. 225–50, VI (1959), pp. 25–56, 233–65; and the relevant chapters of J. Sauvaget, *Alep*, Paris, 1941. On the ʿulamaʾ and the schools of law in Syria see N. Elisseef, *Nūr ad-Dīn*.

Ayyubid architecture is treated by E. Herzfeld, "Damascus: Studies in Architecture," *Ars Islamica*, IX (1942), pp. 1–53, X (1943), pp. 13–70, XI (1946), pp. 1–71, XIII–XIV (1948), pp. 118–38; J. Sauvaget, M. Écochard and J. Sourdel-Thomine, *Les Monuments ayyoubides de Damas*, Paris, 1938–50.

A comprehensive bibliography of works on the Mamluk era in Egypt and Syria is found in I. M. Lapidus, *Muslim Cities in the Later Middle Ages*, Cambridge, Mass., 1967, with supplements in the 2nd edn, Cambridge, 1984.

The history of Egypt under Ottoman rule is given by P. M. Holt, *Egypt and the Fertile Crescent, 1516–1922*, London, 1966; S. J. Shaw, *The Financial and Administrative Organization and Development of Ottoman Egypt, 1517–1798*, Princeton, 1962; *Ottoman Egypt in the Eighteenth Century*, Cambridge, Mass., 1962. The economy of Ottoman Egypt: A. Raymond, *Artisans et commerçants au Caire*, 2 vols., Damascus, 1973–74, and "The Economic Crisis of Egypt in the Eighteenth Century," *The Islamic Middle East, 700–1900: Studies in Economic and Social History*, ed. A. L. Udovitch, Princeton, 1981, pp. 687–707; G. Baer, *Egyptian Guilds in Modern Times*, Jerusalem, 1964.

On Egyptian Islam see A. L. Marsot, "The Ulama of Cairo in the Eighteenth and Nineteenth Centuries," *Scholars, Saints and Sufis*, ed. N. R. Keddie, Berkeley, Calif., 1972, pp. 149–65; M. Winter, *Society and Religion in Early Ottoman Egypt*, New Brunswick, N.J., 1982.

On the Arab provinces under Ottoman Rule see H. Laoust, *Les Gouverneurs de Damas sous les Mamlouks et les premiers Ottomans*, Damascus, 1952; M. A. Bakhit, *The Ottoman Province of Damascus in the Sixteenth Century*, Beirut, 1982; K. K. Barbir, *Ottoman Rule in Damascus 1708–1758*, Princeton, 1980; A. K. Rafeq, *The Province of Damascus, 1723–1783*, Beirut, 1966.

For the ʿulamaʾ and Sufism in Syria see M. Winter, "Sheikh ʿAlī ibn Maymūn and Syrian Sufism in the Sixteenth Century," *Israel Oriental Studies*, VII (1977), pp. 281–308; A. Hourani, "Sheikh Khalid and the Naqshbandi Order," *Islamic Philosophy and the Classical Tradition*, eds. S. M. Stern and V. Brown, Columbia, S.C., 1972, pp. 89–103; J. Voll, "Old ʿUlamaʾ Families and Ottoman Influence in 18th-century Damascus," *The American Journal of Arabic Studies*, III (1975), pp. 48–59.

Palestine has been the subject of U. Heyd, *Ottoman Documents on Palestine, 1552–1615*, Oxford, 1960; A. Cohen and B. Lewis, *Population and Revenue in the Towns of Palestine in the Sixteenth Century*, Princeton, 1978; M. Maʾoz, ed., *Studies on Palestine during the Ottoman Period*, Jerusalem, 1975; A. Cohen, *Palestine in the Eighteenth Century*, Jerusalem, 1973. On Lebanon see K. S. Salibi, *The Modern History of Lebanon*, London, 1965; I. F. Harik, *Politics and Change in a Traditional Society: Lebanon, 1711–1845*, Princeton, 1968.

On Iraq see T. Nieuwenhuis, *Politics and Society in Early Modern Iraq (1802–1831)*, The Hague, 1982; S. H. Longrigg, *Four Centuries of Modern Iraq*, Oxford, 1925.

Chapter 16

The most useful general works on North Africa include J. M. Abun-Nasr, *A History of the Maghrib*, 2nd edn, Cambridge, 1975; A. Laroui, *The History of the Maghrib*, Princeton, 1977; L. Valensi, *On the Eve of Colonialism: North Africa before the French Conquest*, New York, 1977; C. A. Julien, *History of North Africa: Tunisia, Algeria, Morocco, from the Arab Conquest to 1830*, New York, 1970.

The Arab conquests to the thirteenth century: H. R. Idris, *La Berbérie orientale sous les Zīrīdes*, Paris, 1962; G. Marçais, *Les Arabes en Berbérie du XIᵉ au XIVᵉ siècle*, Paris, 1913; M. Talbi, *L'Émirat aghlabide: Histoire politique*, Paris, 1966. For the Fatimids see the previous section on Egypt and Syria. Kharijism has been studied by T. Lewicki, "La Répartition géographique des groupements ibādites dans l'Afrique du Nord au moyen âge," *Rocznik orientalistyczny*, XXI (1957), pp. 301–43, and "The Ibadites in Arabia and Africa," *Journal of World History*, XIII (1971), pp. 51–130.

The origin of the Almoravid movement has recently been reinterpreted by P. F. de Moraes Farias, "The Almoravids: Some Questions Concerning the Character of the Movement during its Periods of Closest Contact with the Western Sudan," *Bulletin de l'Institut français d'Afrique Noire*, XXIX (1967), pp. 794–878; H. T. Norris, "New Evidence on the Life of ʿAbdullāh b. Yāsīn and the Origins of the Almoravid Movement," *JAH*, XII (1971), pp. 255–68; V. Lagardere, "Esquisse de l'organization militaire des Murābitūn à l'époque de Yūsuf b. Tāšfīn, 430 H. / 1039 à 500 H. / 1106," *ROMM*, XXVII (1979), pp. 99–114; N. Levtzion, "ʿAbd Allāh b. Yāsīn and the Almoravids," *Studies in West African Islamic History*, I, ed. J. R. Willis, London, 1979, pp. 78–112.

The impact of the Hilali invasions is much debated: H. R. Idris, "L'Invasion hilālienne et ses conséquences," *Cahiers de civilisation médiévale*, XI (1968), pp. 353–69; J. Poncet, "Prospérité et décadence ifrikiyennes," *Cahiers de Tunisie*, IX (1961), pp. 221–43, and "Le Mythe de la 'catastrophe' hilālienne," *Annales E.S.C.*, XXII (1967), pp. 1099–1120.

On Saharan, North African, and Mediterranean trade see N. Pacha, *Le Commerce au*

Maghreb du XIe au XIVe siècle, Tunis, 1976; J. Devisse, "Routes de commerce et échanges en Afrique Occidentale en relation avec la Méditerranée"; *Revue d'histoire économique et sociale*, L (1972), pp. 42–73, 357–97.

The basic study of Tunisian society from the thirteenth to the sixteenth century is R. Brunschvig, *La Berbérie orientale sous les Hafsides*, 2 vols., Paris, 1940–47. See also L. C. Brown, "The Religious Establishment in Husainid Tunisia," *Scholars, Saints and Sufis*, ed. N. Keddie, Berkeley, Calif., 1972, pp. 47–91; J. Abun-Nasr, "The Beylicate in Seventeenth-Century Tunisia," *IJMES*, VI (1975), pp. 70–93; J. Pignon, "La Milice des Janissaires du Tunis au temps des Deys (1590–1650)," *Cahiers de Tunisie*, IV (1956), pp. 301–26.

For the economic history of Tunisia in the eighteenth and early nineteenth centuries see L. Valensi, "Islam et capitalisme, production et commerce des Chéchias en Tunisie et en France aux XVIIIe et XIXe siècles," *Revue d'histoire moderne et contemporaine*, XVI (1969), pp. 376–400, and *Tunisian Peasants in the Eighteenth and Nineteenth Centuries*, Cambridge, 1985; M. H. Cherif, "Expansion européenne et difficultés tunisiennes de 1815 à 1830," *Annales E.S.C.*, XXV (1961), pp. 714–45; L. C. Brown, *The Tunisia of Ahmad Bey, 837–1855*, Princeton, 1974.

For Algeria under the Turks see P. Boyer, *L'Évolution de l'Algérie médiane*, Paris, 1960, and *La Vie quotidienne à Alger*, Paris, 1964; W. Spencer, *Algiers in the Age of the Corsairs*, Norman, Okla., 1976. On piracy and trade in the Mediterranean from the sixteenth to the nineteenth century see G. Fisher, *Barbary Legend: War, Trade and Piracy in North Africa, 1415–1830*, Oxford, 1957; P. Masson, *Histoire des établissements et du commerce français dans l'Afrique barbaresque (1560–1793)*, Paris, 1903; A. E. Sayous, *Le Commerce des Européens à Tunis*, Paris, 1929.

On Algerian society see P. Boyer, "Contribution à l'étude de la politique religieuse des Turcs dans la Régence d'Alger (XVIe–XIXe siècles)," *ROMM*, I (1966), pp. 11–49. R. Gallissot, *L'Algérie pré-coloniale: Classes sociales en système précapitaliste*, Paris, 1968; "Pre-colonial Algeria," *Economy and Society*, IV (1975), pp. 418–45; J. C. Vatin, "L'Algérie en 1830: Essai d'interprétation des recherches historiques sous l'angle de la science politique," *Revue algérienne*, VII (1970), pp. 977–1058; A. Nouschi, "La vita rurale in Algeria prima de 1830," *Studi Storici*, IV (1963), pp. 449–78.

Morocco's history is covered by the work of H. Terrasse, *Histoire du Maroc*, 2 vols., Casablanca, 1950; E. Lévi-Provençal, *Les Historiens des Chorfa: Essai sur la littérature historique et biographique au Maroc du XVIe au XXe siècle*, Paris, 1922. On the Moroccan economy before the nineteenth century see P. Berthier, *Les Anciennes Sucreries du Maroc*, 2 vols., Rabat, 1966; A. Hammoudi, "Sainteté, pouvoir et société: Tamgrout aux XVIIe et XVIIIe siècles," *Annales E.S.C.*, XXXV (1980), pp. 615–41.

For Moroccan urban society, see K. Brown, *People of Salé*, Manchester, 1976; R. Le Tourneau, *Fès avant le protectorat*, Casablanca, 1949, *Les Villes musulmanes de l'Afrique du Nord*, Algiers, 1957, and *Fez in the Age of the Marinides*, Norman, Okla., 1961; J. S. Gerber, *Jewish Society in Fez, 1450–1700*, Leiden, 1980.

On North African Sufism see A. Bel, *La Religion musulmane en Berbérie*, Paris, 1938; G. Drague, *Esquisse d'histoire religieuse du Maroc: confréries et zaouias*, Paris, 1951; P. J. André, *Contribution à l'études des confréries religieuses musulmanes*, Algiers, 1956; J. Abun-Nasr, *The Tijaniyya*, London, 1965; R. G. Jenkins, "The Evolution of Religious Brotherhoods in North and Northwest Africa 1523–1900," *Studies in West African*

Islamic History, I, ed. J. R. Willis, London, 1979, pp. 40–77; C. Geertz, *Islam Observed*, New Haven, Conn., 1968; V. J. Cornell, "The Logic of Analogy and the Role of the Sufi Shaykh," *IJMES*, xv (1983), pp. 67–93.

Introductory accounts of Muslim Spain include A. Chejne, *Muslim Spain*, Minneapolis, 1974; J. O'Callaghan, *A History of Medieval Spain*, Ithaca, N.Y., 1975; and the classic E. Lévi-Provençal, *Histoire de l'Espagne musulmane*, 3 vols., Paris, 1950–53. Important interpretations of the economic and social bases of Spanish and Muslim civilization are T. Glick, *Irrigation and Society in Medieval Valencia*, Cambridge, Mass., 1970, and *Islamic and Christian Spain in the Early Middle Ages*, Princeton, 1979; P. Guichard, *Structures sociales, orientales et occidentales dans l'Espagne musulmane*, Paris, 1977. See also D. Wasserstein, *The Rise and Fall of the Party-Kings*, Princeton, N.J., 1985.

Muslim urban communities and the supervision of markets are treated in the work of P. Chalmeta Gendrón, *El "señor del zoco" en España*, Madrid, 1973; L. Torres Balbás, "Les Villes musulmanes d'Espagne et leur urbanisation," *AIÉO*, vi (1942–47), pp. 5–30, and "Extensión y demografía de las ciudades hispano musulmanas," *SI*, III (1955), pp. 37–59.

On Islam in Spain see H. Mones, "Le Rôle des hommes de religion dans l'histoire de l'Espagne musulmane jusqu'à la fin du Califat," *SI*, xx (1964), pp. 47–88. For Spanish Sufism see P. Nwyia, *Ibn ʿAbbād de Ronda (1332–1390)*, Beirut, 1961.

For the Reconquista and relations between Muslims and Christians see R. Burns, *Islam under the Crusaders: Colonial Survival in the Thirteenth-Century Kingdom of Valencia*, Princeton, 1973; *The Crusader Kingdom of Valencia: Reconstruction on a Thirteenth-Century Frontier*, 2 vols., Cambridge, Mass., 1967; J. Boswell, *The Royal Treasure: Muslim Communities under the Crown of Aragon in the Fourteenth Century*, New Haven, Conn., 1978; J. Edwards, *Christian Cordoba: The City and Its Region in the Late Middle Ages*, Cambridge, 1982.

On Arabic literature see the contributions of J. Monroe, *The Shuʿubiyya in Al-Andalus: The Risala of Ibn Garcia and Five Refutations*, Berkeley, Calif., 1969, and *Hispano-Arabic Poetry*, Berkeley, Calif., 1974; S. Stern, *Hispano-Arabic Strophic Poetry*, Oxford, 1974; L. Compton, *Andalusian Lyrical Poetry and Old Spanish Love Songs*, New York, 1976. A vivid interpretation of Spanish architecture and its cultural significance is O. Grabar, *The Alhambra*, London, 1978.

Chapter 17

For the dynamics of steppe empires see R. Grousset, *The Empire of the Steppes: A History of Central Asia*, tr. N. Walford, New Brunswick, N.J., 1970; D. Sinor, *Introduction à l'étude de l'Eurasie centrale*, Wiesbaden, 1963 contains ample bibliographies. O. Lattimore, *Inner Asian Frontiers of China*, New York, 1951 is an imaginative interpretation of the formation of nomadism in Inner Asia and its relation to sedentary empires. L. Krader discusses Inner Asian social organization: *Peoples of Central Asia*, Bloomington, Ind., 1963, and *Social Organization of the Mongol-Turkic Pastoral Nomads*, The Hague, 1963.

On the Mongol, Chaghatay, and Timurid periods in Inner Asia see P. Brent, *The Mongol Empire: Genghis Khan, His Triumph and Legacy*, London, 1976; V. V. Bartold, *Histoire des Turcs d'Asie centrale*, Paris, 1945, and *Four Studies on the History of Central*

Asia, tr. V. and T. Minorsky, 3 vols., Leiden, 1956–62; J. A. Boyle, *The Mongol World Empire, 1206–1370*, London, 1977. Two important early histories have been translated: Rashid al-Din Tabib, *The Successors of Genghis Khan*, tr. J. A. Boyle, New York, 1971; M. Haydar (Dughlat), *A History of the Moghuls of Central Asia (Tarikh-i Rashidi)*, tr. E. D. Ross, New York, 1970.

For the Golden Horde see G. Vernadsky, *The Mongols and Russia*, New Haven, Conn., 1953. For the Russian conquest: A. S. Donnelly, *The Russian Conquest of Bashkiria, 1552–1740*, New Haven, Conn., 1968; C. Lemercier-Quelquejay, "Les Missions orthodoxes en pays musulmans de Moyenne et Basse Volga, 1552–1865," *CMRS*, VIII (1967), pp. 363–403; H. Carrère d'Encausse, "Les Routes commerciales de l'Asie Centrale et les tentatives de reconquête d'Astrakhan," *CMRS*, XI (1970), pp. 391–422. For the Crimea see A. Bennigsen *et al.*, *Le Khanat de Crimée dans les archives du Musée du Palais de Topkapi*, Paris, 1978; A. W. Fisher, *The Russian Annexation of the Crimea*, Cambridge, 1970.

On Kazakhs see R. Majerczak, "Renseignements historiques sur les Kazaks ou Kirghizes-Kazaks depuis la formation de la Horde Kazak jusqu'à la fin du XIXᵉ siècle," *Revue du monde musulman*, XLIII (1921), pp. 54–220; A. Hudson, *Kazak Social Structure*, New Haven, Conn., 1938; T. G. Winner, *The Oral Art and Literature of the Kazakhs of Russian Central Asia*, Durham, N.C., 1958; E. Bacon, *Central Asia under Russian Rule*, Ithaca, N.Y., 1966.

Bukhara and the Central Asian Khanates: M. Holdsworth, *Turkestan in the Nineteenth Century: A Brief History of the Khanates of Bukhara, Kokand and Khiva*, London, 1959; H. Carrère d'Encausse, *Réforme et révolution chez les musulmans de l'Empire russe: Bukhara, 1867–1924*, Paris, 1966. On Central Asian culture see E. Knobloch, *Beyond the Oxus: Archaeology, Art and Architecture of Central Asia*, London, 1972; N. Chadwick and V. Zhirmunsky, *Oral Epics of Central Asia*, London, 1969.

On Islam in Inner Asia see H. Algar, "The Naqshbandi Order: A Preliminary Survey of Its History and Significance," *SI*, XLIV (1976), pp. 123–52. Important Russian scholarship on Sufism in Turkestan and Turkmenistan includes S. M. Demidov, *Sufizm v Turkmenii: Evolutsiia i perezhitki* (Sufism in Turkmenia: Evolution and Remnants), Ashkhabad, 1978; M. B. Durdyev, "Dukhovenstvo v sisteme obshchestvennykh institutov turkmen kontsa XIX – nachala XX v." [The Clergy in the System of Social Institutions of the Turkmen at the End of the Nineteenth – beginning of the Twentieth Century], *Vestnik Moskovskogo Universiteta* [Moscow University Review], 1970, pp. 27–42; S. M. Demidov, "Magtymy" [The Magtyms], *Domusul'manskie verovanie i obriady v srednei azii* [Pre-Moslem Beliefs and Rites in Central Asia], Moscow, 1975; V. N. Basilov, "Honour Groups in Traditional Turkmenian Society," *Islam in Tribal Societies: From the Atlas to the Indus*, eds. A. S. Ahmed and D. M. Hart, London, 1984, pp. 220–43.

For the Muslims of China before the Chinese occupation of eastern Turkestan see M. Rossabi, *China and Inner Asia*, New York, 1975, and "The Muslims in the Early Yuan Dynasty," *China under Mongol Rule*, ed. J. Langlois, Princeton, 1981, pp. 257–95; R. Israeli, "The Muslim Minority in Traditional China," *Asian and African Studies*, X (1974–75), pp. 101–26, and "The Muslims under the Manchu Reign in China," *SI*, XLIX (1979), pp. 159–79.

The Khwajas of Kashgar and the nineteenth-century struggle for eastern Turkestan are the subject of T. Saguchi, "The Eastern Trade of the Khoqand Khanat," *Memoirs of the Research Department of the Toyo Bunko*, XXIV (1965), pp. 47–114; H. G. Schwarz, "The Khwajas of Eastern Turkestan," *Central Asiatic Journal*, XX (1976), pp. 266–96; T. Yuan, "Yakub Beg (1820–1877) and the Moslem Rebellion in Chinese Turkestan," *Central Asiatic Journal*, VI (1961), pp. 134–67. On other nineteenth-century Muslim rebellions see R. Israeli, "The Muslim Revival in 19th-Century China," *SI*, XLIII (1976), pp. 119–38; Wen-djang Chu, *The Moslem Rebellion in Northwest China*, 1966.

Chapter 18

The best general history of the Muslims in India is P. Hardy, *The Muslims of British India*, New York, 1973. See also H. G. Behr, *Die Moguln: Macht und Pracht der indischen Kaiser von 1369–1857*, Vienna, 1979. For histories written in the subcontinent see S. M. Ikram, *Muslim Civilization in India*, New York, 1964; M. Mujeeb, *The Indian Muslims*, Montreal, 1967; I. H. Qureshi, *The Muslim Community of the Indo-Pakistan Sub-continent, 610–1947*, Karachi, 1977; S. M. Haq, *Islamic Thought and Movements in the Subcontinent, 711–1947*, Karachi, 1979.

On the Delhi regime see V. D. Mahajan, *The Delhi Sultanate*, Delhi, 1981. Provincial Regimes: S. Dale, *Islamic Society on the South Asian Frontier: The Mappilas of Malabar 1498–1922*, Oxford, 1980; R. M. Eaton, *Sufis of Bijapur 1300–1700: Social Roles of Sufis in Medieval India*, Princeton, 1978; J. F. Richards, *Mughal Administration in Golconda*, London, 1976; A. Karim, *A Social History of the Muslims in Bengal Down to A.D. 1538*, Dacca, 1959.

On Mughal administration the principal works are I. Habib, *The Agrarian System of Mughal India 1556–1707*, Bombay, 1963; W. H. Moreland, *The Agrarian System of Moslem India*, Delhi, 1968; M. Athar ⁽Ali, *The Mughal Nobility under Aurangzeb*, Bombay, 1966; J. F. Richards, *Kingship and Authority in South Asia*, Madison, Wis., 1978.

For Islamic religion and culture see Aziz Ahmad, *Studies on Islamic Culture in the Indian Environment*, Oxford, 1969, and *An Intellectual History of Islam in India*, Edinburgh, 1969; A. Schimmel, *Islam in the Indian Subcontinent*, London, 1980; B. D. Metcalf, ed., *Moral Conduct and Authority: The Place of Adab in South Asian Islam*, Berkeley, Calif., 1984; A. Schimmel, *Mystical Dimensions of Islam*, Chapel Hill, N.C., 1975; J. A. Subhan, *Sufism: Its Saints and Shrines*, Lucknow, 1960; S. A. A. Rizvi, *A History of Sufism in India*, New Delhi, 1978.

On Islam under the Delhi Sultanate the principal contributor is K. A. Nizami, *Some Aspects of Religion and Politics in India during the Thirteenth Century*, Aligarh, 1961, and *Studies in Medieval Indian History and Culture*, Allahabad, 1966. On Sufism in the Mughal period see A. A. Rizvi, *Muslim Revivalist Movements in Northern India in the Sixteenth and Seventeenth Centuries*, Agra, 1965. Sirhindi is the subject of Y. Friedmann, *Shaykh Ahmad Sirhindi: An Outline of His Thought and a Study of His Image in the Eyes of Posterity*, Montreal, 1971. For translations and works concerning Shah Waliallah: Shah Waliullah, *Sufism and the Islamic Tradition: The Lamahat and Sata⁽at of Shah Waliullah*, tr. G. N. Jalbani, London, 1980; S. A. A. Rizvi, *Shah Wali-Allah and His Times: A Study of 18th Century Islam, Politics and Society in India*, Canberra, 1980.

Commerce in India and the Indian Ocean is the subject of M. N. Pearson, *Merchants and Rulers in Gujarat: The Response to the Portuguese in the Sixteenth Century*, Berkeley,

Calif., 1976; A. Das Gupta, *Malabar in Asian Trade: 1740–1800*, Cambridge, 1967, and *Indian Merchants and the Decline of Surat c. 1700–1750*, Wiesbaden, 1979; O. P. Singh, *Surat and Its Trade in the Second Half of the 17th Century*, Delhi, 1977.

On Muslim "sects": S. C. Misra, *Muslim Communities in Gujarat*, Bombay, 1964; A. Nanji, *The Nizari Ismaili Tradition in the Indo-Pakistan Subcontinent*, Delmar, N.Y., 1978.

Indian architecture and art are the subjects of S. C. Welch and M. C. Beach, *Gods, Thrones and Peacocks: Northern Indian Painting from Two Traditions: Fifteenth to Nineteenth Centuries*, New York, 1965; P. Brown, *Indian Architecture: Islamic Period*, Bombay, 1968; G. Hambly, *Cities of Mughal India*, New Delhi, 1977; R. Nath, *History of Sultanate Architecture*, New Delhi, 1978. On Mughal poetry see R. Russell and K. Islam, *Three Mughal Poets: Mir, Sauda, Mir Hasan*, Cambridge, 1968.

The decline of the Mughal empire and the transition to the British era are interpreted in C. A. Bayly, *Rulers, Townsmen, and Bazaars: North Indian Society in the Age of British Expansion*, Cambridge and New York, 1983; R. B. Barnett, *North India between Empires: Awdh, the Mughals, and the British, 1720–1801*, Berkeley, Calif., 1980.

Chapter 19

A survey of Southeast Asian peoples is given by H. Geertz, "Indonesian Cultures and Communities," *Indonesia*, ed. R. T. McVey, New Haven, Conn., 1963, pp. 24–96. Brief historical introductions are to be found in H. J. Benda, "The Structure of Southeast Asian History: Some Preliminary Observations," *Journal of Southeast Asian History*, III (1962), pp. 106–38; W. Roff, "South-East Asian Islam in the Nineteenth Century," *Cambridge History of Islam*, II, Cambridge, 1970, pp. 155–81. For a fuller history see B. H. M. Vlekke, *Nusantara: A History of Indonesia*, The Hague, 1959. On trade and society see J. C. van Leur, *Indonesian Trade and Society*, trs. J. S. Holmes and A. van Marle, The Hague, 1955; B. J. O. Schrieke, *Indonesian Sociological Studies*, 2 vols., The Hague, 1955, 1957; W. F. Wertheim, *Indonesian Society in Transition*, The Hague, 1959.

Origins and diffusion of Islam in Indonesia: C. A. Majul, "Theories on the Introduction and Expansion of Islam in Malaysia," *Sulliman Journal*, XI (1964), pp. 335–98; M. C. Ricklefs, "Six Centuries of Islamization in Java," *Conversion to Islam*, ed. N. Levtzion, New York and London, 1979, pp. 100–28; C. C. Berg, "The Islamisation of Java," *SI*, IV (1955), pp. 111–42; A. H. Johns, "From Coastal Settlement to Islamic School and City: Islamization in Sumatra, the Malay Peninsula and Java," *Hamdard Islamicus*, IV (1981), pp. 3–28.

For Southeast Asian trade see O. W. Wolters, *The Fall of Srivijaya in Malay History*, Ithaca, N.Y., 1970. For Dutch and British commerce and colonial empires see F. S. Gaastra, J. R. Bruijn and I. Schoffer, eds., *Dutch–Asiatic Shipping in the Seventeenth and Eighteenth Centuries*, 3 vols., The Hague, 1979; K. Glamann, *Dutch–Asiatic Trade, 1620–1740*, Copenhagen, 1958; A. Reid, *The Contest for North Sumatra: Atjeh, the Netherlands, and Britain, 1858–1898*, Kuala Lumpur and New York, 1969; J. S. Bastin, *The Changing Balance of the Early Southeast Asian Pepper Trade*, Kuala Lumpur, 1980; J. S. Bastin and R. Roolvink, eds., *Malayan and Indonesian Studies*, Oxford, 1964; J. S.

Furnivall, *Colonial Policy and Practice: A Comparative Study of Burma and Netherlands India*, Cambridge, 1948; *Netherlands India: A Study of Plural Economy*, Cambridge, 1944.

For Java see C. Geertz, *The Religion of Java*, Glencoe, Ill., 1960; B. Anderson, "The Idea of Power in Javanese Culture," *Culture and Politics in Indonesia*, ed. C. Holt, Ithaca, N.Y., 1972, pp. 1–69; S. Moertono, *State and Statecraft in Old Java: A Study of the Later Mataram Period, 16th to 19th Century*, Ithaca, N.Y., 1968.

Minangkabau and the Padri movement have been studied by C. Dobbin, *Islamic Revivalism in a Changing Peasant Economy: Central Sumatra 1784–1847*, London, 1983; P. E. Josselin de Jong, *Minangkabau and Negri Sembilan: Socio-Political Structure in Indonesia*, Leiden, 1951. C. S. Hurgronje, *The Achehnese*, 2 vols., tr. A. W. S. O'Sullivan, Leiden and London, 1906 is the classical study of this north Sumatran Muslim society.

On Sufism there are several articles by A. H. Johns: "Muslim Mystics and Historical Writing," *Historians of South-East Asia*, ed. D. G. E. Hall, London, 1961–62, pp. 37–49, "Islam in Southeast Asia: Reflections and New Directions," *Indonesia*, XIX (1975), pp. 33–55, "Friends in Grace: Ibrahim al-Kurani and ʿAbd al-Raʾuf al-Singkeli," *Spectrum: Essays Presented to Sultan Takdir Alisjahbana on His Seventieth Birthday*, ed. S. Udin, Jakarta, 1978, pp. 469–85.

The history of Malaya is treated by J. Kennedy, *A History of Malaya, A.D. 1400–1959*, London and New York, 1962; K. G. Tregonning, *Papers on Malayan History*, Singapore, 1962; R. O. Winstedt, *The Malays: A Cultural History*, London, 1961, *A History of Classical Malay Literature*, Kuala Lumpur, 1969. For political institutions see J. M. Gullick, *Indigenous Political Systems of Western Malaya*, London, 1965.

Chapter 20

Two good bibliographies are P. E. Ofori, *Islam in Africa South of the Sahara: A Select Bibliographic Guide*, Nendeln, 1977; S. M. Zoghby, *Islam in Sub-Saharan Africa: A Partially Annotated Guide*, Washington, D.C., 1978. Valuable introductory histories include R. A. Oliver and J. D. Fage, *A Short History of Africa*, 3rd edn, Harmondsworth, 1970; *The Cambridge History of Africa*, 8 vols., Cambridge, 1975– ; J. S. Trimingham, *The Influence of Islam upon Africa*, Beirut, 1968. Important collections of articles include I. M. Lewis, ed., *Islam in Tropical Africa*, London, 1966; J. Kritzeck and W. H. Lewis, eds., *Islam in Africa*, New York, 1969. Studies of special topics with African-wide scope are J. N. D. Anderson, *Islamic Law in Africa*, London, 1954; A. G. B. and H. J. Fisher, *Slavery and Muslim Society in Africa: The Institution in Saharan and Sudanic Africa, and the Trans-Saharan Trade*, London, 1970; C. Meillassoux, ed., *L'Esclavage en Afrique pré-coloniale*, Paris, 1975.

For histories of Islam in West Africa see J. S. Trimingham, *A History of Islam in West Africa*, London, New York, 1962; J. D. Fage, *History of West Africa*, Cambridge, 1969; D. McCall and N. Bennett, *Aspects of West African Islam*, Boston, Mass., 1971; C. Meillassoux, *The Development of Indigenous Trade and Markets in West Africa*, London, 1971; J. F. A. Ajayi and M. Crowder, eds., *History of West Africa*, 2 vols., London, 1976; J. R. Willis, ed., *Studies in West African Islamic History*, London, 1979; P. B. Clarke, *West Africa and Islam*, London, 1982. An unusual study of the integration of pagan and Muslim culture in West Africa is R. A. Bravman, *Islamic and Tribal Art in West Africa*, London, 1974. For the Almoravid movement see the bibliography for Chapter 16.

On Mali, an early Muslim empire, see C. Monteil, *Les Empires du Mali*, Paris, 1930; D. T. Niane, *Sundiata: An Epic of Old Mali*, tr. G. D. Pickett, London, 1965; N. Levtzion, *Ancient Ghana and Mali*, London, 1973. For the Songhay empire see J. Boulnois and B. Hama, *L'Empire de Gao*, Paris, 1954.

Timbuktu is the subject of H. M. Miner, *The Primitive City of Timbucktoo*, Garden City, N.Y., 1965; S. M. Cissoko, *Tombouctou et l'empire Songhai*, Dakar, 1976; M. Abitbol, *Tombouctou et les arma*, Paris, 1979; E. N. Saad, *Social History of Timbuktu: The Role of Muslim Scholars and Notables, 1400–1900*, Cambridge, 1983.

For Hausaland from the fourteenth century to the jihad of ʿUthman don Fodio see M. G. Smith, "The Beginnings of Hausa Society, A.D. 1000–1500," *The Historian in Tropical Africa*, eds., J. Vansina, R. Mauny and L. V. Thomas, London, 1964, pp. 339–57; F. Fuglestad, "A Reconstruction of Hausa History before the Jihad," *JAH*, XIX (1978), pp. 319–39; J. E. G. Sutton, "Towards a Less Orthodox History of Hausaland," *JAH*, XX (1979), pp. 179–201; M. Hiskett, "An Islamic Tradition of Reform in the Western Sudan from the Sixteenth to the Eighteenth Century," *BSOAS*, XXV (1962), pp. 577–96.

For Bornu see A. Schultze, *The Sultanate of Bornu*, tr. P. A. Benton, London, 1968; L. Brenner, *The Shehus of Kukawa: A History of the Al-Kanemi Dynasty of Bornu*, Oxford, 1973.

Mauritania: D. G. Lavroff, *Introduction à la Mauritanie*, Paris, 1979; C. C. Stewart with E. K. Stewart, *Islam and Social Order in Mauritania*, Oxford, 1973; H. T. Norris, *Shinqiti Folk Literature and Songs*, Oxford, 1968, and *The Tuaregs: Their Islamic Legacy and Its Diffusion in the Sahel*, Warminster, 1975.

On Muslim merchants and scholars: P. D. Curtin, *Economic Change in Precolonial Africa*, Madison, Wis., 1974; P. E. Lovejoy, "The Role of the Wangara in the Economic Transformation of the Central Sudan in the Fifteenth and Sixteenth Centuries," *JAH*, XIX (1978), pp. 173–93; C. C. Stewart, "Southern Saharan Scholarship and the *Bilad Al-Sudan*," *JAH*, XVII (1976), pp. 73–93. L. O. Sanneh stresses the clerical rather than the commercial groups: *The Jakhanke: The History of an Islamic Clerical People of the Senegambia*, London, 1979.

On Islam in Ghana the principal contribution is N. Levtzion, *Muslims and Chiefs in West Africa*, Oxford, 1968. On Muslims in the Ashanti empire of Ghana see I. Wilks, *The Northern Factor in Ashanti History*, Legon, Ghana, 1961, and *Asante in the Nineteenth Century*, London, 1975.

For Sierra Leone see D. Skinner, "Islam and Education in the Colony and Hinterland of Sierra Leone (1750–1914)," *Canadian Journal of African Studies*, X (1976), pp. 499–520, and "Mande Settlement and the Development of Islamic Institutions in Sierra Leone," *IJAHS*, XI (1978), pp. 32–62.

Important studies of the great eighteenth- and nineteenth-century jihads include J. R. Willis, "Jihad fi Sabil Allah: Its Doctrinal Basis in Islam and Some Aspects of Its Evolution in Nineteenth Century West Africa," *JAH*, VIII (1967), pp. 395–415; M. Hiskett, "The Nineteenth-Century Jihads in West Africa," *The Cambridge History of Africa, 1790–1870*, V, ed. J. E. Flint, Cambridge, 1976, pp. 125–69; M. Last, *The Sokoto*

Caliphate, New York, 1967; H. A. S. Johnston, *The Fulani Empire of Sokoto*, London, 1967; M. Hiskett, *The Sword of Truth: The Life and Times of the Shehu Usuman Dan Fodio*, New York, 1973. For the Sokoto Caliphate: M. G. Smith, *Government in Zazzau, 1800–1950*, London and New York, 1960; R. A. Adeleye, *Power and Diplomacy in Northern Nigeria, 1804–1906*, London, 1971; V. N. Low, *Three Nigerian Emirates*, Evanston, Ill., 1972. On the trade and economy of northern Nigeria in this period see J. P. Smaldane, *Warfare in the Sokoto Caliphate*, Cambridge, 1974; P. E. Lovejoy, "Plantations in the Economy of the Sokoto Caliphate," *JAH*, xix (1978), pp. 341–68.

The eastern offshoots of ʿUthman's jihad are treated in S. Abubakar, *The Lamibe of Fombina: A Political History of Adamawa, 1809–1901*, Zaria, Nigeria, 1977; A. D. Babikir, *L'Empire de Rabeh*, Paris, 1950. On the western offshoots A. H. Ba and J. Daget, *L'Empire peul du Macina*, Paris, 1962.

For the jihads in Senegambia and Mauritania see M. A. Klein, "Social and Economic Factors in the Muslim Revolution in Senegambia," *JAH*, xiii (1972), pp. 419–41; J. R. Willis, "The Torodbe Clerisy: A Social View," *JAH*, xix (1978), pp. 195–212.

For al-Hajj ʿUmar see B. G. Martin, *Muslim Brotherhoods in Nineteenth-Century Africa*, Cambridge, 1976, pp. 68–217. For the Umarian state see B. O. Oloruntimehin, *The Segu Tukulor Empire*, London, 1972; Y. Saint-Martin, *L'Empire toucouleur, 1848–1897*, Paris, 1970; R. L. Roberts, "Production and Reproduction of Warrior States: Segu Bambara and Segu Tokolor, *c.* 1712–1890," *IJAHS*, xiii (1980), pp. 389–419. For comparative purposes see D. Forde and P. M. Kaberry, eds., *West African Kingdoms in the Nineteenth Century*, London, 1967.

The principal contributions to the study of the Senegambian region in the nineteenth century are M. A. Klein, *Islam and Imperialism in Senegal*, Stanford, Calif. and Edinburgh, 1968; Charlotte A. Quinn, *Mandingo Kingdoms of the Senegambia*, Evanston, Ill., 1972; P. D. Curtin, *Economic Change in Procolonial Africa: Senegambia in the Era of the Slave Trade*, Madison, Wis., 1975; D. W. Robinson, *Chiefs and Clerics: Abdul Bokar Kan and Futa Toro, 1853–1891*, Oxford, 1975; T. Diallo, *Les Institutions politiques du Fouta Dyallon au XIXe siècle*, Dakar, 1972. See also L. G. Colvin, "Islam and the State of Kajoor: A Case of Successful Resistance to Jihad," *JAH*, xv (1974), pp. 587–606. The conversion of the Wolof is discussed in L. Behrman, "The Islamization of the Wolof by the End of the Nineteenth Century," *Western African History*, iv, eds. D. McCall, N. Bennett, and J. Butler, New York, 1969, pp. 102–31. On French policy in Senegal at the beginning of the colonial era see G. W. Johnson, *The Emergence of Black Politics in Senegal: The Struggle for Power in the Four Communes, 1900–1920*, Stanford, Calif., 1971.

The principal study of Samory is Y. Person, *Samori: Une révolution dyula*, Dakar, 1968–75.

On Muslim brotherhoods and religious teaching in West Africa see J. M. Abun-Nasr, *The Tijaniyya: A Sufi Order in the Modern World*, London and New York, 1965; B. G. Martin, *Muslim Brotherhoods in Nineteenth-Century Africa*, Cambridge, 1976.

Chapter 21

For overviews of East African history see R. Oliver and G. Matthew, eds., *History of East Africa*, I, Oxford, 1963; V. Harlow and E. M. Chilver, eds., *History of East Africa*, II, Oxford, 1965; *The Cambridge History of Africa, 1050–1600*, III, ed. K. Oliver, Cambridge, 1977; *The Cambridge History of Africa, 1600–1790*, IV, ed. R. Gray, Cambridge, 1975.

On the early history of Muslim settlement see H. N. Chittick, *Kilwa: An Islamic Trading City on the East African Coast*, Nairobi, 1974; P. S. Garlake, *The Early Islamic Architecture of the East African Coast*, Nairobi and London, 1966; G. S. P. Freeman-Grenville, *The Medieval History of the Coast of Tanganyika*, London and New York, 1962. An important revision of the subject is underway. See R. L. Pouwels, "The Medieval Foundations of East African Islam," *IJAHS*, XI (1978), pp. 201–26, 393–409; J. de V. Allen, "Swahili Culture and the Nature of East Coast Settlement," *IJAHS*, XIV (1981), pp. 306–34; J. C. Wilkinson, "Oman and East Africa: New Light on Early Kilwan History from the Omani Sources," *IJAHS*, XIV (1981), pp. 272–305.

On Zanzibar and the development of coastal trade with the interior see C. S. Nicholls, *The Swahili Coast: Politics, Diplomacy and Trade on the East African Littoral, 1798–1856*, London, 1971; L. Farrant, *Tippu Tip and the East African Slave Trade*, London, 1975; N. R. Bennett, *Mirambo of Tanzania ca. 1840–1884*, New York, 1971.

For Ethiopia see J. S. Trimingham, *Islam in Ethiopia*, London, 1965; M. Abir, *Ethiopia: The Era of the Princes*, New York, 1968; J. Cuoq, *L'Islam en Éthiopie des origines au seizième siècle*, Paris, 1981.

On Somalia see I. M. Lewis, *Peoples of the Horn of Africa, Somali, Afar and Saho*, London, 1969; D. D. Laitin, *Polity, Language and Thought: The Somali Experience*, Chicago, 1977; L. V. Cassanelli, *The Shaping of Somali Society: Reconstructing the History of a Pastoral People, 1600–1900*, Philadelphia, Pa., 1982.

For the Sudan see J. S. Trimingham, *Islam in the Sudan*, London, 1965; P. M. Holt and M. W. Daly, *The History of the Sudan from the Coming of Islam to the Present Day*, 3rd edn, London, 1979; Y. F. Hasan, *The Arabs and the Sudan: From the Seventh to the Early Sixteenth Century*, Edinburgh, 1967; R. S. O'Fahey and J. L. Spaulding, *Kingdoms of the Sudan*, London, 1974; R. S. O'Fahey, *State and Society in Dar Fur*, London, 1980.

For African society on the eve of colonialism see E. Colson, "African Society at the Time of the Scramble," *Colonialism in Africa: The History and Politics of Colonialism 1870–1914*, I, eds. L. H. Gann and P. Duignan, Cambridge, 1969, pp. 27–65 and other essays in this volume. On the rise of colonial domination see M. Crowder, "West Africa and the Europeans: Five Hundred Years of Direct Contact," *Colonial West Africa: Collected Essays*, London, 1978, pp. 1–25; P. Ehrensaft, "The Political Economy of Informal Empire in Pre-Colonial Nigeria, 1807–1884," *Canadian Journal of African Studies*, VI (1972), pp. 451–90. The diplomatic background of the European scramble for Africa is included in R. Robinson and J. Gallagher, *Africa and the Victorians*, New York, 1961; J. D. Hargreaves, *Prelude to the Partition of West Africa*, London and New York, 1963.

PART III

Introduction

On the contemporary Islamic world see J. Voll, *Islam: Continuity and Change in the Modern World*, Boulder, Col., 1982; M. Ruthven, *Islam in the World*, New York, 1984.

Chapter 22

Of the general histories of modern Iran, N. R. Keddie, *Roots of Revolution: An Interpretive History of Modern Iran*, New Haven, Conn., 1981 is up-to-date and well balanced. Iran's foreign relations are discussed in M. E. Yapp, *Strategies of British India: Britain, Iran, and Afghanistan, 1798–1850*, Oxford, 1980; R. K. Ramazani, *Iran's Foreign Policy, 1941–1973*, Charlottesville, Va., 1975; S. Chubin and S. Zabih, *The Foreign Relations of Iran*, Berkeley, Calif., 1974; F. Kazemzadeh, *Russia and Britain in Persia, 1864–1914: A Study in Imperialism*, New Haven, Conn., 1968.

On nineteenth-century Iran under the Qajars see S. Bakhash, *Iran: Monarchy, Bureaucracy, and Reform under the Qajars, 1858–1896*, London, 1978; N. R. Keddie, "The Iranian Power Structure and Social Change, 1800–1969: An Overview," *IJMES*, II (1971), pp. 3–20; E. Abrahamian, "Oriental Despotism: The Case of Qajar Iran," *IJMES*, V (1974), pp. 3–31.

Iran's economic history is covered by C. P. Issawi, *The Economic History of Iran, 1800–1914*, Chicago, 1971; A. Ashraf and H. Hekmat, "Merchants and Artisans and the Developmental Processes of Nineteenth-Century Iran," *The Islamic Middle East, 700–1900: Studies in Economic and Social History*, ed. A. L. Udovitch, Princeton, 1981, pp. 725–50.

Iran under the Pahlavis: A. Banani, *The Modernization of Iran, 1921–1941*, Stanford, 1961; E. Abrahamian, *Iran Between Two Revolutions*, Princeton, 1982; J. Bharier, *Economic Development in Iran, 1900–1970*, London, 1971; J. Amuzegar and M. A. Fekrat, *Iran: Economic Development under Dualistic Conditions*, Chicago, 1971. Post-World War II institutions and political struggle are treated in R. W. Cottam, *Nationalism in Iran*, Pittsburgh, Pa., 1964; L. Binder, *Iran: Political Development in a Changing Society*, Berkeley, Calif., 1962; M. Zonis, *The Political Elite of Iran*, Princeton, N.J., 1971; J. A. Bill, *The Politics of Iran: Groups, Classes, and Modernization*, Columbus, Ohio, 1972; S. Zabih, *The Mossadegh Era: Roots of the Iranian Revolution*, Chicago, 1982; E. J. Hooglund, *Land and Revolution in Iran, 1960–1980*, Austin, Texas, 1982.

Relations of ʿulamaʾ and the state are the subject of H. Algar, *Religion and State in Iran, 1785–1906: The Role of the Ulama in the Qajar Period*, Berkeley, Calif., 1969, and "The Oppositional Role of the Ulama in Twentieth-Century Iran," *Scholars, Saints and Sufis*, ed. N. R. Keddie, Berkeley, Calif., 1972, pp. 231–55; N. R. Keddie, *Religion and Rebellion in Iran: The Tobacco Protest of 1891–1892*, London, 1966; H. Algar, *Mirza Malkum Khan: A Study in the History of Iranian Modernism*, Berkeley, Calif., 1973. On the Constitutional Revolution of 1906–11: N. R. Keddie, "Iranian Politics 1900–1905: Background to Revolution," *Middle Eastern Studies*, V (1969), pp. 3–31, 151–67, 234–50; S. Arjomand, "The Shi-ite Hierocracy and the State in Pre-Modern Iran, 1785–1890," *European Journal of Sociology*, XXII (1981), pp. 40–78; S. Akhavi, *Religion and Politics in Contemporary Iran: Clergy–State Relations in the Pahlavi Period*, Albany, N.Y.,

1980; Y. Richard, *Le Shiʿisme en Iran: Imam et révolution*, Paris, 1980; P. J. Chelkowski, ed., *Taʿziyeh, Ritual and Drama in Iran*, New York, 1979; M. M. J. Fischer, *Iran: From Religious Dispute to Revolution*, Cambridge, Mass., 1980; Ayatollah Ruhollah Khomeini, *Islamic Government*, tr. Joint Publications Research Service, New York, 1979.

A number of stimulating assessments of the revolution include the work of S. A. Arjomand, "Shiʿite Islam and the Revolution in Iran," *Government and Opposition*, XVI (1981), pp. 293–316; "Traditionalism in Twentieth-Century Iran" *From Nationalism to Revolutionary Islam*, ed. S. A. Arjomand, London, 1984, pp. 195–232; T. Skocpol, "Rentier State and Shiʿa Islam in the Iranian Revolution," *Theory and Society*, XI (1982), pp. 265–83; N. R. Keddie, "Iranian Revolutions in Comparative Perspective," *American Historical Review*, LXXXVIII (1983), pp. 579–98.

On contemporary social structure see P. W. English, *City and Village in Iran: Settlement and Economy in the Kirman Basin*, Madison, Wis., 1966; J. I. Clarke, *The Iranian City of Shiraz*, Durham, 1963; M. E. Bonine, *Yazd and Its Hinterland: A Central Place System of Dominance in the Central Iranian Plateau*, Austin, Texas, 1975; P. G. Ahrens, *Die Entwicklung der Stadt Teheran. Eine städtebauliche Untersuchung ihrer zukunftigen Gestaltung*, Opladen, 1966. An outstanding book on a declining pastoral society is F. Barth, *Nomads of South Persia: The Basseri Tribe of the Khamseh Confederacy*, Boston, Mass., 1961.

On the place of women in Iranian society see G. Nashat, ed., *Women and Revolution in Iran*, Boulder, Col., 1983; E. Sanasarian, *The Women's Rights Movement in Iran*, New York, 1982; F. Azari, *Women of Iran: The Conflict with Fundamentalist Islam*, London, 1983; A. K. Ferdows, "Women and the Islamic Revolution," *IJMES*, XV (1983), pp. 283–98.

Chapter 23

Turkey's relations with Europe are the subject of M. S. Anderson, *The Eastern Question, 1774–1923*, London, 1966; S. J. Shaw, *Between Old and New: The Ottoman Empire under Sultan Selim III, 1789–1807*, Cambridge, Mass., 1971; C. K. Webster, *The Foreign Policy of Castlereagh, 1812–1815*, London, 1931; H. W. V. Temperley, *The Foreign Policy of Canning, 1822–1827*, London, 1966; C. K. Webster, *The Foreign Policy of Palmerston, 1830–1841*, London, 1951; J. C. Hurewitz, "The Background of Russia's Claims to the Turkish Straits: A Reassessment," *Belleten, Türk Tarih Kurumu*, XXVIII (1964), pp. 459–97; V. J. Puryear, *England, Russia and the Straits Question, 1844–1856*, Berkeley, Calif., 1931; F. E. Bailey, *British Policy and the Turkish Reform Movement: A Study in Anglo-Turkish Relations, 1826–1853*, London, 1942.

On the Crimean War, Russia and the Balkans see B. H. Sumner, *Russia and the Balkans, 1870–1880*, Oxford, 1937; H. Temperley, *England and the Near East: The Crimea*, London, 1936; W. L. Langer, *The Diplomacy of Imperialism, 1890–1902*, 2nd edn, New York, 1960, and *European Alliances and Alignments, 1871–1890*, 2nd edn, New York, 1962; D. Harris, *A Diplomatic History of the Balkan Crisis of 1875–1878: The First Year*, London, 1936; E. M. Earle, *Turkey, the Great Powers, and the Baghdad Railway*, New York, 1935.

World War I and the partition of the Ottoman empire: H. N. Howard, *The Partition of Turkey: A Diplomatic History, 1913–1923*, Norman, Okla., 1931; E. Kedourie, *England and the Middle East: The Destruction of the Ottoman Empire, 1914–1921*, 2nd edn, Hassocks,

1978; F. G. Weber, *Eagles on the Crescent: Germany, Austria and the Diplomacy of the Turkish Alliance, 1914–1918*, Ithaca, N.Y., 1970; C. Jelavich and B. Jelavich, *The Establishment of the Balkan National States, 1804–1920*, Seattle, Wash., 1977; P. Helmreich, *From Paris to Sèvres: The Partition of the Ottoman Empire at the Peace Conference of 1919–1920*, Columbus, Ohio, 1974; H. N. Howard, *Turkey, the Straits and U.S. Policy*, Baltimore, Md., 1974. On the Armenian question see R. G. Hovannisian, *The Armenian Holocaust: A Bibliography Relating to the Deportations, Massacres, and Dispersion of the Armenian People, 1912–1915*, Cambridge, 1980, *Armenia on the Road to Independence*, Berkeley, Calif., 1984, *The Republic of Armenia*, 2 vols., Berkeley, Calif., 1971, 1982.

The development of the Middle Eastern economy: R. Owen, *The Middle East in the World Economy, 1800–1914*, New York, 1981. See also C. Issawi, ed., *The Economic History of Turkey, 1800–1914*, Chicago, 1980, and *The Economic History of the Middle East, 1800–1914*, Chicago, 1966; D. Quataert, *Social Disintegration and Popular Resistance in the Ottoman Empire 1881–1908*, New York, 1983.

On reform and modernization of the Ottoman empire, the most comprehensive surveys are B. Lewis, *The Emergence of Modern Turkey*, 2nd edn, London, 1968; N. Berkes, *The Development of Secularism in Turkey*, Montreal, 1964; R. H. Davison, *Reform in the Ottoman Empire, 1856–1876*, Princeton, 1963; R. Devereaux, *The First Ottoman Constitutional Period: A Study of the Midhat Constitution and Parliament*, Baltimore, Md., 1963; S. Mardin, "Power, Civil Society and Culture in the Ottoman Empire," *Comparative Studies in Society and History*, XI (1969), pp. 258–81.

Works concerning institutional modernization include C. V. Findley, *Bureaucratic Reform in the Ottoman Empire: The Sublime Porte, 1789–1922*, Princeton, 1980; S. S. Omar, "The Majalla," *Law in the Middle East*, I, eds. M. Khadduri and H. J. Liebesny, Washington, D.C., 1956, pp. 292–308; G. Baer, "The Transition from Traditional to Western Criminal Law in Turkey and Egypt," *SI*, XLV (1977), pp. 139–58; A. M. Kazamias, *Education and the Quest for Modernity in Turkey*, Chicago, 1966; S. J. Shaw, "The Origins of Representative Government in the Ottoman Empire: An Introduction to the Provincial Councils, 1839–1876," *Near Eastern Round Table, 1967–1968*, ed. R. B. Winder, New York, 1969, pp. 53–142.

The principal studies of the Ottoman intelligentsia are S. Mardin, *The Genesis of Young Ottoman Thought*, Princeton, 1962; E. E. Ramsaur, *The Young Turks: Prelude to the Revolution of 1908*, Princeton, 1957; F. Ahmad, *The Young Turks: The Committee of Union and Progress in Turkish Politics, 1908–1914*, Oxford, 1969; D. Kushner, *The Rise of Turkish Nationalism, 1876–1908*, London, 1977.

Ottoman ʿulamaʾ and the state are the subject of U. Heyd, "The Ottoman ʿUlemā and Westernization in the Time of Selim III and Mahmud II," *Studies in Islamic History and Civilization*, ed. U. Heyd, Jerusalem, 1961, pp. 63–96; R. L. Chambers, "The Ottoman Ulema and the Tanzimat," *Scholars, Saints and Sufis*, ed. N. R. Keddie, Berkeley, Calif., 1972, pp. 33–46.

For Ataturk and the Turkish Republic see R. D. Robinson, *The First Turkish Republic*, Cambridge, Mass., 1965; Lord Kinross, *Ataturk: The Rebirth of a Nation*, London, 1964; C. Keyder, *The Definition of a Peripheral Economy: Turkey, 1923–1929*, Cambridge, Mass., 1981.

For Turkish politics and economy since World War II see K. H. Karpat, *Turkey's Politics: The Transition to a Multi-party System*, Princeton, 1959, and *Social Change and*

Politics in Turkey: A Structural-historical Analysis, Leiden, 1973; F. Ahmad, *The Turkish Experiment in Democracy, 1950–1975*, Boulder, Col., 1977; E. K. Trimberger, *Revolution from Above*, New Brunswick, N.J., 1978; J. M. Landau, *Radical Politics in Modern Turkey*, Leiden, 1974. On Turkish economic development see B. Berberoglu, *Turkey in Crisis: From State Capitalism to Neo-colonialism*, London, 1982.

On local politics see J. S. Szyliowicz, *Political Change in Rural Turkey: Erdemli*, The Hague, 1966; K. H. Karpat, *The Gecekondu: Rural Migration and Urbanization*, New York, 1976. See also A. P. Sterling, *Turkish Village*, London, 1965; M. Makal, *A Village in Anatolia*, ed. A. P. Stirling, tr. Sir W. Deedes, London, 1954, a touching account of the efforts of a teacher to bring the revolution to rural Turkey; M. E. Meeker, "The Great Family Aghas of Turkey: A Study of a Changing Political Culture," *Rural Politics and Social Change in the Middle East*, eds. R. Antoun and I. Harik, Bloomington, Ind., 1972, pp. 237–66.

The revival of Islam: U. Heyd, *Revival of Islam in Modern Turkey*, Jerusalem, 1968; S. Mardin, "Religion in Modern Turkey," *International Social Science Journal*, xxix (1977), pp. 279–97; J. Landau, "The National Salvation Party in Turkey," *Asian and African Studies*, xi (1976), pp. 1–57; I. Sunar and B. Toprak, "Islam in Politics: The Case of Turkey," *Government and Opposition*, xviii (1983), pp. 421–41.

On the role of women see N. Abadan-Unat, "The Modernization of Turkish Women," *Middle East Journal*, xxxii (1978), pp. 291–306, and *Women in Turkish Society*, Leiden, 1981.

Chapter 24

General histories of Egypt in the nineteenth and twentieth centuries include P. M. Holt, *Egypt and the Fertile Crescent, 1516–1922: A Political History*, London, 1966; J. Marlowe, *A History of Modern Egypt and Anglo-Egyptian Relations, 1800–1956*, 2nd edn, Hamden, Conn., 1965. Collected articles dealing with the social transformation of Egyptian society are found in P. M. Holt, ed., *Political and Social Change in Modern Egypt*, London, 1968; G. Baer, *Studies on the Social History of Modern Egypt*, Chicago, 1969. Also see J. Abu Lughod, *Cairo: 1001 Years of the City Victorious*, Princeton, 1971. The classic description of Egyptian society is E. Lane, *An Account of the Manners and Customs of the Modern Egyptians*, London, 1842, republished as *The Modern Egyptians*, London, 1908.

Books dealing with the economic development of Egypt in the nineteenth century: D. S. Landes, *Bankers and Pashas: International Finance and Economic Imperialism in Egypt*, New York, 1958; E. R. J. Owen, *Cotton and the Egyptian Economy, 1820–1914*, Oxford, 1969; A. Richards, *Egypt's Agricultural Development, 1800–1980: Technical and Social Change*, Boulder, Col., 1982. On the long-range patterns of Egyptian economic development: C. Issawi, "Egypt since 1800: A Study in Lop-sided Development," *Journal of Economic History*, xxi (1961), pp. 1–25; P. O'Brien, "The Long-term Growth of Agricultural Production in Egypt: 1821–1962," *Political and Social Change in Modern Egypt*, ed. P. M. Holt, London, 1968, pp. 162–95; A. Richards, "Growth and Technical Change: 'Internal' and 'External' Sources of Egyptian Underdevelopment, 1800–1914," *Asian and African Studies*, xv (1981), pp. 45–67.

Muhammad ᶜAli and nineteenth-century reforms: P. Gran, *Islamic Roots of Capital-*

ism: Egypt, 1760–1840, Austin, Texas, 1979 is suggestive but not reliable. H. H. Dodwell, *The Founder of Modern Egypt: A Study of Muhammad ʿAli in Egypt*, Cambridge, 1931; H. Rivlin, *The Agricultural Policy of Muhammad ʿAli in Egypt*, Cambridge, Mass., 1961. Muhammad ʿAli's Foreign Policy: V. J. Puryear, *Napoleon and the Dardanelles*, Berkeley, Calif., 1951; Shafik Ghurbal, *The Beginnings of the Egyptian Question and the Rise of Mehmet Ali*, London, 1928. Ismaʿil Pasha and Egypt in the mid-nineteenth century: G. Douin, *Histoire du règne du khédive Ismaʿil*, 3 vols., Rome, 1933–41.

Egypt under British Rule, 1882–1922: A. Scholch, *Egypt for the Egyptians: The Sociopolitical Crisis in Egypt, 1878–1882*, London, 1981; A. L. al-Sayyid Marsot, *Egypt and Cromer: A Study in Anglo-Egyptian Relations*, New York, 1968; J. Berque, *L'Égypte, l'imperialisme et révolution*, Paris, 1967.

For the ʿulamaʾ and Sufism in the nineteenth century: A. L. al-Sayyid Marsot, "The Role of the ʿUlama in Egypt during the Early 19th Century," *Political and Social Change in Modern Egypt*, ed. P. M. Holt, London, 1968, pp. 264–80, and "The Beginnings of Modernization among the Rectors of al-Azhar, 1798–1879," *Beginnings of Modernization in the Middle East*, eds. W. R. Polk and R. L. Chambers, Chicago, 1968, pp. 267–80; F. de Jong, *Turuq and Turuq-linked Institutions in Nineteenth-Century Egypt*, Leiden, 1978; P. Kahle, "Zār-Beschwörungen im Egypten, *Der Islam*, III (1912), pp. 1–41.

Egypt under the Parliamentary Regime: M. Deeb, *Party Politics in Egypt: The Wafd and Its Rivals, 1919–1939*, London, 1979; A. L. al-Sayyid Marsot, *Egypt's Liberal Experiment, 1922–1936*, Berkeley, Calif., 1977. Egyptian Nationalism and Islam in the interwar years: J. Heyworth-Dunne, *Religious and Political Trends: Modern Egypt*, Washington, D.C., 1950; N. Safran, *Egypt in Search of Political Community*, Cambridge, Mass., 1961; C. Wendell, *The Evolution of the Egyptian National Image: From Its Origins to Ahmad Lutfi al-Sayyid*, Berkeley, Calif., 1972; C. D. Smith, *Islam and the Search for Social Order in Modern Egypt*, Albany, N.Y., 1983; Taha Husayn, *Stream of Days: At the Azhar*, 2nd edn, tr. H. Wayment, London,, 1948; P. Cachia, *Taha Husayn: His Place in the Egyptian Literary Renaissance*, London, 1956.

For introductions to modern Egyptian literature see H. Kilpatrick, *The Modern Egyptian Novel*, London, 1974; H. Sakkut, *The Egyptian Novel and Its Main Trends from 1913 to 1952*, Cairo, 1971.

Egypt under Nasser and Sadat: A. Abdel-Malek, *Egypt: Military Society; The Army Regime, the Left and Social Change under Nasser*, tr. C. L. Markmann, New York, 1968, and *Idéologie et renaissance nationale: L'Égypte moderne*, Paris, 1969; R. W. Baker, *Egypt's Uncertain Revolution under Nasser and Sadat*, Cambridge, Mass., 1978. For issues of political economy see J. Waterbury, *The Egypt of Nasser and Sadat: The Political Economy of Two Regimes*, Princeton, 1983; R. Mabro and S. Radwan, *The Industrialization of Egypt, 1939–1973: Policy and Performance*, Oxford, 1976; R. Mabro, *The Egyptian Economy, 1952–1972*, Oxford, 1974; P. K. O'Brien, *The Revolution in Egypt's Economic System: From Private Enterprise to Socialism, 1952–1965*, London, 1966; R. Springborg, *Family, Power and Politics in Egypt: Sayed Bey Marei: His Clan, Clients and Cohorts*, Philadelphia, Pa., 1982.

On rural development see G. Saab, *The Egyptian Agrarian Reform: 1952–1962*, London, 1967; J. Mayfield, *Rural Politics in Nasser's Egypt: A Quest for Legitimacy*, Austin, Texas, 1971; H. Fakhouri, *Kafr el-Elow: An Egyptian Village in Transition*, New

York, 1972; I. Harik, *The Political Mobilization of Peasants: A Study of an Egyptian Community*, Bloomington, Ind., 1974; L. Binder, *In a Moment of Enthusiasm: Political Power and the Second Stratum in Egypt*, Chicago, 1978.

On Islam in the era of Nasser and Sadat see M. Berger, *Islam in Egypt Today: Social and Political Aspects of Popular Religion*, Cambridge, 1970; M. Gilsenan, *Saint and Sufi in Modern Egypt*, Oxford, 1973. On the Muslim Brotherhood see C. Wendell, ed. and tr., *Five Tracts of Hasan al-Banna (1906–1949)*, Berkeley, Calif., 1978; R. P. Mitchell, *The Society of the Muslim Brothers*, London, 1969; S. Qutb, *Social Justice in Islam*, tr. J. B. Hardie, Washington, D.C., 1953.

On the current Islamic revival: S. E. Ibrahim, "Anatomy of Egypt's Militant Islamic Groups," *IJMES*, XII (1980), pp. 423–53; F. El-Guindi, "Veiling *Infitah* with Muslim Ethic: Egypt's Contemporary Islamic Movement," *Social Problems*, XXVIII (1981), pp. 465–85; G. Kepel, *Le Prophète et Pharaon: Les mouvements islamistes dans l'Égypte contemporaine*, Paris, 1984.

Chapter 25

A large literature deals with the diplomatic, economic, and social problems of the Middle East as a whole. Here we shall indicate books which concentrate on the Arab East, though some contain discussions of Iran and Turkey. On the role of the big powers in the nineteenth century and during World War I see the bibliography for Chapter 23. On the Arab world since World War I see B. Lewis, *The Middle East and the West*, New York, 1966; W. R. Polk, *The United States and the Arab World*, Cambridge, Mass., 1969; E. Monroe, *Britain's Moment in the Middle East, 1914–1956*, Baltimore, Md., 1963.

England's role in the partition of the Ottoman empire and its diplomatic relations with France, Sharif Husayn, and the Zionists is the subject of E. Kedourie, *England and the Middle East, 1914–1921*, 2nd edn, Hassocks, 1978, and *The Chatham House Version*, London, 1970; G. Antonius, *The Arab Awakening*, London, 1938. T. E. Lawrence tells his own story in the brilliant *Seven Pillars of Wisdom*, Garden City, N.Y., 1935, and is the subject of a rewarding biography by J. E. Mack, *A Prince of Our Disorder*, Boston, 1976.

On the economic history of the Middle East see R. Owen, *The Middle East in the World Economy*. Three important collections of articles are C. Issawi, ed., *The Economic History of the Middle East, 1800–1914*, Chicago, 1966; A. L. Udovitch, ed., *The Islamic Middle East, 700–1900: Studies in Economic and Social History*, Princeton, 1981; and M. A. Cook, ed., *Studies in the Economic History of the Middle East*, London, 1970. For the development of the region since World War II see C. Issawi, *An Economic History of the Middle East and North Africa*, New York, 1982. From a dependency theory point of view, see S. A. Amin, *The Modernization of Poverty: A Study in the Political Economy of Growth in Nine Arab Countries, 1945–1970*, Leiden, 1974, and *The Arab Economy Today*, London, 1981. On Middle Eastern oil see P. R. O'Dell, *Oil and World Power*, 5th edn, Harmondsworth, 1979; M. Abir, *Oil, Power and Politics*, London, 1974; M. A. Adelman, *The World Petroleum Market*, Baltimore, Md., 1972.

The best general introduction to Arab nationalism and Arab thought is A. Hourani, *Arabic Thought in the Liberal Age*, Cambridge, 1983. This may be supplemented by S. Haim, ed., *Arab Nationalism: An Anthology*, Berkeley, Calif., 1976; H. Sharabi, *Arab*

Intellectuals and the West, 1875–1914, Baltimore, Md., 1970. On Arab nationalism at the time of World War I see Z. N. Zeine, *Arab–Turkish Relations and the Emergence of Arab Nationalism*, Beirut, 1958, and *The Emergence of Arab Nationalism*, Delmar, N.Y., 1973; C. E. Dawn, *From Ottomanism to Arabism: Essays on the Origins of Arab Nationalism*, Urbana, Ill., 1973; and P. S. Khoury, *Urban Notables and Arab Nationalism: The Politics of Damascus, 1860–1920*, Cambridge, 1983.

Arab nationalism in the interwar years: W. Cleveland, *The Making of an Arab Nationalist: Ottomanism and Arabism in the Life and Thought of Sati⁺ al-Husri*, Princeton, 1971. Post-war statements of the Arab position include al-Bazzaz, *Al-Bazzaz on Arab Nationalism*, London, 1965; H. Nuseibeh, *The Ideas of Arab Nationalism*, Ithaca, N.Y., 1956; F. A. Sayegh, *Arab Unity: Hope and Fulfillment*, New York, 1958.

On contemporary Arab ideology and politics see L. Binder, *The Ideological Revolution in the Middle East*, 2nd edn, New York, 1979; M. C. Hudson, *Arab Politics: The Search for Legitimacy*, New Haven, Conn., 1977; F. Ajami, *The Arab Predicament: Arab Political Thought and Practice since 1967*, Cambridge, 1981; A. Abdel-Malek, *La Pensée politique arabe contemporaine*, 3rd edn, Paris, 1980.

On the Salafiya movement see E. Kedourie, *Afghani and ⁺Abduh*, London, 1966; N. R. Keddie, *Sayyid Jamal ad-Din al-Afghani: A Political Biography*, Berkeley, Calif., 1972; C. C. Adams, *Islam and Modernism in Egypt*, London, 1933; M. H. Kerr, *Islamic Reform: The Political and Legal Theories of Muhammad ⁺Abduh and Rashid Rida*, Berkeley, Calif., 1966.

On Islam in the period since World War II see H. A. R. Gibb, *Modern Trends in Islam*, Chicago, 1947; W. C. Smith, *Islam in Modern History*, Princeton, 1977; E. Kedourie, *Islam in the Modern World*, London, 1980; J. J. Donohue and J. L. Esposito, eds., *Islam in Transition: Muslim Perspectives*, New York, 1982.

Studies of the role of Islam in the functioning of contemporary societies include R. Peters, *Islam and Colonialism: The Doctrine of Jihad in Modern History*, The Hague, 1979; E. I. J. Rosenthal, *Islam in the Modern National State*, New York, 1965; S. A. Arjomand, ed., *From Nationalism to Revolutionary Islam*, London, 1984; M. Rodinson, *Islam and Capitalism*, tr. B. Pearce, Austin, Texas, 1978; M. Gilsenan, *Recognizing Islam: Religion and Society in the Modern Arab World*, New York, 1982.

On Arab World politics see W. Laqueur, *The Middle East in Transition*, New York, 1958; M. H. Kerr, *The Arab Cold War: Gamal ⁺Abd al-Nasir and His Rivals*, 3rd edn, London, 1971. The Military in the Middle East: E. Be'eri, *Army Officers in Arab Politics and Society*, tr. D. Ben-Abba, New York, 1969; J. C. Hurewitz, *Middle East Politics: The Military Dimension*, New York, 1969; V. J. Parry and M. E. Yapp, eds., *War, Technology and Society in the Middle East*, London, 1975.

A number of recent works on the social structure of the Arab Middle East are G. Baer, *Population and Society in the Arab East*, tr. H. Szoke, London, 1964; D. Eickelman, *The Middle East: An Anthropological Approach*, Englewood Cliffs, N.J., 1981; A. Hourani, *A Vision of History: Near Eastern and Other Essays*, Beirut, 1961, and *The Emergence of the Modern Middle East*, Berkeley, Calif., 1981.

On land tenure, rural development, and politics see D. Warriner, *Land Reform and Development in the Middle East: A Study of Egypt, Syria and Iraq*, 2nd edn, London, 1962; G. Baer, *Fellah and Townsman in the Middle East*, London, 1982; R. Springborg, "New Patterns of Agrarian Reform in the Middle East and North Africa," *Middle East Journal*,

XXXI (1977), pp. 127–42; R. Antoun and I. Harik, eds., *Rural Politics and Social Change in the Middle East*, Bloomington, Ind., 1972; L. J. Cantori and I. Harik, eds., *Local Politics and Development in the Middle East*, Boulder, Col., 1981. On nomadism see C. Nelson, ed., *The Desert and the Sown: Nomads in the Wider Society*, Berkeley, Calif., 1973.

A number of lively books with insight into the conditions of town and village life include H. Ammar, *Growing Up in an Egyptian Village*, London, 1954; H. Ayrout, *The Egyptian Peasant*, tr. J. Williams, Boston, 1963; Ivo Andrić, *The Bridge on the Drina*, tr. L. Edwards, New York, 1959, is a revealing historical novel about a town in Bosnia under Ottoman rule.

Urbanization is the subject of a brief overview by C. Issawi, "Economic Change and Urbanization in the Middle East," *Middle Eastern Cities*, ed. I. M. Lapidus, Berkeley, Calif., 1969, pp. 102–21; G. H. Blake and R. I. Lawless, eds., *The Changing Middle Eastern City*, New York, 1980; V. F. Costello, *Urbanisation in the Middle East*, Cambridge, 1977.

Introductions to recent changes in Islamic law include N. J. Coulson, *Conflicts and Tensions in Islamic Jurisprudence*, Chicago, 1969; J. N. D. Anderson, *Islamic Law in the Modern World*, Westport, Conn., 1975; N. J. Coulson, *Succession in the Muslim Family*, Cambridge, 1971; H. Liebesny, *The Law of the Near and Middle East*, Albany, N.Y., 1975.

On Arabic literature see the bibliographical review by R. Allen, "Arabic Literature," *The Study of the Middle East*, ed. L. Binder, New York, 1976, pp. 399–453. On poetry see M. Khouri and H. Algar, eds., *An Anthology of Modern Arabic Poetry*, Berkeley, Calif., 1974; S. Jayyusi, *Trends and Movements in Modern Arabic Poetry*, 2 vols., Leiden, 1977; M. Badawi, *A Critical Introduction to Modern Arabic Poetry*, Cambridge, 1976. For drama and theater see T. al-Hakim, *The Sultan's Dilemma in Arabic Writing Today: The Drama*, II, ed. M. Manzalaoui, Cairo, 1968; J. Landau, *Studies in the Arabic Theater and Cinema*, Philadelphia, Pa., 1958.

On the role of women in contemporary Muslim and Middle Eastern societies see E. Fernea, *Guests of the Sheik*, Garden City, N.Y., 1965; L. Beck and N. Keddie, eds., *Women in the Muslim World*, Cambridge, Mass., 1978; James Allman, *Women's Status and Fertility in the Muslim World*, New York, 1978; F. Hussain, *Muslim Women*, London, 1984; J. I. Smith, ed., *Women in Contemporary Muslim Societies*, London, 1980; E. W. Fernea and B. Bezirgan, eds., *Middle Eastern Muslim Women Speak*, Austin, Texas, 1977. On changing Muslim law see J. L. Esposito, *Women in Muslim Family Law*, Syracuse, N.Y., 1982. On the Arab countries see D. J. Gerner-Adams, "The Changing Status of Muslim Women in the Arab World," *Arab Studies Quarterly*, I (1979), pp. 324–53; E. T. Prothro and L. N. Diab, *Changing Family Patterns in the Arab East*, Beirut, 1974. From a feminist point of view there are a number of controversial works, including G. Tillion, *The Republic of Cousins: Women's Oppression in Mediterranean Society*, Thetford, 1966; F. Mernissi, *Beyond the Veil: Male–Female Dynamics in a Modern Muslim Society*, Cambridge, Mass., 1975; N. El-Saadawi, *The Hidden Face of Eve: Women in the Arab World*, tr. S. Hetata, London, 1980; F. A. Sabbah, *Women in the Muslim Unconscious*, New York, 1984.

Nineteenth-century Syrian economic development and political change: M. Ma'oz, *Ottoman Reform in Syria and Palestine, 1840–1861*, Oxford, 1968. Valuable articles on this subject by D. Chevallier, S. Shamir, A. Hourani, and R. S. Salibi are included in *Beginnings of Modernization in the Middle East*, eds. W. R. Polk and R. L. Chambers, Chicago, 1968. On long-term relations of nomadic and settled peoples see N. Lewis, "The Frontier of Settlement, 1800–1950," *The Economic History of the Middle East 1800–1914*, ed. C. Issawi, Chicago, 1966, pp. 258–68.

Syria in the Mandate Period: S. H. Longrigg, *Syria and Lebanon under the French Mandate*, London, 1958; P. S. Khoury, "Factionalism among Syrian Nationalists during the French Mandate," *IJMES*, XIII (1981), pp. 441–69. The rise of the Baᶜth party: J. F. Devlin, *The Baᶜth Party: A History from its Origins to 1966*, Stanford, Calif., 1976; K. S. Abu Jaber, *The Arab Baᶜth Socialist Party: History, Ideology and Organization*, Syracuse, N.Y., 1966.

Independent Syria and the Baᶜth Regime: P. Seale, *The Struggle for Syria: A Study of Post-war Arab Politics, 1945–1958*, London, 1965; N. Van Dam, *The Struggle for Power in Syria: Sectarianism, Regionalism and Tribalism in Politics, 1961–1978*, London, 1979; I. Rabinovich, *Syria under the Bath, 1963–66: The Army–Party Symbiosis*, Jerusalem, 1972. The Baᶜth party machine is treated in R. Hinnebusch, *Party and Peasant in Syria: Rural Politics and Social Change under the Baᶜth*, Cairo, 1979. On Islam and politics in contemporary Syria see H. Batatu, "Syria's Muslim Brethren," *MERIP Reports*, CX (1982), pp. 12–20.

Political Economy and Economic Development: S. Amin, *Irak et Syrie, 1960–1980: Du projet national à la transnationalisation*, Paris, 1982; A. G. Samarbakhsh, *Socialisme en Irak et en Syrie*, Paris, 1980.

Geographical and anthropological studies of Syrian towns and cities include D. Chevallier, *Villes et travail en Syrie du XIXᵉ au XXᵉ siècle*, Paris, 1982; J. Gulick, *Tripoli: A Modern Arab City*, Cambridge, Mass., 1967; L. Sweet, *Tell Toqaan: A Syrian Village*, Ph.D. thesis, University of Michigan, Ann Arbor, 1958.

The single outstanding work on modern Iraq is H. Batatu, *The Old Social Classes and Revolutionary Movements of Iraq*, Princeton, 1978. On contemporary political issues see D. Pool, "From Elite to Class: The Transformation of Iraqi Leadership, 1920–1939," *IJMES*, XII (1980), pp. 331–50; P. A. Marr, "Iraq's Leadership Dilemma: A Study in Leadership Trends, 1948–1968," *Middle East Journal*, XXIV (1970), pp. 283–301; S. Jawad, *Iraq and the Kurdish Question, 1958–1970*, London, 1981; H. Batatu, "Iraq's Underground Shiᶜa Movements: Characteristics, Causes and Prospects," *Middle East Journal*, XXXV (1981), pp. 578–94. On social change in rural areas: R. A. Fernea, *Shaykh and Effendi: Changing Patterns of Authority among the Shabana of Southern Iraq*, Cambridge, Mass., 1969.

On Jordan see P. J. Vatikiotis, *Politics and the Military in Jordan: A Study of the Arab Legion, 1921–1957*, London, 1967; P. Gubser, *Politics and Change in al-Karak, Jordan*, London, 1973; P. Mazur, *Economic Growth and Development in Jordan*, London, 1979.

Lebanon: Nineteenth-century conflict is studied in I. Harik, *Politics and Change in a Traditional Society: Lebanon 1711–1845*, Princeton, 1968; W. R. Polk, *The Opening of South Lebanon, 1788–1840*, Cambridge, Mass., 1963; D. Chevallier, *La Société du Mont Liban à l'époque de la Révolution Industrielle en Europe*, Paris, 1971; L. T. Fawaz, *Merchants and Migrants in Nineteenth-Century Beirut*, Cambridge, Mass., 1983.

Interpretations of the Lebanese political system in the post-war period: M. C. Hudson, *The Precarious Republic: Political Modernization in Lebanon*, New York, 1968;

L. Binder, ed., *Politics in Lebanon*, New York, 1966; R. Owen, ed., *Essays on the Crisis in Lebanon*, London, 1976; D. Gilmour, *Lebanon: The Fractured Country*, Oxford, 1983. The Maronites and the Kata'ib movement are treated in J. P. Entelis, *Pluralism and Party Transformation in Lebanon: Al-Kata'ib, 1936–1970*, Leiden, 1974; S. Joseph, "Muslim–Christian Conflicts: A Theoretical Perspective," *Muslim–Christian Conflicts: Economic, Political and Social Origins*, eds. S. Joseph and B. Pillsbury, Boulder, Col., 1978, pp. 1–60.

Studies of town and village communities include J. Gulick, *Social Structure and Culture Change in a Lebanese Village*, New York, 1955; S. Khalaf and P. Kongstad, *Hamra of Beirut: A Case of Rapid Urbanization*, Leiden, 1973; F. I. al-Khuri, *From Village to Suburb: Order and Change in Beirut*, Chicago, 1975; E. L. Peters, "Aspects of Rank and Status among Muslims in a Lebanese Village," *Mediterranean Countrymen*, ed. J. Pitt-Rivers, Paris, 1963, pp. 159–200.

The most balanced account of Zionist settlement and Arab resistance from World War I to 1950 is J. C. Hurewitz, *The Struggle for Palestine*, New York, 1976. On the Arab Palestinian population in the British mandate period see J. Migdal, ed., *Palestinian Society and Politics*, Princeton, 1980; Y. Porath, *The Emergence of the Palestinian-Arab National Movement, 1918–1929*, London, 1974, and *The Palestinian Arab National Movement: From Riots to Rebellion, 1929–39*, London, 1977; A. Lesch, *Arab Politics in Palestine, 1917–1939: The Frustration of a Nationalist Movement*, Ithaca, N.Y., 1979; Y. N. Miller, *Government and Society in Rural Palestine, 1920–1948*, Austin, Texas, 1985.

Post-1948 Arab–Israeli relations: C. K. Zurayk, *The Meaning of the Disaster*, tr. R. B. Winder, Beirut, 1956; D. Peretz, *Israel and the Palestine Arabs*, Washington, D.C., 1958; W. R. Polk, D. Stamler, and E. Asfour, *Backdrop to Tragedy: The Struggle for Palestine*, Boston, Mass., 1957; W. Khalidi, ed., *From Haven to Conquest: Readings in Zionism and the Palestine Problem*, Beirut, 1971; N. Safran, *The United States and Israel*, Cambridge, Mass., 1963, and *From War to War: The Arab–Israeli Confrontation, 1948–1967*, New York, 1969; I. Lustick, *Arabs in the Jewish State: Israel's Control of a National Minority*, Austin, Texas, 1980; N. Johnson, *Islam and the Politics of Meaning in Palestinian Nationalism*, London, 1982.

On the history of Zionism and Israel: W. Laqueur, *A History of Zionism*, New York, 1972; H. M. Sachar, *A History of Israel: From the Rise of Zionism to Our Time*, New York, 1976; D. Peretz, *The Government and Politics of Israel*, 2nd edn, Boulder, Col., 1983.

Arabian Peninsula: for bibliographical guides see J. D. Anthony, *The States of the Arabian Peninsula and the Gulf Littoral: A Selected Bibliography*, Washington, D.C., 1973; E. A. Nakhleh, "Persian Gulf Studies," *Bulletin of the Middle East Studies Association*, XI (1977), pp. 31–43.

The Gulf region in the nineteenth and early twentieth century, and the role of Great Britain, is covered in A. M. Abu Hakima, *History of Eastern Arabia, 1750–1800: The Rise and Development of Bahrain and Kuwait*, Beirut, 1965; T. E. Marston, *Britain's Imperial Role in the Red Sea Area, 1800–1878*, Hamden, Conn., 1961; J. B. Kelly, *Britain and the Persian Gulf, 1795–1880*, Oxford, 1968; B. C. Busch, *Britain and the Persian Gulf, 1894–1914*, Berkeley, Calif., 1967. For Oman see R. Said-Ruete, *Said bin Sultan (1791–1865): Ruler of Oman and Zanzibar*, London, 1929; R. G. Landen, *Oman since 1856*, Princeton, 1967.

Recent accounts of the Gulf states include J. D. Anthony, *Arab States of the Lower Gulf: People, Politics, Petroleum*, Washington, D.C., 1975; A. J. Cottrell, ed., *The Persian Gulf States: A General Survey*, Baltimore, Md., 1980; T. Niblock, ed., *Social and Economic Development in the Arab Gulf*, New York, 1980; M. W. Khouja and P. G. Saadler, *The Economy of Kuwait: Development and Role of International Finance*, London, 1979; J. E. Peterson, *Oman in the Twentieth Century: Political Foundations of an Emerging State*, London and New York, 1978; J. C. Wilkinson, *Water and Tribal Settlement in South-East Arabia: A Study of the Aflaj of Oman*, Oxford, 1977; J. Townsend, *Oman: The Making of a Modern State*, London, 1977; E. A. Nakhleh, *Bahrain: Political Development in a Modernizing Society*, Lexington, Mass., 1976; F. I. Khuri, *Tribe and State in Bahrain*, Chicago, 1980; R. S. Zahlan, *The Origins of the United Arab Emirates: A Political and Social History of the Trucial States*, London, 1978; R. El-Mallakh, *The Economic Development of the United Arab Emirates*, London, 1981.

For Yemen see R. W. Stokey, *Yemen: The Politics of the Yemen Arab Republic*, Boulder, Col., 1978; A. S. Bujra, *The Politics of Stratification: A Study of Political Change in a South Arabian Town*, Oxford, 1971; C. Makhlouf, *Changing Veils: Women and Modernisation in North Yemen*, Austin, Texas, 1979.

For the Wahhabi movement and the Saʿudi state see C. S. Hurgronje, *Mekka in the Latter Part of the Nineteenth Century*, tr. J. H. Monahan, Leiden and London, 1931; R. B. Winder, *Saudi Arabia in the Nineteenth Century*, New York, 1965; G. Troeller, *The Birth of Saʿudi Arabia: Britain and the Rise of the House of Saʿud*, London, 1976; J. S. Habib, *Ibn Saʿud's Warriors of Islam: The Ikhwan of Najd and Their Role in the Creation of the Saʿudi Kingdom*, Leiden, 1978.

Saʿudi Arabia in contemporary times is the subject of W. A. Beling, ed., *King Faisal and the Modernisation of Saudi Arabia*, London and Boulder, Col., 1980; C. M. Helms, *The Cohesion of Saudi Arabia: Evolution of Political Identity*, London, 1981; R. El-Mallakh, *Saudi Arabia, Rush to Development: Profile of an Energy Economy and Investment*, London, 1982; W. B. Quandt, *Saudi Arabia in the 1980s: Foreign Policy, Security, and Oil*, Washington, D.C., 1981; W. Ochsenwald, "Saudi Arabia and the Islamic Revival," *IJMES*, XIII (1981), pp. 271–86.

For the contemporary life of the bedouin see H. R. P. Dickson, *The Arabs of the Desert: A Glimpse into Badawin Life in Kuwait and Saʿudi Arabia*, 2nd edn, London, 1951; W. Thesiger, *Arabian Sands*, New York, 1959, a great travel adventure.

Chapter 26

An outstanding contribution to the analysis of development in North Africa is E. Hermassi, *Leadership and National Development in North Africa*, Berkeley, Calif., 1972. On North Africa under French rule and the rise of nationalism see J. Berque, *French North Africa: The Maghrib between Two World Wars*, tr. J. Stewart, New York, 1967; R. Le Tourneau, *Évolution politique de l'Afrique du Nord musulmane, 1920–1961*, Paris, 1962; C. R. Ageron, *Politiques coloniales au Maghreb*, Paris, 1972; A. al-Fasi, *The Independence Movements in Arab North Africa*, tr. H. Z. Nuseibeh, Washington, D.C., 1954.

Comparative studies of independent North Africa include M. Brett, ed., *Northern Africa: Islam and Modernization*, London, 1973; M. Halpern, *The Politics of Social Change in the Middle East and North Africa*, Princeton, 1963; D. E. Ashford, *National Development and Local Reform: Political Participation in Morocco, Tunisia, and Pakistan*, Princeton, 1967; I. W. Zartman, ed., *Man, State and Society in the Contemporary Maghrib*, New York, 1973; L. Anderson, *States in the Periphery: Politics and Rural Transformation in Tunisia and Libya, 1850–1980*, forthcoming. On Islam see P. Shinar, "ᶜUlamaᵓ, Marabouts and Government: An Overview of Their Relationships in the French Colonial Maghrib," *Israel Oriental Studies*, x (1980), pp. 211–29.

The imposition of the Tunisian protectorate is the subject of J. Ganiage, *Les Origines du Protectorat français en Tunisie, 1861–1881*, 2nd edn, Tunis, 1968. On French rule in Tunisia see J. Poncet, *La Colonisation et l'agriculture européennes en Tunisie depuis 1881*, Paris, 1961. Tunisian state and society in the late nineteenth century: L. C. Brown, tr., *The Surest Path, by Khayr al-Din al-Tunisi*, Cambridge, Mass., 1967; A. H. Green, *The Tunisian Ulama 1873–1915*, Leiden, 1978.

The Tunisia Nationalist Movement: N. Ziadeh, *Origins of Nationalism in Tunisia*, Beirut, 1969; A. Mahjoubi, *Les Origines du mouvement national en Tunisie (1904–1934)*, Tunis, 1982. A. Memmi, *The Pillar of Salt*, tr. E. Roditi, New York, 1955, is a sensitive novel portraying the impact of colonialism upon a Tunisian Jewish boy. General books on independent Tunisia include C. Micaud *et al.*, *Tunisia: The Politics of Modernization*, New York, 1964; C. H. Moore, *Tunisia since Independence*, Berkeley, Calif., 1965; J. Duvignaud, *Change at Shibeika: Report from a North African Village*, tr. F. Frenaye, Austin, Texas, 1977.

The principal histories of Algeria under French rule are P. Boyer, *L'Évolution de L'Algérie médiane (ancien département d'Alger) de 1830 à 1956*, Paris, 1960; C. R. Ageron, *Histoire de l'Algérie contemporaine (1830–1964)*, Paris, 1966; C. A. Julien, *Historie de l'Algérie contemporaine*, Paris, 1964; C. R. Ageron, *Les Algériens musulmans et la France (1871–1919)*, 2 vols., Paris, 1968.

For Algerian society on the eve of the French invasion see the bibliography to Part II. For the resistance of ᶜAbd al-Qadir see R. Danziger, *Abd al-Qadir and the Algerians*, New York and London, 1977. Later Algerian resistance movements have been studied by A. Nadir, "Les Ordres religieux et la conquête française (1830–1851)," *Revue algérienne des sciences juridiques, politiques et économiques*, IX (1972), pp. 819–68; P. Von Sivers, "The Realm of Justice: Apocalyptic in Algeria (1849–1879)," *Humaniora Islamica*, I (1973), pp. 47–60; F. Colonna, "Cultural Resistance and Religious Legitimacy in Colonial Algeria," *Economy and Society*, III (1974), pp. 233–52; "Saints furieux et saints studieux ou, dans l'Aurès, comment la religion vient aux tribus," *Annales E.S.C.*, xxxv (1980), pp. 642–62; J. Clancy-Smith, "Saints, Mahdis and Arms: Religion and Resistance in Nineteenth-Century North Africa," *Islam, Politics, and Social Movements*, eds. E. Burke and I. M. Lapidus, Berkeley, Calif., forthcoming.

On Muslim culture see H. Masse, "Les Études arabes en Algérie (1830–1930)," *Revue Africaine*, LXXIV (1933), pp. 208–58, 458–505; F. Colonna, *Instituteurs algériens: 1833–1939*, Paris, 1975; J. P. Charnay, *La Vie musulmane en Algérie: d'après la jurisprudence de la première moitié du XXᵉ siècle*, Paris, 1965.

The French colonization and its impact upon the economic well-being of the Muslims: J. Reudy, *Land Policy in Colonial Algeria: The Origins of the Rural Public Domain*, Berkeley, Calif., 1967; M. Launay, *Paysans algériens: La terre, la vigne et les hommes*, Paris, 1963.

The birth of Algerian nationalism: A. Nouschi, *La Naissance du nationalisme algérien*, Paris, 1962; E. Sivan, *Communisme et nationalisme en Algérie, 1920–1962*, Paris, 1976. For Muslim reformism see A. Merad, *Le Reformisme musulman en Algérie de 1925 à 1940*, The Hague, 1967; P. Shinar, "The Historical Approach of the Reformist ᶜUlamaᵓ in the Contemporary Maghrib," *Asian and African Studies*, Jerusalem, VII (1971), pp. 181–210, "Ibadiyya and Orthodox Reformism in Modern Algeria," *Scripta Hierosolymitana*, IX, ed. U. Heyd, Jerusalem, 1961, pp. 97–120, and "Traditional and Reformist Mawlid Celebrations in the Maghrib," *Studies in Memory of Gaston Wiet*, ed. M. Rosen-Ayalon, Jerusalem, 1977, pp. 371–413. For Sufi Islam see J. Carret, *Le Maraboutisme, et les confréries religieuses musulmanes en Algérie*, Algiers, 1959; M. Lings, *A Moslem Saint of the Twentieth Century: Shaikh Ahmad al-ᶜAlawi, His Spiritual Heritage and Legacy*, London, 1961.

The revolutionary struggle: D. Ling, *The Passing of French Algeria*, London, 1966; W. B. Quandt, *Revolution and Political Leadership: Algeria, 1954–1968*, Cambridge, Mass., 1969; D. Ottaway and M. Ottaway, *Algeria: The Politics of a Socialist Revolution*, Berkeley, Calif., 1970; T. Smith, *The French Stake in Algeria, 1945–1962*, Ithaca, N.Y., 1978; Frantz Fanon, *The Wretched of the Earth*, tr. C. Farrington, New York, 1963; I. L. Gendzier, *Frantz Fanon: A Critical Study*, New York, 1973.

Post-independence Algeria: J.-C. Vatin, *L'Algérie politique*, 2nd edn, Paris, 1983; M. Lacheraf, *L'Algérie: Nation et société*, Paris, 1965; A. Gauthier, *L'Algérie: Décolonisation, socialisme, industrialisation*, Montreuil, 1976; M. Lazreg, *The Emergence of Classes in Algeria*, Boulder, Col., 1976; J. R. Nellis, "Socialist Management in Algeria," *Journal of Modern African Studies*, XV (1977), pp. 529–54. On the structure of Algerian society: P. Bourdieu, *The Algerians*, tr. A. C. M. Ross, Boston, 1962, and *Sociologie de l'Algérie*, 3rd edn, Paris, 1963.

The basic structures of Moroccan rural society are treated in a number of brilliant and conflicting works: J. Berque and P. Pascon, *Structures sociales du Haut-Atlas*, 2nd edn, Paris, 1978; E. Gellner, *Saints of the Atlas*, Chicago, 1969, supplemented by *Muslim Society*, Cambridge, 1981; D. F. Eickelman, *Moroccan Islam: Tradition and Society in a Pilgrimage Center*, Austin, Texas, 1976; C. Geertz, H. Geertz, and R. Rosen, *Meaning and Order in Muslim Society: Three Essays in Cultural Analysis*, Cambridge, 1979. Other valuable studies include: V. Crapanzano, *The Hamadsha: A Study in Moroccan Ethnopsychiatry*, Berkeley, 1973; R. Jamous, *Honneur et baraka: Les Structures sociales traditionelles dans le Rif*, Paris, 1981; P. Rabinow, *Symbolic Domination: Cultural Form and Historical Change in Morocco*, Chicago, 1975; D. Hart, *Dadda ᶜAtta and his Four Grandsons: The Socio-Political Organisation of the Ait ᶜAtta of Southern Morocco*, Cambridge, 1981; D. Seddon, *Moroccan Peasants: A Century of Change in the Eastern Rif, 1870–1970*, Kent, 1980. On Islam see the classic E. A. Westermarck, *Ritual and Belief in Morocco*, 2 vols., New Hyde Park, N.Y., 1968.

On Moroccan political society and its response to the French occupation: R. E. Dunn, *Resistance in the Desert: Moroccan Responses to French Imperialism, 1881–1912*, London and Madison, Wis., 1977; E. Burke, *Prelude to Protectorate in Morocco*, Chicago, 1976. See also E. Burke, "Morocco and the Near East: Reflections on Some Basic Differences," *Archives européennes de sociologie*, X (1969), pp. 70–94; D. Seddon, "Tribe and State: 'Approaches to Maghreb History,'" *The Maghreb Review*, II (1977), pp. 23–40.

The French Protectorate is treated in C.-A. Julien, *Le Maroc face aux impérialismes, 1415–1956*, Paris, 1978; R. Landau, *Moroccan Drama, 1900–1955*, San Francisco, Calif., 1978; R. L. Bidwell, *Morocco under Colonial Rule: French Administration of Tribal Areas 1912–1956*, London, 1973; G. Maxwell, *Lords of the Atlas: The Rise and Fall of the House of Glaoua, 1893–1956*, London, 1966. The development of an Islamic-national resistance is covered by A. Laroui, *Les Origines sociales et culturelles du nationalisme marocain (1830–1912)*, Paris, 1977; J. P. Halstead, *Rebirth of a Nation: The Origins and Rise of Moroccan Nationalism, 1912–1944*, Cambridge, Mass., 1967.

For the Moroccan economy see C. F. Stewart, *The Economy of Morocco, 1912–1962*, Cambridge, Mass., 1964; J. L. Miege, *Le Maroc et l'Europe (1830–1894)*, 4 vols., Paris, 1961–63; J. Waterbury, *North for the Trade: The Life and Times of a Berber Merchant*, Berkeley, Calif., 1972.

On the politics of independent Morocco see J. Waterbury, *The Commander of the Faithful: The Moroccan Political Elite*, London, 1970; K. E. Mourad, *Le Maroc à la recherche d'une révolution*, Paris, 1972; I. W. Zartman, *Morocco: Problems of New Power*, New York, 1964.

A good introduction to the historical background of modern Libya is L. Anderson, "Nineteenth-Century Reform in Ottoman Libya," *IJMES*, xvi (1984), pp. 325–48. The Sanusiya are discussed in the classic E. E. Evans-Pritchard, *The Sanusi of Cyrenaica*, Oxford, 1949. On the Qadhdhafi regime see J. L. Wright, *Libya: A Modern History*, Baltimore, Md., 1982.

Chapter 27

For the principal histories of the Muslim populace of India see Part II above. See also S. M. Ikram, *Modern Muslim India and the Birth of Pakistan, 1858–1951*, 2nd edn, Lahore, 1970; A. Ahmad, *Islamic Modernism in India and Pakistan*, London, 1967; A. Ahmad and G. E. von Grunebaum, eds., *Muslim Self-statement in India and Pakistan, 1857–1968*, Wiesbaden, 1970.

The nineteenth-century Muslim reform movements in Bengal: M. A. Khan, *History of the Farāʾidi Movement in Bengal, 1818–1906*, Karachi, 1965; R. Ahmad, *The Bengal Muslims, 1871–1906: A Quest for Identity*, Delhi, 1981; S. Ahmad, *The Muslim Community of Bengal 1884–1912*, Dacca, 1974. On the college of Deoband: B. D. Metcalf, *Islamic Revival in British India: Deoband, 1860–1900*, Princeton, 1982; see also F. Robinson, "The ʿUlamaʾ of Farangi Mahall and Their Adab," *Moral Conduct and Authority*, ed. B. D. Metcalf, Berkeley, Calif., 1984, pp. 152–83.

Indian Muslim modernist movements are treated in D. Lelyveld, *Aligarh's First Generation*, Princeton, 1978; F. Robinson, *Separatism among Indian Muslims: The Politics of the United Provinces' Muslims, 1860–1923*, Cambridge, 1974; G. Minault, *The Khilafat Movement: Religious Symbolism and Political Mobilization in India*, New York, 1982; M. Hasan, ed., *Communal and Pan-Islamic Trends in Colonial India*, New Delhi, 1981. The position of the ʿulamaʾ is explained by P. Hardy, *Partners in Freedom and True Muslims*, Lund, 1971; M. Anwarul Haq, *The Faith Movement of Mawlana Muhammad Ilyas*, London, 1972.

The development of Muslim communalism and Pakistan to 1947: M. Iqbal, *The Reconstruction of Religious Thought in Islam*, Lahore, 1962, and *Poems from Iqbal*, tr. V. G.

Kiernan, London, 1955; P. Moon, *Divide and Quit*, Berkeley, Calif., 1962; D. Gilmartin, "Religious Leadership and the Pakistan Movement in the Punjab," *Modern Asian Studies*, XIII (1979), pp. 485–517.

Muslims in India since partition: T. N. Madan, *Muslim Communities of South Asia*, New Delhi, 1976; R. E. Miller, *Mappila Muslims of Kerala*, Madras, 1976; I. Ahmad, ed., *Family, Kinship and Marriage among Muslims in India*, New Delhi, 1976, *Caste and Social Stratification among Muslims in India*, 2nd edn, New Delhi, 1978, and *Ritual and Religion among Muslims in India*, New Delhi, 1981; G. Krishna, "Indian Muslims in the Nation-Formation Process," *Contributions to South Asian Studies*, 2nd edn, Delhi, 1982, pp. 110–45.

On Pathans and the Northwest Frontier provinces see A. S. Ahmed, *Pukhtun Economy and Society: Traditional Structure and Economic Development in a Tribal Society*, London, 1980; A. S. Ahmed and D. Hart, eds., *From the Atlas to the Indus: The Tribes of Islam*, London, 1981; F. Barth, *Features of Person and Society in Swat*, London, 1981.

Islam and Politics in Pakistan: L. Binder, *Religion and Politics in Pakistan*, Berkeley, Calif., 1961; on Mawdudi see S. A. A. Maudoodi, *First Principles of the Islamic State*, tr. K. Ahmad, Lahore, 1960, and *Towards Understanding Islam*, tr. K. Ahmad, Lahore, 1974; C. J. Adams, "The Ideology of Mawlana Mawdudi," *South Asian Politics and Religion*, ed. D. E. Smith, Princeton, 1966, pp. 371–97.

For Pakistani politics see K. B. Sayeed, *The Political System of Pakistan*, Lahore, 1967; R. S. Wheeler, *The Politics of Pakistan*, Ithaca, N.Y., 1970; S. J. Burki, *Pakistan under Bhutto, 1971–1977*, London, 1980; K. B. Sayeed, *Politics in Pakistan*, New York, 1980; H. Gardezi and J. Rashid, eds., *Pakistan; The Roots of Dictatorship: The Political Economy of a Praetorian State*, London, 1983.

Chapter 28

On Indonesian history see M. C. Ricklefs, *A History of Modern Indonesia, c. 1300 to the Present*, Bloomington, Ind., 1981; H. J. Benda, *The Crescent and the Rising Sun*, Ithaca, N.Y., 1955; "South-East Asian Islam in the Twentieth Century," *Cambridge History of Islam*, II, Cambridge, 1970, pp. 182–208. On Indonesian society see C. Geertz, *The Religion of Java*, Glencoe, Ill., 1960; W. F. Wertheim, *Indonesian Society in Transition: A Study of Social Change*, 2nd edn, The Hague, 1959; J. L. Peacock, *Indonesia: An Anthropological Perspective*, Pacific Palisades, Calif., 1973; J. C. van Leur, *Indonesian Trade and Society*, tr. J. Holmes and A. van Marle, The Hague, 1955. On the rise of the Indonesian nationalist movement see R. Van Niel, *The Emergence of the Modern Indonesian Elite*, The Hague, 1960.

Muslim peasant resistance to Dutch rule is treated in S. Kartodirdjo, *The Peasants' Revolt of Banten in 1888*, Amsterdam, 1966; J. M. Van der Kroef, "Prince Diponegoro: Progenitor of Indonesian Nationalism," *Far Eastern Quarterly*, VIII (1948), pp. 424–50, and "Javanese Messianic Expectations: Their Origin and Cultural Content," *Comparative Studies in Society and History*, I (1959), pp. 299–323.

Muslim reformism is discussed in D. Noer, *The Modernist Muslim Movement in Indonesia, 1900–1942*, Singapore and New York, 1973; J. L. Peacock, *Purifying the Faith: The Muhammadiya Movement in Indonesian Islam*, Menlo Park, Calif., 1978, and

Muslim Puritans: Reformist Psychology in Southeast Asian Islam, Berkeley, Calif., 1978; H. M. Federspiel, *Persatuan Islam: Islamic Reform in Twentieth Century Indonesia*, Ithaca, N.Y., 1970; T. Abdullah, *Schools and Politics: The Kaum Muda Movement in West Sumatra (1927–1933)*, Ithaca, N.Y., 1971.

The relations between religion, national consciousness, and social change are studied in C. Geertz, *The Social History of an Indonesian Town*, Cambridge, Mass., 1965, *Peddlers and Princes*, Chicago, 1963, and *Agricultural Involution: The Process of Ecological Change in Indonesia*, Berkeley, Calif., 1966; D. H. Burger, *Structural Changes in Javanese Society: The Supra-Village Sphere*, Ithaca, N.Y., 1956; B. J. O. Schrieke, *Indonesian Sociological Studies*, 2 vols., The Hague, 1955–57; R. R. Jay, *Religion and Politics in Rural Central Java*, New Haven, Conn., 1963; L. Castles, *Religion, Politics, and Economic Behavior in Java: The Kudus Cigarette Industry*, New Haven, Conn., 1967. J. T. Siegel, *The Rope of God*, Berkeley, Calif., 1969 analyzes the social structure and mentality of Acheh.

The politics of independent Indonesia is covered in G. M. Kahin, *Nationalism and Revolution in Indonesia*, Ithaca, N.Y., 1952; H. Feith, *The Decline of Constitutional Democracy in Indonesia*, Ithaca, N.Y., 1962. On the recent role of Islam see B. J. Boland, *The Struggle of Islam in Modern Indonesia*, The Hague, 1971; M. K. Hassan, *Muslim Intellectual Responses to New Order Modernization in Indonesia*, Kuala Lumpur, 1980; A. A. Samson "Religious Belief and Political Action in Indonesian Islamic Modernism," *Political Participation in Modern Indonesia*, ed. R. W. Liddle, New Haven, 1973, pp. 116–42. On Muslim legal administration see D. S. Lev, *Islamic Courts in Indonesia*, Berkeley, Calif., 1972; D. Noer, *Administration of Islam in Indonesia*, Ithaca, N.Y., 1978.

On Malaysia see W. R. Roff, *The Origins of Malay Nationalism*, New Haven, Conn., 1967; M. Yeger, *Islam and Islamic Institutions in British Malaya: Policies and Implementation*, Jerusalem, 1979; B. W. and L. Y. Andaya, *A History of Malaysia*, London, 1982; J. Nagata, *The Reflowering of Malaysian Islam: Modern Religious Radicals and Their Roots*, Vancouver, 1984. Clive Kessler gives revealing insights into Muslim symbols and politics: *Islam and Politics in a Malay State: Kelantan 1838–1969*, Ithaca, N.Y., 1978.

On the political economy of Malaysia see H. Osman Rani, Jomo Kwame Sundaram, and I. Shari, eds., "Development in the Eighties: With Special Emphasis on Malaysia," *Bangi: Journal Ekonomi Malaysia*, 11, (1981); Hua Wu Yin, *Classical Communalism in Malaysia. Politics in a Dependent Capitalist State*, London, 1983.

Chapter 29

Inner Asia up to the revolution is covered by the general works indicated in Part II. In addition see R. A. Pierce, *Russian Central Asia, 1867–1917: A Study in Colonial Rule*, Berkeley, 1960; S. Becker, *Russia's Protectorates in Central Asia: Bukhara and Khiva, 1865–1924*, Cambridge, Mass., 1968; H. Carrère d'Encausse, "Tsarist Educational Policy in Turkestan, 1867–1917," *Central Asian Review*, XI (1963), pp. 374–94.

A number of general books deal with the Soviet period and the contemporary Muslim population: A. Bennigsen and C. Lemercier-Quelquejay, *Islam in the Soviet Union*, London, 1967; A. Bennigsen, *Les Musulmans oubliés: L'Islam en Union Soviétique*, Paris, 1981. See also H. Carrère d'Encausse, *Decline of an Empire: The Soviet Socialist Republics in Revolt*, tr. M. Sokolinsky and H. A. LaFarge, New York, 1979; S. Akiner, *Islamic Peoples of the Soviet Union*, London and Boston, Mass., 1983.

The jadid movement is treated in S. A. Zenkovsky, *Pan-Turkism and Islam in Russia*, Cambridge, Mass., 1960; C. Lemercier-Quelquejay, "Abdul Kayum al-Nasyri: A Tatar Reformer of the 19th Century," *Central Asian Survey*, 1 (1983), pp. 109–32; A. Bennigsen and C. Lemercier-Quelquejay, *La Presse et le mouvement national chez les Musulmans de Russie avant 1920*, Paris, 1964. On Muslim national communism see A. Bennigsen and C. Lemercier-Quelquejay, *Les Mouvements nationaux chez les Musulmans de Russie*, Paris, 1960; A. Bennigsen and S. E. Wimbush, *Muslim National Communism in the Soviet Union: A Revolutionary Strategy for the Colonial World*, Chicago, 1979.

The revolutionary epoch is treated in A. G. Park, *Bolshevism in Turkestan, 1917–1927*, New York, 1957; R. E. Pipes, *The Formation of the Soviet Union: Communism and Nationalism, 1917–1923*, Cambridge, Mass., 1964; E. E. Bacon, *Central Asians under Russian Rule: A Study in Culture Change*, Ithaca, N.Y., 1966. Controversial but informative accounts are given by B. Hayit, *Turkestan im XX. Jahrhundert*, Darmstadt, 1956, and *Sowjetrussische Orientpolitik am Beispiel Turkestans*, Köln, 1962. Questions of national identity and Soviet policy are treated in E. Allworth, *Uzbek Literary Politics*, The Hague, 1964, *Central Asia: A Century of Russian Rule*, New York, 1967, and *The Nationality Question in Soviet Central Asia*, New York, 1973; J. R. Azrael, ed., *Soviet Nationality Policies and Practices*, New York, 1978.

The impact of Soviet rule upon Muslim populations in terms of education, employment, acculturation, and political relations is the subject of M. Rywkin, *Moscow's Muslim Challenge: Soviet Central Asia*, Armonk, N.Y., 1982. See also W. K. Medlin, W. M. Cave, and F. Carpenter, *Education and Development in Central Asia: A Case Study on Social Change in Uzbekistan*, Leiden, 1971; G. Hodnett, *Leadership in the Soviet National Republics: A Quantitative Study of Recruitment Policy*, Oakville, Ontario, 1978; T. Rakowska-Harmstone, *Russia and Nationalism in Central Asia: The Case of Tadzhikistan*, Baltimore, Md., 1970.

Important recent works in Russian include T. Saidbaev, *Islam i obshchestvo: opyt istoriko-sotsiologicheskogo issledovaniia* [Islam and Society: An Experiment in Historico-Sociological Research], Moscow, 1978; N. Ashirov, *Evoliutsiia islama v SSSR* [The Evolution of Islam in the USSR], Moscow, 1973, and *Islam v SSSR: Osobennosti protsessa sekuliarizatsii v respublikakh sovetskogo vostoka* [Islam in the USSR: The Particularities of the Process of Secularization in the Republics of the Soviet East], Moscow, 1983; S. M. Demidov, *Turkmenskie ovliady* [The Turkmen Evliads], Ashkhabad, 1976.

Two general books on Islam in China are R. Israeli, *Muslims in China: A Study in Cultural Confrontation*, London and Malmo, 1980; J. T. Dreyer, *China's Forty Millions*, Cambridge, Mass., 1976, an account of the minorities policies of the People's Republic of China. For Sinkiang see R. Yang, "Sinkiang under the Administration of Governor Yang Tseng-Hsin, 1911–1928," *Central Asiatic Journal*, VI (1961), pp. 270–316; O. Lattimore, *Pivot of Asia: Sinkiang and the Inner Asian Frontiers of China and Russia*, Boston, Mass., 1950; G. Moseley, *A Sino-Soviet Cultural Frontier: The Ili Kazakh Autonomous Chou*, Cambridge, Mass., 1966.

Chapter 30

For Muslim peoples in West Africa see J. S. Trimingham, *Islam in West Africa*, Oxford, 1959, and *A History of Islam in West Africa*, London, 1962; V. Monteil, *L'Islam noir*,

Paris, 1980; R. L. Moreau, *Africains musulmans: des communautés en mouvement*, Paris, 1982.

For the European scramble for Africa see Part II. A comprehensive survey of the era of colonial rule may be found in L. H. Gann and P. Duignan, eds., *Colonialism in Africa, 1870–1960*, 5 vols., London, 1969–75; M. Crowder, *West Africa under Colonial Rule*, Evanston, Ill., 1968, *West African Resistance: The Military Response to Colonial Occupation*, London, 1971, and *Colonial West Africa: Collected Essays*, London, 1978. A leading French historian is J. Suret-Canale, *French Colonialism in Tropical Africa*, tr. T. Gottheiner, London, 1971, and *Afrique noire: occidentale et centrale*, 3 vols., Paris, 1961–64. On German colonialism there is M. E. Townsend, *The Rise and Fall of the German Colonial Empire, 1884–1914*, New York, 1930.

The transition to independence is treated in T. L. Hodgkin, *Nationalism in Colonial Africa*, New York, 1957; W. H. Morris-Jones and G. Fischer, eds., *Decolonisation and After: The British and French Experience*, London, 1980; J. Hargreaves, *The End of Colonial Rule in West Africa*, London, 1979; E. Mortimer, *France and the Africans 1944–1960: A Political History*, London, 1969; W. J. Foltz, *From French West Africa to the Mali Federation*, New Haven, Conn., 1965. A very brief but effective account of the gaining of independence in French West Africa is I. Wallerstein, "How Seven States Were Born in Former French West Africa," *Africa Report*, VI, iii (1961), pp. 3ff.

On the independent African states see G. M. Carter, ed., *African One-party States*, Ithaca, N.Y., 1962; J. S. Coleman and C. G. Rosberg, eds., *Political Parties and National Integration in Tropical Africa*, Berkeley, Calif., 1964; A. R. Zolberg, *Creating Political Order: The Party-states of West Africa*, Chicago, 1966; L. Kuper and M. G. Smith, eds., *Pluralism in Africa*, Berkeley, Calif., 1969; R. I. Rotberg and A. A. Mazrui, eds., *Protest and Power in Black Africa*, New York, 1970; M. Crowder and O. Ikime, eds., *West African Chiefs: Their Changing Status under Colonial Rule and Independence*, tr. B. Packman, New York, 1970; G. N. Brown and M. Hiskett, eds., *Conflict and Harmony in Education in Tropical Africa*, London, 1975.

Mauritania: F. de Chassey, *Mauritanie 1900–1975: De l'ordre colonial à l'ordre neo-colonial entre Maghreb et Afrique Noire*, Paris, 1978; Chad: A. Le Rouvreur, *Sahéliens et Sahariens du Tchad*, Paris, 1962; J. Le Cornec, *Histoire politique du Tchad, de 1900 à 1962*, Paris, 1963. On Ghana see I. M. Wallerstein, *The Road to Independence: Ghana and the Ivory Coast*, Paris, 1964; D. Austin, *Politics in Ghana, 1946–1960*, London, 1964. An important study of the Muslim populace of Kumasi, Ghana is E. Schildkrout, *People of the Zongo: The Transformation of Ethnic Identities in Ghana*, Cambridge, 1978. On the Muslims in the Volta River region see E. P. Skinner, *The Mossi of the Upper Volta: The Political Development of a Sudanese People*, Stanford, Calif., 1964; J. Adouin, *L'Islam en Haute-Volta à l'époque coloniale*, Abidjan, 1975. For Sierra Leone see B. E. Harrell-Bond, A. M. Howard, and D. E. Skinner, *Community Leadership and the Transformation of Freetown (1801–1976)*, The Hague, 1978; M. Kilson, *Political Change in a West African State: A Study of the Modernization Process in Sierra Leone*, Cambridge, Mass., 1966.

Senegal: E. J. Schumacher, *Politics, Bureaucracy and Rural Development in Senegal*, Berkeley, Calif., 1975; M. Crowder, *Senegal: A Study of French Assimilation Policy*, London, 1967. The Murids have inspired an extensive literature: D. B. Cruise O'Brien, *The Mourides of Senegal: The Political and Economic Organization of an Islamic Brotherhood*,

Oxford, 1971, and *Saints and Politicians: Essays in the Organisation of a Senegalese Peasant Society*, London, 1975; C. T. Sy, *La Confrérie sénégalaise des Mourides*, Paris, 1969; L. C. Behrman, *Muslim Brotherhoods and Politics in Senegal*, Cambridge, Mass., 1970; J. Copans, *Les Marabouts de l'arachide: La Confrérie mouride et les paysans du Senegal*, Paris, 1980.

The history of Nigeria is best introduced by M. Crowder, *The Story of Nigeria*, London, 1977; J. S. Coleman, *Nigeria: Background to Nationalism*, Berkeley, Calif., 1958. For the post-1966 military regimes and political economy see S. K. Panter-Brick, ed., *Nigerian Politics and Military Rule*, London, 1970, and *Soldiers and Oil: The Political Transformation of Nigeria*, London, 1978; R. Melson and H. Wolpe, eds., *Nigeria: Modernization and the Politics of Communalism*, East Lansing, Mich., 1972. See also A. Ozigi and L. Ocho, *Education in Northern Nigeria*, London and Boston, Mass., 1981; M. Bray, *Universal Primary Education in Nigeria: A Study of the Kano State*, London and Boston, Mass., 1981.

On Islam and society in northern Nigeria the principal work is J. N. Paden, *Religion and Political Culture in Kano*, Berkeley, Calif., 1973. This has been followed by more recent studies by Paul Lubeck on the relations of Islam and the political-economic structures of Nigerian society: *Islam and Urban Labor: The Making of a Muslim Working Class in Northern Nigeria*, Princeton, N.J., forthcoming.

Migrant Hausa merchants and workers are treated in the important study of A. Cohen, *Custom and Politics in Urban Africa: A Study of Hausa Migrants in Yoruba Towns*, London, 1969. For Islam among the Yoruba see T. G. O. Gbadamosi, *The Growth of Islam among the Yoruba, 1841–1908*, Atlantic Highlands, N.J., 1978; P. J. Ryan, *Imale, Yoruba Tradition: A Study of Clerical Piety*, Missoula, Mont., 1977. See also S. F. Nadel, *A Black Byzantium: The Kingdom of Nupe in Nigeria*, London, 1942, and *Nupe Religion*, Glencoe, Ill., 1954.

Other studies of Islam in West Africa are P. Alexandre, "A West African Islamic Movement: Hamallism in French West Africa," *Protest and Power in Black Africa*, eds. R. I. Rotberg and A. A. Mazrui, New York, 1970, pp. 497–512; L. Brenner, *West African Sufi: The Religious Heritage and Spiritual Search of Cerno Bokar Saalif Taal*, Berkeley, Calif., 1984; L. Kaba, *The Wahabiyya: Islamic Reform and Politics in French West Africa*, Evanston, Ill., 1974; H. J. Fisher, *Ahmadiyyah: A Study in Contemporary Islam on the West African Coast*, London, 1964.

Chapter 31

Muslim peoples in East Africa are the subject of J. S. Trimingham, *Islam in East Africa*, Oxford, 1964; P. H. Gulliver, ed., *Tradition and Transition in East Africa*, Berkeley, Calif., 1969; A. I. Richards, *The Multicultural States of East Africa*, Montreal, 1969; B. A. Ogot, ed., *Zamani: A Survey of East African History*, 2nd edn, Nairobi, 1974; D. A. Low and A. Smith, eds., *A History of East Africa*, III, Oxford, 1976. See also W. Arens, ed., *A Century of Change in Eastern Africa*, The Hague and Chicago, 1976.

On the Swahili-speaking coastal population see J. W. T. Allen, ed. and tr., *The Customs of the Swahili People*, Berkeley, Calif., 1981. On Zanzibar: N. R. Bennett, *A History of the Arab State of Zanzibar*, London, 1978; A. Clayton, *The Zanzibar Revolution and Its Aftermath*, Hamden, Conn., 1981; "The Zanzibari Revolution: African Protest in a Racially Plural Society," *Protest and Power in Black Africa*, eds. R. I. Rotberg and A. A. Mazrui, New York, 1970, pp. 924–67.

For Tanzania see R. Yeager, *Tanzania: An African Experiment*, Boulder, Col., 1982; J. Iliffe, *A Modern History of Tanganyika*, London, 1979; A. H. Nimtz, Jr., *Islam and Politics in East Africa: The Sufi Order in Tanzania*, Minneapolis, 1980. For Ugandan history and politics see S. R. Karugire, *The Political History of Uganda*, Nairobi, 1979; F. B. Welbourn, *Religion and Politics in Uganda, 1952–1962*, Nairobi, 1965; N. King, A. Kasozi, and A. Oded, *Islam and the Confluence of Religions in Uganda, 1840–1966*, Tallahassee, Fla., 1973; A. Oded, *Islam in Uganda: Islamization through a Centralized State in Pre-Colonial Africa*, New York, 1974. The Asian Muslim minorities are the subject of G. Delf, *Asians in East Africa*, London, 1963.

Somalia: I. M. Lewis, *A Modern History of Somalia: Nation and State in the Horn of Africa*, London, 1980, and "Sufism in Somaliland: A Study in Tribal Islam," *BSOAS*, XVII (1955), pp. 581–602.

The best overview of the history of the Sudan is P. M. Holt and M. W. Daly, *The History of the Sudan from the Coming of Islam to the Present Day*, 3rd edn, London, 1979. See also R. L. Hill, *Egypt in the Sudan, 1820–1881*, London, 1959; P. M. Holt, *The Mahdist State in the Sudan, 1881–1898*, Oxford, 1958; H. Shaked, *The Life of the Sudanese Mahdi*, New Brunswick, N.J., 1978. Sudan under British rule: M. W. Daly, *British Administration and the Northern Sudan, 1917–1924*, Istanbul, 1980; G. Warburg, *Islam, Nationalism and Communism in a Traditional Society: The Case of the Sudan*, London, 1978.

For the politics of independent Sudan see P. K. Bechtold, *Politics in the Sudan: Parliamentary and Military Rule in an Emerging African Nation*, New York, 1976. On Islamic movements see J. S. Trimingham, *Islam in the Sudan*, London, 1965. For the conflict between north and south see D. M. Wai, ed., *The Southern Sudan: The Problem of National Integration*, London, 1973; L. P. Sanderson and N. Sanderson, *Education, Religion and Politics in Southern Sudan, 1899–1964*, London and Khartoum, 1981.

Arab tribal organization: T. Asad, *The Kababish Arabs: Power, Authority and Consent in a Nomadic Tribe*, London and New York, 1970; A. G. M. Ahmad, *Shaykhs and Followers: Political Struggle in the Rufaʿa al-Hoi Nazirate in the Sudan*, Khartoum, 1974.

On Ethiopia see J. S. Trimingham, *Islam in Ethiopia*, London, 1952; R. L. Hess, *Ethiopia: The Modernization of Autocracy*, Ithaca, N.Y., 1970; B. Habte Selassie, *Conflict and Intervention in the Horn of Africa*, New York, 1980; G. K. N. Trevaskis, *Eritrea: A Colony in Transition, 1941–52*, London, 1960.

INDEX

887, 906; East Africa, 534, 853–6, 859, 865, 877; Egypt, 620–2, 625–34; India, 258–9, 435, 450, 452, 462, 564, 566, 720–2, 725–6, 731–4, 736; Inner Asia, 435, 566, 567, 790–3, 797, 799–802, 912; Iran, 587–8, 907; Java, 761–3; Lebanon, 640; Libya, 564, 711–14, 716; and modernism, 557–70, 666, 904; Morocco, 568, 707, 715, 910; North Africa, 258–9, 263, 566–7, 703, 707–8, 887; Ottoman empire, 327, 360, 886; Pakistan, 745, 909; Palestine, 661; Saʿudi Arabia, 566, 667, 679, 763–5, 910; Southeast Asia, 259, 474, 478–9, 567, 757–76, 778, 781–2, 903; Tunisia, 699–700, 716, 901; West Africa, 505, 508, 512–16, 519, 522, 564, 830, 840–1, 846, 849–51, 877; *see also* Quran
religion, popular, 192–24, 222, 223–4, 325, 449, 466, 469, 524–8, 762–3, 793, 812, 876
revivalism, Islamic, xxiii, 883, 908–10, 915; Egypt, 625–7, 633–6, 667, 889–90, 905; North Africa, 901, 905; Southeast Asia, 758–9, 763, 781, 887; Turkey, 613–14; West Africa, 848
Reza Khan, 580–1, 894, 907
ribat (fort), 246, 368, 372, 377
ribat (meeting-house), 168, 170, 174, 353
Rida, Rashid, 666, 688
Rifaʿiya school, 171, 305
Rodrigo, king of Visigoths, 379
Roman empire, *see* Byzantine empire
Romanos I, Byzantine emperor, 304
rubaʿi (quatrain), 156, 319; *see also* poetry (post-ʿAbbasid)
Rudaki, poet, 155
Rukh, Shah, 281
Rumania, 595, 603
Rumi, Mawlana Jalal al-Din, 158, 326
Russia: and Egypt, 628, 631, 652; and Inner Asia, 273, 415, 418, 420–3, 426, 430, 435–6, 551, 557, 564, 567, 573, 784–95; and Iran, 300, 563, 573–6, 578–80, 590; and Ottoman empire, 311, 315, 335, 340–1, 546, 593–6, 597, 601, 731
Russia, Soviet, 653
absorption of Bukhara, 798–9
in Arabian peninsula, 672
in Inner Asia, 795–815, 797–802, 912–13
and Iran, 580–4
and Islam, 810–15, 822, 884, 888, 913, 916
Muslim opposition to, 816–17
Muslim Soviet Socialist Republics, 799, 800–1, 817
Muslims: as political minority, 809–10,

912–13; in work force, 809
state administration, 808, 895
suppression of Islam, 802–3, 806–8, 810–11, 813, 816–17
Rustamid dynasty, 366, 369, 371, 376
Rwanda, 531, 539, 867, 871

Sabah b. Jabr, 677
al-Sabah family, 677–8
Sabaheddin, Prince, 602
Saʿd Zaghlul, 622–3
Sadat, Anwar, 627, 629–34, 636, 904
Saddam Husayn, 655
Saʿdians, 263, 367, 403–5, 411; legitimacy, 403–4
Sadiqi College, 697–9
Sadr al-Din, 285
sadr (religious bureaucrat), 289, 296, 428, 447, 459
Safavid dynasty, 235, 253, 263, 284–6, 424, 426; administration, 265, 289, 295, 542, 571; concept of monarchy, 285–6, 294–5, 302, 404; decline of, 268, 299–302, 310, 342, 906; in Inner Asia, 815; legitimation, 264, 266–7, 285–6, 287–9, 292, 294, 542–3, 544, 572; military organization, 289–90, 295, 299; and Ottoman empire, 310–11, 325, 342, 815; relation to uymaqs, 283, 285, 286, 287–90, 294, 299, 301–2, 541–2, 881; *see also* state and religion, trade (international)
Saffarid dynasty, 131, 134
Safi al-Din, Shaykh, 284
Saghanughu family, 505, 508, 848
al-Saʿid, Sayyid, 864, 871
Saʿid b. Taymur, 677
Said Nursi, *Risale-i Nur*, 613, 901
saints, veneration of, 114–15, 121, 195, 216–18, 235, 254, 377, 428–9, 458, 460, 469, 506–7, 816, 879; opposition to, 462, 563, 673, 688, 707, 722, 793, 854
sajjada nishin (Sufi elite), 262, 724, 739
Salafiya movement, 566, 622, 666, 688, 700, 707–9, 716–17
Salah al-Din (Saladin), 135, 217, 352–4, 358
salat (ritual prayer), 24, 28, 101, 223
Salga, Muhammad, 840–1
Salih b. Tarif, 372
Salihiya, in East Africa, 534, 860, 865
Salim Suwari, al-Hajj, 506
Saljuq dynasty, 135, 137, 143–6, 179, 230, 301, 303, 304, 390, 414, 815; administration, 145, 147–9, 152, 176, 230, 278, 301, 304–5, 308, 316; in Anatolia, 304–6, 316; and Islamic

waqf (endowments) *(cont.)*
618, 632; in India, 459, /25; in Inner
Asia, 421, 424, 785, 788, 797–8, 804,
807, 811; in Iran, 296; in North Africa,
695, 697, 699; in Ottoman empire,
359–61, 598; in Tunisia, 700, 702; in
Turkey, 608, 611, 642
Wasulu, kingdom, 449–50
Wattasid dynasty, 367, 391, 402
wazir/vizier, 72–3, 128–9, 289–90, 317, 518, 530
Weber, Max, 271
West Africa: anti-colonial movements, 826–7;
independence, 828–9; Islam in, 829; *see
also* elites, intelligentsia
Wolofs, 834–7
women: education of, 893–4, 895–7; and
modernization, 635–6, 689, 696, 702–3,
763, 819, 861, 872, 876, 890–9; Quranic
teaching on, 29–31, 35; wearing of veil,
635–6, 688, 697, 808, 892–3, 894, 895

Yahya, Zaydi leader, 669
Yahya b. Ibrahim, 372
Yahya Effendi, Ottoman poet, 320
Yahya Khan, general, 744–5
Yaji, Hausa ruler, 496
Yang Tseng-hsin, 817–18
Ya'qub Beg, 435, 566
al-Yasavi, Shaykh Ahmad, 414, 425
Yasaviya order, 419–20, 425–6, 786
Yazid, Caliph, 59
Yaziji, Nasif, 640
Yemen: early history, 13, 14–17, *see also*
Hadhramaut; Islam in, 672–3, 895
Yemen, Imamate, 668–72
Yemen, People's Democratic Republic of,
671, 672–3
Yemen, South, 671, 672–3, 895
Yemen (Kalb), warring faction, 59, 63, 67,
98, 349, 363, 379
Yoruba, 828–9, 832, 842, 843–7
Young Algerians, 687

Young Bukharans, 792, 798
Young Ottoman movement, 507–8, 561,
600–1, 602–3, 621
Young Tunisians, 566, 699–700, 716
Young Turks, 561–2, 602, 604, 792, 900
Yuan dynasty, 432–3
Yunnan, 435, 566
Yunus, Mahmud, 774
Yunus Emre, Sufi poet, 325
Yusuf Hamadani, 425

Zaghlul, Sa'd, 524
Zahir al-'Umar, 363
zakat (almsgiving), 28, 33, 64, 101, 223, 688
778, 814
zamindars (local notables), 454–5, 464, 466,
719, 721–3
Zands, in Iran, 299–300
Zangid dynasty, 135
Zanj slave labourers, 131
Zanzibar, 529–31, 539, 677, 864–6, 868, 869
zawaya, 255, 257, 500, 510, 833–4
zawiyas, 257, 394, 402, 405, 500, 527, 567,
618, 682, 684, 704, 712, 841
Zayanids, 391
Zaydi dynasty, 219, 669–72
Zaytuna mosque, 569–70, 689, 697–9, 702
Zayyanid family, 410
Zengi, governor of Mosul, 351–2
Zia ul-Haq, General, 744–5, 909
Zia ul-Rahman, General, 747
Zionist movement, 628, 649, 652, 659–62,
667, 714
Zirid family, 366, 370, 373, 377
Ziryab, poet, 380
Ziya Gokalp, 603–4, 609
Zongo, *see* Kumasi, Muslims in
Zoroastrianism, 7–9, 36, 37, 78–9, 92, 175,
286; and diffusion of Islam, 245–6, 297
Zsitva Torak, treaty of, 314
Zubayr, Meccan aristocrat, 56

Index compiled by Meg Davies, Society of Indexers.